EDMUND SPENSER'S POETRY

AUTHORITATIVE TEXTS

CRITICISM

THIRD EDITION

W.W. NORTON & COMPANY, INC.
also publishes

THE NORTON ANTHOLOGY OF AMERICAN LITERATURE
edited by Nina Baym et al.

THE NORTON ANTHOLOGY OF ENGLISH LITERATURE
edited by M. H. Abrams et al.

THE NORTON ANTHOLOGY OF LITERATURE BY WOMEN
edited by Sandra M. Gilbert and Susan Guber

THE NORTON ANTHOLOGY OF MODERN POETRY
edited by Richard Ellmann and Robert O'Clair

THE NORTON ANTHOLOGY OF POETRY
edited by Alexander W. Allison et al.

THE NORTON ANTHOLOGY OF SHORT FICTION
edited by R. V. Cassill

THE NORTON ANTHOLOGY OF WORLD MASTERPIECES
edited by Maynard Mack et al.

THE NORTON FACSIMILE OF
THE FIRST FOLIO OF SHAKESPEARE
prepared by Charlton Hinman

THE NORTON INTRODUCTION TO LITERATURE
edited by Carl E. Bain, Jerome Beaty, and J. Paul Hunter

THE NORTON INTRODUCTION TO THE SHORT NOVEL
edited by Jerome Beaty

THE NORTON READER
edited by Arthur M. Eastman et al.

THE NORTON SAMPLER
edited by Thomas Cooley

THE NORTON ANTHOLOGY OF CONTEMPORARY FICTION
edited by R. V. Cassill

A NORTON CRITICAL EDITION

EDMUND SPENSER'S

POETRY

AUTHORITATIVE TEXTS

CRITICISM

THIRD EDITION

Selected and Edited by

HUGH MACLEAN

PROFESSOR EMERITUS
OF ENGLISH
STATE UNIVERSITY OF
NEW YORK AT ALBANY

ANNE LAKE PRESCOTT

BARNARD COLLEGE,
COLUMBIA UNIVERSITY

W · W · NORTON & COMPANY · *New York* · *London*

The text of this book is composed in Electra
with the display set in Bernhard Modern
Composition by PennSet Inc.
Manufacturing by Courier
Book design by Antonina Krass

Library of Congress Cataloging-in-Publication Data
Spenser, Edmund, 1552?–1599.
[Selections. 1993]
Edmund Spenser's poetry : authoritative texts, criticism /
selected and edited by Hugh Maclean and Anne Lake Prescott.
— 3rd ed.
p.   cm. — (A Norton critical edition)
I. Maclean, Hugh, 1919–   . II. Prescott, Anne Lake, 1936–
III. Title.
PR2352.M3   1993
821'.3—dc20   92-15409

ISBN 0-393-96299-7

W. W. Norton & Company, Inc., 500 Fifth Avenue, New York, N.Y. 10110
W. W. Norton & Company Ltd., 10 Coptic Street, London WC1A 1PU

4   5   6   7   8   9   0

Contents

Criticism

Preface to the Third Edition

Spenser tells quest stories in a way that incorporates the reader, in his or her own quest for understanding, into the fiction's fabric of meaning. His poetry conveys the sense that the protean nature of language itself is always at issue when it is used for mighty purposes. In his work there is proof that self-reflexiveness in poetry need not be the old sterile matter of Narcissus in deathly love with his own image; that in tiny, intense, even joking details of wit the highest seriousness can reside; that allusiveness can be deployed with great originality.

—John Hollander

When the Second Edition of *Edmund Spenser's Poetry* appeared in 1982, it was already clear that something in the nature of a revolution in Spenser studies was taking place, and that new methods of reading texts, often deriving from the critical practice of such postmoderns as Derrida, Foucault, and Lacan—together with other influential captains of literary theory—were challenging earlier assumptions about Spenser's poetry. This revolution has in the last decade or so become an information explosion of enormous and bewildering variety. Regularly stimulated by cool and/or acid critical pronouncements like those of Catherine Belsey ("criticism can no longer be isolated from other areas of knowledge"), or Terry Eagleton, who trashes "a sterile critical formalism, piously swaddled with eternal verities," all of the critical developments touched upon in the Preface to the Second Edition have flowered in profusion. Over the last ten or twelve years, Spenser scholarship has been especially receptive to a new historicism that emphasizes the intertextuality of literary texts and cultural, economic, and political developments at large and the relation of political power to that of the poet. It has also been particularly receptive to a feminist criticism in which the politics of the body is central and potentially controlling. These accents sound also in a decided revival of interest in the pastoral genre, notably its interplay with epic (as in Book VI of *The Faerie Queene*).

Still, "traditional" scholarship of the highest quality holds its ground. Recent work on *Complaints*, for example, reflects an emerging sense that careful re-examination of primary sources may lead to biographical studies more firmly founded than those we know. New attention to Spenser's Ireland and to the poet's prose *View* (not to mention Kilcolman Castle) is relevant too. Solidly professional editorial work flourishes. William Oram and an international group of young scholars have collaborated on a splendid new edition of Spenser's shorter poems. The first complete English translation of Boiardo has recently appeared in an edition distinctly user-friendly for Spenser scholars. Since 1989 other students of Spenser's poetry, "traditional" in methodology and outlook, have produced exciting new studies of feminine patronage in Spenser's time, Tudor royal iconography, *mimesis* in Sidney and Spenser, astrological symbolism in *The Shepheardes Calender*—to choose just four books from the extensive list of such works published in very recent years.

Accordingly, we have made every effort to preserve a sense of balance and proportion in our selection of texts and criticism for this Third Edition, as well as in the revised (or newly provided) Editors' Notes. We have sought neither to turn away from traditional approaches nor uncritically to embrace the new sense of context, the "hermeneutics of suspicion," that has so evidently deepened and expanded understanding of Spenser's mind and art in our time, but principally to recognize incisive and lucid scholarship. In this connection we acknowledge a continuing debt to *The Spenser Encyclopedia* (1990E in our apparatus), so thoughtfully designed to supply the different needs of Spenser scholars, teachers in English studies, and all students or general readers of Spenser's poetry. If the character and content of this Third Edition have been shaped in some important ways by the continuing torrent of newly oriented books and articles, our editorial perceptions have also been regularly steadied by *The Spenser Encyclopedia*, brought forth after many years of devoted labor.

New selections from *The Faerie Queene* include the ninth canto of Book II ("Alma's castle"), not simply to enlarge the range of symbolically central locations or moments available here to students and scholars, but to respond to recent critical attention to bodies masculine, feminine, and politic. Book VI, in earlier editions rather abruptly cut off at x.30, now flows uninterruptedly on to its desperate concluding scene: *the Blatant Beast at terrific large*, the narrator's world brought low by "wicked fate" or "guilt of men." The addition of these cantos (in conjunction with shorter poems retained or newly included in this edition) enables the reader to assess the range and shifting emphases of pastoral elements in the Spenserian canon. To assure these inclusions, given space restrictions, we have felt obliged to abandon IV.x (the Temple of Venus). But we retain the Proem to Book IV so that readers may continue to compare the varied emphases of Spenser's "introductions" to all six books of *The Faerie Queene*.

Major additions to the shorter poems include *Colin Clouts Come Home Againe*, newly recognized for its indications of the poet's struggle to come to terms with the teasing ambiguities of a patronage system that is part and parcel of the great queen's court and to meet the larger challenge of that court's power-system to moral and aesthetic integrity. Colin Clout's doubts and frustrations echo in the pastoral world of Book VI of *The Faerie Queene*. *Amoretti* is here complete (together with *Epithalamion*), annotated to reflect the most recent critical commentary on a sonnet sequence that rewrites Petrarchan tradition; its inclusion will enable readers to recognize the particular elements of Spenser's distinction in this kind, with special relevance to the sonnets of Sidney and Shakespeare. Finally, in the selections from *The Shepheardes Calender* we thought it best to replace the "June" eclogue with ["Morall"] "Februarie," an especially instructive and taking poem in recent years for a wide variety of critics and scholars. To make way for these substantial additions we have dropped, not without pain, *Fowre*

Hymnes from this edition. It is our hope that readers who find special profit and delight in the later stages of *Colin Clouts Come Home Againe* will explore and savor these four moving poems.

Texts of the poems are based on those of the early editions of Spenser's poetry: selections from *The Faerie Queene* on the 1596 text, shorter poems on the texts of the first editions. The editors' aim is to deliver a text that closely follows the substantive form of the early edition in question, that reproduces the spelling and (essentially) the punctuation of that edition, and that introduces only those elements of modernization that seem required to render the text easily accessible to modern readers. Unfamiliar words are glossed in the margins. The Textual Notes provide a list of (chiefly substantive) variants among the early editions of *The Faerie Queene* and the shorter poems.

Not quite as in earlier editions of *Edmund Spenser's Poetry*, an "Editors' Note" accompanies each poem or group of poems. In some ways these continue to serve a principally introductory purpose, dealing with the circumstances of composition, genre, structure, versification; in our edition, however, we have endeavored also to give readers some sense of the range of criticism that has in recent years significantly deepened understanding of Spenser's poetry. Editors' Notes to poems that appeared also in earlier editions have been revised and rewritten. New Editors' Notes are provided for *Colin Clouts Come Home Againe* and for *Amoretti* and *Epithalamion*. Footnotes in the Third Edition have been thoroughly updated and revised, with a view to directing readers' attention to the best in recent criticism. In Editors' Notes and footnotes, full bibliographical data are provided only for books and articles published before 1973 (which are not included in our Selected Bibliography). The 1989 edition of the shorter poems, ed. Oram et al., cited in full in the Selected Bibliography, is referred to in footnotes and headnotes as "Yale." For work published in and after 1973, author's name and publication date must serve, with fuller bibliographical data reserved for the Selected Bibliography.

To select critical materials for this Third Edition has been a difficult task, not least in that we have felt constrained to delete a number of valuable essays included in the Second Edition. We deeply regret all these deletions; given the quality and penetration of so many books and articles published since 1982, space restrictions have forced our hand. Still, of the twenty-five critical interpretations included in this edition, nine survive from the 1982 edition: two brief selections from Roche, one each from Frye, Hamilton, Heninger, Hieatt, Tonkin, MacCaffrey, and Martz. Of selections newly added, one (Woolf) was published in 1948, five others (Cheney, Allen, Nelson, Giamatti, Bond) prior to 1977. Eight of the remaining nine selections have been published since 1980; one (Miller) makes its first appearance in print in the Third Edition. Two authors (Berger, Alpers), represented in the 1982 edition by earlier work, reappear with recent essays on pastoral. We believe that the critical materials included in the Third Edition make up a full and fair sampling of the way we live now, in Spenser studies.

All the selections from Early Critical Views in the 1982 edition are represented again in the Third Edition. "E.K." now appears, however, properly in bed with the *Calender*, and Camden's brief but moving account of Spenser's last years, death, and burial will alert modern readers to the respect and love generally accorded to the man who "surpassed all the English poets of former times." Virginia Woolf's essay on *The Faerie Queene* scarcely suggests the feminist perspective remarked by Fox (1990) in Woolf's notes on Spenser; all the same, the essay is a perceptive response to an initial challenge: how to read Spenser? Helgerson's remarkable essay, on much more than its title appears to promise, and the following essay by Montrose in the context of "a newer historical orientation" together provide another kind of introduction, to larger patterns in Spenser's thoughtful art. Other couplings match Hamilton's comparison of Spenser and Dante with Judith Anderson's exemplary presentment of the "Chaucerian Connection"; Martz and Prescott on *Amoretti*; Miller's Lacanian piece on Colin's vision atop Mount Acidale and Tonkin's quietly authoritative essay on the same scene. We retain the grouping of critical opinions on the House of Busyrane, with Padelford and Lewis bowing out in favor of Susanne Wofford. MacCaffrey keeps company with Berger and Alpers to provide materials for explorative discussion of the pastoral mode. A quartet of lively scholars makes up our "mini-casebook" on *Muiopotmos*. Donald Cheney's essay on the *Mutabilitie Cantos* as "a stylistic tour de force" [and much more] seems to us the most thoughtfully persuasive among a number of penetrating analyses of the *Cantos*. Bart Giamatti's moving chapter on pageantry reminds modern readers of an essential element, sometimes overlooked or neglected, in Spenser's poetry. And William Nelson fittingly concludes these critical speculations with his delightful essay on the playfulness of Spenser—too often silenced by the deathwatch beetle of solemnity. The enlarged Selected Bibliography provides a list of especially rewarding books and articles published since 1973.

The editors gratefully acknowledge their continuing debt to Edwin Greenlaw, Charles G. Osgood, Frederick S. Padelford, and Ray Heffner, editors of *The Works of Edmund Spenser: A Variorum Edition* (*Variorum* in our apparatus; Baltimore: Johns Hopkins UP, 1932–49). Particular thanks are due to the Director of Libraries and her staff at the University Library of the State University of New York at Albany: without their kindly assistance and provision of working space in the University Library, the publication of this Third Edition would at the very least have been long delayed. We also thank Michael Mallik, Elizabeth Lukacs, Claudine Conan, John Mason, and Kathy Thornton, who took time from their studies at Columbia, Barnard, or SUNY-Albany to track down materials in various libraries or to assist in proofreading. Antonia Prescott also helped us with these activities, and to her we give thanks. Robert Clark, on the teaching staff at Barnard, helped bring order to the Selected Bibliography.

We owe special thanks to five scholars whose thoughtful suggestions have significantly contributed to the cast and character of the Third Edition: Elizabeth A. Bieman, A. Leigh DeNeef, Richard Helgerson, Clark Hulse, and Susanne Woods. We wish also to thank A. Kent Hieatt for aid and comfort throughout the assembling of this Third Edition, and, for advice, suggestion, or merely a friendly and knowledgeable ear, Ward Allen, Judith Anderson, Jean Brink, Patrick Cullen, Duk-ae Chung, Heather Dubrow,

Margaret Hannay, and Carol Kaske. Finally, we are deeply grateful to our editor, Carol Bemis, for her steady wisdom, encouraging presence, and patient control throughout the development of this third and most challenging edition of *Edmund Spenser's Poetry*.

It remains only to recall and honor the insight, quality, and grace, over a very long term of years, of a great editor; and to remember with affection and gratitude a scholar whose extraordinary learning, intellectual generosity, and charm brought more than one generation of students to a deeper understanding of our poet. We dedicate this Third Edition to the memory of John Benedict and of William Nelson.

HUGH MACLEAN
ANNE LAKE PRESCOTT

The Texts of
THE POEMS

THE FAERIE
QVEENE.

Diſpoſed into twelue bookes,

Fashioning

XII. Morall vertues.

LONDON
Printed for VVilliam Ponſonbie.
1596.

TO
THE MOST HIGH,
MIGHTIE
And
MAGNIFICENT
EMPRESSE RENOVV-
MED FOR PIETIE, VER-
TVE, AND ALL GRATIOVS
GOVERNMENT ELIZABETH BY
THE GRACE OF GOD QVEENE
OF ENGLAND FRAVNCE AND
IRELAND AND OF VIRGI-
NIA, DEFENDOVR OF THE
FAITH, &c . HER MOST
HVMBLE SERVAVNT
EDMVND SPENSER
DOTH IN ALL HV-
MILITIE DEDI-
CATE, PRE-
SENT
AND CONSECRATE THESE
HIS LABOVRS TO LIVE
VVITH THE ETERNI-
TIE OF HER
FAME.

A Letter of the Authors

EXPOUNDING HIS WHOLE INTENTION IN THE COURSE OF THIS WORKE: WHICH FOR THAT IT GIVETH GREAT LIGHT TO THE READER, FOR THE BETTER UNDER-STANDING IS HEREUNTO ANNEXED.[1]

To the Right noble, and Valorous, Sir Walter Raleigh knight, Lo. Wardein of the Stanneryes, and her Majesties liefetenaunt of the County of Cornewayll.

Sir knowing how doubtfully all Allegories may be construed, and this booke of mine, which I have entituled the Faery Queene, being a continued Allegory, or darke conceit, I have thought good aswell for avoyding of gealous opinions and misconstructions, as also for your better light in reading thereof, (being so by you commanded,) to discover unto you the general intention and meaning, which in the whole course thereof I have fashioned, without expressing of any particular purposes or by-accidents[2] therein occasioned. The generall end therefore of all the booke is to fashion[3] a gentleman or noble person in vertuous and gentle discipline: Which for that I conceived shoulde be most plausible[4] and pleasing, being coloured with an historicall fiction, the which the most part of men delight to read, rather for variety of matter, then for profite of the ensample: I chose the historye of king Arthure, as most fitte for the excellency of his person, being made famous by many mens former workes, and also furthest from the daunger of envy, and suspition of present time.[5] In which I have followed all the antique Poets historicall, first Homere, who in the Persons of Agamemnon and Ulysses hath ensampled a good governour and a vertuous man, the one in his *Ilias*, and the other in his *Odysseis*: then Virgil, whose like intention was to doe in the person of Aeneas: after him Ariosto comprised them both in his Orlando: and lately Tasso dissevered them againe, and formed both parts in two persons, namely that part which they in Philosophy call Ethice, or vertues of a private man, coloured in his Rinaldo: The other named Politice in his Godfredo.[6] By ensample of which excellente Poets, I labour to pourtraict in Arthure, before he was king, the image of a brave knight, perfected in the twelve private morall vertues, as Aristotle

---

1. This "Letter" was appended to the 1590 edition of *The Faerie Queene* (Books I–III) and dropped from the 1596 edition. Such epistolary commentaries were commonly employed by Renaissance poets to explain or defend their purpose and method; cf. Tasso's account of the allegory in his epic poem *Gerusalemme Liberata*, and Sir John Harington's preface to his translation of Ariosto's *Orlando Furioso* (1591), not to mention the "Epistle" and "Argument" prefixed to *The Shepheardes Calender.*
2. Side issues, secondary concerns.
3. I.e., to represent (in a secondary sense, to train or educate).
4. Acceptable, deserving of approval.
5. I.e., not subject to malicious interpretation in terms of contemporary political bias or prejudice.
6. Lodovico Ariosto (1474–1533) was author of the epic romance *Orlando Furioso*, first published in complete form in 1532; Torquato Tasso (1544–95) published his chivalric romance *Rinaldo* in 1562 and the epic *Gerusalemme Liberata* (centered on the heroic figure of Count Godfredo) in 1581.

1

hath devised,[7] the which is the purpose of these first twelve bookes: which if I finde to be well accepted, I may be perhaps encoraged, to frame the other part of polliticke vertues in his person, after that hee came to be king. To some I know this Methode will seeme displeasaunt, which had rather have good discipline delivered plainly in way of precepts, or sermoned at large, as they use, then thus clowdily enwrapped in Allegoricall devises. But such, me seeme, should be satisfide with the use of these dayes, seeing all things accounted by their showes, and nothing esteemed of, that is not delightfull and pleasing to commune sence. For this cause is Xenophon preferred before Plato, for that the one in the exquisite depth of his judgement, formed a Commune welth such as it should be, but the other in the person of Cyrus and the Persians fashioned a governement such as might best be: So much more profitable and gratious is doctrine by ensample, then by rule.[8] So have I laboured to doe in the person of Arthure: whome I conceive after his long education by Timon, to whom he was by Merlin delivered to be brought up, so soone as he was borne of the Lady Igrayne, to have seene in a dream or vision the Faery Queen, with whose excellent beauty ravished, he awaking resolved to seeke her out, and so being by Merlin armed, and by Timon throughly instructed, he went to seeke her forth in Faerye land. In that Faery Queene I meane glory in my generall intention, but in my particular I conceive the most excellent and glorious person of our soveraine the Queene, and her kingdome in Faery land. And yet in some places els, I doe otherwise shadow[9] her. For considering she beareth two persons, the one of a most royall Queene or Empresse, the other of a most vertuous and beautifull Lady, this latter part in some places I doe expresse in Belphoebe, fashioning her name according to your owne excellent conceipt of Cynthia,[1] (Phoebe and Cynthia being both names of Diana.) So in the person of Prince Arthure I sette forth magnificence in particular, which vertue for that (according to Aristotle and the rest)[2] it is the perfection of all the rest, and conteineth in it them all, therefore in the whole course I mention the deedes of Arthure applyable to that vertue, which I write of in that booke. But of the xii. other vertues, I make xii. other knights the patrones, for the more variety of the history: Of which these three bookes contayn three, The first of the knight of the Redcrosse, in whome I expresse Holynes: The seconde of Sir Guyon, in whome I sette forth Temperaunce: The third of Britomartis a Lady knight, in whome I picture Chastity. But because the beginning of the whole worke seemeth abrupte and as depending upon other antecedents, it needs that ye know

---

7. Aristotle does not actually distinguish twelve moral virtues in the *Nicomachaean Ethics*, but medieval and early sixteenth-century commentators, following Aquinas, had so divided them; Spenser's friend Lodowick Bryskett speaks of twelve virtues in his *Discourse of Civill Life*. DeNeef 1990E proposes that since "devise" could then mean "divide," Spenser may refer to Aristotle's division between private and public.
8. This distinction between Xenophon's *Cyropaedia* and Plato's *Republic* recalls Sidney's praise of the poet (who "coupleth the generall notion with the particuler example") at the expense of the philosopher, whose "woordish description . . . dooth neyther strike, pierce, nor possesse the sight of the soule so much as that other dooth."
9. I.e., portray.
1. Raleigh's fragmentary poem *Cynthia* celebrated Queen Elizabeth.
2. I.e., notably, Cicero's *De inventione*, the *Somnium Scipionis* of Macrobius, and (among later commentators on the virtues) the pseudo-Senecan *Formula honestae vitae* written by Martin of Braga in the sixth century.

the occasion of these three knights severall adventures. For the Methode
of a Poet historical is not such, as of an Historiographer.[3] For an Historiographer discourseth of affayres orderly as they were donne, accounting
as well the times as the actions, but a Poet thrusteth into the middest, even
where it most concerneth him, and there recoursing to the thinges forepaste,
and divining of thinges to come, maketh a pleasing Analysis of all. The
beginning therefore of my history, if it were to be told by an Historiographer,
should be the twelfth booke, which is the last, where I devise that the Faery
Queene kept her Annuall feaste xii. dayes, uppon which xii. severall dayes,
the occasions of the xii. severall adventures hapned, which being undertaken
by xii. severall knights, are in these xii books severally handled and discoursed. The first was this. In the beginning of the feast, there presented
him selfe a tall clownishe[4] younge man, who falling before the Queen of
Faries desired a boone (as the manner then was) which during that feast
she might not refuse: which was that hee might have the atchievement of
any adventure, which during that feaste should happen, that being graunted,
he rested him on the floore, unfitte through his rusticity for a better place.
Soone after entred a faire Ladye in mourning weedes, riding on a white
Asse, with a dwarfe behind her leading a warlike steed, that bore the Armes
of a knight, and his speare in the dwarfes hand. Shee falling before the
Queene of Faeries, complayned[5] that her father and mother an ancient
King and Queene, had bene by an huge dragon many years shut up in a
brasen Castle, who thence suffred them not to yssew: and therefore besought
the Faery Queene to assygne her some one of her knights to take on him
that exployt. Presently that clownish person upstarting, desired that adventure: whereat the Queene much wondering, and the Lady much gaincsay-
ing, yet he earnestly importuned his desire. In the end the Lady told him
that unlesse that armour which she brought, would serve him (that is the
armour of a Christian man specified by Saint Paul v. Ephes.)[6] that he could
not succeed in that enterprise, which being forthwith put upon him with
dewe furnitures[7] thereunto, he seemed the goodliest man in al that company, and was well liked of the Lady. And eftesoones[8] taking on him
knighthood, and mounting on that straunge Courser, he went forth with
her on that adventure: where beginneth the first booke, vz.

A gentle knight was pricking on the playne. &c.

The second day ther came in a Palmer bearing an Infant with bloody
hands, whose Parents he complained to have bene slayn by an Enchaun-
teresse called Acrasia: and therefore craved of the Faery Queene, to appoint
him some knight, to performe that adventure, which being assigned to Sir
Guyon, he presently went forth with that same Palmer: which is the be-

---

3. I.e., the method employed by an epic poet is not that of the historian.
4. I.e., of rustic appearance (appropriate to the man brought up in "ploughmans state," I.x.66). Wall
   1986 and 1987 deduces from an astronomical reference in II.ii.46 that Gloriana holds her twelve-
   day feast at Christmastide, traditional time for mumming plays about St. George and, in Arthurian
   literature, for new marvels.
5. Lamented.
6. Cf. the note on I.i.1.
7. Suitable equipment.
8. Forthwith.

ginning of the second booke and the whole subject thereof. The third day
there came in, a Groome who complained before the Faery Queene, that
a vile Enchaunter called Busirane had in hand a most faire Lady called
Amoretta, whom he kept in most grievous torment, because she would not
yield him the pleasure of her body. Whereupon Sir Scudamour the lover
of that Lady presently tooke on him that adventure. But being unable to
performe it by reason of the hard Enchauntments, after long sorrow, in
the end met with Britomartis, who succoured him, and reskewed his love.

But by occasion hereof, many other adventures are intermedled, but
rather as Accidents, then intendments.[9] As the love of Britomart, the overthrow of Marinell, the misery of Florimell, the vertuousnes of Belphoebe,
the lasciviousnes of Hellenora, and many the like.

Thus much Sir, I have briefly overronne to direct your understanding
to the wel-head[1] of the History, that from thence gathering the whole
intention of the conceit, ye may as in a handfull gripe al the discourse,
which otherwise may happily[2] seeme tedious and confused. So humbly
craving the continuaunce of your honorable favour towards me, and
th'eternall establishment of your happines, I humbly take leave.

23. January. 1589.[3]

Yours most humbly affectionate.

Ed. Spenser.

9. I.e., as matters relatively incidental to a central purpose.
1. Source, spring.
2. By chance.
3. I.e., 1590. In England (until 1753), the official year was reckoned from March 25.

The First Booke of The Faerie Queene

Contayning
The Legende of the Knight of the Red Crosse,
or
Of Holinesse

1

Lo I the man, whose Muse whilome° did maske,   formerly
    As time her taught, in lowly Shepheards weeds,[1]
Am now enforst a far unfitter taske.
For trumpets sterne to chaunge mine Oaten reeds,
And sing of Knights and Ladies gentle deeds;
Whose prayses having slept in silence long,
Me, all too meane, the sacred Muse areeds°   counsels
To blazon broad[2] emongst her learnéd throng:
Fierce warres and faithfull loves shall moralize my song.

2

Helpe then, O holy Virgin chiefe of nine,[3]
    Thy weaker° Novice to performe thy will,   too weak
Lay forth out of thine everlasting scryne°   chest for records
The antique rolles, which there lye hidden still,
Of Faerie knights and fairest Tanaquill,[4]
Whom that most noble Briton Prince[5] so long
Sought through the world, and suffered so much ill,
That I must rue his undeservéd wrong:
O helpe thou my weake wit, and sharpen my dull tong.

3

And thou most dreaded impe[6] of highest Jove,
    Faire Venus sonne, that with thy cruell dart
At that good knight so cunningly didst rove,°   shoot

1. On Book I see Brooks-Davies 1990E. Lines 1–4 imitate verses that Servius (fourth century A.D.) says Virgil's first editors removed from the start of the *Aeneid*; medieval and Renaissance manuscripts or editions often quote them. Spenser thus associates his poem with the classical epic and announces his shift from pastoral to heroic poetry. On Virgil's role in Spenser's "idea of the poet," see Neuse 1978; Sessions 1980 shows how the knight's name, George, recalls Virgil's bucolic "Georgics" and thus implies the "labors needed to make an epic hero," labors that "can only be realized with time." Line 5 paraphrases the start of Ariosto's *Orlando Furioso*; on Book I's allusions to Ariosto see especially P. Alpers, *The Poetry of "The Faerie Queene"* (Princeton, 1967) and, for a recent study, Wiggins 1991.
2. I.e., to proclaim.
3. Perhaps Clio, muse of history (see I.xi.5 and III.iii.4). In *The Teares of the Muses* 53, Spenser calls her "eldest Sister" of the nine muses, but in the same poem (457–62) he notes how Calliope can "deifie" mortals and their deeds (cf. *The Shepheardes Calender*, "Aprill" 100, "June" 57). Some critics (e.g., Roche 1989) have made a case for Calliope; others have anticipated the tempered preference of Hamilton 1977 for Clio. Revard 1990E thinks the "unnamed Muse" may be either, while for Anderson 1989 she is a composite.
4. Gloriana, i.e., Elizabeth I. The humanist Vives (1492–1540) thought "Caia Tanaquill," whom legend called the wife of the Roman king Tarquinus Priscus, was the very pattern of a noble queen.
5. I.e., Arthur.
6. Child, i.e., Cupid, god of love.

That glorious fire it kindled in his hart,
Lay now thy deadly Heben° bow apart,   *ebony*
And with thy mother milde come to mine ayde:
Come both, and with you bring triumphant Mart,[7]
In loves and gentle jollíties arrayd,
After his murdrous spoiles and bloudy rage allayd.

4

And with them eke,° O Goddesse heavenly bright,[8]   *also*
Mirrour of grace and Majestie divine,
Great Lady of the greatest Isle, whose light
Like Phoebus lampe throughout the world doth shine,
Shed thy faire beames into my feeble eyne,
And raise my thoughts too humble and too vile,°   *lowly*
To thinke of that true glorious type° of thine,   *pattern*
The argument of mine afflicted° stile: *humble*
The which to heare, vouchsafe, O dearest dred[9] a-while.

Canto I

The Patron of true Holinesse,
Foule Errour doth defeate:
Hypocrisie him to entrappe,
Doth to his home entreate.

1

A Gentle Knight was pricking° on the plaine,   *riding briskly*
Y cladd in mightie armes and silver shielde,[1]
Wherein old dints of deepe wounds did remaine,
The cruell markes of many a bloudy fielde;
Yet armes till that time did he never wield:
His angry steede did chide his foming bitt,
As much disdayning to the curbe to yield:
Full jolly° knight he seemd, and faire did sitt,   *gallant*
As one for knightly giusts° and fierce encounters fitt.   *tourneys*

2

But on his brest a bloudie Crosse he bore,
The deare remembrance of his dying Lord,
For whose sweete sake that glorious badge he wore,
And dead as living[2] ever him adored:
Upon his shield the like was also scored,
For soveraine hope, which in his helpe he had:

7. Mars, god of war, and Venus's lover (Ovid, *Metamorphoses* 4.167–89).
8. I.e., Queen Elizabeth.
9. Object of reverence and awe.
1. Cf. Ephesians 6.11–17: "Put on the whole armour of God, that ye may be able to stand against the wiles of the devil. . . . Above all, taking the shield of faith, wherewith ye shall be able to quench all the fiery darts of the wicked." Redcrosse's armor is that of every Christian. On this scene, see Anderson, pp. 726–32, in this edition.
2. Revelation 1.18: "I am he that liveth, and was dead; and, behold, I am alive for evermore."

Right faithfull true he was in deede and word,
  But of his cheere° did seeme too solemne sad;°   *countenance/grave*
Yet nothing did he dread, but ever was ydrad.°   *dreaded*

3

Upon a great adventure he was bond,
  That greatest Gloriana to him gave,
  That greatest Glorious Queene of Faerie lond,
  To winne him worship,° and her grace to have,   *honor*
  Which of all earthly things he most did crave;
  And ever as he rode, his hart did earne°   *yearn*
  To prove his puissance in battell brave
  Upon his foe, and his new force to learne;
Upon his foe, a Dragon[3] horrible and stearne.

4

A lovely Ladie[4] rode him faire beside,
  Upon a lowly Asse more white then snow,
  Yet she much whiter, but the same did hide
  Under a vele, that wimpled° was full low,   *folded*
  And over all a blacke stole she did throw,
  As one that inly mournd: so was she sad,
  And heavie sat upon her palfrey slow;
  Seeméd in heart some hidden care she had,
And by her in a line° a milke white lambe she lad.°   *leash/led*

5

So pure an innocent, as that same lambe,[5]
  She was in life and every vertuous lore,
  And by descent from Royall lynage came
  Of ancient Kings and Queenes, that had of yore
  Their scepters stretcht from East to Westerne shore,
  And all the world in their subjection held;
  Till that infernall feend with foule uprore
  Forwasted all their land, and them expeld:
Whom to avenge, she had this Knight from far compeld.°   *summoned*

6

Behind her farre away a Dwarfe[6] did lag,
  That lasie seemd in being ever last,

---

3. Cf. Revelation 20.2: ". . . the dragon, that old serpent, which is the devil, and Satan. . . ."
4. I.e., Una, whose name (given in stanza 45) is Latin for "one." She represents Truth, including the true faith of Redcrosse and the true Church. Her "lowly Asse" shows her humility: cf. Jesus' mount in John 12.14 and Matthew 21.5. On the narrative of her love for Redcrosse, see Levin 1991.
5. The lamb indicates Una's Christian significance (cf. John 1.29) as well as her innocent purity; it also recalls the lamb that accompanies the princess whom St. George rescues from a dragon in Caxton's fifteenth-century *Golden Legend* (translated from Voraigne's thirteenth-century *Legenda Aurea*), scoffed at by sterner Protestants but still much read.
6. The dwarf may represent common sense, practical understanding, or reason as it follows and serves faith; cf. Horton 1990E.

Or weariéd with bearing of her bag
Of needments at his backe. Thus as they past,
The day with cloudes was suddeine overcast,
And angry Jove an hideous storme of raine
Did poure into his Lemans lap[7] so fast,
That every wight° to shrowd° it did constrain,   *creature/cover*
And this faire couple eke to shroud themselves were fain.°   *eager*

7

Enforst to seeke some covert nigh at hand,
  A shadie grove not far away they spide,
  That promist ayde the tempest to withstand:
  Whose loftie trees yclad with sommers pride,
  Did spred so broad, that heavens light did hide,
  Not perceable with power of any starre:
  And all within were pathes and alleies wide,
  With footing worne, and leading inward farre:
Faire harbour° that them seemes; so in they entred arre.   *shelter*

8

And foorth they passe, with pleasure forward led,
  Joying to heare the birdes sweete harmony,
  Which therein shrouded from the tempest dred,
  Seemd in their song to scorne the cruell sky.
  Much can° they prayse the trees so straight and hy,[8]   *did*
  The sayling Pine, the Cedar proud and tall,
  The vine-prop Elme, the Poplar never dry,
  The builder Oake, sole king of forrests all,
The Aspine good for staves, the Cypresse funerall.

9

The Laurell, meed° of mightie Conquerours   *reward*
  And Poets sage, the Firre that weepeth still,
  The Willow worne of forlorne Paramours,
  The Eugh° obedient to the benders will,   *yew*
  The Birch for shaftes, the Sallow for the mill,
  The Mirrhe sweete bleeding in the bitter wound,[9]
  The warlike Beech, the Ash for nothing ill,
  The fruitfull Olive, and the Platane° round,   *plane-tree*
The carver Holme,° the Maple seeldom inward sound.   *holly*

7. I.e., into the lap of his mistress, the earth.
8. Chaucer's *Parliament of Fowls* 176–82 is the immediate source for this catalog of trees; the convention has its roots in Ovid's *Metamorphoses* 10.90–105. Spenser's epithets include scriptural and classical associations, e.g., "the Cedar proud and tall" recalls Isaiah 2.13, while "the Cypresse funerall" glances at Ovid's story of Cyparissus (*Metamorphoses* 10.106–42).
9. Sweet gum flows from the tree when its bark is cut; because of its association with Christ's birth and death (Matthew 2.11 and Mark 15.23; cf. the *OED*), myrrh recalls the trees in Paradise and the "tree" on which Christ was crucified. Ovid tells how Myrrha slept with her father and, when turned into a tree, gave birth to Adonis through a rent in her bark (*Metamorphoses* 10.298–514).

10

Led with delight, they thus beguile the way,
  Untill the blustring storme is overblowne;
  When weening° to returne, whence they did stray,   *expecting*
  They cannot finde that path, which first was showne,
  But wander too and fro in wayes unknowne,
  Furthest from end then, when they neerest weene,
  That makes them doubt, their wits be not their owne:
  So many pathes, so many turnings seene,
That which of them to take, in diverse° doubt they been.[1]   *distracting*

11

At last resolving forward still to fare,
  Till that some end they finde or° in or out,   *either*
  That path they take, that beaten seemd most bare,
  And like to lead the labyrinth about;°   *out of*
  Which when by tract° they hunted had throughout,   *track*
  At length it brought them to a hollow cave,
  Amid the thickest woods. The Champion stout
  Eftsoones° dismounted from his courser brave,   *forthwith*
And to the Dwarfe a while his needlesse spere he gave.

12

"Be well aware," quoth then that Ladie milde,
  "Least suddaine mischiefe ye too rash provoke:
  The danger hid, the place unknowne and wilde,
  Breedes dreadfull doubts: Oft fire is without smoke.
  And perill without show: therefore your stroke
  Sir knight with-hold, till further triall made."
  "Ah Ladie," said he, "shame were to revoke
  The forward footing for° an hidden shade: *because of*
Vertue gives her selfe light, through darkenesse for to wade."

13

"Yea but," quoth she, "the perill of this place
  I better wot° then you, though now too late   *know*
  To wish you backe returne with foule disgrace,
  Yet wisedome warnes, whilest foot is in the gate,
  To stay the steppe, ere forcéd to retrate.
  This is the wandring wood, this Errours den,
  A monster vile, whom God and man does hate:
  Therefore I read° beware." "Fly fly," quoth then   *advise*
The fearefull Dwarfe: "this is no place for living men."

---

1. So at the start of the *Inferno*, Dante is lost in a dark wood. The labyrinth of forest paths suggests the bewildering variety of choices in a world of multiplicity and matter.

14

But full of fire and greedy hardiment,°   *boldness*
  The youthfull knight could not for ought be staide,
But forth unto the darksome hole he went,
And lookéd in: his glistring armor made
A litle glooming light, much like a shade,
By which he saw the ugly monster plaine,
Halfe like a serpent horribly displaide,
But th'other halfe did womans shape retaine,[2]
Most lothsom, filthie, foule, and full of vile disdaine.

15

And as she lay upon the durtie ground,
  Her huge long taile her den all overspred,
Yet was in knots and many boughtes° upwound,   *coils*
Pointed with mortall sting. Of her there bred
A thousand yong ones, which she dayly fed,
Sucking upon her poisonous dugs, eachone
Of sundry shapes, yet all ill favoréd:
Soone as that uncouth° light upon them shone,   *unaccustomed*
Into her mouth they crept, and suddain all were gone.

[handwritten margin notes: Cave ↓ Plato ↓ unknown? sexual]

16

Their dam upstart, out of her den effraide,
  And rushéd forth, hurling her hideous taile
About her curséd head, whose folds displaid
Were stretcht now forth at length without entraile.°   *coiling*
She lookt about, and seeing one in mayle
Arméd to point,° sought backe to turne againe;   *completely*
For light she hated as the deadly bale,°   *injury*
Ay wont in desert darknesse to remaine,
Where plaine none might her see, nor she see any plaine.

17

Which when the valiant Elfe perceived, he lept
  As Lyon fierce upon the flying pray,
And with his trenchand° blade her boldly kept   *sharp*
From turning backe, and forcéd her to stay:
Therewith enraged she loudly gan to bray,°   *cry out*
And turning fierce, her speckled taile advaunst,
Threatning her angry sting, him to dismay:
Who nought aghast, his mightie hand enhaunst:°   *raised*
The stroke down from her head unto her shoulder glaunst.

2. On analogues to Spenser's Errour see Pheifer 1984. On occasion the serpent in Eden was depicted with a female head. Errour combines elements from classical and Christian sources: specifically, the snake goddess in Hesiod, *Theogony* 297–300, and (in Revelation 9.7–10) the locusts with men's faces, "hair as the hair of women," and tails "like unto scorpions with stings in their tails." This encounter prefigures the battle with "the dragon, that old serpent," in Canto xi.

18

Much daunted with that dint, her sence was dazd,
   Yet kindling rage, her selfe she gathered round,
   And all attonce her beastly body raizd
   With doubled forces high above the ground:
   Tho° wrapping up her wrethéd sterne arownd,   *then*
   Lept fierce upon his shield, and her huge traine°   *tail*
   All suddenly about his body wound,
   That hand or foot to stirre he strove in vaine:
God helpe the man so wrapt in Errours endlesse traine.[3]

19

His Lady sad to see his sore constraint,
   Cride out, "Now now Sir knight, shew what ye bee,
   Add faith unto your force, and be not faint:
   Strangle her, else she sure will strangle thee."
   That when he heard, in great perplexitie,
   His gall did grate[4] for griefe° and high disdaine,   *anger*
   And knitting all his force got one hand free,
   Wherewith he grypt her gorge° with so great paine,   *throat*
That soone to loose her wicked bands did her constraine.

[handwritten margin note: Strength comes from the female relation]

20

Therewith she spewd out of her filthy maw
   A floud of poyson horrible and blacke,
   Full of great lumpes of flesh and gobbets raw,
   Which stunck so vildly, that it forst him slacke
   His grasping hold, and from her turne him backe:
   Her vomit full of bookes and papers[5] was,
   With loathly frogs and toades, which eyes did lacke,
   And creeping sought way in the weedy gras:
Her filthy parbreake° all the place defiléd has.[6]   *vomit*

[handwritten margin note: Knowledge   Pope?]

21

As when old father Nilus gins to swell
   With timely° pride above the Aegyptian vale,   *seasonal*
   His fattie° waves do fertile slime outwell,   *rich*
   And overflow each plaine and lowly dale:
   But when his later spring gins to avale,°   *subside*
   Huge heapes of mudd he leaves, wherein there breed

---

3. An illustration of Spenser's "emblematic" manner, to which the Spenserian stanza is well suited: eight lines elaborate a striking image, and the Alexandrine (a six-beat line) adds a comment. Redcrosse is now, indeed, a knight errant. For Parker 1979 and Quilligan 1983 (see 80–85), the pun generates allegorical narrative.
4. I.e., his gall bladder (once considered the source of angry emotion) was violently disturbed.
5. I.e., Catholic propaganda directed against Elizabeth I and the established church; by extension, the often virulent literature of religious controversy.
6. Revelation 16.13: "I saw three unclean spirits like frogs come out of the mouth of the dragon, and out of the mouth of the beast, and out of the mouth of the false prophet." The margin of the 1560 Geneva translation identifies them as lying agents of the Pope.

hermes
↓
*Border
idea*

Ten thousand kindes of creatures,[7] partly male
And partly female of his fruitfull seed;
Such ugly monstrous shapes elswhere may no man reed.°   see

22

Coward

The same so sore annoyéd has the knight,
　That welnigh chokéd with the deadly stinke,
　His forces faile, ne can no longer fight.
　Whose corage when the feend perceived to shrinke,
　She pouréd forth out of her hellish sinke
　Her fruitfull curséd spawne of serpents small,
　Deforméd monsters, fowle, and blacke as inke,
　Which swarming all about his legs did crall,
And him encombred sore, but could not hurt at all.

23

Sun

As gentle Shepheard in sweete even-tide,
　When ruddy Phoebus gins to welke° in west,   fade, sink
　High on an hill, his flocke to vewen wide,
　Markes which do byte their hasty supper best;
　A cloud of combrous gnattes do him molest,
　All striving to infixe their feeble stings,

Collective

　That from their noyance he no where can rest,
　But with his clownish° hands their tender wings   rustic
He brusheth oft, and oft doth mar their murmurings.

24

*More
afraid
of
shame
than
danger*

Thus ill bestedd,° and fearefull more of shame,   situated
　Then of the certaine perill he stood in,
　Halfe furious unto his foe he came,
　Resolved in minde all suddenly to win,
　Or soone to lose, before he once would lin;°   cease
　And strooke at her with more then manly force,

*gives
energy*

　That from her body full of filthie sin
　He raft° her hatefull head without remorse;   cut away
A streame of cole black bloud forth gushéd from her corse.

25

Her scattred brood, soone as their Parent deare
　They saw so rudely falling to the ground,
　Groning full deadly, all with troublous feare,
　Gathred themselves about her body round,
　Weening their wonted entrance to have found
　At her wide mouth: but being there withstood
　They flockéd all about her bleeding wound,

7. Ovid, *Metamorphoses* 1.416–37, is the likely source for Spenser's comments on spontaneous generation, although numerous classical writers refer to the fertility of Nile mud, e.g., Plutarch and Diodorus Siculus.

And suckéd up their dying mothers blood,
Making her death their life, and eke her hurt their good.

Mothers
children
age

26

That detestable sight him much amazde,
  To see th'unkindly Impes[8] of heaven accurst,
  Devoure their dam; on whom while so he gazd,
  Having all satisfide their bloudy thurst,
  Their bellies swolne he saw with fulnesse burst,
  And bowels gushing forth: well worthy end
  Of such as drunke her life, the which them nurst;
  Now needeth him no lenger labour spend,
His foes have slaine themselves, with whom he should contend.

27

His Ladie seeing all, that chaunst, from farre
  Approcht in hast to greet his victorie,
  And said, "Faire knight, borne under happy starre,   *Astrology*
  Who see your vanquisht foes before you lye:
  Well worthy be you of that Armoric,°   armor
  Wherein ye have great glory wonne this day,
  And prooved your strength on a strong enimie,   *sexual*
  Your first adventure: many such I pray,
And henceforth ever wish, that like succeed it may."

28

Then mounted he upon his Steede againe,
  And with the Lady backward sought to wend;°   turn, go
  That path he kept, which beaten was most plaine,
  Ne ever would to any by-way bend,
  But still did follow one unto the end,
  The which at last out of the wood them brought.
  So forward on his way (with God to frend)°   as a friend
  He passéd forth, and new adventure sought;
Long way he travelléd, before he heard of ought.

29   *Chance*

At length they chaunst to meet upon the way
  An aged Sire, in long blacke weedes° yclad,   garments
  His feete all bare, his beard all hoarie gray,
  And by his belt his booke he hanging had;
  Sober he seemde, and very sagely sad,°   grave
  And to the ground his eyes were lowly bent,
  Simple in shew, and voyde of malice bad,
  And all the way he prayéd, as he went,
And often knockt his brest, as one that did repent.

8. Unnatural offspring.

mea culpe

30

He faire the knight saluted, louting° low,   *bowing*
  Who faire him quited,° as that courteous was: *responded in kind*
  And after askéd him, if he did know
  Of straunge adventures, which abroad did pas.
  "Ah my deare Sonne," quoth he, "how should, alas,
  Silly° old man, that lives in hidden cell,   *simple*
  Bidding° his beades all day for his trespas,   *telling*
  Tydings of warre and worldly trouble tell?   *Storytelling*
With holy father sits not with such things to mell.°   *meddle*

31

"But if of daunger which hereby doth dwell,
  And homebred evill ye desire to heare,
  Of a straunge man I can you tidings tell,
  That wasteth all this countrey farre and neare."
  "Of such," said he, "I chiefly do inquere,
  And shall you well reward to shew the place,
  In which that wicked wight his dayes doth weare:°   *spend*
  For to all knighthood it is foule disgrace,
That such a curséd creature lives so long a space."

32

"Far hence," quoth he, "in wastfull° wildernesse   *desolate*
  His dwelling is, by which no living wight
  May ever passe, but thorough great distresse."
  "Now," sayd the Lady, "draweth toward night,
  And well I wote,° that of your later° fight   *know/recent*
  Ye all forwearied be: for what so strong,
  But wanting rest will also want of might?
  The Sunne that measures heaven all day long,
At night doth baite° his steedes the Ocean waves emong.   *refresh*

33

"Then with the Sunne take Sir, your timely rest,
  And with new day new worke at once begin:
  Untroubled night they say gives counsell best."
  "Right well Sir knight ye have adviséd bin,"
  Quoth then that aged man; "the way to win
  Is wisely to advise: now day is spent;
  Therefore with me ye may take up your In°   *lodging*
  For this same night." The knight was well content:
So with that godly father to his home they went.

34

A little lowly Hermitage it was,
  Downe in a dale, hard by a forests side,

Far from resort of people, that did pas
In travell to and froe: a little wyde°   apart
There was an holy Chappell edifyde,°   built
Wherein the Hermite dewly wont° to say   was accustomed
His holy things each morne and eventyde:
Thereby a Christall streame did gently play,
Which from a sacred fountaine welléd forth alway.

35

Arrivéd there, the little house they fill,
Ne looke for entertainement, where none was:
Rest is their feast, and all things at their will;
The noblest mind the best contentment has.
With faire discourse the evening so they pas:
For that old man of pleasing wordes had store,
And well could file his tongue as smooth as glas;
He told of Saintes and Popes, and evermore
He strowd° an Ave-Mary[9] after and before.   scattered

Storyteller figure holiness of narrative

36

The drouping Night thus creepeth on them fast,
And the sad humour[1] loading their eye liddes,
As messenger of Morpheus on them cast
Sweet slombring deaw, the which to sleepe them biddes.
Unto their lodgings then his guestes he riddes°:   conducts
Where when all drownd in deadly° sleepe he findes,   deathlike
He to his study goes, and there amiddes
His Magick bookes and arts of sundry kindes,
He seekes out mighty charmes, to trouble sleepy mindes.

37

Then choosing out few wordes most horrible,
(Let none them read) thereof did verses frame,
With which and other spelles like terrible,
He bad awake blacke Plutoes griesly Dame,[2]
And curséd heaven, and spake reprochfull shame
Of highest God, the Lord of life and light;   *myths*
A bold bad man, that dared to call by name
Great Gorgon,[3] Prince of darknesse and dead night,
At which Cocytus quakes, and Styx[4] is put to flight.

9. I.e., a "Hail Mary"; it is now clear that the "beades" of stanza 30 are a rosary.
1. Heavy moisture, i.e., the dew of sleep; Morpheus is the god of sleep.
2. I.e., Proserpine.
3. I.e., Demogorgon, who "the hideous Chaos keepes" (IV.ii.47). Spenser's conception of this figure
   as a mysterious and terrible prince of darkness is probably based on passages in Boccaccio's
   mythography, *De Genealogia Deorum Gentilium* (Venice, 1472; Basel, 1532), one of two such
   works on which Spenser regularly depends; the other is Natalis Comes's *Mythologiae* . . . (Venice,
   1551).
4. Styx, Cocytus, Acheron, Phlegethon, and Lethe are the rivers of Hades. The flies in stanza 38
   suggest Beëlzebub, "Lord of the Flies."

38

And forth he cald out of deepe darknesse dred
  Legions of Sprights, the which like little flyes
  Fluttring about his ever damnéd hed,
  A-waite whereto their service he applyes.
  To aide his friends, or fray° his enimies: *frighten*
  Of those he chose out two, the falsest twoo,
  And fittest for to forge true-seeming lyes;
  The one of them he gave a message too,
The other by him selfe staide other worke to doo.

39

He making speedy way through sperséd° ayre,   *dispersed*
  And through the world of waters wide and deepe,
  To Morpheus house[5] doth hastily repaire.
  Amid the bowels of the earth full steepe,
  And low, where dawning day doth never peepe,
  His dwelling is; there Tethys[6] his wet bed
  Doth ever wash, and Cynthia[7] still doth steepe
  In silver deaw his ever-drouping hed,
Whiles sad Night over him her mantle black doth spred.

40

Whose double gates he findeth lockéd fast,
  The one faire framed of burnisht Yvory,[8]
  The other all with silver overcast;
  And wakefull dogges before them farre do lye,
  Watching to banish Care their enimy,
  Who oft is wont to trouble gentle Sleepe.
  By them the Sprite doth passe in quietly,
  And unto Morpheus comes, whom drownéd deepe
In drowsie fit he findes: of nothing he takes keepe.°   *notice*

41

And more, to lulle him in his slumber soft,
  A trickling streame from high rocke tumbling downe
  And ever-drizling raine upon the loft,
  Mixt with a murmuring winde, much like the sowne°   *sound*
  Of swarming Bees, did cast him in a swowne:°   *swoon*
  No other noyse, nor peoples troublous cryes,
  As still are wont t'annoy the walléd towne,
  Might there be heard: but carelesse Quiet lyes,
Wrapt in eternall silence farre from enemyes.

5. Spenser's primary source for this episode is *Metamorphoses* 11.592–632.
6. The wife of Ocean, in classical tradition; here the ocean.
7. Goddess of the moon.
8. Homer (*Odyssey* 19.562–67) and Virgil (*Aeneid* 6.893–96) refer to the twin portals of Sleep: truthful dreams pass through the gate of horn, false dreams through that of ivory.

42

The messenger approching to him spake,
  But his wast° wordes returnd to him in vaine: *wasted*
  So sound he slept, that nought mought him awake.
  Then rudely he him thrust, and pusht with paine,
  Whereat he gan to stretch: but he againe
  Shooke him so hard, that forcéd him to speake.
  As one then in a dreame, whose dryer braine⁹
  Is tost with troubled sights and fancies weake,
He mumbled soft, but would not all his silence breake.

43

The Sprite then gan more boldly him to wake,
  And threatned unto him the dreaded name
  Of Hecate:¹ whereat he gan to quake,
  And lifting up his lumpish° head, with blame   *heavy*
  Halfe angry askéd him, for what he came.
  "Hither," quoth he, "me Archimago² sent,   *Black angel*
  He that the stubborne Sprites can wisely tame,
  He bids thee to him send for his intent°   *purpose*
A fit false dreame, that can delude the sleepers sent."° *senses*

44

The God obayde, and calling forth straight way
  A diverse° dreame out of his prison darke,   *distracting*
  Delivered it to him, and downe did lay
  His heavie head, devoide of carefull carke,°   *concerns*
  Whose sences all were straight benumbd and starke.°   *rigid*
  He backe returning by the Yvorie dore,
  Remounted up as light as chearefull Larke,
  And on his litle winges the dreame he bore
In hast unto his Lord, where he him left afore.

45

Who all this while with charmes and hidden artes,
  Had made a Lady of that other Spright,
  And framed of liquid ayre her tender partes
  So lively,° and so like in all mens sight,   *lifelike*
  That weaker° sence it could have ravisht quight:³   *too weak*

9. I.e., too dry brain, not saturated with the dew of sleep.
1. The queen of Hades; in Comes, patroness of the black arts and goddess of dreams.
2. As this canto's "Argument" indicates, Archimago signifies hypocrisy, including what many feared was Catholics' willingness to lie about their loyalties. But his name puns on two other Reformation claims: as "arch-magus," he embodies the deluding power of magic (Protestants said Catholic beliefs about the Mass confused religion and magic), and as "arch-image" he represents, in Spenser's Protestant view, an idolatrous worship of saints and images; see, e.g., Cross 1985. The black magician in hermit's disguise is found in medieval romance, but Archimago recalls the disguised hermit in Ariosto's *Orlando Furioso* 2.12–13 and the enchanter Malagigi in Tasso's *Rinaldo* 1.31.
3. The creation of such figures by evil enchanters is a regular feature of medieval romance: Archimago's "new creature" is "borne without her dew," i.e., unnaturally. Spenser may also recall Apollo's creation (*Iliad* 5.449–50) of a phantom resembling Aeneas, or the fashioning by Juno (*Aeneid* 10.637–44) of a shadowy Aeneas, "like dreams that befool the sleeping senses."

The maker selfe for all his wondrous witt,
Was nigh beguiléd with so goodly sight:
Her all in white he clad, and over it
Cast a blacke stole, most like to seeme for Una fit.

46

Now when that ydle° dreame was to him brought,   *unsubstantial*
    Unto that Elfin knight he bad him fly,
    Where he slept soundly void of evill thought,
    And with false shewes abuse his fantasy,°   *imagination*
    In sort as he him schooléd privily:
    And that new creature borne without her dew,
    Full of the makers guile, with usage sly
    He taught to imitate that Lady trew,
Whose semblance she did carrie under feignéd hew.°   *form*

47

Thus well instructed, to their worke they hast,
    And comming where the knight in slomber lay,
    The one upon his hardy head him plast,
    And made him dreame of loves and lustfull play,
    That nigh his manly hart did melt away,
    Bathéd in wanton blis and wicked joy:
    Then seeméd him his Lady by him lay,
    And to him playnd,° how that false wingéd boy   *complained*
Her chast hart had subdewd, to learne Dame pleasures toy.

Fairies cause dreams

48

And she her selfe of beautie soveraigne Queene,
    Faire Venus seemde unto his bed to bring
    Her, whom he waking evermore did weene
    To be the chastest flowre, that ay° did spring   *ever*
    On earthly braunch, the daughter of a king,
    Now a loose Leman° to vile service bound: *paramour*
    And eke the Graces⁴ seeméd all to sing,
    Hymen iō Hymen, dauncing all around,
Whilst freshest Flora⁵ her with Yvie girlond crownd.

Mutability

49

In this great passion of unwonted° lust,   *unaccustomed*
    Or wonted feare of doing ought amis,
    He started up, as seeming to mistrust
    Some secret ill, or hidden foe of his:
    Lo there before his face his Lady is,
    Under blake stole hyding her bayted hooke,

Cryer of lust

4. The Graces are Aglaia, Thalia, and Euphrosyne, who collectively personify grace and beauty. Cf.
   VI.x.21–24.
5. Goddess of flowers and springtime. Cf. E.K.'s Glosse to "March": "the Goddesse of flowres, but
   indede (as saith Tacitus) a famous harlot, which with the abuse of her body having gotten great
   riches, made the people of Rome her heyre. . . ." Ivy is the plant of Bacchus, god of wine.

And as halfe blushing offred him to kis,
With gentle blandishment and lovely looke,
Most like that virgin true, which for her knight him took.

50

All cleane dismayd to see so uncouth° sight,   *unseemly*
And halfe enragéd at her shameless guise,
He thought have slaine her in his fierce despight:°   *indignation*
But hasty heat tempring with sufferance wise,
He stayde his hand, and gan himselfe advise
To prove his sense, and tempt her faignéd truth.
Wringing her hands in wemens pitteous wise,
Tho can° she weepe, to stirre up gentle ruth,°   *did/pity*
Both for her noble bloud, and for her tender youth.

51

And said, "Ah Sir, my liege Lord and my love,
Shall I accuse the hidden cruell fate,
And mightie causes wrought in heaven above,
Or the blind God, that doth me thus amate,°   *dismay*
For° hopéd love to winne me certaine hate?   *instead of*
Yet thus perforce he bids me do, or die.
Die is my dew: yet rew my wretched state
You,[6] whom my hard avenging destinie
Hath made judge of my life or death indifferently.

52

"Your owne deare sake forst me at first to leave
My Fathers kingdome," There she stopt with teares;
Her swollen hart her speach seemd to bereave,
And then againe begun, "My weaker yeares
Captived to fortune and frayle worldly feares,
Fly to your faith for succour and sure ayde:
Let me not dye in languor and long teares."
"Why Dame," quoth he, "what hath ye thus dismayd?
What frayes° ye, that were wont to comfort me affrayd?"   *frightens*

53

"Love of your self," she said, "and deare° constraint   *dire*
Lets me not sleepe, but wast the wearie night
In secret anguish and unpittied plaint,
Whiles you in carelesse sleepe are drownéd quight."
Her doubtfull° words made that redoubted knight   *questionable*
Suspect her truth: yet since no'untruth he knew,
Her fawning love with foule disdainefull spight

---

6. The curious aural effect of lines 6–8 is deliberate; Spenser often invites the reader to take note of the infelicitous expressions employed by evil or foolish figures: cf., for example, III.x.31, and I.iv.50. Here he also parodies Petrarchan clichés.

He would not shend,° but said, "Deare dame I rew,   *reprove*
That for my sake unknowne such griefe unto you grew.

54

"Assure your selfe, it fell not all to ground;
　For all so deare as life is to my hart,
　I deeme your love, and hold me to you bound;
　Ne let vaine feares procure your needlesse smart,
　Where cause is none, but to your rest depart."
　Not all content, yet seemd she to appease°   *cease*
　Her mournefull plaintes, beguiléd of her art,
　And fed with words, that could not chuse but please,
So slyding softly forth, she turnd as to her ease.

55

Long after lay he musing at her mood,
　Much grieved to thinke that gentle Dame so light,°   *frivolous*
　For whose defence he was to shed his blood.
　At last dull wearinesse of former fight
　Having yrockt a sleepe his irkesome spright,°   *mind, spirit*
　That troublous dreame gan freshly tosse his braine,
　With bowres, and beds, and Ladies deare delight:
　But when he⁷ saw his labour all was vaine,
With that misforméd spright he backe returnd againe.

Canto II

The guilefull great Enchaunter parts
The Redcrosse Knight from Truth:
Into whose stead faire falshood steps,
And workes him wofull ruth.°   *harm*

1

By this the Northerne wagoner had set
　His sevenfold teme behind the stedfast starre,¹
　That was in Ocean waves yet never wet,
　But firme is fixt, and sendeth light from farre
　To all, that in the wide deepe wandring arre:
　And chearefull Chaunticlere with his note shrill
　Had warnéd once, that Phoebus fiery carre²
　In hast was climbing up the Easterne hill,
Full envious that night so long his roome did fill.

---

7. I.e., the dream.
1. I.e., the constellation Boötes (the "ox-driver") has "set" the seven stars of "the Plough" (Ursa Major) behind the unmoving North Star. Since Ursa Major itself never "sets," this may mean that Arcturus, chief star in Boötes, has risen and hitched his plow to the North Star in order to start the day's work. If so, with dawn approaching, the time would be early fall, which accords with Eade 1983 (but not 1990E, "Cosmography") on a fall date for I.iii.16. Some linked Arcturus to Arthur, while as a plowman Boötes recalls George, whose name in Greek, *Georgos*, means "earth-tiller." Unlike the sleeping knight, Boötes is steadfast in plowing (cf. Luke 9.62); meanwhile, Archimago will "plow iniquity and sow wickedness" (Job 4.8).
2. The chariot of the sun. Chanticleer is the generic name for a rooster.

2

When those accurséd messengers of hell,
  That feigning dreame, and that faire-forgéd Spright
  Came to their wicked maister, and gan tell
  Their bootelesse° paines, and ill succeeding night: *useless*
  Who all in rage to see his skilfull might
  Deluded so, gan threaten hellish paine
  And sad Prosérpines wrath, them to affright.
  But when he saw his threatning was but vaine,
He cast about, and searcht his balefull° bookes againe.   *deadly*

3

Eftsoones he tooke that miscreated faire,
  And that false other Spright, on whom he spred
  A seeming body of the subtile aire,
  Like a young Squire, in loves and lusty-hed
  His wanton dayes that ever loosely led,
  Without regard of armes and dreaded fight:
  Those two he tooke, and in a secret bed,
  Covered with darknesse and misdeeming° night,   *misleading*
Them both together laid, to joy in vaine delight.

4

Forthwith he runnes with feignéd faithfull hast
  Unto his guest, who after troublous sights
  And dreames, gan now to take more sound repast,°   *repose*
  Whom suddenly he wakes with fearefull frights,
  As one aghast with feends or damnéd sprights,
  And to him cals, "Rise rise unhappy Swaine,
  That here wex° old in sleepe, whiles wicked wights   *grows*
  Have knit themselves in Venus shamefull chaine;
Come see, where your false Lady doth her honour staine."

5

All in amaze he suddenly up start
  With sword in hand, and with the old man went;
  Who soone him brought into a secret part,
  Where that false couple were full closely ment°   *joined*
  In wanton lust and lewd embracément:
  Which when he saw, he burnt with gealous fire,
  The eye of reason was with rage yblent,°   *blinded*
  And would have slaine them in his furious ire,
But hardly° was restreinéd of that aged sire.   *with difficulty*

6

Returning to his bed in torment great,
  And bitter anguish of his guiltie sight,

He could not rest, but did his stout heart eat,
And wast his inward gall with deepe despight,
Yrkesome° of life, and too long lingring night.   *tired*
At last faire Hesperus[3] in highest skie
Had spent his lampe, and brought forth dawning light,
Then up he rose, and clad him hastily;
The Dwarfe him brought his steed: so both away do fly.[4]

7

Now when the rosy-fingred Morning faire,
　　Weary of aged Tithones[5] saffron bed,
　　Had spred her purple robe through deawy aire,
　　And the high hils Titan[6] discoveréd,
　　The royall virgin shooke off drowsy-hed,
　　And rising forth out of her baser° bowre,   *humble*
　　Lookt for her knight, who far away was fled,
　　And for her Dwarfe, that wont to wait each houre;
Then gan she waile and weepe, to see that woefull stowre.°   *plight*

8

And after him she rode with so much speede
　　As her slow beast could make; but all in vaine:
　　For him so far had borne his light-foot steede,
　　Prickéd with wrath and fiery fierce disdaine,
　　That him to follow was but fruitlesse paine;
　　Yet she her weary limbes would never rest,
　　But every hill and dale, each wood and plaine
　　Did search, sore grievéd in her gentle brest,
He so ungently left her, whom she lovéd best.

9

But subtill Archimago, when his guests
　　He saw divided into double parts,
　　And Una wandring in woods and forrests,
　　Th'end of his drift,° he praisd his divelish arts,   *plot*
　　That had such might over true meaning harts;
　　Yet rests not so, but other meanes doth make,
　　How he may worke unto her further smarts:
　　For her he hated as the hissing snake,
And in her many troubles did most pleasure take.

---

3. The evening star; in this context a herald of the morning.
4. That is, Holiness is separated from Truth, through the pernicious influence of indignation and
　　lust (aggravated by false dreams). Fittingly, it is in Canto ii that the duplicitous Archimago divides
　　Una from Redcrosse and Redcrosse from his own better nature; in this he is devilish, a "diabolos"
　　with the forked tongue of slander.
5. Husband of Aurora, goddess of the dawn.
6. The sun.

10

He then devisde himselfe how to disguise;
  For by his mightie science° he could take   *knowledge*
  As many formes and shapes in seeming wise,°   *in appearance*
  As ever Proteus[7] to himselfe could make:
  Sometime a fowle, sometime a fish in lake,
  Now like a foxe, now like a dragon fell,°   *cruel*
  That of himselfe he oft for feare would quake,
  And oft would flie away. O who can tell
The hidden power of herbes, and might of Magicke spell?

11

But now seemde best, the person to put on
  Of that good knight, his late beguiléd guest:
  In mighty armes he was yclad anon,
  And silver shield: upon his coward brest
  A bloudy crosse, and on his craven crest
  A bounch of haires discolourd° diversly: *dyed*
  Full jolly knight he seemde, and well addrest,
  And when he sate upon his courser free,°   *noble*
Saint George himself ye would have deeméd him to be.

12

But he the knight, whose semblaunt° he did beare,   *likeness*
  The true Saint George was wandred far away,
  Still flying from his thoughts and gealous feare;
  Will was his guide, and griefe led him astray.
  At last him chaunst to meete upon the way
  A faithlesse Sarazin° all armed to point,   *Saracen*
  In whose great shield was writ with letters gay
  Sans foy:[8] full large of limbe and every joint
He was, and caréd not for God or man a point.

13

He had a faire companion of his way,
  A goodly Lady clad in scarlot red,[9]
  Purfled° with gold and pearle of rich assay,   *decorated*
  And like a Persian mitre on her hed
  She wore, with crownes and owches° garnishéd,   *brooches*
  The which her lavish lovers to her gave;

7. A sea god who could change himself into many shapes, including that of water and fire (cf. *Odyssey* 4.398–424). Spenser indicates the subtlety and terror of Archimago's magic; but he hints also at its ludicrous aspect.
8. "Faithlessness," or false faith. Although Redcrosse has left Una to follow his will, his "native vertue" (stanza 19) will overcome the furious brutality of Sansfoy.
9. The lady, named in stanza 44, recalls "the purple clothed woman on the seven hills" of Revelation 17.4, who "was arrayed in purple and scarlet colour, and decked with gold and precious stones and pearls, having a golden cup in her hand full of abominations and filthiness of her fornication." She represents false religion, especially what Protestants saw as the pomp and hypocrisy of Rome. D. Waters, *Duessa as Theological Satire* (Columbia, 1970), associates her with the Catholic Mass; but cf. Hume 1990E.

Her wanton palfrey all was overspred
With tinsell trappings, woven like a wave,
Whose bridle rung with golden bels and bosses° brave.   *studs*

14

With faire disport° and courting dalliaunce   *diversion*
    She intertainde her lover all the way:
    But when she saw the knight his speare advaunce,
    She soone left off her mirth and wanton play,
    And bad her knight addresse him to the fray:
    His foe was nigh at hand. He prickt with pride
    And hope to winne his Ladies heart that day,
    Forth spurréd fast: adowne his coursers side
The red bloud trickling staind the way, as he did ride.

15

The knight of the Redcrosse when him he spide,
    Spurring so hote with rage dispiteous,°   *unpitying*
    Gan fairely couch° his speare, and towards ride: *lower*
    Soone meete they both, both fell and furious,
    That daunted with their forces hideous,
    Their steeds do stagger, and amazéd stand,
    And eke themselves too rudely rigorous,
    Astonied° with the stroke of their owne hand,   *stunned*
Do backe rebut,° and each to other yeeldeth land.   *recoil*

16

As when two rams stird with ambitious pride,
    Fight for the rule of the rich fleecéd flocke,
    Their hornéd fronts so fierce on either side
    Do meete, that with the terrour of the shocke
    Astonied both, stand sencelesse as a blocke,
    Forgetfull of the hanging victory:
    So stood these twaine, unmovéd as a rocke,
    Both staring fierce, and holding idely
The broken reliques of their former cruelty.

17

The Sarazin sore daunted with the buffe
    Snatcheth his sword, and fiercely to him flies;
    Who well it wards, and quyteth° cuff with cuff: *returns*
    Each others equall puissaunce envies,
    And through their iron sides with cruell spies°   *glances*
    Does seeke to perce: repining° courage yields   *angry*
    No foote to foe. The flashing fier flies
    As from a forge out of their burning shields,
And streames of purple bloud new dies the verdant fields.

18

"Curse on that Crosse," quoth then the Sarazin,
  "That keepes thy body from the bitter fit;[1]
Dead long ygoe I wote thou haddest bin,
Had not that charme from thee forwarnéd° it: *guarded*
But yet I warne thee now assuréd sitt,
And hide thy head." Therewith upon his crest
With rigour so outrageous he smitt,
  That a large share° it hewd out of the rest,   *piece*
And glauncing downe his shield, from blame°   *harm*
  him fairely blest.°   *preserved*

19

Who thereat wondrous wroth, the sleeping spark
  Of native vertue° gan eftsoones revive,   *power*
And at his haughtie helmet making mark,
So hugely stroke, that it the steele did rive,
And cleft his head. He tumbling downe alive,
With bloudy mouth his mother earth did kis,
Greeting his grave: his grudging° ghost did strive   *complaining*
  With the fraile flesh. at last it flitted is,
Whither the soules do fly of men, that live amis.

20

The Lady when she saw her champion fall,
  Like the old ruines of a broken towre,
Staid not to waile his woefull funerall,
But from him fled away with all her powre;
Who after her as hastily gan scowre,°   *run*
Bidding the Dwarfe with him to bring away
The Sarazins shield, signe of the conqueroure.
  Her soone he overtooke, and bad to stay,
For present cause was none of dread her to dismay.

21

She turning backe with ruefull countenaunce,
  Cride, "Mercy mercy Sir vouchsafe to show
On silly° Dame, subject to hard mischaunce,   *innocent*
And to your mighty will." Her humblesse low
In so ritch weedes and seeming glorious show,
Did much emmove his stout heroicke heart,
And said, "Deare dame, your suddein overthrow
Much rueth° me; but now put feare apart,   *grieves*
And tell, both who ye be, and who that tooke your part."

1. I.e., the throes of death. Sansfoy confuses the sign with the power it signifies and thinks it a
  "charme."

22

Melting in teares, then gan she thus lament;
  "The wretched woman, whom unhappy howre
  Hath now made thrall to your commandément,
  Before that angry heavens list to lowre,°   *frown*
  And fortune false betraide me to your powre,
  Was (O what now availeth that I was!)
  Borne the sole daughter of an Emperour,
  He that the wide West under his rule has,
And high hath set his throne, where Tiberis² doth pas.

23

"He in the first flowre of my freshest age,
  Betrothéd me unto the onely haire°   *heir*
  Of a most mighty king, most rich and sage;
  Was never Prince so faithfull and so faire,
  Was never Prince so meeke and debonaire;°   *gracious*
  But ere my hopéd day of spousall shone,
  My dearest Lord fell from high honours staire,
  Into the hands of his accurséd fone,°   *foes*
And cruelly was slaine, that shall I ever mone.

24

"His blesséd body spoild of lively breath,³
  Was afterward, I know not how, convaid°   *removed*
  And fro me hid: of whose most innocent death
  When tidings came to me unhappy maid,
  O how great sorrow my sad soule assaid.°   *afflicted*
  Then forth I went his woefull corse to find,
  And many yeares throughout the world I straid,
  A virgin widow, whose deepe wounded mind
With love, long time did languish as the striken hind.

25

"At last it chauncéd this proud Sarazin
  To meete me wandring, who perforce me led
  With him away, but yet could never win
  The Fort, that Ladies hold in soveraigne dread.
  There lies he now with foule dishonour dead,
  Who whiles he livde, was calléd proud Sans foy,
  The eldest of three brethren, all three bred
  Of one bad sire, whose youngest is Sans joy,
And twixt them both was borne the bloudy bold Sans loy.⁴

2. The river Tiber, in Rome. The claim to rule "the wide West" contrasts with that of Una's parents,
   whose "scepters stretcht from East to Westerne shore" (I.i.5); Roman Catholic power is fragmentary
   in comparison with the universal Christian truth.
3. I.e., bereft of the breath of life. Duessa's emphasis on inexplicable death and loss associates Rome
   with Christ's dead body. Cf. John 20.2.
4. The three brothers allegorically indicate the degeneration of human institutions progressively
   brought on by spiritual blindness.

"In this sad plight, friendlesse, unfortunate,
  Now miserable I Fidessa dwell,
  Craving of you in pitty of my state,
  To do none° ill, if please ye not do well."   *no*
He in great passion all this while did dwell,
  More busying his quicke eyes, her face to view,
  Then his dull eares, to heare what she did tell;
  And said, "Faire Lady hart of flint would rew°   *pity*
The undeservéd woes and sorrowes, which ye shew.

27

"Henceforth in safe assuraunce may ye rest,
  Having both found a new friend you to aid,
  And lost an old foe, that did you molest:
  Better new friend then an old foe is° said."   *it is*
With chaunge of cheare the seeming simple maid
  Let fall her eyen, as shamefast to the earth,
  And yeelding soft, in that she nought gain-said,
  So forth they rode, he feining seemely merth,
And she coy° lookes: so dainty they say maketh derth.⁵ *modest*

28

Long time they thus together traveiléd,
  Till weary of their way, they came at last,
  Where grew two goodly trees, that faire did spred
  Their armes abroad, with gray mosse overcast.
And their greene leaves trembling with every blast,°   *breeze*
  Made a calme shadow far in compasse round:
  The fearefull Shepheard often there aghast
  Under them never sat, ne wont there sound
His mery oaten pipe, but shund th'unlucky ground.

29

But this good knight soone as he them can° spie,   *did*
  For the coole shade him thither hastly got:
  For golden Phoebus now ymounted hie,
  From fiery wheeles of his faire chariot
Hurléd his beame so scorching cruell hot,
  That living creature mote it not abide;
  And his new Lady it enduréd not.
  There they alight, in hope themselves to hide
From the fierce heat, and rest their weary limbs a tide.° *time*

5. A proverb: "fastidiousness brings poverty"; in this context, Duessa's manner arouses the knight's
   desire, even as her pseudonym, Fidessa ("Faith"), lulls him.

30

Faire seemely pleasaunce each to other makes,
  With goodly purposes° there as they sit: *conversation*
  And in his falséd° fancy he her takes   *deceived*
  To be the fairest wight, that livéd yit;
  Which to expresse, he bends his gentle wit,
  And thinking of those braunches greene to frame
  A girlond for her dainty forehead fit,
  He pluckt a bough; out of whose rift there came
Small drops of gory bloud, that trickled downe the same.[6]

31

Therewith a piteous yelling voyce was heard,
  Crying, "O spare with guilty hands to teare
  My tender sides in this rough rynd embard,°   *imprisoned*
  But fly, ah fly far hence away, for feare
  Least to you hap, that happened to me heare,
  And to this wretched Lady, my deare love,
  O too deare love, love bought with death too deare."
  Astond he stood, and up his haire did hove,°   *rise*
And with that suddein horror could no member move.

32

At last whenas the dreadfull passion[7]
  Was overpast, and manhood well awake,
  Yet musing at the straunge occasion,
  And doubting much his sence, he thus bespake;
  "What voyce of damnéd Ghost from Limbo[8] lake,
  Or guilefull spright wandring in empty aire,
  Both which fraile men do oftentimes mistake,°   *mislead*
  Sends to my doubtfull eares these speaches rare,
And ruefull plaints, me bidding guiltlesse bloud to spare?"

33

Then groning deepe, "Nor damnéd Ghost," quoth he,
  "Nor guilefull sprite to thee these wordes doth speake,
  But once a man Fradubio,[9] now a tree,
  Wretched man, wretched tree; whose nature weake,
  A cruell witch her curséd will to wreake,
  Hath thus transformd, and plast in open plaines,
  Where Boreas[1] doth blow full bitter bleake,

6. The ensuing episode combines elements from Virgil's account of Polydorus, transformed into a
tree that bleeds when Aeneas tears off a branch (*Aeneid* 3.27–42), and from Ariosto's description
of the exchange between Ruggiero and Astolfo, changed into a tree by the enchantress Alcina
(*Orlando Furioso* 6.26–53). See Kennedy 1973 and Scott 1986.
7. Passion of dread.
8. Abode of lost spirits. The name "Limbo lake" may come from Thomas Phaer's 1584 translation
of the *Aeneid* and need not mean a Christian Limbo.
9. "Brother Doubt."
1. The north wind.

And scorching Sunne does dry my secret vaines:
For though a tree I seeme, yet cold and heat me pains."

34

"Say on Fradubio then, or° man, or tree,"   *whether*
  Quoth then the knight, "by whose mischievous arts
  Art thou misshapéd thus, as now I see?
  He oft finds med'cine, who his griefe imparts;°   *makes known*
  But double griefs afflict concealing harts,
  As raging flames who striveth to suppresse."
  "The author then," said he, "of all my smarts,
  Is one Duessa² a false sorceresse,
That many errant° knights hath brought to wretchednesse.   *wandering*

35

"In prime of youthly yeares, when corage hot
  The fire of love and joy of chevalree
  First kindled in my brest, it was my lot
  To love this gentle Lady, whom ye see,
  Now not a Lady, but a seeming tree;
  With whom as once I rode accompanyde,
  Me chauncéd of a knight encountred bee,
  That had a like° faire Lady by his syde,   *similarly*
Like a faire Lady, but did fowle Duessa hyde.

36

"Whose forgéd beauty he did take in hand,³
  All other Dames to have exceeded farre;
  I in defence of mine did likewise stand,
  Mine, that did then shine as the Morning starre:
  So both to battell fierce arraungéd arre,
  In which his harder° fortune was to fall   *too hard*
  Under my speare: such is the dye° of warre: *hazard*
  His Lady left as a prise martiall,°   *spoil of battle*
Did yield her comely person, to be at my call.

37

"So doubly loved of Ladies unlike faire,
  Th'one seeming such, the other such indeede,
  One day in doubt I cast° for to compare,   *resolved*
  Whether° in beauties glorie did exceede;   *which one*
  A Rosy girlond was the victors meede:°   *reward*
  Both seemde to win, and both seemde won to bee,
  So hard the discord was to be agreede.
  Fraelissa° was as faire, as faire mote bee,   *Frailty*
And ever false Duessa seemde as faire as shee.

---

2. I.e., of double essence; two-faced. Appearing after Redcrosse's calamitous distrust of Una, her
name recalls how Archimago's guests are now "divided into double parts" (I.ii.9).
3. I.e., he maintained.

38

"The wicked witch now seeing all this while
  The doubtfull ballaunce equally to sway,
  What not by right, she cast to win by guile,
  And by her hellish science raisd streight way
  A foggy mist, that overcast the day,
  And a dull blast, that breathing on her face,
  Dimméd her former beauties shining ray,
  And with foule ugly forme did her disgrace:°   *disfigure*
Then was she faire alone, when none was faire in place.[4]

39

"Then cride she out, 'Fye, fye, deforméd wight,
  Whose borrowed beautie now appeareth plaine
  To have before bewitchéd all mens sight;
  O leave her soone, or let her soone be slaine.'
  Her loathly visage viewing with disdaine,
  Eftsoones I thought her such, as she me told,
  And would have kild her; but with faignéd paine,
  The false witch did my wrathfull hand withhold;
So left her, where she now is turnd to treén mould.[5]

40

"Thens forth I tooke Duessa for my Dame,
  And in the witch unweeting° joyd long time,   *unwittingly*
  Ne ever wist, but that she was the same,
  Till on a day (that day is every Prime,°   *spring*
  When Witches wont do penance for their crime)
  I chaunst to see her in her proper hew,°   *shape*
  Bathing her selfe in origane and thyme:[6]
  A filthy foule old woman I did vew,
That ever to have toucht her, I did deadly rew.

41

"Her neather partes misshapen, monstruous,
  Were hidd in water, that I could not see,
  But they did seeme more foule and hideous,
  Then womans shape man would beleeve to bee.
  Thens forth from her most beastly companie
  I gan refraine, in minde to slip away,
  Soone as appeard safe opportunitie:
  For danger great, if not assured decay°   *destruction*
I saw before mine eyes, if I were knowne to stray.

4. I.e., when none present was fair; or, perhaps, when none present was fair in place of her.
5. Form of a tree.
6. Herbs valued for their powers of healing skin disorders (such as Duessa's, described in I.viii.47).

42

"The divelish hag by chaunges of my cheare°   *countenance*
    Perceived my thought, and drownd in sleepie night,
    With wicked herbes and ointments did besmeare
    My bodie all, through charmes and magicke might,
    That all my senses were bereavéd quight:
    Then brought she me into this desert waste,
    And by my wretched lovers side me pight,°   *placed*
    Where now enclosd in wooden wals full faste,
Banisht from living wights, our wearie dayes we waste."

43

"But how long time," said then the Elfin knight,
    "Are you in this misforméd house to dwell?"
    "We may not chaunge," quoth he, "this evil plight,
    Till we be bathéd in a living well;⁷
    That is the terme prescribéd by the spell."
    "O how," said he, "mote I that well out find,
    That may restore you to your wonted well?"°   *well-being*
    "Time and suffiséd° fates to former kynd   *satisfied*
Shall us restore, none else from hence may us unbynd."

44

The false Duessa, now Fidessa hight,⁸
    Heard how in vaine Fradubio did lament,
    And knew well all was true. But the good knight
    Full of sad feare and ghastly dreriment,°   *gloom*
    When all this speech the living tree had spent,
    The bleeding bough did thrust into the ground,
    That from the bloud he might be innocent,
    And with fresh clay did close the wooden wound:
Then turning to his Lady, dead with feare her found.

45

Her seeming dead he found with feignéd feare,
    As all unweeting of that well she knew,⁹
    And paynd himselfe with busie care to reare
    Her out of carelesse° swowne. Her eylids blew   *unconscious*
    And dimméd sight with pale and deadly hew
    At last she up gan lift: with trembling cheare°   *demeanor*
    Her up he tooke, too simple and too trew,
    And oft her kist. At length all passéd feare,¹
He set her on her steede, and forward forth did beare.

---

7. I.e., the grace of God. "The water that I shall give him shall be in him a well of water springing
   up into everlasting life" (John 4.14); "And he shewed me a pure river of water of life" (Revelation
   22.1).
8. I.e., called Faith.
9. I.e., feigning ignorance of what she well knew.
1. I.e., having passed all fear.

Canto III

Forsaken Truth long seekes her love,
And makes the Lyon mylde,
Marres blind Devotions mart,° and fals   trade
In hand of leachour vylde.

1

Nought is there under heav'ns wide hollownesse,
 That moves more deare compassion of mind,
 Then beautie brought t'unworthy° wretchednesse   undeserved
 Through envies snares or fortunes freakes unkind:
 I, whether lately through her brightnesse blind,
 Or through alleageance and fast fealtie,
 Which I do owe unto all woman kind,
 Feele my heart perst° with so great agonie,   pierced
When such I see, that all for pittie I could die.

2

And now it is empassionéd so deepe,
 For fairest Unaes sake, of whom I sing,
 That my fraile eyes these lines with teares do steepe,
 To thinke how she through guilefull handeling,°   treatment
 Though true as touch,¹ though daughter of a king,
 Though faire as ever living wight was faire,
 Though nor in word nor deede ill meriting,
 Is from her knight divorcéd in despaire
And her due loves derived° to that vile witches share.   diverted

3

Yet she most faithfull Ladie all this while
 Forsaken, wofull, solitarie mayd
 Farre from all peoples prease,° as in exile,   press, gathering
 In wildernesse and wastfull deserts strayd,
 To seeke her knight; who subtilly betrayd
 Through that late vision, which th'Enchaunter wrought,
 Had her abandond. She of nought affrayd,
 Through woods and wastnesse wide him daily sought;
Yet wishéd tydings none of him unto her brought.

4

One day nigh wearie of the yrkesome way,
 From her unhastie beast she did alight,
 And on the grasse her daintie limbes did lay
 In secret shadow, farre from all mens sight:
 From her faire head her fillet° she undight,°   headband/unfastened
 And laid her stole aside. Her angels face
 As the great eye of heaven shynéd bright,

---

1. I.e., absolutely true, as the touchstone tests the quality of gold.

And made a sunshine in the shadie place;
Did never mortall eye behold such heavenly grace.

5

It fortunéd out of the thickest wood
   A ramping° Lyon rushéd suddainly,   *raging*
   Hunting full greedie after salvage° blood;   *wild*
   Soone as the royall virgin he did spy,
   With gaping mouth at her ran greedily,
   To have attonce devoured her tender corse:
   But to the pray when as he drew more ny,
   His bloudie rage asswagéd with remorse,°   *pity*
And with the sight amazd, forgat his furious forse.[2]

6

In stead thereof he kist her wearie feet,
   And lickt her lilly hands with fawning tong,
   As° he her wrongéd innocence did weet.°   *as though/know*
   O how can beautie maister the most strong,
   And simple truth subdue avenging wrong?
   Whose yeelded pride and proud submission,
   Still dreading death, when she had markéd long,
   Her hart gan melt in great compassion,
And drizling teares did shed for pure affection.

7

"The Lyon Lord of everie beast in field,"
   Quoth she, "his princely puissance doth abate,
   And mightie proud to humble weake does yield,
   Forgetfull of the hungry rage, which late
   Him prickt, in pittie of my sad estate:°   *condition*
   But he my Lyon, and my noble Lord,
   How does he find in cruell hart to hate
   Her that him loved, and ever most adord,
As the God of my life? why hath he me abhord?"

8

Redounding° teares did choke th'end of her plaint,   *overflowing*
   Which softly ecchoed from the neighbour wood;
   And sad to see her sorrowfull constraint°   *distress*
   The kingly beast upon her gazing stood;
   With pittie calmd, downe fell his angry mood.
   At last in close hart shutting up her paine,

2. While lions in *The Faerie Queene* may represent irrationality (Wrath, in I.iv.33, rides "a Lion, loth for to be led"), Una's lion recalls those in medieval romance, e.g., the lion that attends Guy of Warwick, Sir Percival's lion in Malory's *Morte d'Arthur*, and the lions that instinctively revere the virgin heroine of *Bevis of Hampton*. As primate of the beasts, Una's lion represents the force of nature's law, supporting neglected or despised truth. W. Nelson, *The Poetry of Edmund Spenser* (New York, 1963), quotes R. Hooker's "Sermon on Faith in the Elect" (1585–86): "Lions, beasts ravenous by nature, . . . have as it were religiously adored the very flesh of the faithful man" (156).

Arose the virgin borne of heavenly brood,°   *parentage*
And to her snowy Palfrey got againe,
To seeke her strayéd Champion, if she might attaine.°   *overtake*

9

The Lyon would not leave her desolate,
    But with her went along, as a strong gard
    Of her chast person, and a faithfull mate
    Of her sad troubles and misfortunes hard:
    Still° when she slept, he kept both watch and ward,   *always*
    And when she wakt, he waited diligent,
    With humble service to her will prepard:
    From her faire eyes he tooke commaundément,
And ever by her lookes conceivéd her intent.

10

Long she thus traveiléd through deserts° wyde,   *wildernesses*
    By which she thought her wandring knight shold pas,
    Yet never shew of living wight espyde;
    Till that at length she found the troden gras,
    In which the tract° of peoples footing was,   *track*
    Under the steepe foot of a mountaine hore;°   *gray*
    The same she followes, till at last she has
    A damzell spyde slow footing her before,
That on her shoulders sad° a pot of water bore.   *heavy, bent down*

11

To whom approching she to her gan call,
    To weet, if dwelling place were nigh at hand;
    But the rude° wench her answered nought at all,   *ignorant*
    She could not heare, nor speake, nor understand;
    Till seeing by her side the Lyon stand,
    With suddaine feare her pitcher downe she threw,
    And fled away: for never in that land
    Face of faire Ladie she before did vew,
And that dread Lyons looke her cast in deadly hew.[3]

12

Full fast she fled, ne ever lookt behynd,
    As if her life upon the wager lay,[4]
    And home she came, whereas her mother blynd
    Sate in eternall night: nought could she say,
    But suddaine catching hold, did her dismay
    With quaking hands, and other signes of feare:
    Who full of ghastly fright and cold affray,°   *terror*
    Gan shut the dore. By this arrivéd there
Dame Una, wearie Dame, and entrance did requere.°   *request*

3. I.e., made her turn pale as death.
4. I.e., as if her life were at stake.

13

Which when none yeelded, her unruly Page
  With his rude clawes the wicket open rent,
  And let her in; where of his cruell rage
  Nigh dead with feare, and faint astonishment,[5]
  She found them both in darkesome corner pent;
  Where that old woman day and night did pray
  Upon her beades devoutly penitent;
  Nine hundred *Pater nosters* every day,
And thrise nine hundred *Aves* she was wont to say.

14

And to augment her painefull pennance more,
  Thrise every weeke in ashes she did sit,
  And next her wrinkled skin rough sackcloth wore,
  And thrise three times did fast from any bit:°   *bite (of food)*
  But now for feare her beads she did forget.
  Whose needlesse dread for to remove away,
  Faire Una framéd words and count'nance fit:
  Which hardly° doen, at length she gan them pray,   *with difficulty*
That in their cotage small, that night she rest her may.

15

The day is spent, and commeth drowsie night,
  When every creature shrowdéd is in sleepe;
  Sad Una downe her laies in wearie plight,
  And at her feet the Lyon watch doth keepe:
  In stead of rest, she does lament, and weepe
  For the late losse of her deare lovéd knight,
  And sighes, and grones, and evermore does steepe
  Her tender brest in bitter teares all night,
All night she thinks too long, and often lookes for light.

16

Now when Aldeboran was mounted hie
  Above the shynie Cassiopeias chaire,[6]
  And all in deadly sleepe did drownéd lie,
  One knockéd at the dore, and in would fare;
  He knockéd fast, and often curst, and sware,
  That readie entrance was not at his call:
  For on his backe a heavy load he bare
  Of nightly stelths and pillage severall,°   *of various kinds*
Which he had got abroad by purchase° criminall.   *acquisition*

---

5. I.e., amazed and terrified (at the sight of the lion, Una's "Page") to the point of fainting away.
6. Aldebaran is a star in Taurus. If the time is well after midnight, the season would be autumn (see I.ii.1 and Eade 1983). Cassiopeia, Andromeda's mother, boasted of her daughter's beauty, thus offending the Nereids; the gods ordained that Andromeda should be sacrificed to a sea monster (she was saved by Perseus). When Cassiopeia stirred up trouble anew, Poseidon placed her among the stars. Cf. *Metamorphoses* 4.663–803, and Comes, *Mythologiae* 8.6.

17

He was to weete[7] a stout and sturdie thiefe,
  Wont to robbe Churches of their ornaments,
  And poore mens boxes° of their due reliefe,   *almsboxes*
  Which given was to them for good intents;
  The holy Saints of their rich vestments
  He did disrobe, when all men carelesse slept,
  And spoild the Priests of their habiliments,°   *vestments*
  Whiles none the holy things in safety kept;
Then he by cunning sleights in at the window crept.

Satire

18

And all that he by right or wrong could find,
  Unto this house he brought, and did bestow
  Upon the daughter of this woman blind,
  Abessa daughter of Corceca slow,[8]
  With whom he whoredome usd, that few did know,
  And fed her fat with feast of offerings,
  And plentie, which in all the land did grow;
  Ne spared he to give her gold and rings:
And now he to her brought part of his stolen things.

19

Thus long the dore with rage and threats he bet,°   *beat*
  Yet of those fearefull women none durst rize,
  The Lyon frayéd° them, him in to let: *frightened*
  He would no longer stay him to advize,°   *consider*
  But open breakes the dore in furious wize,
  And entring is; when that disdainfull beast
  Encountring fierce, him suddaine doth surprize,
  And seizing cruell clawes on trembling brest,
Under his Lordly foot him proudly hath supprest.

20

Him booteth not resist,[9] nor succour call,
  His bleeding hart is in the vengers° hand,   *avenger's*
  Who streight him rent in thousand peeces small,
  And quite dismembred hath: the thirstie land
  Drunke up his life; his corse left on the strand.°   *ground*
  His fearefull friends weare out the wofull night,

---

7. In fact.
8. Abessa's name (from *abesse*, "to be absent, to lack being") suggests the Augustinian view of evil as ontological deprivation. "Abessa" connotes "abbess" and hence (to Spenser) a monastic withdrawal from both pleasure and active charity. It also implies a clerical absenteeism that impoverishes the congregation (see Gless 1990E, "Abessa," and Walls 1984 on Abessa as the Old Law). Filled with superstitious dread, Corceca ("blindness of heart") recalls Ephesians 4.17–18: "Walk not as other Gentiles walk, in the vanity of their mind, Having the understanding darkened, being alienated from the life of God through the ignorance that is in them, because of the blindness of their heart." Kirkrapine ("church-robber") gives Abessa the plunder that her absence permits him to seize.
9. I.e., it is useless for him to resist.

Ne dare to weepe, nor seeme to understand
  The heavie hap,° which on them is alight,°   *lot/fallen*
Affraid, least to themselves the like mishappen might.

21

Now when broad day the world discovered° has,   *revealed*
  Up Una rose, up rose the Lyon eke,
  And on their former journey forward pas,
  In wayes unknowne, her wandring knight to seeke,
  With paines farre passing that long wandring Greeke,
  That for his love refuséd deitie;[1]
  Such were the labours of this Lady meeke,
  Still seeking him, that from her still did flie,
Then furthest from her hope, when most she weened nie.° *believed near*

22

Soone as she parted thence, the fearefull twaine,
  That blind old woman and her daughter deare
  Came forth, and finding Kirkrapine there slaine,
  For anguish great they gan to rend their heare,
  And beat their brests, and naked flesh to teare.
  And when they both had wept and wayld their fill,
  Then forth they ranne like two amazéd deare,
  Halfe mad through malice, and revenging will,[2]
To follow her, that was the causer of their ill.

23

Whom overtaking, they gan loudly bray,
  With hollow howling, and lamenting cry,
  Shamefully at her rayling all the way,
  And her accusing of dishonesty,°   *unchastity*
  That was the flowre of faith and chastity;
  And still amidst her rayling, she[3] did pray,
  That plagues, and mischiefs, and long misery
  Might fall on her, and follow all the way,
And that in endlesse error° she might ever stray.   *wandering*

24

But when she saw her prayers nought prevaile,
  She backe returnéd with some labour lost;
  And in the way as she did weepe and waile,
  A knight her met in mighty armes embost,°   *encased*
  Yet knight was not for all his bragging bost,°   *boast*
  But subtill Archimag, that Una sought
By traynes° into new troubles to have tost: *deceptive plots*

1. Odysseus, who preferred reunion with his wife, Penelope, to the immortality offered him by Calypso.
2. Desire for revenge.
3. I.e., Corceca.

Of that old woman tydings he besought,
If that of such a Ladie she could tellen ought.

25

Therewith she gan her passion to renew,
　And cry, and curse, and raile, and rend her heare,
　Saying, that harlot she too lately knew,
　That causd her shed so many a bitter teare,
　And so forth told the story of her feare:
　Much seeméd he to mone her haplesse chaunce,
　And after for that Ladie did inquere;
　Which being taught, he forward gan advaunce
His fair enchaunted steed, and eke his charméd launce.

·26

Ere long he came, where Una traveild slow,
　And that wilde Champion wayting her besyde:
　Whom seeing such, for dread he durst not show
　Himselfe too nigh at hand, but turnéd wyde°   *aside*
　Unto an hill; from whence when she him spyde,
　By his like seeming shield, her knight by name
　She weend it was,[4] and towards him gan ryde:
　Approchingnigh, she wist° it was the same,   *believed*
And with faire fearefull humblesse° towards him shee came.   *humility*

27

And weeping said, "Ah my long lackéd Lord,
　Where have ye bene thus long out of my sight?
　Much fearéd I to have been quite abhord,
　Or ought° have done, that ye displeasen might,   *aught*
　That should as death unto my deare hart light:[5]
　For since mine eye your joyous sight did mis,
　My chearefull day is turnd to chearelesse night,
　And eke my night of death the shadow is;
But welcome now my light, and shining lampe of blis."

28

He thereto meeting° said, "My dearest Dame,   *responding in kind*
　Farre be it from your thought, and fro my will,
　To thinke that knighthood I so much should shame,
　As you to leave, that have me lovéd still,
　And chose in Faery court of meere° goodwill,   *pure*
　Where noblest knights were to be found on earth:
　The earth shall sooner leave her kindly° skill   *natural*
　To bring forth fruit, and make eternall derth,
Then I leave you, my liefe,° yborne of heavenly berth.   *beloved*

4. I.e., by his shield, which seemed to be that of Redcrosse, she supposed him to be her own particular
knight.
5. I.e., that should be a deathlike blow to my sad heart.

29

"And sooth to say, why I left you so long,
  Was for to seeke adventure in strange place,
  Where Archimago said a felon strong
  To many knights did daily worke disgrace;
  But knight he now shall never more deface:°   *defame*
  Good cause of mine excuse; that mote° ye please   *may*
  Well to accept, and evermore embrace
  My faithfull service, that by land and seas
Have vowd you to defend, now then your plaint appease."

30

His lovely° words her seemd due recompence   *loving*
  Of all her passéd paines: one loving howre
  For many yeares of sorrow can dispence:°   *make amends*
  A dram of sweet is worth a pound of sowre:
  She has forgot, how many a wofull stowre°   *peril*
  For him she late endured; she speakes no more
  Of past: true is, that true love hath no powre
  To looken backe; his eyes be fixt before.
Before her stands her knight, for whom she toyld so sore.

31

Much like, as when the beaten marinere,
  That long hath wandred in the Ocean wide,
  Oft soust in swelling Tethys saltish teare,[6]
  And long time having tand his tawney hide
  With blustring breath of heaven, that none can bide,
  And scorching flames of fierce Orions hound,[7]
  Soone as the port from farre he has espide,
  His chearefull whistle merrily doth sound,
And Nereus crownes with cups;[8] his mates him pledg around.

32

Such joy made Una, when her knight she found;
  And eke th'enchaunter joyous seemd no lesse,
  Then the glad marchant, that does vew from ground
  His ship farre come from watrie wildernesse,
  He hurles out vowes, and Neptune oft doth blesse:
  So forth they past, and all the way they spent
  Discoursing of her dreadfull late distresse,
  In which he askt her, what the Lyon ment:
Who told her all that fell° in journey as she went.   *happened*

6. I.e., soaked by the ocean's waves; as in I.i.39, Tethys, properly the consort of Oceanus, is identified with the ocean.
7. Sirius, the Dog Star, ascendant in July and August.
8. I.e., the mariners offer libations to Nereus, god of the Aegean Sea.

33

They had not ridden farre, when they might see
  One pricking towards them with hastie heat,
  Full strongly armd, and on a courser free,
  That through his fiercenesse foméd all with sweat,
  And the sharpe yron° did for anger eat,   *bit*
  When his hot ryder spurd his chtrauféd° side;   *heated*
  His looke was sterne, and seeméd still to threat
  Cruell revenge, which he in hart did hyde,
And on his shield *Sans loy*[9] in bloudie lines was dyde.

34

When nigh he drew unto this gentle payre
  And saw the Red-crosse, which the knight did beare,
  He burnt in fire, and gan eftsoones prepare
  Himselfe to battell with his couchéd° speare.   *lowered*
  Loth was that other, and did faint through feare,
  To taste th'untryéd dint of deadly steele;
  But yet his Lady did so well him cheare,
  That hope of new good hap he gan to feele;
So bent° his speare, and spurnd his horse with yron heele.   *aimed*

35

But that proud Paynim° forward came so fierce,   *pagan*
  And full of wrath, that with his sharp-head speare
  Through vainely crosséd[1] shield he quite did pierce,
  And had his staggering steede not shrunke for feare,
  Through shield and bodie eke he should him beare:°   *thrust*
  Yet so great was the puissance of his push,
  That from his saddle quite he did him beare:
  He tombling rudely downe to ground did rush,
And from his goréd wound a well of bloud did gush.

36

Dismounting lightly from his loftie steed,
  He to him lept, in mind to reave° his life,   *take away*
  And proudly said, "Lo there the worthie meed
  Of him, that slew Sansfoy with bloudie knife;
  Henceforth his ghost freed from repining° strife,   *fretful*
  In peace may passen over Lethe lake,[2]
  When mourning altars purgd° with enemies life,   *cleansed*
  The blacke infernall Furies[3] doen aslake°:   *appease*
Life from Sansfoy thou tookst, Sansloy shall from thee take."

9. "Lawlessness"; this figure represents anarchical and even demonic opposition to all forms of man-made, natural, and divine law.
1. I.e., without the power inherent in the faith that Redcrosse's shield symbolizes (see note to I.ii.18).
2. Underworld river of forgetfulness.
3. Spirits of revenge and discord; E.K., glossing "November," calls them "authours of all evill and mischiefe."

37

Therewith in haste his helmet gan unlace,
  Till Una cride, "O hold that heavie hand,
  Deare Sir, what ever that thou be in place:[4]
  Enough is, that thy foe doth vanquisht stand
  Now at thy mercy: Mercie not withstand:°   *deny*
  For he is one the truest knight[5] alive,
  Though conquered now he lie on lowly land,
  And whilest him fortune favour, faire did thrive
In bloudie field: therefore of life him not deprive."

38

Her piteous words might not abate his rage,
  But rudely rending up his helmet, would
  Have slaine him straight: but when he sees his age,
  And hoarie head of Archimago old,
  His hastie hand he doth amazéd hold,
  And halfe ashaméd, wondred at the sight:
  For that old man well knew he, though untold,
  In charmes and magicke to have wondrous might,
Ne ever wont in field, ne in round lists° to fight.   *enclosures for jousting*

39

And said, "Why Archimago, lucklesse syre,
  What doe I see? what hard mishap is this,
  That hath thee hither brought to taste mine yre?
  Or thine the fault, or mine the error is,
  In stead of foe to wound my friend amis?"
  He answered nought, but in a traunce still lay,
  And on those guilefull dazéd eyes of his
  The cloud of death did sit. Which doen away,[6]
He left him lying so, ne would no lenger stay.

40

But to the virgin comes, who all this while
  Amaséd stands, her selfe so mockt° to see   *deceived*
  By him, who has the guerdon° of his guile,   *reward*
  For so misfeigning° her true knight to bee: *falsely pretending*
  Yet is she now in more perplexitie,
  Left in the hand of that same Paynim bold,
  From whom her booteth° not at all to flie;   *avails*
  Who by her cleanly garment catching hold,
Her from her Palfrey pluckt, her visage to behold.

4. I.e., whoever you are.
5. I.e., the one truest knight.
6. I.e., when he had recovered from the swoon.

41

But her fierce servant full of kingly awe
　And high disdaine, whenas his soveraine Dame
　So rudely handled by her foe he sawe,
　With gaping jawes full greedy at him came,
　And ramping on his shield, did weene the same
　Have reft away with his sharpe rending clawes:
　But he was stout, and lust did now inflame
　His corage more, that from his griping pawes
He hath his shield redeemed,° and foorth his swerd he drawes.　　*recovered*

42

O then too weake and feeble was the forse
　Of salvage beast, his puissance to withstand:
　For he was strong, and of so mightie corse,°　　　*body*
　As ever wielded speare in warlike hand,
　And feates of armes did wisely° understand.　　　*skilfully*
　Eftsoones he percéd through his chauféd chest
　With thrilling° point of deadly yron brand,°　　*searching/sword*
　And launcht° his Lordly hart: with death opprest　　*pierced*
He roared aloud, whiles life forsooke his stubborne brest.[7]

43

Who now is left to keepe the forlorne maid
　From raging spoile of lawlesse victors will?
　Her faithfull gard removed, her hope dismaid,
　Her selfe a yeelded pray to save or spill.°　　　*destroy*
　He now Lord of the field, his pride to fill,
　With foule reproches, and disdainfull spight
　Her vildly entertaines,° and will or nill,　　　*deals with*
　Beares her away upon his courser light:
Her prayers nought prevaile, his rage is more of might.

44

And all the way, with great lamenting paine,
　And piteous plaints she filleth his dull° eares,　　　*deaf*
　That stony hart could riven have in twaine,
　And all the way she wets with flowing teares:
　But he enraged with rancor, nothing heares.
　Her servile beast yet would not leave her so,
　But followes her farre off, ne ought he feares,
　To be partaker of her wandring woe,
More mild in beastly kind,° then that her beastly foe.　　　*nature*

7. The force of nature's law is not itself sufficient to resist lawlessness in human society.

Canto IV

To sinfull house of Pride, Duessa
guides the faithfull knight,
Where brothers death to wreak° Sansjoy   avenge
doth chalenge him to fight.

Contrasts w/
Canto 10
Pride Vs.
holiness.

1

Young knight, what ever that dost armes professe,
  And through long labours huntest after fame,
  Beware of fraud, beware of ficklenesse,
  In choice, and change of thy deare lovéd Dame,
  Least thou of her beleeve too lightly blame,
  And rash misweening° doe thy hart remove: misunderstanding
  For unto knight there is no greater shame,
  Then lightnesse and inconstancie in love;
That doth this Redcrosse knights ensample plainly prove.

2

Who after that he had faire Una lorne,°   left
  Through light misdeeming° of her loialtie,   misjudging
  And false Duessa in her sted had borne,
  Calléd Fidess', and so supposd to bee;
  Long with her traveild, till at last they see
  A goodly building, bravely garnishéd,°   adorned
  The house of mightie Prince it seemd to bee:
  And towards it a broad high way that led,
All bare through peoples feet, which thither traveiléd.[1]

3

Great troupes of people traveild thitherward
  Both day and night, of each degree and place,°   rank
  But few returnéd, having scapéd hard,°   with difficulty
  With balefull beggerie, or foule disgrace,
  Which ever after in most wretched case,
  Like loathsome lazars,° by the hedges lay.   lepers
  Thither Duessa bad him bend his pace:
  For she is wearie of the toilesome way,
And also nigh consuméd is the lingring day.

4

A stately Pallace built of squaréd bricke,
  Which cunningly was without morter laid,
  Whose wals were high, but nothing strong, nor thick,
  And golden foile all over them displaid,
  That purest skye with brightnesse they dismaid:
  High lifted up were many loftie towres,
  And goodly galleries farre over laid°   placed above

1. Cf. Matthew 7.13: "For wide is the gate, and broad is the way, that leadeth to destruction, and many there be which go in thereat."

Full of faire windowes, and delightfull bowres;
And on the top a Diall told the timely° howres.[2]   *measured*

5

It was a goodly heape° for to behould,   *building*
  And spake the praises of the workmans wit;°   *skill*
  But full great pittie, that so faire a mould°   *structure*
  Did on so weake foundation ever sit:
  For on a sandie hill, that still did flit,°   *give way*
  And fall away, it mounted was full hie,
  That every breath of heaven shakéd it:
  And all the hinder parts, that few could spie,
Were ruinous and old, but painted cunningly.[3]

6

Arrivéd there they passéd in forth right;
  For still to all the gates stood open wide,
  Yet charge of them was to a Porter hight°   *committed*
  Cald Malvenu,[4] who entrance none denide:
  Thence to the hall, which was on every side
  With rich array and costly arras dight:°   *decked*
  Infinite sorts of people did abide
  There waiting long, to win the wishéd sight
Of her, that was the Lady of that Pallace bright.

7

By them they passe, all gazing on them round.[5]
  And to the Presence° mount; whose glorious vew   *reception chamber*
  Their frayle amazéd senses did confound:
  In living Princes court none ever knew
  Such endlesse richesse, and so sumptuous shew;
  Ne Persia selfe, the nourse of pompous pride
  Like ever saw. And there a noble crew
  Of Lordes and Ladies stood on every side,
Which with their presence faire, the place much beautifide.

2. Medieval and Renaissance allegorists enjoyed imagining evil and good courts or cities (influenced by Augustine's *City of God*). Lucifera's house, particularly its gold-covered wall, recalls Alcina's residence in *Orlando Furioso* 6.59. Cullen 1974 calls it the World, part of the "infernal triad"— World, Flesh, and Devil—that Christians vow at baptism to defy. The clock indicates Time's power over the edifice and its inhabitants, i.e., over the fallen world. An evil parody of Gloriana's Cleopolis and God's New Jerusalem, Lucifera's court opposes the House of Holiness (I.x).
3. The stanza may owe something to Chaucer's House of Fame, founded on ice ("a feble fundament/To bilden on a place hye," 3.1132–33); but the primary reference is to Matthew 7.26–27: "every one that heareth these sayings of mine, and doeth them not, shall be likened unto a foolish man, which built his house upon the sand: And the rain descended, and the floods came, and the winds blew, and beat upon that house: and it fell: and great was the fall of it."
4. The allegorized court-of-love tradition influences Spenser's account of the House of Pride and of the contrasting House of Holiness. Malvenu's name, the opposite of *bienvenu* (welcome) and of *Bel-accueil*, a name often given to the porter in court-of-love allegories, suggests the inhospitality and lovelessness of the House of Pride, where self-love reigns.
5. I.e., the crowd around gazing on them.

8

High above all a cloth of State was spred,
  And a rich throne, as bright as sunny day,
  On which there sate most brave embellishéd
  With royall robes and gorgeous array,
  A mayden Queene, that shone as Titans ray,[6]
  In glistring gold, and peerelesse pretious stone:
  Yet her bright blazing beautie did assay°   *attempt*
  To dim the brightnesse of her glorious throne,
As envying her selfe, that too exceeding shone.

9

Exceeding shone, like Phoebus fairest child,[7]
  That did presume his fathers firie wayne,°   *chariot*
  And flaming mouthes of steedes unwonted° wilde   *unusually*
  Through highest heaven with weaker° hand to rayne; *too weak*
  Proud of such glory and advancement vaine,
  While flashing beames do daze his feeble eyen,
  He leaves the welkin° way most beaten plaine,   *heavenly*
  And rapt° with whirling wheeles, inflames the skyen, *carried away*
With fire not made to burne, but fairely for to shyne.

10

So proud she shynéd in her Princely state,
  Looking to heaven; for earth she did disdayne,
  And sitting high; for lowly° she did hate: *lowliness*
  Lo underneath her scornefull feete, was layne
  A dreadfull Dragon with an hideous trayne,°   *tail*
  And in her hand she held a mirrhour bright,
  Wherein her face she often vewéd fayne,
  And in her selfe-loved semblance tooke delight;
For she was wondrous faire, as any living wight.[8]

11

Of griesly Pluto she the daughter was,
  And sad Proserpina the Queene of hell;
  Yet did she thinke her pearelesse worth to pas
  That parentage, with pride so did she swell,
  And thundring Jove, that high in heaven doth dwell,
  And wield the world, she clayméd for her syre,
  Or if that any else did Jove excell:
  For to the highest she did still aspyre,
Or if ought higher were then that, did it desyre.

6. "Titans ray" refers to the sun's brightness (as is usual in Spenser's work), but it here recalls the Titans' wars, born of rebellious pride, against the rule of the Olympian gods (cf. Hesiod, *Theogony* 617–735).
7. Phaëthon, whose reckless driving of his father's chariot threatened to set the world afire; Jove killed him with lightning (*Metamorphoses* 2.1–400).
8. Like many Renaissance images of pride, in literature and the visual arts, Lucifera holds a mirror, a sign of her vain and worldly nature.

12

And proud Lucifera[9] men did her call,
  That made her selfe a Queene, and crownd to be,
  Yet rightfull kingdome she had none at all,
  Ne heritage of native soveraintie,
  But did usurpe with wrong and tyrannie
  Upon the scepter, which she now did hold:
  Ne ruld her Realmes with lawes, but pollicie,°   *political cunning*
  And strong advizement of six wisards old,
That with their counsels bad her kingdome did uphold.

13

Soone as the Elfin knight in presence came,
  And false Duessa seeming Lady faire,
  A gentle Husher,° Vanitie by name   *usher*
  Made rowme, and passage for them did prepaire:
  So goodly brought them to the lowest staire
  Of her high throne, where they on humble knee
  Making obeyssance, did the cause declare,
  Why they were come, her royall state to see,
To prove° the wide report of her great Majestee.   *confirm*

14

With loftie eyes, halfe loth to looke so low,
  She thankéd them in her disdainefull wise,
  Ne other grace vouchsaféd them to show
  Of Princesse worthy, scarse them bad arise.
  Her Lordes and Ladies all this while devise°   *make ready*
  Themselves to setten forth to straungers sight:
  Some frounce° their curléd haire in courtly guise,   *arrange*
  Some prancke° their ruffes, and others trimly dight   *display*
Their gay attire: each others greater pride does spight.

15

Goodly they all that knight do entertaine,
  Right glad with him to have increast their crew:
  But to Duess' each one himselfe did paine
  All kindnesse and faire courtesie to shew;
  For in that court whylome° her well they knew: *formerly*
  Yet the stout Faerie mongst the middest° crowd   *thickest*
  Thought all their glorie vaine in knightly vew,
  And that great Princesse too exceeding prowd,
That to strange knight no better countenance allowd.[1]

9. Lucifera's name links her with Lucifer (i.e., "light-bearer," recalling his original brightness in Heaven); she rules her usurped realm by "pollicie" and magic rather than by statesmanship allied with true religion. She is presumably the opposite of that other "mayden Queene," Elizabeth, but some suspect that Spenser's satire does not quite exempt his monarch and her court.
1. I.e., while Redcrosse is not taken in by the vanity of Lucifera and her court, he is himself in some degrée vain.

16

Suddein upriseth from her stately place
  The royall Dame, and for her coche doth call:
  All hurtlen° forth, and she with Princely pace,   *rush*
  As faire Aurora in her purple pall,°   *cloak*
Out of the East the dawning day doth call:
  So forth she comes: her brightnesse brode° doth blaze;   *abroad*
  The heapes of people thronging in the hall,
  Do ride each other, upon her to gaze:
Her glorious glitterand° light doth all mens eyes amaze.   *glittering*

17

So forth she comes, and to her coche does clyme,
  Adornéd all with gold, and girlonds gay,
  That seemd as fresh as Flora in her prime,
  And strove to match, in royall rich array,
  Great Junoes golden chaire, the which they say
  The Gods stand gazing on, when she does ride
  To Joves high house through heavens bras-paved way
  Drawne of faire Pecocks, that excell in pride,
And full of Argus eyes their tailes dispredden wide.[2]

18

But this was drawne of six unequall beasts,[3]
  On which her six sage Counsellours did ryde,
  Taught to obay their bestiall beheasts,
  With like conditions to their kinds° applyde: *natures*
  Of which the first, that all the rest did guyde,
  Was sluggish Idlenesse the nourse of sin;
  Upon a slouthfull Asse he chose to ryde,
  Arayd in habit blacke, and amis° thin,   *hood*
Like to an holy Monck, the service to begin.

19

And in his hand his Portesse° still he bare,   *breviary*
  That much was worne, but therein little red,
  For of devotion he had little care,
  Still drownd in sleepe, and most of his dayes ded;
  Scarse could he once uphold his heavie hed,
  To looken, whether it were night or day:
  May seeme the wayne was very evill led,
  When such an one had guiding of the way,
That knew not, whether right he went, or else astray.

2. Ovid (*Metamorphoses* 1.590–726) tells how Juno set the hundred eyes of Argus, killed by Mercury at Jove's command, in her peacock's tail; peacocks symbolize pride.
3. The counselors ride in pairs, on mounts suited to each rider; but the beasts themselves are ill-matched and incongruous, as their differing gaits emphasize. Pictures of the Seven Deadly Sins were common, and it is unlikely that Spenser used a single source; he may have taken details from John Gower's *Mirour de l'Omme* (c. 1380) and from the text and woodcuts of Stephen Bateman's *Cristall Glasse* (1569).

20

From worldly cares himselfe he did esloyne,°   *withdraw*
    And greatly shunnéd manly exercise,
    From every worke he chalengéd essoyne,[4]
    For contemplation sake: yet otherwise,
    His life he led in lawlesse riotise;
    By which he grew to grievous malady;
    For in his lustlesse° limbs through evill guise°   *feeble/living*
    A shaking fever raignd continually:
Such one was Idlenesse, first of this company.

21

And by his side rode loathsome Gluttony,
    Deforméd creature, on a filthie swyne,
    His belly was up-blowne with luxury,
    And eke with fatnesse swollen were his eyne,
    And like a Crane his necke was long and fyne,°   *scrawny*
    With which he swallowd up excessive feast,
    For want whereof poore people oft did pyne;°   *waste away*
    And all the way, most like a brutish beast,
He spuéd up his gorge,[5] that all did him deteast.

22

In greene vine leaves he was right fitly clad;[6]
    For other clothes he could not weare for heat,
    And on his head an yvie girland had,
    From under which fast trickled downe the sweat:
    Still as he rode, he somewhat° still did eat,   *something*
    And in his hand did beare a bouzing can,[7]
    Of which he supt so oft, that on his seat
    His dronken corse he scarse upholden can,
In shape and life more like a monster, than a man.

23

Unfit he was for any worldly thing,
    And eke unhable once° to stirre or go°   *at all/walk*
    Not meet to be of counsell to a king,
    Whose mind in meat and drinke was drownéd so.
    That from his friend he seldome knew his fo:
    Full of diseases was his carcas blew,°   *livid*
    And a dry dropsie[8] through his flesh did flow:
    Which by misdiet daily greater grew:
Such one was Gluttony, the second of that crew.

4. Pleaded exemption.
5. I.e., he vomited up what he had swallowed.
6. The portrait of Gluttony recalls that of Silenus in *Metamorphoses* 4.26–27, 11.90–93, and perhaps also in Virgil, *Eclogue VI*; both poets emphasize the senile grossness of one lost in the anarchy or stupor of drink.
7. Drinking cup.
8. I.e., a thirst-producing dropsy.

24

And next to° him rode lustfull Lechery,   *Lechery*   *after*
  Upon a bearded Goat, whose rugged haire,
  And whally° eyes (the signe of gelosy,)   *wall-eyed, staring*
  Was like the person selfe, whom he did beare:
Who rough, and blacke, and filthy did appeare,
  Unseemely man to please faire Ladies eye;
Yet he of Ladies oft was lovéd deare,
  When fairer faces were bid standen by:°   *away*
O who does know the bent of womens fantasy?

25

In a greene gowne he clothéd was full faire,
  Which underneath did hide his filthinesse,
  And in his hand a burning hart he bare,
  Full of vaine follies, and new fanglenesse:
For he was false, and fraught° with ficklenesse,   *filled*
  And learnéd had to love with secret lookes,
And well could daunce, and sing with ruefulnesse,
  And fortunes tell, and read in loving bookes,[9]
And thousand other wayes, to bait his fleshly hookes.

26

Inconstant man, that lovéd all he saw,
  And lusted after all, that he did love,
  Ne would his looser life be tide to law,
  But joyd weake wemens hearts to tempt and prove
If from their loyall loves he might them move;
  Which lewdnesse fild him with reprochful paine
Of that fowle evill,[1] which all men reprove,
  That rots the marrow, and consumes the braine:
Such one was Lecherie, the third of all this traine.

27

And greedy <u>Avari</u>ce by him did ride,   *Avarice*
  Upon a Camell loaden all with gold;
  Two iron coffers hong on either side,
  With precious mettall full, as they might hold,
And in his lap an heape of coine he told;°   *counted*
  For of his wicked pelfe° his God he made,   *wealth*
And unto hell him selfe for money sold;
  Accuséd usurie was all his trade,
And right and wrong ylike in equall ballaunce waide.[2]

9. I.e., manuals on the art of love (e.g., Ovid's *Ars Amatoria*); or, perhaps, erotic books like Aretino's
   I Modi.
1. I.e., syphilis.
2. I.e., made no distinction between right and wrong.

28

His life was nigh unto deaths doore yplast,
    And thred-bare cote, and cobled shoes he ware,
    Ne scarse good morsell all his life did tast,
    But both from backe and belly still did spare,
    To fill his bags, and richesse to compare;°   *acquire*
    Yet chylde ne kinsman living had he none
    To leave them to; but thorough daily care
    To get, and nightly feare to lose his owne,
He led a wretched life unto him selfe unknowne.°   *solitary*

29

Most wretched wight, whom nothing might suffise,
    Whose greedy lust° did lacke in greatest store,   *desire*
    Whose need had end, but no end covetise,°   *covetousness*
    Whose wealth was want, whose plenty made him pore,
    Who had enough, yet wishéd ever more;
    A vile disease, and eke in foote and hand
    A grievous gout tormented him full sore,
    That well he could not touch, nor go, nor stand:
Such one was Avarice, the fourth of this faire band.

30

And next to him malicious Envie rode,
    Upon a ravenous wolfe, and still did chaw
    Betweene his cankred° teeth a venemous tode,[3]   *infected*
    That all the poison ran about his chaw;°   *jaw*
    But inwardly he chawéd his owne maw°   *entrails*
    At neighbours wealth, that made him ever sad;
    For death it was, when any good he saw,
    And wept, that cause of weeping none he had,
But when he heard of harme, he wexéd wondrous glad.

31

All in a kirtle of discolourd say[4]
    He clothéd was, ypainted full of eyes;
    And in his bosome secretly there lay
    An hatefull Snake, the which his taile uptyes°   *coils*
    In many folds, and mortall sting implyes.°   *enfolds*
    Still as he rode, he gnasht his teeth, to see
    Those heapes of gold with griple° Covetyse,   *greedy*
    And grudgéd at the great felicitie
Of proud Lucifera, and his owne companie.

---

3. In Ovid, *Metamorphoses* 2.768–69, Envy eats "snakes, proper food of her venom."
4. In a multicolored woolen outer garment.

32

He hated all good workes and vertuous deeds,
　　And him no lesse, that any like did use,°   *practice*
　　And who with gracious bread the hungry feeds,[5]
　　His almes for want of faith he doth accuse;
　　So every good to bad he doth abuse:°   *pervert*
　　And eke the verse of famous Poets witt
　　He does backebite, and spightfull poison spues
　　From leprous mouth on all, that ever writt:
Such one vile Envie was, that fifte in row did sitt.[6]

33

And him beside rides fierce revenging Wrath,
　　Upon a Lion, loth for to be led;
　　And in his hand a burning brond° he hath,   *sword*
　　The which he brandisheth about his hed;
　　His eyes did hurle forth sparkles fiery red,
　　And staréd sterne on all, that him beheld,
　　As ashes pale of hew and seeming ded;
　　And on his dagger still his hand he held,
Trembling through hasty rage, when choler° in him sweld.   *anger*

34

His ruffin° raiment all was staind with blood,   *disarranged*
　　Which he had spilt, and all to rags yrent,°   *torn*
　　Through unadvizéd rashnesse woxen wood;°   *mad*
　　For of his hands he had no governement,°   *control*
　　Ne cared for[7] bloud in his avengément:
　　But when the furious fit was overpast,
　　His cruell facts° he often would repent;   *deeds*
　　Yet wilfull man he never would forecast,
How many mischieves should ensue his heedlesse hast.

35

Full many mischiefes follow cruell Wrath;
　　Abhorréd bloudshed, and tumultuous strife,
　　Unmanly° murder, and unthrifty scath,°   *inhuman/harm*
　　Bitter despight, with rancours rusty knife,
　　And fretting griefe the enemy of life;
　　All these, and many evils moe° haunt ire,   *more*
　　The swelling Splene,° and Frenzy raging rife,   *malice*
　　The shaking Palsey, and Saint Fraunces fire:[8]
Such one was Wrath, the last of this ungodly tire.°   *procession*

---

5. I.e., graciously feeds the hungry with bread.
6. Here merely one of Pride's attendants, Envy elsewhere in Spenser's work is a threatening and
   insidious figure, the enemy of true poets. In VI.i.8, the "Blatant Beast" is said to have been sent
   "Into this wicked world . . . To be the plague and scourge of wretched men: / Whom with vile
   tongue and venemous intent / He sore doth wound, and bite, and cruelly torment."
7. I.e., shrank from.
8. Erysipelas, a skin inflammation.

36

And after all, upon the wagon beame
  Rode Sathan, with a smarting whip in hand,
  With which he forward lasht the laesie teme,
  So oft as Slowth still in the mire did stand.
  Huge routs° of people did about them band,   *crowds*
  Showting for joy, and still before their way
  A foggy mist had covered all the land;
  And underneath their feet, all scattered lay
Dead sculs and bones of men, whose life had gone astray.

37

So forth they marchen in this goodly sort,
  To take the solace° of the open aire,   *pleasure*
  And in fresh flowring fields themselves to sport;
  Emongst the rest rode that false Lady faire,
  The fowle Duessa, next unto the chaire
  Of proud Lucifera, as one of the traine:
  But that good knight would not so nigh repaire.°   *approach*
  Him selfe estraunging from their joyaunce vaine,
Whose fellowship seemd far unfit for warlike swaine.

38

So having solacéd themselves a space
  With pleasaunce of the breathing° fields yfed,   *fragrant*
  They backe returnéd to the Princely Place;
  Whereas an errant knight in armes ycled,°   *clad*
  And heathnish shield, wherein with letters red
  Was writ *Sans joy*, they new arrivéd find:
  Enflamed with fury and fiers hardy-hed,°   *audacity*
  He seemd in hart to harbour thoughts unkind,
And nourish bloudy vengeaunce in his bitter mind.[9]

39

Who when the shaméd shield of slaine Sans foy
  He spide with that same Faery champions page,
  Bewraying° him, that did of late destroy   *revealing*
  His eldest brother, burning all with rage
  He to him leapt, and that same envious gage[1]
  Of victors glory from him snatcht away:
  But th'Elfin knight, which ought that warlike wage,[2]
  Disdaind to loose the meed he wonne in fray,
And him rencountring° fierce, reskewd the noble pray.   *engaging in battle*

9. Redcrosse, separated from Una, can resist the "joyaunce vaine" of Lucifera's court, but he is not
   proof against "joylessness," a condition akin to despair; perhaps seeing how sin governs this world
   has plunged the knight into further sadness.
1. Envied pledge.
2. I.e., who owned that shield.

40

Therewith they gan to hurtlen° greedily,   *rush together*
  Redoubted battaile ready to darrayne,°   *prepare*
  And clash their shields, and shake their swords on hy,
  That with their sturre they troubled all the traine;
  Till that great Queene upon eternall paine
  Of high displeasure, that ensewen might,
  Commaunded them their fury to refraine,
  And if that either to that shield had right,
In equall lists they should the morrow next it fight.

41

"Ah dearest Dame," quoth then the Paynim bold,
  "Pardon the errour of enragéd wight,
  Whom great griefe made forget the raines to hold
  Of reasons rule, to see this recreant knight,
  No knight, but treachour full of false despight
  And shamefull treason, who through guile hath slayn
  The prowest° knight, that ever field did fight,   *bravest*
  Even stout Sans foy (O who can then refrayn?)
Whose shield he beares renverst,° the more to heape disdayn.   *reversed*

42

"And to augment the glorie of his guile,
  His dearest love the faire Fidessa loe
  Is there possесséd of the traytour vile,
  Who reapes the harvest sowen by his foe,
  Sowen in bloudy field, and bought with woe:
  That brothers hand shall dearcly well requight
  So be, O Queene, you equall° favour showe."   *impartial*
  Him litle answerd th'angry Elfin knight;
He never meant with words, but swords to plead his right.

43

But threw his gauntlet as a sacred pledge,
  His cause in combat the next day to try:
  So been they parted both, with harts on edge,
  To be avenged each on his enimy.
  That night they pas in joy and jollity,
  Feasting and courting both in bowre and hall;
  For Steward was excessive Gluttonie,
  That of his plenty pouréd forth to all:
Which doen,° the Chamberlain Slowth did to rest them call.   *done*

44

Now whenas darkesome night had all displayd
  Her coleblacke curtein over brightest skye,
  The warlike youthes on dayntie couches layd,

Did chace away sweet sleepe from sluggish eye,
To muse on meanes of hopéd victory.
But whenas Morpheus had with leaden mace
Arrested all that courtly company,
Up-rose Duessa from her resting place,
And to the Paynims lodging comes with silent pace.

45

Whom broad awake she finds, in troublous fit,°   mood
Forecasting, how his foe he might annoy,
And him amoves° with speaches seeming fit: arouses
"Ah deare Sans joy, next dearest to Sans foy,
Cause of my new griefe, cause of my new joy,
Joyous, to see his ymage in mine eye,
And greeved, to thinke how foe did him destroy,
That was the flowre of grace and chevalrye;
Lo his Fidessa to thy secret faith I flye."

46

With gentle wordes he can° her fairely greet,   did
And bad say on the secret of her hart.
Then sighing soft, "I learne that litle sweet
Oft tempred is," quoth she, "with muchell° smart: much
For since my brest was launcht° with lovely dart   pierced
Of deare Sansfoy, I never joyéd howre,
But in eternall woes my weaker° hart   too weak
Have wasted, loving him with all my powre,
And for his sake have felt full many an heavie stowre.°   grief

47

"At last when perils all I weenéd past,
And hoped to reape the crop of all my care,
Into new woes unweeting I was cast,
By this false faytor,° who unworthy ware   impostor
His worthy shield, whom he with guilefull snare
Entrappéd slew, and brought to shamefull grave.
Me silly° maid away with him he bare,   innocent
And ever since hath kept in darksome cave,
For that° I would not yeeld, that° to Sans foy I gave.   because/what

48

"But since faire Sunne hath sperst° that lowring clowd,   dispersed
And to my loathéd life now shewes some light,
Under your beames I will me safely shrowd,
From dreaded storme of his disdainfull spight:
To you th'inheritance belongs by right
Of brothers prayse, to you eke longs° his love.   belongs
Let not his love, let not his restlesse spright

Be unrevenged, that calles to you above
From wandring Stygian shores,[3] where it doth endlesse move."

49

Thereto said he, "Faire Dame be nought dismaid
  For sorrowes past; their griefe is with them gone:
  Ne yet of present perill be affraid;
  For needlesse feare did never vantage° none,   *aid*
  And helplesse° hap it booteth not to mone.   *unavoidable*
  Dead is Sans foy, his vitall paines are past,
  Though greevéd ghost for vengeance deepe do grone:
  He lives, that shall him pay his dewties° last,   *rites*
And guiltie Elfin bloud shall sacrifice in hast."

50

"O but I feare the fickle freakes,"° quoth shee,   *whims*
  "Of fortune false, and oddes of armes in field."
  "Why dame," quoth he, "what oddes can ever bee,
  Where both do fight alike, to win or yield?"
  "Yea but," quoth she, "he beares a charméd shield,
  And eke enchaunted armes, that none can perce,
  Ne none can wound the man, that does them wield."
  "Charmd or enchaunted," answerd he then terce,°   *fiercely*
"I no whit reck, ne you the like need to reherce.°   *recount*

51

"But faire Fidessa, sithens° fortuncs guile,   *since*
  Or enimies powre hath now captivéd you,
  Returne from whence ye came, and rest a while
  Till morrow next, that I the Elfe subdew,
  And with Sans foyes dead dowry you endew."[4]
  "Ay me, that is a double death," she said,
  "With proud foes sight my sorrow to renew:
  Where ever yet I be, my secrete aid
Shall follow you." So passing forth she him obaid.

Canto V

*The faithfull knight in equall field
subdewes his faithlesse foe,
Whom false Duessa saves, and for
his cure to hell does goe.*

1

The noble hart, that harbours vertuous thought,
  And is with child of glorious great intent,
  Can never rest, untill it forth have brought

---

3. The banks of the river Styx, in the underworld.
4. I.e., endow you with the dowry of the dead Sansfoy.

Th'eternall brood of glorie excellent:[1]
Such restlesse passion did all night torment
The flaming corage of that Faery knight,
Devizing, how that doughtie turnament
With greatest honour he atchieven might;
Still did he wake, and still did watch for dawning light.

2

At last the golden Orientall gate
  Of greatest heaven gan to open faire,
And Phoebus fresh, as bridegrome to his mate,
  Came dauncing forth, shaking his deawie haire:
  And hurld his glistring beames through gloomy aire.
Which when the wakeful Elfe perceived, streight way
  He started up, and did him selfe prepaire,
  In sun-bright armes, and battailous° array: warlike
For with that Pagan proud he combat will that day.

3

And forth he comes into the commune hall,
  Where earely waite him many a gazing eye,
To weet° what end to straunger knights may fall.   learn
  There many Minstrales maken melody,
  To drive away the dull melancholy,
And many Bardes, that to the trembling chord
  Can tune their timely° voyces cunningly,   measured
  And many Chroniclers, that can record
Old loves, and warres for Ladies doen by many a Lord.[2]

4

Soone after comes the cruell Sarazin,
  In woven maile all arméd warily,
And sternly lookes at him, who not a pin
  Does care for looke of living creatures eye.
  They bring them wines of Greece and Araby,
And daintie spices fetcht from furthest Ynd,
  To kindle heat of corage privily:°   inwardly
  And in the wine a solemne oth they bynd
T'observe the sacred lawes of armes, that are assynd.[3]

5

At last forth comes that far renowméd Queene,
  With royall pomp and Princely majestie;

1. The view that virtue must be expressed in action is a mark of much Renaissance thought, from Castiglione's *Il Cortegiano* to Milton's *Areopagitica*. Spenser's figure of speech recalls Plato's *Symposium* 206c.
2. Spenser does not distinguish among minstrels, bards, and chroniclers: in the prose *Vewe of the Present State of Irelande*, Irenius speaks of "Bardes or Irishe Cronicles" (1205).
3. The setting and preliminaries to battle accord with precedent in medieval romance: proceedings traditionally began with an oath to observe the laws of arms. Cf. Shakespeare's *Richard II* 1.3.7–10.

She is ybrought unto a paléd° greene,   *fenced*
And placéd under stately canapee,°   *canopy*
The warlike feates of both those knights to see.
On th'other side in all mens open vew
Duessa placéd is, and on a tree
Sans-foy his shield is hangd with bloudy hew:
Both those the lawrell girlonds to the victor dew.

6

A shrilling trompet sownded from on hye,
    And unto battaill bad them selves addresse:
    Their shining shieldes about their wrestes° they tye,   *wrists*
    And burning blades about their heads do blesse,°   *brandish*
    The instruments of wrath and heavinesse:
    With greedy force each other doth assayle,
    And strike so fiercely, that they do impresse
    Deepe dinted furrowes in the battred mayle;
The yron walles to ward their blowes are weake and fraile.

7

The Sarazin was stout, and wondrous strong,
    And heapéd blowes like yron hammers great:
    For after bloud and vengeance he did long.
    The knight was fiers, and full of youthly heat:
    And doubled strokes, like dreaded thunders threat:
    For all for prayse and honour he did fight.
    Both stricken strike, and beaten both do beat,
    That from their shields forth flyeth firie light,
And helmets hewen deepe, shew marks of eithers might.

8

So th'one for wrong, the other strives for right:
    As when a Gryfon[4] seizéd° of his pray,   *in possession*
    A Dragon fiers encountreth in his flight,
    Through widest ayre making his ydle way,
    That would his rightfull ravine° rend away: *booty*
    With hideous horrour both together smight,
    And souce° so sore, that they the heavens affray: *strike*
    The wise Southsayer seeing so sad° sight,   *ominous*
Th'amazéd vulgar tels of warres and mortall fight.

9

So th'one for wrong, the other strives for right,
    And each to deadly shame would drive his foe:
    The cruell steele so greedily doth bight

4. The griffon, referred to by Herodotus (*Histories* 3.116) as guarding deposits of gold in the northern
   parts of Europe, is a monster combining the body of a lion with the head and wings of an eagle;
   "but a griffoun" (as Sir John Mandeville wrote in the fourteenth century) hath a body greater than
   viii Lyons," and is stronger than one hundred eagles (*Travels*, ed. J. Bramont [London, 1928]
   195).

In tender flesh, that streames of bloud down flow,
  With which the armes, that earst° so bright did show,   *at first*
  Into a pure vermillion now are dyde:
  Great ruth in all the gazers harts did grow,
  Seeing the goréd woundes to gape so wyde,
That victory they dare not wish to either side.

10

At last the Paynim chaunst to cast his eye,
  His suddein° eye, flaming with wrathfull fyre,   *darting*
  Upon his brothers shield, which hong thereby:
  Therewith redoubled was his raging yre,
  And said, "Ah wretched sonne of wofull syre,
  Doest thou sit wayling by black Stygian lake,
  Whilest here thy shield is hangd for victors hyre,°   *reward*
  And sluggish german° doest thy forces slake,°   *brother/abate*
To after-send his foe, that him may overtake?[5]

11

"Goe caytive° Elfe, him quickly overtake,   *base*
  And soone redeeme from his long wandring woe;
  Goe guiltie ghost, to him my message make,
  That I his shield have quit° from dying foe."   *taken back*
  Therewith upon his crest he stroke him so,
  That twise he reeléd, readie twise to fall;
  End of the doubtfull battell deeméd tho°   *then*
  The lookers on, and lowd to him gan call
The false Duessa, "Thine the shield, and I, and all."

12

Soone as the Faerie heard his Ladie speake,
  Out of his swowning dreame he gan awake,
  And quickning° faith, that earst was woxen weake,   *vitalizing*
  The creeping deadly cold away did shake:
  Tho moved with wrath, and shame, and Ladies sake,
  Of all attonce he cast° avengd to bee,   *resolved*
  And with so'exceeding furie at him strake,
  That forcéd him to stoupe upon his knee;
Had he not stoupéd so, he should have cloven bee.

13

And to him said, "Goe now proud Miscreant,
  Thy selfe thy message doe° to german deare,   *give*
  Alone he wandring thee too long doth want:
  Goe say, his foe thy shield with his doth beare."
  Therewith his heavie hand he high gan reare,

---

5. Sansjoy's reaction recalls that of Aeneas, who, momentarily inclined to spare the defeated Turnus, is once again roused to fury by the sight of the dead Pallas's sword belt on the shoulder of Turnus (*Aeneid* 12.941–49).

Him to have slaine; when loe a darkesome clowd
Upon him fell: he no where doth appeare,
But vanisht is. The Elfe him cals alowd,
But answer none receives: the darknes him does shrowd.[6]

14

In haste Duessa from her place arose,
  And to him running said, "O prowest° knight,   *bravest*
  That ever Ladie to her love did chose,
  Let now abate the terror of your might,
  And quench the flame of furious despight,
  And bloudie vengeance; lo th'infernall powres
  Covering your foe with cloud of deadly night,
  Have borne him thence to Plutoes balefull bowres.
The conquest yours, I yours, the shield, and glory yours."

15

Not all so satisfide, with greedie eye
  He sought all round about, his thirstie blade
  To bath in bloud of faithlesse enemy;
  Who all that while lay hid in secret shade:
  He standes amazéd, how he thence should fade.
  At last the trumpets Triumph sound on hie,
  And running Heralds humble homage made,
  Greeting him goodly with new victorie,
And to him brought the shield, the cause of enmitie.

16

Wherewith he goeth to that soveraine Queene,
  And falling her before on lowly knee,
  To her makes present of his service seene:°   *proven*
  Which she accepts, with thankes, and goodly gree,°   *favor*
  Greatly advauncing° his gay chevalree.   *praising*
  So marcheth home, and by her takes the knight,
  Whom all the people follow with great glee,
  Shouting, and clapping all their hands on hight,
That all the aire it fils, and flyes to heaven bright.

17

Home is he brought, and laid in sumptuous bed:
  Where many skilfull leaches° him abide,°   *surgeons/attend*
  To salve his hurts, that yet still freshly bled.
  In wine and oyle they wash his woundés wide,
  And softly can embalme° on every side.   *anoint*
  And all the while, most heavenly melody
  About the bed sweet musicke did divide,°   *descant*

6. Spenser might have found in Virgil (or Homer) similar measures taken by a god to protect a favorite
(cf. *Aeneid* 5.810–12; *Iliad* 3.380); more probably the episode is based on Armida's protection of
Rambaldo from the wrath of Tancred, in Tasso, *Gerusalemme Liberata* 7.44–45.

Him to beguile of griefe and agony:
And all the while Duessa wept full bitterly.

18

As when a wearie traveller that strayes
  By muddy shore of broad seven-mouthéd Nile,
  Unweeting of the perillous wandring wayes,
  Doth meet a cruell craftie Crocodile,
  Which in false griefe hyding his harmefull guile,
  Doth weepe full sore, and sheddeth tender teares:
  The foolish man, that pitties all this while
  His mournefull plight, is swallowed up unwares,
Forgetfull of his owne, that mindes anothers cares.[7]

19

So wept Duessa untill eventide,
  That° shyning lampes in Joves high house were light: *when*
  Then forth she rose, ne lenger would abide,
  But comes unto the place, where th'Hethen knight
  In slombring swownd° nigh voyd of vitall spright,   *swoon*
  Lay covered with inchaunted cloud all day:
  Whom when she found, as she him left in plight,
  To wayle his woefull case she would not stay,
But to the easterne coast of heaven makes speedy way.

20

Where griesly Night,[8] with visage deadly sad,
  That Phoebus chearefull face durst never vew,
  And in a foule blacke pitchie mantle clad,
  She findes forth comming from her darkesome mew,°   *cavern*
  Where she all day did hide her hated hew.
  Before the dore her yron charet stood,
  Alreadie harnesséd for journey new;
  And coleblacke steedes yborne of hellish brood,
That on their rustie bits did champ, as they were wood.°   *mad*

21

Who when she saw Duessa sunny bright,
  Adornd with gold and jewels shining cleare,
  She greatly grew amazéd at the sight,
  And th'unacquainted° light began to feare: *unfamiliar*
  For never did such brightnesse there appeare,
  And would have backe retyréd to her cave,

7. A twelfth-century Latin bestiary observes that "hypocritical, dissolute and avaricious people have the same nature as [the crocodile]—also any people who are puffed up with the vice of pride, dirtied with the corruption of luxury, or haunted with the disease of avarice—even if they do make a show of falling in with the justifications of the Law, pretending in the sight of men to be upright and indeed very saintly" (*The Bestiary: A Book of Beasts*, T. H. White, trans. and ed. [New York, 1960] 50).
8. For Night's origin, "age," and appearance, Spenser depends largely on Comes, *Mythologiae* 3.12.

Untill the witches speech she gan to heare,
　Saying, "Yet O thou dreaded Dame, I crave
Abide, till I have told the message, which I have."

22

She stayd, and foorth Duessa gan proceede,
　"O thou most auncient Grandmother of all,
　More old than Jove, whom thou at first didst breede,
　Or that great house of Gods caelestiall,
　Which wast begot in Daemogorgons hall,[9]
　And sawst the secrets of the world unmade,
　Why suffredst thou thy Nephewes° deare to fall　　　　　　*grandsons*
　With Elfin sword, most shamefully betrade?
Lo where the stout Sansjoy doth sleepe in deadly shade.

23

"And him before, I saw with bitter eyes
　The bold Sansfoy shrinke underneath his speare;
　And now the pray of fowles in field he lyes,
　Nor wayld of friends, nor laid on groning beare,[1]
　That whylome was to me too dearely deare.
　O what of Gods then boots it to be borne,
　If old Aveugles sonnes so evill heare?[2]
　Or who shall not great Nightés children scorne,
When two of three her Nephews are so fowle forlorne?

24

"Up then, up dreary Dame, of darknesse Queene,
　Go gather up the reliques of thy race,
　Or else goe them avenge, and let be seene,
　That dreaded Night in brightest day hath place,
　And can the children of faire light deface.°"　　　　　　*destroy*
　Her feeling speeches some compassion moved
　In hart, and chaunge in that great mothers face:
　Yet pittie in her hart was never proved°　　　　　　　　*felt*
Till then: for evermore she hated, never loved.

25

And said, "Deare daughter rightly may I rew
　The fall of famous children borne of mee,
　And good successes, which their foes ensew:°　　　　　　*attend*
　But who can turne the streame of destinee,
　Or breake the chayne of strong necessitee,

9. I.e., in Chaos.
1. I.e., on the bier attended by mourners.
2. I.e., if Aveugle's sons are so evilly treated. Aveugle ("blindness" or "darkness") is the son of Night.

Which fast is tyde to Joves eternall seat?[3]
  The sonnes of Day he favoureth, I see,
  And by my ruines thinkes to make them great:
To make one great by others losse, is bad excheat.°   *gain*

26

"Yet shall they not escape so freely all;
  For some shall pay the price of others guilt:
  And he the man that made Sansfoy to fall,
  Shall with his owne bloud price° that he hath spilt.   *pay for*
  But what art thou, that telst of Nephews kilt?"
  "I that do seeme not I, Duessa am,"
  Quoth she, "how ever now in garments gilt,
  And gorgeous gold arayd I to thee came;
Duessa I, the daughter of Deceipt and Shame."

27

Then bowing downe her agéd backe, she kist
  The wicked witch, saying; "In that faire face
  The false resemblance of Deceipt, I wist°   *knew*
  Did closely lurke; yet so true-seeming grace
  It carried, that I scarse in darkesome place
  Could it discerne, though I the mother bee
  Of falshood, and root of Duessaes race.
  O welcome child, whom I have longd to see,
And now have seene unwares. Lo now I go with thee."

28

Then to her yron wagon she betakes,
  And with her beares the fowle welfavourd° witch: *attractive*
  Through mirkesome° aire her readie way she makes.   *murky, obscure*
  Her twyfold° Teme, of which two blacke as pitch,   *twofold*
  And two were browne, yet each to each unlich,°   *unlike*
  Did softly swim away, ne ever stampe,
  Unlesse she chaunst their stubborne mouths to twitch;
  Then foming tarre,° their bridles they would champe,   *black froth*
And trampling the fine element,[4] would fiercely rampe.

29

So well they sped, that they be come at length
  Unto the place, whereas the Paynim lay,
  Devoid of outward sense, and native strength,
  Coverd with charméd cloud from vew of day,
  And sight of men, since his late luckelesse fray.

---

3. Homer's is the first reference to the "golden rope" of Zeus, suspended from heaven, to which gods, mortals, and the entire universe are attached (*Iliad* 8.18–27). Elsewhere Spenser employs the image to signify the harmony that informs the universe and links the actions of the virtuous (I.ix.1), or, in an opposite sense, to represent the struggle for position and power (II.vii.46–47). Night's language hints at her misconception of cosmic design.
4. I.e., the air.

His cruell wounds with cruddy° bloud congealed,   *clotted*
  They binden up so wisely, as they may,
  And handle softly, till they can be healed:
So lay him in her charet, close in night concealed.

30

And all the while she stood upon the ground,
  The wakefull dogs did never cease to bay,
  As giving warning of th'unwonted sound,
  With which her yron wheeles did them affray,
  And her darke griesly looke them much dismay;
  The messenger of death, the ghastly Owle
  With drearie shriekes did also her bewray;°   *reveal*
  And hungry Wolves continually did howle,
At her abhorréd face, so filthy and so fowle.

31

Thence turning backe in silence soft they stole,
  And brought the heavie corse with easie pace
  To yawning gulfe of deepe Avernus hole.[5]
  By that same hole an entrance darke and bace
  With smoake and sulphure hiding all the place,
  Descends to hell: there creature never past,
  That backe returnéd without heavenly grace;
  But dreadfull Furies, which their chaines have brast,°   *broken apart*
And damnéd sprights sent forth to make ill° men aghast.   *evil*

32

By that same way the direfull dames doe drive
  Their mournefull charet, fild with rusty blood,
  And downe to Plutoes house are come bilive:°   *quickly*
  Which passing through, on every side them stood
  The trembling ghosts with sad amazéd mood,
  Chattring their yron teeth, and staring wide
  With stonie eyes; and all the hellish brood
  Of feends infernall flockt on every side,
To gaze on earthly wight, that with the Night durst ride.

33

They pas the bitter waves of Acheron,[6]
  Where many soules sit wailing woefully,
  And come to fiery flood of Phlegeton,
  Whereas the damnéd ghosts in torments fry,
  And with sharpe shrilling shriekes doe bootlesse cry,
  Cursing high Jove, the which them thither sent.

[handwritten marginalia: descent into hell / Classical & Christian / meld.]

5. A lake near Naples, traditionally an entrance to hell (cf. *Aeneid* 6.200, 239–40). Stanzas 31–35
   owe much to Virgil's account of Aeneas's descent into Hades: even the assertion that "heavenly
   grace" alone assures return from hell has a counterpart in *Aeneid* 6.129–31.
6. Acheron ("stream of woe") and Phlegethon ("flaming") are rivers in Hades.

The house of endlesse paine is built thereby,
In which ten thousand sorts of punishment
The curséd creatures doe eternally torment.

34

Before the threshold dreadfull Cerberus[7]
 His three deforméd heads did lay along,°   *at full length*
 Curléd with thousand adders venemous,
 And lilléd° forth his bloudie flaming tong: *lolled*
 At them he gan to reare his bristles strong,
 And felly gnarre,[8] untill dayes enemy
 Did him appease; then downe his taile he hong
 And suffered them to passen quietly:
For she in hell and heaven had power equally.

35

There was Ixion turnéd on a wheele,
 For daring tempt the Queene of heaven to sin;
 And Sisyphus an huge round stone did reele°   *roll*
 Against an hill, ne might from labour lin;°   *cease*
 There thirstie Tantalus hong by the chin;
 And Tityus fed a vulture on his maw;
 Typhoeus joynts were stretchéd on a gin,°   *rack*
 Theseus condemned to endlesse slouth by law,
And fifty sisters water in leake° vessels draw.[9]   *leaky*

36

They all beholding worldly wights in place,°   *there*
 Leave off their worke, unmindfull of their smart,
 To gaze on them; who forth by them doe pace,
 Till they be come unto the furthest part:
 Where was a Cave ywrought by wondrous art,
 Deepe, darke, uneasie, dolefull, comfortlesse,
 In which sad Aesculapius farre a part
 Emprisond was in chaines remedilesse,
For that Hippolytus rent corse he did redresse.[1]

37

Hippolytus a jolly huntsman was,
 That wont in charet chace the foming Bore;
 He all his Peeres in beautie did surpas,
 But Ladies love as losse of time forbore:

7. The three-headed hound that guards the entrance to hell.
8. I.e., fiercely snarl.
9. Ixion tried to seduce Hera; Sisyphus was notorious for deceit; Tantalus both fed his son to the gods and betrayed their secrets (cf. II.vii.59); Tityus tried to rape Leto; the giant Typhoeus rebelled against the gods; the fifty daughters of Danaus, forced to marry their cousins, killed their husbands on the wedding night. For these figures, Spenser used Comes; for Theseus, cf. *Aeneid* 6.617–18.
1. Aesculapius, the son of Apollo, was god of medical arts. For the story of Hippolytus, Theseus's son, Spenser draws on *Metamorphoses* 15.497–550, and on *Aeneid* 7.765–69; but his primary authority is Boccaccio, *De Genealogia Deorum* 10.50.

His wanton stepdame[2] lovéd him the more,
But when she saw her offred sweets refused
Her love she turnd to hate, and him before
His father fierce of treason false accused,
And with her gealous termes his open° eares abused.   *receptive*

38

Who all in rage his Sea-god syre[3] besought,
  Some curséd vengeance on his sonne to cast:
From surging gulf two monsters straight were brought,
  With dread whereof his chasing steedes aghast,
  Both charet swift and huntsman overcast.
  His goodly corps on ragged cliffs yrent,
  Was quite dismembred, and his members chast
Scattered on every mountaine, as he went,
That of Hippolytus was left no moniment.°   *trace of identity*

39

His cruell stepdame seeing what was donne,
  Her wicked dayes with wretched knife did end,
  In death avowing th'innocence of her sonne.
Which hearing, his rash Syre, began to rend
  His haire, and hastie tongue, that did offend:
  Tho gathering up the relicks of his smart[4]
  By Dianes meanes, who was Hippolyts frend,
  Them brought to Aesculape, that by his art
Did heale them all againe, and joynéd every part.

40

Such wondrous science° in mans wit to raine   *skill*
  When Jove avizd,° that could the dead revive,   *perceived*
  And fates expiréd[5] could renew againe,
  Of endlesse life he might him not deprive,
  But unto hell did thrust him downe alive,
  With flashing thunderbolt ywounded sore:
  Where long remaining, he did alwaies strive
  Himselfe with salves to health for to restore,
And slake the heavenly fire, that ragéd evermore.

41

There auncient Night arriving, did alight
  From her nigh wearie waine, and in her armes
  To Aesculapius brought the wounded knight:
  Whom having softly disarayd of armes,
  Tho gan to him discover° all his harmes,   *reveal*

2. Phaedra.
3. Neptune.
4. I.e., the remains of Hippolytus.
5. I.e., the completed term of life, allotted by fate.

Beseeching him with prayer, and with praise,
   If either salves, or oyles, or herbes, or charmes
   A fordonne° wight from dore of death mote raise,   *undone*
He would at her request prolong her nephews daies.

42

"Ah Dame," quoth he, "thou temptest me in vaine,
   To dare the thing, which daily yet I rew,
   And the old cause of my continued paine
   With like attempt to like end to renew.
   Is not enough, that thrust from heaven dew°   *fitting*
   Here endlesse penance for one fault I pay,
   But that redoubled crime with vengeance new
   Thou biddest me to eeke°? Can Night defray°   *augment/appease*
The wrath of thundring Jove, that rules both night and day?"

43

"Not so," quoth she, "but sith that heavens king
   From hope of heaven hath thee excluded quight,
   Why fearest thou, that canst not hope for thing,
   And fearest not, that more thee hurten might,
   Now in the powre of everlasting Night?
   Goe to then, O thou farre renowméd sonne
   Of great Apollo, shew thy famous might
   In medicine, that else° hath to thee wonne   *already*
Great paines, and greater praise, both never to be donne."°   *ended*

44

Her words prevaild: And then the learnéd leach°   *doctor*
   His cunning hand gan to his wounds to lay,
   And all things else, the which his art did teach:
   Which having seene, from thence arose away
   The mother of dread darknesse, and let stay
   Aveugles sonne there in the leaches cure,
   And backe returning tooke her wonted way,
   To runne her timely° race, whilst Phoebus pure   *measured*
In westerne waves his wearie wagon did recure.°   *refresh*

45

The false Duessa leaving noyous° Night,   *harmful*
   Returnd to stately pallace of dame Pride;
   Where when she came, she found the Faery knight
   Departed thence, albe° his woundés wide   *although*
   Not throughly heald, unreadie were to ride.
   Good cause he had to hasten thence away;
   For on a day his wary Dwarfe had spide,
   Where in a dongeon deepe huge numbers lay
Of caytive° wretched thrals,° that wayléd night and day.   *confined/slaves*

46

A ruefull sight, as could be seene with eie;
  Of whom he learnéd had in secret wise
  The hidden cause of their captivitie,
  How mortgaging their lives to Covetise,
  Through wastfull Pride, and wanton Riotise,
  They were by law of that proud Tyrannesse
  Provokt with Wrath, and Envies false surmise,
  Condemnéd to that Dongeon mercilesse,
Where they should live in woe, and die in wretchednesse.[6]

47

There was that great proud king of Babylon,[7]
  That would compell all nations to adore,
  And him as onely God to call upon,
  Till through celestiall doome° throwne out of dore,   *judgment*
  Into an Oxe he was transformed of yore:
  There also was king Croesus,[8] that enhaunst°   *exalted*
  His heart too high through his great riches store;
  And proud Antiochus,[9] the which advaunst°   *lifted*
His curséd hand gainst God, and on his altars daunst.

48

And them long time before, great Nimrod[1] was,
  That first the world with sword and fire warrayd;°   *made war on*
  And after him old Ninus[2] farre did pas°   *surpass*
  In princely pompe, of all the world obayd;
  There also was that mightie Monarch[3] layd
  Low under all, yet above all in pride,
  That name of native° syre did fowle upbrayd,   *natural*
  And would as Ammons sonne be magnifide,
Till scornd of God and man a shamefull death he dide.

49

All these together in one heape were throwne,
  Like carkases of beasts in butchers stall.
  And in another corner wide were strowne
  The antique ruines of the Romaines fall:

6. Many "wretched thrals" named in stanzas 47–50 appear in Chaucer's "Monk's Tale," itself modeled on Boccaccio's account of the fall of famous men, *De Casibus Illustrium Virorum*; those condemned by Lucifera's law, though, fall because of pride or some other sin.
7. Nebuchadnezzar (cf. Daniel 3–4).
8. A fabulously wealthy king of Lydia, in the sixth century B.C. See Herodotus, *Histories* 1.26–30.
9. Antiochus IV, king of Syria (second century B.C.), who tried to extirpate Judaism; see 1 Maccabees 1.20–24.
1. "A mighty hunter before the Lord" (Genesis 10.9) associated with the Tower of Babel, symbol of boundless human pride.
2. Founder of Nineveh, "an exceeding great city"; its circumference was "a three days' journey" (Jonah 3.3).
3. Alexander the Great, who, after his visit to the Libyan temple of Jupiter Ammon in 331 B.C., was worshipped in some places as Jupiter's son. Arrian's *Life of Alexander* (7.25–27) says he died after a drinking bout.

Great Romulus the Grandsyre of them all,
Proud Tarquin, and too lordly Lentulus,
Stout Scipio, and stubborne Hanniball,
Ambitious Sylla, and sterne Marius,
High Caesar, great Pompey, and fierce Antonius.[4]

50

Amongst these mighty men were wemen mixt,
  Proud wemen, vaine, forgetfull of their yoke:
  The bold Semiramis,[5] whose sides transfixt
  With sonnes owne blade, her fowle reproches spoke;
  Faire Sthenoboea,[6] that her selfe did choke
  With wilfull cord, for wanting° of her will;   *lacking*
  High minded Cleopatra, that with stroke
  Of Aspés sting her selfe did stoutly° kill: *boldly*
And thousands moe the like, that did that dongeon fill.

51

Besides the endlesse routs of wretched thralles,
  Which thither were assembled day by day,
  From all the world after their wofull falles,
  Through wicked pride, and wasted wealthes decay.
  But most of all, which in that Dongeon lay
  Fell from high Princes courts, or Ladies bowres,
  Where they in idle pompe, or wanton play,
  Consuméd had their goods, and thriftlesse howres,
And lastly throwne themselves into these heavy stowres.°   *violent ends*

52

Whose case whenas the carefull Dwarfe had tould,
  And made ensample of their mournefull sight
  Unto his maister, he no lenger would
  There dwell in perill of like painefull plight,
  But early rose, and ere that dawning light
  Discovered had the world to heaven wyde,
  He by a privie Posterne° tooke his flight,   *rear gate*
  That of no envious eyes he mote be spyde:
For doubtlesse death ensewd, if any him descryde.

53

Scarse could he footing find in that fowle way,
  For many corses, like a great Lay-stall°   *heap of trash*
  Of murdred men which therein strowéd lay,
  Without remorse,° or decent funerall: *pity*
  Which all through that great Princesse pride did fall
  And came to shamefull end. And them beside

4. On these leaders see Plutarch's *Lives of the Noble Grecians and Romans.*
5. The wife of Ninus.
6. The wife of Proetus, a king of Argos; her love for the younger Bellerophon led to her death.

Forth ryding underneath the castell wall,
A donghill of dead carkases he spide,
The dreadfull spectacle° of that sad house of Pride.   *sign, example*

Canto VI

From lawlesse lust by wondrous grace
fayre Una is releast:
Whom salvage nation does adore,
and learnes her wise beheast.°   *bidding*

1

As when a ship, that flyes faire under saile,
  An hidden rocke escapéd hath unwares,
  That lay in waite her wrack for to bewaile,[1]
  The Marriner yet halfe amazéd stares
  At perill past, and yet in doubt ne dares
  To joy at his foole-happie° oversight: *lucky*
  So doubly is distrest twixt joy and cares
  The dreadlesse courage of this Elfin knight,
Having escapt so sad ensamples in his sight.

2

Yet sad he was that his too hastie speed
  The faire Duess had forst him leave behind;
  And yet more sad, that Una his deare dreed°   *revered one*
  Her truth had staind with treason so unkind;°   *unnatural*
  Yet crime in her could never creature find,
  But for his love, and for her owne selfe sake,
  She wandred had° from one to other Ynd,°   *would have/Indies*
  Him for to seeke, ne ever would forsake,
Till her unwares the fierce Sansloy did overtake.

3

Who after Archimagoes fowle defeat,
  Led her away into a forrest wilde,
  And turning wrathfull fire to lustfull heat,
  With beastly sin thought her to have defilde,
  And made the vassall of his pleasures vilde.°   *vile*
  Yet first he cast by treatie,° and by traynes,°   *entreaty/trickery*
  Her to perswade, that stubborne fort to yilde:
  For greater conquest of hard love he gaynes,
That workes it to his will, then he that it constraines.

4

With fawning wordes he courted her a while,
  And looking lovely,° and oft sighing sore,   *lovingly*
  Her constant hart did tempt with diverse guile:

1. I.e., to cause her wrack (?). "Bewaile" may be an error: see the Textual Notes.

But wordes, and lookes, and sighes she did abhore,
As rocke of Diamond stedfast evermore.
Yet for to feed his fyrie lustfull eye,
He snatcht the vele, that hong her face before;
Then gan her beautie shine, as brightest skye,
And burnt his beastly hart t'efforce° her chastitye.   *violate*

5

So when he saw his flatt'ring arts to fayle,
    And subtile engines bet from batteree,[2]
    With greedy force he gan the fort assayle,
    Whereof he weend possesséd soone to bee,
    And win rich spoile of ransackt chastetee.
    Ah heavens, that do this hideous act behold,
    And heavenly virgin thus outragéd see,
    How can ye vengeance just so long withhold,
And hurle not flashing flames upon that Paynim bold?

6

The pitteous maiden carefull° comfortlesse,   *full of care*
    Does throw out thrilling shriekes, and shrieking cryes,
    The last vaine helpe of womens great distresse,
    And with loud plaints importuneth the skyes,
    That molten starres do drop like weeping eyes;
    And Phoebus flying so most shamefull sight,
    His blushing face in foggy cloud implyes,°   *enfolds*
    And hides for shame. What wit of mortall wight
Can now devise to quit a thrall[3] from such a plight?

7

Eternall providence exceeding° thought,   *transcending*
    Where none appeares can make her selfe a way:
    A wondrous way it for this Lady wrought,
    From Lyons clawes to pluck the gripéd pray.
    Her shrill outcryes and shriekes so loud did bray,
    That all the woodes and forestes did resownd;
    A troupe of Faunes and Satyres far away
    Within the wood were dauncing in a rownd,
Whiles old Sylvanus slept in shady arber sownd.[4]

2. I.e., his courtly wiles repulsed.
3. Free a slave.
4. The "woodgods" of classical mythology, half human and half goat, engage in "rurall meriment"
    appropriate to rustic England; "Faunes or Sylvanes," according to E.K.'s Glosse to "July," "be of
    Poetes feigned to be Gods of the Woode." "Old Sylvanus," Roman god of fields and forests, loved
    Pomona, goddess of fruit trees. Combining ignorant idolatry with an instinct for natural goodness,
    these figures represent a pre-Christian, or "natural," religion that some in Spenser's day viewed
    with sympathetic interest (D. P. Walker, *The Ancient Theology* [London, 1972]). That their
    appearance puts the "raging" Sansloy to flight suggests a debt to Comes, who, noting the old belief
    that fauns and forest spirits watch over workers in field and forest, says that no event in those areas
    escapes God's attention (*Mythologiae* 10). In other contexts, these figures assume a different
    significance (e.g., III.x.43–51).

8

Who when they heard that pitteous strainéd voice,
 In hast forsooke their rurall meriment,
 And ran towards the far rebownded noyce,
 To weet, what wight so loudly did lament.
 Unto the place they come incontinent:°   *hastily*
 Whom when the raging Sarazin espide,
 A rude, misshapen, monstrous rablement,
 Whose like he never saw, he durst not bide,
But got his ready steed, and fast away gan ride.

9

The wyld woodgods arrivéd in the place,
 There find the virgin dolefull desolate,
 With ruffled rayments, and faire blubbred° face,   *tear-stained*
 As her outragcous foe had left her late,
 And trembling yet through feare of former hate;
 All stand amazéd at so uncouth° sight,   *strange*
 And gin to pittie her unhappie state,
 All stand astonied at her beautie bright,
In their rude eyes unworthie° of so wofull plight.   *undeserving*

10

She more amazed, in double dread doth dwell;
 And every tender part for feare does shake:
 As when a greedic Wolfe through hunger fell°   *cruel*
 A seely° Lambe farre from the flocke does take,   *innocent*
 Of whom he meanes his bloudie feast to make,
 A Lyon spyes fast running towards him,
 The innocent pray in hast he does forsake,
 Which quit° from death yet quakes in every lim   *saved*
With chaunge of feare, to see the Lyon looke so grim.

11

Such fearefull fit assaid° her trembling hart,   *afflicted*
 Ne word to speake, ne joynt to move she had:
 The salvage nation feele her secret smart,
 And read her sorrow in her count'nance sad;
 Their frowning forheads with rough hornes yclad,
 And rusticke horror° all a side doe lay,   *roughness*
 And gently grenning,° shew a semblance glad   *grinning*
 To comfort her, and feare to put away,
Their backward bent knees teach her humbly to obay.[5]

5. I.e., they teach their knees (bent backward like those of a goat) to kneel in humble obedience to
 her.

12

The doubtfull Damzell dare not yet commit
    Her single° person to their barbarous truth,°   *solitary/honesty*
    But still twixt feare and hope amazd does sit,
    Late learnd° what harme to hastie trust ensu'th,   *taught*
    They in compassion of her tender youth,
    And wonder of her beautie soveraine,
    Are wonne with pitty and unwonted ruth,
    And all prostrate upon the lowly plaine,
Do kisse her feete, and fawne on her with countenance faine.°   *glad*

13

Their harts she ghesseth by their humble guise,°   *manner*
    And yieldes her to extremitie of time;[6]
    So from the ground she fearelesse doth arise,
    And walketh forth without suspect of crime:[7]
    They all as glad, as birdes of joyous Prime,°   *springtime*
    Thence lead her forth, about her dauncing round,
    Shouting, and singing all a shepheards ryme,
    And with greene braunches strowing all the ground,
Do worship her, as Queene, with olive girlond cround.[8]

14

And all the way their merry pipes they sound,
    That all the woods with doubled Eccho ring,
    And with their hornéd feet do weare° the ground,   *trample*
    Leaping like wanton kids in pleasant Spring.
    So towards old Sylvanus they her bring;
    Who with the noyse awakéd, commeth out,
    To weet the cause, his weake steps governing,
    And aged limbs on Cypresse stadle° stout,   *staff*
And with an yvie twyne his wast is girt about.

15

Far off he wonders, what them makes so glad.
    Or Bacchus merry fruit they did invent,[9]
    Or Cybeles franticke rites[1] have made them mad;
    They drawing nigh, unto their God present
    That flowre of faith and beautie excellent.
    The God himselfe vewing that mirrhour rare,[2]

6. I.e., to present necessity.
7. I.e., without fear of reproach.
8. Una's loveliness exerts a power unavailable to mere natural beauty; but the satyrs' idolatry shows
they cannot grasp her full significance.
9. I.e., whether they had found the grapes that, as wine, make men merry.
1. The Great Mother Cybele, goddess of Earth and upholder of cities, was a Near Eastern deity
known to the Greeks as Rhea, daughter of Gea and wife of Kronos (Saturn). She was worshipped
with rites led by priests performing orgiastic dances to brass and percussion instruments. For the
Romans (and presumably for Spenser) she was important as patron and symbol of the westward
passage of culture and empire (Hawkins 1981).
2. I.e., that mirror of heavenly beauty.

Stood long amazd, and burnt in his intent;°   *gaze*
  His owne faire Dryope now he thinkes not faire,
And Pholoe fowle, when her to this he doth compaire.[3]

16

The woodborne people fall before her flat,
  And worship her as Goddesse of the wood;
  And old Sylvanus selfe bethinkes° not, what   *concludes*
To thinke of wight so faire, but gazing stood,
  In doubt to deeme her borne of earthly brood;
Sometimes Dame Venus selfe he seemes to see,
  But Venus never had so sober mood;
Sometimes Diana he her takes to bee,
But misseth bow, and shaftes, and buskins° to her knee.   *boots*

17

By vew of her he ginneth to revive
  His ancient love, and dearest Cyparisse,[4]
  And calles to mind his pourtraiture alive,[5]
How faire he was, and yet not faire to this,
  And how he slew with glauncing dart amisse
A gentle Hynd, the which the lovely boy
  Did love as life, above all worldly blisse;
For griefe whereof the lad n'ould° after joy,   *would not*
But pynd away in anguish and selfe-wild annoy.°   *grief*

18

The wooddy Nymphes, faire Hamadryades
  Her to behold do thither runne apace,
  And all the troupe of light-foot Naiades,[6]
Flocke all about to see her lovely face:
  But when they vewéd have her heavenly grace,
They envie her in their malitious mind,
  And fly away for feare of fowle disgrace:
But all the Satyres scorne their woody kind,
And henceforth nothing faire, but her on earth they find.

19

Glad of such lucke, the luckelesse lucky maid,
  Did her content to please their feeble eyes,
  And long time with that salvage people staid,
To gather breath in many miseries.
  During which time her gentle wit she plyes,

3. Dryope was the wife of Faunus; Pholoe a nymph loved by Pan. Spenser apparently considered the
   names of Faunus, Pan, and Sylvanus interchangeable.
4. According to Ovid, Cyparissus, the beloved of Apollo, was changed by the god into a cypress
   (*Metamorphoses* 10.106–42); in Comes's version, he is associated rather with Sylvanus (*Mythologiae*
   5.10).
5. I.e., his appearance when he was alive.
6. Hamadryads are tree nymphs who cannot outlive the trees they inhabit; Naiads are nymphs of
   lakes and rivers, thought to have prophetic powers.

To teach them truth, which worshipt her in vaine,°   *foolishly*
And made her th'Image of Idolatryes;
But when their bootlesse zeale she did restraine
From her own worship, they her Asse would worship fayn.°[7]   *eagerly*

20

It fortunéd a noble warlike knight[8]
    By just occasion to that forrest came,
    To seeke his kindred, and the lignage right,°   *true*
    From whence he tooke his well deservéd name:
    He had in armes abroad wonne muchell fame,
    And fild far landes with glorie of his might,
    Plaine, faithfull, true, and enimy of shame,
    And ever loved to fight for Ladies right,
But in vaine glorious frayes he litle did delight.

21

A Satyres sonne yborne in forrest wyld,
    By straunge adventure as it did betyde,°   *happen*
    And there begotten of a Lady myld,
    Faire Thyamis the daughter of Labryde,
    That was in sacred bands of wedlocke tyde
    To Therion, a loose unruly swayne;[9]
    Who had more joy to raunge the forrest wyde,
    And chase the salvage beast with busie payne,[1]
Then serve his Ladies love, and wast° in pleasures vayne.   *live idly*

22

The forlorne mayd did with loves longing burne,
    And could not lacke° her lovers company,   *be without*
    But to the wood she goes, to serve her turne,
    And seeke her spouse, that from her still does fly,
    And followes other game and venery:[2]
    A Satyre chaunst her wandring for to find,
    And kindling coles of lust in brutish eye,
    The loyall links of wedlocke did unbind,
And made her person thrall unto his beastly kind.

7. Spenser may revise and elaborate a popular emblem (cf. Alciati, *Emblemata* 7) in which an ass
   bearing a statue of Isis thinks the crowd is worshipping him. Spenser's own point is that even well-
   intentioned idolatry confuses the sign or bearer of religious truth with the source of truth, God.
8. I.e., Satyrane (named in stanza 28), whose parentage recalls the theme, common in fairy lore, of
   a mortal's mating with an otherworldly being. He can tame beasts, resist Sansloy (cf. stanzas 43–
   47), and even subdue some monsters (III.vii.29–36); but he is no match for the giantess Argante
   (III.vii.42–43). His natural goodness enables him to protect Una, but he cannot accomplish the
   task assigned to Redcrosse.
9. The names, derived from Greek, indicate each figure's nature: Thyamis, "passion"; Labryde,
   "turbulent" or "greedy"; Therion, "wild beast." "Therion" is also the name of a forester in Philip
   Sidney's *Lady of May*, performed for the queen in 1578 or 1579.
1. I.e., with painstaking care.
2. The term means both "hunting" and "sexual indulgence."

23

So long in secret cabin there he held
  Her captive to his sensuall desire,
  Till that with timely fruit her belly sweld,
  And bore a boy unto that salvage sire:
  Then home he suffred her for to retire,
  For ransome leaving him the late borne childe:
  Whom till to ryper yeares he gan aspire,°   *grow up*
  He noursled up in life and manners wilde,
Emongst wild beasts and woods, from lawes of men exilde.

24

For all he taught the tender ymp,° was but   *child*
  To banish cowardize and bastard° feare;   *base*
  His trembling hand he would him force to put
  Upon the Lyon and the rugged Beare,
  And from the she Beares teats her whelps to teare;
  And eke wyld roring Buls he would him make
  To tame, and ryde their backes not made to beare;
  And the Robuckes in flight to overtake,
That every beast for feare of him did fly and quake.[3]

25

Thereby so fearelesse, and so fell he grew,
  That his owne sire and maister of his guise°   *way of life*
  Did often tremble at his horrid vew,°   *appearance*
  And oft for dread of hurt would him advise,
  The angry beasts not rashly to despise,
  Nor too much to provoke; for he would learne°   *teach*
  The Lyon stoup to him in lowly wise,
  (A lesson hard) and make the Libbard° sterne   *leopard*
Leave roaring, when in rage he for revenge did earne.°   *yearn*

26

And for to make his powre approvéd° more,   *established*
  Wyld beasts in yron yokes he would compell;
  The spotted Panther, and the tuskéd Bore,
  The Pardale° swift, and the Tigre cruell;   *panther*
  The Antelope, and Wolfe both fierce and fell;
  And them constraine in equall teme to draw.[4]
  Such joy he had, their stubborne harts to quell,
  And sturdie courage tame with dreadfull aw,
That his beheast they fearéd, as a tyrans law.

---

3. So Chiron the centaur, half man and half horse, educated Achilles; cf. Pindar's third Nemean Ode, 43 ff.
4. I.e., to draw evenly, in pairs.

27

His loving mother came upon a day
  Unto the woods, to see her little sonne;
  And chaunst unwares to meet him in the way,
  After his sportes, and cruell pastime donne,
  When after him a Lyonesse did runne,
  That roaring all with rage, did lowd requere°   *demand*
  Her children deare, whom he away had wonne:
  The Lyon whelpes she saw how he did beare,
And lull in rugged armes, withouten childish feare.

28

The fearefull Dame all quakéd at the sight,
  And turning backe, gan fast to fly away,
  Until with love revokt° from vaine affright,   *restrained*
  She hardly° yet perswaded was to stay,   *with difficulty*
  And then to him these womanish words gan say;
  "Ah Satyrane, my dearling, and my joy,
  For love of me leave off this dreadfull play;
  To dally thus with death, is no fit toy,
Go find some other play-fellowes, mine own sweet boy."

29

In these and like delights of bloudy game
  He traynéd was, till ryper yeares he raught,°   *attained*
  And there abode, whilst any beast of name
  Walkt in that forest, whom he had not taught
  To feare his force: and then his courage haught°   *high*
  Desird of forreine foemen to be knowne,
  And far abroad for straunge adventures sought:
  In which his might was never overthrowne,
But through all Faery lond his famous worth was blown.

30

Yet evermore it was his manner faire,
  After long labours and adventures spent,
  Unto those native woods for to repaire,°   *return*
  To see his sire and ofspring° auncient.   *origin*
  And now he thither came for like intent;
  Where he unwares the fairest Una found,
  Straunge Lady, in so straunge habiliment,°   *attire*
  Teaching the Satyres, which her sat around,
Trew sacred lore, which from her sweet lips did redound.°   *flow*

31

He wondred at her wisedome heavenly rare,
  Whose like in womens wit he never knew;
  And when her curteous deeds he did compare,

Gan her admire, and her sad sorrowes rew,
Blaming of Fortune, which such troubles threw,
And joyd to make proofe of her crueltie
On gentle Dame, so hurtlesse,° and so trew: *harmless*
Thenceforth he kcpt her goodly company,
And learnd her discipline of faith and veritie.

32

But she all vowd unto the Redcrosse knight,
His wandring perill closely° did lament,   *privately*
Ne in this new acquaintaunce could delight,
But her deare heart with anguish did torment,
And all her wit in secret counsels spent,
How to escape. At last in privie wise⁵
To Satyrane she shewéd her intent;
Who glad to gain such favour, gan devise,
How with that pensive Maid he best might thence arise.°   *depart*

33

So on a day when Satyres all were gone,
To do their service to Sylvanus old,
The gentle virgin left behind alone
He led away with courage stout and bold.
Too late it was, to Satyres to be told,
Or ever hope recover her againe:
In vaine he seekes that having cannot hold.
So fast he carried her with carefull paine,°   *pains*
That they the woods are past, and come now to the plaine.⁶

34

The better part now of the lingring day,
They traveild had, when as they farre espide
A wearie wight forwandring° by the way,   *wandering along*
And towards him they gan in hast to ride,
To weet of newcs, that did abroad betide,
Or tydings of her knight of the Redcrosse.
But he them spying, gan to turne aside,
For feare as seemd, or for some feignéd losse;°   *harm*
More greedy they of newes, fast towards him do crosse.

35

A silly° man, in simple weedes forworne,°   *simple/worn out*
And soild with dust of the long driéd way;
His sandales were with toilesome travell torne,
And face all tand with scorching sunny ray,

5. I.e., secretly.
6. The episode that follows is based on the adventures of Angelica, Sacripante, and Rinaldo, in
Ariosto, *Orlando Furioso* 1.1–2. Spenser, however, plays down Ariosto's characteristically ironic
and mocking tone; further, he leaves unresolved the encounter between Satyrane (who reappears
in Book III) and Sansloy (who appears again in II.ii).

As he had traveild many a sommers day,
Through boyling sands of Arabie and Ynde;
And in his hand a Jacobs staffe,[7] to stay
His wearie limbes upon: and eke behind,
His scrip° did hang, in which his needments he did bind.   *bag*

36

The knight approching nigh, of him inquerd
  Tydings of warre, and of adventures new;
  But warres, nor new adventures none he herd.
  Then Una gan to aske, if ought he knew,
  Or heard abroad of that her champion trew,
  That in his armour bare a croslet° red.   *small cross*
  "Aye me, Deare dame," quoth he, "well may I rew
  To tell the sad sight, which mine eies have red:°   *seen*
These eyes did see that knight both living and eke ded."

37

That cruell word her tender hart so thrild,°   *pierced*
  That suddein cold did runne through every vaine,
  And stony horrour all her sences fild
  With dying fit, that downe she fell for paine.
  The knight her lightly rearéd up againe,
  And comforted with curteous kind reliefe:
  Then wonne from death, she bad him tellen plaine
  The further processe° of her hidden griefe;   *account*
The lesser pangs can beare, who hath endured the chiefe.

38

Then gan the Pilgrim thus, "I chaunst this day,
  This fatall day, that shall I ever rew,
  To see two knights in travell on my way
  (A sory sight) arraunged in battell new,[8]
  Both breathing vengeaunce, both of wrathfull hew:
  My fearefull flesh did tremble at their strife,
  To see their blades so greedily imbrew,°   *thrust*
  That drunke with bloud, yet thristed after life:
What more? the Redcrosse knight was slaine with Paynim knife."

39

"Ah dearest Lord," quoth she, "how might that bee,
  And he the stoutest knight, that ever wonne?"°   *engaged in battle*
  "Ah dearest dame," quoth he, "how might I see
  The thing, that might not be, and yet was donne?"
  "Where is," said Satyrane, "that Paynims sonne,
  That him of life, and us of joy hath reft?"
  "Not far away," quoth he, "he hence doth wonne°   *remain*

7. I.e., a pilgrim's staff.
8. I.e., striking the first blows of their encounter.

Foreby a fountaine, where I late him left
Washing his bloudy wounds, that through the steele were cleft."

40

Therewith the knight thence marchéd forth in hast,
  Whiles Una with huge heavinesse° opprest,   *grief*
  Could not for sorrow follow him so fast;
  And soone he came, as he the place had ghest,
  Whereas that Pagan proud him selfe did rest,
  In secret shadow by a fountaine side:
  Even he it was, that earst would have supprest°   *ravished*
  Faire Una: whom when Satyrane espide,
With fowle reprochfull words he boldly him defide.

41

And said, "Arise thou curséd Miscreaunt,
  That hast with knightlesse guile and trecherous train°   *deceit*
  Faire knighthood fowly shaméd, and doest vaunt
  That good knight of the Redcrosse to have slain:
  Arise, and with like treason now maintain
  Thy guilty wrong, or else thee guilty yield "
  The Sarazin this hearing, rose amain,°   *at once*
  And catching up in hast his three square° shield,   *triangular*
And shining helmet, soone him buckled to the field.

42

And drawing nigh him said, "Ah misbornc° Elfe,   *basely born*
  In evill houre thy foes thee hither sent,
  Anothers wrongs to wrcake upon thy selfe:[9]
  Yet ill thou blamest me, for having blent°   *defiled*
  My name with guile and traiterous intcnt;
  That Redcrosse knight, perdie,° I never slew,   *truly*
  But had he beene, where earst his armes were lent,
  Th'enchaunter vaine his errour should not rew:
But thou his errour shalt, I hope now proven trew."[1]

43

Therewith they gan, both furious and fell,
  To thunder blowes, and fiersly to assaile
  Each other bent° his enimy to quell,   *determined*
  That with their force they perst both plate and maile,
  And made wide furrowes in their fleshes fraile,
  That it would pitty° any living eie.   *bring pity to*
  Large floods of bloud adowne their sides did raile:° *flow*
  But floods of bloud could not them satisfie:
Both hungred after death: both chose to win, or die.

---

9. I.e., to draw upon yourself the consequences of another's wrongs.
1. I.e. [in reference to I.iii.33–39], your experience at my hands shall now, I hope, confirm Archimago's foolishness in venturing to fight me.

44

So long they fight, and fell revenge pursue,
  That fainting each, themselves to breathen let,
  And oft refreshéd, battell oft renue:
  As when two Bores with rancling malice met,
  Their gory sides fresh bleeding fiercely fret,°   *gnaw, tear*
  Til breathlesse both them selves aside retire,
  Where foming wrath, their cruell tuskes they whet,
  And trample th'earth, the whiles they may respire;
Then backe to fight againe, new breathéd and entire.°   *refreshed*

45

So fiersly, when these knights had breathéd once,
  They gan to fight returne, increasing more
  Their puissant force, and cruell rage attonce,
  With heapéd strokes more hugely, then before,
  That with their drerie° wounds and bloudy gore   *gory*
  They both deforméd, scarsely could be known.
  By this sad Una fraught with anguish sore,
  Led with their noise, which through the aire was thrown,
Arrived, where they in erth their fruitles bloud had sown.

46

Whom all so soone as that proud Sarazin
  Espide, he gan revive the memory
  Of his lewd lusts, and late attempted sin,
  And left the doubtfull° battell hastily,   *undecided*
  To catch her, newly offred to his eie:
  But Satyrane with strokes him turning, staid,
  And sternely bad him other businesse plie,
  Then hunt the steps of pure unspotted Maid:
Wherewith he all enraged, these bitter speaches said.

47

"O foolish faeries sonne, what furie mad
  Hath thee incenst, to hast thy dolefull fate?
  Were it not better, I that Lady had,
  Then that thou hadst repented it too late?
  Most sencelesse man he, that himselfe doth hate,
  To love another. Lo then for thine ayd
  Here take thy lovers token on thy pate."
  So they to fight; the whiles the royall Mayd
Fled farre away, of that proud Paynim sore afrayd.

48

But that false Pilgrim, which that leasing° told,   *falsehood*
  Being in deed old Archimage, did stay
  In secret shadow, all this to behold,

And much rejoycéd in their bloudy fray:
But when he saw the Damsell passe away
He left his stond,° and her pursewd apace,   *place*
In hope to bring her to her last decay.°   *destruction*
But for to tell her lamentable cace,
And eke this battels end, will need another place.

Canto VII

*The Redcrosse knight is captive made
By Gyaunt proud opprest,
Prince Arthur meets with Una great-
ly with those newes distrest.*

1

What man so wise, what earthly wit so ware,°   *wary*
   As to descry° the crafty cunning traine,   *discover*
   By which deceipt doth maske in visour faire,
   And cast° her colours dyéd deepe in graine,   *dispose*
   To seeme like Truth, whose shape she well can faine,
   And fitting gestures to her purpose frame,
   The guiltlesse man with guile to entertaine?°   *receive*
   Great maistresse of her art was that false Dame,
The false Duessa, clokéd with Fidessaes name.

2

Who when returning from the drery Night,
   She fownd not in that perilous house of Pryde,
   Where she had left, the noble Redcrosse knight,
   Her hopéd pray, she would no lenger bide,
   But forth she went, to seeke him far and wide.
   Ere long she fownd, whereas he wearie sate,
   To rest him selfe, forehy° a fountaine side,   *near*
   Disarméd all of yron-coted Plate,[1]
And by his side his steed the grassy forage ate.

3

He feedes upon the cooling shade, and bayes°   *bathes*
   His sweatie forehead in the breathing wind,
   Which through the trembling leaves full gently playes
   Wherein the cherefull birds of sundry kind
   Do chaunt sweet musick, to delight his mind:
   The Witch approching gan him fairely greet,
   And with reproch of carelesnesse° unkind   *neglect*

1. Although recognizing the dangers of worldly pride, Redcrosse has been weakened by his struggle
   with Sansjoy; his "carelesnesse" (in a sense other than that intended by Duessa in stanza 3) enthralls
   him to another form of pride and is signaled by the removal of his armor. As Erasmus points out
   in sections 7 and 21 of *Enchiridion* (translated by Tyndale in 1533 as *The Manual of the Christian
   Knight*), we must beware of fleeing vice only to fall into self-congratulatory vanity.

Upbrayd, for leaving her in place unmeet,°   *unfitting*
With fowle words tempring faire, soure gall with hony sweet.

4

Unkindnesse past, they gan of solace treat,°   *speak*
  And bathe in pleasaunce of the joyous shade,
  Which shielded them against the boyling heat,
  And with greene boughes decking a gloomy glade,
  About the fountaine like a girlond made;
  Whose bubbling wave did ever freshly well,
  Ne ever would through fervent° sommer fade: *hot*
  The sacred Nymph, which therein wont to dwell,
Was out of Dianes favour, as it then befell.

5

The cause was this: one day when Phoebe² fayre
  With all her band was following the chace,
  This Nymph, quite tyred with heat of scorching ayre
  Sat downe to rest in middest of the race:
  The goddesse wroth gan fowly her disgrace,°   *scold, revile*
  And bad the waters, which from her did flow,
  Be such as she her selfe was then in place.°   *that place*
  Thenceforth her waters waxéd dull and slow,
And all that drunke thereof, did faint and feeble grow.

6

Hereof this gentle knight unweeting was,   *Spivitual*
  And lying downe upon the sandie graile,°   *pride*   *gravel*
  Drunke of the streame, as cleare as cristall glas;
  Eftsoones his manly forces gan to faile,
  And mightie strong was turnd to feeble fraile.
  His chaungéd powres at first themselves not felt,
  Till crudled° cold his corage° gan assaile,   *congealing/vigor*
  And chearefull° bloud in faintnesse chill did melt,   *lively*
Which like a fever fit through all his body swelt.°   *raged*

7

Yet goodly court he made still to his Dame,
  Pourd out in loosnesse on the grassy grownd,
  Both carelesse of his health, and of his fame:
  Till at the last he heard a dreadfull sownd,
  Which through the wood loud bellowing, did rebownd,
  That all the earth for terrour seemd to shake,
  And trees did tremble. Th'Elfe therewith astownd,°   *amazed*
  Upstarted lightly from his looser make,°   *companion*
And his unready weapons gan in hand to take.

---

2. Diana, goddess of the moon. While this episode seems original with Spenser, lines 8–9 recall Ovid's fountain of Salmacis, whose waters enfeebled those bathing there (*Metamorphoses* 4.286–87).

8

But ere he could his armour on him dight,°   *put*
  Or get his shield, his monstrous enimy
  With sturdie steps came stalking in his sight,
  An hideous Geant horrible and hye,[3]
  That with his talnesse seemd to threat the skye,
  The ground eke gronéd under him for dreed;
  His living like saw never living eye,
  Ne durst behold: his stature did exceed
The hight of three the tallest sonnes of mortall seed.

9

The greatest Earth his uncouth mother was,
  And blustring Aeolus[4] his boasted sire,
  Who with his breath, which through the world doth pas,
  Her hollow womb did secretly inspire,°   *breathe into*
  And fild her hidden caves with stormie yre,
  That she conceived; and trebling the dew time,
  In which the wombes of women do expire,°   *gestate*
  Brought forth this monstrous masse of earthly slime,
Puft up with emptie wind, and fild with sinfull crime.

10

So growen great through arrogant delight
  Of th'high descent, whereof he was yborne,
  And through presumption of his matchlesse might,
  All other powres and knighthood he did scorne.
  Such now he marcheth to this man forlorne,
  And left to losse:° his stalking steps are stayde°   *destruction/steadied*
  Upon a snaggy Oke, which he had torne
  Out of his mothers bowelles, and it made
His mortall mace, wherewith his foemen he dismayde.

11

That when the knight he spide, he gan advance
  With huge force and insupportable mayne,[5]
  And towardes him with dreadfull fury praunce;
  Who haplesse, and eke hopelesse, all in vaine
  Did to him pace, sad battaile to darrayne,°   *undertake*
  Disarmd, disgrast, and inwardly dismayde,

3. This "Geant" (the spelling recalls his mother Gea, "Earth") represents fleshly and irrational presumption, diabolical vainglory that parodies the glory sought by Gloriana's knights. Cf. Maclean 1990E. His physiology and his emergence as the unarmed Redcrosse dallies with Duessa on the grass ("all flesh is grass," says Isaiah 40.6) associate him with monitory earthquakes and hint that he arises from the hero's own swollen lust (see Heninger, pp. 732–41, in this edition, and J. W. Shroeder in *ELH* 29 [1962]). Made of "earthly slime," he is related to his fellow foundling George ("earth-tiller"); like many of Spenser's giants, Orgoglio (Italian for "pride") is the knight's inflated and negative double, the old Adam ("red earth") in humanity that, like classical and biblical giants, seeks to usurp God's place and block or overturn a new dispensation.
4. God of the winds.
5. Irresistible strength.

And eke so faint in every joynt and vaine,
    Through that fraile° fountaine, which him feeble made,   *weakening*
That scarsely could he weeld his bootlesse single blade.[6]

12

The Geaunt strooke so maynly° mercilesse,   *mightily*
    That could have overthrowne a stony towre,
    And were not heavenly grace, that him did blesse,°   *preserve*
    He had beene pouldred° all, as thin as flowre: *pulverized*
    But he was wary of that deadly stowre,°   *peril*
    And lightly lept from underneath the blow:
    Yet so exceeding was the villeins powre,
    That with the wind it did him overthrow,
And all his sences stound,° that still he lay full low.   *stunned*

13

As when that divelish yron Engin[7] wrought
    In deepest Hell, and framd by Furies skill,
    With windy Nitre and quick° Sulphur fraught,°   *inflammable/filled*
    And ramd with bullet round, ordaind to kill,
    Conceiveth fire, the heavens it doth fill
    With thundring noyse, and all the ayre doth choke,
    That none can breath, nor see, nor heare at will,
    Through smouldry cloud of duskish stincking smoke,
That th'onely breath[8] him daunts, who hath escapt the stroke.

14

So daunted when the Geaunt saw the knight,
    His heavie hand he heavéd up on hye,
    And him to dust thought to have battred quight,
    Untill Duessa loud to him gan crye;
    "O great Orgoglio, greatest under skye,
    O hold thy mortall hand for Ladies sake,
    Hold for my sake, and do him not to dye,
    But vanquisht thine eternall bondslave make,
And me thy worthy meed unto thy Leman[9] take."

15

He hearkned, and did stay from further harmes,
    To gayne so goodly guerdon,° as she spake: *reward*
    So willingly she came into his armes,
    Who her as willingly to grace° did take,   *favor*
    And was possesséd of his new found make.°   *companion*
    Then up he tooke the slombred sencelesse corse,
    And ere he could out of his swowne awake,

6. I.e., sword alone, without the aid of armor or shield.
7. I.e., cannon.
8. I.e., the blast alone.
9. I.e., as your mistress.

Him to his castle brought with hastie forse,
And in a Dongeon deepe him threw without remorse.

16

From that day forth Duessa was his deare,
  And highly honourd in his haughtie eye,
  He gave her gold and purple pall° to weare,   *robe*
  And triple crowne¹ set on her head full hye,
  And her endowd with royall majestye:
  Then for to make her dreaded more of men,
  And peoples harts with awfull terrour tye,
  A monstrous beast² ybred in filthy fen
He chose, which he had kept long time in darksome den.

17

Such one it was, as that renowméd Snake³
  Which great Alcides in Stremona slew,
  Long fostred in the filth of Lerna lake,
  Whose many heads out budding ever new,
  Did breed him endlesse labour to subdew:
  But this same Monster much more ugly was;
  For seven great heads out of his body grew,
  An yron brest, and backe of scaly bras,
And all embrewd° in bloud, his eyes did shine as glas.   *stained, defiled*

18

His tayle was stretchéd out in wondrous length,
  That to the house of heavenly gods it raught,°   *reached*
  And with extorted powre, and borrowed strength,
  The ever-burning lamps from thence it brought,
  And prowdly threw to ground, as things of nought;
  And underneath his filthy feet did tread
  The sacred things, and holy heasts° foretaught.   *commaundments*
  Upon this dreadfull Beast with sevenfold head
He set the false Duessa, for more aw and dread.

19

The wofull Dwarfe, which saw his maisters fall,
  Whiles he had keeping of his grasing steed,
  And valiant knight become a caytive° thrall,   *captive*

1. Symbolic of papal power.
2. The description of Duessa's beast echoes passages in Revelation: "I saw a woman sit upon a scarlet coloured beast, full of names of blasphemy, having seven heads and ten horns" (17.3), "behold a great red dragon, having seven heads and ten horns, and seven crowns upon his heads . . . [whose] tail drew the third part of the stars of heaven, and did cast them to the earth . . . [he is] that old serpent, called the Devil, and Satan, which deceiveth the whole world" (12.3–4, 9). Spenser associates this figure with the Roman church. Pictures of the Beast of the Apocalypse regularly illustrate literature on the vices and virtues (cf. R. Tuve, *Allegorical Imagery* [Princeton, 1966] 102–8).
3. To destroy the Lernean hydra, a nine-headed beast of the swamps, was the second of twelve labors assigned to Hercules (also called Alcides). Una is one; the beast is multiple.

When all was past, tooke up his forlorne weed,°　　*equipment*
His mightie armour, missing most at need;
His silver shield, now idle maisterlesse;
His poynant° speare, that many made to bleed,　　*sharp*
The ruefull moniments° of heavinesse,　　*memorials*
And with them all departes, to tell his great distresse.

20

He had not travaild long, when on the way
He wofull Ladie, wofull Una met,
Fast flying from the Paynims greedy pray,°　　*clutch*
Whilest Satyrane him from pursuit did let:°　　*prevent*
Who when her eyes she on the Dwarfe had set,
And saw the signes, that deadly tydings spake,
She fell to ground for sorrowfull regret,
And lively breath her sad brest did forsake,
Yet might her pitteous hart be seene to pant and quake.

21

The messenger of so unhappie newes,
Would faine have dyde: dead was his hart within,
Yet outwardly some little comfort shewes:
At last recovering hart, he does begin
To rub her temples, and to chaufe her chin,
And every tender part does tosse and turne:
So hardly he the flitted life does win,°　　*prevail upon*
Unto her native prison[4] to retourne:
Then gins her grievéd ghost° thus to lament and mourne.　　*spirit*

22

"Ye dreary instruments of dolefull sight,[5]
That doe this deadly spectacle behold,
Why do ye lenger feed on loathéd light,
Or liking find to gaze on earthly mould,°　　*form*
Sith cruell fates the carefull° threeds unfould,　　*full of care*
The which my life and love together tyde?
Now let the stony dart of senselesse cold
Perce to my hart, and pas through every side,
And let eternall night so sad sight fro me hide.

23

"O lightsome day, the lampe of highest Jove,
First made by him, mens wandring wayes to guyde,
When darknesse he in deepest dongeon drove,
Henceforth thy hated face for ever hyde,
And shut up heavens windowes shyning wyde:
For earthly sight can nought but sorrow breed,

4. I.e., the body.
5. I.e., eyes.

And late repentance, which shall long abyde.
Mine eyes no more on vanitie shall feed,
But seeléd up with death, shall have their deadly meed.°"   *reward*

24

Then downe againe she fell unto the ground;
   But he her quickly rearéd up againe:
   Thrise did she sinke adowne in deadly swownd,
   And thrise he her revived with busie paine:
   At last when life recovered had the raine,°   *rule*
   And over-wrestled his strong enemie,
   With foltring tong, and trembling every vaine,
   "Tell on," quoth she, "the wofull Tragedie,
The which these reliques sad present unto mine eie.

25

"Tempestuous fortune hath spent all her spight,
   And thrilling sorrow throwne his utmost dart;
   Thy sad tongue cannot tell more heavy plight,
   Then that I feele, and harbour in mine hart:
   Who hath endured the whole, can heare each part.
   If death it be, it is not the first wound,
   That launchéd° hath my brest with bleeding smart.   *pierced*
   Begin, and end the bitter balefull stound;°   *sorrow*
If lesse, then that I feare, more favour I have found."

26

Then gan the Dwarfe the whole discourse declare,   PAS Machina
   The subtill traines of Archimago old;
   The wanton loves of false Fidessa faire,
   Bought with the bloud of vanquisht Paynim bold:
   The wretched payre transformed to treén mould;[6]
   The house of Pride, and perils round about;
   The combat, which he with Sansjoy did hould;
   The lucklesse conflict with the Gyant stout,
Wherein captived, of life or death he stood in doubt.

27

She heard with patience all unto the end,
   And strove to maister sorrowfull assay,°   *affliction*
   Which greater grew, the more she did contend,
   And almost rent her tender hart in tway;
   And love fresh coles unto her fire did lay:
   For greater love, the greater is the losse.
   Was never Ladie lovéd dearer day,
   Then she did love the knight of the Redcrosse;
For whose deare sake so many troubles her did tosse.

6. Form of a tree.

28

At last when fervent sorrow slakéd was,
  She up arose, resolving him to find
  Alive or dead: and forward forth doth pas,
  All as the Dwarfe the way to her assynd:°   *indicated*
  And evermore in constant carefull mind
  She fed her wound with fresh renewéd bale;
  Long tost with stormes, and bet° with bitter wind,   *buffeted*
  High over hils, and low adowne the dale,
She wandred many a wood, and measurd many a vale.

29

At last she chauncéd by good hap to meet
  A goodly knight,[7] faire marching by the way
  Together with his Squire, arayéd meet:°   *properly*
  His glitterand° armour shinéd farre away,   *glittering*
  Like glauncing light of Phoebus brightest ray;
  From top to toe no place appearéd bare,
  That deadly dint of steele endanger may:
  Athwart his brest a bauldrick° brave he ware,   *shoulder belt*
That shynd, like twinkling stars, with stons most pretious rare.

30

And in the midst thereof one pretious stone
  Of wondrous worth, and eke of wondrous mights,
  Shapt like a Ladies head,[8] exceeding shone,
  Like Hesperus emongst the lesser lights,°   *stars*
  And strove for to amaze the weaker sights;
  Thereby his mortall blade full comely hong
  In yvory sheath, ycarved with curious slights;°   *patterns*
  Whose hilts were burnisht gold, and handle strong
Of mother pearle, and buckled with a golden tong.°   *pin*

31

His haughtie° helmet, horrid° all with gold,   *noble/bristling*
  Both glorious brightnesse, and great terrour bred;
  For all the crest a Dragon[9] did enfold
  With greedie pawes, and over all did spred

---

7. I.e., Prince Arthur, hero of *The Faerie Queene,* in whose person is "sette forth" (as the "Letter to Raleigh" says) "magnificence," a virtue that "according to Aristotle . . . is the perfection of all the rest, and conteineth in it them all." The more usual term was "magnanimity" (greatness of spirit), but Tuve, *Allegorical Imagery* 57–143, describes a tradition of "Christian Magnificence" drawing on Cicero and Macrobius as well as Aristotle; see also Cummings 1987 on patristic and hermetic uses of "magnificence." Derived from British history and legend, Arthur in Book I primarily figures a divine grace that can deliver exhausted wayfaring Christians from evil. Cf. viii.1.
8. *The Faerie Queene.* Geoffrey of Monmouth (c. 1100–54) says Arthur bore the Virgin Mary's image on the inner side of his shield (*Historia Regum Britanniae* 9.4); cf. III.iii.6, note.
9. Geoffrey says a dragon was engraved on Arthur's gold helmet. A dragon was also the ensign of Cadwallader, last king of the Britons, and of the Tudors (to show their Arthurian lineage). In Book I, Arthur's dragon chiefly indicates his power over the evil symbolized by the "great red dragon" of Revelation.

His golden wings: his dreadfull hideous hed
Close couchéd on the bever,° seemed to throw   *visor*
From flaming mouth bright sparkles fierie red,
That suddeine horror to faint harts did show;
And scaly tayle was stretcht adowne his backe full low.

32

Upon the top of all his loftie crest,
  A bunch of haires discolourd° diversly,   *dyed*
With sprincled pearle, and gold full richly drest,
Did shake, and seemed to daunce for jollity,
Like to an Almond tree ymounted hye
On top of greene Selinis[1] all alone,
With blossomes brave bedeckéd daintily;
Whose tender locks do tremble every one
At every little breath, that under heaven is blowne.

33

His warlike shield[2] all closely covered was,
  Ne might of mortall eye be ever seene;
Not made of steele, nor of enduring bras,
Such earthly mettals soone consuméd bene:
But all of Diamond perfect pure and cleene°   *clear*
It framéd was, one massie entire mould,
Hewen out of Adamant° rocke with engines keene,   *diamond-hard*
That point of speare it never percen could,
Ne dint of direfull sword divide the substance would.

34

The same to wight he never wont disclose,
  But° when as monsters huge he would dismay,   *except*
Or daunt unequall armies of his foes,
Or when the flying heavens he would affray;°   *frighten*
For so exceeding shone his glistring ray,
That Phoebus golden face it did attaint,°   *dim, darken*
As when a cloud his beames doth over-lay;
And silver Cynthia wexéd pale and faint,
As when her face is staynd with magicke arts constraint.°   *force*

35

No magicke arts hereof had any might,
  Nor bloudie wordes of bold Enchaunters call,
But all that was not such, as seemd in sight,
Before that shield did fade, and suddeine fall:
And when him list the raskall routes° appall,   *crowds*
Men into stones therewith he could transmew,°   *change*

---

1. Virgil refers to "the city of palms, Selinus," in Asia Minor (*Aeneid* 3.705).
2. Arthur's shield is very like Atlante's in Ariosto, *Orlando Furioso* 2.55–56; but this shield, proof
   against the arts of enchanters, is one of Christian faith (cf. Ephesians 6.16).

And stones to dust, and dust to nought at all;
  And when him list the prouder lookes subdew,
He would them gazing blind, or turne to other hew.°   *form*

36

Ne let it seeme, that credence this exceedes,
  For he that made the same, was knowne right well
  To have done much more admirable deedes.
  It Merlin was, which whylome° did excell   *formerly*
  All living wightes in might of magicke spell:
  Both shield, and sword, and armour all he wrought
  For this young Prince, when first to armes he fell;°   *came*
  But when he dyde, the Faerie Queene it brought
To Faerie lond, where yet it may be seene, if sought.[3]

37

A gentle youth, his dearely lovéd Squire[4]
  His speare of heben° wood behind him bare,   *ebony*
  Whose harmefull head, thrice heated in the fire,
  Had riven many a brest with pikehead square;
  A goodly person, and could menage° faire   *control*
  His stubborne steed with curbéd canon bit,[5]
  Who under him did trample as the aire,[6]
  And chauft, that any on his backe should sit;
The yron rowels into frothy fome he bit.

38

When as this knight nigh to the Ladie drew,
  With lovely° court he gan her entertaine;   *loving*
  But when he heard her answeres loth, he knew
  Some secret sorrow did her heart distraine:°   *oppress*
  Which to allay, and calme her storming paine,
  Faire feeling words he wisely gan display,
  And for her humour fitting purpose faine,[7]
  To tempt the cause it selfe for to bewray;
Wherewith emmoved, these bleeding words she gan to say.

39

"What worlds delight, or joy of living speach
  Can heart, so plunged in sea of sorrowes deepe,
  And heapéd with so huge misfortunes, reach?
  The carefull° cold beginneth for to creepe,   *afflicting*
  And in my heart his yron arrow steepe,
  Soone as I thinke upon my bitter bale°:   *grief*

3. Spenser implies that the virtue and faith figured in Arthur may still flourish in Fairyland's counterpart, Elizabethan England; but Fairyland itself is hard to find, and his tone may include irony.
4. I.e., Timias ("honored").
5. Smooth round bit.
6. I.e., tread lightly and eagerly.
7. I.e., suited his speech and demeanor to her sorrowful mood.

Such helplesse harmes yts better hidden keepe,
  Then rip up° griefe, where it may not availe,   *lay bare*
My last left comfort is, my woes to weepe and waile."

                                40

"Ah Ladie deare," quoth then the gentle knight,
  Well may I weene,° your griefe is wondrous great;   *believe*
  For wondrous great griefe groneth in my spright,
  Whiles thus I heare you of your sorrowes treat.
  But wofull Ladie let me you intrete,
  For to unfold the anguish of your hart:
  Mishaps are maistred by advice discrete,
  And counsell mittigates the greatest smart;
Found never helpe, who never would his hurts impart."

                                41

"O but," quoth she, "great griefe will not be tould,
  And can more easily be thought, then said."
  "Right so," quoth he, "but he, that never would,
  Could never: will to might gives greatest aid."
  "But griefe," quoth she, "does greater grow displaid,
  If then it find not helpe, and breedes despaire."
  "Despaire breedes not," quoth he, "where faith is staid."°   *firm*
  "No faith so fast," quoth she, "but flesh does paire."°   *impair*
"Flesh may empaire," quoth he, "but reason can repaire."

                                42

His goodly reason, and well guided speach
  So deepe did settle in her gratious thought,
  That her perswaded to disclose the breach,
  Which love and fortune in her heart had wrought,
  And said; "Faire Sir, I hope good hap hath brought
  You to inquire the secrets of my griefe,
  Or that your wisedome will direct my thought,
  Or that your prowesse can me yield reliefe:
Then heare the storie sad, which I shall tell you briefe.

                                43

"The forlorne Maiden, whom your eyes have seene
  The laughing stocke of fortunes mockeries,
  Am th'only daughter of a King and Queene,
  Whose parents deare, whilest equall° destinies   *impartial*
  Did runne about,[8] and their felicities
  The favourable heavens did not envy,
  Did spread their rule through all the territories,
  Which Phison and Euphrates floweth by,
And Gehons golden waves doe wash continually.[9]

8. I.e., did revolve.
9. Pison, Gihon, Hiddekel, and Euphrates are the four rivers of Paradise (Genesis 2.10–14).

44

"Till that their cruell curséd enemy,
  An huge great Dragon horrible in sight,
  Bred in the loathly lakes of Tartary,°   *Tartarus (Hell)*
  With murdrous ravine,° and devouring might   *destruction*
  Their kingdome spoild, and countrey wasted quight:
  Themselves, for feare into his jawes to fall,
  He forst to castle strong to take their flight,
  Where fast embard in mightie brasen wall,
He has them now foure yeres[1] besieged to make them thrall.

45

"Full many knights adventurous and stout
  Have enterprizd° that Monster to subdew;   *undertaken*
  From every coast that heaven walks about,
  Have thither come the noble Martiall crew,
  That famous hard atchievements still pursew,
  Yet never any could that girlond win,
  But all still shronke,° and still he greater grew: *quailed, fell back*
  All they for want of faith, or guilt of sin,
The pitteous pray of his fierce crueltie have bin.

46

"At last yledd with farre reported praise,
  Which flying fame throughout the world had spred,
  Of doughtie knights, whom Faery land did raise,
  That noble order hight° of Maidenhed,[2]   *called*
  Forthwith to court of Gloriane I sped,
  Of Gloriane great Queene of glory bright,
  Whose kingdomes seat Cleopolis[3] is red,°   *named*
  There to obtaine some such redoubted knight,
That Parents deare from tyrants powre deliver might.

47

"It was my chance (my chance was faire and good)
  There for to find a fresh unprovéd knight,
  Whose manly hands imbrewed° in guiltie blood   *stained*
  Had never bene, ne ever by his might
  Had throwne to ground the unregarded° right: *unrespected*
  Yet of his prowesse proofe he since hath made
  (I witnesse am) in many a cruell fight;
  The groning ghosts of many one dismaide
Have felt the bitter dint of his avenging blade.

1. The Book of Revelation refers to the dragon's persecution of "the woman clothed with the sun," who "fled into the wilderness, where she had a place prepared of God, that they should feed her there a thousand two hundred and threescore days" (12.1–6).
2. I.e., maidenhood, recalling Queen Elizabeth's virginity; its sign is the head of a maid. The Order parallels England's Order of the Garter, headed by the monarch, in which knights wear insignia that include a figure of George slaying the dragon. On Spenser and chivalric orders, see Leslie 1983.
3. "Famed City" or "City of Fame," counterpart of London (but see I.x.58, note).

48

"And ye the forlorne reliques of his powre,
  His byting sword, and his devouring speare,
  Which have enduréd many a dreadfull stowre,°   *conflict*
  Can speake his prowesse, that did earst you beare,
  And well could rule: now he hath left you heare,
  To be the record of his ruefull losse,
  And of my dolefull disaventurous deare:°   *harm, loss*
  O heavie record of the good Redcrosse,
Where have you left your Lord, that could so well you tosse?°   *wield*

49

"Well hopéd I, and faire beginnings had,
  That he my captive languour should redeeme,[4]
  Till all unweeting, an Enchaunter bad
  His sence abusd, and made him to misdeeme
  My loyalty, not such as it did seeme;
  That rather death desire, then such despight.[5]
  Be judge ye heavens, that all things right esteeme,
  How I him loved, and love with all my might,
So thought I eke of him, and thinke I thought aright.

50

"Thenceforth me desolate he quite forsooke,
  To wander, where wilde fortune would me lead,
  And other bywaies he himselfe betooke,
  Where never foot of living wight did tread,
  That brought not backe the balefull body dead;[6]
  In which him chauncéd false Duessa meete,
  Mine onely° foe, mine onely deadly dread,   *particular*
  Who with her witchcraft and misseeming° sweete,   *deception*
Inveigled him to follow her desires unmeete.°   *improper*

51

"At last by subtill sleights she him betraid
  Unto his foe, a Gyant huge and tall,
  Who him disarméd, dissolute,° dismaid,   *enfeebled*
  Unwares surprinséd, and with mightie mall°   *club*
  The monster mercilesse him made to fall,
  Whose fall did never foe before behold;
  And now in darkesome dungeon, wretched thrall,
  Remedilesse, for aie° he doth him hold;   *ever*
This is my cause of griefe, more great, then may be told."

4. I.e., that he should relieve my condition, captive to sadness (by freeing my parents from the grip
  of the dragon).
5. I.e., I would prefer death to the outrage of being thought disloyal.
6. I.e., that returned alive.

52

Ere she had ended all, she gan to faint:
  But he her comforted and faire bespake,
  "Certes, Madame, ye have great cause of plaint,
  That stoutest heart, I weene, could cause to quake.
  But be of cheare, and comfort to you take:
  For till I have acquit° your captive knight,   *set free*
  Assure your selfe, I will you not forsake."
His chearefull words revived her chearelesse spright,
So forth they went, the Dwarfe them guiding ever right.

Canto VIII

Faire virgin to redeeme her deare
  brings Arthur to the fight:
Who slayes the Gyant, wounds the beast,
  and strips Duessa quight.

1

Ay me, how many perils doe enfold
  The righteous man, to make him daily fall?
  Were not, that heavenly grace doth him uphold,
  And stedfast truth acquite him out of all.
  Her love is firme, her care continuall,
  So oft as he through his owne foolish pride,
  Or weaknesse is to sinfull bands° made thrall: *bonds*
  Else should this Redcrosse knight in bands have dyde,
For whose deliverance she this Prince doth thither guide.

2

They sadly traveild thus, untill they came
  Nigh to a castle builded strong and hie:
  Then cryde the Dwarfe, "lo yonder is the same,
  In which my Lord my liege doth lucklesse lie,
  Thrall to that Gyants hatefull tyrannie:
  Therefore, deare Sir, your mightie powres assay."
  The noble knight alighted by and by[1]
  From loftie steede, and bad the Ladie stay,
To see what end of fight should him befall that day.

3

So with the Squire, th'admirer of his might,
  He marchéd forth towards that castle wall;
  Whose gates he found fast shut, ne living wight
  To ward the same, nor answere commers call.
  Then tooke that Squire an horne of bugle° small,   *wild ox*
  Which hong adowne his side in twisted gold,
  And tassels gay. Wyde wonders over all

---

1. I.e., immediately.

Of that same hornes great vertues weren told,
Which had appróvéd° bene in uses manifold.   *demonstrated*

4

Was never wight, that heard that shrilling sound,
  But trembling feare did feele in every vaine;
  Three miles it might be easie heard around,
  And Ecchoes three answerd it selfe againe:
  No false enchauntment, nor deceiptfull traine
  Might once abide the terror of that blast,
  But presently° was voide and wholly vaine:[2]   *at once*
  No gate so strong, no locke so firme and fast,
But with that percing noise flew open quite, or brast.°   *burst*

5

The same before the Geants gate he blew,
  That all the castle quakéd from the ground,
  And every dore of freewill open flew.
  The Gyant selfe dismaiéd with that sownd,
  Where he with his Duessa dalliance° fownd,   *amorous play*
  In hast came rushing forth from inner bowre,
  With staring countenance sterne, as one astownd,
  And staggering steps, to weet, what suddein stowre°   *disturbance*
Had wrought that horror strange, and dared his dreaded powre.

6

And after him the proud Duessa came,
  High mounted on her manyheaded beast,
  And every head with fyric tongue did flame,
  And every head was crownéd on his creast,
  And bloudie mouthéd with late cruell feast.
  That when the knight beheld, his mightie shild
  Upon his manly arme he soone addrest,°   *placed*
  And at him fiercely flew, with courage fild,
And eger greedinesse° through every member thrild.   *desire*

7

Therewith the Gyant buckled him to fight,[3]
  Inflamed with scornefull wrath and high disdaine,
  And lifting up his dreadfull club on hight,
  All armed with ragged snubbes° and knottie graine,   *snags*
  Him thought at first encounter to have slaine.
  But wise and warie was that noble Pere,
  And lightly leaping from so monstrous maine,°   *power*

2. The magic horn of Astolfo also terrified evildoers (*Orlando Furioso* 15.14), but this one recalls
   the ram's horn of Joshua (Joshua 6.5); it also has the power of those who preach God's word: "their
   sound went into all the earth, and their words unto the ends of the world" (Romans 10.15–18).
3. For now, Redcrosse's vanity resists the power of grace. In the historical allegory, Arthur's encounter
   with Orgoglio suggests Protestant victory over the Roman church; in a wider context, the battle
   shadows that of the Redeemer against the Antichrist.

Did faire avoide the violence him nere;
It booted nought, to thinke, such thunderbolts to beare.

8

Ne shame he thought to shunne so hideous might:
  The idle° stroke, enforcing furious way,   *futile*
  Missing the marke of his misayméd sight
  Did fall to ground, and with his heavie sway°   *force*
  So deepely dinted in the driven clay,
  That three yardes deepe a furrow up did throw:
  The sad earth wounded with so sore assay,°   *assault*
  Did grone full grievous underneath the blow,
And trembling with strange feare, did like an earthquake show.

9

As when almightie Jove in wrathfull mood,
  To wreake° the guilt of mortall sins is bent,   *punish*
  Hurles forth his thundring dart with deadly food,° *feud*
  Enrold in flames, and smouldring dreriment,
  Through riven cloudes and molten firmament;
  The fierce threeforkéd engin° making way,   *weapon*
  Both loftie towres and highest trees hath rent,
  And all that might his angrie passage stay,
And shooting in the earth, casts up a mount of clay.

10

His boystrous° club, so buried in the ground,   *massive*
  He could not rearen up againe so light,°   *easily*
  But that the knight him at avantage found,
  And whiles he strove his combred clubbe to quight° *free*
  Out of the earth, with blade all burning bright
  He smote off his left arme, which like a blocke
  Did fall to ground, deprived of native might;
  Large streames of bloud out of the trunckéd stocke
Forth gushéd, like fresh water streame from riven rocke.

11

Dismaiéd with so desperate deadly wound,
  And eke impatient of[4] unwonted paine,
  He loudly brayd with beastly yelling sound,
  That all the fields rebellowéd againe;
  As great a noyse, as when in Cymbrian plaine[5]
  An heard of Bulles, whom kindly rage[6] doth sting,
  Do for the milkie mothers want complaine,[7]

4. I.e., agonized by.
5. Jutland, once called the Cimbric peninsula after its original inhabitants.
6. I.e., natural passion.
7. I.e., lament the cows' absence.

And fill the fields with troublous bellowing,
The neighbour woods around with hollow murmur ring.

12

That when his deare Duessa heard, and saw
  The evill stownd,° that daungerd her estate,   *peril*
  Unto his aide she hastily did draw
  Her dreadfull beast, who swolne with bloud of late
  Came ramping forth with proud presumpteous gate,
  And threatned all his heads like flaming brands.
  But him the Squire made quickly to retrate,
  Encountring fierce with single° sword in hand,   *only*
And twixt him and his Lord did like a bulwarke stand.

13

The proud Duessa full of wrathfull spight,
  And fierce disdaine, to be affronted so,
  Enforst her purple beast with all her might
  That stop° out of the way to overthroe,   *obstacle*
  Scorning the let° of so unequall foe: *hindrance*
  But nathemore° would that courageous swayne *never the more*
  To her yeeld passage, gainst his Lord to goe,
  But with outrageous strokes did him restraine,
And with his bodie bard the way atwixt them twaine.

14

Then tooke the angrie witch her golden cup,[8]
  Which still she bore, replete with magick artes;
  Death and despeyre did many thereof sup,
  And secret poyson through their inner parts,
  Th'eternall bale of heavie wounded harts:
  Which after charmes and some enchauntments said,
  She lightly sprinkled on his weaker° parts;   *too weak*
  Therewith his sturdie courage soone was quayd,° *daunted*
And all his senses were with suddeine dread dismayd.

15

So downe he fell before the cruell beast,
  Who on his necke his bloudie clawes did seize,
  That life nigh crusht out of his panting brest:
  No powre he had to stirre, nor will to rize.
  That when the carefull° knight gan well avise,° *watchful/notice*
  He lightly left the foe, with whom he fought,
  And to the beast gan turne his enterprise;

8. The golden cup of Revelation 17.4, here signifying the Catholic Mass and what Protestants thought
the false and pseudomagical doctrine of transubstantiation. Duessa's cup recalls that of Circe,
whose drugs turned men to swine (*Odyssey* 10), and of Circe's counterpart, Acrasia (II.i.55); its
antidote is the chalice of Fidelia (I.x.13).

For wondrous anguish in his hart it wrought,
To see his lovéd Squire into such thraldome brought.

16

And high advauncing his bloud-thirstie blade,
  Stroke one of those deforméd heads so sore,
  That of his puissance proud ensample made;[9]
  His monstrous scalpe° downe to his teeth it tore,   *skull*
  And that misforméd shape mis-shapéd more:
  A sea of bloud gusht from the gaping wound,
  That her gay garments staynd with filthy gore,
  And overflowéd all the field around;
That over shoes in bloud he waded on the ground.

17

Thereat he roaréd for exceeding paine,
  That to have heard, great horror would have bred,
  And scourging th'emptie ayre with his long traine,
  Through great impatience° of his grievéd hed   *agony*
  His gorgeous ryder from her loftie sted
  Would have cast downe, and trod in durtie myre,
  Had not the Gyant soone her succouréd;
  Who all enraged with smart and franticke yre,
Came hurtling in full fierce, and forst the knight retyre.

18

The force, which wont in two to be disperst,
  In one alone left° hand he new unites,   *remaining*
  Which is through rage more strong then both were erst;
  With which his hideous club aloft he dites,°   *raises*
  And at his foe with furious rigour smites,
  That strongest Oake might seeme to overthrow:
  The stroke upon his shield so heavie lites,
  That to the ground it doubleth him full low:
What mortall wight could ever beare so monstrous blow?

19

And in his fall his shield, that covered was,
  Did loose his vele by chaunce, and open flew:
  The light whereof, that heavens light did pas,°   *surpass*
  Such blazing brightnesse through the aier threw,
  That eye mote not the same endure to vew.
  Which when the Gyaunt spyde with staring eye,
  He downe let fall his arme, and soft withdrew
  His weapon huge, that heavéd was on hye
For to have slaine the man, that on the ground did lye.

---

9. "And I saw one of [the beast's] heads as it were wounded to death" (Revelation 13.3).

20

And eke the fruitfull-headed° beast, amazed   *many-headed*
  At flashing beames of that sunshiny shield,
  Became starke blind, and all his senses dazed,
  That downe he tumbled on the durtie field,
  And seemed himselfe as conqueréd to yield.[1]
  Whom when his maistresse proud perceived to fall,
  Whiles yet his feeble feet for faintnesse reeld,
  Unto the Gyant loudly she gan call,
"O helpe Orgoglio, helpe, or else we perish all."

21

At her so pitteous cry was much amooved
  Her champion stout, and for to ayde his frend,
  Againe his wonted angry weapon prooved:°   *tried*
  But all in vaine: for he has read his end
  In that bright shield, and all their forces spend
  Themselves in vaine: for since that glauncing° sight,   *dazzling*
  He hath no powre to hurt, nor to defend;
  As where th'Almighties lightning brond does light,
It dimmes the dazéd eyen, and daunts the senses quight.

22

Whom when the Prince, to battell new addrest,
  And threatning high his dreadfull stroke did see,
  His sparkling blade about his head he blest,°   *brandished*
  And smote off quite his right leg by the knee,
  That downe he tombled; as an aged tree,[2]
  High growing on the top of rocky clift,
  Whose hartstrings with keene steele nigh hewen be,
  The mightie trunck halfe rent, with ragged rift
Doth roll adowne the rocks, and fall with fearefull drift.°   *force*

23

Or as a Castle rearéd high and round,
  By subtile engins and malitious slight°   *trickery*
  Is underminéd from the lowest ground,
  And her foundation forst,° and feebled quight,   *shattered*
  At last downe falles, and with her heapéd hight
  Her hastie ruine does more heavie° make,   *forceful*
  And yields it selfe unto the victours might;
  Such was this Gyaunts fall, that seemd to shake
The stedfast globe of earth, as it for feare did quake.

1. Similarly the brightness of Ruggiero's shield, when displayed, overthrows his opponents (*Orlando Furioso* 22).
2. The simile has many classical analogues; see, e.g., *Aeneid* 2.626–31.

24

The knight then lightly leaping to the pray,
  With mortall steele him smot againe so sore,
  That headlesse his unweldy bodie lay,
  All wallowd in his owne fowle bloudy gore,
  Which flowéd from his wounds in wondrous store.
  But soone as breath out of his breast did pas,
  That huge great body, which the Gyaunt bore,
  Was vanisht quite, and of that monstrous mas
Was nothing left, but like an emptie bladder was.

25

Whose grievous fall, when false Duessa spide,
  Her golden cup she cast unto the ground,
  And crownéd mitre rudely threw aside;
  Such percing griefe her stubborne hart did wound,
  That she could not endure that dolefull stound,°   *sorrow*
  But leaving all behind her, fled away:
  The light-foot Squire her quickly turnd around,
  And by hard meanes enforcing her to stay,
So brought unto his Lord, as his deservéd pray.

26

The royall Virgin, which beheld from farre,
  In pensive plight, and sad perplexitie,
  The whole atchievement° of this doubtfull warre,   *course*
  Came running fast to greet his victorie,
  With sober gladnesse, and myld modestie,
  And with sweet joyous cheare him thus bespake;
  "Faire braunch of noblesse, flowre of chevalrie,
  That with your worth the world amazéd make,
How shall I quite° the paines, ye suffer for my sake?   *pay for*

27

"And you³ fresh bud of vertue springing fast,
  Whom these sad eyes saw nigh unto deaths dore,
  What hath poore Virgin for such perill past,
  Wherewith you to reward? Accept therefore
  My simple selfe, and service evermore;
  And he that high does sit, and all things see
  With equall° eyes, their merites to restore,°   *impartial/reward*
  Behold what ye this day have done for mee,
And what I cannot quite, requite° with usuree.°   *repay/interest*

28

"But sith the heavens, and your faire handeling°   *conduct*
  Have made you maister of the field this day,

---

3. I.e., the Squire.

Your fortune maister eke with governing,°   *active control*
And well begun end all so well, I pray,
Ne let that wicked woman scape away;
For she it is, that did my Lord bethrall,
My dearest Lord, and deepe in dongeon lay,
Where he his better dayes hath wasted all.
O heare, how piteous he to you for ayd does call."

29

Forthwith he gave in charge unto his Squire,
    That scarlot whore to keepen carefully;
    Whiles he himselfe with greedie° great desire   *eager*
    Into the Castle entred forcibly,
    Where living creature none he did espye;
    Then gan he lowdly through the house to call:
    But no man cared to answere to his crye.
    There raignd a solemne silence over all,
Nor voice was heard, nor wight was seene in bowre or hall.

30

At last with creeping crooked pace forth came
    An old old man, with beard as white as snow,
    That on a staffe his feeble steps did frame,°   *support*
    And guide his wearie gate both too and fro:
    For his eye sight him failéd long ygo,
    And on his arme a bounch of keyes he bore,
    The which unuséd rust did overgrow:
    Those were the keyes of every inner dore,
But he could not them use, but kept them still in store.

31

But very uncouth sight was to behold,
    How he did fashion his untoward° pace,   *awkward*
    For as he forward mooved his footing old,
    So backward still was turnd his wrincled face,
    Unlike to men, who ever as they trace,°   *walk*
    Both feet and face one way are wont to lead.
    This was the auncient keeper of that place,
    And foster father of the Gyant dead;
His name Ignaro[4] did his nature right aread.°   *indicate*

32

His reverend haires and holy gravitie
    The knight much honord, as beseeméd well,[5]
    And gently askt, where all the people bee,
    Which in that stately building wont to dwell.

---

4. Ignorance, particularly ignorance of the Gospel: his backward-turned face represents preoccupation
   with the Law of the Old Testament.
5. I.e., as was proper.

Who answerd him full soft, he could not tell.
Againe he askt, where that same knight was layd,
Whom great Orgoglio with his puissaunce fell
Had made his caytive thrall; againe he sayde,
He could not tell: ne ever other answere made.

33

Then askéd he, which way he in might pas:
He could not tell, againe he answeréd.
Thereat the curteous knight displeaséd was,
And said, "Old sire, it seemes thou hast not red°   recognized
How ill it sits° with that same silver hed   accords
In vaine to mocke, or mockt in vaine to bee:
But if thou be, as thou art pourtrahéd
With natures pen, in ages grave degree,
Aread° in graver wise, what I demaund of thee."   tell

34

His answere likewise was, he could not tell.
Whose sencelesse speach, and doted° ignorance   senile
When as the noble Prince had markéd well,
He ghest his nature by his countenance,
And calmd his wrath with goodly temperance.
Then to him stepping, from his arme did reach
Those keyes, and made himselfe free enterance.
Each dore he opened without any breach;°   forcing
There was no barre to stop, nor foe him to empeach.°   oppose

35

There all within full rich arayd he found,
With royall arras° and resplendent gold.   tapestry
And did with store of every thing abound,
That greatest Princes presence° might behold.   person
But all the floore (too filthy to be told)
With bloud of guiltlesse babes, and innocents trew,
Which there were slaine, as sheepe out of the fold,
Defiléd was, that dreadfull was to vew,
And sacred° ashes over it was strowéd new.   accursed

36

And there beside of marble stone was built
An Altare, carved with cunning imagery,
On which true Christians bloud was often spilt,
And holy Martyrs often doen to dye,[6]
With cruell malice and strong tyranny:
Whose blessed sprites from underneath the stone
To God for vengeance cryde continually,

---

6. I.e., put to death.

And with great griefe were often heard to grone,
That hardest heart would bleede, to heare their piteous mone.[7]

37

Through every rowme he sought, and every bowr,
  But no where could he find that wofull thrall:
  At last he came unto an yron doore,
  That fast was lockt, but key found not at all
  Emongst that bounch, to open it withall;
  But in the same a little grate was pight,°   *placed*
  Through which he sent his voyce, and lowd did call
  With all his powre, to weet, if living wight
Were houséd therewithin, whom he enlargen° might.   *free*

38

Therewith an hollow, dreary, murmuring voyce
  These piteous plaints and dolours did resound;
  "O who is that, which brings me happy choyce°   *chance*
  Of death, that here lye dying every stound,°   *moment*
  Yet live perforce in balefull darkenesse bound?
  For now three Moones have changéd thrice their hew,°   *shape*
  And have been thrice hid underneath the ground,
  Since I the heavens chearefull face did vew,
O welcome thou, that doest of death bring tydings trew."

39

Which when that Champion heard, with percing point
  Of pitty deare° his hart was thrilléd sore,   *grievous*
  And trembling horrour ran through every joynt,
  For ruth of gentle knight so fowle forlore:°   *lost*
  Which shaking off, he rent that yron dore,
  With furious force, and indignation fell;
  Where entred in, his foot could find no flore,
  But all a deepe descent, as darke as hell,
That breathéd ever forth a filthie banefull smell.

40

But neither darkenesse fowle, nor filthy bands,
  Nor noyous° smell his purpose could withhold,   *poisonous*
  (Entire affection hateth nicer° hands)   *too fastidious*
  But that with constant zeale, and courage bold,
  After long paines and labours manifold,
  He found the meanes that Prisoner up to reare;
  Whose feeble thighes, unhable to uphold

---

7. "I saw under the altar the souls of them that were slain for the word of God, and for the testimony
which they held: And they cried with a loud voice, saying, How long, O Lord, holy and true,
dost thou not judge and avenge our blood on them that dwell on the earth?" (Revelation 6.9–10).
The scriptural echoes in stanzas 35–36 (see cf. Matthew 2.16) reinforce the association of Arthur
with Christ.

His pinéd° corse, him scarse to light could beare,   *wasted*
A ruefull spectacle of death and ghastly drere.°   *wretchedness*

41

His sad dull eyes deepe sunck in hollow pits,
   Could not endure th'unwonted sunne to view;
   His bare thin cheekes for want of better bits,°   *food*
   And empty sides deceivéd° of their dew,   *defrauded*
   Could make a stony hart his hap to rew;
   His rawbone armes, whose mighty brawnéd bowrs°   *muscles*
   Were wont to rive steele plates, and helmets hew,
   Were cleane consumed, and all his vitall powres
Decayd, and all his flesh shronk up like withered flowres.[8]

42

Whom when his Lady saw, to him she ran
   With hasty joy: to see him made her glad,
   And sad to view his visage pale and wan,
   Who earst in flowres of freshest youth was clad.
   Tho° when her well of teares she wasted had,   *then*
   She said, "Ah dearest Lord, what evill starre
   On you hath fround, and pourd his influence bad,
   That of your selfe ye thus berobbéd arre,
And this misseeming hew[9] your manly looks doth marre?

43

"But welcome now my Lord, in wele or woe,
   Whose presence I have lackt too long a day;
   And fie on Fortune mine avowéd foe,
   Whose wrathfull wreakes° them selves do now alay.   *revenges*
   And for these wrongs shall treble penaunce pay
   Of treble good: good growes of evils priefe."°   *experience*
   The chearelesse man, whom sorrow did dismay,
   Had no delight to treaten° of his griefe;   *speak*
His long enduréd famine needed more reliefe.

44

"Faire Lady," then said that victorious knight,[1]
   "The things, that grievous were to do, or beare,
   Them to renew,° I wote, breeds no delight;   *recall*
   Best musicke breeds delight in loathing eare:
   But th'onely good, that growes of passéd feare,

8. Sin has enfeebled and wasted the spirit of Holiness. Breaking down an infernal iron door so as
   mercifully to lead a captive back to the light recalls the Harrowing of Hell as described in the
   apocryphal but popular Gospel of Nicodemus. The belief that while he was dead Christ liberated
   the righteous who lived before his time is, however, older than this composite text from the fourth
   or fifth century. See I.x.40, which explicitly associates the redemption of prisoners with Christ's
   rescue operation.
9. I.e., unseemly appearance.
1. I.e., Arthur, whose tactful speech reflects his courteous recognition of the humiliation felt by the
   exhausted and silent Redcrosse.

Is to be wise, and ware° of like agein.   *wary*
  This dayes ensample hath this lesson deare
  Deepe written in my heart with yron pen,
That blisse may not abide in state of mortall men.

45

"Henceforth sir knight, take to you wonted strength,
  And maister these mishaps with patient might;
  Loe where your foe lyes stretcht in monstrous length,
  And loe that wicked woman in your sight,
  The roote of all your care, and wretched plight,
  Now in your powre, to let her live, or dye."
  "To do her dye," quoth Una, "were despight,°   *spiteful*
  And shame t'avenge so weake an enimy;
But spoile° her of her scarlot robe, and let her fly."   *deprive*

46

So as she bad, that witch they disaraid,
  And robd of royall robes, and purple pall,
  And ornaments that richly were displaid;
  Ne sparéd they to strip her naked all.
  Then when they had despoild her tire° and call,°   *attire/headdress*
  Such as she was, their eyes might her behold,
  That her misshapéd parts did them appall,
  A loathly, wrinckled hag, ill favoured, old,
Whose secret filth good manners biddeth not be told.[2]

47

Her craftie head was altogether bald,
  And as in hate of honorable eld,°   *age*
  Was overgrowne with scurfe and filthy scald;°   *scabby disease*
  Her teeth out of her rotten gummes were feld,°   *fallen*
  And her sowre breath abhominably smeld;
  Her driéd dugs, like bladders lacking wind,
  Hong downe, and filthy matter from them weld;
  Her wrizled° skin as rough, as maple rind,   *wrinkled*
So scabby was, that would have loathd° all womankind.   *disgusted*

48

Her neather parts, the shame of all her kind,
  My chaster° Muse for shame doth blush to write;   *too chaste*
  But at her rompe she growing had behind
  A foxes taile, with dong all fowly dight;°   *smeared*
  And eke her feet most monstrous were in sight;
  For one of them was like an Eagles claw,
  With griping talaunts° armd to greedy fight,   *talons*

---

2. Redcrosse's perception of Duessa's ugliness shows the restored capacity of Holiness to recognize
  falsehood. Alcina is likewise revealed to the disenchanted Ruggiero in *Orlando Furioso* 7.71–73;
  see Revelation 17.16: "these shall hate the whore, and shall make her desolate and naked."

The other like a Beares uneven° paw:[3]   *rough*
More ugly shape yet never living creature saw.

49

Which when the knights beheld, amazd they were,
  And wondred at so fowle deforméd wight.
  "Such then," said Una, "as she seemeth here,
  Such is the face of falshood, such the sight
  Of fowle Duessa, when her borrowed light
  Is laid away, and counterfesaunce° knowne."   *deception*
  Thus when they had the witch disrobéd quight,
  And all her filthy feature° open showne,   *form*
They let her goe at will, and wander wayes unknowne.

50

She flying fast from heavens hated face,
  And from the world that her discovered wide,°   *widely*
  Fled to the wastfull wildernesse apace,
  From living eyes her open shame to hide,
  And lurkt in rocks and caves long unespide.
  But that faire crew of knights, and Una faire
  Did in that castle afterwards abide,
  To rest them selves, and weary powres repaire,
Where store they found of all, that dainty was and rare.

Canto IX

His loves and lignage Arthur tells:
  The knights knit friendly bands:
  Sir Trevisan flies from Despayre,
  Whom Redcrosse knight withstands.

1

O goodly golden chaine,[1] wherewith yfere°   *together*
  The vertues linkéd are in lovely wize:
  And noble minds of yore allyéd were,
  In brave poursuit of chevalrous emprize,°   *enterprise*
  That none did others saféty despize,
  Nor aid envy° to him, in need that stands,   *begrudge*
  But friendly each did others prayse devize
  How to advaunce with favourable hands,
As this good Prince redeemd the Redcrosse knight from bands.

---

3. "And the . . . feet [of the beast] were as the feet of a bear" (Revelation 13.2). Like the fox, falsehood
  is crafty; like eagle and bear, rapacious and brutal.
1. See I.v.25, note. Chaucer, following Boethius, speaks of "the faire cheyne of love" with which
  "the Firste Moevere" linked the elements ("Knightes Tale," 2987–92) and also of love, "that with
  an holsom alliaunce / Halt peples joyned, as hym lest hem gye, / Love, that knetteth lawe of
  compaignie, / And couples doth in vertue for to dwelle" (*Troilus and Criseyde* 3.1746–49).

2

Who when their powres, empaird through labour long,
   With dew repast they had recuréd° well,   *restored*
   And that weake captive wight now wexéd strong,
   Them list no lenger there at leasure dwell,
   But forward fare, as their adventures fell,°   *befell*
   But ere they parted, Una faire besought
   That straunger knight his name and nation tell;
Least so great good, as he for her had wrought,
Should die unknown, and buried be in thanklesse thought.

3

"Faire virgin," said the Prince, "ye me require
   A thing without the compas° of my wit: *scope*
   For both the lignage and the certain Sire,
   From which I sprong, from me are hidden yit.
   For all so soone as life did me admit
   Into this world, and shewéd heavens light,
   From mothers pap I taken was unfit:°   *unsuitably*
   And streight delivered to a Faery knight,
To be upbrought in gentle thewes° and martiall might.   *manners*

4

"Unto old Timon[2] he me brought bylive,°   *immediately*
   Old Timon, who in youthly yeares hath beene
   In warlike feates th'expertest man alive,
   And is the wisest now on earth I weene;
   His dwelling is low in a valley greene,
   Under the foot of Rauran[3] mossy hore,°   *gray*
   From whence the river Dee as silver cleene°   *pure*
   His tombling billowes rolls with gentle rore:
There all my dayes he traind me up in vertuous lore.

5

"Thither the great Magicien Merlin came,
   As was his use, ofttimes to visit me:
   For he had charge my discipline to frame,
   And Tutours nouriture° to oversee.   *training*
   Him oft and oft I askt in privitie,
   Of what loines and what lignage I did spring:
   Whose aunswere bad me still assuréd bee,
   That I was sonne and heire unto a king,
As time in her just terme[4] the truth to light should bring."

2. "Honor." Either the "Faery knight" of stanza 3 (perhaps Malory's Sir Ector) or, more probably, Merlin brought the child to Timon.
3. A hill in western Wales. The Tudors liked to associate their Welsh origin with the semihistorical Arthur.
4. I.e., in due course.

6

"Well worthy impe,"° said then the Lady gent,°   *scion/gentle*
  "And Pupill fit for such a Tutours hand.
  But what adventure, or what high intent
  Hath brought you hither into Faery land,
  Aread° Prince Arthur, crowne of Martiall band?"   *tell*
  "Full hard it is," quoth he, "to read° aright   *discern*
  The course of heavenly cause, or understand
  The secret meaning of th'eternall might,
That rules mens wayes, and rules the thoughts of living wight.[5]

7

"For whither he through fatall° deepe foresight   *prophetic*
  Me hither sent, for cause to me unghest,
  Or that fresh bleeding wound, which day and night
  Whilome° doth rancle in my riven brest,   *incessantly*
  With forcéd fury following his° behest,   *its*
  Me hither brought by wayes yet never found,
  You to have helpt I hold my selfe yet blest."
  "Ah curteous knight," quoth she, "what secret wound
Could ever find,° to grieve the gentlest hart on ground?"   *succeed*

8

"Deare Dame," quoth he, "you sleeping sparkes awake,
  Which troubled once, into huge flames will grow,
  Ne ever will their fervent fury slake,
  Till living moysture into smoke do flow,
  And wasted° life do lye in ashes low.   *consumed*
  Yet sithens° silence lesseneth not my fire,   *since*
  But told it flames, and hidden it does glow,
  I will revele, what ye so much desire:
Ah Love, lay downe thy bow, the whiles I may respire.°   *breathe*

9

"It was in freshest flowre of youthly yeares,
  When courage first does creepe in manly chest,
  Then first the coale of kindly° heat appeares   *natural*
  To kindle love in every living brest;
  But me had warnd old Timons wise behest,°   *bidding*
  Those creeping flames by reason to subdew,
  Before their rage grew to so great unrest,
  As miserable lovers use to rew,
Which still wex old in woe, whiles woe still wexeth new.

10

"That idle name of love, and lovers life,
  As losse of time, and vertues enimy

5. "How unsearchable are his judgments, and his ways past finding out" (Romans 11.33).

I ever scornd, and joyd to stirre up strife,
  In middest of their mournfull Tragedy,
  Ay wont to laugh, when them I heard to cry,
  And blow the fire, which them to ashes brent:°   *burned*
Their God himselfc,[6] grieved at my libertie,
  Shot many a dart at me with fiers intent,
But I them warded all with wary government.°   *self-discipline*

11

"But all in vaine: no fort can be so strong,
  Ne fleshly brest can arméd be so sound,
  But will at last be wonne with battrie long,
  Or unawares at disavantage found;
Nothing is sure, that growes on earthly ground:
  And who most trustes in armc of fleshly might,
  And boasts, in beauties chaine not to be bound,
Doth soonest fall in disaventrous° fight,   *disastrous*
And yeeldes his caytive neck to victours most despight.[7]

12

"Ensample make of him your haplesse joy,
  And of my selfe now mated,° as ye see;   *overcome*
  Whose prouder° vaunt that proud avenging boy   *too proud*
Did soone pluck downe, and curbd my libertie.
For on a day prickt° forth with jollitie   *urged*
  Of looser° life, and heat of hardiment,°   *too loose/boldness*
  Raunging the forest wide on courser frec,
The fields, the floods, the heavens with one consent
Did seeme to laugh on me, and favour mine intent.

13

"For-wearied with my sports, I did alight
  From loftie steed, and downe to sleepe me layd;
  The verdant gras my couch did goodly dight,°   *make*
And pillow was my helmet faire displayd:
Whiles every sencc the humour sweet embayd,°   *pervaded*
  And slombring soft my hart did steale away,
  Me seeméd, by my side a royall Mayd
Her daintie limbes full softly down did lay:
So faire a creature yet saw never sunny day.[8]

14

"Most goodly glee° and lovely blandishment°   *pleasure/flattery*
  She to me made, and bad me love her deare,
  For dearely sure her love was to me bent,

6. I.e., Cupid.
7. I.e., greatest outrage.
8. Celtic folklore or its literary echoes provided Spenser with the outlines of this episode, based on
the liaison established by some elf or fairy with a mortal creature.

As when just time expiréd should appeare.
But whether dreames delude, or true it were,
Was never hart so ravisht with delight,
Ne living man like words did ever heare,
As she to me delivered all that night;
And at her parting said, She Queene of Faeries hight.°   *was called*

15

"When I awoke, and found her place devoyd,°   *empty*
And nought but presséd gras, where she had lyen,
I sorrowed all so much, as earst I joyd,
And washéd all her place with watry eyen.
From that day forth I loved that face divine;
From that day forth I cast° in carefull mind,   *resolved*
To seeke her out with labour, and long tyne,°   *suffering*
And never vow to rest, till her I find,
Nine monethes I seeke in vaine yet ni'll° that vow unbind."   *will not*

16

Thus as he spake, his visage wexéd pale,
And chaunge of hew great passion did bewray;°   *reveal*
Yet still he strove to cloke his inward bale,°   *grief*
And hide the smoke, that did his fire display,
Till gentle Una thus to him gan say;
"O happy Queene of Faeries, that hast found
Mongst many, one that with his prowesse may
Defend thine honour, and thy foes confound:
True Loves are often sown, but seldom grow on ground."

17

"Thine, O then," said the gentle Redcrosse knight,
"Next to that Ladies love, shalbe the place,
O fairest virgin, full of heavenly light,
Whose wondrous faith, exceeding earthly race,
Was firmest fixt in mine extremest case.°   *plight*
And you, my Lord, the Patrone° of my life,   *protector*
Of that great Queene may well gaine worthy grace:
For onely worthy you through prowes priefe°   *trial*
Yf living man mote worthy be, to be her liefe.°"   *loved one*

18

So diversly discoursing of their loves,
The golden Sunne his glistring head gan shew,
And sad remembraunce now the Prince amoves,
With fresh desire his voyage to pursew:
Als° Una earnd° her traveill to renew.   *also/yearned*
Then those two knights, fast friendship for to bynd,
And love establish each to other trew,

Gave goodly gifts, the signes of gratefull mynd,
And eke as pledges firme, right hands together joynd.

19

Prince Arthur gave a boxe of Diamond sure,°   *firm, perfect*
  Embowd° with gold and gorgeous ornament,   *clasped*
  Wherein were closd few drops of liquor pure,[9]
  Of wondrous worth, and vertue excellent,
  That any wound could heale incontinent:°   *forthwith*
  Which to requite, the Redcrosse knight him gave
  A booke, wherein his Saveours testament
  Was writ with golden letters rich and brave;
A worke of wondrous grace, and able soules to save.

20

Thus beene they parted, Arthur on his way
  To seeke his love, and th'other for to fight
  With Unaes foe, that all her realme did pray.°   *prey upon*
  But she now weighing the decayéd plight,
  And shrunken synewes of her chosen knight,
  Would not a while her forward course pursew,
  Ne bring him forth in face of dreadfull fight,
  Till he recovered had his former hew:
For him to be yet weake and wearie well she knew.

21

So as they traveild, lo they gan espy
  An arméd knight towards them gallop fast,
  That seeméd from some fearéd foe to fly,
  Or other griesly thing, that him agast.°   *terrified*
  Still as he fled, his eye was backward cast,
  As if his feare still followed him behind;
  Als flew his steed, as he his bands had brast,°   *burst*
  And with his wingéd heeles did tread the wind,
As he had beene a fole of Pegasus his kind.[1]

22

Nigh as he drew, they might perceive his head
  To be unarmd, and curld uncombéd heares
  Upstaring° stiffe, dismayd with uncouth dread;   *bristling*
  Nor drop of bloud in all his face appeares
  Nor life in limbe: and to increase his feares,
  In fowle reproch of knighthoods faire degree,°   *condition, rank*
  About his neck an hempen rope he weares,

9. Medieval romances allude to such balms and cure-alls. Arthur's "drops of liquor pure" are often taken to signify the Eucharist, but DuRocher 1984 stresses their ability to allay bodily hurt. Redcrosse gives Arthur a New Testament.
1. I.e., of Pegasus's race. Pegasus, the winged horse, is said by Hesiod (*Theogony* 280–81) and Ovid (*Metamorphoses* 4.785–86) to have sprung from Medusa's blood.

That with his glistring armes does ill agree;
But he of rope or armes has now no memoree.

23

The Redcrosse knight toward him crosséd fast,
 To weet, what mister° wight was so dismayd: *kind of*
 There him he finds all sencelesse and aghast,
 That of him selfe he seemd to be afrayd;
 Whom hardly he from flying forward stayd,
 Till he these wordes to him deliver might;
 "Sir knight, aread who hath ye thus arayd,
 And eke from whom make ye this hasty flight:
For never knight I saw in such misseeming° plight."   *unseemly*

24

He answerd nought at all, but adding new
 Feare to his first amazment, staring wide
 With stony eyes, and hartlesse hollow hew,[2]
 Astonisht stood, as one that had aspide
 Infernall furies, with their chaines untide.
 Him yet againe, and yet againe bespake
 The gentle knight; who nought to him replide,
 But trembling every joynt did inly quake,
And foltring tongue at last these words seemd forth to shake.

25

"For Gods deare love, Sir knight, do me not stay;
 For loe he comes, he comes fast after mee."
 Eft° looking backe would faine have runne away;   *again*
 But he him forst to stay, and tellen free
 The secret cause of his perplexitie:
 Yet nathemore° by his bold hartie speach,   *not at all*
 Could his bloud-frosen hart emboldned bee,
 But through his boldnesse rather feare did reach,°   *penetrate*
Yet forst, at last he made through silence suddein breach.

26

"And am I now in safetie sure," quoth he,
 "From him, that would have forcéd me to dye?
 And is the point of death now turnd fro mee,
 That I may tell this haplesse history?"
 "Feare nought:" quoth he, "no daunger now is nye."
 "Then shall I you recount a ruefull cace,"
 Said he, "the which with this unlucky eye
 I late beheld, and had not greater grace
Me reft from it, had bene partaker of the place.[3]

2. I.e., despondent, vacant expression.
3. I.e., would have shared my companion's fate.

27

"I lately chaunst (Would I had never chaunst)
  With a faire knight to keepen companee,
  Sir Terwin hight, that well himselfe advaunst
  In all affaires, and was both bold and free,
  But not so happie as mote happie bee:
  He loved, as was his lot, a Ladie gent,
  That him againe° loved in the least degree: *in return*
  For she was proud, and of too high intent,°   *aspiration*
And joyd to see her lover languish and lament.

28

"From whom returning sad and comfortlesse,
  As on the way together we did fare,
  We met that villen (God from him me blesse°)   *protect*
  That curséd wight, from whom I scapt whyleare,°   *lately*
  A man of hell, that cals himselfe Despaire:[4]
  Who first us greets, and after faire areedes°   *tells*
  Of tydings strange, and of adventures rare:
  So creeping close, as Snake in hidden weedes,
Inquireth of our states, and of our knightly deedes.

29

"Which when he knew, and felt our feeble harts
  Embost° with bale,° and bitter byting griefe,   *exhausted/sorrow*
  Which love had launchéd with his deadly darts,
  With wounding words and termes of foule repriefe,°   *reproach*
  He pluckt from us all hope of due reliefe,
  That earst us held in love of lingring life;
  Then hopelesse hartlesse, gan the cunning thiefe
  Perswade us die, to stint° all further strife: *end*
To me he lent this rope, to him a rustie knife.

30

"With which sad instrument of hastie death,
  That wofull lover, loathing lenger light,
  A wide way made to let forth living breath.
  But I more fearefull, or more luckie wight,
  Dismayd with that deforméd dismall sight,
  Fled fast away, halfe dead with dying feare:
  Ne yet assured of life by you, Sir knight,

4. Redcrosse will now be tempted to despair of God's grace. The theme of despair recurs in many
Renaissance texts, e.g., Skelton's *Magnyfycence*, Sackville's "Induction" in *The Mirror for Magistrates*, and "The Legend of Cordelia" (in the *Mirror*'s 1574 edition), which may have contributed
details to Spenser's Despair and his wasted landscape. The "disease of desperation" was also a
subject for religious and medical works. In *The Anatomy of Melancholy* (1621), Robert Burton
describes it as "a most pernicious sin, wherewith the Devil seeks to entrap men . . . The part
affected is the whole soul, and all the faculties of it" (3.4.2.2). It especially overwhelms the
distressed "if their bodies be predisposed by melancholy, they [be] religiously given, and have
tender consciences" (3.4.2.3).

Whose like infirmitie like chaunce may beare:
But God you never let his charmèd speeches heare."[5]

31

"How may a man," said he, "with idle speach
  Be wonne, to spoyle° the Castle of his health?"   *deprive*
  "I wote," quoth he, "whom triall late did teach,
  That like would not[6] for all this worldés wealth:
  His subtill tongue, like dropping honny, mealt'th°   *melts*
  Into the hart, and searcheth every vaine,
  That ere one be aware, by secret stealth
  His powre is reft,° and weaknesse doth remaine.   *taken away*
O never Sir desire to try° his guilefull traine."   *test*

32

"Certes°," said he, "hence shall I never rest,   *surely*
  Till I that treachours art have heard and tride;
  And you Sir knight, whose name mote° I request,   *might*
  Of grace do me unto his cabin guide."
  "I that hight Trevisan," quoth he, "will ride
  Against my liking backe, to doe you grace:
  But nor for gold nor glee° will I abide   *glitter*
  By you, when ye arrive in that same place;
For lever° had I die, then see his deadly face."   *rather*

33

Ere long they come, where that same wicked wight
  His dwelling has, low in an hollow cave,
  Farre underneath a craggie clift ypight,°   *placed*
  Darke, dolefull, drearie, like a greedie grave,
  That still for carrion carcases doth crave:
  On top whereof aye dwelt the ghastly Owle,
  Shrieking his balefull note, which ever drave
  Farre from that haunt all other chearefull fowle;
And all about it wandring ghostes did waile and howle.

34

And all about old stockes° and stubs of trees,   *stumps*
  Whereon nor fruit, nor leafe was ever seene,
  Did hang upon the ragged rocky knees;°   *crags*
  On which had many wretches hangéd beene,
  Whose carcases were scattered on the greene,
  And throwne about the cliffs. Arrivéd there,
  That bare-head knight for dread and dolefull teene,°   *grief*
  Would faine have fled, ne durst approchen neare,
But th'other forst him stay, and comforted in feare.

5. I.e., may God keep you from ever hearing his enchanted discourse.
6. I.e., would not (again) do the like.

35

That darkesome cave they enter, where they find
  That curséd man, low sitting on the ground,
  Musing full sadly in his sullein mind;
  His griesie° lockes, long growen, and unbound,   *gray*
  Disordred hong about his shoulders round,
  And hid his face; through which his hollow eyne
  Lookt deadly dull, and staréd as astound;
  His raw-bone cheekes through penurie and pine,°   *inner torment*
Were shronke into his jawes, as° he did never dine.   *as if*

36

His garment nought but many ragged clouts,°   *shreds of clothing*
  With thornes together pind and patchéd was,
  The which his naked sides he wrapt abouts;
  And him beside there lay upon the gras
  A drearie corse, whose life away did pas,
  All wallowd in his owne yet luke-warme blood,
  That from his wound yet welléd fresh alas;
  In which a rustie knife fast fixéd stood,
And made an open passage for the gushing flood.

37

Which piteous spectacle, approving° trew   *confirming*
  The wofull tale that Trevisan had told,
  When as the gentle Redcrosse knight did vew,
  With firie zeale he burnt in courage bold,
  Him to avenge, before his bloud were cold,
  And to the villein said, "Thou damnéd wight,
  The author of this fact,° we here behold,   *deed*
  What justice can but judge against thee right,
With thine owne bloud to price° his bloud, here shed   *pay for*
  in sight."

38

"What franticke fit," quoth he, "hath thus distraught
  Thee, foolish man, so rash a doome° to give?[7]   *judgment*
  What justice ever other judgement taught,
  But he should die, who merites not to live?
  None else to death this man despayring drive,
  But his owne guiltie mind deserving death.
  Is then unjust to each his due to give?
  Or let him die, that loatheth living breath?
Or let him die at ease, that liveth here uneath?°   *uneasily*

[handwritten margin notes: "Rep. of the Same", "Char. as Satan", "lies → like truth"]

7. Despair draws his arguments chiefly from classical Stoicism and from sayings in the Old Testament concerning God's justice; he omits mention of God's mercy. That his points are inconsistent (see especially stanza 42) shows despair's final irrationality.

39

"Who travels by the wearie wandring way,
　To come unto his wishéd home in haste,
　And meetes a flood, that doth his passage stay,
　Is not great grace to helpe him over past,
　Or free his feet, that in the myre sticke fast?
　Most envious man, that grieves at neighbours good,
　And fond,° that joyest in the woe thou hast,　　　　　*foolish*
　Why wilt not let him passe, that long hath stood
Upon the banke, yet wilt thy selfe not passe the flood?

40

"He there does now enjoy eternall rest
　And happie ease, which thou doest want and crave,
　And further from it daily wanderest:
　What if some litle paine the passage have,
　That makes fraile flesh to feare the bitter wave?
　Is not short paine well borne, that brings long ease,
　And layes the soule to sleepe in quiet grave?
　Sleepe after toyle, port after stormie seas,
Ease after warre, death after life does greatly please."

41

The knight much wondred at his suddeine° wit,　　　　　*quick*
　And said, "The terme of life is limited,
　Ne may a man prolong, nor shorten it;
　The souldier may not move from watchfull sted,°　　　　　*position*
　Nor leave his stand, untill his Captaine bed."°　　　　　*directs*
　"Who life did limit by almightie doome,"
　Quoth he, "knowes best the termes establishéd;
　And he, that points° the Centonell his roome,°　　　*appoints/station*
Doth license him depart at sound of morning droome.[8]

42

"Is not his deed, what ever thing is donne,
　In heaven and earth? did not he all create
　To die againe? all ends that was begonne.
　Their times in his eternall booke of fate
　Are written sure, and have their certaine date.
　Who then can strive with strong necessitie,
　That holds the world in his° still chaunging state,　　　　　*its*
　Or shunne the death ordaynd by destinie?
When houre of death is come, let none aske whence, nor why.

8. Despair's response paraphrases Cicero's allusion to the advice of Pythagoras (*De Senectute* 20). His soporific invitation to rest, to a parodic Sabbath, is meant to lure Redcrosse into deserting through suicide the fight and labor to which he is committed; but a true pilgrim knight finds full repose only in the New Jerusalem and in God's good time.

43

"The lenger life, I wote the greater sin,
  The greater sin, the greater punishment:
  All those great battels, which thou boasts to win,
  Through strife, and bloud-shed, and avengément,
  Now praysd, hereafter deare thou shalt repent:
  For life must life, and bloud must bloud repay.[9]
  Is not enough thy evill life forespent?°   already spent
  For he, that once hath misséd the right way,
The further he doth goe, the further he doth stray.

[handwritten margin note: Devil quotes scripture here]

44

"Then do no further goe, no further stray,
  But here lie downe, and to thy rest betake,
  Th'ill to prevent, that life ensewen may.[1]
  For what hath life, that may it lovéd make,
  And gives not rather cause it to forsake?
  Feare, sicknesse, age, losse, labour, sorrow, strife,
  Paine, hunger, cold, that makes the hart to quake;
  And ever fickle fortune rageth rife,
All which, and thousands mo° do make a loathsome life.   more

45

"Thou wretched man, of death hast greatest need,
  If in true ballance thou wilt weigh thy state:
  For never knight, that daréd warlike deede,
  More lucklesse disaventures did amate:°   daunt, cast down
  Witnesse the dongeon deepe, wherein of late
  Thy life shut up, for death so oft did call;
  And though good lucke prolongéd hath thy date,°   life span
  Yet death then, would the like mishaps forestall,
Into the which hereafter thou maiest happen fall.

46

"Why then doest thou, O man of sin, desire
  To draw thy dayes forth to their last degree?
  Is not the measure of thy sinfull hire
  High heapéd up with huge iniquitie,
  Against the day of wrath,[2] to burden thee?
  Is not enough, that to this Ladie milde
  Thou falséd hast thy faith with perjurie,
  And sold thy selfe to serve Duessa vilde,°   vile
With whom in all abuse thou hast thy selfe defilde?

9. "Whoso sheddeth man's blood, by man shall his blood be shed" (Genesis 9.6). The stanza's opening lines appear to derive from a poem in *Tottel's Miscellany*, ed. Hyder Rollins (Cambridge, MA, 1965), no. 174. On Despair's manipulative rhetoric and theological sophistication, see Skulsky 1990E.
1. I.e., that the remainder of your life may bring.
2. I.e., Doomsday.

47

"Is not he just, that all this doth behold
    From highest heaven, and beares an equall° eye?   *impartial*
    Shall he thy sins up in his knowledge fold,
    And guiltie be of thine impietie?
    Is not his law, Let every sinner die:
    Die shall all flesh?³ what then must needs be donne,
    Is it not better to doe willinglie,
    Then linger, till the glasse be all out ronne?
Death is the end of woes: die soone, O faeries sonne."

48

The knight was much enmovéd with his speach,
    That as a swords point through his hart did perse,
    And in his conscience made a secret breach,
    Well knowing true all, that he did reherse,°   *recount*
    And to his fresh remembrance did reverse°   *recall*
    The ugly vew of his deforméd crimes,
    That all his manly powres it did disperse,
    As he were charméd with inchaunted rimes,
That oftentimes he quakt, and fainted oftentimes.

49

In which amazement, when the Miscreant
    Perceivéd him to waver weake and fraile,
    Whiles trembling horror did his conscience dant,°   *daunt*
    And hellish anguish did his soule assaile,
    To drive him to despaire, and quite to quaile,°   *be dismayed*
    He shewed him painted in a table° plaine,   *picture*
    The damnéd ghosts, that doe in torments waile,
    And thousand feends that doe them endlesse paine
With fire and brimstone, which for ever shall remaine.⁴

50

The sight whereof so throughly him dismaid,
    That nought but death before his eyes he saw,
    And ever burning wrath before him laid,
    By righteous sentence of th'Almighties law:
    Then gan the villein him to overcraw,°   *exult over*
    And brought unto him swords, ropes, poison, fire,
    And all that might him to perdition draw;
    And bad him choose, what death he would desire:
For death was due to him, that had provokt Gods ire.

3. "All flesh shall perish together, and man shall turn again into dust" (Job 34.15).
4. The persuasive power of images (to which Spenser is alert) caps the sophistical rhetoric of the
   preceding stanzas.

51

But when as none of them he saw him take,
  He to him raught° a dagger sharpe and keene,   *held out*
  And gave it him in hand: his hand did quake,
  And tremble like a leafe of Aspin greene,
  And troubled bloud through his pale face was seene
  To come, and goe with tydings from the hart,
  As it a running messenger had beene.
  At last resolved to worke his finall smart,
He lifted up his hand, that backe againe did start.

52

Which when as Una saw, through every vaine
  The crudled° cold ran to her well of life,[5]   *congealing*
  As in a swowne; but soone relived° againe,   *recovered*
  Out of his hand she snatcht the curséd knife,
  And threw it to the ground, enragéd rife,°   *deeply*
  And to him said, "Fie, fie, faint harted knight,
  What meanest thou by this reprochfull strife?
  Is this the battell, which thou vauntst to fight
With that fire-mouthéd Dragon, horrible and bright?

53

"Come, come away, fraile, feeble, fleshly wight,[6]
  Ne let vaine words bewitch thy manly hart,
  Ne divelish thoughts dismay thy constant spright.
  In heavenly mercies hast thou not a part?
  Why shouldst thou then despeire, that chosen art?
  Where justice growes, there grows eke greater grace,
  The which doth quench the brond of hellish smart,
  And that accurst hand-writing doth deface.°   *blot out*
Arise, Sir knight arise, and leave this cursed place."

54

So up he rose, and thence amounted° streight.   *mounted (his horse)*
  Which when the carle° beheld, and saw his guest   *churl*
  Would safe depart, for all his subtill sleight,
  He chose an halter from among the rest,
  And with it hung himselfe, unbid° unblest.   *not prayed for*
  But death he could not worke himselfe thereby;
  For thousand times he so himselfe had drest,°   *made ready*
  Yet nathelesse it could not doe him die,
Till he should die his last, that is eternally.

5. I.e., her heart.
6. In answer to Despair, Una emphasizes the saving power of God's grace: her language recalls the
  shield of faith by which "ye shall be able to quench all the fiery darts of the wicked" (Ephesians
  6.16) and the significance of Christ's death, "Blotting out the handwriting of ordinances that was
  against us" (Colossians 2.14). Una talks less than Despair, but she acts decisively.

Canto X

Her faithfull knight faire Una brings
to house of Holinesse,
Where he is taught repentance, and
the way to heavenly blesse.°   bliss

1

What man is he, that boasts of fleshly might,
   And vaine assurance of mortality,°   *mortal life*
   Which all so soone, as it doth come to fight,
   Against spirituall foes, yeelds by and by,[1]
   Or from the field most cowardly doth fly?
   Ne let the man ascribe it to his skill,
   That thorough grace hath gainéd victory.
   If any strength we have, it is to ill,
But all the good is Gods, both power and eke will.[2]

2

By that, which lately hapned, Una saw,
   That this her knight was feeble, and too faint;
   And all his sinews woxen weake and raw,°   *unready*
   Through long enprisonment, and hard constraint,
   Which he enduréd in his late restraint,
   That yet he was unfit for bloudie fight:
   Therefore to cherish him with diets daint,°   *dainty*
   She cast to bring him, where he chearen° might,   *be refreshed*
Till he recovered had his° late decayéd plight.   *from his*

3

There was an auntient house[3] not farre away,
   Renowmd throughout the world for sacred lore,
   And pure unspotted life: so well they say
   It governd was, and guided evermore,
   Through wisedome of a matrone grave and hore;°   *gray-haired*
   Whose onely joy was to relieve the needes
   Of wretched soules, and helpe the helpelesse pore:
   All night she spent in bidding of her bedes,[4]
And all the day in doing good and godly deedes.

1. I.e., at once.
2. "For by grace are ye saved through faith; and that not of yourselves: it is the gift of God: Not of works, lest any man should boast" (Ephesians 2.8–9). In the context of Reformation polemic, Spenser's insistence that spiritual victory is due to God, not to human "skill," is a Protestant emphasis.
3. Here, having been brought by faith and hope to acknowledge his sinfulness, Redcrosse is cleansed by penance and instructed in love; then, through contemplation irradiated by mercy, he is granted a vision of the New Jerusalem. Each significant detail of this canto contrasts with one in Canto iv, as the House of Holiness, from which the regenerate perceive Heaven, counters the House of Pride, whose inhabitants fall at last into a grim dungeon.
4. I.e., offering prayers. Unlike Archimago, she prays in private and does good openly; cf. Matthew 6.5–6.

4

Dame Caelia⁵ men did her call, as thought
  From heaven to come, or thither to arise,
  The mother of three daughters, well upbrought
  In goodly thewes,° and godly exercise: *discipline*
  The eldest two most sober, chast, and wise,
  Fidelia and Speranza virgins were,
  Though spousd,° yet wanting wedlocks solemnize;   *bethrothed*
  But faire Charissa to a lovely fere°   *mate*
Was linckéd, and by him had many pledges dere.⁶

5

Arrivéd there, the dore they find fast lockt;
  For it was warely watchéd night and day,
  For feare of many foes: but when they knockt,
  The Porter opened unto them streight way:
  He was an aged syre, all hory gray,
  With lookes full lowly cast, and gate full slow,
  Wont on a staffe his feeble steps to stay,
  Hight Humiltá.⁷ They passe in stouping low;
For streight and narrow was the way, which he did show.⁸

6

Each goodly thing is hardest to begin,
  But entred in a spacious court they see,
  Both plaine, and pleasant to be walkéd in,
  Where them does meete a francklin° faire and free,   *freeman, landowner*
  And entertaines with comely courteous glee,
  His name was Zele, that him right well became,
  For in his speeches and behaviour hee
  Did labour lively to expresse the same,
And gladly did them guide, till to the Hall they came.

7

There fairely them receives a gentle Squire,
  Of milde demeanure, and rare courtesie,
  Right cleanly clad in comely sad° attire;   *sober*
  In word and deede that shewed great modestie,
  And knew his good° to all of each degree,   *proper behavior*
  Hight Reverence. He them with speeches meet
  Does faire entreat; no courting nicetie,°   *affectation*
  But simple true, and eke unfainéd sweet,
As might become a Squire so great persons to greet.

5. "Heavenly."
6. I.e., many children. The daughters' names mean Faith, Hope, and Charity (or "spiritual love"). That Charissa is married and prolific indicates the fruitfulness of this virtue. "And now abideth faith, hope, charity, these three; but the greatest of these is charity" (1 Corinthians 13.13).
7. Humility.
8. "Knock, and it shall be opened unto you" (Matthew 7.7), but "Strait is the gate, and narrow is the way, which leadeth unto life, and few there be that find it" (7.14).

8

And afterwards them to his Dame he leades,
  That aged Dame, the Ladie of the place:
  Who all this while was busie at her beades:
  Which doen, she up arose with seemely grace,
  And toward them full matronely did pace.
  Where when that fairest Una she beheld,
  Whom well she knew to spring from heavenly race,
  Her hart with joy unwonted inly sweld,
As feeling wondrous comfort in her weaker eld.°   *old age*

9

And her embracing said, "O happie earth,
  Whereon thy innocent feet doe ever tread,
  Most vertuous virgin borne of heavenly berth,
  That to redeeme thy woefull parents head,
  From tyrans rage, and ever-dying dread,⁹
  Hast wandred through the world now long a day;
  Yet ceasest not thy wearie soles to lead,
  What grace hath thee now hither brought this way?
Or doen thy feeble feet unweeting° hither stray?   *unwittingly*

10

"Strange thing it is an errant° knight to see   *wandering*
  Here in this place, or any other wight,
  That hither turnes his steps. So few there bee,
  That chose the narrow path, or seeke the right:
  All keepe the broad high way, and take delight
  With many rather for to go astray,
  And be partakers of their evill plight,
  Then with a few to walke the rightest way;
O foolish men, why haste ye to your owne decay?"

11

"Thy selfe to see, and tyred limbs to rest,
  O matrone sage," quoth she, "I hither came,
  And this good knight his way with me addrest,°   *directed*
  Led with thy prayses and broad-blazéd fame,
  That up to heaven is blowne." The auncient Dame
  Him goodly greeted in her modest guise,
  And entertaynd them both, as best became,
  With all the court'sies, that she could devise,
Ne wanted ought, to shew her bounteous or wise.

12

Thus as they gan of sundry things devise,°   *discourse*
  Loe two most goodly virgins came in place,

---

9. I.e., continual fear of death, or fear of eternal death.

Ylinkéd arme in arme in lovely° wise,   *loving*
With countenance demure, and modest grace,
They numbred even steps and equall pace:
Of which the eldest, that Fidelia hight,
Like sunny beames threw from her Christall face,
That could have dazd the rash beholders sight,
And round about her head did shine like heavens light.

13

She was araiéd all in lilly white,
And in her right hand bore a cup of gold,
With wine and water fild up to the hight,
In which a Serpent did himselfe enfold,
That horrour made to all, that did behold;
But she no whit did chaunge her constant mood:°   *expression*
And in her other hand she fast did hold
A booke, that was both signd and seald with blood,
Wherein darke things were writ, hard to be understood.[1]

14

Her younger sister, that Speranza hight,
Was clad in blew, that her beseeméd well;
Not all so chearefull seeméd she of sight,[2]
As was her sister; whether dread did dwell,
Or anguish in her hart, is hard to tell:
Upon her arme a silver anchor lay,
Whereon she leanéd ever, as befell:
And ever up to heaven, as she did pray,
Her stedfast eyes were bent, ne swarvéd other way.[3]

15

They seeing Una, towards her gan wend,
Who them encounters with like courtesie;
Many kind speeches they betwene them spend,
And greatly joy each other well to see:
Then to the knight with shamefast° modestie   *humble*
They turne themselves, at Unaes meeke request,
And him salute with well beseeming glee;
Who faire them quites,° as him beseeméd best,   *responds to*
And goodly gan discourse of many a noble gest.°   *feat of arms*

1. The portraits of Fidelia and Speranza share details with images of faith and hope in emblematic literature and art, notably emblem books like those of Ripa, Alciati, and Whitney. Fidelia's cup recalls Moses's elevation of the brazen serpent (Numbers 21.8–9), which St. John reads typologically as the lifting up of "the Son of man" (John 3.14). Serpents, despite the behavior of one in Eden, can be symbols of healing and—because they cast their skins—of renewal. Jesus says to have the wisdom of the serpent as well as the innocence of the dove (Matthew 10.16). This cup primarily represents Holy Communion, encompassing death and life. She holds the New Testament, "signd and seald" with Christ's blood. Cf. Peter 3.16.
2. I.e., in appearance. Hope includes anxiety.
3. "Which hope we have as an anchor of the soul, both sure and stedfast (Hebrews 6.19).

16

Then Una thus; "But she your sister deare,
  The deare Charissa where is she become?[4]
  Or wants she health, or busie is elsewhere?"
  "Ah no," said they, "but forth she may not come:
  For she of late is lightned of her wombe,
  And hath encreast the world with one sonne more,
  That her to see should be but troublesome."
  "Indeede," quoth she, "that should her trouble sore,
But thankt be God, and her encrease so[5] evermore."

17

Then said the aged Caelia, "Deare dame,
  And you good Sir, I wote that of your toyle,
  And labours long, through which ye hither came,
  Ye both forwearied° be: therefore a whyle   *tired out*
  I read° you rest, and to your bowres recoyle.°"   *advise/retire*
  Then calléd she a Groome, that forth him led
  Into a goodly lodge, and gan despoile°   *disrobe*
  Of puissant armes, and laid in easie bed;
His name was meeke Obedience rightfully ared.°   *understood*

18

Now when their wearie limbes with kindly° rest,   *natural*
  And bodies were refresht with due repast,
  Faire Una gan Fidelia faire request,
  To have her knight into her schoolehouse plaste,
  That of her heavenly learning he might taste,
  And heare the wisedome of her words divine.
  She graunted, and that knight so much agraste,°   *favored*
  That she him taught celestiall discipline,[6]
And opened his dull eyes, that light mote in them shine.

19

And that her sacred Booke, with bloud[7] ywrit,
  That none could read, except she did them teach,
  She unto him discloséd every whit,
  And heavenly documents° thereout did preach,   *teaching*
  That weaker wit of man could never reach,
  Of God, of grace, of justice, of free will,
  That wonder was to heare her goodly speach:
  For she was able, with her words to kill,
And raise againe to life[8] the hart, that she did thrill.°   *pierce*

4. I.e., where is she?
5. I.e., may God increase her in that way.
6. I.e., holy laws.
7. I.e., Christ's blood.
8. "For the letter killeth, but the spirit giveth life" (2 Corinthians 3.6).

20

And when she list poure out her larger spright,[9]
  She would commaund the hastie Sunne to stay,
  Or backward turne his course from heavens hight;
  Sometimes great hostes of men she could dismay,
  Dry-shod to passe, she parts the flouds in tway;
  And eke huge mountaines from their native seat
  She would commaund, themselves to beare away,
  And throw in raging sea with roaring threat.
Almightie God her gave such powre, and puissance great.

21

The faithfull knight now grew in litle space,
  By hearing her, and by her sisters lore,
  To such perfection of all heavenly grace,
  That wretched world he gan for to abhore,
  And mortall life gan loath, as thing forlore,°   *abandoned*
  Greeved with remembrance of his wicked wayes,
  And prickt with anguish of his sinnes so sore,
  That he desirde to end his wretched dayes:
So much the dart of sinfull guilt the soule dismayes.

22

But wise Speranza gave him comfort sweet,
  And taught him how to take assuréd hold
  Upon her silver anchor, as was meet;
  Else had his sinnes so great, and manifold
  Made him forget all that Fidelia told.
  In this distresséd doubtfull agonie,
  When him his dearest Una did behold,
  Disdeining life, desiring leave to die,
She found her selfe assayld with great perplexitie.

23

And came to Caelia to declare her smart,
  Who well acquainted with that commune plight,
  Which sinfull horror[1] workes in wounded hart,
  Her wisely comforted all that she might,
  With goodly counsell and advisement right;
  And streightway sent with carefull diligence,
  To fetch a Leach,° the which had great insight   *physician*
  In that disease of grievéd conscience,
And well could cure the same; His name was Patience.

9. I.e., higher power. The allusions to miraculous events in the Old Testament (Joshua 10.12; 2 Kings 20.10; Judges 7.7; Exodus 14.21–31) are significantly climaxed by a reference to Matthew 21.21: "Jesus answered . . . if ye shall say unto this mountain, Be thou removed, and be thou cast into the sea; it shall be done."
1. I.e., horror of sin.

24

Who comming to that soule-diseaséd knight,
  Could hardly him intreat,° to tell his griefe: *persuade*
  Which knowne, and all that noyd° his heavie spright   *troubled*
  Well searcht, eftsoones he gan apply reliefe
  Of salves and med'cines, which had passing priefe,[2]
  And thereto added words of wondrous might:[3]
  By which to ease he him recuréd briefe,°   *quickly*
  And much asswaged the passion° of his plight,   *suffering*
That he his paine endured, as seeming now more light.

25

But yet the cause and root of all his ill,
  Inward corruption, and infected sin,
  Not purged nor heald, behind remainéd still,
  And festring sore did rankle yet within,
  Close creeping twixt the marrow and the skin.
  Which to extirpe,° he laid him privily   *root out*
  Downe in a darkesome lowly place farre in,
  Whereas he meant his corrosives to apply,
And with streight° diet tame his stubborne malady.   *strict*

26

In ashes and sackcloth he did array
  His daintie corse, proud humors[4] to abate,
  And dieted with fasting every day,
  The swelling of his wounds to mitigate,
  And made him pray both earely and eke late:
  And ever as superfluous flesh did rot
  Amendment readie still at hand did wayt,
  To pluck it out with pincers firie whot,°   *hot*
That soone in him was left no one corrupted jot.

27

And bitter Penance with an yron whip,
  Was wont him once to disple° every day: *discipline*
  And sharpe Remorse his heart did pricke and nip,
  That drops of bloud thence like a well did play;
  And sad Repentance uséd to embay°   *bathe*
  His bodie in salt water smarting sore,
  The filthy blots of sinne to wash away.[5]
  So in short space they did to health restore
The man that would not live, but earst° lay at deathes dore.   *formerly*

2. I.e., surpassing power.
3. As absolution follows confession.
4. I.e., pride.
5. "Wash me throughly from mine iniquity, and cleanse me from my sin" (Psalms 51.2).

28

In which his torment often was so great,
    That like a Lyon he would cry and rore,
    And rend his flesh, and his owne synewes eat.
IIis owne deare Una hearing evermore
His ruefull shriekes and gronings, often tore
Her guiltlesse garments, and her golden heare,
For pitty of his paine and anguish sore;
Yet all with patience wisely she did beare;
For well she wist, his crime could else be never cleare.°   *cleansed*

29

Whom thus recovered by wise Patience,
    And trew Repentance they to Una brought:
    Who joyous of his curéd conscience,
Him dearely kist, and fairely eke besought
Himselfe to chearish, and consuming thought
To put away out of his carefull brest.
By this Charissa, late in child-bed brought,
Was woxen strong, and left her fruitfull nest;
To her faire Una brought this unacquainted guest.[6]

30

She was a woman in her freshest age,[7]
    Of wondrous beauty, and of bountie° rare,   *virtue*
    With goodly grace and comely personage,
That was on earth not easie to compare;
Full of great love, but Cupids wanton snare
As hell she hated, chast in worke and will;
Her necke and breasts were ever open bare,
That ay thereof her babes might sucke their fill;
The rest was all in yellow robes arayéd still.

31

A multitude of babes about her hong,
    Playing their sports, that joyd her to behold,
    Whom still she fed, whiles they were weake and young,
But thrust them forth still, as they wexéd old:
And on her head she wore a tyre° of gold,   *headdress*
Adornd with gemmes and owches° wondrous faire,   *jewels*
Whose passing price uneath was to be told;[8]
And by her side there sate a gentle paire
Of turtle doves, she sitting in an yvorie chaire.

6. "Though I have all faith, so that I could remove mountains, and have not charity, I am nothing" (1 Corinthians 13.2).
7. The description of Charissa includes classical elements: Hymen, the god of marriage, traditionally wore yellow (cf. *Metamorphoses* 10.1), and doves were sacred to Venus. But the love figured in Charissa, "chast in worke and will," is Christian.
8. I.e., whose surpassing value might scarcely be estimated.

32

The knight and Una entring, faire her greet,
  And bid her joy of that her happie brood;
  Who them requites with court'sies seeming meet,°   *appropriate*
  And entertaines with friendly chearefull mood.
  Then Una her besought, to be so good,
  As in her vertuous rules to schoole her knight,
  Now after all his torment well withstood,
  In that sad° house of Penaunce, where his spright   *grave*
Had past the paines of hell, and long enduring night.

33

She was right joyous of her just request,
  And taking by the hand that Faeries sonne,
  Gan him instruct in every good behest,
  Of love, and righteousnesse, and well to donne,⁹
  And wrath, and hatred warély to shonne,
  That drew on men Gods hatred, and his wrath,
  And many soules in dolours° had fordonne:°   *misery/ruined*
  In which when him she well instructed hath,
From thence to heaven she teacheth him the ready path.

34

Wherein his weaker° wandring steps to guide,   *too weak*
  An auncient matrone she to her does call,
  Whose sober lookes her wisedome well descride:°   *revealed*
  Her name was Mercie, well knowne over all,
  To be both gratious, and eke liberall:
  To whom the carefull charge of him she gave,
  To lead aright, that he should never fall
  In all his wayes through this wide worldés wave,
That Mercy in the end his righteous soule might save.

35

The godly Matrone by the hand him beares
  Forth from her presence, by a narrow way,
  Scattred with bushy thornes, and ragged breares,°   *briers*
  Which still before him she removed away,
  That nothing might his ready passage stay:
  And ever when his feet encombred were,
  Or gan to shrinke, or from the right to stray,
  She held him fast, and firmely did upbeare,
As carefull Nourse her child from falling oft does reare.

36

Eftsoones unto an holy Hospitall,°   *retreat, sanctuary*
  That was fore° by the way, she did him bring,   *close*

---

9. I.e., well-doing.

In which seven Bead-men[1] that had vowéd all
Their life to service of high heavens king
Did spend their dayes in doing godly thing:
Their gates to all were open evermore,
That by the wearie way were traveiling,
And one sate wayting° ever them before,   *watching*
To call in commers-by, that needy were and pore.

37

The first of them that eldest was, and best,°   *chief*
Of all the house had charge and governement,
As Guardian and Steward of the rest:
His office was to give entertainement
And lodging, unto all that came, and went:
Not unto such, as could him feast againe,
And double quite,° for that he on them spent,   *repay*
But such, as want of harbour° did constraine: *shelter*
Those for Gods sake his dewty was to entertaine.

38

The second was as Almner° of the place,   *distributor of alms*
His office was, the hungry for to feed,
And thristy give to drinke, a worke of grace:
He feard not once him selfe to be in need,
Ne cared to hoord for those, whom he did breede:[2]
The grace of God he layd up still in store,
Which as a stocke° he left unto his seede;   *resource*
He had enough, what need him care for more?
And had he lesse, yet some he would give to the pore.

39

The third had of their wardrobe custodie,
In which were not rich tyres,° nor garments gay,   *attire*
The plumes of pride, and wings of vanitie,
But clothés meet to keepe keene could° away,   *cold*
And naked nature seemely to aray;
With which bare wretched wights he dayly clad,
The images of God in earthly clay;
And if that no spare cloths to give he had,
His owne coate he would cut, and it distribute glad.

40

The fourth appointed by his office was,
Poore prisoners to relieve with gratious ayd,
And captives to redeeme with price of bras,°   *money*

1. Properly men who pray for others' spiritual welfare, these "Bead-men" are dedicated to serving
   the bodily needs of others. Opposed to the Seven Deadly Sins, they perform the traditional seven
   "Corporal Works of Mercy."
2. I.e., his own family.

From Turkes and Sarazins, which them had stayd;°   *held captive*
And though they faultie were, yet well he wayd,
That God to us forgiveth every howre
Much more then that, why they in bands were layd,   *for which*
And he that harrowd hell with heavie stowre,
The faultie soules from thence brought to his heavenly bowre.

41

The fift had charge sicke persons to attend,
  And comfort those, in point of death which lay;
  For them most needeth comfort in the end,
  When sin, and hell, and death do most dismay
  The feeble soule departing hence away.
  All is but lost, that living we bestow,°   *store up*
  If not well ended at our dying day.
  O man have mind of that last bitter throw;°   *throe*
For as the tree does fall, so lyes it ever low.

42

The sixt had charge of them now being dead,
  In seemely sort their corses to engrave,°   *bury*
  And deck with dainty flowres their bridall bed,
  That to their heavenly spouse[3] both sweet and brave°   *fair*
  They might appeare, when he their soules shall save.
  The wondrous workemanship of Gods owne mould,°   *image*
  Whose face he made, all beasts to feare, and gave
  All in his hand, even dead we honour should.
Ah dearest God me graunt, I dead be not defould.°   *defiled*

43

The seventh now after death and buriall done,
  Had charge the tender Orphans of the dead
  And widowes ayd, least they should be undone:°   *ruined*
  In face of judgement[4] he their right would plead,
  Ne ought the powre of mighty men did dread
  In their defence, nor would for gold or fee
  Be wonne their rightfull causes downe to tread:
  And when they stood in most necessitee,
He did supply their want, and gave them ever free.°   *freely*

44

There when the Elfin knight arrivéd was,
  The first and chiefest of the seven, whose care
  Was guests to welcome, towardes him did pas:
  Where seeing Mercie, that his steps up bare,°   *supported*
  And alwayes led, to her with reverence rare

---

3. I.e., Christ, spouse of the individual soul as well as of the Church (the collective body of all the faithful).
4. I.e., in the court of law.

He humbly louted° in meeke lowlinesse,   *bowed*
And seemely welcome for her did prepare:
For of their order she was Patronèsse,
Albe° Charissa were their chiefest founderesse.   *although*

45

There she awhile him stayes, him selfe to rest,
    That to the rest more able he might bee:
    During which time, in every good behest
    And godly worke of Almes and charitee
    She him instructed with great industree;
    Shortly therein so perfect he became,
    That from the first unto the last degree,
    His mortall life he learnéd had to frame
In holy righteousnesse, without rebuke or blame.

46

Thence forward by that painfull way they pas,
    Forth to an hill, that was both steepe and hy;
    On top whereof a sacred chappell was,
    And eke a litle Hermitage thereby,
    Wherein an aged holy man did lye,
    That day and night said his devotion,
    Ne other worldly busines did apply;°   *pursue*
    His name was heavenly Contemplation;
Of God and goodnesse was his meditation.[5]

47

Great grace that old man to him given had;
    For God he often saw from heavens hight,
    All° were his earthly eyen both blunt° and bad,   *although/dim*
    And through great age had lost their kindly° sight,   *natural*
    Yet wondrous quick and persant° was his spright,   *piercing*
    As Eagles eye, that can behold the Sunne:[6]
    That hill they scale with all their powre and might,
    That his frayle thighes nigh wearie and fordonne°   *exhausted*
Gan faile, but by her helpe the top at last he wonne.

48

There they do finde that godly aged Sire,
    With snowy lockes adowne his shoulders shed,
    As hoarie frost with spangles doth attire
    The mossy braunches of an Oke halfe ded.
    Each bone might through his body well be red,°   *seen*
    And every sinew seene through° his long fast: *in consequence of*

5. In the episode that follows, Spenser may recall the moral refreshment and strength received by
   Ariosto's Rinaldo on the "Hill of Hope" (*Rinaldo* 11.56–65); but the encounter of Redcrosse and
   Contemplation has more consistent religious significance.
6. An attribute of eagles in medieval bestiaries: see Chaucer, *Parliament of Fowls* 330–31: "There
   myghte men the royal egle fynde, / That with his sharpe lok perseth the sonne . . ."

For nought he cared his carcas long unfed;
  His mind was full of spirituall repast,
And pyned° his flesh, to keepe his body low and chast.   *starved*

49

Who when these two approching he aspide,
  At their first presence grew agrievéd sore,
  That forst him lay his heavenly thoughts aside;
  And had he not that Dame respected more,°   *greatly*
  Whom highly he did reverence and adore,
He would not once have movéd for the knight.
  They him saluted standing far afore;°   *before*
  Who well them greeting, humbly did requight,
And askéd, to what end they clomb° that tedious height.   *had climbed*

50

"What end," quoth she, "should cause us take such paine,
  But that same end, which every living wight
  Should make his marke,° high heaven to attaine?   *aim*
  Is not from hence the way, that leadeth right
  To that most glorious house, that glistreth bright
With burning starres, and everliving fire,
  Whereof the keyes are to thy hand behight°   *entrusted*
  By wise Fidelia? she doth thee require,
To shew it to this knight, according° his desire."   *granting*

51

"Thrise happy man," said then the father grave,
  "Whose staggering steps thy steady hand doth lead,
  And shewes the way, his sinfull soule to save.
  Who better can the way to heaven aread,°   *direct*
  Then thou thy selfe, that was both borne and bred
In heavenly throne, where thousand Angels shine?
  Thou doest the prayers of the righteous sead°   *offspring*
  Present before the majestie divine,
And his avenging wrath to clemencie incline.

52

"Yet since thou bidst, thy pleasure shalbe donne.
  Then come thou man of earth,[7] and see the way,
  That never yet was seene of Faeries sonne,
  That never leads the traveiler astray,
  But after labours long, and sad delay,
Brings them to joyous rest and endlesse blis.
  But first thou must a season fast and pray,
  Till from her bands the spright assoiléd° is,   *set free*
And have her strength recured° from fraile infirmitis."   *recovered*

---

7. Contemplation refers to Redcrosse's fleshly humanity but also plays on the etymology of "George," the name by which he identifies him in stanza 61.

53

That done, he leads him to the highest Mount;[8]
  Such one, as that same mighty man of God,
  That bloud-red billowes like a walléd front
  One either side disparted with his rod,
  Till that his army dry-foot through them yod,°   *went*
  Dwelt fortie dayes upon; where writ in stone
  With bloudy letters by the hand of God,
  The bitter doome of death and balefull mone°   *grief*
He did receive, whiles flashing fire about him shone.[9]

54

Or like that sacred hill[1], whose head full hie,
  Adornd with fruitfull Olives all arownd,
  Is, as it were for endlesse memory
  Of that deare Lord, who oft thereon was fownd,
  For ever with a flowring girlond crownd:
  Or like that pleasaunt Mount,[2] that is for ay
  Through famous Poets verse each where° renownd,   *everywhere*
  On which the thrise three learnéd Ladies play
Their heavenly notes, and make full many a lovely lay.

55

From thence, far off he unto him did shew
  A litle path, that was both steepe and long,
  Which to a goodly Citie[3] led his vew;
  Whose wals and towres were builded high and strong
  Of perle and precious stone, that earthly tong
  Cannot describe, nor wit of man can tell;
  Too high a ditty° for my simple song;   *theme*
  The Citie of the great king hight it well,
Wherein eternall peace and happinesse doth dwell.

56

As he thereon stood gazing, he might see
  The blessed Angels to and fro descend
  From highest heaven, in gladsome companee,
  And with great joy into that Citie wend,

8. Cf. that "high mountain" to which the angel carried John "in the spirit" to show him "that great city, the holy Jerusalem, descending out of heaven from God" (Revelation 21.10).
9. I.e., Sinai (Exodus 24.16–18), on which God gave Moses the Ten Commandments; as the still binding "letters" of the Law, the commandments bring death to sinners unless they are released by God's grace working through Christ's sacrifice.
1. I.e., the Mount of Olives, where Christ prayed before his execution; as symbols of peace, olives suggest a redemptive end to the heroics and terror of stanza 53.
2. I.e., Parnassus, abode of the Muses, included here as a forceful claim for the true poet's calling and insight; cf. E.K.'s "Argument" to "October": "Poetrie [is] a divine gift and heavenly instinct not to bee gotten by labour and learning, but adorned with both: and poured into the witte by . . . celestiall inspiration."
3. The New Jerusalem, whose "light was like unto a stone most precious, even like a jasper stone, clear as crystal; . . . and the twelve gates were twelve pearls; every several gate was of one pearl: and the street of the city was pure gold, as it were transparent glass" (Revelation 21.11, 21).

As commonly° as friend does with his frend.   *sociably*
Whereat he wondred much, and gan enquere,
What stately building durst so high extend
Her loftie towres unto the starry sphere,
And what unknowen nation there empeopled° were.   *settled*

57

"Faire knight," quoth he, "Hierusalem that is,
The new Hierusalem, that God has built
For those to dwell in, that are chosen his,
His chosen people purged from sinfull guilt,
With pretious bloud, which cruelly was spilt
On curséd tree, of that unspotted lam,
That for the sinnes of all the world was kilt:[4]
Now are they Saints all in that Citie sam,°   *together*
More deare unto their God, then younglings to their dam."

58

"Till now," said then the knight, "I weenéd well,
That great Cleopolis,[5] where I have beene,
In which that fairest Faerie Queene doth dwell,
The fairest Citie was, that might be seene;
And that bright towre all built of christall cleene,°   *pure*
Panthea,[6] seemd the brightest thing, that was:
But now by proofe all otherwise I weene;
For this great Citie that does far surpas,
And this bright Angels towre quite dims that towre of glas."

59

"Most trew," then said the holy aged man;
"Yet is Cleopolis for earthly frame,°   *structure*
The fairest peece, that eye beholdén can:
And well beseemes all knights of noble name,
That covet in th'immortall booke of fame
To be eternizéd, that same to haunt,°   *frequent*
And doen their service to that soveraigne Dame,
That glorie does to them for guerdon° graunt: *reward*
For she is heavenly borne, and heaven may justly vaunt.[7]

60

"And thou faire ymp, sprong out from English race,
How ever now accompted° Elfins sonne,   *accounted*
Well worthy doest thy service for her grace,°   *favor*

4. "Behold the Lamb of God, which taketh away the sin of the world" (John 1.29).
5. The city of earthly glory; at once an ideal counterpart of Elizabeth's London and a symbolic image of the highest attainment within the reach of the fallen human race unaided by direct divine intervention.
6. The ideal counterpart of either Westminster Abbey or one of Elizabeth's residences near London.
7. I.e., she may justly boast of her heavenly descent.

To aide a virgin desolate foredonne.
But when thou famous victorie hast wonne,
And high emongst all knights hast hong thy shield,
Thenceforth the suit° of earthly conquest shonne,   *pursuit*
And wash thy hands from guilt of bloudy field:
For bloud can nought but sin, and wars but sorrowes yield.

61

"Then seeke this path, that I to thee presage,°   *point out*
Which after all to heaven shall thee send;
Then peaceably thy painefull pilgrimage
To yonder same Hierusalem do bend,
Where is for thee ordaind a blessed end:
For thou emongst those Saints, whom thou doest see,
Shalt be a Saint, and thine owne nations trend
And Patrone: thou Saint George shalt calléd bee,
Saint George of mery England, the signe of victoree."[8]

62

"Unworthy wretch," quoth he, "of so great grace,
How dare I thinke such glory to attaine?"
"These that have it attaind, were in like cace,"
Quoth he, "as wretched, and lived in like paine."
"But deeds of armes must I at last be faine,°   *willing*
And Ladies love to leave so dearely bought?"
"What need of armes, where peace doth ay remaine,"
Said he, "and battailes none are to be fought?
As for loose loves are° vaine, and vanish into nought."   *they are*

63

"O let me not," quoth he, "then turne againe
Backe to the world, whose joyes so fruitlesse are;
But let me here for aye in peace remaine,
Or streight way on that last long voyage fare,
That nothing may my present hope empare."°   *impair*
"That may not be," said he, "ne maist thou yit
Forgo that royall maides bequeathéd care,°   *charge*
Who did her cause into thy hand commit,
Till from her curséd foe thou have her freely quit."°   *released*

8. Although Aelfric's ninth-century *Lives of the Saints* includes St. George, Spenser's conception of
   England's patron saint draws on a tradition stemming from the *Legenda Aurea* (translated by
   Caxton in 1487), an allied pictorial tradition, and suggestions in folklore of the mysterious circumstances attending the infancy and youth of mortals singled out by Providence for a glorious
   destiny; see Maclean 1990E. Spenser's most significant (and Protestant) change was to make George
   a lover and future husband; in older versions, and despite traces of his archaic role as a fertility
   figure, he remains celibate until his martyrdom. Stephen Hawes, too, had combined a dragon
   fight, religious allegory, and love interest (Kaske 1989). Some Protestants, though, viewed George
   with skepticism and thought his cult pagan or "papist" nonsense; thus Barnaby Googe's *Shippe of
   Safegarde* (1569) sets a picture of St. George and the dragon in the Land of Heresy.

64

"Then shall I soone," quoth he, "so God me grace,
  Abet° that virgins cause disconsolate,   *maintain*
  And shortly backe returne unto this place,
  To walke this way in Pilgrims poore estate.
  But now aread, old father, why of late
  Didst thou behight° me borne of English blood,   *call*
  Whom all a Faeries sonne doen nominate?"°   *name, consider*
  "That word shall I," said he, "avouchen° good,   *prove*
Sith to thee is unknowne the cradle of thy brood.

65

"For well I wote, thou springst from ancient race
  Of Saxon kings, that have with mightie hand
  And many bloudie battailes fought in place
  High reard their royall throne in Britane land,
  And vanquisht them, unable to withstand:
  From thence a Faerie thee unweeting reft,°   *stole away*
  There as thou slepst in tender swadling band,
  And her base Elfin brood there for thee left.
Such men do Chaungelings call, so chaunged by Faeries theft.

66

"Thence she thee brought into this Faerie lond,
  And in an heapéd furrow did thee hyde,
  Where thee a Ploughman all unweeting fond,
  As he his toylesome teme that way did guyde,
  And brought thee up in ploughmans state to byde,°   *remain*
  Whereof Georgos he thee gave to name;°.
  Till prickt with courage, and thy forces pryde,
  To Faery court thou cam'st to seeke for fame,
And prove thy puissaunt armes, as seemes thee best became."°   *suited*

67

"O holy Sire," quoth he, "how shall I quight°   *repay*
  The many favours I with thee have found,
  That hast my name and nation red° aright,   *told*
  And taught the way that does to heaven bound?"°   *go*
  This said, adowne he lookéd to the ground,
  To have returnd, but dazéd were his eyne,
  Through passing° brightnesse, which did quite confound   *surpassing*
  His feeble sence, and too exceeding shyne.
So darke are earthly things compard to things divine.

9. Ovid describes the discovery, by an Etrurian ploughman, of Tages, son of the earth; Tages was
destined to instruct his nation in the art of prophecy (*Metamorphoses* 15.558–59). Since George's
name associates him with Adam ("red earth"), to call him *Saint* George shows the sanctification
of fallen and earthly humanity made possible by Christ's victory.

68

At last whenas himselfe he gan to find,°   *recover*
  To Una back he cast him to retire;
  Who him awaited still with pensive mind.
  Great thankes and goodly meed° to that good syre,   *reward*
  He thence departing gave for his paines hyre.[1]
  So came to Una, who him joyed to see,
  And after litle rest, gan him desire,
  Of her adventure mindfull for to bee.
So leave they take of Caelia, and her daughters three.

Canto XI

The knight with that old Dragon fights
two dayes incessantly:
The third him overthrowes, and gayns
most glorious victory.[1]

1

High time now gan it wex° for Una faire,   *become*
  To thinke of those her captive Parents deare,
  And their forwasted kingdome to repaire:[2]
  Whereto whenas they now approchéd neare,
  With hartie words her knight she gan to cheare,
  And in her modest manner thus bespake;
  "Deare knight, as deare, as ever knight was deare,
  That all these sorrowes suffer for my sake,
High heaven behold the tedious toyle, ye for me take.

2

"Now are we come unto my native soyle,
  And to the place, where all our perils dwell;
  Here haunts that feend, and does his dayly spoyle,
  Therefore henceforth be at your keeping[3] well,
  And ever ready for your foeman fell.
  The sparke of noble courage now awake,
  And strive your excellent selfe to excell;
  That shall ye evermore renowméd make,
Above all knights on earth, that batteill undertake."

3

And pointing forth, "lo yonder is," said she,
  "The brasen towre in which my parents deare
  For dread of that huge feend emprisond be,

1. I.e., as recompense for his trouble.
1. On the dragon fight see C. V. Kaske, *SP* 66 (1969), who argues that during the battle George evolves into Christ; Leslie 1983, 105–14, finds him an ordinary Christian now enabled by grace to conquer satanic evil and thus a figure for but not the equivalent of Christ.
2. I.e., to restore to health their kingdom, laid waste by "that old Dragon."
3. I.e., on your guard.

Whom I from far see on the walles appeare,
Whose sight my feeble soule doth greatly cheare:
And on the top of all I do espye
The watchman wayting tydings glad to heare,
That O my parents might I happily
Unto you bring, to ease you of your misery."

4

With that they heard a roaring hideous sound,
  That all the ayre with terrour filléd wide,
  And seemd uneath° to shake the stedfast ground.   *almost*
  Eftsoones that dreadfull Dragon they espide,
  Where stretcht he lay upon the sunny side
  Of a great hill, himselfe like a great hill.
  But all so soone, as he from far descride
  Those glistring armes, that heaven with light did fill,
He rousd himselfe full blith,° and hastned them untill.°   *joyfully/toward*

5

Then bad the knight his Lady yede° aloofe,   *go*
  And to an hill her selfe with draw aside,
  From whence she might behold that battailles proof°   *trial*
  And eke be safe from daunger far descryde:
  She him obayd, and turnd a little wyde.°   *aside*
  Now O thou sacred Muse,°⁴ most learnéd Dame,
  Faire ympe of Phoebus, and his aged bride,
  The Nourse of time, and everlasting fame,
That warlike hands ennoblest with immortall name;

6

O gently come into my feeble brest,
  Come gently, but not with that mighty rage,
  Wherewith the martiall troupes thou doest infest,°   *arouse, inspire*
  And harts of great Heroës doest enrage,
  That nought their kindled courage may aswage,
  Soone as thy dreadfull trompe begins to sownd;
  The God of warre with his fiers equipage°   *equipment*
  Thou doest awake, sleepe never he so sownd,
And scaréd nations doest with horrour sterne astownd.°   *petrify*

7

Faire Goddesse lay that furious fit° aside,   *mood*
  Till I of warres and bloudy Mars do sing,⁵
  And Briton fields with Sarazin bloud bedyde,

---

4. Here Clio, Muse of history. Departing from the tradition that Jove begot the Muses (cf. Hesiod, *Theogony* 53–62), Spenser reads Comes as making Apollo their father (*Mythologiae* 4.10; see Roche 1989, 165).
5. Possibly an allusion to Spenser's intended epic "of politicke vertues in [Arthur's] person, after that hee came to be king" (cf. Hieatt 1988); or the passage may anticipate later portions of *The Faerie Queene*, like Book V.

Twixt that great faery Queene and Paynim king,
That with their horrour heaven and earth did ring,
A worke of labour long, and endlesse prayse:
But now a while let downe that haughtie° string,   *lofty*
And to my tunes thy second tenor[6] rayse,
That I this man of God his godly armes may blaze.°   *proclaim*

8

By this the dreadfull Beast[7] drew nigh to hand,
  Halfe flying, and halfe footing in his hast,
  That with his largenesse measuréd much land,
  And made wide shadow under his huge wast;°   *girth*
  As mountaine doth the valley overcast.
  Approching nigh, he rearéd high afore°   *in front*
  His body monstrous, horrible, and vast,
  Which to increase his wondrous greatnesse more,
Was swolne with wrath, and poyson, and with bloudy gore.

9

And over, all[8] with brasen scales was armd,
  Like plated coate of steele, so couchéd neare,[9]
  That nought mote perce, ne might his corse be harmd
  With dint of sword, nor push of pointed speare;
  Which as an Eagle, seeing pray appeare,
  His aery plumes doth rouze,° full rudely dight,°   *shake/arrayed*
  So shakéd he, that horrour was to heare,
  For as the clashing of an Armour bright,
Such noyse his rouzéd scales did send unto the knight.

dragon ↓

10

His flaggy° wings when forth he did display,   *drooping*
  Were like two sayles, in which the hollow wynd
  Is gathered full, and worketh speedy way·
  And eke the pennes,° that did his pineons bynd,   *feathers, quills*
  Were like mayne-yards, with flying canvas lynd,
  With which whenas him list the ayre to beat,
  And there by force unwonted passage find,
  The cloudes before him fled for terrour great,
And all the heavens stood still amazéd with his threat.

11

His huge long tayle wound up in hundred foldes,
  Does overspred his long bras-scaly backe,

6. I.e., lower strain, perhaps reflecting Plato's distinction (*Republic* 3.399) between the Dorian mode, suited to courageous men in war, and the more restrained Phrygian mode, befitting those engaged in peaceful and sober exertions of the will.
7. Among the references to such creatures in classical and medieval literature, Spenser was most probably influenced by Ovid's account of the "serpent sacred to Mars" which Cadmus overcame (*Metamorphoses* 3.31–94). See also Kaske 1989 on Hawes's dragon.
8. I.e., over the greater part of his body.
9. I.e., closely set.

Whose wreathéd boughts° when ever he unfoldes,   *coils*
And thicke entangled knots adown does slacke,
Bespotted as with shields of red and blacke,
It sweepeth all the land behind him farre,
And of three furlongs does but litle lacke;
And at the point two stings in-fixéd arre,
Both deadly sharpe, that sharpest steele exceeden farre.

12

But stings and sharpest steele did far exceed[1]
    The sharpnesse of his cruell rending clawes;
    Dead was it sure, as sure as death in deed,
    What ever thing does touch his ravenous pawes,
    Or what within his reach he ever drawes.
    But his most hideous head my toung to tell
    Does tremble: for his deepe devouring jawes
    Wide gapéd, like the griesly mouth of hell,
Through which into his darke abisse all ravin° fell.[2]   *prey*

13

And that° more wondrous was, in either jaw   *what*
    Three ranckes of yron teeth enraungéd were,
    In which yet trickling bloud and gobbets raw
    Of late devouréd bodies did appeare,
    That sight thereof bred cold congealéd feare:
    Which to increase, and all atonce to kill,
    A cloud of smoothering smoke and sulphur seare°   *burning*
    Out of his stinking gorge° forth steeméd still,   *maw*
That all the ayre about with smoke and stench did fill.

14

His blazing eyes, like two bright shining shields,
    Did burne with wrath, and sparkled living fyre;
    As two broad Beacons, set in open fields,
    Send forth their flames farre off to every shyre,
    And warning give, that enemies conspyre,
    With fire and sword the region to invade;
    So flamed his eyne with rage and rancorous yre:
    But farre within, as in a hollow glade,
Those glaring lampes were set, that made a dreadfull shade.

15

So dreadfully he towards him did pas,°   *pace*
    Forelifting up aloft his speckled brest,

1. I.e., were far exceeded by.
2. The stanza emphasizes the allegorical significance of this battle, which gathers in all Book I's moral and historical meanings. The fight recalls and re-enacts Christ's victory over sin while also representing the Protestant triumph in England (which Protestants insisted was a recovery of Gospel truth, not an innovation). But the contestants in this encounter are nothing less than Life and Death (see stanza 49, lines 1–3).

And often bounding on the bruséd gras,
As for great joyance of his newcome guest.
Eftsoones he gan advance his haughtie crest,
As chaufféd° Bore his bristles doth upreare,   *angry*
And shoke his scales to battell readie drest;
That made the Redcrosse knight nigh quake for feare,
As bidding bold defiance to his foeman neare.[3]

16

The knight gan fairely couch° his steadie speare,   *rest, aim*
And fiercely ran at him with rigorous might:
The pointed steele arriving rudely theare,
His harder° hide would neither perce, nor bight,   *too hard*
But glauncing by forth passéd forward right;
Yet sore amovéd with so puissant push,
The wrathfull beast about him turnéd light,°   *quickly*
And him so rudely passing by, did brush
With his long tayle, that horse and man to ground did rush.

17

Both horse and man up lightly rose againe,
And fresh encounter towards him addrest:
But th'idle stroke yet backe recoyld in vaine,
And found no place his deadly point to rest.
Exceeding rage enflamed the furious beast,
To be avengéd of so great despight;°   *outrage*
For never felt his imperceable brest
So wondrous force, from hand of living wight;
Yet had he provéd° the powre of many a puissant knight.   *tested*

18

Then with his waving wings displayéd wyde,
Himselfe up high he lifted from the ground,
And with strong flight did forcibly divide
The yielding aire, which nigh too feeble found
Her flitting partes, and element unsound,°   *weak*
To beare so great a weight: he cutting way
With his broad sayles, about him soaréd round:
At last low stouping with unweldie sway,[4]
Snatcht up both horse and man, to beare them quite away.

19

Long he them bore above the subject plaine,[5]
So farre as Ewghen° bow a shaft may send,   *yew*
Till struggling strong did him at last constraine,
To let them downe before his flightés end:

3. I.e., the dragon shook his scales in defiance.
4. I.e., ponderous force.
5. I.e., the plain below.

As hagard° hauke presuming to contend   *wild*
With hardie fowle, above his hable° might,   *powerful*
His wearie pounces° all in vaine doth spend,   *talons*
To trusse° the pray too heavie for his flight;   *seize*
Which comming downe to ground, does free it selfe by fight.

20

He so disseizéd of his gryping grosse,[6]
    The knight his thrillant° speare againe assayd   *piercing*
    In his bras-plated body to embosse,°   *plunge*
    And three mens strength unto the stroke he layd;
    Wherewith the stiffe beame quakéd, as affrayd,
    And glauncing from his scaly necke, did glyde
    Close under his left wing, then broad displayd.
    The percing steele there wrought a wound full wyde,
That with the uncouth° smart the Monster lowdly cryde.   *unfamiliar*

21

He cryde, as raging seas are wont to rore,
    When wintry storme his wrathfull wreck does threat,
    The rolling billowes beat the ragged shore,
    As they the earth would shoulder from her seat,
    And greedie gulfe does gape, as he would eat
    His neighbour element in his revenge:
    Then gin the blustring brethren[7] boldly threat,
    To move the world from off his stedfast henge,°   *axis*
And boystrous battell make, each other to avenge.

22

The steely head stucke fast still in his flesh,
    Till with his cruell clawes he snatcht the wood,
    And quite a sunder broke. Forth flowéd fresh
    A gushing river of blacke goarie blood,
    That drownéd all the land, whereon he stood;
    The streame thereof would drive a water-mill.
    Trebly augmented was his furious mood
    With bitter sense° of his deepe rooted ill,   *feeling*
That flames of fire he threw forth from his large nosethrill.

23

His hideous tayle then hurléd he about,
    And therewith all enwrapt the nimble thyes
    Of his froth-fomy steed, whose courage stout
    Striving to loose the knot, that fast him tyes,
    Himselfe in streighter bandes too rash implyes,[8]
    That to the ground he is perforce constraynd

6. I.e., heavy gripful.
7. I.e., the winds.
8. I.e., too quickly entangles.

To throw his rider: who can° quickly ryse   *did*
  From off the earth, with durty bloud distaynd,°   *stained*
For that reprochfull fall right fowly he disdaynd.

24

And fiercely tooke his trenchand° blade in hand,   *sharp*
  With which he stroke so furious and so fell,
  That nothing seemd the puissance could withstand:
  Upon his crest the hardned yron fell,
  But his more hardned crest was armd so well,
  That deeper dint therein it would not make;
  Yet so extremely did the buffe him quell,°   *dismay*
  That from thenceforth he shund the like to take,
But when he saw them come, he did them still forsake.°   *avoid*

25

The knight was wrath to see his stroke beguyld,°   *foiled*
  And smote againe with more outrageous might;
  But backe againe the sparckling steele recoyld,
  And left not any marke, where it did light;
  As if in Adamant rocke it had bene pight.°   *struck*
  The beast impatient of his smarting wound,
  And of so fierce and forcible despight,°   *injury*
  Thought with his wings to stye° above the ground;   *rise*
But his late wounded wing unserviceable found.

26

Then full of griefe and anguish vehement,
  He lowdly brayd, that like was never heard,
  And from his wide devouring oven sent
  A flake° of fire, that flashing in his beard,   *flash*
  Him all amazd, and almost made affeard:
  The scorching flame sore swingéd° all his face,   *vinged*
  And through his armour all his bodie seard,
  That he could not endure so cruell cace,
But thought his armes to leave, and helmet to unlace.

27

Not that great Champion of the antique world,[9]
  Whom famous Poetes verse so much doth vaunt,
  And hath for twelve huge labours high extold,
  So many furies and sharpe fits did haunt,
  When him the poysoned garment did enchaunt
  With Centaures bloud, and bloudie verses charmed,
  As did this knight twelve thousand dolours° daunt,   *sufferings*
  Whom fyrie steele now burnt, that earst° him armed,   *before*
That erst him goodly armed, now most of all him harmed.

9. Hercules suffered agony when he put on Nessus's robe, soaked in poisoned blood; by the will of
  Jove, he put off mortality and took his place in the stars (*Metamorphoses* 9.134–270).

28

Faint, wearie, sore, emboyléd, grievéd, brent°   *burned*
 With heat, toyle, wounds, armes, smart, and inward fire
 That never man such mischiefes did torment;
 Death better were, death did he oft desire,
 But death will never come, when needes require.
 Whom so dismayd when that his foe beheld,
 He cast to suffer him no more respire,°   *rest, take breath*
 But gan his sturdie sterne° about to weld,°   *tail/lash*
And him so strongly stroke, that to the ground him feld.

29

It fortunéd (as faire it then befell)
 Behind his backe unweeting,° where he stood,   *unnoticed*
 Of auncient time there was a springing well,
 From which fast trickled forth a silver flood,
 Full of great vertues, and for med'cine good.
 Whylome,° before that curséd Dragon got   *formerly*
 That happie land, and all with innocent blood
 Defyld those sacred waves, it rightly hot°   *was called*
The Well of Life,[1] ne yet his° vertues had forgot.   *its*

30

For unto life the dead it could restore,
 And guilt of sinfull crimes cleane wash away,
 Those that with sicknesse were infected sore,
 It could recure, and aged long decay
 Renew, as one were borne that very day.
 Both Silo[2] this, and Jordan did excell,
 And th'English Bath, and eke the german Spau,
 Ne can Cephise, nor Hebrus match this well:
Into the same the knight backe overthrowen, fell.

31

Now gan the golden Phoebus for to steepe
 His fierie face in billowes of the west,
 And his faint steedes watred in Ocean deepe,
 Whiles from their journall° labours they did rest,   *daily*
 When that infernall Monster, having kest°   *cast*
 His wearie foe into that living well,
 Can° high advance his broad discoloured brest,   *did*

1. "And he shewed me a pure river of water of life, clear as crystal, proceeding out of the throne of God and of the Lamb. In the midst of the street of it, and on either side of the river, was there the tree of life, which bare twelve manner of fruits, and yielded her fruit every month; and the leaves of the tree were for the healing of the nations" (Revelation 22.1–2). Well and tree, narrowly interpreted, signify the sacraments of baptism and communion; in a larger sense, both symbolize the power of grace.
2. All these waters were known, either in scripture ("the pool of Siloam" in John 9.7; the cleansing powers of Jordan in 2 Kings 5.10–14), or in classical accounts (the river Cephissus, in Pliny, *Historia Naturalis* 2.106.230; the pure Hebrus, in Horace, *Epistles* 1.16.13), or, in the case of Bath and Spa, for their curative power or their purity.

Above his wonted pitch,° with countenance fell,   *height*
And clapt his yron wings, as victor he did dwell.°   *remain*

32

Which when his pensive Ladie saw from farre,
  Great woe and sorrow did her soule assay,°   *assail*
  As weening that the sad end of the warre,
  And gan to highest God entirely° pray,   *earnestly*
  That fearéd chance from her to turne away;
  With folded hands and knees full lowly bent
  All night she watcht, ne once adowne would lay
  Her daintie limbs in her sad dreriment,
But praying still did wake, and waking did lament.

33

The morrow next gan early to appeare,
  That° Titan[3] rose to runne his daily race;   *when*
  But early ere the morrow next gan reare
  Out of the sea faire Titans deawy face,
  Up rose the gentle virgin from her place,
  And lookéd all about, if she might spy
  Her lovéd knight to move his manly pace:[4]
  For she had great doubt of his saféty,
Since late she saw him fall before his enemy.

34

At last she saw, where he upstarted brave
  Out of the well, wherein he drenchéd lay;
  As Eagle fresh out of the Ocean wave,[5]
  Where he hath left his plumes all hoary gray,
  And deckt himselfe with feathers youthly gay,
  Like Eyas° hauke up mounts unto the skies,   *young*
  His newly budded pineons to assay,
  And marveiles at himselfe, still as he flies:
So new this new-borne knight to battell new did rise.

35

Whom when the damnéd feend so fresh did spy,
  No wonder if he wondred at the sight,
  And doubted, whether his late enemy
  It were, or other new suppliéd knight.
  He, now to prove his late renewéd might,
  High brandishing his bright deaw-burning[6] blade,

3. The sun.
4. I.e., actively recovering.
5. "When the eagle grows old . . . then he goes in search of a fountain, and . . . he flies up to the height of heaven. . . . Then at length, diving down into the fountain, he dips himself three times in it, and instantly he is renewed with a great vigour of plumage and splendor of vision. Do the same thing, O man. . . . Seek for the spiritual fountain of the Lord and . . . then your youth will be renewed like the eagle's" (*The Bestiary, A Book of Beasts* 105–17).
6. I.e., gleaming with "that holy water dew" (stanza 36).

Upon his crested scalpe so sore did smite,
That to the scull a yawning wound it made:
The deadly dint his dulléd senses all dismaid.

36

I wote not, whether the revenging steele
  Were hardned with that holy water dew,
  Wherein he fell, or sharper edge did feele,
  Or his baptizéd hands now greater° grew;   *stronger*
  Or other secret vertue did ensew;
  Else never could the force of fleshly arme,
  Ne molten mettall in his bloud embrew:°   *plunge*
  For till that stownd° could never wight him harme,   *moment*
By subtilty, nor slight,° nor might, nor mighty charme.   *trickery*

37

The cruell wound enragéd him so sore,
  That loud he yelded° for exceeding paine;   *shrieked*
  As hundred ramping Lyons seemed to rore,
  Whom ravenous hunger did thereto constraine:
  Then gan he tosse aloft his stretchéd traine,
  And therewith scourge the buxome° aire so sore,   *unresisting*
  That to his force to yeelden it was faine;°   *forced*
  Ne ought° his sturdie strokes might stand afore,   *anything*
That high trees overthrew, and rocks in peeces tore.

38

The same advauncing high above his head,
  With sharpe intended° sting so rude him smot,   *extended*
  That to the earth him drove, as stricken dead,
  Ne living wight would have him life behot:[7]
  The mortall sting his angry needle shot
  Quite through his shield, and in his shoulder seasd,
  Where fast it stucke, ne would there out be got:
  The griefe thereof him wondrous sore diseasd,°   *troubled*
Ne might his ranckling paine with patience be appeasd.

39.

But yet more mindfull of his honour deare,
  Then of the grievous smart, which him did wring,°   *torment*
  From loathéd soile he can° him lightly reare,   *did*
  And strove to loose the farre infixéd sting:
  Which when in vaine he tryde with struggeling,
  Inflamed with wrath, his raging blade he heft,°   *raised*
  And strooke so strongly, that the knotty string

7. I.e., thought him alive.

Of his huge taile he quite a sunder cleft,
Five joynts thereof he hewd, and but the stump him left.

40

Hart cannot thinke, what outrage, and what cryes,
    With foule enfouldred° smoake and flashing fire,   *black as a thundercloud*
The hell-bred beast threw forth unto the skyes,
That all was coveréd with darknesse dire:
Then fraught with rancour, and engorgéd° ire,   *choking, congested*
He cast at once him to avenge for all,
And gathering up himselfe out of the mire,
With his uneven wings did fiercely fall
Upon his sunne-bright shield, and gript it fast withall.

41

Much was the man encombred with his hold,
    In feare to lose his weapon in his paw,
Ne wist yet, how his talants° to unfold;   *talons*
Nor harder was from Cerberus[8] greedie jaw
To plucke a bone, then from his cruell claw
To reave° by strength the gripéd gage° away: *seize/prize*
Thrise he assayd it from his foot to draw,
And thrise in vaine to draw it did assay,
It booted nought to thinke, to robbe him of his pray.

42

Tho° when he saw no power might prevaile,   *then*
    His trustie sword he cald to his last aid,
Wherewith he fiercely did his foe assaile,
And double blowes about him stoutly laid,
That glauncing fire out of the yron plaid;
As sparckles from the Andvile° use to fly,   *anvil*
When heavie hammers on the wedge are swaid;°   *struck*
Therewith at last he forst him to unty°   *loosen*
One of his grasping feete, him to defend thereby.

43

The other foot, fast fixéd on his shield,
    Whenas no strength, nor stroks mote him constraine
To loose, ne yet the warlike pledge to yield,
He smot thereat with all his might and maine,
That nought so wondrous puissance might sustaine;
Upon the joynt the lucky steele did light,
And made such way, that hewd it quite in twaine;

8. Cf. I.v.34 and note.

The paw yet misséd not his minisht° might,   *lessened*
But hong still on the shield, as it at first was pight.°   *placed*

44

For griefe thereof, and divelish despight,
   From his infernall fournace forth he threw
   Huge flames, that dimméd all the heavens light,
   Enrold in duskish smoke and brimstone blew;
   As burning Aetna from his boyling stew°   *cauldron*
   Doth belch out flames, and rockes in peeces broke,
   And ragged ribs of mountaines molten new,
   Enwrapt in coleblacke clouds and filthy smoke,
That all the land with stench, and heaven with horror choke.

45

The heate whereof, and harmefull pestilence
   So sore him noyd,° that forst him to retire   *troubled*
   A little backward for his best defence,
   To save his bodie from the scorching fire,
   Which he from hellish entrailes did expire.°   *breathe out*
   It chaunst (eternall God that chaunce did guide)
   As he recoyléd backward, in the mire
   His nigh forwearied feeble feet did slide,
And downe he fell, with dread of shame sore terrifide.

46

There grew a goodly tree him faire beside,
   Loaden with fruit and apples rosie red,
   As they in pure vermilion had beene dide,
   Whereof great vertues over all[9] were red°:   *known*
   For happie life to all, which thereon fed,
   And life eke everlasting did befall:
   Great God it planted in that blessed sted°   *place*
   With his almightie hand, and did it call
The Tree of Life, the crime of our first fathers fall.[1]

47

In all the world like was not to be found,
   Save in that soile, where all good things did grow,
   And freely sprong out of the fruitfull ground,
   As incorrupted° Nature did them sow,   *untainted*
   Till that dread Dragon all did overthrow.
   Another like faire tree[2] eke grew thereby,
   Whereof who so did eat, eftsoones did know

9. I.e., everywhere.
1. Adam was expelled from Eden "lest he put forth his hand, and take also of the tree of life, and eat, and live for ever" (Genesis 3.22); his "crime" is responsibility for the consequent denial of this tree (mentioned again in Revelation 22.2) to all humankind.
2. The tree of the knowledge of good and evil.

Both good and ill, O mornefull memory:
That tree through one mans fault hath doen us all to dy.

48

From that first tree forth flowd, as from a well,
  A trickling streame of Balme,[3] most soveraine
  And daintie deare,[4] which on the ground still fell,
  And overflowéd all the fertill plaine,
  As it had deawéd bene with timely° raine: *seasonable*
  Life and long health that gratious° ointment gave,   *full of grace*
  And deadly woundes could heale, and reare againe
  The senselesse corse appointed° for the grave.   *made ready*
Into that same he fell: which did from death him save.

49

For nigh thereto the ever damnéd beast
  Durst not approch, for he was deadly made,[5]
  And all that life preservéd, did detest:
  Yet he it oft adventured° to invade.   *endeavored*
  By this the drouping day-light gan to fade,
  And yeeld his roome to sad succeeding night,
  Who with her sable mantle gan to shade
  The face of earth, and wayes of living wight,
And high her burning torch set up in heaven bright.

50

When gentle Una saw the second fall
  Of her deare knight, who wearie of long fight,
  And faint through losse of bloud, moved not at all,
  But lay as in a dreame of deepe delight,
  Besmeard with pretious Balme, whose vertuous° might   *efficacious*
  Did heale his wounds, and scorching heat alay,
  Againe she stricken was with sore affright,
  And for his safetie gan devoutly pray;
And watch the noyous° night, and wait for joyous day.   *harmful*

51

The joyous day gan early to appeare,
  And faire Aurora from the deawy bed
  Of aged Tithone gan her selfe to reare,
  With rosie cheekes, for shame as blushing red;
  Her golden lockes for haste were loosely shed
  About her eares, when Una her did marke
  Clymbe to her charet, all with flowers spred,

3. The sacrament of communion; more generally, grace. In the Gospel of Nicodemus, Seth heals his father, Adam, with "oil" flowing from "the tree of mercy"; so Christ's blood, in the fullness of time, would restore the descendants of Adam.
4. I.e., choicely precious.
5. I.e., death was his being and essence.

From heaven high to chase the chearelesse darke;
With merry note her loud salutes the mounting larke.

52

Then freshly up arose the doughtie knight,
  All healéd of his hurts and woundés wide,
  And did himselfe to battell readie dight;
  Whose early foe awaiting him beside
  To have devourd, so soone as day he spyde,
  When now he saw himselfe so freshly reare,
  As if late fight had nought him damnifyde,°   *harmed*
He woxe dismayd, and gan his fate to feare;
Nathlesse° with wonted rage he him advauncéd neare.   *nevertheless*

53

And in his first encounter, gaping wide,
  He thought attonce him to have swallowd quight,
  And rusht upon him with outragious pride;
  Who him r'encountring fierce, as hauke in flight,
  Perforce rebutted° backe. The weapon bright   *drove*
  Taking advantage of his open jaw,
  Ran through his mouth with so importune° might,   *violent*
  That deepe emperst his darksome hollow maw,
And back retyrd,° life bloud forth with all did draw.[6]   *withdrawn*

54

So downe he fell, and forth his life did breath,
  That vanisht into smoke and cloudés swift;
  So downe he fell, that th'earth him underneath
  Did grone, as feeble so great load to lift;
  So downe he fell, as an huge rockie clift,
  Whose false° foundation waves have washt away,   *insecure*
  With dreadfull poyse° is from the mayneland rift,   *crash*
  And rolling downe, great Neptune doth dismay;
So downe he fell, and like an heapéd mountaine lay.[7]

55

The knight himselfe even trembled at his fall,
  So huge and horrible a masse it seemed;
  And his deare Ladie, that beheld it all,
  Durst not approch for dread, which she misdeemed,°   *misjudged*
  But yet at last, when as the direfull feend
  She saw not stirre, off-shaking vaine affright,
  She nigher drew, and saw that joyous end:

6. St. George usually wields a spear, but his weapon here recalls the sword issuing from the mouth
of the righteous warrior named "Faithful and True" in Revelation 19.11–16; Redcrosse aims this
sword (usually interpreted as God's Word) at the dragon's mouth, out of which had come destruction
when the Father of Lies spoke through Eden's serpent.
7. That the imagery of fire (dominant in earlier references to the dragon) is absent from this stanza
emphasizes the heroic character of the victory.

Then God she praysd, and thankt her ~~faithfull~~ knight,
That had atchieved so great a conquest by his[8] might.   *Gods*

Canto XII

Faire Una to the Redcrosse knight
betrouthéd is with joy:
Though false Duessa it to barre
her false sleights doe imploy.

1

Behold I see the haven nigh at hand,
  To which I meane my wearie course to bend;
  Vere° the maine shete, and bearc up with[1] the land,   *shift*
  The which afore is fairely to be kend,°   *seen*
  And seemeth safe from stormes, that may offend;
  There this faire virgin wearie of her way
  Must landed be, now at her journeyes end:
  There eke my feeble barke° a while may stay,   *ship*
Till merry wind and weather call her thence away.[2]

2

Scarsely had Phoebus in the glooming East
  Yet harnesséd his firie-footed teeme,
  Ne reard above the earth his flaming creast,
  When the last deadly smoke aloft did steeme,
  That signe of last outbreathéd life did seeme
  Unto the watchman on the castle wall;
  Who thereby dead that balefull Beast did deeme,
  And to his Lord and Ladie lowd gan call,
To tell, how he had seene the Dragons fatall fall.

3

Uprose with hastie joy, and feeble speed
  That aged Sire, the Lord of all that land,
  And lookéd forth, to weet, if true indeede
  Those tydings were, as he did understand,
  Which whenas true by tryall he out fond,°   *found*
  He bad to open wyde his brazen gate,
  Which long time had bene shut, and out of hond[3]
  Proclayméd joy and peace through all his state;
For dead now was their foe, which them forrayéd° late.   *ravaged*

8. I.e., God's might, exerted through Redcrosse; cf. II.i.33.
1. Steer toward.
2. The nautical metaphor with which Spenser opens and concludes this canto (and which recurs at
the end of Book II) is a traditional introductory device; widely employed by classical authors, it
appears also in Dante's *Paradiso* 2.1–15, and in Chaucer's *Troilus and Criseyde* 2.1–7. On Spenser's
unconventional and increasingly discouraged use of it, see Dees 1975.
3. I.e., at once.

4

Then gan triumphant Trompets sound on hie,
  That sent to heaven the ecchoéd report
  Of their new joy, and happie victorie
  Gainst him, that had them long opprest with tort,°   *wrong*
  And fast imprisonéd in siegéd fort.
  Then all the people, as in solemne feast,
  To him assembled with one full consort,°   *company*
  Rejoycing at the fall of that great beast,
From whose eternall bondage now they were releast.

5

Forth came that auncient Lord and aged Queene,
  Arayd in antique robes downe to the ground,
  And sad° habiliments right well beseene°;   *sober/becoming*
  A noble crew about them waited round
  Of sage and sober Peres, all gravely gownd;
  Whom farre before did march a goodly band
  Of tall young men, all hable armes to sownd,[4]
  But now they laurell braunches bore in hand;
Glad signe of victorie and peace in all their land.

6

Unto that doughtie Conquerour they came,
  And him before themselves prostrating low,
  Their Lord and Patrone loud did him proclame,
  And at his feet their laurell boughes did throw.
  Soone after them all dauncing on a row
  The comely virgins came, with girlands dight,
  As fresh as flowres in medow greene do grow,
  When morning deaw upon their leaves doth light:
And in their hands sweet Timbrels° all upheld on hight.   *tambourines*

7

And them before, the fry° of children young   *crowd*
  Their wanton° sports and childish mirth did play,   *frolicsome*
  And to the Maydens sounding tymbrels sung
  In well attunéd notes, a joyous lay,
  And made delightfull musicke all the way,
  Untill they came, where that faire virgin stood;
  As faire Diana in fresh sommers day
  Beholds her Nymphes, enraunged in shadie wood,
Some wrestle, some do run, some bathe in christall flood.

8

So she beheld those maydens meriment
  With chearefull vew; who when to her they came,

---

4. I.e., clash in battle.

Themselves to ground with gratious humblesse bent,
And her adored by honorable name,
Lifting to heaven her everlasting fame:
Then on her head they set a girland greene,
And crownéd her twixt earnest and twixt game;°   *jest, joke*
Who in her selfe-resemblance well beseene,[5]
Did seeme such, as she was, a goodly maiden Queene.

9

And after, all the raskall many° ran,   *multitude*
  Heapéd together in rude rablement,°   *confusion*
  To see the face of that victorious man:
  Whom all admiréd, as from heaven sent,
  And gazd upon with gaping wonderment.
  But when they came, where that dead Dragon lay,
  Stretcht on the ground in monstrous large extent,
  The sight with idle° feare did them dismay,   *baseless*
Ne durst approch him nigh, to touch, or once assay.

10

Some feard, and fled; some feard and well it faynd;°   *concealed*
  One that would wiser seeme, then all the rest,
  Warnd him not touch, for yet perhaps remaynd
  Some lingring life within his hollow brest,
  Or in his wombe might lurke some hidden nest
  Of many Dragonets, his fruitfull seed;
  Another said, that in his eyes did rest
  Yet sparckling fire, and bad thereof take heed;
Another said, he saw him move his eyes indeed.

11

One mother, when as her foolehardie chyld
  Did come too neare, and with his talants play,
  Halfe dead through feare, her litle babe revyld,°   *rebuked*
  And to her gossips° gan in counsell say;   *women friends*
  "How can I tell, but that his talants may
  Yet scratch my sonne, or rend his tender hand?"
  So diversly themselves in vaine they fray;   *frighten*
  Whiles some more bold, to measure him nigh stand,
To prove° how many acres he did spread of land.   *determine*

12

Thus flockéd all the folke him round about,
  The whiles that hoarie° king, with all his traine,   *gray-haired*
  Being arrivéd, where that champion stout
  After his foes defeasance° did remaine,   *defeat*

5. I.e., attractively resembling her real self. Spenser may intend the humor in the following stanzas to "unfigure" the apocalyptic connections he has established between St. George and Christ so that both the hero and the reader can move on (DeNeef 1982, 101–2).

Him goodly greetes, and faire does entertaine,
With princely gifts of yvorie and gold,
And thousand thankes him yeelds for all his paine.
Then when his daughter deare he does behold,
Her dearely doth imbrace, and kisseth manifold.° *many times*

13

And after to his Pallace he them brings,
 With shaumes,° and trompets, and with Clarions sweet; *oboes*
 And all the way the joyous people sings,
 And with their garments strowes the pavéd street:
 Whence mounting up, they find purveyance° meet *provision*
 Of all, that royall Princes court became,° *suited*
 And all the floore was underneath their feet
 Bespred with costly scarlot of great name,° *quality*
On which they lowly sit, and fitting purpose° frame. *discourse*

14

What needs me tell their feast and goodly guize,° *behavior*
 In which was nothing riotous nor vaine?
 What needs of daintie dishes to devize,° *talk*
 Of comely services, or courtly trayne?° *assembly*
 My narrow leaves cannot in them containe
 The large discourse of royall Princes state.
 Yet was their manner then but bare and plaine:
 For th'antique world excesse and pride did hate;
Such proud luxurious pompe is swollen up but late.

15

Then when with meates and drinkes of every kinde
 Their fervent appetites they quenchéd had,
 That auncient Lord gan fit occasion finde,
 Of straunge adventures, and of perils sad,
 Which in his travell him befallen had,
 For to demaund of his renowméd guest:
 Who then with utt'rance grave, and count'nance sad,
 From point to point, as is before exprest,
Discourst his voyage long, according his request.

16

Great pleasure mixt with pittifull° regard, *sympathetic*
 That godly King and Queene did passionate,° *express with feeling*
 Whiles they his pittifull adventures heard,
 That oft they did lament his lucklesse state,
 And often blame the too importune° fate, *severe*
 That heapd on him so many wrathfull wreakes:° *injuries*
 For never gentle knight, as he of late,

So tosséd was in fortunes cruell freakes;
And all the while salt teares bedeawd the hearers cheaks.

17

Then said that royall Pere in sober wise;°   *manner*
  "Deare Sonne, great beene the evils, which ye bore
  From first to last in your late enterprise,
  That I note,° whether prayse, or pitty more: *know not*
  For never living man, I weene, so sore
  In sea of deadly daungers was distrest;
  But since now safe ye seiséd° have the shore,   *attained*
  And well arrivéd are, (high God be blest)
Let us devize of ease and everlasting rest."

18

"Ah dearest Lord," said then that doughty knight,
  "Of ease or rest I may not yet devize;
  For by the faith, which I to armes have plight,
  I bounden am streight after this emprize,°   *enterprise*
  As that your daughter can ye well advize,
  Backe to returne to that great Faerie Queene,
  And her to serve six yeares in warlike wize,
  Gainst that proud Paynim king, that workes her teene:°   *affliction*
Therefore I ought crave pardon, till I there have beene."[6]

19

"Unhappie falles that hard necessitie,"
  Quoth he, "the troubler of my happie peace,
  And vowéd foe of my felicitie;
  Ne I against the same can justly preace:°   *contend*
  But since that band° ye cannot now release,   *bond*
  Nor doen undo; (for vowes may not be vaine)
  Soone as the terme of those six yeares shall cease,
  Ye then shall hither backe returne againe,
The marriage to accomplish vowd betwixt you twain.

20

"Which for my part I covet to performe,
  In sort° as through the world I did proclame,   *manner*
  That who so kild that monster most deforme,
  And him in hardy battaile overcame,
  Should have mine onely daughter to his Dame,°   *wife*
  And of my kingdome heire apparaunt bee:
  Therefore since now to thee perteines° the same,   *belongs*

6. That the marriage of Redcrosse and Una cannot yet be made final signifies that the marriage of
  Christ and the true church will be achieved only at the end of time, at the Day of Judgment.
  Meanwhile, the struggle against evil (and the Roman church) continues.

By dew desert of noble chevalree,
Both daughter and eke kingdome, lo I yield to thee."

21

Then forth he calléd that his daughter faire,
  The fairest Un' his onely daughter deare,
  His onely daughter, and his onely heyre;
  Who forth proceeding with sad sober cheare,°   countenance
  As bright as doth the morning starre appeare
  Out of the East, with flaming lockes bedight,
  To tell that dawning day is drawing neare,
And to the world does bring long wishéd light;
So faire and fresh that Lady shewd her selfe in sight.

22

So faire and fresh, as freshest flowre in May;
  For she had layd her mournefull stole aside,
  And widow-like sad wimple° throwne away,   veil
  Wherewith her heavenly beautie she did hide,
  Whiles on her wearie journey she did ride;
  And on her now a garment she did weare,
  All lilly white, withoutten spot, or pride,°   ornament
  That seemd like silke and silver woven neare,°   closely
But neither silke nor silver therein did appeare.[7]

23

The blazing brightnesse of her beauties beame,
  And glorious light of her sunshyny face
  To tell, were as to strive against the streame.
  My ragged rimes are all too rude and bace,
  Her heavenly lineaments for to enchace.°   be a setting
  Ne wonder; for her owne deare lovéd knight,
  All° were she dayly with himselfe in place,   although
  Did wonder much at her celestiall sight:
Oft had he seene her faire, but never so faire dight.°   adorned

24

So fairely dight, when she in presence came,
  She to her Sire made humble reverence,
  And bowéd low, that her right well became,
  And added grace unto her excellence:
  Who with great wisedome, and grave eloquence
  Thus gan to say. But eare he thus had said,
  With flying speede, and seeming great pretence,°   purpose

7. Una's appearance, reflecting the victory of Protestantism, signifies the mystical union of Christ
and the church: "the marriage of the Lamb is come, and his wife hath made herself ready. And
to her was granted that she should be arrayed in fine linen, clean and white: for the fine linen is
the righteousness of saints" (Revelation 19.7–8). Cf. Revelation 21.2, 11; and the Song of Solomon
4.7: "Thou art all fair, my love; there is no spot in thee."

Came running in, much like a man dismaid,
A Messenger with letters, which his message said.

25

All in the open hall amazéd stood,
    At suddeinnesse of that unwarie° sight,   *unexpected*
    And wondred at his breathlesse hastie mood.
    But he for nought would stay his passage right,°   *direct*
    Till fast° before the king he did alight;   *close*
    Where falling flat, great humblesse he did make,
    And kist the ground, whereon his foot was pight;°   *placed*
    Then to his hands that writ° he did betake,°   *document/deliver*
Which he disclosing,° red thus, as the paper spake.   *unfolding*

26

"To thee, most mighty king of Eden faire,
    Her greeting sends in these sad lines addrest.
    The wofull daughter, and forsaken heire
    Of that great Emperour of all the West:
    And bids thee be advizéd for the best,
    Ere thou thy daughter linck in holy band
    Of wedlocke to that new unknowen guest:
    For he already plighted his right hand
Unto another love, and to another land.

27

"To me sad mayd, or rather widow sad,
    He was affiauncéd long time before,
    And sacred pledges he both gave, and had,
    False erraunt knight, infamous, and forswore:
    Witnesse the burning Altars, which° he swore,   *by which*
    And guiltie heavens of [8] his bold perjury,
    Which though he hath polluted oft of yore,
    Yet I to them for judgement just do fly,
And them conjure° t'avenge this shamefull injury.   *entreat*

28

"Therefore since mine he is, or° free or bond,   *whether*
    Or false or trew, or living or else dead,
    Withhold, O soveraine Prince, your hasty hond
    From knitting league with him, I you aread;°   *advise*
    Ne weene° my right with strength adowne to tread,   *think*
    Through weakenesse of my widowhed, or woe:
    For truth is strong, her rightfull cause to plead,
    And shall find friends, if need requireth soe,
So bids thee well to fare, Thy neither friend, nor foe, Fidessa."

8. I.e., heavens tainted by.

29

When he these bitter byting words had red,
   The tydings straunge did him abashéd make,
   That still he sate long time astonishéd
   As in great muse, ne word to creature spake.
   At last his solemne silence thus he brake,
   With doubtfull eyes fast fixéd on his guest;
   "Redoubted knight, that for mine onely sake
   Thy life and honour late adventurest,°   *hazarded*
Let nought be hid from me, that ought to be exprest.

30

"What meane these bloudy vowes, and idle threats,
   Throwne out from womanish impatient mind?
   What heavens? what altars? what enragéd heates
   Here heapéd up with termes of love unkind,°   *unnatural*
   My conscience cleare with guilty bands would bind?
   High God be witnesse, that I guiltlesse ame.
   But if your selfe, Sir knight, ye faultie find,
   Or wrappéd be in loves of former Dame,
With crime do not it cover, but disclose the same."

31

To whom the Redcrosse knight this answere sent,
   "My Lord, my King, be nought hereat dismayd,
   Till well ye wote by grave intendiment,°   *consideration*
   What woman, and wherefore doth me upbrayd
   With breach of love, and loyalty betrayd.
   It was in my mishaps, as hitherward
   I lately traveild, that unwares I strayd
   Out of my way, through perils straunge and hard;
That day should faile me, ere I had them all declard.

32

"There did I find, or rather I was found
   Of this false woman, that Fidessa hight,
   Fidessa hight the falsest Dame on ground,
   Most false Duessa, royall richly dight,
   That easie was t' invegle° weaker sight: *deceive*
   Who by her wicked arts, and wylie skill,
   Too false and strong for earthly skill or might,
   Unwares me wrought unto her wicked will,
And to my foe betrayd, when least I fearéd ill."

33

Then steppéd forth the goodly royall Mayd,
   And on the ground her selfe prostrating low,
   With sober countenaunce thus to him sayd;

"O pardon me, my soveraigne Lord, to show
The secret treasons, which of late I know
To have bene wroght by that false sorceresse.
She onely she it is, that earst did throw
This gentle knight into so great distresse,
That death him did awaite in dayly wretchednesse.

34

"And now it seemes, that she subornéd hath
This craftie messenger with letters vaine,
To worke new woe and improvided scath,[9]
By breaking of the band betwixt us twaine;
Wherein she uséd hath the practicke paine[1]
Of this false footman, clokt with simplenesse,
Whom if ye please for to discover plaine,
Ye shall him Archimago find, I ghesse,
The falsest man alive; who tries shall find no lesse."

35

The king was greatly movéd at her speach,
And all with suddein indignation fraight,°   *filled*
Bad on that Messenger rude hands to reach.
Eftsoones the Gard, which on his state did wait,
Attacht° that faitor° false, and bound him strait: *seized/imposter*
Who seeming sorely chaufféd° at his band,   *angered*
As chainéd Beare, whom cruell dogs do bait,
With idle force did faine them to withstand,
And often semblaunce made to scape out of their hand.

36

But they him layd full low in dungeon deepe,
And bound him hand and foote with yron chains.
And with continuall watch did warely keepe;
Who then would thinke, that by his subtile trains
He could escape fowle death or deadly paines?[2]
Thus when that Princes wrath was pacifide,
He gan renew the late forbidden banes,°   *banns of marriage*
And to the knight his daughter deare he tyde,
With sacred rites and vowes for ever to abyde.

37

His owne two hands the holy knots did knit,
That none but death for ever can devide;

---

9. I.e., unforeseen harm. J. Miller 1986 notes Redcrosse's evasiveness concerning the past, something
   she says Spenser's not-always-reliable narrator ignores.
1. I.e., cunning pains.
2. "And he laid hold on the dragon, that old serpent, which is the devil, and Satan, and bound him
   a thousand years. And cast him into the bottomless pit, and shut him up, and set a seal upon
   him, that he should deceive the nations no more, till the thousand years should be fulfilled: and
   after that he must be loosed a little season" (Revelation 20.2–3).

His owne two hands, for such a turne° most fit,   *task*
The housling° fire did kindle and provide,   *sacramental*
And holy water thereon sprinckled wide;[3]
At which the bushy Teade° a groome did light,   *torch*
And sacred lampe in secret chamber hide,
Where it should not be quenchéd day nor night,
For feare of evill fates, but burnen ever bright.

38

Then gan they sprinckle all the posts with wine,
And made great feast to solemnize that day;
They all perfumde with frankencense divine,
And precious odours fetcht from far away,
That all the house did sweat with great aray:
And all the while sweete Musicke did apply
Her curious° skill, the warbling notes to play,   *elaborate, exquisite*
To drive away the dull Melancholy;
The whiles one sung a song of love and jollity.[4]

39

During the which there was an heavenly noise
Heard sound through all the Pallace pleasantly,
Like as it had bene many an Angels voice,
Singing before th'eternall majesty,
In their trinall triplicities on hye;[5]
Yet wist no creature, whence that heavenly sweet°   *delight*
Proceeded, yet each one felt secretly
Himselfe thereby reft of his sences meet,°   *proper*
And ravishéd with rare impression in his sprite.

40

Great joy was made that day of young and old,
And solemne feast proclaimd throughout the land,
That their exceeding merth may not be told:
Suffice it heare by signes to understand
The usuall joyes at knitting of loves band.
Thrise happy man the knight himselfe did hold,
Possesséd of his Ladies hart and hand,
And ever, when his eye did her behold,
His heart did seeme to melt in pleasures manifold.

3. Marriages in ancient times were solemnized with sacred fire and water. Plutarch (*Roman Questions* 1) gives four reasons, of which two may especially have interested Spenser: (1) fire is masculine and active, water feminine and passive; (2) as fire and water are most productive in combination, so the joining of male and female in marriage appropriately completes society.
4. Cf. *Epithalamion* 242–60.
5. The song is referable to that sung at the marriage of the Lamb (Revelation 19.6). The "trinall triplicities" are the nine angelic orders, first elaborated in the fifth century A.D. in a work written under the name of Dionysius the Areopagite, enumerated in Dante's *Paradiso* 28, and alluded to by Tasso, *Gerusalemme Liberata* 18.96.

41

Her joyous presence and sweet company
　In full content he there did long enjoy,
　Ne wicked envie, ne vile gealosy
　His deare delights were able to annoy:
　Yet swimming in that sea of blisfull joy,
　He nought forgot, how he whilome had sworne,
　In case he could that monstrous beast destroy,
　Unto his Farie Queene backe to returne:
The which he shortly did, and Una left to mourne.

42

Now strike your sailes ye jolly Mariners,
　For we be come unto a quiet rode,°   *anchorage*
　Where we must land some of our passengers,
　And light this wearie vessell of her lode.
　Here she a while may make her safe abode,
　Till she repairéd have her tackles spent,°   *worn out*
　And wants supplide. And then againe abroad
　On the long voyage whereto she is bent:
Well may she speede and fairely finish her intent.

From The Second Booke of The Faerie Queene

Contayning
The Legend of Sir Guyon
or
Of Temperaunce

1

Right well I wote° most mighty Soveraine,	*know*
That all this famous antique history,	
Of some th'aboundance of an idle braine	
Will judgéd be, and painted forgery,	
Rather then matter of just° memory,	*well-founded*
Sith none, that breatheth living aire, does know,	
Where is that happy land of Faery,	
Which I so much do vaunt, yet no where show,	
But vouch° antiquities, which no body can know.[1]	*affirm*

2

But let that man with better sence advize,°	*consider*
That of the world least part to us is red:°	*known*
And dayly how through hardy enterprize,	
Many great Regions are discoveréd,	
Which to late age[2] were never mentionéd.	
Who ever heard of th'Indian Peru?	
Or who in venturous vessell measuréd	
The Amazons huge river now found trew?	
Or fruitfullest Virginia who did ever vew?[3]	

3

Yet all these were, when no man did them know;	
Yet have from wisest ages hidden beene:	
And later times things more unknowne shall show.	
Why then should witlesse man so much misweene°	*misjudge*
That nothing is, but that which he hath seene?	
What if within the Moones faire shining sphaere?	
What if in every other starre unseene	

1. So too, Ariosto (*Orlando Furioso* 7.1–2) warns that his story may not appeal to the ignorant or foolish and so directs his poem to those with intelligence and insight. The classic study of Book II is H. Berger, *The Allegorical Temper* (New Haven, 1967); see also Graziani 1990E.
2. I.e., to recent times.
3. Sir Walter Raleigh, to whom Elizabeth ("the Virgin Queen") in 1584 granted a patent to establish a "plantation" in America, twice attempted to settle a colony at Roanoke Island in Pamlico Sound. Although the Virginian project was not firmly established until 1607, the Dedication to the 1596 edition of *The Faerie Queene* adds the words "and of Virginia" to her title, which in the 1590 edition reads "Queene of England, France and Ireland." Greenblatt 1980 finds here further evidence that Spenser's epic inscribes hopes, anxieties, and evasions accompanying the start of English colonialism. (Thus one answer to these rhetorical questions might be "kings Atahualpa and Powhatan.") Cain 1978 also associates Book II with the Americas, as does Krier 1990, 79–82.

Of other worldes he happily° should heare?   *by chance*
He wonder would much more: yet such to some appeare.

4

Of Faerie lond yet if he more inquire,
　By certaine signes here set in sundry place
　He may it find; ne let him then admire,°   *wonder*
　But yield his sence to be too blunt and bace,
　That no'te° without an hound fine footing° trace.   *cannot/tracks*
　And thou, O fairest Princesse under sky,
　In this faire mirrhour maist behold thy face,
　And thine owne realmes in lond of Faery,
And in this antique Image thy great auncestry.[4]

5

The which O pardon me thus to enfold
　In covert° vele, and wrap in shadowes light,   *concealing*
　That feeble eyes your glory may behold,
　Which else could not endure those beames bright,
　But would be dazled with exceeding light.
　O pardon, and vouchsafe with patient eare
　The brave adventures of this Faery knight
　The good Sir Guyon gratiously to heare,
In whom great rule of Temp'raunce[5] goodly doth appeare.

Canto I

Guyon by Archimage abusd,°   *deceived*
*　The Redcrosse knight awaytes,*
Findes Mordant and Amavia slaine
*　With pleasures poisoned baytes.*

1

That cunning Architect[1] of cancred° guile,   *malignant*
　Whom Princes late displeasure left in bands,
　For falséd letters and subornéd wile,[2]
　Soone as the Redcrosse knight he understands,
　To beene departed out of Eden lands,
　To serve againe his soveraine Elfin Queene,
　His artes he moves, and out of caytives° hands   *menials'*

---

4. I.e., in Gloriana ("this faire mirrhour") is imaged Queen Elizabeth, and in the whole poem ("this antique Image") England and its ruler's high lineage.
5. "Temperance" infolds or evokes many related words and concepts: to temper (as when we plunge metal alternately into fire and cold water), temperament (the body's balance of humors), temporal (suggesting time and measured tempo), tempest (storms often symbolized the blows of fortune that the temperate and tempered person will meet with fortitude), and what we still call good or bad temper; compare moderate, mode, and mood. On how such concepts relate the body to music and physics, see L. Spitzer, *Classical and Christian Ideas of World Harmony* (Baltimore, 1963).
1. I.e., Archimago, whose escape Spenser has foreshadowed in I.xii.36.
2. I.e., forged letters and perjured deceitfulness.

Himselfe he frees by secret meanes unseene;
His shackles emptie left, him selfe escapéd cleene.

2

And forth he fares full of malicious mind,
  To worken mischiefe and avenging woe,
  Where ever he that godly knight may find,
  His onely hart sore, and his onely foe,
  Sith Una now he algates° must forgoe,   *entirely*
  Whom his victorious hands did earst restore
  To native crowne and kingdome late ygoe:[3]
  Where she enjoyes sure peace for evermore,
As weather-beaten ship arrived on happie shore.

3

Him therefore now the object of his spight
  And deadly food° he makes: him to offend   *feud*
  By forgéd treason, or by open fight
  He seekes, of all his drift° the ayméd end: *plotting*
  Thereto his subtile engins° he does bend,   *machinations*
  His practick° wit, and his faire filéd° tong,   *crafty/smooth*
  With thousand other sleights: for well he kend,°   *knew*
  His credit now in doubtfull ballaunce hong;
For hardly could be hurt, who was already stong.

4

Still as he went, he craftie stales° did lay,   *snares*
  With cunning traines° him to entrap unwares,   *schemes*
  And privie° spials° plast in all his way,   *hidden/spies*
  To weete what course he takes, and how he fares;
  To ketch him at a vantage in his snares.
  But now so wise and warie was the knight
  By triall of his former harmes and cares,
  That he descride, and shonnéd still his slight:°   *trickery*
The fish that once was caught, new bait will hardly bite.

5

Nath'lesse° th'Enchaunter would not spare his paine,   *nevertheless*
  In hope to win occasion to his will;
  Which when he long awaited had in vaine,
  He chaungd his minde from one to other ill:
  For to all good he enimy was still.
  Upon the way him fortunéd to meet,
  Faire marching underneath a shady hill,

3. I.e., lately.

A goodly knight[4] all armd in harnesse meete,°   *proper*
That from his head no place appearéd to his feete.

6

His carriage was full comely and upright,
   His countenaunce demure and temperate,
   But yet so sterne and terrible in sight,
   That cheard his friends, and did his foes amate:°   *dismay*
   He was an Elfin borne of noble state,
   And mickle worship[5] in his native land;
   Well could he tourney and in lists debate,°   *contend*
   And knighthood tooke of good Sir Huons hand,
When with king Oberon he came to Faerie land.[6]

7

Him als° accompanyd upon the way   *also*
   A comely° Palmer,[7] clad in blacke attire,   *seemly, sober*
   Of ripest yeares, and haires all hoarie gray,
   That with a staffe his feeble steps did stire,°   *steer*
   Least his long way his aged limbes should tire:
   And if by lookes one may the mind aread,
   He seemd to be a sage and sober sire,
   And ever with slow pace the knight did lead,
Who taught his trampling steed with equall steps to tread.

8

Such whenas Archimago them did view,
   He weenéd well to worke some uncouth° wile,   *strange*
   Eftsoones untwisting his deceiptfull clew,[8]
   He gan to weave a web of wicked guile,
   And with faire countenance and flattring stile,
   To them approching, thus the knight bespake
   "Faire sonne of Mars, that seeke with warlike spoile,
   And great atchievments great your selfe to make,
Vouchsafe to stay your steed for humble misers° sake."   *wretch's*

4. I.e., Guyon, the knight of Temperance. Guyon does not quite personify Aristotle's temperance, in which no temptation to emotional excess can shake the perfect balance of reason and emotion; rather, he is "continent": apt to be tempted, and therefore needing to restrain his liability to emotional excess or defect. Such a one, says Aristotle, will feel pleasure but will not be led by it (*Ethics* 7.9). Spenser may in fact redefine or question classical temperance; see Stambler 1977 on how he christianizes it and, for an even more skeptical view of the virtue, Silberman 1987. Guyon's name may derive from "Gihon," a river in Eden associated with temperance (A. D. S. Fowler, "The River Guyon," *MLN* 75 [1960]); or it may reflect the equation of "gyon" with "wrestler" in the *Legenda Aurea* (S. Snyder, "Guyon the Wrestler," *RN* 14 [1961]).
5. I.e., much honor.
6. Huon, hero of the thirteenth-century romance *Huon of Bordeaux*, was favored by the fairy king Oberon.
7. A palmer is one who has made a pilgrimage to the Holy Land; the word also meant a schoolroom assistant who corrected students with a swat on the palm. This palmer represents that reasonableness that trails after Truth (cf. Una's dwarf in Book I) but guides the temperate. Guyon follows his measured pace, managing his horse with a balanced precision far from Redcrosse's willfull "pricking" in I.i.1.
8. Ball of thread; i.e., preparing his deceptive plot.

9

He stayd his steed for humble misers sake,
  And bad tell on the tenor of his plaint;
  Who feigning then in every limbe to quake,
  Through inward feare, and seeming pale and faint
  With piteous mone his percing speach gan paint;
  "Deare Lady how shall I declare thy cace,
  Whom late I left in langourous° constraint?   *sorrowful*
  Would God thy selfe now present were in place,
To tell this ruefull tale; thy sight could win thee grace.

10

"Or rather would, O would it had so chaunst,
  That you, most noble Sir, had present beene,
  When that lewd ribauld° with vile lust advaunst°   *ruffian/moved*
  Layd first his filthy hands on virgin cleene,°   *pure*
  To spoile her daintie corse so faire and sheene,°   *bright*
  As on the earth, great mother of us all,
  With living eye more faire was never seene,
  Of chastitie and honour virginall:
Witnesse ye heavens, whom she in vaine to helpe did call."

11

"How may it be," said then the knight halfe wroth,
  "That knight should knighthood ever so have shent?"°   *disgraced*
  "None but that saw," quoth he, "would weene for troth,
  How shamefully that Maid he did torment.
  Her looser° golden lockes he rudely rent,   *unbound*
  And drew her on the ground, and his sharpe sword,
  Against her snowy brest he fiercely bent,
  And threatned death with many a bloudie word;
Toung hates to tell the rest, that eye to see abhord."

12

Therewith amovéd from his sober mood,
  "And lives he yet," said he, "that wrought this act,
  And doen the heavens afford him vitall food?"
  "He lives," quoth he, "and boasteth of the fact,[9]
  Ne yet hath any knight his courage crackt."
  "Where may that treachour then," said he, "be found,
  Or by what meanes may I his footing tract?"°   *trace*
  "That shall I shew," said he, "as sure, as hound
The stricken Deare doth chalenge° by the bleeding wound."   *track*

13

He staid not lenger talke, but with fierce ire
  And zealous hast away is quickly gone

9. I.e., the rape of "that Maid."

To seeke that knight, where him that craftie Squire
Supposd to be.[1] They do arrive anone,
Where sate a gentle Lady all alone,
With garments rent, and haire discheveléd,
Wringing her hands, and making piteous mone;
Her swollen eyes were much disfiguréd,
And her faire face with teares was fowly blubberéd.

14

The knight approaching nigh, thus to her said,
  "Faire Ladie, through foule sorrow ill bedight,[2]
Great pittie is to see you thus dismaid,
And marre the blossome of your beautie bright:
For thy° appease your grief and heavie plight,   *therefore*
And tell the cause of your conceivéd° paine   *evident*
For if he live, that hath you doen despight,°   *wrong*
He shall you doe due recompence againe,
Or else his wrong with greater puissance maintaine."

15

Which when she heard, as in despightfull wise,[3]
  She wilfully her sorrow did augment,
And offred hope of comfort did despise:
Her golden lockes most cruelly she rent,
And scratcht her face with ghastly dreriment,°   *grief*
Ne would she speake, ne see, ne yet be seene,
But hid her visage, and her head downe bent,
Either for grievous shame, or for great teene,°   *anguish*
As if her hart with sorrow had transfixéd beene.[4]

16

Till her that Squire bespake, "Madame my liefe,°   *dear*
  For Gods deare love be not so wilfull bent,
But doe vouchsafe now to receive reliefe,
The which good fortune doth to you present.
For what bootes it to weepe and to wayment,°   *lament*
When ill is chaunst, but doth the ill increase,
And the weake mind with double woe torment?"
When she her Squire heard speake, she gan appease
Her voluntarie° paine, and feele some secret ease.   *willful*

17

Eftsoone she said, "Ah gentle trustie Squire,
  What comfort can I wofull wretch conceave,

1. As Guyon parts company with his guide the Palmer, his just indignation flares into uncontrolled
   anger and haste.
2. I.e., stricken.
3. I.e., in malicious fashion.
4. In her behavior the lady (identified in stanza 21) resembles the enchantress in Trissino's *L'Italia
   Liberata dai Goti* (1548) 4.765 ff.

Or why should ever I henceforth desire,
To see faire heavens face, and life not leave,
Sith that false Traytour did my honour reave?"°   *steal*
"False traytour certes," said the Faerie knight,
"I read° the man, that ever would deceave   *regard*
A gentle Ladie, or her wrong through might:
Death were too little paine for such a foule despight.

18

"But now, faire Ladie, comfort to you make,
And read,° who hath ye wrought this shamefull plight: *tell*
That short° revenge the man may overtake,   *speedy*
Where so he be, and soone upon him light."
"Certes," saide she, "I wote not how he hight,°   *is called*
But under him a gray steede did he wield,°   *control*
Whose sides with dapled circles weren dight;
Upright he rode, and in his silver shield
He bore a bloudie Crosse, that quartred all the field."[5]

19

"Now by my head," said Guyon, "much I muse,°   *wonder*
How that same knight should do so foule amis,
Or ever gentle Damzell so abuse:
For may I boldly say, he surely is
A right good knight, and true of word ywis:°   *surely*
I present was, and can it witnesse well,
When armes he swore, and streight did enterpris°   *undertake*
Th'adventure of the Errant damozell,[6]
In which he hath great glorie wonne, as I heare tell.

20

"Nathlesse he shortly shall againe be tryde,
And fairely quite° him of th'imputed blame,   *acquit*
Else be ye sure he dearely shall abyde,°   *suffer*
Or make you good amendment for the same:
All wrongs have mends, but no amends of shame.
Now therefore Ladie, rise out of your paine,
And see the salving of your blotted name."[7]
Full loth she seemd thereto, but yet did faine;
For she was inly glad her purpose so to gaine.

21

Her purpose was not such, as she did faine,
Ne yet her person such, as it was seene,
But under simple shew and semblant plaine
Lurckt false Duessa secretly unseene,

5. I.e., divided the shield's surface ("field") into quarters.
6. I.e., Una, the wandering maiden.
7. I.e., the vindication of your honor.

As a chast Virgin, that had wrongéd beene:
So had false Archimago her disguisd,
To cloke her guile with sorrow and sad teene;
And eke himselfe had craftily devised
To be her Squire, and do her service well aguised.°   *arrayed*

22

Her late forlorne and naked he had found,
  Where she did wander in waste wildernesse,
  Lurking in rockes and caves farre under ground,
  And with greene mosse covering her nakednesse,
  To hide her shame and loathly filthinesse;
  Sith her Prince Arthur of proud ornaments
  And borrowed beautie spoyld. Her nathelesse
  Th'enchaunter finding fit for his intents,
Did thus revest,° and deckt with due habiliments.°   *reclothe/attire*

23

For all he did, was to deceive good knights,
  And draw them from pursuit of praise and fame,
  To slug in slouth and sensuall delights,
  And end their daies with irrenowméd° shame.   *dishonourable*
  And now exceeding griefe him overcame,
  To see the Redcrosse thus advauncéd hye;[8]
  Therefore this craftie engine° he did frame,   *plot*
  Against his praise to stir up enmitye
Of such, as vertues like mote unto him allye.[9]

24

So now he Guyon guides an uncouth° way   *strange*
  Through woods and mountaines, till they came at last
  Into a pleasant dale, that lowly lay
  Betwixt two hils, whose high heads overplast,°   *looming above*
  The valley did with coole shade overcast;
  Through midst thereof a little river rold,
  By which there sate a knight with helme unlast,
  Himselfe refreshing with the liquid cold,
After his travell long, and labours manifold.

25

"Loe yonder he," cryde Archimage alowd,
  "That wrought the shamefull fact,° which I did shew;   · *deed*
  And now he doth himselfe in secret shrowd,
  To flie the vengeance for his outrage dew;
  But vaine: for ye shall dearely do him rew,[1]
  So God ye speed, and send you good successe;

8. I.e., highly esteemed.
9. I.e., those of similarly virtuous natures, likely to ally themselves with Redcrosse.
1. I.e., make him repent.

Which we farre off will here abide to vew."
So they him left, inflamed with wrathfulnesse,
That streight against that knight his speare he did addresse.°				*direct*

26

Who seeing him from farre so fierce to pricke,
   His warlike armes about him gan embrace,°				*put on*
   And in the rest his readie speare did sticke;
   Tho° when as still he saw him towards pace,				*then*
   He gan rencounter him in equall race.
   They bene ymet, both readie to affrap,°				*strike*
   When suddenly that warriour[2] gan abace°				*lower*
   His threatned speare, as if some new mishap
Had him betidde,° or hidden danger did entrap.				*befallen*

27

And cryde, "Mercie Sir knight, and mercie Lord,
   For mine offence and heedlesse hardiment,°				*boldness*
   That had almost committed crime abhord,
   And with reprochfull shame mine honour shent,°				*disgraced*
   Whiles curséd steele against that badge I bent,
   The sacred badge of my Redeemers death,
   Which on your shield is set for ornament:"
   But his fierce foe his steede could stay uneath,°				*with difficulty*
Who prickt with courage kene, did cruell battell breath.

28

But when he heard him speake, streight way he knew
   His error, and himselfe inclyning sayd;
   "Ah deare Sir Guyon, well becommeth you,
   But me behoveth rather to upbrayd,
   Whose hastie hand so farre from reason strayd,
   That almost it did haynous violence
   On that faire image of that heavenly Mayd,[3]
   That decks and armes your shield with faire defence:
Your court'sie takes on you anothers due offence."

29

So bene they both attone,° and doen upreare				*united*
   Their bevers° bright, each other for to greete;				*visors*
   Goodly comportance° each to other beare,				*behavior*
   And entertaine themselves with court'sies meet.
   Then said the Redcrosse knight, "Now mote I weet,[4]
   Sir Guyon, why with so fierce saliaunce,°				*assault*
   And fell intent ye did at earst me meet;

2. I.e., Guyon, who (if not perfectly temperate) inclines to temperate conduct; his response to the other's "sacred" badge shows how faith and temperance are complementary. Yet, unlike the pagan Sansfoy in I.ii.18, Guyon also knows that St. George's cross is an "ornament," not a "charme."
3. I.e., Gloriana.
4. I.e., may I know.

For sith I know your goodly governaunce,°   *restraint*
Great cause, I weene, you guided, or some uncouth chaunce."

30

"Certes," said he, "well mote I shame to tell
  The fond encheason,° that me hither led.   *occasion*
  A false infamous faitour° late befell   *villain*
  Me for to meet, that seeméd ill bested,°   *beleaguered*
  And playnd of grievous outrage, which he red°   *said*
  A knight had wrought against a Ladie gent;
  Which to avenge, he to this place me led,
Where you he made the marke of his intent,
And now is fled; foule shame him follow, where he went."

31

So can° he turne his earnest unto game,   *did*
  Through goodly handling and wise temperance.
  By this his aged guide in presence came;
  Who soone as on that knight his eye did glance,
  Eft soones of him had perfect cognizance,[5]
  Sith him in Faerie court he late avizd;°   *had seen*
  And said, "Faire sonne, God give you happie chance,
  And that deare Crosse upon your shield devizd,
Wherewith above all knights ye goodly seeme aguizd.°   *equipped*

32

"Joy may you have, and everlasting fame,
  Of late most hard atchiev'ment by you donne,
  For which enrolléd is your glorious name
  In heavenly Registers above the Sunne,
  Where you a Saint with Saints your seat have wonne:
  But wretched we, where ye have left your marke,
  Must now anew begin, like° race to runne;   *similar*
  God guide thee, Guyon, well to end thy warke,
And to the wishéd haven bring thy weary barke."[6]

33

"Palmer," him answeréd the Redcrosse knight,
  "His be the praise, that this atchiev'ment wrought,
  Who made my hand the organ of his might;
  More then goodwill to me attribute nought:
  For all I did, I did but as I ought.
  But you, faire Sir, whose pageant[7] next ensewes,
  Well mote yee thee,° as well can wish your thought,   *thrive*
  That home ye may report thrise happie newes;
For well ye worthie bene for worth and gentle thewes."°   *manners*

5. Upon the Palmer's return the allegiance of Redcrosse and Guyon is "perfectly" confirmed.
6. The prayers and mutual good wishes of Redcrosse and the Palmer may be meant to show that
Guyon is a Christian knight even if temperance is a classical, not theological, virtue. The Palmer
puns on Guyon's name: to "guy" meant to guide or govern, and a "guy" is a ship's guide-rope.
7. I.e., role in life's drama; on how parts of *The Faerie Queene* are like Renaissance pageants, see
Giamatti 1975, chapter 8.

34

So courteous congé° both did give and take,   *farewell*
  With right hands plighted, pledges of good will.
  Then Guyon forward gan his voyage make,
  With his blacke Palmer, that him guided still.
  Still he him guided over dale and hill,
  And with his steedie° staffe did point his way: *steady*
  His race° with reason, and with words his will,   *actions*
  From foule intemperance he oft did stay,
And suffred not in wrath his hastie steps to stray.

[Although the specific assignment by Gloriana of Guyon's quest (to seek out and capture the enchantress Acrasia) is not described until the end of the second canto, the remainder of Canto i illustrates Acrasia's terrible power over her victims. Guyon and the Palmer encounter the dying Amavia, who has stabbed herself for grief at the death of her husband, Mordant, a victim of Acrasia's evil magic; their child, Ruddymane, dabbles his hands in her blood. Having told her story, Amavia dies; Guyon, assisted by the Palmer, buries the couple, taking a sacred oath to avenge their deaths, but he is unable to cleanse the blood from the hands of Ruddymane. Allegorically, this episode emphasizes the destructive power of intemperate passion in fallen and mortal humanity. Leaving the child in the care of Medina, whose character and conduct exemplify the Aristotelian "Golden Mean" between extremes of "defect" and "excess" (represented by Medina's sisters, Elissa and Perissa), Guyon proceeds on his quest. After an interlude in Canto iii, during which the virgin huntress Belphoebe successfully resists the advances of Braggadocchio, a cowardly boaster, Cantos iv–vi chiefly concern the struggles of Guyon against representatives of the "irascible" element in human nature: Furor, Atin, and the brothers Cymochles and Pyrochles. Guyon subdues or successfully resists each of these, but he is not proof against the seductive persuasions of Acrasia's servant Phaedria ("immodest Merth"), who conducts him across her "Idle lake." Guyon does not remain in her company; but he has now been deprived of the Palmer's guidance.]

Canto VII

Guyon findes Mammon in a delve,°   *pit*
Sunning his threasure hore:°   *ancient*
Is by him tempted, and led downe,
To see his secret store.[1]

1

As Pilot well expert in perilous wave,
  That to a stedfast starre his course hath bent,

---

1. Some find in Guyon's visit underground a Christlike or at least virtuous resistance to temptation. Others think he yields to foolhardy curiosity or vain self-reliance. Read 1990 shows how Mammon's house recalls Spanish mines and colonies. In a world where grain should find root, Guyon will go without food (stanza 65); Spenser may ironically elaborate upon Virgil's famous exclamation at the "cursed hunger" for gold that leads to crime (*Aeneid* 3.57) and upon Ovid's lament that a "cursed love of gain" accompanies our iron age of violence and exploitation (*Metamorphoses* 1.131). Heinzelman 1980 notes the scene's complex of allusions to gold and grain. For an overview of this canto, see Prescott 1990E, "Mammon."

When foggy mistes, or cloudy tempests have
  The faithfull light of that faire lampe yblent,°   *obscured*
  And covered heaven with hideous dreriment,
  Upon his card° and compas firmes his eye,   *chart*
  The maisters of his long experiment,°   *experience*
  And to them does the steddy helme apply,
Bidding his wingéd vessell fairely forward fly:

2

So Guyon having lost his trusty guide,
  Late left beyond that Ydle lake, proceedes
  Yet on his way, of none accompanide;
  And evermore himselfe with comfort feedes,
  Of his owne vertues, and prayse-worthy deedes.
  So long he yode,° yet no adventure found,   *went*
  Which fame of her shrill trompet worthy reedes.°   *declares*
  For still he travcild through wide wastfull ground,
That nought but desert wildernesse shewed all around.

3

At last he came unto a gloomy glade,
  Covered with boughes and shrubs from heavens light,
  Whereas he sitting found in secret shade
  An uncouth, salvage,° and uncivile° wight,   *savage/wild*
  Of griesly hew, and fowle ill favoured sight;°   *appearance*
  His face with smoke was tand, and eyes were bleard,
  His head and beard with sout were ill bedight,°   *adorned*
  His cole-blacke hands did seeme to have beene scard
In smithes fire-spitting forge, and nayles like clawes appeard.

4

His yron coate all overgrowne with rust,
  Was underneath envelopéd with gold,
  Whose glistring glosse darkned with filthy dust,
  Well yet appearéd, to have beene of old
  A worke of rich entayle,° and curious° mould,   *carving/intricate*
  Woven with antickes° and wild Imagery: *fantastic figures*
  And in his lap a masse of coyne he told,°   *counted*
  And turnéd upsidowne, to feede his eye
And covetous desire with his huge threasury.

5

And round about him lay on every side
  Great heapes of gold, that never could be spent:
  Of which some were rude owre,° not purifide   *ore*
  Of Mulcibers devouring element;[2]

2. I.e., fire, of which Mulciber (Vulcan) was the god.

Some others were new driven,° and distent°   *beaten/extended*
    Into great Ingoes,° and to wedges square;   *ingots*
    Some in round plates withouten moniment;°   *markings*
    But most were stampt, and in their metall bare
The antique shapes of kings and kesars° straunge and rare.   *emperors*

6

Soone as he Guyon saw, in great affright
    And hast he rose, for to remove aside
    Those pretious hils from straungers envious sight,
    And downe them pouréd through an hole full wide,
    Into the hollow earth, them there to hide.
    But Guyon lightly to him leaping, stayd
    His hand, that trembled, as one terrifyde;
    And though him selfe were at the sight dismayd,
Yet him perforce restraynd, and to him doubtfull sayd.[3]

7

"What are thou man, (if man at all thou art)
    That here in desert hast thine habitaunce,
    And these rich heapes of wealth doest hide apart
    From the worldes eye, and from her right usaunce?"°   *use*
    Thereat with staring eyes fixéd askaunce,[4]
    In great disdaine, he answerd; "Hardy Elfe,
    That darest vew my direfull countenaunce,
    I read° thee rash, and heedlesse of thy selfe,   *consider*
To trouble my still seate, and heapes of pretious pelfe.

8

"God of the world and worldlings I me call,
    Great Mammon,[5] greatest god below the skye,
    That of my plenty poure out unto all,
    And unto none my graces do envye:°   *begrudge*
    Riches, renowme, and principality,
    Honour, estate, and all this worldés good,
    For which men swinck° and sweat incessantly,   *toil*

3. I.e., said to the apprehensive "wight of griesly hew."
4. I.e., with proudly averted eyes.
5. Mammon (from Syriac, "riches") is not simply the god of money or a personification of cupidity; he opposes God as darkness opposes light (cf. Matthew 6.19–24, especially "Ye cannot serve God and mammon"). Hieatt ("Symmetries," 1973) notes that Guyon's visit takes forty stanzas, recalling Christ's forty days in the wilderness and his temptation by Satan (Matthew 4.1–11). Like Christ, Guyon rejects the offer of wealth (stanzas 18, 32, 38), glory (stanza 49), and, possibly, knowledge (stanza 63). Although deprived of the Palmer's aid, and thus relying on "his owne vertues" (stanza 2), Guyon puts up a successful if exhausting resistance and is then tended by an angel (viii.5; cf. Matthew 4.11). But the scriptural background may also include Christ's words on the charitable use of money: "make ye friends with the unrighteous Mammon" (Luke 16.9; see Tyndale's *Parable of the Unrighteous Mammon* [1528]). For all his virtue, Guyon ignores the question of money's right use (cf. Mallette 1989); nor does he engage Mammon's reminder that in a money economy somebody must pay for a knight's equipment.

Fro me do flow into an ample flood,
And in the hollow earth have their eternall brood.°   *breeding place*

9

"Wherefore if me thou deigne to serve and sew,°   *follow*
  At thy commaund lo all these mountaines bee;
  Or if to thy great mind, or greedy vew
  All these may not suffise, there shall to thee
  Ten times so much be numbred francke and free."
  "Mammon," said he, "thy godheades vaunt[6] is vaine,
  And idle offers of thy golden fee;°   *reward*
To them, that covet such eye-glutting gaine,
Proffer thy giftes, and fitter servaunts entertaine.

10

"Me ill besits, that in der-doing armes,[7]
  And honours suit° my vowéd dayes do spend,   *pursuit*
  Unto thy bounteous baytes, and pleasing charmes,
  With which weake men thou witchest, to attend:
  Regard of worldly mucke doth fowly blend,°   *defile*
  And low abase the high heroicke spright,
  That joyes for crownes and kingdomes to contend;
  Faire shields, gay steedes, bright armes be my delight:
Those be the riches fit for an advent'rous knight."

11

"Vaine glorious Elfe," said he, "doest not thou weet,°   *know*
  That money can thy wantes at will supply?
  Shields, steeds, and armes, and all things for thee meet
  It can purvay° in twinckling of an eye;   *provide*
  And crownes and kingdomes to thee multiply.
  Do not I kings create, and throw the crowne
  Sometimes to him, that low in dust doth ly?
  And him that raignd, into his rowme thrust downe,
And whom I lust,° do heape with glory and renowne?"   *choose*

12

"All otherwise," said he, "I riches read,°   *consider*
  And deeme them roote of all disquietnesse;
  First got with guile, and then preserved with dread,
  And after spent with pride and lavishnesse,
  Leaving behind them griefe and heavinesse.[8]
  Infinite mischiefes of them do arize,
  Strife, and debate, bloudshed, and bitternesse,

---

6. I.e., boastful claim to godhead.
7. I.e., It is not fitting for me, engaged in daring deeds of arms.
8. "But they that will be rich fall into temptation and a snare, and into many foolish and hurtful
   lusts, which drown men in destruction and perdition. For the love of money is the root of all evil
   . . ." (1 Timothy 6.9–10).

Outrageous wrong, and hellish covetize,
That noble heart as great dishonour doth despize.

13

"Ne thine be kingdomes, ne the scepters thine;
  But realmes and rulers thou doest both confound,°   *destroy*
  And loyall truth to treason doest incline;
  Witnesse the guiltlesse bloud pourd oft on ground,
  The crownéd often slaine, the slayer cround,
  The sacred Diademe in peeces rent,
  And purple robe goréd with many a wound;
  Castles surprizd, great cities sackt and brent:°   *burned*
So mak'st thou kings, and gaynest wrongfull governement.

14

"Long were to tell the troublous stormes, that tosse
  The private state,° and make the life unsweet: *condition*
  Who° swelling sayles in Caspian sea doth crosse,   *one who with*
  And in frayle wood on Adrian gulfe⁹ doth fleet,
  Doth not, I weene, so many evils meet."
  Then Mammon wexing wroth, "And why then," said,
  "Are mortall men so fond and undiscreet,
  So evill thing to seeke unto their ayd,
And having not complaine, and having it upbraid?"[1]

15

"Indeede," quoth he, "through fowle intemperaunce,
  Frayle men are oft captived to covetise:
  But would they thinke, with how small allowaunce
  Untroubled Nature doth her selfe suffise,
  Such superfluities they would despise,
  Which with sad cares empeach° our native joyes: *hinder*
  At the well head the purest streames arise:
  But mucky filth his braunching armes annoyes,
And with uncomely weedes the gentle wave accloyes.°   *clogs*

16

"The antique° world, in his first flowring youth,[2]   *ancient*
  Found no defect in his Creatours grace,
  But with glad thankes, and unreprovéd° truth,   *blameless*
  The gifts of soveraigne bountie did embrace:
  Like Angels life was then mens happy cace;
  But later ages pride, like corn-fed steed,
  Abusd her plenty, and fat swolne encreace

9. The Adriatic Sea, like the Caspian Sea notorious for storms.
1. I.e., either complain about not having [money], or, if having it, denigrate it. Guyon's reply echoes
  the distinction made by Boethius (c. 475–525) between natural needs and "the superfluity of
  fortune" (*De Consolatione Philosophiae* 2.Prose 5).
2. The classical myth of the golden age recurs in Elizabethan literature, especially in pastoral poetry;
  cf. Ovid, *Metamorphoses* 1.90–112, Virgil's fourth eclogue, and Boethius 2.Metre 5.

To all licentious lust, and gan exceed
The measure of her meane,[3] and naturall first need.

17

"Then gan a curséd hand the quiet wombe
  Of his great Grandmother with steele to wound,
  And the hid treasures in her sacred tombe,
  With Sacriledge to dig. Therein he found
  Fountaines of gold and silver to abound,
  Of which the matter of his huge desire
  And pompous pride eftsoones he did compound;
  Then avarice gan through his veines inspire°   *breathe*
His greedy flames, and kindled life-devouring fire.

18

"Sonne," said he then, "let be thy bitter scorne,
  And leave the rudenesse of that antique age
  To them, that lived therein in state forlorne;
  Thou that doest live in later times, must wage°   *hire out*
  Thy workes for wealth, and life for gold engage.
  If then thee list my offred grace to use,
  Take what thou please of all this surplusage;
  If thee list not, leave have thou to refuse:
But thing refuséd, do not afterward accuse."

19

"Me list not," said the Elfin knight, "receave
  Thing offred, till I know it well be got,
  Ne wote° I, but thou didst these goods bereave   *know*
  From rightfull owner by unrighteous lot,   *division*
  Or that bloud guiltinesse or guile them blot."
  "Perdy°," quoth he, "yet never eye did vew,   *truly*
  Ne toung did tell, ne hand these handled not,[4]
  But safe I have them kept in secret mew,°   *den*
From heavens sight, and powre of all which them pursew."

20

"What secret place," quoth he, "can safely hold
  So huge a masse, and hide from heavens eye?
  Or where hast thou thy wonne,° that so much gold   *dwelling*
  Thou canst preserve from wrong and robbery?"
  "Come thou," quoth he, "and see." So by and by
  Through that thicke covert he him led, and found
  A darkesome way, which no man could descry,°   *discover*
  That deepe descended through the hollow ground,
And was with dread and horrour compasséd around.

3. I.e., her proper limits.
4. Mammon blasphemously echoes 1 Corinthians 2.9, which refers to the wondrous things God has
prepared for those who love him.

21

At length they came into a larger space,
  That stretcht it selfe into an ample plaine,
  Through which a beaten broad high way did trace,
  That streight did lead to Plutoes griesly raine:[5]
  By that wayes side, there sate infernall Payne,
  And fast beside him sat tumultuous Strife:
  The one in hand an yron whip did straine,°   wield
  The other brandishéd a bloudy knife,
And both did gnash their teeth, and both did threaten life.

22

On thother side in one consort° there sate,   company
  Cruell Revenge, and rancorous Despight,
  Disloyall Treason, and hart-burning Hate,
  But gnawing Gealosie out of their sight
  Sitting alone, his bitter lips did bight,
  And trembling Feare still to and fro did fly,
  And found no place, where safe he shroud him might,
  Lamenting Sorrow did in darknesse lye,
And Shame his ugly face did hide from living eye.

23

And over them sad Horrour with grim hew,°   aspect
  Did alwayes sore, beating his yron wings;
  And after him Owles and Night-ravens flew,
  The hatefull messengers of heavy things,
  Of death and dolour telling sad tidings;
  Whiles sad Celeno,[6] sitting on a clift,
  A song of bale and bitter sorrow sings,
  That hart of flint a sunder could have rift:°   torn
Which having ended, after him she flyeth swift.

24

All these before the gates of Pluto lay,
  By whom they passing, spake unto them nought.
  But th'Elfin knight with wonder all the way
  Did feed his eyes, and fild his inner thought.
  At last him to a litle dore he brought,
  That to the gate of Hell, which gapéd wide,
  Was next adjoyning, ne them parted ought:[7]
  Betwixt them both was but a litle stride,
That did the house of Richesse from hell-mouth divide.

5. I.e., Pluto's horrible kingdom; cf. Virgil's description of Hades' gates (*Aeneid* 6.267–81). Spenser's
  description, particularly the personifications in stanza 22, recalls Sackville's "Induction" in *A
  Mirror for Magistrates*.
6. Chief of the harpies, birds with female faces and torsos; in Spenser's time, they were already
  associated with rapacity.
7. I.e., nor did anything separate them.

25

Before the dore sat selfe-consuming Care,
　Day and night keeping wary watch and ward,
　For feare least Force or Fraud should unaware
　Breake in, and spoile° the treasure there in gard:　　　*plunder*
　Ne would he suffer Sleepe once thither-ward
　Approch, albe° his drowsie den were next;　　　　　*although*
　For next to death is Sleepe to be compard:[8]
　Therefore his house is unto his annext;
Here Sleep, there Richesse, and Hel-gate them both betwext.

26

So soone as Mammon there arrived, the dore
　To him did open, and affoorded way;
　Him followed eke Sir Guyon evermore,
　Ne darkenesse him, ne daunger might dismay.
　Soone as he entred was, the dore streight way
　Did shut, and from behind it forth there lept
　An ugly feend, more fowle then dismall day,[9]
　The which with monstrous stalke behind him stept,
And ever as he went, dew° watch upon him kept.[1]　　　*proper*

27

Well hopéd he, ere long that hardy guest,
　If ever covetous hand, or lustfull eye,
　Or lips he layd on thing, that likt° him best,　　　*pleased*
　Or ever sleepe his eye-strings did untye,
　Should be his pray. And therefore still on hye
　He over him did hold his cruell clawes,
　Threatning with greedy gripe to do him dye
　And rend in peeces with his ravenous pawes,
If ever he transgrest the fatall Stygian lawes.[2]

28

That houses forme within was rude and strong,
　Like an huge cave, hewne out of rocky clift,
　From whose rough vaut° the ragged breaches° hong,　　　*vault/fractures*
　Embost with massy gold of glorious gift,°　　　　　*quality*
　And with rich metall loaded every rift,
　That heavy ruine they did seeme to threat;

8. Both Death and Sleep were sons of Night (Hesiod, *Theogony* 211–12).
9. I.e., the day of death.
1. The fiend who follows Guyon recalls the "fury" in the ancient Eleusinian mysteries who followed initiates so as to enforce their observance of ritual procedures; Spenser could have learned about this from Claudian's *De Raptu Proserpinae* (early fifth century A.D.) or Pausanias's *Description of Greece* (second century A.D.).
2. I.e., the laws of the underworld.

And over them Arachne[3] high did lift
Her cunning web, and spred her subtile° net,   *fine-spun*
Enwrappéd in fowle smoke and clouds more blacke then Jet.

29

Both roofe, and floore, and wals were all of gold,
But overgrowne with dust and old decay,
And hid in darkenesse, that none could behold
The hew° thereof: for vew of chearefull day   *condition*
Did never in that house it selfe display,
But a faint shadow of uncertain light;
Such as a lamp, whose life does fade away:
Or as the Moone cloathéd with clowdy night,
Does shew to him, that walkes in feare and sad affright.

30

In all that rowme was nothing to be seene,
But huge great yron chests and coffers strong,
All bard with double bends,° that none could weene°   *bands/expect*
Them to efforce° by violence or wrong;   *force open*
On every side they placéd were along.
But all the ground with sculs was scatteréd,
And dead mens bones, which round about were flong,
Whose lives, it seeméd, whilome° there were shed,   *formerly*
And their vile carcases now left unburiéd.

31

They forward passe, ne Guyon yet spoke word,
Till that they came unto an yron dore,
Which to them opened of his owne accord,
And shewd of richesse such exceeding store,
As eye of man did never see before;
Ne ever could within one place be found,
Though all the wealth, which is, or was of yore,
Could gathered be through all the world around,
And that above were added to that under ground.

32

The charge thereof unto a covetous Spright
Commaunded was, who thereby did attend,
And warily awaited day and night,
From other covetous feends it to defend,
Who it to rob and ransacke did intend.
Then Mammon turning to that warriour, said;
"Loe here the worldés blis, loe here the end,

3. After defeating Arachne in a weaving contest, Minerva turned her into a spider (*Metamorphoses*
6.1–145). Here and in *Muiopotmos* Spenser makes Arachne's own envy cause the change. The
web, spread for the morally unwary, also shows that this wealth is unused; cf. Christ's parable of
the talents in Matthew 25.14–29.

To which all men do ayme, rich to be made:
Such grace now to be happy, is before thee laid."

33

"Certes," said he, "I n'ill° thine offred grace,   *will not accept*
  Ne to be made so° happy do intend: *thus*
  Another blis before mine eyes I place,
  Another happinesse, another end.
  To them, that list, these base regardes° I lend: *concerns*
  But I in armes, and in atchievements brave,
  Do rather choose my flitting houres to spend,
  And to be Lord of those, that riches have,
Then them to have my selfe, and be their servile sclave."

34

Thereat the feend his gnashing teeth did grate,
  And grieved, so long to lacke his greedy pray;[4]
  For well he weenéd,° that so glorious bayte   *supposed*
  Would tempt his guest, to take thereof assay:°   *trial*
  Had he so doen, he had him snatcht away,
  More light then Culver° in the Faulcons fist.   *dove*
  Eternall God thee save from such decay.°   *ruin*
  But whenas Mammon saw his purpose mist,
Him to entrap unwares another way he wist.°   *knew*

35

Thence forward he him led, and shortly brought
  Unto another rowme, whose dore forthright,
  To him did open, as it had beene taught:
  Therein an hundred raunges weren pight,°   *placed*
  And hundred fornaces all burning bright;
  By every fornace many feends did bide,
  Deforméd creatures, horrible in sight,
  And every feend his busie paines applide,
To melt the golden metall, ready to be tride.°   *purified*

36

One with great bellowes gathered filling aire,
  And with forst wind the fewell did inflame;
  Another did the dying bronds° repaire   *embers*
  With yron toungs, and sprinckled oft the same
  With liquid waves, fiers Vulcans rage[5] to tame,
  Who maistring them, renewd his former heat;
  Some scumd the drosse, that from the metall came;

4. I.e., to be so long denied the prey he greedily desired.
5. I.e., fire. To use a god's name as metonymy has ample classical precedent. Stanzas 35–36 are
based on Virgil's account of the Cyclopean forges beneath Mount Etna (*Aeneid* 8.417–54). Mammon's workaholic miners indicate the joylessness of money-grubbing and, perhaps, the vanity of
works without faith: contrast the untoiling lilies of the field in Matthew 6.28.

Some stird the molten owre with ladles great:
And every one did swincke,° and every one did sweat.   *labor*

37

But when as earthly wight they present saw,
  Glistring in armes and battailous° aray,   *warlike*
  From their whot worke they did themselves withdraw
  To wonder at the sight: for till that day,
  They never creature saw, that came that way.
  Their staring eyes sparckling with fervent fire,
  And ugly shapes did nigh the man dismay,
  That were it not for shame, he would retire,
Till that him thus bespake their soveraigne Lord and sire.

38

"Behold, thou Faeries sonne, with mortall eye,
  That° living eye before did never see: *what*
  The thing, that thou didst crave so earnestly,
  To weet, whence all the wealth late shewd by mee,
  Proceeded, lo now is reveald to thee.
  Here is the fountaine of the worldés good:
  Now therefore, if thou wilt enrichéd bee,
  Avise° thee well, and chaunge thy wilfull mood,   *consider*
Least thou perhaps hereafter wish, and be withstood."

39

"Suffise it then, thou Money God," quoth hee,
  "That all thine idle offers I refuse.
  All that I need I have; what needeth mee
  To covet more, then I have cause to use?
  With such vaine shewes thy worldlings vile abuse:°   *deceive*
  But give me leave to follow mine emprise."°   *enterprise*
  Mammon was much displeasd, yet no'te° chuse,   *could not*
  But beare the rigour of his bold mesprise,°   *scorn*
And thence him forward led, him further to entise.

40

He brought him through a darksome narrow strait,
  To a broad gate, all built of beaten gold:
  The gate was open, but therein did wait
  A sturdy villein, striding stiffe and bold,
  As if that highest God defie he would;
  In his right hand an yron club he held,
  But he himselfe was all of golden mould,
  Yet had both life and sence, and well could weld°   *wield*
That curséd weapon, when his cruell foes he queld.

41

Disdayne he calléd was, and did disdaine
  To be so cald, and who so did him call:
  Sterne was his looke, and full of stomacke° vaine,   *arrogance*
  His portaunce° terrible, and stature tall,   *bearing*
  Far passing th'hight of men terrestriall;
  Like an huge Gyant of the Titans race,
  That made him scorne all creatures great and small,
  And with his pride all others powre deface:°   *destroy*
More fit amongst blacke fiendes, then men to have his place.

42

Soone as those glitterand° armes he did espye,   *glittering*
  That with their brightnesse made that darknesse light,
  His harmefull club he gan to hurtle° hye,   *brandish*
  And threaten batteill to the Faery knight;
  Who likewise gan himselfe to batteill dight,°   *prepare*
  Till Mammon did his hasty hand withhold,
  And counseld him abstaine from perilous fight:
  For nothing might abash the villein bold,
Ne mortall steele emperce his miscreated° mould.   *unnatural*

43

So having him with reason pacifide,
  And the fiers Carle° commaunding to forbeare,   *churl*
  He brought him in. The rowme was large and wide,
  As it some Cyeld° or solemne Temple weare: *guildhall*
  Many great golden pillours did upbeare
  The massy roofe, and riches huge sustayne,
  And every pillour deckéd was full deare°   *expensively*
  With crownes and Diademes, and titles vaine,
Which mortall Princes wore, whiles they on earth did rayne.

44

A route° of people there assembled were,   *crowd*
  Of every sort and nation under skye,
  Which with great uprore preacéd° to draw nere   *pressed*
  To th'upper part, where was advauncéd hye
  A stately siege° of soveraigne majestye;   *throne*
  And thereon sat a woman gorgeous gay,[6]
  And richly clad in robes of royaltye,
  That never earthly Prince in such aray
His glory did enhaunce, and pompous pride display.

6. I.e., Philotime (Greek for "love of honor"), named in stanza 49. She resembles Lucifera (I.iv.6–8, 11), daughter of Pluto and Proserpina. Both pervert the ideal exemplified by Gloriana: Lucifera has usurped her power, while Philotime uses pretense and artifice to rule the pushful mobs that crowd her court.

45

Her face right wondrous faire did seeme to bee,
   That her broad beauties beam great brightnes threw
   Through the dim shade, that all men might it see:
   Yet was not that same her owne native hew,°   aspect
   But wrought by art and counterfetted shew,
   Thereby more lovers unto her to call;
   Nath'lesse most heavenly faire in deed and vew
   She by creation was, till she did fall;
Thenceforth she sought for helps, to cloke her crime withall.

46

There, as in glistring glory she did sit,
   She held a great gold chaine ylinckéd well,
   Whose upper end to highest heaven was knit,
   And lower part did reach to lowest Hell;
   And all that preace° did round about her swell,   throng
   To catchen hold of that long chaine, thereby
   To clime aloft, and others to excell:
   That was Ambition, rash desire to sty,°   mount
And every lincke thereof a step of dignity.[7]

47

Some thought to raise themselves to high degree,
   By riches and unrighteous reward,
   Some by close shouldring,° some by flatteree;   thrusting aside
   Others through friends, others for base regard;[8]
   And all by wrong wayes for themselves prepard.
   Those that were up themselves, kept others low,
   Those that were low themselves, held others hard,
   Ne suffred them to rise or greater grow,
But every one did strive his fellow downe to throw.

48

Which whenas Guyon saw, he gan inquire,
   What meant that preace about that Ladies throne,
   And what she was that did so high aspire.
   Him Mammon answeréd; "That goodly one,
   Whom all that folke with such contention,
   Do flocke about, my deare, my daughter is;
   Honour and dignitie from her alone,
   Derivéd are, and all this worldés blis
For which ye men do strive: few get, but many mis.

7. Cf. I.v.25, note. Comes says that the gold chain can signify avarice or ambition, which, though
   powerful, cannot distract good men (*Mythologiae* 2.4). Moore 1975 suggests that Guyon's polite
   rejection of Philotime, while virtuous, shows an aristocratic disdain of the moneyed middle class.
8. I.e., bribes.

49

"And faire Philotimé she rightly hight,°   *is named*
  The fairest wight that wonneth° under skye,   *lives*
  But that this darksome neather world her light
  Doth dim with horrour and deformitie,
  Worthy of heaven and hye felicitie,
  From whence the gods have her for envy thrust:
  But sith thou has found favour in mine eye,
  Thy spouse I will her make, if that thou lust,°   *desire*
That she may thee advance for workes and merites just."

50

"Gramercy° Mammon," said the gentle knight,   *thanks*
  "For so great grace and offred high estate;
  But I, that am fraile flesh and earthly wight,
  Unworthy match for such immortall mate
  My selfe well wote, and mine unequall fate;
  And were I not, yet is my trouth yplight,°   *plighted*
  And love avowd to other Lady late,°   *lately*
  That to remove the same I have no might:
To chaunge love causelesse is reproch to warlike knight."

51

Mammon emmovéd was with inward wrath;
  Yet forcing it to faine,[9] him forth thence led
  Through griesly shadowes by a beaten path,
  Into a gardin goodly garnishéd
  With hearbs and fruits, whose kinds mote not be red:°   *described*
  Not such, as earth out of her fruitfull woomb
  Throwes forth to men, sweet and well savouréd,
  But direfull deadly blacke both leafe and bloom,
Fit to adorne the dead, and decke the drery toombe.[1]

52

There mournfull Cypresse grew in greatest store,
  And trees of bitter Gall, and Heben sad,
  Dead sleeping Poppy, and blacke Hellebore,
  Cold Coloquintida, and Tetra mad,
  Mortall Samnitis, and Cicuta bad,[2]
  With which th'unjust Atheniens made to dy
  Wise Socrates, who thereof quaffing glad
  Pourd out his life, and last Philosophy
To the faire Critias his dearest Belamy.°   *intimate*

9. I.e., concealing his wrath.
1. The Garden of Proserpina combines elements from the *Odyssey* (the Grove of Persephone, 10.509–40), Claudian, *De Raptu Proserpinae* (the tree bearing golden fruit, 2.290–91), and Comes, *Mythologiae* (the identification of Proserpina with Hecate, goddess of poisons, 3.15).
2. These plants either are associated with death or are themselves poisonous; "Cicuta bad" is hemlock (cf. *Phaedo* 117–18).

53

The Gardin of Proserpina this hight;°   *was named*
  And in the midst thereof a silver seat,³
  With a thicke Arber goodly over dight,°   *covered*
  In which she often usd from open heat
  Her selfe to shroud, and pleasures to entreat.°   *indulge in*
  Next thereunto did grow a goodly tree,
  With braunches broad dispred° and body great,   *spread out*
  Clothéd with leaves, that none the wood mote see
And loaden all with fruit as thicke as it might bee.

54

Their fruit were golden apples⁴ glistring bright,
  That goodly was their glory to behold,
  On earth like never grew, ne living wight
  Like ever saw, but° they from hence were sold;°   *unless/taken*
  For those, which Hercules with conquest bold
  Got from great Atlas daughters, hence began,
  And planted there, did bring forth fruit of gold:
  And those with which th'Euboean young man wan°   *won*
Swift Atalanta, when through craft he her out ran.⁵

55

Here also sprong that goodly golden fruit,
  With which Acontius got his lover trew,
  Whom he had long time sought with fruitlesse suit:
  Here eke that famous golden Apple grew,
  The which emongst the gods false Ate threw;
  For which th'Idaean Ladies disagreed,
  Till partiall Paris dempt° it Venus dew,   *adjudged*
  And had of her, faire Helen for his meed,°   *reward*
That many noble Greekes and Trojans made to bleed.⁶

56

The warlike Elfe much wondred at this tree,
  So faire and great, that shadowed all the ground,
  And his broad braunches, laden with rich fee,°   *wealth*

3. On this seat Theseus was sentenced to remain "condemned to endlesse slouth by law" (I.v.35); it may also refer to the forbidden seat of the goddess Demeter in the Eleusinian rites.
4. To fetch the golden apples of the Hesperides (the daughters of Atlas) was the eleventh of Hercules' twelve labors. For Spenser as for Comes (*Mythologiae* 7.7), the apples symbolize avarice and discord.
5. Atalanta promised to wed anyone who could defeat her in a footrace; losers were killed. Hippomenes (or, some said, Melanion of Euboea, an island near Boeotia) won by casting down golden apples to delay her as she swerved to pick them up (*Metamorphoses* 10.560–680).
6. Acontius won Cydippe by the strategic use of an apple (Ovid, *Heroides* 20–21), which Spenser here makes golden. He also identifies Ate, goddess of discord (rather than the Eris of Greek myth), as the divinity who, angered at not having been invited to the wedding of Thetis and Peleus, threw among the invited goddesses a golden apple inscribed "For the fairest." Juno, Minerva, and Venus asked Paris to judge their contest, held on Mount Ida; his award of the apple to Venus, who had promised him Helen, led to the Trojan War.

Did stretch themselves without the utmost bound
Of this great gardin, compast° with a mound,   *surrounded*
Which over-hanging, they themselves did steepe,
In a blacke flood which flowed about it round;
That is the river of Cocytus deepe,[7]
In which full many soules do endlesse waile and weepe.

57

Which to behold, he clomb up to the banke
And looking downe, saw many damnéd wights,
In those sad waves, which direfull deadly stanke,
Plongéd continually of° cruell Sprights,   *by*
That with their pitteous cryes, and yelling shrights,°   *shrieks*
They made the further shore resounden° wide: *echo*
Emongst the rest of those same ruefull sights,
One curséd creature[8] he by chaunce espide,
That drenchéd lay full deepe, under the Garden side.

58

Deepe was he drenchéd to the upmost chin,
Yet gapéd still, as coveting to drinke
Of the cold liquor, which he waded in,
And stretching forth his hand, did often thinke
To reach the fruit, which grew upon the brincke:
But both the fruit from hand, and floud from mouth
Did flie abacke, and made him vainely swinke:
The whiles he sterved° with hunger and with drouth°   *starved/thirst*
He daily dyde, yet never throughly dyen couth.[9]

59

The knight him seeing labour so in vaine,
Askt who he was, and what he ment thereby:
Who groning deepe, thus answerd him againe;
"Most curséd of all creatures under skye,
Lo Tantalus, I here tormented lye:
Of whom high Jove wont whylome feasted bee,[1]
Lo here I now for want of food doe dye:
But if that thou be such, as I thee see,
Of grace I pray thee, give to eat and drinke to mee."

7. A river in Hades, traditionally associated with tears and sorrow.
8. I.e., Tantalus, punished for revealing divine secrets and for killing his son Pelops and serving him
   at a banquet for the gods. On his torment, see *Odyssey* 11.582–92. Boccaccio (*Genealogiae* 1.14)
   and Comes call him a figure for avarice; Ovid (*Ars Amatoria* 2.601–6) and Pindar stress his
   presumption. The setting here recalls Alciati's *Emblemata* 85. Mythographers routinely assumed
   that Tantalus was a real king about whom poets had woven fables; Horace's *Satire* 1.1, from which
   Spenser may have taken details, warns that we should not scoff at him, for avarice may be in us
   too.
9. I.e., could never utterly die.
1. I.e., by whom Jove was formerly feasted.

60

"Nay, nay, thou greedie Tantalus," quoth he,
    "Abide the fortune of thy present fate,
    And unto all that live in high degree,°   *place*
    Ensample be of mind intemperate,
    To teach them how to use their present state."
    Then gan the curséd wretch aloud to cry,
    Accusing highest Jove and gods ingrate,
    And eke blaspheming heaven bitterly,
As authour of unjustice, there to let him dye.

61

He lookt a little further, and espyde
    Another wretch, whose carkasse deepe was drent°   *immersed*
    Within the river, which the same did hyde:
    But both his hands most filthy feculent,°   *befouled*
    Above the water were on high extent,°   *stretched*
    And faynd° to wash themselves incessantly;   *tried*
    Yet nothing cleaner were for such intent,
    But rather fowler seeméd to the eye;
So lost his labour vaine and idle° industry.   *futile*

62

The knight him calling, askéd who he was,
    Who lifting up his head, him answerd thus:
    "I Pilate am the falsest Judge, alas,
    And most unjust, that by unrighteous
    And wicked doome,° to Jewes despiteous°   *judgment/pitiless*
    Delivered up the Lord of life to die,
    And did acquite a murdrer felonous;°   *wicked*
    The whiles my hands I washt in puritie,[2]
The whiles my soule was soyld with foule iniquitie."

63

Infinite moe,° tormented in like paine   *more*
    He there beheld, too long here to be told:
    Ne Mammon would there let him long remaine,
    For terrour of the tortures manifold,
    In which the damnéd soules he did behold,
    But roughly him bespake. "Thou fearefull foole,
    Why takest not of that same fruit of gold,
    Ne sittest downe on that same silver stoole,
To rest thy wearie person, in the shadow coole."[3]

2. I.e., in token of purity. "Pilate . . . took water, and washed his hands before the multitude, saying, I am innocent of the blood of this just person . . ." (Matthew 27.24). On occasion (e.g., in the *Legenda Aurea*) Pilate was said to have avariciously misused public funds.
3. Mammon invites Guyon to yield to sloth (and so to the punishment imposed on Theseus); to accept his offer is perhaps also, symbolically, to probe forbidden mysteries.

64

All which he did, to doe him deadly fall
  In frayle intemperance through sinfull bayt;
  To which if he inclinéd had at all,
  That dreadfull feend, which did behind him wayt,
  Would him have rent in thousand peeces strayt:°   *immediately*
  But he was warie wise in all his way,
  And well perceivéd his deceiptfull sleight,
  Ne suffred lust° his safetie to betray; .   *desire*
So goodly did beguile the Guyler° of the pray.   *deceiver*

65

And now he has so long remainéd there,
  That vitall powres gan wexe both weake and wan,°   *faint*
  For want of food, and sleepe, which two upbeare,
  Like mightie pillours, this fraile life of man,
  That none without the same endurén can.
  For now three dayes of men were full outwrought,°   *completed*
  Since he this hardie enterprize began:
  For thy° great Mammon fairely he besought,   *therefore*
Into the world to guide him backe, as he him brought.

66

The God, though loth, yet was constraind t'obay,
  For lenger time, then that, no living wight
  Below the earth, might suffred be to stay:
  So backe againe, him brought to living light.
  But all so soone as his enfeebled spright°   *spirit*
  Gan sucke this vitall aire into his brest,
  As overcome with too exceeding might,
  The life did flit away out of her nest,
And all his senses were with deadly fit opprest.[4]

Canto VIII

Sir Guyon laid in swowne is by
Acrates sonnes[1] despoyld,
Whom Arthur soone hath reskewéd
And Paynim brethren foyld.

1

And is there care in heaven? and is there love
  In heavenly spirits to these creatures bace,
  That may compassion of their evils move?

---

4. Guyon's faint is in one sense due to his having necessarily lacked "food, and sleepe" for three days. His naturally temperate character, confirmed by continual resistance to Mammon, is for the moment incapable of active expression: like Redcrosse in the dungeon of Orgoglio, he requires the aid of a power higher than his own. Jonah's sojourn in the whale's belly and that of Jesus "in the heart of the earth" (Matthew 12.40) are relevant too.
1. I.e., Pyrochles and Cymochles.

There is: else much more wretched were the cace
Of men, then beasts. But O th'exceeding grace
Of highest God, that loves his creatures so,
And all his workes with mercy doth embrace,
That blessed Angels, he sends to and fro,
To serve to wicked man, to serve his wicked foe.[2]

2

How oft do they, their silver bowers leave,
  To come to succour us, that succour want?°   *need*
How oft do they with golden pineons, cleave
The flitting skyes, like flying Pursuivant,°   *messenger*
Against foule feends to aide us millitant?[3]
They for us fight, they watch and dewly ward,
And their bright Squadrons round about us plant,
And all for love, and nothing for reward:
O why should heavenly God to men have such regard?

3

During the while, that Guyon did abide
  In Mammons house, the Palmer, whom whyleare°   *earlier*
That wanton Mayd[4] of passage had denide,
By further search had passage found elsewhere,
And being on his way, approchéd neare,
Where Guyon lay in traunce, when suddenly
He heard a voice, that calléd loud and cleare,
"Come hither, come hither, O come hastily;"
That all the fields resounded with the ruefull cry.

4

The Palmer lent his eare unto the noyce,
  To weet, who calléd so importunely:°   *urgently*
Againe he heard a more efforcéd° voyce,   *forceful*
That bad him come in haste. He by and by°   *immediately*
His feeble feet directed to the cry;
Which to that shadie delve him brought at last,
Where Mammon earst° did sunne his threasury: *formerly*
There the good Guyon he found slumbring fast
In senselesse dreame; which sight at first him sore aghast.

5

Beside his head there sate a faire young man,
Of wondrous beautie, and of freshest yeares,
Whose tender bud to blossome new began,

2. Cf. Hebrews 1.14: "Are [the angels] not all ministering spirits, sent forth to minister for them who
shall be heirs of salvation?"; and, with reference to the triple temptation of Jesus, Matthew 4.11:
"Then the devil leaveth him, and, behold, angels came and ministered unto him."
3. I.e., by warring on our behalf.
4. I.e., Phaedria.

And flourish faire above his equall peares;[5]
His snowy front° curléd with golden heares,   *forehead*
Like Phoebus face adornd with sunny rayes,
Divinely shone, and two sharpe wingéd sheares,°   *wings*
Deckéd with diverse plumes, like painted Jayes,
Were fixéd at his backe, to cut his ayerie wayes.

6

Like as Cupido on Idaean hill,[6]
    When having laid his cruell bow away,
    And mortall arrowes, wherewith he doth fill
    The world with murdrous spoiles and bloudie pray,
    With his faire mother he him dights° to play,   *prepares*
    And with his goodly sisters, Graces three;[7]
    The Goddesse pleuséd with his wanton play,
    Suffers her selfe through sleepe beguild to bee,
The whiles the other Ladies mind their merry glee.

7

Whom when the Palmer saw, abasht he was
    Through fear and wonder, that he nought could say,
    Till him the child bespoke, "Long lackt, alas,
    Hath bene thy faithfull aide in hard assay,°   *trial*
    Whiles deadly fit thy pupill doth dismay;°   *overcome*
    Behold this heavie sight, thou reverend Sire,
    But dread of death and dolour doe away;
    For life ere long shall to her home retire,
And he that breathlesse seemes, shal corage bold respire.[8]

8

"The charge, which God doth unto me arret,°   *entrust*
    Of his deare safetie, I to thee commend;°   *commit*
    Yet will I not forgoe, ne yet forget
    The care thereof my selfe unto the end,
    But evermore him succour, and defend
    Against his foe and mine: watch thou I pray;
    For evill is at hand him to offend."°   *harm*
    So having said, eftsoones he gan display°   *spread*
His painted nimble wings, and vanisht quite away.

9

The Palmer seeing his left empty place,
    And his slow eyes beguiléd of their sight,
    Woxe° sore affraid, and standing still a space,   *became*

5. I.e., beyond that of other angels in his rank and station.
6. Probably Mount Ida near Troy (not the Mount Ida in Crete), where Paris awarded Venus the golden apple.
7. This view of the Graces as daughters of Venus (not merely her handmaids) may derive from Boccaccio 3.22, or Comes 4.13.
8. I.e., shall regain valiant spirit.

Gaz'd after him, as fowle escapt by flight;
At last him turning to his charge behight,°   *entrusted*
With trembling hand his troubled pulse gan try;
Where finding life not yet dislodgéd quight,
He much rejoyst, and courd° it tenderly,   *protected*
As chicken newly hatcht, from dreaded destiny.

[Directed to the scene by Archimago, Pyrochles and Cymochles are about to despatch the unconscious Guyon, but at this juncture Prince Arthur appears. After a fierce encounter with the brothers he kills them both. Allegorically, the episode recalls Arthur's deliverance of Redcrosse in Book I; but it is significant, and appropriate to the more secular content of Book II, that in this engagement Arthur's shield remains covered, and that the final strokes in the battle are delivered with Guyon's sword. Having recovered consciousness, Guyon proceeds with Prince Arthur to the house of Temperance.]

Canto IX

The house of Temperance, in which
doth sober Alma dwell,
Besiegd of many foes, whom straunger
knightes to flight compell.

1

Of all Gods workes, which do this world adorne,
    There is no one more faire and excellent,
    Then is mans body both for powre and forme,
    Whiles it is kept in sober government;
    But none then it, more fowle and indecent,°   *unseemly*
    Distempred through misrule and passions bace:
    It growes a Monster, and incontinent°   *immediately*
    Doth loose his dignitie and native grace.
Behold, who list, both one and other[1] in this place.

2

After the Paynim brethren[2] conquered were,
    The Briton Prince recov'ring his stolne sword,
    And Guyon his lost shield, they both yfere°   *together*
    Forth passéd on their way in faire accord,
    Till him the Prince with gentle court did bord;°   *accost*
    "Sir knight, mote I of you this curt'sie read,°   *request*
    To weet° why on your shield so goodly scord   *know*
    Beare ye the picture of that Ladies head?
Full lively is the semblaunt,° though the substance dead." *resemblance*

---

1. I.e., Alma's house of Temperance, and Maleger, whose troops besiege it. The house is an allegory of the body, in its proper state of rationally controlled temperance, yet subject to continual attack by (Maleger's) "misrule . . . the negation or perversion of temperance's government" (Rollinson 1990E; also 1987). For Alma see stanza 18 and note. Brooks-Davies 1977 is especially informative on this canto.
2. I.e., Pyrochles and Cymochles.

3

"Faire Sir," said he, "if in that picture dead
    Such life ye read,° and vertue in vaine shew,   *perceive*
    What mote ye weene, if the trew lively-head[3]
    Of that most glorious visage ye did vew?
    But if the beautie of her mind ye knew,
    That is her bountie, and imperiall powre,
    Thousand times fairer then her mortall hew,°   *shape*
    O how great wonder would your thoughts devoure,
And infinite desire into your spirite poure!

4

"She is the mighty Queene of Faerie,
    Whose faire retrait° I in my shield do beare;   *portrait*
    She is the flowre of grace and chastitie,
    Throughout the world renowméd far and neare,
    My liefe, my liege,[4] my Soveraigne, my deare,
    Whose glory shineth as the morning starre,
    And with her light the earth enlumines cleare;
    Far reach her mercies, and her prayses farre,
As well in state of peace, as puissaunce in warre."

5

"Thrise happy man," said then the Briton knight,
    "Whom gracious lot, and thy great valiaunce
    Have made thee souldier of that Princesse bright,
    Which with her bounty and glad countenance
    Doth blesse her servaunts, and them high advaunce.
    How many straunge knight hope ever to aspire,
    By faithfull service, and meet amenance,°   *conduct*
    Unto such blisse? sufficient were that hire°   *reward*
For losse of thousand lives, to dye at her desire."

6

Said Guyon, "Noble Lord, what meed so great,
    Or grace of earthly Prince so soveraine,
    But by your wondrous worth and warlike feat
    Ye well may hope, and easely attaine?
    But were your will, her sold to entertaine,[5]
    And numbred be mongst knights of Maydenhed,
    Great guerdon,° well I wote, should you remaine,   *reward*
    And in her favour high be reckonéd,
As Arthegall, and Sophy now beene honoréd."[6]

3. I.e., the living original.
4. I.e., My beloved, my lord.
5. I.e., to accept her pay (and, in effect, become her soldier).
6. Arthegall, patron of Justice, is the hero of Book V; Sophy (Greek, "wisdom") was perhaps to have been the hero of a later book.

7

"Certes," then said the Prince, "I God avow,
  That sith I armes and knighthood first did plight,
  My whole desire hath beene, and yet is now,
  To serve that Queene with all my powre and might.
  Now hath[7] the Sunne with his lamp-burning light,
  Walkt round about the world, and I no lesse,
  Sith of that Goddesse I have sought the sight,
  Yet no where can her find: such happinesse
Heaven doth to me envy, and fortune favourlesse."

8

"Fortune, the foe of famous chevisaunce°   *enterprise*
  Seldome," said Guyon, "yields to vertue aide,
  But in her way throwes mischiefe and mischaunce,
  Whereby her course is stopt, and passage staid.
  But you faire Sir, be not herewith dismaid,
  But constant keepe the way, in which ye stand;
  Which were it not, that I am else delaid
  With hard adventure, which I have in hand,
I labour would to guide you through all Faery land."

9

"Gramercy Sir," said he, "but mote I weete,
  What straunge adventure do ye now pursew?
  Perhaps my succour,[8] or advizement meete
  Mote stead° you much your purpose to subdew."   *help*
  Then gan Sir Guyon all the story shew
  Of false Acrasia, and her wicked wiles,
  Which to avenge, the Palmer him forth drew
  From Faery court. So talkéd they, the whiles
They wasted had much way, and measurd many miles.

10

And now faire Phœbus gan decline in hast
  His weary wagon to the Westerne vale,
  Whenas they spide a goodly castle, plast
  Foreby° a river in a pleasant dale,   *near*
  Which choosing for that evenings hospitale,°   *lodging*
  They thither marcht: but when they came in sight,
  And from their sweaty Coursers did avale,°   *dismount*
  They found the gates fast barréd long ere night,
And every loup° fast lockt, as fearing foes despight.   *loophole*

---

7. See Textual Notes.
8. I.e., my aid given in your behalf; see II.viii.25 ff.

11

Which when they saw, they weenéd fowle reproch
  Was to them doen, their entrance to forstall,
  Till that the Squire gan nigher to approch;
  And wind° his horne under the castle wall,   *blow*
  That with the noise it shooke, as it would fall:
  Eftsoones forth lookéd from the highest spire
  The watch, and lowd unto the knights did call,
  To weete, what they so rudely did require.
Who gently° answeréd, They entrance did desire.   *courteously*

12

"Fly fly, good knights," said he, "fly fast away
  If that your lives ye love, as meete ye should;
  Fly fast, and save your selves from neare decay,°   *destruction*
  Here may ye not have entraunce, though we would:
  We would and would againe, if that we could;
  But thousand enemies about us rave,
  And with long siege us in this castle hould:
  Seven yeares⁹ this wize they us besiegéd have,
And many good knights slaine, that have us sought to save."

13

Thus as he spoke, loe with outragious cry
  A thousand villeins¹ round about them swarmd
  Out of the rockes and caves adjoyning nye,
  Vile caytive wretches, ragged, rude, deformd,
  All threatning death, all in straunge manner armd,
  Some with unweldy clubs, some with long speares,
  Some rusty knives, some staves in fire warmd.
  Sterne was their looke, like wild amazéd steares,
Staring with hollow eyes, and stiffe upstanding heares.

14

Fiersly at first those knights they did assaile,
  And drove them to recoile: but when againe
  They gave fresh charge, their forces gan to faile,
  Unable their encounter to sustaine;
  For with such puissaunce and impetuous maine°   *force*
  Those Champions broke on them, that forst them fly,
  Like scattered Sheepe, whenas the Shepheards swaine

9. John Upton was the first of Spenser's editors (*The Faerie Queene* 1758) to notice the probable influence on II.ix of the *Commentary* on *The Dream of Scipio*, by the Roman philosopher Macrobius (395–423), who regards the number seven as controlling and regulatory in human life (*Commentary* I.6; tr. and ed. W. H. Stahl [New York, 1952]). The proverbial seven ages of the world, the seven stages of man's life (cf. *As You Like It* 2.7.139–66), and the seven deadly sins are also relevant here. On the heptad in Spenser's poetry, see V. F. Hopper, *Medieval Number Symbolism* (New York, 1938), and, especially Alastair Fowler, *Spenser and the Numbers of Time* (London, 1964).

1. I.e., a mob of brutish rabble: Maleger's forces, representing in the first instance the "passions bace" (1.6).

A Lyon and a Tigre doth espye,
With greedy pace forth rushing from the forest nye.

15

A while they fled, but soone returnd againe
  With greater fury, then before was found;
  And evermore their cruell Capitaine
  Sought with his raskall routs² t'enclose them round,
  And overrun to tread them to the ground.
  But soone the knights with their bright-burning blades
  Broke their rude troupes, and orders° did confound,   *ranks*
  Hewing and slashing at their idle shades;
For though they bodies seeme, yet substance from them fades.

16

As when a swarme of Gnats at eventide
  Out of the fennes of Allan³ do arise,
  Their murmuring small trompets sounden wide,
  Whiles in the aire their clustring army flies,
  That as a cloud doth seeme to dim the skies;
  Ne man nor beast may rest, or take repast,
  For their sharpe wounds, and noyous° injuries,   *annoying*
  Till the fierce Northerne wind with blustring blast
Doth blow them quite away, and in the Ocean cast.

17

Thus when they had that troublous rout disperst,
  Unto the castle gate they come againe,
  And entraunce craved, which was deniéd erst.
  Now when report of that their perilous paine,
  And combrous° conflict, which they did sustaine,   *harassing*
  Came to the Ladies eare, which there did dwell,
  She forth issewéd with a goodly traine
  Of Squires and Ladies equipagéd° well,   *arrayed*
And entertainéd them right fairely, as befell.⁴

18

Alma⁵ she calléd was, a virgin bright;
  That had not yet felt Cupides wanton rage,
  Yet was she wooed of many a gentle knight,

2. I.e., disreputable gang; the *canaille*.
3. The extensive "Bog of Allen," westward from Dublin, lies between Edenderry and Kildare.
4. I.e., as was fitting.
5. Alma's name derives from Italian, "the soul"; and Latin, "nurturing," "gracious." Her castle,
   looking ultimately to scriptural and classical sources (1 Corinthians 6.19; Plato, *Timaeus*), recalls
   earlier English and French allegories of the body as city or castle, e.g., Langland, *Piers Plowman*
   11.2.1–7; Du Bartas, *Divine Weekes* 1.6. Alma herself effectively signifies the rational soul (Latin,
   anima) that orders and controls the body "in accordance with counsel" (Fowler 1964, 86). Her
   guided tour of the body, beginning at stanza 21, reflects Platonic tradition (*Timaeus* 69–73) in the
   ascent from stomach to heart and at length to the head "that all this other worlds worke doth
   excell" (stanza 47). See also Davis 1981, 1990E.

And many a Lord of noble parentage,
  That sought with her to lincke in marriage:
  For she was faire, as faire mote ever bee,
  And in the flowre now of her freshest age;
  Yet full of grace and goodly modestee,
That even heaven rejoycéd her sweete face to see.

19

In robe of lilly white she was arayd,
  That from her shoulder to her heele downe raught,
  The traine whereof loose far behind her strayd,
  Braunchéd° with gold and pearle, most richly wrought,   *embroidered*
  And borne of two faire Damsels, which were taught
  That service well. Her yellow golden heare
  Was trimly woven, and in tresses wrought,
  Ne other tyre° she on her head did weare,   *headdress*
But crownéd with a garland of sweete Rosiere.°   *rosebush*

20

Goodly she entertaind those noble knights,
  And brought them up into her castle hall;
  Where gentle court and gracious delight
  She to them made, with mildnesse virginall,
  Shewing her selfe both wise and liberall:°   *generous*
  There when they rested had a season dew,
  They her besought of favour speciall,
  Of that faire Castle to affoord them vew;
She graunted, and them leading forth, the same did shew.

21

First she them led up to the Castle wall,
  That was so high, as foe might not it clime,
  And all so faire, and fensible° withall,   *fortified*
  Not built of bricke, ne yet of stone and lime,
  But of thing like to that Aegyptian slime,
  Whereof king Nine whilome built Babell towre;[6]
  But O great pitty, that no lenger time
  So goodly workemanship should not endure:
Soone it must turne to earth; no earthly thing is sure.

22

The frame thereof seemd partly circulare,
  And part triangulare, O worke divine;
  Those two the first and last proportions are,
  The one imperfect, mortall, feminine;

6. For Ninus (and Nimrod, "the beginning of [whose] Kingdom was Babel," Genesis 10.10) see I.5.48 and note. The tower of Babel was constructed of "brick for stone, and slime . . . for mortar," (Genesis 11.3); in Spenser's poem, "slime" in the first instance refers to the "dust" and water from which God made man (Genesis 2.7), but incorporates also the "loathly crime / That is ingenerate in fleshly slime" (III.vi.3.4–5; and see I.vii.9.8).

Th'other immortall, perfect, masculine,
And twixt them both a quadrate was the base,
Proportioned equally by seven and nine;
Nine was the circle set in heavens place,
All which compacted made a goodly diapase.[7]

23

Therein two gates[8] were placed seemly well:
The one before, by which all in did pas,
Did th'other far in workmanship excell;
For not of wood, nor of enduring bras,
But of more worthy substance framd it was;
Doubly disparted, it did locke and close,
That when it lockéd, none might thorough pas,
And when it opened, no man might it close,
Still open to their friends, and closéd to their foes.

24

Of hewen stone the porch[9] was fairely wrought,
Stone more of valew, and more smooth and fine,
Then Jet or Marble far from Ireland brought;
Over the which was cast a wandring vine,
Enchacéd° with a wanton yvie twine.   adorned
And over it a faire Portcullis hong,
Which to the gate directly did incline,
With comely compasse, and compacture strong,
Neither unseemely short, nor yet exceeding long.

25

Within the Barbican a Porter[1] sate,
Day and night duely keeping watch and ward,
Nor wight, nor word mote passe out of the gate,
But in good order, and with dew regard;

7. The problems of this stanza are not to be resolved in a footnote, but readers should consult, in chief, Sir Kenelm Digby, *Observations on the 22. Stanza in the 9th Canto of the 2d. Book of Spencers Faery Queen* (London, 1644), and Fowler 1964 (260–88). In brief, earlier critical emphasis on the physical correspondence of circle, triangle, and "quadrate" to the human head, legs, and torso, or (as in Dowden's ultimately Aristotelian approach) to rational soul, vegetative soul, and sensitive soul has given place to an emphasis on Pythagorean and Platonic arithmology and to the symbolic import of seven and nine (the numbers respectively of body and mind, as Digby observes, corresponding to the seven planets and the nine Ptolemaic spheres, as well as the nine orders of angels). Fowler 267 notes that the stanza draws attention "to the *incommensurateness* of mind (circle) and body (triangle) and the difficulty of establishing proportion between them," and that in this connection "the quadrate," which Digby held to mean "the foure principall humours in mans Bodie," recalls Francesco Giorgio (*De harmonia mundi* . . . , Paris, 1545): "we can never make the square commensurate with the circle." Yet the concluding lines of stanza 22 gently draw together the ninth sphere (or *primum mobile*) with that "goodly diapase" or perfect harmony that finally informs the composition of all God's works. Cf. John Dryden, *A Song for St. Cecilia's Day*, 1687 (stanza 1): "From harmony, from heavenly harmony, / This universal frame began. . . . From harmony to harmony / Through all the compass of the notes it ran, / The diapason closing full in man."
8. The mouth and the anus (or "back-gate": 32.7).
9. Porch, vine, "yvie," and portcullis respectively figure the chin, beard, moustache, and well-proportioned nose.
1. The tongue, within the oral cavity.

Utterers of secrets he from thence debard,
Bablers of folly, and blazers° of crime.   *proclaimers*
His larumbell might lowd and wide be hard,
When cause requird, but never out of time;
Early and late it rong, at evening and at prime.°   *sunrise*

26

And round about the porch on every side
    Twise sixteen warders[2] sat, all arméd bright
In glistring steele, and strongly fortifide:
Tall yeomen seeméd they, and of great might,
And were enraungéd ready, still for fight.
By them as Alma passéd with her guestes,
They did obeysaunce, as beseeméd right,
And then againe returnéd to their restes:
The Porter eke to her did lout with humble gestes.[3]

27

Thence she them brought into a stately Hall,[4]
    Wherein were many tables faire dispred,
And ready dight with drapets° festivall,   *coverings*
Against[5] the viaundes should be ministred.
At th'upper end there sate, yclad in red
Downe to the ground, a comely personage,
That in his hand a white rod menagéd,   *wielded*
He Steward was hight Diet; rype of age,
And in demeanure sober, and in counsell sage.

28

And through the Hall there walkéd to and fro
    A jolly yeoman, Marshall of the same,
Whose name was Appetite; he did bestow°   *place*
Both guestes and meate, when ever in they came,
And knew them how to order without blame,
As him the Steward bad. They both attone°   *together*
Did dewty to their Lady, as became;
Who passing by, forth led her guestes anone°   *immediately*
Into the kitchin rowme, ne spard for nicenesse none.[6]

29

It was a vaut ybuilt for great dispence,[7]
    With many raunges reard along the wall;
And one great chimney, whose long tonnell thence,
The smoke forth threw. And in the midst of all

2. The teeth.
3. I.e., bowed with respectful gestures.
4. The throat.
5. I.e., for the time when.
6. I.e., nor [was she] held back by fastidious reserve.
7. I.e., a room with an arched roof, designed for grand hospitality; figuratively, the stomach.

There placéd was a caudron wide and tall,
 Upon a mighty furnace, burning whot,
 More whot, then Aetn', or flaming Mongiball:[8]
 For day and night it brent, ne ceaséd not,
So long as any thing it in the caudron got.

30

But to delay° the heat, least by mischaunce   *temper*
 It might breake out, and set the whole on fire,
 There added was by goodly ordinaunce,
 An huge great paire of bellowes,[9] which did styre
 Continually, and cooling breath inspyre.
 About the Caudron many Cookes accoyld,°   *gathered*
 With hookes and ladles, as need did require;
 The whiles the viandes in the vessell boyld
They did about their businesse sweat, and sorely toyld.

31

The maister Cooke was cald Concoction,[1]
 A carefull man, and full of comely guise:
 The kitchin Clerke, that hight Digestion,
 Did order all th'Achates° in seemely wise,   *provisions*
 And set them forth, as well he could devise.
 The rest had severall offices assind,
 Some to remove the scum, as it did rise;
 Others to beare the same away did mind;
And others it to use according to his kind.

32

But all the liquour, which was fowle and wast,
 Not good nor serviceable else for ought,
 They in another great round vessell plast,
 Till by a conduit pipe it thence were brought:
 And all the rest, that noyous was, and nought,[2]
 By secret wayes, that none might it espy,
 Was close convaid, and to the back-gate brought,
 That clepéd was Port Esquiline,[3] whereby
It was avoided° quite, and throwne out privily.   *removed*

8. Both names refer to Mount Aetna, in Sicily.
9. The lungs.
1. I.e., the first of three digestive processes recognized in early physiology: digestion in the stomach
 and intestines. This was thought to precede a second and a third "concoction" (Spenser's "Digestion" and his minions in stanzas 31–32), which converted, by pancreatic fluid and bile, the "chyme"
 or pulpy matter into the white milky fluid called "chyle," subsequently eliminated through the
 anus.
2. I.e., was harmful, and useless.
3. The anus. Beyond the Esquiline Gate of ancient Rome lay the city garbage dump. "There is
 much lurking humor here, [which] comes out clearly in the end in a moment of purgation, in
 the puns [of lines 8–9]" (Davis 1981). Remarking the absence of the sexual organs from Alma's
 castle, Miller 1988 argues rather that "the genitals are not allegorized *in the same way* as the other
 body organs, within the same metaphysical conceit or figurative 'frame' " (169).

33

Which goodly order, and great workmans skill
  Whenas those knights beheld, with rare delight,
  And gazing wonder they their minds did fill;
  For never had they seene so straunge a sight.
  Thence backe againe faire Alma led them right,
  And soone into a goodly Parlour[4] brought,
  That was with royall arras° richly dight,   *tapestry*
  In which was nothing pourtrahéd, nor wrought,
Not wrought nor pourtrahéd, but easie to be thought.[5]

34

And in the midst thereof upon the floure,
  A lovely bevy of faire Ladies sate,
  Courted of many a jolly Paramoure,
  The which them did in modest wise amate,[6]
  And eachone sought his Lady to aggrate:°   *please*
  And eke emongst them litle Cupid playd
  His wanton sports, being returnéd late
  From his fierce warres, and having from him layd
His cruell bow, wherewith he thousands hath dismayd.

35

Diverse delights they found them selves to please;
  Some song in sweet consort,° some laught for joy,   *harmony*
  Some plaid with strawes, some idly sat at ease;
  But other some could not abide to toy,
  All pleasaunce was to them griefe and annoy:
  This fround, that faund, the third for shame did blush,
  Another seeméd envious, or coy,
  Another in her teeth did gnaw a rush:°   *reed*
But at these straungers presence every one did hush.

36

Soone as the gracious Alma came in place,
  They all attonce out of their seates arose,
  And to her homage made, with humble grace:
  Whom when the knights beheld, they gan dispose
  Themselves to court, and each a Damsell chose:
  The Prince by chaunce did on a Lady light,
  That was right faire and fresh as morning rose,
  But somwhat sad, and solemne eke in sight,°   *appearance*
As if some pensive thought constraind her gentle spright.

4. The heart, seat of the affections.
5. I.e., nothing except that which is easily apprehended by the five senses; see Brooks-Davies 1977 (166).
6. I.e., keep company with.

37

In a long purple pall,° whose skirt with gold,   robe
    Was fretted all about, she was arayd;
    And in her hand a Poplar braunch[7] did hold:
    To whom the Prince in curteous manner said;
    "Gentle Madame, why 'beene ye thus dismaid,
    And your faire beautie do with sadnesse spill?°   spoil
    Lives any, that you hath thus ill apaid?°   pleased
    Or doen you love, or doen you lacke your will?
What ever be the cause, it sure beseemes you ill."

38

"Faire Sir," said she halfe in disdainefull wise,
    "How is it, that this word in me ye blame,
    And in your selfe do not the same advise?°   perceive
    Him ill beseemes, anothers fault to name,
    That may unwares be blotted with the same:
    Pensive I yeeld I am, and sad in mind,
    Through great desire of glory and of fame;
    Ne ought I weene are ye therein behind,
That have twelue moneths[8] sought one, yet no where can her find."

39

The Prince was inly moved at her speach,
    Well weeting trew, what she had rashly° told;   boldly
    Yet with faire samblaunt° sought to hide the breach,   appearance
    Which chaunge of colour did perforce unfold,
    Now seeming flaming whot, now stony cold.
    Tho turning soft aside, he did inquire,
    What wight she was, that Poplar braunch did hold:
    It answered was, her name was Prays-desire,[9]
That by well doing sought to honour to aspire.

40

The whiles, the Faerie knight did entertaine
    Another Damsell of that gentle crew,
    That was right faire, and modest of demaine,°   demeanor
    But that too oft she chaunged her native hew:
    Straunge was her tyre, and all her garment blew,
    Close round about her tuckt with many a plight:°   pleat
    Upon her fist the bird, which shonneth vew,
    And keepes in coverts close from living wight,
Did sit, as yet ashamd, how rude Pan did her dight.[1]

7. The poplar, traditionally sacred to Hercules (cf. II.v.31), is an emblem of heroic aspiration for glory.
8. See Textual Notes.
9. I.e., desire for praise; the "thought of glorie and of fame" (II.xi.31.8) that consistently informs the character of Arthur and inspires his quest for Gloriana.
1. I.e. (probably), maltreat, abuse sexually. The bird of line 7 may be the owl, dove, or wryneck; but no source for the hints in line 9 has been firmly identified.

41

So long as Guyon with her commonéd,°   *conversed*
  Unto the ground she cast her modest eye,
  And ever and anone with rosie red
  The bashfull bloud her snowy cheekes did dye,
  That her became, as polisht yvory,
  Which cunning Craftesman hand hath overlayd
  With faire vermilion or pure Castory.[2]
  Great wonder had the knight, to see the mayd
So straungely passionéd, and to her gently sayd,

42

"Faire Damzell, seemeth, by your troubled cheare,
  That either me too bold ye weene, this wise
  You to molest, or other ill to feare
  That in the secret of your hart close lyes,
  From whence it doth, as cloud from sea arise.
  If it be I, of pardon I you pray;
  But if ought else that I mote not devise,°   *guess*
  I will, if please you it discure,° assay,   *reveal*
To ease you of that ill, so wisely as I may."

43

She answerd nought, but more abasht for shame,
  Held downe her head, the whiles her lovely face
  The flashing bloud with blushing did inflame,
  And the strong passion mard her modest grace,
  That Guyon mervayld at her uncouth° cace: *strange*
  Till Alma him bespake, "Why wonder yee
  Faire Sir at that, which ye so much embrace?
  She is the fountaine of your modestee;
You shamefast are, but Shamefastnesse it selfe is shee."[3]

44

Thereat the Elfe did blush in privitee,
  And turnd his face away; but she the same
  Dissembled faire, and faynd to oversee.°   *overlook*
  Thus they awhile with court and goodly game,
  Themselves did solace each one with his Dame,
  Till that great Ladie thence away them sought,°   *invited*
  To vew her castles other wondrous frame.
  Up to a stately Turret[4] she them brought,
Ascending by ten steps of Alablaster wrought.

2. I.e., red dye derived from the beaver (and thought to have medicinal value).
3. As Arthur appropriately companions "Prays-desire," so "Shamefastnesse," the idea and font of Guyon's modesty, is suitably matched with the temperate knight. At the same time, Brooks-Davies's suggestion that she figures modesty "in its extreme and pre-social form" (1977, 167) gains force by the terms of line 4 and the violence of Guyon's actions at xii.83.
4. The head, to which the spinal cord ascends; "ten steps" may signify completion and perfection (Upton 1758).

45

That Turrets frame most admirable was,
  Like highest heaven compasséd around,
  And lifted high above this earthly masse,
  Which it survewed,° as hils doen lower ground;   *overlooked*
  But not on ground mote like to this be found,
  Not that, which antique Cadmus whylome built
  In Thebes, which Alexander did confound;
  Nor that proud towre of Troy, though richly guilt,
From which young Hectors bloud by cruell Greekes was spilt.[5]

46

The roofe hereof was arched ouer head,
  And deckt with flowers and herbars° daintily;   *arbors*
  Two goodly Beacons, set in watches stead,[6]
  Therein gave light, and flamed continually:
  For they of living fire most subtilly
  Were made, and set in silver sockets bright,
  Covered with lids devized of substance sly,°   *fine*
  That readily they shut and open might.
O who can tell the prayses of that makers might!

47

Ne can I tell, ne can I stay to tell
  This parts great workmanship, and wondrous powre,
  That all this other worlds worke doth excell,
  And likest is unto that heavenly towre,[7]
  That God hath built for his owne blesséd bowre.
  Therein were diverse roomes, and diverse stages,
  But three the chiefest, and of greatest powre,
  In which there dwelt three honorable sages,
The wisest men, I weene, that livéd in their ages.[8]

48

Not he,[9] whom Greece, the Nourse of all good arts,
  By Phœbus doome, the wisest thought alive,

5. The legendary Cadmus, searching for his sister Europa, and directed by the oracle at Delphi, built the fortress called Cadmea on the site of the future city of Thebes, in Boeotia (*Metamorphoses* 3.1–130). Alexander the Great destroyed the city in c. 335 B.C., sparing only the house of Pindar. Astyanax, Hector's son, was thrown from the walls of Troy by the victorious Greeks (*Metamorphoses* 13.415).
6. The eyes serve as watchmen.
7. I.e., the towered "goodly Citie" of the New Jerusalem, revealed to Redcrosse in I.x.55–57.
8. The three wise men respectively figure (1) the creative imagination, of which prescient foresight makes part; (2) the intellective power of the reason, concerned to correlate and assess the significance in present time of evidence provided by the external senses; (3) memory, which retains and records the mass of sense-evidence so provided through time, that its components "may be forth-coming when they are called for by *phantasy* and *reason*" (Burton, *Anatomy of Melancholy* 1.1.2.7). See Brooks-Davies 1977 on stanzas 48–58 in these and other (especially astrological) contexts.
9. Socrates, identified by the Delphian Oracle as the wisest man alive (*Apology* 21a).

Might be compared to these by many parts:
Nor that sage Pylian syre,[1] which did survive
Three ages, such as mortall men contrive,
By whose advise old Priams cittie fell,
With these in praise of pollicies° mote strive.   *statecraft*
These three in these three roomes did sundry° dwell,   *separately*
And counselléd faire Alma, how to governe well.

49

The first of them could things to come foresee:
The next could of things present best advize;
The third things past could keepe in memoree,
So that no time, nor reason could arize,
But that the same could one of these comprize.°   *comprehend*
For thy the first did in the forepart sit,
That nought mote hinder his quicke prejudize:[2]
He had a sharpe foresight, and working wit,
That never idle was, ne once could rest a whit.

50

His chamber was dispainted all within,
With sundry colours, in the which were writ
Infinite shapes of things disperséd thin;
Some such as in the world were never yit,
Ne can devizéd be of mortall wit;
Some daily seene, and knowen by their names,
Such as in idle fantasies doe flit:
Infernall Hags, Centaurs, feendes, Hippodames,
Apes, Lions, Aegles, Owles, fooles, lovers, children, Dames.[3]

51

And all the chamber filléd was with flyes,
Which buzzéd all about, and made such sound,
That they encombred all mens eares and eyes,
Like many swarmes of Bees assembled round,
After their hives with honny do abound:
All those were idle thoughts and fantasies,
Devices, dreames, opinions unsound,
Shewes, visions, sooth-sayes,° and prophesies;   *predictions*
And all that fainéd is, as leasings,° tales, and lies.   *falsehoods*

---

1. Nestor, king of Pylos for three generations (*Iliad* 1.250–52), was senior counsellor to Agamemnon, leader of the Greek forces besieging Troy.
2. I.e., power to forecast and predict.
3. Mythological Centaur (half-man, half-horse) and Hippodame (a slip for "hippotame," or seahorse; or possibly a quiet jest by our poet) keep confused company with figures from the nether regions and the natural world; yet ironic pattern may also be thought to inform the catalog of beings known and fancied merely.

52

Emongst them all sate he, which wonnéd there,
   That hight Phantastes[4] by his nature trew;
   A man of yeares yet fresh, as mote appere,
   Of swarth complexion, and of crabbéd hew,
   That him full of melancholy did shew;
   Bent hollow beetle browes, sharpe staring eyes,
   That mad or foolish seemd: one by his vew
   Mote deeme him borne with ill disposéd skyes,
When oblique Saturne sate in the house of agonyes.

53

Whom Alma having shewéd to her guestes,
   Thence brought them to the second roome, whose wals
   Were painted faire with memorable gestes,°   *deeds*
   Of famous Wisards, and with picturals
   Of Magistrates, of courts, of tribunals,
   Of commen wealthes, of states, of pollicy,
   Of lawes, of judgements, and of decretals;°   *decrees*
   All artes, all science, all Philosophy,
And all that in the world was aye thought wittily.[5]

54

Of those that roome was full, and them among
   There sate a man of ripe and perfect age,
   Who did them meditate all his life long,
   That through continuall practise and usage,
   He now was growne right wise, and wondrous sage.
   Great pleasure had those stranger knights, to see
   His goodly reason, and grave personage,°   *appearance*
   That his disciples both desired to bee;
But Alma thence them led to th'hindmost roome of three.[6]

55

That chamber seeméd ruinous and old,
   And therefore was removéd farre behind,
   Yet were the wals, that did the same uphold,
   Right firme and strong, though somewhat they declind;
   And therein sate an old oldman, halfe blind,
   And all decrepit in his feeble corse,

4. That Phantastes (Greek, "fantasy") appears "mad or foolish," together with his dark complexion and melancholy demeanor, in astrological contexts indicates the influence of the gloomy and "ominous" planet Saturn; yet such natures are also given to "aspiration above the merely sensual to the rational and contemplative" (Fowler 1964, 104). Fowler's astrological commentary on the horoscope of Phantastes casts learned light on Spenser's careful art in this stanza (289–91).
5. I.e., was ever wisely conceived.
6. It was commonly thought that the back of the brain governed memory; appropriately, Memory's chamber is set behind those of his fellow sages, who meditate on the present or look on into the future. As the walls of the somewhat ruinous "hindmost room" stand "Right firme and strong" still, stanzas 55–58 anticipate the account in Canto x of noble deeds and lineage preserved through time "from Brute . . . to Gloriane" (II.x.Arg.). See Evans 1990E: "The whole of *The Faerie Queene* is in fact a great frame of memory . . ." (468).

Yet lively vigour rested in his mind,
  And recompenst him with a better scorse:°   *exchange*
Weake body well is changed for minds redoubled forse.

56

This man of infinite remembrance was,
  And things foregone through many ages held,
  Which he recorded still, as they did pas,
  Ne suffred them to perish through long eld,
  As all things else, the which this world doth weld,°   *control*
  But laid them up in his immortall scrine,°   *chest*
  Where they for ever incorrupted dweld:
  The warres he well remembred of king Nine,
Of old Assaracus, and Inachus divine.[7]

57

The yeares of Nestor nothing were to his,
  Ne yet Mathusalem, though longest lived;[8]
  For he remembred both their infancies:
  Ne wonder then, if that he were deprived
  Of native strength now, that he them survived.
  His chamber all was hangd about with rolles,
  And old records from auncient times derived,
  Some made in books, some in long parchment scrolles,
That were all worme-eaten, and full of canker holes.

58

Amidst them all he in a chaire was set,
  Tossing and turning them withouten end;
  But for he was unhable them to fet,°   *fetch*
  A litle boy did on him still attend,
  To reach, when ever he for ought did send;
  And oft when things were lost, or laid amis,
  That boy them sought, and unto him did lend.
  Therefore he Anamnestes cleped is,
And that old man Eumnestes, by their propertis.[9]

59

The knights there entring, did him reverence dew
  And wondred at his endlesse exercise,
  Then as they gan his Librarie to vew,
  And antique Registers for to avise,°   *notice*
  There chauncéd to the Princes hand to rize,
  An auncient booke, hight *Briton moniments*,°   *records*

7. For Ninus see I.v.48, II.ix.21.6, and notes. The Trojan king Assaracus was Aeneas's great-
grandfather; Inacus the river god, son of Oceanus and Tethys, was the first king of Argos.
8. "All the dayes of Methuselah were nine hundred sixty and nine years" (Genesis 5.27).
9. The aged Eumnestes (Greek, "good memory") is served by Anamnestes (Greek, "the reminder").
On Eumnestes' "immortal scrine," and Spenser's "sense of a literary tradition and of the words
and forms that constitute it," see Anderson 1989 (esp. 17–22).

That of this lands first conquest did devize,
And old division into Regiments,°   *kingdoms*
Till it reducéd was to one mans governments.

60

Sir Guyon chaunst eke on another booke,
That hight *Antiquitie* of *Faerie* lond.
In which when as he greedily did looke,
Th' off-spring° of Elves and Faries there he fond,   *origin*
As it delivered was from hond to hond:
Whereat they burning both with fervent fire,
Their countries auncestry to understond,
Craved leave of Alma, and that aged sire,
To read those bookes; who gladly graunted their desire.

[In Anamnestes' chamber the two knights study their respective ancestries in
the chronicles of British and Elfin kings, Arthur "quite ravisht with delight,"
the sober Guyon pleased and moved too (although he has not finished the
"great and ample volume" called "Antiquitee of Faery Lond" when Alma
summons the pair to supper). Next day, while Arthur remains behind to repel
an attack on the castle by its besiegers (and eventually to destroy Maleger),
Guyon departs with the Palmer to renew his quest.]

Canto XII

Guyon, by Palmers governance,°   *guidance*
passing through perils great,
Doth overthrowe the Bowre of blisse,
and Acrasie[1] defeat.

1

Now gins this goodly frame° of Temperance   *structure*
Fairely to rise, and her adornéd hed
To pricke° of highest praise forth to advance,   *point*
Formerly grounded, and fast setteled
On firme foundation of true bountihed;°   *virtue*
And this brave knight, that for that vertue fights,
Now comes to point of that same perilous sted,[2]
Where Pleasure dwelles in sensuall delights,
Mongst thousand dangers, and ten thousand magick mights.

2

Two dayes now in that sea he sayléd has,
Ne ever land beheld, ne living wight,
Ne ought save perill, still as he did pas:

1. I.e., Acrasia (from Greek, "incontinence"; disorder, lack of harmony), a Circe-like witch who
represents self-indulgent sensuality. On this canto, the longest in *The Faerie Queene*, see Alpers
1990E, "Bower of Bliss," who more than some (e.g., C. S. Lewis, *The Allegory of Love* [Oxford,
1936]) acknowledges the Bower's appeal: Guyon's final deed there, while just, is disturbingly at
odds with the poetry's seductive effect, evoking particularly subjective responses.
2. I.e., now directly approaches that dangerous place.

Tho° when appearéd the third Morrow bright,   *then*
Upon the waves to spred her trembling light,
An hideous roaring farre away they heard,
That all their senses filléd with affright,
And streight they saw the raging surges reard
Up to the skyes, that them of drowning made affeard.[3]

3

Said then the Boteman, "Palmer stere aright,
And keepe an even course; for yonder way
We needes must passe (God to us well acquight,)°   *preserve*
That is the Gulfe of Greedinesse, they say,
That deepe engorgeth all this worldés pray:
Which having swallowed up excessively,
He soone in vomit up againe doth lay,°   *cast*
And belcheth forth his superfluity,
That all the seas for feare do seeme away to fly.

4

"On th'other side an hideous Rocke is pight,
Of mightie Magnes stone,[4] whose craggie clift
Depending° from on high, dreadfull to sight,   *overhanging*
Over the waves his rugged armes doth lift,
And threatneth downe to throw his ragged rift°   *fragment*
On who so commeth nigh; yet nigh it drawes
All passengers, that none from it can shift:
For whiles they fly that Gulfes devouring jawes,
They on this rock are rent, and sunck in helplesse wawes."[5]

5

Forward they passe, and strongly he them rowes,
Untill they nigh unto that Gulfe arrive,
Where streame more violent and greedy growes:
Then he with all his puissance doth strive
To strike his oares, and mightily doth drive
The hollow vessell through the threatfull wave,
Which gaping wide, to swallow them alive,
In th'huge abysse of his engulfing grave,
Doth rore at them in vaine, and with great terror rave.

6

They passing by, that griesly mouth did see,
Sucking the seas into his entralles° deepe,   *inner depths*

3. For the voyage to the Bower of Bliss, Spenser draws primarily on Homer's *Odyssey* and the
   Mythologiae of Comes; he makes use also of the voyage of Carlo and Ubaldo to Armida's bower,
   in Tasso, *Gerusalemme Liberata* 15, and, perhaps, the medieval legend of St. Brandan, of which
   a version appears in the *Legenda Aurea*.
4. I.e., lodestone, supposed to be found in Magnesia (cf. Lucretius, *De Rerum Natura* 6.909–10).
5. I.e., helplessly sunk beneath the waves. The dangers in stanzas 3–8 recall Scylla and Charybdis
   (*Odyssey* 12).

That seemed more horrible then hell to bee,
Or that darke dreadfull hole of Tartare[6] steepe,
Through which the damnéd ghosts doen often creepe
Backe to the world, bad livers[7] to torment:
But nought that falles into this direfull deepe,
Ne that approcheth nigh the wide descent,
May backe returne, but is condemnéd to be drent.°   *drowned*

7

On th'other side, they saw that perilous Rocke,
   Threatning it selfe on them to ruinate,°   *fall crushingly*
   On whose sharpe clifts the ribs of vessels broke,
   And shivered ships, which had bene wreckéd late,
   Yet stuck, with carkasses exanimate°   *lifeless*
   Of such, as having all their substance spent
   In wanton joyes, and lustes intemperate,[8]
   Did afterwards make shipwracke violent,
Both of their life, and fame for ever fowly blent.°   *stained*

8

For thy, this hight The Rocke of vile Reproch,
   A daungerous and detestable place,
   To which nor fish nor fowle did once approch,
   But yelling Meawes,° with Seagulles hoarse and bace,   *gulls*
   And Cormoyrants, with birds of ravenous race,
   Which still sate waiting on that wastfull clift,
   For spoyle of wretches, whose unhappie cace,
   After lost credite and consuméd thrift,
At last them driven hath to this despairefull drift.°   *end*

9

The Palmer seeing them in safetie past,
   Thus said; "Behold th'ensamples in our sights,
   Of lustfull luxurie and thriftlesse wast:
   What now is left of miserable wights,
   Which spent their looser daies in lewd delights,
   But shame and sad reproch, here to be red,°   *perceived*
   By these rent reliques, speaking their ill plights?
   Let all that live, hereby be counselléd,
To shunne Rocke of Reproch, and it as death to dred."

10

So forth they rowéd, and that Ferryman[9]
   With his stiffe oares did brush the sea so strong,

6. I.e., the cavernous entrance to Tartarus (below Hades), where the rebel Titans were punished.
7. I.e., sinners.
8. Lines 5–9 paraphrase Comes 8.12.
9. In *Aeneid* 6.299, the aged and terrible Charon ferries the shades of the dead over the rivers of the underworld. Comes says he signifies confidence in God's mercy, sustaining the spirit of the dying. (3.4).

That the hoare waters from his frigot° ran,   *swift vessel*
And the light bubbles dauncéd all along,
Whiles the salt brine out of the billowes sprong.
At last farre off they many Islands spy,
On every side floting the floods emong:
Then said the knight, "Loe I the land descry,
Therefore old Syre thy course do thereunto apply."

11

"That may not be," said then the Ferryman,
  "Least we unweeting hap to be fordonne:°   *ruined*
For those same Islands, seeming now and than,[1]
Are not firme lande, nor any certein wonne,[2]
But straggling plots, which to and fro do ronne
In the wide waters: therefore are they hight
The wandring Islands. Therefore doe them shonne;
For they have oft drawne many a wandring wight
Into most deadly daunger and distresséd plight.

12

"Yet well they seeme to him, that farre doth vew,
  Both faire and fruitfull, and the ground dispred
With grassie greene of delectable hew,
And the tall trees with leaves apparelléd,
Are deckt with blossomes dyde in white and red,
That mote the passengers thereto allure;
But whosoever once hath fastenéd
His foot thereon, may never it recure,[3]
But wandreth ever more uncertain and unsure.

13

"As th'Isle of Delos whylome° men report   *formerly*
  Amid th' Aegaean sea long time did stray,
Ne made for shipping any certaine port,
Till that Latona[4] traveiling that way,
Flying from Junoes wrath and hard assay,°   *affliction*
Of her faire twins was there deliveréd,
Which afterwards did rule the night and day;
Thenceforth it firmely was establishéd,
And for Apolloes honor highly herriéd."°   *praised*

14

They to him hearken, as beseemeth meete,
  And passe on forward: so their way does ly,

1. I.e., appearing here and there.
2. I.e., fixed place.
3. I.e., repair that error.
4. For the story of Latona (mother of Apollo and Diana), cf. *Metamorphoses* 6.184–218; but Spenser
   probably used Comes, who notes the instability of the island of Delos at that time (9.6). In Spenser's
   day, some still believed in floating islands (for which Herodotus and Pliny gave authority).

That one of those same Islands, which doe fleet°   *float*
In the wide sea, they needes must passen by,
Which seemd so sweet and pleasant to the eye,
That it would tempt a man to touchen there:
Upon the banck they sitting did espy
A daintie damzell, dressing of her heare,
By whom a litle skippet° floting did appeare.   *skiff*

15

She them espying, loud to them can° call,   *did*
Bidding them nigher draw unto the shore;
For she had cause to busie them withall;
And therewith loudly laught: But nathemore
Would they once turne, but kept on as afore:
Which when she saw, she left her lockes undight,
And running to her boat withouten ore,°   *oar*
From the departing land it launchéd light,°   *quickly*
And after them did drive with all her power and might.

16

Whom overtaking, she in merry sort
Them gan to bord, and purpose diversly,⁵
Now faining dalliance and wanton sport,
Now throwing forth lewd words immodestly;
Till that the Palmer gan full bitterly
Her to rebuke, for being loose and light:
Which not abiding, but more scornefully
Scoffing at him, that did her justly wite,°   *censure*
She turnd her bote about, and from them rowéd quite.

17

That was the wanton Phaedria, which late
Did ferry him over the Idle lake:
Whom nought regarding, they kept on their gate,°   *way*
And all her vaine allurements did forsake,
When them the wary Boateman thus bespake;
"Here now behoveth us well to avyse,°   *consider*
And of our safétie good heede to take;
For here before a perlous° passage lyes,   *dangerous*
Where many Mermayds haunt, making false melodies.

18

"But by the way, there is a great Quicksand,
And a whirlepoole of hidden jeopardy,
Therefore, Sir Palmer, keepe an even hand;
For twixt them both the narrow way doth ly."
Scarse had he said, when hard at hand they spy
That quicksand nigh with water coveréd;

5. I.e., to accost, and chat of various things.

But by the checkéd° wave they did descry   *checkered*
It plaine, and by the sea discolouréd:
It calléd was the quicksand of Unthriftyhed.

19

They passing by, a goodly Ship did see,
   Laden from far with precious merchandize,
   And bravely furnishéd, as ship might bee,
   Which through great disaventure, or mesprize,°   *error*
   Her selfe had runne into that hazardize;
   Whose mariners and merchants with much toyle,
   Laboured in vaine, to have recured° their prize,   *recovered*
   And the rich wares to save from pitteous spoyle,
But neither toyle nor travell° might her backe recoyle.°   *effort/draw*

20

On th'other side they see that perilous Poole,
   That calléd was the Whirlepoole of decay,
   In which full many had with haplesse doole°   *grief*
   Beene suncke, of whom no memorie did stay:
   Whose circled waters rapt with whirling sway,[6]
   Like to a restlesse wheele, still running round,
   Did covet, as they passéd by that way,
To draw their boate within the utmost bound
Of his wide Labyrinth, and then to have them dround.

21

But th'heedfull Boateman strongly forth did stretch
   His brawnie armes, and all his body straine,
   That th'utmost sandy breach they shortly fetch,[7]
   Whiles the dred daunger docs behind remaine.
   Suddeine they see from midst of all the Maine,
   The surging waters like a mountaine rise,
   And the great sea puft up with proud disdaine,
To swell above the measure of his guise,°   *custom*
As threatning to devoure all, that his powre despise.

22

The waves come rolling, and the billowes rore
   Outragiously, as they enragéd were,
   Or wrathfull Neptune did them drive before
   His whirling charet, for exceeding feare:
   For not one puffe of wind there did appeare,
   That all the three thereat woxe much afrayd,
   Unweeting, what such horrour straunge did reare.°   *cause*

6. I.e., gripped by rapid whirling waters.
7. I.e., they soon reach the safety of the beach.

Eftsoones they saw an hideous hoast arrayd,
Of huge Sea monsters, such as living sence dismayd.[8]

23

Most ugly shapes, and horrible aspects,
  Such as Dame Nature selfe mote feare to see,
  Or shame, that ever should so fowle defects
  From her most cunning hand escapéd bee;
  All dreadfull pourtraicts of deformitee:
  Spring-headed Hydraes, and sea-shouldring Whales,
  Great whirlpooles, which all fishes make to flee,
  Bright Scolopendraes, armed with silver scales,
Mighty Monoceros, with immeasuréd° tayles.   *enormous*

24

The dreadfull Fish, that hath deserved the name
  Of Death, and like him lookes in dreadfull hew,
  The griesly Wasserman, that makes his game
  The flying ships with swiftnesse to pursew,
  The horrible Sea-satyre, that doth shew
  His fearefull face in time of greatest storme,
  Huge Ziffius, whom Mariners eschew°   *avoid*
  No lesse, then rockes, (as travellers informe,)
And greedy Rosmarines with visages deforme.

25

All these, and thousand thousands many more,
  And more deforméd Monsters thousand fold,
  With dreadfull noise, and hollow rombling rore,
  Came rushing in the fomy waves enrold,
  Which seemed to fly for feare, them to behold:
  Ne wonder, if these did the knight appall;
  For all that here on earth we dreadfull hold,
  Be but as bugs° to fearen babes withall,   *imaginary terrors*
Compared to the creatures in the seas entrall.°   *depths*

26

"Feare nought," then said the Palmer well avized;
  "For these same Monsters are not these in deed,
  But are into these fearefull shapes disguized
  By that same wicked witch, to worke us dreed,
  And draw from on this journey to proceede."
  Tho lifting up his vertuous staffe[9] on hye,

8. Most of the monsters in stanzas 23–24 are found in Pliny's *Natural History* (first century A.D.) or in N. Gesner, *Historia Animalium* (1588). "Whirlpooles," "Scolopendraes," "Monoceros," "Rosmarines" (and the "morse," named after Death), and "Ziffius" are respectively spouting whales, seagoing centipedes or annelid worms, narwhals, walruses, and swordfish. "Wasserman" and "Sea-satyre" may be the dolphin and the seal, but more likely mermen.
9. Ubaldo, in Tasso's *Gerusalemme* 14.73, bears a similar wand. Noting the significance of Ulysses' voyage, Comes (6.6) says that reason restrains instinct just as wild beasts must be held in check.

He smote the sea, which calméd was with speed,
  And all that dreadfull Armie fast gan flye
Into great Tethys bosome,[1] where they hidden lye.

27

Quit° from that daunger, forth their course they kept,   *freed*
  And as they went, they heard a ruefull cry
  Of one, that wayld and pittifully wept,
  That through the sea the resounding plaints did fly:
  At last they in an Island did espy
  A seemely Maiden, sitting by the shore,
  That with great sorrow and sad agony,
  Seeméd some great misfortune to deplore,
And lowd to them for succour calléd evermore.

28

Which Guyon hearing, streight his Palmer bad,
  To stere the boate towards that dolefull Mayd,
  That he might know, and ease her sorrow sad:
  Who him avizing° better, to him sayd;   *counselling*
  "Faire Sir, be not displeasd, if disobayd:
  For ill it were to hearken to her cry;
  For she is inly nothing ill apayd,°   *pleased*
  But onely womanish fine forgery,
Your stubborne° hart t'affect with fraile infirmity.   *firm*

29

"To which when she your courage° hath inclind   *spirit*
  Through foolish pitty, then her guilefull bayt
  She will embosome° deeper in your mind,   *implant*
  And for your ruine at the last awayt."
  The knight was ruléd, and the Boateman strayt
  Held on his course with stayéd° stedfastnesse,   *constant*
  Ne ever shruncke, ne ever sought to bayt°   *rest*
  His tyréd armes for toylesome wearinesse,
But with his oares did sweepe the watry wildernesse.

30

And now they nigh approchéd to the sted,°   *place*
  Where as those Mermayds dwelt: it was a still
  And calmy bay, on th'one side shelteréd
  With the brode shadow of an hoarie hill,
  On th'other side an high rocke touréd still,
  That twixt them both a pleasaunt port they made,
  And did like an halfe Theatre fulfill:

1. I.e., into the depths of the sea (cf. I.i.39, and note).

There those five sisters[2] had continuall trade,°   *occupation*
And used to bath themselves in that deceiptfull shade.

31

They were faire Ladies, till they fondly° strived   *foolishly*
  With th'Heliconian maides[3] for maistery;
  Of whom they over-comen, were deprived
  Of their proud beautie, and th'one moyity°   *half*
  Transformed to fish, for their bold surquedry,°   *presumption*
  But th'upper halfe their hew° retainéd still,   *form*
  And their sweet skill in wonted melody;
  Which ever after they abusd to ill,
T'allure weake travellers, whom gotten they did kill.

32

So now to Guyon, as he passéd by,
  Their pleasaunt tunes they sweetly thus applide;
  "O thou faire sonne of gentle Faery,
  That art in mighty armes most magnifide
  Above all knights, that ever battell tride,
  O turne thy rudder hither-ward a while:
  Here may thy storme-bet vessell safely ride;
  This is the Port of rest from troublous toyle,
The worlds sweet In, from paine and wearisome turmoyle."

33

With that the rolling sea resounding soft,
  In his big base them fitly answeréd,
  And on the rocke the waves breaking aloft,
  A solemne Meane° unto them measuréd,   *tenor*
  The whiles sweet Zephirus[4] lowd whisteléd
  His treble, a straunge kinde of harmony;
  Which Guyons senses softly tickeléd,
  That he the boateman bad row easily,
And let him heare some part of their rare melody.

34

But him the Palmer from that vanity,
  With temperate advice discounselléd,
  That they it past, and shortly gan descry
  The land, to which their course they leveléd;°   *directed*
  When suddeinly a grosse fog over spred
  With his dull vapour all that desert has,

2. Homer's Sirens (*Odyssey* 12) are the ultimate source for these figures, traditionally three in number; these "five sisters" may indicate the five senses. Comes (7.13) identifies Sirens with the lure of voluptuous desire and, more generally, with whatever seduces the irrational part of the soul.
3. I.e., the Muses. This contest is apparently Spenser's own invention.
4. The west wind, associated by Comes with the stimulation of sexual impulses (4.13). Cf. E.K.'s Glosse to "Aprill," which attributes to Zephyrus the "soveraigntye of al flowres and greene herbes, growing on earth."

And heavens chearefull face .envelopéd,
  That all things one, and one as nothing was,
And this great Universe seemd one confuséd mas.

35

Thereat they greatly were dismayd, ne wist
  How to direct their way in darkenesse wide,
  But feard to wander in that wastfull mist,
  For tombling into mischiefe unespide.
  Worse is the daunger hidden, then descride.
  Suddeinly an innumerable flight
  Of harmefull fowles about them fluttering, cride,
  And with their wicked wings them oft did smight,
And sore annoyéd, groping in that griesly night.

36

Even all the nation of unfortunate°   *ill-omened*
  And fatall birds about them flockéd were,
  Such as by nature men abhorre and hate,
  The ill-faste° Owle, deaths dreadfull messengere,   *ugly*
  The hoars Night-raven, trump of dolefull drere,
  The lether-wingéd Bat, dayes enimy,
  The ruefull Strich,° still waiting on the bere,   *screech owl*
  The Whistler° shrill, that who so heares, doth dy,   *plover*
The hellish Harpies, prophets of sad destiny.[5]

37

All those, and all that else does horrour breed,
  About them flew, and fild their sayles with feare:
  Yet stayd they not, but forward did proceed,
  Whiles th'one did row, and th'other stifly steare;
  Till that at last the weather gan to cleare,
  And the faire land it selfe did plainly show.
  Said then the Palmer, "Lo where does appeare
  The sacred° soile, where all our perils grow;   *cursed*
Therefore, Sir knight, your ready armes about you throw."

38

He hearkned, and his armes about him tooke,
  The whiles the nimble boate so well her sped,
  That with her crooked° keele the land she strooke,   *curved*
  Then forth the noble Guyon salliéd,
  And his sage Palmer, that him governéd;
  But th'other by his boate behind did stay.
  They marchéd fairly forth, of nought ydred,°   *afraid*
  Both firmely armd for every hard assay,
With constancy and care, gainst daunger and dismay.

5. Celeno, the harpies' leader in Virgil's *Aeneid*, foretold the future in gloomy terms to Aeneas and his followers (3.225–62).

39

Ere long they heard an hideous bellowing
　　Of many beasts, that roard outrageously,
　　As if that hungers point, or Venus sting
　　Had them enragéd with fell surquedry;°　　　　　　　*arrogance*
　　Yet nought they feard, but past on hardily,
　　Untill they came in vew of those wild beasts:
　　Who all attonce, gaping full greedily,
　　And rearing fiercely their upstarting° crests,　　　　*bristling*
Ran towards, to devoure those unexpected guests.

40

But soone as they approcht with deadly threat,
　　The Palmer over them his staffe upheld,
　　His mighty staffe, that could all charmes defeat:
　　Eftsoones their stubborne courages° were queld,　　　*spirits*
　　And high advauncéd crests downe meekely feld,
　　In stead of fraying,° they them selves did feare,　　*terrifying*
　　And trembled, as them passing they beheld:
　　Such wondrous powre did in that staffe appeare,
All monsters to subdew to him, that did it beare.

41

Of that same wood it framed was cunningly,
　　Of which Caduceus whilome was made,
　　Caduceus the rod of Mercury,[6]
　　With which he wonts° the Stygian realmes invade,　　*is accustomed to*
　　Through ghastly horrour, and eternall shade;
　　Th' infernall feends with it he can asswage,
　　And Orcus[7] tame, whom nothing can perswade,
　　And rule the Furyes, when they most do rage:
Such vertue in his staffe had eke this Palmer sage.

42

Thence passing forth, they shortly do arrive,
　　Whereas the Bowre of Blisse[8] was situate;
　　A place pickt out by choice of best alive,
　　That natures worke by art can imitate:[9]
　　In which what ever in this worldly state
　　Is sweet, and pleasing unto living sense,
　　Or that may dayntiest fantasie aggrate,°　　　　　　*gratify*

---

6. In *Odyssey* 10, Mercury helps Ulysses evade Circe's magic; with his rod, described in *Aeneid*
   4.242–46, he can summon the dead. Comes (5.5) says he represents divine reason and wisdom.
7. I.e., Pluto.
8. For his Bower, Spenser took descriptive details from Tasso's *Gerusalemme Liberata* 15–16, and
   from Tissino's romance, *L'Italia Liberata dai Goti*, he derived certain events and characters,
   including the name "Acratia." Wall 1984 finds parallels with contemporary descriptions of Virginia.
9. I.e., a place selected by the best living artists. In this lovely garden, though, art works by excess
   (stanza 50), not complementing nature but competing with or merely copying it. So too, the Bower
   is not temperance's opposite but its sterile parody.

Was pouréd forth with plentifull dispence,°   *liberality*
And made there to abound with lavish affluence.

43

Goodly it was encloséd round about,
  Aswell their entred guestes to keepe within,
  As those unruly beasts to hold without;
  Yet was the fence thereof but weake and thin;
  Nought feard their force, that fortilage° to win,   *fortress*
  But wisedomes powre, and temperaunces might,[1]
  By which the mightiest things efforcéd bin:[2]
And eke the gate was wrought of substaunce light,
Rather for pleasure, then for battery or fight.

44

Yt framéd was of precious yvory,
  That seemd a worke of admirable wit;
  And therein all the famous history
  Of Jason and Medaea was ywrit[3]
  Her mighty charmes, her furious loving fit,
  His goodly conquest of the golden fleece,
  His falséd faith, and love too lightly flit,
The wondred° Argo, which in venturous peece[4]   *wonderful*
First through the Euxine seas bore all the flowr of Greece.

45

Ye might have seene the frothy billowes fry°   *foam*
  Under the ship, as thorough them she went,
  That seemd the waves were into yvory,
  Or yvory into the waves were sent;
  And other where the snowy substaunce sprent°   *sprinkled*
  With vermell,° like the boyes[5] bloud therein shed,   *vermilion*
  A piteous spectacle did represent,
  And otherwhiles° with gold besprinkeléd;   *elsewhere*
Yt seemd th'enchaunted flame, which did Creüsa[6] wed.

46

All this, and more might in that goodly gate
  Be red;° that ever open stood to all,   *seen*
  Which thither came: but in the Porch there sate
  A comely personage of stature tall,
  And semblaunce° pleasing, more then naturall,   *appearance*

1. I.e., that enclosure, proof against physical force was vulnerable to wisdom and temperance.
2. I.e., are compelled.
3. On Jason's quest (in the ship *Argo*) for the Golden Fleece, and for his subsequent liaison with the sorceress Medea, see the *Argonautica*, by Apollonius of Rhodes (c. 200 B.C.). That the gate is of ivory shows the Bower's falsity; see I.i.40, note.
4. I.e., adventurous vessel.
5. Medea's younger brother Apsyrtus, killed by Jason at her instance, to delay pursuit of the Argonauts.
6. So as to marry Creüsa, Creon's daughter, Jason deserted Medea, who then destroyed Creüsa by sending her a robe that burst into flames when she put it on.

That travellers to him seemd to entize;
His looser° garment to the ground did fall,   *too loose*
And flew about his heeles in wanton wize,
Not fit for speedy pace, or manly exercize.

47

They in that place him Genius[7] did call:
    Not that celestiall powre, to whom the care
    Of life, and generation of all
    That lives, pertaines in charge particulare,
    Who wondrous things concerning our welfare,
    And straunge phantomes doth let us oft forsee,
    And oft of secret ill bids us beware:
    That is our Selfe, whom though we do not see,
Yet each doth in him selfe it well perceive to bee.

48

Therefore a God him sage Antiquity
    Did wisely make, and good Agdistes call:
    But this same was to that quite contrary,
    The foe of life, that good envyes° to all,   *begrudges*
    That secretly doth us procure to fall,
    Through guilefull semblaunts,° which he makes us see.   *illusions*
    He of this Gardin had the governall,°   *management*
    And Pleasures porter was devizd° to bee,   *considered*
Holding a staffe in hand for more formalitee.

49

With diverse flowres he daintily was deckt,
    And strowéd round about, and by his side
    A mighty Mazer° bowle of wine[8] was set,   *maple-wood*
    As if it had to him bene sacrifide;
    Wherewith all new-come guests he gratifide:
    So did he eke Sir Guyon passing by:
    But he his idle curtesie defide,
    And overthrew his bowle disdainfully;
And broke his staffe, with which he charméd semblants sly.[9]

50

Thus being entred, they behold around
    A large and spacious plaine, on every side
    Strowéd with pleasauns, whose faire grassy ground

7. Spenser depends chiefly on Comes 4.3 for his account of Genius, god of generation, for the evil
   spirits that oppose "Agdistes" (stanza 48), and for the use of wine and flowers in his cult. Related
   to the Phrygian Attis, he is traditionally an androgynous deity born of Zeus and Earth. But unlike
   "Old Genius the porter" in III.vi.31, "Pleasures porter" uses illusion to inspire destructive and
   fruitless lust.
8. The cup Circe offers Ulysses in *Odyssey* 10 is a model for this bowl, as well as for the golden cup
   held by Excess (stanza 56): to drink from either is to yield to sensual intemperance. Both vessels
   parody the Christian communion cup and its sacramental wine.
9. I.e., raised deceitful illusions ("guilefull semblaunts").

Mantled with greene, and goodly beautifide
With all the ornaments of Floraes pride,
Wherewith her mother Art, as halfe in scorne
Of niggard° Nature, like a pompous bride   *miserly*
Did decke her, and too lavishly adorne,
When forth from virgin bowre she comes in th'early morne.

51

Thereto the Heavens alwayes Joviall,°   *propitious*
    Lookt on them lovely,° still in stedfast state,   *lovingly*
    Ne suffred storme nor frost on them to fall,
    Their tender buds or leaves to violate,
    Nor scorching heat, nor cold intemperate
    T'afflict the creatures, which therein did dwell,
    But the milde aire with season moderate
    Gently attempred, and disposd so well,
That still it breathéd forth sweet spirit° and holesome smell.   *breath*

52

More sweet and holesome, then the pleasaunt hill
    Of Rhodope,[1] on which the Nimphe, that bore
    A gyaunt babe, her selfe for griefe did kill;
    Or the Thessalian Tempe,[2] where of yore
    Faire Daphne Phoebus hart with love did gore;
    Or Ida, where the Gods loved to repaire,°   *resort*
    When ever they their heavenly bowres forlore;°   *deserted*
    Or sweet Parnasse, the haunt of Muses faire;
Or Eden selfe, if ought with Eden mote compaire.

53

Much wondred Guyon at the faire aspect
    Of that sweet place, yet suffred no delight
    To sincke into his sence, nor mind affect,
    But passéd forth, and lookt still forward right,*   *straight ahead*
    Bridling his will, and maistering his might:
    Till that he came unto another gate;
    No gate, but like one, being goodly dight
    With boughes and braunches, which did broad dilate°   *spread out*
Their clasping armes, in wanton wreathings intricate.

54

So fashionéd a Porch with rare device,
    Archt over head with an embracing vine,
    Whose bounches hanging downe, seemed to entice
    All passers by, to tast their lushious wine,

1. Traditionally, Jove turned the incestuous nymph Rhodope into a mountain in Thrace to punish the pride that had led her to call herself "Juno" and her brother "Jove" (*Metamorphoses* 6.87–89); her "gyaunt babe," sired by Neptune, gave his name to Mount Athos.
2. The valley in Thessaly where Apollo pursued Daphne (*Metamorphoses* 1.452–567).

And did themselves into their hands incline,
As freely offering to be gatheréd:
Some deepe empurpled as the Hyacint,[3]
Some as the Rubine,° laughing sweetly red,   *ruby*
Some like faire Emeraudes,° not yet well ripenéd.   *emeralds*

55

And them amongst, some were of burnisht gold,
So made by art, to beautifie the rest,
Which did themselves emongst the leaves enfold,
As lurking from the vew of covetous guest,
That the weake bowes, with so rich load opprest,
Did bow adowne, as over-burdenéd.
Under that Porch a comely dame did rest,
Clad in faire weedes,° but fowle disorderéd,   *garments*
And garments loose, that seemd unmeet for womanhed.

56

In her left hand a Cup of gold she held,
And with her right the riper° fruit did reach,   *overripe*
Whose sappy liquor, that with fulnesse sweld,
Into her cup she scruzd,° with daintie breach   *squeezed*
Of her fine fingers, without fowle empeach,[4]
That so faire wine-presse made the wine more sweet:
Thereof she usd to give to drinke to each,
Whom passing by she happenéd to meet:
It was her guise,° all Straungers goodly so to greet.   *custom*

57

So she to Guyon offred it to tast;
Who taking it out of her tender hond,
The cup to ground did violently cast,
That all in peeces it was broken fond,°   *found*
And with the liquor stainéd all the lond:
Whereat Excesse exceedingly was wroth,
Yet no'te° the same amend, ne yet withstond,   *could not*
But suffered him to passe, all° were she loth;   *although*
Who nought regarding her displeasure forward goth.

58

There the most daintie Paradise on ground,
It selfe doth offer to his sober eye,
In which all pleasures plenteously abound,
And none does others happinesse envye:
The painted flowres, the trees upshooting hye,
The dales for shade, the hilles for breathing space,

3. The jacinth, a gem of blue (or perhaps of reddish-orange) color.
4. I.e., crushing them daintily with her delicate fingers.

The trembling groves, the Christall⁵ running by;
  And that, which all faire workes doth most aggrace,°   add grace to
The art, which all that wrought, appearéd in no place.⁶

59

One would have thought, (so cunningly, the rude,
  And scornéd parts were mingled with the fine,)
  That nature had for wantonesse ensude°   imitated
  Art, and that Art at nature did repine;°   complain
  So striving each th' other to undermine,
  Each did the others worke more beautifie;
  So diff'ring both in willes, agreed in fine:⁷
  So all agreed through sweete diversitie,
This Gardin to adorne with all varietie.

60

And in the midst of all, a fountaine⁸ stood,
  Of richest substaunce, that on earth might bee,
  So pure and shiny, that the silver flood
  Through every channell running one might see;
  Most goodly it with curious imageree
  Was over-wrought, and shapes of naked boyes,
  Of which some seemd with lively jollitee,
  To fly about, playing their wanton toyes,°   sports
Whilest others did them selves embay° in liquid joyes.   bathe

61

And over all, of purest gold was spred,
  A trayle of yvie in his native hew:
  For the rich mettall was so colouréd,
  That wight, who did not well avised it vew,
  Would surely deeme it to be yvie trew:
  Low his lascivious armes adown did creepe,
  That themselves dipping in the silver dew,
  Their fleecy flowres they tenderly did steepe,
Which° drops of Christall seemd for wantones to weepe.   on which

62

Infinit streames continually did well
  Out of this fountaine, sweet and faire to see,
  The which into an ample laver° fell,   basin
  And shortly grew to so great quantitie,
  That like a little lake it seemd to bee;

5. I.e., the crystal stream.
6. The final lines of stanza 58, and most of stanza 59, echo Tasso, *Gerusalemme Liberata*, 16.9–10; Tasso's Garden of Armida is the primary model for many passages in stanzas 58–88.
7. I.e., at last.
8. Fountain and damsels recall Tasso 15. 55–66. Like Archimago's seemingly pure fountain (I.i.34), and the clear but enervating stream from which Redcrosse drinks (I.vii.2–6), this fountain signifies the insidious attractions of intemperance, particularly sexual desire.

Whose depth exceeded not three cubits hight,[9]
That through the waves one might the bottom see,
All paved beneath with Jaspar shining bright,
That seemd the fountaine in that sea did sayle upright.

63

And all the margent round about was set,
  With shady Laurell trees, thence to defend°   *ward off*
  The sunny beames, which on the billowes bet,°   *beat*
  And those which therein bathéd, mote offend.
  As Guyon hapned by the same to wend,
  Two naked Damzelles he therein espyde,
  Which therein bathing, seeméd to contend,
  And wrestle wantonly, ne cared to hyde,
Their dainty parts from vew of any, which them eyde.

64

Sometimes the one would lift the other quight
  Above the waters, and then downe againe
  Her plong, as over maisteréd by might,
  Where both awhile would coveréd remaine,
  And each the other from to rise restraine;
  The whiles their snowy limbes, as through a vele,
  So through the Christall waves appearéd plaine:
  Then suddeinly both would themselves unhele,°   *disclose*
And th'amarous sweet spoiles to greedy eyes revele.

65

As that faire Starre, the messenger of morne,
  His deawy face out of the sea doth reare:
  Or as the Cyprian goddesse,[1] newly borne
  Of th'Oceans fruitfull froth, did first appeare:
  Such seeméd they, and so their yellow heare
  Christalline humour° droppéd downe apace.   *moisture*
  Whom such when Guyon saw, he drew him neare,
  And somewhat gan relent° his earnest pace,   *slacken*
His stubborne brest gan secret pleasaunce to embrace.

66

The wanton Maidens him espying, stood
  Gazing a while at his unwonted guise;°   *manner*
  Then th'one her selfe low duckéd in the flood,
  Abasht, that her a straunger did avise:°   *regard*
  But th'other rather higher did arise,
  And her two lilly paps aloft displayd,

---

9. About four and a half feet.
1. Aphrodite (Venus), who, says Hesiod (*Theogony* 197), sprang from foam that issued from the
  genitals of Uranos after his son Kronos castrated him and threw the member into the ocean. The
  new goddess came to shore in Cyprus after passing near Cythera.

And all, that might his melting hart entise
   To her delights, she unto him bewrayd:°   *revealed*
The rest hid underneath, him more desirous made.

67

With that, the other likewise up arose,
   And her faire lockes, which formerly were bownd
   Up in one knot, she low adowne did lose:°   *loosen*
Which flowing long and thick, her clothed arownd,
   And th'yvorie in golden mantle gownd:
So that faire spectacle from him was reft,°   *withdrawn*
   Yet that, which reft it, no lesse faire was fownd:
   So hid in lockes and waves from lookers theft,
Nought but her lovely face she for his looking left.

68

Withall she laughéd, and she blusht withall,
   That blushing to her laughter gave more grace,
   And laughter to her blushing, as did fall:
Now when they spide the knight to slacke his pace,
   Them to behold, and in his sparkling face
The secret signes of kindled lust appeare,
   Their wanton merriments they did encreace,
   And to him beckned, to approch more neare,
And shewd him many sights, that courage cold could reare.[2]

69

On which when gazing him the Palmer saw,
   He much rebukt those wandring eyes of his,
   And counseld well, him forward thence did draw.
Now are they come nigh to the Bowre of blis
   Of her fond favorites so named amis:
When thus the Palmer; "Now Sir, well avise;°   *take care*
   For here the end of all our travell° is: *arduous journey*
   Here wonnes° Acrasia, whom we must surprise,   *dwells*
Else she will slip away, and all our drift despise.[3]

70

Eftsoones they heard a most melodious sound,
   Of all that mote delight a daintie eare,
   Such as attonce might not on living ground,
Save in this Paradise, be heard elswhere:
   Right hard it was, for wight, which did it heare,
To read,° what manner musicke that mote bee: *tell*
   For all that pleasing is to living eare,
   Was there consorted° in one harmonee,   *joined*
Birdes, voyces, instruments, windes, waters, all agree.

2. I.e., could arouse sexual desire.
3. I.e., frustrate all our plans.

71

The joyous birdes shrouded in chearefull shade,
　　Their notes unto the voyce attempred° sweet;　　　　　　*attuned*
　　Th'Angelicall soft trembling voyces made
　　To th'instruments divine respondence meet:°　　　　　　*fitting*
　　The silver sounding instruments did meet°　　　　　　　*join*
　　With the base murmure of the waters fall:
　　The waters fall with difference discreet,°　　　　　　　*suitable*
　　Now soft, now loud, unto the wind did call:
The gentle warbling wind low answeréd to all.⁴

72

There, whence that Musick seeméd heard to bee,
　　Was the faire Witch⁵ her selfe now solacing,
　　With a new Lover, whom through sorceree
　　And witchcraft, she from farre did thither bring:
　　There she had him now layd a slombering,
　　In secret shade, after long wanton joyes:
　　Whilst round about them pleasauntly did sing
　　Many faire Ladies, and lascivious boyes,
That ever mixt their song with light licentious toyes.

73

And all that while, right over him she hong,
　　With her false° eyes fast fixéd in his sight,　　　　　　*deceitful*
　　As seeking medicine, whence she was stong,
　　Or greedily depasturing° delight:　　　　　　　　　　　*feeding on*
　　And oft inclining downe with kisses light,
　　For feare of waking him, his lips bedewd,
　　And through his humid eyes did sucke his spright,
　　Quite molten into lust and pleasure lewd;
Wherewith she sighéd soft, as if his case she rewd.°　　　*pitied*

74

The whiles some one did chaunt this lovely lay;⁶
　　"Ah see, who so faire thing doest faine° to see,　　　　*delight*
　　In springing flowre the image of thy day;
　　Ah see the Virgin Rose, how sweetly shee
　　Doth first peepe forth with bashfull modestee,
　　That fairer seemes, the lesse ye see her may;
　　Lo see soone after, how more bold and free

4. This stanza follows (and revises) *Gerusalemme Liberata* 16.12; Spenser adds voices and instruments
　to Tasso's birds and murmuring wind.
5. I.e., Acrasia, whose beauty masks and reinforces her power to immerse her victims in an intem-
　perance that leads at last to bestiality (stanza 39). She has indirectly murdered the parents of the
　"bloody babe" whose wrong Guyon is avenging.
6. The theme of *carpe diem* ("seize the day"), found in Horace and the Latin elegiac poets, appears
　often in Renaissance verse; Spenser follows *Gerusalemme* 16.14–15.

Her baréd bosome she doth broad display;
Loe see soone after, how she fades, and falles away.

75

"So passeth, in the passing of a day,
  Of mortall life the leafe, the bud, the flowre,
  Ne more doth flourish after first decay,
  That earst was sought to decke both bed and bowre,
  Of many a Ladie, and many a Paramowre:°   *lover*
  Gather therefore the Rose, whilest yet is prime,
  For soone comes age, that will her pride deflowre:
  Gather the Rose of love, whilest yet is time,
Whilest loving thou mayst lovéd be with equall crime."°   *sin*

76

He ceast, and then gan all the quire of birdes
  Their diverse notes t'attune unto his lay,
  As in approvance of his pleasing words.
  The constant paire heard all, that he did say,
  Yet swarvéd not, but kept their forward way,
  Through many covert groves, and thickets close,
  In which they creeping did at last display°   *discover*
  That wanton Ladie, with her lover lose,°   *wanton*
Whose sleepie head she in her lap did soft dispose.

77

Upon a bed of Roses she was layd,
  As faint through heat, or dight to[7] pleasant sin,
  And was arayd, or rather disarayd,
  All in a vele of silke and silver thin,
  That hid no whit her alablaster° skin,   *alabaster*
  But rather shewd more white, if more might bee:
  More subtile web Arachne[8] cannot spin,
  Nor the fine nets, which oft we woven see
Of scorchéd deaw, do not in th'aire more lightly flee.°   *float*

78

Her snowy brest was bare to readie spoyle
  Of hungry eies, which n'ote° therewith be fild,   *might not*
  And yet through languour of her late sweet toyle,
  Few drops, more cleare then Nectar, forth distild,
  That like pure Orient perles adowne it trild,°   *trickled*
  And her faire eyes sweet smyling in delight,
  Moystened their fierie beames, with which she thrild
  Fraile harts, yet quenchéd not; like starry light
Which sparckling on the silent waves, does seeme more bright.

7. I.e., prepared for.
8. Cf. II.vii.28 and note.

79

The young man sleeping by her, seemd to bee
   Some goodly swayne of honorable place,°   *rank*
   That certes it great pittie was to see
   Him his nobilitie so foule deface;°   *disgrace*
   A sweet regard, and amiable grace,
   Mixéd with manly sternnesse did appeare
   Yet sleeping, in his well proportiond face,
   And on his tender lips the downy heare
Did now but freshly spring, and silken blossomes beare.

80

His warlike armes, the idle instruments
   Of sleeping praise, were hong upon a tree,
   And his brave shield, full of old moniments,°   *knightly signs*
   Was fowly ra'st,° that none the signes might see;   *razed*
   Ne for them, ne for honour caréd hee,
   Ne ought, that did to his advauncement tend,[9]
   But in lewd loves, and wastfull luxuree,
   His dayes, his goods, his bodie he did spend:
O horrible enchantment, that him so did blend.°   *blind*

81

The noble Elfe, and carefull Palmer drew
   So nigh them, minding nought, but lustfull game,
   That suddein forth they on them rusht, and threw
   A subtile net,[1] which onely for the same
   The skilfull Palmer formally° did frame.   *in exact form*
   So held them under fast, the whiles the rest
   Fled all away for feare of fowler shame.
   The faire Enchauntresse, so unwares opprest,°   *surprised*
Tryde all her arts, and all her sleights, thence out to wrest.° *twist*

82

And eke her lover strove: but all in vaine;
   For that same net so cunningly was wound,
   That neither guile, nor force might it distraine.°   *tear*
   They tooke them both, and both them strongly bound
   In captive bandes, which there they readie found:
   But her in chaines of adamant he tyde;
   For nothing else might keepe her safe and sound,
   But Verdant (so he hight) he soon untyde,
And counsell sage in steed thereof to him applyde.

9. By yielding to intemperance, the youth has betrayed his potential for heroic knightly action; Parker 1987 stresses the political and linguistic implications of his illegible arms. The name "Verdant" suggests captive fertility, a greenness released in the Garden of Adonis (III.vi), while his trance and posture recall the age's often ambivalent pictures of Venus with a sleeping and unarmed Mars.
1. With a net Vulcan trapped his wife Venus and her lover Mars (cf. *Metamorphoses* 4.169–89).

83

But all those pleasant bowres and Pallace brave,°   *splendid*
  Guyon broke downe, with rigour pittilesse;
  Ne ought their goodly workmanship might save
  Them from the tempest of his wrathfulnesse,
  But that their blisse he turned to balefulnesse:
  Their groves he feld, their gardins did deface,
  Their arbers spoyle, their Cabinets° suppresse,   *bowers*
  Their banket houses burne, their buildings race,°   *raze*
And of the fairest late, now made the fowlest place.

84

Then led they her away, and eke that knight
  They with them led, both sorrowfull and sad:
  The way they came, the same retourned they right,
  Till they arrivéd, where they lately had
  Charmed those wild-beasts, that raged with furie mad.
  Which now awaking, fierce at them gan fly,
  As in their mistresse reskew, whom they lad;°   *led*
  But them the Palmer soone did pacify.
Then Guyon askt, what meant those beastes, which there did ly.

85

Said he, "These seeming beasts are men indeed,
  Whom this Enchauntresse hath transforméd thus,
  Whylome her lovers, which her lusts did feed,
  Now turnéd into figures hideous,
  According to their mindes like° monstruous."[2]   *similarly*
  "Sad end," quoth he, "of life intemperate,
  And mournefull meed of joyes delicious:
  But Palmer, if it mote thee so aggrate,°   *please*
Let them returnéd be unto their former state."

86

Streight way he with his vertuous staffe them strooke,
  And streight of beasts they comely men became;
  Yet being men they did unmanly looke,
  And staréd ghastly, some for inward shame,
  And some for wrath, to see their captive Dame:
  But one above the rest in speciall,
  That had an hog beene late, hight Grille[3] by name,
  Repinéd greatly, and did him miscall,°   *abuse*
That had from hoggish forme him brought to naturall.

2. This episode is based on *Odyssey* 10; Comes (6.6) says each man whom Circe enchanted became a beast appropriate to the vice he had favored.
3. "He that is filthy, let him be filthy" (Revelation 22.11). "Grill" is from Greek for "pig." In Plutarch's witty *Whether Beasts Have the Use of Reason* (in his *Moralia*), Grill would rather stay a pig than resume life as a sophist philosopher; he and Ulysses chat about temperance. Spenser probably read Greek, but he could have found Grill in, e.g., Renaissance emblems; see Chaudhuri 1990E, "Grill."

87

Said Guyon, "See the mind of beastly man,
  That hath so soone forgot the excellence
  Of his creation, when he life began,
  That now he chooseth, with vile difference,°   *change*
  To be a beast, and lacke intelligence."
  To whom the Palmer thus, "The donghill kind
  Delights in filth and foule incontinence:
  Let Grill be Grill, and have his hoggish mind,
But let us hence depart, whilest wether serves and wind."

The Third Booke of The Faerie Queene

Contayning
The Legend of Britomartis
or
Of Chastitie

1

It falles° me here to write of Chastity,   *befalls*
  That fairest vertue, farre above the rest;
  For which what needs me fetch from Faery
  Forreine ensamples, it to have exprest?
  Sith it is shrinéd in my Soveraines brest,
  And formed so lively° in each perfect part,   *lifelike*
  That to all Ladies, which have it profest,
  Need but behold the pourtraict° of her hart,   *image*
If pourtrayd it might be by any living art.

2

But living art may not least part expresse,
  Nor life-resembling pencill[1] it can paint,
  All were it Zeuxis or Praxiteles:[2]
  His daedale° hand would faile, and greatly faint,   *skillful*
  And her perfections with his error taint:
  Ne Poets wit, that passeth Painter farre
  In picturing the parts of beautie daint,°   *delicate*
  So hard a workmanship adventure darre,°   *dare*
For fear through want of words her excellence to marre.

3

How then shall I, Apprentice of the skill,
  That whylome° in divinest wits did raine,   *formerly*
  Presume so high to stretch mine humble quill?
  Yet now my lucklesse lot doth me constraine
  Hereto perforce. But O dred Soveraine
  Thus farre forth pardon, sith that choicest wit
  Cannot your glorious pourtraict figure plaine
  That I in colourd showes may shadow° it,   *represent*
And antique° praises unto present persons fit.   *ancient*

4

But if in living colours, and right hew,°   *form*
  Your selfe you covet to see picturéd,
  Who can it doe more lively, or more trew,

1. I.e., the artist's brush that creates "living art"; the conceit recalls DuBellay, *Olive* 19.
2. These Greek artists of the fourth century B.C. epitomized excellence in painting and sculpture respectively.

Then that sweet verse, with Nectar sprinckeléd,
In which a gracious servant[3] picturéd
His Cynthia, his heavens fairest light?
That with his melting sweetnesse ravishéd,
And with the wonder of her beamés bright,
My senses lulléd are in slomber of delight.

5

But let that same delitious° Poet lend   *pleasing*
  A little leave unto a rusticke Muse
To sing his mistresse prayse, and let him mend,
  If ought amis her liking may abuse:°   *offend*
Ne let his fairest Cynthia refuse,
  In mirrours more then one her selfe to see,
But either Gloriana let her chuse,
  Or in Belphoebe fashionéd to bee:
In th'one her rule, in th'other her rare chastitee.[4]

Canto I

*Guyon encountreth Britomart,
  faire Florimell is chaced:
Duessaes traines[1] and Malecastaes
  champions are defaced.°*   *confounded*

1

The famous Briton Prince and Faerie knight,
  After long wayes and perilous paines endured,
Having their wearie limbes to perfect plight°   *health*
  Restord, and sory° wounds right well recured,   *painful*
Of the faire Alma greatly were procured,°   *urged*
  To make there lenger sojourne and abode;
But when thereto they might not be allured,
  From seeking praise, and deeds of armes abrode,
They courteous congé° tooke, and forth together yode.°   *leave/went*

2

But the captived Acrasia he sent,
  Because of travell long, a nigher way,
With a strong gard, all reskew to prevent,
  And her to Faerie court safe to convay,
That her for witnesse of his hard assay,°   *trial*

3. I.e., Sir Walter Raleigh, whose poem *Cynthia* celebrated Queen Elizabeth. See III.v.30, note 1.
4. In the "Letter to Raleigh," Spenser observes that [since] the queen "beareth two persons, the one
of a most royall Queene or Empresse, the other of a most vertuous and beautifull Lady, this latter
part in some places I doe expresse in Belphoebe, fashioning her name according to your owne
excellent conceipt of Cynthia." Commenting on such passages, Fruen 1987 explores Spenser's
"typology" of Elizabeth; for a poststructuralist view see Bellamy 1987. The classic study of Book
III remains *The Kindly Flame* by T. Roche (Princeton, 1964); see also Roche 1990E and the
"General Description" in Berger 1988.
1. I.e., schemes. The reference to Duessa may reflect an abandoned plan for Book III. Stanza 1
refers to Arthur, Guyon, and the latter's defeat of the witch Acrasia; on Alma, see II.ix.

Unto his Faerie Queene he might present:
But he him selfe betooke another way,
To make more triall of his hardiment,°   *courage*
And seeke adventures, as he with Prince Arthur went.

3

Long so they travelléd through wastefull° wayes,   *desolate*
  Where daungers dwelt, and perils most did wonne,°   *abide*
  To hunt for glorie and renowméd praise;
  Full many Countries they did overronne,
  From the uprising to the setting Sunne,
  And many hard adventures did atchieve;
  Of all the which they honour ever wonne,
  Seeking the weake oppresséd to relieve,
And to recover right for such, as wrong did grieve.

4

At last as through an open plaine they yode,
  They spide a knight, that towards prickéd faire,[2]
  And him beside an aged Squire there rode,
  That seemed to couch° under his shield three-square,   *crouch*
  As if that age had him that burden spare,
  And yield it those, that stouter could it wield:
  He them espying, gan himselfe prepare,
  And on his arme addresse° his goodly shield   *make ready*
That bore a Lion passant in a golden field.[3]

5

Which seeing good Sir Guyon, deare besought
  The Prince of grace, to let him runne that turne.
  He graunted: then the Faery quickly raught°   *took up*
  His poinant° speare, and sharpely gan to spurne°   *piercing/spur*
  His fomy steed, whose fierie feete did burne
  The verdant grasse, as he thereon did tread;
  Ne did the other backe his foot returne,
  But fiercely forward came withouten dread,
And bent° his dreadfull speare against the others head.   *aimed*

6

They bene ymet, and both their points arrived,
  But Guyon drove so furious and fell,°   *fiercely*
  That seemed both shield and plate it would have rived;° *pierced*
  Nathelesse it bore his foe not from his sell,°   *saddle*
  But made him stagger, as he were not well:
  But Guyon selfe, ere well he was aware,
  Nigh a speares length behind his crouper° fell,   *crupper*

2. I.e., rode quickly and expertly.
3. I.e. (in heraldry), a lion walking against a gold background; these were the arms of Brute, legendary founder of the British race and ancestor of this knight (III.ix.38–51).

Yet in his fall so well him selfe he bare,
That mischievous mischance his life and limbes did spare.

7

Great shame and sorrow of that fall he tooke;
  For never yet, sith warlike armes he bore,
  And shivering[4] speare in bloudie field first shooke,
  He found himselfe dishonoréd so sore.
  Ah gentlest knight, that ever armour bore,
  Let not thee grieve dismounted to have beene,
  And brought to ground, that never wast before;
  For not thy fault, but secret powre unseene,
That speare enchaunted was, which layd thee on the greene.[5]

8

But weenedst thou[6] what wight thee overthrew,
  Much greater griefe and shamefuller regret
  For thy hard fortune then thou wouldst renew,
  That of a single damzell thou wert met
  On equall plaine, and there so hard beset;
  Even the famous Britomart[7] it was,
  Whom straunge adventure did from Britaine fet,°   bring
  To seeke her lover (love farre sought alas,)
Whose image she had seene in Venus looking glas.[8]

9

Full of disdainefull wrath, he fierce uprose,
  For to revenge that foule reprochfull shame,
  And snatching his bright sword began to close
  With her on foot, and stoutly forward came;
  Die rather would he, then endure that same.
  Which when his Palmer saw, he gan to feare
  His toward perill and untoward blame,[9]
  Which by that new rencounter he should reare:°   cause
For death sate on the point of that enchaunted speare.

---

4. I.e., quivering; or, perhaps, able to splinter whatever it strikes.
5. The spear, "made by Magick art of yore" (iii.60), recalls the one Astolfo gives the warrior-maiden Bradamante in Ariosto, *Orlando Furioso* 23.15. Allegorically, the encounter implies that chastity (which for Spenser includes faithful married sexuality) is even more powerful than temperance.
6. I.e., if you knew.
7. Britomart (Cretan for "sweet maid") represents a chastity fulfilled in marriage, while her name connotes a Briton's martial might. On her nature and role see Anderson 1990E, "Britomart." Described by Callimachus (third century B.C.) as a nymph of Diana, "Britomartis" was also called Dictynna; in ancient Crete, Diana was worshipped under the name Britomartis. Britomart combines elements from several sources: her quest for Arthegall recalls that of Bradamante for Ruggiero in *Orlando Furioso*; her dialogue with her nurse in Canto ii imitates a scene in the pseudo-Virgilian *Ciris*; her courage in Canto xi parallels the victory over fiery lust of the armed virgin Pudicitia ("Chastity") in Prudentius's fourth-century *Psychomachia*; and in conception she resembles Virgil's warrior-maiden Camilla, to whom Spenser refers in iv.2.
8. The crystal ball presented by Merlin to King Ryence; it enabled the viewer to foresee future events (ii.18–21).
9. I.e., his imminent danger and unlucky injury.

10

And hasting towards him gan faire perswade,
 Not to provoke misfortune, nor to weene°   *expect*
 His speares default to mend with cruell blade;
 For by his mightie Science° he had seene   *knowledge*
 The secret vertue° of that weapon keene,   *power*
 That mortall puissance mote not withstond:
 Nothing on earth mote alwaies happie° beene.   *successful*
 Great hazard were it, and adventure fond,°   *foolish*
To loose long gotten honour with one evill hond.°   *action*

11

By such good meanes he him discounselléd,°   *dissuaded*
 From prosecuting his revenging rage;
 And eke the Prince like treaty handeléd,[1]
 His wrathfull will with reason to asswage,
 And laid the blame, not to his carriage,°   *conduct*
 But to his starting steed, that swarved asyde,
 And to the ill purveyance° of his page,   *preparation*
 That had his furnitures° not firmely tyde: *gear*
So is his angry courage fairely pacifyde.

12

Thus reconcilement was betweene them knit,
 Through goodly temperance, and affection chaste,
 And either vowd with all their power and wit,°   *knowledge*
 To let not others honour be defaste,°   *disgraced*
 Of friend or foe, who ever it embaste,°   *dishonored*
 Ne armes to beare against the others syde:
 In which accord the Prince was also plaste,
 And with that golden chaine of concord tyde.
So goodly all agreed, they forth yfere° did ryde.   *together*

13

O goodly usage of those antique times,[2]
 In which the sword was servant unto right;
 When not for malice and contentious crimes,
 But all for praise, and proofe of manly might,
 The martiall brood° accustoméd to fight: *race*
 Then honour was the meed° of victorie,   *reward*
 And yet the vanquishéd had no despight:
 Let later age that noble use envie,°   *imitate*
Vile rancour to avoid, and cruell surquedrie.°   *arrogance*

1. I.e., used similar appeals.
2. The placing of this stanza in the narrative recalls that of Ariosto's apostrophe to the virtues of
ancient knighthood (*Orlando Furioso* 1.22).

14

Long they thus travelléd in friendly wise,
   Through countries waste, and eke well edifyde,°   *built up*
   Seeking adventures hard, to exercise
   Their puissance, whylome full dernely° tryde: *grievously*
   At length they came into a forrest wyde,
   Whose hideous horror and sad trembling sound
   Full griesly° seemed: Therein they long did ryde,   *grim*
   Yet tract° of living creatures none they found,   *track*
Save Beares, Lions, and Buls, which roméd them around.

15

All suddenly out of the thickest brush,
   Upon a milk-white Palfrey° all alone,   *saddle horse*
   A goodly Ladie[3] did foreby° them rush,   *past*
   Whose face did seeme as cleare as Christall stone,
   And eke through feare as white as whalés bone:
   Her garments all were wrought of beaten gold,
   And all her steed with tinsell° trappings shone,   *glittering*
   Which fled so fast, that nothing mote° him hold,   *might*
And scarse them leasure gave, her passing to behold.

16

Still as she fled, her eye she backward threw,
   As fearing evill, that pursewd her fast;
   And her faire yellow locks behind her flew,
   Loosely disperst with puffe of every blast:
   All as a blazing starre[4] doth farre outcast
   His hearie° beames, and flaming lockes dispred,   *hairy*
   At sight whereof the people stand aghast:
   But the sage wisard telles, as he has red,°   *foreseen*
That it importunes° death and dolefull drerihed.°   *portends/misery*

17

So as they gazéd after her a while,
   Lo where a griesly Foster° forth did rush,   *forester*
   Breathing out beastly lust her to defile:
   His tyreling jade[5] he fiercely forth did push,
   Through thicke and thin, both over banke and bush
   In hope her to attaine by hooke or crooke,
   That from his gorie sides the bloud did gush:

3. I.e., Florimel ("flower-honey"); her flight recalls that of the willful Angelica in *Orlando Furioso*
1.33–35. She suggests an evocative but vulnerable and fleeting beauty, object of universal desire.
For a "mythic" interpretation of her role, see N. Frye, *Fables of Identity* (New York, 1963); Roche
(*Flame*, 151–61) says her later adventures reflect the legend that Paris brought an image of Helen,
not the real woman, to Troy.
4. I.e., a comet.
5. I.e., tired nag.

Large were his limbes, and terrible his looke,
And in his clownish° hand a sharp bore speare he shooke.   *rustic*

18

Which outrage when those gentle knights did see,
  Full of great envie° and fell gealosy,°   *indignation/anger*
  They stayd not to avise,° who first should bee,   *consider*
  But all spurd after fast, as they mote fly,
  To reskew her from shamefull villany.
  The Prince and Guyon equally bylive°   *speedily*
  Her selfe pursewd, in hope to win thereby
  Most goodly meede, the fairest Dame alive:
But after the foule foster Timias did strive.

19

The whiles faire Britomart, whose constant mind,
  Would not so lightly follow beauties chace,
  Ne reckt° of Ladies Love, did stay behind,   *cared*
  And them awayted there a certaine space,
  To weet° if they would turne backe to that place: *know*
  But when she saw them gone, she forward went,
  As lay her journey, through that perlous Pace,°   *region*
  With stedfast courage and stout hardiment;
Ne evill thing she feared, ne evill thing she ment.°   *intended*

20

At last as nigh out of the wood she came,
  A stately Castle farre away she spyde,
  To which her steps directly she did frame.
  That Castle was most goodly edifyde,°   *built*
  And plaste for pleasure nigh that forrest syde:
  But faire before the gate a spatious plaine,
  Mantled with greene, itselfe did spredden wyde,
  On which she saw sixe knights, that did darraine°   *prepare*
Fierce battell against one,[6] with cruell might and maine.

21

Mainly° they all attonce upon him laid,   *violently*
  And sore beset on every side around,
  That nigh he breathlesse grew, yet nought dismaid,
  Ne ever to them yielded foot of ground
  All° had he lost much bloud through many a wound,   *although*
  But stoutly dealt his blowes, and every way
  To which he turnéd in his wrathfull stound,°   *assault*
  Made them recoile, and fly from dred decay,°   *destruction*
That none of all the sixe before, him durst assay.°   *engage*

6. I.e., Redcrosse. That Britomart helps him shows how holiness needs chastity. Cf. 1 Corinthians 6.9–20.

22

Like dastard Curres, that having at a bay
  The salvage beast embost° in wearie chace,   *cornered*
  Dare not adventure° on the stubborne pray,   *rush in*
  Ne byte before, but rome from place to place,
  To get a snatch, when turnéd is his face.
  In such distresse and doubtfull° jeopardy,   *fearful*
  When Britomart him saw, she ran a pace°   *quickly*
  Unto his reskew, and with earnest cry,
Bad those same sixe forbeare that single enimy.

23

But to her cry they list° not lenden eare,   *cared*
  Ne ought the more their mightie strokes surceasse,
  But gathering him round about more neare,
  Their direfull rancour rather did encreasse;
  Till that she rushing through the thickest preasse,
  Perforce disparted their compacted gyre,°   *circle*
  And soone compeld to hearken unto peace:
  Tho° gan she myldly of them to inquyre   *then*
The cause of their dissention and outrageous yre.

24

Whereto that single knight did answere frame°;   *make*
  "These sixe would me enforce by oddes of might,
  To chaunge my liefe,° and love another Dame,   *beloved*
  That death me liefer were, then such despight,
  So unto wrong to yield my wrested right:
  For I love one, the truest one on ground,
  Ne list me chaunge; she th'Errant Damzell hight,[7]
  For whose deare sake full many a bitter stownd,°   *attack*
I have endured, and tasted many a bloudy wound."

25

"Certes,"° said she, "then bene ye sixe to blame,   *surely*
  To weene° your wrong by force to justifie: *expect*
  For knight to leave his Ladie were great shame,
  That faithfull is, and better were to die.
  All losse is lesse, and lesse the infamie,
  Then losse of love to him, that loves but one;
  Ne may love be compeld by maisterie;°   *superior force*
  For soone as maisterie comes, sweet love anone°   *at once*
Taketh his nimble wings, and soone away is gone."[8]

7. I.e., Una, the wandering damsel.
8. Lines 7–9 are based on Chaucer's "Franklin's Tale," 764–66.

26

Then spake one of those sixe, "There dwelleth here
    Within this castle wall a Ladie faire,
    Whose soveraine beautie hath no living pere,°   *equal*
    Thereto so bounteous and so debonaire,
    That never any mote with her compaire.
    She hath ordaind this law, which we approve,°   *make good*
    That every knight, which doth this way repaire,°   *travel*
    In case he have no Ladie, nor no love,
Shall doe unto her service never to remove.

27

"But if he have a Ladie or a Love,
    Then must he her forgoe° with foule defame,   *give up*
    Or else with us by dint of sword approve,°   *prove*
    That she is fairer, then our fairest Dame,
    As did this knight, before ye hither came."
    "Perdie,"° said Britomart, "the choise is hard: *indeed*
    But what reward had he, that overcame?"
    "He should advauncéd be to high regard,"
Said they, "and have our Ladies love for his reward.⁹

28

"Therefore aread° Sir, if thou have a love."   *tell*
    "Love have I sure," quoth she, "but Lady none;
    Yet will I not fro mine owne love remove,
    Ne to your Lady will I service done,
    But wreake° your wrongs wrought to this knight alone,   *avenge*
    And prove his cause." With that her mortall speare
    She mightily aventred° towards one,   *thrust*
    And downe him smot, ere well aware he weare,
Then to the next she rode, and downe the next did beare.

29

Ne did she stay, till three on ground she layd,
    That none of them himselfe could reare againe;
    The fourth was by that other knight dismayd,
    All° were he wearie of his former paine,   *although*
    That now there do but two of six remaine;
    Which two did yield, before she did them smight.
    "Ah," said she then, "now may ye all see plaine,
    That truth is strong, and trew love most of might,
That for his trusty servaunts doth so strongly fight."

30

"Too well we see," said they, "and prove° too well   *experience*
    Our faulty weaknesse, and your matchlesse might:

9. These rules anticipate the lady's uncurbed sensuality later in the canto.

For thy,[1] faire Sir, yours be the Damozell,
Which by her owne law to your lot doth light,°   *fall*
And we your liege men faith unto you plight."
So underneath her feet their swords they mard,[2]
And after her besought, well as they might,
To enter in, and reape the dew reward:
She graunted, and then in they all together fared.

31

Long were it to describe the goodly frame,
    And stately port° of Castle Joyeous,   *appearance*
    (For so that Castle· hight by commune name)
    Where they were entertaind with curteous
    And comely glee° of many gracious   *cheer*
    Faire Ladies, and of many a gentle knight,
    Who through a Chamber long and spacious,
    Eftsoones° them brought unto their Ladies sight,   *presently*
That of them cleepéd° was the Lady of delight.[3]   *called*

32

But for to tell the sumptuous aray
    Of that great chamber, should be labour lost:
    For living wit, I weene, cannot display
    The royall riches and exceeding cost,°   *value*
    Of every pillour and of every post;
    Which all of purest bullion framéd were,
    And with great pearles and pretious stones embost,°   *adorned*
    That the bright glister of their beamés cleare
Did sparckle forth great light, and glorious did appeare.

33

These straunger knights through passing, forth were led
    Into an inner rowme, whose royaltee
    And rich purveyance might uneath be red;[4]
    Mote Princes place beseeme so deckt to bee.
    Which stately manner when as they did see,
    The image of superfluous riotize,°   *extravagance*
    Exceeding much the state of meane degree,[5]
    They greatly wondred, whence so sumptuous guize°   *way of life*
Might be maintaynd, and each gan diversely devize.°   *guess*

34

The wals were round about apparelléd
    With costly clothes of Arras and of Toure,°   *Tours*

1. I.e., therefore.
2. I.e., broke or hacked their sword blades, casting them at her feet.
3. I.e., Malecasta ("badly chaste"), whose luxurious castle recalls similar dwellings in medieval romances. Her excess and sensuosity show her affinity with Book II's Acrasia.
4. I.e., the luxurious richness of which might scarcely be described.
5. I.e., medium rank or class.

In which with cunning hand was pourtrahéd
  The love of Venus and her Paramoure°   *lover*
  The faire Adonis, turnéd to a flowre,
  A worke of rare device, and wondrous wit.[6]
  First did it shew the bitter balefull stowre,°   *turmoil*
  Which her assayd with many a fervent fit,
When first her tender hart was with his beautie smit.

35

Then with what sleights and sweet allurements she
  Entyst the Boy, as well that art she knew,
  And wooéd him her Paramoure to be;
  Now making girlonds of each flowre that grew,
  To crowne his golden lockes with honour dew;°   *due*
  Now leading him into a secret shade
  From his Beauperes,° and from bright heavens vew,   *companions*
  Where him to sleepe she gently would perswade,
Or bathe him in a fountaine by some covert° glade.   *secret*

36

And whilst he slept, she over him would spred
  Her mantle, coloured like the starry skyes,
  And her soft arme lay underneath his hed,
  And with ambrosiall kisses bathe his eyes;
  And whilest he bathed, with her two crafty spyes,
  She secretly would search each daintie lim,
  And throw into the well sweet Rosemaryes,
  And fragrant violets, and Pances° trim,   *pansies*
And ever with sweet Nectar she did sprinkle him.

37

So did she steale his heedelesse hart away,
  And joyd his love in secret unespyde.
  But for she saw him bent to cruell play,
  To hunt the salvage beast in forrest wyde,
  Dreadfull° of daunger, that mote him betyde,°   *fearful/befall*
  She oft and oft advized him to refraine
  From chase of greater° beasts, whose brutish pryde° *too great/spirit*
  Mote breede° him scath° unwares: but all in vaine; *bring/harm*
For who can shun the chaunce, that dest'ny doth ordaine?

38

Lo, where beyond he lyeth languishing,°   *suffering*
  Deadly engoréd of a great wild Bore,
  And by his side the Goddesse groveling

6. The myth of Venus and Adonis appears in Ovid, *Metamorphoses* 10.519–739; Spenser also drew on Natalis Comes, the Renaissance mythographer (*Mythologiae* 5.16). This myth is the operative symbol of Book III, which elaborates its various significances in episode, character, and image. Compare Adonis's useless fate here with his fertility in vi.46–49.

Makes for him endlesse mone, and evermore
With her soft garment wipes away the gore,
Which staines his snowy skin with hatefull hew:
But when she saw no helpe might him restore,
Him to a dainty flowre she did transmew,°   transform
Which in that cloth was wrought, as if it lively° grew.   actually

39

So was that chamber clad in goodly wize,
  And round about it many beds were dight,[7]
  As whilome was the antique worldés guize,°   custom
  Some for untimely° ease, some for delight,   unsuitable
  As pleaséd them to use, that use it might:
  And all was full of Damzels, and of Squires,
  Dauncing and reveling both day and night,
  And swimming deepe in sensuall desires,
And Cupid still emongst them kindled lustfull fires.

40

And all the while sweet Musicke did divide°   descant
  Her looser° notes with Lydian[8] harmony;   too loose
  And all the while sweet birdes thereto applide
  Their daintie layes and dulcet melody,
  Ay° caroling of love and jollity,   always
  That wonder was to heare their trim consort.°   harmony
  Which when those knights beheld, with scornefull eye,
  They sdeignéd° such lascivious disport,   disdained
And loathed the loose demeanure° of that wanton sort.   conduct

41

Thence they were brought to that great Ladies vew,
  Whom they found sitting on a sumptuous bed,
  That glistred all with gold and glorious shew,
  As the proud Persian Queenes accustoméd:[9]
  She seemd a woman of great bountihed,°   virtue
  And of rare beautie, saving that askaunce°   sidewise
  Her wanton eyes, ill signes of womanhed,
  Did roll too lightly, and too often glaunce,
Without regard of grace, or comely amenaunce.°   behavior

42

Long worke it were, and needlesse to devize°   describe
  Their goodly entertainement and great glee:

7. I.e., many couches were arranged.
8. In Greek music, the Lydian mode was thought soft, soothing, and pleasant for guests (Plato, *Republic* 3.398); naughty Catullus praises the "laughter" of a "Lydian" lake (*Carmina* 31), but moral Roger Ascham fears that Lydian music will stimulate immorality in youths (*Toxophilus* [1545]).
9. Duessa (I.ii.13) and Lucifera (I.iv.7) are described in similar terms.

She causéd them be led in curteous wize
Into a bowre, disarméd for to bee,
And chearéd well with wine and spiceree:°   *spiced refreshment*
The Redcrosse Knight was soone disarméd there,
But the brave Mayd would not disarméd bee,
But onely vented up her umbriere,[1]
And so did let her goodly visage to appere.

43

As when faire Cynthia, in darkesome night,
 Is in a noyous° cloud envelopéd,   *noxious*
Where she may find the substaunce thin and light,
 Breakes forth her silver beames, and her bright hed
Discovers° to the world discomfited;°   *reveals/dejected*
 Of the poore traveller, that went astray,
With thousand blessings she is heriéd;°   *praised*
 Such was the beautie and the shining ray,
With which faire Britomart gave light unto the day.[2]

44

And eke those six, which lately with her fought,
 Now were disarmd, and did them selves present
Unto her vew, and company unsoght;
 For they all seeméd curteous and gent,
And all sixe brethren, borne of one parent,
 Which had them traynd in all civilitee,°   *courtesy*
And goodly taught to tilt and turnament;[3]
 Now were they liegemen to this Lady free,°   *noble*
And her knights service ought, to hold of her in fee.[4]

45

The first of them by name Cardante hight,[5]
 A jolly person, and of comely vew;°   *appearance*
The second was Parlante, a bold knight,
 And next to him Jocante did ensew;
Basciante did him selfe most curteous shew;
 But fierce Bacchante seemd too fell and keene;
And yet in armes Noctante greater grew:
 All were faire knights, and goodly well beseene,[6]
But to faire Britomart they all but shadowes beene.

---

1. I.e., raised the face guard of her helmet.
2. Cf. *Orlando Furioso*, when Bradamante removes her helmet (32.79–80); see III.ix.20, note.
3. A tilt is an encounter between two mounted knights, armed with spears; a tournament involves a number of knights, armed with spears and swords.
4. I.e., owed her knightly service, as their feudal homage.
5. The knights' names ("watching," "speaking," "jesting," "kissing," "drinking," and "nocturnal activity" [with perhaps a pun on Latin *noceo*, "injure"]) suggest the chronology of seduction in this court-of-love. Similar figures appear in *The Romance of the Rose* and other medieval stories of love by, e.g., Boccaccio and Machaut.
6. I.e., of good appearance.

46

For she was full of amiable° grace,   *pleasing*
  And manly terrour mixéd therewithall,
  That as the one stird up affections bace,
  So th'other did mens rash desires apall,
  And hold them backe, that would in errour fall;[7]
  As he, that hath espide a vermeill° Rose,   *vermilion*
  To which sharpe thornes and breres the way forstall,
  Dare not for dread his hardy hand expose,
But wishing it far off, his idle° wish doth lose.   *futile*

47

Whom when the Lady saw so faire a wight,
  All ignoraunt of her contrary sex,
  (For she her weend a fresh and lusty knight)
  She greatly gan enamouréd to wex,°   *grow*
  And with vaine thoughts her falséd° fancy vex: *deceived*
  Her fickle hart conceivéd hasty fire,
  Like sparkes of fire, which fall in sclender flex,°   *flax*
  That shortly brent° into extreme desire,   *burned*
And ransackt all her veines with passion entire.

48

Eftsoones she grew to great impatience
  And into termes of open outrage brust,[8]
  That plaine discovered° her incontinence,   *revealed*
  Ne reckt she, who her meaning did mistrust;
  For she was given all to fleshly lust,
  And pouréd forth in sensuall delight,
  That all regard of shame she had discust,°   *shaken off*
  And meet° respect of honour put to flight: *proper*
So shamelesse beauty soone becomes a loathly sight.

49

Faire Ladies, that to love captivéd arre,
  And chaste desires do nourish in your mind,
  Let not her fault your sweet affections marre,
  Ne blot the bounty° of all womankind;   *goodness*
  'Mongst thousands good one wanton Dame to find:
  Emongst the Roses grow some wicked weeds;
  For this was not to love, but lust inclind;
  For love does alwayes bring forth bounteous° deeds,   *virtuous*
And in each gentle hart desire of honour breeds.[9]

7. Britomart is woman and warrior: in her the attractiveness of Venus combines with the cool virtue
   of Diana and the might of Minerva (Athena).
8. I.e., broke into openly intemperate terms.
9. An apostrophe to women modeled on *Orlando Furioso* 28.1.

50

Nought so of love this looser° Dame did skill,°   *too loose/understand*
  But as a coale to kindle fleshly flame,
  Giving the bridle to her wanton will,
  And treading under foote her honest name:
  Such love is hate, and such desire is shame.
  Still did she rove at her with crafty glaunce
  Of her false eyes, that at her hart did ayme,
  And told her meaning in her countenaunce;
But Britomart dissembled it with ignoraunce.[1]

51

Supper was shortly dight° and downe they sat,   *set out*
  Where they were servéd with all sumptuous fare,
  Whiles fruitfull Ceres, and Lyaeus fat[2]
  Pourd out their plenty, without spight° or spare:°   *grudge/restraint*
  Nought wanted there, that dainty was and rare;
  And aye the cups their bancks did overflow,
  And aye betweene the cups, she did prepare
  Way to her love, and secret darts° did throw;   *glances*
But Britomart would not such guilfull message know.

52

So when they slakéd had the fervent heat
  Of appetite with meates of every sort,
  The Lady did faire Britomart entreat,
  Her to disarme, and with delightfull sport
  To loose her warlike limbs and strong effort,°   *power*
  But when she mote not thereunto be wonne,
  (For she her sexe under that straunge purport°   *appearance*
  Did use to hide, and plaine apparaunce shonne:)
In plainer wise to tell her grievaunce she begonne.

53

And all attonce discovered her desire
  With sighes, and sobs, and plaints, and piteous griefe,
  The outward sparkes of her in burning fire;
  Which spent in vaine, at last she told her briefe,
  That but if[3] she did lend her short° reliefe,   *immediate*
  And do her comfort, she mote algates° dye.   *altogether*
  But the chaste damzell, that had never priefe°   *experience*
  Of such malengine° and fine forgerie,°   *guile/deceit*
Did easily beleeve her strong extremitie.[4]

1. I.e., pretended not to understand.
2. Ceres (Demeter) was the goddess of earth and its fruits, Lyaeus (Bacchus) the god of wine; i.e., food and drink were plentiful.
3. I.e., unless.
4. The inexperienced Britomart interprets Malecasta's conduct in the light of her own chaste love (cf. Roche, *Flame*, 69).

54

Full easie was for her to have beliefe,
  Who by self-feeling of her feeble sexe,
  And by long triall of the inward griefe,
  Wherewith imperious love her hart did vexe,
  Could judge what paines do loving harts perplexe.°   *torment*
  Who meanes no guile, be guiléd soonest shall,
  And to faire semblaunce doth light faith annexe;°   *add*
  The bird, that knowes not the false fowlers call,
Into his hidden net full easily doth fall.

55

For thy she would not in discourteise wise,
  Scorne the faire offer of good will profest;
  For great rebuke° it is, love to despise,   *shame*
  Or rudely sdeigne a gentle harts request;
  But with faire countenaunce, as beseeméd best,
  Her entertaynd;° nath'lesse she inly deemd   *treated*
  Her love too light, to wooe a wandring guest:
  Which she misconstruing, thereby esteemd
That from like° inward fire that outward smoke had steemd.   *matching*

56

Therewith a while she her flit° fancy fed,   *changeful*
  Till she mote winne fit time for her desire,
  But yet her wound still inward freshly bled,
  And through her bones the false instilléd fire
  Did spred it selfe, and venime close° inspire.   *secretly*
  Tho were the tables taken all away,
  And every knight, and every gentle Squire
  Gan choose his dame with Basciomani° gay,   *hand kissing*
With whom he meant to make his sport and courtly play.

57

Some fell to daunce, some fell to hazardry,°   *dicing*
  Some to make love, some to make meriment,
  As diverse wits to divers things apply;
  And all the while faire Malecasta bent
  Her crafty engins° to her close intent.   *wiles*
  By this th'eternall lampes, wherewith high Jove
  Doth light the lower world, were halfe yspent,
  And the moist daughters of huge Atlas⁵ strove
Into the Ocean deepe to drive their weary drove.°   *flock*

5. As nymphs, the Hyades ("the rainers") wept for their dead brother; now they are seven stars in
Taurus. Comes (4.7) calls them daughters of Atlas, which may be why Spenser gives them a
"drove" as though they were the Hesperides, also daughters of Atlas, who (some said) herded sheep.
It is midnight, which dates the scene near the spring equinox, then March 11.

58

High time it seeméd then for every wight
　　Them to betake unto their kindly° rest;　　　　　　　　*natural*
Eftsoones long waxen torches weren light,
　　Unto their bowres° to guiden every guest:　　　　　　　*chambers*
Tho when the Britonesse saw all the rest
Avoided° quite, she gan her selfe despoile,°　　　　*departed/disrobe*
And safe commit to her soft fethered nest,
　　Where through long watch, and late dayes weary toile,
She soundly slept, and carefull thoughts did quite assoile.°　　　*dispel*

59

Now whenas all the world in silence deepe
　　Yshrowded was, and every mortall wight
Was drowned in the depth of deadly° sleepe,　　　　　*deathlike*
　　Faire Malecasta, whose engrievéd° spright　　　　　*afflicted*
Could find no rest in such perplexéd plight,
Lightly arose out of her wearie bed,[6]
And under the blacke vele of guilty Night,[7]
　　Her with a scarlot mantle coveréd,
That was with gold and Ermines faire envelopéd.

60

Then panting soft, and trembling everie joynt,
　　Her fearfull feete towards the bowre she moved;
Where she for secret purpose did appoynt
　　To lodge the warlike mayd unwisely loved,
And to her bed approching, first she prooved,°　　　　　*tested*
Whether she slept or wakt, with her soft hand
She softly felt, if any member mooved,
　　And lent her wary care to understand,
If any puffe of breath, or signe of sence she fond.

61

Which whenas none she fond, with easie shift,[8]
　　For feare least her unwares she should abrayd,°　　　*awaken*
Th'embroderd quilt she lightly up did lift,
　　And by her side her selfe she softly layd,
Of every finest° fingers touch affrayd;　　　　　　　　*slightest*
Ne any noise she made, ne word she spake,
But inly sighed. At last the royall Mayd
　　Out of her quiet slomber did awake,
And chaungd her weary side, the better ease to take.

6. I.e., from the bed where she had restlessly lain.
7. Night is "guilty" because its dark veil conceals evil things; in Hesiod, *Theogony* 224, Night is the mother of Deceit. Cf. III.iv.55.
8. I.e., moving softly.

62

Where feeling one close couchéd by her side,
  She lightly lept out of her filéd° bed,   *defiled*
  And to her weapon ran, in minde to gride°   *pierce*
  The loathéd leachour. But the Dame halfe ded
  Through suddein feare and ghastly drerihed,°   *horror*
  Did shrieke alowd, that through the house it rong,
  And the whole family° therewith adred,°   *household/terrified*
  Rashly° out of their rouzéd couches sprong,   *hastily*
And to the troubled chamber all in armes did throng.

63

And those six Knights that Ladies Champions,
  And eke the Redcrosse knight ran to the stownd,°   *uproar*
  Halfe armed and halfe unarmd, with them attons:
  Where when confusedly they came, they fownd
  Their Lady lying on the sencelesse grownd;[9]
  On th'other side, they saw the warlike Mayd
  All in her snow-white smocke, with locks unbownd,
  Threatning the point of her avenging blade,
That with so troublous terrour they were all dismayde.

64

About their Lady first they flockt arownd,
  Whom having laid in comfortable couch,
  Shortly they reard out of her frosen swownd;°   *swoon*
  And afterwards they gan with fowle reproch
  To stirre up strife, and troublous contecke broch:[1]
  But by ensample of the last dayes losse,
  None of them rashly durst to her approch,
  Ne in so glorious spoile themselves embosse;°   *cover*
Her succourd eke the Champion of the bloudy Crosse.

65

But one of those six knights, Gardante hight,
  Drew out a deadly bow and arrow keene,
  Which forth he sent with felonous° despight,   *fierce*
  And fell intent against the virgin sheene:°   *fair*
  The mortall steele stayd not, till it was seene
  To gore her side, yet was the wound not deepe,
  But lightly raséd° her soft silken skin,   *grazed*
  That drops of purple bloud thereout did weepe,
Which did her lilly smock with staines of vermeil steepe.[2]

9. I.e., lying senseless on the ground.
1. I.e., instigate troublesome discord.
2. In this castle, even Britomart's chastity is not altogether proof against the ogling stares of lustful admirers.

66

Wherewith enraged she fiercely at them flew,
  And with her flaming sword about her layd,
  That none of them foule mischiefe could eschew,[3]
  But with her dreadfull strokes were all dismayd:
  Here, there, and every where about her swayd°   *swung*
  Her wrathfull steele, that none mote it abide;°   *endure*
  And eke the Redcrosse knight gave her good aid,
  Ay joyning foot to foot, and side to side,
That in short space their foes they have quite terrifide.

67

Tho whenas all were put to shamefull flight,
  The noble Britomartis her arayd,
  And her bright armes about her body dight:°   *put on*
  For nothing would she lenger there be stayd,
  Where so loose life, and so ungentle trade°   *conduct*
  Was usd of Knights and Ladies seeming gent:
  So earely ere the grosse Earthes gryesy shade,[4]
  Was all disperst out of the firmament,
They tooke their steeds, and forth upon their journey went.

Canto II

The Redcrosse knight to Britomart
describeth Artegall:
The wondrous myrrhour, by which she
in love with him did fall.

1

Here have I cause, in men just blame to find,
  That in their proper° prayse too partiall bee,   *own*
  And not indifferent° to woman kind,   *impartial*
  To whom no share in armes and chevalrie
  They do impart,° ne maken memorie   *allow*
  Of their brave gestes° and prowesse martiall;   *exploits*
  Scarse do they spare to one or two or three,
  Rowme in their writs; yet the same writing small
Does all their deeds deface,° and dims their glories all.   *obscure*

2

But by record of antique times I find,
  That women wont in warres to beare most sway,
  And to all great exploits them selves inclind:
  Of which they still the girlond bore away,
  Till envious Men fearing their rules decay,°   *destruction*
  Gan coyne streight° lawes to curb their liberty;   *strict*

3. I.e., none could avoid deadly danger.
4. I.e., the grim shades of night.

Yet sith they warlike armes have layd away,
They have exceld in artes and pollicy,°   *statecraft*
That now we foolish men that prayse gin eke t'envy.[1]

3

Of warlike puissaunce in ages spent,
  Be thou faire Britomart, whose prayse I write,
  But of all wisedome be thou precedent,°   *model*
  O soveraigne Queene, whose prayse I would endite,°   *proclaim*
  Endite I would as dewtie doth excite;°   *move*
  But ah my rimes too rude and rugged arre,
  When in so high an object they do lite,
  And striving, fit to make, I feare do marre:
Thy selfe thy prayses tell, and make them knowen farre.

4

She travelling with Guyon[2] by the way,
  Of sundry things faire purpose° gan to find,   *discourse*
  T'abridg their journey long, and lingring day;
  Mongst which it fell into that Faeries mind,
  To aske this Briton Mayd, what uncouth° wind,   *strange*
  Brought her into those parts, and what inquest°   *quest*
  Made her dissemble her disguiséd kind:°   *nature*
  Faire Lady she him seemd, like Lady drest,
But fairest knight alive, when arméd was her brest.

5

Thereat she sighing softly, had no powre
  To speake a while, ne ready answere make,
  But with hart-thrilling throbs and bitter stowre,°   *inward turmoil*
  As if she had a fever fit, did quake,
  And every daintie limbe with horrour shake;
  And ever and anone the rosy red,
  Flasht through her face, as it had been a flake°   *flash*
  Of lightning, through bright heaven fulminéd;°   *shot forth*
At last the passion past she thus him answeréd.

6

"Faire Sir, I let you weete, that from the howre
  I taken was from nourses tender pap,
  I have beene trainéd up in warlike stowre,°   *combat*
  To tossen° speare and shield, and to affrap°   *wield/strike*
  The warlike ryder to his most mishap;

---

1. Unlike Ariosto (e.g., *Orlando Furioso* 20.1), Spenser seems serious in affirming women's martial
  and political prowess; such praise was not uncommon in this normally patriarchal culture (cf.
  Book III of Castiglione's *Courtier* and John Bale's 1548 edition of Queen Elizabeth's *Godly
  Meditation*) and had classical precedent (cf. Plutarch's "Bravery of Women" in *Moralia*). But in
  V.v.25 Spenser says that good women know they are "borne to base humilitie." Benson 1990E,
  "Women," presents the issues.
2. Apparently a slip on Spenser's part; Redcrosse is meant (cf. stanza 16).

Sithence° I loathéd have my life to lead,   *since then*
As Ladies wont, in pleasures wanton lap,
To finger the fine needle and nyce° thread;   *delicate*
Me lever° were with point of foemans speare be dead.[3]   *rather*

7

"All my delight on deedes of armes is set,
To hunt out perils and adventures hard,
By sea, by land, where so they may be met,
Onely for honour and for high regard,°   *concerns*
Without respect° of richesse or reward.   *care*
For such intent into these parts I came,
Withouten compasse, or withouten card,°   *map*
Far fro my native soyle, that is by name
The greater Britaine,[4] here to seeke for prayse and fame.

8

"Fame blazéd° hath, that here in Faery lond   *proclaimed*
Do many famous Knightes and Ladies wonne,°   *dwell*
And many straunge adventures to be fond,
Of which great worth and worship° may be wonne;   *honor*
Which I to prove, this voyage have begonne.
But mote I weet of you, right curteous knight,
Tydings of one, that hath unto me donne
Late foule dishonour and reprochfull spight,
The which I seeke to wreake,° and Arthegall he hight."[5]   *avenge*

9

The word gone out, she backe againe would call,
As her repenting so to have missayd,[6]
But that he it up-taking ere the fall,
Her shortly answeréd; "Faire martiall Mayd
Certes ye misavuséd° beene, t'upbrayd   *misinformed*
A gentle knight with so unknightly blame:
For weet ye well of all, that ever playd
At tilt or tourney, or like warlike game,
The noble Arthegall hath ever borne the name.[7]

10

"For thy great wonder were it, if such shame
Should ever enter in his bounteous° thought,   *virtuous*
Or ever do, that mote deserven blame:

3. The warrior woman is a traditional literary type; here Spenser may remember Clorinda's training in Tasso's *Gerusalemme Liberata* 2.39–40.
4. I.e., not the "lesser Britaine," or Brittany, in France.
5. Arthegall, destined to marry Britomart, is the hero of Book V ("The Legend of Justice"). Geoffrey of Monmouth's *Historia Regum Britanniae* (c. 1139) refers to "Arthgal of Cargueir, that is now called Warwick" (10.12), but the name also links Arthegall to Arthur, Lord Grey of Wilton, Spenser's chief in Ireland from 1580 to 1582, and to King Arthur. See III.iii.26 and note.
6. I.e., as if she repented having spoken thus wrongly.
7. I.e., has ever been most renowned.

The noble courage° never weeneth ought,   *spirit*
That may unworthy of it selfe be thought.
Therefore, faire Damzell, be ye well aware,°   *wary*
Least that too farre ye have your sorrow sought:
You and your countrey both I wish welfare,
And honour both; for each of other worthy are."

11

The royall Mayd woxe° inly wondrous glad,   *grew*
    To heare her Love so highly magnifide,
    And joyd that ever she affixéd had,
    Her hart on knight so goodly glorifide,
    How ever finely she it faind to hide:
    The loving mother, that nine monethes did beare,
    In the deare closet of her painefull side,
    Her tender babe, it seeing safe appeare,
Doth not so much rejoyce, as she rejoycéd theare.

12

But to occasion° him to further talke,   *induce*
    To feed her humour° with his pleasing stile,   *mood*
    Her list in strifull termes with him to balke,°   *dispute*
    And thus replide, "How ever, Sir, ye file
    Your curteous tongue, his prayses to compile,
    It ill beseemes a knight of gentle sort,
    Such as ye have him boasted, to beguile
    A simple mayd, and worke so haynous tort,°   *wrong*
In shame of knighthood, as I largely° can report.   *at length*

13

"Let be[8] therefore my vengeaunce to disswade,
    And read,° where I that faytour° false may find."   *tell/villain*
    "Ah, but if reason faire might you perswade,
    To slake your wrath, and mollifie° your mind,"   *soften*
    Said he, "perhaps ye should it better find:
    For hardy° thing it is, to weene by might,   *bold*
    That man to hard conditions to bind,
    Or ever hope to match in equall fight,
Whose prowesse paragon[9] saw never living wight.

14

"Ne soothlich° is it easie for to read,°   *truly/know*
    Where now on earth, or how he may be found;
    For he ne wonneth in one certaine stead,°   *place*
    But restlesse walketh all the world around,
    Ay° doing things, that to his fame redound,   *always*
    Defending Ladies cause, and Orphans right,

8. I.e., cease.
9. I.e., the equal of whose prowess.

Where so he heares, that any doth confound°   *persecute*
Them comfortlesse,° through tyranny or might;   *helpless*
So is his soveraine honour raisde to heavens hight."

15

His feeling words her feeble sence much pleased,
And softly sunck into her molten° hart;   *melting*
Hart that is inly hurt, is greatly eased
With hope of thing, that may allegge° his smart;   *alleviate*
For pleasing words are like to Magick art,
That doth the charméd Snake in slomber lay:
Such secret ease felt gentle Britomart,
Yet list the same efforce with faind gainesay;[1]
So dischord oft in Musick makes the sweeter lay.

16

And said, "Sir knight, these idle termes forbeare,
And sith it is uneath° to find his haunt,°   *difficult/abode*
Tell me some markes, by which he may appeare,
If chaunce I him encounter paravaunt;°   *face to face*
For perdie° one shall other slay, or daunt: *surely*
What shape, what shield, what armes, what steed, what sted,
And what so else his person most may vaunt?"°   *display*
All which the Redcrosse knight to point ared,[2]
And him in every part before her fashionéd.

17

Yet him in every part before she knew,
How ever list her now her knowledge faine,°   *hide*
Sith him whilome in Britaine she did vew,
To her revealéd in a mirrhour plaine,
Whereof did grow her first engrafféd° paine,   *implanted*
Whose root and stalke so bitter yet did tast,
That but the fruit more sweetnesse did containe,
Her wretched dayes in dolour she mote wast,
And yield the pray of love to lothsome death at last.

18

By strange occasion she did him behold,
And much more strangely gan to love his sight,
As it in bookes hath written bene of old.
In Deheubarth that now South-wales is hight,
What time king Ryence raigned, and dealéd° right,   *dispensed*
The great Magitian Merlin had devized,
By his deepe science, and hell-dreaded might,

---

1. I.e., yet was pleased to intensify that sensation by pretended disagreement.
2. I.e., exactly described.

A looking glasse,[3] right wondrously aguized,°   *fashioned*
Whose vertues through the wyde world soone were solemnized.

19

It vertue° had, to shew in perfect sight,   *power*
  What ever thing was in the world contaynd,
  Betwixt the lowest earth and heavens hight,
  So that it to the looker appertaynd;
  What ever foe had wrought, or frend had faynd,
  Therein discovered was, ne ought mote pas,
  Ne ought in secret from the same remaynd;
  For thy it round and hollow shapéd was,
Like to the world it selfe, and seemed a world of glas.

20

Who wonders not, that reades° so wonderous worke?   *perceives*
  But who does wonder, that has red° the Towre,   *considered*
  Wherein th'Aegyptian Phao long did lurke
  From all mens vew, that none might her discoure,°   *discover*
  Yet she might all men vew out of her bowre?
  Great Ptolomae[4] it for his lemans° sake   *lover's*
  Ybuilded all of glasse, by Magicke powre,
  And also it impregnable did make;
Yet when his love was false, he with a peaze° it brake.   *blow*

21

Such was the glassie globe that Merlin made,
  And gave unto king Ryence for his gard,°   *protection*
  That never foes his kingdome might invade,
  But he it knew at home before he hard
  Tydings thereof, and so them still debared.
  It was a famous Present for a Prince,
  And worthy worke of infinite reward,
  That treasons could bewray, and foes convince;°   *conquer*
Happie this Realme, had it remainéd ever since.

22

One day it fortunéd, faire Britomart
  Into her fathers closet to repayre;°   *go*
  For nothing he from her reserved apart,
  Being his onely daughter and his hayre:°   *heir*
  Where when she had espyde that mirrhour fayre,
  Her selfe a while therein she vewd in vaine;

3. I.e., a crystal ball. In Chaucer's "Squire's Tale" a "mirror of glas" gives the viewer foreknowledge in matters of love or war; for Dobin 1990 this globe recalls that of Dr. Dee, the astrologer, who told Elizabeth during a famous consultation that her Arthurian lineage legitimated her imperial claims.

4. Ptolemy II (308–246 B.C.), who built the Pharos, Museum, and Library at Alexandria; Arab legend credited him with almost magical ability in working with glass. The next stanza may allude indirectly to recent plots against the queen, such as the 1586 Babington conspiracy, and to the war with Spain.

  Tho her avizing° of the vertues rare,   *thinking*
  Which thereof spoken were, she gan againe
Her to bethinke of, that mote to her selfe pertaine.

23

But as it falleth, in the gentlest harts
  Imperious Love hath highest set his throne,
  And tyrannizeth in the bitter smarts
  Of them, that to him buxome° are and prone:°   *yielding/submissive*
  So thought this Mayd (as maydens use to done)
  Whom fortune for her husband would allot,
  Not that she lusted after any one;
  For she was pure from blame of sinfull blot,
Yet wist° her life at last must lincke in that same knot.   *knew*

24

Eftsoones there was presented to her eye
  A comely knight, all armed in complete wize,
  Through whose bright ventayle° lifted up on hye   *visor*
  His manly face, that did his foes agrize,°   *terrify*
  And friends to termes of gentle truce entize,
  Lookt foorth, as Phoebus face out of the east,
  Betwixt two shadie mountaines doth arize;
  Portly° his person was, and much increast   *dignified*
Through his Heroicke grace, and honorable gest.°   *bearing*

25

His crest was covered with a couchant Hound,
  And all his armour seemed of antique mould,°   *form*
  But wondrous massie and assuréd sound,
  And round about yfrettcd° all with gold,   *adorned*
  In which there written was with cyphers° old,   *letters*
  Achilles armes, which Arthegall did win.
  And on his shield enveloped sevenfold
  He bore a crownéd litle Ermilin,°   *ermine*
That deckt the azure field with her faire pouldred° skin.⁵   *spotted*

26

The Damzell well did vew his personage,°   *image*
  And likéd well, ne further fastned° not,   *fixed on*
  But went her way; ne her unguilty age
  Did weene, unwares, that her unlucky lot
  Lay hidden in the bottome of the pot;
  Of hurt unwist most daunger doth redound:°   *result*

5. Arthegall's helmet displays a greyhound lying down with head alertly raised; his shield's crowned
   ermine signifies royalty and chastity. Ariosto alludes to Mandricardo's winning of Hector's arms
   (*Orlando Furioso* 14.30–31), but for Arthegall to win those of the Greek Achilles is especially apt,
   given the legend that Brute, a Trojan, founded Britain (see ix.46–51). There may also be a
   psychological dynamic implied by this glimpse in a "mirror": Britomart's search will lead her from
   an image of a man to the man himself.

But the false Archer, which that arrow shot
So slyly, that she did not feele the wound,
Did smyle full smoothly at her weetlesse wofull stound.

27

Thenceforth the feather in her loftie crest,
  Ruffëd of⁶ love, gan lowly to availe,°   *bow*
  And her proud portance,° and her princely gest,   *bearing*
  With which she earst tryumphéd, now did quaile:°   *falter*
  Sad, solemne, sowre, and full of fancies fraile
  She woxe; yet wist she neither how, nor why,
  She wist not, silly° Mayd, what she did aile,   *innocent*
  Yet wist, she was not well at ease perdy,°   *certainly*
Yet thought it was not love, but some melancholy.

28

So soone as Night had with her pallid hew
  Defast° the beautie of the shining sky,   *obscured*
  And reft from men the worlds desiréd vew,
  She with her Nourse adowne to sleepe did lye;
  But sleepe full farre away from her did fly:
  In stead thereof sad sighes, and sorrowes deepe
  Kept watch and ward about her warily,
  That nought she did but wayle, and often steepe°   *stain*
Her daintie couch with teares, which closely° she did weepe. *secretly*

29

And if that any drop of slombring rest
  Did chaunce to still° into her wearie spright,   *trickle*
  When feeble nature felt her selfe opprest,
  Streight way with dreames, and with fantasticke sight
  Of dreadfull things the same was put to flight,
  That oft out of her bed she did astart,
  As one with vew of ghastly feends affright:
  Tho gan she to renew her former smart,
And thinke of that faire visage, written in her hart.

30

One night, when she was tost with such unrest,
  Her aged Nurse, whose name was Glauce hight,⁷
  Feeling her leape out of her loathéd nest,
  Betwixt her feeble armes her quickly keight,°   *caught*
  And downe againe in her warme bed her dight;°   *placed*

6. I.e., ruffled by.
7. This episode draws heavily on the pseudo-Virgilian *Ciris*, in which passion leads a princess—less
honorable than Spenser's heroine—to betray her father and kingdom (cf. Ovid, *Metamorphoses*
8); her nurse is the mother of Diana's nymph, Britomartis. Glauce's name (Greek for "gray" and
"owl") suits her age and, the owl being sacred to Athena, associates her charge with the armed
goddess of war, wisdom, and giant killing. The old nurse is a common figure from classical
literature through the Renaissance, usually sympathetic but often amoral: even Glauce acts in
ways of which Guyon's Palmer would disapprove.

"Ah my deare daughter, ah my dearest dread,
What uncouth fit," said she, "what evil plight
Hath thee opprest, and with sad drearyhead°   *grief*
Chaungéd thy lively cheare,° and living made thee dead?   *mood*

31

"For not of nought these suddeine ghastly feares
All night afflict thy naturall repose,
And all the day, when as thine equall peares°   *companions*
Their fit disports with faire delight doe chose,
Thou in dull corners doest thy selfe inclose,
Ne tastest Princes pleasures, ne doest spred
Abroad thy fresh youthes fairest flowre, but lose
Both leafe and fruit, both too untimely shed,
As one in wilfull balc° for ever buriéd.   *grief*

32

"The time, that mortall men their weary cares
Do lay away, and all wilde beastes do rest,
And every river eke his course forbeares,
Then doth this wicked evill thee infest,°   *attack*
And rive with thousand throbs thy thrilléd° brest; *pierced*
Like an huge Aetn' of deepe engulféd griefe,
Sorrow is heapéd in thy hollow chest,
Whence forth it breakes in sighes and anguish rife,
As smoke and sulphure mingled with confuséd strife.

33

"Aye me, how much I feare, least love it bee;
But if that love it be, as sure I read°   *perceive*
By knowen signes and passions, which I see,
Be it worthy of thy race and royall sead,
Then I avow by this most sacred head
Of my deare foster child, to ease thy griefe,
And win thy will: Therefore away doe° dread;   *banish*
For death nor daunger from thy dew reliefe
Shall me debarre, tell me therefore my liefest liefe."°   *beloved*

34

So having said, her twixt her armés twaine
She straightly° straynd, and colléd° tenderly,   *closely/embraced*
And every trembling joynt, and every vaine
She softly felt, and rubbéd busily,
To doe° the frosen cold away to fly;   *cause*
And her faire deawy eies with kisses deare
She oft did bath, and oft againe did dry;
And ever her importund,° not to feare   *urged*
To let the secret of her hart to her appeare.

35

The Damzell pauzd, and then thus fearefully:
  "Ah Nurse, what needeth thee to eke° my paine?   *add to*
  Is not enough, that I alone doe dye,
  But it must doubled be with death of twaine?
  For nought for me but death there doth remaine."
  "O daughter deare," said she, "despaire no whit;
  For never sore, but might a salve obtaine:
  That blinded God, which hath ye blindly smit,
Another arrow hath your lovers hart to hit."

36

"But mine is not," quoth she, "like others wound;
  For which no reason can find remedy."
  "Was never such, but mote the like be found,"
  Said she, "and though no reason may apply
  Salve to your sore, yet love can higher stye,°   *mount*
  Then reasons reach, and oft hath wonders donne."
  "But neither God of love, nor God of sky
  Can doe," said she, "that, which cannot be donne."
"Things oft impossible," quoth she, "seeme, ere begonne."

37

"These idle words," said she, "doe nought asswage
  My stubborne smart, but more annoyance° breed,   *grief*
  For no no usuall fire, no usuall rage°   *passion*
  It is, O Nurse, which on my life doth feed,
  And suckes the bloud, which from my hart doth bleed.
  But since thy faithfull zeale lets me not hyde
  My crime, (if crime it be) I will it reed.°   *tell*
  Nor Prince, nor pere it is, whose love hath gryde° *pierced*
My feeble brest of late, and launchéd° this wound wyde. *inflicted*

38

"Nor man it is, nor other living wight;
  For then some hope I might unto me draw,
  But th'only shade and semblant° of a knight,   *likeness*
  Whose shape or person yet I never saw,
  Hath me subjected to loves cruell law:
  The same one day, as me misfortune led,
  I in my fathers wondrous mirrhour saw,
  And pleaséd with that seeming goodly-hed,° *good appearance*
Unwares the hidden hooke with baite I swallowéd.

39

"Sithens° it hath infixéd faster hold   *Since then*
  Within my bleeding bowels, and so sore
  Now ranckleth in this same fraile fleshly mould,°   *body*

That all mine entrailes flow with poysnous gore,
And th'ulcer groweth daily more and more;
Ne can my running sore find remedie,
Other then my hard fortune to deplore,
And languish as the leafe falne from the tree,
Till death make one end of my dayes and miserie."

40

"Daughter," said she, "what need ye be dismayd,
  Or why make ye such Monster of your mind?
  Of much more uncouth thing I was affrayd;
  Of filthy lust, contrarie unto kind:°   *nature*
  But this affection nothing straunge I find;
  For who with reason can you aye° reprove,   *ever*
  To love the semblant pleasing most your mind,
  And yield your heart, whence ye cannot remove?
No guilt in you, but in the tyranny of love.[8]

41

"Not so th'Arabian Myrrhe[9] did set her mind;
  Nor so did Biblis spend her pining hart,
  But loved their native flesh against all kind,°   *nature*
  And to their purpose uséd wicked art:
  Yet playd Pasiphae a more monstrous part,
  That loved a Bull, and learnd a beast to bee;
  Such shamefull lusts who loaths not, which depart
  From course of nature and of modestie?
Sweet love such lewdnes bands° from his faire companie.   *banishes*

42

"But thine my Deare (welfare thy heart my deare)
  Though strange beginning had, yet fixéd is
  On one, that worthy may perhaps appeare;
  And certes seemes bestowéd not amis:
  Joy thereof have thou and eternall blis."
  With that upleaning on her elbow weake,
  Her alablaster° brest she soft did kis,   *alabaster*
  Which all that while she felt to pant and quake,
As it an Earth-quake were; at last she thus bespake.

43

"Beldame,° your words doe worke me litle ease;   *good mother*
  For though my love be not so lewdly bent,°   *inclined*
  As those ye blame, yet may it nought appease
  My raging smart, ne ought my flame relent,°   *abate*

8. Chaste love accords with reason; yet reason cannot match or control love's power (cf. stanza 36).
9. Yielding to passion for her royal father, and aided by her old nurse, Myrrha conceived Adonis (*Metamorphoses* 10.312–518); Biblis slept with her brother; Queen Pasiphae entered a wooden cow made for her by Daedalus and, impregnated by a handsome bull, bore the Minotaur; cf. Boccaccio, *Genealogiae* 4.9–10.

But rather doth my helpelesse griefe augment.
For they, how ever shamefull and unkind,
Yet did possesse° their horrible intent: *achieve*
Short end of sorrowes they thereby did find;
So was their fortune good, though wicked were their mind.

44

"But wicked fortune mine, though mind be good,
Can have no end, nor hope of my desire,
But feed on shadowes, whiles I die for food,
And like a shadow wexe,° whiles with entire   *become*
Affection, I doe languish and expire.
I fonder, then Cephisus foolish child,[1]
Who having vewéd in a fountaine shere°   *clear*
His face, was with the love thereof beguild;
I fonder love a shade, the bodie farre exild."

45

"Nought like," quoth she, "for that same wretched boy
Was of himselfe the idle Paramoure;
Both love and lover, without hope of joy,
For which he faded to a watry flowre.
But better fortune thine, and better howre,°   *occasion*
Which lov'st the shadow of a warlike knight;
No shadow, but a bodie hath in powre:[2]
That bodie, wheresoever that it light,°   *lodges*
May learnéd be by cyphers,° or by Magicke might.   *astrological signs*

46

"But if thou may with reason yet represse
The growing evill, ere it strength have got,
And thee abandond wholly doe possesse,
Against it strongly strive, and yield thee not,
Till thou in open field adowne be smot.
But if the passion mayster thy fraile might,
So that needs love or death must be thy lot,
Then I avow to thee, by wrong or right
To compasse° thy desire, and find that lovéd knight."   *bring about*

47

Her chearefull words much cheard the feeble spright
Of the sicke virgin, that her downe she layd
In her warme bed to sleepe, if that she might;
And the old-woman carefully displayd°   *arranged*
The clothes about her round with busie ayd;
So that at last a little creeping sleepe
Surprisd her sense: She therewith well apayd,°   *pleased*

1. I.e., Narcissus.
2. I.e., there is no shadow not cast by a body.

The drunken lampe downe in the oyle did steepe,
And set her by to watch, and set her by to weepe.

48

Earely the morrow next, before that day
  His joyous face did to the world reveale,
  They both uprose and tooke their readie way
  Unto the Church, their prayers to appeale,°   *say*
  With great devotion, and with litle zeale:
  For the faire Damzell from the holy herse°   *ceremony*
  Her love-sicke hart to other thoughts did steale;
  And that old Dame said many an idle verse,
Out of her daughters hart fond fancies to reverse.

49

Returnéd home, the royall Infant[3] fell
  Into her former fit; for why, no powre
  Nor guidance of her selfe in her did dwell.
  But th'aged Nurse her calling to her bowre,°   *chamber*
  Had gathered Rew, and Savine, and the flowre
  Of Camphora, and Calamint, and Dill,
  All which she in a earthen Pot did poure,
  And to the brim with Colt wood did it fill,
And many drops of milke and bloud through it did spill.[4]

50

Then taking thrise three haires from off her head,
  Them trebly breaded° in a threefold lace,   *braided*
  And round about the pots mouth, bound the thread,
  And after having whisperéd a space
  Certaine sad words, with hollow voice and bace,
  She to the virgin said, thrise said she it;
  "Come daughter come, come; spit upon my face,
  Spit thrise upon me, thrise upon me spit;
Th'uneven number for this businesse is most fit."

51

That sayd, her round about she from her turnd,
  She turnéd her contrarie to the Sunne,
  Thrise she her turnd contrary, and returnd,
  All contrary, for she the right did shunne,
  And ever what she did, was streight° undonne.   *strictly*
  So thought she to undoe her daughters[5] love:
  But love, that is in gentle brest begonne,

---

3. I.e., noble maiden, princess.
4. These herbs were thought to cool love; milk and blood propitiate Hecate, patroness of black magic.
  Glauce's procedures suggest English witchcraft as well as ancient magic ritual.
5. I.e., her ward's.

No idle charmes so lightly may remove,
That well can witnesse, who by triall it does prove.°   *test*

52

Ne ought it mote the noble Mayd avayle,
  Ne slake the furie of her cruell flame,
But that she still did waste, and still did wayle,
  That through long languour, and hart-burning brame°   *longing*
  She shortly like a pynéd° ghost became,   *wasted*
Which long hath waited by the Stygian strond.[6]
  That when old Glauce saw, for feare least blame
  Of her miscarriage° should in her be fond,   *failure*
She wist not how t'amend, nor how it to withstond.

Canto III

   Merlin bewrayes° to Britomart,   *reveals*
   the state of Artegall.
   And shewes the famous Progeny
   which from them springen shall.

1

Most sacred fire, that burnest mightily
  In living brests, ykindled first above,
Emongst th'eternall spheres and lamping° sky,   *resplendent*
  And thence pourd into men, which men call Love;
  Not that same, which doth base affections move
In brutish minds, and filthy lust inflame,
  But that sweet fit, that doth true beautie love,
  And choseth vertue for his dearest Dame,
Whence spring all noble deeds and never dying fame:[1]

2

Well did Antiquitie a God thee deeme,
  That over mortall minds hast so great might,
To order them, as best to thee doth seeme,
  And all their actions to direct aright;
  The fatall° purpose of divine foresight,   *fated*
Thou doest effect in destinéd descents,°   *lineages*
  Through deepe impression of thy secret might,
  And stirredst up th'Heroes high intents,
Which the late world admyres for wondrous moniments.°   *memorials*

---

6. I.e., who still awaits passage across the Styx on Charon's ferry so as to complete the journey to Hades.
1. In his *Fowre Hymnes*, Spenser develops this distinction between lust and that love which has "true beauty" and "vertue" for its object; in the Book of Chastity he does not, though, disparage sexuality per se.

3

But thy dread darts in none doe triumph more,
  Ne braver° proofe in any, of thy powre   *finer*
  Shew'dst thou, then in this royall Maid of yore,
  Making her seeke an unknowne Paramoure,
  From the worlds end, through many a bitter stowre:°   *encounter*
  From whose two loynes thou afterwards did rayse
  Most famous fruits of matrimoniall bowre,
  Which through the earth have spred their living prayse,
That fame in trompe of gold eternally displayes.

4

Begin then, O my dearest sacred Dame,[2]
  Daughter of Phœbus and of Memorie,
  That doest ennoble with immortall name
  The warlike Worthies, from antiquitie,
  In thy great volume of Eternitie:
  Begin, O Clio, and recount from hence
  My glorious Soveraines goodly auncestrie,
  Till that by dew degrees and long protense,°   *extension*
Thou have it lastly brought unto her Excellence.

5

Full many wayes within her troubled mind,
  Old Glauce cast,° to cure this Ladies griefe: *considered*
  Full many waies she sought, but none could find,
  Nor herbes, nor charmes, nor counsell, that is chiefe
  And choisest med'cine for sicke harts reliefe:
  For thy great care she tooke,[3] and greater feare,
  Least that it should her turne to foule repriefe,°   *reproof*
  And sore reproch, when so her father deare
Should of his dearest daughters hard misfortune heare.

6

At last she her avisd,° that he, which made   *recalled*
  That mirrhour, wherein the sicke Damosell
  So straungely vewéd her straunge lovers shade,
  To weet, the learnéd Merlin,[4] well could tell,
  Under what coast° of heaven the man did dwell,   *region*
  And by what meanes his love might best be wrought:

2. I.e., Clio, muse of history. The nine "Worthies" were Hector, Alexander, Julius Caesar; Joshua, Daniel, Judas Maccabaeus; Arthur, Charlemagne, and Godfrey of Boulogne.
3. I.e., therefore she was much troubled.
4. For Merlin and his prophecies, Spenser drew on Geoffrey's *Historia* and Holinshed's *Chronicles*, although he also used Malory's *Morte d'Arthur* and Camden's *Britanniae.* Geoffrey's tale of the early pagan kings and of "Arthur and the many others that did succeed him after the Incarnation" (1.1) combines invention and legend with material from histories like Bede's *Ecclesiastical History* (731) and William of Malmesbury's history of English kings (c. 1125). The design of this canto follows Ariosto's story of Bradamante's visit to Merlin's tomb, where she learns about the future (*Orlando Furioso* 3).

For though beyond the Africk Ismaell,[5]
Or th'Indian Peru he were, she thought
Him forth through infinite endevour to have sought.

7

Forthwith themselves disguising both in straunge
   And base attyre, that none might them bewray,
   To Maridunum, that is now by chaunge
   Of name Cayr-Merdin[6] cald, they tooke their way:
   There the wise Merlin whylome wont (they say)
   To make his wonne,° low underneath the ground,   *dwelling*
   In a deepe delve,° farre from the vew of day,   *den*
   That of no living wight he mote be found,
When so he counseld with his sprights encompast round.

8

And if thou ever happen that same way
   To travell, goe to see that dreadfull place:
   It is an hideous hollow cave (they say)
   Under a rocke that lyes a little space
   From the swift Barry, tombling downe apace,
   Emongst the woodie hilles of Dynevowre:
   But dare thou not, I charge, in any cace,
   To enter into that same balefull Bowre,°   *cavern*
For fear the cruell Feends should thee unwares devowre.

9

But standing high aloft, low lay thine eare,
   And there such ghastly noise of yron chaines,
   And brasen Caudrons thou shalt rombling heare,
   Which thousand sprights with long enduring paines
   Do tosse,° that it will stonne thy feeble braines,   *stir up*
   And oftentimes great grones, and grievous stounds,°   *outcries*
   When too huge toile and labour them constraines:
   And oftentimes loud strokes, and ringing sounds
From under that deepe Rocke most horribly rebounds.

10

The cause some say is this: A litle while
   Before that Merlin dyde, he did intend,
   A brasen wall in compas to compile°   *build*
   About Cairmardin, and did it commend°   *command*
   Unto these Sprights, to bring to perfect end.
   During which worke the Ladie of the Lake,[7]

5. The African territories held by the Saracens, thought to be descendants of Ishmael.
6. I.e., Carmarthen, in Wales; Merlin's birthplace, according to Geoffrey (6.17). Dynevor Castle, nearby, was the seat of the princes of South Wales.
7. I.e., Nimue; see Malory's *Morte d'Arthur* 4.1.

Whom long he loved, for him in hast did send,
    Who thereby forst his workemen to forsake,
Them bound till his returne, their labour not to slake.°   *slacken*

11

In the meane time through that false Ladies traine,°   *trickery*
    He was surprisd, and buried under beare,°   *tomb*
    Ne ever to his worke returnd againe:
    Nath'lesse those feends may not their worke forbeare,
    So greatly his commaundément they feare,
    But there doe toyle and travell day and night,
    Untill that brasen wall they up doe reare:°   *erect*
    For Merlin had in Magicke more insight,
Then ever him before or after living wight.

12

For he by words could call out of the sky
    Both Sunne and Moone, and make them him obay:
    The land to sea, and sea to maineland dry,
    And darkesome night he eke could turne to day:
    Huge hostes of men he could alone dismay,
    And hostes of men of meanest things could frame,
    When so him list his enimies to fray:°   *terrify*
    That to this day for terror of his fame,
The feends do quake, when any him to them does name.

13

And sooth,° men say that he was not the sonne   *truly*
    Of mortall Syre, or other living wight,
    But wondrously begotten, and begonne
    By false illusion of a guilefull Spright,
    On a faire Ladie Nonne, that whilome hight
    Matilda, daughter to Pubidius,
    Who was the Lord of Mathravall by right,
    And coosen° unto king Ambrosius:[8]   *kinsman*
Whence he induéd° was with skill so marvellous.   *endowed*

14

They here ariving, staid a while without,
    Ne durst adventure rashly in to wend,°   *go*
    But of their first intent gan make new dout
    For dread of daunger, which it might portend:
    Untill the hardie° Mayd (with love to frend)   *bold*
    First entering, the dreadfull Mage° there found   *magician*

8. Matraval was a town in Montgomeryshire, Wales; but Geoffrey gives no such names, and identifies Merlin's sire only as an "incubus daemon" (6.18). This is also Ariosto's version (*Orlando Furioso* 33.9).

Deepe busiéd bout worke of wondrous end,
And writing strange characters in the ground,
With which the stubborn feends he to his service bound.

15

He nought was movéd at their entrance bold:
　For of their comming well he wist afore,
　Yet list them bid their businesse to unfold,
　As if ought in this world in secret store
　Were from him hidden, or unknowne of yore.
　Then Glauce thus, "Let not it thee offend,
　That we thus rashly through thy darkesome dore,
　Unwares° have prest: for either fatall end,[9]   *suddenly*
Or other mightie cause us two did hither send."

16

He bad tell on; And then she thus began:
　"Now have three Moones with borrowed brothers light,
　Thrice shinéd faire, and thrice seemed dim and wan,
　Sith° a sore evill, which this virgin bright   *since*
　Tormenteth, and doth plonge in dolefull plight,
　First rooting tooke; but what thing it mote bee,
　Or whence it sprong, I cannot read aright:
　But this I read, that but if[1] remedee
Thou her afford, full shortly I her dead shall see."

17

Therewith th'Enchaunter softly gan to smyle
　At her smooth speeches, weeting inly well,
　That she to him dissembled womanish guyle,
　And to her said, "Beldame, by that ye tell,
　More need of leach-craft° hath your Damozell,   *medicine*
　Then of my skill: who helpe may have elsewhere,
　In vaine seekes wonders out of Magicke spell."
　Th'old woman wox half blanck,[2] those words to heare;
And yet was loth to let her purpose plaine appeare.

18

And to him said, "If any leaches skill,
　Or other learnéd meanes could have redrest°   *cured*
　This my deare daughters deepe engrafféd° ill,   *implanted*
　Certes I should be loth thee to molest:
　But this sad evill, which doth her infest,
　Doth course of naturall cause farre exceed,

9. I.e., a purpose ordained by fate.
1. I.e., unless.
2. I.e., became somewhat disconcerted.

And houséd is within her hollow brest,
That either seemes some curséd witches deed,
Or evill spright, that in her doth such torment breed."

19

The wisard could no lenger beare her bord,°   *talk*
But brusting° forth in laughter, to her sayd;   *bursting*
"Glauce, what needs this colourable° word,   *deceptive*
To cloke the cause, that hath it selfe bewrayd?
Ne ye faire Britomartis, thus arayd,
More hidden are, then Sunne in cloudy vele;
Whom thy good fortune, having fate obayd,
Hath hither brought, for succour to appele:
The which the powres to thee are pleaséd to revele."

20

The doubtfull° Mayd, seeing her selfe descryde,   *apprehensive*
Was all abasht, and her pure yvory
Into a cleare Carnation suddeine dyde;
As faire Aurora rising hastily,
Doth by her blushing tell, that she did lye
All night in old Tithonus frosen bed,
Whereof she seemes ashaméd inwardly.
But her old Nourse was nought dishartenéd,
But vauntage made of that, which Merlin had ared.°   *said*

21

And sayd, "Sith then thou knowest all our griefe,
(For what doest not thou know?) of grace I pray,
Pitty our plaint, and yield us meet° reliefe."   *suitable*
With that the Prophet still awhile did stay,
And then his spirite thus gan forth display;°   *show*
"Most noble Virgin, that by fatall lore[3]
Hast learned to love, let no whit thee dismay
The hard begin, that meets thee in the dore,
And with sharpe fits thy tender hart oppresseth sore.

22

"For so must all things excellent begin,
And eke enrooted deepe must be that Tree,
Whose big embodied braunches shall not lin,°   *cease*
Till they to heavens hight forth stretchéd bee.
For from thy wombe a famous Progenie
Shall spring, out of the auncient Trojan blood,[4]

3. I.e., fated knowledge.
4. Belief that Britons (Celtic tribes in Britain before the Anglo-Saxon invasions) were descended,
   through Brute, from Aeneas and his Trojans echoes regularly in the age's literature. But doubt
   was growing (the debate was politicized as skeptics affirmed a Germanic heritage with a larger role
   for parliaments). Spenser accepts the legend in II.x.5–13 and III.ix.38–51 but rejects it in his prose
   View; see Anderson 1987.

Which shall revive the sleeping memorie
Of those same antique Peres° the heavens brood,   *champions*
Which Greeke and Asian rivers stainéd with their blood.

23

"Renowméd kings, and sacred Emperours,
    Thy fruitfull Ofspring, shall from thee descend;
    Brave Captaines, and most mighty warriours,
    That shall their conquests through all lands extend,
    And their decayéd kingdomes shall amend:°   *restore*
    The feeble Britons, broken with long warre,
    They shall upreare, and mightily defend
    Against their forrein foe, that comes from farre,
Till universall peace compound° all civill jarre.   *settle*

24

"It was not, Britomart, thy wandring eye,
    Glauncing unwares in charméd looking glas,
    But the streight° course of heavenly destiny,   *strict*
    Led with eternall providence, that has
    Guided thy glaunce, to bring his will to pas:
    Ne is thy fate, ne is thy fortune ill,
    To love the prowest° knight, that ever was.   *bravest*
    Therefore submit thy wayes unto his will,
And do by all dew meanes thy destiny fulfill."

25

"But read,"° said Glauce, "thou Magitian   *tell*
    What meanes shall she out seeke, or what wayes take?
    How shall she know, how shall she find the man?
    Or what needs her to toyle, sith fates can make
    Way for themselves, their purpose to partake?"°   *accomplish*
    Then Merlin thus; "Indeed the fates are firme,
    And may not shrinck, though all the world do shake:
    Yet ought mens good endevours them confirme,
And guide the heavenly causes to their constant terme.[5]

26

"The man whom heavens have ordaynd to bee
    The spouse of Britomart, is Arthegall:[6]
    He wonneth° in the land of Fayeree,   *dwells*
    Yet is no Fary borne, ne sib° at all   *related*
    To Elfes, but sprong of seed terrestriall,

---

5. I.e., fixed outcome. Here and in stanzas 21–22, Merlin assumes that virtuous men and women
   actively cooperate with Providence. Britomart's love for Arthegall, demanding and formative, makes
   part of her divinely appointed destiny.
6. Stanzas 26–28 prepare for the alignment of the Tudors with Britain's ancient rulers that culminates
   at stanza 49, when Arthegall is connected with Arthur, son of Uther Pendragon and Igerne (wife
   of Gorlois). The circumstances of Arthegall's birth and upbringing associate him also with Redcrosse
   (cf. I.x.65–66). Arthur's quest for Gloriana is reflected and balanced by that of Britomart for
   Arthegall.

And whilome by false Faries stolne away,
Whiles yet in infant cradle he did crall;°   *crawl*
Ne other to himselfe is knowne this day,
But that he by an Elfe was gotten° of a Fay.   *begot*

27

"But sooth he is the sonne of Gorlois,
And brother unto Cador Cornish king,[7]
And for his warlike feates renowméd is,
From where the day out of the sea doth spring,
Untill the closure° of the Evening.   *limit*
From thence, him firmely bound with faithfull band,° *bond*
To this his native soyle thou backe shalt bring,
Strongly to aide his countrey, to withstand
The powre of forrein Paynims,° which invade thy land. *pagans*

28

"Great aid thereto his mighty puissaunce,
And dreaded name shall give in that sad day:
Where also proofe of thy prow° valiaunce   *courageous*
Thou then shalt make, t'increase thy lovers pray
Long time ye both in armes shall beare great sway,
Till thy wombes burden thee from them do call,
And his last fate him from thee take away,
Too rathe° cut off by practise criminall   *soon*
Of secret foes, that him shall make in mischiefe° fall. *misfortune*

29

"With thee yet shall he leave for memory
Of his late puissaunce, his Image dead,[8]
That living him in all activity
To thee shall represent. He from the head
Of his coosin Constantius without dread
Shall take the crowne, that was his fathers right,
And there with crowne himselfe in th'others stead:[9]
Then shall he issew forth with dreadfull might,
Against his Saxon foes in bloudy field to fight.

30

"Like as a Lyon, that in drowsie cave
Hath long time slept, himselfe so shall he shake,
And comming forth, shall spred his banner brave
Over the troubled South, that it shall make

7. According to Geoffrey (9.1, 5), Cador helped Arthur fight the Saxons.
8. I.e., Arthegall's son, the image of his deceased father.
9. Constantine, son of Cador, succeeded Arthur; soon he was killed by his nephew Conan (*Historia* 11.4–5). From this point to the end of the canto, Spenser depends heavily on Geoffrey and Holinshed, diverging occasionally to take account of other chroniclers; now and then he departs altogether from these sources (e.g., Conan's wars with the Mercians, in stanza 30; the Saxons' defeat by Careticus, in stanza 33; and the manner of Pellite's death, in stanza 36).

The warlike Mertians[1] for feare to quake:
Thrise shall he fight with them, and twise shall win,
But the third time shall faire accordaunce° make: *agreement*
And if he then with victorie can lin,°   *cease*
He shall his dayes with peace bring to his earthly In.°   *dwelling*

31

"His sonne, hight Vortipore, shall him succeede
  In kingdome, but not in felicity;
  Yet shall he long time warre with happy speed,°   *success*
  And with great honour many battels try:°   *undertake*
  But at the last to th'importunity
  Of froward° fortune shall be forst to yield.   *perverse*
  But his sonne Malgo shall full mightily
  Avenge his fathers losse, with speare and shield,
And his proud foes discomfit in victorious field.

32

"Behold the man, and tell me Britomart,
  If ay° more goodly creature thou didst see;   *ever*
  How like a Gyaunt in each manly part
  Beares he himselfe with portly° majestee,   *dignified*
  That one of th'old Heroés seemes to bee:
  He the six Islands,[2] comprovinciall
  In auncient times unto great Britainee,
  Shall to the same reduce,° and to him call   *restore*
Their sundry kings to do their homage severall.°   *diverse*

33

"All which his sonne Careticus awhile
  Shall well defend, and Saxons powre suppresse,
  Untill a straunger king from unknowne soyle
  Arriving, him with multitude oppresse;
  Great Gormond,[3] having with huge mightinesse
  Ireland subdewd, and therein fixt his throne,
  Like a swift Otter, fell° through emptinesse,   *fierce*
  Shall overswim the sea with many one
Of his Norveyses,° to assist the Britons fone.°   *Norwegians/foes*

34

"He in his furie all shall overrunne,
  And holy Church with faithlesse hands deface,
  That thy sad people utterly fordonne,°   *ruined*
  Shall to the utmost mountaines fly apace:

1. An Anglian tribe, who established the kingdom of Mercia, in south-central England, during the
   sixth century.
2. I.e., Iceland, Norway, the Orkneys, Ireland, Gotland, and Dacia (Denmark).
3. In making Gormond a Norwegian king, Spenser follows the *History of Ireland* by Richard Stanyhurst
   and Edward Campion (included by Holinshed in his *Chronicles*); Geoffrey (11.8) calls him "king
   of the Africans."

Was never so great wast° in any place,   *destruction*
Nor so fowle outrage doen by living men:
For all thy Cities they shall sacke and race,°   *raze*
And the greene grasse, that groweth, they shall bren,°   *burn*
That even the wild beast shall dy in starvéd den.

35

"Whiles thus thy Britons do in languour° pine,   *sorrow*
    Proud Etheldred[4] shall from the North arise,
    Serving th' ambitious will of Augustine,
    And passing Dee with hardy enterprise,
    Shall backe repulse the valiaunt Brockwell twise,
    And Bangor with massacred Martyrs fill;
    But the third time shall rew his foolhardise:°   *folly*
    For Cadwan pittying his peoples ill,
Shall stoutly him defeat, and thousand Saxons kill.

36

"But after him, Cadwallin mightily
    On his sonne Edwin all those wrongs shall wreake;°   *avenge*
    Ne shall availe the wicked sorcery
    Of false Pellite, his purposes to breake,
    But him shall slay, and on a gallowes bleake
    Shall give th'enchaunter his unhappy hire;°   *reward*
    Then shall the Britons, late dismayd and weake,
    From their long vassalage gin to respire,°   *recover*
And on their Paynim foes avenge theirranckled° ire.   *embittered*

37

"Ne shall he yet his wrath so mitigate,
    Till both the sonnes of Edwin he have slaine,
    Offricke and Osricke, twinnes unfortunate,
    Both slaine in battell upon Layburne plaine,
    Together with the king of Louthiane,
    Hight Adin, and the king of Orkeny,
    Both joynt partakers of their fatall° paine: *fated*
    But Penda, fearefull of like desteny,
Shall yield him selfe his liegeman, and sweare fealty.

38

"Him shall he make his fatall Instrument,
    T'afflict the other Saxons unsubdewd;
    He marching forth with fury insolent
    Against the good king Oswald, who indewd°   *invested*
    With heavenly powre, and by Angels reskewd,
    All holding crosses in their hands on hye,
    Shall him defeate withouten bloud imbrewd:°   *spilt*

4. In stanzas 35–39, Spenser alters Geoffrey's names and events to conform with other Welsh and
English sources.

Of which, that field for endlesse memory,
Shall Hevenfield be cald to all posterity.

39

"Where at Cadwallin wroth, shall forth issew,
    And an huge hoste into Northumber lead,
    With which he godly Oswald shall subdew,
    And crowne with martyrdome his sacred head.
    Whose brother Oswin, daunted with like dread,
    With price of silver shall his kingdome buy,°   *ransom*
    And Penda, seeking him adowne to tread,
    Shall tread adowne, and do him fowly dye,⁵
But shall with gifts his Lord Cadwallin pacify.

40

"Then shall Cadwallin dye, and then the raine
    Of Britons eke with him attonce° shall dye;   *forthwith*
    Ne shall the good Cadwallader with paine,
    Or powre, be hable it to remedy,
    When the full time prefixt by destiny,
    Shalbe expird of Britons regiment.°   *rule*
    For heaven it selfe shall their successe envy,
    And them with plagues and murrins° pestilent   *diseases*
Consume, till all their warlike puissaunce be spent.

41

"Yet after all these sorrowes, and huge hills
    Of dying people, during eight yeares space,
    Cadwallader not yielding to his ills,
    From Armoricke,⁶ where long in wretched cace°   *state*
    He lived, returning⁷ to his native place,
    Shalbe by vision staid from his intent:
    For th'heavens have decreéd, to displace
    The Britons, for their sinnes dew punishment,
And to the Saxons over-give° their government.   *give up*

42

"Then woe, and woe, and everlasting woe,
    Be to the Briton babe, that shalbe borne,
    To live in thraldome of° his fathers foe;   *to*
    Late King, now captive, late Lord, now forlorne,
    The worlds reproch, the cruell victors scorne,
    Banisht from Princely bowre° to wastfull° wood: *chamber/desolate*
    O who shall helpe me to lament, and mourne

5. I.e., and Oswin shall defeat Penda (who sought to defeat Oswin) and put him miserably to death.
6. The old name for Brittany, by Spenser's day part of northwestern France.
7. I.e., expecting to return.

The royall seed, the antique Trojan blood,
Whose Empire lenger here, then ever any stood."[8]

43

The Damzell was full deepe empassionéd,°   *moved*
  Both for his griefe, and for her peoples sake,
  Whose future woes so plaine he fashionéd,
  And sighing sore, at length him thus bespake,
  "Ah but will heavens fury never slake,°   *slacken*
  Nor vengeaunce huge relent it selfe at last?
  Will not long misery late° mercy make,   *at length*
  But shall their name for ever be defast,°   *destroyed*
And quite from of the earth their memory be rast?"°   *erased*

44

"Nay but the terme," said he, "is limited,
  That in this thraldome Britons shall abide,
  And the just revolution[9] measuréd,
  That they as Straungers shalbe notifide.°   *known*
  For twise foure hundreth yeares shalbe supplide,
  Ere they to former rule restored shalbee,[1]
  And their importune° fates all satisfide: *grievous*
  Yet during this their most obscuritee,
Their beames shall oft breake forth, that men them faire may see.

45

"For Rhodoricke,[2] whose surname shalbe Great,
  Shall of him selfe a brave ensample shew,
  That Saxon kings his friendship shall intreat:
  And Howell Dha shall goodly well indew
  The salvage minds with skill of just and trew;
  Then Griffyth Conan also shall up reare
  His dreaded head, and the old sparkes renew
  Of native courage, that his foes shall feare,
Least backe againe the kingdome he from them should beare.°   *take*

46

"Ne shall the Saxons selves all peaceably
  Enjoy the crowne, which they from Britons wonne
  First ill, and after ruléd wickedly:
  For ere two hundred yeares be full outronne,
  There shall a Raven[3] far from rising Sunne,
  With his wide wings upon them fiercely fly,

---

8. Reckoning from the arrival of Brute, supposedly in 1132 B.C., to the death of Cadwallader, c. A.D. 690.
9. I.e., exact cycle.
1. I.e., with the reign of Henry VII, who came to the throne in 1485, almost exactly eight hundred years after Cadwallader's death.
2. These Welsh rulers reigned within the period from A.D. 843 to 1136.
3. The (heathen) Danes, who first invaded England in A.D. 787.

And bid his faithlesse chickens overrone
The fruitfull plaines, and with fell cruelty,
In their avenge, tread downe the victours surquedry.°　　　*presumption*

47

"Yet shall a third both these, and thine subdew;
　There shall a Lyon[4] from the sea-bord wood
　Of Neustria come roring, with a crew
　Of hungry whelpes, his battailous° bold brood,　　　*warlike*
　Whose clawes were newly dipt in cruddy° blood,　　　*clotted*
　That from the Daniske Tyrants head shall rend
　Th'usurpéd crowne, as if that he were wood,°　　　*mad*
　And the spoile of the countrey conqueréd
Emongst his young ones shall divide with bountyhed.°　　　*generosity*

48

"Tho when the terme is full accomplishid,
　There shall a sparke of fire,[5] which hath longwhile
　Bene in his ashes rakéd up, and hid,
　Be freshly kindled in the fruitfull Ile
　Of Mona, where it lurkéd in exile;
　Which shall breake forth into bright burning flame,
　And reach into the house, that beares the stile°　　　*title*
　Of royall majesty and soveraigne name;°　　　*reputation*
So shall the Briton bloud their crowne againe reclame.

49

"Thenceforth eternall union shall be made
　Betweene the nations different afore,
　And sacred Peace shall lovingly perswade
　The warlike minds, to learne her goodly lore,°　　　*doctrine*
　And civile armes to exercise no more:
　Then shall a royall virgin[6] raine, which shall
　Stretch her white rod over the Belgicke shore,
　And the great Castle smite so sore with all,
That it shall make him shake, and shortly learne to fall.

50

"But yet the end is not." There Merlin stayd,°　　　*ceased*
　As° overcomen of the spirites powre,　　　*as if*
　Or other ghastly spectacle dismayd,
　That secretly he saw, yet note discoure:[7]
　Which suddein fit, and halfe extatick stoure°　　　*paroxysm*

---

4. William I of Normandy.
5. Henry VII was born in Anglesey (Mona), the last British territory possessed by the Welsh prince Llewelyn ap Griffith under the terms of his treaty with Edward I in 1283.
6. Queen Elizabeth, whose navy turned back the galleons (or "great castles") of the Spanish Armada in 1588, and whose troops (from 1585 onward) were actively engaged in the Low Countries against those of Spain (Castile).
7. I.e., would not reveal.

When the two fearefull women saw, they grew
  Greatly confuséd in behavioure;
  At last the fury° past, to former hew°   *seizure/appearance*
Hee turnd againe, and chearefull looks as earst° did shew.   *before*

51

Then, when them selves they well instructed had
  Of all, that needed them to be inquird,
  They both conceiving hope of comfort glad,
  With lighter hearts unto their home retird;
  Where they in secret counsell close conspird,
  How to effect so hard an enterprize,
  And to possesse° the purpose they desird: *achieve*
  Now this, now that twixt them they did devise,
And diverse plots did frame, to maske in strange disguise.

52

At last the Nourse in her foolhardy wit
  Conceived a bold devise,° and thus bespake;   *plan*
  "Daughter, I deeme that counsell aye most fit,
  That of the time doth dew advauntage take;
  Ye see that good king Uther now doth make
  Strong warre upon the Paynim brethren, hight
  Octa and Oza, whom he lately brake
  Beside Cayr Verolame, in victorious fight,
That now all Britanie doth burne in armés bright.[8]

53

"That therefore nought our passage may empeach,°   *hinder*
  Let us in feignéd armes our selves disguize,
  And our weake hands (whom need new strength shall teach)
  The dreadfull speare and shield to exercize:
  Ne certes daughter that same warlike wize°   *manner*
  I weene, would you misseme°; for ye bene tall,   *not be fitting*
  And large of limbe, t'atchieve an hard emprize,
  Ne ought ye want,° but skill, which practize small *lack*
Will bring, and shortly make you a mayd Martiall.

54

"And sooth, it ought your courage much inflame,
  To heare so often, in that royall hous,
  From whence to none inferiour ye came,
  Bards tell of many women valorous
  Which have full many feats adventurous
  Performd, in paragone° of proudest men: *emulation*
  The bold Bunduca, whose victorious

8. These events, described in Geoffrey (8.23), would have taken place about A.D. 470–80, approximately the supposed time of Arthur.

Exploits made Rome to quake, stout Guendolen,
Renowméd Martia, and redoubted Emmilen.[9]

55

"And that, which more than all the rest may sway,°   *move*
Late dayes ensample, which these eyes beheld,
In the last field before Menevia[1]
Which Uther with those forrein Pagans held,
I saw a Saxon Virgin,[2] the which feld
Great Ulfin thrise upon the bloudy plaine,
And had not Carados her hand withheld
From rash revenge, she had him surely slaine,
Yet Carados himselfe from her escapt with paine."°   *difficulty*

56

"Ah read," quoth Britomart, "how is she hight?"
"Faire Angela," quoth she, "men do her call,
No whit lesse faire, then terrible in fight:
She hath the leading of a Martiall
And mighty people, dreaded more then all
The other Saxons, which do for her sake
And love, themselves of her name Angles call.
Therefore faire Infant her ensample make
Unto thy selfe, and equall courage to thee take."

57

Her harty° words so deepe into the mynd   *spirited*
Of the young Damzell sunke, that great desire
Of warlike armes in her forthwith they tynd,°   *kindled*
And generous stout courage did inspire,
That she resolved, unweeting° to her Sire,   *unknown*
Advent'rous knighthood on her selfe to don,
And counseld with her Nourse, her Maides attire
To turne into a massy habergeon,°   *coat of mail*
And bad her all things put in readinesse anon.

58

Th'old woman nought, that needed, did omit;
But all things did conveniently purvay:°   *provide*
It fortunéd (so time their turne did fit)[3]
A band of Britons ryding on forray°   *a raid*
Few dayes before, had gotten a great pray°   *booty*

9. Boadicea, queen of the Iceni in southeastern England, led a revolt against the Romans in A.D.
   61; Gwendolen, daughter of Corineus, slew her unfaithful husband in battle and ruled Cornwall
   for fifteen years; Marcia, wife of the British king Guithelin, was renowned for learning and statecraft;
   "Emmilen" is perhaps Charlemagne's daughter, but Spenser also gives the name to the mother
   of Sir Tristram (VI.ii.29).
1. St. Davids; cf. Geoffrey 8.16.
2. Angela, identified with the Saxon queen for whom England was named; Spenser invented this
   story or used some now lost source.
3. I.e., events fell out suitably for their needs.

Of Saxon goods, emongst the which was seene
A goodly Armour, and full rich aray,°   *equipment*
Which longed to Angela, the Saxon Queene,
All fretted° round with gold, and goodly well beseene.   *adorned*

59

The same, with all the other ornaments,
  King Ryence causéd to be hangéd hy
  In his chiefe Church, for endlesse moniments°   *memorials*
  Of his successe and gladfull victory:
  Of which her selfe avising° readily,   *calling to mind*
  In th'evening late old Glauce thither led
  Faire Britomart, and that same Armory°   *armor*
  Downe taking, her therein appareléd,
Well as she might, and with brave bauldrick° garnishéd. *shoulder belt*

60

Beside those armes there stood a mighty speare,
  Which Bladud[4] made by Magick art of yore,
  And usd the same in battell aye to beare;
  Sith which it had bin here preserved in store,
  For his great vertues° provéd long afore: *powers*
  For never wight so fast in sell° could sit,   *saddle*
  But him perforce unto the ground it bore:
  Both speare she tooke, and shield, which hong by it:
Both speare and shield of great powre, for her purpose fit.

61

Thus when she had the virgin all arayd,
  Another harnesse,° which did hang thereby,   *set of armor*
  About her selfe she dight, that the young Mayd
  She might in equall armes accompany,
  And as her Squire attend her carefully:
  Tho to their ready Steeds they clombe full light,°   *easily*
  And through back wayes, that none might them espy,
  Covered with secret cloud of silent night,
Themselves they forth convayd, and passéd forward right.

62

Ne rested they, till that to Faery lond
  They came, as Merlin them directed late:
  Where meeting with this Redcrosse knight, she fond
  Of diverse things discourses to dilate,°   *enlarge upon*
  But most of Arthegall, and his estate.°   *condition*
  At last their wayes so fell, that they mote part:
  Then each to other well affectionate,°   *disposed*

4. A British king renowned for his magic. Britomart's arms, Saxon and Celtic in origin, implicitly combine the strengths of both races; in them magic has been sanctified by religious faith.

Friendship professéd with unfainéd hart,
The Redcrosse knight diverst, but forth° rode Britomart.   *forward*

Canto IV

Bold Marinell of Britomart,
    Is throwne on the Rich strond:°   *shore*
Faire Florimell of Arthur is
    Long followed, but not fond.°   *found*

1

Where is the Antique glory now become,°   *gone*
  That whilome wont in women to appeare?
Where be the brave atchievements doen by some?
Where be the battels, where the shield and speare,
And all the conquests, which them high did reare,
That matter made for famous Poets verse,
And boastfull men so oft abasht to heare?
Bene they all dead, and laid in dolefull herse?
Or doen they onely sleepe, and shall againe reverse?°   *return*

2

If they be dead, then woe is me therefore:
  But if they sleepe, O let them soone awake:
For all too long I burne with envy° sore,   *longing*
To heare the warlike feates, which Homere spake
Of bold Penthesilee,[1] which made a lake
Of Greekish bloud so oft in Trojan plaine;
But when I read, how stout Debora strake
Proud Sisera, and how Camill' hath slaine
The huge Orsilochus, I swell with great disdaine.°   *indignation*

3

Yet these, and all that else had puissaunce,
  Cannot with noble Britomart compare,
Aswell for glory of great valiaunce,°   *valor*
As for pure chastitie and vertue rare,
That all her goodly deeds do well declare.
Well worthy stock, from which the branches sprong,
That in late yeares so faire a blossome bare,
As thee, O Queene, the matter° of my song,   *theme*
Whose lignage from this Lady I derive along.°   *throughout*

4

Who when through speaches with the Redcrosse knight,
  She learnéd had th'estate of Arthegall,

---

1. Homer does not mention the Amazon queen Penthesilea, but she appears briefly in *Aeneid* 1.490–95; on Camilla and Orsilochus, see 11.690–98. The Israelite heroine Jaël killed Sisera, a patriotic murder engineered and celebrated by the judge Deborah (Judges 4).

And in each point her selfe informd aright,
A friendly league of love perpetuall
She with him bound, and Congé° tooke withall.   *leave*
Then he forth on his journey did proceede,
To seeke adventures, which mote him befall,
And win him worship° through his warlike deed,   *renown*
Which alwayes of his paines he made the chiefest meed.°   *reward*

5

But Britomart kept on her former course,
Ne ever dofte° her armes, but all the way   *took off*
Grew pensive through that amorous discourse,
By which the Redcrosse knight did earst display°   *set forth*
Her lovers shape, and chevalrous aray;
A thousand thoughts she fashioned in her mind,
And in her feigning fancie did pourtray
Him such, as fittest she for love could find,
Wise, warlike, personable, curteous, and kind.

6

With such selfe-pleasing thoughts her wound she fed,
And thought so to beguile° her grievous smart;   *charm away*
But so her smart was much more grievous bred,
And the deepe wound more deepe engord her hart,
That nought but death her dolour mote depart.°   *remove*
So forth she rode without repose or rest,
Searching all lands and each remotest part,
Following the guidance of her blinded guest,[2]
Till that to the sea-coast at length she her addrest.

7

There she alighted from her light-foot beast,
And sitting downe upon the rocky shore,
Bad her old Squire unlace her lofty creast;°   *helmet*
Tho having vewd a while the surges hore,°   *gray*
That gainst the craggy clifts did loudly rore,
And in their raging surquedry° disdaynd,   *arrogance*
That the fast° earth affronted them so sore,   *firm*
And their devouring covetize restraynd,
Thereat she sighéd deepe, and after thus complaynd.[3]

8

"Huge sea of sorrow, and tempestuous griefe,
Wherein my feeble barke° is tosséd long,   *vessel*
Far from the hopéd haven of reliefe,

2. I.e., Cupid, god of love.
3. The central conceit of Britomart's "complaint" (likening herself to a ship in a storm) appears often in Renaissance love lyrics, most famously in Petrarch's *Rime* 189 (cf. Wyatt's "My galley charged" and *Amoretti* 34). Wofford 1987 argues that Spenser here examines Petrarchism, interiority, and the allegorical representation of human emotion.

Why do thy cruell billowes beat so strong,
And thy moyst mountaines each on others throng,
Threatning to swallow up my fearefull life?
O do thy cruell wrath and spightfull wrong
At length allay, and stint° thy stormy strife,   *cease*
Which in these troubled bowels raignes, and rageth rife.°   *strongly*

9

"For else my feeble vessell crazd,° and crackt   *weakened*
Through thy strong buffets and outrageous blowes,
Cannot endure, but needs it must be wrackt
On the rough rocks, or on the sandy shallowes,
The whiles that love it steres, and fortune rowes;
Love my lewd° Pilot hath a restlesse mind   *unskillful*
And fortune Boteswaine no assurance° knowes,   *certainty*
But saile withouten starres gainst tide and wind:
How can they other do, sith both are bold and blind?

10

"Thou God of winds, that raignest in the seas,
That raignest also in the Continent,°   *land*
At last blow up some gentle gale of ease,
The which may bring my ship, ere it be rent,°   *torn apart*
Unto the gladsome port of her intent:°   *purpose*
Then when I shall my selfe in safety see,
A table° for eternall moniment   *votive tablet*
Of thy great grace, and my great jeopardee,
Great Neptune, I avow to hallow unto thee."

11

Then sighing softly sore, and inly deepe,
She shut up all her plaint in privy° griefe;   *secret*
For her great courage° would not let her weepe,   *spirit*
Till that old Glauce gan with sharpe repriefe,°   *reproof*
Her to restraine, and give her good reliefe,
Through hope of those, which Merlin had her told
Should of her name and nation be chiefe,
And fetch their being from the sacred mould°   *form*
Of her immortall wombe, to be in heaven enrold.

12

Thus as she her recomforted, she spyde,
Where farre away one all in armour bright,[4]

4. I.e., Marinell, whose name expresses his tie to the sea and whose self-absorption precludes love.
Britomart's spear shatters this complacency, the wound opening him to more adult affections. It
is relevant that elsewhere Spenser identifies "Beautie, and money" as "engins" threatening the
"bulwarke of the Sight" (II.xi.9); guarding a "Rich strond," Marinell has the wealth that rivals
beauty as an object of human desire. Men seek beauty, the allegory semisatirically implies, while
women seek riches: "they for love of him would algates dy" (stanza 26). Marinell's opposition to
Britomart thus also figures an obsession with riches at the cost of other loves.

With hastie gallop towards her did ryde;
Her dolour soone she ceast, and on her dight
Her Helmet, to her Courser mounting light:
Her former sorrow into suddein wrath,
Both coosen° passions of distroubled spright,   *kindred*
Converting, forth she beates the dustie path;
Love and despight° attonce her courage kindled hath.   *defiance*

13

As when a foggy mist hath overcast
  The face of heaven, and the cleare aire engrost,°   *thickened*
  The world in darkenesse dwels, till that at last
  The watry Southwinde from the seabord cost
  Upblowing, doth disperse the vapour lo'st,°   *released*
  And poures it selfe forth in a stormy showre;
  So the faire Britomart having disclo'st
  Her clowdy care into a wrathfull stowre,[5]
The mist of griefe dissolved, did into vengeance powre.

14

Eftsoones her goodly shield addressing° faire,   *adjusting*
  That mortall speare she in her hand did take,
  And unto battell did her selfe prepaire.
  The knight approching, sternely her bespake;
  "Sir knight, that doest thy voyage rashly make
  By this forbidden way in my despight,[6]
  Ne doest by others death ensample take,
  I read° thee soone retyre, whiles thou hast might,   *advise*
Least afterwards it be too late to take thy flight."

15

Ythrild° with deepe disdaine of his proud threat,   *deeply moved*
  She shortly thus; "Fly they, that need to fly;
  Words fearen° babes. I meane not thee entreat   *frighten*
  To passe; but maugre° thee will passe or dy."   *in spite of*
  Ne lenger stayd for th'other to reply,
  But with sharpe speare the rest made dearly° knowne.   *resolutely*
  Strongly the straunge knight ran, and sturdily
  Strooke her full on the brest, that made her downe
Decline her head, and touch her crouper with her crowne.[7]

16

But she againe° him in the shield did smite   *in return*
  With so fierce furie and great puissaunce,
  That through his threesquare scuchin° percing quite,   *shield*
  And through his mayléd hauberque,° by mischaunce   *coat of mail*

---

5. I.e., having relieved her gloomy despondency by an outburst of anger.
6. I.e., in scorn of me.
7. I.e., that forced her backward so far that her head touched her horse's back (or crupper).

The wicked steele through his left side did glaunce;
Him so transfixéd she before her bore
Beyond his croupe, the length of all her launce,
Till sadly soucing° on the sandie shore,   *falling*
He tombled on° an heape, and wallowd in his gore.   *in*

17

Like as the sacred Oxe, that carelesse stands,
With gilden hornes, and flowry girlonds crownd,
Proud of his dying honor and deare bands,°   *bonds*
Whiles th' altars fume with frankincense arownd,
All suddenly with mortall stroke astownd,°   *stunned*
Doth groveling fall, and with his streaming gore
Distaines° the pillours, and the holy grownd,   *stains*
And the faire flowres, that deckéd him afore;
So fell proud Marinell upon the pretious shore.

18

The martiall Mayd stayd not him to lament,
But forward rode, and kept her readie way
Along the strond, which as she over-went,°   *traversed*
She saw bestrowéd all with rich aray
Of pearles and pretious stones of great assay,°   *worth*
And all the gravell mixt with golden owre;°   *ore*
Whereat she wondred much, but would not stay
For gold, or perles, or pretious stones an howre,
But them despiséd all; for° all was in her powre.   *although*

19

Whiles thus he lay in deadly stonishment,°   *swoon*
Tydings hereof came to his mothers eare;
His mother was the blacke-browd Cymoent,[8]
The daughter of great Nereus, which did beare
This warlike sonne unto an earthly peare,°   *noble*
The famous Dumarin; who on a day
Finding the Nymph a sleepe in secret wheare,°   *place*
As he by chaunce did wander that same way,
Was taken with her love, and by her closely lay.

20

There he this knight of her begot, whom borne
She of his father Marinell did name,
And in a rocky cave as wight forlorne,
Long time she fostred up, till he became
A mightie man at armes, and mickle° fame   *much*

8. Cymoent (from Greek, "wave") was one of fifty Nereids (sea nymphs). Her son's conception, and
her efforts to preserve him, recall Thetis's futile attempt to make her son, Achilles, invulnerable
(*Metamorphoses* 11.217–65; 13.162–70). Goldberg 1975 shows how Book III indicates maternity's
power to nurture but also to smother offspring in matter: for Marinell, "Cupidity replaces erotic
energy."

Did get through great adventures by him donne:
For never man he suffred by that same
Rich strond to travell, whereas he did wonne,°   *dwell*
But that he must do battell with the Sea-nymphes sonne.

21

An hundred knights of honorable name
He had subdewed, and them his vassals made,
That through all Farie lond his noble fame
Now blazéd° was, and feare did all invade,°   *proclaimed/afflict*
That none durst passen through that perilous glade.
And to advaunce° his name and glorie more,   *heighten*
Her Sea-god syre she dearely° did perswade,°   *boldly/entreat*
T'endow her sonne with threasure and rich store,
Bove all the sonnes, that were of earthly wombes ybore.

22

The God did graunt his daughters deare demaund,
To doen° his Nephew in all riches flow;   *make*
Eftsoones his heapéd waves he did commaund,
Out of their hollow bosome forth to throw
All the huge threasure, which the sea below
Had in his greedie gulfe devouréd deepe,
And him enrichéd through the overthrow
And wreckes of many wretches, which did weepe,
And often waile their wealth, which he from them did keepe.

23

Shortly upon that shore there heapéd was,
Exceeding riches and all pretious things,
The spoyle of all the world, that it did pas
The wealth of th'East, and pompe of Persian kings;
Gold, amber, yvorie, perles, owches,° rings,   *brooches*
And all that else was pretious and deare,°   *valuable*
The sea unto him voluntary brings,
That shortly he a great Lord did appeare,
As was in all the lond of Faery, or elsewheare.

24

Thereto he was a doughtie dreaded knight,
Tryde often to the scath° of many deare,°   *harm/dearly*
That none in equall armes him matchen might,
The which his mother seeing, gan to feare
Least his too haughtie hardines might reare°   *cause*
Some hard mishap, in hazard of⁹ his life:
For thy she oft him counseld to forbeare
The bloudie battell, and to stirre up strife,
But after all his warre, to rest his wearie knife.°   *sword*

9. I.e., to endanger.

25

And for his more assurance,° she inquired   *security*
  One day of Proteus[1] by his mightie spell,°   *magic charm*
  (For Proteus was with prophecie inspired)
  Her deare sonnes destinie to her to tell,
  And the sad end of her sweet Marinell.
  Who through foresight of his eternall skill,°   *knowledge*
  Bad her from womankind to keepe him well:
  For of a woman he should have much ill,
A virgin strange and stout° him should dismay, or kill.   *bold*

26

For thy she gave him warning every day,
  The love of women not to entertaine;°   *accept*
  A lesson too too hard for living clay,
  From love in course of nature to refraine:
  Yet he his mothers lore did well retaine,
  And ever from faire Ladies love did fly;
  Yet many Ladies faire did oft complaine,
  That they for love of him would algates° dy: *entirely*
Dy, who so list for him, he was loves enimy.

27

But ah, who can deceive his destiny,
  Or weene by warning to avoyd his fate?
  That when he sleepes in most security,
  And safest seemes, him soonest doth amate,°   *dismay*
  And findeth dew effect or soone or late.
  So feeble is the powre of fleshly arme.
  His mother bad him womens love to hate,
  For she of womans force did feare no harme;
So weening to have armed him, she did quite disarme.

28

This was that woman, this that deadly wound,
  That Proteus prophecide should him dismay,
  The which his mother vainely° did expound,   *wrongly*
  To be hart-wounding love, which should assay°   *assault*
  To bring her sonne unto his last decay.
  So tickle° be the termes of mortall state,°   *uncertain/condition*
  And full of subtile sophismes, which do play
  With double senses, and with false debate,
T'approve° the unknowen purpose of eternall fate.   *demonstrate*

1. A sea god who could foretell the future and change his shape at will: cf. Ovid, *Metamorphoses* 11.249–56, and Homer, *Odyssey* 4.384 ff.

29

Too true the famous Marinell it fownd,
  Who through late triall, on that wealthy Strond
  Inglorious now lies in senselesse swownd,
  Through heavy° stroke of Britomartis hond.   *grievous*
  Which when his mother deare did understond,
  And heavy tydings heard, whereas she playd
  Amongst her watry sisters by a pond,
  Gathering sweet daffadillyes, to have made
Gay girlonds, from the Sun their forheads faire to shade;

30

Eftsoones both flowres and girlonds farre away
  She flong, and her faire deawy lockes yrent,°   *tore*
  To sorrow huge she turnd her former play,
  And gamesom merth to grievous dreriment:
  She threw her selfe downe on the Continent,°   *ground*
  Ne word did speake, but lay as in a swowne,
  Whiles all her sisters did for her lament,
  With yelling outcries, and with shrieking sowne;°   *sound*
And every one did teare her girlond from her crowne.

31

Soone as she up out of her deadly fit°   *swoon*
  Arose, she bad her charet° to be brought,   *chariot*
  And all her sisters, that with her did sit,
  Bad eke attonce their charets to be sought;
  Tho full of bitter griefe and pensive thought,
  She to her wagon clombe;° clombe all the rest,   *mounted*
  And forth together went, with sorrow fraught.
  The waves obedient to their beheast,°   *bidding*
Them yielded readie passage, and their rage surceast.

32

Great Neptune stood amazéd at their sight,
  Whiles on his broad round backe they softly slid
  And eke himselfe mournd at their mournfull plight,
  Yet wist not what their wailing ment, yet did
  For great compassion of their sorrow, bid
  His mightie waters to them buxome° bee: *yielding*
  Eftsoones the roaring billowes still abid,°   *remained*
  And all the griesly° Monsters of the See   *horrible*
Stood gaping at their gate, and wondred them to see.

33

A teme of Dolphins raungéd in aray,
  Drew the smooth charet of sad Cymoent;
  They were all taught by Triton, to obay

To the long raynes, at her commaundément:
As swift as swallowes, on the waves they went,
That their broad flaggie° finnes no fome did reare,°   *drooping/raise*
Ne bubbling roundell° they behind them sent;   *globule*
The rest of° other fishes drawen weare,   *by*
Which with their finny oars the swelling sea did sheare.°   *cleave*

34

Soone as they bene arrived upon the brim°   *edge*
Of the Rich strond, their charets they forlore,°   *left*
And let their teméd fishes softly swim
Along the margent of the fomy shore,
Least they their finnes should bruze, and surbate° sore   *chafe*
Their tender feet upon the stony ground:
And comming to the place, where all in gore
And cruddy bloud enwallowéd° they found   *tumbled*
The lucklesse Marinell, lying in deadly swound;

35

His mother swownéd thrise, and the third time
Could scarce recovered be out of her paine;
Had she not bene devoyd of mortall slime,°   *clay*
She should not then have bene relivéd° againe,   *revived*
But soone as life recovered had the raine,
She made so piteous mone and deare wayment,°   *lamentation*
That the hard rocks could scarse from teares refraine,
And all her sister Nymphes with one consent°   *harmony*
Supplide her sobbing breaches² with sad complement.

36

"Deare image of my selfe," she said, "that is,
The wretched sonne of wretched mother borne,
Is this thine high advauncement, O is this
Th'immortall name, with which thee yet unborne
Thy Gransire Nereus promist to adorne?
Now lyest thou of life and honor reft;°   *deprived*
Now lyest thou a lumpe of earth forlorne,
Ne of thy late life memory is left,
Ne can thy irrevocable destiny be weft?°   *avoided*

37

"Fond° Proteus, father of false prophecis,   *foolish*
And they more fond, that credit to thee give,
Not this the worke of womans hand ywis,°   *certainly*
That so deepe wound through these deare members drive.
I fearéd love: but they that love do live,
But they that die, doe neither love nor hate.
Nath'lesse to thee thy folly I forgive,

---

2. I.e., the intervals between fits of sobbing.

And to my selfe, and to accurséd fate
The guilt I doe ascribe: deare wisedome bought too late.

38

"O what availes it of immortall seed
  To beene ybred and never borne to die?
  Farre better I it deeme to die with speed,
  Then waste in woe and wailefull miserie.
  Who dyes the utmost dolour doth abye,°   *suffer*
  But who that lives, is left to waile his losse:
  So life is losse, and deathe felicitie.
  Sad life worse then glad death: and greater crosse
To see friends grave, then dead the grave selfe to engrosse.°   *fill*

39

"But if the heavens did his dayes envie,
  And my short blisse maligne,° yet mote they well   *grudge*
  Thus much afford me, ere that he did die
  That the dim eyes of my deare Marinell
  I mote have closéd, and him bed farewell,
  Sith other offices° for mother meet   *services*
  They would not graunt.
  Yet maulgre° them farewell, my sweetest sweet;   *in spite of*
Farewell my sweetest sonne, sith we no more shall meet."

40

Thus when they all had sorrowéd their fill,
  They softly gan to search his griesly wound:
  And that they might him handle more at will,
  They him disarmed, and spredding on the ground
  Their watchet° mantles frindgd with silver round,   *pale blue*
  They softly wipt away the gelly° blood   *clotted*
  From th'orifice; which having well upbound,
  They pourd in soveraine balme, and Nectar good,
Good both for earthly med'cine, and for heavenly food.

41

Tho when the lilly handed Liagore,[3]
  (This Liagore whylome had learnéd skill
  In leaches craft, by great Appolloes lore,°   *teaching*
  Sith her whylome upon high Pindus hill,
  He lovéd, and at last her wombe did fill
  With heavenly seed, whereof wise Paeon sprong)
  Did feele his pulse, she knew their staiéd still
  Some litle life his feeble sprites° emong;   *spirit*
Which to his mother told, despeire she from her flong.

3. From Greek, "white-armed"; Hesiod calls her a Nereid (*Theogony* 257). Spenser seems to have invented his story of the birth of Paeon, physician to the gods; cf. *Iliad* 5.401–2, 899–901.

42

Tho up him taking in their tender hands,
　　They easily unto her charet beare:
　　Her teme at her commaundement quiet stands,
　　Whiles they the corse into her wagon reare,°　　　　　　*raise*
　　And strow with flowres the lamentable beare:[4]
　　Then all the rest into their coches clim,°　　　　　　　*mount*
　　And through the brackish waves their passage sheare;
　　Upon great Neptunes necke they softly swim,
And to her watry chamber swiftly carry him.

43

Deepe in the bottome of the sea, her bowre
　　Is built of hollow billowes heapéd hye,
　　Like to thicke cloudes, that threat a stormy showre,
　　And vauted° all within, like to the sky,　　　　　　　　*arched*
　　In which the Gods do dwell eternally:
　　There they him laid in easie couch well dight;
　　And sent in haste for Tryphon,[5] to apply
　　Salves to his wounds, and medicines of might:
For Tryphon of sea gods the soveraine leach is hight.

44

The whiles the Nymphes sit all about him round,
　　Lamenting his mishap and heavy° plight;　　　　　　　*sad*
　　And oft his mother vewing his wide wound,
　　Curséd the hand, that did so deadly smight
　　Her dearest sonne, her dearest harts delight.[6]
　　But none of all those curses overtooke
　　The warlike Maid, th'ensample of that might,
　　But fairely well she thrived, and well did brooke°　　　*persist in*
Her noble deeds, ne her right course for ought forsooke.

45

Yet did false Archimage[7] her still pursew,
　　To bring to passe his mischievous intent,
　　Now that he had her singled° from the crew　　　　　　*separated*
　　Of courteous knights, the Prince, and Faery gent,°　　*noble*
　　Whom late in chace of beautie excellent
　　She left, pursewing that same foster strong;
　　Of whose foule outrage they impatient,°　　　　　　　*angered*
　　And full of fiery zeale, him followed long,
To reskew her from shame, and to revenge her wrong.

4. I.e., the bier and its sad burden.
5. A sea god skilled in healing; Boccaccio says he was the brother of Aesculapius (*De Genealogia Deorum* 7.36).
6. Thus Marinell disappears from Book III into the recesses of the wild salt sea. He will be cured by Tryphon in IV.xi.7.
7. See note to the "Argument" of III.i.

46

Through thick and thin, through mountaines and through plains,
   Those two great champions did attonce° pursew   *together*
   The fearefull damzell, with incessant paines:
   Who from them fled, as light-foot hare from vew
   Of hunter swift, and sent of houndés trew.
   At last they came unto a double way,
   Where, doubtfull which to take, her to reskew,
   Themselves they did dispart,° each to assay,   *separate*
Whether more happie were, to win so goodly pray.

47

But Timias, the Princes gentle Squire,
   That Ladies love unto his Lord forlent,°   *relinquished*
   And with proud envy,° and indignant ire,   *indignation*
   After that wicked foster fiercely went.
   So beene they three three sundry wayes ybent.°   *turned*
   But fairest fortune to the Prince befell,
   Whose chaunce it was, that soone he did repent,°   *regret*
   To take that way, in which that Damozell
Was fled afore, affraid of him, as feend of hell.

48

At last of her farre off he gainéd vew:
   Then gan he freshly pricke his fomy steed,
   And ever as he nigher to her drew,
   So evermore he did increase his speed,
   And of each turning still kept warie heed:
   Aloud to her he oftentimes did call,
   To doe° away vaine doubt, and needlesse dreed: *banish*
   Full myld to her he spake, and oft let fall
Many meeke wordes, to stay and comfort her withall.

49

But nothing might relent° her hastie flight;   *slacken*
   So deepe the deadly feare of that foule swaine°   *rustic*
   Was carst impresséd in her gentle spright:
   Like as a fearefull Dove, which through the raine,°   *domain*
   Of the wide aire her way does cut amaine,   *rapidly*
   Having farre off espyde a Tassell gent,[8]
   Which after her his nimble wings doth straine,
   Doubleth her haste for feare to be for-hent,°   *seized*
And with her pineons cleaves the liquid firmament.

50

With no lesse haste, and eke with no lesse dreed,
   That fearefull Ladie fled from him, that ment

8. I.e., a male falcon.

To her no evill thought, nor evill deed;
Yet former feare of being fowly shent,°   *disgraced*
Carried her forward with her first intent:
And though oft looking backward, well she vewd,
Her selfe freed from that foster insolent,
And that it was a knight, which now her sewd,°   *pursued*
Yet she no lesse the knight feard, then that villein rude.

51

His uncouth° shield and straunge armes her dismayd,   *unusual*
Whose like in Faery lond were seldome seene,
That fast she from him fled, no lesse affrayd,
Then of wilde beastes if she had chaséd beene:
Yet he her followd still with courage° keene,   *spirit*
So long that now the golden Hesperus[9]
Was mounted high in top of heaven sheene,°   *bright*
And warned his other brethren joyeous,
To light their blesséd lamps in Joves eternall hous.

52

All suddenly dim woxe the dampish ayre,
And griesly shadowes covered heaven bright,
That now with thousand starres was deckéd fayre;
Which when the Prince beheld, a lothfull sight,
And that perforce, for want of lenger light,
He mote surcease his suit,° and lose the hope   *pursuit*
Of his long labour, he gan fowly wyte°   *chide*
His wicked fortune, that had turnd aslope,°   *awry*
And curséd night, that reft from him so goodly scope.°   *desired object*

53

Tho when her wayes he could no more descry,
But to and fro at disaventure° strayd;   *random*
Like as a ship, whose Lodestarre suddenly
Covered with cloudes, her Pilot hath dismayd;
His wearisome pursuit perforce he stayd,
And from his loftie steed dismounting low,
Did let him forage. Downe himselfe he layd
Upon the grassie ground, to sleepe a throw;°   *while*
The cold earth was his couch, the hard steele his pillow.

54

But gentle Sleepe envyde° him any rest;   *grudged*
In stead thereof sad sorrow, and disdaine
Of his hard hap° did vexe his noble brest,   *lot*
And thousand fancies bet his idle braine
With their light wings, the sights of semblants° vaine: *illusions*
Oft did he wish, that Lady faire mote bee

9. The evening star.

His Faery Queene, for whom he did complaine:°   *lament*
    Or that his Faery Queene were such, as shee:
And ever hastie Night he blaméd bitterlie.[1]

55

"Night thou foule Mother of annoyance° sad,   *grief*
    Sister of heavie death, and nourse of woe,
    Which wast begot in heaven, but for thy bad
    And brutish shape thrust downe to hell below,
    Where by the grim floud of Cocytus slow
    Thy dwelling is, in Herebus blacke house[2]
    (Blacke Herebus thy husband is the foe
    Of all the Gods) where thou ungratious,
Halfe of thy dayes doest lead in horrour hideous.

56

"What had th'eternall Maker need of thee,
    The world in his° continuall course to keepe,   *its*
    That doest all things deface,° ne lettest see   *obscure*
    The beautie of his worke? Indeed in sleepe
    The slouthfull bodie, that doth love to steepe
    His lustlesse° limbes, and drowne his baser° mind,   *feeble/too base*
    Doth praise thee oft, and oft from Stygian deepe
    Calles[3] thee, his goddesse in his error blind,
And great Dame Natures handmaide, chearing every kind.

57

"But well I wote, that to an heavy hart
    Thou art the root and nurse of bitter cares,
    Breeder of new, renewer of old smarts:
    In stead of rest thou lendest rayling° teares,   *bitter*
    In stead of sleepe thou sendest troublous feares,
    And dreadfull visions, in the which alive
    The drearie image of sad death appeares:
    So from the wearie spirit thou doest drive
Desiréd rest, and men of happinesse deprive.

58

"Under thy mantle blacke there hidden lye,
    Light-shonning theft, and traiterous intent,
    Abhorréd bloudshed, and vile felony,
    Shamefull deceipt, and daunger imminent;°   *threatening*
    Foule horror, and eke hellish dreriment:[4]

1. Arthur's lament in stanzas 55–60 structurally balances that of Britomart early in the canto; it, too, belongs to the genre of the lover's "complaint," often rendered at night by a forlorn lover (cf. Dido's lament, *Aeneid* 4.522–54). Beauty can distract even the magnanimous mind; yet the scope and reach of this address to night befit a heroic prince.
2. Hesiod says Chaos bore Night and Erebus, who dwell in the underworld (*Theogony* 123, 669–70).
3. I.e., summons thee from Hades, and calls thee his goddess and the handmaid of Dame Nature.
4. The list of Night's offspring is based on Hesiod, *Theogony* 211–25, or Comes, *Mythologiae* 3.12.

All these I wote in thy protection bee,
  And light doe shonne, for feare of being shent:°   *put to shame*
  For light ylike° is lothed of them and thee,   *alike*
And all that lewdnesse° love, doe hate the light to see.   *wickedness*

59

"For day discovers° all dishonest wayes,   *reveals*
  And sheweth each thing, as it is indeed:
  The prayses of high God he faire displayes
  And his large bountie rightly doth areed.°   *show*
  Dayes dearest children be the blesséd seed,
  Which darknesse shall subdew, and heaven win:
  Truth is his daughter; he her first did breed,
  Most sacred virgin, without spot of sin.[5]
Our life is day, but death with darknesse doth begin.

60

"O when will day then turne to me againe,
  And bring with him his long expected light?
  O Titan, haste to reare thy joyous waine:[6]
  Speed thee to spred abroad thy beamés bright,
  And chase away this too long lingring night,
  Chase her away, from whence she came, to hell.
  She, she it is, that hath me done despight:°   *wrong*
  There let her with the damnéd spirits dwell,
And yeeld her roome to day, that can it governe well."

61

Thus did the Prince that wearie night outweare,°   *spend*
  In restlesse anguish and unquiet paine:
  And earely, ere the morrow did upreare
  His deawy head out of the Ocean maine,
  He up arose, as halfe in great disdaine,
  And clombe unto his steed. So forth he went,
  With heavie looke and lumpish° pace, that plaine   *dull*
  In him bewraid great grudge and maltalent:°   *ill will*
His steed eke seemed t'apply° his steps to his intent.°   *suit/spirit*

5. More often Truth is called the daughter of Time.
6. I.e., may the sun soon rise.

Canto V

Prince Arthur heares of Florimell:
    three fosters° Timias wound,   *foresters*
Belphebe finds him almost dead,
    and reareth out of sownd.°   *swoon*

1

Wonder it is to see, in diverse minds,
    How diversly love doth his pageants° play,   *roles*
And shewes his powre in variable° kinds: *various*
    The baser wit,° whose idle thoughts alway   *mind*
    Are wont to cleave unto the lowly clay,
    It stirreth up to sensuall desire,
    And in lewd slouth to wast his carelesse day:
But in brave sprite it kindles goodly fire,
That to all high desert° and honour doth aspire.   *worth*

2

Ne suffereth it uncomely° idlenesse,   *unbecoming*
    In his free thought to build her sluggish nest:
Ne suffereth it thought of ungentlenesse,
    Ever to creepe into his noble brest,
    But to the highest and the worthiest
    Lifteth it up, that else would lowly fall:
    It lets not fall, it lets it not to rest:
It lets not scarse this Prince to breath at all,
But to his first poursuit him forward still doth call.

3

Who long time wandred through the forrest wyde,
    To finde some issue° thence, till that at last   *way out*
He met a Dwarfe, that seemed terrifyde
    With some late perill, which he hardly° past,   *with difficulty*
    Or other accident, which him aghast;°   *terrified*
    Of whom he askéd, whence he lately came,
    And whither now he travelléd so fast:
For sore he swat,° and running through that same   *sweated*
Thicke forest, was bescratcht, and both his feet nigh lame.

4

Panting for breath, and almost out of hart,
    The Dwarfe him answerd, "Sir, ill mote I stay
To tell the same. I lately did depart
    From Faery court, where I have many a day
    Servéd a gentle Lady of great sway,
    And high accompt° through out all Elfin land,   *reputation*
    Who lately left the same, and tooke this way:

Her now I seeke, and if ye understand
Which way she faréd hath, good Sir tell out of hand."[1]

5

"What mister° wight," said he, "and how arayd?"   *kind of*
"Royally clad," quoth he, "in cloth of gold,
As meetest may beseeme a noble mayd;
Her faire lockes in rich circlet be enrold,
A fairer wight did never Sunne behold,
And on a Palfrey rides more white then snow,
Yet she her selfe, is whiter manifold:
The surest signe, whereby ye may her know,
Is, that she is the fairest wight alive, I trow."

6

"Now certes swaine," said he, "such one I weene,
Fast flying through this forest from her fo,
A foule ill favoured° foster, I have seene;   *featured*
Her selfe, well as I might, I reskewd tho,
But could not stay; so fast she did foregoe,°   *go on before*
Carried away with wings of speedy feare."
"Ah dearest God," quoth he, "that is great woe,
And wondrous ruth° to all, that shall it heare.   *grief*
But can ye read Sir, how I may her find, or where?"

7

"Perdy me lever° were to weeten that,"   *rather*
Said he, "then ransome of the richest knight,
Or all the good that ever yet I gat:
But froward° fortune, and too forward Night   *perverse*
Such happinesse did, maulgre, to me spight,[2]
And fro me reft both life and light attone.°   *together*
But Dwarfe aread,° what is that Lady bright,   *explain*
That through this forest wandreth thus alone;
For of her errour° straunge I have great ruth and mone."   *wandering*

8

"That Lady is," quoth he, "where so she bee,
The bountiest° virgin, and most debonaire,   *most virtuous*
That ever living eye I weene did see;
Lives none this day, that may with her compare
In stedfast chastitie and vertue rare,
The goodly ornaments of beautie bright;
And is yclepéd° Florimell the faire,   *called*
Faire Florimell beloved of many a knight,
Yet she loves none but one, that Marinell is hight.

1. I.e., at once.
2. I.e., Fortune and Night, against my will, envied me this happiness.

9

"A Sea-nymphes sonne, that Marinell is hight,
  Of my deare Dame is lovéd dearely well;
  In other none, but him, she sets delight,
  All her delight is set on Marinell;
  But he sets nought at all by Florimell:
  For Ladies love his mother long ygoe
  Did him, they say, forwarne° through sacred spell.   forbid
  But fame° now flies, that of a forreine foe   rumor
He is yslaine, which is the ground of all our woe.

10

"Five dayes there be, since he (they say) was slaine,
  And foure, since Florimell the Court for-went,°   left
  And vowéd never to returne againe,
  Till him alive or dead she did invent.°   find
  Therefore, faire Sir, for love of knighthood gent,
  And honour of trew Ladies, if ye may
  By your good counsell, or bold hardiment,
  Or° succour her, or me direct the way;   either
Do one, or other good, I you most humbly pray ³

11

"So may ye gaine to you full great renowme,
  Of all good Ladies through the world so wide,
  And haply in her hart find highest rowme,
  Of whom ye seeke to be most magnifide:
  At least eternall meede shall you abide."°   await
  To whom the Prince; "Dwarfe, comfort to thee take,
  For till thou tidings learne, what her betide,
  I here avow thee never to forsake.
Ill weares he armes, that nill° them use for Ladies sake."   will not

12

So with the Dwarfe he backe returned againe,
  To seeke his Lady, where he mote her find;
  But by the way he greatly gan complaine
  The want of his good Squire late left behind,
  For whom he wondrous pensive grew in mind,
  For doubt° of daunger, which mote him betide;   fear
  For him he lovéd above all mankind,
  Having him trew and faithfull ever tride,°   proved
And bold, as ever Squire that waited by knights side.

13

Who all this while full hardly was assayd
  Of deadly daunger, which to him betid;°   befell

3. Spenser has allowed an inconsistency between the Dwarfe's account of Florimell's departure from
   the court and the glimpse (at III.i.15–16) of Florimell in flight before Marinell's encounter with
   Britomart.

For whiles his Lord pursewd that noble Mayd,
After that foster fowle he fiercely rid,°   *rode*
To bene avengéd of the shame, he did
To that faire Damzell: Him he chacéd long
Through the thicke woods, wherein he would have hid
His shamefull head from his avengement strong,
And oft him threatned death for his outrageous wrong.

14

Nathlesse the villen° sped him selfe so well,   *churl*
Whether through swiftnesse of his speedy beast,
Or knowledge of those woods, where he did dwell,
That shortly he from daunger was releast,
And out of sight escapéd at the least;°   *last*
Yet not escapéd from the dew reward
Of his bad deeds, which dayly he increast,
Ne ceaséd not, till him oppresséd hard
The heavy plague, that for such leachours is prepard.

15

For soone as he was vanisht out of sight,
His coward courage gan emboldned bee,
And cast° t'avenge him of that fowle despight,   *resolved*
Which he had borne of his bold enimee.
Tho to his brethren came: for they were three
Ungratious children of one gracelesse sire,[4]
And unto them complainéd, how that he
Had uséd bene of that foolehardy Squire;
So them with bitter words he stird to bloudy ire.

16

Forthwith themselves with their sad° instruments   *grievous*
Of spoyle and murder they gan arme bylive,°   *speedily*
And with him forth into the forest went,
To wreake the wrath, which he did earst revive
In their sterne brests, on him which late did drive
Their brother to reproch and shamefull flight:
For they had vowed, that never he alive
Out of that forest should escape their might;
Vile rancour their rude harts had fild with such despight.

17

Within that wood there was a covert glade,
Foreby° a narrow foord, to them well knowne,   *near*
Through which it was uneath° for wight to wade;   *difficult*
And now by fortune it was overflowne:
By that same way they knew that Squire unknowne

---

4. Perhaps signifying the lusts variously of eye, ear, and touch.

Mote algates° passe; for thy themselves they set   *necessarily*
  There in await, with thicke woods over growne,
  And all the while their malice they did whet
With cruell threats, his passage through the ford to let.°   *prevent*

18

It fortunéd, as they devizéd had,
  The gentle Squire came ryding that same way,
  Unweeting of their wile and treason bad,
  And through the ford to passen did assay;
  But that fierce foster, which late fled away,
  Stoutly forth stepping on the further shore,
  Him boldly bad his passage there to stay,
  Till he had made amends, and full restore
For all the damage, which he had him doen afore.

19

With that at him a quiv'ring dart he threw,
  With so fell force and villeinous despighte,
  That through his haberjeon the forkchead flew,
  And through the linkéd mayles° empicrcéd quite,   *armor rings*
  But had no powre in his soft flesh to bite:
  That stroke the hardy Squire did sore displease,
  But more that him he could not come to smite;
  For by no meanes the high banke he could sease,°   *reach*
But laboured long in that deepe ford with vaine disease.°   *distress*

20

And still the foster with his long bore-speare
  Him kept from landing at his wishéd will;
  Anone one sent out of the thicket neare
  A cruell shaft, headed with deadly ill,
  And fetheréd with an unlucky quill;
  The wicked steele stayd not, till it did light
  In his left thigh, and deepely did it thrill:°   *pierce*
  Exceeding griefe that wound in him empight,°   *fixed*
But more that with his foes he could not come to fight.

21

At last through wrath and vengeaunce making way,
  He on the bancke arrived with mickle° paine,   *much*
  Where the third brother him did sore assay,
  And drove at him with all his might and maine
  A forrest bill,[5] which both his hands did straine;
  But warily he did avoide the blow,
  And with his speare requited him againe,
  That both his sides were thrilléd with the throw,°   *thrust*
And a large streame of bloud out of the wound did flow.

5. A digging or pruning implement.

22

He tombling downe, with gnashing teeth did bite
  The bitter earth, and bad to let him in
  Into the balefull house of endlesse night,
  Where wicked ghosts do waile their former sin.
  Tho gan the battell freshly to begin;
  For nathemore for that spectacle bad,
  Did th'other two their cruell vengeaunce blin,°   *cease*
  But both attonce on both sides him bestad,°   *beset*
And load upon him layd,[6] his life for to have had.

23

Tho when that villain he avized,° which late   *perceived*
  Affrighted had the fairest Florimell,
  Full of fiers fury, and indignant hate,
  To him he turnéd, and with rigour° fell   *force*
  Smote him so rudely on the Pannikell,°   *brain pan*
  That to the chin he cleft his head in twaine:
  Downe on the ground his carkas groveling fell;
  His sinfull soule with desperate disdaine,
Out of her fleshly ferme° fled to the place of paine.   *enclosure*

24

That seeing now the onely° last of three,   *solitary*
  Who with that wicked shaft him wounded had,
  Trembling with horrour, as° that did foresee   *as one*
  The fearefull end of his avengement sad,
  Through which he follow should his brethren bad,
  His bootelesse bow in feeble hand upcaught,
  And therewith shot an arrow at the lad;
  Which faintly fluttring, scarce his helmet raught,°   *reached*
And glauncing fell to ground, but him annoyéd naught.

25

With that he would have fled into the wood;
  But Timias him lightly overhent,°   *overtook*
  Right as he entring was into the flood,
  And strooke at him with force so violent,
  That headlesse him into the foord he sent:
  The carkas with the streame was carried downe,
  But th'head fell backeward on the Continent.°   *ground*
  So mischief fel upon the meaners crowne;[7]
They three be dead with shame, the Squire lives with renowne.

26

He lives, but takes small joy of his renowne;
  For of that cruell wound he bled so sore,

6. I.e., assailed him with blows.
7. I.e., on those who intended mischief.

That from his steed he fell in deadly swowne;
Yet still the bloud forth gusht in so great store,
That he lay wallowd all in his owne gore.
Now God thee keepe, thou gentlest Squire alive,
Else shall thy loving Lord thee see no more,
But both of comfort him thou shalt deprive,
And eke thy selfe of honour, which thou didst atchive.

27

Providence heavenly passeth living thought,
  And doth for wretched mens reliefe make way;
  For loe great grace or fortune thither brought
  Comfort to him, that comfortlesse now lay.
  In those same woods, ye well remember may,
  How that a noble huntcresse did wonne,
  She, that base Braggadochio did affray,°   *frighten*
  And made him fast out of the forrest runne;
Belphoebe[8] was her name, as faire as Phoebus sunne.

28

She on a day, as she pursewd the chace
  Of some wild beast, which with her arrowes keene
  She wounded had, the same along did trace
  By tract° of bloud, which she had freshly seene,   *trace*
  To have besprinckled all the grassy greene;
  By the great persue,° which she there perceaved,   *trail of blood*
  Well hopéd she the beast engored had beene,
  And made more hast, the life to have bereaved:
But ah, her expectation greatly was deceaved.

29

Shortly she came, whereas that woefull Squire
  With bloud deforméd,° lay in deadly swownd: *made hideous*
  In whose faire eyes, like lamps of quenchéd fire,
  The Christall humour° stood congealéd rownd;   *fluid*
  His locks, like faded leaves fallen to grownd,
  Knotted with bloud, in bounches rudely ran,
  And his sweete lips, on which before that stownd°   *encounter*
  The bud of youth to blossome faire began,
Spoild of their rosie red, were woxen pale and wan.

30

Saw never living eye more heavy sight,
  That could have made a rocke of stone to rew,
  Or rive in twaine: which when that Lady bright

8. The "Letter to Raleigh" says that Belphoebe at times figures Elizabeth in her character "of a most
vertuous and beautifull Lady." As her name implies, she resembles Diana, lunar goddess of forests
and the hunt; she flourishes in radiant purity, but Britomart is destined to transcend this virginal
chastity through chaste wedded love.

Besides all hope[9] with melting eyes did vew,
All suddeinly abasht she chaungéd hew,
And with sterne horrour backward gan to start:
But when she better him beheld, she grew
Full of soft passion and unwonted smart:
The point of pitty percéd through her tender hart.[1]

31

Meekely she bowéd downe, to weete if life
  Yet in his frosen members did remaine,
  And feeling by his pulses beating rife,°   *strongly*
  That the weake soule her seat did yet retaine,
  She cast to comfort him with busie paine:
  His double folded necke she reard upright,
  And rubd his temples, and each trembling vaine;
  His mayléd haberjeon she did undight,°   *take off*
And from his head his heavy burganet did light.°   *remove*

32

Into the woods thenceforth in hast she went,
  To seeke for hearbes, that mote him remedy;
  For she of hearbes had great intendiment,°   *knowledge*
  Taught of the Nymphe, which from her infancy
  Her nourcéd had in trew Nobility:
  There, whether it divine Tobacco were,
  Or Panachaea, or Polygony,[2]
  She found, and brought it to her patient deare
Who al this while lay bleeding out his hartbloud neare.

33

The soveraigne weede betwixt two marbles plaine° *smooth*
  She pownded small, and did in peeces bruze,°   *break*
  And then atweene her lilly handés twaine,
  Into his wound the juyce thereof did scruze,°   *squeeze*
  And round about, as she could well it uze,
  The flesh therewith she suppled and did steepe,
  T'abate all spasme, and soke the swelling bruze,
  And after having searcht the intuse° deepe,   *contusion*
She with her scarfe did bind the wound from cold to keepe.

34

By this he had sweete life recured° againe,   *recovered*
  And groning inly deepe, at last his eyes,

9. I.e., contrary to expectation.
1. The remainder of this canto adapts Ariosto's account of Angelica and Medoro (*Orlando Furioso* 19.17–42). But Angelica allows Medoro to "gather the first rose," whereas Belphoebe, by nature unaware of what Timias feels, reserves "that dainty Rose" (stanza 51). Especially in the 1596 *Faerie Queene*, Timias represents aspects of Walter Raleigh and his stormy if ostentatiously loving service to the queen. Her fury when he seduced and then secretly married one of her ladies and her partial forgiveness are allegorized in IV.vii–viii; see Oram 1983 and Bednarz 1983.
2. Raleigh introduced tobacco into England in 1584; "panachaea" means an herb with manifold healing properties; polygony is an astringent root.

His watry eyes, drizling like deawy raine,
He up gan lift toward the azure skies,
From whence descend all hopelesse° remedies: *unexpected*
Therewith he sighed, and turning him aside,
The goodly Mayd full of divinities,
And gifts of heavenly grace he by him spide,
Her bow and gilden quiver lying him beside.

35

"Mercy dearc Lord," said he, "what grace is this,
That thou hast shewéd to me sinfull wight,
To send thine Angell from her bowre of blis,
To comfort me in my distresséd plight?
Angell, or Goddesse do I call thee right?
What service may I do unto thee meete,
That hast from darkencsse me returnd to light,
And with thy heavenly salves and med'cines sweetc,
Hast drest my sinfull wounds? I kisse thy blessed feetc."

36

Thereat she blushing said, "Ah gentle Squire,
Nor Goddesse I, nor Angell, but the Mayd,
And daughter of a woody° Nymphe, desire   *of the forest*
No service, but thy safety and ayd;
Which if thou gaine, I shalbe well apayd.
We mortall wights whose lives and fortunes bee
To commun accidcnts still open layd,
Are bound with commun bond of frailtee,
To succour wrctched wights, whom we captivéd see."

37

By this her Damzels, which the former chace
Had undertaken after her, arryved,
As did Belphoebe, in the bloudy place,
And thereby deemd the bcast had bene deprivcd
Of life, whom late their Ladies arrow ryved:°   *pierced*
For thy the bloudy tract they follow fast,
And every one to runne the swiftest stryved;
But two of them the rest far overpast,
And where their Lady was, arrivéd at the last.

38

Where when they saw that goodly boy, with blood
Defowléd, and their Lady dresse his wownd,
They wondred much, and shortly understood,
How him in deadly case° their Lady fownd,   *condition*
And reskewéd out of the heavy stownd.°   *plight*
Eftsoones his warlike courser, which was strayd

Farre in the woods, while that he lay in swownd,
She made those Damzels search, which being stayd,
They did him set thereon, and forth with them convayd.°   *removed*

39

Into that forest farre they thence him led,
Where was their dwelling, in a pleasant glade,
With mountaines round about environéd,
And mighty woods, which did the valley shade,
And like a stately Theatre it made,
Spreading it selfe into a spatious plaine.
And in the midst a little river plaide
Emongst the pumy° stones, which seemd to plaine   *pumice*
With gentle murmure, that his course they did restraine.

40

Beside the same a dainty place there lay,
Planted with mirtle trees and laurels greene,
In which the birds song many a lovely lay
Of gods high prayse, and of their loves sweet teene,°   *sorrow*
As it an earthly Paradize had beene:
In whose encloséd shadow there was pight
A faire Pavilion, scarcely to be seene,
The which was all within most richly dight,
That greatest Princes living it mote well delight.

41

Thither they brought that wounded Squire, and layd
In easie couch his feeble limbes to rest,
He rested him a while, and then the Mayd
His ready wound with better salves new drest;
Dayly she dresséd him, and did the best
His grievous hurt to garish,° that she might,   *cure*
That shortly she his dolour hath redrest,°   *healed*
And his foule sore reducéd° to faire plight: *restored*
It she reducéd, but himselfe destroyéd quight.

42

O foolish Physick, and unfruitfull paine,°   *effort*
That heales up one and makes another wound:
She his hurt thigh to him recured againe,
But hurt his hart, the which before was sound,
Through an unwary dart, which did rebound°   *leap*
From her faire eyes and gracious countenaunce.
What bootes it him from death to be unbound,
To be captivéd in endlesse duraunce°   *captivity*
Of sorrow and despaire without aleggeaunce?°   *alleviation*

43

Still as his wound did gather, and grow hole,
  So still his hart woxe sore, and health decayd:
  Madnesse to save a part, and lose the whole.
  Still whenas he beheld the heavenly Mayd,
  Whiles dayly plaisters to his wound she layd,
  So still his Malady the more increast,
  The whiles her matchlesse beautie him dismayd.
  Ah God, what other could he do at least,
But love so faire a Lady, that his life releast?°   *saved*

44

Long while he strove in his courageous brest,
  With reason dew the passion to subdew,
  And love for to dislodge out of his nest:
  Still when her excellencies he did vew,
  Her soveraigne bounty,° and celestiall hew,°   *goodness/form*
  The same to love he strongly was constraind:
  But when his meane estate he did revew,
  He from such hardy boldnesse was restraind,
And of his lucklesse lot and cruell love thus plaind.

45

"Unthankfull wretch," said he, "is this the meed,
  With which her soveraigne mercy thou doest quight?°   *repay*
  Thy life she savéd by her gracious deed,
  But thou doest weene with villeinous despight,°   *wrong*
  To blot her honour, and her heavenly light.
  Dye rather, dye, then so disloyally
  Deeme of her high desert,° or seeme so light: *worth*
  Faire death it is to shonne more shame, to dy:
Dye rather, dy, then ever love disloyally.

46

"But if to love disloyalty it bee,
  Shall I then hate her, that from deathés dore
  Me brought? ah farre be such reproch fro mee.
  What can I lesse do, then her love therefore,
  Sith I her dew reward cannot restore?
  Dye rather, dye, and dying do her serve,
  Dying her serve, and living her adore;
  Thy life she gave, thy life she doth deserve:
Dye rather, dye, then ever from her service swerve.

47

"But foolish boy, what bootes thy service bace
  To her, to whom the heavens do serve, and sew?
  Thou a meane Squire, of meeke and lowly place,

She heavenly borne, and of celestiall hew.
How then? of all love taketh equall vew:
And doth not highest God vouchsafe to take
The love and service of the basest crew?°   company
If she will not, dye meekly for her sake;
Dye rather, dye, then ever so faire love forsake."

48

Thus warreid° he long time against his will,   struggled
  Till that through weaknesse he was forst at last,
  To yield himselfe unto the mighty ill:
  Which as a victour proud, gan ransack fast
  His inward parts, and all his entrayles wast,
  That neither bloud in face, nor life in hart
  It left, but both did quite drye up, and blast;
  As percing levin,° which the inner part   lightning
Of every thing consumes, and calcineth° by art.   pulverizes

49

Which seeing faire Belphoebe gan to feare,
  Least that his wound were inly well not healed,
  Or that the wicked steele empoysned were:
  Litle she weend, that love he close concealed;
  Yet still he wasted, as the snow congealed,
  When the bright sunne his beams thereon doth beat;
  Yet never he his hart to her revealed,
  But rather chose to dye for sorrow great,
Then with dishonorable termes her to entreat.

50

She gracious Lady, yet no paines did spare,
  To do him ease, or do him remedy:
  Many Restoratives of vertues° rare,   powers
  And costly Cordialles she did apply,
  To mitigate his stubborne mallady:
  But that sweet Cordiall, which can restore
  A love-sick hart, she did to him envy;°   grudge
  To him, and to all th'unworthy world forlore°   forlorn
She did envy that soveraigne salve, in secret store.

51

That dainty Rose,[3] the daughter of her Morne,
  More deare then life she tenderéd, whose flowre
  The girlond of her honour did adorne:
  Ne suffred she the Middayes scorching powre,
  Ne the sharp Northerne wind thereon to showre,

---

3. Stanzas 51–55 emblematically figure virginal chastity: its natural beauty, its divine "root," its
   mysterious influence over earthly rulers, and its power to resist evil. Belphoebe lacks Britomart's
   passionate vigor, but for a sympathetic view of her reserve see Krier 1990.

But lappéd° up her silken leaves most chaire,°   *folded/dear*
When so the froward skye began to lowre:
But soone as calméd was the Christall aire,
She did it faire dispred, and let to florish faire.

52

Eternall God in his almighty powre,
  To make ensample of his heavenly grace,
  In Paradize whilome did plant this flowre,
  Whence he it fetcht out of her native place,
  And did in stocke of earthly flesh enrace,°   *implant*
  That mortall men her glory should admire:
  In gentle Ladies brest, and bounteous race
Of woman kind it fairest flowre doth spire,°   *cause to spring*
And beareth fruit of honour and all chast desire.

53

Faire ympes° of beautie, whose bright shining beames   *children*
  Adorne the world with like to heavenly light,
  And to your willes both royalties and Realmes
  Subdew, through conquest of your wondrous might,
  With this faire flowre your goodly girlonds dight,
  Of chastity and vertue virginall,
  That shall embellish more your beautie bright,
  And crowne your heades with heavenly coronall,
Such as the Angels weare before Gods tribunall.

54

To youre faire selves a faire ensample frame,
  Of this faire virgin, this Belphoebe faire,
  To whom in perfect love, and spotlesse fame
  Of chastitie, none living may compaire:
  Ne poysnous Envy justly can empaire
  The prayse of her fresh flowring Maidenhead;
  For thy she standeth on the highest staire
  Of th'honorable stage of womanhead,
That Ladies all may follow her ensample dead.

55

In so great prayse of stedfast chastity,
  Nathlesse she was so curteous and kind,
  Tempred with grace, and goodly modesty,
  That seeméd those two vertues strove to find
  The higher place in her Heroick mind:
  So striving each did other more augment,
  And both encreast the prayse of woman kind,
  And both encreast her beautie excellent;
So all did make in her a perfect complement.

Canto VI

The birth of faire Belphoebe and
Of Amoret is told.
The Gardins of Adonis fraught
With pleasures manifold.

1

Well may I weene,° faire Ladies, all this while   *expect*
  Ye wonder, how this noble Damozell
  So great perfections did in her compile,°   *heap up*
  Sith that in salvage forests she did dwell,
  So farre from court and royall Citadell,
  The great schoolmistresse of all curtesy:
  Seemeth that such wild woods should far expell
  All civill usage and gentility,
And gentle sprite deforme with rude rusticity.

2

But to this faire Belphoebe in her berth
  The heavens so favourable were and free,
  Looking with myld aspect upon the earth,
  In th'Horoscope of her nativitee,
  That all the gifts of grace and chastitee
  On her they pouréd forth of plenteous horne;
  Jove laught on Venus from his soveraigne see,°   *throne*
  And Phoebus with faire beames did her adorne,[1]
And all the Graces rockt her cradle being borne.

3

Her berth was of the wombe of Morning dew,[2]
  And her conception of the joyous Prime,°   *spring*
  And all her whole creation did her shew
  Pure and unspotted from all loathly crime,
  That is ingenerate in fleshly slime.°   *clay*
  So was this virgin borne, so was she bred,
  So was she traynéd up from time to time,[3]
  In all chast vertue, and true bounti-hed
Till to her dew perfection she was ripenéd.

4

Her mother was the faire Chrysogonee,[4]
  The daughter of Amphisa, who by race

---

1. Spenser seems to imply that Jupiter and Venus were "in trine," an astrological "aspect" thought to confer beauty, grace, fidelity, and honesty on those born under its influence. While the sun's "aspect" is not given, its influence was favorable to fortune and high place.
2. "Thy people shall be willing in the day of thy power, in the beauties of holiness from the womb of the morning: thou hast the dew of thy youth" (Psalms 110.3).
3. I.e., in each stage of her youth. Stars might shape a newborn's character, but they could not take the place of education in virtue.
4. Greek for "golden-born"; "Amphisa" would suggest "double nature" in Greek.

A Faerie was, yborne of high degree,
 She bore Belphoebe, she bore in like cace°   *condition*
 Faire Amoretta in the second place:
 These two were twinnes, and twixt them two did share
 The heritage of all celestiall grace.
 That all the rest it seemed they robbéd bare
Of bountie, and of beautie, and all vertues rare.

5

It were a goodly storie, to declare,
 By what straunge accident faire Chrysogone
 Conceived these infants, and how them she bare,
 In this wild forrest wandring all alone,
 After she had nine moneths fulfild and gone:
 For not as other wemens commune brood,
 They were enwombéd° in the sacred throne   *conceived*
 Of her chaste bodie, nor with commune food,
As other wemens babes, they suckéd vitall blood.

6

But wondrously they were begot, and bred
 Through influence of th'heavens fruitfull ray,
 As it in antique bookes is mentionéd.[5]
 It was upon a Sommers shynie day,
 When Titan faire his beamés did display,
 In a fresh fountaine, farre from all mens vew,
 She bathed her brest, the boyling heat t' allay;
 She bathed with roses red, and violets blew,
And all the sweetest flowres, that in the forrest grew.

7

Till faint through irkesome wearinesse, adowne
 Upon the grassie ground her selfe she layd
 To sleepe, the whiles a gentle slumbring swowne
 Upon her fell all naked bare displayd;
 The sunne-beames bright upon her body playd,
 Being through former bathing mollifide,°   *softened*
 And pierst into her wombe, where they embayd° *suffused*
 With so sweet sence and secret power unspide,
That in her pregnant flesh they shortly fructifide.

8

Miraculous may seeme to him, that reades
 So straunge ensample of conception;
 But reason teacheth that the fruitfull seades
 Of all things living, through impression

5. Stanzas 6–9 (cf. *Metamorphoses* 1.416–37) prepare for the allegory of life processes in the Garden of Adonis. Like other mythographers, Comes associates Adonis with the sun, "sole author of generation" (*Mythologiae* 4.13).

Of the sunbeames in moyst complexion,[6]
Doe life conceive and quickned are by kynd:°   nature
So after Nilus inundation,
Infinite shapes of creatures men do fynd,
Informéd° in the mud, on which the Sunne hath shynd.[7]   formed

9

Great father he of generation
Is rightly cald, th'author of life and light;
And his faire sister[8] for creation
Ministreth matter fit, which tempred right
With heate and humour, breedes the living wight.
So sprong these twinnes in wombe of Chrysogone,
Yet wist° she nought thereof, but sore affright,   knew
Wondred to see her belly so upblone,
Which still increast, till she her terme had full outgone.°   completed

10

Whereof conceiving shame and foule disgrace,
Albe her guiltlesse conscience her cleard,
She fled into the wildernesse a space,
Till that unweeldy burden she had reard,°   brought forth
And shund dishonor, which as death she feard:
Where wearie of long travell,° downe to rest   labor
Her selfe she set, and comfortably cheard;
There a sad cloud of sleepe her overkest,°   covered
And seizéd every sense with sorrow sore opprest.

11

It fortunéd, faire Venus having lost
Her little sonne, the wingéd god of love,
Who for some light displeasure, which him crost,
Was from her fled, as flit° as ayerie Dove,   swift
And left her blisfull bowre of joy above,
(So from her often he had fled away,
When she for ought him sharpely did reprove,
And wandred in the world in strange aray,
Disguized in thousand shapes, that none might him bewray.)[9]

12

Him for to seeke, she left her heavenly hous,
The house of goodly formes and faire aspects,
Whence all the world derives the glorious

6. I.e., in a temperament, or physical constitution, dominated by moist "humors."
7. Cf. I.i.21 and note.
8. I.e., the moon, whose light Plutarch considered favorable to the generation and growth of life in plants and animals (*Isis and Osiris* 41).
9. This episode is based on Tasso's version (in his pastoral drama *Aminta*) of the first *Idyl*, "Love the Runaway," by Moschus (fl. 250 B.C.). In his Glosse to "March," E.K. cites "Moschus his Idyllion of wandering love."

Features of beautie, and all shapes select,
With which high God his workmanship hath deckt;
And searchéd every way, through which his wings
Had borne him, or his tract° she mote detect: *track*
She promist kisses swect, and sweeter things
Unto the man, that of him tydings to her brings.

13

First she him sought in Court, where most he used
  Whylome to haunt, but there she found him not;
But many there she found, which sore accused
  His falsehood, and with foule infamous blot
  His cruell deedes and wicked wyles did spot:
Ladies and Lords she every where mote heare
  Complayning, how with his empoysned shot
  Their wofull harts he wounded had whyleare,
And so had left them languishing twixt hope and feare.

14

She then the Citties sought from gate to gate,
  And every one did aske, did he him see;
And every one her answerd, that too late
  He had him seene, and felt the crueltie
  Of his sharpe darts and whot° artillerie;   *hot*
And every one threw forth reproches rife
  Of his mischievous deedes, and said, That hee
  Was the disturber of all civill life,
The enimy of peace, and author of all strife.

15

Then in the countrey she abroad him sought,
  And in the rurall cottages inquired,
Where also many plaints to her were brought,
  How he their heedlesse harts with love had fyred,
  And his false venim through their veines inspyred;
And eke the gentle shephcard swaynes, which sat
  Keeping their fleecie flockes, as they were hyred,
  She sweetly heard complaine, both how and what
Her sonne had to them doen; yet she did smile thereat.

16

But when in none of all these she him got,
  She gan avize,° where else he mote him hyde: *consider*
At last she her bethought, that she had not
  Yet sought the salvage woods and forrests wyde,
  In which full many lovely Nymphes abyde,
Mongst whom might be, that he did closely lye,[1]
  Or that the love of some of them him tyde:

1. I.e., did secretly lurk.

For thy she thither cast° her course t'apply,   resolved
To search the secret haunts of Dianes company.

17

Shortly unto the wastefull° woods she came,   wild
    Whereas she found the Goddesse with her crew,
    After late chace of their embrewéd° game,   blood-stained
    Sitting beside a fountaine in a rew,°   row
    Some of them washing with the liquid dew
    From off their dainty limbes the dustie sweat,
    And soyle which did deforme their lively hew;
    Others lay shaded from the scorching heat;
The rest upon her person gave attendance great.

18

She having hong upon a bough on high
    Her bow and painted quiver, had unlaste
    Her silver buskins° from her nimble thigh,   high boots
    And her lancke° loynes ungirt, and brests unbraste,   slender
    After her heat the breathing cold to taste;
    Her golden lockes, that late in tresses bright
    Embreaded were for hindring of her haste,[2]
    Now loose about her shoulders hong undight,
And were with sweet Ambrosia all besprinckled light.

19

Soone as she Venus saw behind her backe,
    She was ashamed to be so loose surprized,
    And woxe halfe wroth against her damzels slacke,
    That had not her thereof before avized,°   warned
    But suffred her so carelesly disguized
    Be overtaken. Soone her garments loose
    Upgath'ring, in her bosome she comprized,°   gathered
    Well as she might, and to the Goddesse rose,
Whiles all her Nymphes did like a girlond her enclose.

20

Goodly she gan faire Cytherea[3] greet,
    And shortly askéd her, what cause her brought
    Into that wildernesse for her unmeet,
    From her sweete bowres, and beds with pleasures fraught:
    That suddein change she strange adventure thought.
    To whom halfe weeping, she thus answeréd,
    That she her dearest sonne Cupido sought,
    Who in his frowardnesse from her was fled;
That she repented sore, to have him angeréd.

2. I.e., were braided up to prevent them from hindering her speed.
3. I.e., Venus, who rose from sea foam near Cythera, off the southernmost point of Greece; see
    II.xii.65.

21

Thereat Diana gan to smile, in scorne
  Of her vaine plaint, and to her scoffing sayd;
  "Great pittie sure, that ye be so forlorne
  Of your gay sonne, that gives ye so good ayd
  To your disports: ill mote ye bene apayd."[4]
  But she was more engrievéd, and replide;
  "Faire sister, ill beseemes it to upbrayd
  A dolefull heart with so disdainfull pride;
The like that mine, may be your paine another tide.°   *time*

22

"As you in woods and wanton wildernesse
  Your glory set, to chace the salvage beasts,
  So my delight is all in joyfulnesse,
  In beds, in bowres, in banckets, and in feasts:
  And ill becomes you with your loftie creasts,
  To scorne the joy, that Jove is glad to seeke;
  We both are bound to follow heavens beheasts,°   *commands*
  And tend our charges with obeisance meeke:
Spare, gentle sister, with reproch my paine to eeke.°   *increase*

23

"And tell me, if that ye my sonne have heard,
  To lurke emongst your Nymphes in secret wize;
  Or keepe their cabins: much I am affeard,
  Least he like one of them him selfe disguize,
  And turne his arrowes to their exercize:
  So may he long himselfe full easie hide:
  For he is faire and fresh in face and guize,
  As any Nymph (let not it be envyde.)"°   *grudged*
So saying every Nymph full narrowly she eyde.

24

But Phoebe therewith sore was angeréd,
  And sharply said; "Goe Dame, goe seeke your boy,
  Where you him lately left, in Mars his bed;
  He comes not here, we scorne his foolish joy,
  Ne lend we leisure to his idle toy:°   *play*
  But if I catch him in this company,
  By Stygian lake I vow, whose sad annoy[5]
  The Gods doe dread, he dearely shall abye:°   *pay*
Ile clip his wanton wings, that he no more shall fly."

---

4. I.e., you are ill requited.
5. I.e., grievous affliction.

25

Whom when as Venus saw so sore displeased,
  She inly sory was, and gan relent,
  What she had said: so her she soone appeased,
  With sugred words and gentle blandishment,
  Which as a fountaine from her sweet lips went,
  And welléd goodly forth, that in short space
  She was well pleasd, and forth her damzels sent,
  Through all the woods, to search from place to place,
If any tract of him or tydings they mote trace.

26

To search the God of love, her Nymphes she sent
  Throughout the wandring forrest every where:
  And after them her selfe eke with her went
  To seeke the fugitive, both farre and nere.
  So long they sought, till they arrivéd were
  In that same shadie covert, whereas lay
  Faire Crysogone in slombry traunce whilere:°   *lately*
  Who in her sleepe (a wondrous thing to say)
Unwares had borne two babes, as faire as springing day.

27

Unwares she them conceived, unwares she bore:
  She bore withouten paine, that she conceived
  Withouten pleasure; ne her need implore
  Lucinaes[6] aide: which when they both perceived,
  They were through wonder nigh of sense bereaved,
  And gazing each on other, nought bespake:
  At last they both agreed, her seeming grieved
  Out of her heavy swowne not to awake,
But from her loving side the tender babes to take.

28

Up they them tooke, each one a babe uptooke,
  And with them carried, to be fosteréd;
  Dame Phoebe to a Nymph her babe betooke,
  To be upbrought in perfect Maydenhed,
  And of her selfe her name Belphoebe red:°   *called*
  But Venus hers thence farre away convayd,
  To be upbrought in goodly womanhed,
  And in her litle loves stead, which was strayd,
Her Amoretta cald, to comfort her dismayd.

29

She brought her to her joyous Paradize,
  Where most she wonnes, when she on earth does dwel.

---

6. The goddess of childbirth.

So faire a place, as Nature can devize:
Whether in Paphos,[7] or Cytheron hill,
Or it in Gnidus be, I wote not well;
But well I wote by tryall, that this same
All other pleasant places doth excell,
And calléd is by her lost lovers name,
The Gardin of Adonis,[8] farre renowmd by fame.

30

In that same Gardin all the goodly flowres,
  Wherewith dame Nature doth her beautifie,
  And decks the girlonds of her paramoures,
  Are fetcht: there is the first seminarie°   *seed plot*
Of all things, that are borne to live and die,
  According to their kindes [9] Long worke it were,
  Here to account° the endlesse progenie   *list*
Of all the weedes,° that bud and blossome there;   *plants*
But so much as doth need, must needs be counted° here.   *recounted*

31

It sited was in fruitfull soyle of old,
  And girt in with two walles on either side;
  The one of yron, the other of bright gold,[1]
  That none might thorough breake, nor overstride:
And double gates it had, which opened wide,
  By which both in and out men moten° pas;   *could*
  Th'one faire and fresh, the other old and dride:
Old Genius[2] the porter of them was,
Old Genius, the which a double nature has.

32

He letteth in, he letteth out to wend,
  All that to come into the world desire;

7. Important centers of the cult of Venus were at Paphos (on Cyprus) and at Cnidus, in Asia Minor. The allusion to "Cytheron hill" probably derives from Boccaccio (*Genealogiae* 3.22).
8. In antiquity, a "garden of Adonis" was a pot of quick-growing herbs (see e.g., *Phaedrus* 276b); Erasmus, *Adagia* 1.1.4, says it symbolized what is transitory or fleeting. Spenser's own Garden is in a tradition of earthly paradises such as Homer's Garden of Alcinous (*Odyssey* 7.112–34), Claudian's Cyprian Garden of Venus (*Epithalamion of Honoris and Maria* 49–96), Eden in Dante's *Purgatorio* 28, and Nature's garden in Chaucer's *Parliament of Fowls*. Love allegories like *The Romance of the Rose* and Boccaccio's *Teseide* contributed to the tradition. Spenser consulted all these as well as Comes 5.16.
9. The loose Neoplatonism of stanzas 30–50 reflects a number of texts, particularly the Myth of Er in Plato's *Republic*, the *Enneads* of Plotinus (or Ficino's commentary), and Arthur Golding's translation of the *Metamorphoses* together with his prefatory epistle. Spenser's account develops in four stages: stanzas 30–35 describe, first in symbolic terms, then more concretely, the cyclical process through which all life passes; stanzas 36–38 emphasize how substance survives all changes of form (a stress found also in works by the French poets Ronsard and Du Bartas); stanzas 39–42 acknowledge the power of mutability in this otherwise perfect garden; stanzas 43–50 give a final account of the life process by revising the myth of Venus and Adonis.
1. Probably from Claudian 56–57.
2. Cf. II.xii.47 and note.

A thousand thousand naked babes[3] attend
About him day and night, which doe require,
That he with fleshly weedes° would them attire: clothes
Such as him list, such as eternall fate
Ordainéd hath, he clothes with sinfull mire,[4]
And sendeth forth to live in mortall state,
Till they againe returne backe by the hinder gate.

33

After that they againe returnéd beene,
   They in that Gardin planted be againe;
   And grow afresh, as they had never seene
   Fleshly corruption, nor mortall paine.
   Some thousand yeares so doen they there remaine;
   And then of him are clad with other hew,°   form
   Or sent into the chaungefull world againe,
   Till thither they returne, where first they grew:
So like a wheele around they runne from old to new.[5]

34

Ne needs there Gardiner to set, or sow,
   To plant or prune: for of their owne accord
   All things, as they created were, doe grow,
   And yet remember well the mightie word,
   Which first was spoken by th'Almightie lord,
   That bad them to increase and multiply.[6]
   Ne doe they need with water of the ford,°   stream
   Or of the clouds to moysten their roots dry;
For in themselves eternall moisture they imply.°   contain

35

Infinite shapes of creatures there are bred,
   And uncouth° formes, which none yet ever knew,   strange
   And every sort is in a sundry° bed   separate
   Set by it selfe, and ranckt in comely rew:[7]
   Some fit for reasonable soules t'indew,°   put on
   Some made for beasts, some made for birds to weare,
   And all the fruitfull spawne of fishes hew
   In endlesse rancks along enraungéd were,
That seemed the Ocean could not containe them there.

3. I.e., the "seed principles" of natural life; probably not souls in the religious sense, for reincarnation and pre-existence are not part of Christian doctrine. Cartari, *Imagini degli Dei* (Venice, 1571) 38, has a picture of such "babes" with Time as their porter.
4. I.e., the flesh.
5. As in Plato's Myth of Er (*Republic* 10); cf. Ovid, *Metamorphoses* 15. 165–72.
6. Genesis 1.22: "And God blessed them, saying, Be fruitful, and multiply." To mix scripture and an undoctrinaire Platonism is common in Christian tradition: cf. Golding's prefatory epistle to his translation of the *Metamorphoses*.
7. 1 Corinthians 15.39: "All flesh is not the same flesh: but there is one kind of flesh of men, another flesh of beasts, and another of fishes, and another of birds."

36

Daily they grow, and daily forth are sent
  Into the world, it to replenish more;
  Yet is the stocke not lessenéd, nor spent,
  But still remaines in everlasting store,
  As it at first created was of yore.
  For in the wide wombe of the world there lyes,
  In hatefull darkenesse and in deepe horrore,
  An huge eternall Chaos, which supplyes
The substances of natures fruitfull progenyes.[8]

37

All things from thence doe their first being fetch,
  And borrow matter, whereof they are made,
  Which when as forme and feature it does ketch,[9]
  Becomes a bodie, and doth then invade°   enter
  The state of life, out of the griesly shade.
  That substance is eterne, and bideth° so,   remains
  Ne when the life decayes, and forme does fade,
  Doth it consume, and into nothing go,
But chaungéd is, and often altred to and fro.

38

The substance is not chaunged, nor alteréd,
  But th'only forme and outward fashion;°   appearance
  For every substance is conditionéd°   bound
  To change her hew, and sundry formes to don,
  Meet for her temper and complexion:
  For formes are variable and decay,
  By course of kind,° and by occasion;   nature
  And that faire flowre of beautie fades away,
As doth the lilly fresh before the sunny ray.

39

Great enimy to it, and to all the rest,
  That in the Gardin of Adonis springs,
  Is wicked Time, who with his scyth addrest,°   armed
  Does mow the flowring herbes and goodly things,
  And all their glory to the ground downe flings,
  Where they doe wither, and are fowly mard:
  He flyes about, and with his flaggy° wings   drooping
  Beates downe both leaves and buds without regard,
Ne ever pittie may relent° his malice hard.   soften

8. Boccaccio refers to Chaos in strikingly similar terms (1.2).
9. I.e., when it assumes shape and outline. The word "forme" in stanzas 37–38 seems confusingly
  at odds with the expressions in stanzas 32 and 35.

40

Yet pittie often did the gods relent,
   To see so faire things mard, and spoyléd quight:
   And their great mother Venus did lament
   The losse of her deare brood, her deare delight:
   Her hart was pierst with pittie at the sight,
   When walking through the Gardin, them she spyde,
   Yet no'te she find redresse for such despight.[1]
   For all that lives, is subject to that law:
All things decay in time, and to their end do draw.

41

But were it not, that Time their troubler is,
   All that in this delightfull Gardin growes,
   Should happie be, and have immortall blis:
   For here all plentie, and all pleasure flowes,
   And sweet love gentle fits° emongst them throwes,   *impulses*
   Without fell rancor, or fond gealosie;
   Franckly each paramour his leman° knowes,   *lover*
   Each bird his mate, ne any does envie
Their goodly meriment, and gay felicitie.

42

There is continuall spring, and harvest there
   Continuall, both meeting at one time:
   For both the boughes doe laughing blossomes beare,
   And with fresh colours decke the wanton Prime,[2]
   And eke attonce the heavy trees they clime,
   Which seeme to labour under their fruits lode:
   The whiles the joyous birdes make their pastime
   Emongst the shadie leaves, their sweet abode,
And their true loves without suspition tell abrode.

43

Right in the middest of that Paradise,
   There stood a stately Mount,[3] on whose round top
   A gloomy grove of mirtle trees did rise,
   Whose shadie boughes sharpe steele did never lop,
   Nor wicked beasts their tender buds did crop,
   But like a girlond compasséd the hight,
   And from their fruitfull sides sweet gum did drop,

---

1. I.e., she could not repair that injury. Stanza 42 makes clear, though, that Time's effect on the Garden differs from its effect on our world.
2. I.e., luxuriant spring.
3. The goddess lies with her young lover in terrain representing her own pubic region; myrtle, the plant of Venus growing on the *mons veneris*, parallels the laurel of poetry and conquest that Spenser perhaps ironically placed in the Bower of Bliss (II.xii). The Garden's healthy fruitfulness contrasts with the Bower's infertile voyeurism and artifice. In the 1590 *Faerie Queene* this scene "in the middest of that Paradise" comes at the exact center of Book III.

That all the ground with precious deaw bedight,
Threw forth most dainty odours, and most sweet delight.

44

And in the thickest covert of that shade,
  There was a pleasant arbour, not by art,
  But of the trees owne inclination made,
  Which knitting their rancke° braunches part to part,   *dense*
  With wanton yvie twyne entrayld° athwart,   *interlaced*
  And Eglantine, and Caprifole° emong,   *honeysuckle*
  Fashioned above within their inmost part,
  That nether Phoebus beams could through them throng,
Nor Aeolus sharp blast could worke them any wrong.

45

And all about grew every sort of flowre,
  To which sad lovers were transformd of yore;
  Fresh Hyacinthus,[4] Phoebus paramoure,
  And dearest love,
  Foolish Narcisse, that likes the watry shore,
  Sad Amaranthus,[5] made a flowre but late,
  Sad Amaranthus, in whose purple gore
  Me seemes I see Amintas[6] wretched fate,
To whom sweet Poets verse hath given endlesse date.

46

There wont faire Venus often to enjoy
  Her deare Adonis joyous company,
  And reape sweet pleasure of the wanton boy;
  There yet, some say, in secret he does ly,
  Lappéd in flowres and pretious spycery,
  By her hid from the world, and from the skill°   *knowledge*
  Of Stygian Gods, which doe her love envy;
  But she her selfe, when ever that she will,
Possesseth him, and of his sweetnesse takes her fill.

47

And sooth it seemes they say: for he may not
  For ever die, and ever buried bee
  In balefull night, where all things are forgot;
  All° be he subject to mortalitie,   *although*
  Yet is eterne in mutabilitie,
  And by succession made perpetuall,

4. After accidentally killing the youth Hyacinthus, Apollo made the hyacinth spring from his beloved's
blood and bear the marking "AI AI" ("alas"); see *Metamorphoses* 10.163–219 and, on Narcissus,
3.341–511.
5. Greek for "unfading," a flower traditionally symbolizing eternity.
6. An allusion to Sidney, or perhaps to Thomas Watson's pastoral *Amintae Gaudia*. "Amyntas" is
also a shepherd in Virgil's *Eclogue* 10.

Transforméd oft, and chaungéd diverslie:
For him the Father of all formes[7] they call;
Therefore needs mote he live, that living gives to all.

48

There now he liveth in eternall blis,
  Joying his goddesse, and of her enjoyed:
  Ne feareth he henceforth that foe of his,
  Which with his cruell tuske him deadly cloyd:°   *gored*
  For that wilde Bore,[8] the which him once annoyd,°   *injured*
  She firmely hath emprisonéd for ay,
  That her sweet love his malice mote avoyd,
  In a strong rocky Cave, which is they say,
Hewen underneath that Mount, that none him losen° may.   *set free*

49

There now he lives in everlasting joy,
  With many of the Gods in company,
  Which thither haunt,° and with the wingéd boy   *frequent*
  Sporting himselfe in safe felicity:
  Who when he hath with spoiles and cruelty
  Ransackt the world, and in the wofull harts
  Of many wretches set his triumphes hye,
  Thither resorts, and laying his sad darts
Aside, with faire Adonis playes his wanton parts.

50

And his true love faire Psyche[9] with him playes,
  Faire Psyche to him lately reconcyld,
  After long troubles and unmeet upbrayes,°   *reproaches*
  With which his mother Venus her revyld,°   *scolded*
  And eke himselfe her cruelly exyld:
  But now in stedfast love and happy state
  She with him lives, and hath him borne a chyld,
  Pleasure, that doth both gods and men aggrate,°   *gratify*
Pleasure, the daughter of Cupid and Psyche late.

51

Hither great Venus brought this infant faire,
  The younger daughter of Chrysogonee,[1]

7. Since Venus actively "posseseth" Adonis, her relationship to him may seem like that of form to matter, reversing the tradition that form is male and matter female. But Adonis seems also to represent a formal principle that survives through the very variety it begets on matter.
8. Mythographers identified the boar that killed Adonis as winter, the sun's antagonist and, as such, part of the natural cycle (cf. Comes 5.16). Here it may also suggest the passion and violence that sustain animate life yet require restraint.
9. The story of Cupid and Psyche, representing the soul's purification by trial and misfortune, is told by Apuleius in his second-century novel *Metamorphoses*, trans. W. Adlington as *The Golden Ass* in 1566; the birth of Pleasure shows, says Horton 1991, a Protestant stress on the lawful joys of married sex.
1. I.e., Amoret.

...st and care
...ee,
...hee:
...ndered,°   *cared for*
...asure, to whom shee
...her lessonéd°   *taught*
...odly womanhead.

52

...ect ripenesse grew,
...oble Paragone,°   *model*
...into the worldés vew,
slacke   ...true love alone,
...chaste affectione,
...that doe live on ground.
...came, where many one
...y haveour,° and found   *deportment*
...launchéd° with loves cruell wound.   *pierced*

53

...of them her love did cast,°   *grant*
...oble knight Sir Scudamore,
...loving hart she linkéd fast
...love, t'abide for evermore,
...dearest sake enduréd sore,°   *grievous*
...ole of an hainous enimy;
...would forcéd have to have forlore
...her love, and stedfast loialty,
As ...elsewhere read that ruefull history.

54

But ...I weene, ye first desire to learne,
What end unto that fearefull Damozell,
Which fled so fast from that same foster stearne,
That was to weet, the goodly Florimell;
Who wandring for to seeke her lover deare,
Her lover deare, her dearest Marinell,
Into misfortune fell, as ye did heare,
And from Prince Arthur fled with wings of idle feare.

Canto VII

The witches sonne loves Florimell:
she flyes, he faines° to die.   *desires*
Satyrane saves the Squire of Dames
from Gyants tyrannie.

1

Like as an Hynd forth singled from the heard,
That hath escapéd from a ravenous beast,

Yet flyes away of her owne feet affeard,
And every leafe, that shaketh with the least
Murmure of winde, her terror hath encreast;
So fled faire Florimell from her vaine feare,
Long after she from perill was releast:
Each shade she saw, and each noyse she did heare,
Did seeme to be the same, which she escapt whyleare.[1]

2

All that same evening she in flying spent,
And all that night her course continewéd:
Ne did she let dull sleepe once to relent,°
Nor wearinesse to slacke her hast, but fled
Ever alike, as if her former dred
Were hard behind, her readie to arrest:°
And her white Palfrey having conqueréd
The maistring raines out of her weary wrest,°
Perforce her carriéd, where ever he thought best.

3

So long as breath, and hable° puissance   s
Did native courage unto him supply,
His pace he freshly forward did advaunce,
And carried her beyond all jeopardy,
But nought that wanteth rest, can long aby.°
He having through incessant travell spent
His force, at last perforce a downe did ly,
Ne foot could further move: The Lady gent°   le
Thereat was suddein strooke with great astonishment.°   nay

4

                                                                 entirely
And forst t'alight, on foot mote algates° tare,
A traveller unwonted to such way:
Need teacheth her this lesson hard and rare,   balance
That fortune all in equall launce° doth sway,
And mortall miseries doth make her play.
So long she travelled, till at length she came
To an hilles side, which did to her bewray
A little valley, subject to[2] the same,   spread over
All covered with thick woods, that quite it overcame.°

1. Florimell's flight parallels that of Angelica from Rinaldo in *Orlando Furioso* 1.33–34, which itself
   has models in Horace and Anacreon; but Spenser reserves Angelica's artful sophistication (cf.
   Ariosto 1.50–51) for the false Florimell (cf. viii.5–8).
2. I.e., beneath.

5

Through the tops of the high trees she did descry
    A litle smoke, whose vapour thin and light,
    Reeking° aloft, uprolléd to the sky: *smoking*
    Which chearefull signe did send unto her sight,
    That in the same did wonne some living wight.
    Eftsoones her steps she thereunto applyde,
    And came at last in weary wretched plight
    Unto the place, to which her hope did guyde,
To find some refuge there, and rest her weary syde.

6

There in a gloomy hollow glen she found
    A little cottage, built of stickes and reedes
    In homely wize, and wald with sods around,
    In which a witch did dwell, in loathly weedes,°   *garments*
    And wilfull want, all carelesse of her needes;
    So choosing solitaire to abide,
    Far from all neighbours, that her devilish deedes
    And hellish arts from people she might hide,
And hurt far off unknowne, whom ever she envide.°   *hated*

7

The Damzell there arriving entred in;
    Where sitting on the flore the Hag she found,
    Busie (as seemed) about some wicked gin:°   *scheme*
    Who soone as she beheld that suddein stound,°   *surprising sight*
    Lightly upstarted from the dustie ground,
    And with fell looke and hollow deadly gaze
    Staréd on her awhile, as one astound,°   *stunned*
    Ne had one word to speake, for great amaze,
But shewd by outward signes, that dread her sence did daze.

8

At last turning her feare to foolish wrath,
    She askt, what devill had her thither brought,
    And who she was, and what unwonted° path   *unfamiliar*
    Had guided her, unwelcoméd, unsought?
    To which the Damzell full of doubtfull thought,
    Her mildly answered; "Beldame be not wroth
    With silly° Virgin by adventure brought   *innocent*
    Unto your dwelling, ignorant and loth,°   *reluctant*
That crave but rowme to rest, while tempest overblo'th."

9

With that adowne out of her Christall eyne
    Few trickling teares she softly forth let fall,
    That like two Orient pearles, did purely shyne

Upon her snowy cheeke; and therewithall
She sighéd soft, that none so bestiall,
Nor salvage hart, but ruth° of her sad plight   *pity*
Would make to melt, or pitteously appall;
And that vile Hag, all° were her whole delight   *although*
In mischiefe, was much movéd at so pitteous sight.

10

And gan recomfort her in her rude wyse,
  With womanish compassion of her plaint,
  Wiping the teares from her suffuséd eyes,
  And bidding her sit downe, to rest her faint
  And wearie limbs a while. She nothing quaint°   *fastidious*
  Nor s'deignfull of so homely fashion,
  Sith brought she was now to so hard constraint,
  Sate downe upon the dusty ground anon,
As glad of that small rest, as Bird of tempest gon.°   *passed*

11

Tho gan she gather up her garments rent,°   *torn*
  And her loose lockes to dight in order dew,
  With golden wreath and gorgeous ornament;
  Whom such whenas the wicked Hag did vew,
  She was astonisht at her heavenly hew,°   *appearance*
  And doubted her to deeme an earthly wight,
  But or° some Goddesse, or of Dianes crew,   *either*
  And thought her to adore with humble spright;
T'adore thing so divine as beauty, were but right.

12

This wicked woman had a wicked sonne,
  The comfort of her age and weary dayes,
  A laesie loord,° for nothing good to donne,[3]   *lout*
  But stretchéd forth in idlenesse alwayes,
  Ne ever cast his mind to covet prayse,
  Or ply him selfe to any honest trade,
  But all the day before the sunny rayes
  He used to slug,° or sleepe in slothfull shade: *idle*
Such laesinesse both lewd° and poore attonce him made.   *ignorant*

13

He comming home at undertime,° there found   *noon*
  The fairest creature, that he ever saw,
  Sitting beside his mother on the ground;
  The sight whereof did greatly him adaw,°   *daunt*
  And his base thought with terrour and with aw

3. I.e., good for nothing.

So inly smot, that as one, which had gazed
On the bright Sunne unwares, doth soone withdraw
His feeble eyne, with too much brightnesse dazed,
So staréd he on her, and stood long while amazed.

14

Softly at last he gan his mother aske,
  What mister° wight that was, and whence derived,   *kind of*
  That in so straunge disguizement there did maske,
  And by what accident she there arrived:
  But she, as one nigh of her wits deprived,
  With nought but ghastly lookes him answeréd,
  Like to a ghost, that lately is revived
  From Stygian shores, where late it wanderéd;
So both at her, and each at other wonderéd.

15

But the faire Virgin was so meeke and mild,
  That she to them vouchsaféd to embace
  Her goodly port,[4] and to their senses vild,°   *vile*
  Her gentle speach applide, that in short space
  She grew familiare in that desert° place.   *desolate*
  During which time, the Chorle° through her so kind   *churl*
  And curteise use° conceived affection bace,   *demeanour*
  And cast° to love her in his brutish mind;   *resolved*
No love, but brutish lust, that was so beastly tind.°   *kindled*

16

Closely° the wicked flame his bowels brent,°   *secretly/burned*
  And shortly grew into outrageous fire;
  Yet had he not the hart, nor hardiment,
  As unto her to utter his desire;
  His caytive° thought durst not so high aspire,   *base*
  But with soft sighes, and lovely semblaunces,°   *expressions*
  He weened that his affection entire
  She should aread; many resemblaunces°   *signs of love*
To her he made, and many kind remembraunces.

17

Oft from the forrest wildings° he did bring,   *crab apples*
  Whose sides empurpled were with smiling red,
  And oft young birds, which he had taught to sing
  His mistresse prayses, sweetly caroléd,
  Girlonds of flowres sometimes for her faire hed
  He fine would dight; sometimes the squirell wild

---

4. I.e., she adopted a gently courteous manner toward them.

He brought to her in bands, as conqueréd
To be her thrall, his fellow servant vild;
All which, she of him tooke with countenance meeke and mild.

18

But past awhile, when she fit season° saw	*time*
To leave that desert mansion, she cast	
In secret wize her selfe thence to withdraw,	
For feare of mischiefe, which she did forecast	
Might be by the witch or that her sonne compast:°	*contrived*
Her wearie Palfrey closely, as she might,	
Now well recovered after long repast,	
In his proud furnitures° she freshly dight,	*trappings*
His late miswandred wayes now to remeasure° right.	*retrace*

19

And earely ere the dawning day appeard,	
She forth issewed, and on her journey went;	
She went in perill, of each noyse affeard,	
And of each shade, that did it selfe present;	
For still she fearéd to be overhent,°	*overtaken*
Of that vile hag, or her uncivile sonne:	
Who when too late awaking, well they kent,°	*discovered*
That their faire guest was gone, they both begonne	
To make exceeding mone, as they had bene undonne.	

20

But that lewd° lover did the most lament	*base*
For her depart, that ever man did heare;	
He knockt his brest with desperate intent,	
And scratcht his face, and with his teeth did teare	
His rugged flesh, and rent his ragged heare:	
That his sad mother seeing his sore plight,	
Was greatly woe begon, and gan to feare,	
Least his fraile senses were emperisht° quight,	*enfeebled*
And love to frenzy turnd, sith love is franticke hight.	

21

All wayes she sought, him to restore to plight,	
With herbs, with charms, with counsell, and with teares,	
But tears, nor charms, nor herbs, nor counsell might	
Asswage the fury, which his entrails teares:	
So strong is passion, that no reason heares.	
Tho when all other helpes she saw to faile,	
She turnd her selfe backe to her wicked leares°	*lessons*
And by her devilish arts thought to prevaile,	
To bring her backe againe, or worke her finall bale.°	*harm*

22

Eftsoones out of her hidden cave she cald
  An hideous beast,[5] of horrible aspect,
  That could the stoutest courage have appald;
  Monstrous mishapt, and all his backe was spect°   *speckled*
  With thousand spots of colours queint elect,[6]
  Thereto so swift, that it all beasts did pas:
  Like never yet did living eye detect;
  But likest it to an Hyena was,
That feeds on womens flesh, as others feede on gras.

23

It forth she cald, and gave it streight in charge,
  Through thicke and thin her to pursew apace,
  Ne once to stay to rest, or breath at large,
  Till her he had attaind, and brought in place,[7]
  Or quite devourd her beauties scornefull grace.
  The Monster swift as word, that from her went,
  Went forth in hast, and did her footing trace
  So sure and swiftly, through his perfect sent,°   *scent*
And passing speede, that shortly he her overhent.

24

Whom when the fearefull Damzell nigh espide,
  No need to bid her fast away to flie;
  That ugly shape so sore her terrifide,
  That it she shund no lesse, then dread to die,
  And her flit° Palfrey did so well apply°   *fleet/adapt*
  His nimble feet to her conceivéd feare,
  That whilest his breath did strength to him supply,
  From perill free he her away did beare:
But when his force gan faile, his pace gan wex areare.°   *slacken*

25

Which whenas she perceived, she was dismayd
  At that same last extremitie° full sore,   *adversity*
  And of her safetie greatly grew afrayd;
  And now she gan approch to the sea shore,
  As it befell, that she could flie no more,
  But yield her selfe to spoile of greedinesse.
  Lightly she leapéd, as a wight forlore,
  From her dull horse, in desperate distresse,
And to her feet betooke her doubtfull sickernesse.°   *safety*

5. Stanzas 22–28 are based on the pursuit of Manricardo by a monstrous "orc" in Boiardo, *Orlando Innamorato* (3.3.24 ff.). Medieval bestiaries associate the hyena with changefulness, hypocrisy, sin, and death. In particular, Spenser's beast represents the slander that pursues beauty and undermines reputation.
6. I.e., strangely chosen.
7. I.e., back to the witch's abode.

26

Not halfe so fast the wicked Myrrha[8] fled
  From dread of her revenging fathers hond:
  Nor halfe so fast to save her maidenhed,
  Fled fearefull Daphne on th'Aegaean strond,
  As Florimell fled from that Monster yond,
  To reach the sea, ere she of him were raught:°   *seized*
  For in the sea to drowne her selfe she fond,°   *tried*
  Rather then of the tyrant to be caught:
Thereto feare gave her wings, and neede her courage taught.

27

It fortunéd (high God did so ordaine)
  As she arrivéd on the roring shore,
  In minde to leape into the mighty maine,
  A little boate lay hoving° her before,   *floating*
  In which there slept a fisher old and pore,
  The whiles his nets were drying on the sand;
  Into the same she leapt, and with the ore°   *oar*
  Did thrust the shallop° from the floting strand:
So safetie found at sea, which she found not at land.

28

The Monster ready on the pray to sease,
  Was of his forward° hope deceivéd quight;   *eager*
  Ne durst assay to wade the perlous seas,
  But greedily long gaping at the sight,
  At last in vaine was forst to turne his flight,
  And tell the idle tidings to his Dame:
  Yet to avenge his devilish despight,°   *malice*
  He set upon her Palfrey tired lame,
And slew him cruelly, ere any reskew came.

29

And after having him embowelléd,
  To fill his hellish gorge,° it chaunst a knight   *maw*
  To passe that way, as forth he travelléd;
  It was a goodly Swaine, and of great might,
  As ever man that bloudy field did fight;
  But in vaine sheows,° that wont young knights bewitch,   *pretence*
  And courtly services tooke no delight,
  But rather joyd to be, then seemen sich:°   *such*
For both to be and seeme to him was labour lich.°   *like*

---

8. For Myrrha, see the note on III.ii.41; Daphne, fleeing from Apollo, was turned into a laurel tree
(Ovid, *Metamorphoses* 1.450–567).

30

It was to weete the good Sir Satyrane,
  That raungd abroad to seeke adventures wilde,
  As was his wont in forrest, and in plaine;
  He was all armd in rugged steel unfilde,°   *unpolished*
  As in the smoky forge it was compilde,°   *made*
  And in his Scutchin° bore a Satyres hed: *shield*
  He comming present, where the Monster vilde
  Upon that milke-white Palfreyes carkas fed,
Unto his reskew ran, and greedily him sped.

31

There well perceived he, that it was the horse,
  Whereon faire Florimell was wont to ride,
  That of that feend was rent without remorse.
  Much fearéd he, least ought did ill betide
  To that faire Mayd, the flowre of womens pride;
  For her he dearely lovéd, and in all
  His famous conquests highly magnifide:°   *glorified*
  Besides her golden girdle, which did fall
From her in flight, he found, that did him sore apall.°   *dismay*

32

Full of sad feare, and doubtfull agony,
  Fiercely he flew upon that wicked feend,
  And with huge strokes, and cruell battery
  Him forst to leave his pray, for to attend
  Him selfe from deadly daunger to defend:
  Full many wounds in his corrupted flesh
  He did engrave,° and muchell bloud did spend,   *cut deeply*
  Yet might not do him dye, but aye more fresh
And fierce he still appeard, the more he did him thresh.°   *strike*

33

He wist not, how him to despoile of life,
  Ne how to win the wishéd victory,
  Sith him he saw still stronger grow through strife,
  And him selfe weaker through infirmity;
  Greatly he grew enraged, and furiously
  Hurling his sword away, he lightly lept
  Upon the beast, that with great cruelty°   *ferocity*
  Roréd, and ragéd to be under-kept:°   *held down*
Yet he perforce him held, and strokes upon him hept.

34

As he that strives to stop a suddein flood,
  And in strong banckes his violence enclose,
  Forceth it swell above his wonted mood,

And largely overflow the fruitfull plaine,
That all the countrey seemes to be a Maine,°   *sea*
And the rich furrowes flote, all quite fordonne:°   *ruined*
The wofull husbandman doth lowd complaine,
To see his whole yeares labour lost so soone,
For which to God he made so many an idle boone.°   *prayer*

35

So him he held, and did through might amate:°   *subdue*
So long he held him, and him bet so long,
That at the last his fiercenesse gan abate,
And meekely stoup unto the victour strong:
Who to avenge the implacable° wrong,   *irremediable*
Which he supposéd donne to Florimell,
Sought by all meanes his dolour° to prolong,   *pain*
Sith dint of steele his carcas could not quell:
His maker with her charmes had framéd him so well.

36

The golden ribband, which that virgin wore
About her sclender wast, he tooke in hand,
And with it bound the beast, that lowd did rore
For great despight of that unwonted band,
Yet daréd not his victour to withstand,
But trembled like a lambe, fled from the pray,
And all the way him followd on the strand,
As he had long bene learnéd to obay;
Yet never learnéd he such service, till that day.[9]

37

Thus as he led the Beast along the way,
He spide far off a mighty Giauntesse,[1]
Fast flying on a Courser dapled gray,
From a bold knight, that with great hardinesse
Her hard pursewd, and sought for to suppresse;
She bore before her lap a dolefull Squire,
Lying athwart° her horse in great distresse,   *across*
Fast bounden hand and foote with cords of wire,
Whom she did meane to make the thrall of her desire.

38

Which whenas Satyrane beheld, in hast
He left his captive Beast at liberty,
And crost the nearest way, by which he cast°   *intended*
Her to encounter, ere she passéd by:

---

9. That Satyrane can bind the beast with Florimell's girdle (identified in IV.v.3 as the symbol of chastity) indicates that active virtue can restrain (but not destroy) slander.
1. I.e., Argante, a type of extreme unchastity in women that male vigor alone cannot successfully resist; Anderson 1988 suggests that she may in part parody the queen's "notorious exploitation of courtly flirtation with her younger male courtiers."

resumes importance, although compared to Books I and II, these last two books tend to assign more adventures to a second protagonist (Arthur in Book V, Sir Calepine in Book VI). Every book, furthermore, has appropriately placed and symbolically central moments when the narrative slows and the reader can witness an arrangement of emblematic figures and setting: in Book I, for example, the House of Holiness; in Book VI, Mount Acidale.

Related to the poem's play of analogy, pattern, and discontinuity or deferral, is the Spenserian stanza, suited to Spenser's often emblematic method. Whereas Chaucer's enjambed rhymes, for example, tend to hustle us through a well-plotted story, and whereas the surge of Milton's spacious periods sweeps us along his epic path, the final hexameters of Spenser's stanzas invite us to pause and look around. Donne's lyrics typically marshal a line of pseudological argument; Spenser's stanzas seem more spatial in effect, segments of an elaborate tapestry or pageant. The first eight lines often present a vividly realized visual description, or the illusion of one, and then the last comments on the picture. (Wise readers may often decline to take that comment as the whole truth and nothing but the truth, although many disagree on the precise relation of Spenser the "author" to the poem's narrative voice or voices; cf. Alpers 1977 and Berger 1991.) Within the stanza, moreover, Spenser achieves an astonishing range of effect. He introduces exaggeratedly alliterative language, for example (see I.i.51, or III.x.31), so as to stress the discordant nature of evil or grotesque figures. The varied accents of his pentameters frequently accord with context: note Despair's mesmerizing language in I.ix.46–47, the angel's urgently syncopated summons to the Palmer in II.viii.3, the incantatory rhythms of the nurse's magic spells in III.ii.50–51, or the lines' pitch and roll in almost any account of ships at sea, extending to uneven metrical effects when a shipwreck threatens (II.ii.24; III.14.9).

For Hazlitt, Spenser was "the poet of our waking dreams," whose music lulls the senses. One sees his point, and many have loved an idealistic Spenser who opens magic casements onto a fairyland populated with creatures of fancy given definition by their association with clear-cut good and evil. Yet the poem everywhere also reminds us of this world's noise and bustle: of religious conflict, competition for fame and patronage, discoveries, wars, treasons, the pleasures and failures of the human body, court intrigue, the sorrow and comedy of sexual desire, the search for beauty or money and status, and the dangers to the soul of what Bunyan was to call Vanity Fair. Even when St. George sees the New Jerusalem, this plowman's adopted son stands on solid ground, and although the narrator longs for Eternity (VII.viii), he longs for it while on this earth. If The Faerie Queene has been called a dream-poem, "what the poet dreams of," says Northrop Frye, "is the strenuous effort, physical, mental, and moral, of waking up to one's true humanity."[3] Since modern criticism has often turned from texts to readers, though, it seems right to end this note with the following warning and advice from A. Bartlett Giamatti (1975, 89): "Great poems are not only relevant to readers; readers must strive to become relevant to great poems. In the mediative activity of reading, we expand our humanity by engaging a world wholly new to us." To read The Faerie Queene astutely (even skeptically, when need be), yet with heart and imagination open, is to preserve the freshness of this new world even while making it our own.

---

3. "The Structure of Imagery in The Faerie Queene," UTQ 30 (1961); see pp. 707–16, in this edition.

From The Shepheardes Calender†

To His Booke

Goe little booke:[1] thy selfe present,
As child whose parent is unkent:°   *unknown*
To him that is the president°   *pattern*
Of noblesse and of chevalree,
5 And if that Envie barke at thee,
As sure it will, for succoure flee
    Under the shadow of his wing,[2]
And askéd, who thee forth did bring,
A shepheards swaine saye did thee sing,
10 All as his straying flocke he fedde:
And when his honor has thee redde,°   *seen*
Crave pardon for my hardyhedde.°   *boldness*
    But if that any aske thy name,
Say thou wert base° begot with blame: *lowly*
15 For thy° thereof thou takest shame.   *therefore*
And when thou art past jeopardee,

---

† See Heninger 1988, 1990E, on this "complex poem comprising many distinct but interrelated parts," and the probable relation of its typographical layout to that of *Arcadia* (Venice, 1571) by Jacopo Sannazaro (1456–1530). Luborsky 1980 suggests that "this our newe Poete" (as "E.K." calls Spenser in the dedicatory epistle prefixed to the poem), by his elaborately allusive presentation of the *Calender* "created a new [kind of] book."

1. Spenser echoes Chaucer's expression in *Troilus and Criseyde*, 5.1786 ("Go, litel bok, go litel myn tragedye"), to indicate his literary indebtedness to Chaucer, and to associate himself with the poet whom E.K. calls "the Loadestarre of our Language." At the conclusion of the *Calender*, Spenser again gracefully acknowledges Chaucer's mastery ("Envoy" 8–11). Among the wealth of critical commentary on the *Calender* in variously pastoral contexts, see, among others, A. C. Hamilton, "The Argument of Spenser's *Shepheardes Calender*," *ELH* 29 (1956): 171–82; P. Cullen, *Spenser, Marvell, and Renaissance Pastoral* (Cambridge, MA, 1970); P. Alpers, "The Eclogue Tradition and the Nature of Pastoral," *CE* 34 (1972): 352–71. See also I. MacCaffrey, "Allegory and Pastoral in *The Shepheardes Calender*," *ELH* 31 (1969): 88–109, and Berger 1988 (both excerpted, on pp. 769–78 and 778–87 of this volume), together with Montrose 1979, 1980, and Johnson 1990.

2. I.e., the protective sponsorship of Sir Philip Sidney, "the Noble and Vertuous Gentleman most worthy of all titles both of learning and chevalrie" to whom Spenser dedicates his poem. Writing in October 1579, Spenser remarked to Gabriel Harvey, "As for the twoo worthy Gentlemen, Master Sidney, and Master Dyer, they have me, I thanke them, in some use of familiarity." Yet Spenser throughout his career is well aware of the malicious envy in high places that threatens an aspiring poet: the barking dog of envy (5) anticipates FQ I.iv.32 and the Blatant Beast of Book VI, notably xi.40–41.

But she the way shund nathemore for thy,[2]
But forward gallopt fast; which when he spyde,
His mighty speare he couchéd warily,
And at her ran: she having him descryde,
Her selfe to fight addrest,° and threw her lode aside.   *prepared*

39

Like as a Goshauke, that in foote doth beare
  A trembling Culver,° having spide on hight   *dove*
An Egle, that with plumy wings doth sheare
  The subtile ayre, stouping° with all his might,   *plunging*
The quarrey throwes to ground with fell despight,
  And to the battell doth her selfe prepare:
So ran the Geauntesse unto the fight;
  Her firie eyes with furious sparkes did stare,°   *glitter*
And with blasphemous bannes° high God in peeces tare.[3]   *oaths*

40

She caught in hand an huge great yron mace,
  Wherewith she many had of life deprived,
But ere the stroke could seize° his ayméd place,   *attain*
  His speare amids her sun-broad shield arrived;
Yet nathemore the steele a sunder rived,
  All were the beame° in bignesse like a mast,   *spear*
Ne her out of the stedfast sadle drived,
  But glauncing on the tempred metall, brast°   *burst*
In thousand shivers, and so forth beside her past.

41

Her Steed did stagger with that puissaunt strooke;
  But she no more was movéd with that might,
Then it had lighted° on an aged Oke;   *fallen*
  Or on the marble Pillour, that is pight
Upon the top of Mount Olympus hight,
  For the brave youthly Champions to assay,
With burning charet wheeles it nigh to smite:[1]
  But who that smites it, mars his joyous play,
And is the spectacle of ruinous decay.°   *destruction*

42

Yet therewith sore enraged, with sterne regard
  Her dreadfull weapon she to him addrest,°   *directed*
Which on his helmet martelléd° so hard,   *hammered*
  That made him low incline his lofty crest,
And bowd his battred visour to his brest:

---

2. I.e., but she did not turn aside on that account.
3. I.e., dismember the body of God (in the person of Christ) with once common oaths such as "swounds" ("his wounds") or "sdeath" ("his death").
4. The assumption that Mount Olympus was the site of the Olympic Games appears also in Sidney's *Apologie for Poetrie*, but Spenser may have been misled by phrasing in Comes 5.1.

Wherewith he was so stund, that he n'ote° ryde,   *could not*
But reeléd to and fro from East to West:
Which when his cruel enimy espyde,
She lightly unto him adjoynéd side to syde;

43

And on his collar laying puissant hand,
  Out of his wavering seat him pluckt perforse,°   *forcibly*
Perforse him pluckt, unable to withstand,
Or helpe himselfe, and laying thwart her horse,
In loathly wise like to a carion corse,°   *corpse*
She bore him fast away. Which when the knight,
That her pursewéd, saw, with great remorse°   *compassion*
He neare was touchéd in his noble spright,
And gan encrease his speed, as she encreast her flight.

44

Whom when as nigh approching she espyde,
  She threw away her burden angrily;
For she list° not the battell to abide,   *cared*
But made her selfe more light, away to fly:
Yet her the hardy knight pursewd so nye,
That almost in the backe he oft her strake:
But still when him at hand she did espy,
  She turnd, and semblaunce of faire fight did make;
But when he stayd, to flight againe she did her take.

45

By this the good Sir Satyrane gan wake
  Out of his dreame, that did him long entraunce,
And seeing none in place, he gan to make
Exceeding mone, and curst that cruell chaunce,
Which reft from him so faire a chevisaunce:°   *enterprise*
At length he spide, whereas that wofull Squire,
Whom he had reskewéd from captivaunce
  Of his strong foe, lay tombled in the myre,
Unable to arise, or foot or hand to styre.°   *stir*

46

To whom approching, well he mote perceive
  In that foule plight a comely personage,
And lovely face, made fit for to deceive
Fraile Ladies hart with loves consuming rage,
Now in the blossome of his freshest age:
He reard him up, and loosd his yron bands,
And after gan inquire his parentage,
  And how he fell into that Gyaunts hands,
And who that was, which chacéd her along the lands.°   *countryside*

47

Then trembling yet through feare, the Squire bespake,
  "That Geauntesse Argante is behight,
  A daughter of the Titans which did make
  Warre against heaven, and heapéd hils on hight,
  To scale the skyes, and put Jove from his right:
  Her sire Typhoeus was, who mad through merth,
  And drunke with bloud of men, slaine by his might,
  Through incest, her of his owne mother Earth
Whilome begot, being but halfe twin of that berth.

48

"For at that berth another Babe she bore,
  To weet the mighty Ollyphant⁵ that wrought
  Great wreake° to many errant knights of yore,   *destruction*
  And many hath to foule confusion° brought.   *ruin*
  These twinnes, men say, (a thing far passing thought)
  Whiles in their mothers wombe enclosd they were,
  Ere they into the lightsome° world were brought,   *bright*
  In fleshly lust were mingled both yfere,°   *together*
And in that monstrous wise did to the world appere.

49

"So lived they ever after in like sin,
  Gainst natures law, and good behavioure:°   *conduct*
  But greatest shame was to that maiden twin,
  Who not content so fowly to devoure°   *eagerly enjoy*
  Her native flesh, and staine her brothers bowre,
  Did wallow in all other fleshly myre,
  And suffred beasts her body to deflowre:
  So whot° she burnéd in that lustfull fyre,   *hot*
Yet all that might not slake her sensuall desyre.

50

"But over all the countrey she did raunge,
  To seeke young men, to quench her flaming thrust,°   *thirst*
  And feed her fancy with delightfull chaunge:
  Whom so she fittest finds to serve her lust,
  Through her maine° strength, in which she most doth trust,   *mighty*
  She with her brings into a secret Ile,
  Where in eternall bondage dye he must,
  Or be the vassall of her pleasures vile,
And in all shamefull sort him selfe with her defile.

5. Literally, "elephant"; cf. the "geaunt" named "Sire Olifaunt" in Chaucer's comic "Tale of Sir
   Thopas." The parentage Spenser invents for the twins explains their sexual perversity and monstrous
   pride, vices shared with the Giants and Titans who opposed Zeus's new order.

51

"Me seely° wretch she so at vauntage caught,   *simple*
   After she long in waite for me did lye,
   And meant unto her prison to have brought,
   Her lothsome pleasure there to satisfye;
   That thousand deathes me lever° were to dye,   *rather*
   Then breake the vow, that to faire Columbell
   I plighted have, and yet keepe stedfastly:
   As for my name, it mistreth° not to tell;   *needs*
Call me the Squyre of Dames,[6] that me beseemeth well.

52

"But that bold knight, whom ye pursuing saw
   That Geauntesse, is not such, as she seemed,
   But a faire virgin, that in martiall law,
   And deedes of armes above all Dames is deemed,
   And above many knights is eke esteemed,
   For her great worth; She Palladine is hight:
   She you from death, you me from dread redeemed.
   Ne any may that Monster match in fight,
But she, or such as she, that is so chaste a wight."[7]

53

"Her well beseemes that Quest," quoth Satyrane,
   "But read, thou Squyre of Dames, what vow is this,
   Which thou upon thy selfe hast lately ta'ne?"
   "That shall I you recount," quoth he, "ywis,°   *certainly*
   So be ye pleasd to pardon all amis.
   That gentle Lady, whom I love and serve,
   After long suit and weary servicis,
   Did aske me, how I could her love deserve,
And how she might be sure, that I would never swerve.

54

"I glad by any meanes her grace to gaine,
   Bad her commaund my life to save, or spill.°   *destroy*
   Eftsoones she bad me, with incessaunt paine
   To wander through the world abroad at will,
   And every where, where with my power or skill
   I might do service unto gentle Dames,
   That I the same should faithfully fulfill,
   And at the twelve monethes end should bring their names
And pledges; as the spoiles of my victorious games.

6. The Squire comically exemplifies bondage to conventional love codes; the cynical futility of his "quests" matches the triviality of his lady's commands (cf. *Orlando Furioso* 28).
7. Only Palladine can rout Argante: only true chastity counters perverted lust. Her name suggests "paladin" (a knightly champion) and the giant-fighter Pallas Athena; she may represent an early version of Britomart.

55

"So well I to faire Ladies service did,
  And found such favour in their loving hartes,
  That ere the yeare his course had compassid,°   *completed*
  Three hundred pledges for my good desartes,
  And thrise three hundred thanks for my good partes°   *conduct*
  I with me brought, and did to her present:
  Which when she saw, more bent to eke° my smartes,   *add to*
  Then to reward my trusty true intent,
She gan for me devise a grievous punishment.

56

"To weet, that I my travell should resume,
  And with like labour walke the world around,
  Ne ever to her presence should presume,
  Till I so many other Dames had found,
  The which, for all the suit I could propound,
  Would me refuse their pledges to afford,
  But did abide for ever chast and sound."
  "Ah gentle Squire," quoth he, "tell at one word,
How many foundst thou such to put in thy record?"

57

"In deed Sir knight," said he, "one word may tell
  All, that I ever found so wisely stayd;°   *constant*
  For onely three they were disposd so well,
  And yet three yeares I now abroad have stayd,
  To find them out." "Mote I," then laughing sayd
  The knight, "inquire of thee, what were those three,
  The which thy proffred curtesie denayd?°   *rejected*
  Or ill they seeméd sure avizd to bee,[8]
Or brutishly brought up, that nev'r did fashions see."

58

"The first which then refuséd me," said hee,
  "Certes was but a common Courtisane,
  Yet flat refusd to have a do with mee,
  Because I could not give her many a Jane."°   *coin*
  (Thereat full hartely laughed Satyrane).
  "The second was an holy Nunne to chose,[9]
  Which would not let me be her Chappellane,°   *confessor*
  Because she knew, she said, I would disclose
Her counsell,° if she should her trust in me repose.   *secrets*

8. I.e., either they were foolish.
9. I.e., if you please.

59

"The third a Damzell was of low degree,
  Whom I in countrey cottage found by chaunce;
  Full little weenéd I, that chastitee
  Had lodging in so mcanc a maintenaunce,°   *condition*
  Yet was she faire, and in her countenance
  Dwelt simple truth in seemely fashion.
  Long thus I wooed her with dew observaunce,
  In hope unto my pleasure to have won;
But was as farre at last, as when I first begon.

60

"Safe her, I never any woman found,
  That chastity did for it selfe embrace,
  But were for other causes firme and sound;
  Either for want of handsome° time and place,   *suitable*
  Or else for feare of shame and fowle disgrace.
  Thus am I hopelesse ever to attaine
  My Ladies love, in such a desperate case.
  But all my dayes am like to wast in vaine,
Seeking to match the chaste with th'unchaste Ladies traine."°   *company*

61

"Perdy," said Satyrane, "thou Squire of Dames,
  Great labour fondly° hast thou hent° in hand,   *foolishly/taken*
  To get small thankes, and therewith many blames,
  That may emongst Alcides[1] labours stand."
  Thence backe returning to the former land,°   *place*
  Where late he left the Beast, he overcame,
  He found him not; for he had broke his band,
  And was returned againe unto his Dame,
To tell what tydings of faire Florimell became.

Canto VIII

The Witch creates a snowy Lady,
  like to Florimell,
  Who wronged by Carle° by Proteus saved,   *churl*
  is sought by Paridell.

1

So oft as I this history record,
  My hart doth melt with meere° compassion,   *pure*
  To thinke, how causelesse of her owne accord[1]
  This gentle Damzell, whom I write upon,
  Should plongéd be in such affliction,
  Without all hope of comfort or reliefe,

1. Hercules.
1. I.e., through no culpable action on her part.

That sure I weene, the hardest hart of stone,
  Would hardly find° to aggravate her griefe;   *choose*
For misery craves rather mercie, then repriefe.°   *reproach*

2

But that accursèd Hag, her hostesse late,
  Had so enranckled her malitious hart,
  That she desyrd th'abridgement of her fate,[2]
  Or long enlargement° of her painefull smart.   *increase*
  Now when the Beast, which by her wicked art
  Late forth she sent, she backe returning spyde,
  Tyde with her broken girdle, it a part
  Of her rich spoyles, whom he had earst destroyd,
She weend,° and wondrous gladnesse to her hart applyde. *supposed*

3

And with it running hast'ly to her sonne,
  Thought with that sight him much to have relived;°   *restored*
  Who thereby deeming sure the thing as donne,
  His former griefe with furie fresh revived,
  Much more then earst, and would have algates rived[3]
  The hart out of his brest: for sith her ded
  He surely dempt,° himselfe he thought deprived   *thought*
  Quite of all hope, wherewith he long had fed
His foolish maladie, and long time had misled.

4

With thought whereof, exceeding mad° he grew,   *frenzied*
  And in his rage his mother would have slaine,
  Had she not fled into a secret mew,°   *hiding place*
  Where she was wont her Sprights to entertaine
  The maisters of her art:[4] there was she faine° *accustomed*
  To call them all in order to her ayde,
  And them conjure° upon eternall paine,   *charge*
  To counsell her so carefully° dismayd,   *grievously*
How she might heale her sonne, whose senses were decayd.° *destroyed*

5

By their advise, and her owne wicked wit,
  She there devized a wondrous worke to frame,°   *construct*
  Whose like on earth was never framèd yit,
  That even Nature selfe envide the same,
  And grudged to see the counterfet should shame
  The thing it selfe. In hand she boldly tooke
  To make another like the former Dame,

2. I.e., to shorten the fated term of her life.
3. I.e., entirely torn.
4. The demons who enable her to use magic; in *Macbeth*, the witches call such spirits their "masters" (4.1.63).

Another Florimell, in shape and looke
So lively° and so like, that many it mistooke.   *lifelike*

6

The substance, whereof she the bodie made,
  Was purest snow in massie mould congeald,
  Which she had gathered in a shadie glade
  Of the Riphoean hils,[5] to her reveald
  By errant Sprights, but from all men conceald:
  The same she tempred with fine Mercury,
  And virgin wex, that never yet was seald,
  And mingled them with perfect vermily,°   *vermilion*
That like a lively sanguine° it seemed to the eye.   *blood-red*

7

In stead of eyes two burning lampes she set
  In silver sockets, shyning like the skyes,
  And a quicke moving Spirit did arret°   *assign*
  To stirre and roll them, like a womans eyes;
  In stead of yellow lockes she did devise,
  With golden wyre° to weave her curléd head;   *metallic thread*
  Yet golden wyre was not so yellow thrise°   *by a third*
  As Florimells faire haire: and in the stead
Of life, she put a Spright to rule the carkasse dead.

8

A wicked Spright yfraught° with fawning guile,   *filled*
  And faire resemblance above all the rest,
  Which with the Prince of Darknesse fell somewhile,
  From heavens blisse and everlasting rest;
  Him needed not instruct,[6] which way were best
  Himselfe to fashion likest Florimell,
  Ne how to speake, ne how to use his gest,°   *bearing*
  For he in counterfeisance° did excell,   *deception*
And all the wyles of wemens wits knew passing well.[7]

9

Him shapéd thus, she deckt in garments gay,
  Which Florimell had left behind her late,
  That who so then her saw, would surely say,
  It was her selfe, whom it did imitate,
  Or fairer then her selfe, if ought algate
  Might fairer be. And then she forth her brought

5. Mountains once supposed to be in the wilds of northern Eurasia.
6. I.e., he needed no instruction.
7. The making of the false Florimell, whose pseudo-Petrarchan beauty cloaks immodesty, hints at the danger of magic technology (her ingredients are alchemical and Paracelsean) and of false art that imitates Nature's mere externals; it may also be relevant that mercury was used to cure syphilis. Magic is a dark parody of the poet's art (cf. Gross 1985), although P. Cheney 1988 argues that for Spenser good magic is an analogue of effective poetry.

Unto her sonne, that lay in feeble state;
Who seeing her gan streight° upstart, and thought   *at once*
She was the Lady selfe, whom he so long had sought.

10

Tho fast her clipping twixt his armés twaine,
   Extremely joyéd in so happie sight,
   And soone forgot his former sickly paine;
   But she, the more to seeme such as she hight,
   Coyly rebutted° his embracement light;   *repelled*
   Yet still with gentle countenaunce retained,
   Enough to hold a foole in vaine delight:
   Him long she so with shadowes entertained,
As her Creatresse had in charge to her ordained.

11

Till on a day, as he disposéd was
   To walke the woods with that his Idole faire,
   Her to disport,° and idle time to pas,   *entertain*
   In th'open freshnesse of the gentle aire,
   A knight that way there chauncéd to repaire;°   *go*
   Yet knight he was not, but a boastfull swaine,
   That deedes of armes had ever in despaire,[8]
   Proud Braggadocchio, that in vaunting vaine
His glory did repose,° and credit did maintaine.   *establish*

12

He seeing with that Chorle so faire a wight,
   Deckéd with many a costly ornament,
   Much merveiléd thereat, as well he might,
   And thought that match a fowle disparagement:°   *disgrace*
   His bloudie speare eftsoones he boldly bent
   Against the silly clowne,° who dead through feare,   *rustic*
   Fell streight to ground in great astonishment;
   "Villein," said he, "this Ladie is my deare,
Dy, if thou it gainesay: I will away her beare."

13

The fearefull Chorle durst not gainesay, nor dooe,
   But trembling stood, and yielded him the pray;
   Who finding litle leasure her to wooe,
   On Tromparts steed her mounted without stay,°   *hindrance*
   And without reskew led her quite away.
   Proud man himselfe then Braggadocchio deemed,
   And next to none, after that happie day,

8. I.e., from whom true feats of arms could never be expected. The boaster Braggadocchio and his squire Trompart, whose name suggests "trompeur" (French for "deceiver") and trumpet, have been introduced in II.iii.

Being possesséd of that spoyle, which seemed
The fairest wight on ground, and most of men esteemed.

14

But when he saw himselfe free from poursute,
    He gan make gentle purpose° to his Dame,   *discourse*
    With termes of love and lewdnesse dissolute;
    For he could well his glozing speaches frame
    To such vaine uses, that him best became:
    But she thereto would lend but light regard,
    As seeming sory, that she ever came
    Into his powre, that uséd her so hard,
To reave° her honor, which she more then life prefard.   *take away*

15

Thus as they two of kindnesse° treated long,   *love*
    There them by chaunce encountred on the way
    An arméd knight,[9] upon a courser strong,
    Whose trampling feet upon the hollow lay°   *ground*
    Seeméd to thunder, and did nigh affray
    That Capons° courage: yet he lookéd grim,   *coward*
    And fained to cheare his Ladie in dismay;
    Who seemed for feare to quake in every lim,
And her to save from outrage, meekely prayéd him.

16

Fiercely that stranger forward came, and nigh
    Approaching, with bold words and bitter threat,
    Bad that same boaster, as he mote, on high[1]
    To leave to him that Lady for excheat,[2]
    Or bide° him battell without further treat.°   *endure/parley*
    That challenge did too peremptory seeme,
    And fild his senses with abashment great;
    Yet seeing nigh him jeopardy extreme,
He it dissembled well, and light seemed to esteeme.

17

Saying, "Thou foolish knight, that weenst with words
    To steale away, that I with blowes have wonne,
    And brought throgh points of many perilous swords:
    But if thee list to see thy Courser ronne,
    Or prove thy selfe, this sad° encounter shonne,   *grievous*
    And seeke else° without hazard of thy hed."   *elsewhere*
    At those proud words that other knight begonne
    To wexe exceeding wroth, and him ared°   *told*
To turne his steede about, or sure he should be ded.

9. I.e., Sir Ferraugh, who is not identified until IV.ii.4.
1. I.e., as loudly as he could.
2. I.e., as his property.

18

"Sith then," said Braggadocchio, "needes thou wilt
 Thy dayes abridge, through proofe of puissance,
 Turne we our steedes, that both in equall tilt°   *mounted combat*
 May meet againe, and each take happie chance."
 This said, they both a furlongs mountenance°   *distance*
 Retyrd their steeds, to ronne in even race:
 But Braggadocchio with his bloudie lance
 Once having turnd, no more returnd his face,
But left his love to losse, and fled himselfe apace.

19

The knight him seeing fly, had no regard°   *care*
 Him to poursew, but to the Ladie rode,
 And having her from Trompart lightly reard,°   *taken up*
 Upon his Courser set the lovely lode,
 And with her fled away without abode.°   *delay*
 Well weenéd he, that fairest Florimell
 It was, with whom in company he yode,°   *went*
 And so her selfe did alwaies to him tell;
So made him thinke him selfe in heaven, that was in hell.

20

But Florimell her selfe was farre away,
 Driven to great distresse by Fortune straunge,
 And taught the carefull° Mariner to play,   *full of care*
 Sith late mischaunce had her compeld to chaunge
 The land for sea, at randon° there to raunge: *random*
 Yet there that cruell Queene avengeresse,[3]
 Not satisfide so farre her to estraunge
 From courtly blisse and wonted happinesse,
Did heape on her new waves of weary wretchednesse.

21

For being fled into the fishers bote,
 For refuge from the Monsters crueltie,
 Long so she on the mightie maine did flote,
 And with the tide drove forward careleslie;
 For th'aire was milde, and clearéd was the skie,
 And all his windes Dan° Aeolus did keepe,   *Master*
 From stirring up their stormy enmitie,
 As pittying to see her waile and weepe;
But all the while the fisher did securely sleepe.

22

At last when droncke with drowsinesse, he woke,
 And saw his drover° drive along the streame,   *boat*

3. I.e., the goddess Fortuna (Fortune).

He was dismayd, and thrise his breast he stroke,
For marvell of that accident extreame;
But when he saw that blazing beauties beame,
Which with rare light his bote did beautifie,
He marveild more, and thought he yet did dreame
Not well awakt, or that some extasie°   *madness*
Assotted° had his sense, or dazéd was his eie.   *bewildered*

23

But when her well avizing,° he perceived   *viewing*
  To be no vision, nor fantasticke sight,
  Great comfort of her presence he conceived,
  And felt in his old courage° new delight   *spirit*
  To gin awake, and stirre his frozen spright:
  Tho rudely askt her, how she thither came.
  "Ah," said she, "father, I note read⁴ aright,
  What hard misfortune brought me to the same;
Yet am I glad that here I now in safety am.

24

"But thou good man, sith farre in sea we bee,
  And the great waters gin apace to swell,
  That now no more we can the maine-land see,
  Have care, I pray, to guide the cock-bote° well,   *skiff*
  Least worse on sea then us on land befell."
  Thereat th'old man did nought but fondly° grin,   *foolishly*
  And said, his boat the way could wisely tell:
  But his deceiptfull eyes did never lin,°   *cease*
To looke on her faire face, and marke her snowy skin.

25

The sight whereof in his congealéd flesh,
  Infixt such secret sting of greedy lust,
  That the drie withered stocke it gan refresh,
  And kindled heat, that soone in flame forth brust:°   *burst*
  The driest wood is soonest burnt to dust.
  Rudely to her he lept, and his rough hand
  Where ill became him, rashly would have thrust,
  But she with angry scorne him did withstond,
And shamefully reprovéd for his rudeness fond.

26

But he, that never good nor maners knew,
  Her sharpe rebuke full litle did esteeme;
  Hard is to teach an old horse amble trew.
  The inward smoke, that did before but steeme,
  Broke into open fire and rage° extreme,   *passion*
  And now he strength gan adde unto his will,

4. I.e., cannot tell.

Forcing to doe, that did him fowle misseeme:°   *misbecome*
Beastly he threw her downe, ne cared to spill[5]
Her garments gay with scales of fish, that all did fill.

27

The silly° virgin strove him to withstand,   *innocent*
  All that she might, and him in vaine revild:°   *rebuked*
  She struggled strongly both with foot and hand,
  To save her honor from that villaine vild,
  And cride to heaven, from humane helpe exild.
  O ye brave knights, that boast this Ladies love,
  Where be ye now, when she is nigh defild
  Of filthy wretch? well may shee you reprove
Or falshood or of slouth, when most it may behove.[6]

28

But if that thou, Sir Satyran, didst weete,
  Or thou, Sir Peridure,[7] her sorie state,
  How soone would yee assemble many a fleete,
  To fetch from sea, that ye at land lost late;
  Towres, Cities, Kingdomes ye would ruinate,°   *ruin*
  In your avengement and dispiteous° rage,   *pitiless*
  Ne ought your burning fury mote abate;
  But° if Sir Calidore[8] could it presage,°   *unless/know of*
No living creature could his cruelty asswage.

29

But sith that none of all her knights is nye,
  See how the heavens of voluntary grace,
  And soveraine favour towards chastity,
  Doe succour send to her distresséd cace:
  So much high God doth innocence embrace.°   *protect*
  It fortunéd, whilest thus she stifly strove,
  And the wide sea importunéd long space
  With shrilling shrieckes, Proteus[9] abroad did rove,
Along the fomy waves driving his finny drove.

30

Proteus is Shepheard of the seas of yore,
  And hath the charge of Neptunes mightie heard;
  An aged sire with head all frory° hore,   *frosty*
  And sprinckled frost upon his deawy beard:

5. I.e., nor cared if he stained. Cf. the hermit's assault on Angelica in *Orlando Furioso* 8.30–50.
6. I.e., when it most behooves you to aid her.
7. In the Welsh *Mabinogion* Peredur is the equivalent of Perceval; Geoffrey of Monmouth calls him a knight of the Round Table (9.12); Spenser may have intended him to be the hero of a later book.
8. The hero of Book VI.
9. At III.iv.25 chiefly a seer, Proteus is here the shape-shifting shepherd of the seas (cf. *Odyssey* 4.456–58, and Virgil, *Georgics* 4.387–95, 406–10). To Boccaccio (*Genealogiae* 7.9), his various forms indicate the passions.

Who when those pittifull outcries he heard,
Through all the seas so ruefully resound,
His charet swift in haste he thither steard,
Which with a teeme of scaly Phocas° bound   seals
Was drawne upon the waves, that foméd him around.

31

And comming to that Fishers wandring bote,
   That went at will, withouten carde° or sayle,   chart
He therein saw that yrkesome sight, which smote
   Deepe indignation and compassion frayle°   tender
   Into his hart attonce: streight did he hayle°   drag
The greedy villein from his hopéd pray,
   Of which he now did very litle fayle,
   And with his staffe, that drives his Heard astray,
Him bet so sore, that life and sense did much dismay.

32

The whiles the pitteous Ladie up did ryse,
   Ruffled and fowly raid° with filthy soyle,   smeared
And blubbred face with teares of her faire eyes:
   Her heart nigh broken was with weary toyle,
   To save her selfe from that outrageous spoyle,
But when she lookéd up, to weet, what wight
   Had her from so infamous fact assoyle,°   freed
   For shame, but more for feare of his grim sight,
Downe in her lap she hid her face, and loudly shright.°   shrieked

33

Her selfe not savéd yet from daunger dred
   She thought, but chaunged from one to other feare;
Like as a fearefull Partridge, that is fled
   From the sharpe Hauke, which her attachéd neare,[1]
   And fals to ground, to seeke for succour theare,
Whereas the hungry Spaniels she does spy,
   With greedy jawes her readie for to teare;
   In such distresse and sad perplexity
Was Florimell, when Proteus she did see thereby.

34

But he endevouréd with speeches milde
   Her to recomfort, and accourage bold,
Bidding her feare no more her foeman vilde,
   Nor doubt himselfe; and who he was, her told.
   Yet all that could not from affright her hold,
Ne to recomfort her at all prevayld;
   For her faint heart was with the frozen cold
   Benumbd so inly, that her wits nigh fayld,
And all her senses with abashment° quite were quayld.°   fear/overcome

1. I.e., nearly seized.

35

Her up betwixt his rugged hands he reard,
  And with his frory° lips full softly kist,   *frosty*
  Whiles the cold ysickles from his rough beard,
  Droppéd adowne upon her yvorie brest:
  Yet he himselfe so busily addrest,°   *applied*
  That her out of astonishment° he wrought.   *insensibility*
  And out of that same fishers filthy nest
  Removing her, into his charet brought,
And there with many gentle termes her faire besought.

36

But that old leachour, which with bold assault
  That beautie durst presume to violate,
  He cast° to punish for his hainous fault: *resolved*
  Then tooke he him yet trembling sith of late,
  And tyde behind his charet, to aggrate°   *gratify*
  The virgin, whom he had abusde so sore:
  So draged him through the waves in scornefull state,
  And after cast him up, upon the shore;
But Florimell with him unto his bowre he bore.

37

His bowre is in the bottome of the maine,°   *ocean*
  Under a mightie rocke, gainst which do rave
  The roaring billowes in their proud disdaine,
  That with the angry working of the wave,
  Therein is eaten out an hollow cave,
  That seemes rough Masons hand with engines° keene   *tools*
  Had long while labouréd it to engrave:°   *dig out*
  There was his wonne, ne living wight was seene,
Save one old Nymph, hight Panope[2] to keepe it cleane.

38

Thither he brought the sory Florimell,
  And entertainéd her the best he might
  And Panope her entertaind eke well,
  As an immortall mote a mortall wight,
  To winne her liking unto his delight:
  With flattering words he sweetly wooéd her,
  And offeréd faire gifts t'allure her sight,
  But she both offers and the offerer
Despysde, and all the fawning of the flatterer.

2. From Greek, "all-seeing." Hesiod makes her a nereid (*Theogony* 250), but as an elderly underwater
housekeeper she is Spenser's own creation. In V.iii Florimell, released from watery captivity, will
marry her beloved Marinell.

39

Daily he tempted her with this or that,
  And never suffred her to be at rest:
But evermore she him refuséd flat,
  And all his fainéd kindnesse did detest,
  So firmely she had sealéd up her brest.
Sometimes he boasted, that a God he hight:
  But she a mortall creature lovéd best:
  Then he would make himselfe a mortall wight;
But then she said she loved none, but a Faerie knight.

40

Then like a Faerie knight himselfe he drest;
  For every shape on him he could endew:°   *endow*
  Then like a king he was to her exprest,°   *shown*
  And offred kingdomes unto her in vew,
  To be his Leman° and his Ladie trew: *lover*
  But when all this he nothing saw prevaile,
  With harder meanes he cast her to subdew,
  And with sharpe threates her often did assaile,
So thinking for to make her stubborne courage quaile.

41

To dreadfull shapes he did himselfe transforme,
  Now like a Gyant, now like to a feend,
  Then like a Centaure, then like to a storme,
  Raging within the waves: thereby he weend
  Her will to win unto his wishéd end.
  But when with feare, nor favour, nor with all
  He else could doe, he saw himselfe esteemd,
  Downe in a Dongeon deepe he let her fall,
And threatned there to make her his eternall thrall.

42

Eternall thraldome was to her more liefe,°   *dear*
  Then losse of chastitie, or chaunge of love:
  Die had she rather in tormenting griefe,
  Then any should of falsenesse her reprove,
  Or loosenesse, that she lightly did remove.°   *change*
  Most vertuous virgin, glory be thy meed,
  And crowne of heavenly praise with Saints above,
  Where most sweet hymmes of this thy famous deed
Are still emongst them song, that far my rymes exceed.[3]

---

3. "Beauty is wooed by Proteus, the mutable forms of this life, but . . . beauty and love are above
the physical, mutable realm of Proteus" (Roche, *Flame*, 161–62).

43

Fit song of Angels caroléd to bee;
  But yet what so my feeble Muse can frame,
  Shall be t'advaunce° thy goodly chastitee,   *praise*
  And to enroll thy memorable name,
  In th'heart of every honourable Dame,
  That they thy vertuous deedes may imitate,
  And be partakers of thy endlesse fame.
  It yrkes° me, leave thee in this wofull state,   *grieves*
To tell of Satyrane, where I him left of late.

44

Who having ended with that Squire of Dames
  A long discourse of his adventures vaine,
  The which himselfe, then° Ladies more defames,   *than*
  And finding not th' Hyena to be slaine,
  With that same Squire, returnéd backe againe
  To his first way. And as they forward went,
  They spyde a knight faire pricking on the plaine,
  As if he were on some adventure bent,
And in his port appearéd manly hardiment.

45

Sir Satyrane him towards did addresse,
  To weet, what wight he was, and what his quest:
  And comming nigh, eftsoones he gan to gesse
  Both by the burning hart, which on his brest
  He bare, and by the colours in his crest,
  That Paridell[4] it was. Tho to him yode,°   *went*
  And him saluting,° as beseeméd best,   *greeting*
  Gan first inquire of tydings farre abrode;
And afterwardes, on what adventure now he rode.

46

Who thereto answering, said; "The tydings bad,
  Which now in Faerie court all men do tell,
  Which turnéd hath great mirth, to mourning sad,
  Is the late ruine of proud Marinell,
  And suddein parture of faire Florimell,
  To find him forth: and after her are gone
  All the brave knights, that doen in armes excell,
  To savegard her, ywandred all alone;
Emongst the rest my lot (unworthy) is to be one."

---

4. Paridell's name indicates his descent from the Trojan Paris; see ix.36–37. Comes says, "Nature made [Paris] noble, but a little time joined him with lust" (6.23).

47

"Ah gentle knight," said then Sir Satyrane,
  "Thy labour all is lost, I greatly dread,
  That hast a thanklesse service on thee ta'ne,
  And offrest sacrifice unto the dead:
  For dead, I surely doubt,° thou maist aread   *fear*
  Henceforth for ever Florimell to be,
  That all the noble knights of Maydenhead,
  Which her adored, may sore repent° with me,   *grieve*
And all faire Ladies may for ever sory be."

48

Which words when Paridell had heard, his hew
  Gan greatly chaunge, and seemed dismayd to bee;
  Then said, "Faire Sir, how may I weene it trew,
  That ye doe tell in such uncertaintee?
  Or speake ye of report,° or did ye see   *rumor*
  Just cause of dread, that makes ye doubt so sore?
  For perdie else how mote it ever bee,
  That ever hand should dare for to engore°   *shed*
Her noble bloud? the heavens such crueltie abhore."

49

"These eyes did see, that° they will ever rew   *what*
  T'have seene," quoth he, "when as a monstrous beast
  The Palfrey, whereon she did travell, slew,
  And of his bowels made his bloudie feast:
  Which speaking token[5] sheweth at the least
  Her certaine losse, if not her sure decay:°   *destruction*
  Besides, that° more suspition encreast,   *which*
  I found her golden girdle cast astray,°   *aside*
Distaynd with durt and bloud, as relique of the pray."

50

"Aye me," said Paridell, "the signes be sad,
  And but God turne the same to good soothsay,°   *omen*
  That Ladies safetie is sore to be drad:°   *feared*
  Yet will I not forsake my forward way,
  Till triall doe more certaine truth bewray."
  "Faire Sir," quoth he, "well may it you succeed,
  Ne long shall Satyrane behind you stay,
  But to the rest, which in this Quest proceed
My labour adde, and be partaker of their speed."°   *fortune*

51

"Ye noble knights," said then the Squire of Dames,
  "Well may ye speed in so praiseworthy paine:

5. I.e., eloquent indication.

But sith the Sunne now ginnes to slake his beames,
In deawy vapours of the westerne maine,
And lose° the teme out of his weary waine,   *release*
Mote not mislike° you also to abate   *ill please*
Your zealous hast, till morrow next againe
Both light of heaven, and strength of men relate:°   *bring back*
Which if ye please, to yonder castle turne your gate."°   *steps*

52

That counsell pleaséd well; so all yfere°   *together*
Forth marchéd to a Castle them before,
Where soone arriving, they restrainéd were
Of readie entrance, which ought evermore
To errant knights be commun: wondrous sore
Thereat displeasd they were, till that young Squire
Gan them informe the cause, why that same dore
Was shut to all, which lodging did desire:
The which to let you weet, will further time require.

Canto IX

> Malbecco will no straunge knights host,
>   For peevish gealosie:
> Paridell giusts° with Britomart: *jousts*
>   Both shew their auncestrie.

1

Redoubted knights, and honorable Dames,[1]
To whom I levell° all my labours end,   *direct*
Right sore I feare, least with unworthy blames
This odious argument my rimes should shend,°   *disgrace*
Or ought your goodly patience offend,
Whiles of a wanton Lady I do write,
Which with her loose incontinence doth blend°   *blemish*
The shyning glory of your soveraigne light,
And knighthood fowle defacéd by a faithlesse knight.

2

But never let th'ensample of the bad
Offend the good: for good by paragone°   *comparison*
Of evill, may more notably be rad,°   *perceived*
As white seemes fairer, matcht with blacke attone;°   *together*
Ne all are shaméd by the fault of one:
For lo in heaven, whereas all goodnesse is,
Emongst the Angels, a whole legione
Of wicked Sprights did fall from happy blis;
What wonder then, if one of women all did mis?°   *err*

---

1. Stanzas 1–2 are based on the opening stanzas of Ariosto, *Orlando Furioso* 28.

3

Then listen Lordings, if ye list to weet
   The cause, why Satyrane and Paridell
   Mote not be entertaynd, as seeméd meet,
   Into that Castle (as that Squire does tell.)
   "Therein a cancred° crabbéd Carle does dwell,   *malignant*
   That has no skill° of Court nor courtesie,   *knowledge*
   Ne cares, what men say of him ill or well;
   For all his dayes he drownes in privitie,°   *seclusion*
Yet has full large to live, and spend at libertie.

4

"But all his mind is set on mucky pelfe,°   *lucre*
   To hoord up heapes of evill gotten masse,°   *wealth*
   For which he others wrongs, and wreckes° himselfe;   *harms*
   Yet is he linckéd to a lovely lasse,
   Whose beauty doth her bounty° far surpasse,   *goodness*
   The which to him both far unequall yeares,
   And also far unlike conditions has;
   For she does joy to play emongst her peares,[2]
And to be free from hard restraint and gealous feares.

5

"But he is old, and witheréd like hay,
   Unfit faire Ladies service to supply;
   The privie° guilt whereof makes him alway   *secret*
   Suspect her truth, and keepe continuall spy
   Upon her with his other blinckéd° eye;   *dim*
   Ne suffreth he resort° of living wight   *visiting*
   Approch to her, ne keepe her company,
   But in close bowre her mewes° from all mens sight,   *shuts up*
Deprived of kindly° joy and naturall delight.   *natural*

6

"Malbecco he, and Hellenore she hight,
   Unfitly yokt together in one teeme,[3]
   That is the cause, why never any knight
   Is suffred here to enter, but he seeme
   Such, as no doubt of him he neede misdeeme."°   *suspect*
   Thereat Sir Satyrane gan smile, and say;
   "Extremely mad° the man I surely deeme,   *crazed*
   That weenes with watch and hard restraint to stay°   *restrain*
A womans will, which is disposd to go astray.

2. I.e., to enjoy herself with lively and youthful friends.
3. The jealous old husband, his bored young wife, and the vigorous sophisticate who takes advantage
are literary types familiar since ancient times; cf. Chaucer's "Merchant's Tale." Spenser takes
details from *Orlando Furioso* 32, but the names of Malbecco (Latin *malus* [bad] and Italian *becco*
[goat]: i.e., cuckold), Hellenore, and Paridell parody those of Menelaus, Helen of Troy, and
Helen's abductor, Paris.

7

"In vaine he feares that, which he cannot shonne:
  For who wotes not, that womans subtiltyes
  Can guilen° Argus,[4] when she list misdonne?°   *deceive/misbehave*
  It is not yron bandes, nor hundred eyes,
  Nor brasen walls, nor many wakefull spyes,
  That can withhold her wilfull wandring feet;
  But fast° good will with gentle curtesyes,   *firm*
  And timely service to her pleasures meet
May her perhaps containe, that else would algates fleet."°   *slip away*

8

"Then is he not more mad," said Paridell,
  "That hath himselfe unto such service sold,
  In dolefull thraldome all his dayes to dwell?
  For sure a foole I do him firmely hold,
  That loves his fetters, though they were of gold.
  But why do we devise of others ill,
  Whiles thus we suffer this same dotard old,
  To keepe us out, in scorne of his owne will,
And rather do not ransack all, and him selfe kill?"

9

"Nay let us first," said Satyrane, "entreat
  The man by gentle meanes, to let us in,
  And afterwardes affray with cruell threat,
  Ere that we to efforce it do begin:
  Then if all fayle, we will by force it win,
  And eke reward the wretch for his mesprise,°   *insolence*
  As may be worthy of his haynous sin."
  That counsell pleasd: then Paridell did rise,
And to the Castle gate approcht in quiet wise.

10

Whereat soft knocking, entrance he desyrd.
  The good man selfe, which then the Porter playd,
  Him answeréd, that all were now retyrd
  Unto their rest, and all the keyes convayd
  Unto their maister, who in bed was layd,
  That none him durst awake out of his dreme;
  And therefore them of patience gently prayd.
  Then Paridell began to chaunge his theme,
And threatned him with force and punishment extreme.

---

4. The hundred-eyed monster Juno set to watch Jove's beloved Io (*Metamorphoses* 1.622–723); after
   Mercury lulled him to sleep with music and story, Juno set his eyes in her peacock's tail.

11

But all in vaine; for nought mote him relent,
　And now so long before the wicket fast
　They wayted, that the night was forward spent,[5]
　And the faire welkin° fowly overcast,　　　　　　　　　　*sky*
　Gan blowen up a bitter stormy blast,
　With shoure and hayle so horrible and dred,
　That this faire many° were compeld at last,　　　　　*company*
　To fly for succour to a little shed,
The which beside the gate for swine was orderéd.°　　*prepared*

12

It fortunéd, soone after they were gone,
　Another knight, whom tempest thither brought,
　Came to that Castle, and with earnest mone,°　　　　*plea*
　Like as the rest, late entrance deare besought;
　But like so as the rest he prayd for nought,
　For flatly he of entrance was refusd,
　Sorely thereat he was displeasd, and thought
　How to avenge himselfe so sore abusd,
And evermore the Carle of curtesie[6] accusd.

13

But to avoyde th'intollerable stowre,°　　　　　　　　*storm*
　He was compeld to seeke some refuge neare,
　And to that shed, to shrowd him from the showre,
　He came, which full of guests he found whyleare,°　*already*
　So as he was not let to enter there:
　Whereat he gan to wex exceeding wroth,
　And swore, that he would lodge with them yfere,
　Or them dislodge, all were they liefe or loth;[7]
And so defide them each, and so defide them both.

14

Both were full loth to leave that needfull tent,°　　*shed*
　And both full loth in darkenesse to debate;
　Yet both full liefe him lodging to have lent,
　And both full liefe his boasting to abate;
　But chiefly Paridell his hart did grate,°　　　　　*fret*
　To heare him threaten so despightfully,
　As if he did a dogge to kenell rate,°　　　　　　　*scold*
　That durst not barke; and rather had he dy,
Then when he was defide, in coward corner ly.

---

5. I.e., well advanced. This episode recalls a passage in the *Thebaid* 1.401–81, an epic by the Roman
poet Statius (A.D. 61–c.96), and also Bradamante's actions outside the Castle of Tristan in *Orlando
Furioso* 32.
6. I.e., of discourtesy.
7. I.e., whether they were willing or not.

15

Tho hastily remounting to his steed,
  He forth issewed; like as a boistrous wind,
  Which in th'earthes hollow caves hath long bin hid,
  And shut up fast within her prisons blind,°   *dark*
  Makes the huge element against her kind
  To move, and tremble as it were agast,
  Until that it an issew forth may find;
  Then forth it breakes, and with his furious blast
Confounds both land and seas, and skyes doth overcast.

16

Their steel-hed speares they strongly coucht, and met
  Together with impetuous rage and forse,
  That with the terrour of their fierce affret,°   *encounter*
  They rudely drove to ground both man and horse,
  That each awhile lay like a sencelesse corse.
  But Paridell sore bruséd with the blow,
  Could not arise, the counterchaunge to scorse,[8]
  Till that young Squire him rearéd from below;
Then drew he his bright sword, and gan about him throw.°   *brandish*

17

But Satyrane forth stepping, did them stay
  And with faire treatie° pacifide their ire,   *speech*
  Then when they were accorded° from the fray,   *reconciled*
  Against that Castles Lord they gan conspire,
  To heape on him dew vengeaunce for his hire.°   *reward*
  They bene agreed, and to the gates they goe
  To burne the same with unquenchable fire,
  And that uncurteous Carle their commune foe
To do fowle death to dye, or wrap in grievous woe.

18

Malbecco seeing them resolved in deed
  To flame the gates, and hearing them to call
  For fire in earnest, ran with fearefull° speed,   *full of fear*
  And to them calling from the castle wall,
  Besought them humbly, him to beare with all,[9]
  As ignoraunt of servaunts bad abuse,
  And slacke attendaunce unto straungers call.
  The knights were willing all things to excuse,
Though nought beleved, and entraunce late did not refuse.

8. I.e., to strike back by way of requital.
9. I.e., to bear with him.

19

They bene ybrought into a comely bowre,°   *chamber*
  And served of all things that mote needfull bee;
  Yet secretly their hoste did on them lowre,°   *scowl*
  And welcomde more for feare, then charitee;
  But they dissembled, what they did not see,[1]
  And welcoméd themselves. Each gan undight
  Their garments wet, and weary armour free,
  To dry them selves by Vulcanes flaming light,
And eke their lately bruzéd parts to bring in plight.°   *health*

20

And eke that straunger knight emongst the rest
  Was for like need enforst to disaray:
  Tho whenas vailéd° was her loftie crest,   *lowered*
  Her golden locks, that were in tramels° gay   *plaits*
  Unbounden, did them selves adowne display,
  And raught° unto her heeles; like sunny beames,   *reached*
  That in a cloud their light did long time stay,
  Their vapour vaded,° shew their golden gleames,   *vanished*
And through the persant aire shoote forth their azure streames.[2]

21

She also dofte her heavy haberjeon,°   *coat of mail*
  Which the faire feature of her limbs did hyde,
  And her well plighted° frock, which she did won°   *folded/use*
  To tucke about her short, when she did ryde,
  She low let fall, that flowd from her lanck° syde   *slender*
  Downe to her foot, with carelesse° modestee.   *simple*
  Then of them all she plainly was espyde,
  To be a woman wight, unwist° to bee,   *unknown*
The fairest woman wight, that ever eye did see.

22

Like as Minerva[3] being late returnd
  From slaughter of the Giaunts conqueréd;
  Where proud Encelade, whose wide nosethrils burnd
  With breathéd flames, like to a furnace red,
  Transfixéd with the speare, downe tombled ded
  From top of Hemus, by him heapéd hye;
  Hath loosd her helmet from her lofty hed,

1. I.e., they pretended not to notice his discourtesy.
2. This simile appears in *Orlando Furioso* 32.80 and Tasso's *Gerusalemme* 4.29; cf. *Metamorphoses* 14.767–69 (see also III.i.43). The lady knight is identified in stanza 27.
3. "Bellona" in the 1590 edition. In a Glosse to "October," E.K. identifies Bellona with Pallas (Minerva), "godesse of battaile." Some say Pallas transfixed Enceladus, biggest of the Giants, with her spear; others give the victory to Zeus, who put him under a volcano (often identified as Aetna). But it was Typhoeus, not "proud Encelade," whom Zeus overcame on Mount Haemus in Thrace.

And her Gorgonian[4] shield gins to untye
From her left arme, to rest in glorious victorye.

23

Which whenas they beheld, they smitten were
  With great amazement of so wondrous sight,
  And each on other, and they all on her
  Stood gazing, as if suddein great affright
  Had them surprised. At last avizing° right,   *perceiving*
  Her goodly personage and glorious hew,°   *form*
  Which they so much mistooke, they tooke delight
  In their first errour, and yet still anew
With wonder of her beauty fed their hungry vew.

24

Yet note° their hungry vew be satisfide,   *might not*
  But seeing still the more desired to see,
  And ever firmely fixéd did abide
  In contemplation of divinitie:
  But most they mervaild at her chevalree,
  And noble prowesse, which they had approved,°   *tested*
  That much they faynd° to know, who she mote bee;   *desired*
  Yet none of all them her thereof amoved,°   *stirred*
Yet every one her likte, and every one her loved.

25

And Paridell though partly discontent
  With his late fall, and fowle indignity,
  Yet was soone wonne his malice to relent,°   *soften*
  Through gracious regard of her faire eye,
  And knightly worth, which he too late did try,°   *experience*
  Yet triéd did adore. Supper was dight;°   *set out*
  Then they Malbecco prayd of curtesy,
  That of his Lady they might have the sight,
And company at meat, to do them more delight.

26

But he to shift their curious request,
  Gan causen,° why she could not come in place;   *explain*
  Her craséd° health, her late° recourse to rest,   *infirm/recent*
  And humid evening ill for sicke folkes cace:
  But none of those excuses could take place;[5]
  Ne would they eate, till she in presence came.
  She came in presence with right comely grace,
  And fairely them saluted,° as became,   *greeted*
And shewd her selfe in all a gentle curteous Dame.

4. Minerva wore the snaky-haired head of Medusa, the Gorgon slain by Perseus, on her "aegis,"
(shield or breastplate); see *Metamorphoses* 4.803.
5. I.e., was acceptable.

27

They sate to meat, and Satyrane his chaunce
  Was her before,[6] and Paridell besyde;
  But he him selfe sate looking still askaunce,°   *sidewise*
  Gainst Britomart, and ever closely eyde
  Sir Satyrane, that glaunces might not glyde:
  But his blind eye, that syded Paridell,
  All his demeasnure° from his sight did hyde: *behavior*
  On her faire face so did he feede his fill,
And sent close° messages of love to her at will.   *secret*

28

And ever and anone, when none was ware,
  With speaking lookes, that close embassage° bore,   *message*
  He roved° at her, and told his secret care: *darted*
  For all that art he learnéd had of yore.
  Ne was she ignoraunt of that lewd lore,
  But in his eye his meaning wisely red,
  And with the like him answerd evermore:
  She sent at him one firie dart, whose hed
Empoisned was with privy° lust, and gealous dred.   *secret*

29

He from that deadly throw° made no defence,   *thrust*
  But to the wound his weake hart opened wyde;
  The wicked engine° through false influence,   *device*
  Past through his eyes, and secretly did glyde
  Into his hart, which it did sorely gryde.°   *pierce*
  But nothing new to him was that same paine,
  Ne paine at all; for he so oft had tryde
  The powre thereof, and loved so oft in vaine,
That thing of course[7] he counted,° love to entertaine. *regarded*

30

Thenceforth to her he sought to intimate
  His inward griefe, by meanes to him well knowne,
  Now Bacchus fruit[8] out of the silver plate°   *cup*
  He on the table dasht, as overthrowne,
  Or of the fruitfull liquor overflowne,
  And by the dauncing bubbles did divine,
  Or therein write to let his love be showne;
  Which well she red out of the learnéd line,
A sacrament prophane in mistery of wine.

6. I.e., was to sit opposite her.
7. I.e., as a usual occurrence.
8. I.e., the wine. Paridell's techniques echo Ovid's *Art of Love* and the epistle from Helen to Paris
in his *Heroides* 17.75–90; line 9 suggests that he blasphemously misuses wine in a sort of lustful
anti-eucharist.

31

And when so of his hand the pledge she raught,[9]
  The guilty cup she fainéd to mistake,°   *let slip*
  And in her lap did shed her idle draught,
  Shewing desire her inward flame to slake:°   *relieve*
  By such close signes they secret way did make
  Unto their wils, and one eyes watch escape;
  Two eyes him needeth, for to watch and wake,
  Who lovers will deceive. Thus was the ape,
By their faire handling, put into Malbeccoes cape.[1]

32

Now when of meats and drinks they had their fill,
  Purpose° was movéd by that gentle Dame,   *proposal*
  Unto those knights adventurous, to tell
  Of deeds of armes, which unto them became,°   *happened*
  And every one his kindred, and his name.
  Then Paridell, in whom a kindly° pryde   *natural*
  Of gracious speach, and skill his words to frame
  Abounded, being glad of so fit tyde°   *occasion*
Him to commend to her, thus spake, of all well eyde.

33

"Troy, that art now nought, but an idle name,
  And in thine ashes buried low dost lie,
  Though whilome far much greater then thy fame,
  Before that angry Gods, and cruell skye
  Upon thee heapt a direfull destinie,
  What boots it boast thy glorious descent,
  And fetch from heaven thy great Genealogie,
  Sith all thy worthy prayses being blent,°   *stained*
Their of-spring hath embaste, and later glory shent.° *disgraced*

34

"Most famous Worthy of the world, by whome
  That warre was kindled, which did Troy inflame,
  And stately towres of Ilion whilome
  Brought unto balefull ruine, was by name
  Sir Paris far renowmd through noble fame,
  Who through great prowesse and bold hardinesse,
  From Lacedaemon fetcht the fairest Dame,
  That ever Greece did boast, or knight possesse,
Whom Venus to him gave for meed of worthinesse.[2]

9. I.e., when she reached to take the cup from his hand.
1. I.e., they made a fool of him (as in Chaucer, Introduction to "The Prioress's Tale," 1630).
2. See II.vii.55, note.

35

"Faire Helene, flowre of beautie excellent,
  And girlond of the mighty Conquerours,
  That madest many Ladies deare lament
  The heavie losse of their brave Paramours,
  Which they far off beheld from Trojan toures,
  And saw the fieldes of faire Scamander[3] strowne
  With carcases of noble warrioures,
  Whose fruitless lives were under furrow sowne,
And Xanthus sandy bankes with bloud all overflowne.

36

"From him my linage I derive aright,
  Who long before the ten yeares siege of Troy,
  Whiles yet on Ida he a shepheard hight,
  On faire Oenone got a lovely boy,
  Whom for remembraunce of her passéd joy,
  She of his Father Parius[4] did name;
  Who, after Greekes did Priams realme destroy,
  Gathred the Trojan reliques saved from flame,
And with them sayling thence, to th'Isle of Paros[5] came.

37

"That was by him cald Paros, which before
  Hight Nausa, there he many yeares did raine,
  And built Nausicle by the Pontick[6] shore,
  The which he dying left next in remaine
  To Paridas his sonne.
  From whom I Paridell by kin descend;
  But for faire Ladies love, and glories gaine,
  My native soile have left, my dayes to spend
In sewing° deeds of armes, my lives and labours end."   *following*

38

Whenas the noble Britomart heard tell
  Of Trojan warres, and Priams Citie sackt,
  The ruefull story of Sir Paridell,
  She was empassiond at that piteous act,
  With zelous envy° of Greekes cruell fact,°   *indignation/deed*
  Against that nation, from whose race of old
  She heard, that she was lineally extract:°   *descended*
  For noble Britons sprong from Trojans bold,
And Troynovant[7] was built of old Troyes ashes cold.

---

3. The river Scamander (also called the Xanthus) flowed near Troy.
4. Oenone's son by Paris was named Corythus, but Paridell (or Spenser) changes it to "Parius" to suit his claim to descend from Trojan royalty.
5. An island in the Aegean Sea.
6. The Black Sea.
7. I.e., London, "New Troy."

39

Then sighing soft awhile, at last she thus:
"O lamentable fall of famous towne,
Which raignd so many yeares victorious,
And of all Asie bore the soveraigne crowne,
In one sad night consumd, and throwen downe:
What stony hart, that heares thy haplesse fate,
Is not empierst with deepe compassiowne,.
And makes ensample of mans wretched state,
That floures so fresh at morne, and fades at evening late?

40

"Behold, Sir, how your pitifull complaint°   *lament*
Hath found another partner of your payne:
For nothing may impresse so deare constraint,°   *distress*
As countries cause, and commune foes disdayne.
But if it should not grieve you, backe agayne
To turne your course, I would to heare desyre,
What to Aeneas fell; sith that men sayne
He was not in the Cities wofull fyre
Consumed, but did him selfe to safétie retyre."

41

"Anchyses sonne begot of Venus faire,"
Said he, "out of the flames for safegard fled,
And with a remnant did to sea repaire,
Where he through fatall errour[8] long was led
Full many yeares, and weetlesse° wanderéd   *at random*
From shore to shore, emongst the Lybicke° sands,   *Lybian*
Ere rest he found. Much there he sufferéd,
And many perils past in forreine lands,
To save his people sad from victours vengefull hands.[9]

42

"At last in Latium[1] he did arrive,
Where he with cruell warre was entertaind
Of th'inland folke, which sought him backe to drive,
Till he with old Latinus was constraind,
To contract wedlock:[2] (so the fates ordaind.)
Wedlock contract in bloud, and eke in blood
Accomplishéd, that many deare complaind:
The rivall slaine, the victour through the flood
Escapéd hardly, hardly praisd his wedlock good.

8. I.e., fated wandering; Virgil calls Aeneas "fato profugus" (impelled by fate, *Aeneid* 1.2).
9. Paridell passes rapidly over the earlier wanderings of Aeneas, omitting his love for Dido and descent
   to Hades so as to stress his final romance and resettlement.
1. Land of the Latins. King Latinus gave his daughter Lavinia in marriage to Aeneas (*Aeneid* 7.267–
   74); this precipitated war with the Rutulian leader Turnus, to whom she had been promised.
2. I.e., to ally himself through marriage with Lavinia.

43

"Yet after all, he victour did survive,
    And with Latinus did the kingdome part.°   *divide*
But after, when both nations gan to strive,
    Into their names the title to convart,[3]
His sonne Iülus did from thence depart,
    With all the warlike youth of Trojans bloud,
    And in long Alba[4] plast his throne apart,
    Where faire it florishéd, and long time stoud,
Till Romulus renewing it, to Rome removd."

44

"There there," said Britomart, "a fresh appeard
    The glory of the later world to spring,
And Troy againe out of her dust was reard,
    To sit in second seat of soveraigne king,
    Of all the world under her governing.
But a third kingdome yet is to arise,
    Out of the Trojans scatteréd of-spring,
    That in all glory and great enterprise,
Both first and second Troy shall dare to equalise.°   *equal*

45

"It Troynovant is hight, that with the waves
    Of wealthy Thamis[5] washéd is along,
Upon whose stubborne neck, whereat he raves
    With roring rage, and sore him selfe does throng,°   *press*
That all men feare to tempt his billowes strong,
    She fastned hath her foot, which standes so hy,
    That it a wonder of the world is song
In forreine landes, and all which passen by,
Beholding it from far, do thinke it threates the skye.

46

"The Trojan Brute did first that Citie found,
    And Hygate made the meare° thereof by West,   *boundary*
And Overt gate by North: that is the bound
    Toward the land; two rivers bound the rest.
So huge a scope at first him seeméd best,
    To be the compasse of his kingdomes seat:
    So huge a mind could not in lesser rest,
    Ne in small meares containe his glory great,
That Albion[6] had conquered first by warlike feat."

3. I.e., to claim sole power.
4. Alba Longa, Latium's oldest town, about twenty miles southeast of Rome. On Iulus's move to
   Alba Longa, see Boccaccio (*Genealogiae* 6.54).
5. The Thames, spanned by London Bridge.
6. The island's pre-British name (see Geoffrey 1.16). Dubrow 1990 stresses that it is Britomart, not
   the morally flaccid Paridell, who first recalls the tale's relevance to British history and Troy's rebirth
   in a new empire; Suzuki 1989 (159–73) argues that Spenser reinforces the opposing private and
   public imperatives by making Paridell Ovidian and Britomart Virgilian.

47

"Ah fairest Lady knight," said Paridell,
   "Pardon I pray my heedlesse oversight,
   Who had forgot, that whilome I heard tell
   From aged Mnemon,[7] for my wits bene light.
   Indeed he said (if I remember right,)
   That of the antique Trojan stocke, there grew
   Another plant, that raught° to wondrous hight,   *reached*
   And far abroad his mighty branches threw,
Into the utmost Angle of the world he knew.

48

"For that same Brute, whom much he did advaunce°   *praise*
   In all his speach, was Sylvius his sonne,[8]
   Whom having slaine, through luckles arrowes glaunce
   He fled for feare of that he had misdonne,
   Or else for shame, so fowle reproch to shonne,
   And with him led to sea an youthly trayne,°   *company*
   Where wearie wandring they long time did wonne,
   And many fortunes proved° in th'Ocean mayne,   *experienced*
And great adventures found, that now were long to sayne.

49

"At last by fatall° course they driven were   *fated*
   Into an Island spatious and brode,
   The furthest North, that did to them appeare:
   Which after rest they seeking far abrode,
   Found it the fittest soyle for their abode,
   Fruitfull of all things fit for living foode,
   But wholy wast, and void of peoples trode,°   *footstep*
   Save an huge nation of the Geaunts broode,
That fed on living flesh, and druncke mens vitall blood.

50

"Whom he through wearie wars and labours long,
   Subdewd with losse of many Britons bold:
   In which the great Goëmagot of strong
   Corineus, and Coulin of Debon old
   Were overthrowne, and layd on th'earth full cold,
   Which quakéd under their so hideous masse,
   A famous history to be enrold
   In everlasting moniments of brasse,
That all the antique Worthies merits far did passe.

7. From Greek, "memory."
8. I.e., the son of Sylvius. Stanzas 48–51 rely on Geoffrey 1.3–17, who does not, though, say Brute founded Lincoln.

51

"His worke great Troynovant, his worke is eke
   Faire Lincolne, both renowméd far away,
   That who from East to West will endlong° seeke,   *from end to end*
   Cannot two fairer Cities find this day,
   Except Cleopolis: so heard I say
   Old Mnemon. Therefore Sir, I greet you well
   Your countrey kin,° and you entirely pray   *kinsman*
   Of pardon for the strife, which late befell
Betwixt us both unknowne." So ended Paridell.

52

But all the while, that he these speaches spent,
   Upon his lips hong faire Dame Hellenore,
   With vigilant regard, and dew attent,°   *attention*
   Fashioning worlds of fancies evermore
   In her fraile wit, that now her quite forlore:
   The whiles unwares away her wondring eye,
   And greedy eares her weake hart from her bore:
   Which he perceiving, ever privily
In speaking, many false belgardes° at her let fly.   *loving looks*

53

So long these knights discourséd diversly,
   Of straunge affairs, and noble hardiment,
   Which they had past with mickle jeopardy,
   That now the humid night was farforth spent,
   And heavenly lampes were halfendeale ybrent:[9]
   Which th'old man seeing well, who too long thought
   Every discourse and every argument,
   Which by the houres he measuréd, besought
Them go to rest. So all unto their bowres were brought.

Canto X

Paridell rapeth° Hellenore: *carries off*
   Malbecco her pursewes:
   Findes emongst Satyres, whence with him
      To turne she doth refuse.

1

The morow next, so soone as Phoebus Lamp
   Bewrayéd had the world with early light,   *revealed*
   And fresh Aurora had the shady damp
   Out of the goodly heaven amovéd quight,
   Faire Britomart and that same Faerie knight[1]
   Uprose, forth on their journey for to wend:

9. I.e., half consumed.
1. I.e., Satyrane.

But Paridell complaynd, that his late fight
  With Britomart, so sore did him offend,°   *trouble*
That ryde he could not, till his hurts he did amend.

2

So forth they fared, but he behind them stayd,
  Maulgre° his host, who grudgéd grievously,   *despite*
  To house a guest, that would be needes obayd,
  And of his owne him left not liberty:
  Might wanting measure moveth surquedry.[2]
  Two things he fearéd, but the third was death;
  That fierce youngmans unruly maistery;
  His money, which he loved as living breath;
And his faire wife, whom honest long he kept uneath.°   *with difficulty*

3

But patience perforce he must abie,°   *endure*
  What fortune and his fate on him will lay,
  Fond° is the feare, that findes no remedie;   *foolish*
  Yet warily he watcheth every way,
  By which he feareth evill happen may:
  So th'evill thinkes by watching to prevent;
  Ne doth he suffer her, nor night, nor day,
  Out of his sight her selfe once to absent.
So doth he punish her and eke himselfe torment.

4

But Paridell kept better watch, then hee,
  A fit occasion for his turne to find:
  False love, why do men say, thou canst not see,
  And in their foolish fancie feigne thee blind,
  That with thy charmes° the sharpest sight doest bind,   *spells*
  And to thy will abuse? Thou walkest free,
  And seest every secret of the mind;
  Thou seest all, yet none at all sees thee;
All that is by the working of thy Deitee.

5

So perfect in that art was Paridell,
  That he Malbeccoes halfen eye did wyle,[3]
  His halfen eye he wiléd wondrous well,
  And Hellenors both eyes did eke beguyle,
  Both eyes and hart attonce, during the whyle
  That he there sojournéd his wounds to heale;
  That Cupid selfe it seeing, close did smyle,

2. I.e., excessive power breeds arrogance.
3. I.e., fooled his one good eye. Malbecco's damaged sight matches his idolatry toward wife and money; Gregerson 1991 calls him morally "dyslexic."

To weet how he her love away did steale,
And bad, that none their joyous treason should reveale.

6

The learnéd lover lost no time nor tyde,
  That least avantage mote to him afford,
  Yet bore so faire a saile, that none espyde
  His secret drift,° till he her layd abord.   *aim*
  When so in open place, and commune bord,°   *table*
  He fortuned her to meet, with commune speach
  He courted her, yet bayted° every word,   *spoke softly*
  That his ungentle hoste n'ote him appeach
Of vile ungentlenesse, or hospitages breach.[4]

7

But when apart (if ever her apart)
  He found, then his false engins° fast he plyde,   *wiles*
  And all the sleights unbosomd in his hart;
  He sighed, he sobd, he swownd, he perdy° dyde,   *verily*
  And cast himselfe on ground her fast° besyde: *close*
  Tho when againe he him bethought to live,
  He wept, and wayld, and false laments belyde,°   *counterfeited*
  Saying, but if[5] she Mercie would him give
That he mote algates dye, yet did his death forgive.[6]

8

And otherwhiles with amorous delights,
  And pleasing toyes he would her entertaine,
  Now singing sweetly, to surprise her sprights,
  Now making layes of love and lovers paine,
  Bransles,° Ballads, virelayes,° and verses vaine;   *dances/songs*
  Oft purposes,° oft riddles he devysd,   *word games*
  And thousands like, which flowéd in his braine,
  With which he fed her fancie, and entysd
To take to his new love, and leave her old despysd.

9

And every where he might, and every while
  He did her service dewtifull, and sewed°   *followed*
  At hand with humble pride, and pleasing guile,
  So closely yet, that none but she it vewed,
  Who well perceivéd all, and all indewed.°   *took in*
  Thus finely did he his false nets dispred,
  With which he many weake harts had subdewed
  Of yore, and many had ylike misled:
What wonder then, if she were likewise carriéd?

---

4. I.e., could not accuse him of discourtesy or of conduct unbecoming to a guest.
5. I.e., unless.
6. Spenser parodies medieval and Petrarchan love complaint.

10

No fort so fensible,° no wals so strong,   *fortified*
  But that continuall battery will rive,
  Or daily siege through dispurvayance° long,   *lack of supplies*
  And lacke of reskewes will to parley drive;
  And Peece,° that unto parley eare will give,   *fortress*
  Will shortly yeeld it selfe, and will be made
  The vassall of the victors will bylive:°   *quickly*
  That stratageme had oftentimes assayd
This crafty Paramoure, and now it plaine displayd.

11

For through his traines° he her intrappéd hath,   *wiles*
  That she her love and hart hath wholy sold
  To him, without regard of gaine, or scath,°   *harm*
  Or care of credite, or of husband old,
  Whom she hath vowed to dub a faire Cucquold.
  Nought wants but time and place, which shortly shee
  Devizéd hath, and to her lover told.
  It pleaséd well. So well they both agree;
So readie rype to ill, ill wemens counsels bee.

12

Darke was the Evening, fit for lovers stealth,
  When chaunst Malbecco busie be elsewhere,
  She to his closet° went, where all his wealth   *private room*
  Lay hid: thereof she countlesse summes did reare,°   *take*
  The which she meant away with her to beare;
  The rest she fyred for sport, or for despight;°   *malice*
  As Hellene, when she saw aloft appeare
  The Trojane flames, and reach to heavens hight
Did clap her hands, and joyéd at that dolefull sight.[7]

13

This second Hellene, faire Dame Hellenore,
  The whiles her husband ranne with sory haste,
  To quench the flames, which she had tyned° before,   *kindled*
  Laught at his foolish labour spent in waste;
  And ranne into her lovers armes right fast;
  Where streight embracéd, she to him did cry,
  And call aloud for helpe, ere helpe were past;
  For loe that Guest would beare her forcibly,
And meant to ravish her, that rather had to dy.

14

The wretched man hearing her call for ayd,
  And readie seeing him with her to fly,

---

7. Cf. allusions in *Aeneid* (e.g., 6.517–19) to Helen's conduct when Troy fell.

In his disquiet mind was much dismayd:
But when againe he backward cast his eye,
And saw the wicked fire so furiously
Consume his hart, and scorch his Idoles face,
He was therewith distresséd diversly,
Ne wist he how to turne, nor to what place;
Was never wretched man in such a wofull cace.

15

Ay° when to him she cryde, to her he turnd,   *always*
    And left the fire; love money overcame:
    But when he markéd, how his money burnd,
    He left his wife; money did love disclame:°   *renounce*
    Both was he loth to loose his lovéd Dame,
    And loth to leave his liefest pelfe behind,
    Yet sith he n'ote° save both, he saved that same,   *might not*
    Which was the dearest to his donghill mind,
The God of his desire, the joy of misers blind.

16

Thus whilest all things in troublous uprore were,
    And all men busie to suppresse the flame,
    The loving couple need no reskew feare,
    But leasure had, and libertie to frame
    Their purpost flight, free from all mens reclame;°   *recall*
    And Night, the patronesse of love-stealth faire,
    Gave them safe conduct, till to end they came:
    So bene they gone yfeare,° a wanton paire   *together*
Of lovers loosely knit, where list them to repaire.

17

Soone as the cruell flames yslakéd° were,   *abated*
    Malbecco seeing, how his losse did lye,
    Out of the flames, which he had quencht whylere
    Into huge waves of griefe and gealosye
    Full deepe emplongéd was, and drownéd nye,
    Twixt inward doole° and felonous° despight;   *grief/fierce*
    He raved, he wept, he stampt, he lowd did cry,
    And all the passions, that in man may light,°   *occur*
Did him attonce oppresse, and vex his caytive spright.

18

Long thus he chawd the cud of inward griefe,
    And did consume his gall with anguish sore,
    Still when he muséd on his late mischiefe,
    Then still the smart thereof increaséd more,
    And seemed more grievous, then it was before:
    At last when sorrow he saw booted° nought,   *availed*
    Ne griefe might not his love to him restore,

He gan devise, how her he reskew mought,
Ten thousand wayes he cast in his confuséd thought.

19

At last resolving, like a pilgrim pore,
  To search her forth, where so she might be fond,
  And bearing with him treasure in close° store,   *secret*
  The rest he leaves in ground: So takes in hond
  To seeke her endlong, both by sea and lond.
  Long he her sought, he sought her farre and nere,
  And every where that he mote understond,
  Of knights and ladies any meetings were,
And of eachone he met, he tydings did inquere.

20

But all in vaine, his woman was too wise,
  Ever to come into his clouch° againe,   *grip*
  And he too simple ever to surprise
  The jolly° Paridell, for all his paine.   *gallant*
  One day, as he forpasséd by[8] the plaine
  With weary pace, he farre away espide
  A couple, seeming well to be his twaine,
  Which hovéd° close under a forrest side,   *waited*
As if they lay in wait, or else themselves did hide.

21

Well weenéd he, that those the same mote bee,
  And as he better did their shape avize,
  Him seeméd more their manner did agree;
  For th'one was arméd all in warlike wize,
  Whom, to be Paridell he did devize;°   *guess*
  And th'other all yclad in garments light,
  Discoloured° like to womanish disguise,   *many colored*
  He did resemble° to his Ladie bright;   *liken*
And ever his faint hart much carnéd° at the sight. *yearned*

22

And ever faine° he towards them would goe,   *eagerly*
  But yet durst not for dread approchen nie,
  But stood aloofe, unweeting what to doe;
  Till that prickt forth with loves extremitie,
  That is the father of foule gealosy,
  He closely nearer crept, the truth to weet:
  But, as he nigher drew, he easily
  Might scerne,° that it was not his sweetest sweet, *discern*
Ne yet her Belamour,° the partner of his sheet. *lover*

8. I.e., passed over.

23

But it was scornefull Braggadocchio,
  That with his servant Trompart hoverd there,
  Sith late he fled from his too earnest foe:
  Whom such when as Malbecco spyéd clere,
  He turnéd backe, and would have fled arere;°   *back*
  Till Trompart ronning hastily, him did stay,
  And bad before his soveraine Lord appere:
  That was him loth, yet durst he not gainesay,
And comming him before, low louted° on the lay.°   *bowed/lea*

24

The Boaster at him sternely bent his browe,
  As if he could have kild him with his looke,
  That to the ground him meekely made to bowe,
  And awfull terror deepe into him strooke,
  That every member of his bodie quooke.°   *quaked*
  Said he, "Thou man of nought, what doest thou here,
  Unfitly furnisht with thy bag and booke,
  Where I expected one with shield and spere,
To prove° some deedes of armes upon an equall pere."   *try*

25

The wretched man at his imperious speach,
  Was all abasht, and low prostrating, said;
  "Good Sir, let not my rudenesse be no breach
  Unto your patience, ne be ill ypaid;°   *pleased*
  For I unwares this way by fortune straid,
  A silly Pilgrim driven to distresse,
  That seeke a Lady," There he suddein staid,
  And did the rest with grievous sighes suppresse,
While teares stood in his eies, few drops of bitternesse.

26

"What Ladie, man?" said Trompart, "take good hart,
  And tell thy griefe, if any hidden lye;
  Was never better time to shew thy smart,
  Then now, that noble succour is thee by,
  That is the whole worlds commune remedy."
  That cheareful word his weake hart much did cheare,
  And with vaine hope his spirits faint supply,
  That bold he said; "O most redoubted Pere,
Vouchsafe with mild regard a wretches cace to heare."

27

Then sighing sore, "It is not long," said hee,
  "Sith I enjoyd the gentlest Dame alive;
  Of whom a knight, no knight at all perdee,

But shame of all, that doe for honor strive,
By treacherous deceipt did me deprive;
Through open outrage he her bore away,
And with fowle force unto his will did drive,
Which all good knights, that armes do beare this day;
Are bound for to revenge, and punish if they may.

28

"And you most noble Lord, that can and dare
  Redresse the wrong of miserable wight,
  Cannot employ your most victorious speare
  In better quarrell, then defence of right,
  And for a Ladie gainst a faithlesse knight;
  So shall your glory be advauncéd° much,   *praised*
  And all faire Ladies magnifie your might,
  And eke my selfe, albe I simple such,°
Your worthy paine shall well reward with guerdon rich."

29

With that out of his bouget° forth he drew   *pouch*
  Great store of treasure, therewith him to tempt;
  But he on it lookt scornefully askew,°   *sidelong*
  As much disdeigning to be so misdempt,°   *misjudged*
  Or a war-monger° to be basely nempt;°   *mercenary/named*
  And said, "Thy offers base I greatly loth,
  And eke thy words uncourteous and unkempt;°   *unpolished*
  I tread in dust thee and thy money both,
That, were it not for shame," So turnéd from him wroth.

30

But Trompart, that his maisters humor knew,
  In lofty lookes to hide an humble mind,
  Was inly tickled with that golden vew,
  And in his eare him rounded° close behind.   *whispered*
  Yet stoupt he not, but lay still in the wind,[1]
  Waiting advauntage on the pray to sease;
  Till Trompart lowly to the ground inclind,
  Besought him his great courage° to appease,   *anger*
And pardon simple man, that rash did him displease.

31

Bigge looking like a doughtie Doucepere,[2]
  At last he thus; "Thou clod of vilest clay,
  I pardon yield, and with thy rudenesse beare;
  But weete henceforth, that all that golden pray,
  And all that else the vaine world vaunten° may,   *boast of*

9. I.e., although I am so humble and lowly.
1. I.e. (in a hawking image), he did not swoop down on the prey, but hovered aloft.
2. One of Charlemagne's twelve peers ("les douze pairs").

I loath as doung, ne deeme my dew reward:
Fame is my meed, and glory vertues pray.°   *booty*
But minds of mortall men are muchell mard,
And moved amisse with massie mucks unmeet regard.³

32

"And more, I graunt to thy great miserie
  Gratious respect,° thy wife shall backe be sent,   *attention*
  And that vile knight, who ever that he bee,
  Which hath thy Lady reft, and knighthood shent,°   *disgraced*
  By Sanglamort my sword, whose deadly dent°   *blow*
  The bloud hath of so many thousands shed,
  I sweare, ere long shall dearely it repent;
  Ne he twixt heaven and earth shall hide his hed,
But soone he shall be found, and shortly doen be ded."

33

The foolish man thereat woxe wondrous blith,
  As if the word so spoken, were halfe donne,
  And humbly thankéd him a thousand sith,°   *times*
  That had from death to life him newly wonne.
  Tho forth the Boaster marching, brave begonne
  His stolen steed to thunder furiously,
  As if he heaven and hell would overronne,
  And all the world confound with cruelty,
That much Malbecco joyéd in his jollity.°   *gallant show*

34

Thus long they three together traveiléd,
  Through many a wood, and many an uncouth way,
  To seeke his wife, that was farre wanderéd:
  But those two sought nought, but the present pray,
  To weete the treasure, which he did bewray,°   *reveal*
  On which their eies and harts were wholly set,
  With purpose, how they might it best betray;
  For sith the houre, that first he did them let
The same behold, therewith their keene desires were whet.°   *sharpened*

35

It fortunéd as they together fared,
  They spide, where Paridell came pricking fast
  Upon the plaine, the which himselfe prepared
  To giust with that brave straunger knight a cast,°   *bout*
  As on adventure by the way he past:
  Alone he rode without his Paragone;°   *companion*
  For having filcht her bels, her up he cast

---

3. I.e., men's minds are much marred and misdirected by unbecoming care for cash. The crude alliteration emphasizes Braggadocchio's pompous triviality.

To the wide world, and let her fly alone,
He nould be clogd.[4] So had he servéd many one.

36

The gentle Lady, loose at randon left,
  The greene-wood long did walke, and wander wide
  At wilde adventure, like a forlorne weft,°   *waif*
  Till on a day the Satyres her espide
  Straying alone withouten groome° or guide;   *servant*
  Her up they tooke, and with them home her led,
  With them as housewife ever to abide,
  To milk their gotes, and make them cheese and bred,
And every one as commune good her handeléd.

37

That shortly she Malbecco has forgot,
  And eke Sir Paridell, all° were he deare;   *although*
  Who from her went to seeke another lot,
  And now by fortune was arrivéd here,
  Where those two guilers with Malbecco were:
  Soone as the oldman saw Sir Paridell,
  He fainted, and was almost dead with feare,
  Ne word he had to speake, his griefe to tell,
But to him louted low, and greeted goodly well.

38

And after askéd him for Hellenore,
  "I take no keepe° of her," said Paridell,   *care*
  "She wonneth in the forrest there before."
  So forth he rode, as his adventure fell;
  The whiles the Boaster from his loftie sell°   *saddle*
  Faynd to alight, something amisse to mend;
  But the fresh Swayne would not his leasure dwell,° *await*
  But went his way, whom when he passéd kend,[5]
He up remounted light, and after fained to wend.

39

"Perdy nay," said Malbecco, "shall ye not:
  But let him passe as lightly, as he came:
  For litle good of him is to be got,
  And mickle perill to be put to shame.
  But let us go to seeke my dearest Dame,
  Whom he hath left in yonder forrest wyld:
  For of her safety in great doubt I am,
  Least salvage beastes her person have despoyld:
Then all the world is lost, and we in vaine have toyld."

4. I.e., having taken his pleasure, and not wanting to be weighed down, he went his own way (a hawking image).
5. I.e., when he was sure that Paridell had gone.

40

They all agree, and forward them addrest:
    "Ah but," said craftie Trompart, "weete ye well,
    That yonder in that wastefull wildernesse
    Huge monsters haunt, and many dangers dwell;
    Dragons, and Minotaures, and feendes of hell,
    And many wilde woodmen, which robbe and rend
    All travellers; therefore advise ye well,
    Before ye enterprise that way to wend:
One may his journey bring too soone to evill end."

41

Malbecco stopt in great astonishment,°   *dismay*
    And with pale eyes fast fixéd on the rest,
    Their counsell craved, in daunger imminent.
    Said Trompart, "You that are the most opprest
    With burden of great treasure, I thinke best
    Here for to stay in safetie behind;
    My Lord and I will search the wide forrest."
    That counsell pleaséd not Malbeccoes mind;
For he was much affraid, himselfe alone to find.

42

"Then is it best," said he, "that ye doe leave
    Your treasure here in some securitie,
    Either fast closéd in some hollow greave,°   *thicket*
    Or buried in the ground from jeopardie,
    Till we returne againe in safetie:
    As for us two, least doubt of us ye have,
    Hence farre away we will blindfolded lie,
    Ne privie be unto your treasures grave."[6]
It pleaséd: so he did. Then they march forward brave.

43

Now when amid the thickest woods they were,
    They heard a noyse of many bagpipes shrill,
    And shrieking Hububs them approching nere,
    Which all the forrest did with horror fill:
    That dreadfull sound the boasters hart did thrill,°   *pierce*
    With such amazement, that in haste he fled,
    Ne ever lookéd backe for good or ill,
    And after him eke fearefull Trompart sped;
The old man could not fly, but fell to ground halfe ded.

44

Yet afterwards close creeping, as he might,
    He in a bush did hide his fearefull hed,

6. I.e., and not know where your money is hidden.

The jolly Satyres full of fresh delight,
   Came daunsing forth, and with them nimbly led
   Faire Hellenore, with girlonds all bespred,
   Whom their May-lady they had newly made:
   She proud of that new honour, which they red,°   *declared*
   And of their lovely° fellowship full glade,   *loving*
Daunst lively, and her face did with a Lawrell shade.[7]

45

The silly man that in the thicket lay
   Saw all this goodly sport, and grievéd sore,
   Yet durst he not against it doe or say,
   But did his hart with bitter thoughts engore,
   To see th'unkindnesse° of his Hellenore.   *unnatural conduct*
   All day they dauncéd with great lustihed,
   And with their hornéd feet the greene grasse wore,
   The whiles their Gotes upon the brouzes° fed,   *twigs*
Till drouping Phoebus gan to hide his golden hed.

46

Tho up they gan their merry pypes to trusse,°   *pack*
   And all their goodly heards did gather round,
   But every Satyre first did give a busse°   *kiss*
   To Hellenore: so busses did abound.
   Now gan the humid vapour shed the ground
   With perly deaw, and th'Earthés gloomy shade
   Did dim the brightnesse of the welkin° round,   *heavens*
   That every bird and beast awarnéd made,
To shrowd themselves, while sleepe their senses did invade.

47

Which when Malbecco saw, out of his bush
   Upon his hands and feete he crept full light,
   And like a Gote emongst the Gotes did rush,
   That through the helpe of his faire hornes[8] on hight,
   And misty dampe of misconceiving° night,   *misleading*
   And eke through likenesse of his gotish beard,
   He did the better counterfeite aright:
   So home he marcht emongst the hornéd heard,
That none of all the Satyres him espyde or heard.

48

At night, when all they went to sleepe, he vewd,
   Whereas his lovely wife emongst them lay,

---

7. In I.vi, the satyrs instinctively treat the virtuous Una with admiration (if also with ignorant idolatry); here they instinctively treat Hellenore with delighted sensuality. For Bernard 1989 (98–104), the "erotic nightmare" of this sylvan scene also has echoes of pastoral's "dream of pleasure."
8. The horns of cuckoldry, first sign of his transformation into Jealousy; Spenser modulates from a fabliau to personification allegory by way of pastoral. On the rest of this canto, see P. Alpers, *The Poetry of* The Faerie Queene (Princeton, 1967) 215–28.

Embracéd of a Satyre rough and rude,
Who all the night did minde° his joyous play: *attend to*
Nine times he heard him come aloft ere day,
That all his hart with gealosie did swell;
But yet that nights ensample did bewray,
That not for nought his wife them loved so well,
When one so oft a night did ring his matins bell.

49

So closely as he could, he to them crept,
When wearie of their sport to sleepe they fell,
And to his wife, that now full soundly slept,
He whispered in her eare, and did her tell,
That it was he, which by her side did dwell,
And therefore prayd her wake, to heare him plaine.
As one out of a dreame not wakéd well,
She turned her, and returnéd backe againe:
Yet her for to awake he did the more constraine.

50

At last with irkesome trouble she abrayd;°   *awakened*
And then perceiving, that it was indeed
Her old Malbecco, which did her upbrayd,
With loosenesse of her love, and loathly deed,
She was astonisht with exceeding dreed,
And would have wakt the Satyre by her syde;
But he her prayd, for mercy, or for meed,
To save his life, ne let him be descryde,
But hearken to his lore, and all his counsell hyde.

51

Tho gan he her perswade, to leave that lewd
And loathsome life, of God and man abhord,
And home returne, where all should be renewd
With perfect peace, and bandes of fresh accord,
And she received againe to bed and bord,
As if no trespasse ever had bene donne:
But she it all refuséd at one word,
And by no meanes would to his will be wonne,
But chose emongst the jolly Satyres still to wonne.°   *dwell*

52

He wooéd her, till day spring he espyde;
But all in vaine: and then turnd to the heard,
Who butted him with hornes on every syde,
And trode downe in the durt, where his hore° beard   *gray*
Was fowly dight,° and he of death afeard.   *defiled*
Early before the heavens fairest light
Out of the ruddy East was fully reard,

The heardes out of their foldes were looséd quight,
And he emongst the rest crept forth in sory plight.

53

So soone as he the Prison dore did pas,
  He ran as fast, as both his feete could beare,
  And never lookéd, who behind him was,
  Ne scarsely who before: like as a Beare
  That creeping close, amongst the hives to reare°   *carry off*
  An hony combe, the wakefull dogs espy,
  And him assayling, sore his carkasse teare,
  That hardly he with life away does fly,
Ne stayes, till safe himselfe he see from jeopardy.

54

Ne stayd he, till he came unto the place,
  Where late his treasure he entombéd had,
  Where when he found it not (for Trompart bace
  Had it purloynéd for his maister bad:)
  With extreme fury he became quite mad,
  And ran away, ran with himselfe away:
  That who so straungely had him seene bestad,°   *situated*
  With upstart haire, and staring eyes dismay,
From Limbo lake him late escapéd sure would say.

55

High over hilles and over dales he fled,
  As if the wind him on his winges had borne,
  Ne banck nor bush could stay him, when he sped
  His nimble feet, as treading still on thorne:
  Griefe, and despight, and gealosie, and scorne
  Did all the way him follow hard behind,
  And he himselfe himselfe loathed so forlorne,
  So shamefully forlorne of womankind;
That as a Snake, still lurkéd in his wounded mind.

56

Still fled he forward, looking backward still,
  Ne stayd his flight, nor fearefull agony,
  Till that he came unto a rockie hill,
  Over the sea, suspended dreadfully,
  That living creature it would terrify,
  To looke adowne, or upward to the hight:
  From thence he threw himselfe dispiteously,°   *pitilessly*
  All desperate° of his fore-damnéd spright,   *despairing*
That seemed no helpe for him was left in living sight.

57

But through long anguish, and selfe-murdring thought
   He was so wasted and forpinéd° quight, *enfeebled*
   That all his substance was consumed to nought,
   And nothing left, but like an aery Spright,
   That on the rockes he fell so flit and light,
   That he thereby received no hurt at all,
   But chauncéd on a craggy cliff to light;
   Whence he with crooked clawes so long did crall,
That at the last he found a cave with entrance small.

58

Into the same he creepes, and thenceforth there
   Resolved to build his balefull mansion,
   In drery darkenesse, and continuall feare
   Of that rockes fall, which ever and anon
   Threates with huge ruine him to fall upon,
   That he dare never sleepe, but that one eye
   Still ope he keepes for that occasion;
   Ne ever rests he in tranquillity,
The roring billowes beat his bowre so boystrously.

59

Ne ever is he wont on ought to feed,
   But toades and frogs, his pasture° poysonous, *food*
   Which in his cold complexion° do breed *constitution*
   A filthy bloud, or humour rancorous,
   Matter of doubt and dread suspitious,
   That doth with curelesse care consume the hart,
   Corrupts the stomacke with gall vitious,
   Croscuts the liver with internall smart,
And doth transfixe the soule with deathes eternall dart.

60

Yet can he never dye, but dying lives,
   And doth himselfe with sorrow new sustaine,
   That death and life attonce unto him gives.
   And painefull pleasure turnes to pleasing paine.
   There dwels he ever, miserable swaine,
   Hatefull both to him selfe, and every wight;
   Where he through privy griefe, and horrour vaine,
   Is woxen so deformed, that he has quight
Forgot he was a man, and Gealosie is hight.

Canto XI

Britomart chaceth Ollyphant,
findes Scudamour distrest:
Assayes the house of Busyrane,[1]
where Loves spoyles are exprest.

1

O hatefull hellish Snake, what furie furst
  Brought thee from balefull house of Proserpine,
  Where in her bosome she thee long had nurst,
  And fostred up with bitter milke of tine,°   *affliction*
  Fowle Gealosie, that turnest love divine
To joylesse dread, and mak'st the loving hart
  With hatefull thoughts to languish and to pine,
  And feed it selfe with selfe-consuming smart?
Of all the passions in the mind thou vilest art.

2

O let him far be banishéd away,
  And in his stead let Love for ever dwell,
  Sweet Love, that doth his golden wings embay°   *bathe*
  In blesséd Nectar, and pure Pleasures well,
  Untroubled of vile feare, or bitter fell.°   *rancor*
  And ye faire Ladies, that your kingdomes make
In th'harts of men, them governe wisely well,
  And of faire Britomart ensample take,
That was as trew in love, as Turtle° to her make.°   *dove/mate*

3

Who with Sir Satyrane, as earst ye red,
  Forth ryding from Malbeccoes hostlesse hous,
  Far off aspyde a young man, the which fled
  From an huge Geaunt, that with hideous
  And hatefull outrage long him chacéd thus;
  It was that Ollyphant, the brother deare
  Of that Argante vile and vitious,
  From whom the Squire of Dames was reft whylere;
This all as bad as she, and worse, if worse ought were.

4

For as the sister did in feminine
  And filthy lust exceed all woman kind,
  So he surpasséd his sex masculine,
  In beastly use that I did ever find;°   *hear of*
  Whom when as Britomart beheld behind

1. The name recalls the Egyptian tyrant Busiris, who sacrificed strangers to Zeus; Hercules killed
  him. Like Archimago, Busyrane misuses words (his magic is the dark side of Spenser's own craft);
  true chastity, though, is largely unimpressed by his finally unreal magic. On this episode see
  comments by Roche, Hieatt, and Wofford, pp. 741–52, in this edition.

The fearefull boy so greedily pursew,
She was emmovéd in her noble mind,
T''employ her puissaunce to his reskew,
And prickéd fiercely forward, where she him did vew.

5

Ne was Sir Satyrane her far behinde,
  But with like fiercenesse did ensew° the chace: *follow*
  Whom when the Gyaunt saw, he soone resinde
  His former suit, and from them fled apace;
  They after both, and boldly bad him bace,[2]
  And each did strive the other to out-goe,
  But he them both outran a wondrous space,
  For he was long, and swift as any Roe,°   *deer*
And now made better speed, t''escape his fearéd foe.

6

It was not Satyrane, whom he did feare,
  But Britomart the flowre of chastity;
  For he the powre of chast hands might not beare,
  But always did their dread encounter fly:
  And now so fast his feet he did apply,
  That he has gotten to a forrest neare,
  Where he is shrowded in security.
  The wood they enter, and search every where,
They searchéd diversely, so both divided were.

7

Faire Britomart so long him followéd,
  That she at last came to a fountaine sheare,°   *clear*
  By which there lay a knight[3] all wallowéd°   *grovelling*
  Upon the grassy ground, and by him neare
  His haberjeon, his helmet, and his speare;
  A little off,° his shield was rudely throwne,   *aside*
  On which the wingéd boy in colours cleare
  Depeincted was, full easie to be knowne,
And he thereby, where ever it in field was showne.

8

His face upon the ground did groveling ly,
  As if he had bene slombring in the shade,
  That the brave Mayd would not for courtesy,
  Out of his quiet slomber him abrade,°   *arouse*
  Nor seeme too suddeinly him to invade:°   *intrude on*
  Still as she stood, she heard with grievous throb
  Him grone, as if his hart were peeces made,

2. I.e., challenged him.
3. I.e., Scudamour, whose shield bears Cupid's image; as Amoret's fiancé, he is the courtly embodiment of male desire. The episode that follows is based primarily on Tasso, *Rinaldo* 5.

And with most painefull pangs to sigh and sob,
That pitty did the Virgins hart of patience rob.

9

At last forth breaking into bitter plaintes
    He said; "O soveraigne Lord that sit'st on hye,
    And raignst in blis emongst thy blesséd Saintes,
    How suffrest thou such shamefull cruelty,
    So long unwreakéd° of thine enimy?   *unavenged*
    Or hast thou, Lord, of good mens cause no heed?
    Or doth thy justice sleepe, and silent ly?
    What booteth then the good and righteous deed,
If goodnesse find no grace, nor righteousnesse no meed?

10

"If good find grace, and righteousnesse reward,
    Why then is Amoret in caytive band,[4]
    Sith that more bounteous creature never fared
    On foot, upon the face of living land?
    Or if that heavenly justice may withstand
    The wrongfull outrage of unrighteous men,
    Why then is Busirane with wicked hand
    Suffred, these seven monethes day in secret den
My Lady and my love so cruelly to pen?[5]

11

"My Lady and my love is cruelly pend
    In dolefull darkenesse from the vew of day,
    Whilest deadly torments do her chast brest rend,
    And the sharpe steele doth rive her hart in tway,
    All for she Scudamore will not denay.°   *deny*
    Yet thou vile man, vile Scudamore art sound,
    Ne canst her ayde, ne canst her foe dismay;
    Unworthy wretch to tread upon the ground,
For whom so faire a Lady feeles so sore a wound "

12

There an huge heape of singultes° did opresse   *sobs*
    His strugling soule, and swelling throbs empeach°   *hinder*
    His foltring toung with pangs of drerinesse,°   *grief*
    Choking the remnant of his plaintife speach,
    As if his dayes were come to their last reach.°   *end*
    Which when she heard, and saw the ghastly fit,
    Threatning into his life to make a breach,

4. I.e., captive in bonds.
5. Spenser may pun on "to pen" (to enclose, to write), for Amoret's situation is made of clichés from love poetry (see, e.g., Roche, *Flame*). Readers have disagreed as to whose imagination generates what Britomart sees: is Amoret upset by Scudamour's attempted masculine mastery, or does her own wavering "wit" (stanza 26) make her fear such mastery? Might the lovers' impasse result from some combination of her doubts and his urgency? Her captivity recalls those of Florimell and Pastorella (in Book VI), but her torture also shows how cultural convention can reconstruct the erotic impulse as a cruel prison.

Both with great ruth and terrour she was smit,
Fearing least from her cage the wearie soule would flit.

13

Tho stooping downe she him amovéd light;
  Who therewith somewhat starting, up gan looke,
  And seeing him behind a straunger knight,
  Whereas no living creature he mistooke,[6]
  With great indignaunce he that sight forsooke,
  And downe againe himselfe disdainefully
  Abjecting,° th'earth with his faire forhead strooke: *casting*
  Which the bold Virgin seeing, gan apply
Fit medcine to his griefe, and spake thus courtesly.

14

"Ah gentle knight, whose deepe conceivéd griefe
  Well seemes t'exceede the powre of patience,
  Yet if that heavenly grace some good reliefe
  You send, submit you to high providence,
  And ever in your noble hart prepense,°   *consider*
  That all the sorrow in the world is lesse,
  Then vertues might, and values° confidence,   *valor's*
  For who nill bide the burden of distresse,
Must not here thinke to live: for life is wretchednesse.

15

"Therefore, faire Sir, do comfort to you take,
  And freely read,° what wicked felon so   *tell*
  Hath outraged you, and thrald your gentle make.°   *mate*
  Perhaps this hand may helpe to ease your woe,
  And wreake your sorrow on your cruell foe,
  At least it faire endevour will apply."
  Those feeling wordes so neare the quicke did goe,
  That up his head he rearéd easily,
And leaning on his elbow, these few wordes let fly.

16

"What boots it plaine,° that cannot be redrest,   *to lament*
  And sow vaine sorrow in a fruitlesse eare,
  Sith powre of hand, nor skill of learnéd brest,
  Ne worldly price cannot redeeme my deare,
  Out of her thraldome and continuall feare?
  For he the tyraunt, which her hath in ward°   *control*
  By strong enchauntments and blacke Magicke leare,°   *lore*
  Hath in a dungeon deepe her close embard,
And many dreadfull feends hath pointed° to her gard.   *appointed*

17

"There he tormenteth her most terribly,
  And day and night afflicts with mortall paine,

6. I.e., where he had mistakenly thought no one to be.

Because to yield him love she doth deny,
Once to me yold,° not to be yold againe:[7]   *yielded*
But yet by torture he would her constraine
Love to conceive in her disdainfull brest;
Till so she do, she must in doole° remaine,   *pain*
Ne may by living meanes be thence relest:°   *released*
What boots it then to plaine, that cannot be redrest?"

18

With this sad hersall° of his heavy stresse,°   *account/distress*
The warlike Damzell was empassiond sore,
And said; "Sir knight, your cause is nothing lesse,
Then is your sorrow, certes if not more;
For nothing so much pitty doth implore,
As gentle Ladies helplesse misery.
But yet, if please ye listen to my lore,
I will with proofe of last extremity,[8]
Deliver her fro thence, or with her for you dy."

19

"Ah gentlest knight alive," said Scudamore,
"What huge heroicke magnanimity
Dwels in thy bounteous brest? what couldst thou more,
If she were thine, and thou as now am I?
O spare thy happy dayes, and them apply
To better boot,° but let me dye, that ought;   *advantage*
More is more losse: one is enough to dy."
"Life is not lost," said she, "for which is bought
Endlesse renowm, that more then death is to be sought."[9]

20

Thus she at length perswaded him to rise,
And with her wend, to see what new successe°   *result*
Mote him befall upon new enterprise;
His armes, which he had vowed to disprofesse,°   *renounce*
She gathered up and did about him dresse,
And his forwandred steed unto him got:
So forth they both yfere° make their progresse,   *together*
And march not past the mountenaunce° of a shot,   *distance*
Till they arrived, whereas their purpose they did plot.

21

There they dismounting, drew their weapons bold
And stoutly came unto the Castle gate;
Whereas no gate they found, them to withhold,

---

7. In IV.x, Scudamour tells how he won Amoret and the shield of Love (hence his name) in the Temple of Venus; the story of the wedding, during which Busirane abducts Amoret, is in IV. i.2–4.
8. I.e., to the utmost of my strength and spirit.
9. I.e., that is to be sought even at the risk of death.

Nor ward° to wait at morne and evening late,   *porter*
But in the Porch, that did them sore amate,°   *dismay*
A flaming fire,[1] ymixt with smouldry smoke,
And stinking Sulphure, that with griesly hate
And dreadfull horrour did all entraunce choke,
Enforcéd them their forward footing to revoke.°   *withdraw*

22

Greatly thereat was Britomart dismayd,
    Ne in that stownd° wist, how her selfe to beare;   *crisis*
    For daunger vaine it were, to have assayd
    That cruell element, which all things feare,
    Ne none can suffer to approchen neare:
    And turning backe to Scudamour, thus sayd;
    "What monstrous enmity provoke we heare,
    Foolhardy as th'Earthes children, the which made
Battell against the Gods? so we a God invade.[2]

23

"Daunger without discretion to attempt,
    Inglorious and beastlike is: therefore Sir knight,
    Aread what course of you is safest dempt,°   *judged*
    And how we with our foe may come to fight."
    "This is," quoth he, "the dolorous despight,
    Which earst to you I playnd: for neither may
    This fire be quencht by any wit or might,
    Ne yet by any meanes removed away,
So mighty be th'enchauntments, which the same do stay.°   *support*

24

"What is there else, but cease these fruitlesse paines,
    And leave me to my former languishing?
    Faire Amoret must dwell in wicked chaines,
    And Scudamore here dye with sorrowing."
    "Perdy not so;" said she, "for shamefull thing
    It were t'abandon noble chevisaunce,°   *enterprise*
    For shew of perill, without venturing:
    Rather let try extremities of chaunce,
Then enterpriséd prayse for dread to disavaunce."[3]

25

Therewith resolved to prove her utmost might,
    Her ample shield she threw before her face,

---

1. Stanzas 21–25 adapt Tasso's *Rinaldo* 5.58–61 and *Gerusalemme* 13.34–35. There are similar details in R. Johnson's *Seven Champions of Christendom* (printed c. 1597), notably the fire barrier (found also in fairy stories). Britomart's passage through this fire shows how thoughtful chastity can meet challenges that defeat willful desire.
2. I.e., like the giants attacking Olympus, we attack Vulcan (god of fire and oft-cuckolded husband of Venus; he was also, as in stanza 26, called Mulciber).
3. I.e., than to retreat fearfully from actions deserving praise.

And her swords point directing forward right,
Assayld the flame, the which eftsoones gave place,
And did it selfe divide with equall space,
That through she passéd; as a thunder bolt
Perceth the yielding ayre, and doth displace
The soring clouds into sad showres ymolt;°   *melted*
So to her yold the flames, and did their force revolt.°   *withdraw*

26

Whom whenas Scudamour saw past the fire,
Safe and untoucht, he likewise gan assay,
With greedy will, and envious desire,
And bad the stubborne flames to yield him way:
But cruell Mulciber would not obay
His threatfull pride, but did the more augment
His mighty rage, and with imperious sway
Him forst (maulgre) his fiercenesse to relent,
And backe retire, all scorcht and pitifully brent.

27

With huge impatience he inly swelt,°   *burned*
More for great sorrow, that he could not pas,
Then for the burning torment, which he felt,
That with fell woodnesse° he effiercéd° was,   *madness/enraged*
And wilfully him throwing on the gras,
Did beat and bounse his head and brest full sore;
The whiles the Championesse now entred has
The utmost° rowme, and past the formest dore,   *outermost*
The utmost rowme, abounding with all precious store.

28

For round about, the wals yclothéd were
With goodly arras of great majesty,[4]
Woven with gold and silke so close and nere,
That the rich metall lurkéd privily,
As faining to be hid from envious eye;
Yet here, and there, and every where unwares
It shewd it selfe, and shone unwillingly;
Like a discolourd° Snake, whose hidden snares   *varicolored*
Through the greene gras his long bright burnisht backe declares.

29

And in those Tapets° weren fashionéd   *tapestries*
Many faire pourtraicts, and many a faire feate,
And all of love, and all of lusty-hed,
As seeméd by their semblaunt did entreat;°   *concern*
And eke all Cupids warres they did repeate,

4. The chief literary basis for stanzas 28–46 is *Metamorphoses* 6.103–28; Spenser also consulted the
   mythographers, and there are parallels in Renaissance tapestries, paintings, and court pageantry.

And cruell battels, which he whilome fought
Gainst all the Gods, to make his empire great;
Besides the huge massacres, which he wrought
On mighty kings and kesars,° into thraldome brought.   *emperors*

30

Therein was writ, how often thundring Jove
Had felt the point of his hart-percing dart,
And leaving heavens kingdome, here did rove
In straunge disguize, to slake his scalding smart;
Now like a Ram, faire Helle to pervart,[5]
Now like a Bull, Europa to withdraw:°   *carry off*
Ah, how the fearefull Ladies tender hart
Did lively° seeme to tremble, when she saw   *actually*
The huge seas under her t'obay her servaunts law.

31

Soone after that into a golden showre
Him selfe he chaunged faire Danaë to vew,
And through the roofe of her strong brasen towre
Did raine into her lap an hony dew,
The whiles her foolish garde, that little knew
Of such deceipt, kept th'yron dore fast bard,
And watcht, that none should enter nor issew;
Vaine was that watch, and bootlesse all the ward,°   *guard*
Whenas the God to golden hew° him selfe transfard.   *form*

32

Then was he turnd into a snowy Swan,
To win faire Leda to his lovely° trade: *loving*
O wondrous skill, and sweet wit of the man,
That her in daffadillies sleeping made,
From scorching heat her daintie limbes to shade:
Whiles the proud Bird ruffing° his fethers wyde,   *ruffling*
And brushing his faire brest, did her invade:
She slept, yet twixt her eyelids closely spyde,
How towards her he rusht, and smiléd at his pryde.

33

Then shewd it, how the Thebane Semelee[6]
Deceived of gealous Juno, did require

5. Helle and her brother, Phrixus, whom their stepmother, Ino, meant to sacrifice to Zeus, were
saved when Hermes (Mercury) provided a gold-fleeced flying ram to carry them to safety (although
Helle fell into the sea now called the Hellespont); see Ovid, *Fasti* 3.851–76, and Boccaccio,
Genealogiae 13.68. In 4.68, Boccaccio links the influence of Aries ("the Ram") to the characteristics
of Jove as leader and lover; Spenser combines these to make his own myth.
6. See *Metamorphoses* 3.253–309. Jealous of Semele, Juno took the form of her nurse and urged
her to ask Jove to make love in all his glory; when he did so, Semele was consumed (but the god
placed her embryo son, Bacchus, in his own thigh to gestate).

To see him in his soveraigne majestee,
Armd with his thunderbolts and lightning fire,
Whence dearely she with death bought her desire.
But faire Alcmena[7] better match did make,
Joying his love, in likenesse more entire;°   *perfect*
Three nights in one, they say, that for her sake
He then did put, her pleasures lenger to partake.

34

Twise was he seene in soaring Eagles shape,
And with wide wings to beat the buxome° ayre,   *yielding*
Once, when he with Asterie[8] did scape,
Againe, when as the Trojane boy[9] so faire
He snatcht from Ida hill, and with him bare:
Wondrous delight it was, there to behould,
How the rude Shepheards after him did stare,
Trembling through feare, least down he fallen should,
And often to him calling, to take surer hould.

35

In Satyres shape Antiopa he snatcht:
And like a fire, when he Aegin' assayd:
A shepheard, when Mnemosyné he catcht:
And like a Serpent to the Thracian mayd.[1]
Whiles thus on earth great Jove these pageaunts° playd,   *scenes*
The wingéd boy did thrust into his throne,
And scoffing, thus unto his mother sayd,
"Lo now the heavens obey to me alone,
And take me for their Jove, whiles Jove to earth is gone."

36

And thou, faire Phoebus, in thy colours bright
Wast there enwoven, and the sad distresse,
In which that boy thee plongéd, for despight,
That thou bewrayedst his mothers wantonnesse,
When she with Mars was meynt° in joyfulnesse: *mingled*
For thy he thrild° thee with a leaden dart,   *pierced*
To love faire Daphne, which thee lovéd lesse:[2]
Lesse she thee loved, then was thy just desart,
Yet was thy love her death, and her death was thy smart.

7. Alcmena conceived Hercules when Jove came to her in the form of her husband, Amphitryon. The fusing of three nights into one may reflect the version in Comes 6.1.
8. Fleeing Jove, Asterie became a quail; he then became an eagle.
9. I.e., Ganymede (cf. *Metamorphoses* 10.155–62); often read as describing a homosexual abduction, the myth was sometimes also allegorized as the rapture of mystic contemplation.
1. I.e., Proserpine, known to her Thracian worshippers as Cotytto.
2. On Apollo and Daphne, see *Metamorphoses* 1.450–567. Ovid says Cupid's gold-tipped and lead-tipped arrows inspire love or antipathy respectively; here the "leaden dart" may indicate Apollo's failure in love.

37

So lovedst thou the lusty° Hyacinct,   *handsome*
    So lovedst thou the faire Coronis deare:[3]
    Yet both are of thy haplesse hand extinct,
    Yet both in flowres do live, and love thee beare,
    The one a Paunce,° the other a sweet breare: *pansy*
    For griefe whereof, ye mote have lively seene
    The God himselfe rending his golden heare,
    And breaking quite his gyrlond ever greene,
With other signes of sorrow and impatient teene.°   *woe*

38

Both for those two, and for his owne deare sonne,
    The sonne of Climene[4] he did repent,
    Who bold to guide the charet of the Sunne,
    Himselfe in thousand peeces fondly rent,
    And all the world with flashing fier brent;
    So like,° that all the walles did seeme to flame.   *lifelike*
    Yet cruell Cupid, not herewith content,
    Forst him eftsoones to follow other game,
And love a Shepheards daughter for his dearest Dame.

39

He lovéd Isse for his dearest Dame,[5]
    And for her sake her cattell fed a while,
    And for her sake a cowheard vile became,
    The servant of Admetus cowheard vile,
    Whiles that from heaven he sufferéd exile.
    Long were to tell each other lovely fit,°   *episode of love*
    Now like a Lyon, hunting after spoile,
    Now like a Stag, now like a faulcon flit:
All which in that faire arras was most lively writ.

40

Next unto him was Neptune picturéd,
    In his divine resemblance wondrous lyke:
    His face was rugged, and his hoarie hed
    Droppéd with brackish deaw; his three-forkt Pyke
    He stearnly shooke, and therewith fierce did stryke
    The raging billowes, that on every syde
    They trembling stood, and made a long broad dyke,
    That his swift charet might have passage wyde,
Which foure great Hippodames° did draw in temewise tyde.   *sea horses*

---

3. On Hyacinth see III.vi.45. Coronis, a victim of Apollo's jealous rage, appears in *Metamorphoses*
   2.542–632; Spenser invents her transformation into a sweetbriar.
4. I.e., Phaethon (cf. *Metamorphoses* 2.1–400).
5. Spenser merges two myths: Apollo's appearance as a shepherd to Isse (*Metamorphoses* 6.124) and
   his nine years as an indentured herdsman to Admetus (see Hyginus, *Fabulae* 50).

41

His sea-horses did seeme to snort amayne,°   *violently*
    And from their nosethrilles blow the brynie streame,
    That made the sparckling waves to smoke agayne,
    And flame with gold, but the white fomy creame,
    Did shine with silver, and shoot forth his beame.
    The God himselfe did pensive seeme and sad,
    And hong adowne his head, as he did dreame:
    For privy love his brest empiercéd had,
Ne ought but deare Bisaltis[6] ay could make him glad.

42

He lovéd eke Iphimedia deare,
    And Aeolus faire daughter Arne hight,
    For whom he turnd him selfe into a Steare,
    And fed on fodder, to beguile her sight.
    Also to win Deucalions daughter bright,[7]
    He turned him selfe into a Dolphin fayre;
    And like a wingéd horse he tooke his flight,
    To snaky-locke Medusa to repayre,
On whom he got faire Pegasus, that flitteth in the ayre.

43

Next Saturne[8] was, (but who would ever weene,
    That sullein Saturne ever weend to love?
    Yet love is sullein, and Saturnlike seene,
    As he did for Erigone it prove,)
    That to a Centaure did him selfe transmove.°   *transmute*
    So prooved it eke that gracious God of wine,
    When for to compasse° Philliras hard love,   *achieve*
    He turnd himselfe into a fruitfull vine,
And into her faire bosome made his grapes decline.

44

Long were to tell the amorous assayes,
    And gentle pangues,° with which he makéd meeke   *pangs*
    The mighty Mars, to learne his wanton playes:
    How oft for Venus, and how often eek
    For many other Nymphes he sore did shreek,
    With womanish teares, and with unwarlike smarts,
    Privily moystening his horrid° cheek.   *rough*
    There was he painted full of burning darts,
And many wide woundes launchéd° through his inner parts.   *pierced*

6. I.e., Theophane, changed by Neptune into a ewe that he might, in the form of a ram, outwit
   her suitors (cf. Hyginus, *Fabulae* 88).
7. I.e., Melantho; for these allusions Spenser depends on *Metamorphoses* 6.116–20 and commentaries
   by Boccaccio and Comes.
8. The planet Saturn's influence is stern, ominous, and "crabbed" (cf. *Mutabilitie* vii.52). The stanza
   confuses Bacchus's seduction of Erigone with Saturn's deception of Philyra, mother of the centaur
   Chiron (*Metamorphoses* 6.125–26). A scribal or printer's error may be to blame.

45

Ne did he spare (so cruell was the Elfe)
  His owne deare mother, (ah why should he so?)
  Ne did he spare sometime to pricke himselfe,
  That he might tast the sweet consuming woe,
  Which he had wrought to many others moe.
  But to declare the mournfull Tragedyes,
  And spoiles, wherewith he all the ground did strow,
  More eath° to number, with how many eyes   *easy*
High heaven beholds sad lovers nightly theeveryes.

46

Kings Queenes, Lords Ladies, Knights and Damzels gent°   *noble*
  Were heaped together with the vulgar sort,
  And mingled with the raskall rablement,
  Without respect of person or of port,°   *rank*
  To shew Dan° Cupids powre and great effort: *Master*
  And round about a border was entrayld,°   *entwined*
  Of broken bowes and arrowes shivered short,
  And a long bloudy river through them rayld,°   *flowed*
So lively and so like, that living sence it fayld.

47

And at the upper end of that faire rowme,
  There was an Altar built of pretious stone,
  Of passing valew, and of great renowme,
  On which there stood an Image all alone,
  Of massy gold, which with his owne light shone;
  And wings it had with sundry colours dight,
  More sundry colours, then the proud Pavone[9]
  Beares in his boasted fan, or Iris bright,
When her discolourd° bow she spreds through   *many colored*
    heaven bright.

48

Blindfold he was, and in his cruell fist
  A mortall bow and arrowes keene did hold,
  With which he shot at random, when him list,
  Some headed with sad lead, some with pure gold;
  (Ah man beware, how thou those darts behold)
  A wounded Dragon[1] under him did ly,
  Whose hideous tayle his left foot did enfold,
  And with a shaft was shot through either eye,
That no man forth might draw, ne no man remedye.

9. I.e., the peacock; Iris is goddess of the rainbow. The combination of images recalls Tasso, *Ger-usalemme* 16.24, while the altar suggests idolatry.
1. The blinded dragon is a fitting emblem of love's cruelty and terror; in Apuleius's *Golden Ass*, Psyche's jealous sisters persuade her that her husband Cupid, whom she has not seen by day, is a huge poisonous snake.

49

And underneath his feet was written thus,
  Unto the Victor of the Gods this bee:
And all the people in that ample hous
Did to that image bow their humble knee,
And oft committed fowle Idolatree.
That wondrous sight faire Britomart amazed,
Ne seeing could her wonder satisfie,
But ever more and more upon it gazed,
The whiles the passing° brightnes her fraile sences dazed.   *surpassing*

50

Tho as she backward cast her busie eye,
  To search each secret of that goodly sted,°   *place*
Over the dore thus written she did spye
  Be bold: she oft it over-red,
Yet could not find what sence it figuréd:
But what so were therein or writ or ment,
She was no whit thereby discouragéd
From prosecuting of her first intent,
But forward with bold steps into the next roome went.

51

Much fairer, then the former, was that roome,
  And richlier by many partes° arayd: *degrees*
For not with arras made in painefull° loome,   *painstaking*
But with pure gold it all was overlayd,
Wrought with wilde Antickes,° which their   *grotesque figures*
  follies playd,
In the rich metall, as they living were:
A thousand monstrous formes therein were made,
Such as false love doth oft upon him weare,
For love in thousand monstrous formes doth oft appeare.

52

And all about, the glistring walles were hong
  With warlike spoiles, and with victorious prayes,°   *booty*
Of mighty Conquerours and Captaines strong,
Which were whilome captivéd in their dayes
To cruell love, and wrought their owne decayes:
Their swerds and speres were broke, and hauberques rent;
And their proud girlonds of tryumphant bayes°   *laurels*
Troden in dust with fury insolent,
To shew the victors might and mercilesse intent.

53

The warlike Mayde beholding earnestly
  The goodly ordinance° of this rich place,   *arrangement*

Did greatly wonder, ne could satisfie
Her greedy eyes with gazing a long space,
But more she mervaild that no footings trace,
Nor wight appeared, but wastefull emptinesse,
And solemne silence over all that place:
Straunge thing it seemed, that none was to possesse
So rich purveyance,° ne them keepe with carefulnesse.   *provision*

54

And as she lookt about, she did behold,
How over that same dore was likewise writ,
Be bold, be bold, and every where *Be bold*,
That much she muzed, yet could not construe it
By any ridling skill, or commune wit.
At last she spyde at that roomes upper end,
Another yron dore, on which was writ,
Be not too bold; whereto though she did bend
Her earnest mind, yet wist not what it might intend.[2]

55

Thus she there waited untill eventyde,
Yet living creature none she saw appeare:
And now sad shadowes gan the world to hyde,
From mortall vew, and wrap in darkenesse dreare;
Yet nould° she d'off her weary armes, for feare   *would not*
Of secret daunger, ne let sleepe oppresse
Her heavy eyes with natures burdein deare,
But drew her selfe aside in sickernesse,°   *safety*
And her welpointed° weapons did about her dresse.°   *ready; arrange*

Canto XII

The maske of Cupid,[1] and th'enchaunted
Chamber are displayd,
Whence Britomart redeemes faire
Amoret, through charmes decayd.°   *weakened*

1

Tho when as chearelesse Night ycovered had
Faire heaven with an universall cloud,
That every wight dismayd with darknesse sad,°   *heavy*
In silence and in sleepe themselves did shroud,
She heard a shrilling Trompet sound aloud,

2. Britomart is judiciously "bold," but in his intemperate eagerness Scudamour may be "too bold."
1. This artfully symmetrical "maske" may revise an early work by Spenser such as the "Court of
Cupide" mentioned in the "Epistle" to *The Shepheardes Calender* or the "Pageaunts" noted in the
Glosse to "June." It is a "disguising," or pageant, presented (as IV.i.2–3 confirms) at the wedding
of Amoret and Scudamour. Its personages, structure, and allegory reflect Tudor court entertainments, which fused mythology, romance, and court-of-love allegory. Specifically, Spenser joins
the court-of-love "procession of Cupid" (as in Andreas Capellanus's *De Amore*) to Cupid's "triumph"
with his adherents and victims (cf. Petrarch's *Trionfi*).

Signe of nigh battell, or got victory;
Nought therewith daunted was her courage proud,
But rather stird to cruell enmity,
Expecting ever, when some foe she might descry.

2

With that, an hideous storme of winde arose,
  With dreadfull thunder and lightning atwixt,
  And an earth-quake, as if it streight would lose°   *loosen*
  The worlds foundations from his centre fixt;
  A direfull stench of smoke and sulphure mixt
  Ensewd, whose noyance fild the fearefull sted,°   *place*
  From the fourth houre of night untill the sixt;
  Yet the bold Britonesse was nought ydred,
Though much emmoved, but stedfast still perseveréd.

3

All suddenly a stormy whirlwind blew
  Throughout the house, that clappéd° every dore,   *slammed*
  With which that yron wicket[7] open flew,
  As it with mightie levers had bene tore:
  And forth issewd, as on the ready° flore   *prepared*
  Of some Theatre, a grave personage,
  That in his hand a branch of laurell bore,
  With comely haveour and count'nance sage,
Yclad in costly garments, fit for tragicke Stage.

4

Proceeding to the midst, he still did stand,
  As if in mind he somewhat had to say,
  And to the vulgar° beckning with his hand,   *common people*
  In signe of silence, as to heare a play,
  By lively actions he gan bewray
  Some argument of matter passionéd;[3]
  Which doen, he backe retyréd soft away,
  And passing by, his name discoveréd,
Ease, on his robe in golden letters cypheréd.°   *written*

5

The noble Mayd, still standing all this vewd,
  And merveild at his strange intendiment;°   *purpose*
  With that a joyous fellowship issewd
  Of Minstrals, making goodly meriment,
  With wanton Bardes, and Rymers impudent,
  All which together sung full chearefully
  A lay of loves delight, with sweet concent:°   *harmony*

2. I.e., the "yron dore" in xi.54.
3. I.e., by expressive gestures, he revealed the theme of the coming masque. In Senecan tragedies of the period, dumbshows between the acts indicated the play's progressive action.

After whom marcht a jolly company,
In manner of a maske, enrangéd orderly.

6

The whiles a most delitious harmony,
  In full straunge notes was sweetly heard to sound,
  That the rare sweetnesse of the melody
  The feeble senses wholly did confound,
  And the fraile soule in deepe delight nigh dround:
  And when it ceast, shrill trompets loud did bray,
  That their report° did farre away rebound,   *echo*
  And when they ceast, it gan againe to play,
The whiles the maskers marchéd forth in trim aray.

7

The first was Fancy, like a lovely boy,
  Of rare aspect, and beautie without peare;
  Matchable either to that ympe of Troy,[4]
  Whom Jove did love, and chose his cup to beare,
  Or that same daintie lad, which was so deare
  To great Alcides, that when as he dyde,
  He wailéd womanlike with many a teare,
  And every wood, and every valley wyde
He fild with Hylas name; the Nymphes eke Hylas cryde.[5]

8

His garment neither was of silke nor say,°   *fine wool*
  But painted plumes, in goodly order dight,
  Like as the sunburnt Indians do aray
  Their tawney bodies, in their proudest plight:°   *attire*
  As those same plumes, so seemd he vaine and light,
  That by his gate° might easily appeare;   *gait*
  For still he fared as dauncing in delight,
  And in his hand a windy fan[6] did beare,
That in the idle aire he moved still here and there.

9

And him beside marcht amorous Desyre,
  Who seemd of riper yeares, then th'other Swaine,
  Yet was that other swayne this elders syre,
  And gave him being, commune to them twaine:
  His garment was disguiséd very vaine,[7]
  And his embrodered Bonet sat awry;
  Twixt both his hands few sparkes he close did straine,°   *clasp*

4. I.e., Ganymede, son of Troy's King Tros.
5. Cf. Theocritus, *Idyl* 13. Accompanying his lover Hercules (often called Alcides) on the Argo, the youth Hylas drowned in a spring during shore leave. See also the *Dictionarium* (1553) of C. Estienne, which has the wailing nymphs.
6. I.e., a fan to stir the breeze.
7. I.e., unusually designed for fashionable display.

Which still he blew, and kindled busily,
That soone they life conceived, and forth in flames did fly.

10

Next after him went Doubt, who was yclad
 In a discoloured cote, of straunge disguyse,°   *fashion*
 That at his backe a brode Capuccio° had,   *hood*
 And sleeves dependant Albanese-wyse:[8]
 He lookt askew with his mistrustfull eyes,
 And nicely° trode, as thornes lay in his way,   *delicately*
 Or that the flore to shrinke he did avyse,°   *perceive*
 And on a broken reed he still did stay°   *support*
His feeble steps, which shrunke, when hard theron he lay.

11

With him went Daunger, clothed in ragged weed,°   *garment*
 Made of Beares skin, that him more dreadfull made,
 Yet his owne face was dreadfull, ne did need
 Straunge horrour, to deforme his griesly shade;
 A net in th'one hand, and a rustie blade
 In th'other was, this Mischiefe, that Mishap;
 With th'one his foes he threatned to invade,°   *assault*
 With th'other he his friends ment to enwrap:
For whom he could not kill, he practizd° to entrap.   *plotted*

12

Next him was Feare, all armed from top to toe,
 Yet thought himselfe not safe enough thereby,
 But feard each shadow moving to and fro,
 And his owne armes when glittering he did spy,
 Or clashing heard, he fast away did fly,
 As ashes pale of hew, and wingyheeld;
 And evermore on Daunger fixt his eye,
 Gainst whom he alwaies bent° a brasen shield,   *directed*
Which his right hand unarméd fearefully did wield.

13

With him went Hope in rancke, a handsome Mayd,
 Of chearefull looke and lovely to behold;
 In silken samite° she was light arayd,   *rich cloth*
 And her faire lockes were woven up in gold;
 She alway smyld, and in her hand did hold
 An holy water Sprinckle,[9] dipt in deowe,°   *dew*
 With which she sprinckled favours manifold,
 On whom she list, and did great liking sheowe,
Great liking unto many, but true love to feowe.

8. Hanging down in the Albanian style.
9. An aspergillum, or brush for sprinkling holy water.

14

And after them Dissemblance, and Suspect
  Marcht in one rancke, yet an unequall paire:
  For she was gentle, and of milde aspect,
  Courteous to all, and seeming debonaire,
  Goodly adornéd, and exceeding faire:
  Yet was that all but painted, and purloynd,
  And her bright browes were deckt with borrowed haire:
  Her deedes were forgéd, and her words false coynd,
And alwaies in her hand two clewes° of silke she twynd.   *balls*

15

But he was foule, ill favouréd, and grim,
  Under his eyebrowes looking still askaunce;°   *sideways*
  And ever as Dissemblance laught on him,
  He lowrd° on her with daungerous° eyeglaunce;   *scowled/hard*
  Shewing his nature in his countenance;
  His rolling eyes did never rest in place,
  But walkt each° where, for feare of hid mischaunce,   *every*
  Holding a lattice[1] still before his face,
Through which he still did peepe, as forward he did pace.

16

Next him went Griefe, and Fury matcht yfere;°   *together*
  Griefe all in sable sorrowfully clad,
  Downe hanging his dull head with heavy chere,°   *countenance*
  Yet inly being more, then seeming sad:
  A paire of Pincers in his hand he had,
  With which he pinchéd people to the hart,
  That from thenceforth a wretched life they lad,
  In wilfull languor and consuming smart,
Dying each day with inward wounds of dolours dart.

17

But Fury was full ill appareiléd
  In rags, that naked nigh she did appeare,
  With ghastly lookes and dreadfull drerihed;°   *horror*
  For from her backe her garments she did teare,
  And from her head oft rent her snarléd heare:
  In her right hand a firebrand she did tosse
  About her head, still roming here and there;
  As a dismayéd Deare in chace embost,°   *hard pressed*
Forgetfull of his safety, hath his right way lost.

18

After them went Displeasure and Pleasance,
  He looking lompish and full sullein sad,

1. I.e., a small screen or vizard.

And hanging downe his heavy countenance;
She chearefull fresh and full of joyance glad,
As if no sorrow she ne felt ne drad;°   *feared*
That evill matchéd paire they seemed to bee:
An angry Waspe th'one in a viall had,
Th'other in hers an hony-lady° Bee;   *honey-laden*
Thus marchéd these sixe couples forth in faire degree.°   *order*

19

After all these there marcht a most faire Dame,
Led of two grysie° villeins, th'one Despight,°   *grim/outrage*
The other clepéd° Cruelty by name: *called*
She dolefull Lady, like a dreary Spright,
Cald by strong charmes out of eternall night,
Had deathes owne image figurd in her face,
Full of sad signes, fearefull to living sight;
Yet in that horror shewd a seemely grace,
And with her feeble feet did move a comely pace.

20

Her brest all naked, as net° ivory,   *pure*
Without adorne of gold or silver bright,
Wherewith the Craftesman wonts° it beautify,   *is used to*
Of her dew honour° was despoyléd quight,   *covering*
And a wide wound therein (O ruefull sight)
Entrenchéd deepe with knife acc11rséd keene,
Yet freshly bleeding forth her fainting spright,
(The worke of cruell hand) was to be seene,
That dyde in sanguine red her skin all snowy cleene.

21

At that wide orifice her trembling hart
Was drawne forth, and in silver basin layd,
Quite through transfixed with a deadly dart,
And in her bloud yet steeming fresh embayd:°   *bathed*
And those two villeins, which her steps upstayd,
When her weake feete could scarcely her sustaine,
And fading vitall powers gan to fade,
Her forward still with torture did constraine,
And evermore encreaséd her consuming paine.

22

Next after her the wingéd God himselfe[2]
Came riding on a Lion ravenous,
Taught to abay the menage° of that Elfe,   *control*
That man and beast with powre imperious
Subdeweth to his kingdome tyrannous:
His blindfold eyes he bad a while unbind,

2. I.e., Cupid.

That his proud spoyle of that same dolorous
Faire Dame he might behold in perfect kind;°   *manner*
Which seene, he much rejoycéd in his cruell mind.

23

Of which full proud, himselfe up rearing hye,
  He lookéd round about with sterne disdaine;
  And did survay his goodly company:
  And marshalling the evill ordered traine,°   *assembly*
  With that the darts which his right hand did straine,
  Full dreadfully he shooke that all did quake,
  And clapt on hie his coulourd wingés twaine,
  That all his many° it affraide did make: *company*
Tho blinding him againe, his way he forth did take.

24

Behinde him was Reproch, Repentance, Shame;
  Reproch the first, Shame next, Repent behind:
  Repentance feeble, sorrowfull, and lame:
  Reproch despightfull, carelesse, and unkind;
  Shame most ill favour,° bestiall, and blind: *featured*
  Shame lowrd, Repentance sighed, Reproch did scould;
  Reproch sharpe stings, Repentance whips entwind,
  Shame burning brond-yrons in her hand did hold:
All three to each° unlike, yet all made in one mould.   *each other*

25

And after them a rude confuséd rout°   *mob*
  Of persons flockt, whose names is hard to read:°   *distinguish*
  Emongst them was sterne Strife, and Anger stout,
  Unquiet Care, and fond Unthriftihead,°   *wastefulness*
  Lewd° Losse of Time, and Sorrow seeming dead,   *foolish*
  Inconstant Chaunge, and false Disloyaltie,
  Consuming Riotise,° and guilty Dread   *extravagance*
  Of heavenly vengeance, faint Infirmitie,
Vile Povertie, and lastly Death with infamie.

26

There were full many moe like° maladies,   *similar*
  Whose names and natures I note° readen well;   *cannot*
  So many moe, as there be phantasies
  In wavering wemens wit,° that none can tell,°   *mind/count*
  Or paines in love, or punishments in hell;
  All which disguizéd marcht in masking wise,
  About the chamber with that Damozell,
  And then returnéd, having marchéd thrise,
Into the inner roome, from whence they first did rise.°   *emerge*

27

So soone as they were in, the dore streight way
  Fast lockéd, driven with that stormy blast,
  Which first it opened; and bore all away.
  Then the brave Maid, which all this while was plast
  In secret shade, and saw both first and last,
  Issewéd forth, and went unto the dore,
  To enter in, but found it lockéd fast:
  It vaine she thought with rigorous uprore
For to efforce,° when charmes had coséd it afore.   *force open*

28

Where force might not availe, there sleights and art
  She cast° to use, both fit for hard emprize;   *purposed*
  For thy from that same roome not to depart
  Till morrow next, she did her selfe avize,°   *resolve*
  When that same Maske againe should forth arize.
  The morrow next appeard with joyous cheare,
  Calling men to their daily exercize,
  Then she, as morrow fresh, her selfe did reare°   *arouse*
Out of her secret stand, that day for to out weare.[3]

29

All that day she outwore in wandering,
  And gazing on that Chambers ornament,
  Till that againe the second evening
  Her covered with her sable vestiment,
  Wherewith the worlds faire beautie she hath blent:°   *obscured*
  Then when the second watch was almost past,[4]
  That brasen dore flew open, and in went
  Bold Britomart, as she had late forecast,°   *determined*
Neither of idle shewes, nor of false charmes aghast

30

So soone as she was entred, round about
  She cast her eies, to see what was become
  Of all those persons, which she saw without:
  But lo, they streight were vanisht all and some,[5]
  Ne living wight she saw in all that roome,
  Save that same woefull Ladie,[6] both whose hands
  Were bounden fast, that did her ill become,
  And her small wast girt round with yron bands,
Unto a brasen pillour, by the which she stands.

3. I.e., to pass that day.
4. I.e., just before midnight. The "second watch" began at nine and ended at twelve.
5. I.e., one and all.
6. I.e., Amoret. One can read the pillar to which Amoret is bound as the phallic rigidity that she fears or that Scudamour threatens to exert too masterfully; it detumesces in stanza 37.

31

And her before the vile Enchaunter[7] sate,
  Figuring° straunge characters of his art,   *drawing*
  With living bloud he those characters wrate,
  Dreadfully dropping from her dying hart,
  Seeming transfixéd with a cruell dart,
  And all perforce to make her him to love.
  Ah who can love the worker of her smart?
  A thousand charmes he formerly did prove;°   *try*
Yet thousand charmes could not her stedfast heart remove.

32

Soone as that virgin knight he saw in place,[8]
  His wicked bookes in hast he overthrew,
  Not caring his long labours to deface,[9]
  And fiercely ronning to that Lady trew,
  A murdrous knife out of his pocket drew,
  The which he thought, for villeinous despight,
  In her tormented bodie to embrew:°   *plunge*
  But the stout Damzell to him leaping light,
His cursed hand withheld, and maisteréd his might.

33

From her, to whom his fury first he ment,°   *intended*
  The wicked weapon rashly° he did wrest,   *quickly*
  And turning to her selfe his fell intent,
  Unwares° it strooke into her snowie chest,   *suddenly*
  That little drops empurpled her faire brest.
  Exceeding wroth therewith the virgin grew,
  Albe the wound were nothing deepe imprest,
  And fiercely forth her mortall blade she drew,
To give him the reward for such vile outrage dew.

34

So mightily she smote him, that to ground
  He fell halfe dead; next stroke him should have slaine,
  Had not the Lady, which by him stood bound,
  Dernely° unto her calléd to abstaine,   *dismally*
  From doing him to dy. For else her paine
  Should be remedilesse, sith none but hee,
  Which wrought it, could the same recure againe.[1]

7. I.e., Busyrane.
8. I.e., there.
9. I.e., not caring whether he destroyed his long labors.
1. Amoret's request may hint that Busyrane is in some sense a necessary if distorted aspect of Scudamour and the erotic experience, or that he is that experience as it might seem to the uninitiated.
The fears, if such they be, are movingly resolved in stanza 38 when Amoret finds herself complete
and undamaged.

Therewith she stayd her hand, loth stayd to bee;
For life she him envyde,° and longed revenge to see.   *begrudged*

35

And to him said, "Thou wicked man, whose meed
  For so huge mischiefe, and vile villany
  Is death, or if that ought do death exceed,
  Be sure, that nought may save thee from to dy,
  But if that[2] thou this Dame doe presently°   *at once*
  Restore unto her health, and former state;
  This doe and live, else die undoubtedly."
  He glad of life, that lookt for death but late,
Did yield himselfe right willing to prolong his date.°   *term of life*

36

And rising up, gan streight to overlooke°   *read*
  Those curséd leaves, his charmes backe to reverse;
  Full dreadfull things out of that balefull booke
  He red,° and measured° many a sad verse,   *said/chanted*
  That horror gan the virgins hart to perse,
  And her faire locks up staréd stiffe on end,
  Hearing him those same bloudy lines reherse;°   *recite*
  And all the while he red, she did extend
Her sword high over him, if ought° he did offend.   *in any way*

37

Anon she gan perceive the house to quake,
  And all the dores to rattle round about;
  Yet all that did not her dismaiéd make,
  Nor slacke her threatfull hand for daungers dout,°   *fear*
  But still with stedfast eye and courage stout
  Abode,° to weet what end would come of all.   *waited*
  At last that mightie chaine, which round about
  Her tender waste was wound, adowne gan fall,
And that great brasen pillour broke in peeces small.

38

The cruell steele, which thrild her dying hart,
  Fell softly forth, as of his owne accord,
  And the wyde wound, which lately did dispart°   *cleave*
  Her bleeding brest, and riven bowels gored,[3]
  Was closéd up, as it had not bene bored,
  And every part to safety full sound,
  As she were never hurt, was soone restored:
  Tho when she felt her selfe to be unbound,
And perfect hole, prostrate she fell unto the ground.

2. I.e., unless.
3. I.e., pierced her torn inner parts.

39

Before faire Britomart, she fell prostrate,
   Saying, "Ah noble knight, what worthy meed
   Can wretched Lady, quit from wofull state,
   Yield you in liew of this your gratious deed?
   Your vertue selfe her owne reward shall breed,
   Even immortall praise, and glory wyde,
   Which I your vassall, by your prowesse freed,
   Shall through the world make to be notifyde,°   *proclaimed*
And goodly well advance,° that goodly well was tryde."   *praise*

40

But Britomart uprearing her from ground,
   Said, "Gentle Dame, reward enough I weene
   For many labours more, then I have found,
   This, that in safety now I have you seene,
   And meane° of your deliverance have beene: *means*
   Henceforth faire Lady comfort to you take,
   And put away remembrance of late teene;°   *woe*
   In stead thereof know, that your loving Make,°   *mate*
Hath no lesse griefe enduréd for your gentle sake."

41

She much was cheard to heare him mentiónd,
   Whom of all living wights she lovéd best.
   Then laid the noble Championesse strong hond
   Upon th'enchaunter, which had her distrest
   So sore, and with foule outrages opprest:
   With that great chaine, wherewith not long ygo
   He bound that pitteous Lady prisoner, now relest,
   Himselfe she bound, more worthy to be so,
And captive with her led to wretchednesse and wo.

42

Returning backe, those goodly roomes, which erst
   She saw so rich and royally arayd,
   Now vanisht utterly, and cleane subverst°   *overturned*
   She found, and all their glory quite decayd,°   *destroyed*
   That sight of such a chaunge her much dismayd.
   Thence forth descending to that perlous° Porch,   *perilous*
   Those dreadfull flames she also found delayd,°   *allayed*
   And quenchéd quite, like a consuméd torch,
That erst all entrers wont so cruelly to scorch.

43

More easie issew now, then entrance late
   She found: for now that fainéd° dreadfull flame,   *false*
   Which chokt the porch of that enchaunted gate,

And passage bard to all, that thither came,
Was vanisht quite, as it were not the same,
And gave her leave at pleasure forth to passe.
Th'Enchaunter selfe, which all that fraud did frame,
To have efforst° the love of that faire lasse,   *compelled*
Seeing his worke now wasted deepe engrievéd was.

44

But when the victoresse arrivéd there,
  Where late she left the pensife Scudamore,
  With her owne trusty Squire, both full of feare,
  Neither of them she found where she them lore:°   *left*
  Thereat her noble hart was stonisht sore;
  But most faire Amoret, whose gentle spright
  Now gan to feede on hope, which she before
  Conceivéd had, to see her owne deare knight,
Being thereof beguyld was fild with new affright.

45

But he sad man, when he had long in drede
  Awayted there for Britomarts returne,
  Yet saw her not nor signe of her good speed,°   *success*
  His expectation to despaire did turne,
  Misdeeming sure that her those flames did burne;
  And therefore gan advize° with her old Squire,   *consult*
  Who her deare nourslings losse no lesse did mourne,
  Thence to depart for further aide t'enquire:
Where let them wend at will, whilest here I doe respire.°   *breathe*

[Stanzas 43–45 first appear in the 1596 edition of *The Faerie Queene*. In the
edition of 1590, the following stanzas conclude Book III.]

At last she came unto the place, where late
  She left Sir Scudamour in great distresse,
  Twixt dolour and despight halfe desperate,
  Of his loves succour, of his owne redresse,°   *relief*
  And of the hardie Britomarts successe:
  There on the cold earth him now thrown she found,
  In wilfull anguish, and dead heavinesse,°   *grief*
  And to him cald; whose voices knowen sound
Soon as he heard, himself he rearéd light from ground.

There did he see, that most on earth him joyd,
  His dearest love, the comfort of his dayes,
  Whose too long absence him had sore annoyd,°   *troubled*
  And weariéd his life with dull delayes:
  Straight he upstarted from the loathéd layes,°   *ground*
  And to her ran with hasty egernesse,
  Like as a Deare, that greedily embayes°   *bathes*

In the coole soile,° after long thirstinesse,   *marsh*
Which he in chace enduréd hath, now nigh breathlesse.

Lightly he clipt her twixt his armés twaine,
  And streightly° did embrace her body bright,   *closely*
  Her body, late the prison of sad paine,
  Now the sweet lodge of love and deare delight:
  But she faire Lady overcommen quight
  Of huge affection, did in pleasure melt,
  And in sweete ravishment pourd out her spright:
  No word they spake, nor earthly thing they felt,
But like two senceles stocks in long embracement dwelt.

Had ye them seene, ye would have surely thought,
  That they had beene that faire Hermaphrodite,[4]
  Which that rich Romane of white marble wrought,
  And in his costly Bath causd to bee site:
  So seemd those two, as growne together quite,
  That Britomart halfe envying their blesse,°   *bliss*
  Was much empassiond° in her gentle sprite,   *moved*
  And to her selfe oft wisht like happinesse,
In vaine she wisht, that fate n'ould° let her yet possesse.   *would not*

Thus doe those lovers with sweet countervayle,°   *exchange*
  Each other of loves bitter fruit despoile.
  But now my teme begins to faint and fayle,
  All woxen weary of their journall° toyle: *daily*
  Therefore I will their sweatie yokes assoyle°   *release*
  At this same furrowes end, till a new day:
  And ye faire Swayns, after your long turmoyle,
  Now cease your worke, and at your pleasure play;
Now cease your worke; to morrow is an holy day.

---

4. Cf. *Metamorphoses* 4.285–388. Upon request, the gods fused Salmacis and Hermaphroditus into one creature; on Spenser's use of the resulting figure (often read as symbolizing marriage), see Silberman 1987. D. Cheney, "Spenser's Hermaphrodite and the 1590 *Faerie Queene*," *PMLA* 87 (1972), notes that, suiting the book's "threeness," Britomart's presence leaves us "with an awareness that someone is left over." The decadence perhaps implied by a "rich Romane" with a "costly bath" may further complicate the tone. For the 1596 *Faerie Queene*, to keep the romance going, Spenser undid his lovers' closeness and his narrative's closure so as to send Amoret and Scudamour off into new stories. The genre of romance resists closed endings, as modern moviegoers know from seeing sequels and even "prequels"; cf. Parker 1979.

From The Fourth Booke of the Faerie Queene

Containing
The Legend of Cambel and Telamond[1]
or
of Friendship

1

The rugged forhead that with grave foresight
  Welds° kingdomes causes, and affaires of state,[2]   *manages*
  My looser rimes (I wote) doth sharply wite,°   *blame*
  For praising love, as I have done of late,
  And magnifying lovers deare debate;
  By which fraile youth is oft to follie led,
  Through false allurement of that pleasing baite,
  That better were in vertues discipled,°   *instructed*
Then with vaine poemes weeds to have their fancies fed.

2

Such ones ill judge of love, that cannot love,
  Ne in their frosen hearts feele kindly° flame: *natural*
  For thy° they ought not thing unknowne reprove,   *therefore*
  Ne naturall affection faultlesse blame,
  For fault of few that have abusd the same.
  For it of honor and all vertue is
  The roote, and brings forth glorious flowres of fame,
  That crowne true lovers with immortall blis,
The meed of them that love, and do not live amisse.

3

Which who so list looke backe to former ages,
  And call to count the things that then were donne,
  Shall find, that all the workes of those wise sages,
  And brave exploits which great Heroés wonne,
  In love were either ended or begunne:
  Witnesse the father of Philosophie,[3]
  Which to his Critias, shaded oft from sunne,
  Of love full manie lessons did apply,
The which these Stoicke censours cannot well deny.

1. Nobody named Telamond appears in the poem. Roche, *Flame* 16–17, suggests that the name, "perfect world" (Greek *téleios*, Latin *mundus*), subsumes those of the brothers Priamond, Dyamond, and Triamond, whose story in IV.ii–iii is an allegory of world harmony. There was, moreover, an ancient King Telamon, an Argonaut and friend of Hercules who married the sister of Priam, king of Troy.
2. The forehead may belong to the queen's chief minister, Lord Burleigh, whose displeasure seems to be noted in VI.xii.41; if so, Spenser's unrepentant phrases are surprisingly rash.
3. I.e., Socrates, who discoursed on love to Phaedrus (not Critias) under a plane tree (Plato, *Phaedrus* 229a ff.).

4

To such therefore I do not sing at all,
　　But to that sacred Saint my soveraigne Queene,
　　In whose chast breast all bountie naturall,
　　And treasures of true love enlockéd beene,
　　Bove all her sexe that ever yet was seene;
　　To her I sing of love, that loveth best,
　　And best is loved of all alive I weene:
　　To her this song most fitly is addrest,
The Queene of love, and Prince of peace from heaven blest.

5

Which that she may the better deigne to heare,
　　Do thou dred infant,[4] Venus dearling dove,
　　From her high spirit chase imperious feare,[5]
　　And use of awfull Majestie remove:
　　In sted thereof with drops of melting love,
　　Deawd with ambrosiall kisses, by thee gotten
　　From thy sweete smyling mother from above,
　　Sprinckle her heart, and haughtie courage° soften,　　　　　*nature*
That she may hearke to love, and reade this lesson[6] often.

[The involved structure of Book IV reflects Spenser's examination of the full reach and scope of the traditional virtue of friendship, even as the convolutions befit the romance form's postponement of closure (Parker 1979; for a deconstructionist view of the poem's "endlesse werke," see Goldberg 1981). The first two cantos focus on friendships true and false; the third, with the story of Cambel and the three sons of Agape, explores friendship's larger role in human relationships. The allegorical narrative thenceforth shows how amity informs and steadies "lovers' deare debate" while helping establish social concord and natural harmony. For C. S. Lewis (1936), Books III and IV constitute "a single book on the subject of love" (338); certainly Book IV carries forward the several narrative strands of Book III. Britomart and Arthegall meet and pledge mutual love (Cantos iv, vi). Belphoebe is reconciled to Timias (Canto viii); in Cantos xi–xii, the marriage of Thames and Medway, magnificently celebrated by the world's rivers, leads to the union of Florimell and Marinell, whose wedding is described in Book V. Finally, Scudamour's story of how he conquered "vertuous Amoret" in the Temple of Venus provides an allegorical set-piece retrospectively central not only to this book but to the tapestry of love relationships woven in Books III and IV.]

4. I.e., Cupid.
5. I.e., the power to instill fear and awe.
6. I.e., the lesson to feel love. Spenser appeals over the minister's grave forehead to a queen who, for political (and perhaps personal) reasons, had encouraged a cult of love conflating courtship and courtiership; see, e.g., Montrose 1985, on pp. 686–95 of this edition, and Marotti 1982.

From The Fifth Booke of the Faerie Queene

Contayning
The Legend of Artegall
or
of Justice

1

So oft as I with state of present time,
  The image of the antique world compare,
  When as mans age was in his freshest prime,
  And the first blossome of faire vertue bare,
  Such oddes° I finde twixt those, and these which are,   *difference*
  As that, through long continuance of his course,
  Me seemes the world is runne quite out of square,[1]
  From the first point of his appointed sourse,
And being once amisse growes daily wourse and wourse.

2

For from the golden age, that first was named,
  It's now at earst[2] become a stonie one;
  And men themselves, the which at first were framed
  Of earthly mould, and formed of flesh and bone,
  Are now transforméd into hardest stone:
  Such as behind their backs (so backward bred)
  Were throwne by Pyrrha and Deucalione:[3]
  And if then those may any worse be red,°   *imagined*
They into that ere long will be degenderéd.°   *degenerated*

3

Let none then blame me, if in discipline°   *instruction*
  Of vertue and of civill uses lore,
  I doe not forme them to the common line°   *standard*
  Of present dayes, which are corrupted sore,
  But to the antique use, which was of yore,
  When good was onely for it selfe desyred,

---

1. I.e., has careered away from its first appointed and ordered course. The phrase "out of square" may wittily refer to turning from the *fourth* book. Spenser's account of the world's decay looks to the myth (cf. Ovid's *Metamorphoses* 1.89–151) of a decline from a "golden" age, by way of silver and brass, to a modern time of "hard iron." The mood is darkened also by a once common belief in the deterioration of the created universe. No doubt the wretchedness of Ireland, worsened by bad government, contributed to his pessimism: see the prose *View of the Present State of Ireland*, written c. 1594–97.
2. I.e., at length.
3. Ovid (*Metamorphoses* 1.348–415) tells how Pyrrha and Deucalion, after a flood that destroyed all other human life, were divinely instructed to cast stones behind them, which became people. Spenser's reference to a "stonie" age echoes Ovid's dry comment that this explains the stony character of humanity since the flood.

And all men sought their owne, and none no more;
When Justice was not for most meed outhyred,[4]
But simple Truth did rayne, and was of all admyred.

4

For that which all men then did vertue call,
 Is now cald vice; and that which vice was hight,
 Is now hight vertue, and so used of all:
 Right now is wrong, and wrong that was is right,
 As all things else in time are chaungéd quight.
 Ne wonder; for the heavens revolution
 Is wandred farre from where it first was pight,
 And so doe make contrarie constitution
Of all this lower world, toward his dissolution.

5

For who so list into the heavens looke,
 And search the courses of the rowling spheares,
 Shall find that from the point, where they first tooke
 Their setting forth, in these few thousand yeares
 They all are wandred much; that plaine appeares.
 For that same golden fleecy Ram, which bore
 Phrixus and Helle from their stepdames feares,
 Hath now forgot, where he was plast of yore,
And shouldred hath the Bull, which fayre Europa bore.[5]

6

And eke the Bull hath with his bow-bent horne
 So hardly butted those two twinnes of Jove,
 That they have crusht the Crab, and quite him borne
 Into the great Nemaean lions grove.[6]
 So now all range, and doe at randon rove
 Out of their proper places farre away,
 And all this world with them amisse doe move,
 And all his creatures from their course astray,
Till they arrive at their last ruinous decay.°   destruction

4. I.e., responsive to the largest bribes.
5. In Ptolemaic cosmology, because of the precession of the equinoxes the astrological "signs" of the zodiac no longer correspond to their matching constellations; e.g., when the sun should be in Aries (the Ram) it is in fact in Taurus (the bull). Most people continued to calculate according to signs, not constellations (see Eade 1984, 10–14), but Spenser wryly notes an entropy and disorder paralleling injustice and moral decay here below; cf. *King Lear* 1.2.103–17 and Donne's "First Anniversary" 201–19. For the story of Phrixus and Helle, see III.xi.30. Jove became a bull so as to carry off Europa.
6. That is, the sign Gemini ("the twinnes") has been thrust into the realm of Cancer (the Crab), which in turn has moved along the zodiac into the place of Leo (the Lion). Becoming a swan, Jove begot Castor and Pollux on Leda. To slay the Nemean Lion was the first of Hercules' twelve labors.

7

Ne is that same great glorious lampe of light,
    That doth enlumine all these lesser fyres,[7]
    In better case, ne keepes his course more right,
    But is miscaried° with the other Spheres.   *strayed*
    For since the terme of fourteene hundred yeres,
    That learnéd Ptolomae his hight did take,
    He is declynéd from that marke of theirs,
    Nigh thirtie minutes to the Southerne lake;
That makes me feare in time he will us quite forsake.

8

And if to those Aegyptian wisards old,
    Which in star-read° were wont have best insight,   *astronomy*
    Faith may be given, it is by them told,
    That since the time they first tooke the Sunnes hight,
    Foure times his place he shifted hath in sight,
    And twice hath risen, where he now doth West,°   *set*
    And wested twice, where he ought rise aright.
    But most is Mars amisse of all the rest,
And next to him old Saturne, that was wont be best.[8]

9

For during Saturnes ancient raigne[9] it's sayd,
    That all the world with goodnesse did abound:
    All lovéd vertue, no man was affrayd
    Of force, ne fraud in wight was to be found:
    No warre was knowne, no dreadfull trompets sound,
    Peace universall rayned mongst men and beasts,
    And all things freely grew out of the ground:
    Justice sate high adored with solemne feasts,
And to all people did divide° her dred beheasts.   *dispense*

10

Most sacred vertue she of all the rest,
    Resembling God in his imperiall might;
    Whose soveraine powre is herein most exprest,
    That both to good and bad he dealeth right,
    And all his workes with Justice hath bedight.°   *adorned*
    That powre he also doth to Princes lend,
    And makes them like himselfe in glorious sight,

7. Stars, as well as planets, were thought to reflect solar light. On solar declination see Eade 1984; he doubts Spenser's fears are serious (177).
8. The authority for lines 4–7 is Herodotus, *Histories* 2.142. Before Kepler showed them to be ellipses, planetary orbits were assumed to be normally circular, so observers were puzzled by anomalies in those of Mars and Saturn.
9. I.e., the golden age.

To sit in his owne seate, his cause to end,°   *fulfill*
And rule his people right, as he doth recommend.[1]

11

Dread Soverayne Goddesse,[2] that doest highest sit
    In seate of judgement, in th'Almighties stead,°   *place*
    And with magnificke might and wondrous wit
    Doest to thy people righteous doome aread,°   *proclaim*
    That furthest Nations filles with awfull dread,
    Pardon the boldnesse of thy basest thrall,
    That dare discourse of so divine a read,°   *matter*
    As thy great justice prayséd over all:
The instrument whereof loe here thy Artegall.

[The association of justice with Elizabeth established in the proem leads to the
introduction in V.i of Arthegall, "Champion of true Justice," to whom Astraea
taught "all the discipline" of that virtue. The quest assigned him by Gloriana
is the overthrow of the tyrant Grantorto ("great wrong") and the restoration of
the maiden queen Eirena ("peace," with a pun on "Eire" [Ireland]), a task duly
but incompletely accomplished in V.xii. Structurally, Book V returns to the
linear form of Books I and II. In V.i–iv, Arthegall (aided by his squire Talus,
"an yron man" provided by Astraea) overcomes a succession of arrogant or crass
figures representing various forms of injustice. In V.v he is himself overcome
by Radigund, an Amazon queen who forces him to wear female dress and spin
flax (recalling Hercules' servitude to Omphale). Heartened by her vision in Isis
Church (Canto vii), Britomart kills Radigund, frees Arthegall, and restores male
government. The remainder of Book V (focusing allegorically on foreign policy)
narrates the further adventures of Arthegall, instructed by Queen Mercilla
(equity, or perhaps the mercy that tempers justice), and of Arthur, whose exploits
on behalf of justice are set out in V.viii, x, and xi. Critics have debated the
relation of equity to Spenser's view of female sovereignty and to the politics
allegorized in Book V, notably the anti-egalitarian violence in V.ii and the
suppression of Irish rebels. And many readers are fascinated by the iconography
of Britomart's sojourn in Isis Church, a scene central to the moral, historical,
and psychological allegory in Book V.]

Canto VII

Britomart comes to Isis Church,
    Where shee strange visions sees:
She fights with Radigund, her slaies,
    And Artegall thence frees.

1

Nought is on earth more sacred or divine,
    That Gods and men doe equally adore,
    Then this same vertue, that doth right define:
    For th'hevens themselves, whence mortal men implore

1. Cf. Proverbs 8.15: "By me [i.e., God's wisdom] Kings reign, and princes decree justice."
2. I.e., Queen Elizabeth. "Justice" (stanza 9) is Astraea, who fled in disgust at the iron age; she is
now the constellation (and sign) Virgo. Elizabeth was often praised as a returned Astraea (F. Yeats,
Astraea [London, 1975]).

Right in their wrongs, are ruled by righteous lore
Of highest Jove, who doth true justice deale
To his inferiour Gods, and evermore
Therewith containes° his heavenly Common-weale: *controls*
The skill° whereof to Princes hearts he doth reveale.   *understanding*

2

Well therefore did the antique world invent,°   *feign*
That Justice was a God of soveraine grace,
And altars unto him, and temples lent,°   *gave*
And heavenly honours in the highest place;
Calling him great Osyris, of the race
Of th'old Aegyptian Kings, that whylome were;
With faynéd colours shading[1] a true case:
For that Osyris, whilest he livéd here,
The justest man alive, and truest did appeare.[2]

3

His wife was Isis, whom they likewise made
A Goddesse of great powre and soveraity,
And in her person cunningly did shade
That part of Justice, which is Equity,[3]
Whereof I have to treat here presently.°   *now*
Unto whose temple when as Britomart
Arrivéd, shee with great humility
Did enter in, ne would that night depart;
But Talus mote not be admitted to her part.°   *side*

4

There she receivéd was in goodly wize
Of many Priests, which duely did attend
Uppon the rites and daily sacrifize,
All clad in linnen robes with silver hemd;
And on their heads with long locks comely kemd,°   *combed*
They wore rich Mitres shapéd like the Moone,
To shew that Isis doth the Moone portend;°   *signify*
Like as Osyris signifies the Sunne.
For that they both like race in equall justice runne.[4]

1. I.e., (1) obscuring; (2) "shadowing forth."
2. Plutarch, *De Iside* 13, and Diodorus Siculus, *Bibliotheca Historica* 1.11–22, identify Osiris with the sun and Isis with the moon, and both stress Osiris's justice as king of Egypt. On the relevant iconography see J. Aptekar, *Icons of Justice* (New York, 1967) and Hieatt 1975. For Book V's mythological substructure, Spenser drew on materials merging Greek and biblical story, Egyptian religion, and European dynastic legend; such a heady mixture was used by many in the Renaissance, particularly those who read (with differing degrees of credulity) the forgeries of Annius of Viterbo and the work of Jean Lemaire de Belges. Britomart's sojourn also recalls the initiation of Lucius in Apuleius's *Metamorphoses* 11.4–8.
3. J. E. Phillips, *HLQ* 33 (1970), says, "Justice is the absolute, measure-for-measure equation of exact reward and punishment according to the letter of the law. . . . Equity is the taking into account of the individual circumstances in each case. . . . Mercy or Clemency is the human and divine impulse to forgive."
4. I.e., the courses of sun and moon are equally precise and regular.

5

The Championesse them greeting, as she could,[5]
  Was thence by them into the Temple led;
  Whose goodly building when she did behould,
  Borne uppon stately pillours, all dispred°   *overspread*
  With shining gold, and archéd over hed,
  She wondred at the workemans passing skill,
  Whose like before she never saw nor red;°   *imagined*
  And thereuppon long while stood gazing still,
But thought, that she thereon could never gaze her fill.

6

Thence forth unto the Idoll they her brought,
  The which was framéd all of silver fine,
  So well as could with cunning hand be wrought,
  And clothéd all in garments made of line,°   *linen*
  Hemd all about with fringe of silver twine.
  Uppon her head she wore a Crowne of gold,
  To shew that she had powre in things divine;
  And at her feete a Crocodile was rold,
That with her wreathéd taile her middle did enfold.[6]

7

One foote was set uppon the Crocodile,
  And on the ground the other fast did stand,
  So meaning to suppresse both forgéd guile,
  And open force:[7] and in her other hand
  She stretchéd forth a long white sclender wand.
  Such was the Goddesse; whom when Britomart
  Had long beheld, her selfe uppon the land
  She did prostrate, and with right humble hart,
Unto her selfe her silent prayers did impart.

8

To which the Idoll as it were inclining,
  Her wand did move with amiable looke,
  By outward shew her inward sence desining.°   *indicating*
  Who well perceiving, how her wand she shooke,
  It as a token of good fortune tooke.
  By this the day with dampe° was overcast,   *mist*
  And joyous light the house of Jove forsooke:
  Which when she saw, her helmet she unlaste,
And by the altars side her selfe to slumber plaste.

5. I.e., as she knew how (decorously).
6. On crocodiles see Aptekar, *Icons*, ch. 6. Wearing both gold and silver, the lunar Isis here has solar elements.
7. Cf. I.v.18. C. Davidson in *SP* 66 (1969) argues that this crocodile has "both guile and force"; as equity, Isis restrains practices that threaten justice but that Machiavelli (*The Prince*) thought needed for effective government.

9

For other beds the Priests there uséd none,
  But on their mother Earths deare lap did lie,
  And bake° their sides uppon the cold hard stone,   *harden*
  T'enure them selves to sufferaunce° thereby   *endurance*
  And proud rebellious flesh to mortify.°   *subject*
  For by the vow of their religion
  They tiéd were to stedfast chastity,
  And continence of life, that all forgon,°   *renounced*
They mote the better tend to their devotion.[8]

10

Therefore they mote not taste of fleshly food,
  Ne feed on ought, the which doth bloud containe,
  Ne drinke of wine, for wine they say is blood,
  Even the bloud of Gyants, which were slaine,
  By thundring Jove in the Phlegrean plaine.[9]
  For which the earth (as they the story tell)
  Wroth with the Gods, which to perpetuall paine
  Had damned her sonnes, which gainst them did rebell,
With inward griefe and malice did against them swell.

11

And of their vitall bloud, the which was shed
  Into her pregnant bosome, forth she brought
  The fruitfull vine, whose liquor blouddy red
  Having the mindes of men with fury fraught,
  Mote in them stirre up old rebellious thought,
  To make new warre against the Gods againe:
  Such is the powre of that same fruit, that nought
  The fell contagion may thereof restraine,
Ne within reasons rule, her madding mood containe.

12

There did the warlike Maide her selfe repose,
  Under the wings of Isis[1] all that night,
  And with sweete rest her heavy eyes did close,
  After that long daies toile and weary plight.
  Where whilest her earthly parts with soft delight
  Of sencelesse sleepe did deeply drownéd lie,
  There did appeare unto her heavenly spright
  A wondrous vision, which did close implie[2]
The course of all her fortune and posteritie.

8. For the priests' austere life, see Plutarch, *De Iside* 2.
9. Spenser combines scripture and classical myth. Lines 1–2 echo Genesis 9.4: "But flesh with the life thereof, which is the blood thereof, shall ye not eat"; the rest of the stanza and stanza 11 reflect *Metamorphoses* 1.151–62 and Plutarch, *De Iside* 6.
1. Cf. Psalms 57.1: "in the shadow of thy wings will I make my refuge."
2. I.e., secretly enfold.

13

Her seemed, as she was doing sacrifize
  To Isis, deckt with Mitre on her hed,
  And linnen stole after those Priestés guize,
  All sodainely she saw transfiguréd
  Her linnen stole to robe of scarlet red,[3]
  And Moone-like Mitre to a Crowne of gold,
  That even she her selfe much wonderéd
  At such a chaunge, and joyéd to behold
Her selfe, adorned with gems and jewels manifold.

14

And in the midst of her felicity,
  An hideous tempest seeméd from below,
  To rise through all the Temple sodainely,
  That from the Altar all about did blow
  The holy fire, and all the embers strow
  Uppon the ground, which kindled privily,
  Into outragious flames[4] unwares did grow,
  That all the Temple put in jeopardy
Of flaming, and her selfe in great perplexity.°   *concern*

15

With that the Crocodile, which sleeping lay
  Under the Idols feete in fearelesse bowre,[5]
  Seemed to awake in horrible dismay,
  As being troubled with that stormy stowre;°   *turmoil*
  And gaping greedy wide, did streight devoure
  Both flames and tempest:[6] with which growen great,
  And swolne with pride of his owne peerelesse powre,
  He gan to threaten her likewise to eat;
But that the Goddesse with her rod him backe did beat.

16

Tho turning all his pride to humblesse meeke,
  Him selfe before her feete he lowly threw,
  And gan for grace and love of her to seeke:
  Which she accepting, he so neare her drew,
  That of his game[7] she soone enwombéd grew,
  And forth did bring a Lion of great might;
  That shortly did all other beasts subdew.

3. Scarlet was an imperial color; cf. "Aprill" 57.
4. I.e., flames of desire. "The night before the consummation of her marriage," Olympias, mother of Alexander the Great, "dreamed that a thunderbolt fell upon her body, which kindled a great fire, whose divided flames dispersed themselves all about . . ." (Plutarch, *Lives*, tr. Dryden: "Alexander"). Plutarch adds that "once . . . a serpent was found lying by Olympias as she slept."
5. I.e., fearlessly lay sheltered under the idol's feet.
6. Cf. III.xi.48, and note.
7. I.e., his amorous play.

With that she wakéd, full of fearefull fright,
And doubtfully dismayd through that so uncouth° sight.   *strange*

17

So thereuppon long while she musing lay,
  With thousand thoughts feeding her fantasie,
  Untill she spide the lampe of lightsome day,
  Up-lifted in the porch of heaven hie.
  Then up she rose fraught with melancholy,
  And forth into the lower parts did pas;
  Whereas the Priestes she found full busily
  About their holy things for morrow Mas:[8]
Whom she saluting° faire, faire resaluted was.   *greeting*

18

But by the change of her unchearefull looke,
  They might perceive, she was not well in plight;
  Or that some pensivenesse to heart she tooke.
  Therefore thus one of them, who seemed in sight
  To be the greatest, and the gravest wight,
  To her bespake; "Sir Knight it seemes to me,
  That thorough evill rest of this last night,
  Or ill apayd,° or much dismayd ye be,   *pleased*
That by your change of cheare is easie for to see."

19

"Certes," sayd she, "sith ye so well have spide
  The troublous passion of my pensive mind,
  I will not seeke the same from you to hide,
  But will my cares unfolde, in hope to find
  Your aide, to guide me out of errour blind."
  "Say on," quoth he, "the secret of your hart:
  For by the holy vow, which me doth bind,
  I am adjured,° best counsell to impart   *sworn*
To all, that shall require my comfort in their smart."

20

Then gan she to declare the whole discourse°   *course*
  Of all that vision, which to her appeard,
  As well as to her minde it had recourse.[9]
  All which when he unto the end had heard,
  Like to a weake faint-hearted man he fared,°   *behaved*
  Through great astonishment of that strange sight;
  And with long locks up-standing, stifly stared
  Like one adawéd° with some dreadfull spright.   *terrified*
So fild with heavenly fury,° thus he her behight.°   *frenzy/addressed*

8. I.e., for the first religious observance next day.
9. I.e., as well as she could recall it.

21

"Magnificke Virgin, that in queint° disguise   *strange*
   Of British armes doest maske thy royall blood,
   So to pursue a perillous emprize,
   How couldst thou weene, through that disguizéd hood,°   *covering*
   To hide thy state from being understood?
   Can from th'immortall Gods ought hidden bee?
   They doe thy linage, and thy Lordly brood;°   *race*
   They doe thy sire, lamenting sore for thee;
They doe thy love, forlorne in womens thraldome see.

22

"The end whereof, and all the long event,°   *outcome*
   They doe to thee in this same dreame discover.
   For that same Crocodile doth represent
   The righteous Knight, that is thy faithfull lover,
   Like to Osyris in all just endever.
   For that same Crocodile Osyris is,
   That under Isis feete doth sleepe for ever:
   To shew that clemence oft in things amis,
Restraines those sterne behests, and cruell doomes of his.

23

"That Knight shall all the troublous stormes asswage,
   And raging flames, that many foes shall reare,
   To hinder thee from the just heritage
   Of thy sires Crowne, and from thy countrey deare.
   Then shalt thou take him to thy lovéd fere,°   *mate*
   And joyne in equall portion of thy realme.
   And afterwards a sonne to him shalt beare,
   That Lion-like shall shew his powre extreame:
So blesse thee God, and give thee joyance of thy dreame."[1]

24

All which when she unto the end had heard,
   She much was easéd in her troubles thought,
   And on those Priests bestowéd rich reward:
   And royall gifts of gold and silver wrought,
   She for a present to their Goddesse brought.
   Then taking leave of them, she forward went,
   To seeke her love, where he was to be sought;
   Ne rested till she came without relent°   *delay*
Unto the land of Amazons, as she was bent.

1. Thus together the crocodile Arthegall/Osiris and Britomart/Isis "represent justice and equity and
   will continue the British nation" (T. Dunseath, *Spenser's Allegory of Justice* [Princeton, 1968]
   176). For Aptekar, *Icons* 107, the crocodile also shows "the energy (which resembles, and derives
   from, and in part *is* sexuality) which justice uses and abuses."

From The Sixte Booke of the Faerie Queene

Contayning
The Legend of S. Calidore
or
of Courtesie

1

The waies, through which my weary steps I guyde,
  In this delightfull land of Faery,
  Are so exceeding spacious and wyde,
  And sprinckled with such sweet variety,
  Of all that pleasant is to eare or eye,
  That I nigh ravisht with rare thoughts delight,
  My tedious travell doe forget thereby;
  And when I gin to feele decay of might,
It strength to me supplies, and chears my dulléd spright.

2

Such secret comfort, and such heavenly pleasures,
  Ye sacred imps, that on Parnasso dwell,[1]
  And there the keeping have of learnings threasures,
  Which doe all worldly riches farre excell,
  Into the mindes of mortall men doe well,°   flow
  And goodly fury° into them infuse;   inspiration
  Guyde ye my footing, and conduct me well
  In these strange waies, where never foote did use,°   go, frequent
Ne none can find, but who was taught them by the Muse.[2]

3

Revele to me the sacred noursery
  Of vertue, which with you doth there remaine,
  Where it in silver bowre does hidden ly
  From view of men, and wicked worlds disdaine.
  Since it at first was by the Gods with paine
  Planted in earth, being derived at furst
  From heavenly seedes of bounty° soveraine,   virtue
  And by them long with carefull labour nurst,
Till it to ripenesse grew, and forth to honour burst.

---

1. I.e., the Muses.
2. Such claims are found from classical times on (cf. Lucretius, *De Rerum Natura* 1.925–26, Ariosto, *Orlando Furioso* 1.1–2, and Milton's Muse, who will pursue "Things unattempted yet in prose or rhyme" [*Paradise Lost* 1.16]).

4

Amongst them all growes not a fayrer flowre,
  Then is the bloosme of comely courtesie,[3]
  Which though it on a lowly stalke doe bowre,°   *shelter*
  Yet brancheth forth in brave nobilitie,
And spreds it selfe through all civilitie:°   *civilized life*
  Of which though present age doe plenteous seeme,
  Yet being matcht with plaine Antiquitie,
  Ye will them all but faynéd showes esteeme,
Which carry colours° faire, that feeble eies misdeeme.°   *appearances*
                                            misjudge

5

But in the triall of true curtesie,
  Its now so farre from that, which then it was,
  That it indeed is nought but forgerie,
  Fashioned to please the eies of them, that pas,
  Which see not perfect things but in a glas:[4]
  Yet is that glasse so gay,° that it can blynd   *brilliant*
  The wisest sight, to thinke gold that is bras.
  But vertues seat is deepe within the mynd,
And not in outward shows, but inward thoughts defynd.°   *determined*

6

But where shall I in all Antiquity
  So faire a patterne finde, where may be seene
  The goodly praise of Princely curtesie,
  As in your selfe, O soveraine Lady Queene,
  In whose pure minde, as in a mirrour sheene,°   *bright*
  It showes, and with her brightnesse doth inflame°   *inspire*
  The eyes of all, which thereon fixéd beene;[5]
  But meriteth indeede an higher name:
Yet so from low to high uplifted is your name.

3. Full studies of Book VI are A. Williams, *Flower on a Lowly Stalk* (East Lansing, 1967) and H. Tonkin, *Spenser's Courteous Pastoral* (Oxford, 1972); see also Tonkin 1990E. The "courtesy" Spenser explores owes something to Aristotle on the man "concerned with the pleasures and pains of social life" who "renders to each class what is befitting" (*Nichomachaean Ethics* 4.6), and something to the belief, shared by Chaucer and others, that virtuous conduct, not birth, proves nobility. See also Castiglione's *Courtier* on how a true gentleman acts among rural or "base" people (cf. VI.ix). More significant for Spenser than external etiquette is a sensitive (if sometimes canny) concern for others. True, the story suggests that courtesy most readily graces the wellborn, yet while the pastoral world in which Calidore vacations may support an ideal of contented hierarchy, the poetry also hints at anticourt satire or complaint as well as at the problematic nature of courtesy itself: its need for lies or slippery language and the ease with which it can serve the self. Like St. George, Calidore is potentially implicated in or morally endangered by aspects of the evil he combats.
4. Cf. I Corinthians 13.12: "For now we see through a glass, darkly; but then face to face. . . ."
5. One of Spenser's favorite images, perhaps derived from Ficino's commentary on Plato's *Symposium*; cf. 2 Corinthians 3.18: "But we all, with open face beholding as in a glass the glory of the Lord, are changed into the same image from glory to glory. . . ."

7

Then pardon me, most dreaded Soveraine,
   That from your selfe I doe this vertue bring,
   And to your selfe doe it returne againe:
So from the Ocean all rivers spring,
And tribute backe repay as to their King.
Right so from you all goodly vertues well
Into the rest, which round about you ring.
   Faire Lords and Ladies, which about you dwell,
And doe adorne your Court, where courtesies excell.

[Calidore's quest, described in Canto i as "an endlesse trace," is to find and subdue the Blatant Beast, a many-tongued monster whose poisoned bites afflict men and women in every quarter of the world; as Spenser's most compelling figure for slander, envious backbiting, and badmouthing of all kinds, the Beast is courtesy's chief enemy. Calidore's adventures are the focus of Cantos i–iii, in which a number of episodes illustrate varieties of courtesy and discourtesy; he does not appear in Cantos iv–viii, which explore courtesy through the adventures of other figures, including Arthur, Timias, and Sir Calepine. In Canto ix Spenser resumes Calidore's story: taken by the delights of the pastoral world, the Knight of Courtesy is about to suspend his quest so as to enjoy the pleasures of courtship and the rustic life (some readers have seen his holiday as restorative recreation, others as lax truancy). In the final cantos, perhaps strengthened by a fleeting vision of the Graces, he will move from contemplation to action, from smooth words to the deeds that show courtesy in operation.]

Canto IX

Calidore hostes° with Meliboe   lodges
   and loves fayre Pastorell;
Coridon envies him, yet he
   for ill rewards him well.

1

Now turne againe my teme thou jolly swayne,[1]
   Backe to the furrow which I lately left;
   I lately left a furrow, one or twayne
Unploughed, the which my coulter° hath not cleft: plowshare
Yet seemed the soyle both fayre and frutefull eft,°   moreover
As I it past, that were too great a shame,
That so rich frute should be from us bereft;
   Besides the great dishonour and defame,
Which should befall to Calidores immortall name.[2]

1. Spenser's poetic powers, personified to suit a rustic sojourn and, says DeNeef 1982, to suggest a Virgilian Georgic poetic mode that can mediate between the pastoral and chivalric epic and cultivate the seeds in courtesy's nursery.
2. Calidore (Greek, "beautiful gift," with maybe an overtone of Latin *calidus*, adroit and crafty) may be meant to recall the late Philip Sidney, whom "To His Book," prefaced to the *Calender*, calls the pattern of "noblesse and of chevalree." A case can also be made for the earl of Essex.

2

Great travell hath the gentle Calidore
  And toyle enduréd, sith I left him last
  Sewing° the Blatant beast,[3] which I forbore   *pursuing*
  To finish then, for other present hast.
  Full many pathes and perils he hath past,
  Through hils, through dales, throgh forests, and throgh plaines
  In that same quest which fortune on him cast,[4]
  Which he atchievéd to his owne great gaines,
Reaping eternall glorie of his restlesse° paines.   *unresting*

3

So sharply he the Monster did pursew,
  That day nor night he suffred him to rest,
  Ne rested he himselfe but natures dew,
  For dread of daunger, not to be redrest,
  If he for slouth forslackt° so famous quest.   *neglected*
  Him first from court he to the citties coursed,°   *chased*
  And from the citties to the townes him prest,
  And from the townes into the countrie forsed,
And from the country back to private farmes he scorsed.[5]

4

From thence into the open fields he fled,
  Whereas the Heardes° were keeping of their neat,°   *herdsmen/cattle*
  And shepheards singing to their flockes, that fed,
  Layes of sweete love and youthes delightfull heat:
  Him thether eke for all his fearefull threat
  He followed fast, and chacéd him so nie,
  That to the folds, where sheepe at night doe seat,°   *rest*
  And to the litle cots,° where shepherds lie   *shelters*
In winters wrathfull time, he forcéd him to flie.

5

There on a day as he pursewed the chace,
  He chaunst to spy a sort of shepheard groomes,[6]
  Playing on pypes,° and caroling apace,   *bagpipes*
  The whyles their beasts there in the budded broomes°   *broom plants*

3. Chief model for the monster is the "questing [barking] beast" of Malory's *Morte d'Arthur* (1.19, 10.13), which made a noise of "thirty couple of hounds questing." "Blatant" is from Latin *blaterare*, to babble or talk idly. The beast shares features with the parents named in i.7–8: Cerberus (many-headed hound of Hades) and the Chimera (amalgam of lion, goat, and serpent). In vi.12 Spenser gives as the Beast's parents yet older monsters: "foule Echidna" (a snake goddess) and "Cruell Typhon" (a giant). These monsters, doomed to defeat by Zeus or heroes like Hercules, are in Hesiod's *Theogony*. Looking for historical allegory, Ben Jonson thought the Beast signified "Puritans" (*Complete Poems*, ed. G. Parfitt [Baltimore, 1975] 465); he probably meant radical reformers who called the established church pagan and papist.
4. Fortune is much in evidence in Book VI, suiting a story with parallels in late classical romances such as the third-century *Daphnis and Chloe* by Longus; on Spenser's concept of fortune (often a foe to virtue yet sometimes a mask for providence) see Steppat 1990.
5. I.e., forced it to leave the open country for private estates and farms.
6. I.e., a company of shepherds.

Beside them fed, and nipt the tender bloomes:
For other worldly wealth they caréd nought.
To whom Sir Calidore yet sweating comes,
And them to tell him courteously besought,
If such a beast they saw, which he had thether brought.

6

They answered him, that no such beast they saw,
    Nor any wicked feend, that mote offend
    Their happie flockes, nor daunger to them draw:
    But if that such there were (as none they kend)
    They prayd high God him farre from them to send.
    Then one of them him seeing so to sweat,
    After his rusticke wise,° that well he weend,   *manner*
    Offred him drinke, to quench his thirstie heat,
And if he hungry were, him offred eke to eat.

7

The knight was nothing nice,° where was no need,   *fastidious*
    And tooke their gentle offer: so adowne
    They prayd him sit, and gave him for to feed
    Such homely what,° as serves the simple clowne,°   *thing/rustic*
    That doth despise the dainties of the towne.
    Tho having fed his fill, he there besyde
    Saw a faire damzell, which did weare a crowne
    Of sundry flowres, with silken ribbands tyde,
Yclad in home-made greene that her owne hands had dyde.

8

Upon a litle hillocke she was placed
    Higher then all the rest, and round about
    Environed with a girland, goodly graced,
    Of lovely lasses, and them all without[7]
    The lustie shepheard swaynes sate in a rout,°   *group*
    The which did pype and sing her prayses dew,
    And oft rejoyce, and oft for wonder shout,
    As if some miracle of heavenly hew°   *form*
Were downe to them descended in that earthly vew.

9

And soothly sure[8] she was full fayre of face,
    And perfectly well shapt in every lim,
    Which she did more augment with modest grace,
    And comely carriage of her count'nance° trim,   *demeanor*
    That all the rest like lesser lamps did dim:
    Who her admiring as some heavenly wight,
    Did for their soveraine goddesse her esteeme,

7. I.e., outside the ring of maidens.
8. I.e., truly.

And caroling her name both day and night,
The fayrest Pastorella her by name did hight.°   *call*

10

Ne was there heard, ne was there shepheards swayne
    But her did honour, and eke many a one
    Burnt in her love, and with sweet pleasing payne
    Full many a night for her did sigh and grone:
    But most of all the shepheard Coridon
    For her did languish, and his deare life spend;°   *waste away*
    Yet neither she for him, nor other none
    Did care a whit, ne any liking lend:°   *give*
Though meane her lot, yet higher did her mind ascend.

11

Her whyles Sir Calidore there vewéd well,
    And markt her rare demeanure, which him seemed
    So farre the meane° of shepheards to excell,   *usual average*
    As that he in his mind her worthy deemed,
    To be a Princes Paragone° esteemed,   *consort*
    He was unwares surprisd in subtile bands
    Of the blynd boy,[9] ne thence could be redeemed
    By any skill out of his cruell hands,
Caught like the bird, which gazing still on others stands.[1]

12

So stood he still long gazing thereupon,
    Ne any will had thence to move away,
    Although his quest[2] were farre afore him gon;
    But after he had fed, yet did he stay,
    And sate there still, untill the flying day
    Was farre forth spent, discoursing diversly
    Of sundry things, as fell,° to worke delay;   *befell*
    And evermore his speach he did apply
To th'heards, but meant them to the damzels fantazy.°   *fancy*

13

By this the moystie° night approching fast,   *humid*
    Her deawy humour° gan on th'earth to shed,   *mist*
    That warned the shepheards to their homes to hast
    Their tender flocks, now being fully fed,
    For feare of wetting them before their bed;
    Then came to them a good old aged syre,
    Whose silver lockes bedeckt his beard and hed,

9. I.e., Cupid.
1. I.e., the lark, caught with a net while it stared in fascination at the hawk held by the fowler.
2. I.e., the object of his quest, the Blatant Beast.

With shepheards hooke in hand, and fit attyre,
That wild° the damzell rise; the day did now expyre.   *bade*

14

He was to weet[3] by common voice esteemed
  The father of the fayrest Pastorell,
  And of her selfe in very deede so deemed;°   *considered*
  Yet was not so, but as old stories tell
  Found her by fortune, which to him befell,
  In th'open fields an Infant left alone,
  And taking up brought home, and nourséd well
  As his owne chyld; for other he had none,
That she in tract° of time accompted was his owne.   *course*

15

She at his bidding meekely did arise,
  And streight unto her litle flocke did fare:
  Then all the rest about her rose likewise,
  And each his sundrie sheepe with severall° care   *separate*
  Gathered together, and them homeward bare·
  Whylest everie one with helping hands did strive
  Amongst themselves, and did their labours share,
  To helpe faire Pastorella, home to drive
Her fleecie flocke; but Coridon most helpe did give.

16

But Meliboe[4] (so hight that good old man)
  Now seeing Calidore left all alone,
  And night arrivéd hard at hand, began
  Him to invite unto his simple home;
  Which though it were a cottage clad with lome,°   *clay*
  And all things therein meane, yet better 30
  To lodge, then in the salvage° fields to rome.   *wild*
  The knight full gladly soone agreed thereto,
Being his harts owne wish, and home with him did go.

17

There he was welcomed of that honest syre,
  And of his aged Beldame° homely well;   *wife*
  Who him besought himselfe to disattyre,°   *take off his armor*
  And rest himselfe, till supper time befell.
  By which home came the fayrest Pastorell,
  After her flocke she in their fold had tyde,
  And supper readie dight, they to it fell

3. I.e., in fact.
4. From Greek, "honey-toned"; cf. stanza 26.

With small adoe, and nature satisfyde,
The which doth litle crave contented to abyde.[5]

18

Tho when they had their hunger slakéd well,
  And the fayre mayd the table° ta'ne away,   *food and drink*
  The gentle knight, as he that did excell
  In courtesie, and well could doe and say,
  For so great kindnesse as he found that day,
  Gan greatly thanke his host and his good wife;
  And drawing thence his speach another way,
  Gan highly to commend the happie life,
Which Shepheards lead, without debate° or bitter strife.   *contention*

19

"How much," sayd he, "more happie is the state,
  In which ye father here doe dwell at ease,
  Leading a life so free and fortunate,
  From all the tempests of these worldly seas,
  Which tosse the rest in daungerous disease;°   *distress*
  Where warres, and wreckes, and wicked enmitie
  Doe them afflict, which no man can appease,
  That certes° I your happinesse envie,   *surely*
And wish my lot were plast in such felicitie."

20

"Surely my sonne," then answered he againe,[6]
  "If happie, then it is in this intent,°   *respect*
  That having small, yet doe I not complaine
  Of want, ne wish for more it to augment,
  But doe my self, with that I have, content;
  So taught of nature, which doth litle need
  Of forreine helpes to lifes due nourishment:
  The fields my food, my flocke my rayment breed;
No better doe I weare, no better doe I feed.

21

"Therefore I doe not any one envy,
  Nor am envyde of any one therefore;
  They that have much, feare much to loose thereby,
  And store of cares doth follow riches store.
  The litle that I have, growes dayly more
  Without my care,° but onely to attend it;   *worry*
  My lambes doe every yeare increase their score,
  And my flockes father daily doth amend° it.   *improve*
What have I, but to praise th'Almighty, that doth send it?

5. I.e., nature needs little to be contented.
6. Stanzas 20–25 may be compared to Tasso, *Gerusalemme* 7.8–13.

22

"To them, that list,° the worlds gay showes I leave,   *desire*
    And to great ones such follies doe forgive,°   *leave*
    Which oft through pride do their owne perill weave,
    And through ambition downe themselves doe drive
    To sad decay,° that might contented live.   *ruin*
    Me no such cares nor combrous thoughts offend,°   *disturb*
    Ne once my minds unmovéd quiet grieve,
    But all the night in silver sleepe[7] I spend,
And all the day, to what I list, I doe attend.

23

"Sometimes I hunt the Fox, the vowéd foe
    Unto my Lambes, and him dislodge away;
    Sometime the fawne I practise° from the Doe,   *devise*
    Or from the Goat her kidde how to convay;°   *steal away*
    Another while I baytes and nets display,
    The birds to catch, or fishes to beguyle:
    And when I wearie am, I downe doe lay
    My limbes in every° shade, to rest from toyle,   *any*
And drinke of every brooke, when thirst my throte doth boyle.

24

"The time was once, in my first prime of yeares,
    When pride of youth forth prickéd my desire,
    That I disdained amongst mine equall peares
    To follow sheepe, and shepheards base attire:
    For further fortune then I would inquire.°   *seek*
    And leaving home, to roiall court I sought;°   *went*
    Where I did sell my selfe for yearely hire,
    And in the Princes gardin daily wrought:
There I beheld such vainenesse, as I never thought.

25

"With sight whereof soone cloyd, and long deluded
    With idle hopes, which them doe entertaine,
    After I had ten yeares my selfe excluded
    From native home, and spent my youth in vaine,
    I gan my follies to my selfe to plaine,°   *lament*
    And this sweet peace, whose lacke did then appeare.
    Tho backe returning to my sheepe againe,
    I from thenceforth have learned to love more deare
This lowly quiet life, which I inherite° here."   *possess*

7. I.e., soft and truly enriching sleep (aptly suggesting the moon's influence).

26

Whylest thus he talkt, the knight with greedy eare
   Hong still upon his melting mouth attent;[8]
   Whose sensefull° words empierst his hart so neare,   *sensible*
   That he was rapt with double ravishment,
   Both of his speach that wrought him great content,
   And also of the object of his vew,[9]
   On which his hungry eye was alwayes bent;
   That twixt his pleasing tongue, and her faire hew,°   *form*
He lost himselfe, and like one halfe entrauncéd grew.

27

Yet to occasion meanes, to worke his mind,
   And to insinuate his harts desire,[1]
   He thus replyde; "Now surely syre, I find,
   That all this worlds gay showes, which we admire,
   Be but vaine shadowes to this safe retyre°   *retirement*
   Of life, which here in lowlinesse ye lead,
   Fearelesse of foes, or fortunes wrackfull° yre,   *destructive*
   Which tosseth states, and under foot doth tread
The mightie ones, affrayd of every chaunges dread.

28

"That even I which daily doe behold
   The glorie of the great, mongst whom I won,°   *dwell*
   And now have proved,° what happinesse ye hold   *experienced*
   In this small plot of your dominion,
   Now loath great Lordship and ambition;
   And wish the heavens so much had gracéd mee,
   As graunt me live in like condition;
   Or that my fortunes might transposéd bee
From pitch° of higher place, unto this low degree."   *height*

29

"In vaine," said then old Meliboe, "doe men
   The heavens of their fortunes fault accuse,
   Sith they know best, what is the best for them:
   For they to each such fortune doe diffuse,°   *distribute*
   As they doe know each can most aptly use.
   For not that, which men covet most, is best,
   Nor that thing worst, which men do most refuse;
   But fittest is, that all contented rest
With that they hold: each hath his fortune in his brest.[2]

8. I.e., attentively listened to his sweetly persuasive speech. Alpers 1989 says that Meliboe can be "a pastoral figure," one who speaks with pastoral authority, "because he has been at court" (799, 812).
9. I.e., Pastorella.
1. I.e., to exercise thought, and, subtly, also to satisfy his longing.
2. Cf. Juvenal, *Satire* 10. 417–25, and Chaucer, *Troilus and Criseyde* 4.197–201.

30

"It is the mynd, that maketh good or ill,
   That maketh wretch or happie, rich or poore:
   For some, that hath abundance at his will,
   Hath not enough, but wants in greatest store;
   And other, that hath litle, askes no more,
   But in that litle is both rich and wise.
   For wisedome is most riches; fooles therefore
   They are, which fortunes doe by vowes devize,°   *plan to get*
Sith each unto himselfe his life may fortunize."°   *make fortunate*

31

"Since then in each mans self," said Calidore,
   "It is, to fashion his owne lyfes estate,
   Give leave awhyle, good father, in this shore
   To rest my barcke, which hath bene beaten late
   With stormes of fortune and tempestuous fate,
   In seas of troubles and of toylesome paine,
   That whether quite from them for to retrate
   I shall resolve, or backe to turne againe,
I may here with your selfe some small repose obtaine.

32

"Not that the burden of so bold a guest
   Shall chargefull° be, or chaunge to you at all;   *troublesome*
   For your meane food shall be my daily feast,
   And this your cabin both my bowre and hall.
   Besides for recompence hereof, I shall
   You well reward, and golden guerdon give,
   That may perhaps you better much withall,
   And in this quiet make you safer live."
So forth he drew much gold, and toward him it drive.°   *thrust*

33

But the good man, nought tempted with the offer
   Of his rich mould,° did thrust it farre away,   *dross*
   And thus bespake; "Sir knight, your bounteous proffer
   Be farre fro me, to whom ye ill display
   That mucky masse, the cause of mens decay,
   That mote empaire my peace with daungers dread.
   But if ye algates° covet to assay   *in any case*
   This simple sort of life, that shepheards lead,
Be it your owne: our rudenesse to your selfe aread."°   *take*

34

So there that night Sir Calidore did dwell,
   And long while after, whilest him list remaine,
   Dayly beholding the faire Pastorell,

And feeding on the bayt of his owne bane.°   *ruin*
During which time he did her entertaine
With all kind courtesies, he could invent;
And every day, her companie to gaine,
When to the field she went, he with her went:
So for to quench his fire, he did it more augment.

35

But she that never had acquainted beene
   With such queint° usage, fit for Queenes and Kings,   *elegant*
   Ne ever had such knightly service seene,
   But being bred under base shepheards wings,
   Had ever learned to love the lowly things,
   Did litle whit regard his courteous guize,°   *behavior*
   But caréd more for Colins[3] carolings
   Then all that he could doe, or ever devize:
His layes, his loves, his lookes she did them all despize.

36

Which Calidore perceiving, thought it best
   To chaunge the manner of his loftie looke;°   *appearance*
   And doffing his bright armes, himself addrest°   *clothed*
   In shepheards weed, and in his hand he tooke,
   In stead of steelehead speare, a shepheards hooke,
   That who had seene him then, would have bethought
   On Phrygian Paris[4] by Plexippus brooke,
   When he the love of fayre Oenone sought,
What time the golden apple was unto him brought.

37

So being clad, unto the fields he went
   With the faire Pastorella every day,
   And kept her sheepe with diligent attent,°   *attention*
   Watching to drive the ravenous Wolfe away,
   The whylest at pleasure she mote sport and play;
   And every evening helping them to fold:
   And otherwhiles for need, he did assay
   In his strong hand their rugged teats to hold,
And out of them to presse the milke: love so much could.

38

Which seeing Coridon, who her likewise
   Long time had loved, and hoped her love to gaine,
   He much was troubled at that straungers guize,

---

3. I.e., Colin Clout, the shepherd poet with whom Spenser associates himself; cf. E.K.'s Glosse to "Januarye," in *The Shepheardes Calender.*
4. Paris, a Trojan prince whose abduction of Helen started the Trojan War, was a shepherd when young; asked to award a golden apple to the fairest goddess, he chose Venus (the episode was much mythologized as a choice among lives of contemplation, action, and pleasure; see Stewart 1988). "Plexippus brooke" is Spenser's invention, perhaps derived from a mistaken etymology.

And many gealous thoughts conceived in vaine,
That this of all his labour and long paine
Should reap the harvest, ere it ripened were,
That made him scoule, and pout, and oft complaine
Of Pastorell to all the shepheards there,
That she did love a stranger swayne then him more dere.

39

And ever when he came in companie,
    Where Calidore was present, he would loure,°   *scowl*
    And byte his lip, and even for gealousie
    Was readie oft his owne hart to devoure,
    Impatient of any paramoure:°   *lover*
    Who on the other side did seeme so farre
    From malicing, or grudging his good houre,[5]
    That all he could, he gracéd him with her,
Ne ever shewéd signe of rancour or of jarre.°   *quarrelling*

40

And oft, when Coridon unto her brought
    Or° litle sparrowes, stolen from their nest,   *either*
    Or wanton squirrels, in the woods farre sought,
    Or other daintie thing for her addrest,°   *prepared*
    He would commend his guift, and make the best.[6]
    Yet she no whit his presents did regard,
    Ne him could find to fancie in her brest:
    This newcome shepheard had his market mard.°   *spoiled*
Old love is litle worth when new is more prefard.

41

One day when as the shepheard swaynes together
    Were met, to make their sports and merrie glee,
    As they are wont in faire sunshynie weather,
    The whiles their flockes in shadowes shrouded bee,
    They fell to daunce: then did they all agree,
    That Colin Clout should pipe as one most fit;
    And Calidore should lead the ring, as hee
    That most in Pastorellaes grace did sit.
Thereat frowned Coridon, and his lip closely bit.

42

But Calidore of courteous inclination
    Tooke Coridon, and set him in his place,
    That he should lead the daunce, as was his fashion;
    For Coridon could daunce, and trimly trace[7]
    And when as Pastorella, him to grace,

---

5. I.e., good fortune.
6. I.e., praise it highly.
7. I.e., precisely execute the dance steps.

Her flowry garlond tooke from her owne head,
And plast on his, he did it soone displace,
And did it put on Coridons in stead:
Then Coridon woxe° frollicke, that earst seeméd dead.   *became*

43

Another time, when as they did dispose°   *incline*
  To practise games, and maisteries° to try,   *contests of strength*
  They for their Judge did Pastorella chose;
  A garland was the meed of victory.
  There Coridon forth stepping openly,
  Did chalenge Calidore to wrestling game:
  For he through long and perfect industry,
  Therein well practisd was, and in the same
Thought sure t'avenge his grudge, and worke his foe great shame.

44

But Calidore he greatly did mistake;
  For he was strong and mightily stiffe pight,[8]
  That with one fall his necke he almost brake,
  And had he not upon him fallen light,
  His dearest joynt[9] he sure had broken quight.
  Then was the oaken crowne by Pastorell
  Given to Calidore, as his due right;
  But he, that did in courtesie excell,
Gave it to Coridon, and said he wonne it well.

45

Thus did the gentle knight himselfe abeare°   *conduct*
  Amongst that rusticke rout in all his deeds,
  That even they, the which his rivals were,
  Could not maligne him, but commend him needs:
  For courtesie amongst the rudest breeds
  Good will and favour.[1] So it surely wrought
  With this faire Mayd, and in her mynde the seeds
  Of perfect love did sow, that last° forth brought   *finally*
The fruite of joy and blisse, though long time dearely bought.

46

Thus Calidore continued there long time,
  To winne the love of the faire Pastorell;
  Which having got, he uséd without crime°   *sin*
  Or blamefull blot, but menagéd so well,
  That he of all the rest, which there did dwell,
  Was favouréd, and to her grace commended.

---

8. I.e., solidly built.
9. I.e., presumably, his neck.
1. Calidore uses courtesy to gain the goodwill of others, notably Pastorella. Few Renaissance writers on courtesy blame such social skill, but the hint that charm can be self-serving may suggest courtesy's problematic nature.

But what straunge fortunes unto him befell,
Ere he attained the point by him intended,
Shall more conveniently in other place be ended.

Canto X

Calidore sees the Graces daunce,
*   To Colins melody:*
The whiles his Pastorell is led
*   Into captivity.*

1

Who now does follow the foule Blatant Beast,
    Whilest Calidore does follow that faire Mayd,
    Unmyndfull of his vow and high beheast,°   *command*
    Which by the Faery Queene was on him layd,
    That he should never leave, nor be delayd
    From chacing him, till he had it attchieved?
    But now entrapt of love, which him betrayd,
    He mindeth more, how he may be relieved
With grace from her, whose love his heart hath sore engrieved.

2

That from henceforth he meanes no more to sew°   *pursue*
    His former quest, so full of toile and paine;
    Another quest, another game in vew
    He hath, the guerdon° of his love to gaine: *reward*
    With whom he myndes° for ever to remaine,   *intends*
    And set his rest[1] amongst the rusticke sort,
    Rather then hunt still after shadowes vaine
    Of courtly favour, fed with light° report   *empty*
Of every blaste, and sayling alwaies in the port.[2]

3

Ne certes mote he greatly blaméd be,
    From so high step to stoupe unto so low.
    For who had tasted once (as oft did he)
    The happy peace, which there doth overflow,
    And proved the perfect pleasures, which doe grow
    Amongst poore hyndes,° in hils, in woods, in dales,   *rustics*
    Would never more delight in painted show
    Of such false blisse, as there is set for stales,°   *snares*
T'entrap unwary fooles in their eternall bales.°   *woe*

4

For what hath all that goodly glorious gaze°   *spectacle*
    Like to one sight, which Calidore did vew?

1. I.e., permanently remain.
2. I.e., never setting sail at all.

The glaunce whereof their dimméd eies would daze,°   *dazzle*
That never more they should endure the shew
Of that sunne-shine, that makes them looke askew.°   *asquint*
Ne ought in all that world of beauties rare,
(Save onely Glorianaes heavenly hew
To which what can compare?) can it compare;°   *rival*
The which as commeth now, by course³ I will declare.

5

One day as he did raunge the fields abroad,
   Whilest his faire Pastorella was elsewhere,
   He chaunst to come, far from all peoples troad,°   *track*
   Unto a place, whose pleasaunce did appere
   To passe all others, on the earth which were:
For all that ever was by natures skill
Devized to worke delight, was gathered there,
And there by her were pouréd forth at fill,
As if this to adorne, she all the rest did pill.°   *ransack*

6

It was an hill plaste in an open plaine,
   That round about was bordered with a wood
   Of matchlesse hight, that seemed th'earth to disdaine,
   In which all trees of honour stately stood,
   And did all winter as in sommer bud,
Spredding pavilions for the birds to bowre,°   *shelter*
Which in their lower braunches sung aloud;
And in their tops the soring hauke did towre,°   *perch*
Sitting like King of fowles in majesty and powre.

7

And at the foote thereof, a gentle flud°   *stream*
   His silver waves did softly tumble downe,
   Unmard with ragged mosse or filthy mud,
   Ne mote wylde beastes, ne mote the ruder clowne°   *rustic*
   Thereto approch, ne filth mote therein drowne:°   *fall*
But Nymphes and Faeries by the bancks did sit,
In the woods shade, which did the waters crowne,
Keeping all noysome° things away from it,   *harmful*
And to the waters fall tuning their accents fit.

8

And on the top thereof a spacious plaine
   Did spred it selfe, to serve to all delight,
   Either to daunce, when they to daunce would faine,°   *desire*
   Or else to course about their bases light;⁴
   Ne ought there wanted, which for pleasure might

3. I.e., in due order, properly.
4. In the game of prisoner's base.

Desiréd be, or thence to banish bale:°   *sorrow*
So pleasauntly the hill with equall° hight,   *even*
Did seeme to overlooke the lowly vale;
Therefore it rightly cleepéd° was mount Acidale.[5]   *named*

9

They say that Venus, when she did dispose°   *incline*
  Her selfe to pleasaunce, uséd to resort
  Unto this place, and therein to repose
  And rest her selfe, as in a gladsome port,°   *refuge*
  Or with the Graces there to play and sport;
  That even her owne Cytheron,[6] though in it
  She uséd most to keepe her royall court,
  And in her soveraine Majesty to sit,
She in regard° hereof refusde and thought unfit.   *comparison*

10

Unto this place when as the Elfin Knight
  Approcht, him seeméd that the merry sound
  Of a shrill pipe he playing heard on hight,°   *loudly*
  And many feete fast thumping th'hollow ground,
  That through the woods their Eccho did rebound.
  He nigher drew, to weete what mote it be;
  There he a troupe of Ladies dauncing found
  Full merrily, and making gladfull glee,
And in the midst a Shepheard piping he did see.

11

He durst not enter into th'open greene,
  For dread of them unwares to be descrydc,°   *observed*
  For° breaking of their daunce, if he were seene;   *and for*
  But in the covert of the wood did byde,
  Beholding all, yet of them unespyde.
  There he did see, that pleaséd much his sight,
  That even he him selfe his eyes envyde,
  An hundred naked maidens lilly white,
All raungéd in a ring, and dauncing in delight.

12

All they without were raungéd in a ring,
  And dauncéd round; but in the midst of them
  Three other Ladies did both daunce and sing,
  The whilest the rest them round about did hemme,
  And like a girlond did in compasse stemme:°   *encircle*
  And in the middest of those same three, was placed
  Another Damzell, as a precious gemme,

5. Venus was sometimes called "Acidalia" after a spring in Boeotia where the Graces, her handmaids,
   would bathe. The name may derive from ἀκηδήη, "free from care."
6. Perhaps Cythera; but cf. III. vi. 29.

Amidst a ring most richly well enchaced,°   *adorned*
That with her goodly presence all the rest much graced.

13

Looke how the Crowne, which Ariadne[7] wore
  Upon her yvory forehead that same day,
  That Theseus her unto his bridale bore,
  When the bold Centaures made that bloudy fray
  With the fierce Lapithes, which did them dismay;°   *defeat*
  Being now placéd in the firmament,
  Through the bright heaven doth her beams display,
  And is unto the starres an ornament,
Which round about her move in order excellent.

14

Such was the beauty of this goodly band,
  Whose sundry parts were here too long to tell:
  But she that in the midst of them did stand,
  Seemed all the rest in beauty to excell,
  Crownd with a rosie girlond, that right well
  Did her beseeme. And ever, as the crew°   *company*
  About her daunst, sweet flowres, that far did smell,
  And fragrant odours they uppon her threw;
But most of all, those three did her with gifts endew.

15

Those were the Graces, daughters of delight,
  Handmaides of Venus, which are wont to haunt
  Uppon this hill, and daunce there day and night:
  Those three to men all gifts of grace do graunt,
  And all, that Venus in her selfe doth vaunt,
  Is borrowéd of them. But that faire one,
  That in the midst was placéd paravaunt,°   *pre-eminently*
  Was she to whom that shepheard pypt alone,
That made him pipe so merrily, as never none.[8]

16

She was to weete that jolly Shepheards lasse,[9]
  Which pipéd there unto that merry rout,°   *company*

7. Spenser combines two passages from the *Metamorphoses*. Daughter of King Minos, Ariadne helped Theseus escape Crete after killing the Minotaur hidden in the Labyrinth; finding her abandoned on the isle of Naxos, Dionysus made her his consort and her bridal crown a constellation (VIII.169–82). The battle of Centaurs and Lapithae, which Theseus joined, took place at the wedding of Hippodamia to Pirithous (XII.210–535). On the pastoral dance that forms this royal "Crowne," see the essay by Tonkin, pp. 752–56, in this volume.
8. I.e., as no one had ever piped.
9. In the "Aprill" eclogue of the *Calender*, Colin had called "fayre Elisa" a fourth Grace, but this figure cannot be simply equated with the *Calender*'s Rosalind or with Spenser's wife, and stanza 28 distinguishes her from the queen: as Colin's "love," she figures inspiration as well as divinely "graced" human beauty. Many critics (e.g., Miller 1979 and Bernard 1989, 153–62) detect, in

That jolly shepheard, which there pipéd, was
Poore Colin Clout (who knowes not Colin Clout?)
He pypt apace,° whilest they him daunst about.   *briskly*
Pype jolly shepheard, pype thou now apace
Unto thy love, that made thee low to lout;°   *bow*
Thy love is present there with thee in place,
Thy love is there advaunst° to be another Grace.   *raised*

17

Much wondred Calidore at this straunge sight
  Whose like before his eye had never seene,
  And standing long astonishéd in spright,
  And rapt with pleasaunce, wist not what to weene;°   *think*
  Whether it were the traine° of beauties Queene,   *assembly*
  Or Nymphes, or Faeries, or enchaunted show,
  With which his eyes mote have deluded beene.
  Therefore resolving, what it was, to know,
Out of the wood he rose, and toward them did go.

18

But soone as he appearéd to their vew,
  They vanisht all away out of his sight,
  And cleane were gone, which way he never knew;
  All save the shepheard, who for fell despight°   *anger*
  Of that displeasure, broke his bag-pipe quight,
  And made great mone for that unhappy° turne.   *unlucky*
  But Calidore, though no lesse sory wight,
  For that mishap, yet seeing him to mourne,
Drew neare, that he the truth of all by him mote learne.

19

And first him greeting, thus unto him spake,
  "Haile jolly shepheard, which thy joyous dayes
  Here leadest in this goodly merry make,°   *making*
  Frequented of these gentle Nymphes alwayes,
  Which to thee flocke, to heare thy lovely layes;
  Tell me, what mote these dainty Damzels be,
  Which here with thee doe make their pleasant playes?
  Right happy thou, that mayst them freely see:
But why when I them saw, fled they away from me?"

20

"Not I so happy," answerd then that swaine,
  "As thou unhappy, which them thence didst chace,
  Whom by no meanes thou canst recall againe,

---

the scene's tension between the shepherd's private piping and the knight's bumbling intrusion,
Spenser's increasing doubts concerning his epic vocation. Others (e.g., Alwes 1990) find Colin's
vision relevant to a nation (Ireland, but also England) torn by discourtesy and to a queen forgetful
of poetry's civilizing role.

For being gone, none can them bring in place,
But whom they of them selves list so to grace."
"Right sory I," saide then Sir Calidore,
"That my ill fortune did them hence displace.
But since things passéd none may now restore,
Tell me, what were they all, whose lacke thee grieves so sore."

2 1

Tho gan that shepheard thus for to dilate;°   *discourse*
  "Then wote thou shepheard, whatsoever thou bee,
That all those Ladies, which thou sawest late,
Are Venus Damzels, all within her fee,°   *service*
But differing in honour and degree:
They all are Graces, which on her depend,[1]
Besides a thousand more, which ready bee
Her to adorne, when so she forth doth wend:
But those three in the midst, doe chiefe on her attend.

2 2

"They are the daughters of sky-ruling Jove,
  By him begot of faire Eurynome,[2]
The Oceans daughter, in this pleasant grove,
As he this way comming from feastfull glee,
Of Thetis wedding with Aeacidee,
In sommers shade him selfe here rested weary.
The first of them hight mylde Euphrosyne,
Next faire Aglaia, last Thalia merry:
Sweete Goddesses all three which me in mirth do cherry.°   *cheer*

2 3

"These three on men all gracious gifts bestow,
  Which decke the body or adorne the mynde,
To make them lovely or well favoured show,
As comely carriage, entertainement° kynde,   *manners*
Sweete semblaunt,° friendly offices that bynde,   *demeanor*
And all the complements° of curtesie: *accomplishments*
They teach us, how to each degree and kynde
We should our selves demeane, to low, to hie;
To friends, to foes, which skill men call Civility.

2 4

"Therefore they alwaies smoothly seeme to smile,
  That we likewise should mylde and gentle be,
And also naked are, that without guile
Or false dissemblaunce all them plaine may see,
Simple and true from covert malice free:

---

1. I.e., who belong to her and make part of her retinue.
2. Cf. Hesiod, *Theogony* 907–11; the notion that Jove sired the Graces after the marriage of Thetis to Peleus, son of Aeacus, is Spenser's.

And eke them selves so in their daunce they bore,
  That two of them still froward° seemed to bee,   *turned away*
  But one still towards shewed her selfe afore;°   *in front*
That good should from us goe, then come in greater store.[3]

25

"Such were those Goddesses, which ye did see;
  But that fourth Mayd, which there amidst them traced,°   *danced*
  Who can aread,° what creature mote she bee,   *say*
  Whether a creature, or a goddesse graced
  With heavenly gifts from heven first enraced?°   *implanted*
  But what so sure she was, she worthy was,
  To be the fourth with those three other placed:
  Yet was she certes but a countrey lasse,
Yet she all other countrey lasses farre did passe.

26

"So farre as doth the daughter of the day,[4]
  All other lesser lights in light excell,
  So farre doth she in beautyfull array,
  Above all other lasses beare the bell,[5]
  Ne lesse in vertue that beseemes her well,
  Doth she exceede the rest of all her race,
  For which the Graces that here wont to dwell,
  Have for more honor brought her to this place,
And gracéd her so much to be another Grace.

27

"Another Grace she well deserves to be,
  In whom so many Graces gathered are,
  Excelling much the meane° of her degree;   *average*
  Divine resemblaunce, beauty soveraine rare,
  Firme Chastity, that spight ne blemish dare;[6]
  All which she with such courtesie doth grace,
  That all her peres cannot with her compare,
  But quite are dimméd, when she is in place.
She made me often pipe and now to pipe apace.

28

"Sunne of the world, great glory of the sky,
  That all the earth doest lighten with thy rayes,
  Great Gloriana, greatest Majesty,
  Pardon thy shepheard, mongst so many layes,
  As he hath sung of thee in all his dayes,

3. Cf. "Aprill" 109. See Seneca's skeptical but influential comments on the Graces in *De Beneficiis* I.ii–iii and E. Wind, *Pagan Mysteries in the Renaissance* (New York, 1958), ch. 2.
4. Perhaps the sun, but since it is usually male in English poetry, Spenser may mean the morning star, Venus, which reflects the sun's light; in III.iv.59 Truth is Day's daughter.
5. I.e., take the prize.
6. I.e., that neither malice nor slur may injure.

To make one minime[7] of they poore handmayd,
And underneath thy feete to place her prayse,
That when thy glory shall be farre displayd
To future age of her this mention may be made."

29

When thus that shepheard ended had his speach,
  Sayd Calidore; "Now sure it yrketh° mee,   *pains*
  That to thy blisse I made this luckelesse breach,
  As now the author of thy bale° to be,   *grief*
  Thus to bereave thy loves deare sight from thee:
  But gentle Shepheard pardon thou my shame,
  Who rashly sought that, which I mote not see."
Thus did the courteous Knight excuse his blame,
And to recomfort him, all comely meanes did frame.

30

In such discourses they together spent
  Long time, as fit occasion forth them led;
  With which the Knight him selfe did much content,
  And with delight his greedy fancy fed,
  Both of his words, which he with reason red;°   *spoke*
  And also of the place, whose pleasures rare
  With such regard° his sences ravishéd,   *sight*
  That thence, he had no will away to fare,
But wisht, that with that shepheard he mote dwelling share.

31

But that envenimd sting,[8] the which of yore,
  His poysnous point deepe fixéd in his hart
  Had left, now gan afresh to rancle sore,
  And to renue the rigour of his smart:
  Which to recure, no skill of Leaches° art   *physicians*
  Mote him availe, but to returne againe
  To his wounds worker, that with lovely dart
  Dinting° his brest, had bred his restlesse paine,   *striking*
Like as the wounded Whale to shore flies from the maine.[9]

32

So taking leave of that same gentle swaine,
  He backe returnéd to his rusticke wonne,°   *dwelling*
  Where his faire Pastorella did remaine:
  To whome in sort, as[1] he at first begonne,
  He daily did apply him selfe to donne

7. I.e., a half-note; also a musician's mark placed in a circle to indicate "perfect [triple] time." Weiner 1984 argues that this mere "minime" perfects the dance.
8. I.e., the wound inflicted by Cupid's arrow (1.7; cf. VI.ix. 11.6–9).
9. I.e., from the ocean (natural habitat of the whale). The simile emphasizes love's mysterious and terrible power.
1. I.e., the same as.

All dewfull° service voide of thoughts impure: *due*
Ne any paines ne perill did he shonne,
By which he might her to his love allure,
And liking in her yet untaméd heart procure.

33

And evermore the shepheard Coridon,
   What ever thing he did her to aggrate,°   *please*
   Did strive to match with strong contention,
   And all his paines did closely emulate;
   Whether it were to caroll, as they sate
   Keeping their sheepe, or games to exercize,
   Or to present her with their labours late;
   Through which if any grace chaunst to arize
To him, the Shepheard streight with jealousie did frize.°   *turn cold*

34

One day as they all three together went
   To the greene wood, to gather strawberies,
   There chaunst to them a dangerous accident;
   A Tigre[2] forth out of the wood did rise,
   That with fell clawes full of fierce gourmandize,°   *gluttony*
   And greedy mouth, wide gaping like hell gate,
   Did runne at Pastorell her to surprize:
   Whom she beholding, now all desolate
Gan cry to them aloud, to helpe her all too late.

35

Which Coridon first hearing, ran in hast
   To reskue her, but when he saw the feend,
   Through cowherd feare he fled away as fast,
   Ne durst abide the daunger of the end;
   His life he steeméd dearer then his frend.   *reckoned*
   But Calidore soone comming to her ayde,
   When he the beast saw ready now to rend
   His loves deare spoile, in which his heart was prayde,[3]
He ran at him enraged in stead of being frayde.

36

He had no weapon, but his shepheards hooke,
   To serve the vengeaunce of his wrathfull will,
   With which so sternely he the monster strooke,
   That to the ground astonishéd° he fell;   *stunned*
   Whence ere he could recov'r, he did him quell,°   *kill*

2. Tigers in Spenser's art are regularly fierce, cruel, and "unkind" (*Amoretti* 56; *FQ passim*); notably,
   Maleger rides "a Tygre swift and fierce" as he directs his savage band in "restlesse siege" of Alma's
   castle (II.xi.20.4). But the beast that rises out of this green wood, where strawberry fields recall
   the pastoral bliss of a lost golden age (cf. *Metamorphoses* 1.104), is something more: "the feend"
   who means to have the gentle berry-pickers' souls (cf. I.xi.12.7–9).
3. I.e., his love's dear body (about to be despoiled), where his heart lies captive as booty.

And hewing off his head, [he][4] it presented
Before the feete of the faire Pastorell;
Who scarcely yet from former feare exempted,
A thousand times him thankt, that had her death prevented.

37

From that day forth she gan him to affect,°   *love*
 And daily more her favour to augment;
 But Coridon for cowherdize reject,
 Fit to keepe sheepe, unfit for loves content:
 The gentle heart scornes base disparagement.[5]
 Yet Calidore did not despise him quight,
 But usde him friendly for further intent,
 That by his fellowship, he colour° might   *disguise*
Both his estate, and love from skill° of any wight.   *knowledge*

38

So well he wood her, and so well he wrought her,
 With humble service, and with daily sute,
 That at the last unto his will he brought her;
 Which he so wisely well did prosecute,
 That of his love he reapt the timely frute,[6]
 And joyéd long in close felicity:
 Till fortune fraught with malice, blinde, and brute,°   *insensible*
 That envies lovers long prosperity,
Blew up a bitter storme of foule adversity.

39

It fortuned one day, when Calidore
 Was hunting in the woods (as was his trade)°   *custom*
 A lawlesse people, Brigants hight of yore,
 That never vsde to live by plough nor spade,
 But fed on spoile and booty, which they made
 Upon their neighbours, which did nigh them border,
 The dwelling of these shepheards did invade,
 And spoyld their houses, and them selves did murder;
And drove away their flocks, with other much disorder.[7]

40

Amongst the rest, the which they then did pray,°   *capture*
 They spoyld old Melibee of all he had,
 And all his people captive led away,

4. See Textual Notes.
5. I.e., The true aristocratic temper draws back from union with natures of inferior quality.
6. Coridon had feared such reaping, "ere it ripened were" (VI.ix.38.6); but the courteous knight will taste no wine before its time.
7. Spenser's fable may here reflect the brutal realities of life along the Scottish border (Spenser, *Works*, ed. H. J. Todd [London, 1805], xxxix ff.), and in Ireland. But if these brigands (Ital., "devils") initially recall that other "salvage nation" of VI.viii.35–49, who practice human sacrifice and cannibalism, the naive agreement that seals the doom of Pastorella's rough captors fits well with the traditional emphases of pastoral romance.

Mongst which this lucklesse mayd away was lad,
Faire Pastorella, sorrowfull and sad,
Most sorrowfull, most sad, that ever sight.°   *signed*
Now made the spoile of theeves and Brigants bad,
Which was the conquest of the gentlest Knight,
That ever lived, th'onely° glory of his might.   *chief*

41

With them also was taken Coridon,
And carried captive by those theeves away;
Who in the covert of the night, that none
Mote them descry, nor reskue from their pray,
Unto their dwelling did them close° convay.   *secretly*
Their dwelling in a little Island was,
Covered with shrubby woods, in which no way
Appeard for people in nor out to pas,
Nor any footing fynde for overgrowen gras.

42

For underneath the ground their way was made,
Through hollow caves, that no man mote discover
For the thicke shrubs, which did them alwaies shade
From view of living wight, and covered over:
But darkenesse dred and daily night did hover
Through all the inner parts, wherein they dwelt.
Ne lightned was with window, nor with lover,[8]
But with continuall candlelight, which delt
A doubtfull sense of things, not so well seene, as felt.

43

Hither those Brigants brought their present pray,
And kept them with continuall watch and ward,
Meaning so soone, as they convenient may,
For slaves to sell them, for no small reward,
To merchants, which them kept in bondage hard,
Or sold againe. Now when faire Pastorell
Into this place was brought, and kept with gard
Of griesly theeves, she thought her self in hell,
Where with such damnéd fiends she should in darknesse dwell.

44

But for to tell the dolefull dreriment,
And pittifull complaints, which there she made,
Where day and night she nought did but lament
Her wretched life, shut up in deadly shade,
And waste her goodly beauty, which did fade
Like to a flowre, that feeles no heate of sunne,
Which may her feeble leaves with comfort glade.°   *gladden*

8. I.e., louvre; an opening in the roof to let smoke escape, and to admit light.

But what befell her in that theevish wonne,
Will in an other Canto better be begonne.

Canto XI

The theeves fall out for Pastorell,
Whilest Melibee is slaine:
Her Calidore from them redeemes,
And bringeth backe againe.

1

The joyes of love, if they should ever last,
   Without affliction or disquietnesse,
   That worldly chaunces° doe amongst them cast,   *hazards*
   Would be on earth too great a blessednesse,
   Liker to heaven, then mortall wretchednesse.
   Therefore the wingéd God,[1] to let men weet,
   That here on earth is no sure happinesse,
   A thousand sowres hath tempred with one sweet,
To make it seeme more deare and dainty,° as is meet.   *choice*

2

Like as is now befalne to this faire Mayd,
   Faire Pastorell,[2] of whom is now my song,
   Who being now in dreadfull darknesse layd,
   Amongst those theeves, which her in bondage strong
   Detaynd, yet Fortune not with all this wrong
   Contented, greater mischiefe on her threw,
   And sorrowes heapt on her in greater throng;
   That who so heares her heavinesse,° would rew   *grief*
And pitty her sad plight, so changed from pleasaunt hew.

3

Whylest thus she in these hellish dens remayned,
   Wrappéd in wretched cares and hearts unrest,
   It so befell (as Fortune had ordayned)
   That he, which was their Capitaine profest,
   And had the chiefe commaund of all the rest,
   One day as he did all his prisoners vew,
   With lustfull eyes, beheld that lovely guest,
   Faire Pastorella, whose sad mournefull hew
Like the faire Morning clad in misty fog did shew.

4

At sight whereof his barbarous heart was fired,
   And inly burnt with flames most raging whot,
   That her alone he for his part desired

1. Cupid (in league with Fortune).
2. The episode of Pastorella's captivity derives from Ariosto, *Orlando Furioso* 12.91 ff.

Of all the other pray, which they had got,
And her in mynde did to him selfe allot.
From that day forth he kyndnesse to her showed,
And sought her love, by all the meanes he mote;
With looks, with words, with gifts he oft her wowed:°   *wooed*
And mixéd threats among, and much unto her vowed.

5

But all that ever he could doe or say,
  Her constant mynd could not a whit remove,
  Nor draw unto the lure of his lewd lay,
  To graunt him favour, or afford him love.
  Yet ceast he not to sew° and all waies prove,°   *plead/try*
  By which he mote accomplish his request,
  Saying and doing all that mote behove;[3]
  Ne day nor night he suffred her to rest,
But her all night did watch, and all the day molest.°   *annoy*

6

At last when him she so importune saw,
  Fearing least he at length the raines would lend
  Unto his lust, and make his will his law,
  Sith in his powre she was to foe or frend,[4]
  She thought it best, for shadow to pretend
  Some shew of favour, by him gracing small,[5]
  That she thereby mote either freely wend,°   *go*
  Or at more ease continue there his thrall:
A little well is lent, that gaineth more withall.

7

So from thenceforth, when love he to her made,
  With better tearmes she did him entertaine,
  Which gave him hope, and did him halfe perswade,
  That he in time her joyaunce should obtaine.[6]
  But when she saw, through that small favours gaine,
  That further, then she willing was, he prest,
  She found no meanes to barre him, but to faine
  A sodaine sickenesse, which her sore opprest,
And made unfit to serve his lawlesse mindes behest.

8

By meanes whereof she would not him permit
  Once to approach to her in privity,°   *private*
  But onely mongst the rest by her to sit,
  Mourning the rigour of her malady,

---

3. I.e., that might aptly serve his purpose.
4. I.e., since it was in his power to treat her as foe or friend.
5. I.e., by showing him some slight favor.
6. I.e., when he undertook flattering preliminaries (that might lead "in time" to sexual consummation).

And seeking all things meete for remedy.
But she resolved no remedy to fynde,
Nor better cheare to shew in misery,
Till Fortune would her captive bonds unbynde,
Her sickenesse was not of the body but the mynde.

9

During which space that she thus sicke did lie,
  It chaunst a sort° of merchants, which were wount   *company*
  To skim those coastes, for bondmen° there to buy,   *slaves*
  And by such trafficke after gaines to hunt,
  Arrivéd in this Isle though bare and blunt,
  T'inquire for slaves; where being readie met
  By some of these same theeves at the instant brunt,[7]
  Were brought unto their Captaine, who was set
By his faire patients side with sorrowfull regret.

10

To whom they shewéd, how those marchants were
  Arrived in place, their bondslaves for to buy,
  And therefore prayd, that those same captives there
  Mote to them for their most commodity°   *profit*
  Be sold, and mongst them sharéd equally.
  This their request the Captaine much appalled;
  Yet could he not their just demaund deny,
  And willéd streight the slaves should forth be called,
And sold for most advantage not to be forstalled.[8]

11

Then forth the good old Meliboe was brought,
  And Coridon, with many other moe,
  Whom they before in diverse spoyles had caught:
  All which he to the marchants sale did showe.
  Till some, which did the sundry prisoners knowe,
  Gan to inquire for that faire shepherdesse,
  Which with the rest they tooke not long agoe,
  And gan her forme and feature to expresse,°   *describe*
The more t'augment her price, through praise of comlinesse.

12

To whom the Captaine in full angry wize
  Made answere, that the Mayd of whom they spake,
  Was his owne purchase and his onely prize,[9]
  With which none had to doe, ne ought partake,
  But he himselfe, which did that conquest make;
  Litle for him to have one silly° lasse: *simple*

7. I.e., at the moment of their arrival.
8. I.e., not reserving any slaves from sale.
9. I.e., his booty, reserved for him alone.

Besides through sicknesse now so wan and weake,
That nothing meet in marchandise to passe.[1]
So shewed them her, to prove how pale and weake she was.

13

The sight of whom, though now decayd and mard,
　　And eke but hardly seene by candle-light,
　　Yet like a Diamond of rich regard,° value
　　In doubtfull shadow of the darkesome night,
　　With starrie beames about her shining bright,
　　These marchants fixéd eyes did so amaze,
　　That what through wonder, and what through delight,
　　A while on her they greedily did gaze,
And did her greatly like, and did her greatly praize.

14

At last when all the rest them offred were,
　　And prises° to them placéd at their pleasure, prices
　　They all refuséd in regard of her,[2]
　　Ne ought would buy, how ever prisd with measure,[3]
　　Withouten her, whose worth above all threasure
　　They did esteeme, and offred store of gold.
　　But then the Captaine fraught with more displeasure,
　　Bad them be still, his love should not be sold:
The rest take if they would, he her to him would hold.

15

Therewith some other of the chiefest theeves
　　Boldly him bad such injurie forbeare;
　　For that same mayd, how ever it him greeves,
　　Should with the rest be sold before him theare,
　　To make the prises of the rest more deare.
　　That with great rage he stoutly doth denay;
　　And fiercely drawing forth his blade, doth sweare,
　　That who so hardie hand on her doth lay,
It dearely shall aby,° and death for handsell° pay. pay/reward

16

Thus as they words amongst them multiply,
　　They fall to strokes, the frute of too much talke,
　　And the mad steele about doth fiercely fly,
　　Not sparing wight, ne leaving any balke,[4]
　　But making way for death at large to walke:
　　Who in the horror of the griesly night,
　　In thousand dreadful shapes doth mongst them stalke,

1. I.e., not fit for sale.
2. I.e., on account of her (beauty).
3. I.e., however moderately (the rest were) priced.
4. I.e., leaving anyone untouched (as careless farmers may leave a "balke" or ridge of land unploughed).

And makes huge havocke, whiles the candlelight
Out quenchéd, leaves no skill° nor difference of wight.   *distinction*

17

Like as a sort of hungry dogs ymet
  About some carcase by the common way,
  Doe fall together, stryving each to get
  The greatest portion of the greedie pray;[5]
  All on confiuséd heapes themselves assay,°   *attack*
  And snatch, and byte, and rend, and tug, and teare;
  That who them sees, would wonder at their fray,
  And who sees not, would be affrayd to heare.
Such was the conflict of those cruell Brigants there.

18

But first of all, their captives they doe kill,
  Least they should joyne against the weaker side,
  Or rise against the remnant at their will;
  Old Meliboe is slaine, and him beside
  His aged wife, with many others wide,°   *round about*
  But Coridon escaping craftily,
  Creepes forth of dores, whilst darknes him doth hide,
  And flyes away as fast as he can hye,
Ne stayeth leave to take, before his friends doe dye.

19

But Pastorella, wofull wretched Elfe,[6]
  Was by the Captaine all this while defended,
  Who minding more her safety then himselfe,
  His target° alwayes over her pretended;°   *shield/stretched*
  By meanes whereof, that mote not be amended,
  He at the length was slaine, and layd on ground,
  Yet holding fast twixt both his armes extended
  Fayre Pastorell, who with the selfe same wound
Launcht° through the arme, fell down with him in drerie° swound.   *pierced/bloody*

20

There lay she covered with confuséd preasse°   *heap*
  Of carcases, which dying on her fell.
  Tho when as he was dead, the fray gan ceasse,
  And each to other calling, did compell
  To stay their cruell hands from slaughter fell,
  Sith they that were the cause of all, were gone.
  Thereto they all attonce agreéd well,
  And lighting candles new, gan search anone,
How many of their friends were slaine, how many fone.

5. I.e., the prey for which they greedily fight.
6. I.e., frail creature.

21

Their Captaine there they cruelly found kild,
  And in his armes the dreary[7] dying mayd,
  Like a sweet Angell twixt two clouds uphild:
  Her lovely light was dimméd and decayd,
  With cloud of death upon her eyes displayd;
  Yet did the cloud make even that dimmed light
  Seeme much more lovely in that darknesse layd,
  And twixt the twinckling of her eye-lids bright,
To sparke out litle beames, like starres in foggie night.

22

But when they moved the carcases aside,
  They found that life did yet in her remaine:
  Then all their helpes they busily applyde,
  To call the soule backe to her home againe;
  And wrought so well with labour and long paine,
  That they to life recovered her at last.
  Who sighing sore, as if her hart in twaine
  Had riven bene, and all her hart strings brast,°   *torn*
With drearie drouping eyne lookt up like one aghast.

23

There she beheld, that sore her grieved to see,
  Her father and her friends about her lying,
  Her selfe sole left, a second spoyle to bee
  Of those, that having savéd her from dying,
  Renewed her death by timely death denying:
  What now is left her, but to wayle and weepe,
  Wringing her hands, and ruefully loud crying?
  Ne caréd she her wound in teares to steepe,°   *bathe*
Albe with all their might those Brigants her did keepe.

24

But when they saw her now relived againe,
  They left her so, in charge of one the best
  Of many worst, who with unkind disdaine
  And cruell rigour her did much molest;
  Scarse yeelding her due food, or timely rest,
  And scarsely suffring her infestred° wound,   *infected*
  That sore her payned, by any to be drest.
  So leave we her in wretched thraldome bound,
And turne we backe to Calidore, where we him found.

25

Who when he backe returnéd from the wood,
  And saw his shepheards cottage spoyléd quight,

---

7. I.e., dismal, bloody.

And his love reft away, he wexed wood,°   *frantic*
And halfe enragéd at that ruefull sight,
That even his hart for very fell despight,
And his owne flesh he readie was to teare,
He chauft, he grieved, he fretted, and he sight,°   *groaned*
And faréd° like a furious wyld Beare,   *acted*
Whose whelpes are stolne away, she being otherwhere.[8]

26

Ne wight he found, to whom he might complaine,
  Ne wight he found, of whom he might inquire;
  That more increast the anguish of his paine.
He sought the woods; but no man could see there:
He sought the plaines; but could no tydings heare.
  The woods did nought but ecchoes vaine rebound;
  The playnes all waste and emptie did appeare:
Where wont the shepheards oft their pypes resound,
And feed an hundred flocks, there now not one he found.

27

At last as there he roméd up and downe,
  He chaunst one comming towards him to spy,
  That seemed to be some sorie simple clowne,°   *rustic*
With ragged weedes, and lockes upstaring° hye,   *bristling*
As if he did from some late daunger fly,
  And yet his feare did follow him behynd:
  Who as he unto him approchéd nye,
He mote perceive by signes, which he did fynd,
That Coridon it was, the silly shepherds hynd.

28

Tho to him running fast, he did not stay
  To greet him first, but askt where were the rest;
  Where Pastorell? who full of fresh dismay,
And gushing forth in teares, was so opprest,
That he no word could speake, but smit his brest,
  And up to heaven his eyes fast streming threw.
  Whereat the knight amazed, yet did not rest,
But askt againe, what ment that rufull hew:
Where was his Pastorell? where all the other crew?

29

"Ah well away," sayd he then sighing sore,
  "That ever I did live, this day to see,
  This dismall day, and was not dead before,
Before I saw faire Pastorella dye."

---

8. Classical and scriptural passages echo here: 4–6 recall *Iliad* 1.243, "then thou shalt tear thy heart within thee for anger," and perhaps Joel 2.13; 7–9 look to 2 Samuel 17.8, "they be chafed in their minds, as a bear robbed of of her whelps in the field," perhaps also to *Iliad* 18.318–22.

"Die? out alas!" then Calidore did cry:
"How could the death dare ever her to quell?°   *overcome*
But read° thou shepheard, read what destiny,   *tell*
Or other dyrefull hap from heaven or hell
Hath wrought this wicked deed, doe° feare away, and tell."   *put*

30

Tho when the shepheard breathéd had a whyle,
    He thus began: "Where shall I then commence
This wofull tale? or how those Brigants vyle,
    With cruell rage and dreadfull violence
Spoyld all our cots, and caried us from hence?
    Or how faire Pastorell should have bene sold
To marchants, but was saved with strong defence?
    Or how those theeves, whilest one sought her to hold,
Fell all at ods, and fought through fury fierce and bold.

31

"In that same conflict (woe is me) befell
    This fatall chaunce, this dolefull accident,
Whose heavy tydings now I have to tell.
    First all the captives, which they here had hent,°   *seized*
Were by them slaine by generall consent;
    Old Meliboe and his good wife withall
These eyes saw die, and dearely did lament:
    But when the lot to Pastorell did fall,
Their Captaine long withstood, and did her death forstall.

32

"But what could he gainst all them doe alone?
    It could not boot;° needs mote she die at last: *serve (her)*
I onely scapt through great confusione
    Of cryes and clamors, which amongst them past,
In dreadfull darknesse dreadfully aghast;
    That better were with them to have bene dead,
Then here to see all desolate and wast,
    Despoyléd of those joyes and jollyhead,°   *merriment*
Which with those gentle shepherds here I wont to lead."

33

When Calidore these ruefull newes had raught,°   *grasped*
    His hart quite deaded was with anguish great,
And all his wits with doole° were nigh distraught,   *grief*
    That he his face, his head, his brest did beat,
And death it selfe unto himselfe did threat;
    Oft cursing th'heavens, that so cruell were
To her, whose name he often did repeat;
    And wishing oft, that he were present there,
When she was slaine, or had bene to her succour nere.

34

But after griefe awhile had had his course,
  And spent it selfe in mourning, he at last
  Began to mitigate his swelling sourse,[9]
  And in his mind with better reason cast,
  How he might save her life, if life did last;
  Or if that dead, how he her death might wreake,°   *avenge*
  Sith otherwise he could not mend thing past;
  Or if it to revenge he were too weake,
Then for to die with her, and his lives threed to breake.[1]

35

Tho Coridon he prayd, sith he well knew
  The readie way unto that theevish wonne,
  To wend with him, and be his conduct trew
  Unto the place, to see what should be donne.
  But he, whose hart through feare was late fordonne,°   *overcome*
  Would not for ought be drawne to former drede,
  But by all meanes the daunger knowne did shonne:
  Yet Calidore so well him wrought with meed,[2]
And faire bespoke with words, that he at last agreed.

36

So forth they goe together (God before)
  Both clad in shepheards weeds agreeably,°   *similarly*
  And both with shepheards hookes: But Calidore
  Had underneath, him arméd privily.
  Tho to the place when they approchéd nye,
  They chaunst, upon an hill not farre away,
  Some flockes of sheepe and shepheards to espy;
  To whom they both agreed to take their way,
In hope there newes to learne, how they mote best assay.°   *proceed*

37

There did they find, that which they did not feare,°   *expect*
  The selfe same flocks, the which those theeves had reft
  From Meliboe and from themselves whyleare,
  And certaine of the theeves there by them left,
  The which for want of heards° themselves then kept.   *herdsmen*
  Right well knew Coridon his owne late sheepe,
  And seeing them, for tender pittie wept:
  But when he saw the theeves, which did them keepe,
His hart gan fayle, albe he saw them all asleepe.

9. I.e., began to moderate his grief.
1. Effectively, to defy the Fates by severing the thread of life (spun and measured by Clotho and
Lachesis), an act reserved for Atropos.
2. I.e., (probably) moved him with (promises of) money.

38

But Calidore recomforting° his griefe,   *consoling*
   Though not his feare: for nought may feare disswade;°   *remove*
   Him hardly° forward drew, whereas the thiefe   *boldly*
   Lay sleeping soundly in the bushes shade,
   Whom Coridon him counseld to invade°   *attack*
   Now all unwares, and take the spoyle away;
   But he, that in his mind had closely° made   *secretly*
   A further purpose, would not so them slay,
But gently waking them, gave them the time of day.[3]

39

Tho sitting downe by them upon the greene,
   Of sundrie things he purpose gan to faine;[4]
   That he by them might certaine tydings weene
   Of Pastorell, were she alive or slaine.
   Mongst which the theeves them questionéd againe,
   What mister° men, and eke from whence they were.   *kind of*
   To whom they answered, as did appertaine,[5]
   That they were poore heardgroomes, the which whylere
Had from their maisters fled, and now sought hyre elswhere.

40

Whereof right glad they seemed, and offer made
   To hyre° them well, if they their flockes would keepe: *pay*
   For they themselves were evill° groomes, they sayd,   *unskilled*
   Unwont with heards to watch, or pasture sheepe,
   But to forray the land, or scoure the deepe.
   Thereto they soone agreed, and earnest° tooke,   *pledge*
   To keepe their flockes for litle hyre and chepe:
   For they for better hyre did shortly looke,
So there all day they bode, till light the sky forsooke.

41

Tho when as towards darksome night it drew,
   Unto their hellish dens those theeves them brought,
   Where shortly they in great acquaintance grew,
   And all the secrets of their entrayles[6] sought.
   There did they find, contrarie to their thought,
   That Pastorell yet lived, but all the rest
   Were dead, right so as Coridon had taught:
   Whereof they both full glad and blyth did rest,
But chiefly Calidore, whom griefe had most possest.

3. I.e., greeted them.
4. I.e., began to make conversation.
5. I.e., as suited their disguise.
6. I.e., either (1) their minds, or, more probably, (2) the inner arrangements of their cave.

42

At length when they occasion fittest found,
  In dead of night, when all the theeves did rest
  After a late forray, and slept full sound,
  Sir Calidore him armed, as he thought best,
  Having of late by diligent inquest,°   *search*
  Provided him a sword of meanest sort:
  With which he streight went to the Captaines nest.
  But Coridon durst not with him consort,
Ne durst abide behind, for dread of worse effort.

43

When to the Cave they came, they found it fast:°   *locked*
  But Calidore with huge resistlesse might,
  The dores assayléd, and the locks upbrast.
  With noyse whereof the theefe awaking light,°   *quickly*
  Unto the entrance ran: where the bold knight
  Encountring him with small resistance slew;
  The whiles faire Pastorell through great affright
  Was almost dead, misdoubting least of new[7]
Some uprore were like that, which lately she did vew.

44

But when as Calidore was comen in,
  And gan aloud for Pastorell to call,
  Knowing his voice although not heard long sin,°   *since*
  She sudden was revivéd therewithall,
  And wondrous joy felt in her spirits thrall:°   *thrill*
  Like him that being long in tempest tost,
  Looking each houre into deathes mouth to fall,
  At length espyes at hand the happie cost,°   *coast*
On which he safety hopes, that earst feard to be lost.

45

Her gentle hart, that now long season past
  Had never joyance felt, nor chearefull thought,
  Began some smacke of comfort new to tast,
  Like lyfull heat to numméd senses brought,
  And life to feele, that long for death had sought;
  Ne lesse in hart rejoycéd Calidore,
  When he her found, but like to one distraught
  And robd of reason, towards her him bore,
A thousand times embrast, and kist a thousand more.

46

But now by this, with noyse of late uprore,
  The hue and cry was raységd all about;

7. I.e., fearing lest again.

And all the Brigants flocking in great store,
Unto the cave gan preasse, nought having dout
Of that was doen, and entred in a rout.°   *crowd*
But Calidore in th'entry close did stand,
And entertayning them with courage stout,
Still slew the formost, that came first to hand,
So long till all the entry was with bodies mand.° *piled*

47

Tho when no more could nigh to him approch,
He breathed° his sword, and rested him till day: *rested*
Which when he spyde upon the earth t'encroch,
Through the dead carcases he made his way,
Mongst which he found a sword of better say,° *temper*
With which he forth went into th'open light:
Where all the rest for him did readie stay,
And fierce assayling him, with all their might
Gan all upon him lay: there gan a dreadfull fight.

48

How many flyes in whottest sommers day
Do seize upon some beast, whose flesh is bare,
That all the place with swarmes do overlay,
And with their litle stings right felly° fare; *fiercely*
So many theeves about him swarming are,
All which do him assayle on every side,
And sore oppresse, ne any him doth spare:
But he doth with his raging brond° divide *sword*
Their thickest troups, and round about him scattreth wide.

49

Like as a Lion mongst an heard of dere,
Disperseth them to catch his choysest pray;
So did he fly amongst them here and there,
And all that nere him came, did hew and slay,
Till he had strowd with bodies all the way;
That none his daunger daring to abide,
Fled from his wrath, and did themselves convay
Into their caves, their heads from death to hide,
Ne any left, that victorie to him envide.

50

Then backe returning to his dearest deare,
He her gan to recomfort, all he might,
With gladfull speaches, and with lovely cheare,
And forth her bringing to the joyous light,
Whereof she long had lackt the wishfull sight,
Devized all goodly meanes, from her to drive
The sad remembrance of her wretched plight.

So her uneath[8] at last he did revive,
That long had lyen dead, and made againe alive.

51

This doen, into those theevish dens he went,
  And thence did all the spoyles and threasures take,
  Which they from many long had robd and rent,
  But fortune now the victors meed did make;
  Of which the best he did his love betake;°   *give to*
  And also all those flockes, which they before
  Had reft from Meliboe and from his make,°   *mate*
  He did them all to Coridon restore.
So drove them all away, and his love with him bore.

Canto XII

Fayre Pastorella by great hap°   *chance*
  her parents understands,
Calidore doth the Blatant beast
  subdew, and bynd in bands.

1

Like as a ship, that through the Ocean wyde
  Directs her course unto one certaine cost,°   *coast*
  Is met of many a counter winde and tyde,
  With which her wingéd speed is let° and crost,   *checked*
  And she her selfe in stormie surges tost;
  Yet making many a borde, and many a bay,
  Still winneth way, ne hath her compasse lost:[1]
  Right so it fares with me in this long way,
Whose course is often stayd, yet never is astray.

2

For all that hetherto hath long delayd
  This gentle knight, from sewing° his first quest,   *pursuing*
  Though out of course, yet hath not bene mis-sayd,
  To shew the courtesie by him profest,
  Even unto the lowest and the least.
  But now I come into my course againe,
  To his atchievement of the Blatant beast;
  Who all this while at will did range and raine,
Whilst none was him to stop, nor none him to restraine.

3

Sir Calidore when thus he now had raught
  Faire Pastorella from those Brigants powre,

8. I.e., with difficulty.
1. I.e. (lines 6–7), either (1) reaching many a coast, and (reaching) many (sheltered) bays; or (2) making many a tack, and often turning directly into the wind (as in "turning to bay"), still forges ahead on the correct course.

Unto the Castle of Belgard[2] her brought,
Whereof was Lord the good Sir Bellamoure;
Who whylome was in his youthes freshest flowre
A lustie knight, as ever wielded speare,
And had enduréd many a dreadfull stoure°   encounter
In bloudy battell for a Ladie deare,
The fayrest Ladie then of all that living were.

4

Her name was Claribell,[3] whose father hight
The Lord of Many Ilands, farre renound
For his great riches and his greater might.
He through the wealth, wherein he did abound,
This daughter thought in wedlocke to have bound
Unto the Prince of Picteland[1] bordering nere,
But she whose sides before with secret wound
Of love to Bellamoure empiercéd werc,
By all meanes shund to match with any forrein fere.°   mate

5

And Bellamour againe so well her pleased,
With dayly service and attendance dew,
That of her love he was entyrely seized,
And closely° did her wed, but knowne to few.   secretly
Which when her father understood, he grew
In so great rage, that them in dongeon deepe
Without compassion cruelly hc threw;
Yet did so streightly° them a sunder keepe,   strictly
That neither could to company of th'other creepe.

6

Nathlesse Sir Bellamour, whether through grace[5]
Or secret guifts so with his keepers wrought,
That to his love sometimes he came in place,
Whereof her wombe unwist to wight was fraught,[6]
And in dew time a mayden child forth brought.
Which she streight way for dread least, if her syre
Should know thereof, to slay he would have sought,
Delivered to her handmayd, that for hyre°   payment
She should it cause be fostred under straunge attyre.[7]

2. "Loving look" or "good care" (Ital.). Bellamoure's name in these contexts signifies both "lover of beauty" and "lover of war," as well as "beautiful love." The remainder of Pastorella's story derives chiefly from Boiardo, *Orlando Innamorato* 2.27.25 ff., and in some details from Tasso, *Rinaldo* 11.94.
3. "Bright beauty."
4. I.e., Scotland, home of the Picts.
5. I.e., the persuasive force of his "gentle" character.
6. I.e., without anyone's knowledge she became pregnant.
7. I.e., under false identity.

7

The trustie damzell bearing it abrode
  Into the emptie fields, where living wight
  Mote not bewray the secret of her lode,
  She forth gan lay unto the open light
  The litle babe, to take thereof a sight.
  Whom whylest she did with watrie eyne behold,
  Upon the litle brest like christall bright,
  She mote perceive a litle purple mold,°   *mole*
That like a rose her silken leaves did faire unfold.

8

Well she it markt, and pittiéd the more,
  Yet could not remedie her wretched case,
  But closing it againe like as before,
  Bedeawed with teares there left it in the place:
  Yet left not quite, but drew a litle space
  Behind the bushes, where she her did hyde,
  To weet what mortall hand, or heavens grace
  Would for the wretched infants helpe provyde,
For which it loudly cald, and pittifully cryde.

9

At length a Shepheard, which there by did keepe
  His fleecie flocke upon the playnes around,
  Led with the infants cry, that loud did weepe,
  Came to the place, where when he wrappéd found
  Th'abandond spoyle, he softly it unbound;
  And seeing there, that did° him pittie sore,   *made*
  He tooke it up, and in his mantle wound;
  So home unto his honest wife it bore,
Who as her owne it nurst, and naméd[8] evermore.

10

Thus long continued Claribell a thrall,
  And Bellamour in bands, till that her syre
  Departed life, and left unto them all.
  Then all the stormes of fortunes former yre
  Were turnd, and they to freedome did retyre.°   *return*
  Thenceforth they joyed in happinesse together,
  And livéd long in peace and love entyre,
  Without disquiet or dislike of ether,
Till time that Calidore brought Pastorella thether.

11

Both whom they goodly well did entertaine;
  For Bellamour knew Calidore right well,

---

8. I.e., who thereafter called it her own child.

And lovéd for his prowesse, sith they twaine
Long since had fought in field. Als Claribell
No lesse did tender the faire Pastorell,
Seeing her weake and wan, through durance° long.   *captivity*
There they a while together thus did dwell
In much delight, and many joyes among,
Untill the damzell gan to wex more sound and strong.

12

Tho gan Sir Calidore him to advize°   *consider*
  Of his first quest, which he had long forlore,°   *neglected*
  Ashamed to thinke, how he that enterprize,
  The which the Faery Queene had long afore
  Bequeathed to him, forslackéd had so sore;
  That much he fearéd, least reprochfull blame
  With foule dishonour him mote blot therefore;
  Besides the losse of so much loos° and fame,   *renown*
As through the world thereby should glorifie his name.

13

Therefore resolving to returne in hast
  Unto so great atchievement, he bethought
  To leave his love, now perill being past,
  With Claribell, whylest he that monster sought
  Throughout the world, and to destruction brought.
  So taking leave of his faire Pastorell,
  Whom to recomfort, all the meanes he wrought,
  With thanks to Bellamour and Claribell,
He went forth on his quest, and did, that him befell.

14

But first, ere I doe his adventures tell,
  In this exploite, me needeth to declare,
  What did betide to the faire Pastorell,
  During his absence left in heavy care,°   *sorrow*
  Through daily mourning, and nightly misfare:°   *grief*
  Yet did that aunccient matrone all she might,
  To cherish her with all things choice and rare;
  And her owne handmayd, that Melissa[9] hight,
Appointed to attend her dewly day and night.

15

Who in a morning, when this Mayden faire
  Was dighting° her, having her snowy brest   *dressing*
  As yet not lacéd, nor her golden haire
  Into their comely tresses dewly drest,
  Chaunst to espy upon her yvory chest
  The rosie marke, which she remembred well

9. From Greek ("honeybee"). The priestesses attending the temple of Demeter (Ceres) were so named.

That litle Infant had, which forth she kest,°   *cast*
The daughter of her Lady Claribell,
The which she bore, the whiles in prison she did dwell.

16

Which well avizing,° streight she gan to cast   *perceiving*
  In her conceiptfull° mynd, that this faire Mayd   *clever*
  Was that same infant, which so long sith past
  She in the open fields had loosely layd
  To fortunes spoile, unable it to ayd.
  So full of joy, streight forth she ran in hast
  Unto her mistresse, being halfe dismayd,
  To tell her, how the heavens had her graste,
To save her chylde, which in misfortunes mouth was plaste.

17

The sober mother seeing such her mood,
  Yet knowing not, what meant that sodaine thro,[1]
  Askt her, how mote her words be understood,
  And what the matter was, that moved her so.
  "My liefe," sayd she, "ye know, that long ygo,
  Whilest ye in durance dwelt, ye to me gave
  A little mayde, the which ye chylded[2] tho;
  The same againe if now ye list to have,
The same is yonder Lady, whom high God did save."

18

Much was the Lady troubled at that speach,
  And gan to question streight how she it knew.
  "Most certaine markes," sayd she, "do me it teach,
  For on her brest I with these eyes did vew
  The litle purple rose, which thereon grew,
  Whereof her name ye then to her did give.
  Besides her countenaunce, and her likely hew,[3]
  Matchéd with equall yeares, do surely prieve°   *prove*
That yond same is your daughter sure, which yet doth live."

19

The matrone stayd no lenger to enquire,
  But forth in hast ran to the straunger Mayd;
  Whom catching greedily for great desire,
  Rent up her brest, and bosome open layd,
  In which that rose she plainely saw displayd.
  Then her embracing twixt her armés twaine,
  She long so held, and softly weeping sayd;

1. I.e., that thrilling emotional quiver.
2. I.e., gave birth to.
3. I.e., her similar appearance.

"And livest thou my daughter now againe?
And art thou yet alive, whom dead I long did faine?°   *imagine*

20

Tho further asking her of sundry things,
  And times comparing with their accidents,°   *happenings*
  She found at last by very certaine signes,
  And speaking markes of passéd monuments,[4]
  That this young Mayd, whom chance to her presents
  Is her owne daughter, her owne infant deare.
  Tho wondring long at those so straunge events,
  A thousand times she her embracéd nere,
With many a joyfull kisse, and many a melting teare.

21

Who ever is the mother of one chylde,
  Which having thought long dead, she fyndes alive,
  Let her by proofe of that, which she hath fylde°   *felt*
  In her owne breast, this mothers joy descrive:°   *describe*
  For other none such passion can contrive
  In perfect forme, as this good Lady felt,
  When she so faire a daughter saw survive,
  As Pastorella was, that nigh she swelt°   *fainted*
For passing° joy, which did all into pitty melt.   *surpassing*

22

Thence running forth unto her lovéd Lord,
  She unto him recounted, all that fell:
  Who joyning joy with her in one accord,
  Acknowledged for his owne faire Pastorell.
  There leave we them in joy, and let us tell
  Of Calidore, who seeking all this while
  That monstrous Beast by finall force to quell,°   *kill*
  Through every place, with restlesse paine and toile
Him followed, by the tract° of his outragious spoile.°   *track/ravaging*

23

Through all estates[5] he found that he had past,
  In which he many massacres had left,
  And to the Clergy now was come at last;
  In which such spoile, such havocke, and such theft
  He wrought, that thence all goodnesse he bereft,
  That endlesse were to tell. The Elfin Knight,
  Who now no place besides unsought had left,

4. I.e., recorded events.
5. I.e., the three estates of church, court (subsuming knighthood and the nobility), and commons: all ranks of human life.

At length into a Monastere did light,
Where he him found despoyling all with maine and might.[6]

24

Into their cloysters now he broken had,
　Through which the Monckes he chacéd here and there,
　And them pursued into their dortours° sad,　　　　　*bed-chambers*
　And searchéd all their cels and secrets neare;
　In which what filth and ordure did appeare,
　Were yrkesome to report; yet that foule Beast
　Nought sparing them, the more did tosse and teare,
　And ransacke all their dennes from most to least,
Regarding nought religion, nor their holy heast.°　　　　*vow*

25

From thence into the sacred Church he broke,
　And robd the Chancell, and the deskes downe threw,
　And Altars fouléd, and blasphemy spoke,
　And th'Images for all their goodly hew,
　Did cast to ground, whilest none was them to rew;
　So all confounded and disordered there.
　But seeing Calidore, away he flew,
　Knowing his fatall hand by former feare;
But he him fast pursuing, soone approchéd neare.

26

Him in a narrow place he overtooke,
　And fierce assailing forst him turne againe:
　Sternely° he turnd againe, when he him strooke　　　*fiercely*
　With his sharpe steele, and ran at him amaine
　With open mouth, that seeméd to containe
　A full good pecke within the utmost brim,
　All set with yron teeth in raunges° twaine,　　　　*ranks*
　That terrifide his foes, and arméd him,
Appearing like the mouth of Orcus[7] griesly grim.

27

And therein were a thousand tongs empight,°　　　　*implanted*
　Of sundry kindes, and sundry quality,
　Some were of dogs, that barkéd day and night,
　And some of cats, that wrawling° still did cry,　　*caterwauling*
　And some of Beares, that groynd° continually,　　　*growled*
　And some of Tygres, that did seeme to gren,°　　　　*grin*
　And snar° at all, that ever passéd by:　　　　　　　*snarl*

6. The Beast's assault on and pillage of monastery and "sacred Church" may reflect Spenser's dislike
of overzealous Puritan iconoclasm equally with the poet's antipathy for lax discipline among the
Roman clergy (cf. *Variorum* 6.265–68, 382–88), not to mention his dismay at the destruction of
works of art and personal reputations in the course of violent religious controversy. But see Tonkin,
Pastoral 153: "the Beast's principal evil is his indiscriminate destruction."
7. I.e., Pluto, ruler of Hades.

But most of them were tongues of mortall men,
Which spake reprochfully, not caring where nor when.

28

And them amongst were mingled here and there,
  The tongues of Serpents with three forkéd stings,
  That spat out poyson and gore bloudy gere°   *filth*
  At all, that came within his ravenings,
  And spake licentious words, and hatefull things
  Of good and bad alike, of low and hie;
  Ne Kesars° sparéd he a whit, nor Kings,   *emperors*
  But either blotted them with infamie,
Or bit them with his banefull teeth of injury.°   *insult*

29

But Calidore thereof no whit afrayd,
  Rencountred him with so impetuous might,
  That th'outrage of his violence he stayd,
  And bet° abacke, threatning in vaine to bite,   *forced*
  And spitting forth the poyson of his spight,
  That foméd all about his bloody jawes.
  Tho rearing up his former° feete on hight,   *fore*
  He rampt[8] upon him with his ravenous pawes,
As if he would have rent him with his cruell clawes.

30

But he right well aware°, his rage to ward,   *alert*
  Did cast his shield atweene, and therewithall
  Putting his puissaunce forth, pursued so hard,
  That backeward he enforcéd him to fall,
  And being downe, ere he new helpe could call,
  His shield he on him threw, and fast downe held,
  Like as a bullocke, that in bloudy stall
  Of butchers balefull hand to ground is feld,
Is forcibly kept downe, till he be throughly queld.

31

Full cruelly the Beast did rage and rore,
  To be downe held, and maystred so with might,
  That he gan fret and fome out bloudy gore,
  Striving in vaine to rere him selfe upright.
  For still the more he strove, the more the Knight
  Did him suppresse, and forcibly subdew;
  That made him almost mad for fell despight.
  He grind,[9] hee bit, he scratcht, he venim threw,
And faréd° like a feend, right horrible in hew.   *acted*

8. I.e., reared up threateningly.
9. I.e., gnashed his teeth.

32

Or like the hell-borne Hydra, which they faine
  That great Alcides whilome overthrew,
  After that he had labourd long in vaine,
  To crop his thousand heads, the which still new
  Forth budded, and in greater number grew.[1]
  Such was the fury of this hellish Beast,
  Whilest Calidore him under him downe threw;
  Who nathemore° his heavy load releast,   never
But aye the more he raged, the more his powre increast.

33

Tho when the Beast saw, he mote nought availe,°   effect
  By force, he gan his hundred tongues apply,
  And sharpely at him to revile and raile,
  With bitter termes of shamefull infamy;
  Oft interlacing many a forgéd lie,
  Whose like he never once did speake, nor heare,
  Nor ever thought thing so unworthily:
  Yet did he nought for all that him forbeare,°   spare
But strainéd° him so streightly, that he chokt him neare.   gripped

34

At last when as he found his force to shrincke,
  And rage to quaile,° he tooke a muzzell strong   fail
  Of surest yron, made with many a lincke;
  Therewith he muréd° up his mouth along,   closed
  And therein shut up his blasphemous tong,
  For never more defaming gentle Knight,
  Or unto lovely Lady doing wrong:
  And thereunto a great long chaine he tight,°   tied
With which he drew him forth, even in his own despight.[2]

35

Like as whylome that strong Tirynthian swaine,[3]
  Brought forth with him the dreadfull dog of hell,
  Against his will fast bound in yron chaine,
  And roring horribly, did him compell
  To see the hatefull sunne, that he might tell
  To griesly Pluto, what on earth was donne,
  And to the other damnéd ghosts, which dwell

1. Hercules, grandson of Alcaeus, needed all his wit and skill (and the help of his servant Iolaus) to slay the nine-headed Lernean Hydra, offspring of Typhon and Echidna (Hesiod, *Theogony* 313–15). See also Hyginus, *Genealogiae*, ed. H. J. Rose (Leiden, 1934) 30.64, and Apollodorus, *Bibliotheca*, tr. K. Aldrich (Lawrence, KS, 1975) 2.77–80. The association of Hydra with Hell appears in *Aeneid* 6.576–77.
2. I.e., in spite of his fury.
3. As the last of his twelve "labors" during his period of service to Eurystheus, in Tiryns, Hercules by main force brought the monstrous dog Cerberus, guardian of Hell-gate, into the upper world (*Iliad* 8.368; *Metamorphoses* 6.408–15).

For aye in darkenesse, which day light doth shonne.
So led this Knight his captyve with like conquest wonne.

36

Yet greatly did the Beast repine at those
   Straunge bands, whose like till then he never bore,
   Ne ever any durst till then impose,
   And chaufféd° inly, seeing now no more   *raged*
   Him liberty was left aloud to rore:
   Yet durst he not draw backe; nor once withstand
   The provéd powre of noble Calidore,
   But trembled underneath his mighty hand,
And like a fearefull dog him followed through the land.

37

Him through all Faery land he followed so,
   As if he learnéd had obedience long,
   That all the people where so he did go,
   Out of their townes did round about him throng,
   To see him leade that Beast in bondage strong,
   And seeing it, much wondred at the sight;
   And all such persons, as he earst did wrong,
   Rejoycéd much to see his captive plight,
And much admyred[4] the Beast, but more admyred the Knight.

38

Thus was this Monster by the maystring might
   Of doughty Calidore, supprest and tamed,
   That never more he mote endammadge wight
   With his vile tongue, which many had defamed,
   And many causelesse causéd to be blamed:
   So did he eeke long after this remaine,
   Untill that, whether wicked fate so framed,
   Or fault of men, he broke his yron chaine,
And got into the world at liberty againe.

39

Thenceforth more mischiefe and more scath° he wrought   *harm*
   To mortall men, then he had done before;
   Ne ever could by any more° be brought   *again*
   Into like bands, ne maystred any more:
   Albe that long time after Calidore,
   The good Sir Pelleas him tooke in hand,
   And after him Sir Lamoracke of yore,[5]
   And all his brethren borne in Britaine land;
Yet none of them could ever bring him into band.

4. I.e., wondered at.
5. Sir Pelleas and Sir Lamoracke, knights of Arthur's Round Table, appear in Malory's *Morte d'Arthur*, but neither is there connected with the "questing beast."

40

So now he raungeth through the world againe,
  And rageth sore in each degree and state;[6]
  Ne any is, that may him now restraine,
  He growen is so great and strong of late,
  Barking and biting all that him doe bate,°   *attack*
  Albe they worthy blame, or cleare of crime:
  Ne spareth he most learnéd wits to rate,°   *scold*
  Ne spareth he the gentle Poets rime,
But rends without regard of person or of time.

41

Ne may this homely verse, of many meanest,
  Hope to escape his venemous despite,
  More then my former writs,° all were they cleanest[7]   *writings*
  From blamefull blot, and free from all that wite,°   *blame*
  With which some wicked tongues did it backebite,
  And bring into a mighty Peres displeasure,[8]
  That never so deservéd to endite.[9]
  Therfore do you my rimes keep better measure,
And seeke to please, that now is counted wisemens threasure.

---

6. I.e., in every rank and class of society.
7. See Textual Notes.
8. Presumably Lord Burleigh, the queen's Lord Treasurer, whose displeasure with some aspects of Spenser's earlier work the poet notices in IV.Pr.1.
9. I.e., that never deserved such censure.

Two Cantos of *Mutabilitie*:

WHICH, BOTH FOR FORME AND MATTER, APPEARE
TO BE PARCELL OF SOME FOLLOWING BOOKE OF THE
FAERIE QUEENE

(∵)

*Under the Legend
of
Constancie.* [1]

Canto VI

*Proud Change (not pleasd, in mortall things,
beneath the Moone, to raigne)
Pretends, as well of Gods, as Men,
to be the Soveraine.*

1

What man that sees the ever-whirling wheele
  Of Change, the which all mortall things doth sway,°   *rule*
But that therby doth find, and plainly feele,
  How Mutability[2] in them doth play
Her cruell sports, to many mens decay?°   *destruction*
  Which that to all may better yet appeare,
I will rehearse that whylome° I heard say,   *formerly*
  How she at first her selfe began to reare,
Gainst all the Gods, and th'empire sought from them to beare.° *take away*

2

But first, here falleth fittest to unfold
  Her antique race and linage ancient,
As I have found it registred of old,
  In Faery Land mongst records permanent:
She was, to weet,[3] a daughter by descent
  Of those old Titans,[4] that did whylome strive

---

1. That Spenser meant this fragment for *The Faerie Queene* is probable, given this statement by
   Matthew Lownes (publisher of the 1609 folio), the stanzaic form, the division into cantos, and
   comments in vi.37. For an overview, see Zitner 1990E. For many readers *The Cantos of Mutabilitie*
   bring Spenser's unfinished epic to a fitting close; W. Blissett calls them "a detached retrospective
   commentary on the poem as a whole" ("Spenser's Mutabilitie," *Essays in English Literature from
   the Renaissance to the Victorian Age*, ed. M. Maclure and F. W. Watt [Toronto, 1964]).
2. The power of change, personified by Mutability, is not identical with that of time (cf. stanza 8),
   here imagined as itself subject to change (see vii.47). Astronomical discoveries in the Renaissance
   reinforced classical affirmations that decay is inevitable (e.g. Ovid, *Metamorphoses* 15.237–51,
   and Lucretius, *De Rerum Natura* 5); "the ever-whirling wheele of Change," though, also suggests
   Fortune's wheel.
3. I.e., in fact.
4. The Titans, offspring of Earth, rebelled against their father, Uranos (Sky); their leader Kronos
   (Saturn) castrated Uranos but was himself deposed by his own son Zeus (Jove); see stanza 27 and
   cf. Hesiod, *Theogony* 137–210.

With Saturnes sonne for heavens regiment.°　　　　　　　　*rule*
Whom, though high Jove of kingdome did deprive,
Yet many of their stemme° long after did survive.　　　　　*race*

3

And many of them, afterwards obtained
　Great power of Jove, and high authority;
　As Hecate,[5] in whose almighty hand,
　He plac't all rule and principality,
　To be by her disposéd diversly,
　To Gods, and men, as she them list° divide:　　　　　　　*chose to*
　And drad° Bellona, that doth sound on hie　　　　　　　*dreaded*
　Warres and allarums unto Nations wide,
That makes both heaven and earth to tremble at her pride.

4

So likewise did this Titanesse aspire,
　Rule and dominion to her selfe to gaine;
　That as a Goddesse, men might her admire,°　　　　　　*wonder at*
　And heavenly honours yield, as to them twaine.[6]
　And first, on earth she sought it to obtaine;
　Where she such proofe and sad° examples shewed　　　*grievous*
　Of her great power, to many ones great paine,
　That not men onely (whom she soone subdewed)
But eke all other creatures, her bad dooings rewed.

5

For, she the face of earthly things so changed,
　That all which Nature had establisht first
　In good estate, and in meet° order ranged,　　　　　　*fitting*
　She did pervert, and all their statutes burst:
　And all the worlds faire frame (which none yet durst
　Of Gods or men to alter or misguide)
　She altered quite, and made them all accurst
　That God had blest; and did at first provide
In that still happy state for ever to abide.

6

Ne shee the lawes of Nature onely brake,
　But eke of Justice, and of Policie;°　　　　　　　　　*government*
　And wrong of right, and bad of good did make,
　And death for life exchangéd foolishlie:
　Since which, all living wights have learned to die,
　And all this world is woxen° daily worse.　　　　　　　*grown*
　O pittious worke of Mutabilitie!

5. Hesiod (411–53) calls Hecate the only Titan favored by Zeus; mythographers associated her, as goddess of witches, with Persephone and Hades. Bellona was the Roman goddess of war; in Spenser's *Visions of Bellay*, "Typhoeus sister" seems to be Bellona (the Glosse to "October" 115 identifies Bellona as Athena, but no mythographer thought Athena a Titan).
6. I.e., Hecate and Bellona.

By which, we all are subject to that curse,
And death in stead of life have suckéd from our Nurse.[7]

7

And now, when all the earth she thus had brought
 To her behest,° and thralléd to her might,   *bidding*
 She gan to cast° in her ambitious thought,   *resolve*
 T'attempt the empire of the heavens hight,
 And Jove himselfe to shoulder from his right.
 And first, she past the region of the ayre,
 And of the fire, whose substance thin and slight,
 Made no resistance, ne could her contraire,°   *withstand*
But ready passage to her pleasure did prepaire.

8

Thence, to the Circle of the Moone she clambe,[8]
 Where Cynthia[9] raignes in everlasting glory,
 To whose bright shining palace straight she came,
 All fairely deckt with heavens goodly story;°   *rows (of stars)*
 Whose silver gates (by which there sate an hory
 Old aged Sire, with hower glasse in hand,
 Hight Tyme) she entred, were he liefe or sory:[1]
 Ne staide till she the highest stage° had scand,°   *level/mounted to*
Where Cynthia did sit, that never still did stand.

9

Her sitting on an Ivory throne shee found,
 Drawne of two steeds, th'one black, the other white,[2]
 Environd with tenne thousand starres around,
 That duly her attended day and night;
 And by her side, there ran her Page, that hight
 Vesper, whom we the Evening-starre intend:°   *call*
 That with his Torche, still twinkling like twylight,
 Her lightened all the way where she should wend,
And joy to weary wandring travailers did lend:

10

That when the hardy Titanesse beheld
 The goodly building of her Palace bright,
 Made of the heavens substance, and up-held

---

7. Stanzas 5–6 associate the consequences of Mutability's ambition with those of the Fall.
8. I.e., climbed to the moon's sphere. Stanzas 8–15 recall Phaethon's disastrous ride across the heavens in the sun chariot of his father, Apollo; to save the earth, Jove killed him with a thunderbolt (*Metamorphoses* 2.1–400).
9. Goddess of the moon. Poets often identified Elizabeth with her, so Mutability's behavior may have political resonance; in effect, she tries permanently to eclipse Cynthia. Meyer 1983 deduces from the lunar eclipse on April 14, 1595, a day when the planets were positioned like the gods in this scene who "all ran together" (stanza 15), that Spenser wrote this canto after that date.
1. I.e., whether he were willing or not.
2. Mythographers (e.g., Boccaccio, *Genealogiae* 4.16) say the moon has these horses because she shines sometimes by night and sometimes by day.

With thousand Crystall pillors of huge hight,
Shee gan to burne in her ambitious spright,
And t'envie her that in such glorie raigned.
Eftsoones she cast by force and tortious° might,   *wrongful*
Her to displace; and to her selfe to have gained
The kingdome of the Night, and waters by her wained.°   *moved*

11

Boldly she bid the Goddesse downe descend,
    And let her selfe into that Ivory throne;
    For, shee her selfe more worthy thereof wend,°   *thought*
    And better able it to guide alone:
    Whether to men, whose fall she did bemone,
    Or unto Gods, whose state she did maligne,°   *envy*
    Or to th'infernall Powers, her need give lone[3]
    Of her faire light, and bounty most benigne,
Her selfe of all that rule shee deeméd most condigne.°   *worthy*

12

But shee that had to her that soveraigne seat
    By highest Jove assigned, therein to beare
    Nights burning lamp, regarded not her threat,
    Ne yielded ought for favour or for feare;
    But with sterne countenaunce and disdainfull cheare,°   *aspect*
    Bending her hornéd browes, did put her back:
    And boldly blaming her for comming there,
    Bade her attonce from heavens coast to pack,
Or at her perill bide the wrathfull Thunders wrack.°   *destruction*

13

Yet nathemore° the Giantesse forbare: *not at all*
    But boldly preacing-on,° raught forth her hand   *advancing*
    To pluck her downe perforce° from off her chaire;   *by force*
    And there-with lifting up her golden wand,
    Threatned to strike her if she did with-stand.
    Where-at the starres, which round about her blazed,
    And eke the Moones bright wagon, still did stand,
    All beeing with so bold attempt amazed,
And on her uncouth° habit and sterne looke still gazed.   *strange*

14

Meane-while, the lower World, which nothing knew
    Of all that chauncéd here, was darkned quite;
    And eke the heavens, and all the heavenly crew
    Of happy wights, now unpurvaide° of light,   *deprived*
    Were much afraid, and wondred at that sight;
    Fearing least Chaos broken had his chaine,
    And brought againe on them eternall night:

3. I.e., she must give.

But chiefely Mercury, that next doth raigne,[4]
Ran forth in haste, unto the king of Gods to plaine.°   *complain*

15

All ran together with a great out-cry,
  To Joves faire Palace, fixt in heavens hight;
And beating at his gates full earnestly,
  Gan call to him aloud with all their might,
  To know what meant that suddaine lack of light.
The father of the Gods when this he heard,
  Was troubled much at their so strange affright,
Doubting least Typhon[5] were againe upreared,
Or other his old foes, that once him sorely feared.°   *frightened*

16

Eftsoones the sonne of Maia forth he sent
  Downe to the Circle of the Moone, to knowe
The cause of this so strange astonishment,
  And why shee did her wonted course forslowe;°   *delay*
  And if that any were on earth belowe
That did with charmes or Magick her molest,
  Him to attache,° and downe to hell to throwe: *seize*
  But, if from heaven it were, then to arrest
The Author, and him bring before his presence prest.°   *immediately*

17

The wingd-foot God, so fast his plumes did beat,
  That soone he came where-as the Titanesse
Was striving with faire Cynthia for her seat:
  At whose strange sight, and haughty hardinesse,°   *boldness*
  He wondred much, and feared her no lesse.
Yet laying feare aside to doe his charge,°   *assigned task*
  At last, he bade her (with bold stedfastnesse)
Ceasse to molest the Moone to walke at large,[6]
Or come before high Jove, her dooings to discharge.°   *account for*

18

And there-with-all, he on her shoulder laid
  His snaky-wreathéd Mace,[7] whose awfull power
Doth make both Gods and hellish fiends affraid:
  Where-at the Titanesse did sternely lower,°   *scowl*
  And stoutly answered, that in evill hower
He from his Jove such message to her brought,
  To bid her leave faire Cynthias silver bower;

4. Mercury (Hermes) was the son of Maia (cf. stanza 16); in Ptolemaic astronomy, the planet Mercury's sphere was next beyond the moon's.
5. The giant Typhon (also called Typhoeus) rebelled against Zeus, who then hurled him down to Tartarus (or, some said, piled Mount Aetna on him).
6. I.e., cease to hinder the moon's free movement.
7. I.e., the caduceus. Cf. II.xii.41.

Sith shee his Jove and him esteeméd nought,
No more then Cynthia's selfe; but all their kingdoms sought.

19

The Heavens Herald staid not to reply,
    But past away, his doings to relate
    Unto his Lord; who now in th'highest sky,
    Was placéd in his principall Estate,[8]
    With all the Gods about him congregate:
    To whom when Hermes had his message told,
    It did them all exceedingly amate,°   *dismay*
    Save Jove; who, changing nought his count'nance bold,
Did unto them at length these speeches wise unfold;

20

"Harken to mee awhile yee heavenly Powers;
    Ye may remember since th'Earths curséd seed[9]
    Sought to assaile the heavens eternall towers,
    And to us all exceeding feare did breed:
    But how we then defeated all their deed,
    Yee all doe knowe, and them destroiéd quite;
    Yet not so quite, but that there did succeed
    An off-spring of their bloud, which did alite
Upon the fruitfull earth, which doth us yet despite.°   *disdain*

21

"Of that bad seed is this bold woman bred,
    That now with bold presumption doth aspire
    To thrust faire Phoebe from her silver bed,
    And eke our selves from heavens high Empire,
    If that her might were match to her desire:
    Wherefore, it now behoves us to advise°   *consider*
    What way is best to drive her to retire;
    Whether by open force, or counsell wise,
Areed° ye sonnes of God, as best ye can devise."   *advise*

22

So having said, he ceast; and with his brow
    (His black eye-brow, whose doomefull dreaded beck[1]
    Is wont to wield the world unto his vow,°   *will*
    And even the highest Powers of heaven to check)
    Made signe to them in their degrees to speake:
    Who straight gan cast° their counsell grave and wise.   *consider*

8. I.e., enthroned in his regal aspect.
9. I.e., the giants, who piled Mount Pelion on Mount Ossa to reach Jove (cf. *Metamorphoses* 1.156–62). Spenser seldom distinguishes between Titans and giants, representatives of rebellion against all established order from the cosmological to the political. Mutability herself combines the earthy giants' will to violent revolt with beauty (stanza 31), intellectual poise, and pride suiting a divine Titan.
1. I.e., his feared nod of command.

Meane-while, th'Earths daughter, thogh she nought did reck
Of Hermes message; yet gan now advise,
What course were best to take in this hot bold emprize.°   *undertaking*

23

Eftsoones she thus resolved; that whil'st the Gods
  (After returne of Hermes Embassie)
  Were troubled, and amongst themselves at ods,
  Before they could new counsels re-allie,°   *form again*
  To set upon them in that extasie;°   *astonishment*
  And take what fortune time and place would lend:
  So, forth she rose, and through the purest sky
  To Joves high Palace straight cast° to ascend,   *resolved*
To prosecute her plot: Good on-set boads good end.

24

Shee there arriving, boldly in did pass;
  Where all the Gods she found in counsell close,°   *secret*
  All quite unarmed, as then their manner was.
  At sight of her they suddaine all arose,
  In great amaze, ne wist what way to chose.
  But Jove, all fearelesse, forc't them to aby;°   *remain*
  And in his soveraine throne, gan straight dispose°   *arrange*
  Himselfe more full of grace and Majestie,
That mote encheare° his friends, and foes mote terrifie.   *cheer*

25

That, when the haughty Titanesse beheld,
  All° were she fraught with pride and impudence,   *although*
  Yet with the sight thereof was almost queld;
  And inly quaking, seemed as reft of sense,
  And voyd of speech in that drad° audience;   *dread*
  Until that Jove himself, her selfe bespake:
  "Speake thou fraile woman, speake with confidence,
  Whence art thou, and what doost thou here now make?°   *intend*
What idle errand hast thou, earths mansion to forsake?"

26

Shee, halfe confuséd with his great commaund,
  Yet gathering spirit of her natures pride,
  Him boldly answered thus to his demaund:
  "I am a daughter, by the mothers side,
  Of her that is Grand-mother magnifide°   *glorified*
  Of all the Gods, great Earth, great Chaos child:[2]
  But by the fathers (be it not envide)
  I greater am in bloud (whereon I build)
Then all the Gods, though wrongfully from heaven exiled.

2. Earth is the child of Chaos in Hesiod, *Theogony* 116; Boccaccio terms her "great mother" in *Genealogia* 1.8.

27

"For Titan (as ye all acknowledge must)
　Was Saturnes elder brother by birth-right;
　Both, sonnes of Uranus: but by unjust
　And guilefull meanes, through Corybantes slight,°   *trickery*
　The younger thrust the elder from his right:[3]
　Since which, thou Jove, injuriously hast held
　The Heavens rule from Titans sonnes by might;
　And them to hellish dungeons downe hast feld:
Witnesse ye Heavens the truth of all that I have teld."

28

Whilst she thus spake, the Gods that gave good eare
　To her bold words, and markéd well her grace,
　Beeing of stature tall as any there
　Of all the Gods, and beautifull of face,
　As any of the Goddesses in place,
　Stood all astonied, like a sort° of Steeres;   *herd*
　Mongst whom, some beast of strange and forraine race,
　Unwares° is chaunc't, far straying from his peeres: *unexpectedly*
So did their ghastly gaze bewray° their hidden feares.   *reveal*

29

Till having pauzed awhile, Jove thus bespake;
　"Will never mortall thoughts ceasse to aspire,
　In this bold sort, to Heaven claime to make,
　And touch celestiall seates with earthly mire?
　I would have thought, that bold Procrustes[4] hire,°   *reward*
　Or Typhons fall, or proud Ixions paine,
　Or great Prometheus, tasting of our ire,
　Would have suffized, the rest for to restraine;
And warned all men by their example to refraine:

30

"But now, this off-scum of that curséd fry,[5]
　Dare to renew the like bold enterprize,
　And chalenge th'heritage of this our skie;
　Whom what should hinder, but that we likewise

3. According to Renaissance mythographers, Titan (not normally found in older classical mythology) agreed to abdicate in favor of his younger brother, Kronos (Saturn), on condition that Saturn would swallow his own children and so assure Titan's eventual return to power (Comes 2.1, 6.20). But when Saturn's wife, Rhea, bore Zeus, she fooled her husband into swallowing a stone while her attendants, the Corybantes, beat on shields to drown out the baby's cries. "The younger thrust the elder from his right," though applicable to Saturn and Titan, refers primarily to the later overthrow of Saturn by Zeus. The implications are intriguing, for England, like Olympus, was ruled by a dynasty basing its claim partly on the right of conquest.
4. The robber Procrustes ("the stretcher") made guests fit his bed by cutting or stretching their limbs; Theseus destroyed him. On Typhon, see stanza 15. For trying to rape Hera (Juno), Ixion was bound in Hades to a whirling wheel. Prometheus stole fire from heaven as a gift to mortals; Jove bound him to a cliff, where a vulture daily consumed his liver (it grew again at night). See Ovid 7.438, 3.303, 4.461, and Hesiod, *Theogony* 521–25.
5. I.e., Mutability, this latest example of rebellious presumption.

Should handle as the rest of her allies,
And thunder-drive to hell?" With that, he shooke
His Nectar-deawéd locks, with which the skyes
And all the world beneath for terror quooke,°   *quaked*
And eft° his burning levin-brond° in hand he tooke.   *then/lightning bolt*

31

But, when he lookéd on her lovely face,
  In which, faire beames of beauty did appeare,
  That could the greatest wrath soone turne to grace
  (Such sway° doth beauty even in Heaven beare)   *power*
  He staide his hand: and having changed his cheare,°   *mood*
  He thus againe in milder wise began;
  "But ah! if Gods should strive with flesh yfere,°   *together*
  Then shortly should the progeny of Man
Be rooted out, if Jove should doe still° what he can:[6]   *always*

32

"But thee faire Titans child, I rather weene,°   *suppose*
  Through some vaine errour or inducement light,
  To see that° mortall eyes have never seene;   *that which*
  Or through ensample of thy sisters might,
  Bellona; whose great glory thou doost spight,°   *envy*
  Since thou hast seene her dreadfull power belowe,
  Mongst wretched men (dismaide with her affright)[7]
  To bandie Crownes, and Kingdomes to bestowe:
And sure thy worth, no lesse then hers doth seem to showe.

33

"But wote° thou this, thou hardy Titanesse,   *know*
  That not the worth of any living wight
  May challenge ought in Heavens interesse;[8]
  Much lesse the Title of old Titans Right:
  For, we by Conquest of our soveraine might,
  And by eternall doome of Fates decree,
  Have wonne the Empire of the Heavens bright;
  Which to our selves we hold, and to whom wee
Shall worthy deeme partakers of our blisse to bee.

34

"Then ceasse thy idle claime thou foolish gerle,
  And seeke by grace and goodnesse to obtaine
  That place from which by folly Titan fell;
  There-to thou maist perhaps, if so thou faine°   *desire*
  Have Jove thy gratious Lord and Soveraigne."

6. Psalms 78.38–39: "Yea, many a time turned he his anger away, and did not stir up all his wrath. For he remembered that they were but flesh. . . ."
7. I.e., terror of her.
8. I.e., may lay claim to any part of Heaven's dominion or title.

So, having said, she thus to him replide;
"Ceasse Saturnes sonne, to seeke by proffers vaine
Of idle hopes t'allure mee to thy side,
For to betray my Right, before I have it tride.

35

"But thee, O Jove, no equall° Judge I deeme   *impartial*
  Of my desert, or of my dewfull° Right;   *due*
That in thine owne behalfe maist partiall seeme:
But to the highest him, that is behight
Father of Gods and men by equall might;⁹
To weet, the God of Nature, I appeale."
There-at Jove wexéd wroth, and in his spright
Did inly grudge, yet did it well conceale;
And bade Dan Phoebus Scribe her Appellation° seale.   *appeal*

36

Eftsoones the time and place appointed were,
  Where all, both heavenly Powers, and earthly wights,
  Before great Natures presence should appeare,
  For triall of their Titles and best Rights:
That was, to weet, upon the highest hights
Of Arlo-hill¹ (Who knowes not Arlo-hill?)
That is the highest head (in all mens sights)
Of my old father Mole, whom Shepheards quill
Renowméd hath with hymnes fit for a rurall skill.

37

And, were it not ill fitting for this file,°   *recital*
  To sing of hilles and woods, mongst warres and Knights,
  I would abate the sternenesse of my stile,
  Mongst these sterne stounds° to mingle soft delights;   *clashes*
And tell how Arlo through Dianaes spights
(Beeing of old the best and fairest Hill
That was in all this holy-Islands hights)
Was made the most unpleasant, and most ill.
Meane while, O Clio, lend Calliope thy quill.²

38

Whylome,° when Ireland florishéd in fame   *formerly*
  Of wealths and goodnesse, far above the rest
  Of all that beare the British Islands name,³
  The Gods then used (for pleasure and for rest)

9. I.e., equally powerful over gods as over men. The god of nature, here described as masculine,
   appears in vii.5, as Dame Nature; "Whether she man or woman inly were" is uncertain.
1. Galtymore, a peak in the mountain range near Spenser's estate in Ireland; it overlooked the "Golden
   Vale" of Aherlow. In the person of the shepherd Colin, Spenser mentions "Old father Mole . .
   . that mountain gray" in *Colin Clouts Come Home Againe* 56–59, 104–15.
2. I.e., let Calliope, borrowing the pen of Clio, Muse of history, tell the story of Faunus and Molanna.
3. Spenser observes in *A Vewe of the Present State of Irelande* that "it is Certaine that Irelande hathe
   had the use of lettres verye Ancientlye and longe before Englande" (1246–47).

Oft to resort there-to, when seemed them best:
But none of all there-in more pleasure found,
Then Cynthia;[4] that is soveraine Queene profest°   *acknowledged*
Of woods and forrests, which therein abound,
Sprinkled with wholsom waters, more then most on ground.

39

But mongst them all, as fittest for her game,°   *recreation*
Either for chace of beasts with hound or boawe,
Or for to shroude in shade from Phoebus flame,
Or bathe in fountaines that doe freshly flowe,
Or from high hilles, or from the dales belowe,
She chose this Arlo; where shee did resort
With all her Nymphes enrangéd on a rowe,
With whom the woody Gods did oft consort:
For, with the Nymphes, the Satyres love to play and sport.

40

Amongst the which, there was a Nymph that hight
Molanna;[5] daughter of old father Mole,
And sister unto Mulla,[6] faire and bright:
Unto whose bed false Bregog whylome stole,
That Shepheard Colin dearely° did condole,   *earnestly*
And made her lucklesse loves well knowne to be.
But this Molanna, were she not so shole,°   *shallow*
Were no lesse faire and beautifull then shee:
Yet as she is, a fairer flood may no man see.

41

For, first, she springs out of two marble Rocks,
On which, a grove of Oakes high mounted growes,
That as a girlond seemes to deck the locks
Of som faire Bride, brought forth with pompous°   *magnificent*
      showes
Out of her bowre,° that many flowers strowes: *chamber*
So, through the flowry Dales she tumbling downe,
Through many woods, and shady coverts° flowes   *thickets*
(That on each side her silver channell crowne)
Till to the Plaine she come, whose Valleyes shee doth drowne.

42

In her sweet streames, Diana uséd oft
(After her sweatie chace and toilesome play)
To bathe her selfe; and after, on the soft
And downy grasse, her dainty limbes to lay

4. I.e., Diana, goddess of the forest.
5. The river Behanna, which rises near Galtymore and eventually joins the Funsheon ("Fanchin" in stanza 44).
6. The river Awbeg; it and the Bregoge flowed by Spenser's estate at Kilcolman. On Mulla and Bregog (Irish, "false"), see *Colin Clouts Come Home Againe* 104–55.

In covert° shade, where none behold her may: *secret*
For, much she hated sight of living eye.
Foolish God Faunus, though full many a day
He saw her clad, yet longéd foolishly
To see her naked mongst her Nymphes in privity.[7]

43

No way he found to compasse° his desire.   *accomplish*
 But to corrupt Molanna, this her maid,
 Her to discover for some secret hire:°   *reward*
 So, her with flattering words he first assaid;
 And after, pleasing gifts for her purvaid,°   *provided*
 Queene-apples,[8] and red Cherries from the tree,
 With which he her alluréd and betraid,
 To tell what time he might her Lady see
When she her selfe did bathe, that he might secret° bee. *hidden*

44

There-to hee promist, if she would him pleasure
 With this small boone, to quit° her with a better; *repay*
 To weet, that where-as she had out of measure
 Long loved the Fanchin,[9] who by nought did set her,[1]
 That he would undertake, for this to get her
 To be his Love, and of him likéd well:
 Besides all which, he vowed to be her debter
 For many moe good turnes then he would tell;
The least of which, this little pleasure should excell.

45

The simple maid did yield to him anone;°   *at once*
 And eft him placéd where he close might view
 That° never any saw, save onely one;   *that which*
 Who, for his hire to so foole-hardy dew,
 Was of his hounds devoured in Hunters hew.[2]
 Tho,° as her manner was on sunny day,   *then*
 Diana, with her Nymphes about her, drew
 To this sweet spring; where, doffing her array,
She bathed her lovely limbes, for Jove a likely pray.

7. This episode combines Irish folklore with classical myth, notably the tale of Actaeon, who, while out hunting, inadvertently spied Diana bathing with her nymphs and, turned into a stag by the goddess, was chased and torn apart by his hounds (*Metamorphoses* 3.138–252); and of Arethusa, who, thanks to Diana, escaped the river god Alpheus by becoming a stream that plunges underground to arise again in Sicily (*Metamorphoses* 5.572–641, where the story is told by Calliope; others add that Alpheus follows and rejoins Arethusa).
8. A kind of apple with red flesh; or perhaps a quince. Faunus's temptation of Molanna recalls Satan's temptation of Eve.
9. The river Funsheon.
1. I.e., who cared nothing for her.
2. I.e., who, deservedly rewarded for his foolhardiness, was devoured by his hounds in the slaughter that concludes the hunt.

46

There Faunus saw that pleaséd much his eye,
  And made his hart to tickle in his brest,
  That for great joy of some-what he did spy,
  He could him not containe in silent rest;
  But breaking forth in laughter, loud profest
  His foolish thought. A foolish Faune indeed,
  That couldst not hold thy selfe so° hidden blest,   *thus*
  But wouldest needs thine owne conceit areed.°   *make known*
Babblers unworthy been of so divine a meed.°   *reward*

47

The Goddesse, all abashéd with that noise,
  In haste forth started from the guilty brooke;
  And running straight where-as she heard his voice,
  Enclosed the bush about, and there him tooke,
  Like darréd° Larke; not daring up to looke   *terrified*
  On her whose sight before so much he sought.
  Thence, forth they drew him by the hornes, and shooke
  Nigh all to peeces, that they left him nought;
And then into the open light they forth him brought.

48

Like as an huswife, that with busie care
  Thinks of her Dairie to make wondrous gaine,
  Finding where-as some wicked beast unware°   *unexpectedly*
  That breakes into her Dayr'house, there doth draine
  Her creaming pannes, and frustrate all her paine;
  Hath in some snare or gin° set close behind,   *trap*
  Entrappéd him, and caught into her traine,°   *snare*
  Then thinkes what punishment were best assigned,
And thousand deathes deviseth in her vengefull mind:

49

So did Diana and her maydens all
  Use silly Faunus, now within their baile:°   *custody*
  They mocke and scorne him, and him foule miscall;
  Some by the nose him pluckt, some by the taile,
  And by his goatish beard some did him haile:°   *pull*
  Yet he (poore soule) with patience all did beare;
  For, nought against their wils might countervaile:°   *resist*
  Ne ought he said what ever he did heare;
But hanging downe his head, did like a Mome° appeare.   *fool*

50

At length, when they had flouted him their fill,
  They gan to cast what penaunce him to give.
  Some would have gelt° him, but that same   *castrated*

    would spill°   *destroy*
The Wood-gods breed, which must for ever live:
Others would through the river him have drive,
And duckéd deepe: but that seemed penaunce light;
But most agreed and did this sentence give,
Him in Deares skin to clad; and in that plight,
To hunt him with their hounds, him selfe save how hee might.

51

But Cynthia's selfe, more angry then the rest,
  Thought not enough, to punish him in sport,
  And of her shame to make a gamesome jest;
  But gan examine him in straighter° sort,   *stricter*
  Which of her Nymphes, or other close consort,[3]
  Him thither brought, and her to him betraid?
  He, much affeard, to her confesséd short,°   *soon*
  That 'twas Molanna which her so bewraid.°   *betrayed*
Then all attonce their hands upon Molanna laid.

52

But him (according as they had decreed)
  With a Deeres-skin they covered, and then chast
  With all their hounds that after him did speed;
  But he more speedy, from them fled more fast
  Then any Deere: so sore him dread aghast.°   *terrified*
  They after followed all with shrill out-cry,
  Shouting as they the heavens would have brast:°   *burst*
  That all the woods and dales where he did flie,
Did ring againe, and loud reeccho to the skie.

53

So they him followed till they weary were;
  When, back returning to Molann' againe,
  They, by commaund'ment of Diana, there
  Her whelmed with stones.[4] Yet Faunus (for her paine)°   *trouble*
  Of her beloved Fanchin did obtaine,
  That her he would receive unto his bed.
  So now her waves passe through a pleasant Plaine,
  Till with the Fanchin she her selfe doe wed,
And (both combined) themselves in one faire river spred.

54

Nath'lesse,° Diana, full of indignation,   *nonetheless*
  Thence-forth abandoned her delicious brooke;
  In whose sweet streame, before that bad occasion,
  So much delight to bathe her limbes she tooke:
  Ne onely her, but also quite forsooke

---

3. I.e., secret companion.
4. Thus accounting for the shallowness of the river (stanza 40).

All those faire forrests about Arlo hid,
And all that Mountaine, which doth over-looke
The richest champian that may else be rid,[5]
And the faire Shure,[6] in which are thousand Salmons bred.

55

Them all, and all that she so deare did way,°   *esteem*
 Thence-forth she left; and parting from the place,
 There-on an heavy haplesse curse did lay,
 To weet, that Wolves, where she was wont to space,° *roam*
 Should harboured be, and all those Woods deface,
 And Thieves should rob and spoile that Coast around.
 Since which, those Woods, and all that
  goodly Chase,°   *hunting ground*
 Doth to this day with Wolves and Thieves abound:
Which too-too true that lands in-dwellers since have found.[7]

Canto VII

> *Pealing,° from Jove, to Natur's Bar,*   *appealing*
> *bold Alteration*[1] *pleades*
> *Large Evidence: but Nature soone*
> *her righteous Doome° areads.°* *judgment/delivers*

1

Ah! whither doost thou now thou greater Muse[2]
 Me from these woods and pleasing forrests bring?
 And my fraile spirit (that dooth oft refuse
 This too high flight, unfit for her weake wing)
 Lift up aloft, to tell of heavens King
 (Thy soveraine Sire) his fortunate successe,
 And victory, in bigger° noates to sing,   *louder*
 Which he obtained against that Titanesse,
That him of heavens Empire sought to dispossesse.

2

Yet sith I needs must follow thy behest,
 Doe thou my weaker° wit with skill inspire, *too weak*
 Fit for this turne; and in my feeble brest
 Kindle fresh sparks of that immortall fire,
 Which learnéd minds inflameth with desire
 Of heavenly things: for, who but thou alone,
 That art yborne of heaven and heavenly Sire,
 Can tell things doen in heaven so long ygone;
So farre past memory of man that may be knowne.

---

5. I.e., the richest plain to be seen anywhere.
6. The river Suir, which flows through the Vale of Aherlow.
7. Cf. *Colin Clouts Come Home Againe* 312–19.
1. I.e., Mutability.
2. Probably Clio, but see I.i.2, note 3.

3

Now, at the time that was before agreed,
  The Gods assembled all on Arlo hill;
  As well those that are sprung of heavenly seed,
  As those that all the other world[3] doe fill,
  And rule both sea and land unto their will:
  Onely th'infernall Powers might not appeare;
  Aswell for horror of their count'naunce ill,
  As for th'unruly fiends which they did feare;°   *keep in awe*
Yet Pluto and Proserpina[4] were present there.

4

And thither also came all other creatures,
  What-ever life or motion doe retaine,
  According to their sundry kinds of features;
  That Arlo scarsly could them all containe;
  So full they fillèd every hill and Plaine:
  And had not Natures Sergeant (that is Order)[5]
  Them well disposèd by his busie paine,°   *care*
  And raungèd farre abroad in every border,
They would have causèd much confusion and disorder.

5

Then forth issewed (great goddesse) great dame Nature,[6]
  With goodly port° and gracious Majesty;   *bearing*
  Being far greater and more tall of stature
  Then any of the gods or Powers on hie:
  Yet certes by her face and physnomy,°   *countenance*
  Whether she man or woman inly were,
  That could not any creature well descry:
  For, with a veile that wimpled° every where,   *covered in folds*
Her head and face was hid, that mote to none appeare.

6

That some doe say was so by skill devized,
  To hide the terror of her uncouth° hew,   *strange*
  From mortall eyes that should be sore agrized;°   *horrified*

3. I.e., the earth.
4. Rulers of the underworld.
5. Order is Nature's sergeant, or chief executive attendant, whereas Mutability opposes every law of Nature (vi.5). Significantly, when the seasons and months appear as witnesses at Mutability's own request, they come in proper order and garb; see S. Hawkins, "Mutabilitie and the Cycle of the Months," in W. Nelson, ed., *Form and Convention in the Poetry of Edmund Spenser* (New York, 1961) 76–102.
6. For his "Great dame Nature" Spenser drew on a number of classical and medieval writers (e.g., Plutarch, Boethius, and Jean de Meun), but she chiefly recalls "this noble goddesse Nature" in Chaucer's *Parliament of Fowls* and, probably, "Natura" in the twelfth-century poem *De Planctu Naturae*, by Alain de Lille [Alanus de Insulis], which Chaucer himself cites. Spenser notes both works in stanza 9. The "Nature" to whom all three refer is the natural creative force itself (what philosophers called *Natura naturans*), not the created natural world. Stanzas 5–6 and 13 stress her power, mystery, and paradoxical inclusiveness. Thus she is taller than other gods; she is veiled (to protect mortals from her face's terror or beauty, and perhaps also because we cannot know Nature herself, only her effects); and she encompasses youth and age, being and becoming.

For that her face did like a Lion shew,
That eye of wight could not indure to view:
But others tell that it so beautious was,
And round about such beames of splendor threw,
That it the Sunne a thousand times did pass,°   *surpass*
Ne could be seene, but °like an image in a glass.   *except*

7

That well may seemen true: for, well I weene
  That this same day, when she on Arlo sat,
  Her garment was so bright and wondrous sheene,°   *fair*
  That my fraile wit cannot devize to what
  It to compare, nor finde like stuffe to that,
  As those three sacred Saints,[7] though else most wise,
  Yet on mount Thabor quite their wits forgat,
  When they their glorious Lord in strange disguise
Transfigured sawe; his garments so did daze their eyes.

8

In a fayre Plaine upon an equall° Hill,   *level*
  She placéd was in a pavilion;
  Not such as Craftes-men by their idle° skill   *vain*
  Are wont for Princes states° to fashion: *canopies*
  But th'earth her self of her owne motion,
  Out of her fruitfull bosome made to growe
  Most dainty trees; that, shooting up anon,
  Did seeme to bow their bloosming° heads full lowe,   *blossoming*
For homage unto her, and like a throne did shew.°   *appear*

9

So hard it is for any living wight,
  All her array and vestiments to tell,
  That old Dan Geffrey[8] (in whose gentle spright
  The pure well head of Poesie did dwell)
  In his *Foules parley* durst not with it mel,°   *meddle*
  But it transferd° to Alane, who he thought   *referred*
  Had in his *Plaint of kindes* described it well:
  Which who will read set forth so as it ought,
Go seek he out that Alane where he may be sought.

10

And all the earth far underneath her feete
  Was dight with flowres, that voluntary grew
  Out of the ground, and sent forth odours sweet,
  Tenne thousand mores° of sundry sent and hew,   *plants*
  That might delight the smell, or please the view:

7. Peter, James, and John, to whom Jesus appeared in transfigured brightness: "his face did shine as the sun, and his raiment was white as the light" (Matthew 17.1–8).
8. I.e., Master Geoffrey Chaucer; "Alane" in line 6 is Alain de Lille.

The which, the Nymphes, from all the brooks thereby
Had gathered, which they at her foot-stoole threw;
That richer seemed then any tapestry,
That Princes bowres adorne with painted imagery.

11

And Mole himselfe, to honour her the more,
  Did deck himself in freshest faire attire,
  And his high head, that seemeth alwaies hore
  With hardned frosts of former winters ire,
  He with an Oaken girlond now did tire,°   attire
  As if the love of some new Nymph late seene,
  Had in him kindled youthfull fresh desire,
  And made him change his gray attire to greene;
Ah gentle Mole! such joyance hath thee well beseene.°   provided

12

Was never so great joyance since the day,
  That all the gods whylome assembled were,
  On Haemus hill⁹ in their divine array,
  To celebrate the solemne bridall cheare,
  Twixt Peleus, and dame Thetis pointed° there;   appointed
  Where Phoebus self, that god of Poets hight,
  They say did sing the spousall hymne full cleere,
  That all the gods were ravisht with delight
Of his celestiall song, and Musicks wondrous might.

13

This great Grandmother of all creatures bred
  Great Nature, ever young yet full of eld,°   age
  Still mooving, yet unmovéd from her sted;°   place
  Unseene of any, yet of all beheld;
  Thus sitting in her throne as I have teld,
  Before her came dame Mutabilitie;
  And being lowe before her presence feld,°   prostrated
  With meek obaysance and humilitie,
Thus gan her plaintif Plea, with words to amplifie;

14

"To thee O greatest goddesse, onely° great,   uniquely
  An humble suppliant loe, I lowely fly
  Seeking for Right, which I of thee entreat;
  Who Right to all dost deale indifferently,°   impartially
  Damning all Wrong and tortious° Injurie,   wrongful
  Which any of thy creatures doe to other
  (Oppressing them with power, unequally)°   unjustly

9. The marriage of Peleus and Thetis took place on Mount Pelion; the opening lines in Ovid's account perhaps misled Spenser (cf. *Metamorphoses* 11.229–30).

Sith of them all thou are the equall mother,
And knittest each to each, as brother unto brother.

15

"To thee therefore of this same Jove I plaine,
  And of his fellow gods that faine° to be,   *pretend*
  That challenge° to themselves the whole worlds raign;   *claim*
  Of which, the greatest part is due to me,
  And heaven it selfe by heritage in Fee[1]
  For, heaven and earth I both alike do deeme,
  Sith heaven and earth are both alike to thee;
  And, gods no more then men thou doest esteeme:
For, even the gods to thee, as men to gods do seeme.

16

"Then weigh, O soveraigne goddesse, by what right
  These gods do claime the worlds whole sovcrainty;
  And that° is onely dew unto thy might   *that which*
  Arrogate to themselves ambitiously:
  As for the gods owne principality,°   *sovereignty*
  Which Jove usurpes unjustly; that to be
  My heritage, Jove's self cannot deny,
  From my great Grandsire Titan, unto mee,
Derived by dew descent; as is well knowen to thee.

17

"Yet mauger° Jove, and all his gods beside,   *despite*
  I doe possesse the worlds most regiment;°   *rule*
  As, if ye please it into parts divide,
  And every parts inholders° to convent,°   *tenants/convene*
  Shall to your eyes appeare incontinent.°   *at once*
  And first, the Earth (great mother of us all)
  That only seems unmoved and permanent,
  And unto Mutability not thrall,
Yet is she changed in part, and eeke in generall.[2]

18

"For, all that from her springs, and is ybredde,
  How-ever fayre it flourish for a time,
  Yet see we soone decay; and, being dead,
  To turne again unto their earthly slime:
  Yet, out of their decay and mortall crime,°   *corruption*
  We daily see new creatures to arize;
  And of their Winter spring another Prime,°   *spring*
  Unlike in forme, and changed by strange disguise:
So turne they still about, and change in restlesse wise.

1. I.e., in fee simple, conferring absolute rule.
2. Mutability's arguments and wording in stanzas 17–25 echo Lucretius's *De Rerum Natura* 5, and (particularly) Ovid's *Metamorphoses* 15.

19

"As for her tenants; that is, man and beasts,
   The beasts we daily see massacred dy,
   As thralls and vassalls unto mens beheasts:
   And men themselves doe change continually,
   From youth to eld, from wealth to poverty,
   From good to bad, from bad to worst of all.
   Ne doe their bodies only flit and fly:
   But eeke their minds (which they immortall call)
Still change and vary thoughts, as new occasions fall.

20

"Ne is the water in more constant case;
   Whether those same on high, or these belowe.
   For, th'Ocean moveth stil, from place to place;
   And every River still doth ebbe and flowe:
   Ne any Lake, that seems most still and slowe,
   Ne Poole so small, that can his smoothnesse holde,
   When any winde doth under heaven blowe;
   With which, the clouds are also tost and rolled;
Now like great hills; and, streight,° like sluces,   *immediately*
   them unfold.°   *open*

21

"So likewise are all watry living wights
   Still tost, and turnéd, with continuall change,
   Never abyding in their stedfast plights.°   *conditions*
   The fish, still floting, doe at randon° range,   *random*
   And never rest; but evermore exchange
   Their dwelling places, as the streames them carrie:
   Ne have the watry foules a certaine grange,°   *abode*
   Wherein to rest, ne in one stead° do tarry;   *place*
But flitting still doe flie, and still their places vary.

22

"Next is the Ayre: which who feels not by sense
   (For, of all sense it is the middle meane)[3]
   To flit still? and, with subtill influence
   Of his thin spirit, all creatures to maintaine,
   In state of life? O weake life! that does leane
   On thing so tickle° as th'unsteady ayre;   *uncertain*
   Which every howre is changed, and altred cleane°   *altogether*
   With every blast that bloweth fowle or faire:
The faire doth it prolong; the fowle doth it impaire.

3. I.e., the medium (for all the senses).

23

"Therein the changes infinite beholde,
  Which to her creatures every minute chaunce;
  Now, boyling hot: streight, friezing deadly cold:
  Now, faire sun-shine, that makes all skip and daunce:
  Streight, bitter storms and balefull countenance,
  That makes them all to shiver and to shake:
  Rayne, hayle, and snowe do pay them sad penance,
  And dreadfull thunder-claps (that make them quake)
With flames and flashing lights that thousand changes make.

24

"Last is the fire: which, though it live for ever,
  Ne can be quenchéd quite; yet, every day,
  We see his parts, so soone as they do sever,
  To lose their heat, and shortly to decay;
  So, makes himself his owne consuming pray.
  Ne any living creatures doth he breed:
  But all, that are of others bredd, doth slay;
  And, with their death, his cruell life dooth feed;
Nought leaving but their barren ashes, without seede.

25

"Thus, all these fower (the which the ground-work bee
  Of all the world, and of all living wights)
  To thousand sorts of Change we subject see:
  Yet are they changed (by other wondrous slights)°   *devices*
  Into themselves, and lose their native mights;
  The Fire to Aire, and th' Ayre to Water sheere,°   *clear*
  And Water into Earth: yet Water fights
  With Fire, and Aire with Earth approaching neere:
Yet all are in one body, and as one appeare.[4]

26

"So, in them all raignes Mutabilitie;
  How-ever these, that Gods themselves do call,
  Of them doe claime the rule and soveraraty:
  As, Vesta, of the fire aethereall;[5]
  Vulcan, of this, with us so usuall;
  Ops,[6] of the earth; and Juno of the Ayre;
  Neptune, of Seas; and Nymphes, of Rivers all.
  For, all those Rivers to me subject are:
And all the rest, which they usurp, be all my share.

4. These views derive from Ovid's doctrine of the transmutation of elements (*Metamorphoses* 15.237–49), a position rejected by Lucretius (*De Rerum Natura* 1.780–844).
5. I.e., of celestial fire. Vesta was Roman goddess of the hearth and, more generally, of consecrated fire; Aeneas transported from Troy the eternal flame sacred to her (*Aeneid* 2.296).
6. Roman goddess of fertility and the ground. Mythographers equated her with the Greek Rhea, consort of Kronos (Saturn) and mother of the Olympian gods.

27

"Which to approven° true, as I have told,   *prove*
   Vouchsafe, O goddesse, to thy presence call
   The rest which doe the world in being hold:
   As, times and seasons of the yeare that fall:
   Of all the which, demand in generall,
   Or judge thy selfe, by verdit° of thine eye,   *verdict*
   Whether to me they are not subject all."
      Nature did yeeld thereto; and by-and-by,°   *immediately*
Bade Order call them all, before her Majesty.

28

So, forth issewed the Seasons of the yeare;[7]
   First, lusty Spring, all dight in leaves of flowres
   That freshly budded and new bloosmes did beare
   (In which a thousand birds had built their bowres
   That sweetly sung, to call forth Paramours):
   And in his hand a javelin he did beare,
   And on his head (as fit for warlike stoures)°   *encounters*
   A guilt engraven morion° he did weare;   *helmet*
That as some did him love, so others did him feare.

29

Then came the jolly Sommer, being dight
   In a thin silken cassock° coloured greene,   *cloak*
   That was unlynéd all, to be more light:
   And on his head a girlond well beseene°   *ordered*
   He wore, from which as he had chrauftéd° been   *heated*
   The sweat did drop; and in his hand he bore
   A boawe and shaftes, as he in forrest greene
   Had hunted late the Libbard° or the Bore,   *leopard*
And now would bathe his limbes, with labor heated sore.

30

Then came the Autumne all in yellow clad,
   As though he joyéd in his plentious store,
   Laden with fruits that made him laugh, full glad
   That he had banisht hunger, which to-fore°   *formerly*
   Had by the belly oft him pinchéd sore.
   Upon his head a wreath that was enrold°   *enfolded*
   With eares of corne, of every sort he bore:
   And in his hand a sickle he did holde,
To reape the ripened fruits the which the earth had yold.°   *yielded*

7. The seasons here may owe something to *Metamorphoses* 2.25–30 and 15.199–213, but the procession in stanzas 28–46 has the Renaissance style as described by A. Fowler, *Triumphal Forms* (Cambridge, 1970).

31

Lastly, came Winter cloathed all in frize,°   *rough cloth*
  Chattering his teeth for cold that did him chill,
  Whil'st on his hoary beard his breath did freese;
  And the dull drops that from his purpled bill°   *nose*
  As from a limbeck° did adown distill.   *alembic*
  In his right hand a tippéd staffe he held,
  With which his feeble steps he stayéd still:°   *continually*
  For, he was faint with cold, and weak with eld;
That scarse his looséd limbes he hable was to weld.°   *move*

32

These, marching softly, thus in order went,
  And after them, the Monthes all riding came;[8]
  First, sturdy March with brows full sternly bent,
  And arméd strongly, rode upon a Ram,
  The same which over Hellespontus swam:
  Yet in his hand a spade he also hent,°   *grasped*
  And in a bag all sorts of seeds ysame,°   *together*
  Which on the earth he strowéd as he went,
And fild her womb with fruitfull hope of nourishment.

33

Next came fresh Aprill full of lustyhed,°   *vigor*
  And wanton as a Kid whose horne new buds:
  Upon a Bull[9] he rode, the same which led
  Europa floting through th'Argolick fluds:
  His hornes were gilden all with golden studs,
  And garnishéd with garlonds goodly dight
  Of all the fairest flowres and freshest buds
  Which th'earth brings forth, and wet he seemed in sight
With waves, through which he waded for his loves delight.

34

Then came faire May, the fayrest mayd on ground,
  Deckt all with dainties of her seasons pryde,
  And throwing flowres out of her lap around:
  Upon two brethrens shoulders she did ride,
  The twinnes of Leda;[1] which on eyther side
  Supported her like to their soveraine Queene.
  Lord! how all creatures laught, when her they spide,

8. In stanzas 32–43, Spenser uses Ovid's *Fasti* and *Metamorphoses* for many details. March leads because until 1753 the official year, in England, began on March 25 (date of the Annunciation to Mary), although like traditional almanacs and social custom, *The Shepheardes Calender* starts with January. As in many Books of Hours, the *Calender*'s illustrations include zodiacal signs appropriate for each month; so here, March's ram represents the sign Aries.
9. The constellation Taurus, here identified with the bull in whose shape Jove abducted Europa, bearing her over the Argolic (i.e., Greek) waves.
1. Castor and Pollux, the Gemini.

And leapt and daunc't as they had ravisht° beene!   *enraptured*
And Cupid selfe about her fluttred all in greene.

35

And after her, came jolly June, arrayd
   All in greene leaves, as he a Player were;[2]
   Yet in his time, he wrought° as well as playd,   *worked*
   That by his plough-yrons° mote right well appeare: *ploughshares*
   Upon a Crab[3] he rode, that him did beare
   With crooked crawling steps an uncouth pase,
   And backward yode,° as Bargemen wont to fare   *went*
   Bending their force contrary to their face,
Like that ungracious crew which faines demurest grace.[4]

36

Then came hot July boyling like to fire,
   That all his garments he had cast away:
   Upon a Lyon[5] raging yet with ire
   He boldly rode and made him to obay:
   It was the beast that whylome did forray
   The Nemaean forrest, till th'Amphytrionide
   Him slew, and with his hide did him array;
   Behinde his back a sithe,° and by his side   *scythe*
Under his belt he bore a sickle circling wide.

37

The sixt was August, being rich arrayd
   In garment all of gold downe to the ground:
   Yet rode he not, but led a lovely Mayd[6]
   Forth by the lilly hand, the which was cround
   With eares of corne, and full her hand was found;
   That was the righteous Virgin, which of old
   Lived here on earth, and plenty made abound;
   But, after Wrong was loved and Justice solde,
She left th'unrighteous world and was to heaven extold.°   *raised*

38

Next him, September marchéd eeke on foote;
   Yet was he heavy laden with the spoyle
   Of harvests riches, which he made his boot,°   *booty*
   And him enricht with bounty of the soyle:
   In his one hand, as fit for harvests toyle,

2. I.e., like an actor garbed as a forest spirit or a "savage" man.
3. I.e., Cancer.
4. I.e., like hypocritical courtiers whose fashion of leaving their lord's presence by walking respectfully
   backward hides their true feelings. Bargemen were London's taxidrivers, who as they rowed passengers up and down the Thames of course faced away from the direction in which they were
   going.
5. Leo, here identified with the Nemean lion slain by Hercules, whose reputed father was Amphitryon.
6. I.e., Virgo (Astraea, goddess of justice), who left earth in disgust at the corrupt violence of the
   iron (modern) age; see *Metamorphoses* 1.127–50.

He held a knife-hook; and in th'other hand
A paire of waights,[7] with which he did assoyle°   *determine*
Both more and lesse, where it in doubt did stand,
And equall gave to each as Justice duly scanned.°   *judged*

39

Then came October full of merry glee:
  For, yet his noule was totty of the must,[8]
  Which he was treading in the wine-fats see,[9]
  And of the joyous oyle, whose gentle gust°   *taste*
  Made him so frollick and so full of lust:
  Upon a dreadfull Scorpion[1] he did ride,
  The same which by Dianaes doom unjust
  Slew great Orion: and eeke by his side
He had his ploughing share, and coulter ready tyde.

40

Next was November, he full grosse and fat,
  As fed with lard, and that right well might seeme;
  For, he had been a fatting° hogs of late,   *fattening*
  That yet his browes with sweat, did reek and steem,
  And yet the season was full sharp and breem;°   *cold*
  In planting eeke he took no small delight:
  Whereon he rode, not easie was to deeme;
  For it a dreadfull Centaure[2] was in sight,
The seed of Saturne, and faire Nais, Chiron hight.

41

And after him, came next the chill December:
  Yet he through merry feasting which he made,
  And great bonfires, did not the cold remember;
  His Saviours birth his mind so much did glad:
  Upon a shaggy-bearded Goat[3] he rade,°   *rode*
  The same wherewith Dan Jove in tender yeares,
  They say, was nourisht by th'Idaean mayd;
  And in his hand a broad deepe boawle he beares;
Of which, he freely drinks an health to all his peeres.

42

Then came old January, wrappéd well
  In many weeds to keep the cold away;
  Yet did he quake and quiver like to quell,°   *perish*

7. I.e., scales, representing Libra.
8. I.e., his head was giddy from new wine.
9. I.e., the "sea" of the wine vats.
1. Representing Scorpio. Angry at the hunter Orion's boasts, Earth made a scorpion that killed him, but Diana placed him and the scorpion in the stars; others, whom Spenser here follows, said it was Diana herself who had sent the scorpion (see C. Estienne, *Dictionarum*, "Orion").
2. The centaur Chiron, son of Saturn and Philyra (a Naiad), was stellified as Sagittarius, the archer.
3. Amalthea nurtured the infant Jove with goat's milk on Mount Ida; the goat became the constellation Capricorn (cf. Comes 7.2).

And blowe his nayles to warme them if he may:
For, they were numbd with holding all the day
An hatchet keene, with which he felléd wood,
And from the trees did lop the needlesse spray:°   *branches*
Upon an huge great Earth-pot steane[4] he stood;
From whose wide mouth, there flowéd forth the Romane floud.

43

And lastly, came cold February, sitting
 In an old wagon, for he could not ride;
 Drawne of two fishes[5] for the season fitting,
 Which through the flood before did softly slyde
 And swim away: yet had he by his side
 His plough and harnesse fit to till the ground,
 And tooles to prune the trees, before the pride
 Of hasting Prime did make them burgein° round: *bud*
So past the twelve Months forth, and their dew places found.

44

And after these, there came the Day, and Night,
 Riding together both with equall pase,
 Th'one on a Palfrey blacke, the other white;
 But Night had covered her uncomely face
 With a blacke veile, and held in hand a mace,
 On top whereof the moon and stars were pight,°   *placed*
 And sleep and darknesse round about did trace:°   *walk*
 But Day did beare, upon his scepters hight,
The goodly Sun, encompast all with beamés bright.

45

Then came the Howres, faire daughters of high Jove,[6]
 And timely Night, the which were all endewed
 With wondrous beauty fit to kindle love;
 But they were Virgins all, and love eschewed,
 That might forslack° the charge to them foreshewed *neglect*
 By mighty Jove; who did them Porters make
 Of heavens gate (whence all the gods issued)
 Which they did dayly watch, and nightly wake°   *guard*
By even turnes, ne ever did their charge forsake.

46

And after all came Life, and lastly Death;
 Death with most grim and griesly visage seene,
 Yet is he nought but parting of the breath;
 Ne ought to see, but like a shade to weene,°   *conceive*

---

4. I.e., an earthen water jar, recalling the sign Aquarius, the water bearer; here it originates the river
Tiber.
5. The constellation Pisces.
6. Like Homer (*Iliad* 5.749) and Ovid (*Fasti* 1.125), Spenser has the Hours attend Heaven's gates;
Hesiod, though, says their mother was Themis (*Theogony* 900). Cf. *Epithalamion* 98–102.

Unbodiéd, unsouled, unheard, unseene.
But Life was like a faire young lusty boy,
Such as they faine Dan Cupid to have beene,
Full of delightfull health and lively joy,
Deckt all with flowres, and wings of gold fit to employ.

47

When these were past, thus gan the Titanesse;
    "Lo, mighty mother, now be judge and say,
    Whether in all thy creatures more or lesse
    Change doth not raign and beare the greatest sway:
    For, who sees not, that Time on all doth pray?°   *prey*
    But Times do change and move continually.
    So nothing here long standeth in one stay:
    Wherefore, this lower world who can deny
But to be subject still to Mutabilitie?"

48

Then thus gan Jove; "Right true it is, that these
    And all things else that under heaven dwell
    Are chaunged of Time, who doth them all disseise°   *deprive*
    Of being: But, who is it (to me tell)
    That Time himselfe doth move and still compell
    To keepe his course? Is not that namely wee[7]
    Which poure that vertue° from our heavenly cell,   *power*
    That moves them all, and makes them changéd be?
So them we gods doe rule, and in them also thee."

49

To whom, thus Mutability: "The things
    Which we see not how they are moved and swayd,
    Ye may attribute to your selves as Kings,
    And say they by your secret powre are made:
    But what we see not, who shall us perswade?
    But were they so, as ye them faine to be,
    Moved by your might, and ordred by your ayde;
    Yet what if I can prove, that even yee
Your selves are likewise changed, and subject unto mee?

50

"And first, concerning her that is the first,[8]
    Even you faire Cynthia, whom so much ye make
    Joves dearest darling, she was bred and nurst
    On Cynthus hill,[9] whence she her name did take:
    Then is she mortall borne, how-so ye crake;°   *brag*
    Besides, her face and countenance every day

7. I.e., only we.
8. In the Ptolemaic system, the moon's sphere is nearest to the earth.
9. Traditionally the birthplace of Diana and Apollo, on the island of Delos.

We changéd see, and sundry forms partake,
Now hornd, now round, now bright, now brown and gray:
So that 'as changefull as the Moone' men use to say.

51

"Next, Mercury, who though he lesse appeare
  To change his hew, and alwayes seeme as one;
  Yet, he his course doth altar every yeare,
  And is of late far out of order gone:[1]
  So Venus eeke, that goodly Paragone,°   *model of excellence*
  Though faire all night, yet is she darke all day;
  And Phoebus self, who lightsome is alone,
  Yet is he oft eclipséd by the way,
And fills the darkned world with terror and dismay.

52

"Now Mars that valiant man is changéd most:
  For, he some times so far runs out of square,
  That he his way doth seem quite to have lost,
  And cleane without° his usuall sphere to fare;   *beyond*
  That even these Star-gazers stonisht are
  At sight thereof, and damne their lying bookes:
  So likewise, grim Sir Saturne oft doth spare°   *restrain*
  His sterne aspect, and calme his crabbéd lookes:
So many turning cranks° these have, so many crookes.   *twists*

53

"But you Dan Jove, that only constant are,
  And King of all the rest, as ye do clame,
  Are you not subject eeke to this misfare?°   *deviation*
  Then let me aske you this withouten blame,
  Where were ye borne? some say in Crete by name,
  Others in Thebes, and others other-where;
  But wheresoever they comment° the same,   *invent*
  They all consent that ye begotten were,
And borne here in this world, ne other can appeare.

54

"Then are ye mortall borne, and thrall to me,
  Unlesse the kingdome of the sky yee make
  Immortall, and unchangeable to bee;
  Besides, that power and vertue which ye spake,
  That ye here worke, doth many changes take,
  And your owne natures change: for, each of you
  That vertue have, or° this, or that to make,   *either*

1. Astronomers of the time were finding that their observations did not support the celestial regularity
   assumed by older theory.

Is checkt and changéd from his nature trew,
By others opposition or obliquid view.[2]

55

"Besides, the sundry motions of your Spheares,
    So sundry waies and fashions as clerkes° faine,   *learned men*
    Some in short space, and some in longer yeares;
    What is the same but alteration plaine?
    Onely the starrie skie doth still remaine:
    Yet do the Starres and Signes therein still move,
    And even it self is moved, as wizards saine.[3]
    But all that moveth, doth mutation love:
Therefore both you and them to me I subject prove.

56

"Then since within this wide great Universe
    Nothing doth firme and permanent appeare,
    But all things tost and turnéd by transverse:[4]
    What then should let,° but I aloft should reare   *hinder*
    My Trophee, and from all, the triumph beare?
    Now judge then (O thou greatest goddesse trew!)
    According as thy selfe doest see and heare,
    And unto me addoom that[5] is my dew;
That is the rule of all, all being ruled by you."

57

So having ended, silence long ensewed,
    Ne Nature to or fro[6] spake for a space,
    But with firme eyes affixt, the ground still viewed.
    Meane while, all creatures, looking in her face,
    Expecting° th'end of this so doubtfull case,   *awaiting*
    Did hang in long suspence what would ensew,
    To whether side should fall the soveraigne place:
    At length, she looking up with chearefull view,
The silence brake, and gave her doome in speeches° few.   *phrases*

58

"I well consider all that ye have sayd,[7]
    And find that all things steadfastnes doe hate
    And changéd be: yet being rightly wayd°   *weighed*

---

2. I.e., each planet's "influence" is counteracted and qualified by the relative position of other planets.
3. I.e., as wise men say, even the sphere of the "fixed stars" moves.
4. I.e., haphazardly.
5. I.e., adjudge that which.
6. I.e., for or against.
7. Nature acknowledges cosmic change, but not as a blind "ever-whirling wheele" (vi.1); her words recall, rather, the Garden of Adonis (see III.vi) and the Neoplatonic view that change is a "dilation" or expansion by which being providentially fulfills itself (cf. Plotinus, *Enneads* 3.7.4). Boethius says that the divine thought which directs all being is properly called Providence, but that when it is "referred to things that it moves and regulates, then by men in ancient times it was called destiny [i.e., fate]" (4. Prose 6).

They are not changéd from their first estate;
But by their change their being doe dilate:°   extend
And turning to themselves at length againe,
Doe worke their owne perfection so by fate:
Then over them Change doth not rule and raigne;
But they raigne over change, and doe their states maintaine.

59

"Cease therefore daughter further to aspire,
And thee content thus to be ruled by me:
For thy decay° thou seekst by thy desire;   ruin
But time shall come that all shall changéd bee,
And from thenceforth, none no more change shall see."
So was the Titaness put downe and whist,°   silenced
And Jove confirmed in his imperiall see.°   throne
Then was that whole assembly quite dismist,
And Natur's selfe did vanish, whither no man wist.°   knew

The VIII. Canto, unperfite.°   unfinished

1

When I bethinke me on that speech whyleare,°   earlier
Of Mutability, and well it way:°   consider
Me seemes, that though she all unworthy were
Of the Heav'ns Rule; yet very sooth to say,
In all things else she beares the greatest sway.
Which makes me loath this state of life so tickle,°   uncertain
And love of things so vaine to cast away;
Whose flowring pride, so fading and so fickle,
Short Time shall soon cut down with his consuming sickle.

2

Then gin I thinke on that which Nature sayd,
Of that same time when no more Change shall be,
But stedfast rest of all things firmely stayd
Upon the pillours of Eternity,
That is contrayr to Mutabilitie:
For, all that moveth, doth in Change delight:
But thence-forth all shall rest eternally
With Him that is the God of Sabbaoth hight:[1]
O that great Sabbaoth God, graunt me that Sabaoths sight.[2]

1. I.e., called the Lord of Hosts.
2. I.e., the sight of that day of eternal rest. Spenser probably intended the wordplay implicit in a
spelling that combines "sabaoth" (hosts) and "sabbath" (rest); puns on "sabbath" were not unusual
because some read Elizabeth's name, incorrectly, as Hebrew for "God's rest." In "Our New Poet"
(Essential Articles for the Study of Edmund Spenser [Hamden, 1972]), A. C. Hamilton finds a
reference to that etymology in this line. Spenser's pun would reconcile action and contemplation:
the poet imagines a peace and closure that The Faerie Queene gestures at but never reaches, even
as the reference to "pillours" points past Rome, London, and even Gloriana's Cleopolis, to yet

Editors' Note

On the evidence of his "Letter to Raleigh," Spenser at one time intended *The Faerie Queene* to be a long epic poem centered on the figure of Arthur "before he was king"; its twelve books would have corresponded to "the twelve private morall vertues, as Aristotle hath devised." Spenser further envisioned writing a sequel that would "frame the other part of polliticke vertues in [Arthur's] person, after that hee came to be king." Perhaps, suggests Hieatt (1988), he hoped to follow Malory's *Morte d'Arthur* by having Arthur conquer Rome, a useful fiction on which to base a Protestant epic. That these ambitions were not realized is scarcely surprising; nor does that fact significantly reduce Spenser's achievement. Indeed, many readers have felt that the last stanzas of the fragmentary *Cantos of Mutabilitie* bring the work to as good a resting place as one could desire: there is nothing conclusive, no final tidying of the plot or issues, but rather a prayer, made while the poet is still on the mutable and turbulent earth, for a "sight" that would reconcile his private and public worlds and at last legitimate a repose denied the poem's characters and their creator.

Spenser probably began work on *The Faerie Queene* in 1579 or early 1580. The earliest known allusion to the poem occurs in a letter dated April 2, 1580, from Spenser to his Cambridge associate and friend Gabriel Harvey: "Now, my *Dreames*, and *dying Pellicane*, being fully finished," he writes, "I wil in hande forthwith with my *Faery Queene*, whyche, I praye you hartily send me with al expedition: and your friendly Letters, and long expected Judgement wythal, whyche let not be shorte, but in all pointes suche, as you ordinarilye use, and I extraordinarily desire." Appointed secretary to Lord Grey, Spenser departed for Ireland in the fall of that year; for the next eight years, while he improved his circumstances (acquiring the estate of Kilcolman by 1588 or early 1589), the poem developed under his hand. In *A Discourse of Civil Life* (1606), his fellow civil servant Lodowick Bryskett describes a social gathering that took place near Dublin, perhaps in 1582: invited to speak on how "vertues are to be distinguished from vices," he says, Spenser declined, explaining that he had already

> well entred into . . . a work tending to the same effect, which is in *heroicall verse* under the title of a *Faerie Queene* to represent all the moral vertues, assigning to every vertue a Knight to be the patron and defender of the same, in whose actions and feates of armes and chivalry the operations of that vertue whereof he is the protector, are to be expressed, and the vices and unruly appetites that oppose themselves against the same, to be beaten down and overcome.

That portions of this work were circulating in manuscript during the 1580s is certain, for Abraham Fraunce's *Arcadian Rhetorike*, published in 1588, quotes a stanza (II.iv.35) to exemplify "conceipted kindes of verses."

The first three books of *The Faerie Queene* were registered with the Stationers' Company on December 1, 1589, and published early in the following year, together with a dedication to the queen, an explanatory "Letter to Raleigh," and a number of sonnets addressed to influential persons. Returning to Ireland

---

greater glory in the New Jerusalem. This final response to Mutability also moves beyond Nature's judgment; as Boethius's prayer to an unmoved mover puts it, "In so much is the thing more free from fate, as it holds the more closely to the center of things [i.e., to God]; and if the thing cleaves to the steadfastness of the thought of God, it is free from motion, and overcomes the necessity of fate" (4.Pr.6). It is fitting that the turn to eternity comes in the eighth canto, for in traditional number symbolism the number eight often signified the resurrection that will succeed mortal time.

in early 1591 (as it appears), Spenser once more set to work on the poem: sonnet 80 of *Amoretti* indicates that he had completed three more books of his epic before his marriage to Elizabeth Boyle in the summer of 1594. Early in 1596, Books I–VI were published in London with an embellished dedication to Elizabeth I but without the "Letter" and most of the sonnets. For this edition, the three earlier books underwent some changes, chiefly of punctuation and spelling, and Spenser altered the end of Book III to fit the narrative of Book IV. There is some evidence that he was present during the printing of at least Books IV–VI.[1] As for the *Cantos of Mutabilitie* (first printed in the 1609 edition), there is little reason to doubt that Spenser intended them to be part of *The Faerie Queene*. The date of their composition is unknown, but their substance and tone, together with what may be allusions to astronomical events in April 1595 (Meyer 1983), suggest that they were written during the poet's last years. True, Spenser presumably did not compose *The Faerie Queene* by starting with Book I and working on through to the *Cantos of Mutabilitie*: indeed (if we may rely on his correspondence with Gabriel Harvey), his early aim to "emulate" and even "overgo" Ariosto's *Orlando Furioso* has led to speculation that passages in Books III and IV were composed at a very early stage in the poem's development.

Although the "Letter to Raleigh" is not an altogether reliable guide to the poet's "whole intention," it remains a useful starting point for discussing the poem. Of first importance is Spenser's claim that the work's "generall end" is "to fashion a gentleman or noble person in vertuous and gentle [i.e., noble, 'liberal'] discipline." In one sense, "to fashion" means "to form, frame, make": Spenser "fashions" his poem and its persons, notably Prince Arthur, a "gentleman" in whom is "sette forth magnificence in particular." But the term also means "to present the form of, to represent": Spenser represents in Arthur—and collectively in other knights whose disparate attributes are gathered in him—an ideal nobility combining chivalric and ethical virtues. Finally, in accord with Spenser's conviction (shared with Sir Philip Sidney) that "doctrine by ensample" is more persuasive and hence "profitable" than "good discipline delivered plainly in way of precepts," the pleasing fictions of *The Faerie Queene* will effectively "fashion" readers into "vertuous and gentle" people. Just as the lover in *Amoretti* 8 says to his beautiful lady, "You frame my thoughts and fashion me within," Spenser apparently hoped his poem might exert a shaping power on the reader. *The Faerie Queene* is, among other things, a "courtesy-book" like Castiglione's *Courtier*, which debates and describes the qualities that distinguish "gentle" men and women; but it is a courtesy-book made more effective by imaginatively compelling fictions. The paradox in which Spenser found himself, however, was that although his pedagogical aims included fashioning the reader into a morally informed and astute "gentleman," the reader he most hoped to please was a lady—Queen Elizabeth. Perhaps he meant the phrase "noble person" to leave a little room for her and also for noblewomen like Mary Sidney, countess of Pembroke.

The Faerie Queene's "generall end" is thus multiple: to make a poem, to imagine a hero, and to persuade and move (even, perhaps, to remake) his society's leadership. It is not clear, though, to what degree Spenser maintained that hope. Some (e.g., O'Connell 1977, Cain 1978, Miller 1979, and Bernard 1989) have plausibly described his growing disillusion with epic poetry's effectiveness and with England's receptivity to "fashioning" in any sense beyond the most frivolous; the pastoral delights and lyric pipings of Book VI, particularly, may show Spenser's longing to retreat into a private world (although how—

1. F. B. Evans, "The Printing of Spenser's *Faerie Queene* in 1596," *SB* 18 (1965): 49–67.

and even whether—Tudor England conceived of the difference between public and private realms is itself open to debate). Yet he continued to write; indeed, it is possible that his gloom concerning his role has been exaggerated, or at least read with too much narrative neatness: his early *Shepheardes Calender* is no tissue of youthful illusions, after all, and even the late Book VI and self-pitying *Prothalamion* may include bids for the earl of Essex's further attention and support (cf. Cain 1978, 163; and P. Cheney 1987). Whether Spenser's career would have prospered after Essex's disastrous rebellion in 1601 is another matter, and in 1603 the new monarch, James I, might well have rejected (or arrested) the politically imprudent poet who had turned the king's mother, Mary Stuart, into the vile Duessa.

Spenser acknowledges in the "Letter" that his "Methode" of "continued Allegory, or darke conceit . . . coloured with an historicall fiction" would displease or confuse some readers, and in fact many of his stricter contemporaries spoke scornfully of fiction as a time-wasting, trivial, and even illicit distraction from truth, work, and moral seriousness. Yet Spenser also knows that many readers will reject whatever "is not delightfull and pleasing." Thus the "Methode" of a "Poet historical" is also that of an artist who can begin *in medias res* and is free to feign and embroider.[2] As a "Poet historical," Spenser claims to have followed both antique precedent and the Italian romantic epic. To discuss these models separately is, admittedly, to misrepresent them, for not only are the *Aeneid* and *Orlando Furioso* both epics, they are specifically dynastic epics, celebrating, if with different tonalities and hints of disbelief or even dissent, the lineage and destiny of the poet's tribe and its ruling family. Furthermore, Spenser seems to have accepted the tradition that, on the one hand, read epic poetry allegorically and, on the other, read classical myths as fables allegorizing or embroidering the lives of once living figures. For centuries many had taken the *Aeneid* as an allegory of the human soul's pilgrimage to God, and in the commentary he provided for his translation of the *Orlando Furioso*, Sir John Harington carefully explained what Ariosto had "meant" by his poem.[3] In Spenser's world, then, epic, romance, and allegory could merge with considerable ease. True, Spenser's particular mixture of personifications like Despair and Disdain into allegorical epic and romance makes for a poem quite unlike any of the works cited by the "Letter." Yet knowing something about allegorical and epic traditions will help the reader more fully appreciate their combination in Spenser's poem.

A short definition of allegory might be "a metaphor that continues through a whole text"; the resulting narrative will usually support and reveal other "levels" of meaning (to adopt for the moment a perhaps misleading spatial metaphor). Yet good allegory is not merely didactic or formulaic; it is not literary algebra, a matter of solving equations and finding substitutions so as to locate a political or theological point, even when the topic is politics or theology. At its best, allegory is a resonant and pleasurable way of saying what cannot otherwise be said so well. Beginning readers of Spenser might remember the celebrated reply of one Hollywood director who was asked to identify a film's "message": "When I send a message," he is supposed to have said, "I use Western Union." Spenser had convictions to sustain and arguments to make, but they are implicit in the poetry's effect, not reducible to moral tags discoverable by decoding.

2. In the Renaissance "history was not yet sharply distinguished from "story," so that "historical" could then mean "telling a narrative"; but Spenser's age also assumed that the "stories" by Homer, Virgil, Ariosto, and of course Tasso were based to some extent on real events or people.
3. To read the *Aeneid* as quasi-Christian allegory goes back at least to Augustine; see Fichter 1982, who places Ariosto, Tasso, and Spenser in this line of allegorized dynastic epic.

As early as classical times many had claimed that incredible or even offensive stories about the gods and heroes must conceal moral and cosmological truths hidden by poets under the veil of fable. This conviction was still strong in Elizabethan England, although some continued to hold that such myths were the work of pagan superstition at best and of demons at worst. For instance, when referring in his *Convivio* to Ovid's account of Orpheus, Dante distinguishes between a literal sense, "which is a truth hidden under a beautiful letter," and an allegorical sense, "which is a truth hidden under a beautiful fiction." By Spenser's day a large body of mythographical scholarship had developed, changing with the times (medieval scholars might see a theological allegory where Renaissance ones would see an ethical or physical one) but still claiming that ancient fictions hide useful truths not in conflict with Christianity. Among works especially influential in this regard were Giovanni Boccaccio's *De Genealogia Deorum* (fourteenth century) and Natalis Comes's *Mythologiae* (sixteenth century); Spenser knew both. Such books did much to link certain figures to particular vices, virtues, and even natural forces, with the result that a poet could, with the mere mention of a name, summon up for the informed reader a set of associations: thus Hercules epitomized heroic valor and persuasive eloquence; Marsyas, rash presumption; Midas, rashness and greed; Adonis, the seasonal energy of natural growth. Yet mythographers also allowed for multiple significance: noble Hercules, for example, betrayed himself with drink and passion; and the same hounds who ate their master Acteon after Diana turned him into a stag were allegorized sometimes as a profligate's parasites and sometimes as agents of divine ecstasy. In painting and sculpture, in the pageants and entertainments of court and town, as well as in emblem books like those by Alciati and Geoffrey Whitney, the allegorizing of classical mythology was everywhere in evidence, designed to appeal to a sophisticated reader's or viewer's awareness of both tradition and context.

Another allegorical tradition derived from centuries of Christian biblical commentary (sometimes indebted, directly or indirectly, to Jewish scholarship). As early as the third century, Origen had found literal, moral, and mystical meanings in the Bible; by medieval times there had developed the fourfold method of scriptural interpretation (described by Dante in the "Letter to Can Grande") in which a literal or historical sense was to be distinguished from a spiritual sense comprising allegorical, moral, and anagogical meanings. Especially after the Reformation, many commentators preferred to stress the historical or literal sense; but allegorizing did not cease, if only because certain parts of scripture such as the Song of Solomon were more theologically useful if read "spiritually," because some of the Bible is without doubt allegorical (e.g., Revelation), and because even Protestants continued to read passages in the Old Testament typologically—that is, as mystically foreshadowing events in the life of Christ and his Church. Book I of *The Faerie Queene*, especially, shows how much Spenser was affected by these methods, even if strictly speaking St. George and Arthur, living later than Jesus, cannot be "types" of Christ in the sense that David and Samson were. Spenser's willingness to find allegory in the Bible, moreover, would have been encouraged (as King 1990 has most fully shown) by earlier Reformation poets and dramatists who read much of it, particularly Daniel and Revelation, as anti-Catholic prophecy.

It is hazardous, of course, to read secular literature with the methods of biblical exegesis, and the problem becomes more complex when a poem is, like *The Faerie Queene*, explicitly described by its author as an allegory. Since the poem evidently contains a good deal of historical, topical, moral, and religious allusion, it is tempting to search for consistent and continuous allegorical narratives, and then to wrest a significance from each character and episode that would fit such narratives. A difficulty with this approach is that it can lead to an exaggeration of one aspect of the allegory: topical political allegory, perhaps, or, more insidiously, moral allegory. As Rosamond Tuve has said, "Of all authors, Spenser is done the most harm by translating all 'allegories' into 'moralizations' ";[4] this is especially the case when "moralizations" assume a simple moralism or idealism on the author's part (one effect of recent shifts in Spenser criticism is a greater willingness to find him tough-minded and even Machiavellian in his understanding of how the world works and perhaps must work). Spenser's names seem at first to encourage "moralizations." The giant Orgoglio, for instance, is simply "pride" in Italian; translated into English, he could well appear in a personification allegory like Prudentius's late classical Psychomachia or the late medieval morality play Everyman. Yet to call pride an empty giant, give him a genealogy, make him appear at a certain time and place, and surround him by similes and metaphors is to say something complicated about pride and how we give birth to it.[5]

A sensible approach to The Faerie Queene, then, will not force or reduce the poem's meaning, but will rather allow for the allegory's flexibility and discontinuity. It will take account of the immediate poetic context (and, when possible, the poem's larger cultural situation) and will tolerate seeming—or even real—inconsistency. For example, a humbly amicable lion comes to the aid of the virtuous heroine Una and for a time acts as her protector, perhaps recalling (among other possibilities) the lion that helps bear England's royal coat of arms. But in the House of Pride, Anger rides a lion. How do we tell good lions from bad ones? Sometimes Spenser makes it easy, whether through his narrator's explicit comment, an eventual naming of an unidentified figure, or a developing context; at other times we have to think and feel our way to a more complex judgment. And sometimes we may realize that our difficulty in deciding is part of Spenser's point about his fallen and deceptive world. Thus we may ask why Una's lion eventually comes to grief. Is it, too, subject to gusts of anger that make it vulnerable to its killer's more conscious and strategic wrath? Perhaps. And is there not, on the other hand, something a little heroic about an Anger, deadly sin though it is, that rides so kingly a beast as a lion? To think hard about these two lions is to see certainties fade into a suspicion that Spenser is not as interested in dividing figures into the good and the bad as he is in exploring what he takes to be the nature of things. After some reflection, most of us would probably rather consort with Una than with Anger, but the hero St. George finds himself staring at the latter precisely because he has been unable to recognize the former's unstained fidelity. Nor is he unique, Spenser seems to imply: we all can misunderstand what we experience.

It is precisely this sense of common human confusion that should console the beginning reader of Spenser if he or she becomes puzzled. This is because The Faerie Queene, as a number of its admirers have suggested, is not an illustration of an a priori set of truths that the allegory encodes and conceals and which we are invited to figure out as we read.[6] Its world is more polyvalent

4. Rosemond Tuve, Allegorical Imagery (Princeton, 1966) 333.
5. Spenserians regularly distinguish Spenser's amalgam of personification, exemplum, extended metaphor, walking puns, symbolic landscape, overtone, topicality, and so forth from allegories like Orwell's Animal Farm or Bunyan's Pilgrim's Progress. But even those live as literature because their personifications do more than walk around as promoted nouns or political caricature; see Van Dyke 1985.
6. "The virtues do not define the books which they name or the knights by whom they are defended; the books and the actions of the knights define the virtues, by working them out through the narrative in human terms" (Kathleen Williams, Spenser's Faerie Queene: The World of Glass [London, 1966] xix). Cf. MacCaffrey 1976, part 1.

and opaque than that; in this fairyland, heroes and villains are often somehow related to each other, and even perverted magicians like Archimago and Busirane exert an art that is not the opposite of Spenser's own but a disturbing parody of it. The epic, then, shows the difficulty of seeing, reading, and identifying, of figuring out where and who we are and what we should be doing; it is as much about epistemology as it is about morality, politics, and cosmology.[7] For example, St. George's problem is not that he wants to be bad; his difficulty is that over and over he misreads the world. Moreover, if we read with attention and delight we will often err right along with him. We go right into the Wood of Error with St. George and Una, and it may be that none of us is out of the woods yet. It is this sense of fertile error (fertile because error is what generates the story), this sense of being lost in an endless forest of shifting symbols that we must, but cannot quite, comprehend, that makes it hard for a generous reader harshly to condemn the protagonists for their mistakes. In sum, any reader who is initially confused can remember, first, that Spenser will probably clarify matters a few lines or stanzas later, and, second, that the main character is probably baffled or mistaken too. Offering the beginning reader the popular and curiously postmodern advice to "go with the flow" (the flow of signifiers, the flow of the narrative, the flow of the verse) may itself be to go too far; but there are worse ways of reading Spenser's allegory.

If his allegory presents enjoyable challenges to the reader, not least the challenge to relish ambiguity and slippery language, Spenser's relation to earlier heroic poetry is no less complex. In general terms, the poem is a romantic epic; more precisely, it is a heroic poem showing affinities with classical epic and fruitfully to be associated also with medieval romance, pilgrimage allegory, the Italian epic romances of the fifteenth and sixteenth centuries, and symbolic patterns of heroic imagery in the Bible.[8] The debt to classical epic is particularly obvious: *The Faerie Queene*'s thrust, after an appropriate invocation, "into the middest" of a twelve-part narrative to be centered (says the "Letter") on a magnificently virtuous and active hero, clearly derives from the design of the *Aeneid*. Arthur's role, especially in Book I, as minister of divine grace (to say nothing of the "glory" explicitly associated with the "Faery Queene") shows a Christian emphasis; yet the heroes of classical epic are likewise linked with a divine power and knowledge beyond ordinary mortal reach. Again, in so far as *The Faerie Queene* reminds a nation of its ancient traditions and points the way to an even more glorious future, the poem recalls the *Aeneid*. And not of least importance, especially in Book III, Spenser shows a poetic commitment (whatever his own doubts) to the tradition, so pleasing to Tudor royalty, that his nation was founded by Trojan heroes and had a political and religious claim to its share of Rome's once "universal" empire.

"Fierce warres and faithfull loves shall moralize my song," Spenser promises at the outset (echoing the start of *Orlando Furioso*): the world of *The Faerie Queene* is also that of the medieval romance that Ariosto too evokes, one in which knightly adventures, love in many forms, and every kind of marvel abound. Each book may also show the influence of other works and genres: thus the imagery of Book I draws heavily on the Bible and on medieval or Renaissance pilgrimage allegories like those of Deguileville, Hawes, Cartigny, and Bateman; the hero of Book II particularly recalls the classical Ulysses and

---

7. "Every Book of *The Faerie Queene* is a perceptual experience and in some way treats human perception" (Anderson 1976, 183).

8. To be sure, whether quietly borrowing from his "sources" or more openly alluding to famous texts, Spenser shows such independence that William Nelson calls him "almost perverse in the way he turns his borrowed matter upside down." See *The Poetry of Edmund Spenser* (New York, 1963) 142.

Hercules; and with its brigands, foundlings, and recognition scenes, Book VI owes something to the newly fashionable Alexandrian romance. Indeed, Spenser is adroit at folding genres into each other so as to achieve startling effects and perhaps comment on the social or political "worlds" the genres imply. Note, for example, the remarkable mixture of Chaucerian fabliau and Ovidian seduction at the house of Malbecco (III.x), or the subtle wit of making the courtier Sir Calidore don pastoral shepherd's weeds to conceal his epic chivalric armor (VI.xi). Nevertheless, the poem's landscape is most often one in which knights, ladies, and magicians move against a background of forests, caverns, enchanted trees, giants, strange waters, gardens, castles, and dragons: the appropriate environment, in fact, for a "historye of king Arthure." The narrative pattern is usually that of a knightly quest traced through a series of arduous encounters, dangers, and sometimes apparent defeat, to glorious if sometimes qualified or temporary victory.

As the "Letter" suggests, Spenser was also considerably influenced by the epic romance as it was developed in the Italian Renaissance, particularly by Ariosto and Tasso. Several characters and a number of episodes in *The Faerie Queene* derive from *Orlando Furioso*, and Spenser adopts Ariosto's technique by which several stories proceed at once, interlaced by a single narrative voice (a voice shimmering with skeptical irony in Ariosto's case, although the earnestness of Spenser's own narrator has doubtless been exaggerated).[9] Spenser's debt to Tasso is of another sort: *Gerusalemme Liberata*'s account of how God's champions delivered the beleaguered Holy City must have appealed to Spenser as both Christian and allegorist, and he must have sympathized also with Tasso's view of love as a noble habit of the will, apt to inform and rouse the spirit of heroic aspiration in both men and women. Spenser's affinities with Tasso, in fact, point to a heroic text that for both poets constituted an influence more telling than any other: the Bible. For those who read typologically, the epic quest and travail of Moses prefigured the struggle of Christ, through whose love mortals might see at last the shining New Jerusalem described in Revelation.[1] The gardens and wildernesses, salt seas and crystal streams, heroes and monsters of romance, after all, parallel the symbolic patterns of scripture: Christ is the archetypal liberator of captives and slayer of dragons.

For Spenser, many of these "heroic" strands are collected in the figure of Queen Elizabeth, unnamed in *The Faerie Queene* but sometimes invoked, and figured forth in many of the poem's characters. As a Tudor, she represents a British "race" (we would say nation or tribe) that included her purported ancestor, Arthur; as leader of the English "race" that supplanted the Britons, and as governor of the English Church, she furthers the work of St. George, England's patron saint, by protecting the Gospel against its serpentine foes. Symbolically, to serve the "Faery Queene," whatever doubts or advice the poetry may also subtly indicate concerning the actual government of England, is to proceed out of darkness into light, to fight chaotic disorder and espouse ordered harmony, to escape bondage and enjoy liberty, and—not least—to shine with glory. Had not the queen restored Protestantism and peace to England? And did she not stand between England and Spanish or papal tyranny? So many thought, and thus it is no wonder that *The Faerie Queene*, especially in the early books, can

9. See the essay by Nelson excerpted on pp. 813–22 of this edition. Noting the poem's "undercurrent of innuendos, incongruities, and surprises" and Spenser's gift for hyperbole, grotesque metaphors, and "deadpan understatement," Leonard (1981, 134, 167) calls *The Faerie Queene* "the great comic allegory of the English Renaissance"; and Esolen 1987 suggests that the poem's irony is sometimes meant not to support or subvert an argument but simply to give pleasure.

1. They also parallel, says Demaray 1991, St. George's eastward movement from Error (the serpent Spenser associates with the mud of Egypt's Nile); Spenser thus includes Exodus in a pattern of typological references that takes in Genesis and Revelation.

be read as the poetry of praise (cf. Cain 1978), a major text in the cult that Elizabeth certainly promoted but did not entirely invent. More recently, to be sure, some readers have heard hints of admonishment and even subversion in The Faerie Queene: Spenser's verse seems to respond to tensions between monarchy and aristocracy, to gender issues (many, including perhaps Spenser, would have preferred a male ruler), and to Elizabeth's vaunted virginity, which left England without an heir to stabilize the succession. Gloriana remains the poem's perhaps necessarily elusive heroine, but some (not everyone) would disagree that Spenser was a "pen-pusher" for the Tudor government (Shepherd 1989) or that Arthur's search for her serves "Spenser's complicity with hegemonic powers" (Mueller 1991). Even in the early books, says Anderson 1982, the queen's "bright image" is "complexly shaded" by the irony and ambiguity of Spenser's language. Whatever his repellent harshness toward Ireland in Book V, furthermore, it is not clear that he liked his leaders' Irish policy; and if his fairyland is "a dream of empire" (Murrin 1980), his response to colonial adventuring can be as much anxious as enthusiastic (Read 1990). In other words, The Faerie Queene's relations to court and politics, to power, to the search for patronage, to women, to America, and to church government, are sufficiently complex to show that its often lovely but still vulnerable world is far from serene, subject not only to infestations of giants and monsters but to debate and indecision. Even his heroes, for at least some readers, are not so much exemplars of their respective virtues as they are illustrations of those virtues' limitations or (in the case of St. George) of our human inadequacy.

Structure   As for the structure of *The Faerie Queene*, opinion remains divided over the role assigned to Arthur and over the "Letter"'s allusion to "the twelve private morall vertues, as Aristotle hath devised." Few critics now try to reconcile the poem as we have it to those portions of the "Letter" that deal with the epic's structure; nor, recently, have many shown a perhaps anachronistic desire to find in literary texts the unity so valued by the last few centuries; if Miller (1988) thinks its allegory "organized with reference to the anticipated-but-deferred wholeness," the same critic sees "an internalized iconoclasm that makes the poetry a perpetually self-displacing mode of discourse" (4, 12). Some may still suppose that Spenser planned to make Book XII (or XXIV!) in some sense match and balance Book I and its vision on the Hill of Contemplation. Even those who agree that the romance narrative is inescapable (Parker 1979), that the poem's work of signifying is endless (Goldberg 1981), or that Spenser, knowing that "the final poem is God's," finds pleasure not in stability but in "polyglossal discourse and invention" (Steppat 1990, 324) can nevertheless be tempted to imagine a concluding reunion at Gloriana's court, maybe after some triumph of a matured Arthur. Perhaps such a reunion would have been symbolically linked with that entrance "through the gates into the city" promised by the concluding verses of Revelation. But all this is conjectural. In the meantime, thoughts on what might constitute the poem's structure have varied radically, as witness, e.g., Horton (1978) on the arrangement of virtues, Nohrnberg (1976) on an internal system of analogies, and Alastair Fowler on numerical patterns.[2] Even if Books I–VI incorporate or sustain some larger pattern, though, Spenser did not construct every book on the same plan, although in at least five books the quest of a particular knight is central in the narrative, and although more often than not Prince Arthur performs a rescue in the eighth canto. The development of Books I and II is linear, keyed to the progress of a single hero; that of Books III and IV, in contrast, unfolds spatially from the myth of Venus and Adonis. In Faerie Queene V and VI, forward narrative movement again

2. *Spenser and the Numbers of Time* (London, 1964).

" 'Tis the good

reader that

makes the

good book."

-Ralph Waldo
Emerson

Come tell me, what was sayd of mee:
And I will send more after thee.

IMMERITO.[3]

["E.K."]   *PASTORAL - Rep. of*
Poet who is not
[Dedicatory Epistle to *The Shepheardes Calender*] *properly*
honoured.

To the most excellent and learned both orator and poete, MAYSTER GA-
BRIELL HARVEY,[1] his verie special and singular good frend E. K. com-
mendeth the good lyking of this his labour, and the patronage of the new
Poete.

Uncouthe unkiste, sayde the olde famous Poete Chaucer:[2] whom for his
excellencie and wonderfull skil in making, his scholler Lidgate, a worthy
scholler of so excellent a maister, calleth the Loadestarre of our Language:[3]
and whom our Colin clout in his Aeglogue[4] calleth Tityrus the God of
shepheards, comparing hym to the worthines of the Roman Tityrus Virgile.
Which proverbe, myne owne good friend Ma. Harvey, as in that good old
Poete it served well Pandares purpose, for the bolstering of his baudy bro-
cage,[5] so very well taketh place in this our new Poete, who for that he is
uncouthe (as said Chaucer) is unkist, and unknown to most men, is regarded
but of few. But I dout not, so soone as his name shall come into the
knowledg of men, and his worthines be sounded in the tromp of fame, but
that he shall be not onely kiste, but also beloved of all, embraced of the
most, and wondred at of the best. No lesse I thinke, deserveth his wittinesse[6]
in devising, his pithinesse in uttering, his complaints of love so lovely, his
discourses of pleasure so pleasantly, his pastorall rudenesse,[7] his morall
wisenesse, his dewe observing of Decorum[8] everye where, in personages,
in seasons, in matter, in speach, and generally in al seemely simplycitie
of handeling his matter, and framing his words: the which of many thinges
which in him be straunge, I know will seeme the straungest, the words
them selves being so auncient, the knitting of them so short and intricate,
and the whole Periode and compasse of speache so delightsome for the

---

3. I.e., "The undeserving one."
1. Gabriel Harvey (c. 1545–1630), temperamentally disputatious, but an able rhetorician, was a
   Fellow of Pembroke Hall; he became Spenser's friend at Cambridge. The "Spenser-Harvey correspondence," published in 1580, throws light on Spenser's early interest in quantitative versification in English, and gives some indication of his literary aspirations. On Harvey see Stern 1990E.
   The identity of "E.K." has not been definitively established; probably dedicatory epistle and an
   introductory note (omitted here) on "the generall argument of the whole booke," as well as the
   "glosses" to the several eclogues, reflect a collaborative undertaking by Spenser and Harvey. See
   Heninger 1990E, Schleiner 1990, and Waldman 1991.
2. Cf. Chaucer, *Troilus and Criseyde* 1.809; "Unknowe, unkist, and lost, that is unsought."
3. John Lydgate (c. 1370–c. 1451), in his long didactic poem *The Fall of Princes* 252.
4. I.e., eclogue (from Greek, "selection"), in this context signifying a formal pastoral poem in the
   classical tradition. The spelling adopted by E.K. reflects a mistaken etymology.
5. Pandering.
6. Intelligence, skill.
7. I.e., his deliberately unpolished rustic style.
8. I.e., his concern for what is fitting and proper in this pastoral context.

roundnesse, and so grave for the straungenesse. And firste of the wordes to speake, I graunt they be something hard, and of most men unused, yet both English, and also used of most excellent Authors and most famous Poetes. In whom whenas this our Poet hath bene much traveiled and throughly redd,[9] how could it be, (as that worthy Oratour[1] sayde) but that walking in the sonne although for other cause he walked, yet needes he mought be sunburnt; and having the sound of those auncient Poetes still ringing in his eares, he mought needes in singing hit out some of theyr tunes. But whether he useth them by such casualtye[2] and custome, or of set purpose and choyse, as thinking them fittest for such rusticall rudenesse of shepheards, eyther for that theyr rough sounde would make his rymes more ragged and rustical, or els because such olde and obsolete wordes are most used of country folke, sure I think, and think I think not amisse, that they bring great grace and, as one would say, auctoritie to the verse. For albe amongst many other faultes it specially be objected of Valla against Livie, and of other against Saluste,[3] that with over much studie they affect antiquitie, as coveting thereby credence and honor of elder yeeres, yet I am of opinion, and eke the best learned are of the lyke, that those auncient solemne wordes are a great ornament both in the one and in the other; the one labouring to set forth in hys worke an eternall image of antiquitie, and the other carefully discoursing matters of gravitie and importaunce. For if my memory fayle not, Tullie[4] in that booke, wherein he endevoureth to set forth the paterne of a perfect Oratour, sayth that ofttimes an auncient worde maketh the style seeme grave, and as it were reverend: no otherwise then we honour and reverence gray heares for a certein religious regard, which we have of old age. Yet nether every where must old words be stuffed in, nor the commen Dialecte and maner of speaking so corrupted therby, that as in old buildings it seme disorderly and ruinous. But all as in most exquisite pictures they use to blaze[5] and portraict not onely the daintie lineaments of beautye, but also rounde about it to shadow the rude thickets and craggy clifts, that by the basenesse of such parts, more excellency may accrew to the principall; for oftimes we fynde ourselves, I knowe not how, singularly delighted with the shewe of such naturall rudenesse, and take great pleasure in that disorderly order. Even so doe those rough and harsh termes enlumine and make more clearly to appeare the brightnesse of brave and glorious words. So ofentimes a dischorde in Musick maketh a comely concordaunce:[6] so great delight tooke the worthy Poete Alceus[7] to behold a blemish in the joynt of a wel shaped body. But if any will rashly blame such his purpose in choyse of old and unwonted[8] words, him may I more

---

9. I.e., inasmuch as our poet is widely and thoroughly acquainted (with "those auncient Poetes").
1. I.e., Cicero; cf. De Oratore 2.14.60.
2. Chance.
3. Lorenzo Valla (1405–57) emended the text of Annales, by the Roman historian Titus Livius (59 B.C.–A.D. 17); Sir John Cheke (1514–57), Edward VI's tutor, and professor of Greek at Cambridge, criticized the use of archaic terms by the Roman historian Sallust (86–34 B.C.).
4. I.e., Cicero; cf. De Oratore 3.38.153.
5. Depict.
6. Cf. The Faerie Queene, III.ii.15: "So dischord oft in Musick makes the sweeter lay."
7. Alcaeus, a Greek lyric poet of the seventh century B.C.; cf. Cicero, De Natura Deorum 1.28.79.
8. Unfamiliar.

justly blame and condemne, or[9] of witlesse headinesse[1] in judging, or of heedelesse hardinesse in condemning; for not marking the compasse of hys bent, he wil judge of the length of his cast.[2] For in my opinion it is one special prayse, of many whych are dew to this Poete, that he hath laboured to restore, as to theyr rightfull heritage such good and naturall English words, as have ben long time out of use and almost cleare disherited. Which is the onely cause, that our Mother tonge, which truely of it self is both ful enough for prose and stately enough for verse, hath long time ben counted most bare and barrein of both. Which default when as some endevoured to salve and recure, they patched up the holes with peces and rags of other languages, borrowing here of the french, there of the Italian, every where of the Latine, not weighing how il, those tongues accorde with themselves, but much worse with ours: So now they have made our English tongue, a gallimaufray or hodgepodge of al other speches.[3] Other some not so wel seene[4] in the English tonge as perhaps in other languages, if them happen to here an olde word albeit very naturall and significant, crye out streight way, that we speak no English, but gibbrish, or rather such, as in old time Evanders mother spake.[5] Whose first shame is, that they are not ashamed, in their own mother tonge straungers to be counted and alienes. The second shame no lesse then the first, that what so they understand not, they streight way deeme to be sencelesse, and not at al to be understode. Much like to the Mole in Aesopes fable, that being blynd her selfe, would in no wise be perswaded, that any beast could see. The last more shameful then both, that of their owne country and natural speach, which together with their Nources milk they sucked, they have so base regard and bastard judgement, that they will not onely themselves not labor to garnish and beautific it, but also repine, that of[6] other it shold be embellished. Like to the dogge in the maunger, that him selfe can eate no hay, and yet barketh at the hungry bullock, that so faine would feede: whose currish kind though cannot be kept from barking, yet I conne[7] them thanke that they refraine from byting.

Now for the knitting of sentences, whych they[8] call the joynts and members therof, and for al the compasse of the speach, it is round without roughnesse, and learned wythout hardnes, such indeede as may be perceived of the leaste, understoode of the moste, but judged onely of the learned. For what in most English wryters useth to be loose, and as it were ungyrt, in this Authour is well grounded, finely framed, and strongly trussed up together. In regard whereof, I scorne and spue out the rakehellye route of

---

9. Either.
1. Rashness.
2. I.e., not noting the extent of the artist's purpose, the rash critic foolishly presumes to judge the other's achievement.
3. E.K.'s position recalls that of Sir John Cheke, who observes (in a letter to Sir Thomas Hoby), "our own tongue should be written clean and pure, unmixed and unmangled with borrowing of other tongues."
4. I.e., skilled.
5. Cf. the anecdote in Aulus Gellius (a Latin grammarian of the second century A.D.), *Noctes Atticae* 1.10.2.
6. By.
7. Can.
8. I.e., rhetoricians.

our ragged rymers (for so themselves use to hunt the letter)[9] which without learning boste, without judgement jangle, without reason rage and fome, as if some instinct of Poeticall spirite had newly ravished them above the meanenesse of commen capacitie. And being in the middest of all theyr bravery, sodenly eyther for want of matter, or of ryme, or having forgotten theyr former conceipt, they seeme to be so pained and traveiled in theyr remembrance, as it were a woman in childebirth or as that same Pythia, when the traunce came upon her.

> Os rabidum fera corda domans &c.[1]

Nethelesse[2] let them a Gods name feede on theyr owne folly, so they seeke not to darken the beames of others glory. As for Colin, under whose person the Authour selfe is shadowed, how furre he is from such vaunted titles and glorious showes, both him selfe sheweth, where he sayth.

> Of Muses Hobbin. I conne no skill.   And,
> Enough is me to paint out my unrest, &c.[3]

And also appeareth by the basenesse of the name, wherein, it semeth, he chose rather to unfold great matter of argument covertly, then professing it, not suffice thereto accordingly. Which moved him rather in Aeglogues, then other wise to write, doubting perhaps his habilitie, which he little needed, or mynding to furnish our tongue with this kinde, wherein it faulteth,[4] or following the example of the best and most auncient Poetes, which devised this kind of wryting, being both so base[5] for the matter, and homely for the manner, at the first to trye theyr habilities; and as young birdes, that be newly crept out of the nest, by little first to prove theyr tender wyngs, before they make a greater flyght. So flew Theocritus,[6] as you may perceive he was all ready full fledged. So flew Virgile, as not yet well feeling his winges. So flew Mantuane, as being not full somd.[7] So Petrarque. So Boccace; So Marot, Sanazarus, and also divers other excellent both Italian and French Poetes, whose foting this Author every where followeth, yet so as few, but they be wel sented can trace him out. So finally flyeth this our new Poete, as a bird, whose principals[8] be scarce growen out, but yet as that in time shall be hable to keepe wing with the best.

Now as touching the generall dryft and purpose of his Aeglogues, I mind not to say much, him selfe labouring to conceale it. Onely this appeareth, that his unstayed[9] yougth had long wandred in the common Labyrinth of Love, in which time to mitigate and allay the heate of his passion, or els

---

9. E.K. thrusts at the excessive alliteration that characterized the work of many Elizabethan versifiers; cf. Sidney's allusion (in An Apologie for Poetrie) to "coursing of a Letter, as if they were bound to followe the method of a Dictionary."
1. "Taming the frenzied mouth and savage heart"; cf. Virgil, Aeneid 6.80.
2. Nevertheless.
3. These verses occur in "June" 65, 79.
4. Is deficient.
5. Humble, low.
6. Theocritus of Syracuse, Greek lyric poet of the third century B.C., whose "Idyls" initiated the genre of pastoral poetry, subsequently developed and elaborated by Virgil, Mantuan (Baptista Spagnuoli, 1448–1516, born in Mantua), Petrarch, Boccaccio, Clément Marot (1497–1544), and Jacopo Sannazaro (1458–1530).
7. Fledged.
8. The first two primary feathers of a hawk's wing.
9. Unsteady.

to warne (as he sayth) the young shepheards .s.[1] his equalls and companions of his unfortunate folly, he compiled these xii. Aeglogues, which for that they be proportioned to the state of the xii. monethes, he termeth the SHEPHEARDS CALENDAR, applying an olde name[2] to a new worke. Hereunto have I added a certain Glosse or scholion for thexposition of old wordes and harder phrases: which maner of glosing and commenting, well I wote, wil seeme straunge and rare in our tongue: yet for somuch as I knew many excellent and proper devises both in wordes and matter would passe in the speedy course of reading, either as unknowen, or as not marked, and that in this kind, as in other we might be equal to the learned of other nations, I thought good to take the paines upon me, the rather for that by meanes of some familiar acquaintaunce I was made privie to his counsell and secret meaning in them, as also in sundry other works of his. Which albeit I know he nothing so much hateth, as to promulgate, yet thus much have I adventured upon his frendship, him selfe being for long time furre estraunged, hoping that this will the rather occasion him, to put forth divers other excellent works of his, which slepe in silence, as his Dreames, his Legendes, his Court of Cupide, and sondry others;[3] whose commendations to set out, were verye vayne; the thinges though worthy of many, yet being knowen to few. These my present paynes if to any they be pleasurable or profitable, be you judge, mine own good Maister Harvey, to whom I have both in respect of your worthinesse generally, and otherwyse upon some particular and special considerations voued this my labour, and the may-denhead of this our commen frends Poetrie, himselfe having already in the beginning dedicated it to the Noble and worthy Gentleman, the right worshipfull Ma. Phi. Sidney, a special favourer and maintainer of all kind of learning. Whose cause I pray you Sir, yf Envie shall stir up any wrongful accusasion, defend with your mighty Rhetorick and other your rare gifts of learning, as you can, and shield with your good wil, as you ought, against the malice and outrage of so many enemies, as I know wilbe set on fire with the sparks of his kindled glory. And thus recommending the Author unto you, as unto his most special good frend, and my selfe unto you both, as one making singuler account of two so very good and so choise frends, I bid you both most hartely farwel, and commit you and your most com-mendable studies to the tuicion of the greatest.

Your owne assuredly to be commaunded

E. K.

---

1. *Scilicet*, i.e., namely.
2. I.e., that of *Le Compost et Kalendrier des bergiers*, first published at Paris in 1493; an English translation of the work had been often reprinted by Spenser's time.
3. These poems are lost, although it has been suggested that some part of *The Court of Cupid* may survive in *The Faerie Queene*, III.xii.

Januarye

Argument

In this fyrst Aeglogue Colin cloute[1] a shepheardes boy complaineth him of his unfortunate love, being but newly (as semeth) enamoured of a countrie lasse called Rosalinde: with which strong affection being very sore traveled,[2] he compareth his carefull case[3] to the sadde season of the yeare, to the frostie ground, to the frosen trees, and to his owne winterbeaten flocke. And lastlye, fynding himselfe robbed of all former pleasaunce and delights, hee breaketh his Pipe[4] in peeces, and casteth him selfe to the ground.

COLIN CLOUTE

A Shepheards boye (no better doe him call)
When Winters wastful° spight was almost spent,
All in a sunneshine day, as did befall,
Led forth his flock, that had bene long ypent.°
5 So faynt they woxe,° and feeble in the folde,
That now unnethes° their feete could them uphold.

devastating
pent up
grew
scarcely

1. "A name not greatly used, and yet have I sene a Poesie of M. Skeltons under that title. But indeede the word Colin is Frenche, and used of the French Poete Marot (if he be worthy of the name of a Poete) in a certein Aeglogue. Under which name this Poete secretly shadoweth himself, as sometime did Virgil under the name of Tityrus, thinking it much fitter, then such Latine names, for the great unlikelyhoode of the language" [*E.K.'s Glosse*]. E.K. thus emphasizes Spenser's debt to three areas of pastoral tradition, with particular reference to Virgil's *Eclogue I*, to Clément Marot's *Complaincte de ma Dame Loyse de Savoye*, and to Skelton's *Colin Clout*. Spenser is ordinarily associated also with the figure of Colin in *Colin Clouts Come Home Againe*, and (somewhat less narrowly) with the "jolly shepheard" to whose piping the Graces dance in *The Faerie Queene*, VI.x.15–16. For Patterson 1986 Marot "stood for Spenser as an intermediary between himself and Vergil," serving also as his "model for how to proceed in writing the pastoral of state" (44, 58); see also Montrose 1980. On the reputation of Marot and Skelton in Spenser's time see Prescott 1978, Cheney 1989.
2. Troubled.
3. I.e., his sorrowful plight.
4. I.e., the shepherd's reed pipe or rudimentary flute, in Greek legend the invention of Pan, god of shepherds and pastoral poetry.

All as the Sheepe, such was the shepeheards looke,
For pale and wanne he was, (alas the while,)
May seeme he lovd, or else some care he tooke:[5]
10   Well couth° he tune his pipe, and frame his stile.   *could*
Tho° to a hill his faynting flocke he ledde,   *then*
And thus him playnd,° the while his shepe there fedde.   *lamented*

"Ye Gods of love, that pitie lovers payne,
(If any gods the paine of lovers pitie:)
15   Looke from above, where you in joyes remaine,
And bowe your eares unto my dolefull dittie.
And Pan thou shepheards God,[6] that once didst love,
Pitie the paines, that thou thy selfe didst prove.°   *experience*

"Thou barrein ground, whome winters wrath hath wasted,
20   Art made a myrrhour, to behold my plight:[7]
Whilome° thy fresh spring flowrd, and after hasted   *formerly*
Thy sommer prowde with Daffadillies dight.°   *decked*
And now is come thy wynters stormy state,
Thy mantle mard, wherein thou maskedst late.

25   "Such rage as winters, reigneth in my heart,
My life bloud friesing with unkindly° cold: *unnatural*
Such stormy stoures° do breede my balefull° smart,   *tumults/painful*
As if my yeare were wast,° and woxen old.   *wasted*
And yet alas, but now my spring begonne,
30   And yet alas, yt is already donne.

"You naked trees, whose shady leaves are lost,
Wherein the byrds were wont to build their bowre:
And now are clothd with mosse and hoary frost,
Instede of bloosmes, wherwith your buds did flowre:
35   I see your teares, that from your boughes doe raine,
Whose drops in drery° ysicles remaine.   *dismal*

"All so my lusttull° leafe is drye and sere,   *vigorous*
My timely° buds with wayling all are wasted: *seasonable*
The blossome, which my braunch of youth did beare,
40   With breathéd sighes is blowne away, and blasted
And from mine eyes the drizling teares descend,
As on your boughes the ysicles depend.°   *hang*

"Thou feeble flocke, whose fleece is rough and rent,
Whose knees are weake through fast and evill fare:
45   Mayst witnesse well by thy ill governement,[8]

---

5. I.e., or else he was afflicted by some sorrow.
6. The wood nymph Syrinx, pursued by the amorous Pan, begged her sisters to change her shape
   that she might baffle his desire; she was consequently transformed into a reed (Ovid, *Metamorphoses*
   1.689–712). Cf. also "Aprill" 50–51, and note.
7. Berger 1983, remarking "the continuity binding Colin to Spenser/Immerito" (142), keys his reading
   of "Januarye" to lines 19–20.
8. I.e., by being badly cared for.

Thy maysters mind is overcome with care.
Thou weake, I wanne: thou leane, I quite forlorne:
With mourning pyne I, you with pyning mourne.

"A thousand sithes° I curse that carefull hower,   *times*
50 Wherein I longd the neighbour towne to see:
And eke tenne thousand sithes I blesse the stoure,°   *moment*
Wherein I sawe so fayre a sight, as shee.
Yet all for naught: such sight hath bred my bane.
Ah God, that love should breede both joy and payne.[9]

55 "It is not Hobbinol,[1] wherefore I plaine,
Albee my love he seeke with dayly suit:
His clownish° gifts and curtsies° I disdaine,   *rustic/courtesies*
His kiddes, his cracknelles,° and his early fruit.   *biscuits*
Ah foolish Hobbinol, thy gyfts bene vayne:
60 Colin them gives to Rosalind[2] againe.

"I love thilke° lasse, (alas why doe I love?)   *this*
And am forlorne, (alas why am I lorne?)[3]
Shee deignes° not my good will, but doth reprove,   *accepts*
And of my rurall musick holdeth scorne.
65 Shepheards devise° she hateth as the snake,   *invention*
And laughes the songes, that Colin Clout doth make.

"Wherefore my pype, albee° rude Pan thou please,   *although*
Yet for thou pleasest not, where most I would:
And thou unlucky Muse, that wontst to ease
70 My musing mynd, yet canst not, when thou should:
Both pype and Muse, shall sore the while abye."[4]
So broke his oaten pype, and downe dyd lye.

By that, the welkéd Phoebus[5] gan availe,°   *lower*
His weary waine,° and nowe the frosty Night   *wagon*
75 Her mantle black through heaven gan overhaile.°   *draw over*
Which seene, the pensife boy halfe in despight
Arose, and homeward drove his sonnéd° sheepe,   *sunned*
Whose hanging heads did seeme his carefull case to weepe.

9. The theme recurs throughout the *Calender*: cf. "June" 111–16; the conclusion of "December";
   and, at a higher remove, "October" 91–99.
1. "A fained country name, whereby, it being so commune and usuall, seemeth to be hidden the
   person of some his very speciall and most familiar freend, whom he entirely and extraordinarily
   beloved, as peradventure shall be more largely declared hereafter" [*E.K.'s Glosse*]. In his Glosse
   to "September" 176, E.K. explicitly identifies Hobbinoll as "Mayster Gabriel Harvey."
2. "A feigned name, which being wel ordered, wil bewray the very name of hys love and mistresse,
   whom by that name he coloureth" [*E.K.'s Glosse*]. Citing classical and Renaissance instances,
   E.K. adds, "this generally hath bene a common custome of counterfeicting the names of secret
   Personages." See Mallette 1990E on Rosalind's elusive identity and some readings of her fictional
   role in the *Calender* and *Colin Clout*.
3. "A prety Epanorthosis in these two verses, and withall a Paronomasia or playing with the word"
   [*E.K.'s Glosse*]. The rhetorical figure of epanorthosis "taketh away that that is said, and putteth a
   more meet word in the place" (H. Peacham, *The Garden of Eloquence* [London, 1593] 172);
   paronomasia is a form of pun.
4. I.e., shall dearly pay for that time of failure.
5. I.e., the setting sun.

Colins Embleme.

Anchôra speme.[6]

Februarie

Argument

This Æglogue is rather morall and generall, then bent to any secrete or particular purpose.[1] It specially conteyneth a discourse of old age, in the persone of Thenot an olde Shepheard, who for his crookednesse and unlustinesse, is scorned of Cuddie an unhappy Heardmans boye. The matter very well accordeth with the season of the moneth, the yeare now drouping, and as it were, drawing to his last age. For as in this time of yeare, so then in our bodies there is a dry and withering cold, which congealeth the crudled blood, and frieseth the wetherbeaten flesh, with stormes of Fortune, and hoare frosts of Care. To which purpose the olde man telleth a tale of the

6. "The meaning wherof is, that notwithstande his extreme passion and lucklesse love, yet leaning on hope, he is some what recomforted" [*E.K.'s Glosse*]. For an overview of Spenser's emblems in the *Calender* in sixteenth-century contexts, see Kennedy 1990E.

1. E.K.'s disclaimer has not prevented speculation concerning political or ecclesiastical allegory (see, e.g., Bond 1981, n. 5). Specific allusions, if any, now escape us, but Spenser certainly explores the dynamics of ambition, envy, and repression (Bond, Montrose 1981); hence images such as falling towers and proud peacock tails, which carry both political and psychosexual resonance. As E.K implies, this semicomic study of how youth and age do not comprehend or respect each other fits February, which comes early in the calendar Spenser adopts but late in the equally traditional year that starts in March as the reborn sun comes north for the spring equinox. The year is both old and young (see P. Cullen, *Spenser, Marvell, and Renaissance Pastoral* [Cambridge, MA, 1970]). Tensions between youth and age, ambition and establishment, novelty and antiquity, and desire and limitation parallel cosmological patterns or myths that allow no resolution while time lasts. Most modern critics agree that Spenser does not take sides. The debate is complicated by the debaters' shared longings, if Berger (1989) is right that Thenot is an older Cuddie who cannot give up a dream of lost paradise and so reacts to age with bitterness and envy.

The vocabulary, alliteration, and (usually) four-beat nine-syllable line are meant to sound rustic and "Chaucerian," a style thought suitable for "moral" pastoral commentary on failures of harmony in the body politic (L. Johnson 1990).

Oake and the Bryer, so lively and so feelingly, as if the thing were set forth in some Picture before our eyes, more plainly could not appear.

CUDDIE   THENOT

Ah for pittie, wil rancke° Winters rage,   *violent*
These bitter blasts never ginne t'asswage?°   *lessen*
The kene cold blowes through my beaten hyde,
All as I were through the body gryde.°   *pierced*
5 My ragged rontes[2] all shiver and shake,
As doen high Towers in an earthquake:
They wont in the wind wagge their wrigle° tailes,   *wriggling*
Perke as Peacock: but nowe it avales.[3]

THENOT[4]

Lewdly° complainest thou laesie ladde,   *Ignorantly*
10 Of Winters wracke,[5] for making thee sadde.
Must not the world wend in his commun course
From good to badd, and from badde to worse,
From worse unto that° is worst of all,   *what*
And then returne to his former fall?[6]
15 Who will not suffer° the stormy time,   *endure*
Where will he live tyll the lusty prime°?   *spring*
Selfe° have I worne out thrise threttie° yeares,   *Myself/thirty*
Some in much joy, many in many teares:
Yet never complained of cold nor heate,
20 Of Sommers flame, nor of Winters threat:
Ne ever was to Fortune foeman,°   *enemy*
But gently tooke, that° ungently came.   *whatever*
And ever my flocke was my chiefe care,
Winter or Sommer they mought° well fare.   *could*

CUDDIE

25 No marveile Thenot, if thou can beare
Cherefully the Winters wrathfull cheare:°   *mood*
For Age and Winter accord full nie,
This chill, that cold, this crooked, that wrye.°   *twisted*
And as the lowring Wether lookes downe,
30 So semest thou like good fryday[7] to frowne.
But my flowring youth is foe to frost,
My shippe unwont° in stormes to be tost.   *unused*

2. "Young bullockes" [*E.K.'s Glosse*].
3. Cuddie's calves once wagged their tails proudly but now let them droop, hinting that they and their master suffer "unlustiness" in the cold.
4. "The name of a shepheard in Marot his AEglogues" [*E.K.'s Glosse*]. He means Clément Marot's lament for Louise of Savoy, chief source of Spenser's "November." "Cuddie" is short for Cuthbert, the name of a saint popular in northern England.
5. "Ruine or Violence, whence commeth shipwracke: and not wreake, that is vengeaunce or wrath" [*E.K.'s Glosse*].
6. I.e., circle back to an earlier condition, but the primary meanings of "fall," including musical cadence, a throw at wrestling, the felling of trees, autumn, and the Fall of Man, suggest that although Thenot knows about "lusty prime" his mind dwells on descents, endings, and failures.
7. Good Friday, day of Jesus' crucifixion; Lent usually begins in February.

THENOT

The soveraigne of seas he blames in vaine,
That° once seabeate, will to sea againe.[8]   *who*
35 So loytring live you little heardgroomes,[9]
Keeping your beastes in the budded broomes:[1]
And when the shining sunne laugheth once,
You deemen° the Spring is come attonce.   *believe*
Tho gynne you, fond° flyes, the cold to scorne,   *foolish*
40 And crowing in pypes made of greene corne,[2]
You thinken to be Lords of the yeare.
But eft,° when ye count you freed from feare,   *afterward*
Comes the breme° winter with chamfred° browes,   *chill/wrinkled*
Full of wrinckles and frostie furrowes:
45 Drerily shooting his stormy darte,
Which cruddles the blood, and pricks the harte.
Then is your careless corage accoied,[3]
Your carefull heards with cold bene annoied.
Then paye you the price of your surquedrie,°   *pride*
50 With weeping, and wayling, and misery.

CUDDIE

Ah foolish old man, I scorne thy skill,°   *knowledge*
That wouldest me, my springing youngth to spil.°   *ruin*
I deeme, thy braine emperished bee
Through rusty elde,° that hath rotted thee: *age*
55 Or sicker° thy head veray tottie° is,   *surely/unsteady*
So on thy corbe° shoulder it leanes amisse.   *bent*
Now thy selfe hast lost both lopp and topp,
Als my budding braunch thou wouldest cropp:[4]
But were thy yeares greene, as now bene myne,
60 To other delights they would encline.
Tho° wouldest thou learne to caroll of Love,   *Then*
And hery° with hymnes thy lasses glove.   *praise*
Tho wouldest thou pype of Phyllis° prayse:
But Phyllis is myne for many dayes:
65 I wonne her with a gyrdle° of gelt,°   *sash/gold*

---

8. "Neptune the God of the seas" [*E.K.'s Glosse*]. The lines that follow (35–50) expand Mantuan's
   sixth eclogue 19–25.
9. I.e., thus you young herdsmen live idly; as E.K. notes, this passage paraphrases Chaucer's *House
   of Fame* 1224–26.
1. Broom is a flowering bush.
2. "He compareth careless sluggards or ill husbandmen to flyes [flying insects], that so soone as the
   sunne shineth or yt wexeth any thing warme, begin to flye abroade, when sodeinly they be overtaken
   with cold" [*E.K.'s Glosse*]. The pipes are either made of the stalks of early grain ("corn" in England)
   or, suited to February, blades held between the thumbs and blown on to make noise.
3. I.e., "plucked downe and daunted," says E.K., who calls this passage "A verye excellent and lively
   description of Winter, so as may be indifferently [i.e. equally well] taken, eyther for Old Age, or
   for Winter season" [*Glosse*].
4. "Lopp" and "topp" are a tree's small branches and twigs. Now that Thenot has been pruned by
   age like a tree readied for felling (a task appropriate for February), he in turn would cut off Cuddie's
   new growth; the phallic overtones suggest the anxieties that can accompany generational conflict.
5. "The name of some mayde unknowen, whom Cuddie, whose person is secrete, loved. The name
   is usuall in Theocritus, Virgile, and Mantuane" [*E.K.'s Glosse*], perhaps hinting that in fact Cuddie
   stands for some other figure.

Embost with buegle about the belt.[6]
Such an one shepeheards woulde make full faine:[7]
Such an one would make thee younge againe.

THENOT

Thou art a fon,° of thy love to boste,   *fool*
70   All that is lent to love, wyll be lost.

CUDDIE

Seest, howe brag° yond Bullocke beares,   *boastfully*
So smirke,° so smoothe, his prickéd eares?[8]   *trim*
His hornes bene as broade, as Rainebowe bent,°   *arched*
His dewelap as lythe, as lasse of Kent.
75   See howe he venteth[9] into the wynd.
Weenest of love is not his mynd?
Seemeth thy flocke thy counsell can,[1]
So lustlesse bene they, so weake so wan,
Clothed with cold, and hoary wyth frost.
80   Thy flocks father[2] his corage hath lost:
Thy Ewes, that wont to have blowen bags,[3]
Like wailefull widdowes hangen their crags:°   *necks*
The rather° Lambes bene starved° with cold,   *early/dead*
All for° their Maister is lustlesse and old.   *because*

THENOT

85   Cuddie, I wote thou kenst° little good,   *understand*
So vainely t'advaunce thy headlesse hood.[4]
For Youngth is a bubble blown up with breath,
Whose witt is weakenesse, whose wage is death,
Whose way is wildernesse, whose ynne Penaunce,
90   And stoopegallaunt[5] Age the hoste of Greevaunce.
But shall I tel thee a tale of truth,
Which I cond° of Tityrus[6] in my youth,   *learned*
Keeping his sheepe on the hils of Kent?

6. I.e., embroidered with glass beads on the waistband.
7. I.e., make shepherds well pleased, with a further implication of sexual eagerness.
8. Cuddie's animals have recovered during the debate, for now the bullock pricks up his ears. His erotically alert bull, boasts Cuddie, contrasts with Thenot's listless sheep.
9. I.e., "snuffeth in the wind" [*E.K.'s Glosse*], presumably sensing female scent.
1. I.e., your flock seems to know your secrets.
2. "The ramme" [*E.K.'s Glosse*].
3. I.e., swollen udders.
4. Cuddie's hood is empty because, thinks Thenot, he is brainless.
5. I.e., that which humbles a proudly fashionable youth; sometimes applied to low doors that force one to bend down. The rustic Cuddie is no "gallant," but Thenot's warning is meant generally. E.K. calls the passage a "moral and pithy Allegorie of youth, and the lustes thereof, compared to a wearie wayfaring man" [*Glosse*]. Cf. S. Bateman's *Travayled Pylgrime* (1569), in which a lusty youth crosses a wilderness called Age to lie down with Penance in a bedroom called Pain.
6. "I suppose he meane[s] Chaucer, whose prayse for pleasaunt tales cannot dye, so long as the memorie of hys name shal live, and the name of Poetrie shal endure" [*E.K.'s Glosse*].

CUDDIE

To nought more Thenot, my mind is bent,
95 Then to heare novells of his devise:[7]
They bene so well thewed,[8] and so wise,
What ever that good old man bespake.°   *spoke*

THENOT

Many meete° tales of youth did he make,   *suitable*
And some of love, and some of chevalrie:
100 But none fitter then this to applie.
Now listen a while, and hearken the end.

There grewe an aged Tree on the greene,[9]
A goodly Oake sometime had it bene,
With armes full strong and largely displayd,[1]
105 But of their leaves they were disarayde:°   *stripped*
The bodie bigge, and mightely pight,°   *set*
Throughly rooted, and of wonderous hight:
Whilome° had bene the King of the field,   *Once*
And mochell mast to the husband did yielde,[2]
110 And with his nuts larded° many swine.   *fattened*
But now the gray mosse marred his rine,°   *bark*
His bared boughes were beaten with stormes,
His toppe was bald, and wasted with wormes,
His honor decayed, his braunches sere.
115   Hard by his side grewe a bragging brere,°   *briar*
Which proudly thrust into Th'element,[3]
And seemed to threat the Firmament.
Yt was embellisht with blossomes fayre,
And thereto aye wonned to repayre[4]
120 The shepheards daughters, to gather flowres,
To peinct° their girlonds with his colowres.   *paint*
And in his small bushes used to shrowde°   *shelter*
The sweete Nightingale singing so lowde:
Which made this foolish Brere wexe so bold,
125 That on a time he cast him[5] to scold,
And snebbe° the good Oake, for he was old.[6]   *reprove*
    "Why standst there," quoth he, "thou brutish° blocke?   *stupid*
Nor for fruict, nor for shadowe serves thy stocke:°   *trunk*
Seest, how fresh my flowers bene spredde,

---

7. I.e., new stories devised by him. A "novel" was a short tale.
8. I.e., "full of morall wisenesse" [*E.K.'s Glosse*].
9. As E.K. notes, the fable is closer in style to Aesop. It is, he adds, "excellente for pleasaunt descriptions, being alltogether a certaine Icon or Hypotyposis [vivid description] of disdainfull younkers [youths]" [*Glosse*].
1. I.e., broadly branching outward.
2. I.e., gave many acorns to the farmer.
3. I.e., the air.
4. I.e., were wont to visit; E.K. reads "wonned" as "frequented" [*Glosse*].
5. I.e., he intended, decided.
6. I.e., because the oak was old. E.K. calls his speech "scorneful and very presumptuous" [*Glosse*].

130 Dyed in Lilly white, and Cremsin redde,
    With Leaves engrained° in lusty greene,   *dyed*
    Colours meete to clothe a mayden Queene.[7]
    Thy wast bignes but combers the grownd,[8]
    And dirks° the beauty of my blossomes rownd.   *darkens*
135 The mouldie mosse, which thee accloieth,°   *encumbers*
    My Sinamon smell too much annoieth.
    Wherefore soone I rede° thee, hence remove,   *advise*
    Least thou the price of my displeasure prove."
    So spake this bold brere with great disdaine:
140 Little him answered the Oake againe,
    But yielded, with shame and greefe adawed,[9]
    That of a weede he was overawed.[1]
       Yt chaunced after upon a day,
    The Husbandman selfe° to come that way,   *himself*
145 Of custome for to servewe° his grownd,   *oversee*
    And his trees of state[2] in compasse rownd.
    Him when the spitefull brere had espyed,
    Causlesse complained, and lowdly cryed
    Unto his Lord, stirring up sterne strife:[3]
150 "O my liege Lord,[4] the God of my life,
    Pleaseth you ponder your Suppliants plaint,
    Caused of wrong, and cruell constraint,
    Which I your poore Vassall dayly endure:
    And but° your goodnes the same recure,°   *unless/redress*
155 Am like for desperate doole° to dye,   *pain*
    Through felonous force of mine enemie."
       Greatly aghast with this piteous plea,
    Him rested the goodman on the lea,[5]
    And badde the Brere in his plaint proceede.
160 With painted words tho gan this proude weede,
    (As most usen Ambitious folke:)
    His colowred crime[6] with craft to cloke.
       "Ah my soveraigne, Lord of creatures all,
    Thou placer of plants both humble and tall,
165 Was not I planted of thine owne hand,
    To be the primrose of all thy land,
    With flowring blossomes, to furnish the prime,°   *spring*
    And scarlot berries in Sommer time?

7. Recalling the red-and-white Tudor rose.
8. I.e., your useless bulk merely burdens the ground.
9. I.e., "daunted and confounded" [*E.K.'s Glosse*].
1. See Textual Notes.
2. I.e., "taller trees fitte for timber wood" [*E.K.'s Glosse*]; a "state" was also a statesman.
3. In a Glosse E.K. notes that the phrase is from Chaucer; see the opening of "The Plowman's Tale,"
   then thought authentic.
4. "A maner of supplication, wherein is kindly [naturally] coloured the affection and speache of
   Ambitious men" [*E.K.'s Glosse*].
5. The husbandman sits down on the meadow to listen; in northern dialect a "lea" was a scythe,
   suitable for leaning on but probably not useful in February.
6. The rhetorically disguised ("colowred") crime is slander, of increased legal interest in Spenser's
   day (see F. T. Plucknett, *A Concise History of the Common Law* [London, 1956]) and a major
   theme in his works. The briar commits *scandalum magnatum*: slandering the great.

How falls it then, that this faded Oake,
170 Whose bodie is sere, whose braunches broke,
Whose naked Armes stretch unto the fyre,[7]
Unto such tyrannie doth aspire:
Hindering with his shade my lovely light,
And robbing me of the swete sonnes sight?
175 So beate his old boughes my tender side,
That oft the bloud springeth from wounds wyde:[8]
Untimely my flowres forced to fall,
That bene the honor of your Coronall.°   garland
And oft he lets his cancker wormes° light   caterpillars
180 Upon my braunches, to worke me more spight:
And oft his hoarie locks[9] downe doth cast,
Where with my fresh flowretts bene defast.[1]
For this, and many more such outrage,
Craving your goodlihead° to aswage°   goodness/diminish
185 The ranckorous rigour of his might,
Nought aske I, but onely to hold my right:
Submitting me to your good sufferance,°   permission
And praying to be garded from greevance."
     To this the Oake cast him to replie
190 Well as he couth:[2] but his enemie
Had kindled such coles of displeasure,
That the good man noulde stay his leasure,[3]
But home him hasted with furious heate,
Encreasing his wrath with many a threate.
195 His harmefull Hatchet he hent° in hand,   caught
(Alas, that it so ready should stand)
And to the field alone he speedeth.
(Ay° little helpe to harme there needeth)   Always
Anger nould let him speake to the tree,
200 Enaunter° his rage mought cooled bee: lest
But to the roote bent his sturdy stroke,
And made many wounds in the wast° Oake.   ruined
The Axes edge did oft turne againe,
As halfe unwilling to cutte the graine:
205 Semed, the sencelesse yron dyd feare,
Or to wrong holy eld° did forbeare.°   age/refrain
For it had bene an auncient tree,
Sacred with many a mysteree,
And often crost with the priestes crewe,

---

7. "Metaphorically ment of the bare boughes, spoyled of leaves. This colourably [speciously] he speaketh, as adjudging hym to the fyre" [*E.K.'s Glosse*].
8. "Spoken of a blocke, as it were of a living creature, figuratively, and (as they saye) *kat' eikasmón* [as a comparison]" [*E.K.'s Glosse*].
9. "Metaphorically for withered leaves" [*E.K.'s Glosse*].
1. I.e., by which my new little flowers are destroyed; "defaced" also meant abashed and defamed.
2. I.e., as well as he knew how.
3. I.e., would not wait. It was often said of slander that foolish magistrates act with credulous haste upon hearing it; hence the ass's ears on the judge in the lost but often imitated painting of Calumny by Apelles (fourth century B.C.).

210 And often halowed with holy water dewe.[4]
    But sike° fancies weren foolerie,   such
    And broughten this Oake to this miserye.
    For nought mought they quitten° him from decay:°   deliver/ruin
    For fiercely the good man at him did laye.
215 The blocke oft groned under the blow,[5]
    And sighed to see his neare ouerthrow.
    In fine[6] the steele had pierced his pitth,
    Tho downe to the earth he fell forthwith:
    His wonderous weight made the grounde to quake,
220 Th'earth shronke under him, and seemed to shake.
    There lyeth the Oake, pitied of none.
        Now stands the Brere like a Lord alone,
    Puffed up with pryde and vaine pleasaunce:
    But all this glee had no continuaunce.
225 For eftsones° Winter gan to approche,   soon
    The blustring Boreas[7] did encroche,
    And beate upon the solitarie Brere:
    For nowe no succoure was seene him nere.
    Now gan he repent his pryde to late:
230 For naked left and disconsolate,
    The byting frost nipt his stalke dead,
    The watrie wette weighed downe his head,
    And heaped snowe burdned him so sore,
    That nowe upright he can stand no more:
235 And being downe, is trodde in the durt
    Of cattell, and brouzed, and sorely hurt.
    Such was th'end of this Ambitious brere,
    For scorning Eld[8]

CUDDIE

    Now I pray thee shepheard, tel it not forth:
240 Here is a long tale, and little worth.[9]
    So longe have I listened to thy speche,
    That graffed° to the ground is my breche:°   grafted/rump
    My hartblood is welnigh frorne° I feele,   frozen
    And my galage[1] growne fast to my heele:

---

4. The tree was blessed by the sign of the cross and holy water from a 'crew,' a "pott, wherewith the
   popishe priest used to sprinckle and hallowe the trees from [i.e., against] mischaunce. Such
   blindnesse was in those times, which the Poete supposeth, to have bene the finall decay of this
   auncient Oake" [E.K.'s Glosse]. By associating the oak with practices abolished by the Reformation,
   Spenser hints at historical allegory. The tree resembles one in Lucan's Civil War 1.136–43 (applied
   to Caesar's opponent, Pompey), borrowed by Joachim Du Bellay for Antiquitez 28 (on ancient
   Rome) and then translated by Spenser in The Ruines of Rome (Complaints 1591); the implications
   are thus also geopolitical. Thenot may not understand these ambivalent overtones, thinking the
   tree's fall a disaster for everyone.
5. "A lively figure, which geveth sence and feeling to unsensible [i.e. incapable of sensory perception]
   creatures" [E.K.'s Glosse].
6. I.e., in the end.
7. "The Northerne wynd, that bringeth the moste stormie weather" [E.K.'s Glosse].
8. "And minding (as should seme) to have made ryme to the former verse, he is conningly cutte
   of[f] by Cuddye, as disdayning to here any more" [E.K.'s Glosse]. The slanderous briar is rhetorically effective if foolish; but Thenot's own tale has no impact on Cuddie.
9. I.e., worth little.
1. I.e., "a startuppe [boot; the word also meant upstart] or clownish [rustic] shoe" [E.K.'s Glosse].

245   But little ease of thy lewd° tale I tasted.   *worthless*
      Hye thee home shepheard, the day is nigh° wasted.   *nearly*

Thenots Embleme.

Iddio perche è vecchio,
Fa suoi al suo essempio.[2]

Cuddies Embleme.

Niuno vecchio,
Spaventa Iddio.[3]

Aprill — *Recreate*   ~~Taurus~~

Phoebus

nine muses

Argument   *Elizabeth* 10th May   *recreation of Nature*   *Blason to Elizabeth*

This Aeglogue is purposely intended to the honor and prayse of our most
gracious sovereigne, Queene Elizabeth. The speakers herein be Hobbinoll
and Thenott,[1] *two shepheardes: the which Hobbinoll being before mentioned,*

2. E.K. calls this "a moral of his former tale" and paraphrases the Italian: "God, which is himselfe
   most aged, being before al ages, and without beginninge, maketh those, whom he loveth like to
   himselfe, in heaping yeares unto theyre dayes, and blessing them wyth longe lyfe. . . . So the old
   man checketh the rashheaded boy, for despysing his gray and frostye heares" [*Glosse*].

3. I.e., "No old man fears the Lord" (Italian). Cuddie thus gives a "counterbuff," says E.K., "with
   a byting and bitter proverbe," for "it was an old opinion, and yet is continued in some mens
   conceipt [i.e., thought], that men of yeares have no feare of god at al, or not so much as younger
   folke. For that being rypened with long experience, and having passed many bitter brunts and
   blastes of vengeaunce, they dread no stormes of Fortune, nor wrathe of Gods, nor daunger of
   menne, as being eyther by longe and ripe wisedome armed against all mischaunces and adversitie,
   or with much trouble hardened against all troublesome tydes: lyke unto the Ape, of which is sayd
   in AEsops fables, that oftentimes meeting the Lyon, he was at first sore aghast and dismayed at
   the grimnes[s] and austeritie of hys countenance, but at last being acquainted with his lookes, he
   was so furre from fearing him, that he would familiarly gybe [i.e., joke] and jest with him" [*Glosse*].

1. The name is that of Colin's interlocutor in Marot's *Complaincte de ma Dame Loyse de Savoye*;
   elsewhere in the *Calender* (especially in "Februarie"), Thenot seems to represent the wisdom of
   experience and mature years.

*greatly to have loved Colin, is here set forth more largely, complayning[2] him
of that boyes great misadventure in Love, whereby his mynd was alienate
and with drawen not onely from him, who moste loved him, but also from
all former delightes and studies, aswell in pleasaunt pyping, as conning[3]
ryming and singing, and other his laudable exercises. Whereby he taketh
occasion, for proofe of his more excellencie and skill in poetrie, to recorde a
songe, which the sayd Colin sometime made in honor of her Majestie, whom
abruptely he termeth Elysa.*

THENOT   HOBBINOLL

Tell me good Hobbinoll, what garres° thee greete?°   *makes/weep*
What? hath some Wolfe thy tender Lambes ytorne?
Or is thy Bagpype broke, that soundes so sweete?
Or art thou of thy lovéd lasse forlorne?°   *deserted*

5 Or bene thine eyes attempred° to the yeare,   *attuned*
Quenching the gasping furrowes thirst with rayne?
Like April shoure, so stremes the trickling teares
Adowne thy cheeke, to quenche thy thristye° payne.   *thirsty*

HOBBINOLL

Nor thys, nor that, so muche doeth make me mourne,
10 But for° the ladde,[4] whome long I lovd so deare,   *that*
Nowe loves a lasse, that all his love doth scorne:
He plongd in payne, his tresséd° locks dooth teare.   *curled*

Shepheards delights he dooth them all forsweare,
Hys pleasaunt Pipe, whych made us meriment,
15 He wylfully hath broke, and doth forbeare
His wonted songs, wherein he all outwent.°   *surpassed*

THENOT

What is he for a Ladde,[5] you so lament?
Ys love such pinching payne to them, that prove?°   *feel (it)*
And hath he skill to make[6] so excellent,
20 Yet hath so little skill to brydle love?

2. Lamenting.
3. Learning, studying. "Laudable exercises" are formal expressions of praise: encomiastic poetry. See
   Cain 1978, ch. 1.
4. I.e., Colin, whose love of Rosalind "has broken the bond of friendship, made Hobbinol miserable,
   and halted Colin's own poetry" (L. Johnson 1990, 168).
5. E.K. notes that the expression is "a straunge manner of speaking"; he renders it, "What maner of
   Ladde is he?" [*Glosse*].
6. "To rime and versifye. For in this word making, our olde Englishe Poetes were wont to comprehend
   all the skil of Poetrye, according to the Greeke woorde ποιειν, to make, whence commeth the
   name of Poetes" [*E.K.'s Glosse*].

HOBBINOLL

Colin thou kenst,° the Southerne shepheardes boye:[7] *knowest*
Him Love hath wounded with a deadly darte.
Whilome on him was all my care and joye,
Forcing with gyfts to winne his wanton heart.

25 But now from me hys madding° mynd is starte,° *foolish/broken away*
And woes° the Widdowes daughter of the glenne:[8] *woos*
So nowe fayre Rosalind hath bredde° hys smart, *caused*
So now his frend is chaungéd for a frenne.° *stranger*

THENOT

But if hys ditties bene so trimly dight,[9]
30 I pray thee Hobbinoll, recorde° some one: *sing*
The whiles our flockes doe graze about in sight,
And we close shrowded in thys shade alone.

HOBBINOLL

Contented I: then will I singe his laye[1] *A*
Of fayre Elisa, Queene of shepheardes all: *B*   *Complicated*
35 Which once he made, as by a spring he laye, *A*   *5 tanza*
And tunéd it unto the Waters fall. *B*

"Ye dayntye Nymphs, that in this blesséd Brooke *C*   *—like*
  Doe bathe your brest, *D* *Dimeter*
Forsake your watry bowres, and hether looke, *c*   *rhine*
40 At my request: *D*   *maidens*
And eke you Virgins,[2] that on Parnasse dwell, *B* *like*
Whence floweth Helicon the learnéd well, *B*   *Elizabeth*
  Helpe me to blaze°   *proclaim, depict*
  Her worthy praise,
45 Which in her sexe doth all excell.

---

7. "Seemeth hereby that Colin perteyneth to some Southern noble man . . ." [*E.K.'s Glosse*]. "The Southerne shephearde" may perhaps refer to the earl of Leicester, but Spenser is more probably alluding to his own association with Bishop John Young.

8. "He calleth Rosalind the Widowes daughter of the glenne, that is, of a country Hamlet or borough, which I thinke is rather sayde to coloure and concele the person, then simply spoken. For it is well knowen, even in spighte of Colin and Hobbinoll, that shee is a Gentle woman of no meane house, nor endewed with anye vulgare and common gifts both of nature and manners: but suche indeede, as neede nether Colin be ashamed to have her made knowne by his verses, nor Hobbinol be greved, that so she should be commended to immortalitie for her rare and singular Vertues" [*E.K.'s Glosse*]. E.K. misunderstands the meaning of "glenne" (a wooded mountain valley), which here appears for the first time in English.

9. I.e., neatly made.

1. "A songe. As Roundelayes and Virelayes. In all this songe is not to be respected, what the worthinesse of her Majestie deserveth, nor what to the highnes of a Prince is agreeable, but what is moste comely for the meanesse of a shepheards witte, or to conceive, or to utter. And therefore he calleth her Elysa, as through rudenesse tripping in her name: and a shepheards daughter, it being very unfit, that a shepheards boy brought up in the shepefold, should know, or ever seme to have heard of a Queenes roialty" [*E.K.'s Glosse*].

2. I.e., the nine Muses, described by E.K. as "daughters of Apollo and Memorie, whose abode the Poets faine to be on Parnassus, a hill in Grece, for that in that countrye specially florished the honor of all excellent studies" [*Glosse*]. Properly, Helicon was not a "well," but the mountain that harbored the springs called Hippocrene and Aganippe; medieval tradition (as in Chaucer's *Hous of Fame* 521–22, or *Troilus and Criseyde* 3.1809) accounts for E.K.'s reference.

"Of fayre Elisa be your silver song,   — *daughter of Pan's Syrinx*
  That blessèd wight:
The flowre of Virgins, may shee florish long,
  In princely plight.°   condition
50 For shee is Syrinx daughter without spotte,
  Which Pan the shepheards God of her begot:[3]
    So sprong her grace
    Of heavenly race,
  No mortall blemishe may her blotte.

55 "See, where she sits upon the grassie greene,
    (O seemely sight)
  Yclad in Scarlot like a mayden Queene,
    And Ermines white.
  Upon her head a Cremosin° coronet,   crimson
60 With Damaske roses and Daffadillies set: *red & white*
    Bayleaves betweene,
    And Primroses greene
  Embellish the sweete Violet.

"Tell me, have ye seene her angelick face,
65   Like Phoebe[4] fayre?   *Phoebe — sister to apollo*
  Her heavenly haveour,° her princely grace *Diana*   bearing
    Can you well compare?°   match
  The Redde rose medled° with the White yfere,°   combined/together
  In either cheeke depeincten° lively chere.[5]   depict
70   Her modest eye,   *Cynthia*
    Her Majestie,
  Where have you seene the like, but there?   *sister to apollo*

"I sawe Phoebus thrust out his golden hedde,
    Upon her to gaze:
75 But when he sawe, how broade her beames did spredde,
    It did him amaze.
  He blusht to see another Sunne belowe,   — *blushed*

3. E.K., having briefly summarized Ovid's account of Pan and Syrinx, observes that "here by Pan
and Syrinx is not to bee thoughte, that the shephearde simplye meante those Poetical Gods: but
rather supposing (as seemeth) her graces progenie to be divine and immortall . . . could devise
no parents in his judgement so worthy for her, as Pan the shepheards God, and his best beloved
Syrinx. So that by Pan is here meant the most famous and victorious King, her highnesse Father,
late of worthy memorye K. Henry the eyght. And by that name, oftymes (as hereafter appeareth)
be noted kings and mighty Potentates: And in some place Christ himselfe, who is the verye Pan
and god of Shepheardes" [*Glosse*]. Marot also had alluded to a monarch (Francis I) under the
name of Pan. Johnson 1990 notes "associations [50–54] linking Elisa to the pure bride of the Song
of Solomon 4:7" (165).
4. "The Moone, whom the Poets faine to be sister unto Phoebus, that is the Sunne" [*E.K.'s Glosse*].
Born on Cynthus Hill, in the island of Delos (according to legend), she was known also as Cynthia.
5. "By the mingling of the Redde rose and the White, is meant the uniting of the two principall
houses of Lancaster and of Yorke: by whose longe discord and deadly debate, this realm many
yeares was sore traveiled, and almost cleane decayed. Til the famous Henry the seventh, of the
line of Lancaster, taking to wife the most vertuous Princesse Elisabeth, daughter to the fourth
Edward of the house of Yorke, begat the most royal Henry the eyght aforesayde, in whom was
the firste union of the Whyte Rose and the Redde" [*E.K.'s Glosse*].

Ne durst againe his fyrye face out showe:
    Let him, if he dare,
80   His brightnesse compare
With hers, to have the overthrowe.

"Shewe thy selfe Cynthia with thy silver rayes,
    And be not abasht:
When shee the beames of her beauty displayes,
85   O how art thou dasht?
But I will not match her with Latonaes seede,[6]
Such follie great sorow to Niobe did breede.°   *cause*
    Now she is a stone,
    And makes dayly mone,
90 Warning all other to take heede.

"Pan may be proud, that ever he begot   *Henry VIII*
    Such a Bellibone,°   *fair maid*
And Syrinx rejoyse, that ever was her lot   *Anne Bolyn*
    To beare such an one.
95 Soone as my younglings cryen for the dam,
To her will I offer a milkwhite Lamb:
    Shee is my goddesse plaine,°   *absolute*
    And I her shepherds swayne,
Albee forswonck and forswatt I am.[7]

100 "I see Calliope[8] speede her to the place,   *Muse of epic poetry*
    Where my Goddesse shines:
And after her the other Muses trace,°   *step*
    With their Violines.
Bene they not Bay braunches,[9] which they do beare,
105 All for Elisa in her hand to weare?
    So sweetely they play,
    And sing all the way,
That it a heaven is to heare.

6. Niobe, excessively proud of her fourteen children, presumed to scorn the Titaness Latona, who had given birth only to Apollo and Diana; these two consequently slew all of Niobe's offspring, and Zeus turned her into a stone, from which tears forever flow (cf. Ovid, *Metamorphoses* 6.148–312).
7. I.e., tired from work and bathed in sweat. The expression occurs also in "The Plowman's Tale," a lengthy satire on the clergy, thought at one time to be part of Chaucer's *Canterbury Tales.* Cf. "Envoy" 10 and note.
8. The Muse of epic poetry; "to whome they assigne the honor of al Poetical Invention, and the firste glorye of the Heroicall verse" [*E.K.'s Glosse*]. On the Muses invoked by Colin, "a type of Orpheus," and his encomium's anticipation of "an epic in praise of Elizabeth," see Cain 1978, 14–15.
9. "The signe of honor and victory, and therfore of myghty Conquerors worn in theyr triumphes, and eke of famous Poets, as saith Petrarch in hys Sonets . . ." [*E.K.'s Glosse*].

Masque

"Lo how finely the graces[1] can it foote
110   To the Instrument:
They dauncen deffly,° and singen soote,°   *deftly/sweetly*
    In their meriment.
Wants not a fourth grace, to make the daunce even?
Let that rowme to my Lady be yeven:°   *given*
115   She shalbe a grace,
    To fyll the fourth place,
And reigne with the rest in heaven.[2]

"And whither rennes° this bevie of Ladies bright,   *runs*
    Raungéd in a rowe?
120   They bene all Ladyes of the lake[3] behight,°   *called*
    That unto her goe.
Chloris,[4] that is the chiefest Nymph of al,
Of Olive braunches beares a Coronall:°   *coronet*
    Olives bene for peace,
125   When wars doe surcease:
Such for a Princesse bene principall.°   *princely*

"Ye shepheards daughters, that dwell on the greene,
    Hye you there apace:°   *quickly*
Let none come there, but that Virgins bene,
130   To adorne her grace.
And when you come, whereas shee is in place,
See, that your rudenesse doe not you disgrace:
    Binde your fillets° faste,   *hair ribbons*
    And gird in your waste,
135   For more finesse, with a tawdrie lace.[5]

---

1. "Three sisters, the daughters of Jupiter, whose names are Aglaia, Thalia, Euphrosyne. . . . Whom the Poetes feyned to be the Goddesses of al bountie and comelines, which therefore (as sayth Theodontius) they make three, to wete, that men first ought to be gracious and bountiful to other freely, then to receive benefits at other mens hands curteously, and thirdly to requite them thankfully: which are three sundry Actions in liberalitye. And Boccace saith, that they be painted naked, (as they were indeede on the tombe of C. Julius Caesar) the one having her backe toward us, and her face fromwarde, as proceeding from us: the other two toward us, noting double thanke to be due to us for the benefit, we have done" [*E.K.'s Glosse*].
2. Cf. *The Faerie Queene* VI.x.16 and note.
3. "Ladyes of the lake be Nymphes. For it was an olde opinion amongste the Auncient Heathen, that of every spring and fountaine was a goddesse the Soveraigne. Whiche opinion stucke in the myndes of men not manye yeares sithence, by meanes of certain fine fablers and lowd lyers, such as were the Authors of King Arthure the great and such like, who tell many an unlawfull leasing of the Ladyes of the Lake, that is, the Nymphes. For the word Nymphe in Greeke signifieth Well water, or otherwise a Spouse or Bryde" [*E.K.'s Glosse*]. A "Lady of the Lake" made part of the entertainment presented before Queen Elizabeth at Kenilworth in 1575; such a figure appears also in *Prince Henry's Barriers*, a masque by Ben Jonson presented before the court of King James I. Cf. also *The Faerie Queene* III.iii.10.
4. "The name of a Nymph, and signifieth greenesse, of whome is sayd, that Zephyrus the Westerne wind being in love with her, and coveting her to wyfe, gave her for a dowrie, the chiefedome and soveraigntye of al flowres and greene herbes, growing on earth" [*E.K.'s Glosse*]. The name may also refer to a particular lady in the Queen's retinue.
5. I.e., to present a finer appearance, with a band of lace or silk (sold during the fair of St. Audrey).

"Bring hether the Pincke and purple Cullambine,[6]
    With Gelliflowres:
Bring Coronations, and Sops in wine,
    Worne of Paramoures.°
140 Strowe me the ground with Daffadowndillies,
And Cowslips, and Kingcups, and lovéd Lillies:
    The pretie Pawnce,
    And the Chevisaunce,
Shall match with the fayre flowre Delice.

145 "Now ryse up Elisa, deckéd as thou art,
    In royall aray:
And now ye daintie Damsells may depart
    Echeone her way,
I feare, I have troubled your troupes to longe:
150 Let dame Eliza thanke you for her song.
    And if you come hether,
    When Damsines° I gether,
I will part them all you among."

THENOT

And was thilk same song of Colins owne making?
155 Ah foolish boy, that is with love yblent:°   blinded
Great pittie is, he be in such taking,°   plight
For naught caren, that bene so lewdly bent.[7]

HOBBINOL

Sicker° I hold him, for a greater fon,°   surely/fool
That loves the thing, he cannot purchase.
160 But let us homeward: for night draweth on,
And twincling starres the daylight hence chase.

Thenots Embleme.[8]

O quam te memorem virgo?

Hobbinols Embleme.

165   O dea certe.

6. Spenser's flower passage, deriving in some measure from Marot's *Complaincte de ma Dame Loyse de Savoye* 229–36, in turn influenced Milton's *Lycidas*. "Coronations" are carnations, "sops in wine" clove pinks; the "Pawnce" is the pansy, and the "flowre Delice" [fleur de lis] a variety of iris. The "chevisaunce" has not been satisfactorily identified; it may be a species of wallflower.
7. I.e., for they that are so foolishly inclined are quite heedless.
8. "This Poesye is taken out of Virgile [*Aeneid* I.327–28], and there of him used in the person of Aeneas to his mother Venus, appearing to him in likenesse of one of Dianaes damosells: being there most divinely set forth. To which similitude of divinitie Hobbinoll comparing the excelency of Elisa, and being through the worthynes of Colins song, as it were, overcome with the hugenesse of his imagination, brusteth out in great admiration (O quam te memorem virgo?) being otherwise unhable, then by soddein silence, to expresse the worthinesse of his conceipt. Whom Thenot answereth with another part of the like verse, as confirming by his graunt and approvance, that Elisa is no whit inferiour to the Majestie of her, of whome that Poete so boldly pronounced, O dea certe" [*E.K.'s Glosse*].

October†

Argument

In Cuddie[1] is set out the perfecte paterne of a Poete, whiche finding no maintenaunce of his state and studies, complayneth of the contempte of Poetrie, and the causes thereof: Specially having bene in all ages, and even amongst the most barbarous alwayes of singular accounpt[2] and honor, and being indede so worthy and commendable an arte: or rather no arte, but a divine gift and heavenly instinct not to bee gotten by laboure and learning, but adorned with both: and poured into the witte by a certaine ενθονσιασμòι.[3] *and celestiall inspiration, as the Author hereof els where at large discourseth, in his booke called the English Poete, which booke being lately come to my hands, I mynde also by Gods grace upon further advisement to publish.*

† "This Aeglogue is made in imitation of Theocritus his xvi. Idillion, wherein hee reproved the Tyranne Hiero of Syracuse for his nigardise towarde Poetes, in whome is the power to make men immortal for theyr good dedes, or shameful for their naughty lyfe. And the lyke also is in Mantuane. The style hereof as also that in Theocritus, is more loftye then the rest, and applyed to the heighte of Poeticall witte" [*E.K.'s Glosse*]. In fact, the influence of Theocritus on this eclogue is slight; Spenser's debt to the fifth eclogue of Mantuan (J. Baptista Spagnuoli, 1448–1516) is more significant, in structural outline as well as in detail. The Italian poet's emphasis on the avarice and sloth of his times sounds recurrently also in the "half-bitter, half-nostalgic survey [in "October"] of the decayed state of poetry . . . an embodiment of Spenser's own dilemma" (Heninger 1990E; see also Helgerson 1983, pp. 675–86 of this volume).

1. "I doubte whether by Cuddie be specified the authour selfe, or some other. For in the eyght Aeglogue the same person was brought in, singing a Cantion of Colins making, as he sayth. So that some doubt, that the persons be different" [*E.K.'s Glosse*]. While Cuddie may be identified with one or another of Spenser's contemporaries, it is perhaps more rewarding to recognize the combination in Spenser's personality of elements represented by the frustrated Cuddie (who requires patronage in order to survive), and by the confident Piers, whose idealism cannot be shaken by present trials (and whose promise of future reward concludes this eclogue). But see Hardin 1976, for whom Piers combines idealistic and practical elements.

2. Esteem.

3. "Enthousiasmos," or inspiration. Ultimately derived from Plato's *Ion* 534, and *Phaedrus* 245, the doctrine that poetry is "a divine gift and heavenly instinct" might have been found by E.K. in a number of Renaissance Italian works of literary criticism, e.g., Minturno's *De Poeta* (1559). The "English Poete" has not survived.

iambic pentameter

PIERS   CUDDIE

Cuddie, for shame hold up thy heavye head,
And let us cast° with what delight to chace,   *devise*
And weary thys long lingring Phoebus race.[4]
Whilome° thou wont the shepheards laddes to leade,   *formerly*
5 In rymes, in ridles, and in bydding base:[5]
Now they in thee, and thou in sleepe art dead.

CUDDIE

Piers, I have pypéd erst so long with payne,
That all mine Oten reedes[6] bene rent and wore:
And my poore Muse hath spent her sparéd store,
10 Yet little good hath got, and much lesse gayne.
Such pleasaunce makes the Grashopper so poore,
And ligge so layd,[7] when Winter doth her straine.°   *constrain*

The dapper° ditties, that I wont devise,   *pretty*
To feede youthes fancie, and the flocking fry,[8]
15 Delighten much: what I the bett for thy?[9]
They han° the pleasure, I a sclender prise.   *have*
I beate the bush, the byrds to them doe flye:
What good thereof to Cuddie can arise?

PIERS

Cuddie, the prayse is better, then the price,
20 The glory eke much greater then the gayne:
O what an honor is it, to restraine
The lust of lawlesse youth with good advice:
Or pricke them forth with pleasaunce of thy vaine,°   *poetic vein*
Whereto thou list their traynéd° willes entice.[1]   *allured*

25 Soone as thou gynst to sette thy notes in frame,
O how the rurall routes° to thee doe cleave: *crowds*

---

4. I.e., and pass this long day.
5. The game of prisoner's base; or, possibly, poetical contests.
6. E.K.'s Glosse refers to Virgil's term, "avena" (*Eclogue* 1.2); properly "oats," or "oat stalks," the term signifies in Virgil's (and Ovid's) usage a reed or pipe.
7. "Lye so faynt and unlustie" [*E.K.'s Glosse*]; as in the fable of the ant and the grasshopper.
8. "Frye is a bold Metaphore, forced from the spawning fishes. For the multitude of young fish be called the frye" [*E.K.'s Glosse*].
9. I.e., in what way am I therefore the better?
1. "This place seemeth to conspyre with Plato, who in his first booke de Legibus sayth, that the first invention of Poetry was of very vertuous intent" [*E.K.'s Glosse*]. So in the "Letter to Raleigh," Spenser indicates his concern "to fashion a gentleman or noble person in vertuous and gentle discipline," referring to the pleasing force of "an historicall fiction, the which the most part of men delight to read, rather for variety of matter, then for profite of the ensample"; "doctrine by [fictional] ensample," in fact, is especially "profitable and gratious."

Seemeth thou dost their soule of sence bereave,[2]
All as the shepheard,[3] that did fetch his dame
From Plutoes balefull bowre withouten leave:
His musicks might the hellish hound did tame.   30

CUDDIE

So praysen babes the Peacoks spotted traine,
And wondren at bright Argus blazing eye:[4]
But who rewards him ere the more for thy?[5]
Or feedes him once the fuller by a graine?
Sike° prayse is smoke, that sheddeth° in the skye,   35   *such/is dispersed*
Sike words bene wynd, and wasten soone in vayne.

PIERS

Abandon then the base and viler clowne,[6]
Lyft up thy selfe out of the lowly dust:
And sing of bloody Mars, of wars, of giusts,°   *jousts*
Turne thee to those, that weld° the awful crowne.   40   *bear*
To doubted° Knights, whose woundlesse armour[7] rusts,   *dreaded*
And helmes unbruzéd wexen° dayly browne.   *grow*

There may thy Muse display[8] her fluttryng wing,
And stretch her selfe at large from East to West:
Whither thou list in fayre Elisa rest,   45
Or if thee please in bigger notes to sing,
Advaunce° the worthy whome shee loveth best,[9]   *extol*
That first the white beare to the stake did bring.

2. "What the secrete working of Musick is in the myndes of men, aswell appeareth, hereby, that some of the auncient Philosophers, and those the moste wise, as Plato and Pythagoras held for opinion, that the mynd was made of a certaine harmonie and musicall nombers, for the great compassion and likenes of affection in thone and in the other as also by that memorable history of Alexander: to whom when as Timotheus the great Musitian playd the Phrygian melodie, it is said, that he was distraught with such unwonted fury, that streight way rysing from the table in great rage, he caused himselfe to be armed, as ready to goe to warre (for that musick is very war like:) And immediatly whenas the Musitian chaunged his stroke into the Lydian and Ionique harmony, he was so furr from warring, that he sat as styl, as if he had bene in matters of counsell. Such might is in musick" [E.K.'s Glosse].
3. "Orpheus: of whom is sayd, that by his excellent skil in Musick and Poetry, he recovered his wife Eurydice from hell" [E.K.'s Glosse]. See Yale on the pairing of Orpheus and Colin in the symmetrical patterning of stanzas throughout "October." The "hellish hound" referred to in line 30 is Cerberus, the three-headed hound guarding the gates of Hades (cf. Ovid, Metamorphoses 10.22; Virgil, Georgics 4.483).
4. "Juno to [Argus] committed hir husband Jupiter his Paragon Io, because he had an hundred eyes: but afterwarde Mercury wyth hys Musick lulling Argus aslepe, slew him and brought Io away, whose eyes it is sayd that Juno for his eternall memory placed in her byrd the Peacocks tayle. For those coloured spots indeede resemble eyes" [E.K.'s Glosse]. Cf. Ovid, Metamorphoses 1.622–723.
5. I.e., therefore.
6. I.e., too mean or low rustic. The stanza promises a movement to higher poetic "kinds," i.e., to the genres of tragedy and epic.
7. "Woundlesse armour," E.K. observes, "unwounded in warre, doe rust through long peace" [Glosse].
8. "A poeticall metaphore: whereof the meaning is, that if the Poet list showe his skill in matter of more dignitie, then is the homely Aeglogue, good occasion is him offered of higher veyne and more Heroicall argument, in the person of our most gratious soveraign, whom (as before) he calleth Elisa. Or if mater of knighthoode and chevalrie please him better, that there be many Noble and valiaunt men, that are both worthy of his payne in theyr deserved prayses, and also favourers of hys skil and faculty" [E.K.'s Glosse].
9. I.e., the earl of Leicester, whose heraldic device was a bear and "ragged" staff.

And when the stubborne stroke of stronger stounds,°   *taxing efforts*
50 Has somewhat slackt the tenor of thy string:[1]
Of love and lustihead° tho mayst thou sing,   *pleasure*
And carrol lowde, and leade the Myllers rownde,[2]
All° were Elisa one of thilke same ring.   *although*
So mought our Cuddies name to Heaven sownde.

CUDDIE

55 Indeede the Romish Tityrus,[3] I heare,
Through his Mecaenas left his Oaten reede,
Whereon he earst° had taught his flocks to feede,   *formerly*
And laboured lands to yield the timely eare,
And eft did sing of warres and deadly drede,
60 So as the Heavens did quake his verse to here.[4]

But ah Mecaenas is yclad in claye,
And great Augustus long ygoe is dead:
And all the worthies liggen° wrapt in leade,   *lie*
That matter made for Poets on to play:
65 For ever, who in derring doe[5] were dreade,
The loftie verse of hem was lovéd aye.[6]

But after vertue gan for age to stoupe,
And mighty manhode brought a bedde of ease:[7]
The vaunting Poets found nought worth a pease,°   *pea*
70 To put in preace[8] cmong the learnéd troupe.
Tho gan the streames of flowing wittes to cease,
And sonnebright honour pend in shamefull coupe.[9]

1. I.e., slackened the strings of your lyre, lowering its pitch; "that is when thou chaungest thy verse from stately discourse, to matter of more pleasaunce and delight" [*E.K.'s Glosse*].
2. "A kind of daunce" [*E.K.'s Glosse*].
3. "Wel knowen to be Virgile, who by Mecaenas means was brought into the favour of the Emperor Augustus, and by him moved to write in loftier kinde, then he erst had doen" [*E.K.'s Glosse*]. Cf. *The Faerie Queene* I P 1–4
4. "In these three verses are the three severall workes of Virgile intended. For in teaching his flocks to feede, is meant his Aeglogues. In labouring of lands, is hys Bucoliques. In singing of wars and deadly dreade, is his divine Aeneis figured" [*E.K.'s Glosse*].
5. I.e., daring deeds.
6. "He sheweth the cause, why Poetes were wont be had in such honor of noble men; that is, that by them their worthines and valor shold through theyr famous Posies be commended to al posterities. Wherfore it is sayd, that Achilles had never bene so famous, as he is, but for Homeres immortal verses. Which is the only advantage, which he had of Hector. . . . And that such account hath bene alwayes made of Poetes, aswell sheweth this that the worthy Scipio in all his warres against Carthage and Numantia had evermore in his company, and that in a most familiar sort the good olde Poet Ennius: as also that Alexander destroying Thebes, when he was enformed that the famous Lyrick Poet Pindarus was borne in that citie, not onely commaunded streightly, that no man should upon payne of death do any violence to that house by fire or otherwise: but also specially spared most, and some highly rewarded, that were of hys kinne. So favoured he the only name of a Poete. Whych prayse otherwise was in the same man no lesse famous, that when he came to ransacking of king Darius coffers, whom he lately had overthrowen, he founde in a little coffer of silver the two bookes of Homers works, as layd up there for special jewells and richesse, which he taking thence, put one of them dayly in his bosome, and thother every night layde under his pillowe" [*E.K.'s Glosse*]. E.K. probably drew these materials from Plutarch's *Life of Alexander* or from Boccaccio.
7. I.e., brought into a passive and helpless state through love of luxurious ease; "he sheweth the cause of contempt of Poetry to be idlenesse and basenesse of mynd" [*E.K.'s Glosse*].
8. I.e., to present for competition.
9. ". . . shut up in slouth, as in a coupe or cage" [*E.K.'s Glosse*].

And if that any buddes of Poesie,
Yet of the old stocke gan to shoote agayne:
75   Or° it mens follies mote be forst to fayne,   *either*
And rolle with rest in rymes of rybaudrye:
Or as it sprong, it wither must agayne:
Tom Piper makes us better melodie.[1]

PIERS

O pierlesse Poesye, where is then thy place?
80   If nor in Princes pallace thou doe sitt:
(And yet is Princes pallace the most fitt)
Ne brest of baser birth[2] doth thee embrace.
Then make thee winges of thine aspyring wit,
And, whence thou camst, flye backe to heaven apace.[3]

CUDDIE

85   Ah Percy it is all to weake and wanne,
So high to sore, and make so large a flight:
Her peecéd pyneons[4] bene not so in plight,°   *condition*
For Colin fittes[5] such famous flight to scanne:°   *attempt*
He, were he not with love so ill bedight,°   *afflicted*
90   Would mount as high, and sing as soote as Swanne.[6]

PIERS

Ah fon,° for love does teach him climbe so hie,   *fool*
And lyftes him up out of the loathsome myre:
Such immortall mirrhor,[7] as he doth admire,
Would rayse ones mynd above the starry skie.
95   And cause a caytive corage[8] to aspire,
For lofty love doth loath a lowly eye.

CUDDIE

All otherwise the state of Poet stands,
For lordly love is such a Tyranne fell:
That where he rules, all power he doth expell.[9]

1. "An Ironicall Sarcasmus, spoken in derision of these rude wits, whych make more account of a ryming rybaud, then of skill grounded upon learning and judgment" [*E.K.'s Glosse*]. "Tom Piper" refers to the piper who accompanied the morris dancers. Montrose 1979 notes how lines 67–78 imply that the debasement of poetry results from "political and sociological constraints" upon the poet (46).
2. ". . . the meaner sort of men" [*E.K.'s Glosse*].
3. I.e., turn to a higher "kind" of poetry, inspired by divine love.
4. I.e., imperfect, patched wings: "unperfect skil" [*E.K.'s Glosse*].
5. I.e., it is proper for Colin.
6. "The comparison seemeth to be strange: for the swanne hath ever wonne small commendation for her swete singing: but it is sayd of the learned that the swan a little before hir death, singeth most pleasantly, as prophecying by a secrete instinct her neere destinie . . ." [*E.K.'s Glosse*].
7. "Beauty, which is an excellent object of Poeticall spirites . . ." [*E.K.'s Glosse*]. The lover, contemplating womanly beauty (which reflects immortal and heavenly beauty), is thereby enabled to rise above earthly concerns, and approach more nearly to divine beauty and love. Image and idea recur often in Spenser's work, notably in *Fowre Hymnes*.
8. ". . . a base and abject minde" [*E.K.'s Glosse*].
9. Elizabethan sonneteers regularly make use of the Ovidian conceit that love is an arbitrary tyrant, whose dictates the lover is powerless to resist.

100 The vaunted verse a vacant head demaundes,
    Ne wont with crabbéd care the Muses dwell.
    Unwisely weaves, that takes two webbes in hand.

    Who ever casts to compasse° weightye prise,   *attain*
    And thinks to throwe out thondring words of threate:
105 Let powre in lavish cups and thriftie° bitts of meate,   *nourishing*
    For Bacchus fruite is frend to Phoebus wise.[1]
    And when with Wine the braine begins to sweate,
    The nombers flowe as fast as spring doth ryse.

    Thou kenst not Percie howe the ryme should rage.
110 O if my temples were distaind° with wine,[2]   *stained*
    And girt in girlonds of wild Yvie twine,
    How I could reare the Muse on stately stage,
    And teache her tread aloft in bus-kin[3] fine,
    With queint Bellona[4] in her equipage.

115 But ah my corage cooles ere it be warme,
    For thy, content us in thys humble shade:
    Where no such troublous tydes han us assayde,°   *assailed*
    Here we our slender pipes may safely charme.[5]

                            PIERS

    And when my Cates shall han their bellies layd:[6]
120 Cuddie shall have a Kidde to store his farme.

                    Cuddies Embleme.

            Agitante calescimus illo &c.[7]

1. "In contrast to Piers, who stresses the Apollonian origins of poetry, Cuddie traces poetry to a bacchic root" (Johnson 1990, 83–84). Both Boccaccio (*De Genealogia Deorum* 5.25) and Comes (*Mythologiae* 5.13) note the power of wine to heighten poetic genius.
2. "He seemeth here to be ravished with a Poetical furie. For (if one rightly mark) the numbers rise so ful, and the verse groweth so big, that it seemeth he hath forgot the meanenesse of shephcards state and stile. . . . Wild yvie . . . is dedicated to Bacchus and therefore it is sayd that the Maenades (that is Bacchus franticke priests) used in theyr sacrifice to carry Thyrsos, which were pointed staves or Javelins, wrapped about with yvie" [*E.K.'s Glosse*].
3. The high boot traditionally worn by the actors of Greek tragedy.
4. "Strange Bellona; the goddesse of battaile, that is Pallas, which may therfore wel be called queint for that (as Lucian saith) when Jupiter hir father was in traveile of her, he caused his sonne Vulcane with his axe to hew his head. Out of which leaped forth lustely a valiant damsell armed at all poyntes . . ." [*E.K.'s Glosse*].
5. "Temper and order. For Charmes were wont to be made by verses as Ovid sayth" [*E.K.'s Glosse*]. The passage referred to may be *Amores* 3.7.27–30.
6. I.e., when my goats have been delivered of their young.
7. From Ovid, *Fasti* 6.5: *est deus in nobis; agitante calescimus illo* (There is a god in us, by whose movement we are kept warm). "Hereby is meant, as also in the whole course of this Aeglogue, that Poetry is a divine instinct and unnatural rage passing the reache of comen reason. Whom Piers answereth Epiphonematicos as admiring the excellencye of the skyll whereof in Cuddie hee hadde alreadye hadde a taste" [*E.K.'s Glosse*]. The rhetorical figure "epiphonema" is a brief moralizing summary of what has gone before. Spenser may have intended to assign part of the line from Ovid to Cuddie, the remainder to Piers.

November

Argument

In this xi. Aeglogue he bewayleth the death of some mayden of greate bloud, whom he calleth Dido.[1] The personage is secrete, and to me altogether unknowne, albe of him selfe I often required[2] the same. This Aeglogue is made in imitation of Marot his song, which he made upon the death of Loys the frenche Queene.[3] But farre passing his reache, and in myne opinion all other the Eglogues of this booke.

THENOT   COLIN

Colin my deare, when shall it please thee sing,
As thou were wont songs of some jovisaunce?°   *merriment*
Thy Muse to long slombreth in sorrowing,
Lulléd a sleepe through loves misgovernaunce.
5 Now somewhat sing, whose endles sovenaunce,°   *remembrance*
Emong the shepeheards swaines may aye remaine,
Whether thee list thy lovéd lasse advaunce,°   *praise*
Or honor Pan with hymnes of higher vaine.°   *vein*

COLIN

Thenot, now nis the time of merimake.°   *festivity*
10 Nor Pan to herye,° nor with love to playe: *honor*

---

1. By one reading, Dido represents Queen Elizabeth, "dead" to Leicester and England by virtue of her marriage negotiations with the French Duc d'Alencon (cf. P. McLane, *Spenser's "Shepheardes Calender": A study in Elizabethan Allegory* [Notre Dame, 1961] 47–60). By another, "Dido is . . . an image of Rosalind as Colin would have liked her to be"; further, the "real and therefore mortal . . . Dido's life and character are based" on the pattern of the relatively "ideal and mythic" Elisa [of "Aprill"]: cf. Cullen 91–92n. On the "Dido riddle," see Kay 1990 (31, n.6); D. Cheney 1989 notes the relevance of the "Sieve" portrait of Elizabeth.
2. Requested.
3. Cf. "Januarye," "Argument" and note. In fact, the opening of this eclogue looks rather to Virgil, *Eclogue* V, the model for Marot's poem.

Sike myrth in May is meetest for to make,
Or summer shade under the cocked° haye.   *stacked*
But nowe sadde Winter welkéd[4] hath the day,
And Phoebus weary of his yerely taske,
15 Ystabled hath his steedes in lowlye laye,°   *meadow*
And taken up his ynne in Fishes haske.[5]
Thilke sollein° season sadder plight doth aske,°   *sullen/require*
And loatheth sike delightes, as thou doest prayse:
The mornefull Muse in myrth now list ne maske,
20 As shee was wont in youngth and sommer dayes.
But if thou algate lust light virelayes,[6]
And looser songs of love to underfong°   *undertake*
Who but thy selfe deserves sike Poetes prayse?
Relieve thy Oaten pypes,[7] that sleepen long.

THENOT

25 The Nightingale is sovereigne of song,
Before him sits the Titmose silent bee:[8]
And I unfitte to thrust in skilfull thronge,
Should Colin make judge of my fooleree.
Nay, better learne of hem, that learnéd bee,
30 And han be watered at the Muses well:[9]
The kindlyc dewe drops from the higher tree,
And wets the little plants that lowly dwell.
But if sadde winters wrathe and season chill,
Accorde not with thy Muses meriment,
35 To sadder times thou mayst attune thy quill,°   *pipe*
And sing of sorrowc and dcathes dreeriment.°   *grief*
For deade is Dido, dead alas and drent,°   *drowned*
Dido the greate shepehearde[1] his daughter sheene:°   *fair*
The fayrest May she was that ever went,[2]
40 Her like shee has not left behinde I weene.°   *believe*
And if thou wilt bewayle my wofull tene,°   *grief*
I shall thee give yond Cosset[3] for thy payne:
And if thy rymes as rownd° and rufull bene,   *finished*

4. "Shortned, or empayred. As the moone being in the waine is sayde of Lidgate to welk" [*E.K.'s Glosse*].
5. I.e., the sun's winter course appears to have sunk below the horizon. "A haske is a wicker pad, wherein they use to cary fish" [*E.K.'s Glosse*]. Although the zodiacal sign of Pisces corresponds to February, E.K. observes, "The sonne reigneth . . . in the signe Pisces all November" [*Glosse*]. At line 37 Thenot refers to Dido's death by drowning (not, as in Virgil, by fire). D. Cheney 1989 suggests that these "errors" may deliberately anticipate [in the light of lines 163–202] a rich and paradoxical celebration of renewal" (160).
6. "A light kind of song" [*E.K.'s Glosse*]; e.g., the rondeau.
7. I.e., take up your reed pipe again. Cf. "October" 8 and note.
8. I.e., it is proper that the titmouse (a small bird not unlike the nuthatch) should be silent in the presence of the nightingale.
9. "For it is a saying of poetes, that they have dronk of the Muses well Castalias . . ." [*E.K.'s Glosse*]. The Castalian spring on Mount Parnassus was sacred to Apollo and the Muses (hence called the Castalides).
1. ". . . some man of high degree, and not, as some vainely suppose, God Pan. The person both of the shephearde and of Dido is unknowen, ánd closely buried in the authors conceipt. But out of doubt I am, that it is not Rosalind, as some imagin: for he speaketh soone after of her also" [*E.K.'s Glosse*].
2. I.e., the fairest maiden that ever walked.
3. "A lambe brought up without the dam" [*E.K.'s Glosse*].

As those that did thy Rosalind complayne,
45 Much greater gyfts for guerdon thou shalt gayne,
Then Kidde or Cosset, which I thee bynempt:°   *promised*
Then up I say, thou jolly shepeheard swayne,
Let not my small demaund be so contempt.°   *scorned*

COLIN

Thenot to that I choose, thou doest me tempt,
50 But ah to well I wote my humble vaine,
And howe my rymes bene rugged and unkempt:°   *rough*
Yet as I conne, my conning I will strayne.[4]

A Dirge

"Up then Melpomene thou mournefulst Muse of nyne,[5]
Such cause of mourning never hadst afore:
55 Up grieslie ghostes[6] and up my rufull ryme,
Matter of myrth now shalt thou have no more.
For dead shee is, that myrth thee made of yore.
    Dido my deare alas is dead,
    Dead and lyeth wrapt in lead:
60   O heavie herse,[7]
Let streaming teares be pouréd out in store:
        O carefull verse.

"Shepheards, that by your flocks on Kentish downes abyde,
Waile ye this wofull waste° of natures warke: *devastation*
65 Waile we the wight, whose presence was our pryde:
Waile we the wight, whose absence is our carke.°   *grief*
The sonne of all the world is dimme and darke:
    The earth now lacks her wonted light,
    And all we dwell in deadly night,
70   O heavie herse.
Breake we our pypes, that shrild as lowde as Larke,
        O carefull verse.

"Why doe we longer live, (ah why live we so long)
Whose better dayes death hath shut up in woe?
75 The fayrest floure our gyrlond all emong,
Is faded quite and into dust ygoe.°   *gone*
Sing now ye shepheards daughters, sing no moe
    The songs that Colin made in her prayse,
    But into weeping turne your wanton° layes,   *playful*
80   O heavie herse,

4. I.e., yet as well as I know how, I will exert my skill. The dirge that begins at line 53 recalls, complements, and effectively fulfills the "hints of re-creation" in Colin's lay in "Aprill"; see Johnson 1990, 174.
5. An invocation to Melpomene, "the sadde and waylefull Muse, used of poets in honor of tragedies" [*E.K.'s Glosse*], suitably introduces the elaborately crafted elegy.
6. "The maner of tragicall poetes, to call for helpe of furies and damned ghostes: so is Hecuba of Euripides, and Tantalus brought in of Seneca" [*E.K.'s Glosse*]. E.K. is somewhat confused: the ghost of Tantalus appears in Seneca's *Thyestes*, but it is the ghost of Polydorus that appears in Euripides' *Hecuba*.
7. "The solemne obsequie in funeralles" [*E.K.'s Glosse*].

Now is time to dye. Nay time was long ygoe,
    O carefull verse.

"Whence is it, that the flouret of the field doth fade,
And lyeth buryed long in Winters bale:[8]
85 Yet soone as spring his mantle doth displaye,
It floureth fresh, as it should never fayle?
But thing on earth that is of most availe,°   *worth*
  As vertues braunch and beauties budde,
  Reliven° not for any good.   *revive*
90   O heavie herse,
The braunch once dead, the budde eke needes must quaile,°   *wither*
    O carefull verse.[9]

"She while she was (that was, a woful word to sayne)
For beauties prayse and plesaunce had no pere:
95 So well she couth the shepherds entertayne,
With cakes and cracknells° and such country chere.   *biscuits*
Ne would she scorne the simple shepheards swaine,
  For she would cal hem often heme°   *home*
  And give hem curds and clouted° Creme.   *clotted*
100   O heavie herse,
Als° Colin Cloute she would not once disdayne.   *also*
    O carefull verse.

"But nowe sike happy cheere is turnd to heavie chaunce,
Such pleasaunce now displast by dolors dint:
105 All Musick sleepes, where death doth leade the daunce,
And shepherds wonted solace is extinct.
The blew in black, the greene in gray is tinct,°   *dyed*
  The gaudie girlonds[1] deck her grave,
  The faded flowres her corse embrave.°   *adorn*
110   O heavie herse,
Morne nowe my Muse, now morne with teares besprint.°   *besprinkled*
    O carefull verse.

"O thou greate shepheard Lobbin,[2] how great is thy griefe,
Where bene the nosegays that she dight° for thee,   *made*
115 The colourd chaplets wrought with a chiefe,
The knotted rushrings,[3] and gilte Rosemaree?
For shee deeméd nothing too deere for thee.

8. I.e., winter's harmful power.
9. While lines 83–92 recall Moschus, *Idyl* 3.99–104, there are scriptural echoes too: "For there is hope of a tree, if it be cut down, that it will sprout again, and that the tender branch thereof will not cease. Though the root thereof wax old in the earth, and the stock thereof die in the ground; yet through the scent of water it will bud, and bring forth boughs like a plant. But man dieth, and wasteth away: yea, man giveth up the ghost, and where is he?" (Job 14.7–10).
1. "The meaning is, that the things which were the ornaments of her lyfe are made the honor of her funerall, as is used in burials" [*E.K.'s Glosse*].
2. "The name of a shepherd, which seemeth to have bene the lover and deere frende of Dido" [*E.K.'s Glosse*]. If Dido is to be identified with Queen Elizabeth, "Lobbin" may well refer to her favorite Robert Dudley, earl of Leicester (1531–88), Spenser's patron in 1579–80. "Lobbin," then, might be an anagram for "[R]obbin L."
3. "Agreeable for such base gyftes" [*E.K.'s Glosse*].

Ah they bene all yclad in clay,
One bitter blast blewe all away.
120   O heavie herse,
Thereof nought remaynés but the memoree.
     O carefull verse.

"Ay me that dreerie death should strike so mortall stroke,
That can undoe Dame Natures kindly° course: *natural*
125 The faded lockes[4] fall from the loftie oke,
The flouds° do gaspe, for dryéd is theyr sourse,   *streams*
And flouds of teares flowe in theyr stead perforse.
     The mantled medowes mourne,
     Theyr sondry colours tourne.
130   O heavie herse,
The heavens doe melt in teares without remorse.
     O carefull verse.

[handwritten margin note: a traditional convention; all nature mourns a loved one's death]

"The feeble flocks in field refuse their former foode,
And hang theyr heads, as they would learne to weepe:
135 The beastes in forest wayle as they were woode,°   *mad*
Except the Wolves, that chase the wandring sheepe:
Now she is gon that safely did hem keepe,
     The Turtle° on the baréd braunch,   *turtledove*
     Laments the wound, that death did launch.°   *inflict*
140   O heavie herse,
And Philomele[5] her song with teares doth steepe.
     O carefull verse.

"The water Nymphs, that wont with her to sing and daunce,
And for her girlond Olive braunches beare,
145 Now balefull boughes of Cypres[6] doen advaunce:°   *bring*
The Muses, that were wont greene bayes° to weare,   *laurels*
Now bringen bitter Eldre braunches seare,[7]
     The fatall sisters[8] eke repent,
     Her vitall threde so soone was spent.
150   O heavie herse,
Morne now my Muse, now morne with heavie cheare.°   *mood*
     O carefull verse.

4. "Dryed leaves. As if Nature her selfe bewayled the death of the mayde" [*E.K.'s Glosse*]. Lines 123–42 exemplify a traditional convention of pastoral elegy from the time of Theocritus, that "all nature mourns" the loved one's passing. In *Modern Painters* (5 vols., [London, 1843–60] 3.4), John Ruskin describes the attribution of human capacities to inanimate objects as the "pathetic fallacy": "the extraordinary, or false appearances, when we are under the influence of emotion, or contemplative fancy."
5. "The nightingale: whome the poetes faine once to have bene a ladye of great beauty, till, being ravished by her sisters husbande, she desired to be turned into a byrd of her name" [*E.K.'s Glosse*]. Cf. *Metamorphoses* 6.424–674.
6. "Used of the old paynims in the furnishing of their funerall pompe, and properly the signe of all sorow and heavinesse" [*E.K.'s Glosse*].
7. "So unlucky is the elder that in Langland's *Piers Plowman*, Judas is made to hang himself on an elder tree. . . . The elder is the tree of doom. . . ." (Robert Graves, *The White Goddess* [New York, 1958] 191–92).
8. I.e., the Fates: Clotho, who spins the thread of human life; Lachesis, who measures its length; Atropos, who cuts it with her shears.

"O trustlesse[9] state of earthly things, and slipper° hope   *slippery*
Of mortal men, that swincke° and sweate for nought,   *toil*
155 And shooting wide, doe misse the markéd scope:°   *target*
Now have I learnd (a lesson derely bought)
That nys on earth assuraunce to be sought:
    For what might be in earthlie mould,°   *form*
    That did her buried body hould,
160   O heavie herse,
Yet saw I on the beare° when it was brought   *bier*
        O carefull verse.

"But maugre° death, and dreaded sisters deadly spight,   *in spite of*
And gates of hel, and fyrie fúries[1] forse,
165 She hath the bonds broke of eternall night,
Her soule unbodied of the burdenous corpse.
Why then weepes Lobbin so without remorse?°   *moderation*
    O Lobb, thy losse no longer lament,
    Dido nis dead, but into heaven hent.°   *taken*
170   O happye herse,
Cease now my Muse, now cease thy sorrowes sourse,°   *flow*
        O joyfull verse.

"Why wayle we then? why weary we the Gods with playnts,
As if some evill were to her betight?°   *befallen*
175 She raignes a goddesse now emong the saintes,
That whilome was the saynt of shepheards light:°   *simple*
And is enstalléd nowe in heavens hight.
    I see thee blessed soule, I see,[2]
    Walke in Elisian fieldes[3] so free.
180   O happy herse,
Might I once come to thee (O that I might)
        O joyfull verse.

"Unwise and wretched men to weete whats good or ill,
We deeme of Death as doome of ill desert:[4]
185 But knewe we fooles, what it us bringes until,°   *to*
Dye would we dayly, once it to expert.[5]
No daunger there the shepheard can astert:°   *disturb*
    Fayre fieldes and pleasaunt layes° there bene,   *meadows*
    The fieldes ay fresh, the grasse ay greene:
190   O happy herse,

9. "A gallant exclamation, moralised with great wisedom, and passionate with great affection" [*E.K.'s Glosse*]. The emphasis of lines 153–62 on the "earthlie" context of Colin's dirge to this point dramatically prepares for the change of key, common to classical and Christian elegy, in the remainder of the poem.
1. The three Furies, Tisiphone, Alecto, and Megaera, daughters of Earth (or of Night), dwelt in the depths of Tartarus; they punished men and women in life and after death. E.K. calls them "the authours of all evill and mischiefe" [*Glosse*]. Cf. *Aeneid* 7.324–26.
2. "A lively icon or representation, as if he saw her in heaven present" [*E.K.'s Glosse*].
3. Cf. *The Faerie Queene* IV.x.23.
4. I.e., as an appropriate recompense for an evil or ill-spent life.
5. I.e., to experience. E.K. calls attention to the similar thought in Plato, *Phaedo* (thinking perhaps of 68–69). See Pigman 1985 on the harshness of lines 183–86, not matched in Marot's poem.

Make hast ye shepheards, thether to revert,°   *return*
        O joyfull verse.

"Dido is gone afore (whose turne shall be the next?)
There lives shee with the blessed Gods in blisse,
195 There drincks she Nectar with Ambrosia mixt,[6]
And joyes enjoyes, that mortall men doe misse.
The honor now of highest gods she is,
        That whilome was poore shepheards pryde,
        While here on earth she did abyde.
200   O happy herse,
Ceasse now my song, my woe now wasted° is.   *spent*
        O joyfull verse."

THENOT

Ay francke shepheard, how bene thy verses meint°   *mingled*
With doolful pleasaunce, so as I ne wotte,°   *know*
205 Whether rejoyce or weepe for great constrainte?°   *distress*
Thyne be the cossette, well hast thow it gotte.
Up Colin up, ynough thou mornéd hast,
Now gynnes to mizzle,° hye we homeward fast.   *drizzle*

Colins Embleme.

La mort ny mord.[7]

Death bitest nd.

6. "Feigned to be the drink and food of the gods: ambrosia they liken to manna in Scripture, and nectar to be white like creme . . ." [E.K.'s Glosse].
7. "Which is as much to say as, *death biteth not.* For although by course of nature we be borne to dye, and being ripened with age, as with a timely harvest, we must be gathered in time, or els of our selves fall like rotted ripefruite fro the tree: yet death is not to be counted for evill, nor (as the poete sayd a little before) as doome of ill desert. For though the trespasse of the first man brought death into the world, as the guerdon of sinne, yet being overcome by the death of one that dyed for al, it is now made (as Chaucer sayth) the grene path way to life. So that it agreeth well with that was sayd, that Death byteth not (that is) hurteth not at all" [E.K.'s Glosse]. Spenser acknowledges his debt to Marot, who called himself "Colin," by adopting the French poet's own motto for this eclogue that E.K. so much admires.

December†

Argument

This Aeglogue (even as the first beganne) is ended with a complaynte of Colin to God Pan. Wherein as weary of his former wayes, he proportioneth his life to the foure seasons of the yeare, comparing hys youthe to the spring time, when he was fresh and free from loves follye. His manhoode to the summer, which he sayth, was consumed with greate heate and excessive drouth caused throughe a Comet or blasinge starre, by which hee meaneth love, which passion is comenly compared to such flames and immoderate heate. His riper yeares hee resembleth to an unseasonable harveste wherein the fruites fall ere they be rype. His latter age to winters chyll and frostie season, now drawing neare to his last ende.

The gentle shepheard satte beside a springe,
All in the shadowe of a bushye brere,°   *briar*
That Colin hight, which wel could pype and singe,
For he of Tityrus[1] his songs did lere.°   *learn*
5   There as he satte in secreate shade alone,
   Thus gan he make of love his piteous mone.

"O soveraigne Pan thou God of shepheards all,
Which of our tender Lambkins takest keepe:
And when our flocks into mischaunce mought fall,
10 Doest save from mischiefe the unwary sheepe:
   Als° of their maisters hast no lesse regarde,   *also*
   Then of the flocks, which thou doest watch and ward:

---

† In this final eclogue Spenser closely follows Marot's *Eclogue . . . au Roy* (1539); see, among others, Prescott 1978, Patterson 1986. Johnson 1990 notes the related iconographical functions of the woodcuts for "Januarie" and "December," and their hints of the isolation and sterility associated with Ovid's Narcissus (*Metamorphoses* 3.345–510).

1. See "Februarie," 92 and note.

"I thee beseche (so be thou deigne to heare,
Rude ditties tund to shepheards Oaten reede,
15 Or if I ever sonet[2] song so cleare,
As it with pleasaunce mought thy fancie feede)
    Hearken awhile from thy greene cabinet,°   *bower*
    The rurall song of carefull Colinet.

"Whilome in youth, when flowrd my joyfull spring,
20 Like Swallow swift I wandred here and there:
For heate of heedlesse lust me so did sting,
That I of doubted° daunger had no feare.   *fearful*
    I went° the wastefull woodes and forest wyde,   *walked*
    Withouten dreade of Wolves to bene espyed.

25 "I wont to raunge amydde the mazie thickette,
And gather nuttes to make me Christmas game:°   *pleasure*
And joyéd oft to chace the trembling Pricket,°   *young deer*
Or hunt the hartlesse° hare, til shee were tame.   *timid*
    What wreakéd° I of wintrye ages waste,   *cared*
30 Tho deeméd I, my spring would ever laste.

"How often have I scaled the craggie Oke,
All to dislodge the Raven of her neste:
Howe have I weariéd with many a stroke
The stately Walnut tree, the while the rest
35 Under the tree fell all for nuts at strife:
    For ylike° to me was libertee and lyfe.   *the same*

"And for I was in thilke same looser yeares,[3]
(Whether the Muse so wrought me from my birth,
Or I tomuch beleeved my shepherd peres)
40 Somedele° ybent to song and musicks[4] mirth.   *somewhat*
    A good olde shephearde, Wrenock[5] was his name,
    Made me by arte more cunning in the same.

"Fro thence I durst in derring doe[6] compare
With shepheards swayne, what ever fedde in field:
And if that Hobbinol right judgement bare,°   *held*
45 To Pan his owne selfe pype I neede not yield.
    For if the flocking Nymphes did folow Pan,
    The wiser Muses after Colin ranne.

2. A little poem or song. On the various senses of "thy greene cabinet" (in line 17 [the expression
   is from Marot's *Eclogue . . . au Roy* 1.13]), and their implications for Spenser's stance in pastoral
   contexts, see T. Rosenmeyer, *The Green Cabinet: Theocritus and the European Pastoral Lyric*
   (Berkeley and Los Angeles, 1969), Montrose 1980, Patterson 1986.
3. I.e., since I was in those, my salad days.
4. "That is poetry, as Terence sayth, *Qui artem tractant musicam* ['those who follow poetic art,'
   Terence, *Phormio*, Prologue, 17], speaking of poetes" [*E.K.'s Glosse*].
5. Wrenock is thought to represent Richard Mulcaster (c.1530–1611), Spenser's headmaster at the
   Merchant Taylors' School in London.
6. I.e., daring deeds.

"But ah such pryde at length was ill repayde,
50 The shepheards God (perdie God was he none)
My hurtlesse pleasaunce did me ill upbraide,
My freedome lorne, my life he lefte to mone.[7]
　　Love they him callèd, that gave me checkmate,
　　But better mought they have behote° him Hate.　　　　*named*

55 "Tho gan my lovely Spring bid me farewel,
And Sommer season sped him to display
(For love then in the Lyons house[8] did dwell)
The raging fyre, that kindled at his ray.
　　A comett stird up that unkindly heate,
60　　That reignéd (as men sayd) in Venus[9] seate.

"Forth was I ledde, not as I wont afore,
When choise I had to choose my wandring waye:
But whether luck and loves unbridled lore
Would leade me forth on Fancies bitte to playe,
65　　The bush my bedde, the bramble was my bowre,
　　The Woodes can witnesse many a wofull stowre.°　　　*affliction*

"Where I was[1] wont to seeke the honey Bee,
Working her formall rowmes[2] in Wexen frame:
The grieslie° Todestoole growne there mought I see　　*ugly*
70 And loathéd Paddocks° lording on the same.　　　　*toads*
　　And where the chaunting birds luld me a sleepe,
　　The ghastlie Owle her grievous° ynne doth keepe.　　*dreary*

"Then as the springe gives place to elder time,
And bringeth forth the fruite of sommers pryde:
75 All° so my age now passéd youngthly pryme,　　　　*even*
To thinges of ryper reason selfe° applyed.　　　　　　*itself*
　　And learnd of lighter timber cotes° to frame,　　　*shelters*
　　Such as might save my sheepe and me from shame.°　*disaster*

"To make fine cages for the Nightingale,
80 And Baskets of bulrushes was my wont:
Who to entrappe the fish in winding sale°　　　　　　*net*
Was better seene,° or hurtful beastes to hont?　　　　*skilled*
　　I learnéd als° the signes of heaven to ken,　　　　*also*
　　How Phoebe fayles, where Venus sittes and when.[3]

7. I.e., he did evilly abuse my harmless pleasure; my freedom was lost; he left me a life of lamentation.
8. "He imagineth simply that Cupid, which is Love, had his abode in the whote signe Leo, which is in middest of somer; a pretie allegory, whereof the meaning is that love in him wrought an extraordinarie heate of lust" [*E.K.'s Glosse*].
9. "The goddess of beauty or pleasure. Also a signe in heaven, as it is here taken. So he meaneth that beautie, which hath alwayes aspect to Venus, was the cause of all his unquietnes in love" [*E.K.'s Glosse*].
1. "A fine description of the chaunge of hys lyfe and liking; for all things nowe seemed to hym to have altered their kindly [i.e., natural] course" [*E.K.'s Glosse*]. Cf. "November" 125, and note.
2. I.e., symmetrical compartments.
3. Noting that "Phoebe fayles" refers to the eclipse of the moon, and that "Venus starre" is also called "Hesperus, and Vesper, and Lucifer," E.K. concludes, "All which skill in starres being convenient for shepheardes to knowe, Theocritus and the rest use" [*Glosse*].

85 "And tryéd time⁴ yet taught me greater thinges,
    The sodain rysing of the raging seas:
    The soothe of byrds by beating of their wings,⁵
    The power of herbs, both which can hurt and ease:⁶
    And which be wont t'enrage° the restlesse sheepe,   *arouse*
90 And which be wont to worke eternall sleepe.

    "But ah unwise and witlesse Colin Cloute,
    That kydst° the hidden kinds of many a wede: *knew*
    Yet kydst not ene° to cure thy sore hart roote,   *even*
    Whose ranckling wound as yet does rifelye° bleede.   *copiously*
95 Why livest thou stil, and yet hast thy deathes wound?
    Why dyest thou stil, and yet alive art founde?

    "Thus is my sommer worne away and wasted,
    Thus is my harvest hastened all to rathe:°   *soon*
    The care that budded faire, is burnt and blasted,°   *withered*
100 And all my hopéd gaine is turnd to scathe.°   *loss*
    Of all the seede, that in my youth was sowne,
    Was nought but brakes° and brambles to be mowne.   *bracken*

    "My boughes with bloosmes that crownéd were at firste,
    And promiséd of timely fruite such store,
    Are left both bare and barrein now at erst°   *length*
105 The flattring° fruite is fallen to growND before,   *promising*
    And rotted, ere they were halfe mellow ripe:
    My harvest wast, my hope away dyd wipe.

    "The fragrant flowres,⁷ that in my garden grewe,
110 Bene withered, as° they had bene gathered long.   *as if*
    Theyr rootes bene dryéd up for lacke of dewe,
    Yet dewed with teares they han be ever among.⁸
    Ah who has wrought my° Rosalind this spight,   *in my*
    To spil° the flowres, that should her girlond dight?   *destroy*

115 "And I, that whilome wont to frame° my pype,   *direct*
    Unto the shifting of the shepheards foote:
    Sike follies nowe have gathered as too ripe
    And cast hem out, as rotten and unsoote.°   *unsweet*
    The loser° Lasse I cast° to please nomore,   *fickle/resolve*
120 One⁹ if I please, enough is me therefore.

4. I.e., life's experiences.
5. "A kind of sooth saying used in elder tymes, which they gathered by the flying of byrds: first (as
   is sayd) invented by the Thuscanes [i.e., the Etruscans], and from them derived to the Romanes
   . . ." [E.K.'s Glosse]. Cf. Cicero, De Diviniatione 1.41.
6. "That wonderous thinges be wrought by herbes, aswell appeareth by the common working of them
   in our bodies, as also by the wonderful enchauntments and sorceries that have bene wrought by
   them: insomuch that it is sayde that Circe, a famous sorceresse, turned men into sondry kinds of
   beastes and monsters, and onely by herbes . . ." [E.K.'s Glosse].
7. "Sundry studies and laudable partes of learning, wherein how our poete is seene, be thy witnesse,
   which are privie to his study" [E.K.'s Glosse].
8. I.e., have continually been.
9. I.e., by one view, God; by another and more likely reading, Colin himself.

"And thus of all my harvest hope I have
Nought reapéd but a weedye crop of care:
Which, when I thought have thresht in swelling sheave,
Cockel° for corne, and chaffe for barley bare.°   weeds/bore
125 Soone as the chaffe should in the fan be fynd,[1]
All was blowne away of the wavering wynd.

"So now my yeare drawes to his latter terme,
My spring is spent, my sommer burnt up quite:
My harveste hasts to stirre up winter sterne,
130 And bids him clayme with rigorous rage hys right.
So nowe he stormes with many a sturdy stoure,°   blast
So now his blustring blast eche coste doth scoure.°   scourge

"The carefull cold[2] hath nypt my rugged rynde,
And in my face deepe furrowes eld° hath pight:°   age/placed
135 My head besprent° with hoary frost I fynd,   sprinkled
And by myne eie the Crow his clawe dooth wright.
Delight is layd abedde, and pleasure past,
No sonne now shines, cloudes han all overcast.

"Now leave ye shepheards boyes your merry glee,
140 My Muse is hoarse and weary of thys stounde:°   struggle
Here will I hang my pype upon this tree,
Was never pype of reede did better sounde.
Winter is come, that blowes the bitter blaste,
And after Winter dreerie death does hast.

145 "Gather ye together my little flocke,
My little flock, that was to me so liefe:°   dear
Let me, ah lette me in your folds ye lock,
Ere the breme° Winter breede you greater griefe.   fierce
Winter is come, that blowes the balefull breath,
150 And after Winter commeth timely death.

"Adieu delightes,[3] that lulléd me asleepe,
Adieu my deare, whose love I bought so deare:
Adieu my little Lambes and lovéd sheepe,
Adieu ye Woodes that oft my witnesse were:

---

1. I.e., be made fine; driven off.
2. "For care is sayd to coole the blood" [E.K.'s Glosse].
3. "A conclusion of all, where in sixe verses he comprehendeth briefly all that was touched in this book. In the first verse his delights of youth generally; in the second, his love of Rosalind: in the thyrd, the keeping of sheepe, which is the argument of all Aeglogues: in the fourth, his complaints: and in the last two, his professed friendship and good will to his good friend Hobbinol" [E.K.'s Glosse].

155　Adieu good Hobbinol, that was so true,
　　　Tell Rosalind, her Colin bids her adieu."

Colins Embleme.

[*Vivitur ingenio: caetera mortis erunt.*][4]

[Envoy]†

Loe I have made a Calender for every yeare,
That steele in strength, and time in durance shall outweare:
And if I marked well the starres revolution,
It shall continewe till the worlds dissolution.[1]
5　To teach the ruder shepheard how to feede his sheepe,
And from the falsers° fraud his folded flocke to keepe.　　　　*deceiver's*
　　Goe lyttle Calender, thou hast a free passeporte,
Goe but a lowly gate emongste the meaner sorte.
Dare not to match thy pype with Tityrus hys style,[2]
10　　Nor with the Pilgrim that the Ploughman playde a whyle;[3]
But followed them farre off, and their high steppes adore,
The better please, the worse despise, I ask no more.

Merce non mercede.[4]

Editors' Note

The Shepheardes Calender, first published in 1579, and four times reprinted by 1597, consists of twelve pastoral eclogues, framed by the introductory verses, "To His Booke," and by an envoy (or epilogue) of twelve lines in couplets. The author is identified only as "Immerito," for Spenser's circumstances were by no means those of the privileged courtiers, "Master Sidney, and Master Dyer": is provided with a preface (in the form of a letter addressed to the poet's friend Gabriel Harvey) and an introductory note on the "generall argument," which calls attention to the division of the twelve eclogues into "plaintive," "recreative," or "moral . . . formes or ranckes," and notices the variety of calendrical arrangements adopted in ancient times. There is also a running "Glosse" or detailed commentary on the language, imagery, and allegorical significance of each eclogue. All these elements were provided by one "E.K.," whose identity has not been finally established. A case has been made for (among others)

---

4. Cf. Textual Notes. "The meaning whereof is, that all thinges perish and come to theyr last end, but workes of learned wits and monuments of poetry abide for ever . . ." [*E.K.'s Closse*]. The passage is to be found in "Elegiae in Maecenatem" 37–38, part of the *Appendix Vergiliana*, a collection of minor poems attributed to Virgil in Spenser's time. Modern scholars are generally agreed that "Elegiae in Maecenatum" are not in fact Virgilian.

† "In the epilogue to the *Calender* . . . Spenser speaks in his own voice . . . ," creating "the distance that allows authorial comment about the meaning of his fiction" (Heninger 1990E).

1. At the end of the *Metamorphoses*, Ovid observes that "neither fire nor sword nor consuming time can destroy" his work (15.871–72).

2. I.e., Chaucer's style or manner; probably also, by extension, the achievement of Virgil (cf. "October" 55).

3. I.e., either (1) with the Pilgrim, the role played for a time by the Ploughman, or, more probably, (2) with the Pilgrim, who played the role of a Ploughman for a time. If the latter is correct, line 10 refers to William Langland (c. 1330–c. 1400), author of *The Vision of Piers Plowman*.

4. "For reward [in the sense of substantial and intelligent response] not for hire [or salary]." See also Kennedy 1980, 1990E.

Edward Kirke, Spenser's contemporary at Cambridge; but scholars nowadays prefer to believe that Spenser and Harvey collaborated in some fashion to produce these prefatory materials, or that "the . . . initials are a cover for Spenser himself. . . . [E.K.] functions as one of Spenser's voices in the poem" (Johnson 1990). The glosses are ordinarily printed in full, together with Spenser's eclogues; in this edition, excerpts from the glosses to "Januarye," "Februarie," "Aprill," "October," "November," and "December" have been incorporated in the footnotes. E.K.'s comments are often pedantic (perhaps deliberately so) and occasionally inaccurate (e.g., his insistence on the term "aeglogue"), but they regularly draw attention to the poet's learning and, in particular, to his rhetorical skill; further, they emphasize, either directly or by implication, the poet's serious attention to literary tradition, his loyalty to the "best and most auncient Poetes," and his ability to bring something new and peculiarly English to the genre of pastoral poetry. "So finally flyeth this our new Poete, as a bird, whose principals be scarce growen out, but yet as that in time shall be hable to keepe wing with the best."

Some critics might deplore Spenser's archaisms in the *Calender* (Dr. Johnson's allusion, in 1750, to "studied barbarity," recalled the strictures of Sidney and Ben Jonson); but from the time of the poem's first appearance, while readers were attracted by its range of versification, intrigued by its allegories, or impressed by the poet's vision of his role in society, the most telling critical opinions have emphasized Spenser's independent achievement within the context of poetical tradition, notably that of the pastoral kind. Francis Meres, recalling Theocritus and Virgil, praised "Spencer their imitator in his *Shepheardes Calender* . . . for fine Poeticall invention and most exquisit wit" (*Palladis Tamia*, 1598); while Dryden, observing that England had "produced a third poet in this kind, not inferior to [Theocritus and Virgil]," remarked also that Spenser was "master of our northern dialect, and skilled in Chaucer's English."

One aspect of Spenser's particular relationship to literary tradition is linguistic in character. The experiments with English quantitative verse, in the company of Sidney and Dyer, had interested him; but at length he would exclaim to Harvey, "Why a Gods name may not we, as else the Greekes, have the kingdome of oure owne Language. . . ." In the *Calender*, Spenser was consciously following literary precedent: not many years before, the "Pléiade" (led by Du Bellay and Ronsard), impatient with the continuing dependence of French poetry on an outworn and rigidly authoritative classicism, had encouraged the return to purer classical forms, together with an energetic and explorative use of the vernacular, in order to refresh and invigorate the language. Something of this linguistic nationalism, in an English context, informs Spenser's use of alliterative verse forms, archaic terms, and rustic names; in particular, Colin's name recalls the poetry of Skelton (as well as that of Clément Marot), while Virgil, "the Romish Tityrus," is gracefully drawn into association with an English Tityrus, Chaucer, the "God of shepheards" whom Spenser recalls in "Februarie" and, in "June," acknowledges as his master. So the poet, consciously breaking new ground in his own time, takes care that the classical and English springs of his art shall not be neglected: his originality, never merely novel, truly returns to the sources and origins of relevant tradition.

In its formal aspect also, Spenser's way with traditional materials is neither to follow submissively after literary precedents nor to depart from them altogether, but rather to explore and develop their potential in a fashion appropriate to his circumstances and outlook. The name of his poem Spenser drew from a fifteenth-century French almanac and encyclopedia, *Le Compost et Kalendrier des bergiers* (an English translation of which had been seven times reprinted before 1579); but this work did not otherwise influence *The Shepheardes Calender*, which represents a significant advance within the European development of the pastoral tradition. The pastoral eclogue, in its simplest original form (i.e., the Theocritean idyl of the third century B.C.), presents a dialogue between shepherds, who discourse and sing of love and death, while tending their flocks in a rustic setting. Under Virgil's hand, the thing became a carefully structured artistic creation, typically including disguised allusions to particular poets or leaders of the state; somewhat neglected in medieval times, the Virgilian eclogue was widely imitated by Italian and French Renaissance humanists, notably Petrarch, Boccaccio, and Mantuan, all of whom seized upon the genre as a vehicle for ecclesiastical satire (in the light of that peaceful repose which, in pastoral tradition, recalled the golden age, and also Eden), while they retained its conventional machinery. Spenser's immediate models were, in some particulars, the eclogues of Mantuan and Marot; yet he had Virgil's example in view when he chose the pastoral form for this first earnest of his poetical aspirations: "October" especially reflects his concern to combine a high Virgilian strain with the notes sounded in later vernacular versions of pastoral.

The character of learned commentary on the *Calender* has in this century shifted considerably since the *Variorum* volume of 1942, in which "historical scholarship," primarily concerned with sources, analogues, and the identification of persons shadowed in the poem, bore all the sway. Many leading scholars then and later have subscribed to a philosophically oriented "Christian humanism" that emphasizes the enabling role of classical and Christian tradition in the poet's interlacement of natural, ecclesiastical, and moral elements about the figure of a central poet-pastor, whose expectations and problems in some sense mirror Spenser's own. A. C. Hamilton (owing something to Bush and Woodhouse but rather more to Frye), noting E. K.'s reminder that to the division of the *Calender* into plaintive, recreative, and moral eclogues "every thing herein [may] be reasonably applyed," broke new ground in 1956 with his brisk and telling proposal that the argument of the poem is "the *rejection* of the pastoral life for the truly dedicated life in the world," and that "the patterning of the eclogues . . . provides the developing argument of the poem." Responding directly or indirectly to these emphases, MacCaffrey 1969, Cullen 1970, and Alpers 1972 (and in a distinctive sense Berger 1969, 1988) may be thought to represent a third kind of approach to the poem: a newly critical concern, founded in close reading of the text, with the relation of the *Calender* to pastoral, and the relation of Colin Clout to Spenser.

At the present time the continuing "transformation of [the *Calender*] into a sociopolitical statement" (Heninger 1990E) must be of compelling concern to students of Spenser's art. Deriving from an amalgam of Neomarxist political theory, Derridean deconstruction of literary texts, a "New Historicism" that challenges "assumptions that guarantee a secure distinction between 'literary foreground' and 'political background' " (Greenblatt 1982), and marked by keen sensitivity to the interplay of political power with that of the poet—not forgetting reliance on close reading in the context of reader-response criticism—this critical methodology has paid some rewarding dividends to Spenser scholars of every description. Montrose 1979–80 (and after) is provocative on the symbolic undersong of "Aprill," "October," and much else in the poem; Patterson 1986 is equally provocative and perhaps even more plausible in her reminder of the poet's courage in suggesting (secretly) what is wrong with the political system. In this house, of course, there are many mansions. For Goldberg 1981 the *Calender* is a poem of "fissures, of losses, of disconnections: a jumble of poetic kinds and attitudes, prose and verse, woodcuts and emblematics. All that unites the poet's pleasure to the demands of society is loss." The insistent implication that Spenser and Colin are effectively one may tell truth, although the jointure of poet and persona seems better suited to the later *Colin Clouts Come Home Againe*. Spenser is deeply concerned, to be sure, with the poet's acceptance of his responsibilities, to his craft and to his demanding social role; and he is profoundly troubled, too, by the inequities of an Elizabethan state, so often careless of its more gifted subjects. Still, in "November," noting that Christ's sacrifice has given death new meaning, the poet invites us to smile gently at this self-absorbed shepherd's woe. That Colin, in "December," abandons his art and relapses into self-pitying paralysis reminds the reader that Spenser is not too literally to be identified with the shepherd-poet. In any event, whatever interest of a linguistic, formal, or structural nature the *Calender* has held for its critics, there can be little doubt that the poem's continuing appeal for readers in every age derives in considerable measure from what James Russell Lowell in 1875 called "a variety, elasticity, and harmony of verse most grateful to the ears of man." To represent the *Calender* merely by selections is to obscure Spenser's extraordinary range of versification, which includes accentual alliterative verse, more than one kind of ballad stanza, quatrains, odes, and even an instance of the Italian sestina (employed also by Sidney in the *Arcadia*). Still, the eclogues selected for the present edition illustrate in some degree the variety of effect everywhere informing the *Calender*: the six-line stanza of "Januarye," for example (repeated, appropriately, in "December"), reappears in "October," but with an altered rhyme scheme; the employment, in "Aprill," of linked quatrains to frame the emblematic ode that centers this eclogue, exemplifies the poet's delight in matching rhythmically contrasted forms within the separate eclogues. The dirge in "November," in some ways unique in the *Calender*, recalls (but does not merely repeat) the rhyme scheme and patterning of the "Aprill" ode, managing thereby subtly to prepare the reader, even in the presence of "dreerie death," for the joyful release of this eclogue's concluding stanzas. Alpers 1972 calls the *Calender's* "power as a technical performance . . . essential to its spiritual use—which is to enable men to endure, accept, celebrate . . ."(363).

Spenser's concern with time and its role in the affairs of men and women, continuously apparent over the whole range of his work, shifts from an early emphasis on time defeated (as in *The Ruines of Time*), by way of the steadily more gloomy musings that introduce the later Books of *The Faerie Queene*, to the recognition in the *Cantos of Mutabilitie* that time itself must be shouldered aside by the lovely and terrible Titaness of Change. The allusions to time in the six eclogues reproduced in this volume are for the most part dark enough, notably "November" 81, to say nothing of the poet's uneasy forecast in "To His Booke." But after the onset of winter (with its promise of "timely death") and the self-pitying farewells that wrap up Colin's history, Spenser the maker steps forward to deliver his Envoy: in 1579, the world lay before him, and all things might be possible. His poem promised as much:

> Loe I have made a *Calender* for every yeare,
> That steele in strength, and time in durance shall outweare:
> And if I marked well the starres revolution,
> It shall continewe till the worlds dissolution.

Muiopotmos†

or

The Fate of the Butterflie (Clarion)

To the right worthy and vertuous Ladie; the La: Carey.[1]

Most brave and bountifull La: for so excellent favours as I have received at your sweet handes, to offer these fewe leaves as in recompence, should be as to offer flowers to the Gods for their divine benefites. Therefore I have determined to give my selfe wholy to you, as quite abandoned from my selfe,[2] and absolutely vowed to your services: which in all right is ever held for full recompence of debt or damage to have the person yeelded. My person I wot wel how little worth it is. But the faithfull minde and humble zeale which I beare unto your La: may perhaps be more of price, as may please you to account and use the poore service thereof; which taketh glory to advance your excellent partes and noble vertues, and to spend it selfe in honouring you: not so much for your great bounty to my self, which yet may not be unminded; nor for name or kindreds sake by you vouchsafed, beeing also regardable; as for that honorable name, which yee have by your brave deserts[3] purchast to your self, and spred in the mouths of al men: with which I have also presumed to grace my verses, and under your name to commend to the world this smal Poeme, the which beseeching your La: to take in worth,[4] and of all things therein according to your wonted graciousnes to make a milde construction,[5] I humbly pray for your happines.

Your La: ever
humbly;
E.S.

---

† From Greek *muia* ("fly"), *potmos* ("fate"). Composed probably in 1590, *Muiopotmos* was published a year later, as one of nine mostly earlier poems by Spenser, in *Complaints*: "meditations of the worlds vanitie, verie grave and profitable" ("The Printer to the Gentle Reader"). For a concise overview of the volume's content and character, see Yale 1989; also Maclean 1990E.
1. Lady Elizabeth Carey (1551–1618), to whom Spenser addressed one of the dedicatory sonnets to *The Faerie Queene*, was the second daughter of Sir John Spencer of Althorpe; the poet also praises her as "Phyllis, the floure of rare perfection," in *Colin Clouts Come Home Againe* 541–47.
2. I.e., as having given up all thought of self.
3. I.e., your admirable qualities.
4. I.e., to accept indulgently.
5. I.e., to interpret the poem with judicious reserve.

546

I sing of deadly dolorous debate,
Stired up through wrathfull Nemesis despight,°   *malice*
Betwixt two mightie ones of great estate,
Drawne into armes, and proofe° of mortall fight,   *trial*
5   Through prowd ambition, and hartswelling hate,
Whilest neither could the others greater might
And sdeignfull° scorne endure; that from small jarre°   *haughty/discord*
Their wraths at length broke into open warre.[6]

The roote whereof and tragicall effect,
10 Vouchsafe, O thou the mournfulst Muse of nyne,[7]
That wontst° the tragick stage for to direct,   *are accustomed*
In funerall complaints and waylfull tyne,°   *sorrow*
Reveale to me, and all the meanes detect,°   *reveal*
Through which sad Clarion did at last declyne
15 To lowest wretchednes; And is there then
Such rancour in the harts of mightie men?[8]

Of all the race of silver-wingéd Flies°   *insects*
Which doo possesse the Empire of the aire,
Betwixt the centred earth, and azure skies,
20 Was none more favourable,° nor more faire,   *fortunate*
Whilst heaven did favour his felicities,
Then Clarion, the eldest sonne and haire
Of Muscaroll,[9] and in his fathers sight
Of all alive did seeme the fairest wight.°   *creature*

25 With fruitfull hope his aged breast he fed
Of future good, which his yong toward° yeares,   *promising*
Full of brave courage° and bold hardyhed,°   *spirit/courage*
Above th'ensample of his equall peares,
Did largely promise, and to him forered°   *presaged*
30 (Whilst oft his heart did melt in tender teares)
That he in time would sure prove such an one,
As should be worthie of his fathers throne.

The fresh yong flie, in whom the kindly° fire   *natural*
Of lustfull° youngth began to kindle fast,   *vigorous*
35 Did much disdaine to subject his desire

6. Lines 1–8 recall the opening of the *Iliad*, where Homer describes the enmity between Agamemnon and Achilles; the Greek poet names Apollo as the god who instigated their quarrel. In Spenser's poem "wrathfull Nemesis" reflects *Metamorphoses* 14.694, and Hesiod, *Theogony* 223. The "two mightie ones" (3) may refer to Minerva and Venus (Allen 1956) or to Minerva and Arachne (Morey 1991, acknowledging W. Wells, " 'To Make a Milde Construction': The Significance of the Opening Stanzas of *Muiopotmos*," *SP* 42 [1945]: 544–54).
7. I.e., Melpomene, Muse of tragedy.
8. Cf. *Aeneid* 1.11: "Can the gods be capable of such vindictive rage?" The deliberately high-flown and portentous tone of stanzas 1–2, seeming to promise events of epic proportions, introduces instead a society of insects.
9. From Latin *musca* ("fly"). "Clarion," a trumpet, derives from Latin *clarus* ("bright"; "renowned," thus worthy of Fame's trumpet).

To loathsome sloth, or houres in ease to wast,
But joyed to range abroad in fresh attire;
Through the wide compas of the ayrie coast,°   *region*
And with unwearied wings each part t'inquire°   *explore*
40 Of the wide rule of his renowméd sire.

For he so swift and nimble was of flight,
That from this lower tract° he dared to stie°   *realm/mount*
Up to the clowdes, and thence with pineons light,
To mount aloft unto the Christall skie,
45 To vew the workmanship of heavens hight:
Whence downe descending he along would flie
Upon the streaming rivers, sport to finde;
And oft would dare to tempt° the troublous winde.   *test*

So on a Summers day, when season milde
50 With gentle calme the world has quieted,
And high in heaven Hyperions fierie childe[1]
Ascending, did his beames abroad dispred,
Whiles all the heavens on lower creatures smilde;
Yong Clarion with vauntfull lustie head,[2]
55 After his guize° did cast° abroad to fare;   *custom/resolve*
And theretoo gan his furnitures° prepare.   *equipment*

His breastplate first, that was of substance pure,
Before his noble heart he firmely bound,
That mought his life from yron death assure,
60 And ward his gentle corpes° from cruell wound: *body*
For it by arte was framéd, to endure
The bit of balefull steele and bitter stownd,°   *assault*
No lesse than that, which Vulcane made to shield
Achilles life from fate of Troyan field.[3]

65 And then about his shoulders broad he threw
An hairie hide of some wilde beast, whom hee
In salvage forrest by adventure° slew,   *chance*
And reft° the spoyle his ornament to bee: *took*
Which spredding all his backe with dreadfull vew,°   *appearance*
70 Made all that him so horrible did see,
Thinke him Alcides[4] with the Lyons skin,
When the Naemean Conquest he did win.

Upon his head his glistering Burganet,°   *helmet*
The which was wrought by wonderous device,
75 And curiously engraven, he did set:
The mettall was of rare and passing price;°   *value*

1. I.e., Apollo.
2. I.e., with boastful eagerness.
3. The arming of the hero is a conventional feature of classical epic: cf. *Iliad* 11.15–46, and *Aeneid*
   12.87–89. For the shield of Achilles, cf. *Iliad* 18.478–617.
4. Hercules. Cf. *The Faerie Queene* V.Pr.6, and note.

Not Bilbo[5] steele, nor brasse from Corinth fet,°   *brought*

Nor costly Oricalche° from strange Phoenice;   *brass*

But such as could both Phoebus arrowes ward,

80 And th'hayling darts of heaven beating hard.

Therein two deadly weapons fixt he bore,

Strongly outlancéd° towards either side,   *out-thrust*

Like two sharpe speares, his enemies to gore:

Like as a warlike Brigandine, applyde°   *prepared*

85 To fight, layes forth her threatfull pikes[6] afore,

The engines° which in them sad death doo hyde: *weapons*

So did this flie outstretch his fearefull hornes,

Yet so as him their terrour more adornes.

Lastly his shinie wings as silver bright,

90 Painted with thousand colours, passing farre

All Painters skill, he did about him dight:°   *draw*

Not halfe so manie sundrie colours arre

In Iris[7] bowe, ne heaven doth shine so bright,

Distinguishéd with manie a twinckling starre,

95 Nor Junoes Bird[8] in her ey-spotted traine

So manie goodly colours doth containe.

Ne (may it be withouten perill spoken)

The Archer God, the sonne of Cytheree,[9]

That joyes on wretched lovers to be wroken,°   *avenged*

100 And heapéd spoyles of bleeding harts to see,

Beares in his wings so manie a changefull token.[1]

Ah my liege Lord, forgive it unto mee,

If ought against thine honour I have tolde;

Yet sure those wings were fairer manifolde.

105 Full manie a Ladie faire, in Court full oft

Beholding them, him secretly envide,

And wisht that two such fannes, so silken soft,

And golden faire, her Love would her provide;

Or that when them the gorgeous Flie had doft,

110 Some one that would with grace be gratifide,°   *rewarded*

From him would steale them privily° away,   *secretly*

And bring to her so precious a pray.

Report is that dame Venus on a day,

In spring when flowres doo clothe the fruitful ground,

115 Walking abroad with all her Nymphes to play,

Bad her faire damzels flocking her arownd,

To gather flowres, her forhead to array:

5. Bilbao, on the northern coast of Spain.
6. I.e., the rams with which such small galleys were equipped.
7. Goddess of the rainbow. Cf. *Aeneid* 4.700–701.
8. I.e., the peacock.
9. I.e., Cupid, the son of Venus.
1. I.e., such various patternings.

Emongst the rest a gentle Nymph was found,
Hight° Astery,[2] excelling all the crewe   *named*
120 In curteous usage,° and unstainéd hewe.   *behavior*

Who being nimbler joynted than the rest,
And more industrious, gatheréd more store
Of the fields honour, than the others best;
Which they in secret harts envying sore,
125 Tolde Venus, when her as the worthiest
She praisd, that Cupide (as they heard before)
Did lend her secret aide, in gathering
Into her lap the children of the spring.

Whereof the Goddesse gathering jealous feare,
130 Not yet unmindfull,° how not long agoe   *forgetful*
Her sonne to Psyche[3] secrete love did beare,
And long it close° concealed, till mickle° woe   *secretly/much*
Thereof arose, and manie a rufull teare;
Reason with sudden rage did overgoe,[4]
135 And giving hastie credit to th'accuser,
Was led away of° them that did abuse her.   *by*

Eftsoones° that Damzel by her heavenly might,   *forthwith*
She turned into a wingéd Butterflie,
In the wide aire to make her wandring flight;
140 And all those flowres, with which so plenteouslie
Her lap she filléd had, that bred her spight,
She placéd in her wings, for memorie
Of her pretended crime, though crime none were:
Since which that flie them in her wings doth beare.

145 Thus the fresh Clarion being readie dight,°   *attired*
Unto his journey did himselfe addresse,
And with good speed began to take his flight:
Over the fields in his franke° lustinesse,   *vigorous*
And all the champion° he soaréd light,   *plain*
150 And all the countrey wide he did possesse,
Feeding upon their pleasures bounteouslie,
That none gainsaid, nor none did him envie.

The woods, the rivers, and the medowes green,
With his aire-cutting wings he measured wide,
155 Ne did he leave the mountaines bare unseene,
Nor the ranke grassie fennes° delights untride.   *marshes*
But none of these, how ever sweete they beene,

---

2. Cf. *The Faerie Queene* III.xi.34, and note. Arachne, challenging Pallas Athene's claim to mastery in weaving, made Asterie ("gripped by the struggling eagle") part of her tapestry; cf. *Metamorphoses* 6.108. While Spenser alludes in lines 131–33 to the myth of Cupid and Psyche (see *The Faerie Queene* III.vi.50, and note), the account of the metamorphosis of Astery is essentially his own invention: see Morey 1991.
3. In Greek, "psyche" means both "soul" and "butterfly."
4. I.e., quick rage overcame reason.

Mote please his fancie, nor him cause t'abide:
His choicefull° sense with everie change doth flit.   *fickle*
160 No common things may please a wavering wit.°   *mind*

To the gay gardins his unstaid° desire   *shifting*
Him wholly caried, to refresh his sprights:
There lavish Nature in her best attire,
Powres forth sweete odors, and alluring sights;
165 And Arte with her contending, doth aspire
T'excell the naturall, with made delights:
And all that faire or pleasant may be found,
In riotous excesse doth there abound.

There he arriving, round about doth flie,
170 From bed to bed, from one to other border,
And takes survey with curious busie eye,
Of everie flowre and herbe there set in order;
Now this, now that he tasteth tenderly,
Yet none of them he rudely doth disorder,
175 Ne with his feete their silken leaves deface;°   *harm*
But pastures on the pleasures of each place.

And evermore with most varietie,
And change of sweetnesse (for all change is sweete)
He casts° his glutton sense to satisfie,   *seeks*
180 Now sucking of the sap of herbe most meete,°   *proper*
Or of the deaw, which yet on them does lie,
Now in the same bathing his tender feete:
And then he pearcheth on some braunch thereby,
To weather him, and his moyst wings to dry.

185 And then againe he turneth to his play,
To spoyle° the pleasures of that Paradise:[5]   *ravage*
The wholsome Saulge,° and Lavender still gray,   *sage*
Ranke smelling Rue, and Cummin good for eyes,
The Roses raigning in the pride of May,
190 Sharpe Isope,° good for greene wounds remedies,   *hyssop*
Faire Marigoldes, and Bees alluring Thime,
Sweete Marjoram, and Daysies decking prime.°   *spring*

Coole Violets, and Orpine growing still,[6]
Embathèd Balme, and chearfull Galingale,
195 Fresh Costmarie, and breathfull Camomill,
Dull Poppie, and drink-quickning Setuale,
Veyne-healing Verven, and hed-purging Dill,
Sound Savorie, and Bazill hartie-hale,

---

5. The catalog of plants that follows, in lines 187–200, like that of trees in *The Faerie Queene* I.i.8–
   9, is a literary convention, looking ultimately to *Metamorphoses* 10.90–104.
6. "Orpine" is commonly known in England as "live-long."

Fat Colworts, and comforting Perseline,
200 Colde Lettuce, and refreshing Rosmarine.[7]

And whatso else of vertue good or ill
Grewe in this Gardin, fetcht from farre away,
Of everie one he takes, and tastes at will,
And on their pleasures greedily doth pray.
205 Then when he hath both plaid, and fed his fill,
In the warme Sunne he doth himselfe embay,°   bask
And there him rests in riotous suffisaunce°   abundance
Of all his gladfulnes, and kingly joyaunce.

What more felicitie can fall to creature,
210 Than to enjoy delight with libertie,
And to be Lord of all the workes of Nature,
To raine in th'aire from earth to highest skie,
To feed on flowres, and weeds of glorious feature,
To take what ever thing doth please the eie?
215 Who rests not pleaséd with such happines,
Well worthie he to taste of wretchednes.

commentary

But what on earth can long abide in state?[8]
Or who can him assure of happie day;
Sith morning faire may bring fowle evening late,
220 And least mishap the most blisse alter may?
For thousand perills lie in close° awaite   secret
About us daylie, to worke our decay;°   destruction
That none, except a God, or God him guide,
May them avoyde, or remedie provide.

mutability
Zeu-everything must
come to an end.

225 And whatso heavens in their secret doome°   judgment
Ordainéd have, how can fraile fleshly wight
Forecast, but it must needs to issue come?
The sea, the aire, the fire, the day, the night,
And th'armies of their creatures all and some[9]
230 Do serve to them, and with importune° might   grievous
Warre against us the vassals of their will.
Who then can save, what they dispose to spill?[1]

Not thou, O Clarion, though fairest thou
Of all thy kinde, unhappie happie Flie,
235 Whose cruell fate is woven even now
Of° Joves owne hand, to worke thy miserie: by
Ne may thee helpe the manie hartie vow,
Which thy olde Sire with sacred pietie

---

7. Among the less familiar plants named in this stanza, "galingale" was used as a condiment (e.g.,
   by Chaucer's Cook: cf. *The Canterbury Tales*, "General Prologue" 381); costmary, camomile, and
   vervain are aromatic medicinal herbs; "setuale" is the modern valerian, used as a drug. Colewort
   is a kind of cabbage; perseline either parsley or purslane, a succulent herb.
8. I.e., can long remain secure.
9. I.e., one and all.
1. I.e., what they ordain to destruction. For a discussion of the influence of Calvinist thought on
   Muiopotmos (perhaps by way of Chaucer's "Nun's Priest's Tale"), cf. the essay by J. Anderson in
   JMRS 1 (1971): 89–106.

Hath powred forth for thee, and th'altars sprent:°   *sprinkled*
240 Nought may thee save from heavens avengément.

It fortunéd (as heavens had behight)°   *ordained*
That in this gardin, where yong Clarion
Was wont to solace him,° a wicked wight   *himself*
The foe of faire things, th'author of confusion,
245 The shame of Nature, the bondslave of spight,
Had lately built his hatefull mansion,
And lurking closely, in awayte now lay,
How he might anie in his trap betray.[2]

But when he spide the joyous Butterflie
250 In this faire plot dispacing° too and fro,   *moving*
Fearles of foes and hidden jeopardie,
Lord how he gan for to bestirre him tho,°   *then*
And to his wicked worke each part applie:
His heart did earne° against his hated foe,   *rage*
255 And bowels so with ranckling poyson swelde,
That scarce the skin the strong contagion helde.

The cause why he this Flie so malicéd,
Was (as in stories it is written found)[3]
For that his mother which him bore and bred,
260 The most fine-fingred workwoman on ground,
Arachne, by his meanes was vanquishéd
Of Pallas, and in her owne skill confound,°   *overcome*
When she with her for excellence contended,
That wrought her shame, and sorrow never ended.

265 For the Tritonian Goddesse[4] having hard°   *heard*
Her blazéd° fame, which all the world had filled,   *proclaimed*
Came downe to prove° the truth, and due reward   *test*
For her prais-worthie workmanship to yeild;
But the presumptuous Damzel rashly dared
270 The Goddesse selfe to chalenge to the field,
And to compare° with her in curious° skill   *vie/intricate*
Of workes with loome, with needle, and with quill.°   *spool*

Minerva did the chalenge not refuse,
But deigned with her the paragon to make:[5]
275 So to their worke they sit, and each doth chuse

---

2. The poet spells out the destructive aspects of this "wicked wight," but reserves his name for the crucial encounter with Clarion.
3. Spenser's account of the myth of Arachne differs significantly from that of Ovid (*Metamorphoses* 6.1–145). In the Roman author's poem, Pallas Athene, outraged by the beauty of Arachne's tapestry, and by its truthful depiction of the gods' cheating tricks and riotous life, destroys the work; when Arachne attempts suicide, the goddess, pitying yet stern, transforms the girl into a spider, "and as a spider she works on at her former art of weaving." Spenser's version (259–352) differs chiefly in that a victorious Pallas Athene crowns her work by weaving in the exquisite butterfly that awakens Arachne's rancorous envy, leads to her self-transformation, and accounts for the spider's hatred for the butterfly since that time.
4. According to legend, Pallas Athene was reared by the sea-god Triton.
5. I.e., to accept the (challenge of) comparison.

What storie she will for her tapet° take. — *tapestry*
Arachne figured° how Jove did abuse — *showed*
Europa like a Bull, and on his backe
Her through the sea did beare; so lively seene,
280 That it true Sea, and true Bull ye would weene.° — *suppose*

She seemed still backe unto the land to looke,
And her play-fellowes aide to call, and feare
The dashing of the waves, that° up she tooke — *so that*
Her daintie feete, and garments gathered neare:
285 But (Lord) how she in everie member shooke,
When as the land she saw no more appeare,
But a wilde wildernes of waters deepe:
Then gan she greatly to lament and weepe.

Before the Bull she pictured wingéd Love,
290 With his yong brother Sport, light fluttering
Upon the waves, as each had been a Dove;
The one his bowe and shafts, the other Spring° — *youth*
A burning Teade° about his head did move, — *torch*
As in their Syres new love both triumphing:° — *exulting*
295 And manie Nymphes about them flocking round,
And manie Tritons, which their hornes did sound.

And round about, her worke she did empale° — *enclose*
With a faire border wrought of sundrie flowres,
Enwoven with an Yvie winding trayle:
300 A goodly worke, full fit for Kingly bowres,
Such as Dame Pallas, such as Envie pale,
That al good things with venemous tooth devowres,
Could not accuse. Then gan the Goddesse bright
Her selfe likewise unto her worke to dight.° — *prepare*

305 She made the storie of the olde debate,
Which she with Neptune did for Athens trie:° — *engage in*
Twelve Gods doo sit around in royall state,
And Jove in midst with awfull Majestie,
To judge the strife betweene them stirréd late:
310 Each of the Gods by his like visnomie° — *visage*
Eathe° to be knowen; but Jove above them all, — *easy*
By his great lookes and power Imperiall.

Before them stands the God of Seas in place,
Clayming that sea-coast Citie as his right,
315 And strikes the rockes with his three-forkéd mace;
Whenceforth issues a warlike steed in sight,
The signe by which he chalengeth° the place, — *claims*
That° all the Gods, which saw his wondrous might — *so that*
Did surely deeme the victorie his due:
320 But seldome seene, forejudgment proveth true.

Then to her selfe she gives her Aegide shield,[6]
And steelhed speare, and morion° on her hedd,   *helmet*
Such as she oft is seene in warlicke field:
Then sets she forth, how with her weapon dredd
325   She smote the ground, the which streight foorth did yield
A fruitfull Olyve tree, with berries spredd,
That all the Gods admired; then all the storie
She compast° with a wreathe of Olyves hoarie.   *encircled*

Emongst those leaves she made a Butterflie,
330   With excellent device and wondrous slight,°   *art*
Fluttring among the Olives wantonly,°   *playfully*
That seemed to live, so like it was in sight:
The velvet nap which on his wings doth lie,
The silken downe with which his backe is dight,
335   His broad outstretchéd hornes, his hayrie thies,
His glorious colours, and his glistering° eies.   *shining*

Which when Arachne saw, as overlaid,°   *overwhelmed*
And masteréd with workmanship so rare,
She stood astonied long, ne ought gainesaid,
340   And with fast fixéd eyes on her did stare,
And by her silence, signe of one dismaid,
The victorie did yeeld her as her share:
Yet did she inly fret, and felly° burne,   *fiercely*
And all her blood to poysonous rancor turne.

345   That shortly from the shape of womanhed
Such as she was, when Pallas she attempted,°   *challenged*
She grew to hideous shape of dryrihed,°   *horror*
Pinéd with griefe of follie late repented:
Eftsoones her white streight legs were alteréd
350   To crooked crawling shankes, of marrowe empted,
And her faire face to fowle and loathsome hewe,
And her fine corpes° to a bag of venim grewe.   *body*

This curséd creature, mindfull of that olde
Enfestred grudge, the which his mother felt,
355   So soone as Clarion he did beholde,
His heart with vengefull malice inly swelt,
And weaving straight a net with manie a folde
About the cave, in which he lurking dwelt,
With fine small cords about it stretchéd wide,
360   So finely sponne, that scarce they could be spide.

Not anie damzell, which her° vaunteth most   *herself*
In skilfull knitting of soft silken twyne;
Nor anie weaver, which his worke doth boast
In dieper,[7] in damaske, or in lyne;°   *linen*

6. I.e., her shield with the symbolic and protective device of the "aegis."
7. A fabric patterned with small repeated designs.

365   Nor anie skiled in workmanship embost;[8]
Nor anie skiled in loupes of fingring fine,
Might in their divers cunning° ever dare,   *skill*
With this so curious networke to compare.

     Ne doo I thinke, that that same subtil gin,°   *net*
370   The which the Lemnian God[9] framde craftilie,
Mars sleeping with his wife to compasse in,
That all the Gods with common mockerie
Might laugh at them, and scorne their shamefull sin,
Was like to this. This same he did applie,
375   For to entrap the careles Clarion,
That ranged each where without suspition.

     Suspition of friend, nor feare of foe,
That hazarded° his health, had he at all,   *threatened*
But walkt at will, and wandred too and fro,
380   In the pride of his freedome principall:°   *princely*
Little wist° he his fatall future woe,   *knew*
But was secure, the liker he to fall.
He likest is to fall into mischaunce,
That is regardles of his governaunce.°   *conduct*

385   Yet still Aragnoll[1] (so his foe was hight°)   *named*
Lay lurking covertly him to surprise,
And all his gins that him entangle might,
Drest° in good order as he could devise.   *arranged*
At length the foolish Flie without foresight,
390   As he that did all daunger quite despise,
Toward those parts came flying careleslie,
Where hidden was his hatefull enemie.

     Who seeing him, with secrete joy therefore
Did tickle inwardly in everie vaine,
395   And his false hart fraught with all treasons store,
Was filled with hope, his purpose to obtaine:
Himselfe he close upgathered more and more
Into his den, that his deceiptfull traine°   *snare*
By his there being might not be bewraid,°   *revealed*
400   Ne anie noyse, ne anie motion made.

     Like as a wily Foxe, that having spide,
Where on a sunnie banke the Lambes doo play,
Full closely° creeping by the hinder side,   *secretly*
Lyes in ambushment of° his hopéd pray,   *for*
405   Ne stirreth limbe, till seeing readie tide,[2]

8. I.e., in the art (in embroidery) of richly elaborate decoration.
9. I.e., Vulcan (Hephaestus), who was thrown down from Olympus by Jove; after falling for an entire day, he came to earth on the Aegean isle of Lemnos. For the story of his entrapment of Venus and her lover Mars, cf. *Metamorphoses* 4.176–89.
1. From Latin *aranea* (or perhaps *araneolus*), "spider."
2. I.e., the right moment.

He rusheth forth, and snatcheth quite away
One of the litle yonglings unawares:
So to his worke Aragnoll him prepares.

Who now shall give unto my heavie eyes
410 A well of teares, that all may overflow?
Or where shall I finde lamentable cryes,
And mournfull tunes enough my griefe to show?
Helpe O thou Tragick Muse, me to devise
Notes sad enough, t'expresse this bitter throw:°   *throe*
415 For loe, the drerie stownd° is now arrived,   *moment*
That of all happines hath us deprived.

The luckles Clarion, whether cruell Fate,
Or wicked Fortune faultles him misled,
Or some ungracious blast out of the gate
420 Of Aeoles raine perforce him drove on hed,[3]
Was (O sad hap° and howre unfortunate)   *lot*
With violent swift flight forth cariéd
Into the curséd cobweb, which his foe
Had framéd for his finall overthroe.

425 There the fond° Flie entangled, strugled long,   *foolish*
Himselfe to free thereout; but all in vaine.
For striving more, the more in laces strong
Himselfe he tide, and wrapt his wingés twaine
In lymie° snares the subtill loupes among;   *sticky*
430 That in the ende he breathelesse did remaine,
And all his yougthly forces idly spent,
Him to the mercie of th'avenger lent.°   *gave*

Which when the greisly° tyrant did espie,   *horrible*
Like a grimme Lyon rushing with fierce might
435 Out of his den, he seizéd greedelie
On the resistles pray, and with fell spight,
Under the left wing stroke° his weapon slie   *struck*
Into his heart, that his deepe groning spright
In bloodie streames foorth fled into the aire,
440 His bodie left the spectacle of care.[4]

Editors' Note

That five editions of *The Shepheardes Calender* had appeared by 1597 bears witness to its wide appeal. But a single edition of the *Complaints* volume presumably satisfied even readers eager to assess the quality of Spenser's achievement in the genre of "complaint"; not until the appearance in 1612–13 of Matthew Lownes's folio edition of Spenser's *Works* were all the poems in the

3. I.e., (some blast from the gate) of the kingdom of Aeolus [god of the winds] drove him headlong.
4. So Virgil concludes the *Aeneid*: "[Turnus's] limbs relax and grow cold; and his moaning spirit flies resentfully into the shades" (12.951–52).

first edition of *Complaints* again in print. In Elizabethan times, "complaint" signified a plaintive lyric or narrative poem, expressing grief for unrequited love, the miscarriage of worldly expectation, or the sorrows of the human condition in a fallen world. These accents sound in Spenser's earliest published work, the translations for van der Noot of Petrarch's sixth canzone (from Marot's French translation) and Du Bellay's *Songe*; recurrently in the *Calender* and *The Faerie Queene*; and with special force in the *Cantos of Mutabilitie* (published in 1609), in effect a woman's complaint raised to a higher power, reflecting the poet's dismay in a world "woxen daily worse," governed by "the ever-whirling wheele/Of Change." For Spenser the attraction of complaint is conditioned by his fascination with the impact of worldly change and decay upon the true poet's special insight and social mission. His emphasis often falls less on things hoped for than on things seen: the frustrating counterclaims of love and poetry, hypocrisy victorious while suitors languish, "inconstant mutabilitie" everywhere pressing in upon the poet and his art. Complaint offered an apt vehicle for melancholy comment on the theme, "all that moveth, doth in Change delight" (*Mutabilitie* vii.8.2).

To be sure, the volume has particular interest for students of Spenser's developing command of his art, with special reference to the changes he rings on the genre of complaint, to his craft in translation (notably in *Virgils Gnat*), and, in *Mother Hubberds Tale*, to the attractions of medieval satire for a poet who found the medium of allegorical beast-fable apt for the expression of his own emerging disenchantment with a court where experience and self-interest often seemed to have driven "true courtesy" underground. Still, it is with a shock of real pleasure that many readers, tired with all these melancholy musings, come at length upon the enchanting (and puzzling) *Muiopotmos*, for William Nelson "the lightest and most delicious of Spenser's poems."[1] The poem has something in common with *Virgils Gnat*, but Spenser's achievement in *Muiopotmos* is of another order of magnitude: conception, tone, and management of genre together reflect the poet's easy and innovative command of his craft. For Ralph Waldo Emerson, "Spenser seems to delight in his art for his own skill's sake";[2] and the view that *Muiopotmos* should in the first instance be regarded as a mock-heroic fancy, a playful *jeu d'esprit*, retains a critical half-life still, especially for scholars who stress the poet's ability to employ poetic conventions in his own way, or to illuminate a central theme by the artful combination of seemingly disparate elements.

Another standpoint has been variously represented by those scholars who, struck by the poet's suggestion that Lady Carey should "make a milde construction" of *Muiopotmos*, identify historical personages in the tale of Clarion and Aragnoll. James Russell Lowell had no doubt that "in Clarion the butterfly [Spenser] has symbolized himself"; a number of theories in this kind identify Aragnoll as William Cecil, Lord Burghley, whom the poet covertly criticizes elsewhere in his work. Others prefer to link the earl of Essex or the earl of Oxford with Aragnoll, identifying Clarion as Sir Walter Raleigh or Sir Philip Sidney. So it goes. These schemes are mostly in the dustbin now, recalled, if at all, by Hallett Smith's dry proposal that *Muiopotmos* is "a *prophetic* allegory: that the butterfly represents the scholarly critic who gets caught in the spider-web of extraneous antiquarian, historical, and philosophical learning."[3]

1. William Nelson, *The Poetry of Edmund Spenser* (New York, 1963) 71.
2. Ralph Waldo Emerson, *Works*, ed. E. W. Emerson and W. E. Forbes (Boston, 1846) 7.229.
3. James Russell Lowell, *Complete Writings* (New York, 1904), 16 vols., 4.273. Hallett Smith, "The Use of Conventions in Spenser's Minor Poems," *Form and Convention in the Poetry of Edmund Spenser: Selected Papers from the English Institute*, ed. William Nelson (New York, 1961) 122–45.

Still, Spenser did invite "the right worthy and vertuous" Lady Carey (and by implication his readers) to "make a milde construction . . . of all things [in] . . . this smal Poeme." For some, the tragic undersong of *Muiopotmos* serves a larger allegorical purpose, keyed to the mordant question that concludes the second stanza, recalling the agony of Lear in mid-passage: "Is there any cause in nature that makes these hard hearts?" In 1833 John Wilson read the poem as an allegory of love and death; for D. C. Allen in 1936, Clarion represents the rational soul, drawn down to destruction by the power, or the weakness, of the senses.[4] In this vein, Nelson (as so often) is succinctly persuasive: *Muiopotmos* is "a delightful teaching of the tragic lesson that on earth happiness is its own destruction, that only in heaven or by heavenly intervention is the fruitful olive victorious over chaos and death."[5]

Modern-day scholars have traced other paths into the poem's green wood, still seeking to establish the character of Spenser's vision and to account for his power to refashion myth and make it his own. Anderson 1971 draws attention in particular to the Chaucerian and Calvinist contexts of Spenser's art; Dundas 1975 and 1990E remarks the poet's capacity to transcend the didacticism of mere emblematics and assert the truth of a universe founded on art. Others notice the relation, in this latter regard, of iconographical tradition to Spenser's view of the insidious interplay at Elizabeth's court between fame and envy; and the bearing of that conjunction on the poet's freedom of invention, his delight (especially) in creating his own myths. The story of Arachne is in Ovid, but Spenser's addition of the butterfly in Minerva's web makes new the transformation of an envious Arachne into Aragnoll's ancestor. As for Astery, if her name is Ovidian, and her literary antecedents connected with the myth of Psyche, the nymph in *Muiopotmos* is Spenser's own creation; and the allusion to "her pretended crime, though crime none were," is suited to the poem's larger concerns. Spenser's mythography in *The Faerie Queene* is more ambitious; one thinks of Florimell and Marinell, Faunus and Molanna. But the combination of exquisitely delicate artistry with somber or haunting thematic undertones that informs those extended episodes is displayed with equal art in the microcosm of *Muiopotmos*. Renwick's judgment holds good still: "*Muiopotmos* is Spenser's most original poem."[6]

4. John Wilson, "Spenser," *Blackwood's Magazine* 34 (1833): 824–56; D. C. Allen, "On Spenser's *Muiopotmos*," *SP* 53 (1956): 141–58. See pp. 796–804 in this edition for selections from Allen's and other essays on *Muiopotmos*.
5. Nelson 74.
6. W. L. Renwick, *Edmund Spenser: An Essay on Renaissance Poetry* (London, 1925) 57.

Colin Clouts Come Home Againe

To the Right worthy and noble Knight

Sir Walter Raleigh,[1] Captaine of her Majesties
Guard, Lord Wardein of the Stanneries,
and Lieutenant of the Countie of
Cornwall.

Sir, that you may see that I am not alwaies ydle as yee thinke, though not greatly well occupied, nor altogither undutifull, though not precisely officious,[2] I make you present of this simple pastorall, unworthie of your higher conceipt[3] for the meanesse of the stile, but agreeing with the truth in circumstance and matter. The which I humbly beseech you to accept in part of paiment of the infinite debt in which I acknowledge my selfe bounden unto you, for your singular favours and sundrie good turnes shewed to me at my late being in England, and with your good countenance protect against the malice of evill mouthes, which are alwaies wide open to carpe at and misconstrue my simple meaning. I pray continually for your happinesse. From my house of Kilcolman, the 27. of December. 1591.

Yours ever humbly.
Ed. Sp.

The shepheards boy (best knowen by that name)[4]
That after Tityrus[5] first sung his lay,
Laies of sweet love, without rebuke or blame,

---

1. Raleigh (1554–1618), explorer, soldier, poet, historian, and prototypical courtier, enjoyed the queen's special favor from 1581 until her death in 1603, save for intermittent periods of royal displeasure. At one such juncture, in 1589, while visiting his estates in Ireland, Raleigh met Spenser at Kilcolman; their encounter and subsequent journey to the queen's court at Westminster are described in the poem (56 ff.). The appointment of Raleigh as Lord Warden of the Stanneries (tin mines in Devon and Cornwall) effectively assured him of a considerable income. On Raleigh in the context of Spenser studies, see Mills 1990E and Oram 1990; see also W. Oakeshott, *The Queen and the Poet* (New York, 1961). Shore 1990E provides a useful overview of *Colin Clouts Come Home Againe*, especially of its relation to Spenser's struggle to respond appropriately to the conflicting demands of poetry and public life. See also Bernard 1989, ch. 4, esp. 126–34.
2. I.e., not fastidiously overforward.
3. I.e., higher imaginative insight.
4. *The Shepheardes Calender* had appeared in four editions by 1591; the contemporary association of its author with "Colin Cloute" is remarked in E.K.'s first note to "Januarye," and his note to "September" 176. But Spenser is not literally to be identified with Colin in every sense.
5. Virgil (see E.K.'s Glosse to "October" 55), whose sophisticated eclogues provided Renaissance humanist poets with a pattern for their pastoral poetry.

Sate (as his custome was) upon a day,
5 Charming° his oaten pipe unto his peres,   *playing*
The shepheard swaines that did about him play:
Who all the while with greedie listfull° eares,   *attentive*
Did stand astonisht at his curious skill,
Like hartlesse° deare, dismayd with thunders sound.   *timid*
10 At last when as he pipéd had his fill,
He rested him: and sitting then around,
One of those groomes° (a jolly groome was he,   *shepherds*
As ever pipéd on an oaten reed,
And loved this shepheard dearest in degree,[6]
15 Hight Hobbinol) gan thus to him areed.°   *speak*
   "Colin my liefe,° my life, how great a losse   *dear*
Had all the shepheards nation by thy lacke?
And I poore swaine of many greatest crosse:[7]
That sith thy Muse first since thy turning backe
20 Was heard to sound as she was wont on hye,
Hast made us all so blesséd and so blythe.
Whilest thou wast hence, all dead in dole° did lie: *grief*
The woods were heard to waile full many a sythe,°   *time*
And all their birds with silence to complaine:°   *lament*
25 The fields with faded flowers did seem to mourne,
And all their flocks from feeding to refraine:
The running waters wept for thy returne,
And all their fish with languour did lament:
But now both woods and fields, and floods revive,
30 Sith thou art come, their cause of meriment,
That us late dead, hast made againe alive:
But were it not too painfull to repeat
The passéd fortunes, which to thee befell
In thy late voyage, we thee would entreat,
35 Now at thy leisure them to us to tell."
   To whom the shepheard gently answered thus,
"Hobbin thou temptest me to that I covet:
For a good passéd newly to discus,
By dubble usurie doth twise renew it.
40 And since I saw that Angels[8] blesséd eie,
Her worlds bright sun, her heavens fairest light,
My mind full of my thoughts satietie,[9]
Doth feed on sweet contentment of that sight:
Since that same day in nought I take delight,
45 Ne feeling have in any earthly pleasure,
But in remembrance of that glorious bright,°   *radiance*
My lifes sole blisse, my hearts eternall threasure.
Wake then my pipe, my sleepie Muse awake,
Till I have told her praises lasting long:

6. I.e., most dearly and deeply. Unlike that earlier Hobbinol of the *Calender*, this "jolly groome"
   cannot properly figure Gabriel Harvey, who seems never to have visited Ireland. Yet this Hobbinol
   may well represent "a kindly reaffirmation of Spenser's youthful friendship" (Shore 1990E, 175).
7. I.e., (suffer) the greatest misfortune.
8. I.e., Queen Elizabeth's.
9. I.e., My mind fully gratified by the fullest satisfaction of my thought.

50 Hobbin desires, thou maist it not forsake,°   *avoid*
    Harke then ye jolly shepheards to my song."
      With that they all gan throng about him neare,
    With hungrie eares to heare his harmonie:
    The whiles their flocks devoyd of dangers feare,
55 Did round about them feed at libertie.
      "One day," quoth he, "I sat, (as was my trade)°   *vocation*
    Under the foote of Mole that mountaine hore,[1]
    Keeping my sheepe amongst the cooly shade,
    Of the greene alders by the Mullaes shore:
60 There a straunge shepheard chaunst to find me out,
    Whether alluréd with my pipes delight,
    Whose pleasing sound yshrilléd far about,
    Or thither led by chaunce, I know not right:
    Whom when I askéd from what place he came,
65 And how he hight, himselfe he did ycleepe,°   *call*
    The shepheard of the Océan[2] by name,
    And said he came far from the main-sea deepe.
    He sitting me beside in that same shade,
    Provokéd me to plaie some pleasant fit,°   *song*
70 And when he heard the musicke which I made,
    He found himselfe full greatly pleasd at it:
    Yet aemuling[3] my pipe, he tooke in hond
    My pipe before that aemuléd of many,
    And plaid theron; (for well that skill he cond)°   *knew*
75 Himselfe as skilfull in that art as any.
    He piped, I sung; and when he sung, I piped,
    By chaunge of turnes, each making other mery,
    Neither envying other, nor envied,
    So pipéd we, untill we both were weary."
80   There interrupting him, a bonie° swaine,   *handsome*
    That Cuddy[4] hight, him thus atweene bespake:
    "And should it not thy readie course restraine,
    I would request thee Colin, for my sake,
    To tell what thou didst sing, when he did plaie.
85 For well I weene it worth recounting was,
    Whether it were some hymne, or morall laie,
    Or carol made to praise thy lovéd lasse.[5]
      "Nor of my love, nor of my losse," quoth he,
    "I then did sing, as then occasion fell:
90 For love had me forlorne, forlorne of me,[6]

1. The Ballyhoura hills (Spenser's "Mole") lie to the north of Kilcolman, the poet's residence; the river Awbeg ("Mulla"), rising in the Ballyhoura range, flows southeast past Kilcolman, into the Blackwater and thence to the sea.
2. I.e., Raleigh, familiar with the sea from his West Country birth. In 1585 the queen appointed him vice admiral of Cornwall and Devon.
3. I.e., emulating; desiring to equal or surprise.
4. This "Cuddy" may represent Arthur Hyde, sheriff of Cork, who held lands on the river Funsheon (or Funchin; cf. 301). But efforts to establish originals for the Irish rustics of this poem (unlike the "shepheardes" and "shepheardesses" of Cynthia's court) have not as a rule been fruitful.
5. Lines 86–87 may glance at the *Calender*, in which hymn, moral lay, and carol arguably appear; equally *Colin Clouts Come Home Againe* may be thought to include the three poetic forms (Yale).
6. I.e., love had forsaken me (after) I had forsaken love. See "Colins Embleme" to "June," and E.K.'s *Glosse*.

That made me in that desart chose to dwell.
But of my river Bregogs love I soong,[7]
Which to the shiny Mulla he did beare,
And yet doth beare, and ever will, so long
95   As water doth within his bancks appeare."
      "Of fellowship," said then that bony Boy,
"Record° to us that lovely lay againe: *sing*
The staie° whereof, shall nought these eares annoy,   *continuance*
Who all that Colin makes, do covet faine."
100   "Heare then," quoth he, "the tenor of my tale,
In sort as I it to that shepheard told:
No leasing° new, nor Grandams fable stale,   *falsehood*
But auncient truth confirmed with credence old.
      Old father Mole, (Mole hight that mountain gray
105   That walls the Northside of Armulla dale)[8]
He had a daughter fresh as floure of May,
Which gave that name unto that pleasant vale;
Mulla the daughter of old Mole, so hight
The Nimph, which of that water course has charge,
110   That springing out of Mole, doth run downe right
To Buttevant, where spreading forth at large,
It giveth name unto that auncient Cittie,
Which Kilnemullah clepéd is of old:
Whose ragged ruines breed great ruth and pittie,
115   To travailers, which it from far behold.
Full faine she loved, and was beloved full faine,
Of her owne brother river, Bregog hight,
So hight because of this deceitfull traine,°   *scheme*
Which he with Mulla wrought to win delight.
120   But her old sire more carefull of her good,
And meaning her much better to preferre,[9]
Did thinke to match her with the neighbour flood,
Which Allo hight, Broad water calléd farre:
And wrought so well with his continuall paine,
125   That he that river for his daughter wonne:
The dowre agreed, the day assignéd plaine,
The place appointed where it should be doone.
Nath'lesse the Nymph her former liking held;
For love will not be drawne,° but must be ledde,   *forced*
130   And Bregog did so well her fancie weld,°   *manage*
That her good will[1] he got her first to wedde.
But for her father sitting still on hie,
Did warily still watch which way she went,
And eke from far observed with jealous eie,
135   Which way his course the wanton Bregog bent,

7. The Bregog flows through Spenser's estate, joining the Awbeg at Doneraile. The poet retains the stream's actual name ("deceitful" in Erse), as appropriate to his fable; cf. 117–18. See also *Mutabilitie* vi.40.
8. "Armulla dale" is the valley of the Blackwater ("which Allo hight," 123); Buttevant, some seven miles north of Mallow, on the Blackwater, is about three miles from Kilcolman.
9. I.e., intending to make a more advantageous match for her.
1. I.e., by her consent.

Him to deceive for all his watchfull ward,°   *guard*
The wily lover did devise this slight:°   *trick*
First into many parts his streame he shared,
That whilest the one was watcht, the other might
140 Passe unespide to meete her by the way;
And then besides,° those little streames so broken   *also*
He under ground so closely did convay,
That of their passage doth appeare no token,
Till they into the Mullaes water slide.
145 So secretly did he his love enjoy:
Yet not so secret, but it was descride,
And told her father by a shepheards boy.
Who wondrous wroth for that so foule despight,
In great avenge did roll downe from his hill
150 Huge mightie stones, the which encomber might
His passage, and his water-courses spill.°   *destroy*
So of a River, which he was of old,
He none was made, but scattred all to nought,
And lost emong those rocks into him rold,
155 Did lose his name: so deare his love he bought."
    Which having said, him Thestylis[2] bespake,
"Now by my life this was a mery lay:
Worthie of Colin selfe, that did it make.
But read° now eke of friendship I thee pray,   *tell*
160 What dittie did that other shepheard sing?
For I do covet most the same to heare,
As men use most to covet forreine thing."
"That shall I eke," quoth he, "to you declare.
His song was all a lamentable lay,[3]
165 Of great unkindnesse, and of usage hard,
Of Cynthia the Ladie of the sea,
Which from her presence faultlesse him debard.
And ever and anon with singulfs rife,[4]
He cryéd out, to make his undersong°   *refrain*
170 'Ah my loves queene, and goddesse of my life,
Who shall me pittie, when thou doest me wrong?' "
    Then gan a gentle bonylasse to speake,
That Marin hight, "Right well he sure did plaine:
That could great Cynthia's sore displeasure breake,
175 And move to take him to her grace againe.
But tell on further Colin, as befell
Twixt him and thee, that thee did hence dissuade."[5]
    "When thus our pipes we both had wearied well,"

2. Lodowick Bryskett (c. 1546–1612), Spenser's friend and colleague at Cambridge and in Ireland. His memorial poem to Sidney, "The Mourning Muse of Thestylis," makes part of Spenser's *Astrophel*. See *Amoretti* 33 and note.
3. Several elements in Spenser's poem (pub. 1595) were added after the 1591 dedication to Raleigh (see 432–34; 543 and 564–67; 552–55; and notes). The "lamentable lay" may possibly refer to some part of Raleigh's "The Ocean to Cynthia" (in progress by 1592 but never completed), a substantial poem in various meters designed to "glorify" the queen and to secure her continued favor.
4. I.e., with deep sobs.
5. I.e., turn away (from the narrative, at 80).

Quoth he, "and each an end of singing made,
180 He gan to cast° great lyking to my lore,   *express*
And great dislyking to my lucklesse lot:
That banisht had my selfe, like wight forlore,
Into that waste, where I was quite forgot.
The which to leave, thenceforth he counseld mee,
185 Unmeet for man, in whom was ought regardfull,[6]
And wend with him, his Cynthia to see:
Whose grace was great, and bounty most rewardfull.
Besides her peerlesse skill in making° well   *composing (poetry)*
And all the ornaments of wondrous wit,
190 Such as all womankynd did far excell:
Such as the world admyred and praiséd it:[7]
So what with hope of good, and hate of ill,
He me perswaded forth with him to fare:
Nought tooke I with me, but mine oaten quill:
195 Small needments else need shepheard to prepare.
So to the sea we came; the sea? that is
A world of waters heapéd up on hie,
Rolling like mountaines in wide wildernesse,
Horrible, hideous, roaring with hoarse crie."
200   "And is the sea," quoth Coridon, "so fearfull?"
"Fearful much more," quoth he, "then hart can fear:
Thousand wyld beasts with deep mouthes gaping direfull
Therin stil wait poore passengers to teare.
Who life doth loath, and longs death to behold,
205 Before he die, alreadie dead with feare,
And yet would live with heart halfe stonie cold,
Let him to sea, and he shall see it there.
And yet as ghastly dreadfull, as it seemes,
Bold men presuming[8] life for gaine to sell,
210 Dare tempt that gulf, and in those wandring stremes°   *currents*
Seek waies unknowne, waies leading down to hell.
For as we stood there waiting on the strond,
Behold an huge great vessell to us came,
Dauncing upon the waters back to lond,
215 As if it scornd the daunger of the same;
Yet was it but a wooden frame and fraile,
Glewéd togither with some subtile matter,
Yet had it armes and wings, and head and taile,
And life to move it selfe upon the water.
220 Strange thing, how bold and swift the monster was,
That neither cared for wynd, nor haile, nor raine,
Nor swelling waves, but thorough them did passe
So proudly, that she made them roare againe.
The same aboord us gently did receave,
225 And without harme us farre away did beare,
So farre that land our mother us did leave,

6. I.e., worthy of esteem.
7. I.e., either (1) praised that wit, or (2) praised her "skill in making well."
8. I.e., having the audacity; risking.

And nought but sea and heaven to us appeare.
Then hartlesse quite and full of inward feare,
That shepheard I besought to me to tell,
230 Under what skie, or in what world we were,
In which I saw no living people dwell.
Who me recomforting all that he might,
Told me that that same was the Regiment°   *domain*
Of a great shepheardesse, that Cynthia hight,
235 His liege his Ladie, and his lifes Regent.[9]
'If then,' quoth I, 'a shepheardesse she bee,
Where be the flockes and heards, which she doth keep?
And where may I the hills and pastures see,
On which she useth for to feed her sheepe?'
240 'These be the hills,' quoth he, 'the surges hie,
On which faire Cynthia her heards doth feed:
Her heards be thousand fishes with their frie,
Which in the bosome of the billowes breed,
Of them the shepheard which hath charge in chief,
245 Is Triton blowing loud his wreathéd° horne: *twisted*
At sound whereof, they all for their relief[1]
Wend too and fro at evening and morne.
And Proteus eke with him does drive his heard
Of stinking Seales and Porcpisces° together,   *porpoises*
250 With hoary head and deawy dropping beard,
Compelling them which way he list,° and whether.   *desires*
And I among the rest of many least,
Have in the Ocean charge to me assignd:
Where I will live or die at her beheast,°   *command*
255 And serve and honour her with faithfull mind.
Besides an hundred Nymphs all heavenly borne,
And of immortall race, doo still attend
To wash faire Cynthiaes sheep, when they be shorne,
And fold them up, when they have made an end.
260 Those be the shepheards which my Cynthia serve,
At sea, beside a thousand moe at land:
For land and sea my Cynthia doth deserve
To have in her commandement at hand.'
Thereat I wondred much, till wondring more
265 And more, at length we land far off descryde:
Which sight much gladed me; for much afore
I feard, least land we never should have eyde:
Thereto our ship her course directly bent,
As if the way she perfectly had knowne.
270 We Lunday[2] passe; by that same name is ment

9. I.e., his life's ruler.
1. I.e., their recurrent release from the diurnal round (as watchful concern, equally with "compelling" direction, properly informs pastoral care). Modeling his account of Elizabeth as "great shepheardesse" and queen of the sea on Orpheus's song to the goddess Artemis in Apollonius Rhodius, *Argonautica* (c. third century B.C.), Spenser in 244–51 draws on Homer, *Odyssey* 4.384 ff., Virgil, *Georgics* 4.387–95, and Ovid, *Metamorphoses* 1.330–92 for details that enliven his Triton and Proteus. The conclusion of Wordsworth's sonnet "The world is too much with us" derives from 245.
2. Lundy Island, about twenty miles west of Ilfracombe, Devon.

An Island, which the first to west was showne.
From thence another world of land we kend,
Floting amid the sea in jeopardie,
And round about with mightie white rocks hemd,
275 Against the seas encroching crueltie.
Those same the shepheard told me, were the fields
In which dame Cynthia her landheards fed,
Faire goodly fields, then which Armulla yields
None fairer, nor more fruitfull to be red.°   seen
280 The first to which we nigh approachéd, was
An high headland thrust far into the sea,
Like to an horne, whereof the name it has,[3]
Yet seemed to be a goodly pleasant lea:
There did a loftie mount at first us greet,
285 Which did a stately heape of stones upreare,
That seemd amid the surges for to fleet,°   float
Much greater then that frame, which us did beare:
There did our ship her fruitfull wombe unlade,
And put us all ashore on Cynthias land."
290   "What land is that thou meanst," then Cuddy sayd,
"And is there other, then whereon we stand?"
     "Ah Cuddy," then quoth Colin, "thous a fon,°   fool
That hast not seene least part of natures worke:
Much more there is unkend, then thou doest kon,
295 And much more that does from mens knowledge lurke.
For that same land much larger is then this,
And other men and beasts and birds doth feed:
There fruitfull corne, faire trees, fresh herbage is
And all things else that living creatures need.
300 Besides most goodly rivers there appeare,
No whit inferiour to thy Funchins praise,
Or unto Allo or to Mulla cleare:
Nought hast thou foolish boy seene in thy daies."
     "But if that land be there," quoth he, "as here,
305 And is theyr heaven likewise there all one?[1]
And if like heaven, be heavenly graces there,
Like as in this same world where we do wone?"°   dwell
     "Both heaven and heavenly graces do much more,"
Quoth he, "abound in that same land, then this.
310 For there all happie peace and plenteous store
Conspire in one to make contented blisse:
No wayling there nor wretchednesse is heard,
No bloodie issues[5] nor no leprosies,
No griesly famine, nor no raging sweard,
315 No nightly bodrags, nor no hue and cries;[6]
The shepheards there abroad may safely lie,

3. I.e., the name of Cornwall. The "loftie mount" of 284 is probably St. Michael's Mount, near
   Penzance.
4. I.e., all the same; identified with our own.
5. I.e., (1) sallies, as of rioters and malcontents; (2) discharges of infectious matter, from the physical
   body and also from the "great body" of the state.
6. I.e., no nightly riots, nor loud cries from those who pursue criminals.

On hills and downes, withouten dread or daunger:
No ravenous wolves the good mans hope destroy,
Nor outlawes fell° affray the forest raunger.   *savage*
320 There learnéd arts do florish in great honor,
And Poets wits are had in peerlesse price:°   *value*
Religion hath lay powre to rest upon her,[7]
Advancing vertue and suppressing vice.
For end, all good, all grace there freely growes,
325 Had people grace it gratefully to use:
For God his gifts there plenteously bestowes,
But gracelesse men them greatly do abuse."
      "But say on further," then said Corylas,
"The rest of thine adventures, that betyded."
330   "Foorth on our voyage we by land did passe,"
Quoth he, "as that same shepheard still us guyded,
Untill that we to Cynthiaes presence came:
Whose glorie greater then my simple thought,
I found much greater then the former fame;
335 Such greatnes I cannot compare to ought:
But if I her like ought on earth might read,°   *imagine*
I would her lyken to a crowne of lillies,[8]
Upon a virgin brydes adornéd head,
With Roses dight and Goolds and Daffadillies;
340 Or like the circlet of a Turtle° true,   *turtle-dove*
In which all colours of the rainbow bee;
Or like faire Phebes garlond shining new,
In which all pure perfection one may see.
But vaine it is to thinke by paragone°   *comparison*
345 Of earthly things, to judge of things divine:
Her power, her mercy, and her wisedome, none
Can deeme, but who the Godhead can define.
Why then do I base shepheard bold and blind,
Presume the things so sacred to prophane?
350 More fit it is t'adore with humble mind,
The image of the heavens in shape humane."
      With that Alexis broke his tale asunder,
Saying, "By wondring at thy Cynthiaes praise,
Colin, thy selfe thou mak'st us more to wonder,
355 And her upraising, doest thy selfe upraise.[9]
But let us heare what grace she shewed thee,
And how that shepheard strange, thy cause° advanced?"   *condition*
      "The shepheard of the Ocean," quoth he,
"Unto that Goddesse grace me first enhanced,°   *raised*

---

7. I.e., religion is supported by secular authority.
8. While Spenser preserves the decorum of pastoral praise in 337–51, this series of linked images at
   once highlights Cynthia's "glorie" (and that of Elizabeth, ruler of English church and state) and
   underlines the shepherd-poet's power to celebrate, if not altogether to comprehend, that "image
   of the heavens in shape humane."
9. On the interplay of political power and the poet's powerful art, see Giamatti 1984, Montrose 1986,
   Alwes 1990; and Alpers 1989 (810, 815). Bernard 1989 notices the rhetorical functions of questions
   and interpolations by Colin's "chorus of listeners," chiefly Alexis and Cuddy (127–30).

360 And to mine oaten pipe enclined her eare,
     That she thenceforth therein gan take delight,
     And it desired at timely houres to heare,
     All were my notes but rude and roughly dight.
     For not by measure of her owne great mynd,
365 And wondrous worth she mott° my simple song,   *appraised*
     But joyd that country shepheard ought could fynd
     Worth harkening to, emongst the learned throng."
        "Why," said Alexis then, "what needeth shee
     That is so great a shepheardesse her selfe,
370 And hath so many shepheards in her fee,°   *service*
     To heare thee sing, a simple silly Elfe?°   *creature*
     Or be the shepheards which do serve her laesie,
     That they list not their mery pipes applie?°   *play*
     Or be their pipes untunable and craesie,°   *cracked*
375 That they cannot her honour worthylie?"
        "Ah nay," said Colin, "neither so, nor so:
     For better shepheards be not under skie,
     Nor better hable, when they list to blow
     Their pipes aloud, her name to glorifie.[1]
380 There is good Harpalus[2] now woxen agéd,
     In faithfull service of faire Cynthia:
     And there is Corydon[3] though meanly wagéd,
     Yet hablest wit of most I know this day.
     And there is sad Alcyon[4] bent to mourne,
385 Though fit to frame an everlasting dittie,
     Whose gentle spright for Daphnes death doth tourn
     Sweet layes of love to endlesse plaints of pittie.
     Ah pensive boy pursue that brave conceipt,°   *conception*
     In thy sweet Eglantine of Merifleure,
390 Lift up thy notes unto their wonted height,
     That may thy Muse and mates to mirth allure.
     There eke is Palin[5] worthie of great praise,
     Albe he envie at my rustick quill:
     And there is pleasing Alcon,[6] could he raise
395 His tunes from laies to matter of more skill.
     And there is old Palemon[7] free from spight,
     Whose carefull pipe may make the hearer rew:

---

1. Save for William Alabaster (1567–1640), "knowen yet to few," and Samuel Daniel (1562–1619), "late up sprong," the "shepheards" noted in 380–455 are not in every case certainly identifiable. But see Gaffney 1982.
2. George Turberville (?1540–1610), sometime secretary to the English ambassador to Russia; author of *Epitaphs, Epigrams, Songs, and Sonets* (1567). He comes first by virtue of age, perhaps (and the queen thought well of him).
3. Probably Edward Dyer (d. 1607), "famous for elegy," and close friend to Sir Philip Sidney.
4. Sir Arthur Gorges (?1566–1625), soldier, colonist, and friend to Raleigh. His mourning for the untimely death of his wife, Douglas Howard ("Daphne"), in August 1590 is the principal subject of Spenser's *Daphnaida*. "Eglantine of Merifleure" may be an unfinished poem by Gorges.
5. Perhaps George Peele (?1558–?1597), playwright and composer of entertainments for the queen.
6. Probably Thomas Lodge (?1558–1625), romancer, sonneteer, and much else; the "Induction" to his sonnet sequence *Phillis* (1593) has high praise for Spenser's art.
7. Thomas Churchyard (?1520–1604), "miscellaneous writer," and "hanger-on of the court and the nobility" (*DNB*); but Spenser is gentle with him.

Yet he himselfe may rewéd be more right,
That sung so long untill quite hoarse he grew.
400 And there is Alabaster[8] throughly taught,
In all this skill, though knowen yet to few,
Yet were he knowne to Cynthia as he ought,
His Eliseïs would be redde anew.
Who lives that can match that heroick song,
405 Which he hath of that mightie Princesse made?
O dreaded Dread, do not thy selfe that wrong,
To let thy fame lie so in hidden shade:
But call it forth, O call him forth to thee,
To end thy glorie° which he hath begun: *praise*
410 That when he finisht hath as it should be,
No braver Poeme can be under Sun.
Nor Po nor Tyburs swans[9] so much renowned,
Nor all the brood of Greece so highly praised,
Can match that Muse when it with bayes is crowned,
415 And to the pitch of her perfection raised.
And there is a new shepheard late up sprong,[1]
The which doth all afore him far surpasse:
Appearing well in that well tunéd song,
Which late he sung unto a scornfull lasse.
420 Yet doth his trembling Muse but lowly flie,
As daring not too rashly mount on hight,
And doth her tender plumes as yet but trie,
In loves soft laies and looser thoughts delight.
Then rouze° thy feathers quickly Daniell,   *ruffle*
425 And to what course thou please thy selfe advance:
But most me seemes, thy accent will excell,
In Tragick plaints and passionate mischance.
And there that shepheard of the Ocean is,
That spends his wit in loves consuming smart:
430 Full sweetly tempred° is that Muse of his   *attuned*
That can empierce a Princes mightie hart.
There also is (ah no, he is not now)
But since I said he is, he quite is gone,
Amyntas[2] quite is gone and lies full low,
435 Having his Amaryllis left to mone.
Helpe, O ye shepheards helpe ye all in this.
Helpe Amaryllis this her losse to mourne:
Her losse is yours, your losse Amyntas is,
Amyntas floure of shepheards pride forlorne:
440 He whilest he livéd was the noblest swaine,
That ever pipéd in an oaten quill:
Both did he other, which could pipe, maintaine,

8. William Alabaster, who never completed his *Eliseis,* a Latin epic dedicated to the queen. The only remaining fragment of the work was published in 1979.
9. In this context the swan of Tiber is surely Virgil; that of Po is less certain. Hieatt (correspondence with editors 1990) suggests that "modern Italian poets" may be subsumed under the term.
1. Samuel Daniel. Lines 418–19 presumably refer to the sonnet sequence *Delia* (pub. 1592), which Spenser might have seen in manuscript.
2. Lines 432–43, added to the 1591 version, lament the death of Ferdinando Stanley, Lord Strange, 5th earl of Derby (?1559–94). "Amaryllis" is his wife, Alice Spencer (see 536–71 and note).

And eke could pipe himselfe with passing skill.
And there though last not least is Aetion,[3]
445 A gentler shepheard may no where be found:
Whose Muse full of high thoughts invention,
Doth like himselfe Heroically sound.
All these, and many others mo remaine,
Now after Astrofell[4] is dead and gone:
450 But while as Astrofell did live and raine,
Amongst all these was none his Paragone.
All these do florish in their sundry kynd,
And do their Cynthia immortall make:
Yet found I lyking in her royall mynd,
455 Not for my skill, but for that shepheards sake."
    Then spake a lovely lasse, hight Lucida,
"Shepheard, enough of shepheards thou hast told,
Which favour thee, and honour Cynthia:
But of so many Nymphs which she doth hold
460 In her retinew, thou hast nothing sayd;
That seems, with none of them thou favor foundest,
Or art ingratefull to each gentle mayd,
That none of all their due deserts resoundest."
    "Ah far be it," quoth Colin Clout, "fro me,
465 That I of gentle Mayds should ill deserve:
For that my selfe I do professe to be
Vassall to one,[5] whom all my dayes I serve;
The beame of beautie sparkled from above,
The floure of vertue and pure chastitie,
470 The blossome of sweet joy and perfect love,
The pearle of peerlesse grace and modestie:
To her my thoughts I daily dedicate,
To her my heart I nightly martyrize:
To her my love I lowly do prostrate,
475 To her my life I wholly sacrifice:
My thought, my heart, my love, my life is shee,
And I hers ever onely, ever one:
One ever I all vowéd hers to bee,
One ever I, and others never none."
480   Then thus Melissa said, "Thrise happie Mayd,
Whom thou doest so enforce° to deifie: *strive*
That woods, and hills, and valleyes thou hast made
Her name to eccho unto heaven hie.
But say, who else vouchsaféd° thee of grace?"   *granted*
485   "They all," quoth he, "me gracéd goodly well,
That all I praise, but in the highest place,

3. Probably Michael Drayton (1568–1631), whose *Heroicall Epistles* may have been known to Spenser
    before their publication in 1595.
4. Sir Philip Sidney (1554–86), whose death Spenser laments in *Astrophel* (pub. 1595), appropriately
    concludes the register of "shepheardes" who, while he lived, were not his match. The "shephearde"
    of 455 may arguably be either Sidney or Raleigh; or possibly Spenser acknowledges his debt to
    both.
5. For hints of her identity see E.K.'s Glosses to "Januarye" and "Aprill" (and "June"); both Mallette
    1990E and Heninger 1990E are sensibly cautious. In 477–79, the expressions "ever one . . . One
    ever" English the queen's personal motto, *Semper eadem*. See D. Cheney 1983.

Urania[6] sister unto Astrofell,
In whose brave mynd as in a golden cofer,
All heavenly gifts and riches lockéd are:
490 More rich then pearles of Ynde, or gold of Opher,[7]
And in her sex more wonderfull and rare.
Ne lesse praise worthie I Theana[8] read,°   *name*
Whose goodly beames though they be over dight
With mourning stole of carefull wydowhead,
495 Yet through that darksome vale do glister bright;
She is the well of bountie and brave mynd,
Excelling most in glorie and great light:
She is the ornament of womankind,
And Courts chief garlond with all vertues dight.
500 Therefore great Cynthia her in chiefest grace
Doth hold, and next unto her selfe advance,
Well worthie of so honourable place,
For her great worth and noble governance.
Ne lesse praise worthie is her sister deare,
505 Faire Marian, the Muses onely darling:
Whose beautie shyneth as the morning cleare,
With silver deaw upon the roses pearling.
Ne lesse praise worthie is Mansilia,[9]
Best knowne by bearing up great Cynthiaes traine:
510 That same is she to whom Daphnaida
Upon her neeces death I did complaine.
She is the paterne of true womanhead,
And onely mirrhor of feminitie:
Worthie next after Cynthia to tread,
515 As she is next her in nobilitie.
Ne lesse praise worthie Galathea[1] seemes,
Then best of all that honourable crew,
Faire Galathea with bright shining beames,
Inflaming feeble eyes that her do view.
520 She there then waited upon Cynthia,
Yet there is not her won,° but here with us   *abode*

6. As with the matching catalog of "shepheards," identification of the twelve "Nymphes" in Cynthia's
   retinue is not everywhere beyond question. But Urania is certainly Mary Sidney, countess of
   Pembroke (1561–1621), Sir Philip Sidney's sister to whom the fifteenth dedicatory sonnet prefacing
   The Faerie Queene is dedicated. Devout, learned, and a perceptive patroness of the arts, she was
   considered to exemplify that concern for the threat of "ignorance, the enemie of grace" to "th'
   heavenlie light of knowledge . . . /And the ornaments of Wisdome" attributed to Urania, Muse
   of astronomy (and Christian poetry) in *The Teares of the Muses* 497, 488–89. See Hannay 1990.
7. Traditionally, a region in Arabia (or India) known for its gold, ivory, and sandalwood (Genesis
   10.29; 1 Kings 10.11, 22).
8. Anne Russell, countess of Warwick (1548–1603/4), whose husband had died in 1590. Spenser
   celebrates her exemplary widowhood in *The Ruines of Time* 244–52. In 1596 he dedicated *Fowre
   Hymnes* jointly to her and her sister Margaret, countess of Cumberland (?1560–1616), "Marian"
   in 505–7.
9. The Swedish Helena Snackenborg (d. 1635), marchioness of Northampton. In 1591, twenty years
   after the death of the marquis, she married Sir Thomas Gorges, uncle of Sir Arthur Gorges
   ("Alcyon" in this poem). Spenser dedicated *Daphnaida* to this lady, who was "chief mourner"
   when the queen died in 1603.
1. Frances Howard (d. 1628), wife of Henry Fitzgerald, earl of Kildare. The estate given her in lieu
   of dower included Croom and Adare in the barony of Coshma, southwest from Limerick on the
   river Maigue ("Maa"). One of the dedicatory sonnets prefixed to *The Faerie Queene* is addressed
   to her father, earl of Nottingham.

About the borders of our rich Coshma,
Now made of Maa the Nymph delitious.
Ne lesse praisworthie faire Neæra[2] is,
525 Neæra ours, not theirs, though there she be,
For of the famous Shure, the Nymph she is,
For high desert, advaunst to that degree.
She is the blosome of grace and curtesie,
Adornéd with all honourable parts:
530 She is the braunch of true nobilitie,
Beloved of high and low with faithfull harts.
Ne lesse praisworthie Stella[3] do I read,
Though nought my praises of her needed arre,
Whom verse of noblest shepheard lately dead
535 Hath praised and raised above each other starre.
Ne lesse praisworthic arc thc sistcrs three,
The honor of the noble familie,
Of which I meanest boast my selfe to be,
And most that unto them I am so nie.[4]
540 Phyllis, Charillis, and sweet Amaryllis,
Phyllis the faire, is eldest of the three:
The next to her, is bountifull Charillis.
But th'youngest is the highest in degree.
Phyllis the floure of rare perfection,
545 Faire spreading forth her leaves with fresh delight,
That with their beauties amorous reflexion,
Bereave of sence each rash beholders sight.
But sweet Charillis is the Paragone°   *model*
Of peerlesse price, and ornament of praise,
550 Admyred of all, yet enviéd of none,
Through the myld temperance of her goodly raies.
Thrise happie do I hold thee noble swaine,[5]
The which are of so rich a spoile possest,
And it embracing deare without disdaine,
555 Hast sole possession in so chaste a brest:
Of all the shepheards daughters which there bee,
And yet there be the fairest under skie,

2. Elizabeth Sheffield (d. 1601), second wife of Thomas Butler, tenth earl of Ormonde, who held
lands on the river Suir ("Shure"), near Clonmell, about forty miles from Kilcolman. Sir Philip
Sidney called Ormonde "my professed foe" (Hannay 1990); in any event Spenser addressed one
of the dedicatory sonnets prefixing *The Faerie Queene* to Ormonde.
3. The lady of Sidney's *Astrophel and Stella*; in Spenser's poem not Penelope Devereux, Lady Rich
(?1562–1607), but Sidney's widow, Frances [Walsingham] (1569–1632), subsequently countess of
Essex, to whom Spenser in 1595 dedicated *Astrophel*.
4. Spenser claimed relationship with the Spencers of Althorp, Northamptonshire (see *Prothalamion*
130–31). He dedicated *Muiopotmos* to Elizabeth, Lady Carey (d. 1617/18), the second daughter
of Sir John Spencer; a dedicatory sonnet prefixed to *The Faerie Queene* is also addressed to her.
To the fifth daughter, Anne, Lady Compton and Montegle (d. 1618), he dedicated *Mother
Hubberds Tale*. To the sixth daughter, Alice, Lady Strange (d. 1636/37), he dedicated *The Teares
of the Muses*. She is "highest in degree" (543) because her second husband, Ferdinando Lord
Strange ("Amyntas"), became earl of Derby in 1593; he died in 1594. While Spenser's pastoral
names for the three sisters do not echo those of the classical Graces (Aglaea, Thalia, Euphrosyne),
the poet perhaps expects his readers to recall those personifications of grace and beauty; see *The
Faerie Queene*, VI.x.22–24.
5. Anne Russell's third husband, Robert Sackville (1561–1608/9), subsequently second earl of Dorset,
whom she married in December 1592 (having been "freed from Cupids yoke by fate" [566], when
her second husband, Henry Lord Compton, died in December 1589).

Or that elsewhere I ever yet did see,
A fairer Nymph yet never saw mine eie:
560 She is the pride and primrose of the rest,
Made by the maker selfe to be admired:
And like a goodly beacon high addrest,°   placed
That is with sparks of heavenlie beautie fired.
But Amaryllis, whether fortunate,
565 Or else unfortunate may I aread,°   surmise
That freéd is from Cupids yoke by fate,
Since which she doth new bands adventure dread.
Shepheard what ever thou hast heard to be
In this or that praysd diversly apart,
570 In her thou maist them all assembled see,
And seald up in the threasure of her hart.
Ne thee lesse worthie gentle Flavia,[6]
For thy chaste life and vertue I esteeme:
Ne thee lesse worthie curteous Candida,
575 For thy true love and loyaltie I deeme.
Besides yet many mo that Cynthia serve,
Right noble Nymphs, and high to be commended:
But if I all should praise as they deserve,
This sun would faile me ere I halfe had ended.
580 Therefore in closure of a thankfull mynd,
I deeme it best to hold eternally,
Their bounteous deeds and noble favours shrynd,
Then by discourse them to indignifie."[7]
      So having said, Aglaura him bespake:
585 "Colin, well worthie were those goodly favours
Bestowd on thee, that so of them doest make,
And them requitest with thy thankfull labours.
But of great Cynthiaes goodnesse and high grace,
Finish the storie which thou hast begunne."
590   "More eath,°" quoth he, "it is in such a case   easy
How to begin, then know how to have donne.
For everie gift and everie goodly meed,[8]
Which she on me bestowd, demaunds a day;
And everie day, in which she did a deed,
595 Demaunds a yeare it duly to display.
Her words were like a streame of honny fleeting,
The which doth softly trickle from the hive:
Hable to melt the hearers heart unweeting,°   unaware
And eke to make the dead againe alive.

6. Flavia and Candida have not been identified; these may be "generic" names introduced to fill up the measure of twelve. See *Variorum* VII.1.477.
7. I.e., to dishonor them (since discourse cannot express the quality of their generosity).
8. This second encomiastic passage of praise for Cynthia's "goodnesse and high grace" recalls but overgoes 337–51. As before, the shepherd-poet strives to express her form and function in terms within his pastoral ken; but scriptural echoes now inform the images more evocatively than before. The classical associations of "faire Phebes garland," for instance, give way to the scripturally redolent "fume of Franckincence" (cf. Revelation 8.3–4), while the power of her words not only to melt hearts but to "make the dead againe alive" looks to Proverbs 16.24 and also (Yale) Psalms 119.103. And the speaker (modestly present at the close of the earlier passage) now yields altogether to the vision of Cynthia among "the seats of Angels," magisterially contemplating the timeless divine purpose.

600 Her deeds were like great clusters of ripe grapes,
     Which load the bunches of the fruitfull vine:
     Offring to fall into each mouth that gapes,
     And fill the same with store of timely wine.
     Her lookes were like beames of the morning Sun,
605 Forth looking through the windowes of the East:
     When first the fleecie cattell have begun
     Upon the perléd grasse to make their feast.
     Her thoughts are like the fume of Franckincence,
     Which from a golden Censer forth doth rise:
610 And throwing forth sweet odours mounts fro thence
     In rolling globes up to the vauted° skies.   *vaulted*
     There she beholds with high aspiring thought,
     The cradle of her owne creation:
     Emongst the seats of Angels heavenly wrought,
615 Much like an Angell in all forme and fashion.°"   *kind*
        "Colin," said Cuddy then, "thou hast forgot
     Thy selfe, me seemes, too much, to mount so hie:
     Such loftie flight, base shepheard seemeth° not,   *befits*
     From flocks and fields, to Angels and to skie."
620   "True," answered he, "but her great excellence,
     Lifts me above the measure of my might:
     That being fild with furious insolence,[9]
     I feele my selfe like one yrapt in spright.
     For when I thinke of her, as oft I ought,
625 Then want I words to speake it fitly forth:
     And when I speake of her what I have thought,
     I cannot thinke according to her worth.
     Yet will I thinke of her, yet will I speake,
     So long as life my limbs doth hold together,
630 And when as death these vitall bands shall breake,
     Her name recorded I will leave for ever.
     Her name in every tree I will endosse,°   *inscribe*
     That as the trees do grow, her name may grow:
     And in the ground each where will it engrosse,
635 And fill[1] with stones, that all men may it know.
     The speaking woods and murmuring waters fall,
     Her name Ile teach in knowen termes to frame:
     And eke my lambs when for their dams they call,
     Ile teach to call for Cynthia by name.
640 And long while after I am dead and rotten,
     Amongst the shepheards daughters dancing rownd,
     My layes made of her shall not be forgotten,
     But sung by them with flowry gyrlonds crownd.
     And ye, who so ye be, that shall survive:
645 When as ye heare her memory renewed,
     Be witnesse of her bountie here alive,
     Which she to Colin her poore shepheard shewed."

9. I.e., inspired rapture; poetic "rage." See "October" 108–14; and E.K.'s *Glosse* on the emblem of
     that eclogue.
1. I.e., will write it large and fill in (the characters).

Much was the whole assembly of those heards,
Mooved at his speech, so feelingly he spake:
650 And stood awhile astonisht at his words,
Till Thestylis at last their silence brake,
Saying, "Why, Colin, since thou foundst such grace
With Cynthia and all her noble crew:
Why didst thou ever leave that happie place,
655 In which such wealth might unto thee accrew?
And back returnedst to this barrein soyle,
Where cold and care and penury do dwell:
Here to keep sheepe, with hunger and with toyle,
Most wretched he, that is and cannot tell."[2]
660 "Happie indeed," said Colin, "I him hold,
That may that blesséd presence still enjoy,
Of fortune and of envy uncomptrold,
Which still are wont most happie states t'annoy:
But I by that which little while I prooved:°   *experienced*
665 Some part of those enormities did see,
The which in Court continually hooved,[3]
And followd those which happie seemd to bee.
Therefore I silly° man, whose former dayes   *innocent*
Had in rude fields bene altogether spent,
670 Durst not adventure° such unknowen wayes,   *risk*
Nor trust the guile of fortunes blandishment,
But rather chose back to my sheep to tourne,
Whose utmost hardnesse° I before had tryde,   *roughness*
Then having learnd repentance late, to mourne
675 Emongst those wretches which I there descryde."
"Shepheard," said Thestylis, "it seemes of spight
Thou speakest thus gainst their felicitie,
Which thou enviest, rather then of right[4]
That ought in them blameworthie thou doest spie."
680 "Cause have I none," quoth he, "of cancred will
To quite° them ill, that me demeand so well: *requite*
But selfe-regard of private good or ill,
Moves me of each, so as I found, to tell[5]
And eke to warne yong shepheards wandring wit,
685 Which through report of that lives painted blisse,
Abandon quiet home, to seeke for it,
And leave their lambes to losse misled amisse.
For sooth to say, it is no sort of life,
For shepheard fit to lead in that same place,
690 Where each one seeks with malice and with strife,
To thrust downe other into foule disgrace,
Himselfe to raise: and he doth soonest rise
That best can handle his deceitfull wit,
In subtil shifts, and finest sleights devise,

2. I.e., that cannot express his wretched condition.
3. I.e., lingered (and were tacitly accepted).
4. I.e., rather than justly.
5. I.e., But self-respect [*amour propre*] prompts me to speak of good or ill done to me.

695 Either by slaundring his[6] well deeméd name,
Through leasings° lewd, and fainéd forgerie: *lies*
Or else by breeding° him some blot of blame,   *causing*
By creeping close into his secrecie;
To which him needs, a guilefull hollow hart,
700 Maskéd with faire dissembling curtesie,
A filéd° toung furnisht with tearmes of art,   *smooth*
No art of schoole,[7] but Courtiers schoolery.
For arts of schoole have there small countenance,
Counted but toyes to busie ydle braines,
705 And there professours[8] find small maintenance,
But to be instruments of others gaines.
Ne is there place for any gentle wit,
Unlesse to please, it selfe it can applie:
But shouldred° is, or out of doore quite shit,°   *pushed aside/shut*
710 As base, or blunt, unmeet for melodie.
For each mans worth is measured by his weed,°   *attire*
As harts by hornes, or asses by their eares:
Yet asses been not all whose eares exceed,
Nor yet all harts, that hornes the highest beares.
715 For highest lookes have not the highest mynd,
Nor haughtie words most full of highest thoughts.
But are like bladders blowen up with wynd,
That being prickt do vanish into noughts.
Even such is all their vaunted vanitie,
720 Nought else but smoke, that fumeth soone away:
Such is their glorie that in simple eie
Seeme greatest, when their garments are most gay.
So they themselves for praise of fooles do sell,
And all their wealth for painting on a wall;
725 With price whereof, they buy a golden bell,
And purchace highest rowmes in bowre° and hall: *bedchamber*
Whiles single° Truth and simple honestie   *undivided, one only*
Do wander up and downe despysed of all;
Their plaine attire such glorious gallantry
730 Disdaines so much, that none them in doth call."
    "Ah Colin," then said Hobbinol, "the blame
Which thou imputest, is too generall,
As if not any gentle wit of name,
Nor honest mynd might there be found at all.
735 For well I wot, sith I my selfe was there,
To wait on Lobbin[9] (Lobbin well thou knewest)
Full many worthie ones then waiting were,
As ever else° in Princes Court thou vewest.   *elsewhere*
Of which, among you many yet remaine,
740 Whose names I cannot readily now ghesse:

6. Presumably "his" refers to "other" in 691. But the case might be altered if the (apparently) missing line between 694–95 were to be recovered. See *Variorum* VII.479.
7. I.e., not true learning.
8. I.e., scholar-teachers.
9. Robert Dudley, earl of Leicester (c. 1532–88), in whose household Spenser was employed for a year or so during 1579–80.

Those that poore Sutors papers do retaine,[1]
And those that skill of medicine professe.
And those that do to Cynthia expound
The ledden° of straunge languages in charge:　　　　　*speech*
745　For Cynthia doth in sciences abound,
And gives to their professors stipends large.
Therefore unjustly thou doest wyte° them all,　　　　*blame*
For that which thou mislikedst in a few."
　　"Blame is," quoth he, "more blamelesse generall,
750　Then that which private° errours doth pursew:　　　*individual*
For well I wot, that there amongst them bee
Full many persons of right worthie parts,
Both for report of spotlesse honestie,
And for profession of all learned arts,
755　Whose praise hereby no whit impairéd is,
Though blame do light on those that faultie bee,
For all the rest do most-what° fare amis,　　　　　*mostly*
And yet their owne misfaring will not see:
For either they be pufféd up with pride,
760　Or fraught with envie that their galls do swell,
Or they their dayes to ydlenesse divide,°　　　　　*assign*
Or drownded lie in pleasures wastefull well,
In which like Moldwarps nousling[2] still they lurke,
Unmyndfull of chiefe parts of manlinesse,
765　And do themselves for want of other worke,
Vaine votaries of laesie love professe,
Whose service high so basely they ensew,°　　　　　*pursue*
That Cupid selfe of them ashaméd is,
And mustring all his men in Venus vew,
770　Denies them quite for servitors of his."
　　"And is love then," said Corylas, "once° knowne　　*ever*
In Court, and his sweet lore professéd° there?　　　*recognized*
I weenéd sure he was our God alone:
And only woond° in fields and forests here."　　　　*dwelt*
775　　"Not so," quoth he, "love most aboundeth there.
For all the walls and windows there are writ,°　　　*inscribed*
All full of love, and love, and love my deare,
And all their talke and studie is of it.
Ne any there doth brave or valiant seeme,
780　Unlesse that some gay Mistresse badge° he beares:　　*token*
Ne any one himselfe doth ought esteeme,
Unlesse he swim in love up to the eares.
But they of love and of his sacred lere,°　　　　　*lore*
(As it should be) all otherwise devise,
785　Then we poore shepheards are accustomd here,
And him do sue and serve[3] all otherwise.
For with lewd[4] speeches and licentious deeds,

1. I.e., do keep in mind.
2. I.e., like burrowing moles.
3. I.e., to follow as servant.
4. I.e., unlearned, vulgar; unchaste.

His mightie mysteries they do prophane,
And use his ydle name to other needs,
790 But as a complement for courting vaine.[5]
So him they do not serve as they professe,
But make him serve to them for sordid uses,°   *ends*
Ah my dread Lord, that doest liege° hearts possesse,   *loyal*
Avenge thy selfe on them for their abuses.[6]
795 But we poore shepheards whether rightly so,
Or through our rudenesse into errour led,
Do make religion how we rashly go,[7]
To serve that God, that is so greatly dred;
For him the greatest of the Gods we deeme,[8]
800 Borne without Syre or couples of one kynd,
For Venus selfe doth soly couples seeme,
Both male and female, through commixture joynd.
So pure and spotlesse Cupid forth she brought,
And in the gardens of Adonis nurst:
805 Where growing, he his owne perfection wrought,
And shortly was of all the Gods the first.
Then got he bow and shafts of gold and lead,
In which so fell and puissant he grew,
That Jove himselfe his powre began to dread,
810 And taking up to heaven, him godded° new.   *deified*
From thence he shootes his arrowes every where
Into the world, at randon as he will,
On us fraile men, his wretched vassals here,
Like as himselfe us pleaseth, save or spill.°   *ruin*
815 So we him worship, so we him adore
With humble hearts to heaven uplifted hie,
That to true loves he may us evermore
Preferre,° and of their grace us dignifie:[9]   *raise*
Ne is there shepheard, ne yet shepheards swaine,
820 What ever feeds in forest or in field,
That dare with evil deed or leasing° vaine   *falsehood*
Blaspheme his powre, or termes unworthie yield."[1]
    "Shepheard it seemes that some celestiall rage
Of love," quoth Cuddy, "is breathed into thy brest,

5. I.e., (ironically) merely as mock-courteous ornament for a worthless travesty of courtesy.
6. I.e., corruptions (of Cupid's laws).
7. I.e., either (1) take care that moral scruples moderate rash amorous impulse, or, more probably (2), claim to serve the god of love however rashly we respond to the prick of desire.
8. In Spenser's poetry the figure of Cupid reflects a complex and somewhat contradictory variety of classical and medieval elements, informed (especially in this poem and in "An Hymne in Honour of Love") by "Neoplatonic speculative mythography": see Hyde 1990E. The conception of Cupid as "greatest of the Gods" and "Lord of all the world by right" (880) derives ultimately from Plato, *Symposium* 178a, by way of the *Commentary* on that work by Marsilio Ficino (1433–99) tr. Sears Jayne (Columbia, MO, 1944) 1.2: "Certainly He is great to whose rule men and gods they say are all subject." That Cupid is "borne without Syre" to a Venus "Both male and female" looks probably to Boccaccio, *Genealogia* 3.22, or even to the widely influential *Commentary* by Servius (fourth century A.D.) on the *Aeneid* 2.632. In 807–22 the Cupid of medieval love-literature emerges: pre-eminently a tyrannical figure whose arrows of gold and lead, shot at random, kindle and extinguish love (see *Metamorphoses* 1.469–71), he fiercely triumphs over all lovers, who must serve his pleasure.
9. I.e., And make us worthy of their favor.
1. I.e., or acknowledge (him) in unbefitting language.

825 That powreth forth these oracles so sage,
Of that high powre, wherewith thou art possest.[2]
But never wist I till this present day
Albe of love I alwayes humbly deemed,°   *thought*
That he was such an one, as thou doest say,
830 And so religiously to be esteemed.
Well may it seeme by this thy deep insight,
That of that God the Priest thou shouldest bee:
So well thou wot'st the mysterie of his might,[3]
As if his godhead thou didst present see."
835   "Of loves perfection perfectly to speake,
Or of his nature rightly to define,
Indeed," said Colin, "passeth reasons reach,
And needs his priest t'expresse his powre divine.[4]
For long before the world he was y' bore
840 And bred above in Venus bosome deare:
For by his powre the world was made of yore,
And all that therein wondrous doth appeare.
For how should else things so far from attone°   *agreement*
And so great enemies as of° them bee,   *among*
845 Be ever drawne together into one,
And taught in such accordance to agree?
Through him the cold began to covet heat,
And water fire; the light to mount on hie,
And th'heavie downe to peize°; the hungry t'eat   *sink*
850 And voydnesse to seeke full satietie.
So being former foes, they wexéd friends,
And gan by litle learne to love each other:
So being knit, they brought forth other kynds
Out of the fruitfull wombe of their great mother.[5]
855 Then first gan heaven out of darknesse dread
For to appeare, and brought forth chearfull day:
Next gan the earth to shew her naked head,
Out of deep waters which her drownd alway.
And shortly after everie living wight,
860 Crept forth like wormes out of her slimie nature,
Soone as on them the Suns life giving light,
Had powréd kindly heat and formall feature,
Thenceforth they gan each one his like to love,
And like himselfe desire for to beget,
865 The Lyon chose his mate, the Turtle Dove
Her deare, the Dolphin his owne Dolphinet:
But man that had the sparke of reasons might,

---

2. See 622 and note.
3. I.e., So well you grasp the secret working of his power.
4. Lines 838–94 may be a later addition to the original version of the poem: see R. Ellrodt, *Neoplatonism in the Poetry of Spenser* (Geneva, 1960) 19–23, 222. In this passage Cupid is primarily creator of the world, through the divinely beneficent power of love reconciling all antagonisms, achieving universal concord among discordant opposites that retain their differences within a larger divinely ordered design (cf. "An Hymne in Honour of Love" 57–119). See *Metamorphoses* 1.18–88; and, chiefly, Ficino 1.3, 3.2–3, 6.9, 11; for modern commentary, see Heninger 1974 (149–51). See also Hyde 1990E on Spenser's larger effort to construct "a poetic theodicy of Cupid."
5. I.e., chaos. See Hesiod, *Theogony* 116–22.

More then the rest to rule his passion,
Chose for his love the fairest in his sight,
870   Like as himselfe was fairest by creation.
For beautie is the bayt which with delight
Doth man allure, for to enlarge his kynd,
Beautie the burning lamp of heavens light,
Darting her beames into each feeble mynd:
875   Against whose powre, nor God nor man can fynd
Defence, ne ward the daunger of the wound,
But being hurt, seeke to be medicynd
Of her that first did stir that mortall stownd.[6]
Then do they cry and call to love apace,
880   With praiers lowd importuning the skie,
Whence he them heares, and when he list shew grace,
Does graunt them grace that otherwise would die.
So love is Lord of all the world by right,
And rules the creatures by his powrfull saw:°   *decree*
885   All being made the vassalls of his might,
Through secret sence[7] which therto doth them draw.
Thus ought all lovers of their lord to deeme:
And with chaste heart to honor him alway:
But who so else doth otherwise esteeme,
890   Are outlawes, and his lore do disobay.
For their desire is base, and doth not merit,
The name of love, but of disloyall lust:
Ne mongst true lovers they shall place inherit,°   *receive*
But as Exuls° out of his court be thrust."   *exiles*
895   So having said, Melissa spake at will,
"Colin, thou now full deeply hast divynd:[8]
Of love and beautie and with wondrous skill,
Hast Cupid selfe depainted in his kynd.
To thee are all true lovers greatly bound,
900   That doest their cause so mightily defend:
But most, all wemen are thy debtors found,
That doest their bountie still so much commend."
    "That ill," said Hobbinol, "they him requite,
For having lovéd ever one most dearc:
905   He is repayd with scorne and foule despite,
That yrkes each gentle heart which it doth heare."
    "Indeed," said Lucid, "I have often heard
Faire Rosalind of divers fowly blamed:
For being to that swaine too cruell hard,
910   That her bright glorie else hath much defamed.[9]
But who can tell what cause had that faire Mayd
To use him so that uséd her so well:
Or who with blame can justly her upbrayd,
For loving not? for who can love compell?

6. I.e., did cause that intense inward shock.
7. I.e., deep-rooted physical sensation, stimulating sexual desire; and also intellective and intuitive
   apprehension at a higher spiritual remove. See "An Hymne in Honour of Beautie" 197–203.
8. I.e., intuitively perceived.
9. I.e., that hath much disgraced her otherwise bright honor.

915 And sooth to say, it is foolhardie thing,
    Rashly to wyten° creatures so divine,   *blame*
    For demigods they be and first did spring
    From heaven, though graft° in frailnesse feminine.   *planted*
    And well I wote, that oft I heard it spoken,
920 How one that fairest Helene did revile,[1]
    Through judgement of the Gods to been ywroken°   *revenged*
    Lost both his eyes and so remaynd long while,
    Till he recanted had his wicked rimes,
    And made amends to her with treble praise:
925 Beware therefore, ye groomes, I read betimes,[2]
    How rashly blame of Rosalind ye raise."
        "Ah shepheards," then said Colin, "ye ne weet
    How great a guilt upon your heads ye draw:
    To make so bold a doome° with words unmeet,   *judgement*
930 Of thing celestiall which ye never saw.
    For she is not like as the other crew
    Of shepheards daughters which emongst you bee,
    But of divine regard° and heavenly hew,   *appearance*
    Excelling all that ever ye did see.
935 Not then to her that scornéd thing so base,
    But to my selfe the blame that lookt so hie:
    So hie her thoughts as she her selfe have place,
    And loath each lowly thing with loftie eie.[3]
    Yet so much grace° let her vouchsafe to grant   *favor*
940 To simple swaine, sith her I may not love:
    Yet that I may her honour paravant,°   *pre-eminently*
    And praise her worth, though far my wit above.
    Such grace shall be some guerdon° for the griefe,   *reward*
    And long affliction which I have endured:
945 Such grace sometimes shall give me some reliefe,
    And ease of paine which cannot be recured.[4]
    And ye my fellow shepheards which do see
    And heare the languours of my too long dying,
    Unto the world for ever witnesse bee,
950 That hers I die, nought to the world denying,
    This simple trophe of her great conquest."
        So having ended, he from ground did rise,
    And after him uprose eke all the rest:
    All loth to part, but that the glooming skies
955 Warnd them to draw their bleating flocks to rest.

Editors' Note

Colin Clouts Come Home Againe, for many years relatively neglected by scholars
of Spenser's poetry, has only within the last two decades or so been recognized

1. The Greek poet Stesichorus (c.630–c.555 B.C.), in his poem *Helen* [of Troy], gave an account of
   her marriage to Menelaus for which, according to legend, he was blinded by the gods. He recovered
   only after he recanted that account in another poem, the *Palinode.*
2. I.e., I advise, in good time.
3. I.e., And loathsome (is) each lowly thing that presumes to reach beyond its proper station.
4. I.e., be restored to full health.

as especially important in the context of his developing outlook. Spenser's description of the poem, in the 1591 dedication to Raleigh, as "this simple pastoral," inviting comparison with the complex achievement of *The Shepheardes Calender*, perhaps encouraged earlier critics to speak dismissively of the later work's inconsistencies and "incoherence," or to regard it as something of an afterthought or appendix to the *Calender*. Meyer's full-length study (1969) of *Colin Clout* could still refer to the poem as "a kind of sequel to the *Calender*," while arguing for the unity of Colin's discourse, "crystallized around the theme of love."

But modern scholarship has increasingly reflected the "reorientation of Spenser criticism, toward new methods of interpretation and to other kinds of questions altogether," called for by Michael Murrin in 1973. MacCaffrey 1976, for instance, notices "the formula of 'out-and-back' from which *Colin Clout* derives its tripartite structure"; Burchmore 1977 demonstrates its circular and numerically determined patterning. Others attend chiefly to Colin's progress, either as poet-lover up the Neoplatonic *scala* (Mallette 1979), or as the journey of a poet who seeks to reconcile the demands of poetry and those of public life (Shore 1985, 1990E). Again, Colin's confrontation with how political power functions in his world entails for some Spenser's loss of faith in his own poetical power; by another view, Colin, in some sense strengthened by trial, discovers that his role "is not to confront the fallen world but to recreate the golden one" in poetry (specifically *The Faerie Queene*) that withstands the ravages of time (cf. Shore 1990E). Finally, and perhaps chiefly, a new historicism emphasizing the intertextuality of literary text and that of "history," i.e., "the complex network of institutions, practices, and beliefs that constitute the structure as a whole" (Greenblatt 1982), has pervasively affected the cast and character of present-day Spenser scholarship. New historicists have ministered most strikingly to the big poem and to the *Calender*; but *Colin Clout* resonates in important ways to their emphases, particularly to the manner in which Spenser "by making the poem serve the queen, makes the queen serve the poem" (Montrose 1986; cf. Alwes 1990). The common reader of *Colin Clout* may well find this rich pageant of newsprung critical witness bewildering; but time and patience will show that most of these varied approaches to the poem are in some measure mutually compatible. Certainly the reach and diverse strengths of modern critical response to *Colin Clout* signal a new recognition of its forceful and tart relevance for our own age.

The greater part of the poem was probably completed by 1591. But brief revisions to the two catalogs of shepherd-poets and "gentle Nymphs" at Cynthia's court had been made before the poem was published in 1595; one or two other passages, notably 838–94, may also have been later additions. That the poem dates to the period between 1590 and 1596 (mid-passage in the making of *The Faerie Queene*) is clearly of some importance, bearing significantly on this "greatly expanded pastoral eclogue, [which often] breaks pastoral decorum" (Yale 1989), gathering to itself a variety of other literary kinds, and in particular exploring the poet's role as celebrant of heroic achievement in a court at once golden and corrupt.

As for the verse-form and metrical arrangement, to Shore's succinct commentary on Spenser's deft treatment of these decasyllabic cross-rhymed quatrains one might add only that the interplay of metrical pattern and narrative movement often recalls the art of *The Faerie Queene*, where the poet's control of a demanding stanza form regularly matches language and accent to narrative context. In *Colin Clout* the narrator's first vision of the sea (196–211) is especially instructive in this regard. And the curious effect of the brief encounter between quatrain and terza rima with which the poem opens—a momentary tremor, a certain hesitancy—for this careful poet may anticipate the first clear hint (at 327) that tigers prowl through the strawberry fields of Cynthia's bright court. It's worth noticing too that the poem ends with a passage that pairs the shepherd's "simple trophe" with Rosalind's "great conquest," yet calls attention, by the pause after 951 and the epistrophic "rest . . . rest" that follows, to a yet half sad reluctance that colors the prospect of the poet's return to his epic task.

A discerning critic of Spenser's art has remarked that most people usually enjoy *Colin Clout* more than the *Calender*. To turn from "the confusion of voices in the *Calender* which had been a measure of Colin's alienation" (D. Cheney 1983) to the "dominant presence in *Colin Clout* [of] Colin himself, assured and confident in a poetic role" (Shore 1990E) is at the least initially refreshing, however much the poem may in due course qualify confident expectation. A reader coming to the poem for the first time must be charmed by the opening indication of Colin's power to astonish and disarm that informs the display of his "curious skill" before his rustic audience of shepherds—and women too—each in their several ways keenly attentive to Colin's story, song, or vision. The subsequent account of the singing match with a shepherd of another sort demonstrates Colin's artful control of "auncient truth confirmed with credence old"; scholars as well as rustics can relish the tale of an adventurous sea voyage across the watery wilderness, past headlands resembling now "an horne," now "a goodly pleasant lea," to haven at last in the realm where Cynthia seems to contrive that "all happie peace and plenteous store / Conspire in one to make contented blisse." Yet Spenser devotes a third of his poem to these effects largely to prepare the reader for more demanding kinds and levels of enjoyment, bearing principally on the shepherd-poet's responses to the paradoxical reality of Cynthia's glittering court, where even a Raleigh cannot forever keep his balance. Colin's song of Bregog and Mulla is in one sense a charmingly innocent and "mery lay." Still, to consummate their desire, these lovers must employ the deceit that is Bregog's style, only to be caught and crushed by a watchfully jealous power far greater than their own. In fact the song anticipates those darker aspects of the court, where power and self-interest inevitably hamper, at length all but cancel, the poet's effort to reconcile the demands of poetry and those of the political world. Yet Bregog is not altogether destroyed: if his name is lost, his love lives on, "and ever will, so long / As water does within his bancks appeare"—as in *Mutabilitie* vi. 53, Molanna and her beloved Fanchin are at last made one. The quiet hint at 326–27 of challenges still to come, if it escapes Corylas (eager for more in the adventurous vein), effectively introduces the poem's second movement, in which Spenser will begin to celebrate the "singleness of purpose" under which all forms of love are subsumed (D. Cheney 1983).

Signs of strain thread through this movement; yet the view of its balanced structure advanced by Burchmore remains persuasive, even while the design, like that of the poem, is "finally more cumulative than sequential" (Edwards 1971). Praises for Cynthia enclose praises for her courtly attendants; these in turn enclose the very curious expression of praise for Rosalind (or perhaps Elizabeth Boyle), with its echoes of the queen's motto, *semper eadem*, at the center. This emblematic celebration of queen, court, Rosalind, and the various degrees of love that conjoin them all is finely wrought, if in the total context of the poem its measured patterns of praise form a stranger brooch than a first reading might suggest. In effect, the relatively brief introductory tribute to Cynthia and the extended ode to her that concludes this part of the poem establish her pervasively encompassing presence, made manifest in her "royall mynd," her all but divine perfection, and (principally) her transcendent power to inspire the shepherd-poet "above the measure of [his] might." Each passage leads on to an acknowledgment—briefly by the thoughtful Alexis, more at length by Colin himself—of the pastoral poet's power to "upraise" humble shepherd together with his queen, ensuring their mutually dependent course through time. But yet, it is in the midst of Colin's praise of Rosalind, at the not altogether still center of the poem (477), that Spenser places the motto of his queen—as if to murmur, perhaps, "behold, I show you a mystery."

As Colin calls the roll of Cynthia's attendants, the case is considerably altered. Twelve courtly makers are praised for their several accomplishments in Cynthia's service: Daniel's plaintive verse has particular appeal for Spenser, of course, but it is Alabaster's unfinished "heroic song" *Eliseis* that receives special emphasis, an epic poem that may challenge or surpass those of ancient and modern worlds. If Astrofell remains unmatchable, all these others "do their Cynthia immortall make." That is what matters. There may be a hint of blame, for court or poet, in the comments touching Alabaster, undeservedly obscure; Daniel, too slow to seize his moment; even a great sponsor who "spends his wit in loves consuming smart." Poets who know their quality, all the more in this busy, demanding court that presses in upon them, must not scant their larger responsibilities: time and the hour call them forth.

Not quite in the same way, each of the twelve attendant "Nymphs" mirrors an aspect of Cynthia's full glory; after their fashion, all are Cynthias, all Elizabeths. More to the point, perhaps, they are not simply "ornaments of mankind" but high-mettled women of substance and influence, to the manor born, accustomed to the corridors of power. The poet who expects to hold his place must forever take good care, recognizing as a matter of course "brave minds," "great worth and noble governance," "all honorable parts," and beauty too, while somehow singling out that quality distinguishing each from the rest. The task has its dangers. But Spenser makes a virtue of necessity, employing the formulaic "Ne lesse praise worthie" for each figure after the first, managing for the most part to notice each lady's special gift or virtue—and he retains the formula even for those generic also-rans Flavia and Candida. It is cleverly done. If the strain of repetitive phrase and cadence renders the poet's voice at last a trifle hoarse, the reader is invited to take pleasure in the witty excuses that bring these encomiastics to a close.

But after the careful compliments, and their whispered undersong of the demands made on poor shepherd-poets by the patronage system, the force and passion of the tripartite final movement sound another note altogether. Indignation and rage inform Colin's fierce account of the dark underbelly of Cynthia's court. Only the "blessed presence" herself (perhaps also a handful of reputedly honest figures, tepidly noted at 751–55) can quite withstand envy, guile, and "fortunes blandishment." For the rest, deceitful wit, dissembling courtesy, and the rooted malice that gives life to slander, everywhere drive down "single Truth and simple honestie." Spenser had known in 1579 that the barking dog of envy would surely turn to rend his work; now, years later, the cruel power of slander to destroy a "well deemèd name" carries fearful force, looking on to the Blatant Beast and the end of *The Faerie Queene*.

The roll of blame appropriately turns at last to the vicious abuse at court of love's sacred and mighty mysteries, reaching a bitter climax with that desperate invocation of Cupid, in his most terrible aspect, to hear "poore shepheardes" and in their name be fully avenged. In the elevated account of Love's origin and power that follows, Colin dismissively confirms the exile from Love's court of "outlawes" who flout his "sacred lere": if the shepherd-poet's "divination is essentially poetic" (Shore 1985) and its contexts ultimately NeoPlatonic, it effectively provides a partial response to the grim reckoning of conditions at court, focal center for the world of affairs and of public action, at once invincibly fascinating and profoundly inimical to Spenser's temper, Spenser's vision. Perhaps the demands of poetry and those of public life are, after all, irreconcilable. Yet this poet, buoyed by commitment to the heroic and public ideal personified by his queen, as well as by the private urgencies of his craft and sullen art, may still confirm in his work the poetic allegiance inspired by his monarch's presence. The concluding section of the final movement draws Rosalind together with Colin into these terms of partial reconcilement, after "long affliction . . . some reliefe / And ease of paine which cannot be recured." Near the poem's heart, the reader was assured of Cynthia's survival, her memory renewed by Colin's "layes made of her," voiced "amongst the shepheardes daughters dancing round"; so at last "This simple trophe of her great conquest" will forever conjoin Colin and his Rosalind. And Cynthia too: as Woods perceived in 1977, Rosalind has become for the poet "a type of the Queen, enabling his poetic accomplishment."

In 1974 Kathleen Williams called *Colin Clouts Come Home Againe*

> an astonishingly sure-footed poem which is a kind of pastoral but also a kind of satire and a kind of celebration, with each element somehow undiluted by the others but all working together to make a comprehensive statement about the relations of the poet to the world, of poetry to facts, of retirement to the world of action, of good to evil.

The cool Augustan confidence of this pronouncement isn't likely to satisfy new historicists, for example, who may reasonably object that if *Colin Clout* is indeed a kind of satire, its multiplex tensions send a darker signal, bearing on the poet's continuing sense of alienation within this socio-economic order. As for "celebration," those glooming skies that frown, at the close, on scurrying shepherds and their bleating flocks promise not much more than sporadic relief "of paine which cannot be recured." There can be no doubt that recent tides in critical taste have sharpened our awareness of wearing public pressures on the poet and his work, with special reference to mordant echoes of those pressures in the poetry, perhaps especially in *Colin Clout*. But there is room for celebration too. The divisions of analysis may be bound up and made whole by synthesis, "all working together to make a comprehensive statement." Cheney 1984 has remarked Colin's celebration of "love in all its forms . . . subsumed into a singleness of purpose." In a larger sense, others argue that the completed poem transforms the poet's sense of public failure, enabling him to turn again with fresh resolve to his epic celebration of heroic virtue. And higher yet: for Alpers 1989 *Colin Clout* plays a vital role in the full range of Spenser's achievement, providing "suggestions . . . of poetic authority and of Ireland as the poet's domain," which "the *Mutability Cantos* can be thought to have fulfilled," in turn providing, at last, "a fitting conclusion to *The Faerie Queene*" (815). So, from the charming puzzle of *Colin Clout*, celebrations spring and proliferate. At the very least, the poem, once bruised by neglect, now in age does live again.

Amoretti and Epithalamion

Amoretti†

Sonnet 1

Happy ye leaves¹ when as° those lilly hands,   *when*
Which hold my life in their dead doing² might,
Shall handle you and hold in loves soft bands,
Lyke captives trembling at the victors sight.
5   And happy lines, on which with starry light,
Those lamping° eyes will deigne sometimes to look   *shining*
And reade the sorrowes of my dying spright,°   *spirit*
Written with teares in harts close° bleeding book.   *secret*
And happy rymes bathed in the sacred brooke
10   Of Helicon³ whence she derivéd is,
When ye behold that Angels blesséd looke,
My soules long lackéd foode, my heavens blis.
Leaves, lines, and rymes, seeke her to please alone,
Whom if ye please, I care for other none.°   *none other*

Sonnet 2

Unquiet thought, whom at the first I bred
Of th'inward balc° of my love pinéd° hart:
And sithens° have with sighes and sorrowes fed,   *woe/tormented*
Till greater then my wombe thou woxen° art: *since*
5   Breake forth at length out of the inner part,   *grown*
In which thou lurkest lyke to vipers brood:⁴
And seeke some succour° both to ease my smart   *aid*
And also to sustayne thy selfe with food
But if in presence of that fayrest proud⁵
10   Thou chance to come, fall lowly at her feet:
And with meeke humblesse° and afflicted° mood,   *humility/dejected*
Pardon for thee, and grace for me intreat.

---

† Italian for "little loves."
1. Pages, singly or bound, but also recalling Petrarch's laurel wreath. The pun initiates *Amoretti*'s themes of binding, fame, victory, and time (garlands symbolize both time and eternal glory). Like Petrarch's, the opening sonnet gives an impression of being written after the others and is thus retrospective as well as introductory. See Warkentin 1990E for an overview of *Amoretti* and a history of the Renaissance sonnet sequence.
2. I.e., death-dealing.
3. The Hippocrene Spring on Mount Helicon, sacred to the Muses, inspires poetry, as does Spenser's lady. That she is an "angel" hints at a divine source for both her and these "lines."
4. Vipers were thought to gnaw their way out of their mother, killing her.
5. I.e., proud lady.

Which if she graunt, then live, and my love cherish:
If not, die soone, and I with thee will perish.

Sonnet 3

The soverayne beauty which I doo admyre,[6]
Witnesse the world how worthy to be prayzed:
The light wherof hath kindled heavenly fyre,
In my fraile spirit by her from baseness raysed.
5   That being now with her huge brightnesse dazed,°   *dazzled*
Base thing I can no more endure to view:
But looking still on her I stand amazed,
At wondrous sight of so celestiall hew.°   *figure*
So when my toung would speak her praises dew,[7]
10 It stoppéd is with thoughts astonishment:
And when my pen would write her titles[8] true,
It ravisht is with fancies[9] wonderment:
Yet in my hart I then both speake and write
The wonder that my wit cannot endite.[1]

Sonnet 4

New yeare forth looking out of Janus gate,[2]
Doth seeme to promise hope of new delight:
And bidding th'old Adieu, his passéd date[3]
Bids all old thoughts to die in dumpish° spright.   *sad*
5   And calling forth out of sad Winters night,
Fresh love, that long hath slept in cheerlesse bower:
Wils him awake, and soone about him dight°   *prepare*
His wanton wings and darts of deadly power.[4]
For lusty spring now in his timely howre,
10 Is ready to come forth him[5] to receive:
And warnes the Earth with divers° colord flowre,   *sundry*
To decke hir selfe, and her faire mantle weave.
Then you faire flowre, in whom fresh youth doth raine,
Prepare your selfe new love to entertaine.

6. "Admire" and "wonder at," from Latin *admiror*.
7. That which is due her praiseworthiness or those praises due her.
8. I.e., correct descriptive names; also the lawful claims of a "soverayne" beauty to which witnesses can testify. As often, Spenser's language has legal implications.
9. "Fancy" is our image-making faculty; many viewed it with suspicion as liable to mislead the reason.
1. I.e., express or, more precisely, dictate.
2. Two-faced Janus, bringer of harmony, was god of gates; even before the Julian calendar, his month, January, had replaced March as the start of the Roman year (in Ovid's *Fasti* 1.161–64, Janus explains that midwinter sees the sun renewed). "New yeare," who need not be New Year's Day itself, is too soon for spring, but he looks "forth" toward it. Possibly Spenser means March 25, when the year's number officially changed; this, however, makes "passéd date" (3) hard to identify. In the allegory itself New Year asks Cupid to wake up and meet the coming Spring.
3. Either the recent January 1 or the now elapsed dead of winter; in either case the year's turn teaches the lady to prepare for love.
4. Cupid will put on his wings and the arrows that make us "die" for love.
5. I.e., Cupid.

Sonnet 5

Rudely[6] thou wrongest my deare harts desire,
In finding fault with her too portly° pride: *stately*
The thing which I doo most in her admire,
Is of the world unworthy most envide.[7]
5 For in those lofty lookes is close implide,[8]
Scorn of base things, and sdeigne° of foule dishonor: *disdain*
Thretning rash eies which gaze on her so wide,°   *unrestrainedly*
That loosely they ne° dare to looke upon her.   *not*
Such pride is praise, such portlinesse is honor,
10 That boldned innocence beares in hir eies:
And her faire countenance like a goodly banner,
Spreds in defiaunce of all enemies.
Was never in this world ought° worthy tride,[9]   *anything*
Without some spark of such self-pleasing pride.

Sonnet 6

Be nought° dismayd that her unmovéd mind   *nothing*
Doth still persist in her rebellious pride:
Such love not lyke to lusts of baser kynd,
The harder wonne, the firmer will abide.
5 The durefull[1] Oake whose sap is not yet dride
Is long ere it conceive the kindling fyre:
But when it once doth burne, it doth divide°   *dispense*
Great heat, and makes his flames to heaven aspire.
So hard it is to kindle new desire,
10 In gentle brest that shall endure for ever:
Deepe is the wound that dints the parts entire[2]
With chast affects,° that naught but death can sever.   *desires*
Then thinke not long in taking litle paine,
To knit the knot, that ever shall remaine.[3]

Sonnet 7

Fayre eyes, the myrrour of my mazéd[4] hart,
What wondrous vertue° is contaynd in you,   *power*
The which both lyfe and death forth from you dart
Into the object of your mighty view?[5]
5 For when ye mildly looke with lovely hew,°   *appearance*

---

6. I.e., without learning or sophistication. If not the lover himself, the addressee is a critical bystander, a standard figure in love poetry.
7. I.e., is most envied or denigrated by the unworthy world, or is most unworthily disparaged by the world.
8. I.e., enfolded and included, but also logically necessitated.
9. I.e., attempted; also, experienced and tested.
1. Perhaps "lasting"; but "hard" makes better sense (oak is dense and, when green, slow to burn) and allows wordplay on "harder" and "endure."
2. I.e., that strikes an impression on intact interior organs (such as the heart).
3. I.e., marriage; note the play on "knot" and "not" in 13.
4. I.e., amazed; also, put into a maze or labyrinth. Reflecting and mediating, mirrors fascinated Renaissance love poets, particularly Neoplatonists.
5. Vision was widely believed to emanate from the eye and affect the object viewed; hence the comparison of glances to arrows or lightning.

Then is my soule with life and love inspired:
But when ye lowre, or looke on me askew,
Then doe I die, as one with lightning fyred.
But since that lyfe is more then death desyred,
10 Looke ever lovely, as becomes you best,
That your bright beams of° my weak eies admyred,   *by*
May kindle living fire within my brest.
Such life should be the honor of your light,
Such death the sad ensample° of your might.   *example*

Sonnet 8[6]

More then most faire, full of the living fire
Kindled above unto the maker[7] neere:
No eies but joyes, in which al powers conspire
That to the world naught else be counted deare.
5 Thrugh your bright beams doth not the blinded guest
Shoot out his darts to base affections wound?[8]
But Angels come to lead fraile mindes to rest
In chast desires on heavenly beauty bound.
You frame my thoughts and fashion me within,
10 You stop my toung, and teach my hart to speake,
You calme the storme that passion did begin,
Strong thrugh your cause, but by your vertue weak.[9]
Dark is the world where your light shinéd never;
Well is he borne that may behold you ever.

Sonnet 9

Long-while I sought to what I might compare
Those powrefull eies, which lighten my dark spright,
Yet find I nought on earth to which I dare
Resemble° th'ymage of their goodly light.   *liken*
5 Not to the Sun: for they doo shine by night;
Nor to the Moone: for they are changéd never;
Nor to the Starres: for they have purer sight;
Nor to the fire: for they consume not ever;
Nor to the lightning: for they still° persever;°   *always/continue*
10 Nor to the Diamond: for they are more tender;
Nor unto Christall:[1] for nought may them sever;°   *break*
Nor unto glasse: such basenesse mought° offend her;   *might*
Then to the Maker selfe they likest be,
Whose light doth lighten° all that here we see.[2]   *illuminate*

6. Spenser uses the "Shakespearean" rhyme scheme; this sonnet was probably composed before
 Spenser went to Ireland in 1580; it appears in several manuscript miscellanies (see L. Cummings,
 "Spenser's *Amoretti VIII*: New Manuscript Versions," *SEL* [1964]).
7. I.e., God.
8. The syntax is ambiguous; the sense is that through the lady's eyes Cupid sends wounding arrows
 that create unworthy desires.
9. The storm is strong thanks to her but is moderated by her virtue's power.
1. I.e., quartz, more fragile than diamond and less common than glass.
2. The Bible often compares God to light; Spenser echoes "a light to lighten the gentiles" (Luke
 2.32), said at evening prayer.

Sonnet 10[3]

Unrighteous Lord of love,[4] what law is this,
That me thou makest thus tormented be?
The whiles she lordeth in licentious° blisse[5]   *without regard for rules*   lawless
Of her freewill, scorning both thee and me.
5 See how the Tyrannesse doth joy to see
The huge massácres which her eyes do make:
And humbled harts brings captives unto thee,[6]
That thou of° them mayst mightie vengeance take.   against
But her proud hart doe thou a little shake
10 And that high look, with which she doth comptroll°   dominate
All this worlds pride bow to a baser make,°   mate
And al her faults in thy black booke enroll:
That I may laugh at her in equall sort,
As she doth laugh at me and makes my pain her sport.[7]

Sonnet 11

Dayly when I do seeke and sew° for peace,   sue
And hostages doe offer for my truth:[8]
She cruell warriour doth her selfe addresse
To battell, and the weary war renew'th.
5 Ne wilbe mooved with reason or with rewth,°   pity
To graunt small respit to my restlesse° toile: ceaseless
But greedily her fell° intent poursewth,°   cruel/pursues
Of my poore life to make unpittied spoile.
Yet my poore life, all sorrowes to assoyle,°   release
10 I would her yield,[9] her wrath to pacify:
But then she seekes with torment and turmoyle,
To force me live and will not let me dy.
All paine hath end and every war hath peace,
But mine no price nor prayer may surcease.°   discontinue

Sonnet 12

One day I sought with her hart-thrilling° eies   piercing
To make a truce, and termes to entertaine:[1]
All fearelesse then of so false enimies,
Which sought me to entrap in treasons traine.[2]
5 So as I then disarméd did remaine,
A wicked ambush which lay hidden long
In the close° covert° of her guilefull eyen,   secret/thicket

3. Based on Petrarch *Rime* 121; cf. Wyatt's "Behold, love." Spenser's themes of tyranny and injustice are his own.
4. I.e., Cupid as ruler and lawgiver; the lover asks why he permits subversion.
5. Uncurbed by Cupid's law, the lady follows her own will; the lover does not tax her with overt licentiousness in the modern sense of unchastity.
6. Like a feudal warrior, the lady brings her captives (i.e., lovers' hearts) to present to her lord, Cupid. To imagine erotic pursuit as a war with an armed lady was common.
7. An alexandrine; cf. *Amoretti* 45.
8. I.e., integrity and troth; the lover is like a vanquished leader giving hostages to guarantee a treaty.
9. I.e., give up my life to her.
1. I.e., negotiate a treaty.
2. I.e., a treacherous snare.

Thence breaking forth did thick about me throng.
Too feeble I t'abide the brunt° so strong,   *onslaught*
10 Was forst to yeeld my selfe into their hands:
Who me captiving streight° with rigorous wrong,   *tightly*
Have ever since me kept in cruell bands.
So Ladie now to you I doo complaine,
Against your eies that justice I may gaine.

Sonnet 13

In that proud port,° which her so goodly graceth,   *bearing*
Whiles her faire face she reares up to the skie:
And to the ground her eie-lids low embaseth,°   *lowers*
Most goodly temperature[3] ye may descry,
5 Myld humblesse mixt with awfull° majesty,   *awesome*
For looking on the earth whence she was borne,[4]
Her minde remembreth her mortalitie,
What so is fayrest shall to earth returne.
But that same lofty countenance seemes to scorne
10 Base thing, and thinke how she to heaven may clime:
Treading downe earth as lothsome and forlorne,[5]
That hinders heavenly thoughts with drossy° slime.   *impure*
Yet lowly still vouchsafe to looke on me,
Such lowlinesse shall make you lofty be.

Sonnet 14

Retourne agayne, my forces late dismayd,
Unto the siege by you abandoned quite:
Great shame it is to leave like one afrayd,
So fayre a peece[6] for one repulse so light.
5 Gaynst such strong castles needeth[7] greater might,
Then those small forts which ye were wont belay;[8]
Such haughty mynds enured to hardy° fight,   *bold*
Disdayne to yield unto the first assay.°   *attack*
Bring therefore all the forces that ye may,
10 And lay incessant battery to her heart:
Playnts, prayers, vowes, ruth, sorrow, and dismay,
Those engins can the proudest love convert.°   *turn*
And if those fayle fall downe and dy before her,
So dying live, and living do adore her.

---

3. At its simplest, "temperature" is the right mixture of elements for balance in body, soul, and behavior. Spenser often plays with cognates of "temper" such as "time" (Latin *tempus*), "tempered" (cf. *Amoretti* 21), "temperance," and "tempest" (symbol of time or fortune). His most extensive treatment of these related concepts is Book II of *The Faerie Queene*.
4. She is descended from Adam, made of clay; her "humblesse" recalls Latin *humus*, earth, but her "port" echoes Ovid, who says the gods gave "a face uplifted to the stars" only to humankind (*Metamorphoses* 1.86). The lady tempers this upward-gazing nobility with an awareness of mortality.
5. "Forlorne" suggests both abandoned and lost, a reference to the Fall of Man that also anticipates the lady's leaving earth for Heaven.
6. I.e., fortress. "Piece" was also a decent term for a person of either sex.
7. I.e., there needs.
8. I.e., besiege; it seems the lover has already "belayed" some lesser women. "Belay" also means to make fast, which is the lover's aim.

Sonnet 15[9]

Ye tradefull Merchants that with weary toyle,
Do seeke most pretious things to make your gain:
And both the Indias[1] of their treasures spoile,°   *despoil*
What needeth you to seeke so farre in vaine?
5   For loe my love doth in her selfe containe
All this worlds riches that may farre be found;
If Saphyres, loe her eies be Saphyres plaine,
If Rubies, loe hir lips be Rubies sound:
If Pearles, hir teeth be pearles both pure and round;
10 If Yvorie, her forhead yvory weene,[2]
If Gold, her locks are finest gold on ground;°   *earth*
If silver, her faire hands are silver sheene:°   *shining*
But that which fairest is, but few behold,
Her mind adornd with vertues manifold.

Sonnet 16

One day as I unwarily did gaze
On those fayre eyes my loves immortall light:
The whiles my stonisht° hart stood in amaze,°   *astonished/amazement*
Through sweet illusion[3] of her lookes delight,
5   I mote° perceive how in her glauncing sight,   *could*
Legions of loves[4] with little wings did fly:
Darting their deadly arrowes fyry bright,
At every rash beholder passing by.
One of those archers closely° I did spy,   *covertly*
10 Ayming his arrow at my very hart:
When suddenly with twincle° of her eye,   *blink*
The Damzell broke his misintended dart.
Had she not so doon, sure I had bene slayne,
Yet as it was, I hardly scap't with paine.[5]

Sonnet 17

The glorious pourtraict of that Angels face,
Made to amaze weake mens confuséd skil:
And this worlds worthlesse glory to embase,°   *humble*
What pen, what pencill can expresse her fill?°   *fully*
5   For though he colours could devize at will,
And eke his learnéd hand at pleasure guide,
Least° trembling it his workmanship should spill,°   *lest/ruin*
Yet many wondrous things there are beside.
The sweet eye-glaunces, that like arrowes glide,

---

9. From Desportes, *Diane* 1.32; Spenser adds a couplet on the lady's inwardness. The poem is a
   "blazon," detailing a lady's qualities by a series of comparisons or depictions; some blazons focus
   on one feature, like Maurice Scève's famous poem on his mistress's eyebrow ("Sourcil tractif").
1. The East and West Indies.
2. An imperative: ween (i.e., think) her forehead is ivory.
3. I.e., deceptive appearance; also, perhaps, mockery or teasing.
4. Her eyebeams contain "amoretti."
5. I.e., barely escaped, and only with hurt.

10 The charming smiles, that rob sence from the hart:
    The lovely pleasance[6] and the lofty pride,
    Cannot expresséd be by any art.
    A greater craftesmans hand thereto doth neede,
    That can expresse the life of things indeed.[7]

Sonnet 18

    The rolling wheele that runneth often round,
    The hardest steele in tract of time doth teare:
    And drizling drops that often doe redound,°   *overflow*
    The firmest flint doth in continuance weare.[8]
5   Yet cannot I, with many a dropping teare,
    And long intreaty, soften her hard hart:
    That she will once vouchsafe my plaint to heare,
    Or looke with pitty on my payneful smart.
    But when I pleade, she bids me play my part,
10 And when I weep, she sayes teares are but water:
    And when I sigh, she sayes I know the art,[9]
    And when I waile, she turnes hir selfe to laughter.
    So doe I weepe, and wayle, and pleade in vaine,
    Whiles she as steele and flint doth still remayne.

Sonnet 19

    The merry Cuckow, messenger of Spring,
    His trompet shrill hath thrise already sounded:
    That warnes al lovers wayt upon their king,[1]
    Who now is comming forth with girland crounéd.
5   With noyse whereof the quyre° of Byrds resounded   *choir*
    Their anthemes sweet devizéd of loves prayse,
    That all the woods theyr ecchoes back rebounded,[2]
    As if they knew the meaning of their layes.
    But mongst them all which did Loves honor rayse
10 No word was heard of° her that most it ought,°   *from/owed*
    But she his precept proudly disobayes,
    And doth his ydle[3] message set at nought.
    Therefore O love, unlesse she turne to thee
    Ere Cuckow end, let her a rebell be.[4]

6. I.e., pleasantness; also, a shady garden enclosure for sitting and walking, a contrast with her "lofty pride."
7. Only God or, possibly, the poet has the descriptive power to imitate the lady's essence and movement.
8. I.e., drops that fall continually will wear down flint. Surprise that a lady can resist erosion was common; less so is this one's spirited mockery.
9. It is not clear who speaks: either the lady says the lover knows the art of wooing with sighs or she says she herself sees this art for what it is.
1. I.e., Cupid.
2. Cf. the refrain of *Epithalamion*.
3. I.e., ineffective; and Cupid was said to like idleness.
4. I.e., be legally declared a rebel against Lord Cupid.

Sonnet 20

In vaine I seeke and sew° to her for grace,   *sue*
And doe myne humbled hart before her poure:
The whiles her foot she in my necke doth place,
And tread my life downe in the lowly floure.°   *floor*
5 And yet the Lyon that is Lord of power,
And reigneth over every beast in field,
In his most pride disdeigneth to devoure
The silly lambe that to his might doth yield.[5]
But she more cruell and more salvage wylde,
10 Then either Lyon or the Lyonesse:
Shames not[6] to be with guiltlesse bloud defylde,
But taketh glory in her cruelnesse.
Fayrer then fayrest, let none ever say
That ye were blooded in a yeelded pray.[7]

Sonnet 21

Was it the worke of nature or of Art,
Which tempred so the feature of her face,
That pride and meeknesse mixt by equall part,
Doe both appeare t'adorne her beauties grace?
5 For with mild pleasance, which doth pride displace,
She to her love doth lookers eyes allure:[8]
And with sterne countenance back again doth chace
Their looser lookes that stir up lustes impure.
With such strange termes her eyes she doth inure,[9]
10 That with one looke she doth my life dismay:
And with another doth it streight recure,°   *recover*
Her smile me drawes, her frowne me drives away.
Thus doth she traine[1] and teach me with her lookes,
Such art of eyes I never read in bookes.

Sonnet 22[2]

[center]

This holy season fit to fast and pray,
Men to devotion ought to be inclynd:

[Celebration profane → through sacred]

---

5. Lions were thought magnanimous; see Pliny, *Natural History* 8.19. In famous lines, the Roman poet Martial wrote (*Epigrams* 1.22) that just as lions let hares go, so the great spare the humble. The lover is a "silly" (innocent) lamb, which—he may hope—gives him Christian overtones and a pastoral look.
6. I.e., is not ashamed.
7. Only bad sportsmen kill prey that gives up. It is tempting to read "blooded" as the smearing of a novice hunter with blood from a first kill, but the *OED*'s citations of this sense are modern.
8. I.e., draws observers' eyes to love her.
9. I.e., accustoms her eyes to use peculiar and foreign "terms" (words; also negotiable conditions). "Inure" also meant put into legal effect; once more Spenser describes a private state in the language of public life.
1. Probably "draw along," rather than "educate and discipline," so as to sustain the paradox that her eyes both entice and instruct.
2. The start of a Lenten sequence of forty-seven sonnets (see Editors' Note). Poets like Desportes, whose *Diane* 1.43 *Amoretti* 22 resembles, had promised a temple or sung of love on a holy day (cf. Petrarch, *Rime* 3), so few urbane readers would have found the poem seriously blasphemous.

Therefore, I lykewise on so holy day,[3]
For my sweet Saynt[4] some service fit will find.
5 Her temple fayre is built within my mind,
In which her glorious ymage placéd is,
On which my thoughts doo day and night attend
Lyke sacred priests that never thinke amisse.
There I to her as th'author of my blisse,
10 Will builde an altar to appease her yre:
And on the same my hart will sacrifise,
Burning in flames of pure and chast desyre:
The which vouchsafe O goddesse to accept,
Amongst thy deerest relicks to be kept.

Sonnet 23

Penelope for her Ulisses sake,
Devized a Web her wooers to deceave:
In which the worke that she all day did make
The same at night she did againe unreave:[5]
5 Such subtile craft my Damzell doth conceave,°   *devise*
Th'importune° suit of my desire to shonne:[6]   *importunate*
For all that I in many dayes doo weave,
In one short houre I find by her undonne.
So when I thinke to end that° I begonne,   *what*
10 I must begin and never bring to end:
For with one looke she spils° that long I sponne,[7]   *destroys*
And with one word my whole years work doth rend.[8]
Such labour like the Spyders web I fynd,
Whose fruitlesse worke is broken with least wynd.

Sonnet 24

When I behold that beauties wonderment,
And rare perfection of each goodly part:
Of natures skill the onely complement,
I honor and admire the makers art.
5 But when I feele the bitter balefull° smart,   *deadly*
Which her fayre eyes unwares° doe worke in mee,   *unwittingly*
That death out of theyr shiny beames doe dart,

3. Ash Wednesday, first day of Lent; in 1594 it fell on February 13. The phrasing recalls texts in the prayerbook (Johnson 1990), while the sacrifice and "ire" echo Psalm 51 and the "Commination against Sinners" appointed for this day.
4. By "saint" Protestants often meant anyone assured of salvation; yet together with "ymage," "relicks," and "goddesse," the word can connote "popish" idolatry. Spenser prepares a contrast between *Amoretti* 22's naughty wit and *Amoretti* 68, which redeems erotic "service" by binding human to divine love.
5. During the absence of her husband, Odysseus, Penelope told her suitors that she would choose one of them after finishing a shroud for the hero Laertes; each night she unwove the day's work (Homer, *Odyssey* 2). Spenser's comparison serves his theme of weaving and tying—whether texts or textiles—just as the "web" suggests capture and deception. In *Amoretti* 71 the lady weaves without trickery and the lover is a successful spider.
6. I.e., elude; she imagines a cunning way to evade his desire's urgent pleading.
7. I.e., what I took a long time to spin.
8. This line has fed debate over how the courtship's duration relates to the poetry's time scheme. *Amoretti* 1 need not mark the onset of love, nor must the poems' time parallel that of the lover's suit; but see Kaske 1978.

I thinke that I a new Pandora see,[9]
Whom all the Gods in councell did agree,
10   Into this sinfull world from heaven to send:
That she to wicked men a scourge should bee,
For all their faults with which they did offend.
But since ye are my scourge I will intreat,
That for my faults ye will me gently beat.

Sonnet 25

How long shall this lyke dying lyfe[1] endure,
And know no end of her[2] owne mysery:
But wast and weare away in termes° unsure,   *conditions*
Twixt feare and hope depending° doubtfully?   *suspended*
5   Yet better were attonce to let me die,
And shew the last ensample of your pride:
Then to torment me thus with cruelty,
To prove your powre, which I too wel have tride.°   *experienced*
But yet if in your hardned brest ye hide
10   A close° intent at last to shew me grace: *secret*
Then all the woes and wrecks which I abide,°   *undergo*
As meanes of blisse I gladly wil embrace;
And wish that more and greater they might be,
That greater meede° at last may turne to mee.   *reward*

Sonnet 26[3]

Sweet is the Rose, but growes upon a brere;°   *briar*
Sweet is the Junipere, but sharpe his bough;
Sweet is the Eglantine, but pricketh nere;
Sweet is the firbloome, but his braunches rough.
5   Sweet is the Cypresse, but his rynd is tough,
Sweet is the nut, but bitter is his pill;
Sweet is the broome-flowre, but yet sowre enough;
And sweet is Moly, but his root is ill.[4]
So every sweet with soure is tempred still,°   *always*
10   That° maketh it be coveted the more: *which*
For easie things that may be got at will,
Most sorts of men doe set but little store.
Why then should I accoumpt of little paine,
That endlesse pleasure shall unto me gaine?[5]

9. Pandora, "all-gifted," was forged by Zeus's smith Hephaestus (Vulcan) and graced by all the gods. Angry at the trickster Prometheus for giving mankind fire, Zeus sent her to him and his brother Epimetheus, slyly supplying her with a box enclosing evils and plagues (Hesiod, *Theogony* 507–616, who adds, "This was the origin of the damnable race of women"); some poets used her name to represent perfection, but here she is a scourge. Spenser replaces Zeus's jealous fury at human knowledge with disgust at human sin.
1. I.e., a life that is more like dying.
2. I.e., life's.
3. Yale notes that this flower poem, four sonnets after a reference to Ash Wednesday, balances *Amoretti* 64, four before *Amoretti* 68 and Easter.
4. The black-rooted milky flower that Hermes gave Odysseus as protection against the sorceress Circe (Homer, *Odyssey* 10). For some it signified temperance (*OED*), for others (Alciati 182) learnéd eloquence.
5. I.e., take account of minor pain/work that will gain me endless pleasure.

Sonnet 27

Faire proud, now tell me, why should faire be proud,
Sith° all worlds glorie is but drosse uncleane?   *since*
And in the shade of death it selfe shall shroud,°   *clothe*
How ever now thereof ye little weene.
5 That goodly Idoll now so gay beseene,
Shall doffe her fleshes borowd fayre attyre:[6]
And be forgot as it[7] had never beene,
That many now much worship° and admire.   *honor*
Ne any then shall after it inquire,
10 Ne any mention shall thereof remaine:
But° what this verse, that never shall expyre,   *except*
Shall to you purchas with her thankles paine.[8]
Faire, be no lenger proud of that° shall perish,   *what*
But that which shal you make immortall, cherish.

Sonnet 28

The laurell leafe, which you this day doe weare,
Gives me great hope of your relenting mynd:
For since it is the badg which I doe beare,
Ye bearing it doe seeme to me inclind:[9]
5 The powre thereof, which ofte in me I find,
Let it lykewise your gentle brest inspire
With sweet infusion, and put you in mind
Of that proud mayd, whom now those leaves attyre:
Proud Daphne scorning Phæbus lovely fyre,
10 On the Thessalian shore from him did flee:
For which the gods in theyr revengefull yre
Did her transforme into a laurell tree.
Then fly no more fayre love from Phebus chace,°   *pursuit*
But in your brest his leafe and love embrace.[1]

Sonnet 29

See how the stubborne damzell doth deprave°   *misinterpret*
My simple meaning with disdaynfull scorne:
And by the bay° which I unto her gave,   *laurel*
Accoumpts my selfe her captive quite forlorne.
5 "The bay," quoth she, "is of the victours borne,
Yielded them by the vanquisht as theyr meeds,°   *rewards*

---

6. I.e., her lovely *eidolon* or image that wears flesh like a borrowed dress will have to take it off.
7. Probably "it" is the "Idoll," genderless without its "attyre."
8. I.e., will obtain for you with effort that receives no thanks.
9. In ancient times laurel was worn by victors, but Petrarch, who called his lady Laura, adopted it for poets. Cf. Ronsard, *Astrée* 11, in which the lady wears it to show her power.
1. Ovid (*Metamorphoses* 1.452–567) tells how thanks to divine mercy the nymph Daphne escaped Apollo by becoming a laurel; the god took her foliage as a badge. With only minimal precedent, Spenser mischievously departs from tradition; Cupid had shot Daphne with a leaden arrow of antipathy, so if the lady takes the lover's "leafe and love" into her bosom she too will revise Ovid, letting her pursuer triumph in both love and art.

And they[2] therewith doe poetes heads adorne,
To sing the glory of their famous deedes."
But sith she will the conquest challeng needs,[3]
10 Let her accept me as her faithfull thrall,°   *slave*
That her great triumph which my skill exceeds,
I may in trump of fame blaze° over all.   *proclaim*
Then would I decke her head with glorious bayes,
And fill the world with her victorious prayse.

Sonnet 30[4]

My love is lyke to yse, and I to fyre;
How comes it then that this her cold so great
Is not dissolved through my so hot desyre,
But harder growes the more I her intreat?
5 Or how comes it that my exceeding heat
Is not delayd° by her hart frosen cold: *quenched*
But that I burne much more in boyling[5] sweat,
And feele my flames augmented manifold?
What more miraculous thing may be told,
10 That fire which all thing melts, should harden yse:
And yse which is congeald with sencelesse cold,
Should kindle fyre by wonderfull devyse?°   *contrivance*
Such is the powre of love in gentle° mind,   *noble*
That it can alter all the course of kynd.°   *Nature*

Sonnet 31

Ah why hath nature to so hard a hart,
Given so goodly giftes of beauties grace?
Whose pryde depraves° each other better part,   *spoils*
And all those pretious ornaments deface.[6]
5 Sith to all other beastes of bloody race,
A dreadfull countenaunce she given hath.
That with theyr terrour al the rest may chace,
And warne to shun the daunger of theyr wrath.
But my proud one doth worke the greater scath,°   *harm*
10 Through sweet allurement of her lovely hew:°   *shape*
That she the better may in bloody bath
Of such poore thralls her cruell hands embrew.°   *stain*
But did she know how ill these two accord,
Such cruelty she would have soone abhord.

---

2. Possibly the laurels; more likely the victors, who then in turn crown with bay the poets who will make them famous. Spenser puts into the lady's mouth this useful reminder to the powerful that poets like himself can reward patronage.
3. I.e., since she must needs claim victory.
4. Cf. Petrarch *Rime* 202 and its many offspring noted in the *Variorum*.
5. Yale suggests a pun on boil/Boyle.
6. I.e., defaces; acceptable grammar in Spenser's time.

Sonnet 32

The paynefull° smith with force of fervent heat,   *painstaking*
The hardest yron soone doth mollify,°   *soften*
That with his heavy sledge he can it beat,
And fashion to what he it list apply.[7]
5   Yet cannot all these flames in which I fry,
Her hart more harde then yron soft° awhit: *soften*
Ne all the playnts and prayers with which I
Doe beat on th'andvyle° of her stubberne wit: *anvil*
But still the more she fervent sees my fit,[8]
10   The more she frieseth in her wilfull pryde:
And harder growes the harder she is smit,°   *struck*
With all the playnts which to her be applyde.
What then remaines but I to ashes burne,
And she to stones at length all frosen turne?

Sonnet 33

Great wrong I doe, I can it not deny,
To that most sacred Empresse my dear dred,[9]
Not finishing her Queene of faery,
That mote enlarge her living prayses dead:[1]
5   But lodwick,[2] this of grace to me aread:[3]
Doe ye not thinck th'accomplishment of it,
Sufficient worke for one mans simple head,
All° were it as the rest but rudely writ.   *even*
How then should I without another wit,
10   Thinck ever to endure so tædious toyle?
Sins that this one[4] is tost with troublous fit,
Of a proud love, that doth my spirite spoyle.°   *ravage*
Ceasse then, till she vouchsafe to grawnt me rest,
Or lend you me another living brest.

Sonnet 34[5]

Lyke as a ship that through the Ocean wyde,
By conduct of some star doth make her way,
Whenas a storme hath dimd her trusty guyde,
Out of her course doth wander far astray:

7. I.e., whatever he wants to turn it into and use it for; "apply" had its modern sense but also meant "bend."
8. I.e., my paroxysm of activity, pain, and possibly lunacy; a "fit" was also a section of a poem.
9. Elizabeth I: dear but held in awe, and "Empresse" because she claimed Ireland, France, Virginia, and (like other Renaissance rulers) a share of Rome's ancient *imperium* and later ecclesiastical authority.
1. *Faerie Queene* IV–VI appeared the following year, 1596. It is "her" book because as Gloriana she is its heroine, and it will broaden and preserve her praise after she is dead.
2. Spenser's friend Lodowick Bryskett; sonnet sequences often included poems to friends and public figures. Bryskett has apparently urged Spenser to hurry, but we may hear the poet's own anxiety and the tension between private and public roles.
3. I.e., be so good as to advise me.
4. I.e., this wit, the one in love.
5. Comparing a lover to a storm-tossed sailor who cannot see the guiding stars of his lady's eyes was a famous Petrarchan conceit; cf. *Rime* 189 and Wyatt's "My galley."

5   So I whose star, that wont with her bright ray
    Me to direct, with cloudes is overcast,
    Doe wander now in darknesse and dismay,
    Through hidden perils round about me plast.
    Yet hope I well, that when this storme is past
10 My Helice the lodestar of my life[6]
    Will shine again, and looke on me at last,
    With lovely light to cleare my cloudy grief.
    Till then I wander carefull[7] comfortlesse,
    In secret sorow and sad pensivenesse.

Sonnet 35

    My hungry eyes through greedy covetize
    Still° to behold the object of their paine,   *always*
    With no contentment can themselves suffize: *satisfy*
    But having pine and having not complaine.[8]
5   For lacking it, they cannot lyfe sustayne,
    And having it, they gaze on it the more:
    In their amazement lyke Narcissus vaine
    Whose eyes him starved: so plenty makes me poore.[9]
    Yet are mine eyes so filléd with the store
10 Of that faire sight, that nothing else they brooke,°   *endure*
    But lothe the things which they did like before,
    And can no more endure on them to looke.
    All this worlds glory seemeth vayne to me,
    And all their showes but shadowes saving she.

Sonnet 36

    Tell me when shall these wearie woes have end,
    Or shall their ruthlesse torment never cease:
    But al my dayes in pining languor spend,
    Without hope of aswagement or release:
5   Is there no meanes for me to purchase peace,
    Or make agreement with her thrilling° eyes: *pioroing*
    But that their cruelty doth still increace,
    And dayly more augment my miscryes?
    But when ye have shewed all extremityes,
10 Then thinke how litle glory ye have gayned,
    By slaying him, whose lyfe though ye despyse,
    Mote° have your life in honour long maintayned.   *might*
    But by his death which some perhaps will mone,
    Ye shall condemnéd be of many a one.

6. Helice (which can sound like "Eliza") is a name for Ursa Major and also a city at the foot of
   Helicon. Perhaps that is why Spenser uses it and not "Cynosure" (Ursa Minor), which in fact has
   the pole (or lode) star used in navigation. Chaucer ("Knight's Tale," ed. Robinson, 2059) also
   confuses the names.
7. I.e., full of care.
8. His eyes suffer longingly in seeing the lady who makes them hurt, but they complain when they
   cannot see her.
9. Ovid tells (*Metamorphoses* 3.339–509) how Narcissus so loved his own reflection that he ignored
   the nymph Echo (who faded to a mere voice) and would not eat. Lamenting that "inopem me
   copia fecit" ("plenty makes me poor"), he became a flower—a narcissus.

Sonnet 37

What guyle is this, that those her golden tresses
She doth attyre under a net of gold:
And with sly skill so cunningly them dresses,
That which is gold or heare, may scarse be told?
5 Is it that mens frayle eyes, which gaze too bold,
She may entangle in that golden snare:
And being caught may craftily enfold
Theyr weaker harts, which are not wel aware?
Take heed therefore, myne eyes, how ye doe stare
10 Henceforth too rashly on that guilefull net,
In which if ever ye entrappéd are,
Out of her bands ye by no meanes shall get.
Fondnesse° it were for any being free,[1]   *jolly*
To covet fetters, though they golden bee.

Sonnet 38

Arion, when through tempests cruel wracke,
He forth was thrown into the greedy seas:
Through the sweet musick which his harp did make
Allured a Dolphin him from death to ease.[2]
5 But my rude musick, which was wont to please
Some dainty eares, cannot with any skill
The dreadfull tempest of her wrath appease,
Nor move the Dolphin from her stubborne will,
But in her pride she dooth persever still,
10 All carelesse° how my life for her decayse: *uncaring*
Yet with one word she can it save or spill,°   *destroy*
To spill were pitty, but to save were prayse.
Chose rather to be praysd for dooing good,
Then to be blamed for spilling guiltlesse blood.

Sonnet 39

Sweet smile, the daughter of the Queene of love,[3]
Expressing all thy mothers powrefull art,
With which she wonts to temper° angry Joue,   *moderate*
When all the gods he threats with thundring dart:[4]
5 Sweet is thy vertue,° as thy selfe sweet art,[5]   *power*
For when on me thou shinedst late in sadnesse,
A melting pleasance ran through every part,

1. I.e., anyone being free or, subtly different, any free being.
2. Arion was a famous musician whom sailors robbed and forced into the sea; charmed by his farewell shipboard recital, a passing dolphin carried him to shore, showing the power of song (cf. Herodotus, *Persian Wars* 1.23–24). Here Arion escapes a tempest, not thieves, but storms in turn often symbolized misfortune.
3. I.e., Venus.
4. Thunderbolts, forged by Vulcan for the ruler of the gods.
5. I.e., as thou thyself art sweet.

And me revived with hart-robbing gladnesse.[6]
Whylest rapt with joy resembling heavenly madnes,
10 My soule was ravisht quite as in a traunce:
And feeling thence no more her sorowes sadnesse,
Fed on the fulnesse of that chearefull glaunce.
More sweet than Nectar or Ambrosiall meat,°   food
Seemd every bit which thenceforth I did eat.

Sonnet 40

Mark when she smiles with amiable cheare,°   expression
And tell me whereto can ye lyken it:
When on each eyelid sweetly doe appeare
An hundred Graces as in shade to sit.[7]
5 Lykest it seemeth in my simple wit
Unto the fayre sunshine in somers day:
That when a dreadfull storme away is flit,
Thrugh the broad world doth spred his goodly ray:
At sight whereof each bird that sits on spray,
10 And every beast that to his den was fled,
Comes forth afresh out of their late dismay,
And to the light lift up theyr drouping hed.
So my storme-beaten hart likewise is cheared,
With that sunshine when cloudy looks are cleared.

Sonnet 41

Is it her nature or is it her will,[8]
To be so cruell to an humbled foe?
If nature, then she may it mend with skill:
If will, then she at will may will forgoe.
5 But if her nature and her wil be so,
That she will plague the man that loves her most:
And take delight t'encrease a wretches woe,
Then all her natures goodly guifts are lost.
And that same glorious beauties ydle boast,
10 Is but a bayt such wretches to beguile,
As being long in her loves tempest tost,
She meanes at last to make her piteous° spoyle.   pitiable
O fayrest fayre let never it be named,
That so fayre beauty was so fowly shamed.

---

6. Before William Harvey discovered that blood circulates, it was thought that passions draw it to and from the heart: fear sends blood to succor the constricted organ, but here joy sends it outward—the lover may be flushed with happiness.
7. I.e., as though a hundred Graces were sitting in the shade (as a rule there were three, attending Venus; cf. *Shepheardes Calender* "April" and *Faerie Queene* VI.x.15, 21–24).
8. Will was a psychological faculty needing Reason as a guide lest it become whim, egoism, or unbridled desire; the word had a sexual overtone, so Spenser may delicately imply that his chaste lady makes an eroticized power play.

Sonnet 42

The love which me so cruelly tormenteth,
So pleasing is in my extreamest paine:
That all the more my sorrow it augmenteth,
The more I love and doe embrace my bane.°   *destruction*
5 Ne doe I wish (for wishing were but vaine)
To be acquit° fro my continuall smart: *free*
But joy her thrall for ever to remayne,[9]
And yield for pledge my poore captyvéd hart;
The which that it from her may never start,°   *move*
10 Let her, yf please her, bynd with adamant[1] chayne:
And from all wandring loves which mote pervart[2]
His[3] safe assurance, strongly it restrayne.
Onely let her abstaine from cruelty,
And doe° me not before my time to dy.   *make*

Sonnet 43[4]

Shall I then silent be or shall I speake?
And if I speake, her wrath renew I shall:
And if I silent be, my hart will breake,
Or chokéd be with overflowing gall.
5 What tyranny is this both my hart to thrall,°   *enslave*
And eke my toung with proud restraint to tie;
That nether I may speake nor thinke at all,
But like a stupid stock° in silence die?   *stump*
Yet I my hart with silence secretly
10 Will teach to speak, and my just cause to plead:
And eke mine eies with meeke humility,
Love-learnéd[5] letters to her eyes to read.
Which her deep wit, that true harts thought can spel,°   *read*
Wil soone conceive, and learne to cónstrue well.[6]

Sonnet 44

When those renouméd° noble Peres of Greece,   *renowned*
Thrugh stubborn pride amongst themselves did jar°   *quarrel*
Forgetfull of the famous golden fleece,
Then Orpheus[7] with his harp theyr strife did bar.°   *check*
5 But this continuall cruell civill warre,
The which my selfe against my selfe doe make,
Whilest my weak powres of passions warreid° arre,   *afflicted*

---

9. I.e., rejoice to remain ever her slave.
1. I.e., diamond or, less probably, lodestone.
2. I.e., corrupt; also, turn aside.
3. I.e., his heart's.
4. The first and third quatrains adapt Tasso's "Se taccio, il duol s'avanza."
5. I.e., teach my eyes to send letters taught by love and learnéd concerning it.
6. I.e., comprehend (by making an inward image of what is understood and being affected by it) and interpret.
7. The poet Orpheus was said to have sailed to Argos with Jason's crew of celebrities, singing away their bad temper. The story is told by Apollonius (*Argonautica* 1), but Spenser probably used Natalis Comes *Mythologiae* (Venice, 1551) 7.14.

No skill can stint nor reason can aslake.°   *abate*
But when in hand my tunelesse harp I take,
10   Then doe I more augment my foes despight,°   *scorn*
And griefe renew, and passions doe awake
To battaile fresh against my selfe to fight.
Mongst whome the more I seeke to settle peace,
The more I fynd their malice to increace.

Sonnet 45

Leave lady in your glasse of christall clene,
Your goodly selfe for evermore to vew:
And in my selfe, my inward selfe I meane,
Most lively lyke behold your semblant trew.[8]
5   Within my hart, though hardly it can shew
Thing so divine to vew° of earthly eye,   *sight*
The fayre Idea[9] of your celestiall hew°   *shape*
And every part remaines immortally:
And were it not that through your cruelty,
10   With sorrow dimméd and deformd it were,
The goodly ymage of your visnomy,°   *face*
Clearer then christall would therein appere.
But if your selfe in me ye playne will see,
Remove the cause by which your fayre beames darkned be.[1]

Sonnet 46

When my abodes° prefixéd time is spent,[2]   *visit*
My cruell fayre streight bids me wend my way:
But then from heaven most hideous stormes are sent
As willing me against her will to stay.
5   Whom then shall I or heaven or her obay?
The heavens know best what is the best for me:
But as she will, whose will my life doth sway,
My lower heaven, so it perforce must bee.
But ye high hevens, that all this sorowe see,
10   Sith all your tempests cannot hold me backe:
Aswage your stormes, or else both you and she
Will both together me too sorely wrack.
Enough it is for one man to sustaine
The stormes, which she alone on me doth raine.

Sonnet 47

Trust not the treason of those smyling lookes,
Untill ye have theyr guylefull traynes° well tryde:°   *snares/examined*

8. I.e., see your lifelike resemblance. The paradoxical "semblant trew" implies that the lover's inner
reflection, like poetry, can capture what it imitates better than realistic copying.
9. In diction loosely recalling the Neoplatonic "forms" in God's mind and visible only to the intellect;
this "idea" is the image of the lady in the lover's inmost self, albeit deformed (10) by his grief.
1. An alexandrine.
2. I.e., when my visit's set time is up. A storm gives him a mock-religious excuse to linger, but the
lady rejects this clever nonsense and he obeys.

For they are lyke but unto golden hookes,
That from the foolish fish theyr bayts doe hyde:
5   So she with flattring smyles weake harts doth guyde
Unto her love, and tempte to theyr decay,°   destruction
Whome being caught she kills with cruell pryde,
And feeds at pleasure on the wretched pray:
Yet even whylst her bloody hands them slay,
10 Her eyes looke lovely and upon them smyle:
That they take pleasure in her cruell play,
And dying doe them selves of payne beguyle.[3]
O mighty charm which makes men love theyr bane,[4]
And thinck they dy with pleasure, live with payne.

Sonnet 48

Innocent paper, whom too cruell hand
Did make the matter to avenge her yre:
And ere she could thy cause wel understand,
Did sacrifize unto the greedy fyre.[5]
5   Well worthy thou to have found better hyre,°   payment
Then so bad end for hereticks ordayned:
Yet heresy nor treason didst conspire,
But plead thy maisters cause unjustly payned.[6]
Whom she, all carelesse° of his griefe, constrayned   uncaring
10 To vtter forth the anguish of his hart:
And would not heare, when he to her complayned
The piteous passion° of his dying smart.   suffering
Yet live for ever, though against her will,
And speake her good,[7] though she requite it ill.

Sonnet 49

Fayre cruell, why are ye so fierce and cruell?
Is it because your eyes have powre to kill?
Then know that mercy is the mighties jewell,
And greater glory thinke to save, then spill.[8]
5   But if it be your pleasure and proud will,
To shew the powre of your imperious eyes:
Then not on him that never thought you ill,
But bend your force against your enemyes.
Let them feele th'utmost of your crueltyes,
10 And kill with looks, as Cockatrices[9] doo:
But him that at your footstoole humbled lies,
With mercifull regard, give mercy too.

3. As they die, the hearts elude or charm away pain.
4. I.e., poison; more generally, ruin.
5. Cf. *Amoretti* 22's sacrifice.
6. I.e., tortured into confessing, like a heretic or traitor.
7. I.e., speak well of her; or speak to her benefit.
8. I.e., think you get more glory by preserving than by destroying.
9. Fabulous serpents with lethal eyebeams, born of roosters' eggs.

Such mercy shal you make admyred to be,[1]
So shall you live by giving life to me.

Sonnet 50

Long languishing in double malady,
Of my harts wound and of my bodies griefe,
There came to me a leach° that would apply   *doctor*
Fit medicines[2] for my bodies best reliefe.
5 "Vayne man," quod I, "that hast but little priefe,°   *experience*
In deep discovery of the mynds disease,
Is not the hart of all the body chiefe?
And rules the members as it selfe doth please?[3]
Then with some cordialls[4] seeke first to appease
10 The inward languour of my wounded hart,
And then my body shall have shortly ease:
But such sweet cordialls passe Physitions art."
Then my lyfes Leach[5] doe you your skill reveale,
And with one salve both hart and body heale.

Sonnet 51

Doe I not see that fayrest ymages
Of hardest Marble are of purpose made?[6]
For that they should endure through many ages,
Ne let theyr famous moniments to fade.
5 Why then doe I, untrainde in lovers trade,
Her hardnes blame which I should more commend?
Sith never ought was excellent assayde,
Which was not hard t'atchive and bring to end.[7]
Ne ought so hard, but he that would attend,[8]
10 Mote soften it and to his will allure:
So doe I hope her stubborne hart to bend,
And that it then more stedfast will endure.
Onely my paines wil be the more to get her,
But having her, my joy wil be the greater.

Sonnet 52

So oft as homeward I from her depart,
I goe lyke one that having lost the field,
Is prisoner led away with heavy hart,

1. I.e., shall make you be admired.
2. "Medicine" has two syllables.
3. A lover's view; sager authorities like St. Paul said the head should in turn rule the body.
4. Potions good for the heart (from Latin *cor*, heart).
5. I.e., the lady.
6. I.e., are not the fairest statues deliberately made of the hardest marble?
7. I.e., nothing excellent was ever attempted that was not hard to accomplish.
8. I.e., pay attention and apply himself; the word also means "wait," anticipating *Amoretti* 67's paradox that the pursuit of love succeeds better if the lover stops trying so hard (a strategy that this lover has not yet tried).

Despoyld of warlike armes and knowen shield.[9]
5   So doe I now my selfe a prisoner yeeld,
To sorrow and to solitary paine:
From presence of my dearest deare exylde,
Longwhile alone in languor to remaine.
There let no thought of joy or pleasure vaine,
10   Dare to approch, that may my solace breed:
But sudden° dumps[1] and drery sad disdayne   *unpremeditated*
Of all worlds gladnesse more my torment feed.
So I her absens will my penaunce[2] make,
That of her presens I my meed° may take.   *reward*

Sonnet 53

The Panther knowing that his spotted hyde
Doth please all beasts, but that his looks them fray:°   *terrify*
Within a bush his dreadfull head doth hide,
To let them gaze whylest° he on them may pray.°[3]   *until/prey*
5   Right so my cruell fayre with me doth play,
For with the goodly semblant° of her hew°   *image/form*
She doth allure me to mine owne decay,°   *ruin*
And then no mercy will unto me shew.
Great shame it is, thing so divine in view,°   *appearance*
10   Made for to be the worlds most ornament,
To make the bayte her gazers to embrew:
Good shames to be to ill an instrument.[4]
But mercy doth with beautie best agree,
As in theyr maker[5] ye them best may see.

Sonnet 54

Of this worlds Theatre in which we stay,[6]
My love lyke the Spectátor ydly sits,
Beholding me that all the pageants play,
Disguysing diversly my troubled wits.
5   Sometimes I joy when glad occasion fits,
And mask[7] in myrth lyke to a Comedy:
Soone after when my joy to sorrow flits,
I waile and make my woes a Tragedy.
Yet she beholding me with constant eye,[8]
10   Delights not in my merth nor rues° my smart:°   *pities/hurt*

9. I.e., recognized coat of arms.
1. Doleful pieces of music.
2. Such "penance" suits Lent, although as yet the lover makes no explicit connection between human and divine love.
3. See Pliny, *Natural History* 8.23. "Panther" usually meant a spotted leopard.
4. I.e., it shames goodness (or goodness is ashamed) to be evil's instrument.
5. I.e., God.
6. A favorite Renaissance theme derived in part from Lucian's *Menippos* and further popularized by Erasmus's *Praise of Folly* (Norton ed., 28); cf. Shakespeare, *As You Like It* 2.7.139.
7. Put on a mask; also, act in a masque, an élite entertainment with symbolic costumes or "guises." If the lover plays comedies when happy and tragedies when sad, his masks dramatize as much as they conceal.
8. Noteworthy in that women were often called inconstant; Elizabeth I defied the same stereotype with her motto *semper eadem*: "ever the same."

But when I laugh she mocks, and when I cry
She laughes, and hardens evermore her hart.
What then can move her? if nor merth nor mone,°   *moan*
She is no woman, but a sencelesse stone.[9]

Sonnet 55[1]

So oft as I her beauty doe behold,
And therewith doe her cruelty compare,
I marvaile of what substance was the mould°   *material*
The which her made attonce so cruell faire.
5 Not earth; for her high thoghts more heavenly are,
Not water; for her love doth burne like fyre:
Not ayre; for she is not so light or rare,[2]
Not fyre; for she doth friese with faint desire.
Then needs another Element inquire
10 Whereof she mote be made; that is the skye.
For to the heaven her haughty lookes aspire:
And eke her mind is pure immortall hye.
Then sith to heaven ye lykened are the best,
Be lyke in mercy as in all the rest.

Sonnet 56

Fayre ye be sure,° but cruell and unkind,   *surely*
As is a Tygre that with greedinesse
Hunts after bloud, when he by chance doth find
A feeble beast, doth felly° him oppresse.   *cruelly*
5 Fayre be ye sure, but proud and pittilesse,
As is a storme, that all things doth prostrate:
Finding a tree alone all comfortlesse,
Beats on it strongly it to ruinate.
Fayre be ye sure, but hard and obstinate,
10 As is a rocke amidst the raging floods:
Gaynst which a ship of succour desolate,[3]
Doth suffer wreck both of her selfe and goods.
That ship, that tree, and that same beast am I,
Whom ye doe wreck, doe ruine, and destroy.[4]

Sonnet 57

Sweet warriour[5] when shall I have peace with you?
High time it is, this warre now ended were:
Which I no lenger can endure to sue,°   *wage*
Ne your incessant battry more to beare:

9. Some readers (e.g., Martz 1970, pp. 804–9, in this volume) note in this sonnet a friendly wit that lightens the tone; the lover's seeming anger at his failure to move the lady may be more role-playing for her entertainment.
1. The sonnet relies on the theory that the world is made of four elements: earth, air, fire, and water.
2. I.e., rarefied; Spenser puns on "light," which can mean sexually lax.
3. I.e., utterly without help.
4. These *vers rapportés* summarize the images in reverse order.
5. A famous Petrarchan oxymoron; cf. *Rime* 17, "O dolce mia guerrera."

5 So weake my powres, so sore my wounds appeare,
That wonder is how I should live a jot,
Seeing my hart through-launchéd° every where   *pierced*
With thousand arrowes, which your eies have shot:
Yet shoot ye sharpely still, and spare me not,
10 But glory thinke[6] to make these cruel stoures.°   *battles*
Ye cruell one, what glory can be got,
In slaying him that would live gladly yours?
Make peace therefore, and graunt me timely grace,[7]
That al my wounds wil heale in little space.[8]

Sonnet 58
By her that is most assured to her selfe.[9]

Weake is th'assurance that weake flesh reposeth
In her[1] owne powre, and scorneth others ayde:
That soonest fals when as she most supposeth
Her selfe assurd, and is of nought affrayd.
5 All flesh is frayle, and all her strength unstayd,
Like a vaine[2] bubble blowen up with ayre:
Devouring tyme and changeful chance haue prayd°   *ravaged*
Her glories pride that none may it repayre.
Ne none so rich or wise, so strong or fayre,
10 But fayleth trusting on his owne assurance:
And he that standeth on the hyghest stayre
Fals lowest: for on earth nought hath enduraunce.
Why then doe ye proud fayre, misdeeme so farre,
That to your selfe ye most assuréd arre?

Sonnet 59[3]

Thrise happie she, that is so well assured
Unto her selfe and setled so in hart:
That nether will for better be allured
Ne feard° with worse to any chaunce to start,[4]   *affrighted*
5 But like a steddy ship doth strongly part
The raging waves and keepes her course aright:
Ne ought for tempest doth from it depart,
Ne ought for fayrer weathers false delight.
Such selfe assurance need not feare the spight

6. I.e., you think it glorious.
7. I.e., pity me before I perish; *Amoretti*'s religious overtones permit "grace" also to suggest, now or in retrospect, God's redeeming mercy.
8. I.e., soon.
9. A puzzle. Does "by" mean "concerning," or is the poem said "by" the lady speaking "to herself"? Possibly, the title was intended for the following poem; see Yale for further speculation. The speaker's thoughts on human frailty echo biblical passages such as Isaiah 40.6–7 and 1 Corinthians 10.12.
1. I.e., the flesh's.
2. Both empty and proud; cf. Orgoglio in *Faerie Queene* I.vii–viii.
3. Either the lady's reply or the lover's new perspective. The lady herself is now a ship with an internal guidance system to steady her during fortune's storms or diversions.
4. Obscurely put; the sense is that no misfortune will make her swerve.

10 Of grudging foes, ne favour seek of friends:
But in the stay[5] of her owne stedfast might,
Nether to one her selfe nor other bends.
Most happy she that most assured doth rest,
But he most happy who such one loves best.

Sonnet 60

They that in course of heavenly spheares are skild,
To every planet point° his sundry° yeare:[6] ·················· *appoint/particular*
In which her[7] circles voyage is fulfild,
As Mars in three score yeares doth run his spheare.
5 So since the wingéd God his planet cleare,
Began in me to move, one yeare is spent:[8]
The which doth longer unto me appeare,
Then al those fourty which my life outwent.[9]
Then by that count, which lovers books invent,
10 The spheare of Cupid fourty yeares containes,
Which I have wasted in long languishment,
That seemd the longer for my greater paines.
But let my loves fayre Planet short her wayes
This yeare ensuing,° or else short my dayes.[1] ·················· *following*

Sonnet 61

The glorious image of the makers beautie,
My soverayne saynt, the Idoll of my thought,[2]
Dare not henceforth above the bounds of dewtie,
'I''accuse of pride, or rashly blame for ought.
5 For being as she is divinely wrought,
And of the brood of Angels hevenly borne:
And with the crew of blesséd Saynts upbrought,
Each of which did her with theyr guifts adorne;[3]
The bud of joy, the blossome of the morne,
10 The beame of light, whom mortal eyes admyre:
What reason is it then but she should scorne
Base things that to her love too bold aspire?

5. I.e., guidance and support. A "stay" is a ship's rope.
6. I.e., one full revolution around the earth in the geocentric system. Spenser gives Mars an orbit of sixty years, not the correct seventy-nine, perhaps because he has spent sixty sonnets warring for the lady.
7. I.e., the sphere's; some said the crystal spheres that held the planets were guided by sirens or other beings imagined as female.
8. Spenser jokingly invents a planetary sphere for Cupid—the lover's body; it has been turning for a year.
9. I.e., went through. Spenser must have been about forty in 1594 (for the relevance of his age, see Cheney 1983); forty also recalls Lent and the Israelite trek to the Promised Land.
1. The lady, too, has a sphere. The lover asks her to shorten its orbit—to hurry; then Cupid and she will come into planetary conjunction. Or else, he says, she will shorten his days by killing him with grief.
2. Lines 1–2 are the object of the imperative "dare" in 3: he orders himself not to accuse or blame his saint.
3. A beneficent Pandora; the hint of preexistence is so unorthodox that we may think this semi-Platonic "Idoll" not the lady herself but an aspect of her.

Such heavenly formes ought rather worshipt be,[4]
Then dare be loved by men of meane degree.

Sonnet 62

The weary yeare his race now having run,
The new begins his compast course[5] anew:
With shew of morning mylde he hath begun,
Betokening peace and plenty to ensew.°   *follow*
5 So let us, which° this chaunge of weather vew,   *who*
Chaunge eeke our mynds and former lives amend,
The old yeares sinnes forepast let us eschew,
And fly the faults with which we did offend.
Then shall the new yeares joy forth freshly send,
10 Into the glooming° world his gladsome ray: *dark*
And all these stormes which now his beauty blend,°   *pollute*
Shall turne to caulmes and tymely cleare away.
So, likewise love, cheare you your heavy spright,
And chaunge old yeares annoy to new delight.

Sonnet 63[6]

After long stormes and tempests sad assay,[7]
Which hardly[8] I enduréd heretofore,
In dread of death and daungerous dismay,
With which my silly° barke was tosséd sore:°   *frail/grievously*
5 I doe at length descry the happy shore,
In which I hope ere long for to arryve:
Fayre soyle it seemes from far and fraught° with store°   *laden/plenty*
Of all that deare and daynty is alyve.
Most happy he that can at last atchyve
10 The joyous safety of so sweet a rest:[9]
Whose least delight sufficeth to deprive
Remembrance of all paines which him opprest.
All paines are nothing in respect of[1] this,
All sorrowes short that gaine eternall blisse.

Sonnet 64[2]

Comming to kisse her lyps, (such grace I found)
Me seemd I smelt a gardin of sweet flowres:

4. "Worship" could then mean honor, but as in *Amoretti* 22 Spenser plays for one reason or another
   with the idolatry and image-worship that Protestants condemned.
5. I.e., his curved path; Spenser almost certainly means it is March 25, start of the new civil year,
   also called "Lady Day" in honor of the angel's annunciation to Mary that she was to bear Jesus.
6. Cf. *Amoretti* 34; the expectation of safe harbor rewrites Petrarchan tradition.
7. I.e., assault; also trial and testing.
8. I.e., barely and with hardship.
9. Cf. *Epithalamian* 424. Here and in *Faerie Queene* VII.8.2 Spenser may pun on "Elizabeth" in
   the then common if mistaken belief (see e.g., Camden, *Remains Concerning Britain* [1605; 1974]
   102) that it is Hebrew for Lord's (Eli) rest (Sabbath): Elizabeth = "eternall bliss."
1. I.e., compared to; also, in view of (Latin *respectare*, see).
2. The manner is that of the Bible's Song of Solomon, usually read as a duet by Christ and his
   Church (the body of believers). Greeting a lady on the lips was common, so this kiss may be sweet
   but circumspect, suiting an unbetrothed virgin.

That dainty odours from them threw around,
For damzels fit to decke their lovers bowres.
5 Her lips did smell lyke unto Gillyflowers,[3]
Her ruddy cheekes lyke unto Roses red:
Her snowy browes lyke budded Bellamoures,[4]
Her lovely eyes lyke Pincks but newly spred,
Her goodly bosome lyke a Strawberry bed,
10 Her neck lyke to a bounch of Cullambynes:°   columbines
Her brest lyke lillyes, ere theyr leaves be shed,
Her nipples[5] lyke yong blossomd Jessemynes:°   jasmines
Such fragrant flowres doe give most odorous smell,
But her sweet odour did them all excell.

Sonnet 65

The doubt which ye misdeeme,° fayre love, is vaine,   misconceive
That fondly° feare to loose your liberty,   foolishly
When loosing one, two liberties ye gayne,
And make him bond that bondage earst dyd fly.
5 Sweet be the bands, the which true love doth tye,
Without constraynt or dread of any ill:[6]
The gentle° birde feeles no captivity   noble
Within her cage, but singes and feeds her fill.
There pride dare not approch, nor discord spill°   destroy
10 The league twixt them,[7] that loyal love hath bound:
But simple truth and mutuall good will
Seekes with sweet peace to salve each others wound:[8]
There fayth doth fearlesse dwell in brasen towre,
And spotlesse pleasure builds her sacred bowre.

Sonnet 66

To all those happy blessings which ye have,
With plenteous hand by heaven upon you thrown,
This one disparagement° they to you gave,   disgrace
That ye your love lent to so meane a one.
5 Yee whose high worths surpassing paragon   comparison
Could not on earth have found one fit for mate,
Ne but in heaven matchable to none,
Why did ye stoup unto so lowly state?°[9]   rank
But ye thereby much greater glory gate,
10 Then had ye sorted° with a princes pere: mated

3. A variety of pink, smelling of clove.
4. Unidentified; the name means "beautiful love."
5. Later Elizabethan necklines sometimes revealed much of the bosom, a fashion favored by the queen and connoting virginity (J. Nunn, *Fashion in Costume* [New York, 1984] 39).
6. The claim that love liberates even as it binds parallels a belief that God's "service is perfect freedom" (Morning Prayer's Collect for Peace).
7. I.e., those whom: the lovers.
8. Wounds suffered, presumably, in the wars of fear and longing.
9. I.e., you whose incomparable worthiness could not have found anyone on earth suitable as a mate, you who are fit to be matched only with someone in Heaven, why did you lower yourself to one of my rank? If it is Good Friday, the lady's love for an inferior becomes more poignant as a recollection of Christ's gift of himself to others.

For now your light doth more it selfe dilate,°   *enlarge*
And in my darknesse greater doth appeare.
Yet since your light hath once elumind me,
With my reflex yours shall encreaséd be.[1]

Sonnet 67[2]

Lyke as a huntsman after weary chace,
Seeing the game from him escapt away,
Sits downe to rest him in some shady place,
With panting hounds beguiléd of their pray:
5 So after long pursuit and vaine assay,°   *attempt*
When I all weary had the chace forsooke,
The gentle deare returnd the selfe-same way,
Thinking to quench her thirst at the next° brooke.   *nearby*
There she beholding me with mylder looke,[3]
10 Sought not to fly, but fearelesse still did bide:
Till I in hand her yet halfe trembling tooke,
And with her owne goodwill hir fyrmely tyde.[4]
Strange thing me seemd to see a beast so wyld,
So goodly wonne with her owne will beguyld.[5]

Sonnet 68

Most glorious Lord of lyfe that on this day,[6]
Didst make thy triumph over death and sin:
And having harrowd hell didst bring away
Captivity thence captive[7] us to win:
5 This joyous day, deare Lord, with joy begin,
And grant that we for whom thou diddest dye,
Being with thy deare blood clene washt from sin,
May live for ever in felicity.
And that thy love we weighing worthily,
10 May likewise love thee for the same againe:
And for thy sake that all lyke deare didst buy,[8]
With love may one another entertayne.

1. Without radiation of his own, the lover will reflect and thus add to her glory. It is the first full moon after the equinox (then March 11) that determines the date of Easter, so the lady's "dilation" of light suits the season.
2. Unlike other sonneteers, the lover catches the deer; cf. Petrarch, *Rime* 190 and Wyatt, "Whoso list." Some compare *Amoretti* 67 to Tasso's "Questa fera gentil" (Dasenbrock 1991). For an analogous poem by Marguerite de Navarre, scriptural echoes, and a context for the deer, see Prescott 1985, excerpted on pp. 809–13 of this edition.
3. Who has a milder look is unclear: the hunter is less predatory and the deer less wild. The ambiguity suits Spenser's view of love and theology: no effort can compel love or God.
4. The tying of a half-trembling deer implies betrothal to a lady still nervous about her new life. Deer were often netted, not shot, at the end of the hunt.
5. Cf. 4, where the dogs are beguiled (cheated, tricked); the word acknowledges her complexity, just as "will" may tactfully hint that sexual desire encouraged her surrender.
6. Easter, March 31 in 1594. Lines 1–12 incorporate many phrases from the Bible and prayerbook (see *Variorum*).
7. Cf. "led captivity captive," Psalms 68 and Ephesians 4.8. Before the resurrection, Christ sacked ("harrowed") Hell to free those destined for or worthy of salvation.
8. I.e., redeemed all alike lovingly, and at great cost.

So let us love, deare love, lyke as we ought,[9]
Love is the lesson which the Lord us taught.

Sonnet 69[1]

The famous warriors of the anticke world,
Used Trophees to erect in stately wize:°   *manner*
In which they would the records have enrold,
Of theyr great deeds and valarous emprize.°   *undertaking*
5   What trophee then shall I most fit devize,
In which I may record the memory
Of my loves conquest, peerelesse beauties prise,
Adorned with honour, love, and chastity.
Even this verse vowd to eternity,
10   Shall be thereof immortall moniment:
And tell her prayse to all posterity,
That may admire such worlds rare wonderment:°   *marvel*
The happy purchase° of my glorious spoile,°   *acquisition/plunder*
Gotten at last with labour and long toyle.[2]

Sonnet 70

Fresh spring the herald of loves mighty king,
In whose cote-armour[3] richly are displayd
All sorts of flowers the which on earth do spring
In goodly colours gloriously arrayd:
5   Goe to my love, where she is carelesse layd,
Yet in her winters bowre not well awake:
Tell her the joyous time wil not be staid
Unlesse she doe him by the forelock take.[4]
Bid her therefore her selfe soone ready make,
10   To wayt on love[5] amongst his lovely crew:
Where every one that misseth then her make,°   *mate*
Shall be by him amearst° with penance dew.   *punished*
Make hast therefore sweet love, whilest it is prime,°   *spring*
For none can call againe the passéd time.

Sonnet 71

I joy to see how in your drawen work,[6]
Your selfe unto the Bee ye doe compare;
And me unto the Spyder that doth lurke,
In close awayt° to catch her unaware.   *ambush*

9. I.e., as we should and as we owe. The couplet anticipates the gospel reading for the June 11 wedding day (Kaske 1977).
1. Spenser can still adapt Petrarchan poets; cf. Du Bellay, *Olive* 34.
2. He did not, strictly, win the lady, yet Paul calls Christ's resurrection our "victory" (1 Corinthians 15) and the lover may not be wholly deluded.
3. A herald's formal costume; Spring precedes Cupid to announce his decrees.
4. Opportunity is proverbially bald behind: grab his forelock as he passes or miss your chance.
5. I.e., to attend and serve Cupid (who since the betrothal may more clearly remind us of *Amoretti* 68's Lord of Life).
6. Tapestry work done by drawing out threads to form patterns.

5   Right so your selfe were caught in cunning snare
    Of a deare foe, and thrallèd° to his love: *enslaved*
    In whose streight° bands ye now captivéd are   *tight*
    So firmely, that ye never may remove.
    But as your worke is woven all about[7]
10 With woodbynd flowers and fragrant Eglantine:[8]
    So sweet your prison you in time shall prove,°   *find*
    With many deare delights bedeckéd fyne.
    And all thensforth eternall peace shall see,
    Betweene the Spyder and the gentle Bee.

Sonnet 72[9]

    Oft when my spirit doth spred her bolder winges,
    In mind to mount up to the purest sky:
    It down is weighd with thoght of earthly things
    And clogd with burden of mortality,[1]
5   Where when that soverayne beauty it doth spy,
    Resembling heavens glory in her light:
    Drawne with sweet pleasures bayt, it back doth fly,
    And unto heaven forgets her former flight.
    There my fraile fancy fed with full delight,
10 Doth bath in blisse and mantleth most at ease:[2]
    Ne thinks of other heaven, but how it might
    Her harts desire with most contentment please.
    Hart need not wish none other happinesse,
    But here on earth to have such hevens blisse.

Sonnet 73[3]

    Being my selfe captyvéd here in care,
    My hart, whom none with servile bands can tye,
    But the fayre tresses of your golden hayre,
    Breaking his prison forth to you doth fly.
5   Lyke as a byrd that in ones hand doth spy
    Desiréd food, to it doth make his flight:
    Even so my hart, that wont on your fayre eye
    To feed his fill, flyes backe unto your sight.
    Doe you him take, and in your bosome bright,
10 Gently encage, that he may be your thrall:
    Perhaps he there may learne with rare delight,
    To sing your name and prayses over all.
    That it hereafter may you not repent,
    Him lodging in your bosome to have lent.

7. See Textual Notes.
8. I.e., sweetbriar (wild rose), like woodbind (honeysuckle) an emblem of pleasing entanglement. Both lovers weave well; cf. *Amoretti* 23. D. Cheney suggests that "bee" and "*spider*" allude to Boyle and *Sp*enser (cf. *RenQ* 39 [1986]: 800).
9. The opening lines adapt Tasso's "L'alma vaga"; the anti-Platonic conclusion may be less a rejection of Heaven than a claim that divinely sanctioned love embodies it on earth.
1. A common emblematic image; cf. Alciati 121. Often the winged figure with a clog (a weighted chain) symbolized ambition hampered by poverty.
2. I.e., stretches wings and legs to ease them (a term from hawking).
3. An increasingly free adaptation of Tasso's "Donna, poichè fortuna."

Sonnet 74

Most happy letters framed by skilfull trade,
With which that happy name[4] was first desynd:
The which three times thrise happy hath me made,
With guifts of body, fortune and of mind.
5 The first my being to me gave by kind,°   nature
From mothers womb derived by dew descent,
The second is my sovereigne Queene most kind,
That honour and large richesse to me lent.
The third my love, my lives last ornament,
10 By whom my spirit out of dust was raysed:
To speake her prayse and glory excellent,
Of all alive most worthy to be praysed.
Ye three Elizabeths for ever live,
That three such graces did unto me give.[5]

Sonnet 75

One day I wrote her name upon the strand,°   beach
But came the waves and washéd it away:
Agayne I wrote it with a second hand,
But came the tyde, and made my paynes his pray.°   prey
5 "Vayne man," sayd she, "that doest in vaine assay   *beloved*
A mortall thing so to immortalize,
For I my selve shall lyke to this decay,
And eek my name bee wypéd out lykewize."
"Not so," quod I, "let baser things devize°   contrive
10 To dy in dust, but you shall live by fame:
My verse your vertues rare shall eternize,
And in the hevens wryte your glorious name.
Where whenas death shall all the world subdew,
Our love shall live, and later life renew."

Sonnet 76[6]

Fayre bosome fraught with vertues richest tresure,
The neast of love, the lodging of delight:
The bowre of blisse,[7] the paradice of pleasure,
The sacred harbour of that hevenly spright:
5 How was I ravisht with your lovely sight,
And my frayle thoughts too rashly led astray?
Whiles diving deepe through amorous insight,
On the sweet spoyle of beautie they did pray.
And twixt her paps° like early fruit in May,   nipples

---

4. I.e., the nine letters of "Elizabeth"; cf. *Amoretti* 63, note 9.
5. Cf. *Amoretti* 40. The implied image of Spenser encircled by Elizabeths like Venus amidst her
   Graces is curious and perhaps not without humor.
6. *Amoretti* 76 and 77 derive loosely from Tasso's "Il seno di madonna."
7. A contrast with the deceptive bower in *Faerie Queene* II.x. Severer readers have taken the thoughts
   here and in *Amoretti* 77 as signs of lapse or (Marotti 1982) aggression; the lover only calls them
   rash (possibly because premature) and could cite in their defense Proverbs 5.19: "Let [your wife]
   be as the loving hind . . . let her breasts satisfy thee at all times."

10   Whose harvest seemd to hasten now apace:
      They loosely did theyr wanton winges display,
      And there to rest themselves did boldly place.
      Sweet thoughts I envy your so happy rest,
      Which oft I wisht, yet never was so blest.

Sonnet 77

      Was it a dreame, or did I see it playne,
      A goodly table of pure yvory:
      All spred with juncats,° fit to entertayne   *delicacies*
      The greatest Prince with pompous roialty?
5   Mongst which there in a silver dish did ly
      Twoo golden apples of unvalewd° price: *inestimable*
      Far passing those which Hercules came by,
      Or those which Atalanta did entice. [8]
      Exceeding sweet, yet voyd of sinfull vice,
10   That many sought yet none could ever taste,
      Sweet fruit of pleasure brought from paradice
      By Love himselfe and in his garden plaste.
      Her brest that table was so richly spredd,
      My thoughts the guests, which would thereon have fedd.

Sonnet 78

      Lackyng my love I go from place to place,
      Lyke a young fawne that late hath lost the hynd: [9]
      And seeke each where, where last I sawe her face,
      Whose ymage yet I carry fresh in mynd. [1]
5   I seeke the fields with her late footing synd, [2]
      I seeke her bowre with her late presence deckt,
      Yet nor in field nor bowre I her can fynd:
      Yet field and bowre are full of her aspect.
      But when myne eyes I thereunto direct,
10   They ydly back returne to me agayne,
      And when I hope to see theyr trew obiect,
      I fynd my selfe but fed with fancies vayne.
      Ceasse then myne eyes, to seeke her selfe to see,
      And let my thoughts behold her selfe in mee.

8. On an island garden west of North Africa grew golden apples guarded by a dragon and tended by
   the Hesperides, daughters of the evening star Hesperus (alternatively, of Atlas); Hercules stole some
   as one of his labors. Atalanta would marry only a man able to outrace her (losers were executed).
   Venus gave Hippomenes three gold apples with which to distract her while she ran; he won (Ovid,
   Metamorphoses 10).
9. The huntsman of *Amoretti* 67 is now a deer; cf. Horace's comparison of his timidly unwilling
   Chloë to a trembling fawn seeking its mother (*Odes* 1.23).
1. If Spenser still wants us to remember the church calendar, he may also hope we recall that while
   sometimes impatiently awaiting the return of their absent bridegroom (Christ), Christians harbor
   the Spirit inside them (John 14.16). In any case, Spenser reworks a Petrarchan theme of absence.
2. I.e., bearing signs (footprints) of her recent presence, perhaps with overtones of the vestigial "signs"
   of God still legible in the natural world; see E. Curtius, *European Literature and the Latin Middle
   Ages* (Princeton, 1953) ch. 16.

Sonnet 79

Men call you fayre, and you doe credit° it,   *believe*
For that your selfe ye dayly such doe see:
But the trew fayre,° that is the gentle wit,   *beauty*
And vertuous mind, is much more praysd of° me.   *by*
5 For all the rest, how ever fayre it be,
Shall turne to nought and loose that glorious hew:°   *appearance*
But onely that[3] is permanent and free
From frayle corruption, that doth flesh ensew.°   *attend*
That is true beautie: that doth argue you
10 To be divine and borne of heavenly seed:
Derived from that fayre Spirit,[4] from whom al true
And perfect beauty did at first proceed.
He onely fayre, and what he fayre hath made,
All other fayre lyke flowres untymely fade.[5]

Sonnet 80[6]

After so long a race as I have run
Through Faery land, which those six books compile,°   *comprise*
Give leave to rest me being halfe fordonne,°   *exhausted*
And gather to my selfe new breath awhile.
5 Then as a steed refreshéd after toyle,
Out of my prison I will breake anew:
And stoutly° will that second worke assoyle,°   *boldly/release*
With strong endevour and attention dew.
Till then give leave to me in pleasant mew[7]
10 To sport my muse, and sing my loves sweet praise:
The contemplation of whose heavenly hew,
My spirit to an higher pitch will rayse.
But let her prayses yet be low and meane,[8]
Fit for the handmayd of the Faery Queene.

Sonnet 81[9]

Fayre is my love, when her fayre golden heares,
With the loose wynd ye waving chance to marke:[1]
Fayre when the rose in her red cheekes appeares,
Or in her eyes the fyre of love does sparke.
5 Fayre when her brest lyke a rich laden barke,

3. I.e., that true beauty of wit and mind. See Yale for other ways of sorting out the syntax.
4. I.e., God as the Holy Spirit.
5. I.e., only God is beautiful—he and the things he has made beautiful (or made beautifully); all other beauty fades too soon, like flowers.
6. *Amoretti* 80 helps date the composition of *Faerie Queene* IV–VI, although Spenser may have revised before publication in 1596; apparently in 1594 he hoped, or wished to seem he hoped, to write *Faerie Queene* VII–XII.
7. I.e., confinement; also a cage for a molting hawk as it grows new feathers.
8. I.e., common, but also moderate (as in "golden mean") and temperate; cf. *Faerie Queene* VI.x.28 and note.
9. Spenser adapts Tasso's "Bella è la donna mia," adding his own conclusion.
1. I.e., when you happen to notice her hair waving in the loose wind; evidently her hair is also loose, as suited unwed women.

With pretious merchandize she forth doth lay:
Fayre when that cloud of pryde, which oft doth dark
Her goodly light, with smiles she drives away.
But fayrest she, when so she doth display
10 The gate with pearles and rubyes richly dight:°   *adorned*
Throgh which her words so wise do make their way
To beare the message of her gentle spright:
The rest be works of natures wonderment,
But this the worke of harts astonishment.

Sonnet 82

Joy of my life, full oft for loving you
I blesse my lot, that was so lucky placed:
But then the more your owne mishap I rew,
That are so much by so meane love embased.°   *degraded*
                                                      equitable
5 For had the equall° hevens so much you graced
In this as in the rest, ye mote invent
Som hevenly wit, whose verse could have enchased[2]
Your glorious name in golden moniment.
But since ye deignd so goodly to relent
10 To me your thrall, in whom is little worth,
That little that I am, shall all be spent,
In setting your immortall prayses forth.
Whose lofty argument uplifting me,
Shall lift you up unto an high degree.

Sonnet 83[3]

My hungry eyes, through greedy covetize,
Still° to behold the object of theyr payne: *always*
With no contentment can themselues suffize,°   *satisfy*
But having pine, and having not complayne.
5 For lacking it, they cannot lyfe sustayne,
And seeing it,[4] they gaze on it the more:
In theyr amazement lyke Narcissus vayne
Whose eyes him starved: so plenty makes me pore.
Yet are myne eyes so filléd with the store
10 Of that fayre sight, that nothing else they brooke:°   *endure*
But loath the things which they did like before,
And can no more endure on them to looke.
All this worlds glory seemeth vayne to me,
And all theyr shewes but shadowes saving° she.   *except*

---

2. I.e., put in a setting, like a jewel, so as to show it to advantage; the word also meant to enclose.
3. Almost identical to *Amoretti* 35; the repetition may be an error, but it fits some numerological schemes (e.g., Thompson 1985) and perhaps the meaning shifts with the situation: does a text change when its context changes?
4. In *Amoretti* 35 the eyes "have"; here they "see," perhaps a quasi-Neoplatonic shift from desire for possession to enraptured contemplation.

Sonnet 84[5]

Let not one sparke of filthy lustfull fyre[6]
Breake out, that may her sacred peace molest:
Ne one light glance of sensuall desyre
Attempt to work her gentle mindes unrest.
5 But pure affections bred in spotlesse brest,
And modest thoughts breathd from wel tempred sprites,
Goe visit her in her chast bowre of rest,
Accompanyde with ángelick delightes.
There fill your selfe with those most joyous sights,
10 The which my selfe could never yet attayne:
But speake no word to her of these sad plights,
Which her too constant stiffenesse doth constrayn.°
Onely behold her rare perfection,[7]
And blesse your fortunes fayre election.

Sonnet 85

The world that cannot deeme° of worthy things,   judge
When I doe praise her, say I doe but flatter:
So does the Cuckow, when the Mavis[8] sings,
Begin his witlesse note apace to clatter.
5 But they that skill not of so heavenly matter,
All that they know not, envy or admyre,
Rather then envy let them wonder at her,
But not to deeme of her desert aspyre.[9]
Deepe in the closet of my parts entyre,°   interior
10 Her worth is written with a golden quill:
That me with heavenly fury[1] doth inspire,
And my glad mouth with her sweet prayses fill.
Which when as fame in her shrill trump shal thunder,
Let the world chose to envy or to wonder.

Sonnet 86

Venemous toung tipt with vile adders sting,
Of that selfe kynd with which the Furies fell
Theyr snaky heads doe combe, from which a spring
Of poysoned words and spitefull speeches well:[2]

5. The opening adapts Tasso, "Uom di non pure fiamme."
6. I.e., a sexual urge that ignores her virtue, spirit, or feelings; as he elsewhere makes clear, Spenser did not disdain physical desire except when misdirected or untimely.
7. In Elizabethan verse the suffix "-tion" was often disyllabic.
8. I.e., song thrush. Now engaged to be married, the lover denigrates the traditionally adulterous cuckoo that in *Amoretti* 19 was Spring's messenger.
9. The lover says that those ignorant of heavenly matters respond to what they do not understand with either wonder or envy; so let them wonder at rather than envy the lady, and not try to judge her merit.
1. I.e., divine madness, Platonic language for inspiration infused by the Muses; cf. Plato's *Phaedrus.* Here it comes from something written (we are not told by whom) inside the poet.
2. Spenser merges the Furies (Hades' enforcers, the Erinyes) with a common image of Envy as a snaky-haired hag chewing a viper and spewing slander (cf. Ovid, *Metamorphoses* 2.760 ff. and Alciati, *Emblemata* 71). Perhaps Spenser was slandered to Elizabeth Boyle, but he may also need to find new causes for the pain that sonnet sequences fed on. If the religious subtext still operates, readers can recall that Jesus told his followers to expect slander.

5 Let all the plagues and horrid paines of hell,
    Upon thee fall for thine accurséd hyre:°   *punishment*
    That with false forgéd° lyes, which thou didst tel,   *feigned*
    In my true love did stirre up coles of yre,
    The sparkes whereof let kindle thine own fyre,
10 And catching hold on thine owne wicked hed
    Consume thee quite, that didst with guile conspire
    In my sweet peace such breaches to have bred.
    Shame be thy meed,° and mischiefe thy reward,   *payment*
    Dew° to thy selfe that it for me prepard.[3]   *due*

Sonnet 87

Since I did leave the presence of my love,
Many long weary dayes I have outworne:
And many nights, that slowly seemd to move
Theyr sad protract° from evening untill morne.   *duration*
5 For when as day the heaven doth adorne,
    I wish that night the noyous° day would end: *vexatious*
    And when as night hath us of light forlorne,°   *deprived*
    I wish that day would shortly reascend.
    Thus I the time with expectation spend,
10 And faine° my griefe with chaunges to beguile,   *desiring*
    That[4] further seemes his terme still to extend,
    And maketh every minute seeme a myle.
    So sorrow still° doth seeme too long to last,   *always*
    But joyous houres doo fly away too fast.

Sonnet 88

Since I have lackt the comfort of that light,
The which was wont to lead my thoughts astray,
I wander as in darknesse of the night,
Affrayd of every dangers least dismay.°   *threat*
5 Ne ought I see, though in the clearest day,
    When others gaze upon theyr shadowes vayne:[5]
    But th'onely[6] image of that heavenly ray,
    Whereof some glance doth in mine eie remayne.
    Of which beholding the Idæa playne,
10 Through contemplation of my purest part,
    With light thereof I doe my selfe sustayne,
    And thereon feed my love-affamisht hart.

---

3. I.e., the shame you prepared for me is due instead to you. The phrasing recalls the psalms, e.g., Psalms 57, in which David says his slanderers will fall into the traps they set for him.

4. I.e., my effort to elude my sorrow by changing my desires seems only to extend its duration; if we take "faine" as "feign," he means he pretends to delude grief by looking for change.

5. The shadows are "vayne" because made by mere physical light; cf. Plato's allegory in which those who prefer appearance watch shadows on a firelit cave wall (*Republic* 7). The lady's light is transcendently real; with sparkles of it still in his eyes, the lover can see her divine form when he looks in his soul, feeding his heart. For religious parallels, cf. "in thy light shall we see light" (Psalms 36.9) and eating in memory of the absent beloved at Communion.

6. I.e., but only the image.

But with such brightnesse whylest I fill my mind,
I starve my body and mine eyes doe blynd.

Sonnet 89[7]

Lyke as the Culver° on the baréd bough,   dove
Sits mourning for the absence of her mate:
And in her songs sends many a wishfull vow,
For his returne that seemes to linger late.
5   So I alone now left disconsolate,
Mourne to my selfe the absence of my love:
And wandring here and there all desolate,
Seek with my playnts to match that mournful dove:
Ne joy of ought that under heaven doth hove°   abide
10   Can comfort me, but her owne joyous sight:
Whose sweet aspect° both God and man can move,   sight
In her unspotted pleasauns[8] to delight.
Dark is my day, whyles her fayre light I mis,
And dead my life that wants° such lively blis.   lacks

[Anacreontics]†

[1]

In youth, before I waxéd old,
The blynd boy, Venus baby,
For want of cunning made me bold,
In bitter hyve to grope for honny.

5
But when he saw me stung and cry,
He tooke his wings and away did fly.

[2][1]

As Diane hunted on a day,
She chaunst to come where Cupid lay,
his quiver by his head:
10   One of his shafts she stole away,

---

7. Doves symbolize fidelity, and if betrothed the lovers are now legally "mated." The bare branch suggests winter; perhaps, despite the June date of *Epithalamion*, Spenser refers to the Advent season of waiting, or at least to chilly weather, so as to recall a liturgical circle that bends back toward its cold beginning.
8. I.e., pleasantness; also a garden's pleasure area. Dove and garden together recall the longing lovers in the Song of Solomon: there the groom is a singing dove (2.12) and the bride an enclosed garden (4.12).
† In the first edition these lyrics lack titles and any indication that they are separate poems. Many call them "Anacreontics" because they resemble poems wrongly ascribed to Anacreon (sixth century B.C.), servant of the dictator Polycrates and singer of boys and wine, who died at eighty-five after, some said, choking on a grape seed. Henri Estienne's 1554 edition of *Anacreontea* started a fashion for them. True, a wine-and-roses manner and a taste for self-consciously exquisite erotic anecdotes preceded the recovery of "Anacreon," and Spenser adapts two epigrams by the older poet Clément Marot. Nevertheless, the Anacreontics signal stylish and learned elegance.
1. Based on Marot's "L'Enfant Amour" (Mayer ed. #63).

And one of hers did close° convay,   *secretly*
   into the others stead:°   *place*
     With that love wounded my loves hart,
     but Diane beasts with Cupids dart.[2]

[3][3]

15 I Saw in secret to my Dame,
    How little Cupid humbly came:
    and sayd to her, "All hayle, my mother."
  But when he saw me laugh, for shame
  His face with bashfull blood did flame,
20   not knowing Venus from the other.
"Then never blush, Cupid," quoth I,
  "for many have erred in this beauty."[4]

[4][5]

Upon a day, as love lay sweetly slumbring
    all in his mothers lap:
25 A gentle Bee with his loud trumpet murm'ring,
    about him flew by hap.°   *chance*
Whereof when he was wakened with the noyse,
    and saw the beast so small:
"Whats this," quoth he, "that gives so great a voyce,
30   that wakens men withall?
In angry wize° he flyes about,   *manner*
    and threatens all with corage stout.°   *doughty*

To whom his mother closely° smiling sayd,   *privately*
    twixt earnest and twixt game:
35 "See thou thy selfe likewise art lyttle made,
    if thou regard° the same.   *behold*
And yet thou suffrest neyther gods in sky,
    nor men in earth to rest:
But when thou art disposéd cruelly,
40   theyr sleepe thou doost molest.
Then eyther change thy cruelty,
    or give lyke leave unto the fly."[6]

Nathlesse the cruell boy not so content,
    would needs the fly pursue:
45 And in his hand with heedlesse hardiment,°   *boldness*

---

2. Cupid shot the lady's heart with the huntress Diana's arrow (making her chaste), whereas Diana shot animals with Cupid's arrow (inflaming them sexually). "Beasts" is the object of the understood "wounded."
3. A close translation of Marot's "Amour trouva celle" (Mayer ed. #106).
4. I.e., have mistaken my lady for Venus. "Quoth" then sounded like "quote" and the first syllable of "beauty" could be pronounced "bo," as in French, so the rhyme works.
5. The story of Cupid and the bee was popular. Renaissance versions derive finally from a poem by Bion or Moschus once attributed to Theocritus, or from an ancient imitation first printed in the 1554 *Anacreontea*. Spenser follows Tasso's "Mentre in grembo" for two stanzas and then, with a glance at Ronsard and others, goes his own way (J. Hutton, "Cupid and the Bee," *PMLA* 56 [1941]: 1036–58).
6. A "fly" was any winged insect.

him caught for to subdue.
But when on it he hasty hand did lay,
   the Bee him stung therefore:
"Now out alasse," he cryde, "and welaway,"[7]
50   I wounded am full sore:
The fly that I so much did scorne,
   hath hurt me with his little horne."

Unto his mother straight he weeping came,
   and of his griefe complayned:
55 Who could not chose° but laugh at his fond game,   *choose*
   though sad to see him pained.
"Think now," quod she, "my sonne how great the smart
   of those whom thou dost wound:
Full many thou hast prickéd to the hart,
60   that pitty never found:[8]
Therefore henceforth some pitty take,
   when thou doest spoyle° of lovers make."   *pillage*

She tooke him streight full pitiously lamenting,
   and wrapt him in her smock:
65 She wrapt him softly, all the while repenting,[9]
   that he the fly did mock.
She drest his wound and it embaulmed[1] wel
   with salve of soveraigne might:
And then she bathed him in a dainty well,
70   the well of deare delight.
Who would not oft be stung as this,
   to be so bathed in Venus blis?

The wanton boy was shortly wel recured°   *recovered*
   of that his malady:
75 But he soone after fresh againe enured°   *commenced*
   his former cruelty.
And since that time he wounded hath my selfe
   with his sharpe dart of love:
And now forgets the cruell carelesse elfe
80   his mothers heast° to prove.°   *bidding/do*
So now I languish till he please
   my pining anguish to appease.

7. "Out alas" and "welaway" were common expressions of anguish.
8. I.e., who never had mercy from you.
9. In modern grammar a misplaced participle; it is Cupid who repents.
1. I.e., annointed with ointment.

Epithalamion†

[1]

Ye learned sisters[1] which have oftentimes
Beene to me ayding, others to adorne:
Whom ye thought worthy of your gracefull rymes,
That even the greatest did not greatly scorne
5 To heare theyr names sung in your simple layes,
But joyéd in theyr prayse.[2]
And when ye list your owne mishaps to mourne,
Which death, or love, or fortunes wreck did rayse,
Your string could soone to sadder tenor° turne,
10 And teach the woods and waters to lament
Your dolefull dreriment.°
Now lay those sorrowfull complaints aside,
And having all your heads with girland crownd,
Helpe me mine owne loves prayses to resound,°
15 Ne let the same of° any be envide:
So Orpheus[3] did for his owne bride,
So I unto my selfe alone will sing,
The woods shall to me answer and my Eccho ring.

[2]

Early before the worlds light giving lampe,
20 His golden beame upon the hils doth spred,
Having disperst the nights unchearefull dampe,
Doe ye awake, and with fresh lusty hed,[4]
Go to the bowre° of my belovéd love,   chamber
My truest turtle dove,
25 Bid her awake; for Hymen[5] is awake,
And long since ready forth his maske to move,
With his bright Tead° that flames with many a flake,°   torch/spark
And many a bachelor to waite on him,
In theyr fresh garments trim.
30 Bid her awake therefore and soone her dight,°   dress
For lo the wishéd day is come at last,
That shall for al the paynes and sorrowes past,
Pay to her usury of long delight:
And whylest she doth her dight,
35 Doe ye to her of joy and solace° sing,   pleasure
That all the woods may answer and your eccho ring.

---

† Literally, Greek for "before the bedchamber," the first known use of the term in English. Warkentin 1990E, "Amoretti, Epithalamion," comments on structure, mythic resonances, originality, and tone.
1. The nine Muses.
2. E.g., "Aprill" in *The Shepheardes Calender* and much of *The Faerie Queene*, notably the proems. Lines 7–11 may refer to poems in *Complaints* such as *The Ruines of Time*.
3. Cf. *Amoretti* 40; the singer Orpheus moved Pluto to release the dead Eurydice, but he lost her again when he disobeyed a promise not to look back as he led her home.
4. I.e., vigor.
5. The torchbearing god of marriage who presided over weddings; cf. Catullus, *Carmina* 61.1–15.

margin glosses: tenor° mood   dreriment° grief   resound° celebrate   of° by

[3]

Bring with you all the Nymphes that you can heare[6]
Both of the rivers and the forrests greene:
And of the sea that neighbours to her neare,
40 Al with gay girlands goodly wel beseene.[7]
And let them also with them bring in hand,
Another gay girland
For my fayre love of lillyes and of roses,
Bound truelove wise with a blew silke riband.[8]
45 And let them make great store of bridale poses,°   *posies*
And let them eeke° bring store of other flowers   *also*
To deck the bridale bowers.
And let the ground whereas her foot shall tread,
For feare the stones her tender foot should wrong
50 Be strewed with fragrant flowers all along,
And diapred lyke the discolored mead.[9]
Which done, doe at her chamber dore awayt,
For she will waken strayt,°   *straightway*
The whiles doe ye this song unto her sing,
55 The woods shall to you answer and your Eccho ring.

(margin, handwritten: Bring flowers)

[4]

Ye Nymphes of Mulla[1] which with carefull heed,
The silver scaly trouts doe tend full well,
And greedy pikes which use therein to feed,
(Those trouts and pikes all others doo excell)
60 And ye likewise which keepe the rushy lake,
Where none doo fishes take,
Bynd up the locks the which hang scatterd light,
And in his waters which your mirror make,
Behold your faces as the christall bright,
65 That when you come whereas my love doth lie,
No blemish she may spie.
And eke ye lightfoot mayds which keepe the deere,[2]
That on the hoary mountayne use to towre,[3]
And the wylde wolves which seeke them to devoure,[4]
70 With your steele darts doo chace from comming neer
Be also present heere,
To helpe to decke her and to help to sing,
That all the woods may answer and your eccho ring.

(margin, handwritten: Flows near Castle Kilcolman)

6. I.e., that can hear you.
7. I.e., attractively adorned.
8. Symbolizing the fidelity of true love.
9. I.e., diversely adorned like the varicolored meadows.
1. The river Awbeg, near Spenser's Irish estate of Kilcolman; cf. *Mutabilitie* vi.41.
2. Cf. Textual Notes.
3. A hawking term meaning "to soar"; here, "to frequent high places."
4. Cf. *Mutabilitie* vi.55 and note.

[5]

Wake, now my love, awake;[5] for it is time,
75 The Rosy Morne long since left Tithones[6] bed,
    All ready to her silver coche to clyme,
    And Phoebus gins to shew his glorious hed.
    Hark how the cheerefull birds do chaunt theyr laies
    And carroll of loves praise.
80 The merry Larke hir mattins° sings aloft,   *morning song*
    The thrush replyes, the Mavis descant playes,[7]
    The Ouzell° shrills, the Ruddock° warbles soft,   *blackbird/robin*
    So goodly all agree with sweet consent,
    To this dayes merriment.
85 Ah my deere love why doe ye sleepe thus long,
    When meeter° were that ye should now awake,   *more fitting*
    T'awayt the comming of your joyous make,°   *mate*
    And hearken to the birds lovelearnéd song,
    The deawy leaves among.
90 For they of joy and pleasance to you sing,
    That all the woods them answer and theyr eccho ring.

[6]

My love is now awake out of her dreame,
    And her fayre eyes like stars that dimméd were
    With darksome cloud, now shew theyr goodly beams
    More bright then Hesperus[8] his head doth rere.
    Come now ye damzels, daughters of delight,
    Helpe quickly her to dight,
    But first come ye fayre houres[9] which were begot
    In Joves sweet paradice, of Day and Night,
100 Which doe the seasons of the yeare allot,
    And al that ever in this world is fayre
    Doe make and still° repayre.   *continually*
    And ye three handmayds of the Cyprian Queene,[1]
    The which doe still adorne her beauties pride,
105 Helpe to addorne my beautifullest bride:
    And as ye her array, still throw betweene°   *at intervals*
    Some graces to be seene,
    And as ye use to Venus, to her sing,
    The whiles the woods shal answer and your eccho ring.

5. Cf. the Song of Solomon 2.10–13; the Song was read as an allegory of the love between Christ
   and "the faithful soule or his Church . . . appointed to be his spouse" (headnote in the Geneva
   translation). The Elizabethan prayerbook says marriage was "instituted of God in paradise" and
   signifies "the mystical union, that is betwixt Christ and his Church."
6. The husband of Aurora, goddess of the dawn; cf. Homer, *Iliad* 11.1–2.
7. I.e., the thrush carols the melody. Such bird consorts were conventional in medieval poetry; cf.
   Chaucer's *Romance of the Rose* 655–68.
8. The evening star, usually but not always Venus; as in *Prothalamion* 164, Spenser associates
   Hesperus with the morning star (usually Venus).
9. On the Hours, see *Mutabilitie* vii.45; cf. Comes (*Mythologiae* 4.16), who says the Hours control
   the seasons and preserve natural beauty. See also A. K. Hieatt, *Short Time's Endless Monument*
   (New York, 1960) 32–41.
1. I.e., the Graces (Aglaia, Euphrosyne, and Thalia), attendant on Venus, who was born from the
   sea near Cyprus.

[7]

110 Now is my love all ready forth to come,
Let all the virgins therefore well awayt,
And ye fresh boyes that tend upon her groome
Prepare your selves; for he is comming strayt.
Set all your things in seemely good aray
115 Fit for so joyfull day,
The joyfulst day that ever sunne did see.
Faire Sun, shew forth thy favourable ray,
And let thy lifull° heat not fervent be   *life-giving*
For feare of burning her sunshyny face,
120 Her beauty to disgrace.°   *mar*
O fayrest Phoebus, father of the Muse,[2]
If ever I did honour thee aright,
Or sing the thing, that mote° thy mind delight, *might*
Doe not thy servants simple boone° refuse,   *request*
125 But let this day let this one day be myne,
Let all the rest be thine.
Then I thy soverayne prayses loud wil sing,
That all the woods shal answer and theyr eccho ring.

[8]

Harke how the Minstrels gin to shrill aloud
130 Their merry Musick that resounds from far,
The pipe, the tabor, and the trembling Croud,[3]
That well agree withouten breach or jar.°   *discord*
But most of all the Damzels doe delite,
When they their tymbrels° smyte,   *tambourines*
135 And thereunto doe daunce and carrol sweet,
That all the sences they doe ravish quite,
The whyles the boyes run up and downe the street,
Crying aloud with strong confuséd noyce,
As if it were one voyce.
140 *Hymen iö Hymen, Hymen*[4] they do shout,
That even to the heavens theyr shouting shrill
Doth reach, and all the firmament doth fill,
To which the people standing all about,
As in approvance doe thereto applaud
145 And loud advaunce her laud,[5]
And evermore they *Hymen Hymen* sing,
That al the woods them answer and theyr eccho ring.

---

2. Usually Spenser agrees with Hesiod (*Theogony* 77) in making Jove the Muses' sire; to call Apollo their father may show the influence of some other source but is typical of his willingness to modify established myth.
3. I.e., bagpipe (cf. *The Faerie Queene* VI.x.18), drum, and fiddle, used in Irish popular music.
4. The ritual cry at Roman weddings; cf. Catullus, *Carmina* 61.
5. I.e., sing her praises.

[9]

Diana (handwritten annotation)

Loe where she comes along with portly° pace,   *stately*
Lyke Phoebe[6] from her chamber of the East,

bride arriving (handwritten annotation)

150 Arysing forth to run her mighty race,[7]
Clad all in white, that seemes° a virgin best.   *suits*
So well it her beseemes that ye would weene
Some angell she had beene.
Her long loose yellow locks lyke golden wyre,
155 Sprinckled with perle, and perling[8] flowres a tweene,
Doe lyke a golden mantle her attyre,
And being crownéd with a girland greene,
Seeme lyke some mayden Queene.[9]
Her modest eyes abashéd to behold
160 So many gazers, as on her do stare,
Upon the lowly ground affixéd are.
Ne dare lift up her countenance too bold,
But blush to heare her prayses sung so loud,
So farre from being proud.[1]
165 Nathlesse° doe ye still loud her prayses sing.   *nevertheless*
That all the woods may answer and your eccho ring.

[10]

Tell me ye merchants daughters did ye see
So fayre a creature in your towne before,
So sweet, so lovely, and so mild as she,

praising thru physical attributes (handwritten annotation)

170 Adornd with beautyes grace and vertues store,°   *wealth*
Her goodly eyes lyke Saphyres shining bright,
Her forehead yvory white,
Her cheekes lyke apples which the sun hath rudded,°   *reddened*
Her lips lyke cherryes charming men to byte,
175 Her brest like to a bowle of creame uncrudded,°   *uncurdled*
Her paps lyke lyllies budded,
Her snowie necke lyke to a marble towre,[2]
And all her body like a pallace fayre,
Ascending uppe with many a stately stayre,
180 To honors seat and chastities sweet bowre.[3]
Why stand ye still ye virgins in amaze,
Upon her so to gaze,
Whiles ye forget your former lay to sing,
To which the woods did answer and your eccho ring.

6. Diana, virgin goddess of the moon.
7. In Psalm 19 the sun rises like "a bridegroom coming out of his chamber, and rejoiceth as a strong man to run a race." Wishing, as in *The Faerie Queene* III, to indicate female chastity's mysterious power, Spenser changes the mighty racer's gender.
8. Winding; or perhaps lacework flowers.
9. Perhaps gracefully recalling Elizabeth I; cf. *Amoretti* 74.
1. In the first sixty sonnets of *Amoretti* the lover had often complained of his lady's cruel pride.
2. "Thy neck is as a tower of ivory" (Song of Solomon 7.4); the allusion well concludes a catalog of attractions drawing on classical and Renaissance conventions, for it points to a beauty yet more powerful and directive. Comparing a woman to a building or city (or vice versa) was traditional.
3. I.e., to the head, seat of reason and of the higher faculties generally.

[11]

185 But if ye saw that which no eyes can see,
The inward beauty of her lively spright,[4]
Garnisht with heavenly guifts of high degree,
Much more then would ye wonder at that sight,
And stand astonisht lyke to those which red°   saw
190 Medusaes mazeful hed.[5]
There dwels sweet love and constant chastity,
Unspotted fayth and comely womanhood,
Regard of honour and mild modesty,
There vertue raynes as Queene in royal throne,
195 And giveth lawes alone.
The which the base affections[6] doe obay,
And yeeld theyr services unto her will,
Ne thought of thing uncomcly° ever may   unbecoming
Thereto approch to tempt her mind to ill.
200 Had ye once seene these her celestial threasures,
And unrevealéd pleasures,
Then would ye wonder and her prayses sing,
That al the woods should answer and your echo ring.

[12]

Open the temple gates unto my love,
205 Open them wide that she may enter in,[7]
And all the postes adorne as doth behove,[8]
And all the pillours deck with girlands trim,
For to recyve this Saynt[9] with honour dew,
That commeth in to you.
210 With trembling steps and humble reverence,
She commeth in, before th'almighties vew,
Of her ye virgins learne obedience,
When so ye come into those holy places,
To humble your proud faces;
215 Bring her up to th'high altar, that she may
The sacred ceremonies there partake,
The which do endlesse matrimony make,
And let the roring Organs loudly play
The praises of the Lord in lively notes,
220 The whiles with hollow throates

---

4. I.e., living spirit; soul.
5. All who looked directly at Medusa, a Gorgon whose hair Athena had turned to serpents, became stone: see Ovid, *Metamorphoses* 4. 780–81. The "mazeful" head bears a snaky labyrinth and puts the viewer into an *amaze*ment of thought. The shocking simile hints that spiritual beauty can beget awed fear (Young 1973) and that erotic desire can include anxiety.
6. I.e., the lower passions.
7. "Open yee the gates, that the righteous nation which keepeth the truth may enter in" (Isaiah 26.2). Cf. Psalms 14.7, often read as referring to Christ.
8. I.e., adorn the doorposts, as is fitting. Symbolic decoration of doorposts (e.g., with myrtle, sacred to Venus) was common at ancient weddings. Spenser comfortably mixes classical and Christian elements (cf. 242–60, 409–26), although (says Wall 1988) the poem's biblical and liturgical echoes also allow him to revise and "overgo" the classical epithalamic tradition.
9. In Protestant terminology, a "saint" was anyone assured of salvation.

The Choristers the joyous Antheme sing,
That al the woods may answere and their eccho ring.

[13]

the ceremony

Behold whiles she before the altar stands
Hearing the holy priest that to her speakes
225 And blesseth her with his two happy hands,[1]
How the red roses flush up in her cheekes,
And the pure snow with goodly vermill° stayne,   *the blushes/colours*   vermilion
Like crimsin dyde in grayne,[2]
That even th'Angels which continually,
230 About the sacred Altare doe remaine,
Forget their service and about her fly,
Ofte peeping in her face that seemes more fayre,
The more they on it stare.
But her sad° eyes still fastened on the ground,   grave
235 Are governéd with goodly modesty,
That suffers not one looke to glaunce awry,
Which may let in a little thought unsownd.°   immodest
Why blush ye love to give to me your hand,
The pledge of all our band?°   bond
240 Sing ye sweet Angels, Alleluya sing,
That all the woods may answere and your eccho ring.

[14]

Now al is done; bring home the bride againe,
Bring home the triumph of our victory,   *Rats! Why is getting the bride a victory?!*
Bring home with you the glory of her gaine,[3]
245 With joyance bring her and with jollity.
Never had man more joyfull day then this,
Whom heaven would heape with blis.
Make feast therefore now all this live long day,
This day for ever to me holy is,
250 Poure out the wine without restraint or stay,   *Getting drunk at the reception*
Poure not by cups, but by the belly full,
Poure out to all that wull,°   will
And sprinkle all the postes and wals with wine,[4]
That they may sweat, and drunken be withall.
255 Crowne ye God Bacchus with a coronall,°   garland
And Hymen also crowne with wreathes of vine,
And let the Graces daunce unto the rest;
For they can doo it best:
The whiles the maydens doe theyr carroll sing,
260 To which the woods shal answer and theyr eccho ring.   *June II*

1. I.e., hands that bestow happiness by virtue of the priest's blessing.
2. I.e., thoroughly; fast.
3. I.e., the glory of having gained her.
4. A traditional practice at Roman weddings.

[15]

Ring ye the bels,[5] ye yong men of the towne,
And leave your wonted° labors for this day: *usual*
This day is holy; doe ye write it downe,
That ye for ever it remember may.
265 This day the sunne is in his chiefest hight,
With Barnaby the bright,[6]
From whence declining daily by degrees,
He somewhat loseth of his heat and light,
When once the Crab behind his back he sees.[7]
270 But for this time it ill ordainéd was,
To chose the longest day in all the yeare,
And shortest night, when longest fitter weare:
Yet never day so long, but late° would passe.
Ring ye the bels, to make it weare away,
275 And bonefiers make all day,
And daunce about them, and about them sing
That all the woods may answer, and your eccho ring.

[16]

Ah when will this long weary day have end,
And lende me leave to come unto my love?
280 How slowly do the houres theyr numbers spend?
How slowly does sad Time his feathers move?
Hast thee O fayrest Planet[8] to thy home
Within the Westerne fome:
Thy tyred steedes long since have need of rest.
285 Long though it be, at last I see it gloome,°   *grow dark*
And the bright evening star with golden creast
Appeare out of the East.
Fayre childe of beauty, glorious lampe of love
That all the host of heaven in rankes doost lead,
290 And guydest lovers through the nightes dread,
How chearefully thou lookest from above,
And seemst to laugh atweene thy twinkling light
As joying in the sight

5. Perhaps an artful "change ringing," not a mere random if enthusiastic ringing of bells. In either case, the poem will become steadily quieter.
6. St. Barnabas's Day, June 11, was the summer solstice in the old calendar; bells and bonfires had long greeted the solstice (or Midsummer's Day, June 24); but many now called them "papist," and in England the fun was dying out (D. Cressy, *Bonfires and Bells* [Berkeley, 1989]). Chinitz 1991 shows how lines 263–64 fall at the poem's "golden section" (the point at which dividing the poem would give two parts with a ratio equaling that of the larger part to the whole); such a proportion, thought pleasing to eye and mind, contributes to a poetic structure that "imitates" the cosmos.
7. On the solstice the sun is about to quit the "house" of Gemini (the Twins) for Cancer (the Crab) and daylight will slowly diminish; he will see the Crab at his back because in the old system he daily travels 359° while the fixed stars turn a full 360°, allowing the zodiac's houses one by one to overtake him. Or, because the houses no longer in fact coincide with their constellations, Spenser may mean that Sol is leaving Cancer (cf. *The Faerie Queene* V. Pr.).
8. I.e., the sun, in the Ptolemaic system a planet circling the earth.

Of these glad many which for joy doe sing,
295 That all the woods them answer and their echo ring.

[17]

Now ceasse ye damsels your delights forepast;
Enough is it, that all the day was youres:
Now day is doen, and night is nighing fast:
Now bring the Bryde into the brydall boures.
300 Now night is come, now soone her disaray,°   undress
And in her bed her lay;
Lay her in lillies and in violets,
And silken courteins over her display,
And odourd° sheetes, and Arras coverlets.[9]   perfumed
305 Behold how goodly my faire love does ly
In proud humility;
Like unto Maia,[1] when as Jove her tooke,
In Tempe, lying on the flowry gras,
Twixt sleepe and wake, after she weary was,
310 With bathing in the Acidalian brooke.
Now it is night, ye damsels may be gon,
And leave my love alone,
And leave likewise your former lay to sing:
The woods no more shal answere, nor your echo ring.

[18]

315 Now welcome night, thou night so long expected,
That long daies labour doest at last defray,°   pay for
And all my cares, which cruell love collected,
Hast sumd in one, and cancelléd for aye:
Spread thy broad wing over my love and me,
320 That no man may us see,
And in thy sable mantle us enwrap,
From feare of perrill and foule horror free.
Let no false treason seeke us to entrap,
Nor any dread disquiet once annoy
325 The safety of our joy:
But let the night be calme and quietsome,
Without tempestuous storms or sad afray:°   fear
Lyke as when Jove with fayre Alcmena lay,
When he begot the great Tirynthian groome:
330 Or lyke as when he with thy selfe did lie,
And begot Majesty.[2]

9. Fine tapestry spreads.
1. Loveliest of Atlas's seven daughters (later stellified as the Pleiades), Maia bore Mercury (Hermes)
   to Jove; allusions to Tempe and "the Acidalian brooke" may derive from a hint in Comes,
   Mythologiae 5.5). Since it is now night, the refrain fittingly shifts to the negative; see Editors'
   Note.
2. Tradition calls Hercules (who dwelt at Tiryns, in Argolis) the son of Jove and Alcmena: cf.
   Metamorphoses 9.23–26. Spenser says Majesty's parents were Jove and Night, but Ovid identifies
   them as Honor and Reverence (*Fasti* 5.23).

And let the mayds and yongmen cease to sing:
Ne let the woods them answer, nor theyr eccho ring.

[19]

Let no lamenting cryes, nor dolefull teares,
335 Be heard all night within nor yet without:
Ne let false whispers, breeding hidden feares,
Breake gentle sleepe with misconceivéd dout.°   *fear*
Let no deluding dreames, nor dreadful sights
Make sudden sad affrights;
340 Ne let housefyres, nor lightnings helpelesse harmes,
Ne let the Pouke,[3] nor other evill sprights,
Ne let mischivous witches with theyr charmes,
Ne let hob Goblins, names whose sence we see not,
Fray° us with things that be not.   *terrify*
345 Let not the shriech Oule,[4] nor the Storke be heard:
Nor the night Raven that still° deadly yels,   *continually*
Nor damnéd ghosts cald up with mighty spels,
Nor griesly vultures make us once affeard:
Ne let th'unpleasant Quyre of Frogs still croking
350 Make us to wish theyr choking.
Let none of these theyr drery accents sing;
Ne let the woods them answer, nor theyr eccho ring.

[20]

But let stil Silence trew night watches keepe,
That sacred peace may in assurance rayne,
355 And tymely sleep, when it is tyme to sleepe,
May poure his limbs forth on your pleasant playne,
The whiles an hundred little wingéd loves,[5]
Like divers fethered doves,
Shall fly and flutter round about your bed,
360 And in the secret darke, that none reproves,
Their prety stealthes shal worke, and snares shal spread
To filch away sweet snatches of delight,
Conceald through covert night.
Ye sonnes of Venus, play your sports at will,
365 For greedy pleasure, carelesse of your toyes,°   *amorous dallying*
Thinks more upon her paradise of joyes,
Then what ye do, albe it good or ill.
All night therefore attend your merry play,
For it will soone be day:

3. Puck (Hobgoblin or Robin Goodfellow) was usually thought a malicious spirit. On Spenser's
wishes, with analogues in other epithalamia, see Editors' Note; they may also echo the traditional
pre-Reformation blessing of the bed in which the priest banishes illusory demons (Prescott 1985).
4. Screech owls and ravens are birds of ill omen. The stork is listed with these and other "unclean"
birds in Deuteronomy 14.12–18; Ovid says it "claps its rattling bill" (*Metamorphoses* 6.97).
5. I.e., little cupids ("amoretti"), playful figures in the Anacreontic style that flutter often in Renaissance love poems. Spenser may remember Du Bellay's *Epithalame* 307–10. Doves (358) are
sacred to Venus.

370 Now none doth hinder you, that say or sing,
    Ne will the woods now answer, nor your Eccho ring.

[21]

Who is the same, which at my window peepes?
Or whose is that faire face, that shines so bright,
Is it not Cinthia,[6] she that never sleepes,
375 But walkes about high heaven al the night?
O fayrest goddesse, do thou not envy
My love with me to spy:
For thou likewise didst love, though now unthought,[7]
And for a fleece of woll,° which privily,   wool
380 The Latmian shephard once unto thee brought,
His pleasures with thee wrought.
Therefore to us be favorable now;
And sith of wemens labours thou hast charge,[8]
And generation goodly dost enlarge,
385 Encline thy will t'effect our wishfull vow,
And the chast wombe informe with timely seed,   *impregnating.*
That may our comfort breed:
Till which we cease our hopefull hap[9] to sing,
Ne let the woods us answere, nor our Eccho ring.

[22]

390 And thou great Juno, which with awful might   awe-inspiring
The lawes of wedlock still dost patronize,
And the religion° of the faith first plight   sanctity
With sacred rites hast taught to solemnize:
And eeke for comfort often calléd art
395 Of women in their smart,°   pains
Eternally bind thou this lovely° band,   loving
And all thy blessings unto us impart.
And thou glad Genius,[1] in whose gentle hand,
The bridale bowre and geniall bed[2] remaine,
400 Without blemish or staine,
And the sweet pleasures of theyr loves delight
With secret ayde doest succour and supply,
Till they bring forth the fruitfull progeny,
Send us the timely fruit of this same night.
405 And thou fayre Hebe,[3] and thou Hymen free,

6. Goddess of the moon, Diana.
7. I.e., not thought of. Cynthia loved Endymion, a shepherd whom Jove put into perpetual sleep;
   he lies in a cave on Mount Latmus, in Asia Minor, where she can kiss him. Some said she had
   children by him; others read the sleep and kisses as religious contemplation or astronomical
   discovery (Comes, *Mythologiae* 4.8). Virgil (*Georgics* 3.391–93) says Pan gave the fleece, but
   Spenser follows later mythography.
8. Both Diana and Juno were invoked as Lucina, goddess who "brings to light" and thus presides
   over childbirth.
9. I.e., the lot for which we hope.
1. The god of birth and generation; cf. *The Faerie Queene* II.xii.47, note, and III.vi.31–32.
2. I.e., generative as well as pleasant bed (with a play on the god's name).
3. Daughter of Juno, and cupbearer to the gods; Spenser, following Ovid and Renaissance mythographers, regards her as goddess of youth and rejuvenation (cf. *Metamorphoses* 9.397–401).

Grant that it may so be.
Til which we cease your further prayse to sing,
Ne any woods shal answer, nor your Eccho ring.

[23]

And ye high heavens, the temple of the gods,
410 In which a thousand torches flaming bright
Doe burne, that to us wretched earthly clods,
In dreadful darknesse lend desiréd light;
And all ye powers which in the same[4] remayne,
More then we men can fayne,°   *imagine*
415 Poure out your blessing on us plentiously,
And happy influence upon us raine,
That we may raise a large posterity,
Which from the earth, which they may long possesse,
With lasting happinesse,
420 Up to your haughty pallaces may mount,
And for the guerdon° of theyr glorious merit   *reward*
May heavenly tabernacles there inherit,
Of blessed Saints for to increase the count.
So let us rest, sweet love, in hope of this,[5]
425 And cease till then our tymely joyes to sing,
The woods no more us answer, nor our eccho ring.

[24]

Song[6] made in lieu of many ornaments, A
With which my love should duly have bene dect,° B   *adorned*
Which cutting off through hasty accidents, A
430 Ye would not stay your dew time to expect,° B   *await*
But promist both to recompens, A
Be unto her a goodly ornament, A
And for short time an endlesse moniment. A   *memorial*

Editors' Note

The sonnet sequence *Amoretti* and the marriage ode *Epithalamion* were published together in 1595, a circumstance supporting the belief that the poems
refer specifically and consistently to Spenser's courtship of Elizabeth Boyle and
their marriage (his second), at Cork, in the summer of 1594. Doubtless some
sonnets were written earlier (*Amoretti* 8 before 1580) and addressed to some
other woman or women. Nevertheless, the reference in *Amoretti* 74 to a beloved
named Elizabeth, a pattern of calendrical allusions in the sonnets that situate
the betrothal in the spring of 1594, and the mention in *Epithalamion* of the

---

4. I.e., in the heavens. "Powers" may refer both to the ninefold angelic hierarchy and to stellar "influences" on us.
5. The rhyme is defective; see Editors' Note. The prayer for children echoes the marriage service.
6. The envoy addresses the poem itself, the tangled syntax eventuating in a syntactically ambiguous imperative ordering it to be both decoration and "moniment" (the word means memorial, but can connote a warning).
7. Perhaps alluding to an unexpected change in wedding plans, but see Editors' Note.

summer solstice (then June 11) make it probable that during 1594 Spenser composed new verses and reworked old ones so as to make two cycles of poetry for his new wife.

Any poet with Spenser's ambitions was likely to try his hand at love sonnets. The influence of Petrarch's *Rime* had touched English poetry some years earlier, notably the lyrics of Wyatt and Surrey, and the appearance in 1582 of Thomas Watson's *Hekatompathia* had indicated a renewed interest in Petrarchan modes by younger English poets. But the Petrarchan sonnet cycle in English became fashionable with the posthumous appearance in 1591 of Philip Sidney's *Astrophil and Stella*: Daniel's *Delia*, Constable's *Diana*, Drayton's *Idea's Mirror*, and Lodge's *Phillis* are merely the best known among the sequences published before 1595. English love poets (like those in Italy and France) were struck by Petrarch's linked arrangement of economically rhymed sonnets, by his delicate fusing of Neoplatonism with physical desire, by his use of the "conceit" (an ingenious and elaborate metaphor central to the structure of the poem) as an instrument with which to convey love's paradoxical nature, by his significant repetitions or puns, by his sense of a divided self, and perhaps by his association of political concerns with the discourse of erotic longing. Moreover, in recent years some critics, particularly "new historicists," have argued that Petrarchan language played a part in England's political life as the queen and those who sought her favor collaborated in refashioning her as a mistress to be courted and her courtiers as lovelorn wooers.[1] *Amoretti*'s contribution to this mythmaking is unclear, although sonnets 33 and 80 refer, a little nervously, to the queen and sonnet 74 praises her (but not as a Petrarchan beloved). Indeed, one can read the sequence as a vacation from the epic task of public praise, advice, and reimagining: Bernard 1989 calls this "pastoral of love" the "purification of eros in a pastoral oasis of contemplation" (176).

Each of the more gifted English sonneteers, of course, developed an individual manner, occasionally making sturdy if unconvincing denials of Petrarch's influence. Although Spenser adopts a number of Petrarchan conceits, his own approach is especially individual; even his rhyme scheme is neither quite the Italian (ending as it does with an often snappy couplet) nor the "Shakespearean" form established by Surrey. What most sets *Amoretti* apart, though, is its redirecting of desire away from an unobtainable mistress to a woman the poet can marry and whose own erotic nature can be aroused without dishonor. Spenser thus applies Reformation thought on sex and marriage to Petrarchan tradition, for Protestants tended to elevate married sexuality above celibacy. It is appropriate, therefore, that Spenser concludes his sonnet sequence not with longer poetic complaint (as had, for example, Daniel and Lodge), but with a nuptial song.

Both sequence and epithalamion, moreover, are structured in ways that underline this rewriting of tradition. *Amoretti* is in some sense a lyric garland (note Spenser's punning references to leaves), not least because the verse alludes at times to the circling year. Alexander Dunlop[2] has shown how these allusions give *Amoretti* coherence. His argument recognizes that Elizabethan England had at least two calendars: one, the calendar of social custom and almanacs, began on January 1, while the other, the calendar of the civil year, started on March 25 (date, traditionally, of the angel's annunciation to Mary; the church calendar itself, however, begins in late autumn with Advent). If, as we are

---

1. Marotti 1982; cf. Leonard Forster, *The Icy Fire: Five Studies in European Petrarchism* (Cambridge, 1969), ch. 4, and Louis A. Montrose, "Celebration and Insinuation," *Renaissance Drama* 8 (1977): 3–35.
2. 1980; see also "The Unity of Spenser's *Amoretti*," *Silent Poetry*, ed. Alastair Fowler (London, 1970) 153–69.

invited to do, we imagine sonnet 22 being said on Ash Wednesday, then 68, celebrating Easter, comes after precisely the right number of sonnets to parallel Lent's forty days of deprivation together with its Sundays. Amoretti is thus in one regard a triptych: twenty-one sonnets precede a Lenten sequence that is followed by a second group of twenty-one. Furthermore, if the new year referred to in sonnet 62 is the one beginning on March 25, this identifies the year as 1594, when Easter indeed fell six days later, on March 31 (see Amoretti 68). Some critics (e.g., Kaske 1978) deny that the sonnets' implied time scheme refers to a segment of one year, while others have sought to expand Dunlop's discovery by elaborating some larger pattern that would incorporate Epithalamion (e.g., Thompson 1985, Fukuda 1988) or by tracing further connections with the church calendar (Prescott 1985, Johnson 1990); it may be no coincidence, for example, that there are eighty-nine sonnets in the sequence and eighty-nine sets of readings for special days in the Elizabethan Book of Common Prayer.

Do such number games matter? Yes, and precisely because the Petrarchan tradition that Spenser both assumes and subverts had long postulated a division between human and divine love. Even if one believes, as subtler Christians often have, that what Dante called "the love that moves the sun and the other stars" also moves mortals to seek joy (and babies) from human embraces, most sonneteers adopted a version of that love that was inspiring but forbidden. Petrarch's Laura and Sidney's Stella, for example are married: their poet-lovers condemn themselves to a passion that must remain sexually barren even if productive of verses. Ronsard and Desportes, on the other hand, were in clerical orders and could not marry anyone. Petrarch's followers, and it was hard to write love sonnets and not follow him, dealt with this poetically useful frustration in imaginative ways, allegorizing it, regendering it, politicizing it, satirizing it, and occasionally reworking it in homoerotic terms. But English poets labored under the additional burden of belatedness, of struggling not merely to repeat what had already been said abroad. Spenser's answer was to address his sequence to someone he might lawfully love and marry. Hence the significance of his references to the Christian liturgy. Liturgical references were by no means new in the Petrarchan tradition, but the lovers created by Petrarch, Du Bellay, Desportes, and the others finally cannot reconcile love for God with sexual longing for the women they love. Sidney put the matter well in his seventy-first sonnet: his reason tells him that the lady's goodness inspires a love of virtue—"But ah, Desire still cries 'Give me some food.' " Spenser's lover can hope to satisfy that hunger through a legitimate and earthly consummation of his passion, which is why the Easter sonnet, 68, records both Christ's victory over death and the poet's triumph over the tradition Petrarch had fathered. The calendrical subtext, moreover, helps explain the lonely anxiety of Amoretti's closing sonnets: according to both the prayerbook and Christian history, after Easter comes a time of waiting, separation, and sorrow. To be sure, other Renaissance sonnet sequences often stop inconclusively (Neely 1978), if only because writers find blocked desire more useful than gratification—bliss can silence a lover.

Amoretti thus sets sexuality in a larger scheme of love, particularly love that is open to the paradoxical sacrifice and recovery of the self, to humility that triumphs, to unearned grace that follows defeat, and to bonds that both tie and liberate. But the religious component in Spenser's love poetry by no means renders it serene. Quite the contrary. Recent critics, like Loewenstein 1987, have found in Spenser's sonnets and their often "unquiet thought" (Amoretti 2) an acknowledgment that love includes narcissism, manipulation, and an aggressive reach for mastery; at the very least the sequence now seems to have a tension that older critics found missing (cf. J. Miller 1979). Spenser creates this complexity in part though a polyvalent imagery that helps tie the sonnets together while allowing their implications to develop dynamically; readers might note, particularly, how he variously treats eyes, smiles, food, birds, war, pride, the language of law, and—perhaps most significantly—binding, weaving, and enclosure. More than in some other sequences, furthermore, there is narrative interest as we wait for the lady to transcend her "pride" or hesitations and for the lover to find that his pushy method of courtship, although often charming, must fail. As he rests for a while from pursuit (*Amoretti* 67), the lady softens and, despite her residual fear of change, allows herself to be caught by love ("her owne will"). Some see in this gift of herself evidence that she thinks the lover has at last become worthy of her; others believe the poetry undercuts confidence in effort and self-improvement: a "critique—a Christian critique— of pagan self-sufficiency is at the center of the poet's argument" (Turner 1988, 295).

[margin note: The plot]

These are serious matters, but *Amoretti* has not ceased to seem charming and even funny (see Martz 1961, on pp. 804–9 of this edition, and Bieman 1984). Johnson 1990 shows how dazzling its wordplay can be, and there is delicious comedy as the middle-aged lover courts an apparently spirited younger woman who refuses to take his histrionics seriously—if indeed he means them seriously—and who can tease him as the two bend over her embroidery (*Amoretti* 71), force him out of the house and into the rain (*Amoretti* 46), and dispute his understanding of his own emblem, the laurel (*Amoretti* 29). Modern feminist scholarship has encouraged us to look at older love poetry with a wary eye, but it is still possible to think that even the more conventionally Petrarchan sonnets need not be read solemnly: although identifying the tone of Renaissance poetry is difficult, Spenser's love poetry is more engaging if the possibility of affectionate humor is allowed. A little exaggerated Petrarchism might amuse a clever young woman, Spenser may have felt, and so to add color and variety he wove some well-made conceits into the earlier part of his wreath, conceits that his own poetry then establishes are not adequate to express love's depth.

After *Amoretti*, the 1595 volume offers four untitled poems in a style called "Anacreontic." Kaske 1978 intriguingly suggests that their sexual innuendo answers the sonnets' expressions of desire. Yet the Roman poet Claudian had opened his epithalamion with similarly smiling erotic verses, and Neely 1978 notes that English sonneteers like Daniel (and later Shakespeare) likewise used more lighthearted poetry as a transition to a longer poem. It may be that, aside from their possible role in some larger numerical pattern, Spenser's fashionably mannered lyrics are meant to imitate Claudian's model or to ease our way to a new flavor or mood, like a sorbet between courses or an entr'acte between two parts of a play.

[margin note: Epithalamion] The magnificent marriage ode, *Epithalamion*, follows next, and despite the separate title page it seems reasonable to assume that the marriage celebrated is the same one anticipated by *Amoretti*. Thomas Greene[3] has described how this modified canzone is related to a classical and Renaissance "epithalamic" convention most influentially represented by the sixty-first and sixty-fourth odes of the Roman poet Catullus. Spenser is remarkably innovative, however, in simultaneously playing the roles of bridegroom, poet, and master of ceremonies, an accumulation of functions that may add to the poem's tonality of celebratory triumph. And, once again, the poem's structure helps Spenser situate human

---

3. *Comparative Literature* 9 (1957): 215–28; see also Dubrow 1990E.

love both in a fallen world of time and in a universe governed by a divine love that subsumes and validates the fertile sexuality of loving marriage. As A. Kent Hieatt[4] has shown, the poem is built in terms of temporal divisions: the twenty-four stanzas "are associated with the personified Hours who attend the bride"; the changed refrain in stanza 17 and the mention of nightfall in line 300 divide the poem so as to parallel the proportion of light and darkness in southern Ireland on June 11 (Spenser's calculation is off by a few minutes, but so was that of Renaissance almanacs); and there are 365 "long lines" of five feet or more.

Another aspect of Hieatt's proposal bears on the "envoy" and the apparent marring of Spenser's rhyme scheme by the omission of a short line following line 424. Hieatt suggests that Spenser deliberately introduces these features, recognizing that (in the Ptolemaic system) when the sphere of the fixed stars completes its geocentric orbit of 360 degrees, the sun still falls short by 1 degree. Spenser, says Hieatt, "ostensibly ends his poem in its 359th long line [i.e., line 426], symbolizing in one way the incomplete circle of the sun at the time when the heavenly hours and the celestial sphere are completing theirs, but . . . the envoy, adding six more long lines, expresses symbolically what this daily incompleteness of the sun entails: the creation of the measure of the solar years of 365 days, symbolized by the poem including its [envoy]" (46). As for the irregularity after line 424, there are 68 short lines in the poem (corresponding to the total of seasons, months, and weeks); just as the "symbolic lack at the annual level" is made good by the 6 long lines of the envoy, so the short 431st line, "But promist both to recompens," dramatically makes Spenser's poetic circle just. Spenser's temporal allusions, then, register the flaws in the fallen world of time and death; but the poem suggests several consolations: love, babies, God's "heavenly tabernacles," and poetry.

Set against these parallels with time's circles is a carefully wrought symmetry. Hieatt suggests that the stanzas are paired, one with thirteen, two with fourteen, and so forth; many prefer the argument of Max Wickert[5] for a bilateral symmetry. The poem moves like a pageant or wedding procession from the bride's home to the town and church and eventually to the couple's bedchamber; and it does so by crossing concentric sets of images and evocations. Spenser begins with darkness, silence, and the naming of mythological figures; gradually as the sun rises the human community gathers to witness the wedding and to revel afterward; finally, well after sunset, the newlyweds are alone and the mythological and cosmological references reappear. At the center is the ceremony itself, complete with angels (no mere "amoretti" [little Cupids], but perhaps showing what amoretti can become).

As with *Amoretti*, however, recent criticism has noted how Spenser summons—if only to exorcise—the feelings of loss, aggressiveness, and anxiety that can accompany transition and initiation, especially when the liminal moment involves sexuality. The custom according to which a new husband carries his bride over the threshold recalls this ancient suspicion that even a happy wedding entails dangers hard to describe explicitly. Spenser's equivalent strategy is to evoke and then shoo away grotesque fantasy figures (stanza 19) and to employ images that are not wholly comfortable (e.g., likening himself in stanza 1 to Orpheus, who lost his wife, or the association in stanza 11 of his bride's stunning virtue with the petrifying power of Medusa). There is often, says Schenck 1988, a little elegy even in epithalamia; so too, Anderson 1984 insists

4. *Short Time's Endless Monument* (New York, 1960).
5. "Structure and Ceremony in Spenser's *Epithalamion*," ELH 35 (1968): 135–57.

that Spenser's great poem is not merely cheerful, and Loewenstein 1986 explores its "uncanny poetics." For many readers, of course (as for these critics), Spenser's awareness that human love can mix with fear, cruelty, grief, or deceit makes his affirmations of its beauty and legitimacy all the more powerfully moving.

Prothalamion†

1

Calme was the day, and through the trembling ayre,
Sweete breathing Zephyrus did softly play,
A gentle spirit, that lightly did delay°   *temper*
Hot Titans beames, which then did glyster° fayre: *shine*
5 When I whom sullein care,
Through discontent of my long fruitlesse stay
In Princes Court, and expectation vayne
Of idle hopes, which still doe fly away,
Like empty shaddowes, did aflict my brayne,[1]
10 Walkt forth to ease my payne
Along the shoare of silver streaming Themmes,
Whose rutty° Bancke, the which his River hemmes, *rooty*
Was paynted all with variable° flowers,   *various*
And all the meades adornd with daintie gemmes,
15 Fit to decke maydens bowres,
And crowne their Paramours,°   *lovers*
Against the Brydale day, which is not long:[2]
 Sweete Themmes runne softly, till I end my Song

2

There, in a Meadow, by the Rivers side,
20 A Flocke of Nymphes I chauncéd to espy,
All lovely Daughters of the Flood° thereby,   *river*
With goodly greenish locks all loose untyde,
As each had bene a Bryde,
And each one had a little wicker basket,
25 Made of fine twigs entrayléd° curiously,   *interlaced*

---

† The term, which signifies "a preliminary nuptial song," is invented by Spenser, who subtitles his poem, "a spousall verse." On the genre's tradition, see D. S. Norton, "The Tradition of Proth-alamia," *English Studies in Honor of James Southall Wilson* (Charlottesville, VA, 1951) 223–41. See also H. Smith, "The Use of Conventions in Spenser's Minor Poems," *Form and Convention in the Poetry of Edmund Spenser,* ed. W. Nelson (New York, 1961) 142–44. Bjorvand 1990E attends in historical contexts chiefly to thematic and structural aspects of the poem. P. Cheney 1990 argues that *Prothalamion* "functions as a [humanist] defense of Spenser's career." For Schenck 1988 the poem, "obsessed with the issue of literary patronage," remains "indispensable to a full acount of Spenser's poetic career."
1. The acquisition of an estate, and a certain social standing, in Ireland scarcely alleviated Spenser's continued longing for advancement at the court of Queen Elizabeth, in Westminster.
2. I.e., in anticipation of the bridal day, which is not far off. On the "fullness of Spenser's great refrain" see Fowler 1975 (79–80); also Hollander 1987. For comment on tensive irregularities in the refrain and their relevance to Spenser's presentation of "disappointed courtier [-poet] with . . . an occasion to celebrate," see H. Berger, Jr., "Spenser's *Prothalamion*: An Interpretation," *Essays in Criticism* 15 (1965), 363–80.

In which they gathered flowers to fill their flasket:°   *basket*
And with fine Fingers, cropt full feateously[3]
The tender stalkes on hye.
Of every sort, which in that Meadow grew,
30   They gathered some; the Violet pallid blew,
The little Dazie, that at evening closes,
The virgin Lillie, and the Primrose trew,
With store° of vermeil° Roses,   *abundance/scarlet*
To decke their Bridegromes posies,°   *bouquets*
35   Against the Brydale day, which was not long:
     Sweete Themmes runne softly, till I end my Song.

(handwritten margin note: They were gathering flowers)

3

With that, I saw two Swannes of goodly hewe,°   *appearance*
Come softly swimming downe along the Lee;[4]
Two fairer Birds I yet did never see:
40   The snow which doth the top of Pindus[5] strew,
Did never whiter shew,
Nor Jove himselfe when he a Swan would be
For love of Leda, whiter did appeare:[6]
Yet Leda was they say as white as he,
45   Yet not so white as these, nor nothing neare;
So purely white they were,
That even the gentle streame, the which them bare,
Seemed foule to[7] them, and bad his billowes spare°   *forbear*
To wet their silken feathers, least they might
50   Soyle their fayre plumes with water not so fayre
And marre their beauties bright,
That shone as heavens light,
Against their Brydale day, which was not long:
     Sweete Themmes runne softly, till I end my Song.

(handwritten margin note: The brides are white swans, comparable to none)

4

55   Eftsoones° the Nymphes, which now had Flowers their fill,   *presently*
Ran all in haste, to see that silver brood,[8]
As they came floating on the Christal Flood.
Whom when they sawe, they stood amazéd still,
Their wondring eyes to fill,

---

3. I.e., and with a delicate touch, plucked most dextrously. Fowler 1975 explores emblematic, mythological, and philosophical dimensions of flower gathering.

4. Flocks of swans were regularly to be seen on the Thames in Spenser's time; these two represent the brides-to-be, Elizabeth and Catherine Somerset, daughters of Edward Somerset, earl of Worcester. While "Lee" may refer generically to [any] "river, stream" (or, in the form "lea," to a grassland or meadow), Hieatt 1991 (in correspondence) makes a case for the river Lea, which enters the Thames from the north between Poplar and Canning Town; by this reading the swans swim upstream from the mouth of the Lea to the eastern border of the city of London at the Tower, and thence to Essex House.

5. "Pindus" properly refers to the mountainous western boundary of the Thessalian plain, in Greece. Ovid often alludes to Pindus's height (e.g., *Metamorphoses* 2.225); for Spenser, the mountain has mythical associations as well. Cf. *The Faerie Queene* III.iv.41.

6. Cf. *Metamorphoses* 6.109; and *The Faerie Queene* III.xi.32. Schenck 1988 finds a hint of Leda, "raped rather than wedded," in the "dirtied swans" of 50–51.

7. I.e., compared with.

8. I.e., that silvery pair of noble lineage.

60 Them seemed they never saw a sight so fayre,
Of Fowles so lovely, that they sure did deeme
Them heavenly borne, or to be that same payre
Which through the Skie draw Venus silver Teeme,[9]
For sure they did not seeme
65 To be begot of any earthly Seede,
But rather Angels or of Angels breede:°   race
Yet were they bred of Somers-heat[1] they say,
In sweetest Season, when each Flower and weede°   plant
The earth did fresh aray,
70 So fresh they seemed as day,
Even as their Brydale day, which was not long:
Sweete Themmes runne softly, till I end my Song.

5

Then forth they all out of their baskets drew,
Great store of Flowers, the honour° of the field,   glory
75 That to the sense did fragrant odours yeild,
All which upon those goodly Birds they threw,
And all the Waves did strew,
That like old Peneus Waters[2] they did seeme,
When downe along by pleasant Tempes shore
80 Scattred with Flowres, through Thessaly they streeme,
That they appeare through Lillies plenteous store,
Like a Brydes Chamber flore:
Two of those Nymphes, meane while, two Garlands bound,
Of freshest Flowres which in that Mead° they found,   meadow
85 The which presenting all in trim Array,
Their snowie Foreheads[3] therewithall they crownd,
Whil'st one did sing this Lay,
Prepared against that Day,
Against their Brydale day, which was not long:
90   Sweete Themmes runne softly, till I end my Song.

6

"Ye gentle Birdes, the worlds faire ornament,
And heavens glorie, whom this happie hower
Doth leade unto your lovers blisfull bower,
Joy may you have and gentle hearts content
95 Of your loves couplement:°   union
And let faire Venus, that is Queene of love,
With her heart-quelling Sonne upon you smile,
Whose smile they say, hath vertue° to remove   power
All Loves dislike, and friendships faultie guile

9. Traditionally, the chariot of Venus was drawn through the air by swans; cf. *Metamorphoses* 10.717–
   18.
1. Spenser puns on the ladies' surname.
2. The Peneus river flows through the vale of Tempe, in Thessaly, between Mount Ossa and Mount
   Olympus to the sea; Spenser probably recalls Catullus, *Odes* 64.278–88.
3. I.e., those of the swans.

100 For ever to assoile.[4]
Let endlesse Peace your steadfast hearts accord,°   *harmonize*
And blesséd Plentie wait upon your bord,°   *table*
And let your bed with pleasures chast abound,
That fruitfull issue may to you afford,[5]
105 Which may your foes confound,
And make your joyes redound,°   *overflow*
Upon your Brydale day, which is not long:
 Sweete Themmes run softlie, till I end my Song."

7

So ended she; and all the rest around
110 To her redoubled that her undersong,[6]
Which said, their bridale daye should not be long.
And gentle Eccho from the neighbour ground,
Their accents did resound.
So forth those joyous Birdes did passe along,
115 Adowne the Lee, that to them murmurde low,
As he would speake, but that he lackt a tong,
Yet did by signes his glad affection show,
Making his streame run slow.
And all the foule which in his flood did dwell
120 Gan flock about these twaine, that did excell
The rest, so far, as Cynthia[7] doth shend°   *shame, overgo*
The lesser starres. So they enrangéd° well,   *ordered*
Did on those two attend,
And their best service lend,°   *give*
125 Against their wedding day, which was not long:
 Sweete Themmes run softly, till I end my song.

8

At length they all to mery London came,
To mery London, my most kyndly Nurse,
That to me gave this Lifes first native sourse:
130 Though from another place I take my name,
An house of auncient fame.[8]

---

4. I.e., has power to remove all cause for aversion in love, and to dispel forever the offensive guile that may undermine friendship. Venus appears as beneficent overseer of marriage in Claudian, *Epithalamium de Nuptiis Honorii Augusti* 190–287; and (with her son) in Statius, *Silvae* 1.2.162–93.
5. I.e., be given.
6. I.e., re-echoed the refrain of her song. Fowler 1975 comments on the functions of this "anomalous" stanza, which breaks the zodiacal sequence and is otherwise formally exceptional, within the poem's larger pattern.
7. I.e., Diana, goddess of the moon, called Cynthia from Mount Cynthus (on the island of Delos), her birthplace. The customary allusion to Queen Elizabeth, whose surpassing brightness dims that of her attendants, is implicit here.
8. Born and bred in London, Spenser associates himself with the Spencers of Althorp in Northamptonshire (cf. also *Colin Clouts Come Home Againe* 536–55), who claimed descent from the ancient house of Despencer.

There when they came, whereas those bricky towres,[9]
The which on Themmes brode aged backe doe ryde,
Where now the studious Lawyers have their bowers
135 There whylome° wont the Templer Knights to byde,   *formerly*
Till they decayd[1] through pride:
Next whereunto there standes a stately place,[2]
Where oft I gaynéd giftes and goodly grace
Of that great Lord, which therein wont to dwell,
140 Whose want too well now feeles my freendles case:
But Ah here fits° not well   *suits*
Olde woes but joyes to tell
Against the bridale daye, which is not long:
    Sweete Themmes runne softly, till I end my Song.

9

145 Yet therein now doth lodge a noble Peer,[3]
Great Englands glory and the Worlds wide wonder,
Whose dreadfull name, late through all Spaine did thunder,
And Hercules two pillors standing neere,
Did make to quake and feare:
150 Faire branch of Honor, flower of Chevalrie,
That fillest England with thy triumphs fame,
Joy have thou of thy noble victorie,
And endlesse happinesse of thine owne name
That promiseth the same:[4]
155 That through thy prowesse and victorious armes,
Thy country may be freed from forraine harmes:
And great Elisaes glorious name may ring
Through al the world, filled with thy wide Alarmes,
Which some brave muse may sing
160 To ages following,[5]
Upon the Brydale day, which is not long:
    Sweete Themmes runne softly, till I end my Song.

---

9. I.e., the Temple, between Fleet Street and the north bank of the Thames; originally the London residence of the Knights Templar. When that order was suppressed by Edward II, the property passed to the Knights of St. John, and was subsequently leased to the students of English common law. The estate was formally granted to the lawyers by James I. See Manley 1982 on "the symbiotic relation [in *Prothalamion*] between poetry and the city," which in some sense balances "the tide of mutability" (226–27).
1. I.e., until their downfall.
2. I.e., Leicester House, London residence of "that great Lord" the earl of Leicester, Spenser's patron in 1579–80. When, after the earl's death in 1588, the estate passed into the possession of Robert Devereux, second earl of Essex, the building was called Essex House.
3. I.e., the earl of Essex, who (together with Sir Walter Raleigh) had in June 1596, overwhelmed a Spanish fleet at Cadiz, plundered the city, and forced the destruction of forty-odd merchantmen together with their enormously valuable cargoes. Cadiz lies some fifty miles northwest from the Straits of Gibraltar, anciently known as the Pillars of Hercules.
4. I.e., punningly, that promises to be happy ("heureux") and glorious.
5. I.e., through all the world, everywhere touched by your active and wide-ranging spirit, which some gifted poet [e.g., Spenser] may celebrate for times to come.

10

From those high Towers, this noble Lord issuing,
Like Radiant Hesper[6] when his golden hayre
165 In th'Ocean billowes he hath Bathéd fayre,
Descended to the Rivers open viewing,
With a great traine ensuing.[7]
Above the rest were goodly to bee seene
Two gentle Knights[8] of lovely face and feature
170 Beseeming well the bower of anie Queene,
With gifts of wit and ornaments of nature,
Fit for so goodly stature:
That like the twins of Jove[9] they seemed in sight,
Which decke the Bauldricke of the Heavens bright.[1]
175 They two forth pacing to the Rivers side,
Received those two faire Brides, their Loves delight,
Which at th'appointed tyde,°   *time*
Each one did make his Bryde,
Against their Brydale day, which is not long:
180   Sweete Themmes runne softly, till I end my Song.

Editors' Note

Early and late, rivers run through the poetic landscape of Spenser's verse, watering and refreshing all that country. One thinks first, perhaps, of the magnificent concourse of streams from all the world, gathered for the wedding of Medway and Thames, and celebrated in *The Faerie Queene* IV.xi; yet the earliest poems of the *Complaints* volume abound in riverine allusion, and Spenser takes care that Colin's ode to Elisa in the "Aprill" eclogue of *The Shepheardes Calender* should be "tuned [to] the waters fall" of streams and springs in nature as well as those derived from classical sources. The tale of Mulla and Bregog, in *Colin Clouts Come Home Againe*, and the related account of Faunus and Molanna, in the *Cantos of Mutabilitie*, bear witness to the poet's continuing fascination with river lore. But pride of place in this context must be granted to the "spousall verse" that celebrates "silver streaming Themmes" while a discontented narrator pays somewhat equivocal court to the social occasion for which *Prothalamion* was composed.

On November 8, 1596, Elizabeth and Catherine Somerset, the daughters of Edward Somerset, fourth earl of Worcester, were married to (respectively) Henry Guildford and William Petre. The wedding took place at Essex House, in the Strand, in London. The poet may have been acquainted with relatives of the brides' family; but his sponsorship by the earl of Essex (who was linked to the Somersets by blood and amity) probably explains how Spenser came to write *Prothalamion*. There were plenty of precedents for such a poem. Spenser seems to have known two Latin poems, William Leland's *Cygnea Cantio*, published in 1545, and William Camden's *De Connubio Tamis et Isis*, published in 1586; as well as an English poem by one W. Vallans, *A Tale of Two*

---

6. I.e., Hesperus, the morning star in this context; see *Aeneid* 8.589–91.
7. I.e., attended by an extensive retinue.
8. The bridegrooms-to-be, Henry Guildford and William Petre.
9. I.e., Castor and Pollux, the Gemini.
1. I.e., the zodiac (regarded as a belt studded with stars).

Swannes, which appeared in 1590. In a letter of 1580, Spenser speaks to Gabriel Harvey of his intention "to sette forth a booke . . . whyche I entitle *Epithalamion Thamesis*"; this was to have been a topographic and antiquarian poem, describing "the marriage of the Thames," together with an account of "all the rivers throughout Englande, whyche came to the wedding."[1] Vallans, in his preface to A *Tale of Two Swannes*, states that he has "seen [*Epithalamion Thamesis*] in Latine verse";[2] but that poem now is lost. Nor has an independent English version survived. Presumably the original project was subsumed by the larger plan of *The Faerie Queene*, emerging triumphantly in Book IV.

But if *Prothalamion* has something in common with the poems by Camden and Vallans, it is of course much more than a further instance of a relatively minor poetic kind. The poem has been fortunate in its modern critics. While *The Faerie Queene* and the *Calender* have been virtually overwhelmed by avalanches of scholarly opinion, ranging from the soberly conservative to the red shift of outflying philosophies, the 180 lines of *Prothalamion* have stirred the careful attention of a discerning few. In 1951 Hallett Smith noticed Spenser's individualized employment of conventions that mark other river-poems, effectively extending and focusing the compass of the genre by the introduction of some features from Chaucerian complaint, and by allusive reference to "lively current matters of interest." More recent scholarship, taking its cue from Berger and Fowler, has recognized the importance of the poem's occasion, and of the tensions (reflected in the shifting ambiguities of the refrain) between the poet-persona's "sullein care" and the presumably joyful occasion he celebrates. Some prefer, not unpersuasively, to read *Prothalamion* chiefly as complaint, dominantly elegiac in character; or, brushing aside the shows and "verbal trickery" of this marriage ceremony, to stress the disenchantment of a poet made fierce by a patronage system that fosters economic inequities. Per contra, the poem (in Fowler's philosophy) "resolves complaint into formal order," transmutes plaintive into the festive; for another student of the poem, the allegorical vision of *Prothalamion* at last overgoes the allegorical method of *The Faerie Queene*, beckoning readers to complete the quest for Gloriana. And Berger 1965 shines still: in *Prothalamion*, "poetry has done its work and made a symbolic form which infolds all such occasions and manifests their true importance. The very shortness of time enchases the human triumph . . ." (378–79). That the actions of men and women in time may be at once poignant and nobly in accord with larger patterns of order is the humanistic thought that informs such expressions as "Against the Brydale daye, which is not long," as well as the reminder that these four young lovers are to be joined together "at th'appointed tyde." Even the sardonic and threatening contexts of T. S. Eliot's *The Wasteland*, after all, do not altogether silence the timeless beauty of that mysterious refrain. As Norman Maclean murmurs at the end of his finest story, "Eventually, all things merge into one, and a river runs through it."[3]

---

1. *Three proper and wittie familiar Letters* . . . (London, 1580).
2. W. Vallans, Preface, "A Tale of Two Swannes" [1590], John Leland, *Itinerary*, ed. Thomas Hearne (London, 1744), 9 vols.; 5.vi–vii.
3. *A River Runs Through It, and Other Stories* (Chicago and London, 1976).

Textual Notes

In this edition, the text of *The Faerie Queene* is based on that of the 1596 edition, in a microfilm copy of the volume (STC 23082) in the Huntington Library; the text of the *Cantos of Mutabilitie* is based on that of the 1609 edition, in a microfilm copy of the *Cantos* in the Newberry Library copy. Texts of the minor poems are based on the first editions of each work in microfilm copies of the volumes in the Huntington Library or (in the case of *Amoretti*) on the *Variorum*. References to other editions in the list of variants are made to copies of the 1590 and 1609 editions of *The Faerie Queene* in the New York Public Library; to a microfilm copy of the 1611 edition of Spenser's *Works* in the Library of the University of Washington; and to microfilm copies of the 1581, 1586, 1591, and 1597 editions of *The Shepheardes Calender* in the Huntington Library. A very few variants from the 1617 edition of Spenser's *Works* are noted: these are drawn from the relevant lists of variants in the *Variorum* edition.

The text of Spenser's poetry in this edition has been "updated" as follows: (1) italicized proper names are given in roman type; (2) the use of "i," "u," and "v," is regularized to conform with modern practice; (3) the ampersand is replaced by "and"; (4) diphthongs are replaced by separate characters; (5) quotations are punctuated in accord with modern practice; (6) the silent "e" is substituted for the apostrophe in such words as "ador'd" and "perceiv'd"; (7) accents are inserted over final "ed" and "es" to indicate the sounding of the extra syllable. Some textual peculiarities of the minor poems (e.g., the combination of upper- and lower-case type for the names of characters in *The Shepheardes Calender*, and at line beginnings throughout the *Amoretti*) have also been regularized.

The problem of deciding on an authoritative text for *The Faerie Queene* is complicated by the fact that Books I–III in the edition of 1596 differ considerably, in respect of substantives as well as accidentals, from the text of the 1590 edition. Further, some of the corrections noted in the list of "Faults Escaped" ("F.E.") appended to the 1590 edition were made part of subsequent editions, but others were not incorporated into the text in any of the early editions. While a number of substantive revisions seem certainly to reflect Spenser's hand, it is difficult to be sure of the degree to which the punctuation and spelling of 1596 reflect the poet's own preferences. Spenser's editors have responded variously to this challenge: Morris, for example (in his edition of 1869), adheres to the 1590 text, while Dodge (in 1908) retains the spelling of that edition but considers the substantive readings of the 1596 text to be "generally authoritative." The greater number of modern editors, however, base their texts on that of 1596: as the *Variorum* editors observe, "the text of 1596 shows sufficient alteration for the better to justify the opinion that Spenser was responsible for an incidental revision," and further, "the 1596 quarto has the authority of the last edition in Spenser's lifetime." It has seemed to the present editors that the purposes of this Norton Critical Edition will be best served by a text based on that of 1596.

In view particularly of the "updating" of quotational punctuation in this edition, the textual notes are confined chiefly to substantive departures from the basic texts and significant substantive variants in the early quartos, the 1609 folio of *The Faerie Queene*, and the 1611 volume of Spenser's *Works*. The first reading given for each entry in the textual notes is that which has been adopted for the text of this edition. In the list of variants, "*1590 etc.*" indicates an identical reading in all four of the early editions of *The Faerie Queene*; "*1596 etc.*" an identical reading in the editions of 1596, 1609, and 1611. With a few exceptions, substantive variants appearing only in the edition of 1611 are not included in these textual notes. Whether or not a correction indicated in "F.E." is made in one or more of these early editions, the present edition excludes those corrections that are not clearly of substantive significance, or which evidently refer to a compositor's error in the edition of 1590. Thus, the correction of "sire" to "fire," in I.v.40.9, is excluded; that of "seene" to "seeme," in I.vii.36.1, is also excluded; that of "murmuring" to "murmur ring," in I.viii.11.9, is included in the list of variants. Errors clearly resulting from a compositor's mistake, such as the inversion of a letter, or the omission of a letter (where the meaning is not affected) are excluded. Save for a very few of the most helpful substantive emendations proposed by scholars and editors from the time of John Hughes, no attempt is made in the list of variants to take account of the wide range of conjectural readings, for which the student is referred to the various textual appendices of the Variorum edition.

The punctuation and spelling of *The Faerie Queene* in the present edition closely follow the text of the 1596 edition (given those alterations imposed by the "updating" of quotational punctuation). Occasionally the punctuation of another among the early editions is silently substituted for the punctuation of 1596, where the clarity of Spenser's text is thereby helped on without substantive alteration of the meaning of the passage in question. The textual notes in the present edition do not, as a rule, take account of the large number of variants in punctuation and spelling between 1590 and 1596. However, several of the more significant punctuational variants among the four early editions that bear substantively upon the text are included (e.g., I.xi.6.5–6; III.v.37.2). The textual notes also include a few spelling variants of particular interest, such as the preference of the 1596 text (e.g., at I.v.15.2) for "thirstie" to the "thristy" of 1590, the substitution in 1596 of "am" for the eye-rhyme "ame" of 1590 (e.g., at I.v.26.6), or the consequences for the text of the failure, in 1609, to recognize syllabic "es" (e.g., at I.v.23.8, or I.x.34.8). In the case of the minor poems, finally, for which textual problems are generally less challenging than they are where *The Faerie Queene* is concerned, departures of punctuation or spelling (other than obvious compositorial errors, or the "crowding off" of punctuation, as in the *Amoretti* and *Epithalamion* of 1595) from the texts of the first editions, together with significant variants in later editions, are included. In the case of *Amoretti* and *Epithalamion*, we give only those variants that might possibly affect a reading, for the typesetters of the 1595 volume imposed, in Spenser's absence, punctuation that the *Variorum* calls "inflexible and ill-considered" and Yale calls "chaotic." Like the *Variorum* editors, whose edition is the basis of our own, we sometimes prefer the 1611 or 1617 punctuation and, although rarely, further modernize it; occasionally we restore the punctuation of 1595 or 1611. Not all such changes are noted here. The aim throughout has been to clarify the text for modern readers without altering the meaning and character of Spenser's text.

THE FAERIE QUEENE

A Letter of the Authors . . .

Line 8. by accidents *1590.*

Dedication
The dedication to the edition of 1590 reads: TO THE MOST MIGHTIE AND MAGNIFICENT EMPRESSE ELIZABETH, BY THE GRACE OF GOD QUEENE OF ENGLAND, FRANCE AND IRELAND DEFENDER OF THE FAITH &c. Her most humble Servant: *Ed. Spenser.*

Book I
Proem 1.2. taught, *1590, 1609, 1611;* taught *1596.*
Proem 4.5. my *1596 etc.;* mine *1590.*
i.Arg.3. *entrappe 1590; entrape 1596; entrap 1609, 1611.*
i.2.1. But *1596 etc.;* And *1590.*
i.5.1. an innocent *1596;* and innocent *1590;* an Innocent *1609, 1611.*
i.9.6. sweete bleeding *1590, 1596;* sweet, bleeding *1609, 1611.*
i.10.4. They *1590, 1609, 1611;* The *1596.*
i.12.5. stroke *F.E.;* hardy stroke *1590 etc.*
i.15.6. poisonous *1596 etc.;* poisnous *1590.*
i.21.5. spring *F.E.;* ebbe *1590 etc.;* to avale *F.E., 1596 etc.;* t'avale *1590.*
i.28.8 passed *1590;* passeth *1596 etc.*
i.30.9. sits *1590, 1596;* fits *1609, 1611.*
i.31.6. you *1596 etc.;* thee *1590.*
i.42.8. sights *F.E., 1596 etc.;* sighes *1590.*
i.46.7. usage *1590, 1596;* visage *1609, 1611.*
i.48.9. her with Yvie *1590;* her Yvie *1596 etc.*
i.50.3. thought have *1590, 1596;* thought t'have *1609, 1611.*
i.53.6. since no'untruth *1590, 1596;* sith n'untruth *1609, 1611.*
ii.6.2. his guiltie sight *1590 etc.;* this guiltie sight *1758 conj. Upton.*
ii.8.9. loved *1590, 1609, 1611;* lovest *1596.*
ii.16.5. Astonied both *1590, 1596;* Astonied, both *1609, 1611.*
ii.16.8. idely *1590, 1596;* idlely *1609, 1611.*
ii.17.5. cruell spies *F.E.;* cruelties *1590 etc.*
ii.17.9. dies *1590, 1596;* die *1609, 1611.*
ii.22.5. your *1596 etc.;* thy *1590.*
ii.27.9. so dainty *1590, 1596;* so, Dainty *1609, 1611.*
ii.29.1. can *1590, 1596;* gan *1609, 1611.*
ii.29.2. shade him thither hastly *1590;* shade thither hastly *1596;* shadow thither hast'ly *1609, 1611.*
ii.29.3. ymounted *F.E.;* that mounted *1590 etc.*
ii.40.1. Thens *F.E., 1609, 1611;* Then *1590, 1596.*
ii.40.2. unweeting *1590;* unweening *1596 etc.*
ii.41.5. Thens *F.E., 1609, 1611;* Then *1590, 1596.*
ii.45.6. up gan lift *1590, 1596;* gan uplift *1609, 1611.*
iii.1.4. Through *1590, 1596;* By *1609, 1611.*
iii.28.9. liefe *1590, 1596;* life *1609, 1611.*
iii.29.9. defend, now *1596 etc.;* defend. Now *1590.*
iii.34.9. spurnd *1596 etc.;* spurd *1590.*

iii.36.7. mourning *1590, 1609, 1611;* morning *1596.*
iii.38.7. that *F.E.;* the *1590 etc.*
iii.44.7. feares, *1590, 1596;* feares *1609, 1611.*
iv.3.5. case *F.E., 1596 etc.;* care *1590.*
iv.11.3. worth *1590, 1609, 1611;* wroth *1596.*
iv.12.2. a Queene *1590, 1609, 1611;* Queene *1596.*
iv.12.7. Realmes *1596 etc.;* Realme *1590.*
iv.16.3. hurtlen *1590, 1596;* hurlen *1609, 1611.*
iv.16.9. glitterand *1590;* glitter and *1596 etc.*
iv.20.3 From *1590;* For *1596 etc.*
iv.22.8. corse *F.E., 1596 etc.;* course *1590.*
iv.23.7. dry dropsie *1590 etc.;* dire dropsie *1758 conj. Upton.*
iv.27.4. mettall full, *1590, 1596;* mettall, full *1609, 1611.*
iv.30.4 chaw *1590, 1596;* jaw *1609, 1611.*
iv.32.9. fifte *F.E.;* first *1590 etc.*
iv.45.5. of my new joy *F.E., 1609, 1611;* of new joy *1590, 1596.*
v.1.9. did he wake *1590, 1609, 1611;* did wake *1596.*
v.2.5. hurld *F.E.;* hurls *1590 etc.*
v.7.9. helmets hewen deepe *1596 etc.;* hewen helmets deepe *1590.*
v.15.2. thirstie *1596 etc.;* thristy *1590.*
v.17.4. wash his woundes *1590, 1596;* washen his wounds *1609, 1611.*
v.23.8 Nightes *1590, 1596;* Nights drad *1609, 1611.*
v.24.9. for *1590;* and *1596 etc.*
v.26.6. am *1596 etc.;* ame *1590.*
v.35.5. thirstie *1596 etc.;* thristy *1590.*
v.35.9. leake *F.E., 1596 etc.;* lete *1590.*
v.38.6. cliffs *F.E.;* clifts *1590 etc.*
v.41.2. nigh *1590;* high *1596 etc.*
v.51.5. that *F.E.;* the *1590 etc.*
vi.1.3. "The use of 'bewaile' is either very forced (? suggested by the consequences of a wreck), or it is a mere error" *(O.E.D.). Church, in 1758, proposed* assaile.
vi.1.5. in *F.E.;* it *1590 etc.*
vi.5.5. win *1590;* with *1596 etc.*
vi.8.7. misshapen *1609, 1611;* mishappen *1590;* mishapen *1596.*
vi.12.3. twixt *1590, 1596;* through *1609, 1611.*
vi.14.2. doubled *1590, 1596;* double *1609, 1611.*
vi.15.2. Or *1590;* Of *1596 etc.*
vi.23.8. noursled *1596 etc.;* nousled *1590.*
vi.25.9. earne *1590, 1596;* yearne *1609, 1611.*
vi.26.5. fierce and fell *F.E., 1596 etc.;* swift and cruell *1590.*
vi.26.9. as a tyrans *1590;* as tyrans *1596;* as proud tyrants *1609, 1611.*
vi.38.8. thristed *1590, 1596;* thirsted *1609, 1611.*
vi.39.7. quoth he *1596 etc.;* qd. she *1590.*
vi.44.1. fell *1596 etc.;* full *1590.*
vi.47.8. they to *1590;* they two *1596 etc.*
vii.5.9. drunke thereof, did *1596 etc.;* drinke thereof, do *1590.*
vii.18.4. brought *1596 etc.;* braught *1590.*
vii.18.5. nought *1596 etc.;* naught *1590.*
vii.20.3. the *1596 etc.;* that *1590.*
vii.22.9. sad sight fro *1596 etc.;* sad fro *1590.*

vii.32.8. Whose *1596 etc.*; Her *1590*.
vii.37.7. trample *1596 etc.*; amble *1590*.
vii.43.4. whilest *1596*; whiles *1590*; whil'st *1609, 1611*.
vii.43.5. runne *F.E., 1596 etc.*; come *1590*.
vii.47.3. hands *F.E., 1596 etc.*; hand *1590*.
vii.48.9. have you *1596 etc.*; have yee *1590*.
viii.Arg.3. the *F.E.*; that *1590 etc.*
viii.3.1. the *1596 etc.*; his *1590*.
viii.10.3. avantage *1596 etc.*; advantage *1590*.
viii.11.9. murmur ring *F.E.*; murmuring *1590 etc.*
viii.14.4. inner *1590, 1596*; inward *1609, 1611*.
viii.21.5. their *1590 etc.*; his *1758 conj. Church*.
viii.24.6. his *1596 etc.*; her *1590*.
viii.27.7. eyes *1596 etc.*; eye *1590*.
viii.33.5. sits *1590*; fits *1596 etc.*
viii.41.7. and helmets *1590, 1609, 1611*; helmets *1596*.
viii.44.4. delight *1590 etc.*; dislike *1734 conj. Jortin*.
ix.Arg.2. bands *F.E., 1596 etc.*; hands *1590*.
ix.8.9. the *F.E., 1596 etc.*; that *1590*.
ix.9.5. Timons *F.E., 1596 etc.*; Cleons *1590*.
ix.12.9. on *F.E., 1609, 1611*; at *1590, 1596*.
ix.13.1. For-wearied *1596*; For wearied *1590*; Fore-wearied *1609, 1611*.
ix.15.8. vow *1596 etc.*; vowd *1590*.
ix.18.9. as *1590*; the *1596 etc.*
ix.19.7. his *F.E., 1596 etc.*; this *1590*.
ix.33.3. ypight *1596 etc.*; yplight *1590*.
ix.34.6. cliffs *F.E.*; clifts *1590 etc.*
ix.46.7. falsed *1596 etc.*; falsest *1590*.
ix.52.1. saw *1596 etc.*; heard *1590*.
ix.53.1. feeble *1590*; seely *1596*; silly *1609, 1611*.
x.15.4. well *1596 etc.*; for *1590*.
x.15.9. gan *1590, 1596*; can *1609, 1611*.
x.16.8. her *F.E.*; be *1590 etc.*
x.20.5. *This line, omitted in 1590 and 1596, appears first in 1609.*
x.27.6. His bodie in salt water smarting sore *1596 etc.*; His blamefull body in salt water sore *1590*.
x.34.8. worldes *1590, 1596*; worlds *1609, 1611*.
x.36.6. Their *1609, 1611*; There *1590, 1596*.
x.36.9. in commers-by *1609, 1611*; in-commers by *1590, 1596*.
x.38.1. as *1590, 1596, 1611*; an *1609*.
x.50.1 she *1590, 1609, 1611*; he *1596*.
x.52.1. since *1590, 1596*; sith *1609, 1611*.
x.52.6. Brings *1609, 1611*; Bring *1590, 1596*.
x.57.5. pretious *F.E.*; piteous *1590 etc.*
x.59.2. frame *F.E.*; fame *1590 etc.*
x.61.3. thy *1590, 1609, 1611*; to thy *1596*.
x.62.4. (Quoth he) as wretched, and liv'd in like paine *1596 etc.*; As wretched men, and lived in like paine *1590*.
x.62.8. and battailes none are to be fought *1596 etc.*; and bitter battailes all are fought *1590*.
x.62.9. are vaine *1596 etc.*; they' are vaine *1590*.
x.64.7. doen *1590, 1609, 1611*; doen then *1596*.
x.65.3. place *1596 etc.*; face *1590*.

xi.2.4. at *F.E., 1596 etc.*; it *1590*.
xi.3. *This stanza first appears in 1596.*
xi.5.1. his *F.E.*; this *1590 etc.*
xi.6.5. aswage, *1590, 1596*; asswage; *1609, 1611*.
xi.6.6. sownd; *1590, 1596*; sound, *1609, 1611*.
xi.6.9. scared *F.E.*; feared *1590 etc.*
xi.8.7. vast *1609, 1611*; vaste *1590*; wast *1596*.
xi.11.5. as *F.E.*; all *1590 etc.*
xi.26.6. swinged *1590, 1596*; singed *1609, 1611*.
xi.27.2. vaunt *1590*; daunt *1596 etc.*
xi.30.5. one *F.E.*; it *1590 etc.*
xi.37.2. yelded *1590, 1596*; yelled *1609, 1611*.
xi.39.4. sting *1590*; string *1596 etc.*
xi.39.7. string *1590*; sting *1596 etc.*
xi.39.8. a *1590, 1596*; in *1609, 1611*.
xi.41.4. Nor *1609, 1611*; For *1590, 1596*.
xi.51.2. the *1590*; her *1596 etc.*
xi.51.7. spred, *1758 conj. Church*; spred; *1590 etc.*
xi.51.8. darke; *1758 conj. Church*; darke, *1590 etc.*
xii.3.5. fond *1590*; found *1596 etc.*
xii.7.3. sung *1596 etc.*; song *1590*.
xii.11.5. talants *F.E., 1611*; talents *1590, 1596, 1609*.
xii.16.1. pleasure *1590*; pleasures *1596 etc.*
xii.17.1. that *1590*; the *1596 etc.*
xii.21.7. that dawning day is drawing neare *1590*; the dawning day is dawning neare *1596 etc.*
xii.27.7. of *1590*; and *1596 etc.*
xii.28.7. her *1590*; his *1596 etc.*
xii.32.5. t'invegle *F.E.*; to invegle *1590 etc.*
xii.34.2. vaine *F.E., 1596 etc.*; faine *1590*.
xii.37.6. the *1590, 1596*; a *1609, 1611*.
xii.38.3. frankencense *1596 etc.*; frankincense *1590*.
xii.40.9. His *1590*; Her *1596 etc.*

Book II
i.1.7. caytives *1590, 1596*; caytive *1609, 1611*.
i.2.7. native *1590*; natives *1596 etc.*
i.3.2. food *1590, 1596*; feud *1609*; feude *1611*.
i.3.9. be *1590, 1596*; he *1609, 1611*.
i.0.5. faine *1590, 1609, 1611*; a faire *1596*.
i.10.5. corse *1596 etc.*; corps *1590*.
i.16.1. liefe *1596 etc.*; life *1590*.
i.18.6. did he *1596 etc.*; he did *1590*.
i.29.1. attone *1596 etc.*; at one *1590*.
i.31.2. handling *1590, 1609, 1611*; handing *1596*.
i.33.8. thrise *F.E.*; these *1590 etc.*
vii.4.4. yet *1590*; it *1596 etc.*
vii.4.8. upsidowne *1596 etc.*; upside downe *1590*.
vii.7.3. heapes *1596 etc.*; hils *1590*.
vii.10.1. besits *1590, 1596*; befits *1609, 1611*.
vii.12.9. as *1596 etc.*; in *1590*.
vii.18.2. that antique *1590, 1609, 1611*; antique *1596*.
vii.21.5. infernall *1596 etc.*; internall *1590*.
vii.24.7. ought *1596 etc.*; nought *1590*.
vii.37.1. as *1596 etc.*; an *1590*.
vii.40.5. As if *1590, 1609, 1611*; As *1596.*/ that *F.E.*; the *1590 etc.*
vii.40.7. But *1596 etc.*; And *1590.*/ golden *1596 etc.*; yron *1590*.

vii.41.3.   his   *1590*; to   *1596 etc.*
vii.52.6.   With which   *1734 conj. Jortin*;
  Which with   *1590, 1596*; Which-
  with   *1609, 1611.*
vii.60.4.   intemperate   *1596 etc.*; more
  temperate   *1590.*
vii.64.9.   of the   *1596 etc.*; of his *1590.*
viii.3.8.   Come hither, come hither *1596*;
  Come hether, come hether *1590*; Come
  hither, hither *1609, 1611.*
ix.Arg.4.   *flight   1590; fight   1596 etc.*
ix.5.7.   amenaunce   *1596 etc.*;
  amenance   *1590.*
ix.7.5.   Now hath   *1596 etc.*; Seven
  times   *1590. The 1596 etc. revisions of 7.5–
  6 and 38.9 bring these passages into consistency with I.ix.15.9.*
ix.7.6.   Walkt round   *1596 etc.*; Hath
  walkte   *1590.*
ix.9.1.   weete   *1751 conj. Birch*; wote   *1590
  etc.*
ix.16.8.   wind with blustring   *1590*; wind
  blustring   *1596.*
ix.19.9.   crowned   *F.E., 1596 etc.*;
  crownd   *1590.*
ix.20.6.   There   *1596 etc.*; Then   *1590.*
ix.21.3.   fensible   *1596 etc.*; sensible   *1590.*
ix.22.9.   diapase; Diapase   *F.E., 1611*;
  Dyapase   *1590, 1596, 1609.*
ix.31.4.   th'Achates   *1609, 1611*; the
  cates   *1590, 1596.*
ix.38.9.   twelve moneths   *1596 etc.*; three
  years   *1590.*
ix.41.7.   Castory.   *F.E.*; lastery   *1590*;
  lastery.   *1596.*
ix.49.9.   could   *1596 etc.*; would   *1590.*
xii.Arg.1.   *by   1596 etc.*; through *1590.*
xii.Arg.2.   *passing through   1596 etc.*;
  through passing   1590.
xii.1.6.   for that   *F.E.*; for this   *1590 etc.*
xii.13.9.   honor   *1596 etc.*; temple *1590.*
xii.15.1.   can   *1590, 1596*; gan   *1609, 1611.*
xii.20.8.   their   *1590*; the   *1596 etc.*
xii.21.1.   th'heedfull   *1596 etc.*;
  th'earnest   *1590.*
xii.27.4.   the resounding   *1590, 1596*;
  resounding   *1609, 1611.*
xii.32.4.   That   *1590, 1609, 1611*;
  Thou   *1596.*
xii.39.8.   upstarting   *1596 etc.*;
  upstaring   *1590.*
xii.48.7.   of this   *1596 etc.*; oft his *1590.*
xii.51.1.   Thereto   *1596 etc.*;
  Therewith   *1590.*
xii.52.9.   *Eden* selfe, if   *1590*; *Eden*,
  if   *1596*; *Eden*, if that   *1609, 1611.*
xii.57.9.   nought   *1590*; not   *1596 etc.*
xii.60.5.   curious   *1590, 1596*; pure *1609*,
  1611.
xii.61.8.   tenderly   *1596 etc.*;
  fearefully   *1590.*
xii.73.1.   that   *1590, 1596*; the   *1609, 1611.*
xii.81.4.   the   *1596 etc.*; that   *1590.*
xii.83.7.   spoyle   *1590*; spoyld   *1596 etc.*

Book III
Proem 1.2.   That   *1596 etc.*; The   *1590.*
Proem 4.2.   Your selfe you   *1596 etc.*; Thy
  selfe thou   *1590.*
i.Arg.3.   *Malecastaes   F.E.*;
  Materastaes   1590 etc.
i.7.2.   sith   *1590, 1596*; since   *1609, 1611.*
i.14.8.   creatures   *1596 etc.*; creature *1590.*
i.21.9.   sixe before, *1590, 1596*; sixe,
  before   *1609, 1611.*
i.30.6.   mard   *F.E.*; shard   *1590 etc.*
i.31.6.   of many   *1590*; many   *1596 etc.*

i.41.8.   lightly   *1609, 1611*; highly *1590*,
  1596.
i.47.7.   which   *1596 etc.*; that   *1590.*
i.56.8.   *Basciomani   1596 etc.*;
  Bascimano   1590.
i.60.8.   wary   *1609, 1611*; weary   *1590*,
  1596.
i.60.9.   fond   *1590, 1596*; fand   *1609, 1611.*
ii.4.1.   Guyon   *should read*   Redcrosse.
ii.8.5.   Which I to prove,   *1596 etc.*; Which
  to prove, I   *1590.*
ii.9.7.   well of all,   *1590, 1596*; well, of
  all   *1609, 1611.*
ii.30.5.   in her warme bed her dight   *1596
  etc.*; her in her warme bed dight   *1590.*
ii.36.1.   others   *1596 etc.*; other   *1590.*
ii.37.2.   For no   *1590 etc.*; For know *1758
  conj. Upton.*
ii.49.7.   a earthen   *1590, 1596*; an
  earthen   *1609, 1611.*
iii.1.1.   Most   *1590, 1596*; Oh   *1609, 1611.*
iii.4.8.   protense   *1590*; pretence *1596 etc.*
iii.15.3.   to unfold   *1590, 1596*; unfold *1609*,
  1611.
iii.22.9.   *Greeke   1590; Greece   1596 etc.*
iii.29.1.   With   *1590*; Where   *1596 etc.*
iii.35.1.   thy   *1590*; the   *1596 etc.*
iii.37.7.   their   *1590*; the   *1596 etc.*
iii.43.9.   of the earth   *F.E.*; th'earth   *1590
  etc.*
iii.44.5.   yeares shalbe   *1590*; shalbe *1596*;
  shall be full   *1609, 1611.*
iii.44.6.   to   *1596 etc.*; unto their *1590.*
iii.50.9.   Hee   *F.E.*; Shee   *1590*; She *1596
  etc./*looks as earst   *1609*; looks   *1590, 1596.*
iii.51.9.   disguise   *1590*; devise   *1596 etc.*
iii.53.3.   (whom need new strength shall
  teach)   *1596 etc.*; (need makes good schol-
  lers) teach   *1590.*
iv.6.9.   her   *1590, 1596*; had   *1609, 1611.*
iv.8.4.   Why   *1590*; Who   *1596 etc.*
iv.8.9.   these   *1596 etc.*; thy   *1590.*
iv.15.6.   speare   *1609, 1611*; speares *1590*,
  1596.
iv.33.4.   raynes   *1590*; traines   *1596 etc.*
iv.39.9.   sith we no more shall meet *1596
  etc.*; till we againe may meet *1590.*
iv.59.5.   Dayes dearest children   *1596 etc.*;
  The children of day   *1590.*
v.Arg.4.   *sownd   1590, 1596; swound   1609*,
  1611.
v.3.2.   that at   *1590, 1596*; at the *1609*,
  1611.
v.5.5.   A   *1590*; And   *1596 etc.*
v.11.1.   ye   *1590*; you   *1596 etc.*
v.37.2.   undertaken after her,   *1590*; undertaken after her   *1596*; undertaken, after
  her   *1609, 1611.*
v.37.6.   follow   *1596 etc.*; followd *1590.*
v.38.9.   forth with   *1590, 1609, 1611*;
  forthwith   *1596.*
v.39.9.   his   *1596 etc.*; their   *1590.*
v.40.4.   loves sweet   *1596 etc.*; sweet
  loves   *1590.*
v.40.9.   living   *1596 etc.*; liking   *1590.*
v.44.7.   revew   *1590*; renew   *1596 etc.*
v.52.6.   admire: *1609, 1611*; admyre *1590*;
  admire   *1596.*
vi.3.9.   was   *1596 etc.*; were   *1590.*
vi.6.5.   his   *1590, 1596*; his hot   *1609*,
  1611.
vi.12.4.   beautie   *1590*; beauties *1596 etc.*
vi.25.5.   Which as   *1609, 1611*; From
  which   *1590, 1596.*
vi.26.4.   To seeke the fugitive, both farre and
  nere.   *1609*; To seeke the fugitive.   *1590*;

To seeke the fugitive, both farre and nere, 1596.

vi.28.6. thence   1590; hence   1596 etc.

vi.40.6. spyde   1590 etc.; saw   1758 conj. Church.

vi.42.5. heavy   1596 etc.; heavenly 1590.

vi.45.4. *This half-line first appears in* 1609.

vii.9.3. two   1590 etc.; to   1715 conj. Hughes.

vii.13.6. had   1596 etc.; hath   1590.

vii.18.5. be by the witch or that   1908 conj. Dodge; by the witch or by   1590; be the witch or that   1596 etc.

vii.19.6. her   1590, 1596; that 1609, 1611.

vii.22.4. Monstrous mishapt   1596 etc.; Monstrous, mishapt   1590.

vii.34.2. enclose   1590 etc.; constraine 1758 conj. Church; containe   1908 conj. Dodge.

vii.43.7. saw, with great remorse   1609, 1611; saw with great remorse,   1590, 1596.

vii.45.1. the good   1590; good   1596 etc./ wake   1590, 1596; awake 1609, 1611.

vii.18.4. And many hath to foule 1596 etc.; Till him Chylde Thopas to   1590.

vii.49.5. staine   1590; straine   1596 etc.

vii.50.2. thrust   1590; thurst   1596 etc.

vii.58.3. a do   1596; adoe   1590; a-do   1609, 1611.

viii.2.7. broken   1596 etc.; golden 1590.

viii.5.1. advise   1596 etc.; device 1590.

viii.7.4. a womans   1596 etc.; to womens   1590.

viii.20.2. Fortune   1596; fortune 1590, 1609, 1611.

viii.23.9. am   1596 etc.; ame   1590.

viii.30.3. frory   1590, 1596; frowy 1590, 1596.

viii.33.9. thereby   1596 etc.; her by 1590.

viii.49.4. his   1590, 1596; a   1609, 1611.

ix.4.5. her   1590, 1596; his   1609, 1611.

ix.13.9. And so defide them each 1590; And defide them each   1596; And them defied each   1609, 1611.

ix.14.7. to kenell   1596 etc.; in kenell 1590.

ix.22.1. Minerva   1596 etc.; Bellona 1590.

ix.24.5. But most   1590, 1609, 1611; But   1596.

ix.27.5. that   1596 etc.; with   1590.

ix.48.6. to sea   1590, 1609, 1611; to the sea   1596.

x.8.9. take to   1596 etc.; take with 1590.

x.13.8. would beare   1596 etc., did beare   1590.

x.18.4. Then 1596   etc.; So   1590.

x.27.2. Sith   1590, 1596; Since 1609, 1611.

x.31.3. with thy   1596 etc.; that with 1590.

x.31.7. vertues pray   1596; vertuous pray   1590; vertues pay 1609, 1611.

x.39.7. am   1596 etc.; ame   1590.

x.40.3. wastefull   1596 etc.; faithfull 1590.

x.46.6. th'Earthes   1590, 1596; the Earthes   1609, 1611.

x.53.8. with life away   1590, 1596; away with life   1609, 1611.

xi.2.3. golden   1609, 1611; golding 1590, 1596.

xi.4.4. that I did ever   1596 etc.; all, that I ever   1590.

xi.4.9. him did   1596 etc.; did him 1590.

xi.9.6. hast thou,   1609, 1611; hast, thou   1590, 1596.

xi.12.1. singultes   1609, 1611; singulfes   1590, 1596.

xi.19.9. death   1590 etc.; life   1734 conj. Jortin.

xi.22.8. Foolhardy as th'Earthes children, the which made   1596; Foolhardy, as the

Earthes children, which made   1590; Foole-hardy, as th'Earthes children, the which made 1609, 1611.

xi.23.5. This is   1590, 1609, 1611; This   1596.

xi.26.7. with imperious sway   1590; imperious sway   1596; his imperious sway   1609, 1611.

xi.27.7. entred   1596 etc.; decked 1590.

xi.28.8. Like a   1596 etc.; Like to a 1590.

xi.33.9. her   1590, 1596; his   1609, 1611.

xi.39.6. each   1596 etc.; his   1590.

xi.39.8. Stag   1734 conj. Jortin; Hag 1590 etc.

xi.49.8. ever more   1609, 1611; evermore   1590, 1596.

xii.5.7. concent   1590, 1609, 1611; consent   1596.

xii.7.8. wood   1596 etc.; word   1590.

xii.9.3. other   1609, 1611; others 1590, 1596.

xii.12.3. and   1596 etc.; or   1590.

xii.12.6. wingyheeld   1596 etc.; winged heeld   1590.

xii.18.8. hony-lady   1590 etc.; hony-laden   1758 conj. Upton.

xii.23.5. his right hand   F.E., 1609, 1611; his right   1590, 1596.

xii.26.6. All   1590; And   1596 etc.

xii.26.7. with that   1596 etc.; by the 1590.

xii.27.3. and bore all away   1596 etc.; nothing did remayne   1590.

xii.33.3. her selfe   1596 etc.; the next 1590.

xii.34.4. her   1609, 1611; him   1590, 1596.

xii.41.7. *The line as it stands is an alexandrine:* Church (1758) *suggested that* prisoner *should be omitted;* Upton (1758) *proposed to eliminate either* prisoner *or* Lady.

xii.42.2. She   1596 etc.; He   1590.

xii.42.4. She   F.E., 1596 etc.; He 1590.

xii.42.5. her   F.E., 1596 etc.; him 1590.

Book IV

Proem 1.2 Welds   1596; Wields 1609, 1611

Book V

Proem 2.2 at   1596, 1609; as   1611, 1715 Hughes

Proem 11.2 stead   1609, 1611; place 1596

vii.6.9 with her   1596, 1609, 1611; with his   1855 conj. Child

vii.20.7 up standing, stifly   1596, 1609, 1611; upstanding stifly   1758 conj. Upton

Book VI

ix.6.5. him   1609, 1611; them   1596.

ix.26.1. eare   1596; care   1609, 1611.

ix.26.4. rapt   1596, 1611; wrapt 1609.

ix.36.8. Oenone   1715 corr. Hughes; Benone   1596 etc.

ix.46.5. dwell   1611; well   1596, 1609.

x.2.9. in the port   1609, 1611; on the port   1596.

x.4.9. now, by course   1596; now by course,   1609, 1611.

x.24.7. froward   1611; forward 1596, 1609.

x.32.6. impure: 1609, 1611; impare 1596.

x.35.3. cowherd   1596; coward   1609, 1611.

x.36.6. head, he [it] presented   1758 conj. Church; head, it presented   1596 etc.

x.37.3. cowherdize   1596; cowardize   1609, 1611.

x.42.1. For   1596 etc.; Far   1758 conj. Upton.

x.44.3. Where   1596; (Where   1609, 1611.

x.44.7. glade.   1596; glade)   1609, 1611.

x.44.8. But *1596*; And *1609, 1611*.
xii.12.8. loos *1596*; praise *1609, 1611*.
xii.41.3. cleanest *1715 conj. Hughes*; clearest *1596 etc.*

Cantos of Mutabilitie
vi.4.5. And *1609*; At *1909 conj. Smith*.
vi.10.1. That *1609*; Tho *1715 conj. Hughes*.
vi.38.2. wealths *1609*; wealth *1715 conj. Hughes*.
vii.2.3. feeble *1715 conj. Hughes*; sable *1609 etc.*

vii.9.7. kindes *1609*; kinde *1758 conj. Upton*.
vii.10.4. mores *1609*; more *1715 conj. Hughes*.
vii.16.3. thy *1609*; my *1611*.
vii.28.3. did beare *1609*; beare *1611*.
vii.41.5. rade; rode *1609, 1611*. *The spelling adopted is warranted by the O.E.D.*
vii.55.7. saine *1609*; faine *1611*.
viii.2.8. Sabbaoth *1609*; Sabaoth *1611*.
viii.2.9. Sabbaoth *1609*; Sabaoth *1611*./ Sabaoths *1609, 1611*; Sabbath's *1758 conj. Upton*.

THE SHEPHEARDES CALENDER

To His Booke
12. my *1579, 1581, 1586, 1591, 1597*; thy *1611*.
Januarye
28. yeare *1579, 1581, 1586, 1591*; yeares *1597, 1611*.
34. bloosmes *1579*; blosomes *1581*; blossomes *1586 etc.*
37. All so *1579, 1581*; Also *1586 etc.*
49. hower, *1581 etc.*; hower. *1579*.
Aprill
8. thristye *1579*; thirstie *1581 etc.*
36. tuned *1579, 1581, 1611*; turned *1586, 1591, 1597*.
39. Forsake *1581 etc.*; For sake *1579*.
64. angelick *1579*; angelike *1581, 1586, 1591*; angellike *1597*; angel-like *1611*.
135. finesse *1579, 1581, 1586, 1591*; finenesse *1597, 1611*.
143. Chevisaunce, *1597, 1611*; Chevisaunce. *1579, 1581, 1586, 1591*.
144. Delice. *1611*; Delice, *1579, 1581, 1586, 1591, 1597*.
Februarie
17. threttie *1579*; thirtie *1581, 1586, 1591, 1597, 1611*.
87. Youngth *1579, 1581*; ynough *1586, 1591, 1597*; youth *1611*.
137. Wherefore soone I rede thee, hence remove *1579, 1581, 1586, 1591, 1597*; Wherefore I rede thee hence to remove *1611*.
142. overawed *1579, 1581, 1943 Osgood* [*on the authority of 1579*]; overcrawed *1586, 1591, 1597, 1611, 1910 Sélincourt* [*"the Northern form of 'Overcrowed' "*].
152. constraint *1579, 1581, 1586, 1591, 1597*; complaint *1611*.
176. wounds *1579, 1597, 1611*; woundes *1581, 1586, 1591*.
238. Eld *1579, 1581, 1586*; Eld. *1591, 1597, 1611*; Eld - *1715 Hughes*.
October
Arg.[p.524]. whiche *1581 etc.*; whishe *1579*.
Arg.[p.524]. ἐυθουσιασμὸ *1579*;

Kithousiasmos *1581, 1586, 1591, 1597*; Enthousiasmos *1611*.
2. chace, *1597, 1611*; chace: *1579, 1581, 1586, 1591*.
6. dead. *1597, 1611*; dead? *1579, 1581, 1586, 1591*.
39–40. giusts, . . . crowne. *1579*; guists, . . . crowne. *1581, 1586, 1591*; gusts, . . . crowne, *1611*.
79. thy *1586 etc.*; the *1579, 1581*.
96a. CUDDIE. omitted *1579, 1581*.
100. demaundes, . . . dwell. *1910 Sélincourt*; demaundes. . . . dwell, *1579, 1581, 1586, 1591, 1597*; demands, . . . dwell: *1611*.
November
15. Ystabled *1579, 1581, 1586, 1591*; Ystablished *1597*; Ystablisht *1611 etc.*
23. sike *1579, 1581, 1586, 1591*; like *1597, 1611 etc.*
53. mourn(e)fulst *1579, 1581, 1586, 1591*; mournful(l) *1597, 1611 etc.*
178. thee *1579, 1581, 1586, 1591*; the *1597, 1611 etc.*
December
Arg.[p.537] riper *1579, 1581, 1586, 1591*; ripest *1597, 1611 etc.*
18. rurall *1579, 1581*; laurell *1586, 1591*; lawrell *1597, 1611 etc.*
29. wreaked *1579, 1581, 1586, 1591, 1597*; recked *1611 etc.*
43. derring doe *1908 conj. Dodge*; derring to *1579 etc.*
75. All so *1586 etc.*; Also *1579, 1581*
84. Phoebe *1579, 1581, 1586, 1591*; Phoebus *1597, 1611 etc.*
98. to *1579, 1581, 1586, 1597, 1617*; too *1591, 1611*
103. with *1579, 1581*; and *1586 etc.*
127. his *1579, 1581, 1586, 1591*; my *1597, 1611 etc.*
146. so *1579, 1581, 1586, 1591*; most *1597, 1611 etc.*
157. *The emblem is omitted in all texts before 1715:* "J. Hughes brilliantly restored the missing Emblem from the Gloss" (*Var.*).

MUIOPOTMOS

34. youngth *1910 Selincourt*; yonght *1591*; youth *1611, 1617*
149. champion he *1591*; champaine o're he *1611, 1617*
254. earne *1591*; yearne *1611, 1617*

299. Yvie winding *1591*; Ivie-winding *1611, 1617*
335. hayrie *1591*; ayrie *1611, 1617*
392. hatefull *1591*; fatal *1611, 1617*
420. Of *1591*; On *1611, 1617*

COLIN CLOUTS COME HOME AGAINE

1. knowen *1611 etc.*; knowne *1595*.
44. delight, *1611 etc.*; delight. *1595*.
88. losse *1595*; Lass *1611 etc.*
91. chose *1595*; choose *1611 etc.*
117. owne *1595, 1611, 1617*; one *1619*.

310. fee *1595, 1611*; see *1617, 1619*.
382. Corydon though *1750 Hughes*; a Corydon though *1595*; Corydon, but *1611 etc.*, *1715 Hughes*.
401. this *1595*; his *1611 etc.*

440. in 1595; on 1611 etc.
487. Urania 1611 etc.; Uriana 1595.
502. worthie of so 1595 rev.; worthie she of
so 1595 unrev., 1611 etc.; worthy she
so, 1715 etc. Hughes.
567. which she 1595 rev., 1750 Hughes;
which he 1595 unrev., 1715 Hughes;
which, he 1611 etc.
600. clusters 1611 etc., 1715 etc. Hughes;
glusters 1595.
601. bunches 1595, 1611 etc., 1715 etc.
Hughes; braunches 1869 Morris/Hales,
1908 Dodge, 1910, 1912 de Sélincourt.
670. Durst 1611 etc.; Darest 1595.

757. fare 1611 etc.; far 1595.
775. [Line indented, 1611 etc.; not indented,
1595].
776. [Line indented, 1595; not indented,
1611 etc.].
805. growing, he 1611 etc.; growing
he 1595.
860. her 1595; their 1611 etc.
861. life giving 1617, 1619; like
giving 1595, 1611.
884. the creatures 1611 etc.; their
creatures 1595.
912. used 1595; loved 1611 etc.

AMORETTI

Sonnet 6
5. Oake, . . . dride, 1595; Oake . . .
dride 1611.
11. wound, 1595; wound 1611.
Sonnet 8
1. fire, 1595; fire 1611.
3. conspire, 1595; conspire 1611.
6. wound: 1595; wound? 1611.
13. world, 1595; world 1611.
14. borne, 1595; borne 1611.
Sonnet 14
6. small forts 1595; forces, 1611.
Sonnet 15
3. treasures 1595; treasure 1611.
Sonnet 16
3. amaze 1595; a maze 1611.
Sonnet 18
10. sayes 1595; sayes, 1611.
11. sayes 1595; sayes, 1611.
Sonnet 19
9. all, 1595; all 1611.
Sonnet 20
13. fayrest . . . say, 1595; fayrest, . . .
say 1611.
Sonnet 21
6. love 1611; loves 1595.
Sonnet 26
14. gaine 1617; gaine. 1595, 1611.
Sonnet 27
13. lenger 1595; longer 1611.
Sonnet 28
10. flee 1617; flie 1595, 1611.
Sonnet 33
11. sins 1595; sith 1611.
Sonnet 36
4. release: 1595, 1611; release? Variorum.
8. miseryes? 1617; miseryes 1595, 1611.
Sonnet 39:
4. dart. 1595; dart; 1611.
Sonnet 40
14. sunshine 1595; sun shine 1611.
Sonnet 42
11–12. pervart his safe assurance,; pervart, his
safe assurance 1595; pervart, in safe
assurance 1611, 1617.

Sonnet 44
2. amongst 1595; among 1611.
5. continuall cruell 1595; continuall,
cruell, 1611.
11–12. awake 1611; awake, 1595.
Sonnet 46
2. my way 1595; away 1611.
11. she Variorum; she, 1595;
shee, 1611.
Sonnet 53:
6. semblant 1595; semblance 1611.
10. ornament, 1617; ornament: 1595,
1611.
11. embrew, 1595; embrew: 1611.
Sonnet 55
12. mind 1595; love 1611, 1617.
Sonnet 57
3. lenger 1595; longer 1611.
Sonnet 58
8. glories 1595; glorious 1611, 1617.
14. arre? 1617; arre. 1595, 1611.
Sonnet 66
13. enlumind 1595, 1611;
enlightened 1617.
Sonnet 67
2. escapt 1595; escape away 1611
12. goodwill 1595; good will 1611.
Sonnet 71
9. about 1595 and all early editions. Many
modern editors (see Variorum's textual notes)
emend to above so as to have a rhyme; but
about better suits the sense and Elizabethan
embroidery.
Sonnet 78
7. her can 1595; can her 1611, 1617.
Sonnet 84
6. sprites 1595; spirits 1611.
8. angelick 1595; Angel-like 1611.
Sonnet 85
3. does 1595; doth 1611.
14. chose 1595; chuse 1611.
Sonnet 89
3. vow 1617; vew 1595, 1611.

ANACREONTICS

1. waxed 1595; wexed 1611, 1617.
2. blynd 1595; blinded 1611, 1617.
55. chose 1595; chuse 1611, 1617.

EPITHALAMION

15. envide: 1611; envide, 1595.
22. awake, 1611; awake 1595.
33. delight: 1611; delight, 1595.
61. take, 1611; take. 1595.
67. deere 1910 conj. Sélincourt;
dore 1595, 1611.
105. bride: 1611; bride 1595.
116. see. 1611; see 1595.

129. aloud 1611; aloud, 1595.
158. Queene. 1611; Queene, 1595.
209. you. 1611; you, 1595.
214. faces; 1611; faces 1595.
215. may 1611; may, 1595.
218. play 1617; play; 1595; play, 1611.
220. throates 1611; throates. 1595.
237. unsownd. 1611; unsownd, 1595.

239. band? *1617;* band, *1595;*
  band. *1611.*
290. nightes *1715 conj. Hughes;*
  nights *1595;* nights sad *1611.*
304. coverlets. *1611;* coverlets, *1595.*

310. brooke. *1611;* brooke *1595.*
341. Pouke *1862 corr. Collier;*
  Ponke *1595, 1611.*
385. thy *1611;* they *1595.*
411. clods, *1611;* clods: *1595.*

PROTHALAMION

3. delay *1596, 1611, 1617;* allay *1715*
conj. Hughes.
102. your *1611, 1617;* you *1596.*

175. pacing *1596;* pasing *1611, 1617;*
passing *1679, 1715 Hughes.*

CRITICISM

Early Critical Views

WILLIAM CAMDEN

[The Death of Spenser]†

The rebellion in Ireland now flamed forth dangerously, as I will declare anon, after I shall first have related what countrymen of ours of worthiest memorie died this yeere [1598/9]. And they were no more than 3, except the Lord Burghley already mentioned: and those three of the number of the most learned, and no lesse renowned than Fame that blazed them.

The first was Thomas Stapleton, Doctor of Divinitie, brought up in New Colledge at Oxford, and ordinarie professor of Divinity and controversies in the Universitie of Douay. . . . Another was Richard Cosins a Cambridge man, Doctor of Law, Deane of the Arches. . . . The third was Edmund Spenser, a Londoner by birth, and a Scholler also of the University of Cambridge, borne under so favourable an aspect of the Muses, that he surpassed all the English poets of former times, not excepting even Chaucer himselfe, his Country man. But by a fate peculiar to Poets, he alwaies struggled with poverty, though he were Secretary to the Lord Grey, Lord Deputy of Ireland. For scarce had hee there gotten a solitary place and leisure to write, when hee was by the Rebels cast out of his dwelling, despoyled of his goods, and returned into England, a poore man, where shortly after hee dyed, and was interred at Westminster, neere to Chaucer, at the charges of the Earle of Essex, his Hearse being carried by Poets, and mournefull Verses and Poems thrown into his Tombe.

JOHN HUGHES

[Remarks on *The Faerie Queene* and *The Shepheardes Calender*]‡

By what has been offer'd in the foregoing Discourse on Allegorical Poetry, we may be able, not only to discover many Beauties in the *Fairy Queen*,

---

† From *Annales, or The History of the most Renowned and Victorious Princesse Elizabeth, late Queen of England . . . written in Latin and translated into English, by R. N[orton] . . .* [London] 1635. Camden (1551–1623), antiquary and historian, was also the author of *Britannia* (1586), a Latin topographical history of England (first English tr. 1610), dedicated to Lord Burleigh.
‡ From Hughes's "Remarks on the *Fairy Queen*," and "Remarks on the *Shepherd's Calendar*," in volume 1 of his edition of Spenser's *Works*, 5 vols. (London, 1715).

but likewise to excuse some of its Irregularities. The chief Merit of this Poem consists in that surprizing Vein of fabulous Invention, which runs thro it, and enriches it every where with Imagery and Descriptions more than we meet with in any other modern Poem. The Author seems to be possess'd of a kind of Poetical Magick; and the Figures he calls up to our View rise so thick upon us, that we are at once pleased and distracted by the exhaustless Variety of them; so that his Faults may in a manner be imputed to his Excellencies: His Abundance betrays him into Excess, and his Judgment is overborne by the Torrent of his Imagination.

That which seems the most liable to Exception in this Work, is the Model of it, and the Choice the Author has made of so romantick a Story. The several Books appear rather like so many several Poems, than one entire Fable: Each of them has its peculiar Knight, and is independent of the rest; and tho some of the Persons make their Appearance in different Books, yet this has very little Effect in connecting them. Prince Arthur is indeed the principal Person, and has therefore a share given him in every Legend; but his Part is not considerable enough in any one of them: He appears and vanishes again like a Spirit; and we lose sight of him too soon, to consider him as the Hero of the Poem.

These are the most obvious Defects in the Fable of the *Fairy Queen*. The want of Unity in the Story makes it difficult for the Reader to carry it in his Mind, and distracts too much his Attention to the several Parts of it; and indeed the whole Frame of it wou'd appear monstrous, if it were to be examin'd by the Rules of Epick Poetry, as they have been drawn from the Practice of Homer and Virgil. But as it is plain the Author never design'd it by those Rules, I think it ought rather to be consider'd as a Poem of a particular kind, describing in a Series of Allegorical Adventures or Episodes the most noted Virtues and Vices: to compare it therefore with the Models of Antiquity, wou'd be like drawing a Parallel between the Roman and the Gothick Architecture. In the first there is doubtless a more natural Grandeur and Simplicity: in the latter, we find great Mixtures of Beauty and Barbarism, yet assisted by the Invention of a Variety of inferior Ornaments; and tho the former is more majestick in the whole, the latter may be very surprizing and agreeable in its Parts.

It may seem strange indeed, since Spenser appears to have been well acquainted with the best Writers of Antiquity, that he has not imitated them in the Structure of his Story. Two Reasons may be given for this: The first is, That at the time when he wrote, the Italian Poets, whom he has chiefly imitated, and who were the first Revivers of this Art among the Moderns, were in the highest vogue, and were universally read and admir'd. But the chief Reason was probably, that he chose to frame his Fable after a Model which might give the greatest Scope to that Range of Fancy which was so remarkably his Talent. There is a Bent in Nature, which is apt to determine Men that particular way in which they are most capable of excelling; and tho it is certain he might have form'd a better Plan, it is to be question'd whether he cou'd have executed any other so well.

It is probably for the same reason, that among the Italian Poets, he rather follow'd Ariosto, whom he found more agreeable to his Genius, than Tasso, who had form'd a better Plan, and from whom he has only borrow'd some particular Ornaments; yet it is but Justice to say, that his Plan is much more regular than that of Ariosto. In the *Orlando Furioso*, we every where meet with an exuberant Invention, join'd with great Liveliness and Facility of Description, yet debas'd by frequent Mixtures of the comick Genius, as well as many shocking Indecorums. Besides, in the Huddle and Distraction of the Adventures, we are for the most part only amus'd with extravagant Stories, without being instructed in any Moral. On the other hand, Spenser's Fable, tho often wild, is, as I have observ'd, always emblematical: And this may very much excuse likewise that Air of Romance in which he has follow'd the Italian Author. The perpetual Stories of Knights, Giants, Castles, and Enchantments, and all that Train of Legendary Adventures, wou'd indeed appear very trifling, if Spenser had not found a way to turn them all into Allegory, or if a less masterly Hand had fill'd up his Draught. But it is surprizing to observe how much the Strength of the Painting is superior to the Design. It ought to be consider'd too, that at the time when our Author wrote, the Remains of the old Gothick Chivalry were not quite abolish'd: It was not many Years before, that the famous Earl of Surry, remarkable for his Wit and Poetry in the Reign of King Henry the Eighth, took a romantick Journey to Florence, the Place of his Mistress's Birth, and publish'd there a Challenge against all Nations in Defence of her Beauty. Justs and Turnaments were held in England in the Time of Queen Elizabeth. Sir Philip Sidney tilted at one of these Entertainments, which was made for the French Ambassador, when the Treaty of Marriage was on foot with the Duke of Anjou: and some of our Historians have given us a very particular and formal Account of Preparations, by marking out Lists, and appointing Judges, for a Tryal by Combat, in the same Reign, which was to have decided the Title to a considerable Estate; and in which the whole Ceremony was perfectly agreeable to the fabulous Descriptions in Books of Knight-Errantry. This might render his Story more familiar to his first Readers; tho Knights in Armour, and Ladies Errant are as antiquated Figures to us, as the Court of that time wou'd appear, if we cou'd see them now in their Ruffs and Fardingales.

There are two other Objections to the Plan of the *Fairy Queen*, which, I confess, I am more at a loss to answer. I need not, I think, be scrupulous in mentioning freely the Defects of a Poem, which, tho it was never suppos'd to be perfect, has always been allow'd to be admirable.

The first is, that the Scene is laid in Fairy-Land, and the chief Actors are Fairies. The Reader may see their imaginary Race and History in the Second Book, at the end of the Tenth Canto: but if he is not prepar'd before-hand, he may expect to find them acting agreeably to the common Stories and Traditions about such fancy'd Beings. Thus Shakespear, who has introduc'd them in his *Midsummer-Night's Dream*, has made them speak and act in a manner perfectly adapted to their suppos'd Characters; but the Fairies in this Poem are not distinguish'd from other Persons. There is this Misfortune likewise attends the Choice of such Actors, that having been accustom'd to conceive of them in a diminutive way, we find it difficult to raise our Ideas, and to imagine a Fairy encountring with a Monster or a Giant. Homer has pursu'd a contrary Method, and represented his Heroes above the Size and Strength of ordinary Men; and it is certain that the

Actions of the *Iliad* wou'd have appear'd but ill proportion'd to the Characters, if we were to have imagin'd them all perform'd by Pigmies.

But as the Actors our Author has chosen, are only fancy'd Beings, he
might possibly think himself at liberty to give them what Stature, Customs
and Manners he pleas'd. I will not say he was in the right in this: but it is
plain that by the literal Sense of Fairy-Land, he only design'd an Utopia,
an imaginary Place; and by his Fairies, Persons of whom he might invent
any Action proper to human Kind, without being restrain'd, as he must
have been, if he had chosen a real Scene and historical Characters. As for
the mystical Sense, it appears both by the Work it self, and by the Author's
Explanation of it, that his Fairy-Land is England, and his Fairy-Queen,
Queen Elizabeth; at whose Command the Adventure of every Legend is
suppos'd to be undertaken.

The other Objection is, that having chosen an historical Person, Prince
Arthur, for his principal Hero; who is no Fairy, yet is mingled with them:
he has not however represented any part of his History. He appears here
indeed only in his Minority, and performs his Exercises in Fairy-Land, as
a private Gentleman; but we might at least have expected, that the fabulous
Accounts of him, and of his Victories over the Saxons, shou'd have been
work'd into some beautiful Vision or Prophecy: and I cannot think Spenser
wou'd wholly omit this, but am apt to believe he had done it in some of
the following Books which were lost.

*   *   *

I have not yet said any thing concerning Spenser's Versification; in which,
tho he is not always equal to hismelf, it may be affirm'd, that he is superior
to all his Cotemporaries, and even to those that follow'd him for some
time, except Fairfax,[1] the applauded Translator of Tasso. In this he com-
mendably study'd the Italians, and must be allow'd to have been a great
Improver of our English Numbers: Before his time, Musick seems to have
been so much a Stranger to our Poertry, that, excepting the Earl of Surry's
Lyricks, we have very few Examples of Verses that had any tolerable Cadence. In Chaucer there is so little of this, that many of his Lines are not
even restrain'd to a certain Number of Syllables. Instances of this loose
Verse are likewise to be found in our Author, but it is only in such Places
where he has purposely imitated Chaucer, as in the second Eclogue, and
some others. This great Defect of Harmony put the Wits in Queen Elizabeth's Reign upon a Design of totally changing our Numbers, not only
by banishing Rhime, but by new moulding our Language into the Feet
and Measures of the Latin Poetry. Sir Philip Sidney was at the Head of
this Project, and has accordingly given us some Hexameter and Pentameter
Verses in his *Arcadia*. But the Experiment soon fail'd; and tho our Author,
by some Passages in his Letters to Mr. Harvey, seems not to have disapprov'd
it, yet it does not appear by those Poems of his, which are preserv'd, that
he gave it any Authority by his Example.

As to the Stanza in which the *Fairy Queen* is written, tho the Author
cannot be commended for his Choice of it, yet it is much more harmonious
in its kind than the Heroick Verse of that Age. It is almost the same with

1. Edward Fairfax (c. 1575–1635) translated Tasso's *Gerusalemme Liberata* in 1600 (under the title
"Godfrey of Bulloigne") [*Editors*].

what the Italians call their *Ottave Rime*, which is us'd both by Ariosto and Tasso, but improv'd by Spenser, with the Addition of a Line more in the Close, of the Length of our Alexandrines. The Defect of it, in long or narrative Poems, is apparent. The same Measure, closed always by a full Stop, in the same Place, by which every Stanza is made as it were a distinct Paragraph, grows tiresom by continual Repetition, and frequently breaks the Sense, when it ought to be carry'd on without Interruption. With this Exception, the Reader will however find it harmonious, full of well-sounding Epithets, and of such elegant Turns on the Thought and Words, that Dryden himself owns he learn'd these Graces of Verse chiefly from our Author; and does not scruple to say, that in this Particular *only Virgil surpass'd him among the Romans, and only Mr. Waller among the English.*

* * *

In the Remarks on the *Fairy Queen*, I have chiefly consider'd our Author as an Allegorical Writer; and his Poem as fram'd after a Model of a particular kind. In some of his other Writings, we find more Regularity, tho less Invention. There seems to be the same difference between the *Fairy Queen* and the *Shepherd's Calendar*, as between a Royal Palace and a little Country Seat. The first strikes the Eye with more Magnificence; but the latter may perhaps give the greatest Pleasure. In this Work the Author has not been misled by the Italians; tho Tasso's *Aminta*[2] might have been at least of as good Authority to him in the Pastoral, as Ariosto in the greater kind of Poetry. But Spenser rather chose to follow Nature it self, and to paint the Life and Sentiments of Shepherds after a more simple and unaffected manner.

The two things which seem the most essential to Pastoral, are Love, and the Images of a Country Life: and to represent these, our Author had little more to do, than to examine his own Heart, and to copy the Scene about him; for at the time when he wrote the *Shepherd's Calendar*, he was a passionate Lover of his Rosalind: and it appears that the greatest part of it, if not the whole, was compos'd in the Country on his first leaving the University; and before he had engag'd in Business, or fill'd his Mind with the Thoughts of Preferment in a Life at Court. Perhaps too there is a certain Age most proper for Pastoral Writing; and tho the same Genius shou'd arise afterwards to greater Excellencies, it may grow less capable of this. Accordingly in the Poem call'd *Colin Clout's come home again*, which was written a considerable time after, we find him less a Shepherd than at first: He had then been drawn out of his Retirement, had appear'd at Court, and been engag'd in an Employment which brought him into a Variety of Business and Acquaintance, and gave him a quite different Sett of Ideas. And tho this Poem is not without its Beauties; yet what I wou'd here observe is, that in the Pastoral Kind it is not so simple and unmix'd, and consequently not so perfect as the *Eclogues*, of which I have perhaps given the Reason.

But I am sensible that what I have mention'd as a Beauty in Spenser's Pastorals, will not seem so to all Readers; and that the Simplicity which appears in them may be thought to have too much of the *Merum Rus*.[3] If

2. A pastoral drama composed in 1573 [*Editors*].
3. "Real country" (in the sense of mere, absolute rusticity) [*Editors*].

our Author has err'd in this, he has at least err'd on the right hand. The true Model of Pastoral Writing seems indeed not to be yet fix'd by the Criticks; and there is room for the best Judges to differ in their Opinions about it: Those who wou'd argue for the Simplicity of Pastoral, may say, That the very Idea of this kind of Writing is the Representation of a Life of Retirement and Innocence, made agreeable by all those Pleasures and Amusements, which the Fields, the Woods, and the various Seasons of the Year afford to Men, who live according to the first Dictates of Nature, and without the artificial Cares and Refinements, which Wealth, Luxury, and Ambition, by multiplying both our Wants and Enjoyments, have introduc'd among the Rich and the Polite: That therefore as the Images, Similies, and Allusions are to be drawn from the Scene; so the Sentiments and Expressions ought no where to taste of the City, or the Court, but to have such a kind of plain Elegance only, as may appear proper to the Life and Characters of the Persons introduc'd in such Poems: That this Simplicity, skilfully drawn, will make the Picture more natural, and consequently more pleasing: That even the low Images in such a Representation are amusing, as they contribute to deceive the Reader, and make him fancy himself really in such a Place, and among such Persons as are describ'd; the Pleasure in this case being like that express'd by Milton of one walking out into the Fields:

> ————Who long in populous Cities pent,
> Where Houses thick, and Sewers annoy the Air,
> Forth issuing on a Summer's Morn to breathe
> Among the pleasant Villages and Farms
> Adjoin'd, from each thing met conceives Delight;
> The Smell of Grain, or tedded Grass, or Kine,
> Or Dairy, each rural Sight, each rural Sound.[4]

This indeed seems to be the true Reason of the Entertainment which Pastoral Poetry gives to its Readers: for as Mankind is departed from the Simplicity, as well as the Innocence, of a State of Nature, and is immers'd in Cares and Pursuits of a very different kind; it is a wonderful Amusement to the Imagination, to be sometimes transported, as it were, out of modern Life, and to wander in these pleasant Scenes which the Pastoral Poets provide for us, and in which we are apt to fancy our selves reinstated for a time in our first Innocence and Happiness.

Those who argue against the strict Simplicity of Pastoral Writing, think there is something too low in the Characters and Sentiments of mere Shepherds, to support this kind of Poetry, if not rais'd and improv'd by the Assistance of Art; or at least that we ought to distinguish between what is simple, and what is rustick, and take care that while we represent Shepherds, we do not make them Clowns: That it is a Mistake to imagine that the Life of Shepherds is incapable of any Refinement, or that their Sentiments may not sometimes rise above the Country. To justify this, they tell us, that we conceive too low an Idea of this kind of Life, by taking it from that of modern Shepherds, who are the meanest and poorest sort of People among us. But in the first Ages of the World it was otherwise; that Persons of Rank

4. *Paradise Lost* 9.445–51 [Editors].

and Dignity honour'd this Employment; that Shepherds were the Owners of their own Flocks; and that David was once a Shepherd, who became afterwards a King, and was himself too the most sublime of Poets. Those who argue for the first kind of Pastoral, recommend Theocritus as the best Model; and those who are for the latter, think that Virgil, by raising it to a higher Pitch, has improv'd it. I shall not determine this Controversy, but only observe, that the Pastorals of Spenser are of the former kind.

It is for the same Reason that the Language of the *Shepherd's Calendar*, which is design'd to be rural, is older than that of his other Poems. Sir Philip Sidney however, tho he commends this Work in his *Apology for Poetry*, censures the Rusticity of the Stile as an Affectation not to be allow'd. The Author's profess'd Veneration for Chaucer partly led him into this; yet there is a difference among the Pastorals, and the Reader will observe, that the Language of the Fifth and Eighth is more obsolete than that of some others; the reason of which might be, that the Design of those two Eclogues being Allegorical Satire, he chose a more antiquated Dress, as more proper to his Purpose. But however faulty he may be in the Excess of this, it is certain that a sprinkling of the rural Phrase, as it humours the Scene and Characters, has a very great Beauty in Pastoral Poetry; and of this any one may be convinc'd, by reading the Pastorals of Mr Philips,[5] which are written with great Delicacy of Taste, in the very Spirit and Manner of Spenser.

Having said that Spenser has mingled Satire in some of his Eclogues, I know not whether this may not be another Objection to them: it may be doubted whether any thing of this kind shou'd be admitted to disturb the Tranquillity and Pleasure which shou'd every where reign in Pastoral Poems; or at least nothing shou'd be introduc'd more than the light and pleasant Railleries or Contentions of Shepherds about their Flocks, their Mistresses, or their Skill in piping and singing. I cannot wholly justify my Author in this, yet must say that the Excellency of the Moral in those Pastorals does in a great measure excuse his trangressing the strict Rules of Criticism. Besides, as he design'd under an Allegory to censure the vicious Lives of bad Priests, and to expose their Usurpation of Pomp and Dominion, nothing cou'd be more proper to this purpose than the Allegory he has chosen; the Author of our Holy Religion having himself dignify'd the Parable of a good Shepherd; and the natural Innocence, Simplicity, Vigilance, and Freedom from Ambition, which are the Characters of that kind of Life, being a very good Contrast to the Vices and Luxury, and to that Degeneracy from their first Pattern, which the Poet wou'd there reprehend. * * *

5. Ambrose Philips (c. 1675–1749) [*Editors*].

SAMUEL TAYLOR COLERIDGE
[Spenser's Art]†

There is this difference, among many others, between Shakspeare and Spenser:—Shakspeare is never colored by the customs of his age; what appears of contemporary character in him is merely negative; it is just not something else. He has none of the fictitious realities of the classics, none of the grotesquenesses of chivalry, none of the allegory of the middle ages; there is no sectarianism either of politics or religion, no miser, no witch, —no common witch,—no astrology—nothing impermanent of however long duration; but he stands like the yew-tree in Lorton vale, which has known so many ages that it belongs to none in particular; a living image of endless self-reproduction, like the immortal tree of Malabar. In Spenser the spirit of chivalry is entirely predominant, although with a much greater infusion of the poet's own individual self into it than is found in any other writer. He has the wit of the southern with the deeper inwardness of the northern genius.

No one can appreciate Spenser without some reflection on the nature of allegorical writing. The mere etymological meaning of the word, allegory,—to talk of one thing and thereby convey another,—is too wide. The true sense is this,—the employment of one set of agents and images to convey in disguise a moral meaning, with a likeness to the imagination, but with a difference to the understanding,—those agents and images being so combined as to form a homogeneous whole. This distinguishes it from metaphor, which is part of an allegory. But allegory is not properly distinguishable from fable, otherwise than as the first includes the second, as a genus its species; for in a fable there must be nothing but what is universally known and acknowledged, but in an allegory there may be that which is new and not previously admitted. The pictures of the great masters, especially of the Italian schools, are genuine allegories. Amongst the classics, the multitude of their gods either precluded allegory altogether, or else made every thing allegory, as in the Hesiodic Theogonia; for you can scarcely distinguish between power and the personification of power. The Cupid and Psyche of, or found in, Apuleius, is a phenomenon. It is the Platonic mode of accounting for the fall of man. The Battle of the Soul by Prudentius[1] is an early instance of Christian allegory.

Narrative allegory is distinguished from mythology as reality from symbol; it is, in short, the proper intermedium between person and personification. Where it is too strongly individualized, it ceases to be allegory; this is often felt in the Pilgrim's Progress, where the characters are real persons with nicknames. Perhaps one of the most curious warnings against another attempt at narrative allegory on a great scale, may be found in Tasso's account of what he himself intended in and by his Jerusalem Delivered.

---

† From the third in "A Course of Lectures" (1818); the published versions of these lectures are based on notes arranged by H. N. Coleridge. Cf. Coleridge's Miscellaneous Criticism, ed. T. M. Raysor (Cambridge, MA, 1936) 32–38.
1. Latin (Christian) poet of the fourth century A.D. [Editors].

As characteristic of Spenser, I would call your particular attention in the first place to the indescribable sweetness and fluent projection of his verse, very clearly distinguishable from the deeper and more interwoven harmonies of Shakspeare and Milton. This stanza is a good instance of what I mean:—

> Yet she, most faithfull ladie, all this while
> Forsaken, wofull, solitarie mayd,
> Far from all peoples preace, as in exile,
> In wildernesse and wastfull deserts strayd
> To seeke her knight; who, subtily betrayd
> Through that late vision which th' enchaunter wrought,
> Had her abandond; she, of nought affrayd,
> Through woods and wastnes wide him daily sought,
> Yet wished tydinges none of him unto her brought.
>
> [*F.Q.*, I.iii.3]

2. Combined with this sweetness and fluency, the scientific construction of the metre of the Faery Queene is very noticeable. One of Spenser's arts is that of alliteration, and he uses it with great effect in doubling the impression of an image:—

> In *w*ildernesse and *w*astful deserts
> Through *w*oods and *w*astnes *w*ilde,—
> They passe the bitter *w*aves of Acheron,
> Where many soules sit *w*ailing *w*oefully,
> And come to *f*iery *f*lood of *Ph*legeton,
> Whereas the damned ghosts in torments fry,
> And with sharp shrilling shrieks doth bootlesse cry,—&c.
>
> [*F.Q.*, I.v.33]

He is particularly given to an alternate alliteration, which is, perhaps, when well used, a great secret in melody:—

> A *r*amping *l*yon *r*ushed *s*uddenly,—
> And *s*ad to *s*ee her *s*orrowful constraint,—
> And on the grasse her *d*aintie *l*imbes *d*id *l*ay,—&c.
>
> [*F.Q.*, I.iii.5]

You can not read a page of the Faery Queene, if you read for that purpose, without perceiving the intentional alliterativeness of the words; and yet so skilfully is this managed, that it never strikes any unwarned ear as artificial, or other than the result of the necessary movement of the verse.

3. Spenser displays great skill in harmonizing his descriptions of external nature and actual incidents with the allegorical character and epic activity of the poem. Take these two beautiful passages as illustrations of what I mean:—[Quotes from I.ii.1–2, and I.v.2].

Observe also the exceeding vividness of Spenser's descriptions. They are not, in the true sense of the word, picturesque; but are composed of a wondrous series of images, as in our dreams. Compare the following passage

with any thing you may remember in *pari materia*[2] in Milton or
Shakspeare:—[Quotes I.vii.31–32].

4. You will take especial note of the marvellous independence and true
imaginative absence of all particular space or time in the Faery Queene.
It is in the domains neither of history or geography; it is ignorant of all
artificial boundary, all material obstacles; it is truly in land of Faery, that
is, of mental space. The poet has placed you in a dream, a charmed sleep,
and you neither wish, nor have the power, to inquire where you are, or
how you got there. It reminds me of some lines of my own:—

> Oh ! would to Alla !
> The raven or the sea-mew were appointed
> To bring me food !—or rather that my soul
> Might draw in life from the universal air !
> It were a lot divine in some small skiff
> Along some ocean's boundless solitude
> To float forever with a careless course
> And think myself the only being alive ![3]

Indeed Spenser himself, in the conduct of his great poem, may be represented under the same image, his symbolizing purpose being his mariner's
compass:—

> As pilot well expert in perilous wave,
> That to a stedfast starre his course hath bent,
> When foggy mistes or cloudy tempests have
> The faithfull light of that faire lampe yblent,
> And coverd Heaven with hideous dreriment;
> Upon his card and compas firmes his eye,
> The maysters of his long experiment,
> And to them does the steddy helme apply,
> Bidding his winged vessell fairely forward fly.
> [II.vii.1]

So the poet through the realms of allegory.

5. You should note the quintessential character of Christian chivalry in
all his characters, but more especially in his women. The Greeks, except,
perhaps, in Homer, seem to have had no way of making their women
interesting, but by unsexing them, as in the instances of the tragic Medea,
Electra, &c. Contrast such characters with Spenser's Una, who exhibits no
prominent feature, has no particularization, but produces the same feeling
that a statue does, when contemplated at a distance:—

> From her fayre head her fillet she undight,
> And layd her stole aside : her angels face,
> As the great eye of Heaven, shyned bright,

<hr>

2. I.e., "in similar vein" [*Editors*].
3. From Coleridge's drama *Remorse* 4.3 [*Editors*].

And made a sunshine in the shady place ;
Did never mortal eye behold such heavenly grace.
[I.iii.4]

6. In Spenser we see the brightest and purest form of that nationality which was so common a characteristic of our elder poets. There is nothing unamiable, nothing contemptuous of others, in it. To glorify their country—to elevate England into a queen, an empress of the heart—this was their passion and object; and how dear and important an object it was or may be, let Spain, in the recollection of her Cid,[4] declare! There is a great magic in national names. What a damper to all interest is a list of native East Indian merchants! Unknown names are non-conductors; they stop all sympathy. No one of our poets has touched this string more exquisitely than Spenser; especially in his chronicle of the British Kings,[5] and the marriage of the Thames with the Medway,[6] in both which passages the mere names constitute half the pleasure we receive. To the same feeling we must in particular attribute Spenser's sweet reference to Ireland:—

Ne thence the Irishe rivers absent were;
Sith no lesse famous than the rest they be, &c.

*   *   *   *   *   *   *   *

And Mulla mine, whose waves I whilom taught to weep.
[IV.xi.40–41]

And there is a beautiful passage of the same sort in the Colin Clout's Come Home Again:—

"One day," quoth he, "I sat, as was my trade,
Under the foot of Mole," &c.   [56–57]

Lastly, the great and prevailing character of Spenser's mind is fancy under the conditions of imagination, as an ever-present but not always active power. He has an imaginative fancy, but he has not imagination, in kind or degree, as Shakspeare and Milton have; the boldest effort of his powers in this way is the character of Talus.[7] Add to this a feminine tenderness and almost maidenly purity of feeling, and above all, a deep moral earnestness which produces a believing sympathy and acquiescence in the reader, and you have a tolerably adequate view of Spenser's intellectual being.

---

4. Rodrigo Diaz de Bivar, "el Cid" (c. 1030–99), national hero of Spain [Editors].
5. The Faerie Queene II.x [Editors].
6. The Faerie Queene IV.xi [Editors].
7. Arthegall's servant, "made of yron mould," in The Faerie Queene V [Editors].

Twentieth-Century Criticism

VIRGINIA WOOLF

The Faery Queen†

The Faery Queen, it is said, has never been read to the end; no one has ever wished *Paradise Lost*, it is said, a word longer;[1] and these remarks however exaggerated probably give pleasure, like a child's laugh at a ceremony, because they express something we secretly feel and yet try to hide. Dare we then at this time of day come out with the remark that *The Faery Queen* is a great poem? So one might say early rising, cold bathing, abstention from wine and tobacco are good; and if one said it, a blank look would steal over the company as they made haste to agree and then to lower the tone of the conversation. Yet it is true. Here are some general observations made by one who has gone through the experience, and wishes to urge others, who may be hiding their yawns and their polite boredom, to the same experience.

The first essential is, of course, not to read *The Faery Queen*. Put it off as long as possible. Grind out politics; absorb science; wallow in fiction; walk about London; observe the crowds; calculate the loss of life and limb; rub shoulders with the poor in markets; buy and sell; fix the mind firmly on the financial columns of the newspapers, weather; on the crops; on the fashions. At the mere mention of chivalry shiver and snigger; detest allegory; revel in direct speech; adore all the virtues of the robust, the plain spoken; and then, when the whole being is red and brittle as sandstone in the sun, make a dash for *The Faery Queen* and give yourself up to it.

But reading poetry is a complex art. The mind has many layers, and the greater the poem the more of these are roused and brought into action. They seem, too, to be in order. The faculty we employ upon poetry at the first reading is sensual; the eye of the mind opens. And Spenser rouses the eye softly and brilliantly with his green trees, his pearled women, his crested and plumed knights. (Then we need to use our sympathies, not the strong passions, but the simple wish to go with our knight and his lady to feel their heat and cold, and their thirst and hunger.) And then we need movement. Their figures, as they pass along the grass track, must reach a hovel

† "The Faery Queen" (pp. 24–30) from *The Moment and Other Essays* by Virginia Woolf, copyright 1948 by Harcourt Brace Jovanovich, Inc. and renewed 1976 by Harcourt Brace Jovanovich, Inc. and Marjorie T. Parsons. Reprinted by permission of the publishers, Harcourt Brace Jovanovich, Inc. and The Hogarth Press.

1. It was Dr. Samuel Johnson (1709–84) who observed in "Milton," in *The Lives of the Most Eminent English Poets* (1783), "None ever wished it longer than it is" [*Editors*].

or a palace or find a man in weeds reading his book. That too is gratified. And then living thus with our eyes, with our legs and arms, with the natural quiet feelings of liking and disliking tolerantly and gently excited, we realise a more complex desire that all these emotions should combine. There must be a pervading sense of belief, or much of our emotion will be wasted. The tree must be part of the knight; the knight of the lady. All these states of mind must support one another, and the strength of the poem will come from the combination, just as it will fail if at any point the poet loses belief.

But it may be said, when a poet is dealing with Faery Land and the supernatural people who live there, belief can only be used in a special sense. We do not believe in the existence of giants and ogres, but in something that the poet himself believed them to represent. What then was Spenser's belief, when he wrote his poem? He has himself declared that the "general intention and meaning" of *The Faery Queen* was "to fashion a gentleman or noble person in virtuous and noble discipline." It would be absurd to pretend that we are more than intermittently conscious of the poet's meaning. Yet as we read, we half consciously have the sense of some pattern hanging in the sky, so that without referring any of the words to a special place, they have that meaning which comes from their being parts of a whole design, and not an isolated fragment of unrelated loveliness. The mind is being perpetually enlarged by the power of suggestion. Much more is imagined than is stated. And it is due to this quality that the poem changes, with time, so that after four hundred years it still corresponds to something which we, who are momentarily in the flesh, feel at the moment.

The question asks itself, then, how Spenser, himself imprisoned in so many impediments of circumstance, remote from us in time, in speech, in convention, yet seems to be talking about things that are important to us too? Compare, for example, his perfect gentleman with Tennyson's Arthur.[2] Already, much in Tennyson's pattern is unintelligible; an easy butt for satire. Among living writers again, there is none who is able to display a typical figure. Each seems limited to one room of the human dwelling. But with Spenser, though here in this department of our being, we seem able to unlock the door and walk about. We miss certain intensities and details, but on the other hand we are uncabined. We are allowed to give scope to a number of interests, delights, curiosities, and loves that find no satisfaction in the poetry of our own time. But though it would be easy to frame a reason for this and to generalise about the decay of faith, the rise of machines, the isolation of the human being, let us, however, work from the opposite point of view. In reading *The Faery Queen* the first thing, we said, was that the mind has different layers. It brings one into play and then another. The desire of the eye, the desire of the body, desires for rhythm, movement, the desire for adventure—each is gratified. And this gratification depends upon the poet's own mobility. He is alive in all his parts. He scarcely seems to prefer one to another. We are reminded of the old myth of the body which has many organs, and the lesser and the obscure are as important as the kingly and important.

Here at any rate the poet's body seems all alive. A fearlessness, a simplicity

2. I.e., King Arthur, in Tennyson's *Idylls of the King* [Editors].

that is like the movement of a naked savage possesses him. He is not merely a thinking brain; he is a feeling body, a sensitive heart. He has hands and feet, and, as he says himself, a natural chastity, so that some things are judged unfit for the pen. "My chaster muse for shame doth blush to write." In short, when we read *The Faery Queen*, we feel that the whole being is drawn upon, not merely a separate part.

To say this is to say that the conventions that Spenser uses are not enough to cut us off from the inner meaning. And the reason soon makes itself apparent. When we talk of the modern distaste for allegory, we are only saying that we prefer our qualities in another form. The novelist uses allegory; that is to say, when he wishes to expound his characters, he makes them think; Spenser impersonated his psychology. Thus if the novelist now wished to convey his hero's gloom, he would tell us his thoughts; Spenser creates a figure called Despair. He has the fullest sense of what sorrow is. But he typifies it; he creates a dwelling, an old man who comes out of the house and says I cannot tell; and then the figure of Despair with his beautiful elegy. Instead of being prisoned in one breast we are shown the outer semblance. He is working thus on a larger, freer, more depersonalised scale. By making the passions into people, he gives them an amplitude. And who shall say that this is the less natural, the less realistic? For the most exact observer has to leave much of his people's minds obscure.

Once we get him out of his private mythology, there is no mythology which can personify his actions. We wish to convey delight and have to describe an actual garden, here and now; Spenser at once calls up a picture of nymphs dancing, youth, maidens crowned. And yet it is not pictorial merely. Nothing is more refreshing, nothing serves more to sting and revive us than the spray of fresh hard words, little colloquialisms, tart green words that might have been spoken at dinner, joining in easily with the more stately tribe. But such externality is impossible to us, because we have lost our power to create symbols. Spenser's ability to use despair in person depends on his power to create a world in which such a figure draws natural breath, living breath. He has his dwelling at the centre of a universe which offers him the use of dragons, knights, magic; and all the company that exist about them; and flowers and dawn and sunset. All this was still just within his reach. He could believe in it, his public could believe in it, sufficiently to make it serviceable. It was, of course, just slipping from his grasp. That is obvious from his own words. His poem, he says, will be called the abundance of an idle brain. His language, too, oddly compounded of the high flown and the vernacular, was just then at the turn. On the one hand we have the old smooth conventions—Tithonus, Cynthia, Phoebus, and the rest; on the other fry and rascal and losel,[3] the common speech that was current on the lips of the women at the door. He was not asking the reader to adopt an unnatural pose; only to think poetically. And the writer's faith is still effective. We are removed 400 years from Spenser; and the effort to think back into his mood requires some adjustment, some

---

3. I.e., worthless person [*Editors*].

oblivion; but there is nothing false in what is to be done; it is easier to read Spenser than to read William Morris.[4]

The true difficulty lies elsewhere. It lies in the fact that the poem is a meditation, not a dramatisation. At no point is Spenser under the necessity of bringing his characters to the surface; they lack the final embodiment which is forced so drastically upon the playwright. They sink back into the poet's mind and thus lack definition. He is talking about them; they are not using their own words. Hence the indistinctness which leads, as undoubtedly it does lead, to monotony. The verse becomes for a time a rocking horse; swaying up and down; a celestial rocking horse, whose pace is always rhythmical and seemly, but lulling, soporific. It sings us to sleep; it lulls the teeth of the wind. On no other terms, however, could we be kept in being. And to compensate we have the quality of that mind; the sense that we are confined in one continuous consciousness, which is Spenser's; that he has saturated and enclosed this world, that we live in a great bubble blown from the poet's brain. Yet if it ignores our own marks, houses, chimneys, roads, the multitudinous details which serve like signposts or features to indicate to us where our emotions lie, it is not a private world of fantasy. Here are the qualities that agitate living people at the moment; spite, greed, jealousy, ugliness, poverty, pain; Spenser in his poet's castle was as acutely aware of the rubs and tumbles of life as the living, but by virtue of his poetry blew them away into the higher air. So we feel not shut in, but freed; and take our way in a world which gives expression to sensation more vigorously, more exactly than we can manage for ourselves in the flesh. It is a world of astonishing physical brilliance and intensity; sharpened, intensified as objects are in a clearer air; such as we see them, not in dreams, but when all the faculties are alert and vigorous; when the stuffing and the detail have been brushed aside; and we see the bone and the symmetry; now in a landscape, in Ireland or in Greece; and now when we think of ourselves, under the more intense ray of poetry; under its sharper, its lovelier light.

RICHARD HELGERSON

[The New Poet Presents Himself]†

Among his immediate contemporaries, Spenser was doubly unique. Not only was he the best poet, he was the only poet of distinctly laureate ambition. Other men did, of course, write verse. But he alone presented himself as a poet, as a man who considered writing a duty rather than a distraction. With the exception of a few rare and little-respected hirelings, Spenser's literary contemporaries were gentlemen for whom poetry was a mere ribbon in the cap of youth, a ribbon which, if paraded too ostenta-

---

4. English poet and craftsman (1834–96); Woolf may refer to some parts of *The Earthly Paradise*, a cycle of twenty-four versified medieval tales [*Editors*].

† From *Self-Crowned Laureates: Spenser, Jonson, Milton, and the Literary System* by Richard Helgerson, 55–100. The essay has been slightly condensed. Copyright © 1983 The Regents of the University of California. Reprinted by permission.

tiously, threatened to expose its wearer to ridicule and shame. Their poetic self-indulgence (for self-indulgence it was generally admitted to be) was, in consequence, usually of short duration and was marked, whatever its duration, by much self-conscious defensiveness, leading quite often to repentance. A Sidney, a Lodge, or a Harington might defend poetry in the highest terms, proclaiming its divine origin and advertising its civilizing effect, but when these men spoke of their own work it was either with humorous and graceful disdain or with some more serious uncertainty. At such moments, the various elevated notions of the poet as counselor of kings and monarch of all sciences, as first bringer-in of civility, best teacher of virtue, and most potent inspirer of courage—notions that had filled their defenses of poesy, their apologies, and their honest excuses—failed them, leaving no refuge but self-depreciation or recantation. * * * And often the repentant admission of self-destructive prodigality was coupled with a condemnation of poetry, or of the wit that made it possible, or of the love that inspired it. * * * Whether their excuse was "the unnoble constitution of the age that denies us fit employments" or the overmastering sway of some amorous passion, they did agree that poetry required an excuse, and most felt that the best proof of contrition was a promise not to offend in like sort again—a promise that they usually kept.[1]

But so long as Englishmen offered their poems as mere "idle toys proceeding from a youngling frenzy," England could hardly hope to have a poet of the laureate sort. . . .[2]

How then did he manage to distinguish himself as laureate from his amateur coevals? At first glance, particularly when the glance is taken in retrospect, the formula for his success seems absurdly simple. It consisted of two steps. The first was publicly to abandon all social identity except that conferred by his elected vocation. He ceased to be Master Edmund Spenser of Merchant Taylors' School and Pembroke College, Cambridge, and became Immerito, Colin Clout, the New Poet. No other writer of his generation was willing to take such a step. His contemporaries all hung on to some higher hope or expectation. But where they were lowered by poetry, Spenser, who never tired of insisting on his personal humility, was raised by it. This strategy had, of course, a certain autobiographical plausibility. Unlike Sidney, heir apparent to the earldoms of Leicester and Warwick, or Harington, the Queen's godson, or even Lodge, son of a knighted Lord Mayor of London, Spenser was, whatever his connection with the Spencers of Althorp, a gentleman only by education. He had attended Merchant Taylors' School as a "poor scholar," and Cambridge as a sizar. In presenting himself as a shepherd-poet, he suffered no major *déclassement*.

The second step was the accomplishment of virtuous action through poetry. Though the poet may not himself be an actor in the world, his poetry does make others act. Having abandoned his own public pretension to gentility and its obligations, he proposes nevertheless that "the general

1. For a fuller discussion of this pattern and its place in the lives and works of Spenser's contemporaries, see my *Elizabethan Prodigals* (Berkeley: Univ. of California Press, 1976).
2. Thomas Watson, *Hekatompathia or Passionate Centurie of Love*, ed. S. K. Heninger, Jr. (Gainesville, Florida: Scholars' Facsimiles, 1964), p. 5.

end" of his major work is "to fashion a gentleman or noble person in virtuous and gentle discipline." Now other writers, of course, also argued for the didactic value of their work, but rarely did they go beyond expressing the self-defeating hope that other young gentlemen might learn from the poet's experience to avoid the like excess. The lesson of poetry was thus to stay away from poetry and from everything associated with it. * * * But not only did Spenser maintain his view with a resolutely sage seriousness, as Sidney never did, he also illustrated it triumphantly in the first three books of *The Faerie Queene*.

Yet skirting about the periphery is a slight, but ominous, reminder of the more usual Elizabethan estimate of poetry and its relation to the active life of public service. It emerges most clearly in the dedicatory sonnet to Lord Burghley, the leader of the Queen's government and a man notoriously unsympathetic to poets and to poetry.

> To you right noble Lord, whose carefull brest
> To menage of most grave affaires is bent,
> And on whose mightie shoulders most doth rest
> The burdein of this kingdomes governement,
> As the wide compasse of the firmament,
> On Atlas mighty shoulders is upstayd;
> Unfitly I these ydle rimes present,
> The labor of lost time, and wit unstayd.

Confronted with the statesmanlike gravity of Lord Burghley, Spenser forces himself back into the mold of the prodigal poet, the unstaid wit whose work is the product of idleness and lost time. The pressure on Spenser to define himself and his work in these conventional terms was considerable, for they provided, as I have been arguing, the clearest and most widely understood notion of what a poet was and did. The triumphant realization of another idea of the poet in the first three books of *The Faerie Queene* can hardly be appreciated without some sense of those pressures. * * *

As everyone knows, the publication of *The Shepheardes Calender* was a carefully planned literary event. Not merely another collection of poems, the *Calender* marked the debut of the New Poet. The argument supposed by the poems and by E. K.'s introduction to them was already familiar in 1579 and was to become still more familiar in the decade between this promise and its realization in the first books of *The Faerie Queene*. England lacked a poet. "There are many versifiers," as one contemporary remarked, "but no poet."[3] Italy and France had theirs, as did Greece and Rome before them. Why not England? The English language was as fit for poetry, the glory of the English nation as worthy of celebration. Yet there was no English Homer or Virgil, no English Ariosto or Ronsard. Englishmen could, of course, look back to Chaucer, but Chaucer had lived in a time and written in a language too remote from their own to be more than a distant inspiration. But now, at last, the English Poet had appeared. His fledgling work could not yet fully validate his claim to laureate greatness,

---

3. *Sola quia interea nullum paris Anglia vatem? / Versifices multi, nemo poeta tibi est.* C. Downhale in Watson's *Hekatompathia*, p. 12.

and so his identity, like that of a still unproven knight of chivalric romance, was for a time to remain hidden. But he was, E. K. assured his audience, clearly beginning in the right way, with the pastoral,

> following the example of the best and most ancient poets, which devised this kind of writing . . . So flew Theocritus, . . . Virgil, . . . Mantuan, . . . Petrarch . . . Boccace . . . Marot, Sanazarus, and also diverse other excellent both Italian and French poets. . . . So finally flyeth this our new poet, as a bird, whose principals be scarce grown out, but yet as that in time shall be able to keep wing with the best.

An extraordinary claim, but there was much in the volume to support it. Not only do the poems contain, as Sidney was to say, "much poetry, . . . indeed worthy the reading," they constitute a deliberate *défense et illustration*[4] of the English language—a restoration of true English diction and a display of the range of poetic forms that English could handle.

Yet for all its pretension and real accomplishment, the book is rife with intimations of failure, breakdown, and renunciation—intimations that arise most often in conjunction with the commonplace Elizabethan notion of the poet as a youth beguiled by love. Even E. K., in defining "the general drift and purpose of [these] eclogues," falls back on the usual etiology and the usual defense: "Only this appeareth," he tells us, "that his unstaid youth had long wandered in the common Labyrinth of Love, in which time to mitigate and allay the heat of his passion, or else to warn (as he saith) the young shepherds . . . his equals and companions of his unfortunate folly, he compiled these xii eclogues." Here too poetry derives from the youthful folly of love and serves either to relieve its author of the effects of that folly or to warn others against it. But if this cure prove successful, why should he ever write again? What is to be his new source of inspiration and what is to be his purpose? These are not questions that occur to E. K. He is content to repeat the commonplace without considering its implications. But clearly they do occur to Spenser. He knows his power and has no hesitation in declaring it. He does not, however, know quite how else to use it, or whether indeed it can be put to any further use. Though *The Shepheardes Calender* is meant to distinguish the New Poet from all other writers of English verse, it finds no role for him to play other than the familiar self-defeating one that limited the poetic careers of all his contemporaries.

The series opens with Colin Clout, "under whose person," as we are repeatedly told, "the author self is shadowed," breaking his pipe and abandoning his muse, and it ends twelve eclogues later with a near echo of this gesture of renunciation, as Colin declares his muse hoarse and weary and

---

4. The phrase echoes the title of the "manifesto," *Deffence et illustration de la langue françoise*, composed in c. 1553 by Joachim du Bellay (1522–60), one of a group of young French poets (the "Pléiade") who wished to enrich and elevate the French language [*Editors*].

hangs his pipe upon a tree.[5] Whatever may be true of Spenser, Colin seems destined for no further accomplishment. There is no prospect here of a tomorrow promising "fresh woods, and pastures new," as there will be in Milton's pastoral of poetic self-consecration. On the contrary, having wasted his year on the love that began in January, Colin will have no second chance. Winter has come again, "And after Winter commeth timely death." His experience thus confirms that common moral admonition so fundamental to the Elizabethan pattern of a poetic career: "All the delights of love, wherein wanton youth walloweth," as E. K. puts it in glossing the March eclogue, "be but folly mixed with bitterness, and sorrow sauced with repentance." The pattern finds perhaps its most explicit application to poetry midway through the *Calender* in the June eclogue, where Colin talks of how he sang of love until

> yeeres more rype,
> And losse of her, whose love as lyfe I wayd,
> Those weary wanton toyes away did wype.
> (ll. 46–48)

* * *

Yet played against this conventional image of wanton youth is a suggestion of responsibility neglected—responsibility that in Colin's case is specifically poetic. Love may inspire lyric poetry, but it keeps the poet from other, more worthy, kinds—didactic, panegyric, historical, and divine. * * * The *Shepheardes Calender* thus contains a forceful critique of the conventional poet-as-lover, revealing that poetry written under such a guise is solipsistic, self-indulgent, and fruitless—that it leads inevitably to its own renunciation. Though the point is hardly less familiar than the role itself, we may be surprised to find it here in the book that launched the New Poet. We may be still more surprised to find it associated particularly with the New Poet's pastoral persona, Colin Clout. A great many other works of Spenser's generation teach the same lesson, but they usually announce, not the author's consecration of himself to poetry, but rather his renunciation of poetry in favor of some more serious pursuit. Spenser also talks of more serious pursuits, but these too, as I have said, are literary. Are we then to conclude that in the end Spenser separates himself from Colin, "cast[ing] off his shepherd's weeds," to "emerge as England's heroic poet"?[6] E. K. does deliver a clarion blast worthy of such an epiphany, but the poems fail to echo it. On the contrary, they express, along with a towering ambition and a sense of unique poetic power, much uncertainty about both the practical and the moral implications of a poetic vocation.

Particularly in the October eclogue, the one that deals most directly with these matters, we find a formidable array of barriers in the way of a modern poet. In the first place, poetry does not pay. Unlike a pastime, a vocation requires financial support. "But ah Mecoenas is yclad in claye" (l. 61).

5. John W. Moore, Jr., "Colin Breaks His Pipe: A Reading of the 'January' Eclogue," *ELR*, 5 (1975), 3–24, reviews previous criticism of this aspect of *The Shepheardes Calender* and suggests that the January eclogue and, more particularly, Colin's breaking of his pipe with which it ends "introduces us to the issue which gives unity to the *Calender*"—the nature of Colin's poetic vocation and the question of his fitness for it. I agree and would further suggest that the series as a whole fails either to resolve the issue or to answer the question.
6. A. C. Hamilton, "The Argument of Spenser's *Shepheardes Calender*," *ELH*, 23 (1956), 175.

And were money forthcoming, support of another, still more vital, sort would nevertheless be lacking. As an art of imitation, heroic poetry requires heroic models. But "great Augustus long ygoe is dead: / And all the worthies liggen wrapt in leade" (11. 62–63). In a stooped and fallen age, poetry must either follow fashion and "rolle with rest in rymes of rybaudrye" or "it wither must agayn" (11.73–78). In the Renaissance, such complaints are legion. E. K. tells us that Spenser borrowed his from Mantuan and Theocritus. But they are no less relevant for that. If Spenser was to "emerge as England's heroic poet," he did need money and he did need to believe that his age was capable of something approaching heroic accomplishment. Not that the age had to furnish all his material. The true poet makes his time as well as mirrors it, for he is the repository of "a certain . . . celestial inspiration." Such, E. K. tells us, was the argument of Spenser's own "book called the *English Poet*." But in the October eclogue, inspiration is a matter more of uncertainty than of confident assertion. We have already noticed what short work Cuddie makes of Piers's argument that love and the "immortall mirrhor" of beauty should raise the poet's mind "above the starry skie." Cuddie's own claim for Bacchic inspiration fares no better; his comically bombastic, mock-heroic flight ends, rather, with an inglorious fall: "But ah my corage cooles ere it be warme" (1. 115).

*   *   *

Lacking financial support, at odds with his age, unsure of his inspiration, the New Poet seems less securely set on his way than E. K. would have us think. And underlying his particular uncertainties is a more general and more serious doubt, that poetry of the sort that he was prepared to write could, whatever his inspiration, ever be lifted to the vatic heights of religious, political, and moral perfection.

*   *   *

Yet, though he did not earn his living by writing, he, rather than [Ben] Jonson, deserves to be called England's first professed, if not fully professional, poet. Through all the years of minor civic occupation, and well past the age when most men of his generation stopped writing, he pursued his poetic ambition. So that in 1590 he could complete his imitation of Virgil and emerge indeed as his nation's heroic poet, as the first English laureate.

> Lo I the man, whose Muse whilome did maske,
> As time her taught in lowly Shepheards weeds,
> Am now enforst a far unfitter taske,
> For trumpets sterne to chaunge mine Oaten reeds.

To leap, as I must now do, from the beginning of Spenser's poetic career to its end is to leave out much of the most important part. I count on the reader's acquaintance with the great accomplishment of the 1580s, the first books of *The Faerie Queene*, to keep the picture I am drawing from distortion. In these books there is little of the struggle between the love poet and the vatic poet that we have observed in *The Shepheardes Calender*. Both dissolve into the poem, which contains the passion of the one and the vision of the other in a romance that is also a prophecy. Of the poet's self we hear only the humble fear that he may prove unworthy of his great argument or that his audience may mistake his work for mere "painted forgery, . . . th' aboundance of an idle brain." But these are minor doubts. Properly understood, the poem justifies both itself and its maker. This self-justifying union does not, however, hold together. Although the last books show no radical change in character and certainly no lessening of poetic power, the two poets, or the two ideas of poetry, no longer cohere. The private poet rebels against his public duty; the public poet can find no use for his private inspiration. * * *

Nor is it surprising, given what may well have been a double sense of failure—the practical failure of the policies he favored and the moral failure of the beauty he celebrated—that Spenser should have wearied of his epic task. Through the first books of *The Faerie Queene* fatigue had been the greatest burden, ease after toil the greatest temptation. Redcross was overcome when, like Diana's nymph, he "sat downe to rest in middest of the race" (I.vii.5); Guyon weakened when he heard fair ladies singing of "the Port of rest from troublous toil" (II.xii.32); and even Britomart could be surprised, though not tempted, when "through . . . weary toil she soundly slept" (III.i.58). And most often, as in each of these instances, sensual pleasure combines with rest to oppose heroic activity. So in the Bower of Bliss, Verdant, the green youth (think of Spenser talking of "the greener times of [his] youth" when he wrote his hymns of Love and Beauty), sleeping in the arms of Acrasia, emblematically represents the courtly lovers, and by extension the courtly makers, the prodigal love poets, of Spenser's generation.[7]

* * *

In two of the *Amoretti* he refers to his unfinished poem, and each time it is with a sense of weariness. "Taedious toyle," he calls it. The two sonnets do, however, divide on the question of what relation his private love has to his public poetic duty, one taking the position that Cuddie had argued in the October eclogue, the other agreeing with Piers. In *Amoretti* 33 love cancels duty while in *Amoretti* 80 it raises the poet's "spirit to an higher pitch," thus preparing him to return to *The Faerie Queene* with renewed inspiration. But even here, the amorous resting place is sharply cut off from the world of "strong endevour"; it is a "pleasant mew" where he can "sport [his] muse and sing [his] loves sweet praise," a "prison" from which he "will break anew." The "anew" refers, I would suspect, to his first escape from the prison of private poetry in the early 1580s. But this second time he seems not to have made good his promised escape, at least not as a poet. In *Amoretti* 80 he says that his work on *The Faerie Queene* is "halfe fordonne," six books having been completed. Though he had still some five years to live, he seems never to have finished another. His last "useful" work was not a poem but, rather, a treatise on the *Present State of Ireland*. Thus the end of his literary career does have the bifurcated look that we

---

7. Though Spenser does not identify himself with Verdant or with any other victim of Acrasia's sensuality, there is an echo of the conflict central to Spenser's laureate self-presentation in the violence of Guyon's destruction of the Bower of Bliss. Here the poet apparently felt compelled to overreact. His integrity and perhaps the integrity of the very culture that he, as laureate, sought to embody depended on it. For a discussion of the threat posed by Acrasia and the Bower of Bliss, see Stephen Greenblatt, *Renaissance Self-Fashioning from More to Shakespeare* (Chicago: Univ. of Chicago Press, 1980), pp. 157–192.

observe in the careers of his contemporaries. Once again poetry serves the truant passion of love, while expository and argumentative prose does the work of the active world.

The split was never, of course, absolute or irrevocable. In *Prothalamion*, the last of Spenser's minor poems and perhaps, depending on the date one assigns to the Mutability Cantos, the last poem he wrote, he casts a valedictory glance back over his career—his birth in London, his service to Leicester, his "long fruitless stay" at court—with the regretful air of a man who would still join in the affairs of the great world if the great world would have him. When he says that "some brave muse may sing" the glories of the new champion, Essex, it is hard to tell whether he is putting himself definitively out of contention or bidding for the job. But in the refrain, with its insistence that the day is short and that his song will continue only while the Thames runs softly, we hear the sound of an ending, an impending withdrawal from the public world that this poem still celebrates. Spenser's magnificently unique "both/and," which had made it possible for him to be England's New Poet, had not wholly given way to the familiar "either/or," but disappointment was clearly pushing in that direction.

If he were to satisfy through poetry the humanist expectation that learning would be turned to the useful work of the world, he had to command the respect and attention of those in power. By the time he finished Book VI, Spenser evidently felt he had lost both. The result was a renewed self-consciousness about his role as poet and a backward and inward turn toward "the sacred noursery of vertue," which is both garden and mind. In making this turn, Spenser once again opened the breach between the poet of the inner pastoral world and the poet of heroic accomplishment, between the love poet and the laureate.

The center of Spenser's retreat is found in canto x of Book VI, where he and we and Calidore surprise Colin Clout on Mt. Acidale. Calidore and his creator, the epic poet, have wandered far out of the way of duty (the image and the judgment are Spenser's, and he applies them equally to both knight and poet), only to encounter in the secretmost recesses of the pastoral land an image of themselves. For Calidore, that image is the ideal vision of the courtesy which he is meant to embody. For the poet, it is Colin Clout, in whose guise he had formerly masked. Some critics would argue that this meeting merely reunites the pastoral and the epic strains of Spenser's poetry after the arid division of Book V, while others would claim, rather, that it presents once again what has always been united, though now one side and now the other may have predominated. But such arguments neglect the dramatic construction of the episode and indeed of the whole of Book VI. Calidore comes on the scene as an intruder, an outsider whose very presence causes Colin's vision to dissolve. Moreover, the knight of courtesy fails to understand what he has seen and must have it explained to him by the shepherd-poet. And yet, even given the didactic explanation, Calidore's experience on Mt. Acidale, unlike Redcross's in the House of Holiness, seems not to contribute to his formation as a knight. It neither enhances his courtesy, which was innate, nor moves him to heroic action. On the contrary, he remains in seclusion until called forth by the brigands' destruction of his pastoral retreat.[8] * * *

Though in a more subtle way, the scene on Mt. Acidale bears still further testimony to the disjunction between the two sides of Spenser's poetic identity, for it is here that the union of heroic activity and amorous contemplation breaks down. They had been joined in the figure of the Faerie Queene, "in whose fair eyes," as Harvey wrote, "love linked with virtue sits,"[9] and throughout the poem, devotion to Gloriana had directed and inspired the accomplishment of the epic poet. She had raised his thoughts "too humble and too vile" and provided "the argument of [his] afflicted style." She had been to him, as the various proems proclaim, the "mirror and grace of majesty," the living image of "Faerie lond," the model of rule and chastity, "the Queene of love, and Prince of peace," the "Dread Soveraign Goddesse" whose justice informs his discourse, the source from which "all goodly vertues well." From the April eclogue, where the shepherds' queen, Eliza, figured as a fourth Grace and where Hobbinoll and Thenot lamented that Colin's private love had turned him from the singing of such songs, devotion to the Queen had been Spenser's touchstone of poetic responsibility. What then are we to think when in the midst of The Faerie Queene Colin and the Graces reappear in a scene closely reminiscent of the April eclogue, with "a country lasse" in the place of the Queen, particularly when Spenser himself calls attention to the substitution? The form of his remark is, naturally enough, an apology. "Pardon thy shepheard," he begs of the great Gloriana, "to make one minime of thy poore handmayd" (VI.x.28). But this self-conscious plea only compounds the fault by breaking the fiction and revealing the historical Spenser behind the pastoral mask of Colin Clout. As in the Amoretti, the poet speaks in his own person to associate visionary delight with his private love and wearisome duty with the Faerie Queene.[1] Here the dissociation between his pastoral and his heroic personae is very nearly complete. The conclusion of Book VI makes it still more so. The epic poet ends with the bitter regret that because of the Blatant Beast—the image of the great world's hostility to heroic accomplishment—poetry must be reduced to mere pleasure. "Seeke to please," he tells his verse, "that now is counted wisemens threasure." But for Colin on Mt. Acidale—a place designed "to serve all delight"—pleasure had been sufficient unto itself.

Whether by accident or design, the final shape of Spenser's career resembles the shape of old Melibee's. Each begins with the pastoral and then, as Melibee says, "When pride of youth forth pricked [his] desire," each attaches himself to the court and its public concerns. But after years "excluded from native home," each ruefully returns to the pastoral world (VI.ix.24—25). As Isabel MacCaffrey has remarked, "Spenser evidently

8. For the opposing argument—i.e., that Calidore does undergo an education in true courtesy on Mt. Acidale—see Humphrey Tonkin, Spenser's Courteous Pastoral (Oxford: Clarendon Press, 1972), pp. 111–155. [See pp. 752–56 in this volume—Editors.]
9. Gabriel Harvey printed in the Variorum, III, 186.
1. Cf. VI.proem.1.

attached important meanings to this pattern."[2] It recurs, as she notes, in *Colin Clouts Come Home Againe*, and the title of that poem might well serve as the heading to the final chapter of Spenser's creative life. In his last works, in Book VI of *The Faerie Queene*, in the *Amoretti* and the *Epithalamion*, in the hymns of Divine Beauty and Love, and, to an extent, in the two Mutability Cantos, particularly in their setting on Arlo Hill, Spenser does come home, as he did in the last section of *Colin Clout*. He comes home to the pastoral, the personal, and the amorous. That these are also among his most resonant works, among those which engage the cosmic shape of things most confidently, is testimony to the poetic richness of that home. Whatever the laureate's obligations to the public world, it is in this private realm that he finds the source of his inspiration. And though Spenser's turning back to the self and the secret springs of poetry may be in part the result of that unhappy encounter with the world represented by the threatening of the Blatant Beast, it is no repentance. Unlike the other poets of his generation, Spenser responds to such pressure not by re-nouncing, but rather by reaffirming, the value of poetry. The sometimes hostile active world belongs, he lets us see, to the realm of mutability. Poetry alone has access to the unchanging forms of moral and aesthetic perfection, to "the sacred noursery of vertue" whose ways "none can find, but who was taught them by the Muse" (VI.proem. 2–3). Others may have claimed for poetry a similar superiority to those "serving sciences" that depend on nature rather than on the grace of inspiration, but only Spenser turned that claim into a career. He thus gave to the idea of the laureate poet a local habitation and a name. The "Edmund Spenser" of literary history—"the New Poet," the "first . . . great reformer," "our Virgil"—was for later writers perhaps Spenser's most significant creation. It is in this sense that he particularly deserves to be called "the poets' poet."

If there is any tendency toward repentance at the end of his career, what he repents is not poetry but his engagement with the active world. Melibee may speak for this side of Spenser when he castigates the vanity of the court and regrets that he "spent [his] youth in vaine" seeking public position. As in *Colin Clouts Come Home Againe*, the great world is presented as a place of hollow aspiration and inevitable repentance, a place opposed to the virtuous tranquillity of the pastoral world. But this is only one side of Spenser, and, even at the end, perhaps not the dominant one. Whatever his ultimate disillusionment with the active life, Spenser never unequi-vocally restricts the poet to private contemplation. The poet's pastoral mask is, after all, a mask. Though he may, by virtue of his gift and his art, present himself as a native resident of the land of poetry, he is by education, if not by birth, a gentleman, a man of whom public service is rightfully expected.

The Hermit, another retired wiseman in Book VI, but one "of gentle race," better represents the doubleness of Spenser's view. He too "from all this worlds incombrance did himselfe assoyle," but only after dutifully

---

2. Isabel MacCaffrey, *Spenser's Allegory: The Anatomy of Imagination* (Princeton: Princeton Univ. Press, 1976), pp. 366–370. The examples of retirement mentioned in my next few paragraphs were suggested by MacCaffrey.

spending his youth and strength in the "worlds contentious toyle" (VI.v.37). Thus the undercurrent of irony in the exchange between Melibee and Calidore in praise of the shepherd's life. "Fittest is," as Melibee says, "that all contented rest / With that they hold" (VI.ix.29). The shepherd's life may fit Melibee, but not Calidore, who holds and is held by duty of his knighthood. The laureate is both contemplative shepherd and questing knight. In this he resembles Redcross, the "clownishe younge man," raised as a ploughman, who takes on the armor of heroic endeavor but who will, as Contemplation tells him, one day "wash thy hands from guilt of bloudy field: / For bloud can nought but sin, and war but sorrowes yield" (I.x.60).[3] What kept Spenser from something like the Hermit's open declaration of retirement from "this worlds incombrance" was, I suppose, the fear that such promptings might be only the counsel of Despair, "Sleepe after toyle, port after stormie seas, / Ease after warre, death after life does greatly please" (I.ix.40). In no book of *The Faerie Queene* is the lure of the private world more attractive than in the last, but in none are the warnings against resting in "middest of the race" more pressing. For Spenser, the Christian humanist, the race was never clearly over, so he could never join the Roman Horace in saying of his public poetic duties, *Non eadem est aetas, non mens.*[4]

Spenser's idea of a poet was finally an unstable but necessary union of two ideas, embodied in two roles—shepherd and knight, Colin and Calidore—neither of which could be renounced in favor of the other. The first gained him a place in the genus *poetae* as it was understood by his generation. The second defined him as the unique English member of the species of professed national poets. Without the first he would have been no poet at all, however much public verse he had written. Without the second he would have been able to make of poetry no more than a diversion of youth. But not even Spenser could maintain the precarious equilibrium that had made possible his extraordinary accomplishment of the 1580s, an equilibrium that depended on both roles being subsumed by the poem. Nor could his successors achieve anything approaching that balance. They did not really try. Men like Daniel and Drayton professed themselves poets and stuck to their profession more easily because Spenser had been there first. But while they recognized, praised, and relied on his achievement of a literary career, they neither followed nor dared approve his mixing of the two roles. They wrote in both the pastoral and the heroic guise, but they kept the two nicely separated. A similar hardening of generic distinctions was in process in Italy and France, and it is not surprising that English poets should have responded to it. What is surprising is that, without denying either the humanist or the romantic sides of his cultural and literary heritage and in a country that had known no major poet for two hundred years, Spenser could have created a body of work sufficient to give form and substance to an ideal that other men entertained only in the realm of

---

3. Donald Cheney has suggested the connection between the poet and the Redcross Knight in *Spenser's Image of Nature: Wild Man and Shepherd in "The Faerie Queene"* (New Haven: Yale Univ. Press, 1966), pp. 18–22.
4. "My years, my mind, are not the same": Horace, *Epistle* I.i.4.

hypothetical speculation. Despite the pressures of his generation, Spenser took poetry beyond repentance and, in so doing, gave England its first laureate poet.

LOUIS ADRIAN MONTROSE

[The Elizabethan Subject and the Spenserian Text]†

The study of English Renaissance literature has of late been characterized by a renewed interest in questions of "history." In literary studies, "history" has traditionally meant the literary and intellectual histories that, in combination with techniques of close reading, still form the dominant modes of analysis; or, the now-tarnished "world picture" approach that read complex literary works against a supposedly stable, coherent, and transparent "historical background" that enshrined the political and social orthodoxies of the age; or, the erudite but sometimes eccentric detective work of scholars who, treating texts as ciphers, sought to argue one-to-one correspondences between fictional characters and actions, on the one hand, and specific historical persons and events, on the other. Though sometimes reproducing the shortcomings of the older modes of historical criticism, but also often appropriating their labors to good effect, the newer historical orientation is new in its refusal of traditional distinctions between literature and history, between text and context; new in resisting a traditional opposition of the privileged individual—whether an author or a work—to a world "outside." * * * Integral to this ["new historicism"] is a realization and acknowledgment that the critic's own text is as fully implicated in such an interplay as are the texts under study . . . [and] a renunciation of the illusory quest of an older historical criticism to recover objective, authentic, or stable "meanings."

* * *

Tudor somatic[1] symbolism was culture-specific in two fundamental and interrelated ways: if dominant structures of thought and belief privileged the body of the prince in relation to the body of the subject, they also privileged the male body in relation to the female body. The versions of woman produced by such discourses as those of medicine, law, religion, and domestic economy were almost invariably imperfect versions of man —constitutionally colder, weaker, less stable than he. Almost all modes of authority, domestic as well as public, were invested in positions occupied by men: fathers, husbands, masters, teachers, preachers, magistrates, and lords. The Elizabethan gender-system combined principles of hierarchy and reciprocity, distinguishing male and female as superior and inferior, and interrelating them as complementary. Gender categories interacted with many others—notably those of social estate, age, occupation, and marital status, as well as with religious, economic, educational, and regional

---

† From *Literary Theory/Renaissance Texts*, ed. Patricia Parker and David Quint (Baltimore, 1985) 303–40. The essay has been slightly condensed. Reprinted by permission of The Johns Hopkins University Press.
1. I.e., "of or pertaining to the body; corporeal" (*OED*) [*Editors*].

distinctions—to produce multiple and shifting coordinates of identity and relationship within which the process of subjectification—the ideological work of fashioning and refashioning selves—was performed.

* * *

In this sense, of course, Elizabeth Tudor was herself a gendered and socially situated subject. Women were, at least in theory, excluded from the public domain. By virtue of the body politic that she had acquired at her coronation, Queen Elizabeth was the exception to this rule. However, because she nevertheless remained a woman in her body natural, she represented an affront to those very principles of hierarchy of which she was the guardian. As the anomalous ruler of a society that was pervasively patriarchal in its organization and distribution of authority, the unmarried woman at the society's symbolic center embodied a challenge to the homology between hierarchies of rule and of gender. A range of strategies was generated by means of which this ideological dissonance, this contradiction in the cultural logic, could be variously articulated and obfuscated, contained and exploited.

* * *

The authorized version of the queen—variously instantiated in homilies, proclamations, speeches, pageants, and icons—did not go uncontested. * * * Let me cite two brief examples, one courtly in origins, the other rural. When, in 1619, Ben Jonson told William Drummond that Queen Elizabeth had "had a Membrana on her which made her uncapable of man, though for her delight she tried many," he was only repeating gossip that, apparently, had already been in circulation at the Elizabethan court before the Armada.[2] If some thought the queen uncapable, others were quite convinced of her capabilities. Thus, in 1580, an Essex laborer named Thomas Playfere was convicted of rumoring that the queen had two children by the earl of Leicester; a year later, a certain Henry Hawkins bettered the report: "the earl hath five children by the queen, and she never goeth on progress but to be delivered."[3] Indictments of aristocratic and courtly immorality are implicit in many extant examples of popular and rural sedition of the period. * * * The fragmentary record suggests that the Elizabethan discourse of sedition often combines religious heterodoxy and a skeptical and materialist attitude toward the authorizing fictions of power with a venerable tradition of misogyny. Like the bawdy subplot of some romantic comedy, a predominantly oral and often scurrilous counter-discourse carnivalized the official cult of mystical royal virginity by insisting upon the physicality of the royal body, the carnal inclinations of the queen.

The collective discourse of Elizabethan power that we call "Queen Elizabeth" was [thus] traversed by multiple and potentially antagonistic strategies. The historical subject, Elizabeth Tudor, was no more than a

2. See "Ben Jonson's Conversations with William Drummond of Hawthornden," in *Ben Jonson*, ed. C. H. Herford and Percy Simpson, 11 vols. (Oxford: Clarendon Press, 1925–52), 1.142, and the editorial note on 166.
3. For Playtere, see F. G. Emmison, *Elizabethan Life: Disorder* (Chelmsford, England: Essex County Council, 1970), 42; for Hawkins, see *Calendar of State Papers: Domestic*, vol. 148, item 34 (Thomas Scot to the earl of Leicester, March 1581). For several other examples, see Emmison, 41–42.

privileged agent in the production of the royal image. At a fundamental level, all Elizabethan subjects may be said to have participated in a ceaseless and casual process of producing and reproducing "The Queen" in their daily practices—in their prayers, their gossip, their fantasies. But she was also rather more systematically and consciously fashioned by those Elizabethan subjects who were specifically engaged in production of the texts, icons, and performances in which the queen was variously represented to her people, to her court, to foreign powers, and (of course) to Elizabeth herself. * * * It is in this sense that the ruler and the ruled, the queen and the poet, are construable as subjects differentially shaped within a shared conjuncture of language and social relations, and jointly reshaping that conjuncture in the very process of living it.

Few Elizabethan subjects publicly claimed for themselves a more exalted role in the shaping of this conjuncture than did Edmund Spenser. In "A letter of the Authors, expounding his whole intention in the course of this worke," addressed to Sir Walter Ralegh and printed in the first edition of *The Faerie Queene* in 1590, Spenser declares that "the generall end . . . of all the booke is to fashion a gentleman or noble person in vertuous and gentle discipline." This process of fashioning is at once the book's subject and its object: by the rhetorically effective fashioning of artificial persons, the poet may arouse in his readers a process of emulation; the fashioning of the text and in the text may induce a refashioning in and of its audience, a refashioning that can make the gentry truly gentle and the powerful virtuous. The writer who claimed so central a place for himself in literary history and in his own society was of relatively humble origins. It was only by virtue of his M. A. that Spenser, the son of a London artisan, could begin to sign himself a gentleman, and it was by means of his subsidized education and his verbal skill that he gained the aristocratic patronage, state employment, and Irish property that gave substance to his social pretensions. Though acclaimed as a poet and—given his urban, artisan origins—relatively successful in his bid for advancement, Spenser nevertheless always remained on the social and economic as well as on the geographic margins of that community of privilege whom he addressed and presumed to fashion in his poetry.

* * * Combining classical and biblical traditions of inspired and prophetic speech with emergent notions of an autonomous fictional space, Spenser synthesizes a new Elizabethan author-function. The "Laureate" authorial persona that Richard Helgerson sees as emergent in Spenser (and fully developed, a generation later, in Jonson) not only professionalizes poetry, it authenticates through print the subjectivity of a writer whose class position might otherwise have rendered him merely the anonymous functionary of his patron.[4] In claiming the originative status of an "Author," a writer claims the authority to direct and delimit the interpretive activity of that elite community of readers by whom he himself is authorized to write. Spenser's authorial self-fashioning proceeds by the constitution of the writer

---

4. See Richard Helgerson, *Self-Crowned Laureates: Spenser, Jonson, Milton and the Literary System* (Berkeley and Los Angeles: University of California Press, 1983). [See pp. 675–86 in this volume—*Editors.*]

as a subject of and in his own discourse; and also by the insertion of his text into the economy of courtly service and reward—that is, by its constitution as a *book*, a tangible commodity that functions as a vehicle of the writer's social and material advancement.

* * *

The Shepheardes Calender, like the first edition of *The Faerie Queene* (1590), exemplifies the Elizabethan printed book in its tendency toward the proliferation and contamination of genres, toward the inclusion within its covers of a variety of discursive forms characterized by distinctive modes of address to readers. Here I am thinking not only of the multiple poetic forms and styles included within the eclogues but also of such discursive genres as the title page; the address "To His Booke" by "Immerito"; the Epistle, Generall argument, and glosses by "E. K."; the glosses to the individual eclogues; the emblems, woodcuts, and envoy. In such print-specific genres, Elizabethan literary texts manifest a tendency toward the elaboration rather than the effacement of their status as social—and not merely literary—productions. The "apparatus" of *The Shepheardes Calender* is, then, as significant in the constitution of its rhetorical effects, its "meaning," as is the poetry itself. *The Shepheardes Calender* is ostentatiously designed to inaugurate Spenser's career as "our new Poete" (Epistle), and Elizabethan writer capable of shaping the native language into a national vision. The book's reflexive strategies are aimed at instituting it as the founding text of a new English literary canon.

Within the text, the encomiastic song that is the centerpiece of the *Aprill* eclogue is attributed to Colin Clout, "under whose person the Author selfe is shadowed" (Epistle). Colin is in fact absent from the eclogue, withdrawn into melancholy owing to unrequited love. His song is sung by another shepherd for a rapt audience of his peers. All their talk is of Colin; all their admiration is for his skill in making. The eclogue frame thus provides the poem with its own reception: Spenser/Colin's royal encomium is already in circulation, being reproduced and doing its work in society, which is to advertise the author as much as it is to celebrate the monarch.

Colin's song fuses imperial Virgilian, sacred Gospel, and erotic Ovidian traditions into a pastoral consecration of the English, Protestant, and Tudor present. As the gloss points out, the poem appropriates literary traditions for contemporary social uses. An Ovidian etiological myth is reworked into a Tudor genealogical myth: Elisa is "*Syrinx* daughter without spotte, / Which *Pan* the shepheards God of her begot" (Aprill, 50–51). Working here as a kind of referential fiction, pointing outward beyond the poem and its mythographic and literary traditions to concrete historical subjects, the gloss provides an exact correspondence between Pan and "the most famous and victorious King, her highnesse Father, late of worthy memorye K. Henry the eyght." But if Elisa is in some sense to be identified with Elizabeth Tudor, governor of the English church and state, she is also to be identified with a queen already textualized as the gendered and idealized personification of the state, shaped by Elizabethan poets, artisans, preachers, councillors—and by Elizabeth Tudor herself—and functioning as a focus for the collective energies of Elizabethan subjects. In Ovid's text, the outcome of the love chase is the nymph's transformation into the reeds from which Pan, the "shepheards God" (Januarye, 17), fashions his pipes. In the Ovidian logic of Spenser's poem, Elisa becomes a personification of pastoral poetry; she embodies the literary mode of the poem in which she exists. Ultimately, the queen and her various representations are appropriated and recreated in the specificity of Spenser's text as the figurative offspring of the shepherd/poet (himself identified with Pan) and his pastoral muse. Colin's encomium methodically rehearses the poetic engendering of the royal image: The first stanza is an invocation of the Muses; the second stanza expresses the conception of an image through a genealogical procreation myth; in the third stanza, the unfolding of the image commences with the imperative, "See, where she sits upon the grassie greene" (55); in the final stanza, Colin bids his perfected image to go forth into the world, to be received by the queen: "Now ryse up *Elisa*, decked as thou art,/In royall array" (145–46), "Let dame *Eliza* thanke you for her song" (150).[5]

The genealogical myth is repeated in the central stanza of the song: [see lines 91–99]. The pastoral poet now includes himself within the frame of the image that he is making; this "overlaboured and sunneburnt" (Gloss) rustic bears witness to a Nativity that he himself has brought to pass. Colin offers a lamb to an infant mother-goddess; Spenser offers a pastoral to a queen. The subject's *gift*—both his talent and his offering—is his ability to make the cultural forms in which royal power is not only celebrated but may actually be effected. By representing itself as an offering to a royal persona produced within it, the poem displays itself in a paradoxical relationship to the structures of power: The cultural work of the subject/poet, his informing power, contributes to the legitimation and implementation of the social and political order within which he himself is subjected. By calling attention to its mediatory relationship to the traditional conventions, and devices of poetic discourse, on the one hand, and to the social conditions of its own production, on the other, the song of Colin/Spenser works not simply as a royal encomium but as a contextualization from within (so to speak) of its own encomiastic project.

 * * * The subjectivity fabricated by Spenser in writing—his "Author selfe," as E. K. so nicely puts it in the Epistle to *The Shepheardes Calender*— achieves its uncertain sense of mastery, of authorship and authority, not by means of a static analogy with the monarch but rather in an interplay between submission and resistance to the project of royal celebration which ostensibly defines it. By "resistance" I do not mean to suggest any concerted program of sedition, of political opposition or subversion. Rather, it is a matter of the text registering the felt but perhaps not consciously articulated contradiction between Spenser's exalted self-representation as an Author and his subjection to the authority of an other, the contradiction between a specific authorial ideology—that of "the Laureate"—and the social conditions of literary production within which that ideology may be realized in Spenser's historical moment and from his

---

5. These lines make orthographically explicit the lay's transformation of Eliza into Elisa: the original printed text consistently distinguishes between Elisa as the subject of the song and Eliza as the subject to whom the song is offered, between the royal image of Colin's own making and the collective royal image embodied in the queen.

social position within it. In Spenser's text, the refashioning of an Elizabethan subject as a laureate poet is dialectically related to the refashioning of the queen as the author's subject.

* * *

The poet returns to the theory of Elizabethan representation in the proem to Book 3, "contayning the Legend of Britomartis, or Of Chastitie"—a private virtue of obvious political significance in Elizabethan England, and here personified in a female hero. In the opening lines of this book, the poet preemptively asks himself why he has not personified this virtue in Elizabeth herself, and answers that because the queen's virtue and beauty are perfect they are unrepresentable by painters and poets, except by a series of accommodations and displacements. The proem's address to the sovereign concludes by revising the strategy expounded in the "Letter to Ralegh" [see stanzas 4–5]. The process by which Spenser makes the identification of his sovereign with Belphoebe is noteworthy not only for its idiosyncratic representation of the doctrine of the queen's two bodies but for its appropriation of Ralegh as a mediatory figure. It is not Queen Elizabeth but rather Ralegh's Cynthia whose image is split in the mirror of Spenser's poem; and both poets' source is in a complex history of literary and mythographic forms. Thus, in the movement of the proem to Book 3 from the queen to her representations, from referentiality to intertextuality, the male subject/poet puts into question the female monarch's claim to shape herself and her subjects, to personify the principle and power of form. What the poet conventionally deprecates as his inability to produce an adequate reflection of the glorious royal image is the methodical process of fragmentation and refraction by which the text appropriates that image, imposing upon it its own specificity.

Gloriana, the Faery Queen in whose service her knights are fashioned, does not appear as a character in the narrative, whereas Belphoebe is a conspicuous presence in the middle books. I would suggest that this is so at least in part because the beautiful and virtuous lady is more manipulable by the conventions of literary representation—notably those associated with Petrarchism—than is the empress, that erotic conventions structure Elizabethan relations of power in ways advantageous to the writing subject. Petrarchan conventions and the lineaments of the Petrarchan persona are ubiquitous in the courtly culture of the Renaissance. Petrarchism is one of the discourses in which a recognizably modern mode of subjectivity—an introspective egocentricity founded upon the frustration and sublimation of material desires—is first articulated and actively cultivated. The Petrarchan persona is a distinctly masculine subject explicitly fashioned in relation to a feminine other. (It is also, of course, a male subject whose refinements of style and sensibility implicitly mark him off from the common run of men.) The Petrarchan lover worships a deity of his own making and under his own control; he masters his mistress by inscribing her within his text, where she is repeatedly put together and taken apart—and, sometimes, killed.

Such Petrarchan strategies are evident in the extended blason that introduces Belphoebe into The Faerie Queene in Book 2, canto 3. This, the

longest character description in the entire poem, repeatedly insinuates a
current of sensuality and erotic arousal into its encomium of militant
chastity:

> And in her hand a sharpe bore-speare she held,
>   And at her backe a bow and quiver gay,
>   Stuft with steele-headed darts, wherewith she queld
>   The savage beastes in her victorious play,
>   Knit with a golden bauldricke, which forelay
> Athwart her snowy brest, and did divide
> Her daintie paps; which like young fruit in May
> Now little gan to swell, and being tide,
> Through her thin weed their places only signified.
>   (29)

This rhetorical play between the prohibition and provocation of desire is
observable not only in the composition of stanzas but within individual
lines. For example, in the comparison of her blushing cheeks to "roses in
a bed of lillies shed" (22), the internal rhyme of "bed" and "shed" imparts
to the description of her maidenly modesty a subliminal suggestion of her
defloration.

Perhaps the most remarkable feature of the blason of Belphoebe is its
impairment by one of the poem's very rare unfinished lines, this occurring
in the final alexandrine of stanza 26:

> So faire, and thousand thousand times more faire
>   She seemed, when she presented was to sight,
>   And was yclad, for heat of scorching aire,
>   All in a silken Camus lylly whight,
>   Purfled upon with many a folded plight,
> Which all above besprinckled was throughout
> With golden aygulets, that glistred bright,
> Like twinckling starres, and all the skirt about
> Was hemd with golden fringe
>
> Below her ham her weed did somewhat traine,
>   And her streight legs most bravely were embayld
>   In gilden buskins of costly Cordwaine,
>   All bard with golden bendes, which were entayld
>   With curious antickes, and full faire aumayld:
> Before they fastned were under her knee
> In a rich Jewell, and therein entrayld
> The ends of all their knots that none might see,
> How they within their fouldings close enwrapped bee.
>   (26–27)

The conspicuous gap at the center of the blason coincides with a conspicuous silence about the center of the body it describes. Moving downward,
the narrator's gaze skirts the fringes of Belphoebe's secret parts, displacing
them into an intricate description of the "rich Jewell" in which the "knots"
of her buskins are "entrayld . . . that none might see."

* * * As the royal body is handled ambivalently throughout the blason,

so here in particular the symbolic locus of royal power is less a source of the (male) subject's security than an oblique threat to that security.

The narrative within which the blason is incongruously placed concerns the mock-heroic misadventures of the cowardly knight Braggadocchio and his wily servant Trompart. They happen upon Belphoebe while she is hunting in the forest; her description proceeds as Braggadocchio lies hidden in a bush—a debased, voyeuristic surrogate for the male reader. Enkindled with lust, Braggadocchio tries to assault Belphoebe; she threatens him with her boarspear, then turns and disappears from the book. I think this bald summary of the plot sufficient to indicate that the episode is a parodic rewriting of the episode of Diana and Actaeon in *Metamorphoses*, Book 3. * * * Spenser's descriptive dismemberment of Belphoebe conspicuously avoids the danger inhering in the royal body—the body of a virgin goddess and mother. The poet at once evokes and suppresses the darker aspect of the virtuous and beautiful lady, her vengeful power to deform or even destroy her devotees.

[The myth's] political import is made explicit in the mythographic commentary of George Sandys's 1632 translation of Ovid: "This fable was invented to show us how dangerous a curiosity it is to search into the secrets of Princes, or by chance to discover their nakednesse."[6] To "discover" the nakedness of the prince is both to locate and to reveal—to demystify—the secrets of state. This exegesis is obviously especially resonant when the prince is a woman whose cult has appropriated the mythology of Diana. In Spenser's blason, the poet protects himself by conspicuously censoring himself, marking the constraint upon his text with a lacuna.

* * *

Stephen Greenblatt sees Spenser's self-fashioning as accomplished through symbolic and physical acts of regenerative violence, enacted against those objectified agents of disorder who threaten a civilization that is centered upon Spenser's sovereign. According to Greenblatt, "Spenser sees human identity as conferred by loving service to legitimate authority, to the yoked power of God and the state.[7] "The Faerie Queene is . . . wholly wedded to the autocratic ruler of the English state" (174). It will by now be obvious that in my own view, Spenser's relationship to royal authority is more equivocal, and the ideological situation is more complicated, than Greenblatt here suggests. Greenblatt bases his conclusions on an analysis of the episode of Guyon's destruction of The Bower of Bliss and his binding of its proprietress, the enchantress Acrasia, in Book 2, canto 12. He states the interpretive problem of the canto as "why the particular erotic appeal of the Bower—more intense and sustained than any comparable passage in the poem—excites the hero's destructive violence" (171). But does not the *particularity* of the Bower's intense erotic appeal itself pose a prior interpretive problem—namely, the problem of the implicitly gendered position from which most commentators have read the episode? To write as a male reader, identifying unselfconsciously with Guyon's position, with Guyon's gaze, leads to a misrecognition of the gender-specific character of

6. George Sandys, *Ovid's Metamorphosis Englished, Mythologiz'd and Represented in Figures* (Oxford, 1632), 151–52.
7. *Renaissance Self-Fashioning from More to Shakespeare* (Chicago and London, 1980) 222.

the self-fashioning process figured in Guyon's violent repression of his own sexual arousal. What is being fashioned here is not merely a civilized self but a male subject, whose self-defining violence is enacted against an objectified other who is specifically female. This female other is represented as threatening the male subject with more than sexual enthrallment: the climactic image of the bare bosomed witch cradling the slumbering youth in her lap makes it evident that she is also threatening him with maternal engulfment.

The troubling mixtures of attraction and repulsion, desire and fear, aroused in the descriptions of both Belphoebe and Acrasia have their source in the same cultural complex. The curious affinity between these two female figures subverts their ostensible antithesis. This mode of Spenserian allegory has its culture-specific and culturally pervasive grounding in that familiar repertoire of gendered royal images produced and reproduced throughout the reign of Elizabeth: the vestal virgin, consecrated to the service of God; the beautiful mistress, desired by but necessarily forbidden to her courtiers; the thrifty spouse, married to her nation; the loving and selfless mother, dedicated to her subjects' welfare. The social and psychological potency of such images was generated in an interplay between the public and domestic domains. If I say that the *sexual* politics of Elizabethan representation were also a sexual *politics*, I mean to suggest the interpenetration and mutual contamination of sexual and political codes. This culture-specific discourse of power is the cognitive, communicative, and coercive medium in which an Elizabethan subject like Edmund Spenser has been engendered; it is the native language in which he has learned to think, speak, and write of sovereignty and subjection. In a brilliant analysis, Greenblatt assimilates Acrasia, the alien female other, to various forms of ethnic otherness, Amerindian and Irish. At this level, as in the Armada portraits, the queen is clearly the focus of a collective English civilization with which her subjects may readily identify themselves. Within a different configuration of power relations, however, the male/poet/subject may appear to be constituted not in any unequivocal act of self-devotion to the embodiment of the state but instead in the very tension between his impulse to worship and his internal resistance to such an impulse. Within this configuration of relation and identity, the stance of The Faerie Queene toward what Greenblatt calls "the autocratic ruler" of the Elizabethan state becomes necessarily ambivalent—alternately or simultaneously adoring and contestatory—because, for the male subject, the authority and the other are now one and the same.

* * *

In the Spenserian text, and elsewhere, we can observe a mode of contestation at work within the Elizabethan subject's very gesture of submission to the official fictions. We might call this mode of contestation *appropriative*, for it does not repudiate the given fictions of power but rather works within and through them, reinscribing them in the culture as the fictions of the speaking or writing subject.

* * *

* * * This is not to deny that there exists an authority "beyond the poem," but it is to *un*fix that authority, to put into question its absolute claims upon the subjects who produce the forms in which it authorizes itself. It is precisely by calling attention to its own processes of *re*presentation that Spenser's art calls into question the status of the authority it represents. In the process of representing the queen within his discourse, the subject is in some very limited but nevertheless quite real sense also constituting the sovereignty in relation to which his own subjection and subjectivity are constituted. Every representation of power is also an appropriation of power. Thus, Spenser's text may be said to constitute the identity of its Subject/ Author in an interplay between the subject's gestures of subjection and the author's gestures of authority—in those paradoxical celebrations of power that, in making the poem serve the queen, make the queen serve the poem.

A. BARTLETT GIAMATTI

Pageant, Show, and Verse†

In his *Observations on the Fairy Queen of Spenser* (1752), Thomas Warton remarks:

> We should remember that, in this age allegory was applied as the subject and foundation of public shews and spectacles, which were exhibited with a magnificence superior to that of former times. The virtues and vices, distinguished by their representative allegorical types, were frequently personified and represented by living actors. These figures bore a chief part in furnishing what they called *pageaunts*; which were then the principal species of entertainment and were shewn, not only in private, or upon the stage, but very often in the open streets for solemnising public occasions, or celebrating any grand event. . . . [Spenser's] peculiar mode of allegorizing seems to have been dictated by those spectacles, rather than by the fictions of Ariosto. (1807 edition, II,74–75; 76)

Warton, as so often, touches on something very important for *The Faerie Queene*. Certainly there had been pageants before the time of Spenser. In Volume I of the *Variorum* edition of Spenser, the reader will find enumerated the spectacles involving St. George, the dragon, and the King's daughter and her lamb that were presented before or by Henry V and Edward III and that are so reminiscent of the opening and the ending of the first book of *The Faerie Queene*. But Elizabeth's reign saw pageantry, and the enthusiasm for pageantry, reach its peak. Of course, the taste for pageantry did not pass with the coming of a new century and new monarch. * * * The spectacles so crucial to the formation of *The Faerie Queene*, and

† From *Play of Double Senses: Spenser's "Faerie Queene"* (Englewood Cliffs, NJ, 1975), pp. 78–93. The original footnotes have been slightly edited. Reprinted by permission of The Estate of A. Bartlett Giamatti and Mildred Marmur Associates, Ltd.

its audience, were those, however, that greeted England's queen wherever she went.[1]

On the innumerable progresses by and pageants for Elizabeth, we can note only two and consider them emblematic of the form and spirit of the rest. These two are the series of images that greeted her on the day before her coronation, held on Sunday, January 15, 1559, and the spectacles presented during her nineteen-day visit to her favorite, the Earl of Leicester, at Kenilworth Castle in July of 1575. In his *Chronicles of England, Scotland and Ireland*, Raphael Holinshed tells of Elizabeth's progress through London to Westminster on January 14, 1559. Holinshed compares London to "a stage" (London edition, 1808, IV, 159f.)—a crucial element in the idea of pageantry. At Fanchurch, a child sang and Elizabeth saw two figures, representing Henry VII and his wife Elizabeth, daughter of Edward IV. This pageant represented "The uniting of the two houses of Lancaster and York," the union of the White and the Red roses after the War of the Roses. The chronicler explains the significance of this scene:

It was devised, that like as Elizabeth was the first occasion of concord, so she another Elizabeth, might mainteine the same among hir subjects, so that unitie was the end whereat the whole devise shot . . .

In a kingdom divided by religious dissension, disturbed by the questions of royal legitimacy and (increasingly) of royal succession, and threatened from beyond the channel, concord and unity were overriding concerns of the people and their monarch. Concord and unity, as we know and will see, were also the concern of Elizabeth's greatest poets.

At Cornhill, she saw a pageant on "The seat of worthy government"; at Cheape, two shows: Promises of God to People, and A Flourishing Commonwealth. The last representation came at Fleetstreet. Here was a pageant showing Deborah (Judges, 4–5) as a good ruler consulting with her people, another reminder by the citizens of London to their future Queen of their hopes for her and for themselves. At Temple Bar, there was another oration from a child, verses in Latin and English from "Gogmagog the Albion and Corineus the Briton, two giants" that explained the whole procession, and farewell verses from children. Then Elizabeth went to Westminster where, next day, she took the crown. Deborah had come, the heir to Brut and Arthur, she who would be in the next forty-odd years celebrated under many guises, among them Astraea, the virgin of Justice who fled the earth when the Golden Age ended, and Belphoebe and Gloriana, the Faery Queen.

The passage through London was very much of the people, a progress which displayed their desires for peace and which drew its figures and significance from British and Biblical history. The glittering royal visit to Leicester's Kenilworth Castle in Warwickshire from Saturday, July 9, to

1. On Pageantry, see Sidney Anglo, *Spectacle, Pageantry and Early Tudor Policy* (Oxford, 1969); David Bergeron, *English Civic Pageantry, 1558–1642* (London, 1971); for a fine overview of where this impulse went, in the drama, see E. Waith, "Spectacles of State," *Studies in English Literature* XIII, 2 (1973), pp. 317–30. Neither Anglo nor Bergeron is concerned to know precisely what the word "pageant" meant.

Wednesday, July 27, 1575, was a very different occasion. It was aristocratic, chivalric, and complex. A retainer of Leicester's, one Robert (?) Laneham, has left us a famous account of the Queen's visit in his *Letter* (ed. F. J. Furnivall, The New Shakespeare Society [London, 1890]), and there we can see the Queen did not lack for the more traditional amusements and delights, such as morris dancing, bearbaiting, an Italian tumbler, and a play by the Coventry Men. But tournaments, knightings, and "literary" pageants were in the main fare. * * *

Yet while the mythological and literary pageants of Kenilworth are more sophisticated than the spectacles presented to Elizabeth in London in 1559, the earlier series of images, enacted as Holinshed said upon the "stage" of the city, is closer to the original meaning (and spirit) of the word *pageant*.

A word of disputed origin, *pageant* derives immediately from the late Middle English *pagyn*, which was contemporary with the Anglo-Latin *pagina*. It is a word with four primary and several secondary meanings. A pageant is (1) a scene acted on a stage, a usage applied particularly to the Mystery Plays (late fourteenth century) with (a) the figurative meaning of a part in the drama of life. This primary meaning is implicit in Holinshed's account of Elizabeth's progress in 1559, and both primary and figurative senses exist in Duke Senior's famous words in *As You Like It*:

> This wide and universal theater
> Presents more woeful pageants than the scene
> Wherein we play in.
>
> (II,vii,137–39)

There is also another subsidiary meaning from the late fourteenth century, *pageant* as (b) a deceit or trick, the meaning conveyed by the Venetian Senator when he says in *Othello* that the Turks only feign an attack on Rhodes:

> 'Tis a pageant
> To keep us in false gaze.
> (I,iii,18–19)

The second and third primary meanings of pageant shade into one another. A *pageant* was (2) a stage or platform on which a scene was acted or a tableau presented; it was also (3) any kind of show, device, or temporary structure, exhibited as a feature of a public triumph or celebration, carried on a moving car or erected on a fixed stage. The last primary meaning, which continues 1b and to which we will return, is *pageant* as (4) an empty show, a spectacle without substance or reality.

With the meanings of pageant before us, let us go back to meaning 1a —a scene acted on a stage, used with special reference to Mystery Plays. The Chester Mysteries were called *pagina prima, pagina secunda*, and so on, after the Anglo-Latin root *pagina* for pageant. But Latin *pagina* is also the root of English *page*, and thus *pageant* and *page* derive from the same Latin word. And, etymology aside, it is certainly true that the content of a public spectacle, particularly in procession, is similar to the content displayed and bound in a book.

Pageantry is a way of writing—one can "write" a pageant because pageantry is a language. It is a way of talking about intensely private concerns in a public manner—as in 1559 the people of London spoke to Elizabeth in the streets about their deepest concerns. A single scene or stage, a pageant, is a static moment, but pageants in a series present cumulative and enriching perspectives, as do stanzas in a poem or pages in sequence in a book. Shakespeare, who understood the nuances (and visual uses) of the word *pageant* so well, also perceived the link between *pages* and *pageant*, the way spectacle is a public form of writing (and reading) [cites *Richard III* 4.4.84–85]. * * *

To consider pageantry as a public language signifying private concerns is to approach an idea of allegory. For allegory is a way of talking about substances by way of surfaces, a means of focusing on the private, inner, and hidden through the public, available, and open. Such an approach to allegory (or to pageantry) means we must always absorb the surface, the literal level, in order to penetrate to the substance. We must learn to read the public writing of pageantry in order to grasp the common but submerged private significance. In allegory or in pageantry, the surface is never sacrificed to the substance; surface is, rather, at the service of substance. We must learn, as spectators, as readers, to read back from what is available to what is hidden. We must learn to read out of and into ourselves.

Spenser used the term "pageant" in a variety of ways. In his gloss to *"Many Graces"* in the "June" eclogue, E. K., annotator of *The Shepheardes Calender*, says that Spenser wrote a work called *Pageaunts*. It is now lost, but one can assume that some of it made its way into *The Faerie Queene*. In the epic, there are numerous individual pageants: the procession of the Seven Deadly Sins (I,iv,18–37), the Masque of Busirane (III,xii,6–25), Mutability's progress of seasons, months, hours, life, and death (VII,vii,28–41), to name but a few. But we are urged to see whole books as pageants as well. Redcross says to Guyon and the Palmer:

> His be the praise, that this atchiev'ment wrought,
> Who made my hand the organ of His might:
> More then goodwill to me attribute nought;
> For all I did, I did but as I ought.
> But you, faire sir, whose pageant next ensewes,
> Well mote yee thee. . . .
>
> (II,i,33)

Book II and Book I are by implication pageants, and immediately after Redcross's words, at II,i,36, Guyon's adventure begins with one of those "sad pageaunts of mens miseries," the tableau of Mordant, Amavia, and Ruddymane. Later in the poem, the poet muses.

> Wonder it is to see in diverse mindes
> How diversly Love doth his pageaunts play,
> And shewes his powre in variable kindes.
>
> (III,v,1)

Not only is variability and diversity always the subject of the poem, but the matter of Books III and IV is precisely the multiple forms of Love in progressive pageant before (and within) the reader's mind. * * * Finally, however, it is the epic that is the great pageant. To borrow Shakespeare's phrase, the dedicatory sonnets are only the "flattering index" to the public, triumphal procession of England and her founding heroes.

In the *Amoretti*, his sonnet sequence published in 1595, Spenser presents his most traditional and interesting use of the word pageant. This is the first eight lines of sonnet 54:

> Of this worlds theatre in which we stay,
> My love, lyke the spectator, ydly sits,
> Beholding me, that all the pageants play,
> Disguysing diversly my troubled wits.
> Sometimes I joy, when glad occasion fits,
> And maske in myrth lyke to a comedy:
> Soone after, when my joy to sorrow flits,
> I waile, and make my woes a tragedy.

Through the image of the theater, and in the writing of pageants-pages, we catch the sense of "play," of pretense and illusion that animates the whole poem. *The Faerie Queene* is a spectacle of the various moods and modes of a man's life in the theater of the world. Here we, the reader-spectator, sit watching our private self, our inner being, figured forth in public, and readily understandable, terms.

Thus far we have focused on pageants-pages as a public language that is significant and truly indicative of private concerns. I have suggested that pageantry is like allegory, a surface spectacle leading and urging us through itself to hidden areas of individual moral concern. In this way, Spenser's "spectacular" way of writing, his allegorical mode, is admirably summed up by Isis' gesture to Britomart. The idol, inclining her wand,

> with amiable looke,
> By outward shew her inward sense desining.
>
> (V, vii, 8)

Her outward signs truly reveal her inward sense, just as the poet tells the reader that

> Of Faery Lond yet if he more inquyre,
> By certein signes, here sett in sondrie place,
> He may it fynd.
>
> (II, proem 4)

So pageantry is itself a system of signs, a language, revealing inward sense.

Such a view, however, is only part of the story. From the beginning, pageant also conveyed those subsidiary and, in the sixteenth century, primary meanings of deceit, of empty show, of hollow or false spectacle. This, for instance, is Juliet's meaning when she hears Romeo has wounded Tybalt, and she calls her beloved "Despised substance of divinest show" (III, ii, 77). All pageants are shows, but not all shows are true or wholesome, and thus not all pageants are edifying or trustworthy. Let us recall that Puck also produced "pageants," which only proved "What fools these mortals be" (*Midsummer Night's Dream*, III, ii, 115).

Pageants can be empty or deceptive as pages (or books) can be deceiving or misleading, as language itself, notoriously unstable, can destroy as well as create. We must school ourselves to recognize the difference between a surface, a pageant, or a word that celebrates something real, and a surface, a show, or a word that only hides a deceptive or empty core. We need to learn, finally, how far to trust pages, or books, or any form of language, by reading the procession of images with an eye to distinguishing surface which misleads from surface which reflects substance.

In *The Faerie Queene*, Spenser gives us ample evidence of the deceptive side of pageantry, ample warning about trusting anyone's pages or words. The word "show" conveys constantly the deceptive side of public activity, or social behavior. [cites V.v.35, II.v.34] * * * It is a constant motif in *The Faerie Queene . . .* that the trickster is tricked, that falsity always contaminates its source, and that vice is its own reward. The easy moralism of this motif is always qualified, however, by the constant, underlying implication that only evil will defeat evil in this world, that, finally, good is powerless to do more than stand by and watch, and hope.

Of course, we can do more than stand passively by. We can actively press the issue and probe appearances with the mind. Indeed, we must. True Courtesy, for instance, must always distrust show. Therefore, when Calidore sees the sight on Mount Acidale and does not understand it,

> Whether it were the traine of Beauties Queene,
> Or nymphes, or faeries, or enchaunted show,
> With which his eyes mote have deluded beene.
> Therefore resolving, what it was, to know
>
> (VI,x,17)

he presses strenuously towards it, only to have the vision disappear. The rhyme (and episode) are instructive: (enchanted) "show" is rhymed with "know"—the possibility of falsity impels one, properly, to certainty, and yet the quest for knowledge, tragically, leads to loss.

The Knight of Courtesy's instinctive distrust of vanity and appearances results in the shattering of one of the most authentic moments of vision in the poem, and yet Calidore was in a sense correct. One must see face to face, for so much of the world of the poem is reflected through a glass darkly.

> Her purpose was not such as she did faine,
> Ne yet her person such as it was seene;
> But under simple shew and semblant plaine
> Lurkt false Duessa secretly unseene,
> As a chaste virgin, that had wronged beene;
> So had false Archimago her disguysed,
> To cloke her guile with sorrow and sad teene;
> And eke himselfe had craftily devisd
> To be her squire, and do her service well aguised.
>
> (II,i,21)

This pair, whose essence is falsity and whose goal is division and decay, is everywhere. The spirit of Archimago and Duessa is as ubiquitous in this world as their chivalric trappings are commonplace. It is precisely because what they represent is so commonplace, so much a part of us, that one must guard against show. With Arthur, we as readers must learn when to begin "to doubt [our] dazeled sight" (II,xi,40), for as the poet constantly tells us and shows us, "forged things do fairest shew" (IV,v,15). * * *

Like the world, the poem is full of beauty but also of "an outward shew of things that onely seeme" (*Hymn in Honour of Beautie*, 1,1.91). Thus the poem warns against the poem itself. While like Arthur, gazing at the Faery Queen's image emblazoned on Guyon's shield, we should see the "vertue in vaine shew" (II,ix,3), we must also remember this grand pageant of pages can be seen as only a "painted forgery" (II, proem 1). Even Spenser, recognizing how impossible it is to figure forth the glory of his queen, begs her pardon with an ambiguous term:

> That I in coloured showes may shadow itt,
> And antique praises unto present persons fitt.
> (III, proem 3)

The poet is always aware that his poem, like that other artifact, Acrasia's Island, may only "painted colours shew" (II,vi,29), though he hopes, like Calidore, our sojourn in the genuine world of Faery will render us wise: never more to delight

> in painted show
> Of such false blisse, as there is set for stales,
> T' entrap unwary fooles in their eternall bales.
> (VI,x,3)

Pageant in *The Faerie Queene*, or pageant as *The Faerie Queene*, means both images of the truth and deceptive illusion. So pageantry leads us back to that dual impulse within the poem and * * * within all epic. But even more, it leads us back to the dual nature of the reader and of reading. As we move through the pages and the pageant proceeds before us, as what happens without also happens within, the reader is a spectator or *voyeur* and protagonist. As a spectator, the reader must shape himself for moral action; as a *voyeur*, he must learn to become a *voyant*, that is, learn to pass from spying at the edges, like Calidore, to seeing at the core, like Colin Clout. As we watch versions of the truth pass publicly without, we need to learn to recognize the private, personal truth within. Great poems are not only relevant to readers; readers must strive to become relevant to great poems. In the mediative activity of reading, we expand our humanity by engaging a world wholly new to us.

The double thrust of pageantry is the dual impulse of the poem. As pageant gives either wholesome spectacle or empty show, so the poem, like daylight, "doth discover bad or good" (VI,viii,51) in us, in the world. Made of words, the poem, like the prophecies of Proteus, is ambiguous:

> So tickle be the terms of mortall state
> And full of subtile sophismes, which doe play

With double sences, and with false debate,
T' approve the unknowen purpose of eternall fate.
(III,iv,28)

In his pageants, and pages, the poet plays "with double sences" because
that is his sense of the way life plays with us. And because of these mutable
"termes of mortall state," he will finally cry at the end that Mutability's
sway

makes me loath this state of life so tickle,
And love of things so vaine to caste away.
(VII,viii,1)

Because of language's, and life's, "tickleness," its instability, the poet by
the end will have lost faith in the power of pageants to please and to indicate
permanence, and will crave a Sabbath's sight, which is true, a Sabbath's
site which is unchanging.

The poet will lose faith in the power of language to encompass and
maintain a vision of ideal truth. He will never doubt that his picture of the
antique time offers a better guide to life than the present scene but, as
Harry Berger has done so much to remind us, Spenser will find it increasingly difficult to maintain his pageants.[2] He tells us in the proem (1) to
Book V that "the world is runne quite out of square":

Right now is wrong, and wrong that was is right,
As all things else in time are chaunged quight.
Ne wonder; for the heavens revolution
Is wandred farre from where it first was pight,
And so doe make contrarie constitution
Of all this lower world, toward his dissolution.
(V, proem 4)

Images fail. We cannot depend upon a public language if the public is
depraved and the language is unstable. To escape the terror and frustration
of the play of double senses, the poet goes inward. He places the sources
of ethical wisdom less and less in the public vocabulary of pageantry and
more and more within man, within the manageable world of his private
self. [cites V.i.7, ii.47] * * * The Faerie Queene enacts before us that gradual
loss of faith in public norms which eventually darkens the view of Jacobean
dramatists, for instance, where the only choices to be made and acts to be
pursued are desperate and private ones. Finally, Milton may have borrowed
extensively from Spenser for his gardens and his heavens, but it was Spenser's
deepening moral inwardness and his unshakable Christian convictions that
attracted Milton most.

In the fifth stanza of the proem to Book VI we are told that Courtesy
today is

nought but forgerie
Fashion'd to please the eies of them that pas,
Which see not perfect things but in a glas.

2. Books decline in length after II, sharply after III.

Now Courtesy is simply chic, and only important to those who see indirectly rather than face to face. It is interesting only to the *voyeurs*, not the seers:

> But Vertues seat is deepe within the mynd,
> And not in outward shows, but inward thoughts defyned.
>
> (VI, proem 5)

All is forgery that is not within. The mind is the source and seat of virtue; there exists no longer a public system to communicate a common morality, no longer an "outward shew . . . inward sense desining" (V,vii,8). Spenser has come to the end of pageantry as it extends to allegory, and Book VI is not "allegorical" in the way earlier books were. No great pools of significance gathered around a Despair, or Charissa, or Mammon, or Alma, or Garden of Venus and Adonis, or Busirane, or marriage of rivers; now a story after the courtesy books and Greek Romances, with one great vision but all ethical wisdom, all virtue, deep in the minds of solitary hermits and shepherds. Only the Blatant Beast remains as an impulse from the earlier parts of the poem. And this remnant of the pageantry of the past serves only to embody the harsh truth that no matter how deep in the mind the line of conscience or the doom of right, no matter how far into the self one drives the self, language always bears within it the seeds of monstrosity as well as beauty. As long as men use words, they must risk letting slip the Beast.

Perhaps this view of pageantry and pages overstresses the dark side of Spenser's sense of language. What, after all, kept him writing with any sense of accomplishment if his view of the present state of life was so melancholy, and his faith in words to sustain a better vision so frail? Why did not he cease before he did?

The answer may be partly that for Spenser, in his own particular form of exile in Ireland, writing had become somehow synonymous with living. The long poem, instinct with a better time, peopled with the glistening creations of his imagination, sustained him despite the profound disappointments and frustrations of creating and living. To stop one would have meant stopping the other. That the attraction of ceasing was strong is attested by the temptation to give in that assails his epic protagonists; that he saw no final reconciliation of the images in his head and what he saw around him, or even what he could write, is evident from his own words and from the fact that all ideal moments of vision vanish and all the lovely ladies and brave knights meet only to part with promises of future bliss.

The poem must have filled his life as he put all his humanity into it; its ideal landscapes must have become the far country of his mind, deep in the interior of his being. Certainly he saw the poet as a gardener, working the soil of the soul, a sovereign planter reordering his own inner paradise. From the beginning of his career, Spenser had understood what it meant to write a verse; that is, he knew the English word *verse* was derived from Latin *versus*, the past participle of *vertere*, "to turn," meaning the turn of a plow, a furrow, line or row. Hence (as we know from pageant and page), a line of verse was the mark of the poet on the page, similar to the mark of cultivation made by the ploughman in the earth. If a page is a plot of land, growing its vine-trellis of writing, Spenser is the careful husbandman, tending, pruning, arranging.

Spenser began early to exploit the radical meaning of "verse." In *The Shepheardes Calender*, after Cuddie sings a complex *sestina* composed by Colin Clout, Perigot says:

> O Colin, Colin, the shepheards joye,
> How I admire ech turning of thy verse!
> ("August," ll. 190–91)

Later he muses on how difficult it is to cram every furrow with the seeds of all he knows. In the midst of narrating the marriage of Thames and Medway, the poet pauses:

> How can they all in this so narrow verse
> Contayned be, and in small compasse hild?
> (IV,xi,17)

And yet the small space, or the container, rammed with life's plenitude and energy, is the basic image of *The Faerie Queene*, and here the "narrow verse," the furrow, swells with the names of rivers, is irrigated with the very stuff of life.

Finally, the poet-planter wished to leave no plot unturned.

> Now turne againe my teme, thou jolly swayne,
> Back to the furrow which I lately left;
> I lately left a furrow, one or twayne,
> Unplough'd, the which my coulter hath not cleft:
> Yet seem'd the soyle both fayre and frutefull eft,
> As I it past, that were too great a shame,
> That so rich frute should be from us bereft.
> (VI,ix,1)

He then returns to the story of Calidore; he returns to his main "plot."

Spenser did not stop writing for the reason that cultivation of his poem was cultivation of his mind. Public language could become increasingly difficult to sustain; the conviction would grow that virtue lived only deep within the individual mind. But he would never abandon language, or the mind itself. He continued to sow in that green place, continued to turn the soil of his page, and as long as he did, there could be, in the mind and in the poem:

> continuall spring, and harvest there
> Continuall, both meeting at one tyme.
> (III,vi,42)

THOMAS P. ROCHE, JR.

[The Elizabethan Idea of Allegory]†

Allegorical reading (or more simply allegory) is a form of literary criticism with a metaphysical basis. It postulates a verbal universe at every point correspondent with the physical world in which we live, that is, a Realistic view of language. The history of allegorical interpretation of the Bible and secular literature is too long and complicated to relate here, but by the time of the sixteenth century allegory had attached itself firmly to the image of the universe created by Ptolemy and Dionysius the Areopagite and familiarly known as the "Elizabethan world picture." According to this theory there are in reality three worlds: the *sublunary*, the fallen world in which we live, subject to change and decay; the *celestial*, the unchanging world of the planets and stars; the *supercelestial*, the dwelling of angels and the Godhead. These three worlds are held together by God's Love and are analogically correspondent. Thus, in the sublunary world fire burns, while in the celestial world its analogue the sun not only burns but by its burning nourishes life, and in the supercelestial world the seraphim burn with love for their Creator.[1] The three worlds are a progression away from the material and toward the spiritual, and just as our image of the purely spiritual seraphim is drawn from our knowledge of the visible fire and sun, so too is our knowledge of universal truths drawn (in part) from our reading of the imitation of the visible worlds. Pico makes this quite clear in the introduction to his *Heptaplus*:

> For euen as the . . . three worlds being girt and buckled with the bands of concord doe by reciprocall libertie, interchange their natures; the like do they also by their appellations. And this is the principle from whence springeth & groweth the discipline of allegoricall sense. For it is certaine that the ancient fathers could not conueniently haue represented one thing by other figures, but that they had first learned the secret amity and affnitie of all nature. Otherwise there could bee no reason, why they should represent this thing by this forme, and that by that, rather then otherwise. But hauing the knowledge of the vniuersall world, and of euery part thereof, and being inspired with the same spirit, that not onely knoweth all things: but did also make all things: they haue oftentimes, and very fitly figured the natures of the

---

† From *The Kindly Flame: A Study of the Third and Fourth Books of Spenser's "Faerie Queene"* (Princeton, N.J., 1964), Introduction. Copyright © 1964 by Princeton University Press. Reprinted by permission of Princeton University Press.

1. *Iohannis Pici Mirandvlae . . . omnia . . . opera*, Venice, 1557, sig. **4. "Elemetaris urit: coelestis uiuificat: supercoelestis amat." The quotation may also be found on p. 188 of *De Hominis Dignitate, Heptaplus, De Ente et Uno*, ed. Eugenio Garin, Florence, 1942.

one world, by that which they knew to bee correspondent thereto
in the others.[2]

The basis of allegorical reading is this analogical nature of the universe.
In an hierarchical universe where each thing has a fixed place the relationship of any two things in the same world or sphere may adumbrate the
relationship of two other things in another world or sphere. The original
pair do not lose their identity or relationship by such adumbration; they
simply call attention to other possible relationships through the fact that
they themselves are related in such a way. The analogies are validated by
the fact that the whole hierarchical structure with its often unseen web of
interrelationships is contained within the mind of God, Who sees the
relationship of all things one to another. In allegorical reading a further
step is taken: since words represent things, words must represent this basic
analogical relationship.

The whole matter will be made clearer by returning to Harington's *Apology for Poetry*. Immediately following his definition of allegory is an example: "*Perseus* sonne of *Iupiter* is fained by the Poets to haue slaine *Gorgon*,
and after that conquest atchieued, to haue flowen vp to heauen." Harington
gives an euhemeristic interpretation as the "Historicall sence" and continues
with several more senses:

> Morally it signifieth thus much, *Perseus* a wise man, sonne of
> *Iupiter* endewed with vertue from aboue, slayeth sinne and vice,
> a thing base & earthly; signified by *Gorgon*, and so mounteth vp
> to the skie of vertue: It signifies in one kinde of Allegorie thus
> much; the mind of man being gotten by God, and so the childe
> of God killing and vanquishing the earthlinesse of this Gorgonicall
> nature, ascendeth vp to the vnderstanding of heauenly things, of
> high things, of eternal things; in which cõtemplacion cõsisteth
> the perfection of man: this is the natural allegory, because mã
> [is] one of the chiefe works of nature: It hath also a more high
> and heauenly Allegorie, that the heauenly nature, daughter of
> *Iupiter*, procuring with her continuall motion, corruption and
> mortality in the inferiour bodies, seuered it selfe at last from these
> earthly bodies, and flew vp on high, and there remaineth for euer.
> It hath also another Theological Allegorie; that the angelicall
> nature, daughter of the most high God the creator of all things;
> killing & ouercomming al bodily substance, signified by *Gorgon*,
> ascended into heauen: the like infinite Allegories I could pike out
> of other Poeticall fictions, saue that I would auoid tediousnes.[3]

---

2. The translation is that of the English translator of Pierre de la Primaudaye, *The French Academie*,
London, 1618, p. 671. De la Primaudaye in his discussion of the division of the universal world
simply translates the second proemium to Pico's *Heptaplus*. The original Latin text is on sig. **4
of the Venice, 1557, edition and on p. 192 of the Garin edition. The passage also occurs in
Fornari's *Della Espositione Sopra L'Orlando furioso Parte Seconda*, Florence, 1550, vol. 2, p. 3.
3. Harington, *Orlando Furioso*, 1591, sig. Piiij–Piiijᵛ. Reprinted in Smith, vol. 2, pp. 202–203. For
an earlier interpretation of the Perseus myth that follows the method employed by Harington but
finds different meanings see Giovanni Boccaccio, *Genealogie Deorum Gentilium*, ed. Vincenzo
Romano, 2 vols., Bari, 1951, vol. I, p. 19 (Book I, chap. 3).

The final, almost parenthetical comment is worth the consideration of
any one piecing out the Elizabethan idea of allegory. Many poetical fictions
adumbrate more than one allegorical meaning, and these meanings, as the
Perseus example shows, need not conform totally with every detail in the
narrative (vehicle of the continued metaphor). Perseus, the son of Jupiter,
may become in an allegorical reading the *daughter* of God, as in the "more
high and heauenly Allegorie." Perseus is not the name or personification
of the heavenly or the angelical natures; he is an allegorical representation
of these beings because in his narrative he is the offspring (not son or
daughter) of Jupiter, and hence because of the poetic statement of this
particular adventure the whole statement may adumbrate these and any
other heavenly mysteries that follow this particular pattern. There is no
relation between narrative statement and allegorical meaning except the
"secret amity and affinitie of all nature." When the structural patterns of
the narrative coincide with the structural patterns of any other events of
nature or supernature, we as readers are entitled to view the conformity or
analogy as an allegorical meaning.

* * *

NORTHROP FRYE

The Structure of Imagery in *The Faerie Queene*†

To demonstrate a unity in *The Faerie Queene*, we have to examine the
imagery of the poem rather than its allegory. It is Spenser's habitual technique, developing as it did out of the emblematic visions he wrote in his
nonage, to start with the image, not the allegorical translation of it, and
when he says at the beginning of the final canto of Book II:

> Now ginnes this goodly frame of Temperaunce
> Fayrely to rise

one feels that the "frame" is built out of the characters and places that
are clearly announced to be what they are, not out of their moral or historical shadows. Spenser prefaces the whole poem with sonnets to possible
patrons, telling several of them that they are in the poem somewhere,
not specifying where: the implication is that for such readers the allegory
is to be read more or less *ad libitum*. Spenser's own language about allegory, "darke conceit," "clowdily enwrapped," emphasizes its deliberate
vagueness. We know that Belphoebe refers to Elizabeth: therefore, when
Timias speaks of "her, whom the hevens doe serve and sew," is there, as
one edition suggests, a reference to the storm that wrecked the Armada? I
cite this only as an example of how subjective an allegorical reading can
be. Allegory is not only often uncertain, however, but in the work of one
of our greatest allegorical poets it can even be addled, as it is in *Mother*

† From "The Structure of Imagery in *The Faerie Queene*," *UTQ* 30 (1961): 109–27. Reprinted by
permission of University of Toronto Press.

Hubberds Tale, where the fox and the ape argue over which of them is more like a man, and hence more worthy to wear the skin of a lion. In such episodes as the legal decisions of Artegall, too, we can see that Spenser, unlike Milton, is a poet of very limited conceptual powers, and is helpless without some kind of visualization to start him thinking. I am far from urging that we should "let the allegory go" in reading Spenser, but it is self-evident that the imagery is prior in importance to it. One cannot begin to discuss the allegory without using the imagery, but one could work out an exhaustive analysis of the imagery without ever mentioning the allegory.

Our first step is to find a general structure of imagery in the poem as a whole, and with so public a poet as Spenser we should hardly expect to find this in Spenser's private possession, as we might with Blake or Shelley or Keats. We should be better advised to look for it in the axioms and assumptions which Spenser and his public shared, and which form the basis of its imaginative communication.[1] Perhaps the *Mutabilitie Cantos*, which give us so many clues to the sense of *The Faerie Queene* as a whole, will help us here also.

The action of the *Mutabilitie Cantos* embraces four distinguishable levels of existence. First is that of Mutability herself, the level of death, corruption, and dissolution, which would also be, if this poem were using moral categories, the level of sin. Next comes the world of ordinary experience, the nature of the four elements, over which Mutability is also dominant. Its central symbol is the cycle, the round of days, months, and hours which Mutability brings forth as evidence of her supremacy. In the cycle there are two elements: becoming or change, which is certainly Mutability's, and a principle of order or recurrence within which the change occurs. Hence Mutability's evidence is not conclusive, but could just as easily be turned against her. Above our world is upper nature, the stars in their courses, a world still cyclical but immortal and unchanged in essence. This upper world is all that is now left of nature as God originally created it, the state described in the Biblical story of Eden and the Classical myth of the Golden Age. Its regent is Jove, armed with the power which, in a world struggling against chaos and evil, is "the right hand of justice truly hight." But Jove, however he may bluster and threaten, has no authority over Mutability; that authority belongs to the goddess Nature, whose viceroy he is. If Mutability could be cast out of the world of ordinary experience, lower and upper nature would be reunited, man would re-enter the Golden Age, and the reign of "Saturn's son" would be replaced by that of Saturn. Above Nature is the real God, to whom Mutability appeals when she brushes Jove out of her way, who is invoked in the last stanza of the poem, and who appears in the reference to the Transfiguration of Christ like a mirage behind the assembly of lower gods.

Man is born into the third of these worlds, the order of physical nature which is theologically "fallen" and under the sway of Mutability. But though

---

1. In what follows the debt is obvious to A. S. P. Woodhouse, "Nature and Grace in *The Faerie Queene*," *ELH* (Sept. 1949), but there are some differences of emphasis owing to the fact that I am looking for a structure of images rather than of concepts.

in this world he is not of it: he really belongs to the upper nature of which he formed part before his fall. The order of physical nature, the world of animals and plants, is morally neutral: man is confronted from his birth with a moral dialectic, and must either sink below it into sin or rise above it into his proper human home. This latter he may reach by the practice of virtue and through education, which includes law, religion, and everything the Elizabethans meant by art. The question whether this "art" included what we mean by art, poetry, painting, and music, was much debated in Spenser's day, and explains why so much of the criticism of the period took the form of apologetic. As a poet, Spenser believed in the moral reality of poetry and in its effectiveness as an educating agent; as a Puritan, he was sensitive to the abuse and perversion of art which had raised the question of its moral value in the first place, and he shows his sense of the importance of the question in his description of the Bower of Bliss.

Spenser means by "Faerie" primarily the world of realized human nature. It is an "antique" world, extending backward to Eden and the Golden Age, and its central figure of Prince Arthur was chosen, Spenser tells us, as "furthest from the daunger of envy, and suspition of present time." It occupies the same space as the ordinary physical world, a fact which makes contemporary allusions possible, but its time sequence is different. It is not timeless: we hear of months or years passing, but time seems curiously foreshortened, as though it followed instead of establishing the rhythm of conscious life. Such foreshortening of time suggests a world of dream and wishfulfilment, like the fairylands of Shakespeare's comedies. But Spenser, with his uneasy political feeling that the price of authority is eternal vigilance, will hardly allow his virtuous characters even to sleep, much less dream, and the drowsy narcotic passages which have so impressed his imitators are associated with spiritual peril. He tells us that sleep is one of the three divisions of the lowest world, the other two being death and hell; and Prince Arthur's long tirade against night (III.iv) would be out of proportion if night, like its seasonal counterpart winter, did not symbolize a lower world than Faerie. The vision of Faerie may be the *author's* dream, as the pilgrimage of Christian is presented as a dream of Bunyan, but what the poet dreams of is the strenuous effort, physical, mental, and moral, of waking up to one's true humanity.

In the ordinary physical world good and evil are inextricably confused; the use and the abuse of natural energies are hard to distinguish, motives are mixed and behaviour inconsistent. The perspective of Faerie, the achieved quest of virtue, clarifies this view. What we now see is a completed moral dialectic. The mixed-up physical world separates out into a human moral world and a demonic one. In this perspective heroes and villains are purely and simply heroic and villainous; characters are either white or black, for the quest or against it; right always has superior might in the long run, for we are looking at reality from the perspective of man as he was originally made in the image of God, unconfused about the difference between heaven and hell. We can now see that physical nature is a source of energy, but that this energy can run only in either of two opposing directions: toward its own fulfilment or towards its own destruction. Nature says to Mutability:

"For thy decay thou seekst by thy desire," and contrasts her with those who, struggling out of the natural cycle, "Doe worke their owne perfection so by fate."

Spenser, in Hamlet's language, has no interest in holding the mirror up to nature unless he can thereby show virtue her own feature and scorn her own image. His evil characters are rarely converted to good, and while there is one virtuous character who comes to a bad end, Sir Terpine in Book V, this exception proves the rule, as his fate makes an allegorical point about justice. Sometimes the fiction writer clashes with the moralist in Spenser, though never for long. When Malbecco offers to take Hellenore back from the satyrs, he becomes a figure of some dignity as well as pathos; but Spenser cannot let his dramatic sympathy with Malbecco evolve. Complicated behaviour, mixed motives, or the kind of driving energy of character which makes moral considerations seem less important, as it does in all Shakespeare's heroes, and even in Milton's Satan—none of this could be contained in Spenser's framework.

The Faerie Queene in consequence is necessarily a romance, for romance is the genre of simplified or black and white characterization. The imagery of this romance is organized on two major principles. One is that of the natural cycle, the progression of days and seasons. The other is that of the moral dialectic, in which symbols of virtue are parodied by their vicious or demonic counterparts. Any symbol may be used ambivalently, and may be virtuous or demonic according to its context, an obvious example being the symbolism of gold. Cyclical symbols are subordinated to dialectical ones; in other words the upward turn from darkness to dawn or from winter to spring usually symbolizes the lift in perspective from physical to human nature. Ordinary experience, the morally neutral world of physical nature, never appears as such in The Faerie Queene, but its place in Spenser's scheme is symbolized by nymphs and other elemental spirits, or by the satyrs, who may be tamed and awed by the sight of Una or more habitually stimulated by the sight of Hellenore. Satyrane, as his name indicates, is, with several puns intended, a good-natured man, and two of the chief heroes, Redcrosse and Artegall, are explicitly said to be natives of this world and not, like Guyon, natives of Faerie. What this means in practice is that their quests include a good deal of historical allegory.

In the letter to Raleigh Spenser speaks of a possible twenty-four books, twelve to deal with the private virtues of Prince Arthur and the other twelve with the public ones manifested after he was crowned king. But this appalling spectre must have been exorcized very quickly. If we look at the six virtues he did treat, we can see that the first three, holiness, temperance, and chastity, are essentially private virtues, and that the next three, friendship, justice, and courtesy, are public ones. Further, that both sets seem to run in a sort of Hegelian progression. Of all public virtues, friendship is the most private and personal; justice the most public and impersonal, and courtesy seems to combine the two, Calidore being notable for his capacity for friendship and yet able to capture the Blatant Beast that eluded Artegall. Similarly, of all private virtues, holiness is most dependent on grace and revelation, hence the imagery of Book I is Biblical and apocalyptic, and introduces the theological virtues. Temperance, in contrast, is a virtue shared by the enlightened heathen, a prerequisite and somewhat pedestrian virtue (Guyon loses his horse early in the book and does not get it back until Book V), hence the imagery of Book II is classical, with much drawn from the *Odyssey* and from Platonic and Aristotelian ethics. Chastity, a virtue described by Spenser as "farre above the rest," seems to combine something of both. The encounter of Redcrosse and Guyon is indecisive, but Britomart, by virtue of her enchanted spear, is clearly stronger than Guyon, and hardly seems to need Redcrosse's assistance in Castle Joyeous.

We note that in Spenser, as in Milton's *Comus*, the supreme private virtue appears to be chastity rather than charity. Charity, in the sense of Christian love, does not fit the scheme of *The Faerie Queene*: for Spenser it would primarily mean, not man's love for God, but God's love for man, as depicted in the *Hymn of Heavenly Love*. Charissa appears in Book I, but her main connexions are with the kindliness that we associate with "giving to charity"; Agape appears in Book IV, but is so minor and so dim-witted a character that one wonders whether Spenser knew the connotations of the word. Hence, though Book I is the only book that deals explicitly with Christian imagery, it does not follow that holiness is the supreme virtue. Spenser is not dealing with what God gives to man, but with what man does with his gifts, and Redcrosse's grip on holiness is humanly uncertain.

In one of its aspects *The Faerie Queene* is an educational treatise, based, like other treatises of its time, on the two essential social facts of the Renaissance, the prince and the courtier. The most important person in Renaissance society to educate was the prince, and the next most important was the courtier, the servant of the prince. Spenser's heroes are courtiers who serve the Faerie Queene and who metaphorically make up the body and mind of Prince Arthur. To demonstrate the moral reality of poetry Spenser had to assume a connexion between the educational treatise and the highest forms of literature. For Spenser, as for most Elizabethan writers, the highest form of poetry would be either epic or tragedy, and the epic for him deals essentially with the actions of the heroic prince or leader. The highest form of prose, similarly, would be either a Utopian vision outlined in a Platonic dialogue or in a romance like Sidney's *Arcadia,* or a description of an ideal prince's ideal education, for which the classical model was Xenophon's *Cyropaedia.* Spenser's preference of Xenophon's form to Plato's is explicit in the letter to Raleigh. This high view of education is inseparable from Spenser's view of the relation between nature and art. For Spenser, as for Burke centuries later, art is man's nature. Art is nature on the human plane, or what Sidney calls a second nature, a "golden" world, to use another phrase of Sidney's, because essentially the same world as that of the Golden Age, and in contrast to the "brazen" world of physical nature. Hence art is no less natural than physical nature—the art itself is nature, as Polixenes says in *The Winter's Tale*—but it is the civilized nature appropriate to human life.

Private and public education, then, are the central themes of *The Faerie Queene.* If we had to find a single word for the virtue underlying all private education, the best word would perhaps be fidelity: that unswerving loyalty to an ideal which is virtue, to a single lady which is love, and to the demands of one's calling which is courage. Fidelity on the specifically human plane of endeavour is faith, the vision of holiness by which one lives; on the natural plane it is temperance, or the ability to live humanely in the physical world. The corresponding term for the virtue of public education is, perhaps, concord or harmony. On the physical plane concord is friendship, again the ability to achieve a human community in ordinary life; on the specifically human plane it is justice and equity, the foundation of society.

In the first two books the symbolism comes to a climax in what we may call a "house of recognition," the House of Holiness in Book I and the House of Alma in Book II. In the third the climax is the vision of the order of nature in the Gardens of Adonis. The second part repeats the same scheme: we have houses of recognition in the Temple of Venus in Book IV and the Palace of Mercilla in Book V, and a second *locus amoenus* vision in the Mount Acidale canto of Book VI, where the poet himself appears with the Graces. The sequence runs roughly as follows: fidelity in the context of human nature; fidelity in the context of physical nature; fidelity in the context of nature as a whole; concord in the context of physical nature; concord in the context of human nature; concord in the context of nature as a whole. Or, abbreviated: human fidelity, natural fidelity, nature; natural concord, human concord, art. Obviously, such a summary is unacceptable as it stands, but it may give some notion of how the books are related and of how the symbolism flows out of one book into the next one.

The conception of the four levels of existence and the symbols used to represent it come from Spenser's cultural tradition in general and from the Bible in particular. The Bible, as Spenser read it for his purposes, describes how man originally inhabited his own human world, the Garden of Eden, and fell out of it into the present physical world, which fell with him. By his fall he lost the tree and water of life. Below him is hell, represented on earth by the kingdoms of bondage, Egypt, Babylon, and Rome, and symbolized by the serpent of Eden, otherwise Satan, otherwise the huge water-monster called Leviathan or the dragon by the prophets. Man is redeemed by the quest of Christ, who after overcoming the world descended to hell and in three days conquered it too. His descent is usually symbolized in art as walking into the open mouth of a dragon, and when he returns in triumph he carries a banner of a red cross on a white ground, the colours typifying his blood and flesh. At the end of time the dragon of death is finally destroyed, man is restored to Eden, and gets back the water and tree of life. In Christianity these last are symbolized by the two sacraments accepted by the Reformed Church, baptism and the Eucharist.

The quest of the Redcross knight in Book I follows the symbolism of the quest of Christ. He carries the same emblem of a red cross on a white ground; the monster he has to kill is "that old dragon" (quatrain to Canto xi; cf. Rev. xii, 9) who is identical with the Biblical Satan, Leviathan, and serpent of Eden, and the object of killing him is to restore Una's parents, who are Adam and Eve, to their kingdom of Eden, which includes the entire world, now usurped by the dragon. The tyranny of Egypt, Babylon, and the Roman Empire continues in the tyranny of the Roman Church, and the Book of Revelation, as Spenser read it, prophesies the future ascendancy of that church and its ultimate defeat in its vision of the dragon and Great Whore, the latter identified with his Duessa. St. George fights the dragon for three days in the garden of Eden, refreshed by the water and tree of life on the first two days respectively.

But Eden is not heaven: in Spenser, as in Dante, it is rather the summit of purgatory, which St. George goes through in the House of Holiness. It is the world of recovered human nature, as it originally was and still can be when sin is removed. St. George similarly is not Christ, but only the English people trying to be Christian, and the dragon, while he may be part of Satan, is considerably less Satanic than Archimago or Duessa, who survive the book. No monster, however loathsome, can really be evil: for evil there must be a perversion of intelligence, and Spenser drew his dragon with some appreciation of the fact mentioned in an essay of Valéry, that in poetry the most frightful creatures always have something rather childlike about them:

> So dreadfully he towards him did pas,
> Forelifting up aloft his speckled brest,
> And often bounding on the brused gras,
> As for great joyance of his newcome guest.   (I, xi, 15)

Hence the theatre of operations in the first book is still a human world. The real heaven appears only in the vision of Jerusalem at the end of the tenth canto and in a few other traces, like the invisible husband of Charissa and the heavenly music heard in the background of the final betrothal. Eden is within the order of nature but it is a new earth turned upward, or sacramentally aligned with a new heaven. The main direction of the imagery is also upward: this upward movement is the theme of the House of Holiness, of the final quest, and of various subordinate themes like the worship of Una by the satyrs.

We have spoken of the principle of symbolic parody, which we meet in all books of *The Faerie Queene*. Virtues are contrasted not only with their vicious opposites, but with vices that have similar names and appearances. Thus the golden mean of temperance is parodied by the golden means provided by Mammon; "That part of justice, which is equity" in Book V is parodied by the anarchistic equality preached by the giant in the second canto, and so on. As the main theme of Book I is really faith, or spiritual fidelity, the sharpest parody of this sort is between Fidelia, or true faith, and Duessa, who calls herself Fidessa. Fidelia holds a golden cup of wine and water (which in other romance patterns would be the Holy Grail, though Spenser's one reference to the Grail shows that he has no interest in it); Duessa holds the golden cup of the Whore of Babylon. Fidelia's cup also contains a serpent (the redeeming brazen serpent of Moses typifying the Crucifixion); Duessa sits on the dragon of the Apocalypse who is metaphorically the same beast as the serpent of Eden. Fidelia's power to raise the dead is stressed; Duessa raises Sansjoy from the dead by the power of Aesculapius, whose emblem is the serpent. Of all such parodies in the first book the most important for the imagery of the poem as a whole is the parody of the tree and water of life in Eden. These symbols have their demonic counterparts in the paralysed trees of Fradubio and Fraelissa and in the paralysing fountain from which St. George drinks in the seventh canto.

Thus the first book shows very clearly what we have called the subordinating of cyclical symbols to dialectical ones: the tree and water of life, originally symbols of the rebirth of spring, are here symbols of resurrection, or a permanent change from a life in physical nature above the animals to life in human nature under God. The main interest of the second book is also dialectical, but in the reverse direction, concerned with human life in the ordinary physical world, and with its separation from the demonic world below. The Bower of Bliss is a parody of Eden, and just as the climax of Book I is St. George's three-day battle with the dragon of death, so the narrative climax of Book II is Guyon's three-day endurance in the underworld. It is the climax at least as far as Guyon's heroism is concerned, for it is Arthur who defeats Maleger and it is really the Palmer who catches Acrasia. * * *

Having outlined the dialectical extremes of his imagery, Spenser moves on to consider the order of nature on its two main levels in the remaining books. Temperance steers a middle course between care and carelessness, jealousy and wantonness, miserliness and prodigality, Mammon's cave and Acrasia's bower. Acrasia is a kind of sinister Venus, and her victims, Mordant wallowing in his blood, Cymochles, Verdant, have something of a dead, wasted, or frustrated Adonis about them. Mammon is an old man with a daughter, Philotime. Much of the symbolism of the third book is based on these two archetypes. The first half leads up to the description of the Gardens of Adonis in Canto vi by at least three repetitions of the theme of Venus and Adonis. First we have the tapestry in the Castle Joyeous representing the story, with a longish description attached. Then comes the wounding of Marinell on his "precious shore" by Britomart (surely the most irritable heroine known to romance), where the sacrificial imagery, the laments of the nymphs, the strewing of flowers on the bier are all conventional images of Adonis. Next is Timias, discovered by Belphoebe wounded in the thigh with a boar-spear. Both Belphoebe and Marinell's mother Cymoent have pleasant retreats closely analogous to the Gardens of Adonis. In the second half of the book we have three examples of the old man and young woman relationships: Malbecco and Hellenore, Proteus and Florimell, Busirane and Amoret. All these are evil: there is no idealized version of this theme. The reason is that the idealized version would be the counterpart to the vision of charity in the *Hymn of Heavenly Love*. That is, it would be the vision of the female Sapience sitting in the bosom of the Deity that we meet at the end of the *Hymn to Heavenly Beauty*, and this would take us outside the scope of *The Faerie Queene*, or at any rate of its third book.

The central figure in the third book and the fourth is Venus, flanked on either side by Cupid and Adonis, or what a modern poet would call Eros and Thanatos. Cupid and Venus are gods of natural love, and form, not a demonic parody, but a simple analogy of Christian love, an analogy which is the symbolic basis of the *Fowre Hymnes*. Cupid, like Jesus, is lord of gods and creator of the cosmos, and simultaneously an infant, Venus' relation to him being that of an erotic Madonna, as her relation to Adonis is that of an erotic Pièta. Being androgynous, she brings forth Cupid without male assistance;[2] she loses him and goes in search of him, and he returns in triumph in the great masque at the end as lord of all creation.

The Garden of Adonis, with its Genius and its temperate climate, is so carefully paralleled to the Bower of Bliss that it clearly represents the reality of which the Bower is a mirage. It presents the order of nature as a cyclical process of death and renewal, in itself morally innocent, but still within the realm of Mutability, as the presence of Time shows. Like Eden, it is a paradise: it is nature as nature would be if man could live in his proper human world, the "antique" Golden Age. It is a world where substance is constant but where "Forms are variable and decay"; and hence it is closely connected with the theme of metamorphosis, which is the central symbol of divine love as the pagans conceived it.

* * *

Just as Book III deals with the secular and natural counterpart of love, so Book VI deals with the secular and natural counterpart of grace. The word grace itself in all its human manifestations is a thematic word in this book, and when the Graces themselves appear on Mount Acidale we find ourselves in a world that transcends the world of Venus:

> These three to men all gifts of grace do graunt,
> And all that Venus in herself doth vaunt
> Is borrowed of them   (VI.x.15)

The Graces, we are told, were begotten by Jove when he returned from the wedding of Peleus and Thetis. This wedding is referred to again in the *Mutabilitie Cantos* as the most festive occasion the gods had held before the lawsuit of Mutability. For it was at this wedding that Jove was originally "confirmed in his imperial see": the marriage to Peleus removed the threat to Jove's power coming from the son of Thetis, a threat the secret of which only Prometheus knew, and which Prometheus was crucified on a rock for not revealing. Thus the wedding also led, though Spenser does not tell us this, to the reconciling of Jove and Prometheus, and it was Prometheus, whose name traditionally means forethought or wisdom, who, according to Book II, was the originator of Elves and Fays—that is, of man's moral and conscious nature. There are still many demonic symbols in Book VI, especially the attempt to sacrifice Serena, where the custom of eating the flesh and giving the blood to the priests has obvious overtones of parody. But the centre of symbolic gravity, so to speak, in Book VI is a pastoral Arcadian world, where we seem almost to be entering into the original home of man where, as in the child's world of Dylan Thomas's *Fern Hill*, it was all Adam and maiden. It is no longer the world of Eros; yet the sixth book is the most erotic, in the best sense, of all the books in the poem, full of innocent nakedness and copulation, the surprising of which is so acid a test of courtesy, and with many symbols of the state of innocence and of possible regeneration like the Salvage Man and the recognition scene in which Pastorella is reunited to her parents.

---

2. This detail is not in *The Faerie Queene*: see *Colin Clouts Come Home Againe* 800 ff. [*Editors*].

Such a world is a world in which the distinction between art and nature is disappearing because nature is taking on a human form. In the Bower of Bliss the *mixing* of art and nature is what is stressed: on Mount Acidale the art itself is nature, to quote Polixenes again. Yet art, especially poetry, has a central place in the legend of courtesy. Grace in religion implies revelation by the Word, and human grace depends much on good human words. All through the second part of *The Faerie Queene*, slander is portrayed as the worst enemy of the human community: we have Ate and Sclaunder herself in Book IV, Malfont with his tongue nailed to a post in Mercilla's court, as an allegory of what ought to be done to *other* poets; and finally the Blatant Beast, the voice of rumour full of tongues. The dependence of courtesy on reasonable speech is emphasized at every turn, and just as the legend of justice leads us to the figure of the Queen, as set forth in Mercilla, who manifests the order of society, so the legend of courtesy leads us to the figure of the poet himself, who manifests the order of words.

When Calidore commits his one discourteous act and interrupts Colin Clout, all the figures dancing to his pipe vanish. In Elizabethan English a common meaning of art was magic, and Spenser's Colin Clout, like Shakespeare's Prospero, has the magical power of summoning spirits to enact his present fancies, spirits who disappear if anyone speaks and breaks the spell. Nature similarly vanishes mysteriously at the end of the *Mutabilitie Cantos*, just as the counterpart to Prospero's revels is his subsequent speech on the disappearance of all created things. Colin Clout, understandably annoyed at being suddenly deprived of the company of a hundred and four naked maidens, destroys his pipe, as Prospero drowns his book. Poetry works by suggestion and indirection, and conveys meanings out of all proportion to its words; but in magic the impulse to complete a pattern is very strong. If a spirit is being conjured by the seventy-two names of God as set forth in the *Schemhamphoras*, it will not do if the magician can remember only seventy-one of them. At the end of the sixth book the magician in Spenser had completed half of his gigantic design, and was ready to start on the other half. But the poet in Spenser was satisfied: he had done his work, and his vision was complete.

A. C. HAMILTON

[The Cosmic Image: Spenser and Dante]†

* * *

* * * I shall analyse an episode from Spenser's poem, the most obvious choice being the opening episode in which the Red Cross Knight defeats Error. I shall compare it, since we have been considering the art of reading allegory, to the opening episode of Dante's *Commedia*. These are the only two major classics in modern literature which were conceived by their

† From *The Structure of Allegory in "The Faerie Queene"* (Oxford, 1961), chapter 1. (The original footnotes have been slightly edited.) Reprinted by permission of Oxford University Press.

authors as allegories; yet, strangely enough, they have never been brought into any significant relationship.

* * *

Unless these poets write a common language of allegory, there is little we may ever understand about the genre; but if they do, comparison of the opening episodes of each poem should be mutually illuminating. At first the differences in matter and method may seem too striking. Dante's Wood is nasty, brutish, rough (to adapt Hobbes's relevant phrase), and fills his heart with fear; Spenser's is a pleasant Wood where the knight and his lady are beguiled with delight. Dante describes in concrete and very real terms a man of flesh and blood who is defeated by fear and doubt until Virgil aids him; Spenser uses allegorical devices of a chivalric combat between an armed knight and a monster which personifies Error. But such differences are not essential. Spenser's Wood is also dark, for the enshrouding trees 'heauens light did hide, / Not perceable with power of any starre' and leads to the monster's 'darksome hole'.[1] That Beatrice sends Virgil to aid Dante, and that Una accompanies her knight, reflect rather differences of religious faith than of poetical method. (The differences of method are more apparent than real, but I leave this point until later.) Moreover, these differences do not rule out striking similarities. In larger terms each episode presents an image of one lost in a Wood where he confronts certain monsters (Dante's three beasts, Spenser's threefold enemy in the woman-serpent with her brood) and is overcome by error and doubt. Dante is driven back into the dark pass where he struggles with death until Beatrice aids him: Spenser's knight wanders until he comes to the dark den where he is almost slain before Una aids him. (The donna . . . beata e bella and the 'louely Ladie' clearly suggest God's grace.) Then both begin their Exodus—the one treading that pass which had allowed none to go alive ('che non lasciò già mai persona viva') and the other taking by-ways 'where neuer foot of liuing wight did tread' (I. vii. 50)—until they are restored to the heavenly Jerusalem. Essentially, then, each episode is an initiation: the candidate wanders in a labyrinth or maze which prepares him for his salvation. It initiates the poet also by committing him to his kind of allegory. Further, it initiates the reader by offering a brief allegory of what is to come, and by teaching him the art of reading allegory.

The literal level of an allegory seems the most difficult to read properly. Does the fiction exist in its own right, or is it a veil which must be torn aside to reach the allegorical levels beneath? The latter has been the usual fashion in which to read not only Spenser, as we have seen, but also Dante. Modern Dante criticism recognizes, however, that the Commedia does not respond to such allegorizing. On this subject Professor Hatzfeld writes:

> In passages where . . . the allegorical sense is the literal one,
> the reader is even less entitled to ask extratextual and biographical
> questions, such as whether the dark wood means heresy, or for-
> nication, or pursuit of worldly honors in Dante's life, or whether

1. All references are to the opening episode of each poem, unless indicated otherwise. For Dante, I cite the edition of La Divina Commedia, ed. C. H. Grandgent (New York, rev. ed., 1933).

questions refer only to potentialities, namely, Dante's life as raw
material, and abandon the actually achieved world of Dante's
poetical symbolism. In other words, the new Dante interpretation
makes a strong point of the fact that Dante in his poetry (not in
his prose) overcomes the usual mediaeval allegorism and fuses
personal, theological, political, moral, even astronomical elements into symbols of a decidedly poetical and not didactic
quality.[2]

But not modern Spenser criticism where, as we have seen, the poem's literal
level is still translated into moral precept and historical example. We are
told that in the episode of the Wandering Wood, the knight is Holiness,
Una is Truth, Error is obvious error: *ergo*, the episode means that Holiness
defeats Error with the aid of Truth. We are told this by the critics, not by
Spenser who does not name the knight, nor the lady, and describes the
monster in very real terms. Again without support from the text, we are
told that the knight is England, Una is the true Church, Error is the Church
of Rome: *ergo*, the episode means that England passed successfully through
the dangers of Reformation.[3] Since both poems share a similar critical
history—contemporary praise for their profound meaning, the neo-classical
eclipse, the romantic age's rejection of the allegory for lyrical beauty (Liv-
ingston Lowes on Spenser, Croce on Dante), and yesterday's search for
hidden meanings—probably Spenser criticism needs to catch up.

What seems so perverse about translating the literal level is that Spenser,
like Dante, labours to render the fiction in its own right. It is an image
presented in realistic and visual detail. There is the precise physical detail
of the monster's huge tail wound about the knight's body, his strangling
her gorge, her filthy vomit, the serpents swarming about his legs, and the
final gruesome beheading. There is the exact rendering of the monster
'vpon the durtie ground', her brood 'sucking vpon her poisonous dugs', her
vomit 'full of great lumpes of flesh and gobbets raw'. The details are immediately repulsive to all the senses: to the *sight* with the monster half-
serpent, half-woman, and her deformed brood sucking up her blood; to the
hearing with the monster's loud braying and her brood 'groning full deadly';
to the *smell* with the 'deadly stinke' of her vomit; to the *taste* with the
violent spewing of the flood of poison; and to the *touch* with the monster's
tail strangling him. The realism of the episode is enforced by its dramatic
action: the monster's brood creeping into her mouth 'and suddain all were
gone', her rushing forth and retreating before the knight, the brilliant chia-
roscuro effect of the knight's armour which casts 'a litle glooming light,
much like a shade' into Error's dark hole, the brood with 'bowels gushing
forth'. This monster has all the terrible reality of a nightmare, and even
Fuseli who saw the nightmare could complain that 'when Spenser dragged
into light the entrails of the serpent slain by the Red Knight, he dreamt a
butcher's dream and not a poet's'.[4] Clearly the poet labours to make us see.
His whole effort is to render a clearly-defined, exact, and visual image. No

2. Helmut Hatzfeld, "Modern Dante Criticism", *Comparative Literature*, iii (1951), 297–298.
3. See *Var. Sp.* i. 422 f., 449 f.
4. See E. C. Mason, *The Mind of Henry Fuseli* (London, 1951), p. 217.

less than with Dante, Spenser's reader must respect the primacy and integrity of the poem's literal level.

Whatever the differences of their critical traditions, both poets clearly demand that the reader focus upon this literal level. For Dante it may be enough to point * * * to Holy Scripture with its insistence upon the literal level. For the Renaissance poet there is the classically-derived doctrine that the poet gathers precept and example into a poetic image which he makes us see; and behind this doctrine is the neo-Platonic faith that if man once sees virtues and vices, he will embrace the one and shun the other. For the Protestant poet there is also the renewed emphasis upon the Bible's literal sense. But they may share a simpler basis for insisting upon the literal level of their poems. Ever since Plato, poets have recognized that they deliver fiction rather than truth or morality. In the *Convivio* Dante claims that 'the literal sense ought always to come first, as being that sense in the expression of which the others are all included, and without which it would be impossible and irrational to give attention to the other meanings, and most of all to the allegorical'. Further, the highest allegorical sense, the anagogic, sustains and illuminates the literal by seeing in it the poem's total meaning: 'this occurs when a writing is spiritually expounded, which even in the literal sense by the things signified likewise gives intimation of higher matters belonging to the eternal glory'.[5] The corresponding Renaissance claim is Sidney's doctrine that 'in Poesie, looking but for fiction [that is, *only* for fiction and not allegorical truth], they [the readers] shal vse the narration but as an imaginatiue groundplot of a profitable inuention'.[6] Since the fiction is the groundplot for readers of both Dante and Spenser, to strip it away leaves the poem barren. As readers we must respect what they have given us. To read their allegories we must accept as given that Dante's matter is a history of what happened to him, and that Spenser's 'History' (he insists upon the term) is 'matter of iust memory' (II. Pr. I).

But how may we understand their opening episodes? Not according to the usual medieval or Renaissance theories of allegory: these, with their stress upon levels of allegorical meaning, only distract. If we seek more clear authority for the art of reading than the *Letter to Can Grande* and the *Apology for Poetry* provide, we must begin with the poems themselves, with the fact that each within its tradition is a separate kind of allegory which demands its own kind of reading. And this provides the clue we need. The opening episode of each poem defines the art of reading the allegory. The initiation which is described here both separates and joins: it separates the candidate from us, from our way of life, and enters him upon a pilgrimage which is treated in the rest of the poem. It follows that there are two ways of understanding. The first is outward, that extrinsic meaning which relates the episode (and the poem) to our world; the second is intrinsic, that inner coherence which binds all parts of the poem. Allegory's unique power is achieved through the contrapuntal relationship between the poem's world and our world, and by the centripetal relationship

---

5. *Convivio*, trans. W. W. Jackson (Oxford, 1909), p. 74. See also his letter to Can Grande in *The Letters of Dante*, trans. Paget Toynbee (Oxford, 1920).
6. See the Ponsonby edition (ed. A. S. Cook [Boston, 1890], p. 36), whose version is here less elegant but more explicit.

of its parts. More comprehensively and significantly than other genres, it points beyond itself and also to itself. The brazen world of fallen nature and the poem's golden world, reality and the ideal, fact and fiction become united in our reading.

In their opening episodes both poets exploit the metaphor of the labyrinth or maze, of one wandering lost in a Wood where he encounters beasts. Dante's source has been found in Horace's *Satires*,[7] Spenser's in medieval romance; but the more likely source is Holy Scripture. There we learn that Wisdom (with whom Beatrice and Una are identified) 'wil walke with him [her lover] by crooked waies, and bring him vnto feare, and dread, and torment him with her discipline vntill shee haue tried his soule, and haue proued him by her iudgementes. Then will she returne the streight way vnto him, and comfort him, and shew him her secrets.'[8] But the metaphor is universal, too centrally archetypal to be traced to any source. Or if any, it is that of Christ who, after His baptism, entered the Wilderness where He was with the wild beasts during his initiation into the role of Redeemer. (Dante's baptism is signified by the metaphor of the lake in which he struggles, the knight's baptism by the spiritual armour which he dons.) The Renaissance poet may mingle classical myth with Scripture: the labyrinthine wood with the monster in the middle invokes the myth of Theseus who enters the labyrinth to slay the Minotaur in the middle, and is guided out by Ariadne's thread. He may do so because Christ is the true Theseus who slew monsters, and the Word is 'the thread that will direct us through the winding and intricate labyrinths of this life'.[9]

Singleton has shown Dante's complex use of this metaphor, how it is designed to locate us by showing the way of our life.[1] It is *our* life, as Dante's opening line suggests, but his experience in the Wood is unique. He becomes lost only when he separates himself from the common herd, from our life, through love of Beatrice. As Christian alone in the City of Destruction knows that he bears upon his back the burden which plunges him deeper into hell, Dante in the Dark Wood is forced by the beasts back into the darkness.[2] In the beginning when he is with us, he is nameless; he may begin to find himself only by losing himself, that is, by finding himself lost; and finally Beatrice will restore him to himself, and name him Dante. As in Bunyan where the pilgrim in our city is anonymous—after he enters the way of salvation he is named Christian—and in Spenser where the knight is not named until after he endures the first test. We may say, then, that Dante's poem arises out of its opening episode: once he

7. J. H. Whitfield, *Dante and Virgil* (Oxford, 1949), p. 74. Cf. Upton: 'what are these trees and labyrinths [of the Wandering Wood], but the various amusements and errors of human life? So Horace and Dante apply the similitude' (*Spenser's 'Faerie Queene'*, ii. 339).

8. Eccles. iv. 17–18. The Genevan version (London, 1580) which I cite throughout this study. The tropological significance of Spenser's episode, then, is that given by Fulke Greville to Sidney's *Arcadia*: 'his end in them was not vanishing pleasure alone, but morall Images, and Examples, (as directing threds) to guide every man through the confused *Labyrinth* of his own desires, and life' (*Life of Sir Philip Sidney*, ed. Nowell Smith [Oxford, 1907], p. 223).

9. Alexander Ross, *Mystagogus Poeticus* (London, 1647), p. 254.

1. C. S. Singleton, *Dante Studies*, I (Cambridge, Mass., 1954), p. 7.

2. Francis Fergusson acutely remarks of Dante's experience: 'once in the terror of the Dark Wood, he had to explore the full import of that experience before his spirit was free to take another direction'. *Dante's Drama of the Mind* (Princeton, 1953), p. 5.

realizes the horror of our way of life, he is prepared to be initiated into a new way of life.

Spenser also exploits the metaphor in order to locate us within our world. When the knight has been chosen by Una and the Faery Queen, he goes out 'to winne him worship, and her grace to haue' until the tempest drives every one into hiding: 'euery wight to shrowd it did constrain, / And this faire couple eke to shroud themselues were fain.' All seek the shady grove where 'all within were pathes and alleies wide, / With footing worne, and leading inward farre.' The ominous phrase, 'so in they entred arre', announces the beginning of his initiation (literally, *inire*, to enter in). Within the Wood they no longer lead their way, but passively are led: 'led with delight' they 'wander too and fro in wayes vnknowne':

> That path they take, that beaten seemd most bare,
> And like to lead the labyrinth about;
> Which when by tract they hunted had throughout,
> At length it brought them to a hollow caue,
> Amid the thickest woods.

This is the path which 'euery wight' takes, but none returns. In the first stage of the initiation the candidates (both Dante and Spenser's knight) wander as we do in our life.

In the second stage they are proven worthy of being chosen. To pass this test separates them from us. In Canto II Dante's spirit is so overwhelmed by cowardice that he withdraws from what he has begun. Virgil abjures him:

> L'anima tua è da viltate offesa,
> La qual molte fïate l'omo ingombra,
> Sì che d'onrata impresa lo rivolve,
> Come falso veder bestia, quand' ombra.

Dante is freed from all doubts of his worthiness only after he is told by Virgil how Beatrice cares for him. Only through faith in her compassion may he enter upon his journey. (These doubts recur at the beginning of his final ascent, the 'dubbi' of *Paradiso* IV, but Beatrice herself is there to resolve them.) In Spenser the knight wanders lost (that is, he is overcome by Error) and in doubt—'the place vnknowne and wilde, / Breedes dreadfull doubts'—until he so persists that he sees Error herself. The battle with this monster is described in terms of her labyrinthine tail which 'her den all ouerspred, / Yet was in knots and many boughtes vpwound, / Pointed with mortall sting', for this is the labyrinth which he must overcome. In the encounter his courage is first overcome—l'anima tua è da viltate offesa— and he retreats. Only when the lady intercedes with the injunction: 'add faith vnto your force, and be not faint', does he slay the monster. Then the brood, the doubts bred by the earlier experience in the Wood, 'him encombred sore'—la qual molte fïate l'omo ingombra—but with the death of Error they cannot hurt him and only destroy themselves. Spenser's remark during the battle, 'God helpe the man so wrapt in *Errours* endlesse traine', points to our life here: this monster will devour us, as she devours all who take the beaten path to her den, unless God helps us. But when God intercedes through the Lady, the knight may go 'forward on his way (with God to frend)'. Then he is no longer led by the path, but keeps it:

> That path he kept, which beaten was most plaine,
> Ne euer would to any by-way bend,
> But still did follow one vnto the end.

(The straight march of the concluding line demonstrates his victory over the labyrinth.) In Una's address to him:

> Well worthy be you of that Armorie,
> Wherein ye haue great glory wonne this day,
> And proou'd your strength on a strong enimie,
> Your first aduenture,

the repetition of 'you' and 'your' emphasizes that the battle proves him worthy his armour.[3] (Yet worthy only within his armour: 'that Armorie, / Wherein ye haue great glory wonne': at first he uses 'all his force' to free himself from the monster, but defeats her only when he 'strooke at her with *more then manly force*'.) His worthiness which is sealed by his faith sets him apart from us, even as Dante is commended by the Virgin as 'il tuo fedele'. Through this victory over the world, that is, over our way of life, both Dante and Spenser's knight are initiated into their pilgrimage.

Dante's poetic method may seem to differ radically from Spenser's. Dante renders the experience directly as his own; he describes dramatically and concretely the fear and agony which he suffers in the Wood. In contrast, Spenser leaves the given for the less real: rather than describe a man in error and doubt, he shows a wandering knight battling with Error. These are the terms in which C. S. Lewis has taught us to regard allegory.[4] And such abstract personification, we say, is alien to the reality of Dante's poem. But what, in fact, does Spenser do? In similarly dramatic and concrete terms, he shows a man confronting a monster; and in the immediate visual terms which we have noted earlier, he describes the physical impact of the battle. His 'Allegoricall deuices' serve to sharpen the sense of reality; they add to it; and render it more 'real'. Spenser's metaphor is overt: to yield to the world is to wander in an enchanting Wood; to seek the way out—how difficult it is to avoid metaphor!—is to battle a woman serpent. Dante's metaphor is half-submerged, but it is no less present. Beatrice sees Dante struggling with death: 'non vedi tu la morte che 'l combatte / Su la fiumana ove 'l mar non ha vanto.' This is the sea which Dante struggles to leave:

---

3. It is evident that the episode also proves Spenser worthy of his role as England's heroic poet. The catalogue of trees which he so carefully elaborates in stanzas 8 and 9 imitates Chaucer's *Parlement of Foules*, 169–82. It indicates that he now wears the mantle as England's poet. Behind both poets' use of the catalogue is Ovid's account of Orpheus, the archetype of the inspired poet, moving trees with his music. The power of Orpheus descends now to Spenser as he begins to create his faery land. Spenser's imitation of Chaucer is all the more apt since the poet in the *Parlement* enters a delightful Wandering Wood where he is overcome by error: 'no wit hadde I, for errour, for to chese, / To entre or flen, or me to save or lese' (146-7). Cf. Affrican's rebuke in 155-6. Since Chaucer is indebted to Dante's opening episode (see J. A. W. Bennett, *The Parlement of Foules* [Oxford, 1957], pp. 63–65), there is a nice historical connexion between Spenser and Dante.
4. *The Allegory of Love* (Oxford, 1936), pp. 44f.

> E come quei che, con lena affannata,
> Uscito fuor del pelago a la riva,
> Si volge a l'acqua perigliosa e guata;

and Virgil, in the lines quoted previously, sees Dante's spirit *encumbered* with cowardice, *stricken* by doubts. Once Dante accepts Virgil as his guide, the beast no longer forces him back into the dolorous pass. In effect he has 'slain' the beast. Metaphorically? yes. But it is all metaphor: the Dark Wood, the beasts, even (though in a different way) Hell itself, the Wandering Wood, the monster with her brood, the dungeon of Orgoglio. Dante's three beasts are emblems of the three stages of his journey through Hell. Spenser's monster is an emblem of Error; but what does Error signify? Not vice, nor any simple psychological state such as we meet in the personifications of other poets. Error is all that which stands between the knight and his entering upon his salvation, that is, Hell itself and the death which he must suffer before he may be reborn. The dragon-figure suggests this all-encompassing significance, as it does again in the knight's final antagonist. More simply, Error is what Dante means by the Dark Wood and the three beasts.

Spenser's treatment is more sophisticated largely because his age allowed him to be.[5] For one thing, his knight is more obviously an ideal pattern of what man should be. His entrance into the enchanting wood where he slays the woman serpent invokes the analogy to Adam who, at the beginning of his quest, entered the Garden of Eden where the enchantress Eve joined with the serpent conspired his fall. (Eden was traditionally linked with the labyrinth,[6] and in medieval-Renaissance iconography the woman-serpent is the common emblem for Satan.) As Adam was tempted by the fruit of the knowledge of good and evil, the knight is first overcome by the serpent's vomit 'full of bookes and papers'. Through faith, however, the knight defeats the serpent-Eve and enters the path which leads to his salvation. But in one way Spenser's treatment is more primitive than Dante's. He uses the symbol of the cave which traditionally signifies rebirth. Yet surely Dante's metaphor of the struggle in the water suggests another primitive metaphor, such as that used in *Beowulf* where the hero grapples with the sea monster.

Besides this significant pointing to our world, the initiation described in

5. His elaborate personification follows Renaissance convention, and in this matter it is pertinent to refer to Harington's preference for Ariosto's personification over Dante's. 'This description of the monster of covetousnesse, is (in my fancy) very well handled by mine Author, far beyond the like in *Dant* who maketh her onely like a Wolfe, pined with famine; But *Ariosto* goeth farder, and more significantly, describing her first to be ugly, because of all vices it is the most hatefull; eares of an asse, being for the most part ignorant, or at the least carelesse of other mens good opinions; a Wolfe in head and breast, namely ravenous and never satisfied; a Lions grisly jaw, terrible and devouring; a Foxe in all the rest, wyly and craftie, and timerous of those that are stronger then himselfe; all which applications are so proper and so plaine, as it is needlesse to stand upon them.' *Orlando Furioso* (London, 1634), p. 213.
6. Cf. Bartas' account of Adam in the Garden of Eden: 'musing, anon through crooked Walks he wanders, / Roundwinding rings, and intricate Meanders, / False-guiding paths, doubtfull beguiling strays, / And right-wrong errors of an end-less Maze' (*Diuine Weeks and Workes*, trans. Sylvester (London, 1633), p. 86). Milton's Adam relates how he 'stray'd I knew not whither' at his creation until in vision God comes as his 'Guide / To the Garden of bliss'. Once in the garden he is so overcome by its delight that 'here had new begun / My wandring, had not hee who was my Guide / Up hither, from among the Trees appeer'd / Presence Divine' (*Paradise Lost*, viii. 283, 298–9, 311–14). This is the Red Cross Knight's state of innocence in which he conquers the labyrinth 'with God to frend'.

the opening episode of each poem points inward to the poem's world. In Dante, as Mr. Singleton has shown, it serves as prologue.[7] The three beasts represent the three stages of descent into Hell, Beatrice reveals the role which the poem fulfils, and Dante's journey here corresponds to his journey through Hell. Thus it stands by itself as a brief epic, a 'dumb show' revealing the argument of the drama which will unfold. Virgil saves Dante from the beasts, as later he will guide him through Hell. It is Beatrice who persuades him to begin his journey, as later she brings him to his final salvation. Spenser's opening episode points inward in the same significant way to the world of his poem. The woman-serpent is later revealed as Duessa, the 'goodly Lady' with 'her neather partes misshapen, monstruous', and by the composite symbol of Duessa upon the Dragon. The knight's victory over Error is an emblem, then, of his final victory over Duessa and the Dragon. Here Una reveals the role which the poem fulfils, as later she prepares the knight to battle the Dragon by leading him to the house of Holiness where he is confirmed in faith. As Dante leaves the labyrinth to enter the descending circles of Hell, the knight leaves the Wood only to lose faith in Una through Archimago's false vision, and to wander lost, 'all in amaze' upon that path which leads him into Orgoglio's dungeon. After his rescue by Arthur, as he girds himself for the second stage of his journey—it is also an ascent through Purgatory—he meets Despair. By using the same allegorical language, Spenser places the two scenes in close correspondence. As Error is 'a monster vile, whom God and man does hate', Despair is 'a man of hell', a 'Snake in hidden weedes'. The one lives in a 'darksome hole' in the thickest woods, the other in a 'darkesome caue' among 'old stockes and stubs of trees'.[8] Again the knight must enter the cave and fight the monster. But while the first struggle was outward and physical, this is inward and spiritual. It takes place within his conscience; therefore the labyrinth he treads is intellectual. Error's vomit of books and papers appears in Despair's learning. Earlier he wanders in a maze until Error's 'huge traine / All suddenly about his body wound', now he wonders in amazement until Despair's arguments charm him in 'his guilefull traine'. Against Error Una urges him to 'shew what ye bee': now she reminds him what he is, one chosen by God. As before, she offers faith, that is, faith in God's mercy. Each encounter tests the knight: the earlier proves him worthy his armour, the later to be worthy as one chosen by God.

More than this, we may say, in Singleton's phrase, that Spenser's opening scene also 'figured and forecast, as well as any single scene might do, the whole configuration of the journey beyond'. The knight's token entrance into the cave—he only looks in—is fulfilled later when he descends into the dark depths of Orgoglio's dungeon. Through Una's intercession again, he is redeemed when Arthur makes his deep descent to restore him to light. Later he pays tribute to her 'whose wondrous faith, exceeding earthly race, / Was firmest fixt in mine extremest case.' Then in his last battle he 'descends' into the cave: his sword plunges into the Dragon's mouth which

7. *Dante Studies*, pp. 5–6.
8. Cf. I.i.13 and I.ix.28; I.i.14 and I.ix.34, 35. After the knight defeats Error, 'then mounted he vpon his Steede againe': after he defeats Despair, 'vp he rose, and thence amounted streight' (I.i.28; I.ix.54).

'wide gaped, like the griesly mouth of hell'. As he slays Error by adding faith to his force, here his 'baptized hands' wielding 'his godly armes' defeat the Dragon. The first battle against the Dragon initiates his fall: this last battle initiates him to that restored state signified by his marriage to Una. In the cycle of fall and ascent he progresses from light to darkness to light. But with this difference: that 'his glistring armor made / A litle glooming light, much like a shade' as he peers into Error's cave, while at the end 'those glistring armes . . . heauen with light did fill' (I.xi.4). The opening episode which shows his primal state of innocence becomes a measure of his later descent into sin, and a promise of his final ascent.

The two kinds of reading which we have applied to Dante and Spenser, the one pointing outward to our world, and the other turning inward to the poem's world focus in our single vision of the poem as fiction. That fiction is 'an ideal space', as Curtius terms Dante's poem,[9] or a 'golden world' in Sidney's phrase. Though allegory usually suggests a way of writing in which one thing is said but another is meant, our poets tell 'of Forests, and inchantments drear, / Where *more* is meant then meets the ear.'[1] We read the fiction not by translating, but by retaining the fiction as metaphor. Earlier poets had written fiction, but for Dante and Spenser both the matter and form of their poetry were transformed by Holy Scripture. Mr. Singleton has convinced us that Dante imitates Scripture: 'the literal sense is given as an historical sense standing in its own right, like Milton's, say—Not devised in order to convey a hidden truth, but given in the focus of single vision'.[2] Here Spenser's kind of allegory may seem antithetical to Dante's. Dante moves towards greater reality as his poem proceeds: Spenser moves in an unreal world of giants and dragons where Dr. Johnson would never stub his toe. But what does this difference amount to? Dante's fiction is that his matter is fact; Spenser's fiction is that his matter is romance. The one establishes the illusion of historical reality, the other of faery land. For both poets, their fiction is a metaphor of Holy Scripture. Dante's position is clear; but what of Spenser? To consider briefly the knight's final battle against the Dragon. We say that here Spenser exploits the allegorical devices of the armed knight facing a fire-breathing Dragon while his lady retires to a hill. But where is the truth of this fiction? It is not the moral truth that Holiness defeats Sin or Death, or the historical fact that England defeats the powers of Antichrist. Its truth is given by Holy Scripture. The knight's three-day battle in Eden against the Dragon in order to release Una's parents, Adam and Eve, imitates Christ's harrowing hell, His three-day descent through which mankind is restored to the Tree and Well of Life. The fiction of both poets, then, whether it is given as an historical sense or as romance, is a metaphor of Holy Scripture. Once we see that each poet writes metaphor, then one poem becomes a metaphor of the other. And it is this fact which allows them to be compared.

Once we allow that in reading Spenser's poem we should focus upon the image, rather than upon some idea behind the image, our understanding

---

9. *European Literature and the Latin Middle Ages*, trans. Trask (New York, 1953), p. 18.
1. *Il Penseroso*, 119–20.
2. *Dante Studies*, p. 15.

gathers around our response to the poem's literal level because it arises from it. Our sense of that other reality to which the poem points, by first pointing to itself, grows from our sense of the poem's reality. We may be said to understand—literally to under-stand—the poem because we bear the whole poem in our response. That response is integrated because the intense delight given by the poem determines, at the same time, our understanding of its meaning. Our delight and understanding being integrated, our aware-ness of the literal and allegorical levels is continuous and simultaneous, and our vision of the poem whole. This simple, yet radical, alteration of focus may be achieved by reading the poem not for its hidden truth but rather for its fiction. Instead of treating the narration as a veil to be torn aside for the hidden meaning, we should allow Sidney's art of reading poetry by using the narration 'but as an imaginatiue groundplot of a prof-itable inuention'. Once we allow this art of reading, then Spenser's allegory need not be read as a complicated puzzle concealing riddles which confuse the reader in labyrinths of error, but as an unfolding drama revealing more and greater significance as it brings the reader full understanding of its complex vision.

JUDITH H. ANDERSON

"A Gentle Knight was pricking on the plaine": The Chaucerian Connection†

A subject I have wanted to broach for some years now is the opening line of the first canto of the first Book of *The Faerie Queene*: "A Gentle Knight was pricking on the plaine."[1] I doubt the Spenserian exists who has not heard colleagues declare, "I could never get over, or never forgive Spenser, his opening line." Yet Spenserians themselves, as if conspiring to accept the poet's insensitivity to his own words, have totally ignored the "hard begin" of Spenser's best-known Book. Surely it is time that we consider the meaning of this remarkable line—or at least the nature of its meaning—in a properly open and scholarly context.

The problem in the line centers on the word "pricking," which has, of course, the perfectly straightforward, innocent meaning, "To spur or urge a horse on; to ride fast," and the *OED* rightly cites Spenser's line as an instance of this meaning.[2] I am unpersuaded, however, that this is the full range of the word's meaning in this line. My argument that it is not the full range will be circumstantial and eventually circuitous, but such is the difference between lexical definition and poetic usage: literature—especially poetry and even more especially Spenser—is contextual, that is, circum-stantial in the extreme.

---

† Reprinted from *English Literary Renaissance* 15:2 (1985), 166–74, with the permission of the editors.
1. All Spenserian references are to *The Works of Edmund Spenser: A Variorum Edition*, ed. Edwin A. Greenlaw et al., 11 vols. (Baltimore, Md., 1932–1957), cited as *Var.*; *The Faerie Queene* is cited as *FQ*.
2. *OED*, s.v. Prick v, 11.

The word "pricking," already conspicuous as the first verbal action in the very first line of Spenser's story, occurs in a context designed to render its meaning specifically problematical. "Pricking" emphatically means *fast* riding, even galloping, rather than ambling. It causes some logical distraction, not to mention visual consternation, to learn that "faire beside" the pricking knight a lovely lady rode "Vpon a lowly Asse" and that "by her" side she in turn led a white lamb on a leash and that lagging, but still within sight, a dwarf, loaded down with sleeping bags and provisions, followed on foot. The time is out of joint, or if not the narrative time, then surely the narrative distance and rate. Within the first stanza of canto i alone, the knight's pricking or spurring on his steed is also narratively discontinuous with the steed's displeasure at the "foming bitt." The steed's disdaining control suggests that restraining pressure is being or at least could be applied to the reins and thus that Redcrosse's rear view mirror might eventually show him that he has outpricked Una, her lamb, and her dwarf—left them, I might add allegorically, in his dust.

Besides being narratively incongruous, the word "pricking" has, like the word "shroud" five stanzas later, a resonance and potentially a doubleness of signification that words like "trot," "gallop," or "amble" simply lack.[3] To begin again with the OED, the verb "prick" has also the *figurative* meaning "To drive or urge as with a spur; to impel . . . stimulate, provoke."[4] This meaning commonly carries a generalized association with the agency of nature, appetite, or desire. One of Chaucer's best-known lines in the first sentence of *The Canterbury Tales* describes the lovesick little birds that sleep all night with open eye—"So prycketh hem nature in her corages" —and it thereby affords both an example in point and an instance of the fertile and fundamentally Chaucerian association of such pricking with courage or "corage," the seat of vitality, spirit, lustiness, and vigor.[5]

Although the primary source of the lover's song in Spenser's Temple of Venus is Lucretius' hymn to the Goddess of Love, Lucretian sentiments merge more than once with Chaucerian memories:

> the merry birds, thy prety pages
> Priuily *pricked* with thy *lustfull* powres,
> Chirpe loud to thee out of their leauy cages,
> And thee their mother call to coole their kindly rages.
> (IV.x.45: my emphasis)[6]

Spenser's lines recall the earlier English poet's association of sexual appetite and desire with nature's pricking. Statistically, the greatest numbers of forms of the word "prick" occur in Spenser's second and fourth Books, and it is reasonable that they should do so. Book II is centrally concerned with the tempering of appetite, and Book IV, with the frustration and fulfillment of

---

3. Cf. *FQ* I.i.8. OED, s.v. *Shroud v¹*, 2c, 3–7.
4. OED, s.v. *Prick v*, 10.
5. OED, s.v. *Courage sb*, 1, 3, 4. Unless otherwise specified, all Chaucerian references are to *The Works 1532*, supplemented by material from the editions of 1542, 1561, 1598, and 1602 (London, 1969): I have changed the solidi to commas and expanded the contractions in Thynne's text.
6. See Lucretius, *De Rerum Natura*, trans. W. H. D. Rouse (London, 1924), pp. 2–4, esp. 11.12–13, 18—20 of Book I. Cf: also J. A. W. Bennett, *The Parlement of Foules: An Interpretation* (Oxford, 1957), pp. 119–20.

desire and, more fundamentally, with the natural force and energy of which love is in good part an expression.

Even at a glance through the Spenser *Concordance*, however, two occurrences of the word "prick" in Book I are particularly striking, both for the suggestiveness of their immediate verbal contexts and for their Chaucerian flavor or resonance. Conveniently, these occurrences associate the Redcrosse Knight with Prince Arthur, an association eventually to prove of some interest for a reading of the first line of canto i in this Book. In canto ix, Arthur comments on the circumstances that led to his dream of the Queen of Fairies:

> It was in freshest flowre of youthly yeares,
>   When *courage* first does creepe in manly chest,
> Then first the coale of kindly heat appeares
> To kindle loue in euery liuing brest
>   (I.ix.9: my emphasis)

Nearing the dream itself, Arthur explains how on that fateful day he was "prickt forth with iollitie / Of looser life, and heat of hardiment" (12). Arthur's comments align "courage" and "iollitie of looser life" with the force that "pricks" him into his experience, the dream of an elf queen. Like *courage, jollity* is a richly suggestive word meaning cheerfulness, pleasure, bravery, or lust.[7] Interestingly, it occurs in Chaucer's *Sir Thopas* (lxxxiv^v) and, in adjectival form—"Full iolly knight he seemd"—in the first stanza of Spenser's story that begins with a description of Redcrosse's "pricking on the plaine." The second occurrence of the word "prick" in Book I that is particularly striking comes in canto x when Contemplation describes Redcrosse's route from plowman's state to Faerie court: "Till prickt with courage, and thy forces pryde, / To Faery court thou cam'st to seeke for fame" (66). Here again the word "prickt" is aligned with richly charged words—"courage" and "forces pryde"—implying prowess and desire.

A seemingly inevitable extension of lexical meanings of the word "prick" is persuasively documented by Eric Partridge in *Shakespeare's Bawdy*.[8] Counting substantive and verbal examples, Partridge finds that *prick* appears as a pun eight times in Shakespeare's works. Perhaps the most familiar instance of this Shakespearean pun occurs when Mercutio observes in *Romeo and Juliet*, "the bawdy hand of the dial is now upon the prick of noon" (2.4.112–13).[9] And somewhere elusively, richly, naughtily, and comically in-between Chaucer's description of those little lovesick birds pricked "in her corages" by nature and Shakespeare's more pointed bawdy is Chaucer's notoriously persistent employment of the verb "prick" in the Tale of Sir Thopas; for example:

> Sir Thopas fyl in loue longyng,
> And whan he herde the throstel syng
> He pricked as he were wode
> His faire stede in his prickyng

---

7. *OED*, s.v. *Jollity*, 1, 3, 5.
8. *Shakespeare's Bawdy*, rev. ed. (New York, 1969), p. 167 (*prick*, n., v.; *prick out*), p. 176 (*rose*), p. 153 (*needle*).
9. *The Riverside Shakespeare*, ed. G. Blakemore Evans et al. (Boston, Mass., 1974).

> So swette, that men might him wring
> His sydes were al blode.
> Sir Thopas eke so wery was
> For prickyng on the softe gras
> So fiers was his corage
> That doun he layde him in that place (lxxxiv^v)

to dream of the elf queen who will be his "lemman," he hopes, and will sleep, oddly enough, under his "gore." Inspired, or at least awakened, by the dream, Sir Thopas climbs gracelessly into his saddle and once more "pricketh ouer style and stone / An Elfe quene for to espye." Examples could be multiplied—mercilessly.

For a reader of Chaucer, the word "pricking" has special resonance and, given a suitable context, a particularly strong, metrically mnemonic potential for association with the Tale of Sir Thopas. Excepting the *Treatise on the Astrolabe*, in which *prick* has technically delimited meanings, forms of this word occur eight times in *Sir Thopas*, more often than in any other Chaucerian piece. In view of the relatively short tale in which they occur—roughly two hundred lines—the association of pricking with *Sir Thopas* is readily available, always possible where relevant, and irresistible when invited.

Spenser's own knowledge of Chaucer's Tale of Sir Thopas is indisputable, and the ease, detail, and pervasiveness of his borrowings indicate a thorough assimilation of it. In the March Eclogue of *The Shepheardes Calender*, a tale about two comic boors, he uses one of the two (or more) forms of the tail-rhyme stanza found in *Sir Thopas*, and throughout *The Faerie Queene*, he takes individual words or phrases from it—for example, the Squire of Dame's phrase "many a lane" in Book III (vii.58) and the Giant Disdain's jacket of "checklaton" in Book VI (vii.43).[1] Spenser finds the name Ollyphant in *Sir Thopas*, plausibly also the name Blandamour (spelled Blayndamour in Thynne's *Thopas*) and perhaps, by way of Ollyphant's name, the inspiration for Lust's elephantine ears.[2] In addition, of course, there is mention of Sir Thopas as the confounder of Ollyphant in the 1590, though not in the 1596, edition.[3] And finally, there is Prince Arthur's dream of the Faerie Queene in Book I, for which *Sir Thopas* offers as close a source or analogue as decades of researchers determined to find a more dignified candidate have been able to unearth.[4] I shall return somewhat later to Arthur's dream, which, to my mind, *Sir Thopas* underlies but underlies complexly, for it seems to me most unlikely that Spenser missed the outrageous humor in a Chaucerian tale he knew so well—humor, incidentally,

---

1. The March Eclogue rhymes aabccb. In Thynne's edition, the first stanza of *Sir Thopas* rhymes aabaab; ll. 79ff. rhyme aac/bccb; ll. 142ff. rhyme aabccb. (Thynne's l. 142 is l. 146 in Donaldson's 2nd edition and l. 857 in Robinson's 2nd edition.) See *Var.* III, p. 267; VI, pp. 225–26, and A. Kent Hieatt, *Chaucer, Spenser, Milton: Mythopoeic Continuities and Transformations* (Montreal, 1975), pp. 19–24. (On p. 23, Hieatt mistakenly assumes that the rhyme scheme of *Sir Thopas* is uniform.)
2. *Var.* IV, pp. 170–71.
3. *FQ* III.vii.48,l. 4; *Var.* III, p. 412.
4. Edwin Greenlaw, "Britomart at the House of Busirane," *Studies in Philology*, 26 (1929), 124–27, suggests that *Arthur of Little Britain* is the source of Prince Arthur's dream in *The Faerie Queene*. A glance at Arthur's dreams in chapters 16 and 46 of *Little Britain* will show that, while they might be a distant analogue to Spenser's episode, they are an unlikely source: *The History of the Valiant Knight Arthur of Little Britain*, trans. John Bourchier, Lord Berners ([1555?]; rpt. 1814).

to which Wyatt, Lyly, Drayton, and Shakespeare all responded.[5] Nor do I think the view that Spenser either ignored this humor or simply moralized it out of existence is adequate to the subtlety of *The Faerie Queene*. At present, however, let me return to the opening of Spenser's first canto to ask what sense a distant echo of *Sir Thopas*—an available resonance, as I have termed it—would make here and in the subsequently unfolding context of Redcrosse's story.

To begin with, a reader who considers the possibility of an echo can do little more with it than we already have: that is, to notice resonance and discontinuities and to be puzzled. A similar effect occurs a few stanzas later when a sudden rainstorm is poured by an angry Jove "into his Lemans lap": we have questions and hints, not answers. But once we have grasped the relation of Archimago to Redcrosse and the specifically erotic nature of the dream Archimago provokes, the incongruous—indeed disunified—aspects of our initial impression of Redcrosse become increasingly significant. Increasingly, we realize their potential. Archimago, persistently termed the old man or aged sire, is no more an exclusively external tempter of Redcrosse than the nature of old Adam—the old man as opposed to the new—is external to mankind. The dream Archimago provokes rises out of Redcrosse's own nature, and it reveals the knight's failure to reconcile the pricking of his "corage" with his faith, the force and the energy of his human nature with the form and purity of truth. The word "prick"—conspicuous in the first line of Redcrosse's story and discontinuous with the immediate narrative context—foreshadows this larger, moral discrepancy, making it both more comprehensible and more inevitable—perversely enough, more natural.

Prince Arthur's dream of the Faerie Queene adds another dimension to our initial impression of Redcrosse. As Patricia Parker has shown, Arthur's dream is loaded with verbal memories of Redcrosse's earlier dream of a false Una.[6] Within Spenser's first Book itself, therefore, an element of parody, asking interpretation, underlies Arthur's dream. Allusions to three of Chaucer's stories increase the parody and simultaneously our awareness of the human complexity—possible futility and positive comedy—that underlie and enrich the ideal vision. Perhaps the most striking of the Chau-

---

5. See Josephine Waters Bennett, *The Evolution of "The Faerie Queene"* (1942). New York, 1960), pp. 11–15. For Drayton, see also *Works*, ed. J. William Hebel (Oxford, 1961), I, 88–91; V, 11–12. My understanding of Shakespeare's appreciation of Chaucer's humor in *Sir Thopas* has been influenced by E. Talbot Donaldson's lecture on A *Midsummer Night's Dream*, "The Embarrassments of Art": Mary Flexner Lectures, Bryn Mawr College, 1981. (*MND* is indebted to Lyly's *Endymion*, whose comic Sir Thopas derives from Chaucer's.) While Josephine Waters Bennett (p. 15) does not suppose Spenser unaware of Chaucer's humor in *Sir Thopas*, she observes that Gabriel Harvey considered *Sir Thopas* "morall" and that Harvey so labeled it in his marginalia: *Gabriel Harvey's Marginalia*, ed. G. C. Moore Smith (Stratford-upon-Avon, Eng., 1913), p. 228. She also suggests that Harvey's understanding of *Sir Thopas* was influenced by *The Faerie Queene* (p. 19, n. 32). Unfortunately, however, Bennett misinterprets Harvey's marginalium ("morall") on "Chaucers Tale" in Speght 1598, taking it to refer to *Sir Thopas* rather than to the *Melibeus*. But it is the *Melibeus* that is consistently labeled "Chaucers Tale" in both Speght and the earlier Thynne family of editions. With equal consistency *Sir Thopas* is called "The Rime of Sir Thopas." Bennett's error could be passed over in silence, had not J. A. Burrow recently revived it and implied that it validated a strictly "morall" interpretation of *Sir Thopas* by Spenser: "Sir Thopas in the Sixteenth Century," in *Middle English Studies Presented to Norman Davis*, ed. Douglas Gray and E. G. Stanley (Oxford, 1983), pp. 81–88, esp. p. 87.
6. Patricia A. Parker, *Inescapable Romance: Studies in the Poetics of a Mode* (Princeton, N.J., 1979), pp. 83—86.

cerian allusions in Arthur's experience is to the Tale of Sir Thopas, but there are also pervasive recollections of Chaucer's *Troilus* and one strong echo of the Wife of Bath's Prologue. The recollections of *Troilus* glance at a love story with a bright beginning and a blighted end.[7] The echo of the Wife's Prologue—"no fort can be so strong / Ne fleshly brest can armed be so sound, / But will at last be wonne with battrie long" (11)—recalls her mock harangue on behalf of hapless husbands one through three: "She may no while in chastite abyde / That is assayled on euery syde . . . men may nat kepe a castel wal / It may so long assayled be ouer all" (xli).[8] The memory of Chaucer in Spenser's lines glances both at the failure of human virtue and at the comic vitality of a thoroughly untamed virago.

Far from undermining Arthur's ideal vision, the delicate layering of parody that underlies it strengthens and deepens our awareness of its human significance. Much the same kind of ironic resonance and specifically Chaucerian parody underlie both outset and end of *The Faerie Queene*, both the gentle knight's "pricking on the plaine" and the poet's farewell to this world and this poem in the final stanzas of the Mutability Cantos. Like Arthur's dream, the Chaucerian resonance that thus frames the poem we have is informed with the ambivalent potency of the physical world, the potency of natural appetite and natural time.

In the interest of a specifically Spenserian closure, which is, like circle and cycle, properly circuitous, I would extend these observations on the Chaucerian frame of *The Faerie Queene* to the Chaucerian character of Spenser's poetical career as he himself evidently framed it. Spenser's poetic debut, *The Shepheardes Calender*, like his finale, *The Faerie Queene*, recalls Chaucer at its outset and again at its end, and together these two poems, one pastoral and one epic, enclose the poet's progress. In *The Calender*, Immerito's initial address and final farewell to his poem—"Goe little booke" and "Goe lyttle Calender"—allude simply and unmistakably to Chaucer's *Troilus*:

> Go lytel booke, go my lytel tregedye
> . . . .
> But subiecte ben vnto al poesye
> And kysse the steppes, where as thou seest pace
> Of Vergyl, Ovyde, Homer, Lucan, and Stace. (ccxviii^v)

Spenser similarly cautions his *Calender* not to match with the "poesye" of his predecessors "But [to] followe them farre off, and their high steppes adore."

In the penultimate stanza of the Mutability Cantos, as John Pope has recently written, Spenser's profoundly ambiguous lines on the doubleness of mankind's condition again recall the ending of Chaucer's *Troilus*.[9] But they do so more subtly and richly. Condemning the world in lines which

---

7. See *Troilus and Criseyde*, lxxi–lxxii (Bk. I.183–239, 316–57, in Donaldson's or Robinson's 2nd edition).
8. *Var.* I, p. 267.
9. "The Existential Mysteries as Treated in Certain Passages of Our Older Poets," in *Acts of Interpretation: The Text in Its Contexts 700–1600*, ed. Mary J. Carruthers and Elizabeth D. Kirk (Norman, Okla., 1982), pp. 345–47, 360–62. Pope quotes E. Talbot Donaldson's "Ending of 'Troilus,' " in *Speaking of Chaucer* (London, 1970), p. 98: "All the illusory loveliness of a world which is man's only reality is expressed in the very lines that reject that loveliness."

"poignantly enhance the very thing that he is repudiating," Chaucer cautions "yonge fresshe folkes, he or she" to think "al nys but a fayre / This worlde that passeth sone, as floures fayre" (ccxviii^v).[1] Spenser's lines speak similarly of loveliness and loss, of pleasure and futility:

> Which makes me loath this state of life so tickle (,)
> And loue of things so vaine to cast away;[2]
> Whose flowring pride, so fading and so fickle,
> Short *Time* shall soon cut down with his consuming sickle.

Thus alluding at once to the ending of Chaucer's *Troilus* and recalling, through the fact of such allusion, the end of Spenser's own *Calender*, the final stanzas of Mutability come full circle, even as they signal the conscious nature of the poet's intention to end.[3] These stanzas simultaneously continue and conclude, defeat time and acknowledge it.[4] Their irreducible ambiguity is far distant from the narrative discontinuities at the outset of the poem, but circuitously, through a matrix of association and resonance, they lead us back to beginnings.

S. K. HENINGER, JR.

[Orgoglio]†

The modern tendency to dissociate the "historical" and the "moral" allegory in *The Faerie Queene* can easily lead to a perversion of Spenser's purpose. Any dichotomy between history and morality would have been offensive to Elizabethans, whose very reason for studying the past was the hope of finding some ethical norm. As Richard Harvey flatly stated, "the most morals [is] the best History."[1] Protestants especially stressed this moralistic view of history, and furthermore argued that the future would unfold in strict accord with the prophecies set down in the Revelation of St. John. Therefore future events would also be largely determined by the ethical insight which the Apocalypse provided. Spenser adhered to this

---

1. Quotation earlier in this sentence is from E. T. Donaldson, ed., *Chaucer's Poetry: An Anthology for the Modern Reader*, 2nd ed. (New York, 1975), p. 1144.

2. I have eliminated the comma after *tickle* in *Var*. In these profoundly ambiguous lines, *loath* is either an adjective or a verb and *vain* is either an adjective modifying *love* or *things* or is an adverb modifying the infinitive *to cast*: for further discussion, see my *Growth of a Personal Voice: "Piers Plowman" and "The Faerie Queene"* (New Haven, Conn., 1976), pp. 200–02; cf. pp. 48–49.

3. My position is at variance with Jonathan Goldberg's deconstructive sense of Spenser's helplessness—indeed, his dark despair—in the face of time: *Endlesse Worke: Spenser and the Structures of Discourse* (Baltimore, Md., 1981). I should add that Goldberg's subtle and provocative book has greatly renewed interest, including my own, in the relation of Spenser to Chaucer.

4. In this context, the combination of "flowring pride" with "consuming sickle" also recalls the sequence in the Gardens of Adonis from "that faire flowre of beautie [that] fades away" to "wicked *Time*, who with his scyth addrest, / Does mow the flowring herbes and goodly things" (III.vi.38–39). Susan Hodges has suggested to me that the phrase "Short *Time*" in the penultimate alexandrine of the Mutability Cantos echoes as well the richly ambiguous conclusion of *Epithalamion*: "And for short time an endlesse moniment."

† From "The Orgoglio Episode in *The Faerie Queene*," *ELH* 26 (1959): 171–87. The original footnotes have been slightly edited. Reprinted by permission of The Johns Hopkins University Press.

1. *Philadelphus, or A Defence of Brutes, and the Brutans History* (London, 1593), G 3.

prevailing attitude, and in *The Faerie Queene* he hoped to produce convincing testimony that history and morality are indeed but different statements of the same truth. He is explicit on this point in the Proem to Book I; drawing from "the antique rolles" of England (I. proem. 2. 4), he promises that "fierce warres and faithfull loves shall moralize my song" (I. proem. 1. 9).

At his best, Spenser succeeds in contriving poetry which satisfies the special function of the poet to synthesize history and morality—to provide a "continued Allegory," as Spenser says in his letter to Raleigh. And Spenser is at his best in describing the capture of the Red Crosse Knight by the Giant Orgoglio. Although the meaning is complex, each of the intricate details subsists within the same allegorical continuum. Since this episode is the nadir of Red Crosse's fortunes and the turning-point of Book I, it is a stringent test for the coadunating faculty of Spenser's imagination.

Most readers begin their interpretation of Orgoglio by following the linguistic clue that he must be an embodiment of pride. The name would be most immediately meaningful as the Italian word for "pride, disdaine, haughtines,"[2] closely related to Spanish *orgullo* and French *orgueil*. Since the root is common to the Romance Languages, the appellation would associate the Giant with Rome and Catholicism. We must note, however, that the Giant is not specifically called "Orgoglio" until after he has overcome Red Crosse. We hear the name only when Duessa approaches him with the proposition that he make Red Crosse his bondslave and take her for his paramour (I. vii. 14. 4–9). Therefore the starting-point for an interpretation of this episode does not lie in the meaning of the name "Orgoglio."

A more fundamental point-of-beginning will be found in the genealogical mythus which Spenser provides for the Giant. Here, as he often does, Spenser first suggests the significance of the character.

> The greatest Earth his uncouth mother was,
> And blustring Aeolus his boasted sire,
> Who with his breath, which through the world doth pas,
> Her hollow womb did secretly inspire,
> And fild her hidden caves with stormie yre,
> That she conceiv'd.   (I. vii. 9. 1–6)

When Orgoglio interrupts the dalliance of Red Crosse and Duessa beside the magic fountain, Spenser devotes one stanza to physical description of the Giant, and then carefully relates his parentage [in sts. 9–10]. Spenser expressly states that Orgoglio has been generated by a boisterous wind blowing through caves in the earth. By the principles of Renaissance meteorology, this origin identifies him as an earthquake. Gabriel Harvey had cited this scientific theory in a letter to Spenser:

> The Materiall Cause of Earthquakes . . . is no doubt great aboundance of wynde, or stoare of grosse and drye vapors, and spirites,

2. Giovanni Florio, *A worlde of Wordes, or dictionarie in Italian and English* (London, 1598), p. 248.

fast shut up, & as a man would saye, emprysoned in the Caves,
and Dungeons of the Earth.[3]

No Elizabethan would have missed the transparent mythologizing, the
obvious implication that Orgoglio is the mythical embodiment of an
earthquake.

This conclusion is supported by much of Orgoglio's physical description.
His entrance is heralded by "a dreadfull sownd":

> Which through the wood loud bellowing, did rebownd,
> That all the earth for terrour seemd to shake,
> And trees did tremble.   (I. vii. 7. 5–7)

And when he walks, "the ground eke groned under him for dreed" (I. vii.
8. 6). During the battle with Red Crosse, "the Geaunt strooke so maynly
mercilesse,/That could have overthrowne a stony towre" (I. vii. 12. 1–2).
In the next canto, when Prince Arthur comes to liberate Red Crosse, the
Giant's club misses the Prince and digs into the ground:

> The sad earth wounded with so sore assay,
> Did grone full grievous underneath the blow,
> And trembling with strange feare, did like an earthquake show.
>   (I. viii. 8. 7–9)

After a violent battle, Prince Arthur finally slays Orgoglio, whose fall "seemd
to shake/The stedfast globe of earth, as it for feare did quake" (I. viii. 23.
8–9).

Since Orgoglio is the personification of an earthquake, what significance
would this have for Spenser's audience? The occasion of Gabriel Harvey's
long letter to Spenser was the terrifying earthquake of 6 April 1580, and
this was an event which few Englishmen forgot. It was so frightening that
a special order of prayer was decreed "upon Wednesdayes and Frydayes,
to avert and turne Gods wrath from us, threatned by the late terrible earthquake, to be used in all parish churches."[4] Sermons for a long time thereafter
cited the earthquake as an admonition "to amende our evill life, to reforme
our wicked conversation, to be renewed in the spirite of the inwarde man,
and to be heavenly minded."[5] Here is a vivid example of moral instruction
derived from historical incident.

When Orgoglio is seen as an earthquake, and therefore as a visitation of
God's wrath to warn man to repentance, this gives allegorical meaning to
the opening stanzas of Canto VII. There the Dwarf has just led Red Crosse
from the House of Pride, and the Knight is resting beside a spring when
Duessa arrives. Cajoled by her, the Knight relaxes in the physical pleasantness of the glade and indulges his sensual appetites. When he quenches
his thirst from the stream, which has magical powers to enervate any man
who drinks of it, "mightie strong was turnd to feeble fraile" (I. vii. 6. 5).
But the Knight continues his sinful relations with Duessa (I. vii. 7. 1–3);

---

3. *Three proper, and wittie, familiar Letters* (London, 1580), B4ᵛ.
4. *Liturgies and Occasional Forms of Prayer Set Forth in the Reign of Queen Elizabeth* (Parker
Society, 1847), p. 464.
5. Abraham Fleming, *A Bright Burning Beacon* (London, 1580), E1–E1ᵛ.

and in this weakened condition, unready in the midst of sensual pleasure, the Knight is attacked by Orgoglio and easily captured.

This spring with its magical properties is a truncated version of the Salmacis story that Ovid had related in the *Metamorphoses* (IV. 285 ff.). Salmacis was the nymph of a fountain in Caria, a vain and slothful girl who never joined her sister-nymphs in the sylvan activities led by Diana. When youthful Hermaphroditus bathed himself in her waters, Salmacis was so undone by passion that she intertwined her body with his and prayed to the gods "that this same wilfull boy and I may never parted bee."[6] The gods capriciously consented to this unusual request, as Ovidian gods so often do, and their bodies were fused as one. When Hermaphroditus realized that his masculinity had been diluted to half its former strength, he also prayed for a boon:

> That whoso commes within this Well may so bee weakened there,
> That of a man but halfe a man he may fro thence retire.[7]

The gods were again compliant, and thenceforth whoever drank from Salmacis' spring lost his strength.

Spenser has used only so much of Ovid's legend as he needs. He has eliminated Hermaphroditus completely, and attributes the enervating properties of the water solely to the displeasure of Diana when the indolent Salmacis showed indifference to the chase (I. vii. 5. 1–9). Ovid has never had more ardent disciples than the Elizabethans, however, and to Spenser's audience this enchanted spring would inevitably recall Salmacis.

Since myth was a form of history, it also was subject to moral interpretation; and the venerated tradition of moralizing Ovid would bring with Salmacis' story a moralized meaning. As Golding summarized it in the epistle preceding his translation of the *Metamorphoses*:

> Hermaphrodite and Salmacis declare that idlenesse
> Is cheefest nurce and cherisher of all volupteousnesse,
> And that voluptuous lyfe breedes sin: which linking all
>   toogither
> Make men too bee effeminate, unweeldy, weake and lither.[8]

The interlude beside the fountain shows Red Crosse being both idle and voluptuous, and Spenser focuses the moral significance of this episode by connecting it with the history of Salmacis. The sinfulness of this dalliance with Duessa makes Red Crosse a proper victim for the Giant, the agent of God's wrath, that inevitably follows. Orgoglio wages battle "as when almightie Jove in wrathfull mood,/To wreake the guilt of mortall sins is bent" (I. viii. 9. 1–2).

The interpretation of an earthquake as a warning to repentance was of course based on the Holy Scriptures. Often in the Bible the anger of God descends upon sinful men in the form of an earthquake, but nowhere more terrifyingly than in the Revelation of St. John. The Book of Revelation

---

6. I quote from the translation of Arthur Golding (1567) reprinted as *Shakespeare's Ovid*, ed. W. H. D. Rouse (London, 1904), p. 91, line 461.
7. *Ibid.*, p. 91, lines 477–478.
8. P. 3, lines 113–116.

provided many of the central doctrines for the new militant Protestantism, and recent scholarship has shown its formative influence on Book I of *The Faerie Queene*.[9] Therefore by turning to it we can perhaps fit the Orgoglio episode into the larger framework of allegory based on the Apocalypse.

In the Book of Revelation earthquakes occur as visitations upon the wicked most prominently as the climaxes of three separate but interrelated series of prophecies leading up to the final Day of Judgment: the opening of the seven seals on the book of God (vi. 1–viii. 1), the trumpetings of the seven angels (viii. 2–xi. 19), and the vials poured by seven angels into the air (xvi. 1–xvi. 21). These key passages agree that the Last Judgment will be heralded by an earthquake destroying the world. Moreover, Protestant scholiasts derived their theories of damnation and redemption from the Book of Revelation. With this gloss, for example, Heinrich Bullinger amplified the meaning of the seven seals:

> In the opening of the seven seales, there is severally accompted and reckned up, what and how greate evils should come upon men from the which not somuch as the faithfull living in this world, should be free. Wares, slaughters, famine, pestilences are recyted, and such other lyke plagues: Agayne persecutions, seditions, and (a great deale worse then all these) yᵉ seducyng, and distroying of men through corrupt doctryne. . . .
>   . . . In the calamities, troubles, evils, and corruptions declared hitherto, the Aungel of God is brought in, who marketh the elect of God, in theyr foreheades: and all they through the goodnes and custodye of God, are saved from perdition.[1]

Doomsday will engulf all men, the righteous with the wicked; but the elect shall be saved by the Angel of God and brought to Heaven.

The process of Red Crosse's redemption can be easily traced in the Orgoglio episode. Through his relations with Duessa, the Knight has been guilty of carnality; and even worse, as Bullinger said, he has been seduced by "corrupt doctryne." When Orgoglio brings in Judgment Day, the Knight therefore finds himself helpless in the dungeon beneath the afflictions of his sins. During the battle with the Giant, however, we have been told that Red Crosse is blessed with "heavenly grace" (I. vii. 12. 3); he is one of the elect. So now that he has felt the wrathful hand of God, the Knight is ready for his spiritual rebirth. The Squire's magic horn which automatically opens the gates of Orgoglio's stronghold is a clear-cut analogue to the archangel's trumpet which will open graves on Doomsday. Prince Arthur then enters as the Angel of God who has come to mark the elect and save him from damnation. When the Prince finds Red Crosse, he is "a ruefull spectacle of death" (I. viii. 40. 9). Spenser graphically describes him as a long-dead corpse: "His sad dull eyes [are] deepe sunck in hollow pits"; he

---

9. See particularly Josephine W. Bennett, *The Evolution of "The Faerie Queene"* (Univ. of Chicago Press, 1942), pp. 109–119; and John E. Hankins, "Spenser and the Revelation of St. John," *PMLA*, LX (1945), 364–381.

1. *A hundred sermons vpon the Apocalipse* (2nd ed.; London, 1573), A6ᵛ–A7. See also Franciscus Junius, *The apocalyps . . . With a briefe and methodical exposition* (Cambridge, 1596), p. 76; and *The Bible* (London, 1603), with comm. of Junius on Revelation [STC 2190], fol. 113.

has "bare thin cheekes" and "rawbone armes"; "all his vitall powres/ [Are] Decayd, and all his flesh shronk up like withered flowers" (I. viii. 41. 1–9). Nevertheless, Arthur retrieves Red Crosse from the perdition of the dungeon (which had "no flore,/ But [was] all a deepe descent, as darke as hell" [I. viii. 39. 7–8]), and brings the Knight back to Una.

When we read Orgoglio as the earthquake heralding the Last Judgment, the significance of the Giant's falling upon Red Crosse becomes evident. The Knight has succumbed to fleshly temptation, for which he must be punished. The wages of sin are death, and so in Orgoglio's tomb-like dungeon the Knight undergoes a literal mortification of the flesh. There he lies helpless, until Divine grace lifts the soul and reunites it with Divinity. In Spenser's words, "This good Prince [Arthur] redeemd the *Redcrosse* knight from bands" (I. ix. 1. 9), where "redeemd" should be read with Christian connotations.

Now the introductory stanza of Canto VIII becomes intelligible as an explication of the allegory:

> Ay me, how many perils doe enfold
> The righteous man, to make him daily fall?
> Were not, that heavenly grace doth him uphold,
> And stedfast truth acquite him out of all.
> Her love is firme, her care continuall,
> So oft as he through his owne foolish pride,
> Or weaknesse is to sinfull bands made thrall.
>
> (I. viii. 1. 1–7)

Red Crosse, "the righteous man" before us, has been shown beset by temptation in the grove of Salmacis, which exemplifies the "many perils" which daily surround us; and he has "fallen," re-enacting the drama of Original Sin. He is not lost, however: Red Crosse is rescued from eternal damnation in the dungeon of Orgoglio by Prince Arthur, or "heavenly grace," and reunited with Una, or "stedfast truth." She is constant even though he is led into sin by "his owne foolish pride, / Or weaknesse." Orgogolio, of course, must be equated with the "sinful bands" which have enthralled the Knight, just as "bands" = Orgoglio in I. ix. 1. 9.

Prince Arthur properly interprets Red Crosse's capture as a warning to reform his sinful ways: Arthur knows that "th'only good, that growes of passed feare, / Is to be wise, and ware of like again" (I. viii. 44. 5–6). From this experience he also draws the conclusion "that blisse may not abide in state of mortall men" (I. viii. 44. 9), presumably because all men are touched with Original Sin. But Red Crosse is now eligible for bliss because he no longer exists as a "mortal" man. He has undergone the mortification of Orgoglio's dungeon. This episode is indeed the turning-point of Book I, because from his experience with Orgoglio the Knight emerges as a soul that has subordinated the flesh. In consequence, he is no longer tempted by sins induced by the senses. He still must battle the intellectual crime of hopelessness, though;[2] so in Canto IX the Knight encounters Despair, a sin of the soul, who almost succeeds in having him commit self-murder. But Una dramatically stops the suicide, and then leads Red Crosse to the

---

2. This allegory is explicated in the introductory stanza of Canto X (I. x. 1. 1–5).

House of Holiness, where after the proper instruction and repentance he is shown the New Jerusalem.

In this allegory which outlines the steps to salvation, Orgoglio is an earthquake serving to chastise Red Crosse for his sinfulness, epitomized by his idleness and lechery beside the magic spring. And simultaneously he serves a closely related strand of allegory by representing the destruction of the world on Judgment Day, when only the elect of God will be retrieved from perdition.

This is but one facet of the Giant's allegorical function, however; and when Red Crosse first lies vanquished and Duessa calls the Giant by name, "Orgoglio," a wholly new complex of associations is brought in. Spenser shifts gears, as it were, changing the emphasis from religio-moral to religio-political instruction. There is no discontinuity at this point, because the new phase grows smoothly out of what has gone before. The Revelation of St. John is still the basic text. Now, however, an exposé of Catholic corruption becomes the predominant occupation of the allegory. Protestants had read the Revelation not only as a guide-book along the narrow path to Heaven, but also as a prophecy of world-wide misery propagated by Catholic emperors and prelates. They were the Antichrist. The afflictions disclosed beneath the seven seals and contained in the seven vials of plague—the "wares, slaughters, famine, pestilences . . . persecutions, seditions and . . . distroying of men through corrupt doctryne"—all this suffering was directly attributable to the Pope and his viceroys. More precisely, Mary's marriage to Philip had oppressed England as tyrannously as Orgoglio had imprisoned Red Crosse. So at this point in his narrative Spenser speaks with the indignant voice of an anti-Catholic propagandist.

Now not only the meaning, but the imagery itself derives from the Book of Revelation. Duessa is clearly labelled as the Whore of Babylon, and she triumphantly rides upon the seven-headed Beast. At this point Orgoglio, as Duessa's consort, does become an embodiment of pride—the pride of Catholic despots, of the Pope, of Antichrist.[3]

In addition to leading the Christian toward the New Jerusalem, St. John's Apocalypse was also intended to encourage the faithful in their resistance to the pagan tyranny of Rome. It therefore had political implications. A blasphemous government, because of its efforts to eliminate godliness from the individual heart, was inevitably damned; in view of the promised Armageddon, it was just as inevitably doomed to destruction. And since the Apocalypse does not deal with what God in Christ has already done, but with what is yet to come to insure the establishment of His kingdom, each generation rightly interprets the Revelation according to its own milieu. To St. John writing in Patmos, Babylon was classical Rome in its hedonistic

---

3. Many details of Cantos VII and VIII identify Orgoglio with the Antichrist as conceived by Protestants. He dresses Duessa in the gold and purple of the Babylonian Whore (I. vii. 16.3), he sets the triple crown of the hated Papacy upon her head (I. vii. 16.4), and he provides her with the seven-headed scarlet-colored Beast (I. vii. 16.6–9 ff.). The gorgeous trappings of his palace (I. viii. 35. 1–4) suggest the decadent splendor of Babylon and Rome. The floor is covered "with bloud of guiltlesse babes, and innocents trew" (I. viii. 35.6); and the souls of martyrs are discovered beneath a sacrificial altar (I. viii. 36.1–9). These evidently are the same victims of Antichrist revealed beneath the fifth seal in the Book of Revelation (vi. 9–11). See Hankins, "Spenser and Revelation of St. John," pp. 365, 378.

power, and the Revelation was a promise of its demolition. To Spenser and his contemporaries, Babylon was figured in the Church at Rome, and the Revelation was a promise of the overthrow of Catholic might. In our own times, the number of the Beast has been found to fit Hitler.

Certainly in Spenser's day it was common to correlate St. John's Revelation with current events. When Franciscus Junius' commentary on the apocalypse was printed in English, the titlepage advertised it as "a little treatise, applying the words of S. John to our last times that are full of spirituall and corporall troubles and divisions in Christendom." Sir John Napier in his *Plaine discouery of the whole Reuelation of S. Iohn* (1593) printed in parallel columns (1) the text of the Apocalypse, (2) a prose paraphrase of the text, and (3) historical information that supported his interpretation.

When viewed in the light of contemporary history, the victory of Prince Arthur over Orgoglio becomes the victory of pious Protestantism over corrupt Catholicism. The Giant is finally overthrown by the God-given brightness of Arthur's visage and armor (I. viii. 19. 1 ff.), the sight of which leaves Orgoglio powerless: "for he has read his end / In that bright shield" (I. viii. 21. 4–5). God in this way expresses His incontrovertible will. At this point Duessa throws aside her golden cup and mitre, and attempts to escape (I. viii. 25. 1–3)—symbolically announcing the defeat of the Babylonian Whore, the consort of Antichrist, the personification of the Church at Rome. She is brought to triumphant Prince Arthur (I. viii. 25. 9), and in the presence of all, her true vile nature is exposed (I. viii. 46. 1 ff.). As a perfect gloss on this action, we may note Bullinger's explanation of God's purpose in transmitting the Apocalypse:

> Especially he sheweth the judgement (that is to witte, ye punishement) of the harlot in purple, (I meane of the Pope and the beast) to be seene. First he brought foorth an honest & noble matrone, to weete, the very spouse of Christ. Now as it were by opposition he setteth against her a proude whore, that false new start up Romishe Church, who extolling her selfe braggeth more of her outwarde apparence then of inward furniture. And he affirmeth y^t she shall perish for her great offences.[4]

The intended contrast between Una and Duessa is equally obvious. One of Spenser's intentions was, therefore, a confident re-statement of the Apocalypse in his own terms. Orgoglio is the incarnation of Catholic pride and tyranny, which in the end will be overcome and completely destroyed by Prince Arthur, the allegorical complex representing English Protestantism. When Red Crosse succumbs to the power of Orgoglio, Spenser reveals the incapacity of the individual soul if it succumbs to the sensuality and materialism of popish Rome.

We must not forget, however, that Spenser's vehicle was Italian romance. He was not attempting to imitate the Bible nor a polemical pamphlet. And so perhaps by concentrating on Orgoglio's significance we have distorted

4. *Hundred Sermons*, B1^v.

the Giant's true character—that is, we have dealt with his meaning to the detriment of his actual appearance in the story. In fact, Spenser has done an admirable job of sublimating the serious argument so that on the level of simple narrative-plot Orgoglio is quite convincing in his role of giant in a fairy-tale. He carries his heavy allegorical burden without impairing the childlike wonder and excitement which attends the adventure.

When creating a fairy-tale villain such as Orgoglio, Spenser of course had a rich tradition to draw upon, a tradition which had flourished in folklore, classical mythology, and romance. Here properly we look for Orgoglio's literary antecedents. Spenser labelled him a "Giant," and this would place him under the onus of numerous myths about Giants and Titans related most prominently by Hesiod[5] and Ovid.[6] These malicious superhumans were the offspring of Uranus (Heaven) and Ge (Earth), and they were most infamous for the battles which they had waged against the rightful gods.[7]

As C. W. Lemmi has noted,[8] Orgoglio shows a striking resemblance to the Giants described by Natalis Comes. Springing from the basest Element, Earth, the Giants were not accustomed to the virtues of moderation and justice. Instead, they were partial to sensuality and anger, and they dared attack even Jove himself. Natalis Comes asserts that the Giants were no different from rash men who, driven by a craze for wealth and power, flout all Divinity and attempt to take religion into their own hands. So in the Giants, Spenser happily found an embodiment for the Antichrist which would nonetheless accord with his mise en scène of Italian romance. Orgoglio, by being a Giant, is automatically endowed with the vices that Protestant England attributed to Catholic despots; and yet, on the non-allegorical level he convincingly performs in the romance as the wicked ogre who imprisons the hero.

* * *

Spenser has crowded much into this episode. He had looked into three areas of history—into classical mythology, the Book of Revelation, and recent politics—and in each he found the same archetypal pattern of evil predominating for awhile, but finally being overcome by Divine beneficence. Spenser thought (perhaps wishfully) that he had found an ethical norm, and this moral provides the theme for the Orgoglio episode.

Spenser presents his theme by progressively augmenting the initial statement that Orgoglio is an earthquake. He becomes a warning to repentance, the destruction of the world heralding the Last Judgment, physical death preparing for the resurrection, the Antichrist who brings misery to mankind, the embodiment of Catholic tyranny. In the Giants of mythology Spenser found a solvent to fuse all these constituent meanings into a single unified

5. *Theogony*, 133 ff., 183 ff., 617 ff.
6. *Metamorphoses*, tr. Golding, p. 24, lines 171 ff. [I. 151 ff.].
7. Spenser makes numerous references to "the *Titans*, that whylome rebelled/Gainst highest heauen" (V. i. 9.6–7), and he presents many of his vicious and villainous characters in this form: Lucifera (I. iv. 8.5 ff.), Disdaine (II. vii. 41.6—8, VI. vii. 41.1 ff.), Argante (III. vii. 47.2 ff.) and Ollyphant (III. xi. 3.3 ff.), Care (IV. v. 37.1–2), Geryoneo (V. x. 8.6. ff.), Grantorto (V. xii. 15.1–9), and Change (VII. vi. 2.5 ff.).
8. "The Symbolism of the Classical Episodes in *The Faerie Queene*," *PQ*, VIII (1929), 275–276. See Natalis Comes, *Mythologiae* (Padua, 1616), p. 344 [VI. xxi].

character, so that as the episode proceeds they function simultaneously and consistently. As Spenser controls the conditions, various properties of Orgoglio are activated at different moments—but the total Orgoglio is always present at least latently. Therefore when Prince Arthur releases Red Crosse from Orgoglio's dungeon, the complex of meaning must include the simple fairy-tale rescue of the hero from the villain's den, the religio-moral salvation of the elect on Doomsday, and the religio-political deliverance of mankind from Spanish bigotry. To isolate historical or moral allegory is to decompose Spenser's compound.

READINGS OF THE HOUSE OF BUSYRANE

THOMAS P. ROCHE, JR.: [Love, Lust, and Sexuality]†

* * *

Busyrane is trying to transfer Amoret's love for Scudamour to himself by charms, but the conventional romance structure of this episode should not blind us to its real meaning. He is literally trying to kill Amoret. His love is not sexual but destructive—destructive of the will to love within Amoret herself. Amoret is afraid of the physical surrender which her marriage to Scudamour must entail. The wedding mask crystallizes this fear, and she turns from a joyful acceptance to a cold rejection of the claims of the physical. This is why Busyrane is the great enemy to chastity; he represents a negative force of which chastity is the positive ideal. He represents the negation of chastity, and this for Spenser did not mean lust.

Although Spenser gives no iconographical details to identify his Busyrane, we may learn much from the etymology of his name. Warton suggested long ago that Busyrane is derived from Busiris, "The king of Egypt, famous for his cruelty and inhospitality."[1] Warton, I believe, is correct. The history of Busiris is too complicated to relate. It must suffice to say that Busiris originally was the location of the chief tomb of Osiris, and that in later writers Busiris became the king of the place where Osiris was killed. The complicated traditions agree that Busiris is a location or an agent of sacrificial destruction and is associated with the sacrifice of Osiris.[2] The connection may seem remote, but we must recall the identification of Britomart and Arthegall with Isis and Osiris in Book V and remember that Britomart triumphs over Busyrane before she encounters Arthegall. Even more im-

† From The Kindly Flame: A Study of the Third and Fourth Books of Spenser's "Faerie Queene" (Princeton, 1964), chapter 1. Copyright © 1964 by Princeton University Press. Reprinted by permission of Princeton University Press.

1. Var., 3.287.

2. See Sir Ernest A. T. Wallis Budge, Osiris and the Egyptian Resurrection, 2 vols., London, 1911. Ancient writers who deal with this story include Plutarch, Diodorus Siculus, Apollodorus, Isocrates, Herodotus, and Ovid. See also Heywood's dumbshow in The Brazen Age, Dramatic Works of Thomas Heywood, ed. John Pearson, 6 vols., London, 1874, vol. 3, p. 183; Ralegh, The History of the World, London, 1614, sig. S2ᵛ; Paradise Lost, 1. 307, and Isabel Rathborne, The Meaning of Spenser's Fairyland, pp. 86–90. Professor Rosemond Tuve has kindly pointed out to me the significant appearance of Busiris in Christine de Pisan, The Epistle of Othea to Hector, ed. James D. Gordon, Philadelphia, 1942, pp. 68–69.

portant is Ovid's retelling of the Busiris legend in the first book of the *Ars Amatoria*. This relates Busiris to the qualities I have been trying to establish as the traits of Busyrane:

"If you are wise, cheat women only, and avoid trouble; keep faith save for this one deceitfulness. Deceive the deceivers; they are mostly an unrighteous sort; let them fall into the snare which they have laid. Egypt is said to have lacked the rains that bless its fields, and to have been parched for nine years, when Thrasius approached Busiris, and showed that Jove could be propitiated by the outpoured blood of a stranger. To him said Busiris, 'Thou shalt be Jove's first victim, and as a stranger give water unto Egypt.' Phalaris too roasted in his fierce bull the limbs of Perillus, its maker first made trial of his ill-omened work. Both were just; for there is no juster law than that contrivers of death should perish by their own contrivances. Therefore, that perjuries may rightly cheat the perjured, let the woman feel the smart of a wound she first inflicted."[3]

Ovid's ironic advice to his hypothetical lover throws a new light on the Busiris legend and brings us back to Warton's suggested etymology. These lines betray an attitude toward love and women; it is the same attitude that underlies the conceit of love as war, and it is of particular interest that the well-known Ovidian treatise should link this attitude with the figure of Busiris. Here, it would appear, is the nexus between the conventional figure of Busiris and Spenser's Busyrane; here is the deceit, the sadism, and the destruction, which we associate with Amoret's plight.

But there are further possibilities in Busyrane's name, possibilities that suggest the sixteenth century usage of the word *abuse* as imposture, illusage, delusion. For example, Sidney's sentence from the *Arcadia* quoted in the OED is entirely appropriate: "Was it not enough for him to have deceived me, and through the deceit abused me, and after the abuse forsaken me?" or we might use the obsolete form *abusion*, which the OED defines as "perversion of the truth, deceit, deception, imposture," giving as an example Spenser's lines, "Foolish delights and fond Abusions, Which do that sence besiege with fond illusions." All of these meanings are implicit in the etymology of Busyrane—the illusion, the deceit, the sadism, the destruction.

What then does this make of Busyrane? Is he not the abuse of marriage just as his house is the objectification of Amoret's fears of marriage? He is the abuse of marriage because his mask of Cupid presents an image of marriage as a sacrifice just as Busiris was a place of sacrifice. He is an abuse of marriage because the mind he possesses cannot distinguish between the act of marriage and adulterous love. He is an abuse of marriage because the falsity of his view of love can lead only to lust or death. His power is derived from the *abusion* of the mind in distorting the image of love. The meaning he presents to the wedding guests is trivial, at the most, lust; the meaning he presents to Amoret is the sacrifice of personal integrity. Lust is the least complex of his perversions; he is the image of love distorted in the mind, distorted by lascivious anticipation or horrified withdrawal. He

3. Ovid, *Ars Amatoria*, Book I. 643–658.

becomes the denial of the unity of body and soul in true love. And in all these respects he is the chief adversary of Britomart as the knight of chastity. Britomart's response to the mask and to Busyrane is that of the intelligent moral reader, who can detect the difference between true and false love.

This interpretation of Busyrane and his power over Amoret explains why Scudamour cannot rescue her. Amoret's fears are based on moral and physical grounds. Scudamour can dispel neither. Unwillingly he is the cause of these fears, and any attempt on his part to dispel them would be self-defeating since it would mean her eventual surrender, the basis of her fears. Britomart, on the other hand, can attack these fears on both the moral and physical grounds. As a woman she understands Amoret's attitude toward the physical side of love, and as the exemplar of chastity she is able to make the moral distinction between marriage and adulterous love. Her entry through the wall of flame gives her an intimate knowledge of the House of Busyrane, and her understanding finally allows her to release Amoret from her fears.

* * *

A. KENT HIEATT: [Sexual Adventurism]†

* * *

Most centrally * * * this Masque of Cupid as it relates to Amoret marshals the temptations and horrors of the life of loose sexual commitments, of frequent passion, and of angling for domination of a lover and for deception of a husband or other lovers, as these activities would be seen by a chaste woman, fully committed to one man but tortured by his jealous and insistent dominance over her, as over a sexual prize— a woman, that is, with whom he should have gently and gradually created an entirely different kind of relationship. Such love * * * is really hate, close to the state of the Knight's Tale's Cupid, 'out of alle charitee'. The adulterous temptations begin for Amoret in the fancy and the artificially stoked desire of a life of ease and leisure. They progress through the doubt, dangers, and fearful delights of secret assignations and amours. Such love dangles hopes, but less often satisfactions, before its victims. All of these concepts, personified, pass before us in turn in the Masque of Cupid. Dissemblance and Suspect, Grief and Fury, Displeasure and Pleasure, attend on an unfaithful beloved and a jealous lover. Despite and Cruelty are the lot of an unfaithful wife as conceived by Amoret but also of Amoret herself, a chaste woman, who insists on maintaining her chastity in spite of all temptations and the provocations of a jealous and dominating lover: her heart is taken from her body and bedevilled, yet she will not surrender her love. Like Florimell, she remains love's martyr. As for the remaining figures of the Masque, a woman's ultimate fate in a life of superficial adultery, is, in Amoret's vision, not orgasmic bliss among lusty satyrs but rather something belonging to middle-class ideas, like the final stages of Hogarth's 'Marriage à la Mode',

† From *Chaucer Spenser Milton: Mythopoeic Continuities and Transformations* (Montreal and London, 1975), chapter 8. Reprinted by permission of the publisher, McGill-Queen's University Press.

or, less familiarly but more accurately, like what is warned against in certain Continental and English morality plays and interludes:[1] Reproach, Repentance, Shame, Strife, Anger, Care, Unthriftihead, Loss of Time, Sorrow, Change, Disloyalty, Riotise, Dread, Infirmity, Poverty, and Death with Infamy.

All, or almost all, the figures in the Masque exist in Amoret's imagination, but this imagination is one that bodies forth the real consequences of a certain course of action for a chaste woman to whom frivolous surrender has for the first time become a live option, so that she knows what it is to waver ('wavering' being equivocally applied to both 'wemen' and 'wit'):

> There were full many moe like maladies,
> Whose names and natures I note readen well;
> So many moe, as there be phantasies
> In wavering wemens wit, that none can tell,
> Or paines in love, or punishments in hell.
>
> [xii. 26]

These are quite different from the images of Hellenore's mind, facilely submitting to the Love God's pains and fashioning worlds of fancies 'In her fraile wit' (ix. 52). They are also different from the counterfeits which are the stock-in-trade of the spirit who had fallen with the Prince of Darkness and who animates the body of the false Florimell: he 'all the wyles of wemens wits knew passing well' (viii. 8).

Amoret's torturer, an element in Scudamour himself, is a destroyer of the concord between man and wife. The most advanced embodiment of this concord in *The Faerie Queene* is the relation in V.vii between Britomart-Isis-moon and Artegall-Osiris-crocodile-sun in the Temple of Isis, running 'in equal justice' and achieving a freely offered and freely accepted love and friendship * * * . Certainly then, the explanation of this torturer's name—Busirane—suggested by Professor Roche,[2] is the most apposite one. The key to Roche's etymological explanation is the association of 'Busiris' with the death of Osiris. In the light of Spenser's usual masterful way with mythology, the partly contradictory late Classical and post-Classical lore concerning these two figures, the town of Busiris, and Typhon * * * would have easily permitted him to identify the murderer of Osiris as Busiris. 'Busiris' in this sense, then, furnishes the root of the name 'Busirane', although this name no doubt embodies other phonetic felicities.

* * *

One further reason for believing that in the House of Busirane Amoret is being importuned unintentionally by the masterful practices of her husband to turn from her constant love of him to the life of sexual adventurism is that a kind of reduplicative allegory overtakes Amoret in Book IV. While Britomart sleeps, Amoret is captured by Lust himself—Lust who 'could

---

1. John Rastell's *Calisto and Melebea* is an English example. Jean Bretog, *Tragedie françoise à huict personnages: traictant de l'amour d'un serviteur envers sa maitress, et de tout ce qui en advint* (Lyon, 1571; Chartres, 1831) is closer to what is meant here, although of little literary significance. Less to the point but far better than either of these, and well worth translating into English, is the work published as *De Spiegel der Minnen door Colijn van Rijssele*, ed. Margaretha W. Immink (Utrecht, 1913).
2. Thomas P. Roche, Jr., *The Kindly Flame* (Princeton, 1964), p. 81.

awhape an hardy hart' (vii. 5): that is, who ostensibly is powerful enough to stupefy a strong heart with fear but in fact (considering the singularity of this image) is strong enough to snatch the strongest hearts, just as the Love God joys to see Amoret's heart removed from her bosom and carried before her in the Masque of Cupid. * * * Amoret, like Aemylia, is not simply preyed on by a lustful being, but is herself in some fashion invaded by desire, although she will not perform the acts which desire calls for. She successfully resists both importunities—those of Busirane and Lust— and is finally rescued by the chaste amity of Britomart in the one case and by Belphoebe's virginity in the other.

* * * It is probably true that this episode of Amoret, Timias, and Belphoebe in Book IV is required by Spenser's emergency measures in squaring the accounts of his friend Ralegh with the Queen after the revelation of Ralegh's relations with Elizabeth Throgmorton, but it is equally true that Spenser would not have chosen Amoret for this ambiguous role unless she had been suitable for it. She is readied for pleasure, not overpudicity. Spenser is apparently saying to the Queen that her maid of honour and her favourite Ralegh were touched, but not dominated by, Lust. So with Amoret. In the House of Busirane she is being driven by her lover to become part of the usual courtly round of love that Spenser so strongly condemns elsewhere:

> And is love then (said Corylas) once knowne
> In Court, and his sweet lore professed there?
> I weened sure he was our God alone:
> And only wonned in fields and forests here,
>   Not so (quoth he) love most aboundeth there.
> For all the walls and windows there are writ,
> All full of love, and love, and love my deare,
> And all their talke and studie is of it,
> Ne any there doth brave or valiant seeme,
> Unlesse that some gay Mistresse badge he beares:
> Ne any one himselfe doth ought esteeme,
> Unlesse he swim in love up to the eares.
> But they of love and of his sacred lere,
> (As it should be) all otherwise devise,
> Then we poore shepheards are accustomd here,
> And him do sue and serve all otherwise,
> For with lewd speeches and licentious deeds,
> His mightie mysteries they do prophane,
> And use his ydle name to other needs,
> But as a complement for courting vaine,
> So him they do not serve as they professe,
> But make him serve to them for sordid uses,
> Ah my dread Lord, that doest liege hearts possesse,
> Avenge thy selfe on them for their abuses.
>   [Colin Clouts Come Home Againe, 771–94]

The allegory of Lust in Book IV is simply an intensification of what we have already seen in the House of Busirane. For purposes of Spenser's defending his friend and patron, and Elizabeth Throgmorton, and of maintaining the allegorical locus of Amoret, it was not intended that Timias and Amoret should be punished, but that the unclean cleaving thing, amorous desire without constancy to one lover, should be extirpated.

The friendship which Britomart brings to Amoret is what reverses the charms of Busirane, so that Amoret's wound becomes whole and the chains drop from her body, in the inner room where the magician had held her in thrall. Busirane must not be destroyed (III.xii. 34) because he is a part of Scudamour. As a masterful principle of hate, he is ready to destroy Amoret finally (xii. 32), and he wounds Britomart superficially as the masterful principle of Malecasta had done in canto i. In Book IV Britomart and Amoret now go forth in amity, in spite of Amoret's suspicions of what she takes to be a male's intentions—suspicions which are soon allayed in the formation of the first four-group of that book, with Britomart as knight to Amoret and as lady to another knight, so that they may all be lodged in a castle with a custom. * * *

SUSANNE LINDGREN WOFFORD:
[The Bold Reader in the House of Busyrane]†

* * *

In the final episodes of Book III, Britomart is confronted with a figure of the male artist who is inscribed deep within her mind, an artist/magician whom she resists and overcomes. Her exploring of the House of Busyrane is glossed by Spenser as an activity like reading, and like other inner worlds, the House of Busyrane is treated as textual space, furnished with a multiplicity of intertextual references. Britomart serves as a reader who is urged by Busyrane in his inscriptions to be bold but not too bold in her interpretations. Her imagined depth of character is represented in the text by means of the analogy established between her and the imagined figure of the reader whom she resembles.

With its three chambers, the House of Busyrane resembles in structure the picture of the human mind given in the House of Alma. There we learned that the mind's three chambers correspond to the faculties of Foresight, Reason and Memory (II,ix,49). The mind Britomart explores in III,xi–xii is a tortured version of this temperate mind, though it too contains in its own way the shows and visions of Phantastes, the "wisards" (here evil) of the chambers of reason, and the library of memory, here a library containing mostly Ovid and Petrarch, but also fragments of the works of other love poets. The place that Britomart explores, then, serves as a figure for an imaginative mind, either Britomart's own which she explores and then purges, or Amoret's, or Busyrane's, a horrific version of her author's mind.

The episode of the House of Busyrane notoriously calls out for multiple readings, as an allegory of female fantasy ("So many moe, as there be

† From "Gendering Allegory: Spenser's Bold Reader and the Emergence of Character in *The Faerie Queene* III," *Criticism* 30 (1988):1–21. Original footnotes have been reduced and slightly edited. Reprinted by permission of the Wayne State University Press.

phantasies/In wauering wemens wit" [III,xii,26])[1] and as an allegory of male violence against women, of the kinds of torture to which males have subjected females in their literary and erotic imaginings.[2] If the House represents her own mind, Britomart can be understood to be exploring the sources of her own imagination and therefore of her quest in the previous male poetry that has penned women in stereotypes revealed in the House as torturing and pornographic. Finding his love behind the wall of fire, Scudamour laments, "Why then is Busirane with wicked hand/ Suffred . . . My Lady and my loue so cruelly to pen?" (III,xi,10). The pun in this repeated line (to pen is to write about and to pen up) suggests that to write of women at all may be to pen them into some stereotype or allegorization: the line suggests that any male poet—and perhaps any poet—will run this risk, that to use words to describe an other is necessarily to reduce him or her to some limiting image or form.[3]

The torment that Busyrane's version of courtly love produces in the theater of canto 12 is appropriately enough the forced revelation of the inner self in this abusive world. Such forced revelation, Spenser's poem suggests, objectifies and freezes, leaving only the reified image of the heart, but bringing no emotion with it. In spite of this violence, Amoret remains closed to Busyrane, resistant, her innerness as character inviolate. In refusing to give in to Busyrane, she refuses to become object of this torturing, reifying love poetry. Britomart, a knight who can rescue Amoret partly because she herself is also a woman, represents in her heroic energy and power a choice on Spenser's part: here he reverses the male poetic tradition of making women serve only as the passive objects of erotic poetry. In different ways, Britomart and Amoret struggle against this male tradition, personified by Busyrane, a perverse figure of the poet who tries to place them in a stereotypically "male" poetry.

Like Merlin, Busyrane is presented writing "characters," letters which magically bind and unbind the daemonic figures before him:

> And her before the vile Enchaunter sate,
> Figuring straunge characters of his art,
> With liuing blood he those characters wrate,
> Dreadfully dropping from her dying hart. . . .
>   (III,xii,31)

Busyrane's magic letters, written in blood, serue to transform women (in this case, Amoret) into allegorical figures. The literalization of writing with

---

1. See Thomas Roche, Jr., *The Kindly Flame: A Study of the Third and Fourth Books of Spenser's Faerie Queene* (Princeton, 1964), pp. 72–87, as a representative of the line of argument which concludes "the mask that takes place at the House of Busyrane is Amoret's interpretation of the wedding mask" (p. 77). See Maureen Quilligan, *Milton's Spenser* (Ithaca, 1983) p. 198, for a feminist version of this interpretation.
2. For an example of this interpretation, see Harry Berger, Jr., "Busirane and the War Between the Sexes: An Interpretation of *The Faerie Queene* III, xi–xii," *English Literary Renaissance*, 1 (1971). See also Lauren Silberman, 1986, pp. 266–67, who argues that Amoret is able to elude Busyrane's "forcible troping" because Busirane's sadomasochism is "an archetypal dualism" of the sort that Spenser seeks to transcend in his own poetic language.
3. Spenser may even bring a third pun to the fore by punning on the link between pen and phallus and thereby suggesting that the male poet at issue here not only pens up his female characters in these stereotypes or allegorical figures but abuses them as he does so.

"liuing blood" marks out the implicit violence of his poetic praxis, and shows that Busyrane's art functions by denying the woman any interiority. Though Merlin's plot does so benignly, both Merlin and Busyrane pen the female character into a specific plot that depends not only on female stereotypes but also on making female characters serve allegorical ends.

Spenser isolates one aspect of his art and represents it in the figure of Busyrane, while Britomart in her victory is associated with another incipient aspect of his own technique, one which, at this moment in the dialectic, points the way out of allegory. In his highly allegorical house, where all human emotions are represented in reified terms, and where even figures of speech have become objectified and frozen in time, Busyrane comes to stand for the potential abuses of allegory itself. In this limit case, it is allegory that is challenged here, not simply the failures of courtly love as an imaginative scheme. Allegory in its most extreme form is the pen from which Britomart strives to save the daemonic Amoret, a rescue that can only be partially successful, as both endings of the story suggest.

In this self-interrogation, then, Spenser looks at Busyrane's art from the point of view of a woman and condemns it. He uses a more fictional mode of writing to challenge and reveal the limitations of allegory in its most static and extreme form. The struggle between Britomart and Busyrane— a struggle in which Britomart defends herself as well as Amoret—suggests that the dialectic of allegory and fiction is not a comfortable nor perhaps even a resolvable one. Spenser's self-interrogations in other Books of *The Faerie Queene* are also uncomfortable; what is distinctive here is not the intensity of the self-doubt, but the aesthetic and gender-specific formulations that Spenser gives to the uncertainty and ideological tension at the heart of his poetics.

The nearly obsessive puns on "read" in cantos 11 and 12 prepare the reader for the emphasis on interpretation. Britomart is consistently represented in the House as a reader of allegory. A typical case occurs in canto 11 where she sees the Idol of Cupid and then encounters the first of the inscriptions on the House itself:

> Tho as she backward cast her busie eye,
> To search each secret of that goodly sted
> Ouer the dore thus written she did spye
> *Be Bold*: she oft and oft it ouer-red,
> Yet could not find what sense it figured:
> But what so were therein or writ or ment,
> She was no whit thereby discouraged
> From prosecuting of her first intent,
> But forward with bold steps into the next roome went.
> (III,xi,50)

Here Britomart stands in the same place as the reader, who also over-reads (in both senses) and yet cannot easily interpret these passages. Who wrote "Be Bold" over the door? Busyrane, to encourage his innocent victims? The author, eager for Britomart to discover and unmask Busyrane? The conventions of society and literature which encourage the chaste woman to continue to be bold at this stage of a courtship? Britomart cannot find what sense it figures, but her uncertainty does not keep her from prosecuting her first intent; the reader goes with her into the next room.

Britomart is represented as a reader when she views the Ovidian tapestries, when she studies the Idol of Cupid, and when she watches the Masque of Cupid, but, as the previous example suggested, she is most particularly so in her efforts to "read" the House itself. In the second chamber she is everywhere encouraged to be bold, but only at the far end of the chamber is she told to "be not too bold."

> And as she lookt about, she did behold,
> How ouer that same dore was likewise writ,
> *Be bold, be bold,* and euery where *Be bold,*
> That much she muz'd, yet could not construe it
> By any ridling skill, or commune wit.
> At last she spyde at that roomes vpper end,
> Another yron dore, on which was writ,
> *Be not too bold;* whereto though she did bend
> Her earnest mind, yet wist not what it might intend.
>   (III, xi, 54)

Words like "construe" and "writ" once again emphasize that Britomart and the reader interpret in parallel here. She "bends" her mind to interpret this last command, but she still cannot understand the warning in the inscription. If Busyrane represents at least an aspect of her society's conventions about love, Britomart is being told here exactly how much demystification she should indulge in: the female character is to be drawn in by the snare of "be bold," only to be stopped at the final chamber and prevented from seeing the inmost workings of the male mind. Busyrane blocks her way: when she first tries to enter the chamber, she finds the door locked (III, xii, 27) and has to use "sleights and art" to find a way in.[4]

When she finally does enter the inmost chamber, disobeying the injunction over the door, Britomart finds the male abuser of her fantasy, a figure of the male poet who has drawn her into a pornographic love poem (a love poetry that abuses women by literalizing the cliches of Petrarchan sonnets).[5] She opposes the kind of eroticism represented by Busyrane's reifying art, forcing him "his charmes backe to reuerse" (III, xii, 36), but she also opposes Busyrane by entering the chamber in the first place. Britomart succeeds in rescuing Amoret then, precisely because she is "too bold" in prosecuting her first intent: she is not stopped by the male commands that would pen her into the second room, nor is she stopped because she is unable to reach a conclusive interpretation of the inscription.

This final scene can be understood metaphorically as a figurative representation or animation of the struggle between one type of male poet and a female character whom his poetry would control or destroy. Spenser's narrator is left in an ambiguous position: to the extent that he attempts to

---

4. See Lesley Brill, "Chastity as Ideal Sexuality in the Third Book of *The Faerie Queene,*" *Studies in English Literature,* 11 (1971) for an interpretation of the "Be Bold, Be Bold" inscription that links it to Britomart's lament in III, iv, 9. See Iris Tilman Hill, "Britomart and Be Bold, Be Bot Too Bold," *ELH,* 38 (1971), 173–78, for an interpretation of the inscription as an explicit allusion to the myth of Venus and Adonis.

5. See Mark Rose, *Heroic Love* (Cambridge, 1968) pp. 121 ff., on the tortures in the house of Busyrane as literalizations of the conventions of Petrarchan sonnets.

attach specific allegorical meanings to Britomart's quest, he is allied with Busyrane, even as he represents Britomart's victory over the evil magician sympathetically. Throughout this episode Britomart as character makes such allegorizing more and more difficult. Moreover, she searches out the character who, fictionally speaking, created this section of the plot, and overthrows him, thereby undoing—"reversing," as Spenser says—the plot. Spenser the author in these scenes brings to the surface an evil anti-type to what we should imagine to be the ideal figure of the poet, but here as elsewhere (most notably in the case of Archimago), the poem reveals an uncomfortable liaison between Spenser's poetry and the evil form of art that it attempts to exorcise.

In the 1590 ending of Book III, Britomart brings Amoret out of the House to the embrace of Scudamour, metaphorically making possible the consummation of their marriage as their two bodies blend into one. In the moment of this much desired embrace, the readers see Amoret's more partial side, one reason why she may have been "penned" by Busyrane. As Donald Cheney has shown, the Ovidian subtext of the Hermaphrodite story, to which Spenser explicitly alludes in several lines, speaks of the losses as well as the gains in such an embrace.[6] As Amoret and Scudamor become Scudamoret, the emblem of marriage in the figure of the Hermaphrodite, they also make evident their daemonic nature. Their embrace represents both a gain and a loss: they are reunited, but for them, as for Malbecco, the process of becoming an emblem brings also a loss of human form.

Although this embrace produces the much desired ending of the story, Britomart is excluded from it and from the closure it produces. She stands outside, as does the reader, "halfe enuying their blesse" (III,xii,46a). Britomart is alien in their highly conventional world: as heroine of an epic-romance, she stands outside the lyric; as protonovelistic heroine with her own originality and force of character, she stands outside the allegorical tableau they create. She attempts to read it, she half envies them its relative simplicity, but finally she is left outside it.

Britomart stands outside this closural embrace of Scudamoret particularly because she has stood against one version of the male poet, and thereby resisted the type of conventional characterization of love in which he had attempted to entangle her. Amoret and Scudamour, on the other hand, have clearly not left their conventionality behind.[7] Their daemonic nature is not something Britomart can rescue them from, and they blend together to produce an emblem to balance the emblem of jealousy which begins the episode (III,xi,1–2). Amoret and Scudamour are characters who cannot escape destructive conventionality because they partly symbolize it—or at least, they symbolize the allegorical fragmentation of characteristics that produces in the individual (though not necessarily in the composite) a less complicated picture of human action than does a more multiple characterization. Given such fragmentation, it takes many daemonic or part-ial characters to create a complex analysis, while the individual daemon re-

6. See Donald Cheney, "Spenser's Hermaphrodite and the 1590 *Faerie Queene*," PMLA, 87 (1972).
7. Cheney, "Spenser's Hermaphrodite," stresses the Petrarchan clichés in the rhymes of stanza 44a, and suggests that Scudamour cannot transcend the Petrarchan problematic on his own.

mains penned in his or her limited, "obsessive" identity. In the conclusion to Book III, then, Spenser opposes two methods of achieving a complexity of character and of moral analysis while revealing through the dialectic between them the limitations and powers of each. Each mode alone allows for a less complex "analysis" than does the dialectical combination of the two.

The figurative struggle between a female character and an evil male artist, then, points to a struggle between modes of writing, modes which in this episode are associated with male and female perspectives. Britomart stands against one version of allegory itself, and rescues Amoret from it; afterwards, she stands outside the allegorical representation of the promised marriage, and finds it only half satisfying. In her gesture of liberation, she moves against one version of male authority, positing an alternative female authority that reverses the male plot and creates a different kind of female character.

The interpretive openness of the poem in general, and especially of this episode, stands as an image of that aspect of Britomart which is not "penned" up in her allegorical significance: she has an openness of character that leads her into unexpected adventures and makes her respond in unpredictable ways. She tries to live up to an ideal, which in her quest she may also adumbrate—hence her function in the allegory—but she also has a character which cannot be contained by that or any other closural allegorical significance. Only in the figure of the reader are her two roles able to merge, but to the extent that she becomes a figure of reading she is excluded from what she reads. Britomart's wholeness as a reader, and by extension our own, is gained at the expense of a coherent allegorical or ideological structure within which she herself is a signifier.

In Book III Spenser exposes the epistemological dilemma present throughout his poem through the sexual tension which animates the narrative: this sexual tension undermines the absoluteness of the authority of the narrative voice. Spenser's narrator may tell his readers what his allegory means, but his readers continually find that his inscribed interpretations do not reflect the experience of the characters in their dimension as characters. In Book III Spenser uses female characters to dramatize this disjunction; moreover, Britomart's actions, in serving to tie the idea of depth of character to the figure of the reader, suggest that the interpreter of Spenser also necessarily takes up an oppositional position, searching for the countertext, and reading against as well as with the allegory.

In the 1596 ending of Book III, Spenser again suggests that his own narrative strategies may defile the characters whose virtues he wishes to represent and to praise. As Amoret comes out of the House hoping to see her knight, Spenser tells us that "Being thereof beguyld," she "was fild with new affright" (III,xii,44). Amoret's "perfect hole," her healed inner self, is both "filled" and "defiled" with fright once again, for the denial of closure is a torture to her daemonic self. It constitutes yet another version of the frozen postures of delay that she has experienced within the House. The word "beguyld" associates Spenser's narrative art with Busyrane's imagistic and theatrical art; Spenser's art can either fill or defile, the danger being that these two may amount to the same thing. Breaking off closure is a defiling of the allegorical figure at the same time as it may allow the filling in of the character. As in every case of broken endings that Spenser provides, the lack of plot closure re-emphasizes that there can be no absolute closure to the allegory. Spenser's poem may desire to reach that promised end, but until that time it acts out the impossibility of expressing absolute meaning in a poem. In Book III, Spenser dramatizes this impossibility as the disjunction between the male meanings imposed by narrator or magician and the female understandings represented and acted upon within the story as story, as Britomart, being too bold for the allegory, steps forward to save Amoret from the tortures her author had devised.

HUMPHREY TONKIN

[Pastorella and the Graces]†

* * *

The Dance of the Graces is the intellectual and poetic centre of the Legend of Courtesy. We have already traced the gradual 'rarefication' of Spenser's story—from the cruelties of the outside world, to the shepherds' country, to the Golden World. Within this Golden World, we move swiftly from fairy dance, to Dance of the Graces, to the central, all-important figure of the shepherd maid who is both Colin Clout's mistress and also has the appearance and the substance of a goddess. Everything in Spenser's poetic repertoire contributes to make this almost schizophrenic vision credible. Even the dance itself does not exist in isolation, but at the top of an ascending series. Early in Canto ix, Pastorella sits in the centre of the shepherds' 'rout' just as the central figure of the Dance of the Graces is surrounded by the circling dancers. In both cases the ladies surrounding the central figure are likened to a garland. Later, the shepherds dance to Colin Clout's pipe and again Pastorella is the foremost dancer. While it may be illegitimate categorically to associate the figure of Pastorella with the figure in the centre of the circling dancers on Mount Acidale, such parallels make the Dance of the Graces an all-inclusive vision which embraces and contains these lesser emblems of order. The range of association which the Dance embodies is well expressed in the stanzas describing the Graces and explaining Colin Clout's role.

> Those were the Graces, daughters of delight,
> Handmaides of *Venus*, which are wont to haunt
> Uppon this hill, and daunce there day and night:
> Those three to men all gifts of grace do graunt,
> And all, that *Venus* in her selfe doth vaunt,
> Is borrowed of them. But that faire one,
> That in the midst was placed paravaunt,

---

† From *Spenser's Courteous Pastoral: Book Six of "The Faerie Queene"* (Oxford, 1972), chapter 5. Reprinted by permission of Oxford University Press.

Was she to whom that shepheard pypt alone,
That made him pipe so merrily, as never none.

She was to weete that jolly Shepheards lasse,
Which piped there unto that merry rout,
That jolly shepheard, which there piped, was
Poore *Colin Clout* (who knowes not *Colin Clout?*)
He pypt apace, whilest they him daunst about.
Pype jolly shepheard, pype thou now apace
Unto thy love, that made thee low to lout;
Thy love is present there with thee in place,
Thy love is there advaunst to be another Grace.

(VI. X. 15–16)

The introduction of the author's own *persona* into the world he creates is of course a convention of pastoral. Even in its simplest form the convention has a far-reaching effect on the relation of author and reader to the work, since it blurs the distinction between the poet and his own creation much as the comments of a character on the play he is a part of change the relationship between audience and play. Sometimes (as in Sidney's *Arcadia*, for instance) the author's *persona* plays only a very minor role. But in Spenser's poem the poet's fictional self is piping not for some minor shepherds' dance but for the dance which sums up and epitomizes many of the principal themes of the work—just *how* principal we shall see as this study progresses. The dancers dance to Colin's music: it is he who orders and controls them. In a sense, the relation of the dance to Colin is like the relation of the poem to Spenser. We are confronted in this beautiful scene with the spectacle of the poet creating, the poem coming into being. But, paradoxically, the poem which here comes into being is the poem which contains that poem: the whole is contained in the part.

This, though, is not the end of the complexity. Colin does not pipe to an abstraction or a vision, but to an earthly girl, to his own mistress. She and the shepherd are the two static figures amidst, or beside, the swirling dancers. While we are told that she is an earthly girl, she is nevertheless as ethereal as the other dancers: she disappears as they do, thereby suggesting not only that poetic inspiration is elusive and obscure, but that love, too, is uncertain and fleeting. Or perhaps just as Colin is a fictional Spenser, Colin's love for the girl is a fictional representation of the poet's relation to the controlling idea of his poem, round which he shapes and orders the subsidiary images and themes. If this is so, then the girl in the centre of the dance is the flower of courtesy itself.

The final line of the passage, 'Thy love is there advaunst to be another Grace', introduces another dimension to the paradox. Not only does the dance revolve round the central figure, the poem round the central emblem, but there is also a mysterious relationship between the various revolving circles. This was suggested to us in the stanzas immediately preceding those I have just quoted. Somehow, we know not how (but we believe it), a simple shepherd girl *is* another Grace, *is* the flower of courtesy. Spenser deliberately keeps her position ambiguous (the whole dance depends on such ambiguity): she is another Grace and more than another Grace and worthy to be another Grace. The remark 'And all, that Venus in her selfe doth vaunt / Is borrowed of them' has, I think, an intentional double meaning: either Venus borrows her grace from the Graces, or we borrow from Venus grace *through* the Graces. In other words, we are either watching a dance of four Graces (who epitomize the grace of Venus, since Venus borrows grace from them) or watching a dance of three Graces with Venus in the centre (in which event Venus's grace is passed down to us through the three Graces who surround her).

This ambiguity is mirrored in the visual ambiguities which confront us early on in the episode. I asserted that we see the Dance through Calidore's eyes. Calidore is able to follow and understand the pattern of the hundred maidens who hem the central dancers, but the precise configuration of these central damsels escapes him. When we are told that Colin's mistress was 'as a precious gemme, / Amidst a ring most richly well enchaced', what precisely does this mean in visual terms? Are the three Graces smaller stones surrounding the greater (in which event Colin's mistress is in the centre) or do they correspond to the circle of the ring (in which event Colin's mistress is a fourth member of the same circle)? Is she, in other words, Venus or a fourth Grace? The ambiguity is visual as well as conceptual. By associating Colin's mistress with Venus, Spenser makes the Graces (emblems of courtesy, according to Colin) her handmaids; by associating her with a fourth Grace, he makes her the means by which Venus's powers descend to us. She is thus both the epitome of courtesy and the source of courtesy; and the dance becomes the dance of courtesy, bound together by the love which emanates from Venus.

At stanza 17 the enchantment evaporates. Calidore steps into the ring and the dancers vanish 'all away out of his sight'. This is the climax of Calidore's intrusions—the third and most cataclysmic. One would like to think that Calidore had learned from his previous intrusions. But at first there is precious little evidence that he has. His manner is inappropriately hearty: 'Haile jolly shepheard, which thy joyous dayes / Here leadest in this goodly merry make, / Frequented of these gentle Nymphes alwayes.' As Colin Clout, recovering his composure, explains, regrettably things are not quite as simple as that: the Graces only come when they, and not we, choose. You can't have miracles to order.

Calidore's reaction is again curiously inappropriate. As with Calepine and Serena, he blames the whole incident on 'my ill fortune', and presses Colin for an explanation. The figures Calidore has seen, says Colin, are the Graces, who 'on men all gracious gifts bestow/ Which decke the body or adorne the mynde'—

> As comely carriage, entertainment kynde,
> Sweete semblaunt, friendly offices that bynde,
> And all the complements of curtesie:
> They teach us, how to each degree and kynde
> We should our selves demeane, to low, to hie;
> To friends, to foes, which skill men call Civility.
>   (VI. X. 23)

All this has been made clear to us in the preceding sections of the book, especially in those episodes involving Calidore. But Colin's attention now shifts to the central figure. Again Spenser avoids precise definition:

> So farre as doth the daughter of the day,
> All other lesser lights in light excell,
> So farre doth she in beautyfull array,
> Above all other lasses beare the bell. . . .

> Another Grace she well deserves to be,
> In whom so many Graces gathered are,
> Excelling much the meane of her degree;
> Divine resemblance, beauty soveraine rare,
> Firme Chastity, that spight ne blemish dare;
> All which she with such courtesie doth grace,
> That all her percs cannot with her compare,
> But quite are dimmed, when she is in place.
> She made me often pipe and now to pipe apace.
>   (VI. x. 26–27)

The final line is both a comment on the poem and a suggestion about its inspiration. The romantic reader, anxious to read the poem as a kind of confessional, might choose to call this 'Grace' Spenser's own Elizabeth Boyle. Others, taking their cue from the *Shepheardes Calender*, may call her Rosalind. But perhaps it would be both truer to the spirit of the poem and more immediately relevant to its theme to call her that inspiration which brought the poem into being, the '*Idea* or fore-conceit' out of which the poet fashioned the work of art.

Almost in the same breath, Spenser turns to the Queen. Perhaps (he seems to say), even so all-embracing and transcendent a vision as this might be misconstrued in a poem ostensibly in praise of the Queen herself. The central figure of the dance, an all-inclusive symbol of virtue, has usurped the position normally allotted the sovereign, who cannot by any stretch of the imagination be incorporated into the dance as Spenser has described it. In turning to the Queen, the poet employs the traditional idea that thus Gloriana's handmaid will be eternized in verse. If Colin's mistress is indeed another Grace, then the Queen is her Venus.

Calidore's reply to Colin's explanation is both illuminating and perplexing. For the first time, he is driven to an admission not simply of 'lucklessness' but of imperfection. He has, he says, 'rashly sought that, which I mote not see'. What is this thing which Calidore 'mote not see', and what effect will it have upon him? Colin's explanation of the significance of the Graces may only be a kind of rationalization of a vision essentially irrational, a quality which somehow lies outside the range of the questing knight, the man of action. If so, then there remains a further question, ultimately the most important. Can this vision be translated into action? To this question we must return.

In the presence of such strange knowledge, and overcome by the beauty of the place in which it was vouchsafed him, Calidore is reluctant to leave—'Thence, he had no will away to fare / But wisht, that with the shepheard he mote dwelling share.' This chance remark reminds us that it was actually the sight of beauty that kept Calidore among the shepherds: he saw Pastorella and he elected to stay. Soon the shepherds' world will disappear as the vision of the Graces disappeared. In each case Calidore stands before these creations of the imagination much as the reader stands before the work of art. If Colin is the poet and the dance is his poetry, Calidore represents ourselves, the readers, in our fumbling efforts to understand the incomprehensible and our insistence on pat answers.

The perceptive reader will recognize that this puts Spenser's audience uncomfortably close to Mirabella and the Salvage Nation, or to Amoret in the House of Busyrane. Like Calidore, these characters did not understand the nature of poetic truth. Their inability to understand metaphor is linked with Calidore's inability to comprehend the nature of the dance. Thus, not only is Spenser's own *persona*, Colin Clout, brought within the scope of the poem, but so are we. The Dance of the Graces is the most important statement of a persistent theme in Book VI, the relation between poetry and society. Behind that stand two other related themes: the nature of fiction and our response to art. Book VI is a poem talking about itself.

Though Calidore does appear to learn from his conversation with Colin Clout, his incursion on the Golden World of Mount Acidale destroys the vision. Not only must we recognize the limitations of Calidore in ourselves, but we must also understand that Calidore, all unwittingly, repeatedly does what the Beast does intentionally: he breaks in and destroys. Book VI is the only book the object of whose quest is all around us. We must travel to Canto XII to meet Acrasia or Grantorto, but the Blatant Beast races through the world of the Legend of Courtesy like an ever-present and vulgar philistinism—not merely outside us but within us all.

* * *

DAVID LEE MILLER

Spenser and the Gaze of Glory†

For what hath all that goodly glorious gaze
Like to one sight, which Calidore did vew?
—*The Faerie Queene* VI.x.4

"Gaze" is both a noun and a verb. For Spenser, the noun refers not just to the act of looking but also to the thing looked at. The semantics of the word imply a continuity between the two, a phenomenology of spectacle in which things are not passively "there" but offer themselves actively to be seen, as in a theater. Spenser identifies this imaginary theater with the imperial splendor and pretentions of Elizabeth's royal court, to which he

† Revised by the author for the present volume. An earlier version of this essay was delivered at the annual meeting of the Modern Language Association, December 1990. Remarks on Spenser's "Loe" are adapted from "The Writing ~~Thing~~," *Diacritics* 20.4 (Winter 1990): 17–29. Reprinted by permission of The Johns Hopkins University Press.

will contrast the dance of the Graces on Mount Acidale. There is a sense, however, in which "that goodly glorious gaze" cannot be apprehended directly, like a concrete person or situation—a sense in which, finally, it refers neither to a particular action of looking nor to a particular thing seen, but to the visual milieu itself, the imaginary arena of seeing-and-being-seen within which concrete persons and situations appear. Because this space belongs to the imagination, it may at any moment concentrate its allure in whatever image attracts our attention, or diffuse its origin in every real or fancied source of the attention we solicit. Like that elusive figure of courtly glory, the fairy queen herself, the Gaze is sought everywhere but found nowhere.

In *Ambition and Privilege*, Frank Whigham characterizes the royal court as an arena haunted by this elusive Gaze.[1] And in their accounts of Spenser's career, Louis Montrose and Richard Helgerson clarify the way Spenser's quest for public recognition engaged both the "literary system" of Elizabethan England and the system of courtly patronage that supported it.[2] Yet precisely because the Gaze is so elusive, it partly escapes historical study. Our own history and criticism, written to engage a modern audience, are themselves constructed as objects for the Gaze. So indeed are we, to the extent that we seek one another as social creatures. We may not be courtiers, but the ideologies that have justified literary teaching and scholarship, and the histories that have oriented them, are at once the products and the media of an imperial Gaze. The giant forms that people these discourses have names like "England" and "America," "the Renaissance" and "the Enlightenment"—names that serve to consolidate a vast geopolitical and transhistorical theater of recognition. Within that theater we call on the idealized presences of the past to lend us their immortal substance, and to memorialize the character in which we would appear to ourselves, to each other and the world.

In apprehending Spenser, then, we too are captivated by the phenomenology of spectacle: an image of ourselves informs the way we choose to read. My purpose in this essay is therefore twofold: it is to discuss Spenser's literary emergence into the Elizabethan imperial Gaze, but also to describe how Spenser's emergence as an object for this Gaze confirms our own. I will pursue this double purpose by commenting briefly on three passages that correspond to crucial moments in Spenser's career. These are the conclusion of his first published poem, *The Shepheardes Calender*; the beginning of his major work, *The Faerie Queene*; and the climactic episode of that work, the dance of the Graces on Mount Acidale in Book VI, canto x. The first two of these show us Spenser's emergence as the courtier-poet Montrose and Helgerson describe; the last, however, stages what may be Spenser's yearning to withdraw from the imperial Gaze. At once ecstatic and nostalgic, Colin's vision of the Graces dancing around a mysterious country lass seems to offer an alternative theater, "deep within the mind," for a disclosure untainted by the motives of publicity. Yet as appealing as this episode is, I want to inquire, with as much skepticism as sympathy,

1. Frank Whigham, *Ambition and Privilege: The Social Tropes of Elizabethan Courtesy Theory* (Berkeley: U of California P, 1984). See especially 37–39.
2. See, e.g., the articles excerpted for this edition, pp. 686–95 and 675–86 [*Editors*].

into the source of its appeal, and to ask what image of ourselves we are drawn toward by the seductive mystery of Colin Clout's revery.

Let us begin with the envoy to *The Shepheardes Calender*. In signaling that the poem is ending, these verses mark a threshold. Just at its edge, where the glosses to "December" end and the envoy begins, we find the word "Loe." With this rhetorical gesture, sometimes designated by the heraldic term *mise en abŷme*, the text points to itself: "Loe I have made a Calender for every yeare." But if we pause over the moment of this utterance, the "now" of the poet's "Loe," it turns out to be a confusion of times. There is first of all the imaginary moment of the finishing touch, in which the maker stands back from his work to declare with profound satisfaction, "There, it's finished forever!" But this imaginary scene is complicated by its rhetorical aspect, for the poet is addressing readers who are not present as he writes. He is addressing the future—addressing *us*, across the centuries, to declare that his calendar rises above time to measure every year. This illusion of spanning the centuries works by ignoring the difference between the moment of writing and that of reading: these two historical moments coalesce in a single imaginary moment of mutual witness. The illusion is supported by the placement of the line at the threshold of closure, where it announces that we too have "finished" the poem. Compare the prologue verses, in which the poet speaks not to the reader but to the "little booke" itself—written but not yet read—and waits nervously to hear what the world will say. The envoy forgets this distinction between making and reading in order to sponsor an utterly impossible moment in which we as readers are "there" with the author, stepping back to admire the poem we have all just completed.

Such are the rhetorical illusions by which the poet offers himself and his text to our gaze: reading and writing disappear into each other; 1579 and 1992 come face to face in a moment that transcends history. Yet in order for this fantasy to be complete, there is another, more fundamental illusion we must accept: the presence of the text as an object. Reading takes place over time, and consumes energy. A text as strange as *The Shepheardes Calender* takes a long time to read, and consumes a great deal of energy. Can we ever say we are *done*? In a sense, perhaps—if we read it through once from beginning to end, as the prologue and envoy together seem to imply. But having finished such a reading, can we point to the poem— Lo and behold!—as if it were present to our appreciative gaze?

No. What we can point to in that way is simply the word "Loe." Through synecdoche (the substitution of part for whole) this word seems to point beyond itself to the whole of which it is part. The illusion works because we do have some sense, however vague, of the text as a whole. And yet insofar as it works, it turns synecdoche around, substituting not the part for the whole but the whole for the part. This is the only way the imaginary moment of closure can both contain the completed work as an object we stand back to recognize *and* be contained *by* the work as a single moment of reading, a single word or line. The text, in other words, evokes itself as something closed off, complete, present to be looked at or pointed to, not just when it uses a part to signify the whole, but when it prompts us see the whole *instead of* the part. This rhetorical stutter-step is so important because the signified wholeness of the work is exactly what we never can *finish* reading, never can see all at once. It is the very thing that cannot become an object for the Gaze.

We can grasp this particular illusion more clearly, perhaps, by breaking it down in a very literal-minded way. Is the envoy part of the poem, or not? If it is, then the poem is not finished yet when the envoy says "Loe"—there are still twelve lines and a motto left to read. But if the envoy is not part of the poem, what is it? This same question can be asked about many other pieces of the original text, with its entourage of glosses, notes, epistles, arguments, mottos, and emblems. If all these things somehow belong to the poem yet are not part of it, what are they? We might compare them to a picture frame, which is neither part of the picture nor separate from it, but serves to define and enclose the picture. Spenser's text "frames" itself as if it, too, were set off for the eye like a picture. It does this by distinguishing its imaginary form (what we call the "work" or the "poem") from the textual apparatus that surrounds it. In much the same way, athletes and politicians refer to themselves in the third person, as though "Bo Jackson" and "Richard Nixon" were shimmering giant forms distinct from the mortal men who bear their names. This self-doubling is carried out more subtly in Spenser's text, but we can detect it here at the margin that divides the "poem" from its frame. It appears, for instance, in the discrepancy between the present tense implicit in "Loe" and the past perfect tense of "I have made": the difference between these two tenses is the difference between text and poem. No calendar can chart a moment in which they coincide, yet together these alternatives make up the surreptitious movement by which the text points to its imaginary presence, shuttling itself backward to forecast and forward to recollect an unreal but familiar *now*.

The author, the work, and their moment of presence are fictions, woven with great subtlety by the rhetoric of grammar. They seem so plausible, so familiar, because they echo our sense of our own presence as witnesses. The imaginary *now* of the text coincides with and lends substance to the equally fictitious *now* in which we read. Perhaps the most unsettling implication of this argument is that we ourselves, like the author and the work, are never entirely *there*, fully present to ourselves or others, in any one moment of existence—unless by way of illusions like those we have traced in Spenser's text. Author, reader, work, and the fanciful chronology they share make up a sort of interdependent fictional community, a knot of mutually supportive fantasies that emerge from the text by bearing imaginary witness to one another.

Spenser repeats the "Loe" that closes *The Shepheardes Calender* in the first words of *The Faerie Queene*: "Lo I the man." In the shift from "I have made" to "I the man," we glimpse with special clarity the createdness of the author *as* author—made by what he has made. The "I" is therefore identified by what he has written ("the man, whose Muse whilome did maske"), and by what he is about to write ("now enforst a far unfitter taske"). Before he wrote he was no one, the empty *I* of the *Calender*'s "Immerito." But between prologue and envoy, the *I* of Immerito gains merit. Hence the concluding motto, *Merce non mercede*, revises the pseudonym in offering to exchange the poem for the *merce* Immerito has acquired. Now, however, even as he steps out from behind the mask of obscurity to collect the reward of fame his text has created, the poet is demeaned again by the epic scale of the task ahead. In the execution of that task his "I" will once again be filled and emptied. To judge from the way the poem will end, alienated from the imperial Gaze in which it had sought its glorified reflection, this may be the only "wisemens threasure" (VI.xii.41) produced by textual work: a plenty that impoverishes the worker, expanding his fame to the far reaches of an imperial future while reducing him to the wisp of a vertical stroke.

The proper name of this worker was "Spenser." Derived by way of the older form "Despencer" from the French *despencier*, this name refers to the household office of presiding over the "spence," the buttery or cellar. Spenser's contemporaries sometimes referred to him punningly as "the Muses' dispenser." In such puns, the man and his name disappear into the act of writing: Spenser, de-Spenser, dispenser, a name that empties itself.

If author, reader, and work bear witness to one another, then when one dissolves the others must fade with it. A textual analysis that picks apart the illusion of presence as I have tried to do with Spenser's "Loe" may therefore seem perverse. We have an understandable affection for readerly images that answer our need for self-recognition, and an aversion to the thought that what we recognize as ourselves may be a deeply internalized illusion. The more alienated we are from the public life of our culture, the more we fall back on the reality of individual experience.

This may be why Colin Clout's vision on Mount Acidale has had so much appeal for modern readers. Our preoccupation with the dance of the Graces testifies to the power of our belief in, and our need for, a uniquely personal space of refuge—a space that, however besieged, remains finally uncontaminated by the alienating conditions of social and political life in a consumer paradise haunted by the specters of war, poverty, plague, famine, rape, terrorism, and genocide. Hence the modernist reading of Colin's vision celebrates a retreat from politics into the quiet harbor of intimacy. In the latest, and in some ways the most attractive, version of this reading, Theresa Krier hears Spenser voicing "a need more clearly to demarcate boundaries between political and private . . . and to mediate these two spheres with a more subtle and delicate practice of courtly manners than was available in much of Book V."[3] Clearly this view of Book VI speaks to our desire for socially intimate spaces in which to recover a candor absent from public life. If, as Krier suggests, the encounter between Tristram and Calidore in canto ii "transcends defense by acknowledging it, making possible the full witness and radiant disclosure of identity," then it enacts a wish we share with Spenser: a wish to domesticate the alienating Gaze of a social order we no longer believe in. Retreating into the more manageable confines of the personal, we transform the Gaze into what Leo Braudy calls "the social version of a love that absolves the loved one of all fault, restoring integrity and wholeness."[4]

3. Theresa M. Krier, *Gazing on Secret Sights: Spenser, Classical Imitation, and the Decorums of Vision* (Ithaca: Cornell UP, 1990) 223. Subsequent quotations from 230, 225.
4. Leo Braudy, *The Frenzy of Renown: Fame and Its History* (New York: Oxford UP, 1986) 7.

The problem with reading Spenser on the common ground of this desire is its limited capacity, indeed its refusal, to reckon how thoroughly the most private of spaces is pervaded by the public discourses privacy seeks to exclude. The modernist reading has cherished Book VI as a blessed relief from what Krier calls "the unwieldy social structures and the darker vision of Book V," a retreat from "political structures" to "the social premises and relations that underlie those structures." The deft negotiation of social relations may foster satisfying moments of intimacy, and perhaps this is the only justification it requires. But negotiation—even the negotiation of *otium*—cannot transcend the relations it negotiates, and it certainly cannot produce an epiphany of the personal subject, a "radiant disclosure of identity." Drawn by this fantasy of radiant epiphany, the modernist reading distinguishes so firmly between political structures and "the social premises and relations that underlie those structures" that it fails to recognize how political structures enclose, sustain, and enter into the spaces of personal intimacy precisely by way of those same premises and relations.

When critical judgments about fictional courtesy appear generous and perceptive—as they do in many accounts of Book VI—they do so in the same way as Calidore himself: on the basis of a retreat from "politics"— that realm of bad faith and abusive judgments—to a more manageable theater of sociality, the small circle of the personal. Yet much modern criticism has found Calidore's tact wanting, and this record of conflicting judgments must give us pause: in an important sense, it reenacts the central dilemma of Book VI, for it reintroduces precisely the element of public judgment, with all its multiple and conflicting assumptions about value, which the retreat into intimacy had sought to escape. In a pattern that pervades both the narrative and the criticism of Book VI, every effort to retreat from public scrutiny prompts an invasion by that scrutiny in another form.

The invidious eye that embodies this invasive scrutiny cannot be evaded: its elusiveness is only the other side of its omnipresence. It may seem to be decisively embodied in the queen, who is indeed a privileged wielder of the imperial Gaze. But the concentration of political regard in a preeminent figure coexists in sixteenth-century England with a relative destabilization of social and economic status. The same forces of historical change that made status more attainable for "new men" (or for the "new Poet") under the Tudor monarchs, also rendered status *as such* less secure: they tended to erode the illusion that the social and economic hierarchy was transcendent, unchanging, and divinely ordained. Whigham suggests that this relative destabilizing of the social hierarchy tended to undermine the myth of a supreme witness, embodied in the crown, whose recognition guaranteed one's status. The Gaze thus came to seem less transcendent, less securely anchored in the pinnacle of the hierarchy. It came to be felt instead as socially immanent, instanced in all the particular others who surround the individual, but anchored in none of them.

This evanescence of the social witness, corresponding to a dispersal of the origin and guarantee of status, appears in Book VI as the Blatant Beast, a figure of rumor who charges in from nowhere to inflict his wound and

vanishes just as quickly. It appears also in the Hermit's advice to Calepine
and Serena after they have been bitten by the Beast:

> The best (sayd he) that I can you advize
> Is to avoide the occasion of the ill:
> For when the cause, whence evill doth arize,
> Removed is, th'effect surceaseth still.
>
> (vi. 14)

The hermit's conflation of cause and occasion reflects an unhappy sense
that with slander, the occasion *is* the cause. The bleak counsel that
follows—abstain from pleasure, restrain your will, subdue desire, bridle
delight, scant your diet, shun secrecy—is profoundly defensive. The sheer
hedonism of Mount Acidale is so attractive because it concentrates and
restores like a gift all the pleasure, privacy, and relieved escape from censure
that the hermit here so austerely repudiates.

Damaged reputations are represented in Book VI as wounded bodies.
This body metaphor is important because it supports the notion of the
subject's social being as something integral, capable of appearing as an
object for the Gaze. The Blatant Beast is Gloriana's dark side because we
fear the wounding power of the Gaze as much as we seek its approval. In
a historical context marked not only by the increased preeminence of the
crown but also by a destabilizing of social status, the wounding or exposure
of one's imaginary social self is perhaps no more threatening than its fragmentation, its dispersal in the multiple mirrors of public discourse, where
the unity and stability of an imaginary body are exactly what reputation
cannot secure. Strange then as it may seem, canto viii's dreadful image of
Serena stripped before the gourmandizing gaze of the cannibals may express
desire as well as horror. Hence, perhaps, the giddy mixture of hilarity and
paranoia that marks the tone of the episode: it offers a peculiar intensification
of that imaginary presence before the objectifying Gaze which is feared but
also desired. We might, for instance, compare the way John Donne in his
religious poems seems drawn to fantasies of exposure, humiliation, punitive
violence, and even ravishing, in an intensely charged personal encounter
with God.

Serena's nakedness is sharply contrasted with that of the maidens on
Mount Acidale. The clearing in which Colin Clout pipes differs from the
other invaded hollows of Book VI because what appears to Colin is precisely
not another person but something else: whatever it is another person's
intrusion instantly dispels. This something is signified by nakedness not as
exposure, but as an ideal of pure unselfconscious display, free of all reticence
or alienation before the Gaze of the other. Yet as John Guillory remarks,
for the reader "that presence is already *there* and not here."[5] The Graces
dance naked, but we as readers are clothed in self-consciousness, able to
recognize but not experience the sheer candor of Edenic innocence. The
episode thus alludes to an experience it cannot render: in Guillory's words
again, "we do not hear what Colin Clout sings, only that he is singing."
Yet if we cannot as readers or social beings join the visionary dance, this

---

5. John Guillory, *Poetic Authority: Spenser, Milton, and Literary History* (New York: Columbia UP,
   1983) 43.

does not mean we have never experienced such freedom. We know it from our dreams. There and only there do we cease to exist *for others* and experience instead something like pure being. Whigham observes that to be strikingly unselfconscious in a courtly milieu would be a sign not of candor but of power, a way of embodying for an audience the supreme indifference of the imaginary Other. To dream, however, is not to signify or allude to the candor of Edenic innocence but to *become its subject.*

When Colin tries to identify the country lass at the center of the dance, she takes on the mysterious quality of a dream figure, at once vague and vivid, concretely herself and obscurely something much more:

> Who can aread, what creature she mote be,
> Whether a creature, or a goddess graced
> With heavenly gifts from heaven first enraced?
> But what so sure she was, she worthy was,
> To be the fourth with those three other placed:
> Yet she all other countrey lasses farre did passe.
>
> (x. 23)

Like Shakespeare's dream weaver Bottom, Colin seems at once baffled by what he wants to say and absolutely sure of it.

One thing is certain about Colin's mistress: she is not Gloriana. The fairy queen came once to Arthur in a dream (I.ix), but since then he has sought her in the public world of action and reputation. Elsewhere in Book I the Graces dance to Redcrosse in a dream, but they lead forth a demon spirit as the false image of Una, his bride (i. 48). This repudiation of dream in Book I is part of Spenser's effort to invest Queen Elizabeth as a symbol of Protestant nationalism with all the cryptic glamor of the dreamed other, at once bride, church, and personal truth: a woman clothed with the sun. By the mid 1590s, however, Spenser's dream of the fairy queen is drawing closer to Shakespeare's: a lunar dowager who withers out young men's revenues. In Book VI, then, Spenser detaches Elizabeth from the feminine figure his dreams embrace. Arthur the last time we see him is sleeping once more, his nap interrupted like Colin's vision. Sleep now looks like the only way he can find the fairy queen.

This alienation from public life leads to a powerful investment in the emergent social ideal of personal privacy.[6] In effect Spenser undoes the "Loe" that staged his epiphany to the imperial Gaze, and seeks instead a private arena to which he can summon the self he has labored to fashion ("who knowes not Colin Clout?"). In Book VI therefore he turns toward the provisional enclosures of personal intimacy. He seeks to endow these spaces with the magnetism of the unconscious self, the subject in us that dreams at the origin of all desire and for whose loss the conscious mind feels a deep nostalgia.

When he links the absolute privacy of dreams to the social space of personal intimacy in this way, Spenser helps to sanction one of our culture's most powerful myths: the myth of a personal core which, however fragile,

6. On the changing status of privacy, see A *History of Private Life*, vol. 3: *The Passions of the Renaissance*, ed. Roger Chartier, trans. Arthur Goldhammer (Cambridge: Harvard UP, 1989).

exists outside of and prior to the order of politics. Such a myth is not without value, as a consolation for political alienation and as a basis for personal intimacy. But at the present historical moment—a time, for instance, when both feminism and psychoanalysis have labored to retrace persistently mis-recognized connections between political structures, "the social premises and relations that underlie those structures," and the intimate spaces of personal subjectivity—we may feel some ambivalence about the fascination Book VI has exercised over a generation of readers. We may wish to seek a stricter, less accommodating account of its poetic magic. To do so is not to deny its appeal but, in good Spenserian fashion, to be "wary wise" about just what in us responds to such an appeal. It is to be uneasy, perhaps, about the vision of ourselves to which Colin's piping calls us.

DONALD CHENEY

The Titaness Put Down†

By their relation to the six completed Books of *The Faerie Queene*, the *Cantos of Mutabilitie* invite consideration as a coda summarizing and restating the meaning of the poem. Though some critics have found logical or numerological significance in their attribution to a central position in some seventh Book,[1] they are so different stylistically from what has gone before that attempts to extrapolate any further development of the poem seem largely futile.[2] What is particularly novel is their adoption of an Ovidian prosopopoeia (in VII.vi.1–35) so extended as to entail a unique degree of dramatic irony; readers have variously assessed the tone in ac-cordance with their predilections for a sentimental or a doctrinal reading of Spenser. It is enlightening to consider this fragment in relation to the motifs treated in earlier chapters of this study, in an attempt to suggest the balance of emphases maintained through Spenser's dialectic.

The program of the *Cantos* is enunciated in their opening stanza:

> What man that sees the euer-whirling wheele
>   Of *Change*, the which all mortall things doth sway,
>   But that therby doth find, and plainly feele,
>   How *MVTABILITY* in them doth play
>   Her cruell sports, to many mens decay?
>   Which that to all may better yet appeare,
>   I will rehearse that whylome I heard say,
>   How she at first her selfe began to reare,
> Gainst all the Gods, and th'empire sought from them to beare.
>
> (VII.vi.1)

† From *Spenser's Image of Nature: Wild Man and Shepherd in "The Faerie Queene"* (New Haven, 1966) 239–47. The original footnotes have been slightly edited. Reprinted by permission of the Yale University Press.
1. See Alastair Fowler, "Numerical Composition in *The Faerie Queene*," *Journal of the Warburg and Courtauld Institutes* 25 (1962): 199–239 (repr. in *Spenser and the Numbers of Time* [London, 1964] 24–33).
2. See Northrop Frye, "The Structure of Imagery in *The Faerie Queene*," *UTQ* 30 (1961): 111.

The process of personification is deftly illustrated in the transition from abstract to proper noun. The impersonal relative pronoun "which" in the second line may refer to the wheel of Change, but the logic of the metaphor makes it more likely that Change is swaying mortal things. By the middle of the stanza mutability has received a weak personification (as seen in the "Her" of line 5); but since the poet is still appealing to human experience of the phenomenon, the noun is felt to be essentially abstract. In offering his twice-told legend of mutability, however, Spenser gives substance and human shape to the abstraction. The legendary status which he bestows on her—"Her antique race and linage ancient"—is further expressed in terms of this same controlling irony: though all is flux, her genealogy has been preserved "In *Faery* Land mongst records permanent."

Mutabilitie is therefore a product of the allegorical imagination, as much so as Isis and Osiris were in Spenser's description (V.vii.1ff.) of their worship. She derives from the race of Titans, who figure in Spenser's references as the irrational, anarchic generation which preceded the Olympian pantheon. Like her sisters, Hecate and Bellona, she is associated with the dark, destructive, intuitive forces within the personality. Her proud rebellion against divine authority inevitably bears overtones of Satan's and Adam's. At the same time, the power and authority of the Titans, delegated to them by Jove after his mastery of them (VII.vi.3), suggest the limitations of the fallen world:

> O pittious worke of MVTABILITIE!
> By which, we all are subject to that curse,
> And death in stead of life haue sucked from our Nurse.
> (VII.vi.6)

The terms of Mutabilitie's initial presentation imply two contrary emphases. On the one hand it is true that she is seen here in her largest dimensions, that Spenser presents her "darkest implications"[3] in describing her ancestry and her assault on the heavens. But the very superhuman and supernatural scope of her ambition subjects her to a consequent loss in imaginative power. The first half of canto vi is in effect a statement of the problem in semantics which Mutabilitie's challenge involves. The Olympians are being challenged in two senses simultaneously. As astronomical figures within the circle of Creation, they are to some extent subject to change, both in terms of their regularly changing positions and shapes in the heavens, and in their more alarmingly erratic behavior, as Spenser lamented earlier (V.Proem). As anthropomorphic deities they are burdened with the frailties of human imagination in this same way.[4] But as images of man's positive impulses to control and order they are as much a part of his universe as his negative, demonic, "lower" impulses. Mutabilitie's principal claim here remains moot, but she does succeed in demonstrating that Jove is "no equall judge."

The tone of this first third of the *Cantos* is thus one of a detached, ironic

3. Sherman Hawkins, "Mutabilitie and the Cycle of the Months," in *Form and Convention in the Poetry of Edmund Spenser*, English Institute Essays (New York, 1961), 84.
4. In this Spenser may be indebted to Lucretius or Bruno (*Spaccio de la Bestia Trionfante*), both of whom stressed the "bestial" elements of classical myth.

wit. After the appeal to human experience in the opening lines, there is no further attempt to make her meaningful in human terms. She has, indeed, left the human world and ascended to dizzying heights of abstraction. Conventional formulae, appropriate to the style and subject of this heroic quest, provide ironic commentary on her absurdity. She has climbed to the moon, "Where *Cynthia* raignes in euerlasting glory";[5]

> And by her side, there ran her Page, that hight
> *Vesper*, whom we the Euening-starre intend:
> That with his Torche, still twinkling like twylight,
> Her lightened all the way where she should wend,
> And ioy to weary wandring trauailers did lend:
> (VII.vi.9)

The moon and planets continue to exist; the reader has no serious doubt as to any physical change in the constitution of the cosmos. Mutabilitie is arguing that the planets should henceforth be read as symbols not of changeless order, but of Change itself. The amazement with which the Olympians react to her presence seems a result less of her monstrosity than of her resemblance to themselves:

> Whil'st she thus spake, the Gods that gaue good eare
> To her bold words, and marked well her grace,
> Beeing of stature tall as any there
> Of all the Gods, and beautifull of face,
> As any of the Goddesses in place,
> Stood all astonied, like a sort of Steeres;
> Mongst whom, some beast of strange and forraine race,
> Vnwares is chaunc't, far straying from his peeres:
> So did their ghastly gaze bewray their hidden feares.
> (VII.vi.28)

It is her beauty which conquers at this first interview: a beauty which inspires Jove to mellowness, but which also suggests the close family relationship between the Olympians and their excluded cousins.

The debate between Mutabilitie and Jove is thus controlled by its conflicting levels of meaning. As a dispute between opposing branches of the descendants of Uranus, it quickly resolves itself into a search for a competent forum. As a challenge to the "heavenly" (or ideal) status of celestial bodies, it questions the inherent dignity of gods so extensively created in the image of man. Jove's posturings are made to seem merely bombastic, the futile efforts of a tyrant and usurper to appeal to conservative values. Mutabilitie's chief advantage over him is her singleness of meaning. Her name expresses her nature fully and directly, whereas the names of the gods are emblems to be unfolded—proper names pretending to abstract values. Ultimately the Olympians and the Titans are equally the creatures of the human imagination; but Mutabilitie's dominance here suggests that the legendary figure loses his claim to a role as symbol of permanence in proportion as

---

5. To a contemporary reader, of course, these formulae might bear an added relevance to his queen, Ralegh's Cynthia, whose motto, *Semper eadem*, could represent a further gesture of defiance to Mutabilitie's claims.

he is shaped and defined in human terms, by the proliferation of legend. Mutabilitie is temporarily the stronger for her lack of circumstantial history; what eventually silences her is the contradiction inherent in her claim to omnipotence. Her role may be conceived rather as that of antithesis in an unending dialectical struggle; and it is thus that Nature will finally define her.

The Nature to whom she submits her appeal constitutes a new concept within the world previously adumbrated by the *Cantos*. Jove had seemed supreme, the equivalent even of the Christian God in proportion as Mutabilitie had suggested parallels with Satan and Adam. But now Mutabilitie introduces a broader context:

> But to the highest him, that is behight
> Father of Gods and men by equall might;
> To weet, the God of Nature, I appeale.
> (VII.vi.35)

It would be difficult to find in classical myth any authority for the cosmology which is being presented here. It does not help particularly to cite, as commentators have done,[6] the Homeric Hymn in which Jupiter is described as a supreme god of universal nature, both male and female in his embodiment of active and passive principles; for Mutabilitie's point here is precisely that the Jove of these cantos is not such a god. Rather, the God of Nature to which she refers is superior to men and the Olympians alike; as she confesses later, "even the gods to thee, as men to gods do seeme" (VII.vii.15). When classical writings refer to a single supreme God of Nature, they generally do so without prejudice to the Olympian pantheon. Spenser's Nature, as his reference to Alanus hints (VII.vii.9), brings the reader back to the world of allegorical personification introduced in the opening stanzas of the *Cantos*. Her veiled face, like Una's or that of Venus (with its similar hint of hermaphroditism, IV.x.40–41), suggests the dazzling brilliance of the transfigured Christ: her radiance combines the worlds of Pagan and Neoplatonic conventions, to produce a nexus of meaning characteristic of Spenser's syncretism. But her obscure form enables her to approach the paradoxes traditionally assigned to the Christian God:

> Great Nature, euer young yet full of eld,
> Still moouing, yet vnmoued from her sted;
> Vnseene of any, yet of all beheld.
> (VII.vii.13)

In the orderly pageants assembled by Mutabilitie as a demonstration of her case, Spenser demonstrates simultaneously the arguments for and against the dominance of Change in man's world. Not only the completeness of her cyclical parades (which anatomize change so fully as to suggest the pattern which informs it) but the individual forms within them—the tropes which hearken back to the traditional human search for order within Nature—lead the reader, as spectator and judge alongside Nature herself, to the conclusion that

6. *Variorum* 6, 281–82.

> . . . being rightly wayd
> They are not changed from their first estate;
> But by their change their being doe dilate:
> And turning to themselues at length againe,
> Doe worke their owne perfection so by fate:
> Then ouer them Change doth not rule and raigne;
> But they raigne ouer change, and doe their states maintaine.
>
> (VII.vii.58)[7]

Yet Spenser has preceded this climactic scene on Arlo Hill with a definition of the world in which the confrontation is to take place. The pastoral
and comic interlude at the end of canto vi constitutes a crucial element in
the tripartite structure of the *Cantos*. The lower style contrasts with the
heroic terms of Mutabilitie's quest; the effect is not simply to deflate Mutabilitie herself by parodying her folly in the voyeurism of Faunus, but to
give a new, humbler reality to her sublunary existence. The heroic style
in the first half of the canto had shown a continual risk of degenerating
into mock-epic, for the titaness (rather like Milton's Satan) had been manipulating abstractions too broad and slippery for her control. But in the
Faunus episode Mutabilitie is no longer an active character; rather, she
figures indirectly and thematically, scaled down to the level of an Ovidian
metamorphosis. Here Cynthia appears in another aspect, as Diana, driven
by the sniggering bestiality of Faunus into a destruction of her terrestrial
bower. Like Astraea, she abandons the stony world of man, leaving behind
a wilderness as the more accurate pattern of man's habitat:

> Them all, and all that she so deare did way,
>   Thence-forth she left; and parting from the place,
>   There-on an heauy haplesse curse did lay,
>   To weet, that Wolues, where she was wont to space,
>   Should harbour'd be, and all those Woods deface,
>   And Thieues should rob and spoile that Coast around.
>   Since which, those Woods, and all that goodly Chase,
>   Doth to this day with Wolues and Thieues abound:
> Which too-too true that lands in-dwellers since haue found.
>
> (VII.vi.55)

In this tragicomic incident the catastrophes are averted: Faunus' punishment
recalls Actaeon's but stops short of his death; Molanna's stoning does not
keep her from a watery union with the Fanchin. Spenser is demonstrating
here a highly dexterous control of his subject matter, to the extent that it
seems pompous to speak of a serious meaning to the episode. He has reduced
the scope of man's subjection to change to the level of the housewife crying
over spilt milk in her dairy (VII.vi.48), and to the uncomfortable but
unsurprising reality of a savage wilderness surrounding man's efforts at
civilization. The figure of the poet, lamenting this as "too-too true," provides a graceful frame for the whole canto, and defines the human relevance
of the pageants which follow in canto vii.

The overall effect of the *Cantos* is that of a stylistic tour de force, for
the triadic narrative pattern (epic, pastoral, didactic synthesis) is vastly en-

---

7. This aspect of the *Cantos* has been traced in detail by Hawkins, "Mutabilitie," pp. 76–102.

riched and complicated by a delicately ironic balance of tone within each of these three sections. At no point is the reader permitted to forget the mixture of opposing attitudes with which Mutabilitie is being viewed. One pole of this opposition is the Christian *contemptus mundi*, the feeling of exhaustion and disdain for this world and intense longing for the combination of absolute delight and absolute rest to be found through death in the "Sabaoths sight" hinted by Nature. At the other pole is the artist's delight in the inexhaustible variety and movement of his creation: a delight which is apparent from the moment he begins to unfold his legend, in the effortless tracery of his stanza as in the *copia* with which character, incident, and theme are anatomized. It seems supremely appropriate that the poem should begin and end with a celebration of the seasonal and diurnal cycles, in imitation of the larger creation:

> Loe I haue made a Calendar for euery yeare,
> That steele in strength, and time in durance shall outweare.
> (S.C. Dec. 235–36)

The poet's triumph over a recalcitrant reality lies in his imitation of its complexity, in his celebration of the endless pattern of oppositions by which the worlds of physical nature and of man's moral nature are to be conceived. Critics who tend to dismiss Spenser's allegory as an incomplete or onesided presentation of reality seem radically insensitive to this aspect of the poem. It is the poem's richness, its refusal to reduce its world to any neat conceptual pattern, or to exclude any discordant impulse when it arises, which must in the end constitute its chief claim to imaginative validity.

VIEWS OF PASTORAL

ISABEL MacCAFFREY: [The Shepheardes Calender]†

To read the large-scale masterpieces of Elizabethan literature with something of the agility they assume and demand is an art which must be self-consciously cultivated by us today. *The Shepheardes Calender*, an early, relatively brief essay in a complex mode, provides exercise for our wit in smaller compass. We ought, I believe, to bring to it something of the same resources that we bring to Spenser's larger work. As Ernest de Sélincourt wrote, "It lies along the high-road that leads him to Faery land."[1] It is the product of the same sensibility, and in it we can discern the special proclivities of the poet's imagination: the preference for radical allegory and "iconographical ambiguity";[2] the search for a form that will contain variety and unify it without violating its subtle life-patterns; the exploitation of a

---

† From "Allegory and Pastoral in *The Shepheardes Calender*," *ELH* (1969): 88–109. (The original footnotes have been slightly edited.) Reprinted by permission of The Johns Hopkins University Press.

1. "Introduction," *The Poetical Works of Edmund Spenser*, ed. J. C. Smith and E. de Sélincourt (Oxford Standard Authors, London, 1961), p. xx.
2. C. S. Lewis's useful term for the Renaissance way of reading images, *Studies in Medieval and Renaissance Literature* (Cambridge, 1966), p. 160.

setting that can also serve as a complex controlling metaphor. The great invention of Faerie Land is anticipated by Spenser's evocation of the archetypal hills, valleys, woods, and pastures of the *Calender*.

*   *   *

While it is, I believe, essential to assume that *The Shepheardes Calender* makes sense as a whole, many readings of it, though subtly argued, in the end ignore certain of its elements that may not conform to the proposed pattern. A. C. Hamilton's discussion of the poet's "effort to find himself," R. A. Durr's distinction "between the flesh and the spirit, *amor carnis* and *amor spiritus*," M. C. Bradbrook's thesis that Spenser deals with "the pursuit of honour, surveyed from what was traditionally the lowest of human occupations"—all of these accounts and others, offer us valuable perspectives on Spenser's themes.[3] But all underestimate the power of the poet's imagination, its world-making energy, its drive toward comprehensiveness, its urge to include rather than to exclude meanings.

This energy is visible at the start in Spenser's very choice of forms. His "originality" lay in combining a group of eclogues with a calendar framework, that is, variety with unity.[4] It is a typically Spenserian invention: the two forms neutralize each other's disadvantages and cooperate to produce a structure that uniquely combines symbolic range and resonance with the most fundamental ordering pattern in our experience, the life-cycle itself. The etymology of *eclogue* encourages us to view the separate poems as independent "selections"; the calendar offers the limitation of a circumscribing frame at once linear and cyclical. In consequence, the *Calender* already exhibits the formal paradoxes that confront us in infinite recombination in *The Faerie Queene*: discontinuous continuity, multiple reference, analogical relationships that point simultaneously to likeness and to unlikeness.

These paradoxes are set in motion and contained by the pastoral paradigm, which is to some degree implied by both of the poem's formal components, eclogue and calendar. Development of the implications of pastoral in the early Renaissance had brought it to a point of relative sophistication which was exploited and then notably extended in Spenser's poem. It is important to realize that by the 1570's, the paradigm was not confined exclusively to idyllic themes. Originating in the impulse to criticize artificial and corrupt urban civilization, the pastoral "world" itself was soon infected by that corruption and became in turn the object of critical scrutiny. In the eclogues of Mantuan and Barnabe Googe, the pastoral metaphor is microcosmic, and the preoccupations of fallen man, as well as his vision of unfallen bliss, can be accommodated within it. So, in the *Calender*, Spenser's imagined world includes storms and sunshine, friendly and hostile landscapes, benevolent and ravenous animals, good and bad shepherds, high and low personages. The poet has chosen not to limit himself to the merely idyllic version of pastoral. This choice is reflected in the formal

3. Essays cited are *seriatim*: A. C. Hamilton. "The Argument of Spenser's *Shepheardes Calender*," *ELH*, XXIII (1956), 171–82; R. A. Durr, "Spenser's Calendar of Christian Time," *ELH*, XXIV (1957), 269–95; M. C. Bradbrook, "No Room at the Top: Spenser's Pursuit of Fame," *Elizabethan Poetry*, ed. J. R. Brown and Bernard Harris (London, 1960), pp. 91–109.
4. The generic traditions are outlined by S. K. Heninger, Jr., "The Implications of Form for *The Shepheardes Calender*," *SR*, IX (1962), 309–21.

range of the *Calender*. The decorum of the convention dictated that it move, stylistically, in a temperate zone between the heights of epic and tragedy, and the depths of satirical comedy; the range was wide enough, however, to permit excursions into both these extreme borderlands, as the *Maye* and *October* eclogues demonstrate. The twin concepts of the calendar, with its changing seasons and months, and of the eclogue-group, with its changing metrical and tonal patterns, thus combine with the multiple references of sophisticated pastoral to compose a design of rich potentiality. Above all, this complex literary paradigm offers a context hospitable to allegory; as A. C. Hamilton has said, "the most obvious parallel between the *Calender* and [*The Faerie Queene*] is that each is radically allegorical."[5]

We have to ask, then, what the nature and concern of the allegory may be; and the answer must resemble the answers we devise in commenting on the much more complex allegory of the later poem. Paul McLane has observed that Colin Clout's career is like that of "the main characters of the *Faerie Queene*, most of whom lead a double or triple life on the various levels of the poem."[6] Though the metaphor of "levels" is, I believe, one that we ought to discard in speaking of allegory, McLane's point concerning the multiple life of Colin can be extended to all the major images of the *Calender*. An obvious example is provided by the avatars of Pan, who figures as Henry VIII, as the "God of shepheards all," and as Christ, "the onely and very Pan, then suffering for his flock."[7] These meanings are not equally valid or ultimate, metaphysically, but they are equally potent in the poem, and they imply each other. We lose something by insisting on any single meaning of a Spenserian image, for the reason that all the meanings are related to and shed light on each other. The "statement" incarnate in each thus includes a comment on the relationship of a particular imagining to congruent ones. The *Calender*, like *The Faerie Queene*, is encyclopedic in its design, for Spenser's imagination (like Milton's) is most at home when it is working in a context that can include, or at least allude to, the entire cosmic order. The poem's concern is the nature of human life—our life's shape and quality, its form, its content or "feel," and ultimately its relation to the one life outside and beyond it.

It is this effort at comprehensiveness that makes us uneasy with any single formula for the *Calender*'s meaning, whether religious, social, or metaphysical. Boccaccio's defense of the poet's fictions includes the remark that images are used to "make truths . . . the object of strong intellectual effort and various interpretation."[8] Pope, who thought *The Shepheardes Calender* "sometimes too allegorical," praised the poem's basic metaphor because it allowed Spenser to expose "to his readers a view of the great and little worlds, and their various changes and aspects."[9] He is speaking of the pastoral which, like the calendar frame, encourages, indeed demands, variety of reference; in Puttenham's famous phrase, it was devised "to insinuate

---

5. The *Structure of Allegory in "The Faerie Queene"* (Oxford, 1961), p. 47.
6. *Spenser's "Shepheardes Calender": A Study in Elizabethan Allegory* (Notre Dame, 1961), p. 323.
7. The text of *The Shepheardes Calender* quoted in this essay is that of the Oxford one-volume edition, cited in Note 1. Citations will be to line numbers for the poem, page numbers for prose and gloss. References to Pan are in *Aprill*, p. 434; *December*, 7; *Maye*, p. 439.
8. *Boccaccio on Poetry*, ed. C. G. Osgood (Library of Liberal Arts, New York, 1956), p. 60.
9. *Discourse on Pastoral Poetry*; *Variorum*, p. 574.

and glaunce at greater matters," which, as W. L. Renwick pointed out in the commentary to his edition, could refer to several kinds of subject. "Since all personal and contemporary affairs were proper subject for Pastoral, the interpretation of the simple allegory is various: the shepherds are poets, scholars, governors, ecclesiastics, by a series of easy allusions."[1] All of these matters, in Spenser's imagination, involved each other; each area of "meaning" overlaps with the others, and each alone can offer only an incomplete statement concerning human life.

Renaissance and medieval ontology provided, of course, a rationale for a literature of multiple significances. In a world of concentric realities, a single metaphor could touch several circumferences in one trajectory; intersecting a number of different but analogous worlds, it could speak of church, of state, of poetry, of the individual soul's destiny, of divine providence as manifested in the cosmic pattern. It is well to remind ourselves of this relationship between the literature and the "world picture" of the Elizabethans, for although it has now become a cliché, it lends point to the choice of allegory as the vehicle for major works by Spenser and others, as well as to the development of a drama with broad symbolic resources. For Spenser, the interlocking complexities of reality could only be rendered accurately in a sequence of metaphors susceptible of simultaneous reference—that is, the continued metaphor of allegory.

The Shepheardes Calender, then, as Spenser's first attempt to devise a "visionary geography,"[2] must be read as an anticipation of his greatest work. The formal differences between the two poems are, of course, obvious. The continuousness of the metaphor in the *Calender* is not that of narrative; the poem "has a situation but no plot."[3] The ground-metaphor of *The Faerie Queene* is the chivalric world of Faerie Land, a place where lives unfold and journeys are traced. Time dominates the *Calender* not as the medium of narrative, but as a geometric pattern which may be described schematically as a circle intersected by linear tracks. The space of the poem is an imagined space whose emblematic features conform to the particular circumstances of each eclogue and are related to those of other eclogues, both adjacent and remote. All of them are drawn from the body of images loosely contained within the pastoral paradigm, but spatial continuity, like narrative line, is not to be insisted upon. The description of the structure by W. W. Greg is still the most comprehensive and objective:

> The architectonic basis of Spenser's design consists of the three Colin eclogues standing respectively at the beginning, in the middle, and at the close of the year. These are symmetrically arranged . . . [and supported] by two subsidiary eclogues, those of April and August, in both of which another shepherd sings one of Colin's lays. . . . It is upon this framework that are woven the various moral, polemical, and idyllic themes which Spenser introduces.[4]

1. *The Shepherd's Calendar*, pp. 164–165.
2. C. S. Lewis, *The Allegory of Love* (Oxford, 1948), p. 260. Lewis points out the necessity of an imagined "world" for fully developed allegory.
3. Durr, "Spenser's Calendar of Christian Time," p. 284.
4. *Pastoral Poetry and Pastoral Drama* (London, 1906), p. 91.

In this geometrical structure, the poem's meaning is figured. As almost every recent critic has said, that meaning somehow concerns man's relation to the cycle of nature.[5] Spenser is considering the degree to which "natural" terms must enter into a definition of what man is; we are made aware of the pattern of human life as biologically cyclical, but also as spiritually transcendent in various directions: hence the design of linear or vertically oriented images intersecting the circular ground-plan. "Man is part of nature, but this world's brief beauty gives him less than he asks, and though he loves it he needs to look beyond it. . . . For us the natural cycle is in itself the way of death, and we will gain life only by looking to the cycle's source."[6]

The character whose life is defined by these patterns, as Greg's description properly points out, is Colin Clout. Yet exclusive concentration on Colin may obscure Spenser's purpose; if this hero is a pilgrim, he never attains the Heavenly City, and it is left to other voices to define for us the alternatives to the life within "nature" figured by Colin's career. His life is congruent with the circle's movement toward "experience" and imminent death. He is an antihero, his unredeemed existence tracing a movement which defines the failure of man to realize his *own* nature. Colin recognizes that submission to the seasonal round has led only to death: "So now my yeare drawes to his latter terme" (*Dec.* 127); his life has passed like a dream, and bidding adieu to the "delightes, that lulled me asleepe" (151), he is left alone in a winter landscape.

Colin's uncompleted quest for understanding is expressed in the poem by a sequence of changes in the relationship between nature and man, devised with a good deal of subtlety by Spenser to provide simultaneously a commentary upon and a critique of the macrocosm / microcosm analogy at the root of the pastoral paradigm. The *Calender* begins in January, principally so that Spenser may stress the circular pattern by framing his poem with "winter" ecologues.[7] Since *Januarye* is also the first stage in Spenser's critique of his analogical base, we must see man and nature in it as congruent. Hence, when the poem begins, the protagonist has already suffered disillusionment as the result of love-longing; "his carefull case" resembles "the sadde season of the yeare," as the Argument painstakingly indicates. In fact, we are to see Colin in unwounded innocence only through the reminiscences of other shepherds. The Colin of *Januarye*, however, is still a *literary* innocent; in making his comparison between careful case and sad season, he uses the metaphor of the mirror,[8] indicating that for him the macrocosm still reflects accurately the little world of man, offering valid analogies for his inner state:

5. See Durr, "Spenser's Calendar," pp. 290–99; and Hamilton's discussion of the theme of "the dedicated life where man does not live according to Nature but seeks escape out of Nature," "The Argument," pp. 175–76.
6. Kathleen Williams, *Spenser's World of Glass* (Berkeley and Los Angeles, 1966), p. 203. Miss Williams' succinct pages on the *Calender* in this book outline a view of the poem close to the one I am arguing in many respects.
7. Heninger discusses this aspect of the structure, "a pattern repeated endlessly throughout eternity," in "The Implications of Form," p. 317.
8. For an excellent analysis of these stanzas of *Januarye*, see Hallett Smith, *Elizabethan Poetry* (Cambridge, Mass., 1952), p. 35.

> And from mine eyes the drizling teares descend,
> As on your boughes the ysicles depend. (41–42)

In *December*, Colin reflects on life and death, finally recognizing, and despairingly accepting, the fundamental incongruity of man and nature. His Muse is "hoarse and weary"; his pipe is hung up on a tree (140–41).

> And I, that whilome wont to frame my pype,
> Vnto the shifting of the shepheards foote:
> Sike follies nowe haue gathered as too ripe
> And cast hem out, as rotten and vnsoote.
>   (115–18)

Those aspects of his life which indicate its congruence with nature are unsatisfying or inadequate to the demands made upon them. The old Colin is wise in nature's ways; he has learned "the soothe of byrds" and "the power of herbs," yet this knowledge is of no avail in curing his "ranckling wound."

> But ah vnwise and witlesse *Colin cloute*,
> That kydst the hidden kinds of many a wede:
> Yet kydst not ene to cure thy sore hart roote,
> Whose ranckling wound as yet does rifelye bleede.
>   (91–94)

The metaphor of unripeness, which Milton was later to develop in the opening lines of *Lycidas*, insists that fulfilment for man cannot be looked for within the cycle.

> The flatring fruite is fallen to grownd before,
> And rotted, ere they were halfe mellow ripe.
>   (106–7)

The life of Colin Clout, then, traces for us the line of human life as it diverges psychologically from the life of nature, while remaining physically bound to it. The event which allows this divergence to manifest itself is a familiar one in pastoral poetry from Theocritus to Marvell. It is love, the disturber of pastoral harmony, a metaphor for the troubling of human life which we call sin—that is, the dominance of passion. It is, as Colin says, the result of pride: "But ah such pryde at length was ill repayde" by Cupid (*Dec.* 49). In consequence the orderly cycle of human life is turned awry, its promise blasted. * * * Images of tempest, drought, insomnia, and withered grass became appropriate figures for man's fallen state, the seasons' difference that signifies the penalty of Adam. In the Argument to *December* Colin's "summer" is meteorologically described: "which he sayth, was consumed with greate heate and excessiue drouth caused throughe a Comet or blasinge starre, by which he meaneth loue, which passion is comenly compared to such flames and immoderate heate." Colin himself repeats the point:

> A comett stird vp that vnkindly heate,
> That reigned (as men sayd) in *Venus seate*.
>   (59–60)

The congruence between man's nature and external nature is violently reestablished in a baleful conjunction of planets and passions; the analogy becomes a kind of parody upon the harmonious prelapsarian unity. * * * Sin * * * condemns man to live in an unsheltered world, hostile and uncongenial, characterized by unhappy love, alienation from God, and finally, the despair of December. * * * The notion of an environment that is hostile to man is, of course, one of the insights of experience, which moves from "soft" to "hard" pastoral. Spenser traces this process in the dialogue between youth and age in Februarie; and it is figuratively reiterated by Colin, looking back over his life [quotes December 67–72]. The emblem of an orderly nature that offers a model for man gives way to the décor of death. In fact, Nature is a threat to man, who must assume with respect to it an attitude of constant vigilance. The darkest eclogue [of the Calender] is September where the theme of the watchful shepherd is presented in the fable of Roffyn and the wolf. * * *

[But] immediately following the nadir of September, the Calender takes an upward turn. If we look at the structure as a whole, not merely at the Colin "plot," we can observe Spenser causing his form to cooperate with his theme. As E.K. observes, October and Nouember are in a higher mood than any of the eclogues that preceded them (with the exception of the Aprill lay). We ought to take seriously his epithet for October, "loftye", high flight is the motif of both these poems, "vertical" imagery prevails, and both anticipate escape from that wheel of "miseree" to which September saw men bound. Yet both poems belong to "the cold season," and thus mark, structurally, a divergence between the declining seasonal round and the uplifting powers of the human imagination. Though both include laments—for the decay of poetry and the death of Dido—both also show the means of transcendence and escape from these disasters. Within "nature," spring follows the cold season; within human life, there is a movement not identical, but analogous. In Nouember, the pattern is familiar, inevitable in a Christian pastoral elegy: La mort ny mord, death is "the grene path way to lyfe." In October, the solution is secular and less final, but it turns on a similar paradox: love, the source of human distress and a figure for man's fall into sin, is at the same time the pathway to regained Paradise. The design of the two poems is the same—out of suffering springs joy and release—and both are thus "answers" to Diggon's question, "What shall I doe?" in September; both demonstrate that escape from the wheel is possible. The impeccable poetic logic supports E.K.'s description of the Calender as "finely framed, and strongly trussed vp together."

The poem's final movement, then, as Durr has said, "declares that man cannot, like the other creatures, live his life in accordance with the seasonal round."[9] But Spenser's analysis of human life involves neither an ascetic disdain for the pleasures of the temporal world, nor a "rejection" of pastoral. Rather, those pleasures are defined and confirmed with relation to an ultimately religious sanction; and the power of the pastoral paradigm is reaffirmed as having metaphorical validity. Like Milton in Lycidas, Spenser forces upon us the unwilling recognition that we can never regain Paradise

9. "Spenser's Calendar," p. 290.

literally. * * * The meaning of both *Lycidas* and *The Shepheardes Calender* concerns the need for us to accept a nonliteral, invisible reality[1] as the one most relevant to us as human beings. This reality, in both poems, is defined in the Christian terms conventional for pastoral elegy; in *October*, it is accessible, as well, to the poetic imagination. Awareness of a nonliteral realm of experience can be made to enlighten our *earthly* lives. * * *

※ ※ ※

The lay of *Aprill*, the third of Colin's songs, is designed, like those in *August* and *Nouember*, to confirm Piers' claim in *October* that love, seconded by imagination, can lift us out of the cycle of death. All three poems offer visions of a world in which reality corresponds to human desires. All are elaborate in form, their higher mood surpassing the reach of ordinary shepherds' wit. In celebrating Eliza, Rosalind, and Dido, Colin must keep decorum with themes that transcend the natural order as he observes it in "reality" in many of the other eclogues. The fox of *Maye*, the wolf of *September*, the "Ambitious brere" of *Februarye*, the lowly pastors of *Iulye*, the disharmonies of *Iune*—all these manifest the nature of fallen being. But *Aprill* and *August* offer visions of possibility, and *Nouember* a glimpse of actuality that transcends all human potentiality. Bacon was later to disparage poets for submitting "the shows of things to the desires of the mind," but as both Sidney and Spenser affirm, those desires themselves bear witness to the presence of a realm of being inadequately figured by the shows of things.

All three of Colin Clout's songs are monuments of wit and demonstrations of its capacities; the *Aprill* lay is, in addition, Spenser's most eloquent depiction of a monument of power, a model that refers to our life on earth. It is a vision of perfection within fallen nature that can be effected by exercising another kind of art. Once our world has become the prey of sin, nature can be restored to something like its original purity only with the aid of civilization, that "nurture" regularly opposed in Elizabethan debates to unaltered "nature." The arts of government can unite antagonists and create another Eden, at least a demi-paradise—the garden of the world, as Elizabeth's poets were fond of calling her kingdom. This world is presented in *Aprill*, where the lay's formal artifice can be taken as a symbol of all the artful patterns that bring order out of chaos. *Aprill* speaks of the work of art, be it a commonwealth, a dance, or a poem; *October* speaks of the maker, "the perfect paterne of a Poete" (p. 456). He can create on earth a mirror, fragile but exact, of the world not as it is but as it might be. The making of golden worlds is the chief function assigned to poetry by Sidney; and it lies behind Piers' description of the poet's heavenly goal in *October*:

> Then make thee winges of thine aspyring wit,
> And, whence thou camst, flye backe to heaven apace.
> (83–4)

In *Nouember* we contemplate the true heavenly garden; in *Aprill* we see a fictive version of its earthly counterpart, transient but potent, created by

---

1. I prefer these terms, vaguer but more comprehensive, to Durr's exclusively religious vocabulary which reduces too radically, in my opinion, the implications of Spenser's metaphors.

poet and queen.[2] Colin's art cooperates with that of "our most gracious souereigne" to produce a golden world in imagination; and this world is capable, as the Envoy to the *Calender* insists, of surviving every catastrophe except the final one: "It shall continewe till the worlds disolution."

The microcosmic character of the lay of *Aprill* hardly requires elaboration. The images create a comprehensive harmony that extends from the flowers on the green to golden Phoebus and silver Cynthia, removed from their "natural" orbits, like the Sun in Donne's *The Sunne Rising*, to circle this little cosmos and do homage to its sustaining power. Here, as in Eden, spring and autumn dance hand in hand and flowers of all seasons blossom together to deck Eliza, whose complexion predictably unites "the Redde rose medled with the White yfere" (68). Joining classical and native strains, as later they were to be joined in *Epithalamion*, nymphs of Helicon dance beside Ladies of the Lake and "shepheards daughters, that dwell on the greene" (127)—the two latter groups figuring, it has been suggested, a union of the spirits of water and land.[3] The "chiefest Nymph" brings the final tribute: a coronal of olive branches, signifying the surcease of war, Eliza's establishment of the Peaceable Kingdom, the Golden Age restored. The *Aprill* lay, though not composed in the heroic mode prescribed by Piers in *October*, speaks of the subjects there recommended, and is presided over by Calliope (100). The epic poet is to turn to

> those, that weld the awful crowne,
> To doubted Knights, whose woundlesse armour rusts,
> And helmes vnbruzed wexen dayly browne.
>
> (Oct., 40–42)

Another incarnation of Elizabeth, Mercilla in *Faerie Queene* V, is also a peaceable ruler; at her feet is a sword "Whose long rest rusted the bright steely brand" (V. ix. 30). The sterner style of epic demands images like those of the rusted armour or sword; and those images, too, remind us that epic treats of life in a harsh and threatened fallen world, where the sword may at any moment be drawn. For the homely yet courtly vision of high pastoral, the coronal of olive is more decorous. Yet both images project an ideal that was often referred to by writers on the arts of government. Spenser's version of it in *Aprill* is a world of possibility created by poetry; Castiglione celebrates princely virtue in *The Courtier* in a congruent allusion:

> That vertue, which perhaps among all the matters that belong unto man is the chiefest and rarest, that is to say, the manner and way to rule and to raigne in the right kinde. Which alone were sufficient to make men happie, and to bring once againe into the world the golden age, which is written to have beene when Saturnus raigned in the olde time.[4]

---

2. "Colin's two songs in the *Calender*, the praise of Elisa and the lament for Dido, give between them the whole situation." Williams, *idem*.
3. W. F. Staton, Jr., "Spenser's 'April' Lay as a Dramatic Chorus," *SP*, LIX (1962), 115. Warton was the first to note the similarity between *April* and the royal entertainments; *Variorum*, pp. 284–85.
4. *The Book of the Courtier*, tr. Thomas Hoby (Everyman's Library, London, 1943), p. 273.

Pastoral imagery finds a new sanction in figuring this happy state, as in *Nouember* its validity was to be confirmed in another direction. The more one reads *The Shepheardes Calender*, the more one is struck by the force of Hallett Smith's judgment that "the pastoral idea, in its various ramifications, *is* the *Calender*."[5] The pastoral paradigm, in the service of a potent and resourceful imagination, proves itself to be a flexible expressive instrument. The serious use of pastoral in the Renaissance, by Spenser and others, received, of course, support from its presence in the Bible and from the central paradox of Christianity where low degree is exalted. So the humblest genre can figure the highest matters. This paradox is exploited by Spenser in a secular context in *Aprill*, where the greatest personage of the land enters the shepherds' country world and hallows it. In turn, that world itself provides emblems supremely apt for figuring the special graces of her reign. There is a union of estates, a little mirror of Gloriana's England—appropriately enough, if we recall that on the twenty-third of the month was celebrated the feast of England's patron saint.

Having tested for himself the resources of one of the basic metaphors of his tradition, Spenser laid aside his pastoral pipe for a time. Already, the queen of shepherds was being metamorphosed into the queen of faerie. Yet pastoral was not abandoned for good; it is absorbed into Faerie Land itself, making an essential contribution to the vast landscape of *The Faerie Queene*. And in one of his last poems, *Colin Clouts Come Home Againe*, Spenser produced a classic example of the pastoral paradigm. Yet in the end, the interest for us of *The Shepheardes Calender* lies not in the pastoral "matter," but in the mode of its handling. De Sélincourt's view of the poem as embodying "a world of Spenser's own" strikes the most relevant note.[6] Formally and thematically, it stands as a characteristic product of this poet's imagination, which from the beginning was a maker of worlds. The *Calender* is an ambitious, encyclopedic allegory, controlled by a metaphor that is capable of sustaining a complex *significatio*. Spenser's powers were to develop far beyond the point which they had attained in 1579; particularly in the matter of inventing a narrative, he had much to learn. Yet this early work, especially as it offered an opportunity to explore the imagined landscape of an allegorical country, can be seen as an essential prologue to the bold inventions of *The Faerie Queene*, where the romantic world of the medieval storytellers is transformed into a visionary geography of unsurpassed flexibility, enchantment, and expressive power.

HARRY BERGER, JR.: ["The Paradise Principle":
Approaches to *The Shepheardes Calender*]†

Spenser's *Shepheardes Calender* is self-amused pastoral, a critical and comically squint reenactment of attitudes, topics, and norms characteristic of

5. *Elizabethan Poetry*, p. 46.
6. "Introduction," p. xx.
† From "Introduction to *The Shepheardes Calender*," *Revisionary Play: Studies in the Spenserian Dynamics* by Harry S. Berger 277–89. The essay has been slightly condensed. Copyright © 1988 The Regents of the University of California. Reprinted by permission.

a traditional literary mode. If it is "about" the limits of conventionally defined pastoral assumptions and points of view, it is equally "about" forms of sensibility and responses to life restricted enough to fit within those narrow bounds. The fundamental object of Spenser's criticism is the longing for paradise as the psychological basis of the pastoral retreat from life. He presents this longing in dialectical form, inflected either toward wish-fulfilling fantasy or toward bitter rejection of the world that falls short of such fantasy. These two inflections are causally interdependent and mu-tually intensifying: the mind schooled to expect a perfect world of gold or green responds to actuality by painting it pure black and running back to paradise. The longing for paradise is thus expressed in disappointed as well as in unrealistic expectations. I shall borrow some terms from E. K., the speaker whose dedicatory letter, arguments, and glosses frame the eclogues, and call these two inflections the *recreative* and *plaintive* attitudes. The recreative attitude is voiced by those speakers who have found paradise or who are in it and see no reason for leaving it. The plaintive attitude is voiced by those speakers who have lost it, either through thwarted love or through experience of the actual world and its vicissitudes. These attitudes often wear moral disguises—that is, the idyllic is set up as the ideal, what *could* be is converted to what *should* be—and this mystification provides the model compared to which actuality is found wanting.

I shall refer to this recreative/plaintive dynamic as the "paradise *princi-ple*." I do this partly to highlight its kinship to the more familiar pleasure principle, partly to suggest its motivating character as the shaping cause of what appears as a structure, when the *Calender* is approached in synchronic perspective, and as a process or sequence, when it is viewed in diachronic perspective. The structure is a polarity of recreative and plaintive attitudes that may in any instance take the disjunctive form of a conflict or the conjunctive form of ambivalence. The sequence may be variously viewed as an obsessively repeated alternation between paradisal expectations and bitterness, or as a "fall" from the first to the second followed by an effort to return. My reading of the *Calender* will avail itself of both perspectives, but since (as will gradually become clear) the structural view of the paradise principle is closer than the sequential view to recent interpretive trends, I shall generally focus on synchronic polarities before turning to the various aspects of diachronic organization.

We often encounter in both *The Faerie Queene* and the minor poems figures who display various aspects of Spenser's psychology of the have-not. Some examples are Clarion's foe Aragnoll, Mother Hubberd's Fox and Ape, Malbecco, Busirane, Envy, the Blatant Beast, Dame Mutabilitie, and the speaker (not necessarily the author) in several poems, including Book V and the *Mutabilitie Cantos*.[1] Spenser depicts the plaintive condition of the have-not as self-willed submission to Tantalean bitterness and pain in response to loss, deprivation, and the inability to appease the "infinite desyre" of eros. Some offered prospect or hope of paradisal bliss arouses a longing for quick and complete possession that is marked as self-defeating in its hybristic excess, a premature and unrealistic compulsion to assimilate

1. The original list of examples includes figures from poems not represented in this volume; they are omitted here. [*Editors*].

(and so to destroy) the desired other. This longing for what is unattainably beyond and for what has been irretrievably lost furrows the have-not's spirit with parallel competing impulses: to re-create, worship, replace, disparage, oppress, repress, violate, devour, destroy the loved and hated other or the deprived self. Behind all his have-nots, Spenser traces the lineaments of the paradise principle.

I propose to show that the spirit of the have-not is dramatized in the *Calender* as the plaintive condition. Furthermore, I shall argue that Spenser locates this condition not merely—not even primarily—in his pastoral speakers but in the tradition of received opinion that shapes their culture, norms, and expectations. Few readers now seriously challenge the thesis that the *Calender* is a critique of the great variety of literary traditions and conventions it imitates, and I shall demonstrate that this critique draws much of its power from the *Calender*'s preliminary sketch of the profound and complex portrayal of human motives we tend with greater ease to associate with Spenser's "mature" work. Thus the two basic premises of my argument are (1) that the paradise principle as the source of both the have-not response and the futile attempts to restore and return to the lost paradise is the organizing motif of the *Calender* and (2) that the paradise principle so conceived is the organizing motif of the literary tradition that Spenser's first complete published work imitates, sums up, and deconstructs. These premises are so closely related to the particular view I take toward Spenser's pastoral speakers, their obligation to and divergence from positions developed by other commentators is so problematical, and their applicability to other pastoral poets is so important to demonstrate to reinforce the present reading that consideration must be given to all these topics. The remainder of this introductory section will be devoted to this task.

The account of the paradise principle with which Renato Poggioli begins the earliest of his three classic studies of pastoral, *The Oaten Flute*, is paradigmatic of a view of pastoral that has prevailed until fairly recently:

> The psychological root of pastoral is a double longing after innocence and happiness, to be recovered not through conversion or regeneration, but merely through a retreat. By withdrawing not from the world, but from "the world," pastoral man tries to achieve a new life in imitation of the good shepherd of herds, rather than of the Good Shepherd of the Soul. . . . [Contrary to the Christian ideal] the pastoral ideal shifts on the quicksands of wishful thought. Wishful thinking is the weakest of all moral and religious resorts; but it is the stuff dreams, especially daydreams, are made of. Mankind had not to wait for Freud to learn that poetry itself is made of that stuff. . . . it is easier to reach moral truth and peace of mind . . . by abandoning the strife of civil and social living and the ordeal of human fellowship for a solitary existence, in communion with nature and with the company of one's musings and thoughts.[2]

2. *The Oaten Flute* (Cambridge: Harvard University Press, 1975), 1–2. This view has been reaffirmed by John D. Bernard in "'June' and the Structure of Spenser's *Shepheardes Calender*," *Philological Quarterly* 60 (1981): 305–22.

Insofar as Poggioli is judging rather than merely describing the pastoral mode and its practitioners, his account is a little unfair to those poets who share his critical insights and make the dangers or limits of the pastoral ideal their subject. Had it been voiced unambiguously as a paraphrase of a critical tradition *in* pastoral—as a set of themes dramatized by Virgil, Chaucer, Spenser, Shakespeare, Cervantes, Marvell, Milton, Pope, Yeats, and others—Poggioli's statement could hardly be improved.

Poggioli makes it clear that the pastoral impulse is entertained *in absentia* by minds encumbered with "the world"—that, as Frank Kermode put it, "the first condition of Pastoral is that it is an urban product."[3] Other writers make it equally clear that escapism is not the only motive, and Peter Marinelli has concisely summarized this view:

> To arrive in Arcadia . . . is merely to have one's problems sharp-
> ened by seeing them magnified in a new context of simplicity,
> by seeing Art against Nature and . . . being forced to conclusions
> about them. The issues of the great world or of adulthood are
> transported into Arcadia or into the magic gardens of childhood
> as to a place and time in which they may be better scrutinized
> . . . and the process may result in a clarification of the motives
> that bred the desire for escape in the first place. . . . Those who
> complain of the vitiation of pastoral by the introduction of . . .
> foreign or extraneous elements that cloud its pristine loveliness,
> fail to realize that a note of criticism is inherent in all pastoral
> from the beginning of its existence. It is latent in the form in its
> very desire for movement away from an unsatisfactory time and
> place to another time and place that is imagined to be superior.
> Satire, moralizing and allegory are merely the inborn tendencies
> of pastoral rendered overt and explicit.[4]

When Marinelli speaks of clarifying the motives "that bred the desire for escape," he makes a move toward recognizing a type of pastoral that is reflexive in critically examining its own basis. This differs from the type the passage centers on, that is, pastoral that criticizes the extrapastoral world. Writers on pastoral have tended to identify the reflexive critique with post-Renaissance developments in the mode.[5] * * *

That pastoral has its own peculiar powers that modern critics have in-sufficiently appreciated is a leading theme in Paul Alpers's earlier studies of the mode. In "The Eclogue Tradition and the Nature of Pastoral," Alpers notes that the "soft" view (e.g., Poggioli's) that mistakenly identifies "pas-toralism with a simple lyricism" tends to generate its equally misleading "polar opposite—a 'hard view.' . . . The soft and hard views of pastoral, antithetical though they are, have one thing in common. Neither takes pastoral nature seriously as a home for the human spirit."[6] Alpers goes on

---

3. *English Pastoral Poetry* (London: George G. Harrap, 1952), 14.
4. *Pastoral* (London: Methuen, 1971), 11–12.
5. Berger also notices "interesting moments of reflexive criticism in older pastoral" remarked by Harold Tolliver, *Pastoral Forms and Attitudes* (Berkeley, 1971). [*Editors*].
6. *College English* 34 (1972): 352–53.

to argue that Spenser does take "both 'soft' and 'hard' views of nature seriously, because he takes literally . . . the idea that there is a proportion between man and nature." He asserts that this idea "is basic to Renaissance pastoral and represents a fundamental point of difference between it and ancient pastoral, where life in nature is an ethical alternative, one possibility for the good life. In Renaissance pastoral, with its Christian perspective, man's life has an inherent relation to nature" (p. 364). But Renaissance pastoral shares with its classical predecessors at least one important characteristic:

> The eclogue tradition shows us that the pastoral is not merely, or even primarily, a matter of projecting worlds, real or imaginary, golden or savage. At the center of pastoral is the shepherd-singer. The great pastoral poets are directly concerned with the extent to which song that gives present pleasures can confront and, if not transform and celebrate, then accept and reconcile man to the stresses and realities of his situation. (p. 353)

While I agree with Alpers on many points and find his critique especially valuable, my view of pastoral differs from his in its general orientation, and the differences are sharper when we come to *The Shepheardes Calender*. I am more inclined than Alpers to see Spenser as a "metapastoralist," that is, as a poet who dramatizes the limits of traditional pastoral because he is attracted to the mode and wants to revise rather than to discard it. Consequently my judgment of Spenser's achievement in the *Calender* is more positive than that of Alpers, for whom Spenser fails where Virgil and Milton succeed (pp. 366 ff.). Furthermore, I would argue against the position that "the skeptical view of the pastoral tradition" had to wait for romantic or modern pastoralists. I have learned from Alpers, however, that reflexive criticism is a property of Virgilian pastoral. I think pastoral that criticizes itself rather than (or as well as) the great world is an enduring element of the mode, and I shall try in this essay to substantiate the assertion that reflexive criticism is fundamental to Spenser's pastoral. The assertion itself is by no means original, and a summary of some of the recent commentators to whose work I am indebted will suggest the extent and the limits of the debt.

William Nelson was one of the first to establish the principle that the debates in the *Calender* were not one-sided, a principle implying that the author is not easily identified with any particular speaker or position: "As Spenser uses it, the dialogue of a pastoral poem is not a Socratic demonstration but a valid disagreement in which the speakers explore what may best be said on either part."[7] Nelson argued convincingly that the debates center on a small cluster of contraries, centered on the youth-age antithesis, each of which "recurs often enough to give unity to the whole." Subsequent criticism may occasionally have questioned the assertion that the speakers explored "what may *best* be said," but Nelson's reduction of the diversity of matter and mode to this principle of balanced antithesis has largely been

7. *The Poetry of Edmund Spenser: A Study* (New York: Columbia University Press, 1963), 39.

accepted, especially since the principle he casually sketched out was later developed in considerable detail by Patrick Cullen.[8]

* * *

A more genuinely dialectical view of the conflict between soft and hard pastoral is set forth in Isabel MacCaffrey's "Allegory and Pastoral in *The Shepheardes Calender*."[9] For MacCaffrey Spenser implies that the "naive [or soft] version of the pastoral metaphor inadequately expresses reality" because it posits an idyllic congruence between man and nature, microcosm and macrocosm, which experience belies. The natural cycle in its literal form is an inadequate model because it is either false or unsatisfying—false in that "the orderly cycle of human life is [often] turned awry, its promise blasted," and unsatisfying in that "submission to the seasonal round" leads "only to death." To presuppose a benign or paradisal congruence of the natural and human cycles produces false expectations because "man must suffer inevitable outrage from the forces released in nature at the Fall"— passion, corruption, death—"and against these forces there is no remedy within nature itself." The *Calender* thus moves from soft to hard pastoral and beyond: while it teaches us to abandon our condemnation by sin "to live in an unsheltered world, hostile and uncongenial," it does not advocate rejecting either pastoral or temporal pleasures. "Rather those pleasures are defined and confirmed with relation to an ultimate religious sanction." Hence for MacCaffrey Spenser's sophisticated pastoral transcends both soft and hard versions in shifting the reference of soft pastoral from earth to heaven and from nature to spirit, that is, from literal to metaphoric significant: "the power of the pastoral paradigm is reaffirmed as having *metaphorical* validity"; in other words, its meaning "concerns the need for us to accept a nonliteral invisible reality as the one most relevant to us as human beings."

John Moore gives the MacCaffrey argument a more uncompromisingly religious turn in a reading of the *Januarye* eclogue using the same dialectical scheme.[1] He defines Colin's "spiritual odyssey" as a progress "from allegiance to Pan, the nature God, to the real Pan, the real All, Christ." As a pagan nature god Pan presides over values and expectations that are out of touch with the realities of the fallen world and that leave his devotee unprepared to cope with pain and loss. Colin "must seek his values not in the temporary and fragile beauty of nature's spring, but in the enduring beauty of heaven's eternal springtime, the nonvisible world of the infinite. By doing this he will not define human happiness in terms of an earthly harvest but will seek a heavenly harvest free of mutability" (pp. 22–23). Moore's argument is structured according to the same three-stage model as MacCaffrey's: (1) a naive or soft or pagan or idyllic view of the man-nature relation precedes (2) a fall into hard actuality for which stage 1 left the neophyte unprepared, but in the crucible of bitter experience (3) the mind may yet find "transcendence and escape from . . . disasters" by soaring on "the uplifting powers of the human imagination" (MacCaffrey), toward the

8. *Spenser, Marvell, and Renaissance Pastoral* (Cambridge: Harvard University Press, 1970). Berger summarizes and comments on distinctive features of Cullen's argument (omitted here). [*Editors*].
9. See pp. 769–78 in this volume.
1. "Colin Breaks His Pipe: A Reading of the 'January' Eclogue," *English Literary Renaissance* 5 (1975): 22.

heavenly harvest and a "spring-like birth of a better set of values" (Moore, 23). Both critics see the *November* eclogue as a critical moment in which nature's imagery is metaphorically turned against itself and transcendentalized.

Readings of this sort prompted Alpers to call much recent commentary "portentous" and to censure allegorical critics for overlooking "what Hallett Smith calls 'the verve of the poetry' " (Alpers, 363). Alpers applies to Spenser the lesson he learned from Theocritus and Virgil: pastoral speakers and singers are "men who fully 'realize their own natures,' while still bound, and accepting their bondage, to the earth" (p. 362). His view of nature consequently differs from that exemplified by MacCaffrey and Moore: since in Renaissance pastoral "man's life has an inherent relation to nature," poetry can answer "to permanent realities of nature and human nature," and "the severities and disappointments" expressed by "the pastoral of winter" can be taken to "register a coming to terms with reality and not merely a negative process of disillusionment" (Alpers, 364). When Colin hangs up his pipe, for example, "he is neither expressing despair nor confessing failure," for "this is the traditional act of an old shepherd who submits to the nature of things" (pp. 365–66). On this basis Alpers criticizes the allegorists not only because they are "serious at the expense of poetic surface" but also because, identifying pastoral "with naive idyllicism," they assume that the poet intended pastoral nature to be transcended in the reader's search for more serious messages (pp. 361–62).

I think something can be learned from both sides in this argument by isolating positive insights from those that seem less tenable. MacCaffrey's is, as Alpers noted, one of the more forceful and intelligent statements of the position he criticizes. The link she draws between the theme of false expectations and the limits of "naive idyllicism" strikes me as an important connection, one that can be further developed by separating it from her somewhat inconsistent emphasis on the role Spenser assigns to nature. The account is inconsistent because the accent on fallen nature as a source of the problem conflicts logically with any attempt to root the negative consequences of the naively idyllic attitude within the attitude itself. In her account nature per se is thematized by the *Calender,* and the various senses she assigns to the term compose a set of imaged places and processes, a "macrocosm," "the world of nature," all of them inadequate to the human spirit's desire for transcendence and the imagination's preference for metaphor, which is never "found in nature."[2] Alpers objects to her emphasis on allegory as a visionary mode that adumbrates invisible reality through metaphorical fictions: "The notion that poetry serves human needs only by transcending nature comes from thinking of pastoral solely as a matter of images and projected worlds" (p. 362).

This criticism seems justified to me, for if it is the case—as I maintain —that the *Calender* dramatizes the causal relation between soft expectations and an excessively pessimistic or defeatist reaction to problematical aspects of nature (*and* culture), then in positing the Fall as the cause of nature's hostility, MacCaffrey's argument digresses from the dramatic point. It il-

---

2. See MacCaffrey, *Spenser's Allegory: The Anatomy of Imagination* (Princeton: Princeton University Press, 1976), 25 and Introduction (passim).

lustrates that the visualizing or topographic tendency Alpers criticizes has often encouraged serious-minded readers of the *Calender* to take two further steps: (1) to assume that something called "nature" exists "in" the "world" of the poem, that the speakers are to be imagined as "in" that preexisting natural world, and that it can be described apart from their descriptions of it; (2) to assume that nature exists in two forms, unfallen and fallen, and that the Golden Age is a prelapsarian state identical to Eden. The eclogues proper, however, contain few unmediated references to nature as setting or process. Since all but twenty-five lines are assigned to pastoral speakers, these assumptions make it difficult to focus steadily on—or rather to listen carefully to—the speakers' responses to what they take to be "nature." This is why Alpers's insistence on the primacy of speakers and song in pastoral is a useful corrective. It shifts our attention "to such topics as voice, *tradition*, self-representation, self-reflexiveness, and the community implied by song," as he himself puts it in *The Singer of the "Eclogues."*[3] I have italicized the term *tradition* because of its importance to my reading. I shall try to demonstrate that the paradise associated with the paradise principle has nothing to do with the original pleasance created by God. Rather it is the product of the Muses—that is, of the literary elders, the tradition— and what it delineates is not the prelapsarian state but a set of paradisal expectations implanted by tradition in the pastoral mind. This thesis leads me to uphold against Alpers MacCaffrey's emphasis on the limits of naive idyllicism, but only as corrected by Alpers's emphasis on the representation of pastoral speakers and singers.

Alpers's brilliant insight into the soft and hard views of pastoral—that the former both precedes and generates the latter—uncovers the presence of the paradise principle in recent criticism. In denying the same insight to Spenser, however, he deprives himself of a valuable guide to interpretation of the *Calender*. He agrees with the commentators he criticizes that the *Calender* moves toward a positive resolution, though his sense of that resolution differs substantially from theirs. This marks the point of departure for the reading I shall give in these essays. I shall argue that Spenser does *not* take "pastoral nature seriously as a home for the human spirit," and that although he does take soft and hard pastoral seriously, it is to suggest their limits and show why they make traditional pastoral a home from which a pastoral adequate to the needs of the human spirit must be weaned. In other words, I shall defend the position that Spenser's view of soft and hard pastoral is the same as Alpers's and therefore that Alpers's conclusions about the *Calender*, and his evaluation of it, are represented in the *Calender* and have been targeted in advance. There is plenty of evidence in the eclogues to support the idea that their dominant theme is the power of the paradise principle—the power, that is, of the self-perpetuating dialectic between soft and hard perspectives—to promote disillusionment and to inhibit "a coming to terms with reality." Mantuanesque (or any other) bitterness is produced not by the limitations of the "fallen" world but by those of the golden-world attitude. It may therefore be inadvisable to continue thinking of the recreative and plaintive attitudes as "soft" and "hard"

3. *The Singer of the "Eclogues": A Study of Virgilian Pastoral* (Berkeley: University of California Press, 1979), 6; italics mine.

pastoral, since the adjectives seem to have attached themselves firmly to nature. I propose replacing them by the terms *sweet* and *bitter* to distinguish them as attitudes that speak only secondarily to nature as such but primarily to the paradisal expectation and disillusionment of Spenser's pastoral speakers.

My thesis is that such reflexive issues are central to *The Shepheardes Calender* as a whole, that problems about "art" and problems about "life" are handled together under the same set of ethicopsychological premises, and that these premises are articulated primarily in the presentation of what may be called Spenser's drama of literary imitation. At the heart of the drama is the dialogue, or convergence, or collision, of old with young, ancient with modern, past with present. The literary withdrawal the poet depicts as prompted by paradisal influence is characteristically a "return to"—that is, an imitation of—a set of *topoi*, of "places" as well as conventions, authenticated by their durability. The new poet treasures the beauty or value of these ideal "places" as much as he fears their dangers and temptations. The aesthetic power of his literary models threatens to reduce him either to silence or to the status of an epigone, an ape not of nature but of art. He must criticize and reject the received form of the art he would embrace; otherwise, trying to revise the form, he will succeed only in repeating it. The problematic of imitation and that of the paradise principle converge in the new poet's dramatization of belatedness. His way of breaking free of what he constitutes as his tradition is to encapsulate it in a critical profile, to activate its conventions and to reenact its characteristic "moves" so as to bring out the complexity of attitude implicit in but flattened under the conventional surface. In thus showing how an attitude toward art implicates an attitude toward life, he doesn't merely criticize the tradition; he gives it new energy and meaning.

A clue to the particular form this sympathetic criticism takes in the great metapastoralists may be drawn from Humphrey Tonkin's distinction between the satiric and the romantic functions of pastoral:

> Its first function is satiric: it serves as a device for criticism. It distances the writer from his own milieu and forms a base from which to attack its standards or lack of standards. The eclogue is its special vehicle. Its second function is as a means of articulating moral or spiritual aspirations. It creates a world where the conflicts and pettinesses of ordinary life are eliminated, where all investments have returns, and where actions have desired results. Love is untrammelled, and belief suffers no contradiction. . . . These two devices are not mutually exclusive. Pastoral satire depends on an awareness of the virtues of the pastoral existence, while pastoral romance at least supposes the existence elsewhere of urban and courtly corruption. Most pastoral works involve a combination of satiric and romantic ingredients, some leaning towards the former and some towards the latter.[4]

4. *Spenser's Courteous Pastoral: Book Six of the "Faerie Queene"* (London: Oxford University Press, 1972), 282–83.

By rejoining these two functions, directing them back toward each other, we may effect a more complete closure of pastoral's reflexive critique than Tonkin's account suggests, one that will allow us to capitalize on his illuminating remark that "the pastoral *world*" is to be distinguished from "pastoral *works*, which are often concerned with the disintegration of this world" (p. 283). This world, "this country of beautiful landscape and simple emotions" which "often has an air of fantasy" and is "a retreat into the imagination rather than an escape to the country" (p. 283), is generated and integrated by the romantic function. And the object of the *Calender* poet's criticism (whether satiric or, more genially, parodic) is precisely this function. Tonkin suggests that the disintegration of which he speaks involves the transition from childhood and sexual innocence to manhood and sexuality, and his discussion implies what other scholars have stated—that love is an outside intruder separating us from idyllic nature and the Golden Age (pp. 283–84). But I think that the pastoral criticism is inflected differently: it asserts that the disintegration of the golden world and the plaintive response to love and experience are consequences of the very "retreat into the imagination" that produced that world. Romantic expectations are the source of failure and premature bitterness. And since poetic conventions are in turn the source of romantic expectations, the pastoral critique is first and foremost a critique of pastoral.

PAUL ALPERS: [Spenser's Domain of Lyric]†

This essay seeks to explain, more precisely than is usual and in terms appropriate to literary history, the importance to Elizabethan poetry of Edmund Spenser's *The Shepheardes Calender.* * * *

In some ways it is easy to see why *The Shepheardes Calender* was an event. It was the first set of English pastorals in the European tradition, and in emulating Virgil's *Eclogues,* it self-consciously inaugurated a poetic career on the model of Virgil's—one that would move from a book of eclogues to a national epic. The very success of this project has encouraged modern scholars to turn away from asking why *The Shepheardes Calender* made such a difference when it appeared and to treat it mainly as a prototype of *The Faerie Queene*: most studies since 1950 have emphasized the young poet's epic striving, moral vision, and allegorical technique.[1] Recent studies by younger scholars have sought to give a more precisely historical account of *The Shepheardes Calender.* They have drawn attention to what one might call the problematics of a poetic career in Elizabethan England; to the effects on Spenser of being a courtier and depending on patronage; and in general to the way various social pressures and realities make their presence

† From "Pastoral and the Domain of Lyric in *The Shepheardes Calender,*" *Representations* 12 (1985): 83–100. The original footnotes have been slightly revised. © 1985 by the Regents of the University of California. Reprinted by permission.
1. The best of these studies, to my mind, is Isabel G. MacCaffrey, "Allegory and Pastoral in *The Shepheardes Calender,*" *ELH* 36 (1969): 88–109.

felt in the poem.[2] This kind of historical account has brought out the difficulties and dilemmas of Spenser's literary endeavor in a way that makes his literary achievement all the more impressive. If you assume that in any place or at any time, Renaissance poets could write good pastorals, *The Shepheardes Calender* may appear to you no better than it did to Dr. Johnson, who mocked its "studied barbarity."[3] But the poem was not, so to speak, just there to be written. On the contrary, writing pastorals both required and enabled Spenser to overcome—and helped English poetry break the grip of—the difficulties that attended writing lyric poems in mid-sixteenth-century England.

To understand the significance of Spenser's writing a book of Virgilian eclogues, we need to imagine what a young English poet, around 1575, would have conceived a poem and a book of poems to be. To do so, we must overcome our tendency to think of lyric as the normal mode of nondramatic or nonheroic poetry. We assume this for a number of reasons—first of all, the still-determining heritage of Romanticism, but also many aspects of Renaissance poetry: the older view of Elizabethan poets as "a nest of singing birds"; the preeminence of sonnets among Shakespeare's nondramatic poems and among the poems that still matter by Sidney, Fulke Greville, and others; the centrality of major lyrics in the literary achievement of Donne, Herbert, Herrick, Marvell, and Milton. But what conception of and models for the vernacular lyric would have been available to the young Spenser? Essentially two kinds of poem—the courtly love lyric and the short poem of moral observation or counsel—and a handful of volumes in which these had appeared: Tottel's *Miscellany* of 1557 (in which the poems of Sir Thomas Wyatt and the earl of Surrey were first published) and poetic collections in the '60s and '70s by the likes of Barnabe Googe, George Turberville, and George Gascoigne. Quite aside from questions of quality and range, these poems were compromised by the double apology with which they characteristically appeared: the apology for dealing with matters of love and the apology for appearing in print. Wyatt and Surrey had no choice in the matter, being dead when Richard Tottel published their poems, but both Googe—who anticipated Spenser by trying his hand at eclogues—and Gascoigne, much the finest poet of his generation, disclaimed responsibility for the publication of their poems. * * *

If we view *The Shepheardes Calender* as a mid-Tudor collection of short poems, we find a number of resemblances to its immediate predecessors. Its poems, like Gascoigne's, are presented by a friend of the poet, who is known to us only by his initials. Like Tottel's *Miscellany*, it begins with a poem in which the lover's wintry condition is contrasted with the emerging spring season. It shares major themes with its predecessors—notably the

2. See especially the remarkable articles by Louis Adrian Montrose: " 'The perfecte paterne of a Poete': The Poetics of Courtship in *The Shepheardes Calender,*" *Texas Studies in Literature and Language* 21 (1979): 34–67; " 'Eliza, Queene of shepheardes' and the Pastoral of Power," *English Literary Renaissance* 10 (1980): 153–82; "Of Gentlemen and Shepherds: The Politics of Elizabethan Pastoral Form," *ELH* 50 (1983): 415–59. See also Richard Helgerson, "The New Poet Presents Himself: Spenser and the Idea of a Literary Career," *PMLA* 93 (1978): 893–911; David L. Miller, "Authorship, Anonymity, and *The Shepheardes Calender,*" *Modern Language Quarterly* 40 (1979): 219–36.

3. From *The Rambler* 37 (24 July 1750), in *The Works of Samuel Johnson* (New Haven, 1958–), vol. 3, *The Rambler* (vol. 1), ed. W. J. Bate and Albrecht B. Strauss (1969), 203.

frustrations and wastefulness of love and the conflict between youthful impulse and the moral wisdom and severity of age. Recognizing such likenesses gives a more precise form to our initial question: what difference did it make, in 1579, for a writer of short poems to present himself as a writer of pastorals?

It was certainly important that Spenser was the first Englishman to emulate ancient and modern writers of what was a prestigious kind of poetry. Spenser's E.K. may be as unknowable as Gascoigne's G.T. and H.W., and he may equally be a mask of the poet himself. But he appears not in the character of a courtier who has passed around certain poems and shared certain experiences, but as an editor who can place the poet in relation to his European predecessors and who can annotate each of his eclogues. *The Shepheardes Calender* thus has the appearance of humanist editions of the Greek and Latin classics and of modern classics like Petrarch's *Rime* and Ariosto's *Orlando Furioso*. The volume accordingly gives no sign of diffidence about appearing in print. Print was the humanist's medium, and publication was consistent with E.K.'s hailing the author as "our new poet," as opposed to the pejorative epithet of "rhymer."

What concerns us, however, is not E.K.'s publicity but the way such claims and ambitions affect the poems themselves. Writing Virgilian pastorals made a decisive difference because it meant representing a world of shepherd-singers and representing yourself, the poet, as one of them. Spenser's lyric predecessors characteristically represent themselves as courtiers. This is manifestly the case with Wyatt and Surrey: whatever the relation of their poems to actual experience and situations, the speakers of these poems appear in the character of courtiers. Gascoigne, though socially more marginal than Wyatt and Surrey, also writes as a courtier. He presents his poems as written to various ladies or for various friends on various amatory or social occasions, and the poems characteristically end with a "device" or "posy." His greatest poem, "Gascoigne's Woodmanship," is addressed to his patron and represents an actual social occasion as an allegory of his failure as a courtier. Spenser's life and career were in a number of ways different from Gascoigne's, but he too was a courtier in the sense that he sought in the court itself or in noble households the patronage that would establish him as a public servant. What then does it mean for such a courtier-poet to write pastorals? More than one recent critic has answered this question by turning to the most important Elizabethan statement of a courtly aesthetic, *The Arte of English Poesie*, attributed to George Puttenham and probably written earlier than 1589, when it was published.[4] Puttenham argues that pastoral is not a primitive but a sophisticated form of poetry. Poets, he says, devised eclogues

> not of purpose to counterfait or represent the rusticall manner of
> loues and communication: but vnder the vaile of homely persons,

---

4. Recent attention to Puttenham owes much to Daniel Javitch, *Poetry and Courtliness in Renaissance England* (Princeton, 1978). Javitch's positive account of Puttenham's aesthetic—his book is in some ways what the sixteenth century would have called an "apology" for him—has prompted the more skeptical and ironic views of Montrose (above, note 2) and, among others, Frank Whigham, *Ambition and Privilege: The Social Tropes of Elizabethan Courtesy Theory* (Berkeley, 1984).

and in rude speeches to insinuate and glaunce at greater matters, and such as perchance had not bene safe to haue beene disclosed in any other sort, which may be perceiued by the Eglogues of *Virgill*, in which are treated by figure matters of greater importance than the loues of *Titirus* and *Corydon*.[5]

Prompted by Puttenham's awareness of the danger of glancing at greater matters, critics have argued that Spenser's pastoral personages, far from being a sign of poetic autonomy, bear witness to the social pressures on poetic utterance.

But the relevant passages in *The Shepheardes Calender* are bolder than Puttenham's remark leads us to expect. * * * Spenser's represented shepherds are neither completely autonomous—free just because they are literary—nor entirely the creatures of the courtier's situation. There is a genuine doubleness about them, a mixture of outspokenness and diffidence, that E.K. indicates in discussing why one speaks of great matters in pastoral verse. He says that his author's rejection of "glorious showes" "appeareth by the basenesse" of his pastoral pseudonym, Colin Clout, "wherein, it semeth, he chose rather to vnfold great matter of argument couertly, then professing it, not suffice thereto accordingly." By this last phrase he means: if the poet professed it, i.e., professed to deal with great matters, he might not "suffice thereto." Where Puttenham views the pastoral mask as a way of dealing with social danger, E.K. looks to it for rhetorical adequacy.

We can restate E.K.'s claim of rhetorical sufficiency by saying that speaking through shepherds enabled Spenser to speak out in a relatively full and uncompromised way. I mean "relatively" in a precise sense—relative to the character of the figures represented. The literary shepherd's sufficiency to great matters is due to his simplicity and innocence. These confer on him a moral authority, which can take, through the image of the Good Shepherd, a religious or ecclesiastical form. The shepherd's simple character also manifests itself in forthright, energetic speech, which sometimes appears as blunt moralizing and sometimes as a quasi-biblical eloquence. * * * But the shepherd's simplicity, the source of his moral and poetic strength, is coextensive with his vulnerability and powerlessness. Thus built into the very figure through whom the poet expresses his vision or his complaints, there is an acknowledgment that limits their force and that backs away from—indeed does not even consider—the kind of challenge to authority that in real life was expressed by [Sidney's] letter to the queen objecting to her proposed marriage to the duc d'Alençon. Spenser dedicated *The Shepheardes Calender* to [Sidney] but the very terms on which he gave voice to his allegiances also produced the quietism that ends most of the eclogues that comment on the public world.

* * *

Spenser conceived *The Shepheardes Calender* in terms of roles for literary shepherds made available to him by his European and English predecessors. By conceiving lyrical speakers in this way, he was able to deal with the

5. George Puttenham, *The Arte of English Poesie*, ed. Gladys Doidge Willcock and Alice Walker (Cambridge, 1936), book 1, chap. 18, 38.

problem—which is hard for us to imagine as a problem—of motivating serious lyrics. Apart from the official critical hierarchies, which gave most prestige to narrative and dramatic poems, the work of Spenser's contemporaries reveals a pressure to justify or account for lyical utterance. Gascoigne's *100 Sundry Flowers* begins with a prose tale, "The Adventures of Master F.J.," in which the various moves in an entangled tale of seduction prompt and explain some dozen lyrics, on whose rhetorical efficacy G.T., the author's friend, makes knowing comments. The lyrics that follow F.J.'s tale are frequently introduced by substantial accounts of the circumstances that gave rise to them. "Gascoigne's Woodmanship," which seems self-sufficient to us, is introduced by ten lines of prose that not only explain the circumstances of the poem but motivate it as Gascoigne's response to his patron's teasing. The lyrics of the *Arcadia* are prompted by love pursuits and entanglements that, though fictional, are imagined in full social and dramatic detail. Sidney's attention to situation can extend to surprisingly minute points. * * * When we see Gascoigne and Sidney so attentive to and concerned with the social motives to lyric, we can understand the advantage of pastoral speakers like those of *The Shepheardes Calender*. Just as for the humanist poet writing eclogues was its own justification, so the fictions and conventions of pastoral resolve problems of motivating lyric utterance. A literary shepherd is by definition a singer, and pastoral poems are characteristically singing contests or funeral songs or songs in praise of a ruler or love laments.

* * *

Performance of known poems and kinds of poems is a main and sometimes sufficient motive to lyric in *The Shepheardes Calender*. The April lay celebrating "*Eliza*, Queene of shepheardes" is said to be a poem that Colin Clout wrote in his carefree youth and that is now performed by his friend Hobbinoll. This eclogue, the fourth in *The Shepheardes Calender*, can also be seen as Spenser's performance of the kind of imperial, golden-age pastoral invented by Virgil in *his* fourth eclogue. There is a similar association of imitation and performance in the November eclogue, a pastoral elegy based on a poem by the sixteenth-century French poet, Clément Marot. Within the November eclogue this elegy is conceived as a performance: it is uttered by Colin Clout in response to a request for a song; it is rhetorically lofty, in highly wrought stanzas; and it laments a communal, not a private, loss. It seems equally appropriate to consider Spenser a performer in this poem, since Colin Clout is a role he has created for himself and since he himself is producing a version not simply of his immediate source, the poem by Marot, but of a known and important kind of poem, the pastoral elegy.

The idea of performance extends to more than explicitly performed songs and conscious imitations. Any segment of a poem can emerge as a set piece, and some, like the elaborate stanzas of "April" and "November," invite such treatment. In "April," for example, one finds stanzas devoted to Eliza's birth, to her costume, to the dance of the Graces, and to the flowers gathered for her. The following stanza shows the performative principle involved:

> *Pan* may be proud, that euer he begot
>   such a Bellibone,
> And *Syrinx* reioyse, that euer was her lot
>   to beare such an one.
> Soone as my younglings cryen for the dam,
> To her will I offer a milkwhite Lamb:
>   Shee is my goddesse plaine,
>   And I her shepherds swayne,
> Albee forswonck and forswatt I am.
> (lines 91–99)

E.K. says the name Bellibone is "homely spoken," and we can extend this observation to the clinching phrase, "forswonck and forswatt"; to the represented gift offering; and to the two short lines near the end, in which queen and suitor are acknowledged with lovely plainness. Everything about the stanza depends on conceiving the speaker as a rustic. What is revealing is that he is more rustic here than elsewhere in the poem: that is, the stanza is based on a distinct role, separately performed, within the conspicuous performance of the whole poem.

Used as we are to the lyrics of later poets, we may feel that such a stanza is too sharply set off, too much a set piece: in the greatest lyrics, freshly adopted roles are compatible with the felt continuity of the speaker. But discovering such flexible role playing and capacity for vocal performance was crucial for the English lyric. A stanza in "June" represents this aspect of *The Shepheardes Calender*:

> *Colin*, to heare thy rymes and roundelayes,
> Which thou were wont on wastfull hylls to singe,
> I more delight, then larke in Sommer dayes:
> Whose Echo made the neyghbour groues to ring,
> And taught the byrds, which in the lower spring
> Did shroude in shady leaues from sonny rayes,
> Frame to thy songe their cherefull cheriping,
> Or hold theyr peace, for shame of thy swete layes.
> ("June," lines 49–56)

The lyricism here directly derives from pastoral role playing. The stanza is pastoral, because it imagines song as produced by responsive listening—a fiction of pastoral, with its song contests, echoing woods, and the like, that corresponds to the fact that poets wrote pastorals in responsive imitation and modification of their predecessors. The fullness of lyrical effect is due to the fact that the shepherd's responsive listening has led him to take on not one but two roles—that of Colin Clout, the master singer, and of the lark, both of whom can be imagined to have made the groves to ring and taught the birds to frame their own responsive song.

By writing a book of eclogues, conceived as the performance of pastoral roles, Spenser created what I would like to call a "domain of lyric." In using this term, I am trying to meet Louis Adrian Montrose's argument that when critics speak of Spenser's work in terms of "aesthetic space," they ignore what is specifically historical and cultural about his or any Elizabethan writer's poetic project.[6] The way to avoid this charge—which is certainly justified in a number of cases—is not to oppose the historical and the aesthetic but to recognize that the claim to relative autonomy, by means of something that looks like aesthetic "space," was Spenser's historical (and therefore, indeed, problematic) aim in *The Shepheardes Calender*. I think "domain" takes cultural and ideological elements into account, because it conceives "aesthetic space" in terms of rule and authority. One of the age's most famous lyrics, by Sir Edward Dyer—a courtier close to Sidney and known to Spenser—begins, "My mind to me a kingdom is." Sidney's *Arcadia*, according to the opening sentences of the romance, is the province of singers because of its governance. Sidney says the muses chose Arcadia as "their chiefest repairing place" principally because of the "moderate and well tempered minds of the people," which are due to the fact that "the good minds of the former princes had set down good laws."[7] Spenser did not feel his own domain of song needed such precise social specifications, just as neither he nor E.K. offers anything like Sidney's explanation that the Arcadian shepherds are good singers because they "were not such base shepherds as we commonly make account of, but the very owners of the sheep themselves" and furthermore were infiltrated by gentlemen poets, whose contributions raised the general level of performance. These are not surprising remarks for a gentleman of rank, but they are for a pastoral poet, who, one would think, will find it difficult to take on the roles and voices of his represented shepherds if even their fictional world is invaded by these social anxieties.

Spenser could establish his domain of lyric because his literary assumptions and practices gave *The Shepheardes Calender* a certain distance from courtly and social accountability. A third reason Sidney gives for the excellence of Arcadian singers is that "the presence of their own duke . . . animated the shepherds the more exquisitely to seek a worthy accomplishment of his good liking." This explanation is consistent with the fact that the major pastorals contemporary with *Arcadia* and *The Shepheardes Calender*—Sidney's *Lady of May*, Peele's *Arraignment of Paris*, Lyly's *Gallathea*—were masques or plays written to entertain the queen. Spenser's main audience, however, was not the monarch who bestows favor, nor even the court as a whole, but what print alone could provide—a heterogeneous group of knowledgeable readers. For a number of reasons, including his social origins and his education, he was responsive to and felt empowered by another world than the court, the world of learning represented by his university and European humanism. Nor should we think, as traditional views of tradition tell us, that humanism in general or pastoral poetry in particular was enabling in any simple way, as if Spenser were the passive beneficiary of something already in place. Quite the contrary, Spenser's own innovations—notably the device of the calendar, but also his

6. Montrose, "Of Gentlemen and Shepherds," 451–52.
7. Sir Philip Sidney, *The Countesse of Pembroke's Arcadia (The Old Arcadia)*, ed. Jean Robertson (Oxford, 1973), 4. The next quotation is from the paragraph introducing the first set of eclogues; *ibid.*, 56.

evident intent to "overgo" his sixteenth-century predecessors[8]—show that he was conscious of staking out his claim in the world of European letters. By the modest boldness everywhere evident in *The Shepheardes Calender*, Spenser achieved a qualified but nonetheless genuine independence, of which the legal concept of *demesne* (= "domain") is a suggestive representation. According to F. W. Maitland, the term is

> applied either to the absolute ownership of the king, or to the tenure of the person who held land to his own use, mediately or immediately from the king. . . . In every case the ultimate (free) holder, the person who *stands at the bottom of the scale*, who seems most like an owner of the land, and who *has a general right of doing what he pleases* with it, is said to hold the land in demesne.[9]

Whatever the degree of Spenser's freedom to poetize and possess his own space, the problem of social authority clings to and haunts *The Shepheardes Calender*. Its confidence in poetic tradition can be thought to give it a certain distance from the pressures of an immediate courtly audience, but the humanist tradition was itself founded on the ideal of the learned man as the counselor of princes. This ideal and its problematic relation to courtly realities had motivated the greatest English creation of imaginative space before *The Faerie Queene*—More's Utopia, a literary domain if there ever was one. *The Shepheardes Calender* certainly did not undo the work of decades that turned English humanists, as G. K. Hunter has argued of Lyly, from princely counselors to marginal entertainers.[1] Lyly was not without his own pretensions to moral authority, but the brittle brilliance of his writing was inadequate to them. Spenser's vastly greater talent was adequate to and enabled by the range of performance required by a prestigious form of poetry. He was therefore able to achieve, as his contemporaries immediately recognized, a kind of *literary* authority.

Like the metaphor of a poetic domain, "literary authority" is a thoroughly ambiguous term. The humanist claim is that literary prowess gives one cultural, social, and political authority. On the other hand, literary authority can be seen as merely literary, confined to the world of letters. Whatever its scope and powers, the idea of literary authority is crucial to the epoch of Sidney, Marlowe, and Shakespeare and, later, of Ben Jonson, Donne (praised by his elegist Thomas Carew for ruling "the universal

---

8. The most important of these were the neo-Latin poet Baptistus Mantuanus (known in England as "Mantuan") and Clément Marot, a Protestant and the leading poet of the court of François Ier. Mantuan published (1498) a book of *Eclogues* (ten in number, like those of his fellow Mantuan, Virgil) that became famous all over Europe and was a standard school text. Spenser imitates some of these poems in the July, September, and October eclogues of *The Shepheardes Calender*. Marot translated Virgil's *Eclogue* 1 and wrote four vernacular eclogues of his own, two of which (written in the 1530s) Spenser imitates in his "November" and "December" eclogues.

　　I take the word *overgo* from Gabriel Harvey, who spoke of Spenser's ambition to "emulate" and "overgo" Ariosto's *Orlando Furioso* in *The Faerie Queene*. This remark appears in a piece of literary publicity Spenser and Harvey promulgated in 1580: *Three Proper, and wittie, familiar Letters: Lately passed betwene two Vniuersitie men*, in Spenser, *Poetical Works*, ed. J. C. Smith and E. de Sélincourt (Oxford, 1912), 628.

9. Cited in *OED*; italics mine.

1. G. K. Hunter, *John Lyly: The Humanist as Courtier* (Cambridge, Mass., 1962), chap. 1; reprinted in Paul J. Alpers, ed., *Elizabethan Poetry: Modern Essays in Criticism* (New York, 1967).

monarchy of wit"), and Milton. Spenser's claim to full cultural authority was to be made in *The Faerie Queene*, but in *The Shepheardes Calender* he had already achieved—and for the first time in English—a kind of lyric authority. First of all, the work itself is a complete and substantial book of short poems that stands on its own terms. This will fail to impress us only if we forget the problems of motivating lyric that we have seen in Gascoigne, with his elaborations and evasions, and in Sidney with his romance narration and his self-conscious staging and justifying of his eclogues. *The Shepheardes Calender* appeals for its justification only to what it is, an eclogue book, and its supporting device, the calendar, is enabling and enhancing. If it begins with a diffident bid for Sidney's protection, in the author's poem "To his book," it concludes with an envoi that repeats Horace's proud claim: "Loe I haue made a Calender for euery yeare, / That steele in strength, and time in durance shall outweare."

The literary achievement Spenser claims for his book manifests itself in the lyric authority of his pastoral self-representation, Colin Clout. In the first half of *The Shepheardes Calender*, Colin appears divided against himself: once the master poet, he is now reduced by love to the complaining monotony of the January eclogue and the uneven eloquence he displays in "June." But in "August," his sestina, though not sung by him, expresses his love woes in a form as highly wrought as the youthful celebration of Eliza in "April." Colin's sestina leads to the two final eclogues, in both of which he himself is the singer and which sum up what E.K. called the "plaintive" aspect of the whole sequence. "November" expresses an impersonal grief, uses the most elaborate and lofty stanza in all the eclogues, and is consciously in a main tradition of European poetry. In "December," Colin Clout rehearses his life and love-suffering and uses a native form—the six-line stanza that was common in mid-Tudor lyric—to express his own particular grief and loss. Both poems combine strong feeling with moral awareness and formal control. "November" endows the technical fanciness and impersonal moralizing of Colin's elegy with the passionate feeling E.K. admires in his commentary. In "December," Colin takes a fuller and more accepting view of his plight—and utters a richer and more various complaint—than he does in "January," the opening poem, in which he is mired in his wretchedness.

Colin Clout's emergence as the singer of the two concluding poems—as the master singer in "November" and as, in a sense, master of himself in "December"—might lead us to speak, in a general way, of his lyric authority. But I think the term has a more precise meaning, because these two poems speak to two of the main cultural pressures on the mid-Tudor lyric, the disparagement of love and the moral conflict between youth and age. This conflict is the subject of the February eclogue and underlies the ecclesiastical debate in "May." But in the second half of the work, authoritative old shepherds give way to shepherds who are past youthful innocence, but who do not step into the old shepherd's role of fixed moral authority. Diggon Davy in "September," Cuddie in "October," and Colin Clout himself are all speakers whose experience has thwarted them: Diggon as a seeker of ecclesiastical vocation, Cuddie as an ambitious and noble-spirited poet, Colin as a pastoral philosopher and singer. For each of them,

Spenser seeks to develop a rhetoric that combines, rather than opposes, imagination and moral awareness, emotional energy and the felt lessons of experience. Where Diggon Davy and Cuddie appear in dialogues with other shepherds, Colin's two songs are self-sufficient monodies. The pastoral assumption that song can resolve or at least fully voice distress becomes a source of poetic authority in these poems. They turn the moral and cultural oppositions that in other writers compromise lyric into sources of lyrical accomplishment. Like Sidney's double sestina, they endow the expression of loss with what has the feeling of lyric presence. But where this sense of presence in Sidney's poem is a function of the verse form itself, in the last two eclogues of *The Shepheardes Calender* it attaches itself to the first-person speaker. Sidney too had a pastoral pseudonym, but it was Colin Clout who became a figure, even a name to reckon with, in Elizabethan culture.

MUIOPOTMOS: A MINI-CASEBOOK

D. C. ALLEN: [The Butterfly-Soul]†

The literal reading of the "Muiopotmos" may now be made with a certain assurance. The butterfly Clarion, unaware of his symbolic history and of the great cause between Venus and Minerva, is slain by the spider who is well tutored in traditional antipathy. A conflict on high affects the humble ones below. The moral may be pondered: when great men or goddesses quarrel, lesser innocents suffer. This may be all that the poem means; but I am inclined to think that it has a higher seriousness than this, that it is an allegorical account of the eternal struggle between Good and Evil, and, on a subordinate plane, between Wisdom and Pleasure as partisans of these great forces. To discover this seriousness we can make an excursion into the history of the legend of Cupid and Psyche to which Spenser alludes. * * * The myth of Cupid and Psyche, hallowed by the Platonic associations of its author, was read during the Renaissance as an allegory of the rational soul bound in marriage to Divine Love but disturbed in its marital duties by the lower levels of the mind. * * *

The Psyche legend, like that of the Phoenix, was one of the few pagan myths accepted by early Christians. The myth is represented on many Christian monuments, gravestones, catacomb frescoes, and sarcophagi; and the Christian Psyche is usually painted with the wings of a butterfly.[1] The reason for these symbolic wings is that the Greeks represented the human soul as a butterfly. * * * Spenser had only to look up the word for "soul" in any Greek lexicon such as the 1586 edition of Scapula's dictionary to read: "ψυχή, spiritus, flatus . . . Item papilio."

The title, then, is not so ironic as it seems, for "πότμο," as Spenser

† From "*Muiopotmos*, or The Fate of the Butterflie," *Image and Meaning* (Baltimore, 1968) 20–41. The essay has been slightly condensed. Reprinted by permission of The Johns Hopkins University Press.

1. M. Collingnon, *Essai sur les Monuments Grecs et Romains relatifs au Mythe de Psyché* (Paris, 1877).

surely knew, was reserved by the Greeks for the fatal destiny of great heroes: "πότμον ἐπισπειν," as Homer is accustomed to say. On the literal level there is irony, but it washes away as the allegory unfolds. The clear soul, faultless and sinless, sponsored by piety and wisdom (Minerva), yet ballasted and weighed down by the senses (Venus), can come through spiritual heedlessness into the web of evil. For this tragedy, "πότμο" is an exact term and Melpomene the proper Muse. * * * Patterned after this garden of the fleshly way of life, the "gay gardins" where Clarion wanders are those in which Art aspires

> T'excell the naturall, with made delights:
> And all that faire or pleasant may be found
> In riotous excess doth there abound. (166–68)

The permissible world of experience is left behind, and Clarion yields to the senses. As yet he has not sinned, but his spiritual weakness will carry him into the web of evil. Spenser now begins to warn the reader, to suggest by adjectives that the butterfly-soul is in trouble. Clarion has a "curious busie eye" (171); he attempts to satisfy "his glutton sense" (179); he preys "greedily" (204) on the flowers, and then he rests in "riotous suffisaunce" (207). The hero, in spite of his Christian armor and the good hopes of his "Sire," is slipping into heedlessness. The butterfly soul that cannot distinguish between "flowres" and "weed of glorious feature" will easily succumb to the eye-sins that hide behind "what ever thing doth please the eie."

It is just at this point, too, that Clarion is doomed, for we are instantly informed that Jove has woven the fate of the butterfly. "Heavens avengement," "πότμο," is at hand. Both Destiny and Providence are aware that the butterfly must fall. "Careles Clarion" (375) flutters sinward while Spenser provides us with two passages that comment on his "unstald desire" and the heedless independence that is mutually possessed by the butterfly and the Red Cross Knight. Directed by desire, reckless Clarion feeds hither and yon in the garden of sensation,

> And whatso else of vertue good or ill
> Grewe in this Gardin, fetcht from farre away,
> Of everie one he takes. (201–203)

His inability on this fair morning to distinguish between good and evil, his love of foreign pleasures (any normal Englishman would see the fault in this), his eagerness to possess all that the spring brought forth comes, perhaps, from the spiritual vanity that ruined the Red Cross Knight. This suggestion is strengthened by a suite of lines that ushers in the actual tragedy,

> [Clarion] walkt at will, and wandred too and fro,
> In the pride of his freedome principall:
> Litle wist he his fatall future woe,
> But was secure, the liker he to fall.
> He likest is to fall into mischaunce,
> That is regardles of his gouvernaunce. (379–84)

This is a poetical restatement of the advice given by St. Paul to the men of Corinth, when he reminded the Church of the pride that brought Lucifer down and would overthrow them, too. "Let him that thinketh he standeth take heed lest he fall." Through heedlessness as much as through the "troublous winde," through pride of self-surety as much as through the hate of the spider, Clarion, brightest and fairest of souls, descends to the realm of the senses. With this fall, we return to a Christian reading of the Psyche myth.

It is time now, since the cue has been heard, for Aragnoll, son of Arachne and foe by tradition of Minerva's butterfly, to enter. Thanks to Job 8:14 (His trust shall be like the spider's web) and Isaiah 59:5 (They have eaten the eggs of asps and woven the webs of spiders), Aragnoll and his house embodied a Christian symbolism that associated them with impiety, heresy, hypocrisy, worldliness, and the very Devil himself. * * * An early commentary on the eleventh century *Physiologus* of Theobaldus combines all of these meanings into a spiritual discourse on the nature of Aragnoll.

> The Devil catches us as if we were flies; he is always putting traps, nets, and loops in our way so that he can take us through sin. When he takes someone in mortal sin, then he eviscerates and deprives them of grace unless the sinner is rescued by confession and penitence. So the chief snare of the devil is man's own will and it is only by repentance that he can avoid it. The spider fears the sun just as the devil fears the Holy Church and the just man, who can also be compared to the sun. Usually the spider weaves his web at night; so the devil weaves his when the just man is less watchful.[2]

Thus Aragnoll, the destroyer of the butterfly-soul, is unmasked.

RONALD B. BOND: [The Workings of Envy]†

* * *

Allen's interpretation is paradoxically reductive in that it enlarges the meaning of the poem to a point where more exact analysis has seemed redundant. I want to suggest, however, that as well as being a story embodying disillusionment, as well as being about the fall, "Muiopotmos" is an allegorical story about the workings of envy. Even the normal rivalry between art and nature becomes in this poem part of a spirit of contentiousness which permeates Clarion's world. In considering this competitiveness, we should recall that one of the most frequently used synonyms for *invidia* is *aemulatio*. Cooper's *Thesaurus* defines *aemulor* thus: "With a certayne enuy and ambition to indeuour to passe & excell an other man: to folowe, or study

---

2. Auber, *Histoire et Théorie du Symbolisme Religeux* (Paris, 1884), III. 496.
† From *"Invidia* and the Allegory of Spenser's *Muiopotmos,"* English Studies in Canada 2 (1976): 144–155. The original footnotes have been reduced and edited. Reprinted by permission of *English Studies in Canada* and the author.

to be like an other: to imitate or counterfaite."[1] The first meaning given here, the common one, lies behind Spenser's use of conceptual cognates for the central idea of envy: witness the prominence of words such as "contend," "challenge," and "excell" in the poem.

Spenser's primary allegorical symbol for envy in the poem is Aragnoll. With considerable cumulative force Spenser calls him "a wicked wight / The foe of faire things, th'author of confusion, / The shame of Nature, the bondslaue of spight" (243–45). Traditionally spiders and scorpions had been associated not just with evil in general, but specifically with the envious and detracting. Aragnoll's web is linked with another significant trap, more-over, in the simile which compares the spider's web with Vulcan's net [369–74]. Vulcan, his forge, and his home on Mount Aetna had become con-venient symbols for jealousy and *invidia*, and it is unlikely, therefore, that Spenser's recollection of Vulcan at this juncture is simply fortuitous.

The conjunction of the envious spider with the poem's prominent weav-ing image suggests that a further moralization may apply. Drawing on the literal and derived meanings of the Latin verb *texere*, from which our words "text" and "textile" come, and on the fact that *exordium* can mean either the warp of a web, or the beginning of a speech, Erasmus had written about the nature of the spider and its human counterparts in "Ex se fingit velut araneus," one of the *Adagia*. Included under the rubric "Inconstantiae perfidiae versutiae," the passage suggests that, as the spider brings its web out of itself, so detractors spin their insubstantial tales. I would suggest, then, that the whole weight of the iconographical tradition which associates envy and detraction with spiders lies behind Spenser's poem. To regard Aragnoll as Satan simply because the spider is "traditionally an obnoxious creature"[2] is surely to assume too readily the correctness of Allen's thesis and to make Spenser unnecessarily oblivious to aspects of his culture lesser writers did not ignore.

But what of the spider's victim? He is not just a butterfly, he is a butterfly called Clarion [i.e., trumpet]. * * * The trumpet's designation as Fame's instrument is a commonplace: the Pléiade poets extolled Homer as the "Buccinateur" of Achilles' praise;[3] Valeriano and Ripa both affiliate *tuba* and *fama*, and there are many iconographic representations of Fame's clarion;[4] Puttenham says that poets are "in deede the trumpetters of all praise,"[5] while E.K., in the letter to Harvey, assures us that Spenser will be raised from oblivion when his praises have been broadcast in the "tromp of fame." In the light of this image's conventionality, it is reasonable to assume that in naming his butterfly, Spenser used metonymy, fully ex-pecting his readers to identify properly the nuances of Clarion's name.

---

1. Cooper, *Thesaurus Linguae Romanae et Britanniae* (1565; facs rpt Menston 1969), s.v. *aemulor*. The confusion between *in bono* and *in malo* senses of emulation is noted frequently by late medieval exegetes, particularly when glossing 1 Corinthians 13:4 where Paul includes among the attributes of charity the phrase, "charitas non aemulatur." Commentators distinguished between the meaning of *aemulor* here and its other meaning exemplified in 1 Corinthians 14:1.
2. Franklin E. Court, "The Theme and Structure of Spenser's *Muiopotmos*," *SEL* 10 (1970), p. 12.
3. *Variorum Spenser*, VIII. 297.
4. See Guy de Tervarent, *Attributs et symboles dans l'art profane 1450–1600*: Diction langue perdu (Geneva, 1958–59), col. 397.
5. George Puttenham, *The Arte of English Poesie*, ed. G. D. Willcock and Alice Walker (Folcroft, Pa., 1969), p. 15.

If we think of Clarion as representing the man hungry for fame, many of the poem's details have additional significance. The gathering of flowers to make a garland for Venus is itself germane to the quest for fame and should be compared with Serena's picking of flowers in book VI of *The Faerie Queene*: in both cases, envy's incursions are not long in coming. The praise and "blazed fame" (266) accorded Arachne, moreover, prompt Minerva's descent to earth and finally provoke the presumptuous Arachne's challenge. The happiest consequence of treating Clarion in this way, however, is that throughout the whole of Spenser's work and, indeed, most of Renaissance poetry, the famous man, recipient of worldly praise, is most susceptible to envy. * * *

The historical pressures which complement this philosophical theme add another dimension to the fact that Clarion is a butterfly. "Muiopotmos," published in 1591 after Spenser's visit to England, reflects the same disillusionment with the court and courtiers which we find in "Colin Clouts Come Home Againe" and parts of "Mother Hubberds Tale," and the butterfly who is first envied "in Court" (105) epitomizes, in fact, the vain trifling activity in which courtiers were engaged. In late Elizabethan and Jacobean literature the comparison between courtiers and butterflies becomes a commonplace to be repeated in satires such as *The Scourge of Villanie, Skialetheia, The Time's Whistle*; it is repeated in Marston's *Antonio and Mellida*; both Dekker and Nashe use it.[6] But surely Clarion is the most conspicuous (and perhaps the first) example of this tendency to identify the butterfly with the courtier: decked in all his finery, he is a pregnant reminder of the fame-thirsty courtier who is brought low by his own carelessness and his rivals' envy.

ROBERT A. BRINKLEY: [The Politics of Metamorphosis][†]

If the Arachne-Pallas episode in *Muiopotmos* rereads Ovid in terms of the Elizabethan court, if it uses a reading of Ovid to read the art of the Fairy Queen, the butterfly in *Muiopotmos* involves a rereading of Vergil as well. * * *

Muiopotmos concludes with a fresco from the *Aeneid*; Clarion dies as Turnus dies: "His deepe groning spright/In Bloudie streames foorth fled into the aire,/His bodie left the spectacle of care" (ll. 438–40). Like Turnus, Clarion's corpse is a Vergilian sign: as a spectacle, the corpse represents care (in Vergil, *cura*), but what the corpse also represented in the *Aeneid* was the careful labor (the labors of Aeneas, of Caesar and of Vergil) for which—like force in Homer—mortal things are indices. In *Muiopotmos*, on the other hand, as a spectacle of care, Clarion, a parody of a hero, is

6. For Marston, see *The Poems*, ed Arnold Davenport (Liverpool 1961), p 121 and *The Works*, ed A.H. Bullen (London 1887); Everard Guilpin, *Skialetheia* (1598), Shakespeare Association Facsimiles No. 2 (Oxford 1931), sig. B4ᵛ; R.C., Gent., *The Time's Whistle: or New Daunce of Seven Satires and Other Poems*, ed. J.M. Cowper, EETS os 48, p 136; for Nashe and Dekker, see the reference in John Carey, "Sixteenth and Seventeenth Century Prose," *English Poetry and Prose*, 1540–1674, ed Christopher Ricks (London 1970), pp 381–82.
† From Robert A. Brinkley, "Spenser's *Muiopotmos* and the Politics of Metamorphosis," *ELH* 48 (1981): 668–76. The essay has been slightly condensed. Reprinted by permission of The Johns Hopkins University Press.

an index only of envy. Turnus is killed by Aeneas, the founder of the Roman world. Clarion is killed by a spider, a rival victim. The hero's fate—drained of meaning—has become no more relevant than an insect's.

Such insignificance involves political perspectives. William Nelson suggests that in Muiopotmos Spenser "directs his readers to sit in a godlike seat, to look upon the little world of butterflies and spiders so that he may understand how Olympus sees mankind."[1] The poem recreates us both as gods and insects, and for Spenser's immediate audience, the Elizabethan court, the poem mirrors positions at court. Courtiers may take a godlike perspective and regard Clarion and Aragnoll as insects; courtiers may identify themselves with the insect world and discover that they themselves participate in epic parodies. As gods we celebrate the artistry which produces Clarion and Aragnoll; as insects we feel diminished by that artistry. Yet Spenser's poem may involve a third perspective as well, that of a reader-narrator who, by understanding the fate of the butterfly, absents himself from that fate.

In Muiopotmos, Pallas's artistry recreates the artistry of the poem, but as Vergil's temple in the Georgics centers on an image of Caesar, so Spenser's text in Muiopotmos centers on an image of Elizabeth. As such the focus of his epyllion recreates the focus of The Faerie Queene, a poem consecrated "to live with the eternitie of her fame," * * * [and] even as the mortalia in Vergil's temple are glorifications, so Spenser's epic parodies are frescoes which decorate his poem and glorify the power of his Queen. That the parodies glorify Spenser's own power seems to me less clear. * * * The narrator observes, wanders in, and explores a poetic domain which he claims to have discovered. He rarely seems in possession of it. At times he seems possessed by it, but possessed, in particular, by its foreignness: "My weary steps I guyde/In this delightfull land of Faery . . . straunge waies," Spenser writes (VI, Proem, i). In the Mutability Cantos he explicitly separates his own vision from the vision he relates. In Muiopotmos he finds himself driven toward a conclusion which he does not seek but which the poem's creativity requires. While we may interpret such a stance as mere convention, if we imagine a master rhetorician behind this convention, manipulating our responses, we create a figure for the poet which the poetry itself does not envision. * * * Spenser pictures himself wandering through a landscape of recreations, an explorer of a metamorphic world, who encounters parodies but is not recreated as one of them. Rather than become a sign in the text of the poem, the narrator who reads what he envisions and relates what he reads, makes of his poem an index of his freedom to read—even as what he reads is an index of the presence of the Fairy Queen. The narrator who reads distinguishes himself both from the characters in his poem and from his poetry's metamorphic force. Unlike Arachne or the butterfly, Spenser is not a figure in Pallas's text. Having become its narrator, he evades the politics which has silenced them.

1. William Nelson, The Poetry of Edmund Spenser (New York and London, 1963), p. 72.

ANDREW D. WEINER: [Butterflies, Men,
and the Narrator in *Muiopotmos*]†

* * *

The problem may be stated simply enough: if we accept Allen's notion
(however modified) of the butterfly as the rational soul, we must then
proceed to see in his destruction either a just punishment for his "fall,"
the unjustness of a universe that destroys what is beautiful, fragile, and
innocent for no good reason, or blind chance randomly striking out against
a handy target. In any case, though, the equation of the butterfly with the
soul creates a problem of poetic representation. After all, a butterfly, whatever meaning we may impose upon it, *is* an irrational creature of the "lower
order," and it is not likely to be able to act other than naturally. * * *

If, however, the butterfly is an emblem of the soul, he must be doing
something wrong to merit the destruction the gods visit upon him—if we are
not to be left with the blinded Gloucester's despairing analogy: "As flies to
wanton boys are we to the'gods;/They kill us for their sport" (*King Lear*,
IV.i.36–37). On other occasions, the narrator apparently adopts this position
and, consequently, we are offered (more or less simultaneously) another vision of the psyche's decline and fall. That the butterfly can be a representation of the soul is clear. * * * [But] if commentaries on the legend of Cupid
and Psyche attest to the symbolic meaning of the butterfly, marginal illustrations in medieval and Renaissance manuscripts—at least as late as the Gri-
mani Breviary—abound in butterflies, frequently full of sound and fury, yet
apparently signifying absolutely nothing. With little effort, one finds them
(in the pages of Lilian Randall's census of *Images in the Margins of Gothic
Manuscripts*) sitting still, flying, or being held on strings; fighting men with
swords and bucklers, being shot at by men with crossbows and by centaurs,
or having shawms blown at them; riding in carts; being pursued by women,
nude men, and apes; ringing bells; and being viewed as lunch by storks.[1]

In the fifteenth century, butterflies leave the margins and move into
panel paintings as well. In addition to being presented more or less inno-
cently for decorative purposes, as in the Louvre portrait of an Este Princess
by Pisanello or the Baldovinetti Annunciation (c. 1460) in the Uffizi, there
are Renaissance butterflies whose meaning is precisely that they mean
nothing.[2] * * *

If we now return to consider Spenser's ambiguous butterfly not as a
necessary fixed emblem for the human soul, the rock upon which we must
build an allegory, but as a "creature wilde" by whom man "in somme
thinges may be taughte," * * * we must first decide whether the fate of the
butterfly in fact has the slightest relevance for us. The narrator seems to

† From Andrew D. Weiner, "Spenser's *Muiopotmos* and the Fates of Butterflies and Men," *JEGP*
84 (1985): 203–20. Copyright © 1985 by the Board of Trustees of the University of Illinois.
Reprinted by permission.

1. Lilian M. C. Randall, *Images in the Margins of Gothic Manuscripts* (Berkeley: Univ. of California
Press, 1966), pp. 62, 74, 76, 136, 146–47, 166, and 227.
2. For Pisanello, see Enio Sindona, *Pisanello* (New York: Harry N. Abrams, 1963), Plate 104. For
Baldovinetti, see Paolo Lecaldano, *I Grandi Maestri della Pittura Italiana Del Quattrocento*, II
(Milan: Rizzoli Editore, 1963), Plate 52.

think so, but if we look at him objectively we might well wonder how objectively he is looking at the butterfly. His description of Clarion arming himself to fly abroad may serve as a possible test. While it may begin as a light parody of an epic arming scene, this description (along with the butterfly's "furnitures") quickly becomes too bizarre to comprehend. Clarion's breastplate "of substance pure" is perhaps easily allegorized as the soul guarding itself with righteousness (cf. Ephesians 6:14), although "righteousness" is perhaps not most optimistically viewed as

> framed, to endure
> The bit of balefull steele and bitter stownd,
> No lesse than that, which *Vulcane* made to sheild
> *Achilles* life from fate of *Troyan* field.   (ll. 61–64)

From this point, the narrator's hold on reality seems to become increasingly tenuous. What are we to do with a butterfly who wears "about his shoulders broad" the "hairie hide of some wilde beast, whom hee / In saluage forrest by aduenture slew" (ll. 65–67), and what are we to think about those who, seeing him "so horrible," believe him to be "*Alcides* with the Lyons skin / When the *Naemean* Conquest he did win" (ll. 70–72)? Displaying no sense of the incongruity of his description, the narrator goes on to talk about Clarion's "glistering Burganet" that "could both *Phoebus* arrowes ward, / And th'hayling darts of heauen beating hard" (ll. 79–80). Nor is it easier to accept his comparison of the butterfly's antennae, those "two deadly weapon's fixt," to the "threatfull pikes" of a "warlike Brigandine," which this "flie" outstretched "so as him their terrour more adornes" (ll. 81, 84–85, 87–88). Not only is it hard to see in this an allegory of the soul— Dante's "angelic butterfly / that flieth to judgment without defence"—it is hard to see anything that can possibly be taken as seriously as the narrator quite obviously does.

* * * We are more likely, it seems to me, to get a sense of what *Muiopotmos* is about by considering the butterfly as if it were merely a butterfly and the narrator as though he were a Chaucerian narrator and not Colin Clout in disguise. * * * Like Sir Terwin, who also loves in vain a lady who "ioyd to see her lover languish and lament" (*Faerie Queene*, I.ix.27), the narrator seems to see the world through the eyes of that "Cursed wight," the "man of hell, that cals himselfe *Despaire*" (I.ix.28). All "hope of due reliefe" (I.ix.29) has evidently been plucked from him, and the fate of the butterfly is for him a confirmation of this state of affairs.

Instead of seeing the butterfly's death as totally unrelated to his own or as emblematic of the transitoriness of earthly things—like the love over which "The Archer God . . . /That ioyes on wretched louers to be wroken,/ and heaped spoyles of bleeding harts to see" (ll. 98–100) presides—he takes it as a sign of the destruction that will come to all "fraile, fleshly wight[s]" (l. 225). Una's consolation to another "fraile, feeble, fleshly wight" (*Faerie Queene*, I.ix.53) suffering at the hands of *Despaire*, "In heauenly mercies hast thou not a part?" (I.ix.53), is evidently beyond his comprehension since the only "grace" of which he can conceive is the grace to be gained by stealing Clarion's wings and bringing "So precious a pray" (ll. 110,112) to his love.

If the narrator's psychological state explains *why* he has misunderstood his story, it does not explain *how* he "misread" the events he saw—a butterfly flying through a garden until he became entangled in a spider's web and perished. To say that he turned a simple narrative into an allegory, while true, does not explain how he came to do such a bad job of it. After all, he too presumably had the emblem books and the commentators to tell him how to interpret: what went wrong? * * * Calvin notes that God, "to manifest his perfection in the whole structure of the universe, and daily place himself in our view," has forever engraved his "glory . . . in characters so bright, so distinct, and so illustrious" on all of his works that "none, however dull and illiterate, can plead ignorance as their excuse."[3] As he goes on to add, however, "Bright . . . as is the manifestation which God gives both of himself and his immortal kingdom in the mirror of his works, so great is our stupidity, so dull are we in regard to these bright manifestations, that we derive no benefit from them" (I.v.ii). * * *

Protestant exegetics thus downgrades allegory to the status of "examples or similitudes borrowed of strange matters" or excludes it altogether. As Tyndale comments, "Allegories prove nothing."[4]

The narrator's attempt to find meaning in the life and death of the butterfly is doomed to failure from the beginning. As he seeks to understand allegorically the connection between the butterfly's fate and his own and to comprehend the cause of its fall, his only chance of success lies in his coming to recognize that he must fail. Yet despite his confusion—he vacillates between feeling that the butterfly has done nothing to deserve its fate and assuming that everything it did must have been wrong—he never seems able to confess to himself or to us that he has not the faintest notion why the butterfly died or what its death might mean. The narrator, hoping to find some visible cause for the butterfly's fate, tries his best to condemn the insect for doing what it was created to do, to "cast his glutton sense to satisfy" (l. 179). But if so strict a moralist as Calvin would not find fault in the butterfly's enjoyment in the garden, why should we?

AMORETTI

LOUIS MARTZ: [Amoretti]†

* * *

But what of the other alleged disproportions and inconsistencies in the sequence [e.g., in particular, J. W. Lever's opinion that "the sonnets show

---

3. Jean Calvin, *The Institutes of the Christian Religion*, trans. Henry Beveridge (Grand Rapids, Mich., Wm. B. Eerdmans, 1970), I.vi.1. I cite Calvin simply as a representative of Reformed Protestant opinion in the second half of the sixteenth century, not to suggest that Spenser was a Calvinist.
4. William Tyndale, "Prologue to Leviticus," in Tyndale's *Doctrinal Treatises and Introductions to Different Portions of the Holy Scriptures*, ed. Henry Walter (Cambridge: Cambridge Univ. Press, 1848), p. 425.
† From "The *Amoretti*: 'Most Goodly Temperature,' " *Form and Convention in the Poetry of Edmund Spenser*, ed. W. Nelson (New York, 1961) 146–68. Used by permission of the publisher, Columbia University Press.

irreconcilable inconsistencies in the presentation of the heroine"[1]]? These too, I feel, tend to disappear within a dominant tone of assurance and poise and mutual understanding that controls the series. This peculiar and highly original relationship between the lover and his lady may be our best key to the whole sequence. It involves a variety of closely related issues: how does the lover characterize himself? what attitudes does he adopt toward the lady? what sort of audience does she provide? how does she receive his addresses? It is worth while to examine first the nature of this lady, for she talks and acts more than most of these heroines do. Most Petrarchan ladies, as Pope might say, "have no characters at all"; and even Sidney's Stella, though she comes to display considerable adroitness in damping her lover's ardors, remains for most of the sequence a black-eyed effigy around which Astrophel performs his brilliant Portrait of the Lover as a very young dog.

But Spenser's lady has a very decided and a very attractive character.[2] First of all, it is clear that the lover's tributes to "her mind adornd with vertues manifold" (Sonnet 15), her "deep wit" (Sonnet 43), her "gentle wit, and vertuous mind" (Sonnet 79), her "words so wise," "the message of her gentle spright" (Sonnet 81)—it is clear that all these tributes to her mental powers are very well deserved. Quite early in the sequence, in the paired Sonnets 28 and 29, we find the lady wittily turning the tables on her lover in a dialogue that throws a bright light on their peculiar relationship. In Sonnet 28 the lover has noticed that she is wearing a laurel leaf, and this sign, he says, "gives me great hope of your relenting mynd," since it is the poet's own symbol; he goes on to warn her of the fate that befell proud Daphne when she fled from the god of poetry, and he ends with the witty turn:

> Then fly no more fayre love from Phebus chace,
> but in your brest his leafe and love embrace.

Then in Sonnet 29 the lady pertly carries on this play of wit:

> See how the stubborne damzell doth deprave
>   my simple meaning with disdaynfull scorne:
>   and by the bay which I unto her gave,
>   accoumpts my selfe her captive quite forlorne.
> The bay (quoth she) is of the victours borne,
>   yielded them by the vanquisht as theyr meeds,
>   and they therewith doe poetes heads adorne,
>   to sing the glory of their famous deedes.

All right, he says, since she claims the conquest, "let her accept me as her faithfull thrall":

> Then would I decke her head with glorious bayes,
>   and fill the world with her victorious prayse.

I do not see how this interchange can be taken as anything but smiling and good-humored, yes, even humorous, in our sense of the word. The phrase

1. J. W. Lever, *The Elizabethan Love Sonnet* (London, 1956), 99–136.
2. See Hallett Smith, *Elizabethan Poetry* (Cambridge: Harvard Univ. Press, 1952), 166–167.

"stubborne damzell" tells us a great deal about the poet's tone here: it is intimate, smiling, affectionate, respectful, reproachful, and courtly, all at once: it strikes exactly the tone that an older man, of experience and wisdom (someone a bit like Emma's Mr. Knightley) might adopt toward a bright and beautiful and willful young lady for whom he feels, not awe, but deep admiration and affection. It is an attitude that also implies considerable hope and confidence that his suit will in time be rewarded. It is an attitude that finds a fulfillment and perfect counterpart later on, after his acceptance, in the gentle wit of Sonnet 71, which even Mr. Lever takes as "affectionate banter" (p. 130). This is the sonnet where the lady, in a witty reversal of the poet's complaints, has woven into her embroidery a fable of the Bee and the Spyder; the poet picks up the imagery with joy and develops it with a deeply affectionate humor. Indeed, throughout the sequence she is certainly one of the most smiling and "chearefull" ladies to appear in any English sequence, and I doubt that her smiles are outdone anywhere on the Continent. Sonnets 39 and 40, wholly devoted to her smiling and her "amiable cheare," are only the most sustained of many indications of her "sweet eye-glaunces" and her "charming smiles" (Sonnet 17). In view of this it is hard to see why readers have insisted upon taking the whole sequence so solemnly. Sonnet 16, very early in the game, is enough in itself to tell us otherwise, with its playful, deliberately hyperbolic, and clearly smiling use of the Alexandrian Cupid:

> One day as I unwarily did gaze
>> on those fayre eyes my loves immortall light:
>> the whiles my stonisht hart stood in amaze,
>> through sweet illusion of her lookes delight;
> I mote perceive how in her glauncing sight,
>> legions of loves with little wings did fly:
>> darting their deadly arrowes fyry bright,
>> at every rash beholder passing by.
> One of those archers closely I did spy,
>> ayming his arrow at my very hart:
>> when suddenly with twincle of her eye,
>> the Damzell broke his misintended dart.
> Had she not so doon, sure I had bene slayne,
>> yet as it was, I hardly scap't with paine.

Now the meaning of "twincle" as a wink, a nod, a hint, was current in Elizabethan usage; a damsel with a twinkle would seem to hold here every modern connotation. At the same time, the strong colloquialism of the last two lines seems to warn us with a similar twinkle not to take this lover's professions of grief too solemnly.

But what then shall we make of Mr. Lever's eighteen excommunicated sonnets, along with others of this kind, where the lady commits those "huge massacres" with her eyes, and as a "cruell warriour"

> greedily her fell intent poursewth,
> Of my poore life to make unpittied spoile.
>> (Sonnet 11)

Many of these are done with such extravagant exaggeration of the conventional poses that they strike me as close to mock-heroic. These are the conventions of love, the poet seems to say; these are the usual rituals of courtship; he will gladly pay these tributes, and even overpay them, since this is what his delightful damsel seems to expect, and she thoroughly deserves this state; at the same time a girl of her deep wit will know exactly how to take them, in the spirit offered. She can be expected to respond with a smile and a witty rejoinder, as she does in Sonnet 18, herself outdoing the Petrarchan poses:

> But when I pleade, she bids me play my part,
> and when I weep, she sayes teares are but water:
> and when I sigh, she sayes I know the art,
> and when I waile, she turnes hir selfe to laughter.

We can begin to see, then, the kind of relationship in which these charges of cruelty are uttered; we can begin to anticipate the sort of tone that the lover will tend to adopt in paying his conventional tributes.

Spenser's title is in itself a clue: *Amoretti*, the diminutive form, implying a relationship of intimate affection; it might be translated as: "intimate little tokens of love."[3] At the same time, the Italian title seems to draw a special attention to the great Continental tradition from which the sequence takes its themes, its imagery, its form. A complete definition might read: *Amoretti*, "intimate little tokens of love made out of ancient materials deriving, primarily, from Italy."

And so we have: [Quotes Sonnet 10].

The tone here is very hard to describe. It would be too much to call it parody, and yet the postures seem to be deliberately judged by the presence of some degree of smiling. It would be too much to call the sonnet comic, and yet, if we temper the term rightly, there is an element of comedy here, though not so broad as in the sonnet with the "twincle." At the same time, of course, a great many of these sonnets of complaint are delivered in a straightforward manner, and others allow little more than the glimmer of a smile to break through in the last line or two. I am arguing only that the series is frequently touched with an element that we might call humor, parody, or comedy; it is a light touch, but it is, I think, sovereign. Among the sixty sonnets that comes within the first year of courtship, it is possible to single out at least fifteen that seem clearly to display this transforming humor (for example: Sonnets 10, 12, 16, 18, 20, 24, 26, 28, 29, 30, 32, 33, 37, 43, 46, 48, 50, 57); and their presence is bound to have considerable effect upon our reading of all the other sonnets of complaint. As prime examples I would instance Sonnet 30, where Spenser drives into absurdity the old Petrarchan cliché: "My love is lyke to yse, and I to fyre"; or Sonnet 32, where the homely image of the "paynefull smith" beating the iron with "his heavy sledge" prepares the way for an account of how the lover's "playnts and prayers" beat futilely "on th'andvyle of her stubberne wit";

> What then remaines but I to ashes burne,
> and she to stones at length all frosen turne?

3. This translation was suggested by my friend Thomas Bergin.

Lines such as these, so close to parody, need not be taken as utterly inconsistent with those other sonnets, such as 7, 8, and 9, where the poet praises his lady's angelic virtue, with that famous tribute to her eyes:

> Then to the Maker selfe they likest be,
>   whose light doth lighten all that here we see.
>   (Sonnet 9)

Does the opening line of the next sonnet (10)—"Unrighteous Lord of love what law is this, / That me thou makest thus tormented be?"—conflict with that exalted view of the lady? On the contrary, the poet seems to be making a clear distinction between those essential qualities deriving from the heavenly Maker, and those "cruelties" demanded by conventional Cupid, the unrighteous Lord of love, the adversary of the "glorious Lord of lyfe" who in Sonnet 68 teaches the lovers that devout lesson of love.

*   *   *

In Sonnet 45 we have, fully developed, the view that her essential being is belied by her proud and tyrannic aspects; here the lover, with a tone of excessive courtesy, urges the lady to stop looking in her mirror, "Your goodly selfe for evermore to vew," and instead to seek within her lover's "inward selfe" the image of her "semblant trew": [Quotes the remainder of the sonnet].

In still other sonnets the lover attempts to make a virtue of necessity by converting her twofold aspect into an example of "most goodly temperature": "Myld humblesse mixt with awfull majesty" (Sonnet 13):

> Was it the worke of nature or of Art,
>   which tempred so the feature of her face,
>   that pride and meeknesse mixt by equall part,
>   doe both appeare t'adorne her beauties grace?
>   (Sonnet 21)

In short, the sonnets that deal with the proud and cruel fair form an indispensable part of the series; they represent the due and proper acknowledgment of all the usual forms of tribute:

> Bring therefore all the forces that ye may,
>   and lay incessant battery to her heart,
>   playnts, prayers, vowes, ruth, sorrow, and dismay,
>   those engins can the proudest love convert.
> And if those fayle fall downe and dy before her,
>   so dying live, and living do adore her.

Sonnet 14 thus foretells the use of every possible mode of Petrarchan approach, and the series thoroughly fulfills the promise, in many various modes: exalted, solemn, tender, touched with the edge of a smile, tinged with a hint of wit, or broadly comic.

Then, as we come close to the point where the lover discovers his acceptance, we find the rich variety of all the earlier sonnets summed up for us in Sonnet 54, which is perhaps more important than any other individual sonnet for an understanding of the sequence:

> Of this worlds Theatre in which we stay,
> My love lyke the Spectator ydly sits
> beholding me that all the pageants play,
> disguysing diversly my troubled wits
> Sometimes I joy when glad occasion fits,
> and mask in myrth lyke to a Comedy:
> soone after when my joy to sorrow flits,
> I waile and make my woes a Tragedy.

Those lines provide the best possible answer to any who might doubt the presence of mirth and comedy in the sequence; but more important is the way in which this sonnet indicates the complete recognition of the lover that he is deliberately playing many parts, staging "all the pageants" in an ancient festival of courtship, adopting all the masks that may catch his lady's eye and prove his devotion.

> Yet she beholding me with constant eye,
> delights not in my merth nor rues my smart:
> but when I laugh she mocks, and when I cry
> she laughes, and hardens evermore her hart.
> What then can move her? if nor merth nor mone,
> she is no woman, but a sencelesse stone.

* * *

Most goodly temperature indeed: in that one phrase Spenser has given us the best possible account of the *Amoretti*, as he leads us back to the ancient roots and affiliations of the word *temperature: temperatura, temperatus, temperatio*; signifying, in the terms of my Latin dictionary: a due mingling, fit proportion, proper combination, symmetry, a regulating power, an organizing principle.

ANNE LAKE PRESCOTT:
[Allegorical Deer and *Amoretti* 67]†

As the huntsman of *Amoretti* 67 sits resting in the shade, alone with his hounds and the approaching hind, he is in fact accompanied by the literary ghosts of deer and hunters past. One hunter is Petrarch, of course (see *Rime* 190), and, although less often noted, Tasso's "fera gentil" (a wild animal now tame enough to be caught) is probably around somewhere.[1] But behind Petrarch and Tasso lies an immense body of literature comparing a relationship to that of hunter and hunted. Renaissance readers would know the most famous deer. One appears in Horace's lovely reassurance to Chloë, a poem sometimes cited as a source for *Am.* 78 but with a fawn more closely resembling the beguiled and trembling hind of *Am.* 67 observed at an earlier stage in the process of persuasion. "You avoid me," he tells the

---

† From "The Thirsty Deer and the Lord of Life: Some Contexts for *Amoretti* 67–70," *Spenser Studies* 6 (1985): 33–76. This excerpt has been somewhat revised and the notes severely minimized. Sources for information on deer, their symbolism, and hunting poems are cited in the original article. I quote the Bible in the 1560 Geneva translation. Reprinted by permission of the author and AMS Press, Inc.

1. Dasenbroek 1991 briefly discusses "Questa fera gentil" in the context of Spenser's quarrel with Petrarchism.

girl, "like a fawn seeking its timid mother on the pathless mountains, not without vain fear of the breezes and forest; if the coming spring rustles the light leaves or the green lizards disturb the bramble, the fawn trembles in heart and limb. Yet I do not chase you in order to mangle you like a fierce tiger or Gaetulian lion. Cease then at last to follow your mother, now that you are ready (tempestiva) for a man" (Odes 3.23).

Despite Horace's seductive mildness, hunting imagery like this hints at an anxiety about captivity and dismemberment. Deer are not wrong to tremble, after all, and the ancient metaphor touches on one of Amoretti's major themes: a (supposedly) feminine fear of imprisonment and wounding that must be put by when it is timely to do so. Indeed the hunt in Am. 67 may itself be "timely," because the capture, death, or even sighting of deer has often meant, at least in literary texts, a new beginning. True, such moments of transition can be unhappy. When Virgil compares the lovelorn Dido to a pierced hind wandering in anguish through the city (Aeneid 4.66–73), he indicates something about the cost of refounding a dynasty, for her lover Aeneas must choose between two quarries: the stricken deer and the Italic shores. Dido finds just what many animals fear—death—and in Italy the hero will again have trouble with deer when the killing of a pet fawn starts a war between the natives and the Trojans, a savagery once more associating empire with blood and sorrow.

Renaissance English poetry is likewise crowded with deer, sometimes indicating the poet and sometimes the object of his desire, while puns on deer/dear or hart/heart proliferated so that sometimes it is difficult to know if the author intends his metaphor as anatomical imagery, hunting allegory, or both. Among the hundreds of Renaissance (and medieval) hunting poems there may be several in which the hunter chases the deer with dogs, gives up, sits down by water to rest, and then finds that the deer comes to him to be bound. So far, however, I have found only one precedent for Am. 67 that contains all these elements. It is the sixth lyric in the Chansons spirituelles (1547) of Marguerite de Navarre, sister of King Francis I, grandmother of Henry IV (Sir Burbon in Book V of The Faerie Queene), and famous in England.[2] In it a young hunter asks a happy and wise old woman if the deer he seeks is in that forest, for he is willing to devote all his strength to hunting it. He is a bad hunter, she replies, for this deer is not to be captured by hard work, well-equipped hounds, and fancy paraphernalia. Rather, she informs the at first skeptical huntsman, if he will merely rest by a spring and spread the net of a humble heart, the deer will turn back and let itself be caught by love. Marguerite makes it clear that the deer in her witty evangelical allegory is the crucified Christ (the next song in the volume is, like Am. 68, a Resurrection poem). Some readers have also found the deer in Am. 67 Christlike, and this poem may offer further evidence that they are right—and also support a reading of Amoretti that stresses the utterly free nature of the lady's surrender, not the merit, education, or psychological development of the lover/speaker.[3]

Like Marguerite, moreover, Spenser may want us to recall some biblical harts and hinds, all thought by one or another authority to represent Christ,

2. Ed. Georges Dottin (Geneva, 1971) 17–20.
3. DeNeef 1982, 67, and Bernard 1989, 174, call her behavior Christlike.

the Christian, or the Church, and by some to signify more than one of these. These deer, to be sure, have shifty and multiple identities. Harts in one translation are hinds in another, and it can sometimes be difficult to divide the deer from the goats. In any case, though, deer had a reputation for habits that explain their usefulness to scriptural exegesis, art, and poetry. Even after the Reformation, when biblical commentary had for some time been sobering up after what now seemed its allegorical excesses, the purported behavior of deer remained familiar. As almost any reader of classical science, the church fathers, and bestiaries knew, deer are thirsty by nature. Their thirst increases after contact with their mortal enemies, serpents, which they force from their holes with saliva or warm breath and then either snuffle up in their nostrils and swallow (from hatred or as rejuvenating medicine) or trample under foot. Snake-killing is thirsty work; so, filled with venom, deer race to a spring or brook whose waters will refresh and renew them. Deer move quickly, leaping on the hills and rocky places. Although timid, they may be lured by music. Extremely long-lived, they know that to eat dittany will make an arrow fall out. They cross a wide river by swimming in single file, each deer's head resting on the rump of the preceding one; when the leader is exhausted it retires to the rear of the line and the next one takes over. Spenser would have come across this deer lore in any number of places, while for advice on how to catch them he could have consulted George Gascoigne's *Noble art of venerie* (1575), which also suggests uses for leftover bits of animal (dried deer pizzle, for example, helps stop bleeding) and gives the proper time to hunt each sort of deer: as a hind, the lady of *Am.* 67 is indeed in season in late March, at least if she is "fatte or in good plight."[4]

Of all biblical deer the one with the most obvious significance to a lover with respectable intentions is that in Proverbs 5.18–19: "Let thy fountaine be blessed, and rejoyce with the wife of thy youth. Let her be as the loving hinde and pleasant roe: let her breasts satisfie thee at all times, and delite in her love continually." The Geneva editors say merely that this shows that "God blesseth mariage and curseth whordome," but to the church fathers the loving hind was above all a symbol of Christ or of Christian love and celestial contemplation. God tells us to bear each other's burdens (see Galatians 6.2), says Augustine, and since deer do just that when crossing a river, perhaps Solomon was thinking of their habits when he wrote Proverbs 5.19.[5] Other commentators agreed; Ambrose, for example, calls the deer our lover, Christ (*PL* 14.849–50), and Origen says it signifies the love of a God who makes us not his servants but his friends (*PG* 87^1.1266).

Also relevant to *Am.* 67, despite their gender, are the amorous roes and harts of the Song of Solomon (e.g., 2.9: "My welbeloved is like a roe, or a yong heart"). The wedding of such a hart (usually allegorized as Christ) to his beloved bride sanctifies human unions and the love that sustains or inspires them. More of a puzzle is Psalm 22, the psalm Christ quoted from the cross and which was assumed to foretell the crucifixion. The psalmist was, says the headnote in the Geneva Bible, "past all hope" but now

4. Sigs. C4ff, P7^v; listed under Turberville in Pollard and Redgrave but ascribed to Gascoigne.
5. *Patrologia Latina*, ed. J. P. Migne (Paris, 1844–64) 40.80–81, henceforth *PL*; *PG* is *Patrologia Graeca*, ed. J. P. Migne (Paris, 1857–86).

"recovereth him self from the bottomles pit of tentations and groweth in hope," just as Christ "shulde marvelously, and strangely be dejected and abased, before his Father shulde raise and exalte him againe." The psalm, assigned in the Edward VI prayerbook for Good Friday, is certainly about a victim; is it also about a deer? Many thought it was, for its traditional title is "The Hind of the Morning" (probably in fact referring to the name of the tune). As Richard Sampson's 1539 commentary on the first fifty psalms put it, Christ is not absurdly called a hart or hind, for as deer snuffle up serpents and kill them, so Christ killed the serpent when he harrowed Hell and freed the human race from captivity (cf. Am. 68).

Commentators on deer, however, more often liked to cite Psalm 42, which for centuries had been sung at baptismal ceremonies on Easter Saturday (the day to which Am. 67 corresponds in Spenser's calendrical scheme); in its opening verse David's soul groans for God just as "When lyke in chase the hunted Hynde the water brookes doth glad desire."[6] The thirsty deer's gender varied from psalter to psalter, so like Matthew Parker, whose 1567 translation I quote, Spenser may well have imagined a panting hind. In any case, this deer, too, was associated with Christ, although it more often represented apostles, saints, and the faithful. Like many exegetes, Augustine is content to equate it with the faithful, especially those penitents who have killed the serpents of vice and now race to the waters of baptism and the fountains of life. Let us love like deer, he urges, who help each other (PL 36.464–67). John Chrysostom, whose writings may have influenced The Faerie Queene, goes further. In an impassioned meditation of the sort that earned him his name "Golden Mouth," he turns over and over to this verse. The implied serpents are vices, and we too should eat the "intelligible serpent" so as to acquire a holy thirst. After all, we are contracted to God, having promised to cherish him more than others and to burn with love. So when in the forum you see silver or golden clothes or other wealth, say to yourself, "Just a little while ago I sang, 'As the hart thirsts . . .'" (PG 55.155ff). In other words, the verse is a mnemonic to recall a contract, an engagement; as in the Song of Solomon and Proverbs 5.19 the deer is our partner in a love affair. Reformation commentary, however, tended to stress the exiled David's longing for water as a metaphor for his frustrated desire to worship in the temple. Perhaps this reading has some relevance to Am. 67, for Spenser's lovers are indeed soon found at public worship, probably in the next sonnet with its liturgical rhythms and certainly in the Epithalamion. The point, says Calvin, is to remind us that we are not to live in spiritual isolation, ignoring ceremonies and the congregation: "For he biddeth us not clymb straight up into heaven, but favouring our weaknes, he commeth down neerer untoo us" (Commentaries, trans. A. Golding, 1571). To Calvin, the deer is the suffering historical David, not Christ, but this argument, too, moves the discouraged human lover toward union with a beloved who comes voluntarily and whose love is not private and separate but sociable, joining the soul, in the words of Am. 70, to Love's "lovely crew."

One discussion of the thirsty deer seems particularly germane to Spenser:

6. Bieman 1983 and Johnson 1991 also hear an echo of Psalm 42 in Am. 67.

Victorinus Strigelius's often delightful *A proceeding in the harmonie of King David's harpe* (trans. R. Robinson, 1582 to 1598). The commentary on Psalm 42 (1593) paraphrases the opening verse in words that strikingly anticipate Spenser's own: "As the Hart in *chase* fleeth, and in *long pursute* made *wearie*, doth most greedily covet and *thirst* after the lively running springs," so I thirst not for puddles but for "springs of livelie Water" (my italics). This curative water is true consolation, the forgiveness of sin through Christ, for "The acknowledgement of Gods presence in calamaties, and the hope of the very last deliveraunce and of eternall salvation, doo call back languishing soules, as it were from the jawes of hel, and effectually heale the woundes of the hart." Sometimes, he adds, we feel abandoned (cf. the end of *Amoretti*), but we must learn to wait.

It seems clear, then, that *Am.* 67 resonates with scriptural echoes, all the more audible because Psalm 42 had long been associated with the evening before Easter. But why should Spenser think of a captured deer and not some other pre-Easter symbol? To provide a pastoral moment, maybe, or to help show up Petrarch. To sound again the theme of binding and loosing, of constraint that is liberating because freely chosen and mutual. Also, I think, to acknowledge that erotic love is like divine love also in its experience of pain and sacrifice. Spenser's sonnet nowhere mentions the dismemberment Marguerite's deer will experience, but the implication may be there, and feminine anxieties (whether widespread in real life is probably beside the point) about the consequences of even loving capture certainly receive sympathetic exploration in Books III and IV of *The Faerie Queene*. By accepting the risk of suffering, either as physical intrusion and later parturition or, also scary, as the penetration of an emotional and psychological perimeter, and by taking on an inevitable sense of some loss, the half-trembling deer assures for herself and for others—her lover, her family—a future triumph over doubt, bondage, and fear. It is hard to imagine what deeper or wiser compliment a poet could give a young woman.

WILLIAM NELSON

[Hobgoblin and Apollo's Garland]†

To Drayton's "grave moral" and Milton's "sage and serious" Spenser I would add, not altogether as a footnote, a playful one. The idea that whatever is comic about *The Faerie Queene* is so despite its author no doubt continues to prevail. Yet at least since the time of Upton some readers have been moved to laugh with Spenser rather than at him, and in recent years the response has been common enough to generate a number of essays with such titles as "Spenser's High Comedy," "His Earnest unto Game: Spenser's Humor in *The Faerie Queene*," [and] "Spenserian Humor: *Faerie Queene III* and *IV*." It has even been proposed that mirthlessness is the quality not

† From *Fact or Fiction: The Dilemma of the Renaissance Story-Teller* (Cambridge, MA, 1973) 74–91. Reprinted by permission of Harvard University Press, Copyright © 1973 by the President and Fellows of Harvard College.

of the poet but of his scholarly commentators. Perhaps the wind is shifting.

I am indebted to these studies for many of the examples I shall cite. But I am concerned particularly with the kind of playfulness in which the player mocks his own role. Much of what is remarked as humorous in *The Faerie Queene* is an integral part of its fictional stuff. When, for example, Spenser makes fun of Braggadocchio or shows us those fair ladies vainly trying to put on the girdle of chastity the comedy arises within the story: the characters are ridiculed, but the tale is not. I wish here to draw attention to Spenser's jesting, not at the characters and their actions but at his own fiction, mockery deliberately designed to undermine the narrative illusion. The difference between the two kinds of jest is like that between our laughter at and with Falstaff, in whom we do believe, and our laughter at Chaucer's Sir Thopas, in whom we do not. Of course, *The Faerie Queene* is not an outright burlesque like "The Tale of Sir Thopas." But there is burlesque in it, and recognition of that quality should temper and refine our reading of the poem. Spenser's story is indeed enchanting, like a child's fairy tale or a fantastic dream, yet it is a child's tale told to mature and sophisticated adults, a dream in broad daylight. Spenser's friend, the learned Gabriel Harvey, returned an early draft of the poem to him with the comment that it seemed Hobgoblin had run away with the garland from Apollo.[1] I think Hobgoblin stands for the fanciful fiction, Apollo's garland for the meed of a deeply moral poet writing in the great heroic tradition. I am here concerned only with Hobgoblin. I take as my text the comment of R. W. Church in the English Men of Letters series: "It has been said that Spenser never smiles. He not only smiles with amusement or sly irony; he wrote what he must have laughed at as he wrote, and meant us to laugh at."[2]

What he wrote was a heroic poem of high moral purpose, certainly not a laughing matter for the Renaissance. But it was also a narrative fiction dealing with brave knights' and ladies' gentle deeds, a tale typical of what Dean Colet called the "blotterature" of ignorant and misguided ages. In the glow of Renaissance self-esteem, chivalric story was an absurd, dead fashion, worthy only of such mocking uses as Ariosto made of it. "King Arthur's knights long since are fled," wrote Thomas Howell in 1581.[3] * * * Sidney himself was rather more indulgent, for in defense of fiction he argued that *Orlando Furioso* or "honest King Arthur would be more pleasing to a soldier than a discourse concerning the quiddity of *ens*.[4]

* * *

Spenser, nevertheless, elected this outmoded kind of story for his most ambitious undertaking. He had good reasons for doing so, some of which he lists himself. The example of Vergil taught him, as it taught Ronsard, to choose his hero from his nation's ancient past. Arthur's name was known to all, yet so little was recorded about him historically, particularly before his accession to the throne, that the poet was free to make fictions, precisely the activity that defined him as a poet. "Fierce warres and faithfull loves"

1. *The Works of Edmund Spenser, A Variorum Edition. The Prose Works* (Baltimore, Md., Johns Hopkins Press, 1949), p. 472.
2. R. W. Church, *Spenser* (London, Macmillan, 1906; 1st ed., 1879), p. 141.
3. Quoted by Charles Bowie Millican, *Spenser and the Table Round* (Cambridge, Mass., Harvard University Press, 1932), p. 183, from *Howell His Devises* (1581).
4. Philip Sidney, *An Apology for Poetry*, ed. Geoffrey Shepherd (London, T. Nelson, 1965), p. 127.

provided appropriate metaphors for the conflicts and attractions central to the moral problems with which he was concerned. And despite such mockery and abuse as I have cited, the chivalric tradition carried with it an atmosphere of golden antiquity, of "beautiful old rhyme / In praise of ladies dead and lovely knights." (If not *The Faerie Queene* what could Shakespeare have been thinking of?) Samuel Daniel would have others "Sing of Knights and Palladines / In aged accents and untimely words / Paint shadowes in imaginary lines, / Which well the reach of their high wits records."[5] Queen Elizabeth's Accession Day festivities continued to honor, at least ceremonially, the outworn ritual of tilt and tournament. In later centuries, the influence of *The Faerie Queene* itself and the search for some equivalent of the moribund pastoral made of the tales of ladies, of knights, and their impossible adventures a kind of golden literary world. But the ambivalence of Renaissance attitudes with respect to the chivalric tradition is illustrated dramatically in Shakespeare's *Troilus and Cressida* when noble Hector's storybook challenge to single combat for the honor of a fair lady provokes both admiration for a knightly gesture and Achilles' comment, " 'Tis trash."

Spenser is not like Shakespeare's Achilles, but he too recognizes the absurdity of chivalric narrative and from time to time exposes it to his own amusement and that of his readers. He confronts literary convention with the world as it is, not by means of guffaw, but by a subtle use of devices common to all burlesque, hyperbole, bathos, and patent illogic. That many passages in *The Faerie Queene* are hyperbolic, bathetic, and illogical, few would deny. The question remains, however, whether they are so because of the poet's naïveté or because of his sophistication. It is not a question that can be answered definitively, for it is not given to us to recapture fully the mood in which a work centuries old was written and read. Furthermore, the attempt to answer it is by its nature self-defeating. All dissection injures its subject, and of all subjects literary tone must be the most delicate. Who has ever laughed at a dissected joke?

A test case may serve to focus the issue. In the course of the climactic battle between St. George and the dragon, a battle fraught with the most profound moral and religious significance, the knight wounds his adversary under the wing:

> Forth flowed fresh
> A gushing river of blacke goarie blood,
> That drowned all the land, whereon he stood;
> The streame thereof would drive a water-mill.
> (I.xi.22)

In the Ovidian battle which Spenser appears to have been imitating, the monster's hemorrhage merely dyes the grass red. (*Metamorphoses*, III.85–86.) Does Spenser's passage lie within the fictional convention of desperate encounters, so that the hyperbole of the bloody river and the incongruity of the water mill are not parody but failure of taste, or is he mocking that convention at the same time as he makes use of it? If Chaucer were the author, the question would be easy to resolve. In the "Knight's Tale"

5. Samuel Daniel, *Delia*, Sonnet XLVI.

the sworn friends Palamon and Arcite agree to settle their competition for the love of Emily by mortal combat. They chivalrously arm each other and then chivalrously hack at each other. Perhaps this teeters on the boundary between fictional gallantry and burlesque of it. The story continues:

> Up to the ancle foghte they in hir blood.
> And in this wise I lete hem fightyng dwelle,
> And forth I wole of Theseus yow telle.
>
> (ll. 1660–2)

The blood tide is rather too high, the transition too abrupt. We are not disposed to take "Up to the ancle foghte they in hir blood" as inept hyperbole because we know that Chaucer is neither stupid nor lacking in a sense of the ridiculous. Nor can we dismiss the "Knight's Tale" as mere burlesque, like the "Tale of Sir Thopas." In the delicate balance that Chaucer achieves, the reader accepts the chivalric convention at the same time that he recognizes its absurdity. But Spenser's reputation labors under those heavy Miltonic epithets. He is a self-confessed allegorist dedicated to a moral purpose, a method and end we have been taught to regard as grimly humorless. The contrast of *The Faerie Queene* with *Orlando Furioso* reinforces our prejudice: the English poet borrows episode and rhetoric from the Italian but not his mood, and sometimes he seems to miss or (as I think) to ignore Ariosto's jokes. We read the *Orlando* as a delicious Renaissance entertainment; because *The Faerie Queene* is so very different, some critics are led to think of it as a late flowering of a decayed tradition rather than as a poem of the High Renaissance deliberately dressed in an outworn fashion.

* * *

Among the many voices of *The Faerie Queene* is one which tells its story as though it were written by a poet of long ago, ancient and therefore good, simple, and credulous, a lover of the fair and the brave. Often this speaker does not fully understand the tale he tells; sometimes he distorts its meaning. His language is marked by archaisms, his story by the clichés of medieval romance. He is not unlike the figure of the poet Gower whom Shakespeare puts forward as the "presenter" of *Pericles*—that "mouldy" tale as Ben Jonson called it. Behind this poet-narrator stands Spenser himself, making his presence felt from time to time in order to remind the reader that he has only suspended his disbelief, that the tale of heroes and heroines, monsters and witches, however profound its significance may be, is nevertheless only a tale. This he does typically in those passages in which the story is most characteristically old-fashioned.

Among the most conspicuous features of medieval narrative is its pretense that it is indeed historically true, based upon authoritative documents or reports. Rabelais mocks this pretense in *Gargantua*; Boiardo and Ariosto, in their *Orlandos*; More, in *Utopia*; Cervantes, in *Don Quixote*. Professor Robert Durling remarks on humorous pseudodocumentation in Boiardo and Ariosto, but Spenser, he says, "uses the mention of supposed sources of the poem . . . to lend authority, plausibility, or an aura of antiquity to the story—never for humorous effect."[6] Like most absolutes, I doubt that

6. Robert Durling, *The Figure of the Poet in Renaissance Epic* (Cambridge, Mass., Harvard University Press, 1965), p. 224.

this one can be sustained. The key passage in which Spenser defends the historical truth of his story is the Prologue to Book II. As More had done before him, Spenser pretends to be disturbed by the idea that some readers may doubt his veracity:

> That all this famous antique history,
> Of some th'aboundance of an idle braine
> Will judged be, and painted forgery,
> Rather then matter of just memory.

He is forced to admit that the "antiquities" he cites as authority are hard to come by. Yet the Amazon River and Virginia really were there before they were found, and other populated regions, perhaps even those in outer space, no doubt await other explorers. Therefore, he argues, Fairyland exists because it has not yet been discovered. The logical absurdity should warrant at least a smile.

Sometimes the reader is invited to verify the truth of the tale himself. Should he happen by the region of Merlin's cave (its location is precisely given though not easy to find) he must not attempt to enter its recesses "For feare the cruell Feendes should thee unwares devowre" (III.iii.8). Rather, Spenser advises, he should put his ear to the ground so that he can hear the dreadful noises within. A similar effect is produced by the testimony to the historical reality of Arthur's sword. After Arthur's death, we are told,

> the Faerie Queene it brought
> To Faerie lond, where yet it may be seene, if sought.
> (I.vii.36)

Had the poet stopped with "where yet it may be seene" the reader might well have taken it as the usual coin of chivalric narrative designed, as Durling suggests, to lend an aura of antiquity to the story. But the addition of "if sought" must make him wonder how to go about the seeking.

No chivalric tale can properly be without its desperate encounters between knight and knight or knight and horrid beast. Sparks fly, armor plate is riven, blood flows in torrents. There are many such battles in The Faerie Queene, and C. S. Lewis thinks that Spenser does this kind of thing very badly.[7] But perhaps that usually admirable critic failed to distinguish between bad writing and something that verges on parody. I let pass the dragon's blood-operated water mill, for some may think it intended seriously. But there can be no difference of opinion about Corflambo's recognition of his defeat by Arthur:

> ere he wist, he found
> His head before him tombling on the ground.
> (IV.viii.45)

Or Artegall's conquest of Grantorto:

> Whom when he saw prostrated on the plaine,
> He lightly reft his head, to ease him of his paine.
> (V.xii.23)

7. C. S. Lewis, The Allegory of Love (Oxford, Oxford University Press, 1936; reprinted 1958), p. 347.

Or Britomart's overthrow of Sir Scudamour:

> to the ground she smote both horse and man;
> Whence neither greatly hasted to arise,
> But on their common harmes together did devise.
>
> (IV.vi.10)

Or Radigund's escape from Artegall's huge stroke:

> had she not it warded warily,
> It had depriv'd her mother of a daughter.
>
> (V.iv.41)

Or the desperate fight between that virago and Britomart:

> [they] spared not
> Their dainty parts, which Nature had created
> So faire and tender, without staine or spot,
> For other uses, then they them translated;
> Which they now hackt and hewd, as if such use they hated.
>
> (V.vii.29)

Mocking the precision of a grocery clerk, Spenser says that the maw of the Blatant Beast has the capacity of "A full good pecke within the utmost brim" (VI.xii.26). Orgoglio's yell of pain when Arthur cuts off his left arm is likened, oddly enough, to the bellow of a herd of sexually excited bulls (I.viii.11). A few stanzas after the amputation of that left member the giant returns to the fray:

> The force, which wont in two to be disperst
> In one alone left hand he now unites.
>
> (I.viii.18)

Evidently Spenser is lightheartedly willing to undermine with a pun the seriousness of these combats even though they must signify the desperate struggles of the soul.

The most desperate of these is surely that of the Red Cross Knight against the powers that would destroy him. The subtle Archimago is a formidable magician indeed, capable of transforming himself into a dragon, of course, but also into fish, fowl, or fox, forms so terrifying

> That of himselfe he oft for feare would quake,
> And oft would flie away.
>
> (I.ii.10)

And the story of the final battle with the satanic dragon—that in which the water mill passage occurs—is handled no more respectfully. If one wishes to find a prime example of the comparison of great things to small, there can be few more striking instances than the likening of the "well of life" which can restore the dead and wash away the guilt of sinful crime to the "English *Bath* and eke the german *Spau*" (I.xi.30). When the newborn knight rises from immersion in that well he wounds his adversary with his sword, hardened, Spenser suggests, by holy water dew. The dragon, dazed and terribly angered, roars and renews the attack:

> Then gan he tosse aloft his stretched traine,
> And therewith scourge the buxome aire so sore,
> That to his force to yeelden it was faine.
>
> (I.xi.37)

The "buxome" gives it away. No doubt the obedient air did yield, as it does to the tail of my kitten.

Other examples of what must be deliberate bathos and incongruity are easy to find. The cosmic challenge of Mutability to the principle of constancy in the world takes the form of a motion at law, so that the ruler of Olympus is constrained to bid Dan Phoebus (who here becomes court clerk) to "Scribe her Appellation seale" (VII.vi.35). The list of "idle fantasies" that flit in the chamber of Phantastes in the House of Alma includes supernatural creatures, beasts, birds, and human beings graded in anticlimax:

> Infernall Hags, *Centaurs*, feendes, *Hippodames*,
> Apes, lyons, Aegles, Owles, fooles, lovers, children, Dames.
>
> (II.ix.50)

The cannibal nation, having made captive the sleeping Serena, debates as to whether to eat her at once or let her sleep her fill, deciding on the latter course by cookbook logic: "For sleepe they sayd would make her battill [fatten, as for the table] better" (VI.viii.38). When the naked girl is rescued at the critical moment by Sir Calepine, she says not a word to him. Her silence Spenser explains by describing her mood as "unwomanly" (VI.viii.51). As for Calepine himself, since the great work by Calepino was so well known to all Europe that his name had become a common noun, he must have meant "dictionary" or "thesaurus" to Spenser's reader, rather more specifically than "Webster" does to us. I do not quite get the force of this joke, but it must be a joke because among the other characters in this sixth book are Aldus and his son Aldine, as who should say, Sir Clarendon Press.

* * *

Overt jests at the expense of the fiction are not to be found in every stanza or in every canto of *The Faerie Queene*. They are nevertheless common enough to warn the reader that the naïveté of the narrator is a deliberately assumed pose, that Spenser is playing a part and expects his audience to know it. Nowhere does this mock naïveté appear more strikingly than in the story which is formally (though in form only) the principal action of the whole poem, the enamorment of Prince Arthur and his quest for Gloriana, Queen of the Fairies (I.ix.8–15). If Spenser was to pose as a medieval storyteller, what better choice of tale could he have made than one so typically medieval that Chaucer made fun of himself by telling it? Arthur's resemblance to the absurd Sir Thopas is unmistakable. Both chastely reject love; both on a day ride out hunting. Arthur is "prickt forth with jolitee of looser life"; Thopas pricks forth both north and east and falls into a love-longing. For Arthur, all nature laughs; for Thopas the herbs spring and the birds sing. Both weary of their sportful pricking and dismount to lie down on the soft grass. Arthur uses his helmet as pillow, an uncomfortable practice which Chaucer tells us (though not in the immediate context) is also Thopas'. The Prince dreams that the Queen of Fairies lies down beside him and makes him "Most goodly glee and lovely blandishment." Sir Thopas has a similar dream: a fairy queen shall be his leman and lie beneath his cloak. On waking, both heroes resolve to find their dream loves and their search takes them both to the country of Faery. And nothing more is heard of either quest. Though both poems are aborted, surely for different reasons, each has room for development of the story but neither makes use of it. In Spenser's version Chaucer's tail rhyme— "drasty ryming" (as the Host calls it)—is turned into the Spenserian stanza; obvious banalities are eliminated. Yet although the new version surely signifies the seductive power upon noble youth of a dream of glory, the story itself remains puerile, the characters unrealized, the events barely recounted, their sequence unmotivated. Since we recognize the similarity of the tale of Arthur's dream to that of Sir Thopas, many of Spenser's contemporaries must also have recognized it.

For some modern readers it is intolerable to believe that the central action of a poem of such manifest seriousness as *The Faerie Queen* could derive from a patent joke. Yet Spenser not only read "Sir Thopas," but he read it attentively, for he refers to Thopas and the giant Ollyphant elsewhere in his poem, and in his treatise on Ireland he discourses learnedly, though no doubt erroneously, on the resemblance of Thopas' costume to the dress of Irish horsemen.[8] One scholar attempts to resolve the dilemma by suggesting that Spenser took Chaucer's tale in dead earnest; lacking humor himself, he found no humor in it. Another concludes that since "Thopas" is funny, Spenser's source must have been some other medieval story, no doubt one of the kind that Chaucer burlesques. Another argues that, since the tale of Arthur's enamorment plainly derives from "Sir Thopas," it must be the residue of an earlier draft of *The Faerie Queene*, one without pretensions to didactic purpose and written at the time Spenser was proposing to "overgo" Ariosto rather than to fashion a gentleman or noble person in virtuous and gentle discipline. But it is inconceivable that any normally intelligent adult could take Chaucer's story seriously, almost as inconceivable as that a scholar should think that he did. Similar tales are of course to be found in medieval literature—why else should Chaucer have ridiculed them?—but Spenser had no need to seek elsewhere for his matter. And whether or not the story of Arthur's falling in love and vowing his great quest is part of the debris of an earlier version of *The Faerie Queene*, the poet did include it in the work which he presented so proudly to Queen Elizabeth. If narrative of this kind is what Gabriel Harvey objected to when he described that draft of the poem that Spenser sent him in 1580 as "Hobgoblin runne away with the garland from Apollo" the criticism still holds for the work as we have it. Spenser's imitation of the Thopas story, coupled with his mocking use of the clichés of chivalric narrative, leads to the conclusion that he found nothing incompatible in the association of an absurd tale and a deeply moral significance.

As Curtius shows, the Middle Ages did not doubt that jest and earnest

---

8. Edmund Spenser, A *View of the Present State of Ireland*, lines 2177ff.

could live together.[9] Prudentius finds it appropriate for St. Lawrence on the gridiron to suggest to his executioners that since he has been cooked on one side they have the opportunity of deciding whether the rare or the well-done is more savory. Hagiographers enliven their accounts of the saints with reports of how they miraculously make broken bottles whole or end a plague of insects by excommunicating them. In heroic poetry, too, comedy had its license, given authority by Servius' judgment that the story of Dido in the fourth book of the *Aeneid* is almost wholly comic in style, naturally, says Servius, since its subject is love. To Curtius' medieval examples I would add a Renaissance one: the episode in Canto IX of Camoens' *Lusiads* which concerns the delicious isle on which Thetys and her nubile nymphs provide sexual reward for the comically eager sailors of Vasco da Gama's heroic expedition. Camoens explains at last that the isle is not an isle and the nymphs not nymphs:

> For these fair Daughters of the Ocean,
> Thetys and the Angellick pensil'd Isle,
> Are nothing but sweet Honour, which These wan;
> With whatsoever makes a life not vile.
> The priviledges of the Martial Man,
> The Palm, the Lawrell'd Triumph, the rich spoile;
> The Admiration purchac't by his sword;
> These are the joys, this Island doth afford.
> (IX.89)[1]

The equation of sexual satisfaction with "sweet Honour" and "Lawrell'd Triumph" is exactly that of Arthur's dream of Gloriana.

Much of the harshest criticism of *The Faerie Queene* arises from its failure to meet expectations bred by the tradition of the novel. Spenser's stories do not hang together very well, narrative threads are left untied, episodes succeed each other apparently at haphazard, characters lack recognizable humanity. To counter such charges, one apologist invokes a theory of successive careless revisions. Another attempts to discover a formal dramatic structure in the text, a construction I doubt it will bear. Yet another accounts for the inconsequence of the narrative by describing *The Faerie Queene* as a dream poem, and indeed the story has the apparent formlessness of a dream without the excuse that its maker is asleep. Some single out Britomart as truly flesh and blood, usually on the ground that she undergoes a jealous tantrum, but I am not convinced, for all that, that she is tangible. *The Faerie Queene* is not of the genre of *Pamela*, *War and Peace*, or even Tolkien's *Lord of the Ring*. As the poet declares in his letter to Ralegh, he has embodied his instruction in a fiction because the example of great poets has sanctioned it and because it is "the use of these days" to demand delightfulness. But he is quite aware, and wants the reader to be quite aware, that the tale is merely a tale, an old-fashioned and most improbable one. Hence the note of parody and burlesque which deliberately breaks into the narrative enchantment.

9. E. R. Curtius, *European Literature and the Latin Middle Ages*, tr. W. R. Trask (New York, Pantheon Books, 1953), Excursus IV.
1. Luis de Camoens, *The Lusiads*, tr. Sir Richard Fanshawe, ed. Geoffrey Bullough (Carbondale, Ill., Southern Illinois University Press, 1963).

The parodic quality in the narrative of *The Faerie Queene* is quite different from that of *Orlando Furioso*. Unlike Spenser's poem, Ariosto's could never be misunderstood, even by the dullest reader, for a straightforward example or imitation of the tradition it burlesques. Spenser's reader is indeed absorbed, as the poet himself claims to be, by that delightful land of Faery. But it can be delightful only if he does not really believe in those awful monsters, witches, and bloody combats. So from time to time he is nudged awake, though only tentatively, for the transitions are almost imperceptible, the narrative flow resumes, and the wounded illusion heals itself. Those moments should suffice, I think, to remove him just so far from the fiction that he is at once seduced by it and amused by his own seduction. Perhaps such a mood is set by the deliberately quaint "pricking" and "yclad" of the very first lines of the first canto. If the play of diction is so responded to, the reader will not trouble to inquire how that poor lamb kept pace with the Red Cross Knight and Una; nor will he feel inclined to suppose that, since it is never seen again, Una must have cooked it for supper.

A Chronology of Spenser's Life

1552   Probable date of his birth in London.

1561–69   At the Merchant Taylors' School (founded in 1561), under its first headmaster, the famous educator Richard Mulcaster. Contributes a number of verse translations to Jan van der Noodt's *Theatre [of]* . . . *voluptuous Worldlings*, published in 1569.

1569–76   At Cambridge as a "sizar" of Pembroke Hall; friendship with Gabriel Harvey. Graduates a Bachelor of Arts in 1573; a Master of Arts in 1576.

1578   Secretary to John Young (formerly master of Pembroke), bishop of Rochester, in Kent.

1579   First marriage, to Machabyas Chylde. Associated with Sir Philip Sidney and his circle; for a time in the employ of Robert Dudley, earl of Leicester. Publication of *The Shepheardes Calender*.

1580   Publication of correspondence between Spenser and Harvey (five letters, two by Spenser). At work on *The Faerie Queene*. Appointed secretary to the lord deputy of Ireland, Lord Grey of Wilton, with whom he departs for Ireland in August.

1581   Awarded the post of clerk in chancery for faculties, a sinecure previously held by Lodowick Bryskett, clerk of the council in Munster; retains the post until 1588.

1582   Leases the property of New Abbey, in County Kildare; a commissioner of muster for the county in 1583 and 1584.

1584   Appointed deputy to Lodowick Bryskett.

1588   Occupies Kilcolman, an estate of some three thousand acres, situated between Limerick and Cork, in Munster.

1589   To England, and the court of Queen Elizabeth, with Sir Walter Raleigh (proprietor of Inchiquin, an estate of forty-two thousand acres thirty miles southeast of Kilcolman). *The Faerie Queene* I–III entered in the Stationers' Register, December.

1590   Publication of *The Faerie Queene* I–III together with the *Letter to Raleigh*.

1591   Grant from the queen of an annual pension of £50, for life. Publication of *Daphnaida* and *Complaints*. Returns to Ireland, probably in the spring.

1594   Probable date of marriage to Elizabeth Boyle, in Cork.

1595   Publication of *Colin Clouts Come Home Againe*, and of *Amoretti* and *Epithalamion*.

1596   Publication of *The Faerie Queene* I–VI; *Fowre Hymnes*; and

823

Prothalamion. Probably in England to oversee the printing of at least the later books of *The Faerie Queene*.

1598 The prose tract, *A Vewe of the present state of Irelande* (first published in 1633); entered in the Stationers' Register, April. Insurrection in northern and western Ireland spreads into Munster; Kilcolman sacked by the rebels. Spenser takes refuge in Cork, whence he carries letters from Sir Thomas Norris, lord president of Munster, to the Privy Council in London (arriving on 24 December).

1599 Spenser dies in Westminister, 13 January; he is buried in Westminster Abbey.

1609 Publication of *The Faerie Queene* together with the *Cantos of Mutabilitie*.

Selected Bibliography

The Works of Edmund Spenser: A Variorum Edition, ed. E. Greenlaw, C. G. Osgood, F. M. Padelford, et al., 9 vols. (Baltimore: Johns Hopkins, 1932–49), takes account of textual variants in the early editions, notes preferred readings and emendations in later editions, and provides extensive selections from the whole range of criticism of Spenser's poetry. While the critical approaches that dominate these volumes are now somewhat outmoded, the edition remains a valuable resource, especially for information bearing on scriptural and classical sources of elements in Spenser's poetry. The most significant early edition of Spenser's complete works is that edited by John Hughes (London, 1715). Important later editions of the works include H. J. Todd's eight-volume edition (London, 1805); the single-volume edition by R. E. Neil Dodge (Cambridge, MA: Houghton, 1908); and the edition compiled by J. E. Smith and E. de Selincourt (Oxford: Clarendon, 1909–10).

The most useful modern editions of The Faerie Queene are those by A. C. Hamilton (London and New York: Longman, 1977) and by Thomas P. Roche, assisted by C. Patrick O'Donnell, Jr. (New York: Penguin, 1978). Both editions include Two Cantos of Mutabilitie. Among important earlier editions of The Faerie Queene, that by John Upton (London, 1758) is often brilliantly penetrating. Sheldon P. Zitner's edition of The Mutabilitie Cantos (London: Nelson, 1968) is notable for its wide-ranging introduction and full annotation.

The Yale Edition of the Shorter Poems of Edmund Spenser, ed. William A. Oram, Einar Bjorvand, Ronald Bond, Thomas H. Cain, Alexander Dunlop, and Richard Schell (New Haven and London: Yale, 1989), attends authoritatively to all of Spenser's "minor poems," from the "emblematic translations" in A Theatre for Worldlings to Prothalamion, together with a group of "Commendatory Sonnets" and "fragments." The volume satisfies a long-felt need in the field. W. L. Renwick's earlier editions of Complaints, Daphnaida and Other Poems and The Shepherd's Calendar [sic] (London: Scholartis, 1928, 1929, 1930) remain useful still.

Bibliographies include F. I. Carpenter, A Reference Guide to Edmund Spenser (Chicago: U of Chicago P, 1923; New York: Peter Smith, 1950); Dorothy R. Atkinson, Edmund Spenser: A Bibliographical Supplement (Baltimore: Johns Hopkins UP, 1937 [covering the period 1923–37]); and Waldo F. McNeir and Foster Provost, Edmund Spenser: An Annotated Bibliography 1937 1972 (Pittsburgh. Duquesne UP, 1975). Among pre-1973 collections of criticism, Essential Articles for the Study of Edmund Spenser, ed. A. C. Hamilton (Hamden, CT: Shoe String, 1972) is still enormously helpful. Charles Grosvenor Osgood's Concordance to the Poems of Edmund Spenser (Washington: The Carnegie Institution of Washington, 1915; Gloucester, MA: Peter Smith, 1963) retains its value. The fullest biography remains that by A. C. Judson, The Life of Edmund Spenser (Baltimore: Johns Hopkins UP, 1945).

The appearance in 1990 of The Spenser Encyclopedia, ed. A. C. Hamilton [General Editor], Donald Cheney, W. F. Blissett, David A. Richardson, and William W Barker (Toronto and London: U of Toronto P and Routledge), has happily fulfilled the editors' resolve to produce a major work that should "compile essential scholarship for critics writing on Spenser . . . provide an authoritative source of information for teachers in English studies, and . . . give students and general readers a comprehensive reference book about Spenser" (General Editor's Introduction, xi). The volume draws together articles by four hundred-odd contributors from twenty countries on every aspect of the poet's life, work, literary inheritance, and responses to cultural change. Individual bibliographies and some fifty pages of illustrations supplement and support the articles themselves.

Spenser Studies: A Renaissance Poetry Annual (Pittsburgh: U of Pittsburgh P, 1980–82; New York: AMS Press, 1983–) includes essays on Spenser and related Renaissance subjects. Spenser Newsletter, published thrice yearly at various universities (most recently The University of North Carolina at Chapel Hill), includes reviews, abstracts, and reports on Spenser scholarship and criticism, including regular accounts of papers and discussion by members of The Spenser Society at the Annual Convention of the Modern Language Association of America. The Newsletter also publishes reports of programs presented by members of The Spenser Society at annual meetings of the International Association of Mediaeval Studies, held at Western Michigan University in Kalamazoo, Michigan. Somewhat more extensive reports of Spenser at Kalamazoo for 1977–79 have been made available (in microfiche) by David Richardson, Department of English, Cleveland State University, Cleveland, OH 44115; for 1982–84 similar reports were published by Francis G. Greco, Department of English, Clarion University of Pennsylvania, Clarion, PA 16214.

The lists below do not include books or articles published before 1973, periodical articles reprinted (complete or in part) in this Third Edition, or critical studies primarily concerned with works by Spenser not included in this Third Edition. To save space, we have reluctantly omitted a number of interesting pieces, including short or seemingly peripheral articles, articles now substantially incorporated in books, and works in foreign languages or in journals difficult to find in the United States. We also omit publishers' names for books and full titles for many journals, taking our abbreviations from the *Directory of Periodicals*. Serious students of Spenser will explore the older criticism cited in the works listed here and consult the Modern Language Association bibliographies. Following is a list of journal abbreviations used:

AnM *Annuale Mediaevale*
CahiersE *Cahiers Elisabéthains*
CE *College English*
CentR *Centennial Review*
C&L *Christianity & Literature*
CL *Comparative Literature*
CLS *Comparative Literature Studies*
CML *Classical and Modern Literature*
CRCL *Canadian Review of Comparative Literature*
CritI *Critical Inquiry*
DR *Dalhousie Review*
EIC *Essays in Criticism*
EIRC *Explorations in Renaissance Culture*
ELH *English Literary History*
ELN *English Language Notes*
ELR *English Literary Renaissance*
ELWIU *Essays in Literature*
ES *English Studies*
ESC *English Studies in Canada*
HLQ *Huntington Library Quarterly*
HSL *University of Hartford Studies in Literature*
JAAC *Journal of Aesthetics and Art Criticism*
JDJ *John Donne Journal*
JEGP *Journal of English and Germanic Philology*
JES *Journal of European Studies*
JHI *Journal of the History of Ideas*
JMRS *Journal of Medieval and Renaissance Studies*
JNT *Journal of Narrative Technique*
JWCI *Journal of the Warburg and Courtauld Institutes*
LIT *Literature Interpretation Theory*
L&P *Literature & Psychology*
LOS *Literary Onomastic Studies*
M&H *Medievalia et Humanistica*

MLQ *Modern Language Quarterly*
MLR *Modern Language Review*
MLS *Modern Language Studies*
MP *Modern Philology*
MSE *Massachusetts Studies in English*
N&Q *Notes and Queries*
NLH *New Literary History*
NM *Neuphilologische Mitteilungen*
NOR *New Orleans Review*
PAPA *Publications of the Arkansas Philological Association*
PBSA *Papers of the Bibliographical Society of America*
PLL *Papers on Language and Literature*
PMLA *Publications of the Modern Language Association*
PQ *Philological Quarterly*
Ren&R *Renaissance & Reformation*
RenP *Renaissance Papers*
RenQ *Renaissance Quarterly*
RES *Review of English Studies*
SAQ *South Atlantic Quarterly*
SCJ *Sixteenth Century Journal*
SCRev *South Central Review*
SEL *Studies in English Literature*
SIcon *Studies in Iconography*
SLitI *Studies in the Literary Imagination*
SN *Studia Neophilologica*
SoQ *Southern Quarterly*
SoR *Southern Review*
SoRA *Southern Review (Australia)*
SP *Studies in Philology*
SSt *Spenser Studies*
TSLL *Texas Studies in Literature and Language*
UTQ *University of Toronto Quarterly*
YES *Yearbook of English Studies*
YR *Yale Review*

SPENSER'S POETRY: COLLECTIONS OF CRITICISM

Bloom, Harold, ed. *Modern Critical Views: Edmund Spenser*. New York, 1986.
Frushell, Richard C., and Bernard J. Vondersmith, eds. *Contemporary Thought on Edmund Spenser*. Carbondale, IL, 1975.
Hamilton, A. C., gen. ed., with Donald Cheney, W. F. Blissett, David A. Richardson, and William W. Barker. *The Spenser Encyclopedia*. Toronto, 1990. This bibiography does not list individual articles.
Kennedy, Judith M., and James A. Reither, eds. *A Theatre for Spenserians*. Toronto and Buffalo, 1973.
Logan, George M., and Gordon Teskey, eds. *Unfolded Tales: Essays on Renaissance Romance*. Ithaca, NY, 1989. Individual articles on Spenser are noted separately in this bibliography.

SPENSER'S POETRY: GENERAL STUDIES

Adler, Doris. "Imaginary Toads in Real Gardens," ELR 11 (1981): 235–60.
Attridge, Derek. *Well-Weighed Syllables: Elizabethan Verse in Classical Metres*. Cambridge, England, 1974.
Berek, Peter. "Interpretation, Allegory, and Allegoresis." CE 40 (1978): 117–32.
Berger, Harry, Jr. *Revisionary Play: Studies in Spenserian Dynamics*. Berkeley, 1988.
Bernard, John. *Ceremonies of Innocence: Pastoralism in the Poetry of Edmund Spenser*. Cambridge, England, 1989.
Berry, Philippa. *Of Chastity and Power: Elizabethan Literature and the Unmarried Queen*. London, 1989.

Bieman, Elizabeth. *Plato Baptized: Towards the Interpretation of Spenser's Mimetic Fictions.* Toronto, 1988.

Cheney, Donald. "Spenser's Fortieth Birthday and Related Fictions." *SSt* 4 (1983): 3–31.

Cooper, Helen. *Pastoral: Medieval into Renaissance.* Totowa, NJ, 1977.

Craig, Joanne. " 'Double Nature': Augmentation in Spenser's Poetry." *ESC* 9 (1983): 383–91.

———. "The Queen, Her Handmaid, and Spenser's Career." *ESC* 12 (1986): 255–68.

Dasenbrock, Reed Way. *Imitating the Italians: Wyatt, Spenser, Synge, Pound, Joyce.* Baltimore, 1991.

DeNeef, A. Leigh. *Spenser and the Motives of Metaphor.* Durham, NC, 1982.

Eade, J. C. *The Forgotten Sky: A Guide to Astrology in English Literature.* Oxford, 1984.

Esolen, Anthony. "The Disingenuous Poet Laureate: Spenser's Adoption of Chaucer." *SP* 87 (1990): 285–311.

Ettin, Andrew V. *Literature and the Pastoral.* New Haven, 1984.

Evett, David. *Literature and the Visual Arts in Tudor England.* Athens, GA, 1990.

Ferry, Anne. *The Art of Naming.* Chicago, 1989.

Fox, Alice. *Virginia Woolf and the English Renaissance.* Oxford, 1990.

Fried, Debra. "Spenser's Caesura." *ELR* 11 (1981): 261–80.

Giamatti, A. Bartlett. *Exile and Change in Renaissance Literature.* New Haven, 1984.

———. "A Prince and Her Poet." *YR* 73 (1984): 321–37.

Grant, Patrick. *Images and Ideas in Literature of the English Renaissance.* London, 1979.

Helgerson, Richard. *Self-Crowned Laureates: Spenser, Jonson, Milton and the Literary System.* Berkeley, 1983.

Heninger, S. K., Jr. *Sidney and Spenser: The Poet as Maker.* Philadelphia, 1989.

———. *Touches of Sweet Harmony: Pythagorean Cosmology and Renaissance Poetics.* San Marino, CA, 1974.

Herendeen, Wyman H. *From Landscape to Literature: The River and the Myth of Geography.* Pittsburgh, 1986.

Hieatt, Constance B. "Stooping at a Simile: Some Literary Uses of Falconry." *PLL* 19 (1983): 339–60.

Hulse, Clark. "Spenser, Bacon, and the Myth of Power." IN Heather Dubrow and Richard Strier, eds. *The Historical Renaissance.* Chicago, 1988. 315–46.

———. "Spenser and the Myth of Power." *SP* 85 (1988): 378–89.

Hume, Anthea. *Edmund Spenser: Protestant Poet.* Cambridge, England, 1984.

Hyde, Thomas. *The Poetic Theology of Love: Cupid in Renaissance Literature.* Newark, 1986.

Iser, Wolfgang. "Spenser's Arcadia: The Interrelation of Fiction and History." IN Mihai Spariosu, ed. *Mimesis in Contemporary Theory.* Philadelphia, 1984. 109–40.

Jardine, Lisa, and Anthony Grafton. " 'Studied for Action': How Gabriel Harvey Read His Livy." *Past and Present* 129 (1990): 30–78.

King, John N. *Spenser's Poetry and the Reformation Tradition.* Princeton, 1990.

———. *Tudor Royal Iconography.* Princeton, 1989.

Krier, Theresa M. *Gazing on Secret Sights: Spenser, Classical Imitation, and the Decorums of Vision.* Ithaca, NY, 1990.

MacLure, Millar. "Spenser's Images of Society." *DR* 63 (1983): 22–33.

Mallette, Richard. *Spenser, Milton, and Renaissance Pastoral.* Lewisburg, PA, 1981.

May, Steven W. *The Elizabethan Courtier Poets. The Poems and Their Contexts.* Columbia, MO, 1991.

McCoy, Richard C. *The Rites of Knighthood: The Literature and Politics of Elizabethan Chivalry.* Berkeley, 1989.

Miller, David L. " 'The Pleasure of the Text': Two Renaissance Versions." *NOR* 9 (1982): 50–55.

———. "Spenser's Vocation, Spenser's Career." *ELH* 50 (1983): 197–231.

———. "The Writing Thing." *Diacritics* 20 (1990): 17–29.

Miller, Jacqueline T. *Poetic License: Authority and Authorship in Medieval and Renaissance Contexts.* Oxford, 1986.

Miskimin, Alice S. *The Renaissance Chaucer.* New Haven, 1975.

Neuse, Richard. "Milton and Spenser: The Virgilian Triad Revisited." *ELH* 45 (1978): 606–39.

Norbrook, David. *Poetry and Politics in the English Renaissance.* London, 1984.

Oram, William A. "Elizabethan Fact and Spenserian Fiction." *SSt* 4 (1983): 33–47.

———. "Spenser's Raleghs." *SP* 87 (1990): 341–62.

Patterson, Annabel. *Fables of Power: Aesopian Writing and Political History.* Durham, NC, 1991.

Prescott, Anne Lake. *French Poets and the English Renaissance: Studies in Fame and Transformation.* New Haven, 1978.

Quint, David. *Origin and Originality in Renaissance Literature: Versions of the Source.* New Haven, 1983.

Richardson, David A. "Duality in Spenser's Archaisms." *SLitI* 11 (1978): 81–98.

Rosenberg, Donald M. *Oaten Reeds and Trumpets: Pastoral and Epic in Virgil, Spenser, and Milton.* Lewisburg, PA, 1981.

Shepherd, Simon. *Spenser.* Atlantic Highlands, NJ, 1989.

Shire, Helena. *A Preface to Spenser.* London and New York, 1978.

Shore, David R. *Spenser and the Poetics of Pastoral: A Study of the World of Colin Clout.* Kingston, Canada, 1985.

Sinfield, Alan. *Literature in Protestant England, 1560–1660.* Totowa, NJ, 1983.

Steadman, John M. *The Lamb and the Elephant: Ideal Imitation and the Context of Renaissance Allegory*. San Marino, CA, 1974.

Stewart, Stanley. "Spenser and the Judgment of Paris." *SSt* 9 (1988): 161–209.

Strier, Richard. "Divorcing Poetry from Politics—Two Versions: Clark Hulse and Andrew Weiner on Spenser." *SP* 85 (1988): 407–11.

Tosello, Matthew. "Spenser's Silence About Dante." *SEL* 17 (1977): 59–66.

Tung, Mason. "Spenser's 'Emblematic Imagery.' " *SSt* 5 (1985): 185–207.

Wall, John N. *Transformations of the Word: Spenser, Herbert, Vaughan*. Athens, GA, 1988.

Weatherby, Harold L. "Two Images of Mortalitie: Spenser and Original Sin." *SP* 85 (1988): 321–52.

Webster, John. " 'The Methode of a Poete': An Inquiry into Tudor Conceptions of Poetic Sequence." *ELR* 11 (1981): 22–43.

Woods, Susanne. "Aesthetic and Mimetic Rhythms in the Versification of Gascoigne, Sidney, and Spenser." *SLitI* 11 (1978): 31–44.

THE FAERIE QUEENE: GENERAL

Alpers, Paul. "Narration in *The Faerie Queen*." *ELH* 44 (1977): 19–39.

———. "Spenser's Poetic Language." IN Anthony C. Yu, ed. *Parnassus Revisited: Modern Critical Essays on the Epic Tradition*. Chicago, 1973.

Anderson, Judith H. "The Antiquities of Fairyland and Ireland." *JEGP* 86 (1987): 199–214.

———. *The Growth of a Personal Voice*: Piers Plowman *and* The Faerie Queene. New Haven, 1976.

Barkan, Leonard. *Nature's Work of Art: The Human Body as Image of the World*. New Haven, 1975. Ch. 5.

Bednarz, James P. "Ralegh in Spenser's Historical Allegory." *SSt* 4 (1983): 49–70.

Bellamy, Elizabeth J. *Translations of Power: Narcissism and the Unconscious in Epic History*. Ithaca, NY, 1992. Ch. 5.

———. "The Vocative and the Vocational: The Unreadability of Elizabeth in *The Faerie Queene*." *ELH* 54 (1987): 1–30.

Benson, Pamela J. "Rule, Virginia: Protestant Theories of Female Regiment in *The Fairie Queene*." *ELR* 15 (1985): 277–92.

Berger, Harry, Jr. " 'Kidnapped Romance': Discourse in *The Faerie Queene*." IN Logan and Teskey, 208–56.

———. "Narrative as Rhetoric in *The Faerie Queene*." *ELR* 21 (1991): 3–48.

Berman, Ruth. "Blazonings in *The Faerie Queene*." *CahiersE* 23 (1983): 1–14.

Blissett, William. "Caves, Labyrinths, and *The Faerie Queene*." IN Logan and Teskey, 281–311.

Bowman, Mary R. " 'She There as Princess Rained': Spenser's Figure of Elizabeth." *RenQ* 43 (1990): 509–28.

Brand, C. P. "Tasso, Spenser, and the *Orlando Furioso*." IN Julius A. Molinaro, ed. *Petrarch to Pirandello: Studies in Italian Literature in Honor of Beatrice Corrigan*. Toronto, 1973. 95–110.

Brinkley, Robert A. "Spenser's Gardens of Adonis: The Nature of Infinity." *MSE* 4.4 (1974): 3–16.

Brooks-Davies, Douglas. *The Mercurian Monarch: Magical Politics from Spenser to Pope*. Manchester, England, 1983.

Brown, James Neil. The Unity of *The Faerie Queene*, Books I–V." *SoRA* 10 (1977): 3–21.

Burrow, Colin. "Original Fictions: Metamorphoses in *The Faerie Queene*." IN Charles Martindale, ed. *Ovid Renewed*. Cambridge, MA, 1988. 99–119.

Buxton, John. " 'Certaine Signes Here Set in Sundry Place': Spenser's Advice to His Readers." *RES* 34 (1983): 395–402.

Cain, Thomas H. *Praise in* The Faerie Queene. Lincoln, NB, 1978.

Cavanagh, Sheila T. " 'Beauties Chace': Arthur and Women in *The Faerie Queene*." IN Christopher Baswell and William Sharpe, eds. *The Passing of Arthur: New Essays in Arthurian Tradition*. New York, 1988. 207–18.

Cheney, Donald. "Envy in the Midst of the 1596 *Faerie Queene*." IN Bloom, *Spenser*, 267–83.

Christian, Margaret. " 'The ground of Storie': Genealogy in *The Faerie Queene*." *SSt* 9 (1988): 61–79.

Cincotta, Mary Ann. "Reinventing Authority in *The Faerie Queene*." *SP* 80 (1983): 25–52.

Cook, Timothy. "Gabriel Harvey, 'Pasquill,' Spenser's Lost *Dreames*, and *The Faerie Queene*." *YES* 7 (1977): 75–80.

Crampton, Georgia Ronan. *The Condition of Creatures: Suffering and Action in Chaucer and Spenser*. New Haven, 1974.

Cullen, Patrick. *Infernal Triad: The Flesh, the World, and the Devil in Spenser and Milton*. Princeton, 1974.

Cummings, Robert. "Spenser's 'Twelve Private Morall Virtues.' " *SSt* 8 (1987): 35–59.

Davies, Stevie. *The Feminine Reclaimed: The Idea of Woman in Spenser, Shakespeare and Milton*. Lexington, KY, 1986.

Dees, Jerome S. "The Ship Conceit in *The Faerie Queene*: 'Conspicuous Allusion' and Poetic Structure." *SP* 72 (1975): 208–25.

Demaray, John G. *Cosmos and Epic Representation: Dante, Spenser, Milton, and the Transformation of Renaissance Heroic Poetry*. Pittsburgh, 1991.

Dobin, Howard. *Merlin's Disciples: Prophecy, Poetry, and Power in Renaissance England.* Stanford, CA, 1990.

Dundas, Judith. *The Spider and the Bee: The Artistry of Spenser's* Faerie Queene. Urbana, IL, 1985.

Edwards, Calvin R. "The Narcissus Myth in Spenser's Poetry." *SP* 74 (1977): 63–88.

Esolen, Anthony M. "Irony and the Pseudo-Physical in *The Faerie Queene.*" *SSt* 8 (1987): 61–78.

Estrin, Barbara L. *The Raven and the Lark: Lost Children of the English Renaissance.* Lewisburg, PA, 1985.

Ettin, Andrew V. "The Georgics in *The Faerie Queene.*" *SSt* 3 (1982): 57–71.

Fichter, Andrew. *Poets Historical: Dynastic Epic in the Renaissance.* New Haven, 1982.

Fowler, Alastair. "Emanations of Glory: Neoplatonic Order in Spenser's *Faerie Queene.*" IN Kennedy and Reither, 53–82.

———. "Spenser and War." IN J. R. Mulryne and Margaret Shewring, eds., *War, Literature and the Arts in Sixteenth-Century Europe.* New York, 1989. 147–64.

———. "Spenser's Names." IN Logan and Teskey, 32–48.

Frantz, David O. *Festum Voluptatis: A Study of Renaissance Erotica.* Columbus, OH, 1989. Ch. 8.

Fruen, Jeffrey P. " 'True glorious type': The Place of Gloriana in *The Faerie Queene.*" *SSt* 7 (1986): 147–73.

Frye, Northrop. *The Secular Scripture: A Study of the Structure of Romance.* Cambridge, MA, 1976.

Fumerton, Patricia. "Relative Means: Spenser's Style of 'Discordia Concors.' " *PLL* 24 (1988): 3–22.

Giamatti, A. Bartlett. *Play of Double Senses: Spenser's* Faerie Queene. Englewood Cliffs, NJ, 1975.

———. "Primitivism and the Process of Civility in Spenser's *Faerie Queene.*" IN F. Chiapelli, ed. *First Images of America: The Impact of the New World on the Old.* Berkeley, 1976. 71–82.

Goldberg, Jonathan. *Endlesse Worke: Spenser and the Structures of Discourse.* Baltimore, 1981.

Gottfried, Rudolf B. "Spenser Recovered: The Poet and Historical Scholarship." IN Frushell and Vondersmith, 61–78.

Gray, J. C. "Bondage and Deliverance in the *Faerie Queene*: Varieties of a Moral Imperative." *MLR* 70 (1975): 1–12.

Gregerson, Linda. "Protestant Erotics: Idolatry and Interpretation in Spenser's *Faerie Queene.*" *ELH* 58 (1991): 1–34.

Gross, Kenneth. *Spenserian Poetics: Idolatry, Iconoclasm, and Magic.* Ithaca, NY, 1985.

Guillory, John. *Poetic Authority: Spenser, Milton, and Literary History.* New York, 1983.

Hamilton, A. C. "On Annotating Spenser's *Faerie Queene*: A New Approach to the Poem." IN Frushell and Vondersmith, 41–60.

———. "Our New Poet: Spenser, 'well of English undefyld.' " IN Kennedy and Reither, 101–23.

Harder, Kelsie B. "The Allegorical Sign in *The Faerie Queene.*" *LOS* 14 (1987): 125–38.

Heberle, Mark. "Pagans and Saracens in Spenser's *The Faerie Queene.*" IN Cornelia Moore and Raymond A. Moody, eds. *Comparative Literature East and West: Traditions and Trends.* Honolulu, 1989. 81–87.

Helgerson, Richard. *Forms of Nationhood: The Elizabethan Writing of England.* Chicago, 1992. 25–62.

Heninger, S. K., Jr. "The Aesthetic Experience of Reading Spenser." IN Frushell and Vondersmith, 79–98.

———. "Spenser, Sidney, and Poetic Form." *SP* 88 (1991): 140–52.

Hieatt, A. Kent. *Chaucer, Spenser, Milton: Mythopoeic Continuities and Transformations.* Montreal, 1975.

———. "The Passing of Arthur in Malory, Spenser, and Shakespeare: The Avoidance of Closure." IN Christopher Baswell and William Sharpe, eds. *The Passing of Arthur: New Essays in Arthurian Tradition.* New York, 1988. 173–92.

———, and T. P. Roche, Jr. "The Projected Continuation of *The Fairie Queene*: Rome Delivered." *SSt* 8 (1987): 331–34.

Hinton, Stan. "The Poet and His Narrator: Spenser's Epic Voice." *ELH* 41 (1974): 165–81.

Horton, Ronald Arthur. *The Unity of The Faerie Queene.* Athens, GA, 1978.

Imbrie, Ann E. " 'Playing Legerdemaine with the Scripture': Parodic Sermons in *The Faerie Queene.*" *ELR* 17 (1987): 142–55.

Javitch, Daniel. *Poetry and Courtliness in Renaissance England.* Princeton, 1978.

Kane, Sean. *Spenser's Moral Allegory.* Toronto, 1989.

Keach, William. *Elizabethan Erotic Narratives: Irony and Pathos in the Ovidian Poetry of Shakespeare, Marlowe, and Their Contemporaries.* New Brunswick, NJ, 1977.

Kendrick, Walter M. "Earth of Flesh, Flesh of Earth: Mother Earth in *The Faerie Queene.*" *RenQ* 27 (1974): 533–48.

Kipling, Gordon. *The Triumph of Honour: Burgundian Origins of the Elizabethan Renaissance.* Leiden, Netherlands, 1977. Ch. 8.

Klein, Joan Larsen. "The Anatomy of Fortune in Spenser's *Faerie Queene.*" *AnM* 14 (1973): 74–95.

Kouwenhoven, Jan K. *Apparent Narrative as Thematic Metaphor: The Organization of The Faerie Queene.* Oxford, 1983.

Leggatt, Alexander. "Embarrassment in *The Faerie Queene.*" *EIC* 38 (1988): 114–30.

Lenz, Joseph M. *The Promised End: Romance Closure in the Gawain-poet, Malory, Spenser, and Shakespeare.* New York, 1986 (American University Studies ser. 4, vol. 38). Ch. 3.

Leonard, Frances McNeely. *Laughter in the Courts of Love: Comedy in Allegory, from Chaucer to Spenser*. Norman, OK, 1981.

Leslie, Michael. *Spenser's 'Fierce Warres and Faithfull Loves': Marital and Chivalric Symbolism in The Faerie Queene*. Cambridge, England, 1983.

———. "Edmund Spenser: Art and *The Faerie Queene*." *Proceedings of the British Academy* 76 (1991): 73–107.

Lockerd, Benjamin G., Jr. *The Sacred Marriage: Psychic Integration in The Faerie Queene*. Lewisburg, PA, 1987.

McCabe, Richard A. "The Masks of Duessa: Spenser, Mary Queen of Scots, and James VI." *ELR* 17 (1987): 224–42.

———. *The Pillars of Eternity: Time and Providence in The Faerie Queene*. Dublin, 1989.

MacCaffrey, Isabel G. *Spenser's Allegory: The Anatomy of Imagination*. Princeton, 1976.

MacLachlan, Hugh. " 'In the Person of Prince Arthur': Spenserian *Magnificence* and the Ciceronian Tradition." *UTQ* 46 (1976): 125–46.

Maresca, Thomas E. *Three English Epics: Studies of* Troilus and Criseyde, The Faerie Queene, *and* Paradise Lost. Lincoln, NB, 1979.

Marquis, Paul A. "Problems of Closure in *The Faerie Queene*." *ESC* 16 (1990): 149–63.

Merriman, James Douglas. "The Arthur of *The Faerie Queene*." IN his *The Flower of Kings: A Study of the Arthurian Legend in England*. Lawrence, KA, 1973. 15–33.

Meyer, Russell J. The Faerie Queene: *Educating the Reader*. New York, 1992.

Miller, David Lee. *The Poem's Two Bodies: The Poetics of the 1590* Faerie Queene. Princeton, 1988.

Mills, Jerry Leath. "Spenser's Letter to Raleigh and the Averroistic *Poetica*." *ELN* 14 (1977): 246–49.

Mueller, Robert J. " 'Infinite Desire': Spenser's Arthur and the Representation of Courtly Ambition. *ELH* 58 (1991): 747–71.

Murrin, Michael. "Spenser's Fairyland." IN his *The Allegorical Epic: Essays in Its Rise and Decline*. Chicago, 1980. 131–52.

———. "The Varieties of Criticism." *MP* 70 (1973): 342–56.

Nohrnberg, James. *The Analogy of* The Faerie Queene. Princeton, 1976.

O'Connell, Michael. *Mirror and Veil: The Historical Dimension of Spenser's* Faerie Queene. Chapel Hill, NC, 1977.

Paglia, Camille A. "Spenser and Apollo: *The Faerie Queene*." IN her *Sexual Personae: Art and Decadence from Nefertiti to Emily Dickinson*. London and New Haven, 1990. 170–93.

Parker, Patricia A. *Inescapable Romance: Studies in the Poetics of a Mode*. Princeton, 1979.

Patrides, C. A. "The Achievement of Edmund Spenser." *YR* 69 (1980): 427–43.

———. "Spenser: The Contours of Allegorical Theology." *CentR* 26 (1982): 17–32.

Provost, Foster. "Treatments of Theme and Allegory in Twentieth-Century Criticism of *The Faerie Queene*." IN Frushell and Vondersmith, 1–40.

Quilligan, Maureen. "The Comedy of Female Authority in *The Faerie Queene*." *ELR* 17 (1987): 156–71.

———. "Feminine Endings: The Sexual Politics of Sidney's and Spenser's Rhyming." IN Anne Haselkorn and Betty S. Travitsky, eds. *The Renaissance Englishwoman in Print: Counterbalancing the Canon*. Amherst, MA, 1990. 311–26.

———. *The Language of Allergory: Defining the Genre*. Ithace, NY, 1979.

———. *Milton's Spenser: The Politics of Reading*. Ithaca, NY, 1983.

Rajan, Balachandra. *The Form of the Unfinished: English Poetics from Spenser to Pound*. Princeton, 1985.

Roberts, Gareth. The Faerie Queene. Buckingham, England, and Bristol, PA, 1992.

Roche, Thomas P., Jr. "Spenser's Muse." IN Logan and Teskey, 162–88.

Ross, Charles. "The Grim Humor of Spenser's *Faerie Queene*: Women and Laughter in a Renaissance Epic." *Humor Research* 2 (1989): 153–64.

Røstvig, Maren-Sofie. "Canto Structure in Tasso and Spenser. *SSt* 1 (1980): 177–200.

Sandler, Florence. "The Faerie Queene: An Elizabethan Apocalypse." IN C. A. Patrides and Joseph Wittreich, eds. *The Apocalypse in English Renaissance Thought and Literature*. Ithaca, NY, 1984. 148–74.

Sessions, William A. "Spenser's Georgics." *ELR* 10 (1980): 202–38.

Shaheen, Naseeb. *Biblical References in The Faerie Queene*. Memphis, TN, 1976.

———. "The 1590 and 1596 Texts of *The Faerie Queene*." *PBSA* 74 (1980): 57–63.

Staton, Shirley F. "Reading Spenser's *Faerie Queene*—in a Different Voice." IN Carole Levin and Jeanie Watson, eds. *Ambiguous Realities: Women in the Middle Ages and Renaissance*. Detroit, 1987. 145–62.

Steadman, John M. "The Arming of an Archetype: Heroic Virtue and the Conventions of Literary Epic." IN Norman T. Burns and Christopher J. Reagan eds. *Concepts of the Hero in the Middle Ages and the Renaissance*. Albany, NY, 1975.

———. *Nature into Myth: Medieval and Renaissance Moral Symbols*. Pittsburgh, 1979.

Steppat, Michael. *Chances of Mischief: Variations of Fortune in Spenser*. Cologne, Germany, 1990.

Suzuki, Mihoko. *Metamorphoses of Helen: Authority, Difference, and the Epic*. Ithaca, NY, 1989.

Thickstun, Margaret Olofson. *Fictions of the Feminine: Puritan Doctrine and the Representation of Women*. Ithaca, NY, 1988.

Tonkin, Humphrey. *The Faerie Queene*. London, 1989.

Ulreich, John C., Jr. "Making Dreams Truths, and Fables Histories: Spenser and Milton on the Nature of Fiction." *SP* 87 (1990): 363–77.

Van Dyke, Carolynn. *The Fiction of Truth: Structures of Meaning in Narrative and Dramatic Allegory.* Ithaca, NY, 1985.

Wall, John N., Jr. "Orion's Flaming Head: Spenser's *Faerie Queene*, II.ii.46 and the Feast of the Twelve Days of Christmas." *SSt* 7 (1986): 93–101.

———. "Orion Once More: Revisiting the Sky over Faerieland." *SSt* 8 (1987): 311–23.

Webster, John. "Oral Form and Written Craft in Spenser's *Faerie Queene*." *SEL* 16 (1976): 75–93.

West, Michael. "Spenser's Art of War: Chivalric Allegory, Military Technology, and the Elizabethan Mock-Heroic Sensibility." *RenQ* 41 (1988): 654–704.

———. "Spenser and the Renaissance Ideal of Christian Heroism." *PMLA* 88 (1973): 1013–32.

Williams, Arnold. "The Uses of Myth: Spenser's *Faerie Queene*." *Indiana Social Studies Quarterly* 28 (1975–76): 38–49.

Williams, Kathleen. "Spenser and the Metaphor of Sight." IN J. A. Ward, ed. *Renaissance Studies in Honor of Carroll Camden* [Rice University Studies 60] 1974. 153–69.

Wilson, Rawdon. "Images and 'Allegoremes' of Time in the Poetry of Spenser." *ELR* 4 (1974): 56–82.

Wilson, Robert R. "Narrative Allusiveness: The Interplay of Stories in Two Renaissance Writers, Spenser and Cervantes." *ESC* 12 (1986): 138–62.

Wittreich, Joseph Anthony, Jr. *Visionary Poetics: Milton's Tradition and His Legacy*, San Marino, CA, 1979.

Wofford, Susanne Lindgren. *The Choice of Achilles: The Ideology of Figure in the Epic*. Stanford, CA, 1992. Chs. 4–5.

Woods, Susanne. "Spenser and the Problem of Women's Rule." *HLQ* 48 (1985): 141–58.

THE FAERIE QUEENE: BOOK I

Allen, Margaret J. "The Harlot and the Mourning Bride." IN Jane Campbell and James Doyle, eds. *The Practical Vision: Essays in English Literature in Honour of Flora Roy.* Waterloo, Ontario, 1978. 11–28.

Barney, Stephen A. "The Knight at One: *The Faerie Queene*, Book One." IN his *Allegories of History, Allegories of Love.* Hamden, CT, 1979. 105–43.

Beecher, Donald. "The Anatomy of Melancholy in Book I of *The Faerie Queene*." *Ren&R* 12.2 (1988): 85–99.

———. "Spenser's Redcrosse Knight: Despair and the Elizabethan Malady." *Ren&R* 11.1 (1987): 103–20.

Bellamy, Elizabeth Jane. "The Broken Branch and the 'Liuing Well': Spenser's Fradubio and Romance Error in *The Faerie Queene*." *RenP* 1985: 1–12.

Brooks-Davies, Douglas. *Spenser's* Faerie Queene: *A Critical Commentary on Books I and II*. Manchester, England, 1977.

Bulger, Thomas R. "Classical Vision and Christian Revelation: Spenser's Use of Mythology in Book I of *The Faerie Queene*." *Greyfriar* 23 (1982): 5–25.

Crossett, John M., and Donald V. Stump. "Spenser's Inferno: The Order of the Seven Deadly Sins as the Palace of Pride." *JMRS* 14 (1984): 203–18.

Cunningham, Merrilee. "The Interpolated Tale in Spenser's *The Faerie Queene*. Book I," *SCB* [now *SCRev*] 43 (1983): 99–104.

Davis, Walter R. "Arthur, Partial Exegesis, and the Reader." *TSLL* 18 (1977): 553–76.

Doerksen, Daniel W. "'All the Good Is God's': Predestination in Spenser's *Faerie Queene*, Book I." *C&L* 32 (1983): 11–18.

DuRocher, Richard J. "Arthur's Gift, Aristotle's Magnificence, and Spenser's Allegory: A study of *Faerie Queene* 1.9.19." *MP* 82 (1984): 185–90.

Gilman, Ernest B. *Iconoclasm and Poetry in the English Reformation.* Chicago, 1986.

Heath-Stubbs, John. "The Hero as a Saint: St. George." IN Hilda Ellis Davidson, ed. *The Hero in Tradition and Folklore.* London, 1984. 1–15.

Jordan, Richard Douglas. "Una Among the Satyrs: *The Faerie Queene* 1.6." *MLQ* 38 (1977): 123–31.

Kamholtz, Jonathan Z. "Spenser and Persepctive." *JAAC* 39 (Fall 1980): 59–66.

Kaske, Carol V. "How Spenser Really Used Stephen Hawes in the Legend of Holiness." IN Logan and Teskey, 118–36.

———. "Spenser's Pluralistic Universe: The View from the Mount of Contemplation (F.Q. I.x)." IN Frushell and Vondersmith, 121–49.

Kennedy, William J. "Rhetoric, Allegory, and Dramatic Modality in Spenser's Fradubio Episode." *ELR* 3 (1973): 351–68.

Klein, Joan Larsen. "From Errour to Acrasia." *HLQ* 41 (1978): 173–99.

Knapp, Jeffrey. "Error as a Means of Empire in *The Faerie Queene* 1." *ELH* 54 (1987): 801–34.

Levin, Richard A. "The Legende of the Redcrosse Knight and Una, or Of the Love of a Good Woman." *SEL* 31 (1991): 1–24.

Maier, John R. "Sansjoy and the *Furor Melancholicus*." *MLS* 5 (1975): 78–87.

Mallette, Richard. "The Protestant Art of Preaching in Book One of *The Faerie Queene*." *SSt* 7 (1986): 3–25.

Miller, Jacqueline T. "The Omission in Red Cross Knight's Story: Narrative Inconsistencies in *The Faerie Queene*." *ELH* 53 (1986): 279–88.

O'Connor, John J. "Terwin, Trevisan, and Spenser's Historical Allegory." *SP* 87 (1990): 328–40.

Pearson, D'Orsay W. "Spenser's Labyrinth—Again." *SIcon* 3 (1977): 70–88.

Pheifer, J. D. "Errour and Echidna in *The Faerie Queene*: A Study in Literary Tradition." IN John Scattergood, ed. *Literature and Learning in Medieval and Renaissance England: Essays Presented to Fitzroy Pyle*. Dublin, 1984. 127–74.

Pollock, Zailig. "The Dragon, the Lady, and the Dragon Lady in Book I of *The Faerie Queene*." *ESC* 7 (1981): 270–81.

Prescott, Anne Lake. "Spenser's Chivalric Restoration: From Bateman's Travayled Pylgrime to the Redcrosse Knight." *SP* (1989): 166–97.

Reid, Robert L. "Spenserian Psychology and the Structure of Allegory in Books 1 and 2 of *The Faerie Queene*." *MP* 79 (1982): 359–75.

Roche, Thomas P., Jr. "The Menace of Despair and Arthur's Vision, *Faerie Queene* I.9." *SSt* 4 (1983): 71–92.

Rose, Mark. *Spenser's Art: A Companion to Book 1 of* The Faerie Queene. Cambridge, MA, 1975.

Rudat, Wolfgang. "Spenser's 'Angry Ioue': Vergilian Allusion in the First Canto of *The Faerie Queene*." *CML* 3.2 (1983): 89–98.

Scott, Shirley Clay. "From Polydorus to Fradubio: The History of a Topos." *SSt* 7 (1986): 27–57.

Skulsky, Harold. "Spenser's Despair Episode and the Theology of Doubt." *MP* 78 (1981): 227–42.

Smith, Eric. "*The Faerie Queene*, Book I." IN his *Some Versions of the Fall: The Myth of the Fall of Man in English Literature*. Pittsburgh, 1973.

Teskey, Gordon. "From Allegory to Dialectic: Imagining Error in Spenser and Milton." *PMLA* 101 (1986): 9–23.

Walls, Kathryn. "Abessa and the Lion: *The Faerie Queene*, I.3.1–12." *SSt* 5 (1984): 3–30.

Weatherby, Harold L. " 'Pourd out in loosnesse.' " *SSt* 3 (1982): 73–85.

———. "The True Saint George." *ELR* 17 (1987): 119–41.

———. "What Spenser Meant by Holiness: Baptism in Book One of *The Faerie Queene*." *SP* 84 (1987): 286–307.

Wells, R. Headlam. "Spenser's Christian Knight: Erasmian Theology in *The Faerie Queene*, Book I." *Anglia* 97 (1979): 350–66.

Wiggins, Peter DeSa. "Spenser's Use of Ariosto: Imitation and Allusion in Book I of *The Faerie Queene*." *RenQ* 44 (1991): 257–79.

Williams, Franklin B., Jr. "The Iconography of Una's Lamb." *PBSA* 74 (1980): 301–5.

See also Grant, under "General Studies."

THE FAERIE QUEENE: BOOK II

Anderson, Judith H. " 'Myn Auctor': Spenser's Enabling Fiction and Eumnestes' 'Immortal Scrine.' " IN Logan and Teskey, 16–31.

Bean, John C. "Cosmic Order in *The Faerie Queene*: From Temperance to Chastity." *SEL* 17 (1977): 67–79.

Davis, Walter R. "The Houses of Mortality in Book II of *The Faerie Queene*." *SSt* 2 (1981): 121–40.

Dauber, Antoinette B. "The Art of Veiling in the Bower of Bliss." *SSt* 1 (1980): 163–75.

Doerksen, Daniel W. "Recharting the Via Media of Spenser and Herbert." *Ren&R* 8 (1984): 215–25.

Downing, Crystal Nelson. "The 'Charmes Backe to Reverse': Deconstructing Architectures in Book II and III of *The Faerie Queene*." *Comitatus* 13 (1982): 64–83.

Edwards, Karen L. "On Guile and Guyon in *Paradise Lost* and *The Faerie Queene*." *PQ* 64 (1985): 83–97.

Gohlke, Madelon S. "Embattled Allegory: Book II of *The Faerie Queene*." *ELR* 8 (1978): 123–40.

Greenblatt, Stephen. "To Fashion a Gentleman: Spenser and the Destruction of the Bower of Bliss." IN his *Renaissance Self-Fashioning: From More to Shakespeare*. Chicago, 1980. 157–92.

Hawkins, Harriett. " 'Of Their Vain Contest': Poetic and Critical Deadlocks in *Paradise Lost* and Spenser's Bower of Bliss." IN her *Poetic Freedom and Poetic Truth: Chaucer, Shakespeare, Marlowe, Milton*. Oxford, 1976.

Heinzelman, Kurt. *The Economics of the Imagination*. Amherst, MA, 1980. Ch. 2.

Hieatt, A. Kent. "A Numerical Key for Spenser's *Amoretti* and Guyon in the House of Mammon." *YES* 3 (1973): 14–27.

———. "Three Fearful Symmetries and the Meaning of *Faerie Queene* II." IN Kennedy and Reither, 19–52.

Jordan, Richard Douglas. "*The Faerie Queene*, II.ix,22: The Missing Link." *RES* 31 (1980): 436–40.

———. *The Quiet Hero: Figures of Temperance in Spenser, Donne, Milton, and Joyce*. Washington, D.C., 1989. Ch. 2.

Kaske, Carol V. "Augustinian Psychology in *The Faerie Queene*, Book II." *HSL* 15–16 (1984): 93–98.

———. " 'Religious Reuerence Doth Buriall Teene': Christian and Pagan in *The Faerie Queene*, II.i–ii." *RES* 30 (1979): 129–43.

Macfie, Pamela Royston. "Text and Textura: Spenser's Arachnean Art." IN David Allen and Robert A. White, eds. *Traditions and Innovations: Essays on British Literature of the Middle Ages and the Renaissance.* Newark, NJ, 1990. 88–96.

MacLachlan, Hugh. "The 'carelesse heauens': A Study of Revenge and Atonement in *The Faerie Queene.*" *SSt* 1 (1980): 135–61.

———. "The Death of Guyon and the Elizabethan Book of Homilies." *SSt* 4 (1983): 93–114.

Mallette, Richard. "The Protestant Ethics of Love in Book II of *The Faerie Queene.*" *C&L* 38.3 (1989): 45–64.

Mills, Jerry Leath. "Prudence, History, and the Prince in *The Faerie Queene*, Book II." *HLQ* 41 (1978): 83–101.

———. "Spenser, Lodowick Bryskett, and the Mortalist Controversy: *The Faerie Queene*, II.ix.22." *PQ* 52 (1973): 173–86.

———. "Spenser and the Numbers of History: A Note on the British and Elfin Chronicles in *The Faerie Queene.*" *PQ* 55 (1976): 281–87.

Murrin, Michael. "The Rhetoric of Fairyland." IN Thomas O. Sloan and Raymond B. Waddington, eds. *The Rhetoric of Renaissance Poetry from Wyatt to Milton.* Berkeley, 1974. 73–95.

Okerlund, Arlene N. "Spenser's Wanton Maidens: Reader Psychology and the Bower of Bliss." *PMLA* 88 (1973): 62–68.

Parker, Patricia. "Suspended Instruments: Lyric and Power in the Bower of Bliss." IN her *Literary Fat Ladies: Rhetoric, Gender, Property.* London and New York, 1987. 54–66.

Pollock, Zailig. "Concupiscence and Intemperance in The Bower of Bliss." *SEL* 20 (1980): 43–58.

Read, David T. "Hunger of Gold: Guyon, Mammon's Cave, and the New World Treasure." *ELR* 20 (1990): 209–32.

Rollinson, Philip. "Arthur, Maleger, and the Interpretation of *The Faerie Queene.*" *SSt* 7 (1986): 103–21.

Rooks, John. "Art, Audience, and Performance in the Bowre of Bliss." *MLS* 18.2 (1988): 23–36.

Rossi, Joan Warchol. "'Britons Moniments': Spenser's Definition of Temperance in History." *ELR* 15 (1985): 42–58.

Schleiner, Winfried. "Divina Virago: Queen Elizabeth as an Amazon." *SP* 75 (1978): 163–80.

Silberman, Lauren. "*The Faerie Queene*, Book II and the Limitations of Temperance." *MLS* 17 (1987): 9–22.

Stambler, Peter. "The Development of Guyon's Christian Temperance." *ELR* 7 (1977): 51–89.

Swearingen, Roger C. "Guyons' Faint." *SP* 74 (1977): 165–85.

Wall, John N., Jr. "'Fruitfullest Virginia': Edmund Spenser, Roanoke Island, and the Bower of Bliss." *RenP* 1984: 1–17.

Wells, Robin Headlam. "Spenser and the Politics of Music." *HLQ* 52 (1989): 447–68.

Wright, Lloyd A. "Guyon's Heroism in the Bower of Bliss." *TSLL* 15 (1974): 597–603.

THE FAERIE QUEENE: BOOK III

Anderson, Judith H. "Arthur, Argante, and the Ideal Vision: An Exercise in Speculation and Parody." IN Christopher Baswell and William Sharpe, eds. *The Passing of Arthur: New Essays in Arthurian Tradition.* New York, 1988. 193–206.

———. "'In liuing colours and right hew': The Queen of Spenser's Central Books." IN Maynard Mack and George deForest Lord, eds. *Poetic Traditions of the English Renaissance.* New Haven, 1982. 47–66.

Barkan, Leonard. *The Gods Made Flesh: Metamorphosis and the Pursuit of Paganism.* New Haven, 1986.

Bean, John C. "Making the Daimonic Personal: Britomart and Love's Assault in *The Faerie Queene.*" *MLQ* 40 (1979): 237–55.

Benson, Pamela J. "Florimell at Sea: The Action of Grace in *Faerie Queene*, Book III." *SSt* 6 (1985): 83–94.

Berleth, Richard J. "Heavens Favorable and Free: Belphoebe's Nativity in *The Faerie Queene.*" *ELH* 40 (1973): 479–500.

Blackburn, William. "Spenser's Merlin." *Ren&R* 4 (1980): 179–98.

Boehrer, Bruce Thomas. "'Carelesse modestee': Chastity as Politics in Book III of *The Faerie Queene.*" *ELH* 55 (1988): 555–73.

Brill, Lesley W. "Battles That Need Not Be Fought: *The Faerie Queene*, III.i." *ELR* 5 (1975): 198–211.

Broaddus, James W. "Renaissance Psychology and Britomart's Adventures in *Faerie Queene* III." *ELR* 17 (1987): 186–206.

Bulger, Thomas. "Britomart and Galahad." *ELN* 25 (1987): 10–17.

Burchmore, David W. "The Unfolding of Britomart: Mythic Iconography in *The Faerie Queene.*" *RenP* 1977: 11–28.

Champagne, Claudia M. "Wounding the Body of Woman in Book III of *The Faerie Queene.*" *LIT* 2 (1990): 95–115.

Cheney, Patrick. "'And Doubted Her to Deeme an Earthly Wight': Male Neoplatonic 'Magic' and the Problem of Female Identity in Spenser's Allegory of the Two Florimells." *SP* 86 (1989): 310–40.

———. " 'Secret powre unseene': Good Magic in Spenser's Legend of Britomart." *SP* 85 (1988): 1–28.

Crampton, Georgia Ronan. "Spenser's Lyric Theodicy: The Complaints of *The Faerie Queene*, III.iv." *ELH* (1977): 205–21.

de Gerenday, Lynn. "The Problem of Self-Reflective Love in Book III of *The Faerie Queene*." *L&P* 26 (1976): 37–48.

Donno, Elizabeth Story. "The Triumph of Cupid: Spenser's Legend of Chastity." *YES* 4 (1974): 37–48.

Dubrow, Heather. "The Arraignment of Paridell: Tudor Historiography in *The Faerie Queene*, III.ix." *SP* 87 (1990): 312–27.

Frantz, David O. "The Union of Florimell and Marinell: The Triumph of Hearing." *SSt* 6 (1985): 115–27.

Fumerton, Patricia. *Cultural Aesthetics: Renaissance Literature and the Practice of Social Ornament.* Chicago, 1991. 50–66.

Gardner, Helen. "Some Reflections on the House of Busyrane." *RES* 34 (1983): 403–13.

Geller, Lila. "Venus and the Three Graces: A Neoplatonic Paradigm for Book III of *The Faerie Queene*." *JEGP* 75 (1976): 56–74.

Goldberg, Jonathan. "The Mothers in Book III of *The Faerie Queene*." *TSLL* 17 (1975): 5–26.

Greenfield, Sayre N. "Reading Love in the Geography of *The Faerie Queene*, Book Three." *PQ* 68 (1989): 424–42.

Grund, Gary R. "The Queen's Two Bodies: Britomart and Spenser's *Faerie Queene*, Book III." *CahiersE* 20 (1981): 11–33.

Haskin, Dayton W. "Visionary Experience in Spenser." *Thought* 54 (1979): 365–75.

Horton, Ronald. "The Argument of Spenser's Garden of Adonis." IN Kenneth R. Bartlett, Konrad Eisenbichler, and Janice Liedl, eds. *Love and Death in the Renaissance.* Ottowa, 1991. 61–72.

Hughes, Felicity A. "Psychological Allegory in *The Faerie Queene* III.xi–xii." *RES* 29 (1978): 129–46.

Johnson, William C. " 'God' as Structure in Spenser's Garden of Adonis." *ES* 63 (1982): 301–7.

Maclean, Hugh. " 'Restlesse anguish and unquiet paine': Spenser and the Complaint, 1579–90." IN Jane Campbell and James Doyle, eds. *The Practical Vision: Essays in English Literature in Honour of Flora Roy.* Waterloo, Ontario, 1978. 29–47.

Milne, Fred L. "The Doctrine of Act and Potency: A Metaphysical Ground for Interpretation of Spenser's Garden of Adonis Passages." *SP* 70 (1973): 279–87.

Murtaugh, Daniel M. "The Garden and the Sea: The Topography of *The Faerie Queene*, III." *ELH* 40 (1973): 325–38.

Nestrick, William V. "Spenser and the Renaissance Mythology of Love." *Literary Monographs* 6 (1975): 37–50.

Neuse, Richard T. "Planting Words in the Soul: Spenser's Socratic Garden of Adonis." *SSt* 8 (1987): 79–100.

Rapaport, Herman. "The Phenomenology of Spenserian Ekphrasis." IN Bruce Henricksen, ed. *Murray Krieger and Contemporary Critical Theory.* New York, 1986. 157–75.

Silberman, Lauren. "The Hermaphrodite and the Metamorphosis of Spenserian Allegory." *ELR* 17 (1987): 207–23.

———. "Singing Unsung Heroines: Androgynous Discourse in Book III of *The Faerie Queene*." IN Margaret W. Ferguson, Maureen Quilligan, and Nancy J. Vickers, eds. *Rewriting the Renaissance: The Discourses of Sexual Difference in Early Modern Europe.* Chicago, 1986. 259–71.

———. "Spenser and Ariosto: Funny Peril and Comic Chaos." *CLS* 25 (1988): 23–34.

Sims, Dwight J. "Cosmological Structure in *The Faerie Queene*, Book III." *HLQ* 40 (1977): 99–116.

———. "The Syncretic Myth of Venus in Spenser's Legend of Chastity." *SP* 71 (1974): 427–50.

Thaon, Brenda. "Spenser's Neptune, Nereus, and Proteus: Renaissance Mythography Made Verse." IN Richard J. Schoeck, ed. *Acta Conventus Neo-Latini Bononiensis.* Binghamton, NY, 1985. 630–37.

Vance, Eugene. "Chaucer, Spenser, and the Ideology of Translation." *CRCL* 8 (1981): 217–38.

Waswo, Richard. "The History That Literature Makes." *NLH* 19 (1988): 541–64.

Wiggins, Peter DeSa. "Spenser's Anxiety." *MLN* 103 (1988): 75–86.

Wofford, Susanne L. "Britomart's Petrarchan Lament: Allegory and Narrative in *The Faerie Queene* III, iv." *CL* 39 (1987): 28–57.

THE FAERIE QUEENE: BOOK V

Borris, Kenneth. *Spenser's Poetics of Prophecy in* The Faerie Queene *V.* Victoria, Canada (English Literary Studies, Monograph Series 52, 1991).

Cavanagh, Sheila T. "Ideal and Practical Justice: Artegall and Arthur in *Faerie Queene Five*." *RenP* 1984: 19–28.

Gallagher, Lowell. *Medusa's Gaze: Casuistry and Conscience in the Renaissance.* Stanford, CA, 1991. 123–271.

Goldberg, Jonathan. *James I and the Politics of Literature.* Baltimore, 1983. 1–17.

Hardin, Richard. *Civil Idolatry: Desacralizing and Monarchy in Spenser, Shakespeare, and Milton.* Newark, DE, 1992.

Miskimin, Alice. "Britomart's Crocodile and the Legends of Chastity." *JEGP* 77 (1978): 17–36.
Stump, Donald V. "Isis Versus Mercilla: The Allegorical Shrines in Spenser's Legend of Justice." *SSt* 3 (1982): 87–98.
Waters, D. Douglas. "Spenser and the 'Mas' at the Temple of Isis." *SEL* 19 (1979): 43–53.
Yates, Frances. *Astraea: The Imperial Theme in the Sixteenth Century*. London, 1975.

THE FAERIE QUEENE: BOOK VI

Alpers, Paul. "Spenser's Late Pastorals." *ELH* 56 (1989): 797–817.
Alwes, Derek B. " 'Who knowes not Colin Clout?': Spenser's Self-Advertisement in *The Faerie Queene*, Book 6." *MP* 88 (1990): 26–42.
Anderson, Judith H. "What Comes after Chaucer's 'But': Adversative Constructions in Spenser." IN Mary J. Carruthers and Elizabeth D. Kirk, eds. *Acts of Interpretation . . . in Honor of E. Talbot Donaldson*. Norman, OK, 1982. 105–18.
Archer, Mark. "The Meaning of 'Grace' and 'Courtesy': Book VI of *The Faerie Queene*." *SEL* 27 (1987): 17–34.
Bellamy, Elizabeth J. "Colin and Orphic Interpretation: Reading Neoplatonically on Spenser's Acidale." *CLS* 27 (1990): 172–92.
Belt, Debra. "Hostile Audiences and the Courteous Reader in *The Faerie Queene*, Book VI." *SSt* 9 (1988): 107–35.
Blitch, Alice Fox. "Proserpina Preserved: Book VI of *The Faerie Queene*." *SEL* 13 (1973): 15–30.
Bond, Ronald B. "Vying with Vision: An Aspect of Envy in *The Faerie Queene*." *Ren&R* 8 (1984): 30–38.
Borris, Kenneth. "Fortune, Occasion, and the Allegory of the Quest in Book Six of *The Faerie Queene*." *SSt* 7 (1986): 123–45.
Cheney, Patrick. "Spenser's Dance of the Graces and Tasso's Dance of the Sylvan Nymphs." *ELN* 22 (1984): 5–9.
———, and P. J. Klemp. "Spenser's Dance of the Graces and the Ptolemaic Universe." *SN* 56 (1984): 27–33.
DeNeef, A. Leigh. "Ploughing Virgilian Furrows: The Genres of *Faerie Queene* VI." *JDJ* 1 (1982): 151–66.
Dixon, Michael F. N. "Fairy Tale, Fortune, and Boethian Wonder: Rhetorical Structure in Book VI of *The Faerie Queene*." *UTQ* 44 (1975): 141–65.
Doyle, Charles Clay. "As Old Stories Tell: Daphnis and Chloe and the Pastoral Episode of *The Faerie Queene* Book VI." *Neohelicon* 5.2 (1977): 51–70.
Geller, Lila B. "Spenser's Theory of Nobility in Book VI of *The Faerie Queene*." *ELR* 5 (1975): 49–57.
Green, Paul D. "Spenser and the Masses: Social Commentary in *The Faerie Queene*." *JHI* 35 (1974): 389–406.
Hannay, Margaret. " 'My Sheep are Thoughts': Self-Reflexive Pastoral in *The Faerie Queene*, Book VI." *SSt* 9 (1988): 137–59.
Keaney, Winifred Gleeson. "A Courtly Paradox in Book VI of Spenser's *Faerie Queene*." IN Nathaniel B. Smith and Joseph T. Snow, eds. *The Expansion and Transformations of Courtly Literature*. Athens, GA, 1980. 185–203.
Lupton, Julia Reinhard. "Home-Making in Ireland: Virgil's Eclogue I and Book VI of *The Faerie Queene*." *SSt* 8 (1987): 119–45.
Miller, David L. "Abandoning the Quest." *ELH* 46 (1979): 173–92.
Miller, Jacqueline T. "The Courtly Figure: Spenser's Anatomy of Allegory." *SEL* 31 (1991): 51–68.
Montrose, Louis Adrian. "Gifts and Reasons: The Contexts of Peele's *Araygnement of Paris*." *ELH* 47 (1980): 433–61.
Morgan, Gerald. "Spenser's Conception of Courtesy and the Design of *The Faerie Queene*." *RES* 32 (1981): 17–36.
Panja, Shormishtha. "A Self-Reflexive Parable of Narration: *The Faerie Queene* VI." *JNT* 15 (1985): 277–88.
Rowe, George E. "Privacy, Vision, and Gender in Spenser's Legend of Courtesy." *MLQ* 50 (1989): 309–36.
Rusche, Harry. "The Lesson of Calidore's Truancy." *SP* 76 (1979): 149–61.
Snare, Gerald. "The Poetics of Vision: Patterns of Grace and Courtesy in *The Faerie Queene*, VI." *RenP*: 1974, 1–8.
Stewart, Stanley. "Sir Calidore and 'Closure,' " *SEL* 24 (1984): 69–86.
Trainer, Michael. " 'The thing S. Paule ment by . . . the courteousness that he spake of': Religious Sources for Book VI of *The Faerie Queene*." *SSt* 8 (1987): 147–74.
Weiner, Andrew D. "Spenser and the Myth of Pastoral." *SP* 85 (1988): 390–406.
Weiner, Seth. "Minims and Grace Notes: Spenser's Acidalian Vision and Sixteenth-Century Music." *SSt* 5 (1985): 91–112.
Wells, Robin Headlam. "Spenser and the Courtesy Tradition: Form and Meaning in the Sixth Book of *The Faerie Queene*." *ES* 58 (1977): 221–29.
Woods, Susanne. "Closure in *The Faerie Queene*." *JEGP* 76 (1977): 195–216.
See also Ettin and Mallette, under "General Studies."

CANTOS OF MUTABILITIE

Campbell, Marion. "Spenser's *Mutabilitie Cantos* and the End of *The Faerie Queene.*" *SoR* 15 (1982): 46–59.

Chambers, Jane. "Divine Justice, Mercy, and Love: The 'Mutabilitie' Subplot and Spenser's Apocalyptic Theme." *ELWIU* 8 (1981): 3–10.

Davidson, Arnold E. "Dame Nature's Shifting Logic in Spenser's *Cantos of Mutabilitie.*" *NM* 83 (1982): 451–56.

Doyle, Charles Clay. "*Daphnis and Chloe* and the Faunus Episode in Spenser's *Mutability.*" *NM* 74 (1973): 163–68.

Grimm, Nadine G. "Mutabilitie's Plea before Dame Nature's Bar." *Comitatus* 17 (1986): 22–34.

Hawkins, Peter S. "From Mythography to Myth-Making: Spenser and the Magna Mater Cybele." *SCJ* 12 (1981): 51–64.

Holohan, Michael. " 'Iamque opus exegi': Ovid's Changes and Spenser's Brief Epic of Mutability." *ELR* 6 (1976): 244–70.

Meyer, Russell J. " 'Fixt in heauens hight': Spenser, Astronomy, and the Date of the *Cantos of Mutabilitie.*" *SSt* 4 (1983): 115–29.

Weatherby, Harold L. "The Old Theology: Spenser's Dame Nature and the Transfiguration." *SSt* 5 (1985): 113–42.

Wells, Robin Headlam. "Semper Eadem: Spenser's 'Legend of Constancie.' " *MLR* 73 (1978): 250–55.

THE SHEPHEARDES CALENDER

Adler, Doris. "The Riddle of the Sieve: The Siena Sieve Portrait of Queen Elizabeth." *RenP* 1978: 1–10.

Alpers, Paul. "Pastoral and the Domain of Lyric in Spenser's *Shepheardes Calender.*" *Representations* 12 (1985): 83–100.

Bond, Ronald B. "Supplantation in the Elizabethan Court: The Theme of Spenser's February Eclogue." *SSt* 2 (1981): 55–65.

Brown, James Neil. "A Note on Symbolic Numbers in Spenser's 'Aprill.' " *N&Q* 27 (1980): 301–4.

Cheney, Donald. "The Circular Argument of *The Shepheardes Calender.*" IN Logan and Teskey, 137–61.

Cheney, Patrick. " 'The Nightingale is Sovereigne of Song': The bird as a sign of the Virgilian Orphic Poet in *The Shepheardes Calender.*" *JMRS* 21 (1991): 29–57.

Davies, H. Neville. "Spenser's *Shepheardes Calender*: The Importance of November." *CahiersE* 20 (1981): 35–48.

Doebler, Bettie Anne. "Venus-Humanitas: An Iconic Elizabeth." *JES* 12 (1982): 233–48.

Goldberg, Jonathan. "Colin to Hobbinol: Spenser's Familiar Letters." *SAQ* 88 (1989): 107–126.

———. *Voice Terminal Echo: Postmodernism and English Renaissance Texts.* New York and London, 1986. Ch. 3.

Greene, Roland. "*The Shepheardes Calender*, Dialogue, and Periphrasis." *SSt* 8 (1987): 1–33.

Halpern, Richard. *The Poetics of Primitive Accumulation: English Renaissance Culture and the Genealogy of Capital.* Ithaca, NY, 1991. 176–214.

Hardin, Richard F. "The Resolved Debate of Spenser's 'October.' " *MP* 73 (1976): 257–63.

Heninger, S. K., Jr. "The Typographical Layout of Spenser's *Shepheardes Calender.*" IN Karl Josef Höltgen, Peter M. Daly, and Wolfgang Lottes, eds. *Word and Visual Imagination.* Erlangen, Germany, 1988. 33–71.

Herman, Peter. "*The Shepheardes Calender* and Renaissance Antipoetic Sentiment." *SEL* 32 (1992): 15–33.

Hoffman, Nancy Jo. *Spenser's Pastorals:* The Shepheardes Calender *and "Colin Clout."* Baltimore, 1977.

Johnson, Lynn Staley. The Shepheardes Calender: *An Introduction.* University Park, PA, 1990.

Kay, Dennis. *Melodious Tears: The English Funeral Elegy from Spenser to Milton.* Oxford, 1990.

Kennedy, Judith M. "The Final Emblem of *The Shepheardes Calender.*" *SSt* 1 (1980): 95–106.

Kennedy, William J. "The Virgilian Legacies of Petrarch's *Bucolicum Carmen* and Spenser's *Shepheardes Calender.*" IN Anthony L. Pellegrini, ed. *The Early Renaissance: Virgil and the Classical Tradition.* Binghamton, NY, 1985. 79–106.

Lambert, Ellen Zetzel. *Placing Sorrow: A Study of the Pastoral Convention from Theocritus to Milton.* Chapel Hill, NC, 1976.

Lasater, Alice E. "The Chaucerian Narrator in Spenser's *Shepheardes Calender.*" *SoQ* 12 (1974): 189–201.

Luborsky, Ruth Samson. "The Allusive Presentation of *The Shepheardes Calender.*" *SSt* 1 (1980): 29–67.

———. "The Illustrations of *The Shepheardes Calender.*" *SSt* 2 (1981): 3–53.

Marx, Steven. *Youth Against Age: Generational Strife in Renaissance Poetry; With Special Reference to Edmund Spenser's* The Shepheardes Calender. New York, 1985.

McCanles, Michael. "*The Shepheardes Calender* as Document and Monument." *SEL* 22 (1982): 5–19.

McNeir, Waldo F. "The Drama of Spenser's *Shepheardes Calender.*" *Anglia* 95 (1977): 34–59.

Miller, David L. "Authorship, Anonymity, and *The Shepheardes Calender.*" *MLQ* 40 (1979): 219–36.

Montrose, Louis Adrian. " 'Eliza, Queene of shepheardes,' and the Pastoral of Power." *ELR* 10 (1980): 153–82.

———. "Interpreting Spenser's February Eclogue: Some Contexts and Implications." *SSt* 2 (1981): 67–74.

———. " 'The perfecte paterne of a Poete': The Poetics of Courtship in *The Shepheardes Calender.*" *TSLL* 21 (1979): 34–67.

Moore, John W., Jr. "Colin Breaks His Pipe: A Reading of the 'January' Ecologue." *ELR* 5 (1975): 3–24.

Patterson, Annabel. "Couples, Canons, and the Uncouth: Spenser-and-Milton in Educational Theory." *CritI* 16 (1990): 773–93.

———. "Re-Opening the Green Cabinet: Clément Marot and Edmund Spenser." *ELR* 16 (1986): 44–70.

Pigman, G. W. III. *Grief and English Renaissance Elegy.* Cambridge, England, 1985.

Rambuss, Richard. "The Secretary's Study: The Secret Designs of *The Shepheardes Calender.*" *ELH* 59 (1992): 313–35.

Richardson, J. M. *Astrological Symbolism in Spenser's* The Shepheardes Calender: *The Cultural Background of a Literary Text.* Lewiston, NY, 1989.

Sacks, Peter M. *The English Elegy: Studies in the Genre from Spenser to Yeats.* Baltimore, 1985. Ch. 2.

Schleiner, Louise. "Spenser and Sidney on the Vaticinium." *SSt* 6 (1985): 129–45.

———. "Spenser's 'E.K.' as Edmund Kent (Kenned / of Kent): Kyth (Couth), Kissed, and Kunning-Conning." *ELR* 20 (1990): 374–407.

Shawcross, John T. "Probability as Requisite to Poetic Delight: A Re-View of the Intentionality of *The Shepheardes Calender.*" *SP* 87 (1990): 120–27.

Smith, Bruce R. "On Reading *The Shepheardes Calender.*" *SSt* 1 (1980): 69–93.

Spiegel, Glenn S. "Perfecting English Meter: Sixteenth-Century Criticism and Practice." *JEGP* 79 (1980): 192–209.

Steinberg, Theodore L. "E.K.'s *Shepheardes Calender* and Spenser's." *MLS* 3 (1973): 46–58.

Thornton, Bruce. "Rural Dialectic: Pastoral, Georgic, and *The Shepheardes Calender.*" *SSt* 9 (1988): 1–20.

Tylus, Jane. "Spenser, Virgil, and the Politics of Poetic Labor." *ELH* 55 (1988): 53–77.

Waldman, Louis. "Spenser's Pseudonym 'E.K.' and Humanist Self-Naming." *SSt* 9 (1988): 21–31.

Waters, D. Douglas. "Spenser and Symbolic Witchcraft in *The Shepheardes Calender.*" *SEL* 14 (1974): 3–15.

See also Berger, Cooper, Ettin, King, Mallette, and Shore, under "General Studies."

MUIOPOTMOS

Brink, Jean R. "Who Fashioned Edmund Spenser? The Textual History of *Complaints.*" *SP* 88 (1991): 153–68.

Dundas, Judith. "*Muiopotmos:* A World of Art." *YES* 5 (1975): 30–38.

Hulse, Clark. *Metamorphic Verse: The Elizabethan Minor Epic.* Princeton, 1981.

Kearns, Terrance Brophy. "Rhetorical Devices and the Mock-Heroic in Spenser's 'Muiopotmos.' " *PAPA* 9.2 (1983): 58–66.

Morey, James H. "Spenser's Mythic Adaptations in *Muiopotmos.*" *SSt* 9 (1988): 49–60.

See also Grant and Heninger, under "General Studies," and Macfie, under "*The Faerie Queene*: Book II."

COLIN CLOUTS COME HOME AGAINE

Burchmore, David W. "The Image of the Centre in *Colin Clouts Come Home Againe.*" *RES* 28 (1977): 393–406.

Gaffney, Carmel. "Colin Clouts Come Home Againe." Diss., Edinburgh University, Edinburgh, 1982.

Williams, Kathleen. "The Moralized Song: Some Renaissance Themes in Pope." *ELH* 41 (1974): 578–601.

See also Bernard, Cheney, DeNeef, MacCaffrey, Mallette, Oram, Shepherd, and Shore, under "General Studies"; Bednarz, under "*The Faerie Queene*: General"; Alpers and Alwes, under "*The Faerie Queene*: Book VI"; Cooper, Hoffman, and Mallette, under "*The Shepheardes Calender.*"

AMORETTI AND EPITHALAMION

Allman, Eileen Jorge. "*Epithalamion's* Bridegroom: Orpheus-Adam-Christ." *Renascence* 32 (1980): 240–47.

Anderson, Douglas. " 'Unto My Selfe Alone': Spenser's Plenary Epithalamion." *SSt* 5 (1985): 149–66.

Baker-Smith, Dominic. "Spenser's 'Triumph of Marriage,' " *Word and Image* 4 (1988): 310–16.

Bates, Catherine. "The Politics of Spenser's *Amoretti*." *Criticism* 33 (1991): 73–90.

Bieman, Elizabeth. " 'Sometimes I . . . mask in myrth lyke to a Comedy: Spenser's *Amoretti*." *SSt* 4 (1983): 131–41.

Brown, James Neil. " 'Lyke Phoebe': Lunar Numerical and Calendrical Patterns in Spenser's *Amoretti*." *Gypsy Scholar* 1 (1973): 5–15.

Chinitz, David. "The Poem as Sacrament: Spenser's *Epithalamion* and the Golden Section." *JMRS* 21 (1991): 251–68.

Dubrow, Heather. A *Happier Eden: The Politics of Marriage in the Stuart Epithalamion*. Ithaca, NY, 1990.

Dunlop, Alexander. "The Drama of *Amoretti*." *SpStud* 1 (1980): 107–20.

Fukuda, Shokachi. "The Numerological Patterning of *Amoretti* and *Epithalamion*." *SSt* 9 (1988): 33–48.

Gibbs, Donna. *Spenser's* Amoretti: A *Critical Study*. Aldershot, England, 1990.

Hunter, G. K. "Spenser's *Amoretti* and the English Sonnet Tradition." IN Kennedy and Reither, 124–44.

Johnson, William C. *Spenser's* Amoretti: *Analogies of Love*. Lewisburg, PA, 1990.

Kaske, Carol V. "Spenser's *Amoretti* and *Epithalamion* of 1595: Structure, Genre, and Numerology." *ELR* 8 (1978): 271–95.

Kuin, Roger. "The Gaps and the Whites: Indeterminacy and Undecideability in the Sonnet Sequences of Sidney, Spenser, and Shakespeare." *SSt* 8 (1987): 251–85.

Loewenstein, Joseph. "Echo's Ring: Orpheus and Spenser's Career." *ELR* 16 (1986): 287–302.

———. "A Note on the Structure of Spenser's *Amoretti*: Viper Thoughts." *SSt* 8 (1987): 311–23.

Marotti, Arthur F. " 'Love is Not Love': Elizabethan Sonnet Sequences and the Social Order." *ELH* 49 (1982): 396–428.

Miola, Robert S. "Spenser's Anacreontics: A Mythological Metaphor." *SP* 77 (1980): 50–66.

Neely, Carol Thomas. "The Structure of English Renaissance Sonnet Sequences." *ELH* 45 (1978): 359–89.

Pearcy, Lee T. "A Case of Allusion: Stanza 18 of Spenser's 'Epithalamion' and Catullus 5." *CML* 1 (1981): 243–54.

Quitslund, Jon A. "Spenser's *Amoretti* VIII and Platonic Commentaries on Petrarch." *JWCI* 36 (1973): 256–76.

Schenck, Celeste. " 'Sacred Ceremonies': Spenser's *Epithalamion* and *Prothalamion*." IN her *Mourning and Panegyric: The Poetics of Pastoral Ceremony*. University Park, PA, 1988. 55–72.

Thompson, Charlotte. "Love in an Orderly Universe: A Unification of Spenser's *Amoretti*, 'Anacreontics,' and *Epithalamion*." *Viator* 16 (1985): 277–335.

Turner, Myron. "The Imagery of Spenser's *Amoretti*." *Neophil* 72 (1988): 284–99.

Villeponteaux, Mary A. " 'With her own will beguyld': The Captive Lady in Spenser's *Amoretti*." *EIRC* 14 (1988): 29–39.

Warkentin, Germaine. "Spenser at the Still Point: A Schematic Device in 'Epithalamion.' " IN H. B. de Groot and Alexander Leggatt, eds. *Craft and Tradition: Essays in Honour of William Blissett*. Calgary, 1990. 47–57.

Wells, R. Headlam. "Poetic Decorum in Spenser's *Amoretti*." *CahiersE* 25 (1984): 9–21.

Young, Frank B. "Medusa and the *Epithalamion*: A Problem in Spenserian Imagery." *ELN* 11 (1973): 21–29.

See also Bernard, Dasenbrook, J. Miller, and Wall, under "General Studies"; Hieatt, under "*The Faerie Queene*: Book II."

PROTHALAMION

Cheney, Patrick. "The Old Poet Presents Himself: *Prothalamion* as a Defense of Spenser's Career." *SSt* 8 (1987): 175–209.

Fowler, Alastair. "Spenser's *Prothalamion*." IN his *Conceitful Thought: The Interpretation of English Renaissance Poems*. Edinburgh, 1975. 59–86.

Herendeen, Wyman. "Spenserian Specifics: Spenser's Appropriation of a Renaissance Topos." *M&H* 10 (1981): 159–88.

Manley, Lawrence. "Spenser and the City: The Minor Poems." *MLQ* 43 (1982): 203–27.

Patterson, Sandra R. "Spenser's *Prothalamion* and the Catullan Epithalamic Tradition." *Comitatus* 10 (1979–80): 97–106.

Prager, Carolyn. "Emblem and Motion in Spenser's *Prothalamion*." *SIcon* 2 (1976): 114–20.

West, Michael. "Prothalamia in Propertius and Spenser." *CL* 26 (1974): 346–53.

See also Helgerson, under "General Studies"; Cain, under "*The Faerie Queene*: General"; Schenck, under "*Amoretti* and *Epithalamion*"; and Williams, under "*Colin Clouts Come Home Againe*."

NORTON CRITICAL EDITIONS

MILL On Liberty edited by David Spitz
MILTON Paradise Lost edited by Scott Elledge Second Edition
Modern Irish Drama edited by John P. Harrington
MORE Utopia translated and edited by Robert M. Adams Second Edition
NEWMAN Apologia Pro Vita Sua edited by David J. DeLaura
NEWTON Newton edited by I. Bernard Cohen and Richard S. Westfall
NORRIS McTeague edited by Donald Pizer Second Edition
Restoration and Eighteenth-Century Comedy edited by Scott McMillin Second Edition
RICH Adrienne Rich's Poetry and Prose edited by Barbara Charlesworth Gelpi and
Albert Gelpi
ROUSSEAU Rousseau's Political Writings edited by Alan Ritter and translated by
Julia Conaway Bondanella
ST. PAUL The Writings of St. Paul edited by Wayne A. Meeks
SHAKESPEARE Hamlet edited by Cyrus Hoy Second Edition
SHAKESPEARE Henry IV, Part I edited by James L. Sanderson Second Edition
SHAW Bernard Shaw's Plays edited by Warren Sylvester Smith
SHELLEY Frankenstein edited by Paul Hunter
SHELLEY Shelley's Poetry and Prose selected and edited by Donald H. Reiman and
Sharon B. Powers
SMOLLETT Humphry Clinker edited by James L. Thorson
SOPHOCLES Oedipus Tyrannus translated and edited by Luci Berkowitz and
Theodore F. Brunner
SPENSER Edmund Spenser's Poetry selected and edited by Hugh Maclean and
Anne Lake Prescott Third Edition
STENDHAL Red and Black translated and edited by Robert M. Adams
STERNE Tristram Shandy edited by Howard Anderson
STOKER Dracula edited by Nina Auerbach and David Skal
STOWE Uncle Tom's Cabin edited by Elizabeth Ammons
SWIFT Gulliver's Travels edited by Robert A. Greenberg Second Edition
SWIFT The Writings of Jonathan Swift edited by Robert A. Greenberg and William B. Piper
TENNYSON In Memoriam edited by Robert H. Ross
TENNYSON Tennyson's Poetry selected and edited by Robert W. Hill, Jr.
THACKERAY Vanity Fair edited by Peter Shillingsburg
THOREAU Walden and Resistance to Civil Government edited by William Rossi
Second Edition
TOLSTOY Anna Karenina edited and with a revised translation by George Gibian
Second Edition
TOLSTOY Tolstoy's Short Fiction edited and with revised translations by Michael R. Katz
TOLSTOY War and Peace (the Maude translation) edited by George Gibian Second Edition
TOOMER Cane edited by Darwin T. Turner
TURGENEV Fathers and Sons translated and edited by Michael R. Katz
VOLTAIRE Candide translated and edited by Robert M. Adams Second Edition
WASHINGTON Up from Slavery edited by William L. Andrews
WATSON The Double Helix: A Personal Account of the Discovery of the Structure of DNA
edited by Gunther S. Stent
WHARTON Ethan Frome edited by Kristin O. Lauer and Cynthia Griffin Wolff
WHARTON The House of Mirth edited by Elizabeth Ammons
WHITMAN Leaves of Grass edited by Sculley Bradley and Harold W. Blodgett
WILDE The Picture of Dorian Gray edited by Donald L. Lawler
WOLLSTONECRAFT A Vindication of the Rights of Woman edited by Carol H. Poston
Second Edition
WORDSWORTH The Prelude: 1799, 1805, 1850 edited by Jonathan Wordsworth,
M. H. Abrams, and Stephen Gill